I Guarantee You Will Pass the CPA Exam or your money back* with the Bisk CPA Review . . .the Choice of Gold Medal Winners

AMERICA'S BEST CPA REVIEW SINCE 1971

D1622018

Dear Future CPA:

Your selection of a CPA Review is critical, given the expense, time and effort you will devote to preparing for the nation's most difficult, professional certification exam. **Bisk CPA Review** was the choice of Gold Medal Winners, Paul Ito and Stephanie Seiberg (featured on the opposite page). They achieved the highest test scores in the nation and won the prestigious Elijah Watt Sells Award Gold Medal. In the last 8 years, the University of South Florida, which uses Bisk materials, was ranked more often than any other university as one of the top 5 schools in the nation for students with advanced degrees passing all sections taken on the CPA Exam. Plus, Bisk materials are used by the "Big 5" accounting firms; we are an exclusive provider to one and a preferred provider to the other four. We are ready to put **you** on the fast track to exam success, too.

The award-winning Bisk CPA Review includes

- **Money Back Guarantee** – Pass the CPA Exam with the **Bisk CPA Review** or your money back!*
- **Online CPA Review** – Join our structured "online review" and interact directly with faculty and fellow students via the Internet...no classroom attendance is required. **Register now at www.cpaexam.com/book31 for your online demo.**
- **CD-ROM** – Multimedia video, audio and animated graphics enhance your learning experience within an easy-to-use webstyle interface. Let Bisk Personal Trainer develop a customized study plan just for you.
- **Video** – Intensive and Hot•Spots™ Video Series, boost confidence and add crucial points to your exam scores.
- **Audios** – Bisk Audio Tutor adds 10-15 hours per week to your study program while you're "on the go".
- **Books** – Feature our famed Solutions Approach™ for solving all types of exam problems quickly, easily and accurately.
- **Toll-Free Help Line** – Speak one-on-one with our CPA Review experts whenever you need guidance.
- **Internet Services** – Visit our web site at **www.cpaexam.com/book31** for FREE demos and promotions, career guidance, CPA exam study tips, our online catalogue, new product updates...and much more.
- **Earn up to 12 College Credits with Bisk CPA Review** – Call for details!
- **Meet the 150 Hour Rule and Beyond** – Take undergraduate courses or earn your MBA, online!

Now is the time to set your CPA Review game plan. To introduce you to **Bisk CPA Review's** winning combination of quality products, personalized customer service and exceptional value, I've enclosed a set of **Bisk CPA Review discount coupons** at the back of this textbook, **saving you up to $200.00**. **Free demos** of our Online CPA Review, CD-ROM and video products are also available... see the enclosed request form or visit our web site at **www.cpaexam.com/book31.**

To redeem your **discount coupons**, or to get **free demos**, call
1-888-CPA-BISK, fax to 1-800-345-8273 or send email to
info@cpaexam.com.

Good luck on the CPA exam! I look forward to welcoming you as a fellow CPA, and fulfilling your accounting, graduate and continuing professional education needs in the years to come.

Sincerely,

Nathan M Bisk

Nathan M. Bisk, JD, CPA (FL)
Publisher & Editor-in-Chief

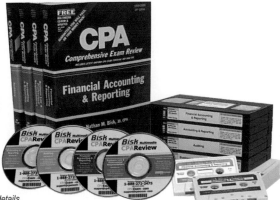

*Call for complete details.

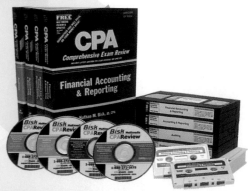

BISK is with you every step of your career...

BA + CPA + CPE + MBA = $$

Increase your income and opportunity

CPA REVIEW

CPE

MBA

Bisk CPA Review makes you a CPA

America's Best CPA Review since 1971, Bisk offers the only CPA Review materials available in your personal choice of learning formats — Online, CD-ROM, Video, Audio or Textbooks...and a free personal help line. Study with Bisk CPA Review and we guarantee that you will pass the CPA Exam, or you get your money back.* Take advantage of Bisk CPA Review as soon as you begin your accounting studies. Our materials and "Solutions Approach™" will help you score higher on your college exams, and prepare for the CPA exam.

Bisk helps you earn your undergraduate degree online with Saint Leo University ... no classroom attendance required

Bisk, in association with the University Alliance (a Bisk Education Network) and Saint Leo University, makes available online Bachelor's degrees in Accounting, Business Administration, Computer Information Systems (CIS), Criminology, and Associate's degrees in Liberal Arts and Business Administration. Utilizing Internet and multimedia technology, no classroom attendance is required.

Bisk low cost CPE meets your mandatory requirements

With over 300 multimedia programs in taxation, accounting & auditing, business & industry and computer training, Bisk is the largest provider of online and multimedia CPE in the country. From candidate to practitioner, you still select the program format that best meets your individual needs and preferences. Over 175,000 CPAs, firms, corporations, universities, state & federal agencies, and the "Big 5", use our programs to satisfy mandatory CPE requirements...**try our CPE programs Risk-Free!**

Now Bisk offers you the opportunity to earn your accredited MBA online from Regis University ... with no classroom attendance required

Bisk has developed, with nationally renowned Regis University, one of the first available multimedia Online MBA Programs for adult professionals around the world. The Regis University Online MBA Program is the largest in the nation. Earn your MBA degree in less than 2 years, with no classroom attendance required.

Bisk puts you out in front of your peers with a Certificate in Project Management from Villanova University

Bisk delivers online the Villanova University Certificate in Project Management. Called the "skill-set for the new millennium", with a thorough grasp of project management, you can enhance your value to the organization.

Call now or visit our web sites for free demo programs –

CPA Review: 1-888-CPA-BISK
www.cpaexam.com/book31

CPE: 1-888-CPE-BISK
www.cpeasy.com/book31

Online Degree and Certificate Programs University Alliance: 1-888-622-7344
www.universityalliance.com/book31

Call for details.

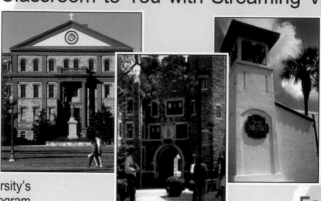

CPA

Comprehensive Exam Review

Financial Accounting & Reporting

Nathan M. Bisk, J.D., C.P.A.

ACKNOWLEDGEMENTS

EDITORIAL BOARD

CONTRIBUTING EDITORS

We wish to thank the **American Institute of Certified Public Accountants** and other organizations for permission to reprint or adapt the following copyright © materials:

1. Uniform CPA Examination Questions and Unofficial Answers, Copyright © American Institute of Certified Public Accountants, Inc., Harborside Financial Center, 201 Plaza Three, Jersey City, NJ 07311-3881.

2. Accounting Research Bulletins, APB Opinions, Audit and Accounting Guides, Auditing Procedure Studies, Risk Alerts, Statements of Position, and Code of Professional Conduct, Copyright © American Institute of Certified Public Accountants, Inc., Harborside Financial Center, 201 Plaza Three, Jersey City, NJ 07311-3881.

3. FASB Statements, Interpretations, Technical Bulletins, and Statements of Financial Accounting Concepts , Copyright © Financial Accounting Standards Board, 401 Merrit 7, P.O. Box 5116, Norwalk, CT 06856.

4. GASB Statements, Interpretations, and Technical Bulletins, Copyright © Governmental Accounting Standards Board, 401 Merritt 7, P.O. Box 5116, Norwalk CT 06856-5116.

5. Statements on Auditing Standards, Statements on Standards for Consulting Services, Statements on Responsibilities in Personal Financial Planning Practice, Statements on Standards for Accounting and Review Services, Statements on Quality Control Standards, Statements on Standards for Attestation Engagements, and Statements on Responsibilities in Tax Practice, Copyright © American Institute of Certified Public Accountants, Inc., Harborside Financial Center, 201 Plaza Three, Jersey City, NJ 07311-3881.

6. ISB Standards, Copyright © Independence Standards Board, 6th Floor, 1211 Avenue of the Americas, New York, NY 10036-8775

PREFACE

Our texts provide comprehensive, complete coverage of all the topics tested on all four sections of the CPA Examination, including **Business Law & Professional Responsibilities, Financial Accounting & Reporting, Accounting & Reporting,** and **Auditing**. Used effectively, our materials will enable you to achieve maximum preparedness for the Uniform CPA Examination. Here is a brief summary of the **features** and **benefits** that our texts will provide for you:

1. **Information on the Closed Exam** . . . Beginning with the May 1996 Exam, the Uniform CPA Examination is non-disclosed. See Appendix B for a full discussion of this issue. This edition contains up-to-date coverage, including complete coverage of all exam changes. This edition also includes all the latest pronouncements of the AICPA and FASB, the current tax rates, governmental and nonprofit accounting, and other topics that are tested on the CPA exam. Our coverage is based on the most recent **AICPA Content Specification Outlines for the Uniform CPA Exam.**

2. **Separate and Complete Volumes** . . . Each volume includes text, multiple choice and other objective questions with solutions, plus essays and problems where appropriate for that section of the CPA exam. There is no need to refer to any other volume.

3. **More than 2,600 Pages of Text** . . . Including a selection of more than 3,200 recent CPA Examination questions, problems, and essays with Unofficial Answers. Solving these questions and problems under test conditions with immediate verification of results instills confidence and reinforces our **SOLUTIONS APPROACH**™ to solving exam questions.

4. **Complete Coverage** . . . No extra materials required. We discuss and explain all important AICPA, FASB, GASB, and ISB pronouncements, including all significant ARBs, APBs, SASs, SSARs, SFACs, and FASB materials. We also cite and identify all authoritative sources including the dates of all AICPA Questions and Unofficial Answers covered in our materials.

5. **Detailed Summaries** . . . We set forth the significant testable concepts in each CPA exam topic. These highly readable summaries are written in complete sentences using an outline format to facilitate rapid and complete comprehension. The summaries isolate and emphasize topics historically tested by the CPA examiners.

6. **Emphasis on "How to Answer Questions" and "How to Take the Exam"** . . . We teach you to solve problem, essay, and objective questions using our unique and famous **SOLUTIONS APPROACH**™.

7. **Discussion and Development of** . . . AICPA grading procedures, grader orientation strategies, examination confidence, and examination success.

8. **Unique Objective Question Coverage and Unofficial Answers Updated** . . . We explain *why* the multiple choice alternatives are either right or wrong. Plus, we clearly indicate the changes that need to be made in the Unofficial Answers to correctly reflect current business and tax laws and AICPA, FASB, GASB, and other authoritative pronouncements.

9. **Writing Skills** . . . Financial Accounting & Reporting, Auditing, and Business Law & Professional Responsibilities contain a section to help you brush up on your writing skills for the CPA exam.

10. **Indexes** . . . We have included a comprehensively compiled index for easy topic reference in all four sections.

11. **Trend Analysis of Recent Exams** . . . We include short summaries of all essays and problems given on the most recent exams, to assist you in accurately pinpointing topics tested most frequently.

12. **Diagnostic Exam to Test Your Present Level of Knowledge** . . . And we include a **Final Exam** to test your exam preparedness under actual exam conditions. These testing materials are designed to help you single out for concentrated study the exam topic areas in which you are dangerously deficient.

Our materials are designed for the candidate who has previously studied accounting. Therefore, the rate at which a candidate studies and learns (not merely reads) our material will depend on a candidate's background and aptitude. Candidates who have been out of school for a period of years might need more time to study than recent graduates. The point to remember is that all the material you will need to know to pass the exam is here. All you need to do is apply yourself and learn this material at a rate that is appropriate to your situation. **As a final thought**, keep in mind that test confidence gained through disciplined preparation equals success.

iv

YOU WILL LEARN FROM OUR OUTSTANDING EXPERTS ... WITHOUT LEAVING YOUR HOME OR OFFICE.

Consulting Editor

MORTIMER M. CAPLIN, LL.B., J.S.D., LL.D., is a senior partner with the Washington D.C. law firm of Caplin and Drysdale. He served as Commissioner of the Internal Revenue Service and as a member of the President's Task Force on Taxation. He received the Alexander Hamilton Award (the highest award conferred by the Secretary of the Treasury) for outstanding and unusual leadership during service as a U.S. Commissioner of Internal Revenue. For more than 25 years, Mr. Caplin has been in private practice with his present law firm, and has served as adjunct professor for the University of Virginia Law School. He is a nationally acclaimed author of numerous articles on tax and corporate matters.

Consulting Editor

RICHARD M. FELDHEIM, M.B.A., J.D., LL.M., C.P.A. (NY), is a New York CPA as well as an attorney in New York and Arizona. He holds a Masters in Tax Law from New York University Law School. Mr. Feldheim is a member of the New York State Society of CPAs, AICPA, New York State Bar Association, Association of the Bar of the City of New York, Arizona Bar, and American Bar Association. His background includes practice as both a CPA with Price Waterhouse & Co. and as a Senior Partner with the Arizona law firm of Wentworth & Lundin. He has lectured for the AICPA, the Practicing Law Institute, Seton Hall University, and the University of Arizona.

Consulting Editor

WILLIAM J. MEURER, CPA (FL), is former Managing Partner for both the overall operations in Central Florida and the Florida Audit and Business Advisory Services sector of Arthur Andersen LLP. During his 35-year career with the firm, Mr. Meurer developed expertise in several industries, including high technology, financial services, real estate, retailing/distribution, manufacturing, hospitality, professional services, and cable television. A graduate of Regis University, he is a member of both the American Institute of CPAs and the Florida Society of CPAs.

Consulting Editor

THOMAS A. RATCLIFFE, Ph.D., C.P.A. (TX), is Dean of the Sorrell College of Business Administration and Eminent Scholar in Accounting and Finance at Troy State University. He has published more than 100 technical works in accounting and auditing and serves as consultant to several CPA firms. He received the Alabama Society of CPAs Outstanding Discussion Leader Award for six years (this award is now named the Thomas A. Ratcliffe Outstanding Discussion Leader Award) and the 1991 Outstanding Accounting Educator Award. Dr. Ratcliffe is 2001-2002 President of the Alabama Society of CPAs, serves on several committees, and is a past Council Representative. He was the 1991 President of the Southeast Alabama Chapter.

Consulting Editor

C. WILLIAM THOMAS, M.B.A., Ph.D., C.P.A. (TX), currently serves as J.E. Bush Professor and former Chair of the Department of Accounting and Business Law at Baylor University. He is a member of the AICPA, the Texas Society of CPAs, the Central Texas Chapter of CPAs, and the American Accounting Association, where he is past Chair for the Southwestern Regional Audit Section. Professor Thomas is a nationally known author and has extensive experience in Auditing CPA Review. In addition, he has received recognition for special audit education and curriculum projects he developed for Coopers & Lybrand. His background includes public accounting experience with KPMG Peat Marwick.

CHANGE ALERTS

SFAS 141, Business Combinations

In June 2001, the FASB issued SFAS 141, *Business Combinations*, requiring that the purchased method of accounting be used for all business combinations initiated after June 30, 2001. Use of the pooling-of-interests method Is prohIbIted. This statement supersedes APB Opinion No. 16, *Business Combinations*, and SFAS 38, *Accounting for Preacquisition Contingencies of Purchased Enterprises*.

Many of the provisions related to the application of the purchase method were not changed. However, accounting for business combinations is changed by this statement in the following significant respects:

- The purchase method is the only method of accounting for business combinations

- Intangible assets must be recognized as assets apart from goodwill if they meet one of two criteria: (1) the contractual-legal criterion or (2) the separability criterion. Previously, separate recognition of intangible assets was required when they could be identified and named.

- Additional disclosures are required, including the primary reasons for the combination and the allocation of the purchase price paid to the assets and liabilities assumed by major balance sheet caption.

- When the amounts of goodwill and intangible assets acquired are significant, disclosure of additional information is required, such as the amount of goodwill by reportable segment and the amount of the purchase price assigned to each major intangible asset class. (Chapter 20)

SFAS 142, Goodwill and Other Intangible Assets

In June 2001, the FASB issued SFAS 142, *Goodwill and Other Intangible Assets*, changing the accounting for goodwill from an amortization method to an impairment-only approach. Amortization of goodwill, including goodwill recorded in past business combinations, ceases upon adoption of SFAS 142, on or about January 1, 2002. (Chapter 5)

SFAS 143, Accounting for Asset Retirement Obligations

In June 2001, the FASB issued SFAS 143, *Accounting for Asset Retirement Obligations*. SFAS 143 is first eligible to be tested on the May 2002 exam; however, due to the specialized nature of its content, SFAS 143 is beyond the likely scope of future exams. SFAS 143 addresses accounting for costs and liabilities related to tangible long-term asset retirement. While it applies to all entities, the statement was developed to address oil and gas producing companies in particular. SFAS 143 is effective for fiscal years beginning after June 15, 2002, with earlier application encouraged. (Chapter 7)

SFAS 144, *Accounting for the Impairment or Disposal of Long-Lived Assets*

In October 2001, the FASB issued SFAS 144, *Accounting for the Impairment or Disposal of Long-Lived Assets*. This statement amends APB Opinion 30, *Reporting the Results of Operations—Reporting the Effects of Disposal of a Segment of a Business, and Extraordinary, Unusual and Infrequently Occurring Events and Transactions,* and ARB 51, *Consolidated Financial Statements.* SFAS 144 supercedes SFAS 121, *Accounting for the Impairment of Long-Lived Assets and for Long-Lived Assets to Be Disposed of* and EITF Issue No. 95-18, *Accounting and Reporting for a Discontinued Business Segment When the Measurement Date Occurs after the Balance Sheet Date but Before the Issuance of Financial Statements.* As this guidance is effective for fiscal periods beginning after December 15, 2001, with early application encouraged, SFAS 144 is eligible to be tested starting with the **May 2002** exam. Superceded guidance is also eligible to be tested on the May 2002 exam.

FINANCIAL ACCOUNTING & REPORTING

VOLUME I of IV

TABLE OF CONTENTS

QUICK TEXT REFERENCE

The editors strongly recommend that candidates read the entire **Getting Started** and **Practical Advice** sections of this volume, unless they have already read these sections in the *Financial Accounting & Reporting* volume. The references on this page are only intended for conveniently relocating selected parts of the volume. Add items to this list that you find yourself revisiting frequently.

VIDEOTAPE CROSS REFERENCE

The videotapes are designed to supplement all of our study packages. They contain concise, informative lectures, as well as CPA exam tips, tricks, and techniques to help you learn the material needed to pass the exam. The **HotSpots**™ videotapes concentrate on particular topics. Use them to study the areas that are most troubling for you. Each one of the **Intensive** video programs covers one of the four exam sections. The **Intensive** videotapes are designed for final, intensive review, after you already have done considerable work. Alternatively, the **Intensive** videotapes may be used as both a preview and a final review. Please see the information in the **Getting Started** section of this volume for a discussion on integrating videos into your study plan. This information is accurate as we go to press, but it is subject to change without notice.

Video Title	Text Chapters	Approx. Time
HotSpots™ Assets	2, 4, 5	4:15
HotSpots™ Inventory	3	2:25
HotSpots™ Bonds & Other Liabilities	6, 7	4:00
HotSpots™ Leases & Pensions	8, 9	2:50
HotSpots™ Owners' Equity	10	2:50
HotSpots™ Revenue Recognition & Income Statement Presentation	11, 12	3:00
HotSpots™ FASB 109: Accounting for Income Taxes	13	2:00
HotSpots™ FASB 95: Statement of Cash Flows	14	2:00
HotSpots™ EPS & Everything Else	15 - 18	3:00
HotSpots™ Consolidations	19, 20	5:00
HotSpots™ Governmental & Nonprofit Accounting	21 - 23	5:40
HotSpots™ Cost & Managerial Accounting	24 - 26	3:20
HotSpots™ General Taxation	27, 29	3:00
HotSpots™ Individual Taxation	27	3:00
HotSpots™ Property Taxation	28	2:30
HotSpots™ Corporate Taxation	29	3:20
HotSpots™ Partnerships & Other Tax Topics	30	3:00
HotSpots™ Audit Planning & Standards	31, 32	3:05
HotSpots™ Internal Control	33, 34	2:10
HotSpots™ Audit Evidence	35, 36	2:25
HotSpots™ EDP Auditing & Statistical Sampling	37, 38	2:50
HotSpots™ Standard Audit Reports	39	2:55
HotSpots™ Other Reports, Reviews & Compilations	40, 41	1:50
HotSpots™ Contracts	44	2:35
HotSpots™ Sales	45	2:00
HotSpots™ Commercial Paper & Documents of Title	46	2:00
HotSpots™ Secured Transactions	47	1:10
HotSpots™ Bankruptcy & Suretyship	48, 49	1:30
HotSpots™ Business Organizations	50 - 53	2:15
HotSpots™ Government Regulation of Business	54, 55	1:20
HotSpots™ Real Property, Personal Property & Insurance	56, 57	1:45
HotSpots™ Professional & Legal Responsibilities	42, 43	1:30

Intensive Video Review	FARE	ARE	AUD	BLPR	Total
Text Chapters	1 - 20	21 - 30	31 - 41	42 - 57	
Approximate Time	6:00	6:00	3:30	3:30	19:00

Using Videos to Study

Actively watch video classes, taking notes and answering questions as if it were a live class. If the lecturer recommends you to work an example as the video plays, write the numbers in the viewer guide, rather than merely following along. If the lecturer instructs you to stop the tape to answer questions, stop the tape. If the lecturer advises you to take notes, personalize your copy of the viewer guide. The lecturers provide these instructions with the insight gained from years of CPA review experience.

Each of the Hot•Spot™ videotapes concentrates on a few topics. Use them to help you study the areas that are most troubling for you. If you are strong in a topic, watching the video and answering the questions may be sufficient review. If your strength is moderate in a topic, you should probably read the related text before watching the video. If you are weak in a topic, one successful strategy is to watch the video (including following all of the lecturer's instructions), read the book, and then watch the video again.

Each of the Intensive videotapes are designed for a final, intensive review, after a candidate has already done considerable work. If time permits, use the Intensive tapes at both the very beginning (for an overview) and set them aside until the final review in week 19. They contain concise, informative lectures, as well as CPA exam tips, tricks, and techniques that will help you to learn the material needed to pass the exam.

FYI: The Hot*Spot and Intensive videotapes have similar content as the audio and online video lectures, but they are not exactly the same.

FOREWORD: GETTING STARTED

STEP ONE: **READ PART ONE OF THE PRACTICAL ADVICE SECTION**

Part One of the **Practical Advice** section (Appendix B) is designed to familiarize you with the CPA Examination. Included in **Practical Advice** are general comments about the exam, a schedule of exam dates, addresses and numbers of state boards of accountancy, and attributes required for exam success.

STEP TWO: **TAKE THE DIAGNOSTIC EXAMS**

The diagnostic exam in this foreword is designed to help you determine your strong and weak areas. This in turn will help you design your personalized training plan so that you spend more time in your weak areas and do not waste precious study time in areas where you are already strong. You can take the exams using either the books or CPA Review Software for Windows™. The books provide you with a worksheet that makes self-diagnosis fast and easy. CPA Review Software for Windows will automatically score your exams for you and give you a personalized analysis of your strong and weak areas.

NOTE: If you took a previous CPA exam and passed some but not all the sections, also analyze these exam sections to help you determine where you need to concentrate your efforts this time.

NOTE: If you purchase a package that includes software, you will also want to go through all of the software tutorials prior to beginning intensive study. They are each only a few minutes long, but they are loaded with valuable information. There is simply no better way to prepare yourself to study.

STEP THREE: **DEVELOP A PERSONALIZED TRAINING PLAN**

Based on the results from your diagnostic exams, develop your personalized training plan. If you are taking the exam for the first time, and you are the "average" CPA candidate, we recommend that you train for 20 weeks at a minimum of 20 hours per week. This level of intensity should increase during the final four weeks of your training and peak at a minimum of 40 hours the final week before the exam. Designed to complete your study program, our Intensive Video Series is a concentrated and effective "cram course" that targets the information you must know to pass. The videos will refresh your memory on subjects you covered weeks earlier and clarify topics you haven't yet fully grasped.

If you took the exam previously and did not condition (you still have to take all four sections), and you are the "average" CPA candidate, we recommend that you train for 12 weeks at a minimum of 20 hours per week. Again, this level of intensity should increase during the final four weeks of your training and peak during the final week before the exam. If you have conditioned (you have to take three or less sections), you can adjust these guidelines accordingly.

You may wonder what we mean by an "average" candidate. We are referring to a candidate who is just finishing or has just finished his or her academic training, attended a school that has a solid accounting curriculum, and received above average grades in accounting and business law courses. (An "average" candidate's native language is English.) Remember, "average" is a benchmark. Many candidates are not "average," so adjust your training plan accordingly.

TIME AVAILABILITY

	MON	TUES	WED	THURS	FRI	SAT	SUN
1:00 AM							
2:00 AM							
3:00 AM							
4:00 AM							
5:00 AM							
6:00 AM							
7:00 AM							
8:00 AM							
9:00 AM							
10:00 AM							
11:00 AM							
12:00 PM							
1:00 PM							
2:00 PM							
3:00 PM							
4:00 PM							
5:00 PM							
6:00 PM							
7:00 PM							
8:00 PM							
9:00 PM							
10:00 PM							
11:00 PM							
12:00 AM							

How to Find 20 Hours a Week to Study

The typical CPA candidate is a very busy individual. He or she goes to school and/or works full or part time. Some candidates have additional responsibilities such as a spouse, children, a house to take care of—the list can go on and on. Consequently, your first reaction may be, "I don't have 20 hours a week to devote to training for the CPA exam." Using the chart on the previous page, we will show you how to "find" the time that you need to develop your training schedule.

1. Keeping in mind what you would consider to be a typical week, first mark out in black the time that you know you won't be able to study. For example, mark an "X" in each block which represents time that you normally sleep, have a class, work, or have some other type of commitment. Be realistic.

2. Next, in a different color, put a "C" in each block that represents commute time, an "M" in each block that represents when you normally eat, and an "E" in each block that represents when you exercise.

3. Now pick one hour each day to relax and give your mind a break. Write "BREAK" in one block for each day. Do not skip this step. By taking a break, you will study more efficiently and effectively.

4. In a third color, write "STUDY" in the remaining blocks. Count the "STUDY" blocks. Are there 20? If not, count your "C", "M", and "E" blocks; if needed, these blocks of time can be used to gain additional study time by using Bisk Education CPA Review audio tapes and videotapes. For example, our audios are ideal for candidates on the go, you can listen to them whenever you're in the car or exercising and gain valuable study time each week.

5. If you still do not have 20 "STUDY" blocks, and you scored 70% or more on your diagnostic exams, you may still be able to pass the exam even with your limited study time. If, however, you scored less than 70% on your diagnostic exams, you have 2 options: (1) re-prioritize and make a block that has an "X" in it available study time; or (2) concentrate on conditioning (passing some but not all of the sections) instead of on passing the entire exam. Before you choose to condition, check with your state board about the details. A drastic solution is to skip the managerial portion of the ARE section of the exam if you are extremely pressed. Ordinarily, we do not recommend this strategy.

How to Allocate Your 20 Weeks

Develop your overall training plan. We outline a recommended training plan based on 20 hours per week and 20 weeks of study. The time allocated to each topic was based on the length of the chapter, the difficulty of the material, and how heavily the topic is tested on the exam (refer to the exam specifications and our frequency analysis found in the **Practical Advice** section of your book). Keep in mind that this plan is for the "average" CPA candidate. You should customize this plan based on the results of your diagnostic exams and level of knowledge in each area tested. **Warning:** When studying, be careful not to fall into the trap of spending too much time on an area that is rarely tested on the exam. **NOTE:** For each week listed below there are corresponding Hot•Spot videos and audio tapes for more in-depth study. Call 1-888-CPA-BISK.

Recommended Training Plan (all 4 sections)*

		Hours
Week 1:	READ **GETTING STARTED** AND **PRACTICAL ADVICE** SECTIONS	1
	TAKE DIAGNOSTIC EXAMS	10
	GET ORGANIZED	2
	READ **ACCOUNTING FOR 5%** SECTION	1
	CHAPTER 1—OVERVIEW OF FINANCIAL ACCOUNTING & REPORTING	2
	CHAPTER 2—CASH, SHORT-TERM INVESTMENTS, & RECEIVABLES	4

* Candidates should make modifications to suit their individual circumstances. For instance, this training plan repeats Chapter 21. Candidates may not need to return to Chapter 21, particularly those who took a governmental accounting course.

		Hours
WEEK 2:	CHAPTER 2—CASH, SHORT-TERM INVESTMENTS & RECEIVABLES	3
	CHAPTER 3—INVENTORIES	5
	CHAPTER 4—PROPERTY, PLANT & EQUIPMENT	5
	CHAPTER 5—INTANGIBLES, R&D COSTS & OTHER ASSETS	4
	CHAPTER 6—BONDS	3
WEEK 3:	WEEKLY REVIEW OF WEEKS 1 - 2	2
	CHAPTER 6—BONDS	2
	CHAPTER 7—LIABILITIES	6
	CHAPTER 8—LEASES	5
	CHAPTER 9—PENSIONS & OTHER POSTRETIREMENT BENEFITS	5
WEEK 4:	WEEKLY REVIEW OF WEEKS 1 - 3	1
	CHAPTER 10—OWNERS' EQUITY	7
	CHAPTER 31—STANDARDS & RELATED TOPICS	4
	CHAPTER 32—PLANNING	6
	CHAPTER 33—INTERNAL CONTROL: GENERAL	2
WEEK 5:	WEEKLY REVIEW OF WEEKS 1 - 4	2
	CHAPTER 33—INTERNAL CONTROL: GENERAL	4
	CHAPTER 34—INTERNAL CONTROL: TRANSACTION CYCLES	4
	CHAPTERS 35—EVIDENCE & PROCEDURES	6
	CHAPTERS 36—AUDIT PROGRAMS	4
WEEK 6:	WEEKLY REVIEW OF WEEKS 1 - 5	2
	CHAPTER 11—REPORTING THE RESULTS OF OPERATIONS	11
	CHAPTER 37—AUDIT SAMPLING PROCEDURES	3
	CHAPTER 38—AUDITING EDP SYSTEMS	4
WEEK 7:	WEEKLY REVIEW OF WEEKS 1 - 6	1
	CHAPTER 12—REVENUE & EXPENSE RECOGNITION: SPECIAL AREAS	6
	CHAPTER 39—REPORTS ON AUDITED FINANCIAL STMTS	9
	CHAPTER 40—OTHER TYPES OF REPORTS	4
WEEK 8:	WEEKLY REVIEW OF WEEKS 1 - 7	2
	CHAPTER 13—ACCOUNTING FOR INCOME TAXES	5
	CHAPTER 14—STATEMENT OF CASH FLOWS	7
	CHAPTER 15—FINANCIAL STATEMENT ANALYSIS & EPS	4
	CHAPTER 40—OTHER TYPES OF REPORTS	2
WEEK 9:	WEEKLY REVIEW OF WEEKS 1 - 8	2
	CHAPTER 16—FINANCIAL REPORTING & CHANGING PRICES	2
	CHAPTER 17—FOREIGN OPERATIONS	3
	CHAPTER 18—PARTNERSHIPS & PERSONAL F/S	3
	CHAPTER 19—INVESTMENTS IN EQUITY SECURITIES	3
	CHAPTER 41—OTHER PROFESSIONAL SERVICES	7
WEEK 10:	WEEKLY REVIEW OF WEEKS 1 - 9	2
	OVERALL REVIEW OF AUDITING	3
	CHAPTER 20—CONSOLIDATED F/S	12
	CHAPTER 21—GOVERNMENTAL OVERVIEW	3

		Hours
Week 11:	OVERALL REVIEW OF FINANCIAL ACCOUNTING & REPORTING	6
	CHAPTER 22—GOVERNMENTAL FUNDS & ACCOUNT GROUPS	7
	CHAPTER 42—ACCOUNTANT'S PROFESSIONAL RESPONSIBILITIES	3
	CHAPTER 43—ACCOUNTANT'S LEGAL RESPONSIBILITIES	4
Week 12:	WEEKLY REVIEW OF WEEKS 1 - 11	4
	CHAPTER 21—GOVERNMENTAL OVERVIEW	3
	CHAPTER 23—NONPROFIT ACCOUNTING	7
	CHAPTER 44—CONTRACTS	6
Week 13:	WEEKLY REVIEW OF WEEKS 1 - 12	4
	CHAPTER 24—DECISION MAKING	4
	CHAPTER 25—COST ACCOUNTING	4
	CHAPTER 44—CONTRACTS	2
	CHAPTER 45—SALES	6
Week 14:	WEEKLY REVIEW OF WEEKS 1 - 13	3
	CHAPTER 27—DECISION MAKING	1
	CHAPTER 26—PLANNING & CONTROL	5
	CHAPTER 28—FEDERAL TAXATION: PROPERTY	5
	CHAPTER 46—NEGOTIABLE INSTRUMENTS	3
	CHAPTER 47—SECURED TRANSACTIONS & DOCUMENTS OF TITLE	3
Week 15:	WEEKLY REVIEW OF WEEKS 1 - 14	3
	CHAPTER 27—FEDERAL TAXATION: INDIVIDUALS	10
	CHAPTER 48—BANKRUPTCY	4
	CHAPTER 49—DEBTORS, CREDITORS & GUARANTORS	3
Week 16:	WEEKLY REVIEW OF WEEKS 1 - 15	3+
	CHAPTER 29—FEDERAL TAXATION: CORPORATIONS	10
	CHAPTER 50—AGENCY	3
	CHAPTER 51—PARTNERSHIPS	4
Week 17:	WEEKLY REVIEW OF WEEKS 1 - 16	4+
	CHAPTER 30—FEDERAL TAXATION: PARTNERSHIPS & OTHER TOPICS	10
	CHAPTER 52—CORPORATIONS	3
	CHAPTER 53—ESTATES & TRUSTS	3
Week 18:	WEEKLY REVIEW OF WEEKS 1 - 17	2+
	CHAPTER 54—EMPLOYMENT & ENVIRONMENTAL REGULATION	2
	CHAPTER 55—FEDERAL SECURITIES REGULATION	4
	CHAPTER 56—REAL & PERSONAL PROPERTY	4
	CHAPTER 57—FIRE & CASUALTY INSURANCE	1
	OVERALL REVIEW OF ACCOUNTING & REPORTING	4
	OVERALL REVIEW OF BUSINESS LAW & PROFESSIONAL RESPONS.	3
Week 19:	REVIEW AREAS IN WHICH YOU STILL FEEL WEAK	20+
Week 20:	TAKE FINAL EXAMS UNDER EXAM CONDITIONS	10
	DO FINAL REVIEWS	10+

Your Personalized Training Plan:

WEEK	TASK	DIAGNOSTIC SCORE	EST. HOURS	DATE COMPLETE	CHAPTER SCORE	FINAL SCORE
1						
2						
3						
4						
5						
6						
7						
8						
9						

WEEK	TASK	DIAGNOSTIC SCORE	EST. HOURS	DATE COMPLETE	CHAPTER SCORE	FINAL SCORE
10						
11						
12						
13						
14						
15						
16						
17						

WEEK	TASK	DIAGNOSTIC SCORE	EST. HOURS	DATE COMPLETE	CHAPTER SCORE	FINAL SCORE
18						
19						
20						

STEP FOUR: READ THE REST OF THE PRACTICAL ADVICE SECTION

Part Two of the **Practical Advice** section of the book will familiarize you with how the CPA examination is graded and tell you how you can earn extra points on the exam simply by knowing what the grader is going to seek. In addition, in Part Three we explain our Solutions Approach™, an approach that will help you maximize your grade. In Part Four, we discuss examination strategies. In Part Five, we provide information on the AICPA exam content specifications and point distribution.

STEP FIVE: INTEGRATE YOUR REVIEW MATERIALS

In this step, we demonstrate how to integrate the Bisk Education CPA Review products to optimize the effectiveness of your training plan. Find and read the section that corresponds to the package that you purchased. (To facilitate easy reference to your package guidance, you may want to strike through the sections corresponding to other packages.)

VIDEOTAPES

The videotapes are designed to supplement all of the study packages. Note how we recommend using the audiotapes in the following review plans. These recommendations also apply to the videotape programs. FYI: The videotapes have similar content as the online video lectures, but they are not exactly the same. Each of the Hot•Spot™ videotapes concentrates on a few topics. Use them to help you study the areas that are most troubling for you. Each of the Intensive videotapes are designed for a final, intensive review, after a candidate has already done considerable work. If time permits, use the Intensive tapes at both the very beginning (for an overview) and set them aside until the final review in week 19. They contain concise, informative lectures, as well as CPA exam tips, tricks, and techniques that will help you to learn the material needed to pass the exam.

ONLINE PACKAGE: BOOKS, VIDEO LECTURES, AND CPA SOFTWARE FOR WINDOWS

This is our most comprehensive review package. This combination provides the personal advice, discipline, and camaraderie of a classroom setting with the convenience of self-study. It is intended for those candidates who want to make sure that they pass the exam the **first** time. By using this package, you are eligible to qualify for Bisk Education's money-back guarantee. Contact a customer representative for details on the components of this package. Contact your online faculty advisor if you have questions about integrating your materials after viewing the web site guidance. The editors strongly recommend that candidates working full-time take a maximum of 2 sections per six-week session.)

BOOKS, AUDIOTAPES, AND CPA REVIEW SOFTWARE FOR WINDOWS

This is our most comprehensive self-study review package. This combination is designed expressly for the serious CPA candidate. It is intended for those candidates who want to make sure that they pass the exam the **first** time (or *this* time, if you have already taken the exam). In addition, by using this package, you are eligible to qualify for Bisk Education's money-back guarantee.

How to Use This Package:

1. First take the diagnostic exams using CPA Review Software for Windows™. CPA Review Software for Windows™ automatically scores your exams and tells you what your strong and weak areas are.

In chapters where you are strong (i.e., you scored 65% or better on the diagnostic exam):

2. Answer the objective questions using CPA Review Software for Windows™.

3. Read the subsections of the chapter that correspond to your weak areas.

4. Listen to the audiotape for topics covered in this chapter to reinforce your weak areas and review your strong areas.

5. Now, using CPA Review Software for Windows™, answer the objective questions that you previously answered incorrectly. If you answer 70% or more of the questions correctly, you are ready to move to the next chapter. If you answer less than 70% of the questions correctly, handle this chapter as if you scored less than 65% on the diagnostic exam.

6. Answer the related essay questions.

In chapters where you are weak (i.e., you scored less than 65% on the diagnostic exam):

2. Read the chapter in the book.

3. Listen to the audiotape lectures on topics covered in the chapter.

4. Re-read the subsections of the chapter that correspond to your weak subtopics.

5. Using CPA Review Software for Windows™, answer the objective questions for this chapter. If you answer 70% or more of the questions correctly, you are ready to move on to the next chapter. If you get less than 70% of the questions correct, review the subtopics where you are weak. Then answer the questions that you previously answered incorrectly. If you still do not get at least 70% correct, check the exam specification and frequency charts in the Practical Advice section to find out how heavily the area is tested. If this is an area that is heavily tested, continue reviewing the material and answering multiple choice questions until you can answer at least 70% correctly. Allocate more time than you originally budgeted, if necessary. If this is not a heavily tested area, move on, but make a note to come back to this area later as time allows.

6.   Answer the related essay questions.

BOOKS AND CPA REVIEW SOFTWARE FOR WINDOWS™

This combination allows you to use the books to review the material and CPA Review Software for Windows™ to practice exam questions. You can also use the books to practice exam questions when you do not have access to a computer. In addition, by using this package, you are eligible to qualify for Bisk Education's money-back guarantee.

How to Use This Package:

1.   Take the diagnostic exams using CPA Review Software for Windows™. CPA Review Software for Windows automatically scores your exams and tells you what your strong and weak areas are.

In chapters where you are strong (i.e., you scored 65% or better on the diagnostic exam):

2.   Answer the objective questions using CPA Review Software for Windows™.

3.   Read the subsections of the chapter that correspond to your weak areas.

4.   Now using CPA Review Software for Windows™, answer the objective questions that you previously answered incorrectly. If you answer 70% or more of the questions correctly, you are ready to move on to the next chapter. If you answer less than 70% of the questions correctly, handle this chapter as if you scored less than 65% on the diagnostic exam.

5.   Answer the related essay questions.

In chapters where you are weak (i.e., you scored less than 65% on the diagnostic exam):

2.   Read the chapter in the book.

3.   Using CPA Review Software for Windows™, answer the objective questions for this chapter. If you answer 70% or more of the questions correctly, you are ready to move on to the next chapter. If you get less than 70% of the questions correct, review the subtopics where you are weak. Then answer the questions that you previously answered incorrectly. If you still do not get at least 70% correct, check the exam specification and frequency charts in the Practical Advice section to find out how heavily the area is tested. If this is an area that is heavily tested, continue reviewing the material and answering multiple choice questions until you can answer at least 70% correctly. Allocate more time than you originally budgeted, if necessary. If this is not a heavily tested area, move on, but make a note to come back to this area later as time allows.

4.   Answer the related essay questions.

BOOKS AND AUDIOTAPES

This combination is designed for the candidate who does not have access to a computer to study, who spends time commuting or doing other activities that could take valuable time away from studying, and for those who like to reinforce what they read by listening to a lecture on tape.

How to Use This Package:

1.   Take the diagnostic exams found in your book. Using the worksheets provided, score your exams to determine your strong and weak areas.

In chapters where you are strong (i.e., you scored 65% or better on the diagnostic exam):

2. Do the objective questions for that chapter. Using the worksheet provided, analyze your strong and weak areas.

3. Read the subsections of the chapter that correspond to your weak subtopics.

4. At this point, listen to the audiotape on topics covered in this chapter to reinforce weak areas and review strong areas.

5. Answer the objective questions that you previously answered incorrectly. If you answer 70% or more of the questions correctly, you are ready to move on to the next chapter. If you answer less than 70% of the questions correctly, handle this chapter as if you scored 65% or less on the diagnostic exam.

6. Answer at least one essay question (if there are any) and review any other essay questions and solutions.

In chapters where you are weak (i.e., you scored less than 65% on the diagnostic exam):

2. First read the chapter in the book.

3. Now listen to the audiotape lectures covering topics in this chapter.

4. Re-read the subsections of the chapter that correspond to your weak subtopics.

5. Do the objective questions and score yourself using the worksheet provided. If you answer 70% or more of the questions correctly, you are ready to move on to the next chapter. If you answer less than 70% of the questions correctly, review the subtopics that are still giving you trouble. Then answer the questions that you have previously answered incorrectly. If you still do not get at least 70% of the questions correct, check the exam specification and frequency charts in the Practical Advice section to find out how heavily this area is tested. If this is an area that is heavily tested, continue reviewing the material and answering questions until you can answer at least 70% of them correctly. Allocate more time than you originally budgeted for if necessary. If this area is not heavily tested, move on, but make a note to come back to this topic later as time allows.

6. Answer at least one essay question (if there are any) and review any other essay questions and solutions.

STEP SIX: USE THESE HELPFUL HINTS AS YOU STUDY

♦   SPEND YOUR WEEKLY REVIEW TIME EFFECTIVELY. DURING EACH WEEKLY REVIEW:

Answer the objective questions that you previously answered incorrectly or merely guessed correctly.

Read through your notes.

Pick one essay question or problem to work. (Do not wait until the end of your 20 weeks to attempt the essay questions.) Read the other essay and problem questions and solutions.

Go through your flashcards.

♦ DO NOT MARK THE OBJECTIVE QUESTION ANSWERS IN THE BOOK.

Do not circle the answer to objective questions in the book. You should work every multiple-choice question at least twice and you do not want to influence your later answers by knowing how you previously answered the question.

♦ MARK THE OBJECTIVE QUESTIONS THAT YOU ANSWER INCORRECTLY OR MERELY GUESS CORRECTLY.

This way you know to answer this question again at a later time.

♦ MAKE NOTES AS YOU STUDY

Make notes and/or highlight when you read the chapters in the book. When possible, make notes when you listen to the tapes. You will find these very useful for weekly reviews and your final review.

♦ MAKE FLASHCARDS

Make flashcards for topics that are heavily tested on the exam or that are giving you trouble. By making your own flashcards, you can tailor them to your individual learning style and problem areas. You will find these very useful for weekly reviews and your final review. Replace flashcards of information you know with new material as you progress through your study plan. Keep these handy and review them when you are waiting in line or on hold. This will turn nonproductive time into valuable study time. Review your complete set during the last two weeks before the exam.

♦ EFFECTIVELY USE THE VIDEOTAPES

Watch the videotapes in an environment without distractions. Be prepared to take notes and answer questions just as if you were attending a live class. Frequently, the instructors will have you stop the tape to work a question on your own. This means a 2-hour tape may take 2½ hours or more to view.

♦ EFFECTIVELY USE THE AUDIOTAPES

Use these tapes to turn nonproductive time into valuable study time. For example, play the tapes when you are commuting, exercising, getting ready for school or work, doing laundry, etc. The tapes will help you to memorize and retain key concepts. They will also reinforce what you have read in the books. Get in the habit of listening to the tapes whenever you have a chance. The more times that you listen to each tape, the more familiar you will become with the material and the easier it will be for you to recall it during the exam.

STEP SEVEN: IMPLEMENT YOUR TRAINING PLAN

This is it! You are primed and ready. You have decided which training tools will work best for you and you know how to use them. As you implement your personalized training plan, keep yourself focused. Your goal is to obtain a grade of 75 or better on each section and, thus, pass the CPA exam. Therefore, you should concentrate on learning new material and reviewing old material only to the extent that it helps you reach this goal. Also, keep in mind that now is not the time to hone your procrastination skills. Utilize the personalized training plan that you developed in step three so that you do not fall behind schedule. Adjust it when necessary if you need more time in one chapter or less time in another. Refer to the AICPA content specification and the frequency analysis to make sure that the adjustment is warranted. Above all else, remember that passing the exam is an **attainable** goal. Good luck!

***

DIAGNOSTIC EXAMINATION

NUMBER 1 MULTIPLE CHOICE QUESTIONS (120 to 150 minutes)

1. What is the underlying concept that supports the immediate recognition of a contingent loss?
a. Substance over form
b. Consistency
c. Matching
d. Conservatism   (11/94, FAR, #3, 5268)

2. One of the elements of a financial statement is comprehensive income. Comprehensive income excludes changes in equity resulting from which of the following?
a. Loss from discontinued operations
b. Prior period error correction
c. Dividends paid to stockholders
d. Unrealized loss on investments in noncurrent marketable equity securities
          (5/95, FAR, #2, 5538)

3. According to the FASB conceptual framework, the usefulness of providing information in financial statements is subject to the constraint of
a. Consistency.
b. Cost-benefit.
c. Reliability.
d. Representational faithfulness.
          (11/95, FAR, #2, 6084)

4. The following information pertains to Grey Co. at December 31, 2003:

Checkbook balance	$12,000
Bank statement balance	16,000
Check drawn on Grey's account, payable to a vendor, dated and recorded 12/31/03 but not mailed until 1/10/04	1,800

On Grey's December 31, 2003 balance sheet, what amount should be reported as cash?
a. $12,000
b. $13,800
c. $14,200
d. $16,000   (5/94, FAR, #12, amended, 4827)

5. A company decided to change its inventory valuation method from FIFO to LIFO in a period of rising prices. What was the result of the change on ending inventory and net income in the year of the change?

	Ending inventory	Net income
a.	Increase	Increase
b.	Increase	Decrease
c.	Decrease	Decrease
d.	Decrease	Increase

          (11/95, FAR, #9, 6091)

6. Walt Co. adopted the dollar-value LIFO inventory method as of January 1, 2004, when its inventory was valued at $500,000. Walt's entire inventory constitutes a single pool. Using a relevant price index of 1.10, Walt determined that its December 31, 2004, inventory was $577,500 at current year cost, and $525,000 at base year cost. What was Walt's dollar-value LIFO inventory at December 31, 2004?
a. $525,000
b. $527,500
c. $552,500
d. $577,500   (5/95, FAR, #11, amended, 5547)

7. Herc Co.'s inventory at December 31, 2003, was $1,500,000, based on a physical count priced at cost, and before any necessary adjustment for the following:

- Merchandise costing $90,000, shipped F.O.B. shipping point from a vendor on December 30, 2003, was received and recorded on January 5, 2004.
- Goods in the shipping area were excluded from inventory although shipment was not made until January 4, 2004. The goods, billed to the customer F.O.B. shipping point on December 30, 2003, had a cost of $120,000.

What amount should Herc report as inventory in its December 31, 2003 balance sheet?
a. $1,500,000
b. $1,590,000
c. $1,620,000
d. $1,710,000   (11/94, FAR, #13, amended, 5278)

8. Which of the following statements are correct when a company applying the lower-of-cost-or-market method reports its inventory at replacement cost?

I. The original cost is less than replacement cost.
II. The net realizable value is greater than replacement cost.

a. I only
b. II only
c. Both I and II
d. Neither I nor II   (11/94, FAR, #14, 5279)

9. Drew Co. uses the average cost inventory method for internal reporting purposes and LIFO for financial statement and income tax reporting. At December 31, 2002, the inventory was $375,000 using average cost and $320,000 using LIFO. The unadjusted credit balance in the LIFO Reserve account on December 31, 2002, was $35,000. What adjusting entry should Drew record to adjust from average cost to LIFO at December 31, 2002?

		Debit	Credit
a.	Cost of Goods Sold	$55,000	
	Inventory		$55,000
b.	Cost of Goods Sold	$55,000	
	LIFO Reserve		$55,000
c.	Cost of Goods Sold	$20,000	
	Inventory		$20,000
d.	Cost of Goods Sold	$20,000	
	LIFO Reserve		$20,000

(11/93, PI, #19, amended, 4388)

10. Estimates of price-level changes for specific inventories are required for which of the following inventory methods?
a. Conventional retail
b. Dollar-value LIFO
c. Weighted average cost
d. Average cost retail   (11/93, Theory, #3, 4508)

11. Jones Wholesalers stocks a changing variety of products. Which inventory costing method will be most likely to give Jones the lowest ending inventory when its product lines are subject to specific price increases?
a. Specific identification
b. Weighted average
c. Dollar-value LIFO
d. FIFO periodic   (11/92, Theory, #15, 3448)

12. Theoretically, which of the following costs incurred in connection with a machine purchased for use in a company's manufacturing operations would be capitalized?

	Insurance on machine while in transit	Testing and preparation of machine for use
a.	Yes	Yes
b.	Yes	No
c.	No	Yes
d.	No	No

(5/95, FAR, #12, 5548)

13. Turtle Co. purchased equipment on January 2, 2001, for $50,000. The equipment had an estimated five-year service life. Turtle's policy for five-year assets is to use the 200% double-declining depreciation method for the first two years of the asset's life, and then switch to the straight-line depreciation method. In its December 31, 2003 balance sheet, what amount should Turtle report as accumulated depreciation for equipment?
a. $30,000
b. $38,000
c. $39,200
d. $42,000   (5/94, FAR, #18, amended, 4833)

14. On January 1, 1998, Crater Inc. purchased equipment having an estimated salvage value equal to 20% of its original cost at the end of a 10-year life. The equipment was sold December 31, 2002, for 50% of its original cost. If the equipment's disposition resulted in a reported loss, which of the following depreciation methods did Crater use?
a. Double-declining-balance
b. Sum-of-the-years'-digits
c. Straight-line
d. Composite (5/93, Theory, #27, amended, 4215)

15. A machine with a 5-year estimated useful life and an estimated 10% salvage value was acquired on January 1, 1999. On December 31, 2002, accumulated depreciation, using the sum-of-the-years'-digits method, would be
a. (Original cost less salvage value) multiplied by 1/15.
b. (Original cost less salvage value) multiplied by 14/15.
c. Original cost multiplied by 14/15.
d. Original cost multiplied by 1/15.
(5/92, Theory, #16, amended, 2709)

16. During 2003, Burr Co. had the following transactions pertaining to its new office building:

Purchase price of land	$ 60,000
Legal fees for contracts to purchase land	2,000
Architects' fees	8,000
Demolition of old building on site	5,000
Sale of scrap from old building	3,000
Construction cost of new building (fully completed)	350,000

In Burr's December 31, 2003 balance sheet, what amounts should be reported as the cost of land and cost of building?

	Land	Building
a.	$60,000	$360,000
b.	$62,000	$360,000
c.	$64,000	$358,000
d.	$65,000	$362,000

(5/91, PI, #24, amended, 0931)

17. During 2004, Jase Co. incurred research and development costs of $136,000 in its laboratories relating to a patent that was granted on July 1, 2004. Costs of registering the patent equaled $34,000. The patent's legal life is 17 years, and its estimated economic life is 10 years. In its December 31, 2004 balance sheet, what amount should Jase report as patent, net of accumulated amortization?

a. $ 32,300
b. $ 33,000
c. $161,500
d. $165,000   (5/95, FAR, #13, amended, 5549)

18. Roro Inc. paid $7,200 to renew its only insurance policy for three years on March 1, 2005, the effective date of the policy. At March 31, 2005, Roro's unadjusted trial balance showed a balance of $300 for prepaid insurance and $7,200 for insurance expense. What amounts should be reported for prepaid insurance and insurance expense in Roro's financial statements for the three months ended March 31, 2005?

	Prepaid insurance	Insurance expense
a.	$7,000	$300
b.	$7,000	$500
c.	$7,200	$300
d.	$7,300	$200

(5/95, FAR, #14, amended, 5550)

19. On January 2, 2003, Rafa Co. purchased a franchise with a useful life of ten years for $50,000.

An additional franchise fee of 3% of franchise operation revenues must be paid each year to the franchisor. Revenues from franchise operations amounted to $400,000 during 2003. In its December 31, 2003 balance sheet, what amount should Rafa report as an intangible asset-franchise?

a. $33,000
b. $43,800
c. $45,000
d. $50,000   (5/94, FAR, #20, amended, 4835)

20. On July 1, 2004, Eagle Corp. issued 600 of its 10%, $1,000 bonds at 99 plus accrued interest. The bonds are dated April 1, 2004 and mature on April 1, 2014. Interest is payable semiannually on April 1 and October 1. What amount did Eagle receive from the bond issuance?

a. $579,000
b. $594,000
c. $600,000
d. $609,000
    (5/95, FAR, #19, amended, amended, 5555)

21. On January 2, 2004, Nast Co. issued 8% bonds with a face amount of $1,000,000 that mature on January 2, 2010. The bonds were issued to yield 12%, resulting in a discount of $150,000. Nast incorrectly used the straight-line method instead of the effective interest method to amortize the discount. How is the carrying amount of the bonds affected by the error?

	At December 31, 2004	At January 2, 2010
a.	Overstated	Understated
b.	Overstated	No effect
c.	Understated	Overstated
d.	Understated	No effect

(5/95, FAR, #20, amended, 5556)

22. On December 30, 2002, Fort Inc. issued 1,000 of its 8%, 10-year, $1,000 face value bonds with detachable stock warrants at par. Each bond carried a detachable warrant for one share of Fort's common stock at a specified option price of $25 per share. Immediately after issuance, the market value of the bonds without the warrants was $1,080,000 and the market value of the warrants was $120,000. In its December 31, 2002 balance sheet, what amount should Fort report as bonds payable?

a. $1,000,000
b. $ 975,000
c. $ 900,000
d. $ 880,000   (11/93, PI, #33, amended, 4402)

23. On July 31, 2003, Dome Co. issued $1,000,000 of 10%, 15-year bonds at par and used a portion of the proceeds to call its 600 outstanding 11%, $1,000 face value bonds, due on July 31, 2013, at 102. On that date, unamortized bond premium relating to the 11% bonds was $65,000. In its 2003 income statement, what amount should Dome report as gain or loss, before income taxes, from retirement of bonds?
a. $ 53,000 gain
b. $0
c. $(65,000) loss
d. $(77,000) loss
(11/94, FAR, #42, amended, 5304)

24. Cali Inc. had a $4,000,000 note payable due on March 15, 2005. On January 28, 2005, before the issuance of its 2004 financial statements, Cali issued long-term bonds in the amount of $4,500,000. Proceeds from the bonds were used to repay the note when it came due. How should Cali classify the note in its December 31, 2004 financial statements?
a. As a current liability, with separate disclosure of the note refinancing
b. As a current liability, with no separate disclosure required
c. As a noncurrent liability, with separate disclosure of the note refinancing
d. As a noncurrent liability, with no separate disclosure required
(5/95, FAR, #5, amended, 5541)

25. During January 2002, Haze Corp. won a litigation award for $15,000 which was tripled to $45,000 to include punitive damages. The defendant, who is financially stable, has appealed only the $30,000 punitive damages. Haze was awarded $50,000 in an unrelated suit it filed, which is being appealed by the defendant. Counsel is unable to estimate the outcome of these appeals. In its 2002 financial statements, Haze should report what amount of pretax gain?
a. $15,000
b. $45,000
c. $50,000
d. $95,000
(11/92, PII, #53, amended, 3387)

26. In its 2003 financial statements, Cris Co. reported interest expense of $85,000 in its income statement and cash paid for interest of $68,000 in its cash flow statement. There was no prepaid interest or interest capitalization either at the beginning or end of 2003. Accrued interest at December 31, 2002, was $15,000. What amount should Cris report as accrued interest payable in its December 31, 2003 balance sheet?
a. $ 2,000
b. $15,000
c. $17,000
d. $32,000
(11/94, FAR, #18, amended, 5282)

27. On January 2, 2005, Marx Co. as lessee signed a five-year noncancelable equipment lease with annual payments of $200,000 beginning December 31, 2005. Marx treated this transaction as a capital lease. The five lease payments have a present value of $758,00 at January 2, 2005, based on interest of 10%. What amount should Marx report as interest expense for the year ended December 31, 2005?
a. $0
b. $48,400
c. $55,800
d. $75,800
(5/96, FAR, #4, amended, 6277)

28. In the long-term liabilities section of its balance sheet at December 31, 2002, Mene Co. reported a capital lease obligation of $75,000, net of current portion of $1,364. Payments of $9,000 were made on both January 2, 2003, and January 2, 2004. Mene's incremental borrowing rate on the date of the lease was 11% and the lessor's implicit rate, which was known to Mene, was 10%. In its December 31, 2003 balance sheet, what amount should Mene report as capital lease obligation, net of current portion?
a. $66,000
b. $73,500
c. $73,636
d. $74,250
(5/94, FAR, #25, amended, 4840)

29. A company with a defined benefit pension plan must disclose in the notes to its financial statements a reconciliation of
a. The vested and nonvested benefit obligation of its pension plan with the accumulated benefit obligation.
b. The accrued or prepaid pension cost reported in its balance sheet with the pension expense reported in its income statement.
c. The accumulated benefit obligation of its pension plan with its projected benefit obligation.
d. The funded status of its pension plan with the accrued or prepaid pension cost reported in its balance sheet.
(5/95, FAR, #57, 5593)

30. The following information pertains to Hall Co.'s defined-benefit pension plan at December 31, 2004:

Unfunded accumulated benefit obligation $25,000
Unrecognized prior service cost 12,000
Net periodic pension cost 8,000

Hall made no contributions to the pension plan during 2004.

At December 31, 2004, what amount should Hall record as additional pension liability?
a. $ 5,000
b. $13,000
c. $17,000
d. $25,000   (11/95, FAR, #14, amended, 6096)

31. The following information pertains to Kane Co.'s defined benefit pension plan:

Prepaid pension cost, January 1, 2004 $ 2,000
Service cost 19,000
Interest cost 38,000
Actual return on plan assets 22,000
Amortization of unrecognized prior
    service cost 52,000
Employer contributions 40,000

The fair value of plan assets exceeds the accumulated benefit obligation. In its December 31, 2004 balance sheet, what amount should Kane report as unfunded accrued pension cost?
a. $45,000
b. $49,000
c. $67,000
d. $87,000   (5/95, FAR, #18, amended, 5554)

32. The following information pertains to Gali Co.'s defined benefit pension plan for 2004:

Fair value of plan assets, beginning
    of year $350,000
Fair value of plan assets, end of year 525,000
Employer contributions 110,000
Benefits paid 85,000

In computing pension expense, what amount should Gali use as actual return on plan assets?
a. $ 65,000
b. $150,000
c. $175,000
d. $260,000   (5/95, FAR, #39, amended, 5575)

33. The stockholders' equity section of Brown Co.'s December 31, 2004, balance sheet consisted of the following:

Common stock, $30 par, 10,000 shares
    authorized and outstanding $300,000
Additional paid-in capital 150,000
Retained earnings (deficit) (210,000)

On January 2, 2005, Brown put into effect a stock-holder-approved quasi-reorganization by reducing the par value of the stock to $5 and eliminating the deficit against additional paid-in capital. Immediately after the quasi-reorganization, what amount should Brown report as additional paid-in capital?
a. $ (60,000)
b. $150,000
c. $190,000
d. $400,000   (11/95, FAR, #25, amended, 6107)

34. Selected information from the accounts of Row Co. at December 31, 2005, follows:

Total income since incorporation $420,000
Total cash dividends paid 130,000
Total value of property dividends
    distributed 30,000
Excess of proceeds over cost of
    treasury stock sold, accounted
    for using the cost method 110,000

In its December 31, 2005, financial statements, what amount should Row report as retained earnings?
a. $260,000
b. $290,000
c. $370,000
d. $400,000   (5/96, FAR, #1, amended, 6274)

35. Nest Co. issued 100,000 shares of common stock. Of these, 5,000 were held as treasury stock at December 31, 2003. During 2004, transactions involving Nest's common stock were as follows:

May 3   — 1,000 shares of treasury stock
                were sold.
August 6   — 10,000 shares of previously
                unissued stock were sold.
November 18 — A 2-for-1 stock split took effect.

Laws in Nest's state of incorporation protect treasury stock from dilution. At December 31, 2004, how many shares of Nest's common stock were issued and outstanding?

	Shares	
---	Issued	Outstanding
a.	220,000	212,000
b.	220,000	216,000
c.	222,000	214,000
d.	222,000	218,000

(11/95, FAR, #18, amended, 6100)

36. East Co. issued 1,000 shares of its $5 par common stock to Howe as compensation for 1,000 hours of legal services performed. Howe usually bills $160 per hour for legal services. On the date of issuance, the stock was trading on a public exchange at $140 per share. By what amount should the additional paid-in capital account increase as a result of this transaction?
a. $135,000
b. $140,000
c. $155,000
d. $160,000   (11/94, FAR, #28, 5291)

37. Wand, Inc., has adopted FASB Statement No. 144, *Accounting for the Impairment or Disposal of Long-Lived Assets.* On October 1, 2003, Wand Inc. committed itself to a formal plan to sell its Kam division's assets. Wand estimated that the loss from the disposal of assets in February 2004 would be $25,000. Wand also estimated that Kam would incur operating losses of $100,000 for the period of October 1, through December 31, 2003, and $50,000 for the period January 1, 2004, through February 28, 2004. These estimates were materially correct. Disregarding income taxes, what should Wand report as loss from discontinued operations in its comparative 2003 and 2004 income statements?

	2003	2004
a.	$175,000	$0
b	$125,000	$ 50,000
c.	$100,000	$ 75,000
d.	$0	$175,000

(11/94, Theory, #52, amended, 5313)

38. In open market transactions, Gold Corp. simultaneously sold its long-term investment in Iron Corp. bonds and purchased its own outstanding bonds. The broker remitted the net cash from the two transactions. Gold's gain on the purchase of its own bonds exceeded its loss on the sale of the Iron bonds. Gold should report the
a. Net effect of the two transactions as an extraordinary gain.
b. Net effect of the two transactions in income before extraordinary items.
c. Effect of its own bond transaction gain in income before extraordinary items, and report the Iron bond transaction as an extraordinary loss.
d. Effect of its own bond transaction as an extraordinary gain, and report the Iron bond transaction loss in income before extraordinary items.
(11/95, FAR, #41, 6123)

39. For interim financial reporting, a company's income tax provision for the second quarter of 2002 should be determined using the
a. Effective tax rate expected to be applicable for the full year of 2002 as estimated at the end of the first quarter of 2002.
b. Effective tax rate expected to be applicable for the full year of 2002 as estimated at the end of the second quarter of 2002.
c. Effective tax rate expected to be applicable for the second quarter of 2002.
d. Statutory tax rate for 2002.
(11/93, Theory, #31, amended, 4536)

40. Rill Co. owns a 20% royalty interest in an oil well. Rill receives royalty payments on January 31 for the oil sold between the previous June 1 and November 30, and on July 31 for oil sold between the previous December 1 and May 31. Production reports show the following oil sales:

June 1, 2003—November 30, 2003	$300,000
December 1, 2003—December 31, 2003	50,000
December 1, 2003—May 31, 2004	400,000
June 1, 2004—November 30, 2004	325,000
December 1, 2004—December 31, 2004	70,000

What amount should Rill report as royalty revenue for 2004?
a. $140,000
b. $144,000
c. $149,000
d. $159,000   (11/95, FAR, #30, amended, 6112)

41. The following data pertains to Pell Co.'s construction jobs, which commenced during 2002:

	Project 1	Project 2
Contract price	$420,000	$300,000
Costs incurred during 2002	240,000	280,000
Estimated costs to complete	120,000	40,000
Billed to customers during 2002	150,000	270,000
Received from customers during 2002	90,000	250,000

If Pell used the completed-contract method, what amount of gross profit (loss) would Pell report in its 2002 income statement?
a. $ (20,000)
b. $0
c. $340,000
d. $420,000   (5/93, PI, #38, amended, 4079)

42. The following information pertains to a sale of real estate by Ryan Co. to Sud Co. on December 31, 2001:

Carrying amount		$2,000,000
Sales price:		
Cash	$ 300,000	
Purchase money mortgage	2,700,000	3,000,000

The mortgage is payable in nine annual installments of $300,000 beginning December 31, 2002, plus interest of 10%. The December 31, 2002 installment was paid as scheduled, together with interest of $270,000. Ryan uses the cost-recovery method to account for the sale. What amount of income should Ryan recognize in 2002 from the real estate sale and its financing?

a. $570,000
b. $370,000
c. $270,000
d. $0   (5/91, PI, #50, amended, 1317)

43. On its December 31, 2004, balance sheet, Shin Co. had income taxes payable of $13,000 and a current deferred tax asset of $20,000 before determining the need for a valuation account. Shin had reported a current deferred tax asset of $15,000 at December 31, 2003. No estimated tax payments were made during 2004. At December 31, 2004, Shin determined that it was more likely than not that 10% of the deferred tax asset would not be realized. In its 2004 income statement, what amount should Shin report as total income tax expense?

a. $ 8,000
b. $ 8,500
c. $10,000
d. $13,000   (11/95, FAR, #36, amended, 6118)

ITEMS 44 AND 45 are based on the following:

Zeff Co. prepared the following reconciliation of its pretax financial statement income to taxable income for the year ended December 31, 2004, its first year of operations:

Pretax financial income	$160,000
Nontaxable interest received on municipal securities	(5,000)
Long-term loss accrual in excess of deductible amount	10,000
Depreciation in excess of financial statement amount	(25,000)
Taxable income	$140,000

Zeff's tax rate for 2004 is 40%.

44. In its 2004 income statement, what amount should Zeff report as income tax expense—current portion?

a. $52,000
b. $56,000
c. $62,000
d. $64,000   (11/95, FAR, #37, amended, 6119)

45. In its December 31, 2004, balance sheet, what should Zeff report as deferred income tax liability?

a. $2,000
b. $4,000
c. $6,000
d. $8,000   (11/95, FAR, #38, amended, 6120)

46. As a result of differences between depreciation for financial reporting purposes and tax purposes, the financial reporting basis of Noor Co.'s sole depreciable asset, acquired in 2004, exceeded its tax basis by $250,000 at December 31, 2004. This difference will reverse in future years. The enacted tax rate is 30% for 2004, and 40% for future years. Noor has no other temporary differences. In its December 31, 2004 balance sheet, how should Noor report the deferred tax effect of this difference?

a. As an asset of $75,000
b. As an asset of $100,000
c. As a liability of $75,000
d. As a liability of $100,000
          (5/95, FAR, #16, amended, 5552)

47. For the year ended December 31, 2004, Tyre Co. reported pretax financial statement income of $750,000. Its taxable income was $650,000. The difference is due to accelerated depreciation for income tax purposes. Tyre's effective income tax rate is 30%, and Tyre made estimated tax payments during 2004 of $90,000. What amount should Tyre report as current income tax expense for 2004?

a. $105,000
b. $135,000
c. $195,000
d. $225,000   (5/95, FAR, #41, amended, 5577)

48. Quinn Co. reported a net deferred tax asset of $9,000 in its December 31, 2003 balance sheet. For 2004, Quinn reported pretax financial statement income of $300,000. Temporary differences of $100,000 resulted in taxable income of $200,000 for 2004. At December 31, 2004, Quinn had cumulative taxable differences of $70,000. Quinn's effective income tax rate is 30%. In its December 31, 2004 income statement, what should Quinn report as deferred income tax expense?
a. $12,000
b. $21,000
c. $30,000
d. $60,000   (5/95, FAR, #42, amended, 5578)

49. Which of the following information should be disclosed as supplemental information in the statement of cash flows?

	Cash flow per share	Conversion of debt to equity
a.	Yes	Yes
b.	Yes	No
c.	No	Yes
d.	No	No

           (5/95, FAR, #49, 5585)

ITEMS 50 AND 51 are based on the following:

In preparing its cash flow statement for the year ended December 31, 2004, Reve Co. collected the following data:

Gain on sale of equipment	$ (6,000)
Proceeds from sale of equipment	10,000
Purchase of A.S. Inc. bonds (par value $200,000)	(180,000)
Amortization of bond discount	2,000
Dividends declared	(45,000)
Dividends paid	(38,000)
Proceeds from sale of treasury stock (carrying amount $65,000)	75,000

In its December 31, 2004 statement of cash flows,

50. What amount should Reve report as net cash used in investing activities?
a. $170,000
b. $176,000
c. $188,000
d. $194,000   (5/95, FAR, #47, amended, 5583)

51. What amount should Reve report as net cash provided by financing activities?
a. $20,000
b. $27,000
c. $30,000
d. $37,000   (5/95, FAR, #48, amended, 5584)

52. Fara Co. reported bonds payable of $47,000 at December 31, 2002, and $50,000 at December 31, 2003. During 2003, Fara issued $20,000 of bonds payable in exchange for equipment. There was no amortization of bond premium or discount during the year. What amount should Fara report in its 2003 statement of cash flows for redemption of bonds payable?
a. $ 3,000
b. $17,000
c. $20,000
d. $23,000   (5/94, FAR, #50, amended, 4865)

53. The following data pertain to Cowl Inc. for the year ended December 31, 2004:

Net sales	$ 600,000
Net income	150,000
Total assets, January 1, 2004	2,000,000
Total assets, December 31, 2004	3,000,000

What was Cowl's rate of return on assets for 2004?
a. 5%
b. 6%
c. 20%
d. 24%   (11/95, FAR, #60, amended, 6142)

54. Ute Co. had the following capital structure during 2001 and 2002:

Preferred stock, $10 par, 4% cumulative, 25,000 shares issued and outstanding	$ 250,000
Common stock, $5 par, 200,000 shares issued and outstanding	1,000,000

Ute reported net income of $500,000 for the year ended December 31, 2002. Ute paid no preferred dividends during 2001 and paid $16,000 in preferred dividends during 2002. In its December 31, 2002, income statement, what amount should Ute report as earnings per share?
a. $2.42
b. $2.45
c. $2.48
d. $2.50   (11/95, FAR, #45, amended, 6127)

55. Financial statements prepared under which of the following methods include adjustments for both specific price changes and general price-level changes?
a. Historical cost/nominal dollar
b. Current cost/nominal dollar
c. Current cost/constant dollar
d. Historical cost/constant dollar
           (11/95, FAR, #57, 6139)

56. Fogg Co., a U.S. company, contracted to purchase foreign goods. Payment in foreign currency was due one month after the goods were received at Fogg's warehouse. Between the receipt of goods and the time of payment, the exchange rates changed in Fogg's favor. The resulting gain should be included in Fogg's financial statements as a(an)
a. Component of income from continuing operations.
b. Extraordinary item.
c. Deferred credit.
d. Component of other comprehensive income.
(11/95, FAR, #32, amended, 6114)

57. During 2004, Young and Zinc maintained average capital balances in their partnership of $160,000 and $100,000, respectively. The partners receive 10% interest on average capital balances, and residual profit or loss is divided equally. Partnership profit before interest was $4,000. By what amount should Zinc's capital account change for the year?
a. $ 1,000 decrease
b. $ 2,000 increase
c. $11,000 decrease
d. $12,000 increase
(11/95, FAR, #23, amended, 6105)

58. When the equity method is used to account for investments in common stock, which of the following affect(s) the investor's reported investment income?

	A change In market value of investee's common stock	Cash dividends from investee
a.	Yes	Yes
b.	Yes	No
c.	No	Yes
d.	No	No

(5/96, FAR, #2, 6275)

ITEMS 59 AND 60 are based on the following:

On January 2, 2004, Pare Co. purchased 75% of Kidd Co.'s outstanding common stock. Selected balance sheet data at December 31, 2004, is as follows:

	Pare	Kidd
Total assets	$420,000	$180,000
Liabilities	$120,000	$ 60,000
Common stock	100,000	50,000
Retained earnings	200,000	70,000
	$420,000	$180,000

During 2004, Pare and Kidd paid cash dividends of $25,000 and $5,000, respectively, to their shareholders. There were no other intercompany transactions.

59. In its December 31, 2004, consolidated statement of retained earnings, what amount should Pare report as dividends paid?
a. $ 5,000
b. $25,000
c. $26,250
d. $30,000   (11/95, FAR, #49, amended, 6131)

60. In Pare's December 31, 2004, consolidated balance sheet, what amount should be reported as minority interest in net assets?
a. $0
b. $ 30,000
c. $ 45,000
d. $105,000   (11/95, FAR, #50, amended, 6132)

OTHER OBJECTIVE FORMAT QUESTIONS

NUMBER 2 (15 to 25 minutes)

ITEMS 61 THROUGH 64 are based on the following:

Camp Co. purchased various securities during 2004 to be classified as held-to-maturity securities, trading securities, or available-for-sale securities.

ITEMS 61 THROUGH 64 describe various securities purchased by Camp. For each item, select the appropriate category for each security. A category may be used once, more than once, or not at all.

Categories
(H) Held-to-maturity.
(T) Trading.
(A) Available-for-sale.

ITEMS 65 THROUGH 70 are based on the following:

The following information pertains to Dayle Inc.'s portfolio of marketable investments for the year ended December 31, 2004:

	Cost	Fair value, 12/31/03	2004 activity Purchases	2004 activity Sales	Fair value, 12/31/04
Held-to-maturity securities					
Security ABC			$100,000		$ 95,000
Trading securities					
Security DEF	$150,000	$160,000			155,000
Available-for-sale securities					
Security GHI	190,000	165,000		$175,000	
Security JKL	170,000	175,000			160,000

Security ABC was purchased at par. All declines in fair value are considered to be temporary.

ITEMS 65 THROUGH 70 describe amounts to be reported in Dayle's 2004 financial statements. For each item, select the correct numerical response. An amount may be selected once, more than once, or not at all. Ignore income tax considerations.

65. Carrying amount of security ABC at 12/31/04.

66. Carrying amount of security DEF at 12/31/04.

67. Carrying amount of security JKL at 12/31/04.

ITEMS 68 THROUGH 70 require a second response. For each item, indicate whether a gain (G) or a loss (L) is to be reported.

68. Recognized gain or loss on sale of security GHI.

61. Debt securities bought and held for the purpose of selling in the near term.

62. U.S. Treasury bonds that Camp has both the positive intent and the ability to hold to maturity.

63. $3 million debt security bought and held for the purpose of selling in three years to finance payment of Camp's $2 million long-term note payable when it matures.

64. Convertible preferred stock that Camp does not intend to sell in the near term.

69. Unrealized gain or loss to be reported in 2004 income statement.

70. Unrealized gain or loss to be reported at December 31, 2004, in accumulated other comprehensive income.

Answer List	
(A) $0	(G) $100,000
(B) $ 5,000	(H) $150,000
(C) $10,000	(I) $155,000
(D) $15,000	(J) $160,000
(E) $25,000	(K) $170,000
(F) $95,000	

(11/95, FAR, #61-70, amended)

NUMBER 3 (15 TO 25 MINUTES)

On January 2, 2003, Quo Inc., hired Reed to be its controller. During the year, Reed, working closely with Quo's president and outside accountants, made changes in accounting policies, corrected several errors dating from 2002 and before, and instituted new accounting policies.

Quo's 2003 financial statements will be presented in comparative form with its 2002 financial statements.

REQUIRED:

ITEMS 71 THROUGH 80 represent Quo's transactions. List A represents possible classifications of these transactions as: a change in accounting principle, a change in accounting estimate, a correction of an error in previously presented financial statements, or neither an accounting change nor an accounting error.

List B represents the general accounting treatment required for these transactions. These treatments are:

- Cumulative effect approach—Include the cumulative effect of the adjustment resulting from the accounting change or error correction in the 2003 financial statements, and do **not** restate the 2002 financial statements.
- Retroactive restatement approach—Restate the 2002 financial statements and adjust 2002 beginning retained earnings if the error or change affects a period prior to 2002.
- Prospective approach—Report 2003 and future financial statements on the new basis, but do **not** restate 2002 financial statements.

For each item, select one from List A and one from List B.

<u>List A (Select one)</u>
A. Change in accounting principle.
B. Change in accounting estimate.
C. Correction of an error in previously presented financial statements.
D. Neither an accounting change nor an accounting error.

<u>List B (Select one)</u>
X. Cumulative effect approach.
Y. Retroactive restatement approach.
Z. Prospective approach.

ITEMS TO BE ANSWERED:

71. Quo manufactures heavy equipment to customer specifications on a contract basis. On the basis that it is preferable, accounting for these long-term contracts was switched from the completed-contract method to the percentage-of-completion method.

72. As a result of a production breakthrough, Quo determined that manufacturing equipment previously depreciated over 15 years should be depreciated over 20 years.

73. The equipment that Quo manufactures is sold with a five-year warranty. Because of a production breakthrough, Quo reduced its computation of warranty costs from 3% of sales to 1% of sales.

74. Quo changed from LIFO to FIFO to account for its finished goods inventory.

75. Quo changed from FIFO to average cost to account for its raw materials and work in process inventories.

76. Quo sells extended service contracts on its products. Because related services are performed over several years, in 2003 Quo changed from the cash method to the accrual method of recognizing income from these service contracts.

77. During 2003, Quo determined that an insurance premium paid and entirely expensed in 2002 was for the period January 1, 2002, through January 1, 2004.

78. Quo changed its method of depreciating office equipment from an accelerated method to the straight-line method to more closely reflect costs in later years.

79. Quo instituted a pension plan for all employees in 2003 and adopted Statement of Financial Accounting Standards No. 87, Employers' Accounting for Pensions. Quo had not previously had a pension plan.

80. During 2003, Quo increased its investment in Worth Inc. from a 10% interest, purchased in 2002, to 30%, and acquired a seat on Worth's board of directors. As a result of its increased investment, Quo changed its method of accounting for investment in subsidiary from the cost method to the equity method.

(5/94, FAR, #61-70, amended 4938-4947)

PROBLEM/ESSAY QUESTIONS

NUMBER 4 (30 to 40 minutes)

Deck Co. has just hired a new president, Palmer, and is reviewing its employee benefit plans with the new employee. For current employees, Deck offers a compensation plan for future vacations. Deck also provides post-employment benefits to former or inactive employees.

On the date of Palmer's hire, Palmer entered into a deferred compensation contract with Deck. Palmer is expected to retire in ten years. The contract calls for a payment of $150,000 upon termination of employment following a minimum three-year service period. The contract also provides that interest of 10% compounded annually, be credited on the amount due each year after the third year.

REQUIRED:

a. Give an example of post-employment benefits. State the conditions under which Deck is required to accrue liabilities for compensated absences and post-employment benefits. State Deck's disclosure requirements if these conditions, in full or in part, are not met.

b. Describe the general accrual period for amounts to be paid under a deferred compensation contract. State the theoretical rationale for requiring accrual of these liabilities and related expenses.

c. Prepare a schedule of the expense and accrued liability related to Palmer's deferred compensation agreement to be reported in Deck's financial statements for the first four years of the contract.
(5/96, FAR, #16, 6289)

NUMBER 5 (15 to 25 minutes)

On September 1, 2002, Plains Corp. acquired all of Sox Corp.'s outstanding stock for cash. The fair value of Sox's net assets was less than the purchase price but greater than the net carrying amount. During November 2002, Plains sold goods to Sox at a price that included its normal markup. At December 31, 2002, 20% of these goods remained in Sox's inventory. The separate legal entities were maintained and Sox uses push-down accounting for its separate financial statements.

REQUIRED:

Ignore income tax considerations when answering all questions.

a. 1. Specify three reasons for preparing consolidated financial statements that present operating results, cash flows, and financial position as if a parent company and its subsidiaries were a single entity.

2. What changes in Plains' September 1, 2002 consolidated balance sheet will result from this acquisition?

3. In preparing Plains' December 31, 2002 consolidated financial statements, what adjustments or eliminations are required as a consequence of the intercompany sales?

b. In preparing separate financial statements immediately after acquisition (September 1, 2002), what is the effect of the purchase on the balance sheet of:

1. Plains?
2. Sox (which uses push-down accounting)? (5/92, Theory, #4, amended, 6197)

ANSWERS TO MULTIPLE CHOICE QUESTIONS

1. d	6. b	11. c	16. c	21. b	26. d	31. a	36. a	41. a	46. d	51. d	56. a
2. c	7. d	12. a	17. a	22. c	27. d	32. b	37. d	42. d	47. c	52. b	57. a
3. b	8. b	13. b	18. b	23. a	28. b	33. c	38. d	43. c	48. c	53. b	58. d
4. b	9. d	14. c	19. c	24. c	29. d	34. a	39. b	44. b	49. c	54. b	59. b
5. c	10. b	15. b	20. d	25. a	30. c	35. a	40. c	45. c	50. a	55. c	60. b

---

ANSWERS TO OTHER OBJECTIVE FORMAT QUESTIONS

61.	T	66.	I	71.	A,Y	76.	C,Y
62.	H	67.	J	72.	B,Z	77.	C,Y
63.	A	68.	D,L	73.	B,Z	78.	A,X
64.	A	69.	B,L	74.	A,Y	79.	D,Z
65.	G	70.	C,L	75.	A,X	80.	D,Y

ANSWERS TO PROBLEM/ESSAY QUESTIONS

SOLUTION 4 EMPLOYEE BENEFITS (10 points total)

a. (3 points) An example of post-employment benefits offered by employers is continuation of health care benefits. Deck is required to accrue liabilities for compensated absences and post-employment benefits if all of the following conditions are met:

- The obligation is attributable to employees' services already rendered,
- The employees' rights accumulate or vest,
- Payment is probable, and
- The amount of the benefits can be reasonably estimated.

If an obligation cannot be accrued solely because the amount cannot be reasonably estimated, the financial statements should disclose that fact.

b. (3 points) Estimated amounts to be paid under a deferred compensation contract should be accrued over the period of an employee's active employment from the time the contract is signed to the employee's full eligibility date. The theoretical rationale for accrual of these obligations to be paid in the future is that accrual matches the cost of the benefits to the period in which services are rendered, and results in recognition of a measurable liability.

c. (4 points)

Deck Co.
Schedule of Deferred Compensation Amounts

For the year ended	Accrued liability	Deferred compensation expense
12/31/X1	$ 50,000	$50,000 [a]
12/31/X2	$1000,000	$50,000
12/31/X3	$ 150,000	$50,000
12/31/X4	$ 165,000	$15,000 [b]

[a] $150,000 ÷ 3 (straight-line method)
[b] $150,000 x 10%

SOLUTION 5 CONSOLIDATED FINANCIAL STATEMENTS (10 points total)

a. 1. (3 points) Consolidated operating results, cash flows, and financial position are prepared, as if a parent company and its subsidiaries are a single entity, to provide information that:

- Reflects the operating results, financial status, and central management ties that bind the companies into a **single economic and financial unit.**
- Is **representationally faithful and fair**, without the biases caused by exclusions or netting of data.
- Is **comparable** with information about other economic entities regardless of the companies' legal framework.
- Is **relevant and complete for investors** and other parties basing decisions on the data.

2. (2 points) Plains' September 1, 2002, consolidated balance sheet is changed by **Including all of Sox's identifiable assets and liabilities at their fair values**, and **cash is decreased by the purchase price**. The **excess of purchase price over the fair value of the net assets acquired is reported as goodwill.**

3. (2 points) The effect of the intercompany sales is eliminated from Plains' December 31, 2002, consolidated financial statements by:

- **Reducing sales by the amount of the intercompany sales.**
- **Reducing ending inventory by the markup on goods sold by Plains and still held by Sox.**
- **Reducing cost of goods sold for the difference between the amounts of the two previous adjustments.**

b. 1. (1 point) The effects on Plains' September 1, 2002, balance sheet are the **establishment of an investment in Sox** and a **decrease in cash equal to the purchase price.**

2. (2 points) Using push-down accounting, all of **Sox's assets and liabilities**, including goodwill, are **restated to reflect their fair values on** **September 1, 2002. The retained earnings balance is eliminated. Additional paid-in capital is adjusted** for the difference arising from the restatement of the asset and liability balances and the elimination of retained earnings.

PERFORMANCE BY SUBTOPICS

Diagnostic exam question numbers corresponding to each chapter of the Financial Accounting & Reporting text are listed below. To assess your preparedness for the CPA Exam, record the number and percentage of questions you correctly answered in each topic area. Multiple choice questions and items in the other objective format questions each are worth one point. The points for problem and essay questions are indicated. The point distribution approximates that of the exam.

The numbers in parenthesis refer to the question numbers and corresponding explanations in the related chapters. We strongly recommend that candidates not spend much time on the answers to specific questions that they answered incorrectly on the diagnostic exam, particularly at the beginning of their review. Instead, study the related chapter.

Chapter 1: An Overview of Financial Accounting & Reporting

Question #	Correct √
1 (4)	
2 (7)	
3 (18)	
# Points	3

Correct _____
% Correct _____

Chapter 2: Cash, Short-Term Investments & Receivables

Question #	Correct √
4 (4)	
61 (2-2, 1)	
62 (2-2, 2)	
63 (2-2, 3)	
64 (2-2, 4)	
65 (2-2, 5)	
66 (2-2, 6)	
67 (2-2, 7)	
68 (2-2, 8)	
69 (2-2, 9)	
70 (2-2, 10)	
# Points	11

Correct _____
% Correct _____

Chapter 3: Inventory

Question #	Correct √
5 (13)	
6 (19)	
7 (3)	
8 (34)	
9 (15)	
10 (14)	
11 (26)	
# Points	7

Correct _____
% Correct _____

Chapter 4: Property, Plant & Equipment

Question #	Correct √
12 (3)	
13 (38)	
14 (31)	
15 (36)	
16 (5)	
# Points	5

Correct _____
% Correct _____

Chapter 5: Intangible Assets, R&D Costs & Other Assets

Question #	Correct √
17 (2)	
18 (29)	
19 (8)	
# Points	3

Correct _____
% Correct _____

Chapter 6: Bonds

Question #	Correct √
20 (29)	
21 (20)	
22 (44)	
23 (32)	
# Points	4

Correct _____
% Correct _____

Chapter 7: Liabilities

Question #	Correct √
24 (8)	
25 (49)	
26 (20)	
No. 4 (10 points)	
# Points	13

Correct _____
% Correct _____

Chapter 8: Leases

Question #	Correct √
27 (21)	
28 (3)	
# Points	2

Correct _____
% Correct _____

Chapter 9: Pensions & Other Postretirement Benefits

Question #	Correct √
29 (32)	
30 (25)	
31 (12)	
32 (7)	
# Points	4

Correct _____
% Correct _____

Chapter 10: Owners' Equity

Question #	Correct √
33 (20)	
34 (43)	
35 (42)	
36 (10)	
# Points	4

Correct _____
% Correct _____

Chapter 11: Reporting the Results of Operations

Question #	Correct √
37 (15)	
38 (26)	
39 (94)	
71 (11-3, 1)	
72 (11-3, 2)	
73 (11-3, 3)	
74 (11-3, 4)	
75 (11-3, 5)	
76 (11-3, 6)	
77 (11-3, 7)	
78 (11-3, 8)	
79 (11-3, 9)	
80 (11-3, 10)	
# Points	13

Correct _____
% Correct _____

Chapter 12: Revenue & Expense Recognition: Special Areas

Question #	Correct √
40 (39)	
41 (23)	
42 (17)	
# Points	3

Correct _____
% Correct _____

Chapter 13: Accounting for Income Taxes

Question #	Correct √
43 (35)	
44 (17)	
45 (18)	
46 (23)	
47 (33)	
48 (30)	
# Points	6

Correct _____
% Correct _____

Chapter 14: Statement of Cash Flows

Question #	Correct √
49 (8)	
50 (13)	
51 (14)	
52 (25)	
# Points	4

Correct _____
% Correct _____

Chapter 15: Financial Statement Analysis & EPS

Question #	Correct √
53 (27)	
54 (33)	
# Points	2

Correct _____
% Correct _____

Chapter 16: Financial Reporting & Changing Prices

Question #	Correct √
55 (1)	
# Points	1

Correct _____
% Correct _____

Chapter 17: Foreign Operations

Question #	Correct √
56 (12)	
# Points	1

Correct _____
% Correct _____

Chapter 18: Partnership & Personal Financial Statements

Question #	Correct √
57 (8)	
# Points	1

Correct _____
% Correct _____

Chapter 19: Investments in Equity Securities

Question #	Correct √
58 (13)	
# Points	1

Correct _____
% Correct _____

Chapter 20: Consolidated F/Ss

Question #	Correct √
59 (9)	
60 (10)	
No. 5 (10 pts)	
# Points	12

Correct _____
% Correct _____

CHANGE ALERT

SFAC 7, *USING CASH FLOW INFORMATION AND PRESENT VALUE IN ACCOUNTING MEASUREMENTS*

SFAC 7, *Using Cash Flow Information and Present Value in Accounting Measurements,* was issued by the FASB as a general guide for standards makers to use in deliberations involving interest computations. This concept statement does not alter any existing authoritative standard. SFAC 7 provides a framework for using future cash flows as the basis for accounting measurements at initial recognition or fresh-start measurements and for the interest method of amortization; general principles to govern the use of present value, especially when the amount of future cash flows and/or their timing are uncertain. It also provides a common understanding of the objective of present value in accounting measurements.

CHAPTER 1

AN OVERVIEW OF FINANCIAL ACCOUNTING & REPORTING

CHAPTER 1

AN OVERVIEW OF FINANCIAL ACCOUNTING & REPORTING

I. THE ENVIRONMENT OF ACCOUNTING

A. FINANCIAL ACCOUNTING DEFINED

Accounting is a service activity. Its function is to provide quantitative information, primarily financial in nature, about economic entities that is intended to be useful in making economic decisions—in making reasoned choices among alternative courses of action. In financial accounting, these objectives are met primarily by the presentation of financial statements. Financial statements purport to present in a condensed form the economic events affecting an entity during a specific period of time and the cumulative effect of such events. The most important criterion to meet in a financial statement presentation is that the information provided be useful for decision making. Examples of useful information include information that helps a user of the financial statements predict cash flows and earning power, as well as information that increases management's ability to use resources efficiently and to understand contingencies that may have an effect on future operations.

B. UNDERLYING ENVIRONMENTAL ASSUMPTIONS

Accounting operates in an environment almost as varied as the many types of entities which accounting serves. To provide a basis for comparison, it has been necessary to formulate certain underlying environmental assumptions on which financial accounting theory is based. The most important of these assumptions are as follows:

1. **ECONOMIC ENTITY ASSUMPTION** In order to properly report those economic events affecting an entity, the specific economic entity must be defined and separated from other entities. A distinction is also made between a business concern and its owners.

2. **GOING CONCERN ASSUMPTION** The business is not expected to liquidate in the near future. Where there is a reasonable expectation of an upcoming liquidation, the going concern assumption is abandoned. Liquidation accounting, characterized by the use of net realizable values rather than historical costs, is then employed.

3. **UNIT-OF-MEASURE ASSUMPTION** Monetary units are used for the measurement and reporting of economic activity. Costs incurred at different points in time are intermingled in the accounts and, thus, it must be assumed that the purchasing power of the dollar remains constant over time. In past years, a high rate of inflation made this assumption questionable. SFAS 89, *Financial Reporting and Changing Prices*, encourages enterprises to issue voluntary supplementary reports based on current costs and dollars of constant purchasing power. This information is to be furnished in addition to the usual historical cost financial statements.

4. **PERIODICITY ASSUMPTION** This assumption recognizes the necessity of providing financial accounting information on a periodic, timely basis, so that it is useful in decision making.

C. BASIC ACCOUNTING PRINCIPLES

Based upon these underlying environmental assumptions, a set of basic accounting principles has evolved. These assumptions and principles are implemented through the use of the basic accounting model, upon which the accounting for most profit-oriented entities is based. This model is composed of three main submodels, each focusing on a different aspect of the economic activities of an enterprise.

1. **HISTORICAL COST** Assets acquired, as well as liabilities incurred by an enterprise, are recorded at cost. Cost is generally defined as the cash equivalent amount that would be paid

in an arm's-length transaction. When costs benefit more than one period, they must be apportioned among the periods benefited. This is accomplished through depreciation or amortization.

2.   **REVENUE REALIZATION** Revenue is generally recognized when both of the following conditions are met:

   a.   The earnings process is complete or virtually complete.

   b.   An exchange has taken place. This implies that revenues are usually recognized at the point of sale. Under certain conditions, however, revenue recognition takes place on a different basis, such as a percentage-of-completion, production, installment, or cost recovery basis.

3.   **MATCHING** For income to be stated fairly, all expenses incurred in generating the revenues for a period must be recognized in that same period.

4.   **OBJECTIVITY** Accounting data should be both (a) objectively determined and (b) verifiable. While this does not preclude the use of estimates, they must be verifiable in the sense that an independent, knowledgeable person would find such estimates reasonable.

5.   **MATERIALITY** The relative importance of data, the cost-benefit relationship of additional accuracy, and the possible confusion resulting from the use of too much detail are considerations that must be weighed in determining the materiality of accounting information. When an item is immaterial, good accounting theory can be abandoned.

6.   **CONSISTENCY** The usefulness of accounting information is enhanced when the information is presented in a manner consistent with that used in prior periods. This provides for interperiod comparability and the identification of trends. Consistency in the application of accounting principles also prevents income manipulation by management.

7.   **FULL DISCLOSURE** Financial statements should be presented in a manner that will reasonably assure complete and understandable communication of all relevant accounting information useful for decision making. When the nature of relevant information is such that it cannot appear in the accounts, this principle dictates that such relevant information be included in the accompanying notes to the financial statements.

8.   **CONSERVATISM** Where use of the most appropriate accounting treatment is uncertain, when making estimates, or when data conflicts, the favored accounting treatment should be that which understates rather than overstates income or net assets. Conservatism, however, should not be used in place of a more conceptually sound approach when the difference in results is of a material nature.

D.   **ACCOUNTING MODEL**

1.   **FINANCIAL POSITION** Assets = Liabilities + Owners' equity. The financial position submodel purports to present the economic resources, the economic obligations, and the resulting residual interest in the assets of the entity to its owners. This information is reported by means of a balance sheet.

2.   **RESULTS OF OPERATIONS** Revenues – Expenses = Net income. The purpose of the results of operations submodel is to report on the relative success of the profit-directed activities of an entity. The revenues obtained through the sale of goods and services are compared to the expenses incurred in providing those goods and services. The resulting difference is the operating income or loss for the period. To arrive at net income, gains, losses, and the effect of accounting changes must be incorporated into the submodel. The results of operations submodel is formally represented by the income statement.

3. **STATEMENT OF CASH FLOWS** Cash flows from operating activities +(−) Cash flows from investing activities +(−) Cash flows from financing activities = Change in cash. The objective of this submodel is to provide information about the cash receipts and cash payments of an entity during the period. The statement of cash flows reports the net cash provided or used by operating, investing, and financing activities, and the aggregate effect of those flows on cash during the period.

II. FINANCIAL POSITION—BALANCE SHEET

A. DESCRIPTION

The balance sheet presents the assets, liabilities, and owners' equity of an entity at a specific point in time, measured in conformity with generally accepted accounting principles (GAAP).

B. FORMAT

The formats most commonly used are the account format and the report format.

EXHIBIT 1 ♦ BALANCE SHEET FORMATS (ASSUMED AMOUNTS)

Account Format		Report Format	
Assets $50,000	Liabilities $35,000	Assets	$50,000
		Liabilities	$35,000
	Owners' equity $15,000		
		Owners' equity	$15,000

C. VALUATION

1. **ASSETS**

   a. **HISTORICAL COST** The acquisition cost less depreciation or amortization to date. While this method of valuation is both verifiable and systematic, it often fails to reflect either the current value of the asset or changes due to the purchasing power of the dollar.

   b. **MARKET VALUE** The hypothetical selling price that could be obtained in an arm's-length transaction.

   c. **REPLACEMENT COST** Attempts to value assets on the basis of their current replacement cost. Current replacement cost is defined as the price of a new, similar item after allowance for use and depreciation. This method is used in the primary financial statements only in certain cases where the utility of inventory items has diminished.

   d. **PRICE-LEVEL ADJUSTED** Historical cost adjusted to reflect changes in the general purchasing power of the dollar.

   e. **DISCOUNTED CASH FLOWS** Valuation of assets in terms of the present value of the future benefits associated with the ownership of the asset. Notes receivable and bond investments are valued at present value upon acquisition.

2. **LIABILITIES** Liabilities are valued at their current debt equivalent. For long-term liabilities this implies discounting to their present value the future sums required to satisfy the liability. Due to materiality considerations, short-term liabilities are usually presented at their face amount.

3. **OWNERS' EQUITY** Owners' equity is a residual amount obtained by subtracting total liabilities from total assets. Consequently, the valuation of owners' equity depends on the amounts presented for assets and liabilities.

D.   ELEMENTS

1.   ASSETS   Assets are defined by SFAC 6 as probable future economic benefits obtained or controlled by a particular entity as a result of past transactions or events.   Assets are classified in their order of liquidity and intended use.

a.   CURRENT ASSETS   Current Assets are assets that are reasonably expected to be converted into cash or used during the normal operating cycle of the business or one year, whichever is longer.

b.   INVESTMENTS   Investments are assets that are held for control, appreciation, regular income, or a combination of the above. Examples include stocks, bonds, subsidiaries, land held as a future plant site, and the cash surrender value of life insurance. Also in this category are special purpose funds such as bond sinking funds and plant expansion funds.

c.   OPERATIONAL ASSETS   Operational Assets are assets that are directly used by the enterprise in generating revenues. Operational assets are classified as tangible or intangible. Tangible assets have physical substance. Intangible assets do not have physical existence, but, nevertheless, represent a future economic benefit due to the exclusive rights that they convey to their owners.   Intangible assets can have unlimited legal lives, or their lives may be restricted by law.

d.   VALUATION ACCOUNTS   Valuation accounts are reductions or increases in an asset account to reflect adjustments beyond the historical cost or carrying amount of the asset. Valuation accounts are part of the related asset; they are neither assets nor liabilities in their own right.

2.   LIABILITIES   Liabilities are defined by SFAC 6 as probable future sacrifices of economic benefits arising from present obligations of a particular entity to transfer assets or provide services to other entities in the future as a result of past transactions or events. Liabilities are classified according to their due date as either current or long-term.

a.   CURRENT LIABILITIES   Current liabilities are obligations whose liquidation is expected to require the use of existing current assets or the creation of other current liabilities.

b.   LONG-TERM LIABILITIES   Long-term liabilities are obligations not requiring the use of existing current assets or the creation of current liabilities for their extinguishment.

c.   VALUATION ACCOUNTS   Valuation accounts may increase or decrease the carrying amount of a liability. Examples include the premium or discount on outstanding bonds payable. Valuation accounts are part of the related liability; they are neither assets nor liabilities in their own right.

3.   OWNERS' EQUITY   Owners' Equity is defined by SFAC 6 as the residual interest in the assets of an entity that remains after deducting its liabilities.

a.   EQUITY OF BUSINESS ENTERPRISES   The major distinguishing characteristic of the equity of a business enterprise is that it may be increased through investments of assets by owners who also may receive distributions of assets from the entity.

(1)   An equity interest derives its value from being a potential source of distribution of cash or other assets to its owner. In case of liquidation, all liabilities must be satisfied first.

(2)   Equity is originally created by the initial investment of the enterprise owners. Subsequent investments by the owners, or the admission of new owners, increase equity, while distributions to owners decrease it.

(3) Equity is also changed as a result of the operating activities of the enterprise and other events and circumstances affecting it. This combined effect constitutes comprehensive income.

b. **PROPRIETORSHIP** Proprietorship's equity consists of a single proprietor's equity account.

c. **PARTNERSHIP** Partnership's equity consists of one capital account for each partner. Each individual partner's capital account records his or her investment and subsequent allocations of income and withdrawals.

d. **CORPORATION** Corporation's equity consists of several accounts that are segregated according to source.

(1) **CONTRIBUTED CAPITAL**

(a) Par or stated value represents minimum legal required capital as determined by articles of incorporation and state law.

(b) Additional paid-in capital reflects the amount received in excess of the par or stated value of the stock at the time of issuance.

(2) **RETAINED EARNINGS** Retained earnings are accumulated earnings less losses and dividends. They represent resources retained by the entity for use in expansion and growth.

(3) **ACCUMULATED OTHER COMPREHENSIVE INCOME** SFAS 115, *Accounting for Certain Investments in Debt and Equity Securities*, requires adjustments to available-for-sale securities. A valuation or contra asset account must be used to reflect the decrease of the investment market value. The corresponding debit is shown as unrealized capital in other comprehensive income. SFAS 52, *Foreign Currency Translation*, also requires that certain translation adjustments be reported in other comprehensive income. In addition, SFAS 87, *Employers' Accounting for Pensions*, also requires that adjustments from recognizing certain additional pension liabilities be reported in other comprehensive income.

e. **NET ASSETS** The net assets of a nonprofit organization represent a residual, but are not an ownership interest.

f. **COMPREHENSIVE INCOME** Comprehensive income is the change in equity, from transactions and other events and circumstances from nonowner sources, of a business enterprise during a period.

E. **OFF-BALANCE-SHEET-RISK**
Off-balance-sheet-risk of accounting loss is the risk of accounting loss from a financial instrument that exceeds the amount recognized for the instrument in the balance sheet. Examples include standby loan commitments written, options, letters of credit, and noncancelable operating leases with future minimum lease commitments. Recent pronouncements attempt to eliminate off-balance-sheet-risk by requiring that more risks are reflected within the balance sheet.

III. **REPORTING OF OPERATIONS—INCOME STATEMENT**

A. **DESCRIPTION**
The income statement for a period presents the revenues, expenses, gains, losses, and net income (net loss) recognized during the period and thereby presents an indication, in conformity with GAAP, of the results of the enterprise's profit-directed activities during the period.

B.   FORMAT
Two basic formats are used to present the income statement.

1.   **SINGLE-STEP FORMAT** Focuses on two classifications of items: revenues and expenses. All revenues are added together to arrive at a total revenue figure. The sum of all expenses is subtracted from this figure. The resultant amount is "Income Before Extraordinary Items."

2.   **MULTIPLE-STEP FORMAT** Focuses on multiple classifications of revenue and expense items. This format is characterized by several intermediate subtotals, such as gross margin and operating income, which together produce "Income Before Extraordinary Items."

EXHIBIT 2 ♦ INCOME STATEMENT FORMATS (ASSUMED AMOUNTS)

SINGLE-STEP FORMAT			MULTIPLE-STEP FORMAT		
Revenues:			Net sales	$500,000	
Sales revenue	$500,000		Less CGS	350,000	
Other revenues, gains	20,000		Gross margin		$150,000
Total revenues		$520,000	Less operating exp.		
Expenses:			Selling	80,000	
CGS	350,000		Administrative	30,000	
Selling	80,000		Total operating exp.		110,000
Administrative	30,000		Operating income		40,000
Other expenses, losses	10,000		Other revenues, gain	20,000	
Income taxes	5,000		Other exp., losses	10,000	10,000
Total expenses		475,000	Income before taxes & extraordinary items		50,000
Income before extraordinary items		45,000	Income taxes		5,000
			Income before extraordinary items		45,000
Extraordinary gain, net of $1,200 applicable taxes		7,000	Extraordinary gain, net of $1,200 applicable taxes		7,000
Net income		$ 52,000	Net income		$ 52,000

C.   ELEMENTS

1.   **REVENUES** Revenues are defined by SFAC 6 as inflows or other enhancements of assets of an entity or settlements of its liabilities (or a combination of both) during a period from delivering or producing goods, rendering services, or other activities that constitute the entity's ongoing major or central operations.

a.   **INFLOWS** Revenues represent actual or expected cash inflows (or equivalents) resulting from the entity's major or central operations.

b.   **RECOGNITION** Revenues are usually recognized at the point of sale, in conformity with the basic accounting principle of revenue realization. Several exceptions to this principle are permitted under very specific circumstances.

(1)   **PERCENTAGE-OF-COMPLETION METHOD** For long-term construction contracts, revenue may be recognized during the earnings process (i.e., before the earnings process is virtually complete) in order to enhance the interperiod comparability of the financial statements.

(2)   **PRODUCTION BASIS** This method recognizes revenue at the point of production when the units are homogeneous, there is a relatively stable market, and any

selling costs are nominal. It is applicable to metals and farm products with assured sales prices.

(3) **INSTALLMENT BASIS** Where final collection of the proceeds of a sale or rendering of services is doubtful, revenue is recognized as cash is received by applying the gross margin ratio to the proceeds received.

(4) **COST-RECOVERY BASIS** This method defers the recognition of revenue until cash payments by the buyer exceed the seller's cost of the merchandise sold. After all costs have been recovered, any additional cash collections are included in income. Per APB 10, this method should only be used to account for sales in which there is no reasonable basis for estimating collectibility.

2. **EXPENSES** Expenses are defined by SFAC 6 as outflows or other use of assets or incurrence of liabilities (or a combination of both) from delivering or producing goods, rendering services, or carrying out other activities that constitute the entity's ongoing major or central operations during a period.

   a. **OUTFLOWS** Expenses represent actual or expected cash outflows (or equivalents) resulting from the entity's major or central operations.

   b. **RECOGNITION** Expenses are generally recognized in accordance with one of three principles.

   (1) **ASSOCIATING CAUSE AND EFFECT** Some costs are presumed to be directly related to specific revenues. Examples are cost of goods sold and sales commissions.

   (2) **SYSTEMATIC AND RATIONAL ALLOCATION** If a direct association between costs and revenues is not apparent, costs must be allocated on a systematic and rational basis among the periods benefited. Depreciation of fixed assets, amortization of intangible assets, and allocation of prepaid rent and insurance are applications of this principle.

   (3) **IMMEDIATE RECOGNITION** Costs that are deemed to provide no discernible future benefits are expensed in the current period. Likewise, costs recorded as assets in prior periods that no longer have discernible benefits are expensed in the current period.

3. **GAINS AND LOSSES** Gains and losses are defined by SFAC 6 as increases (or decreases) in equity—i.e., net assets—from peripheral or incidental transactions of an entity and from all other transactions and other events and circumstances affecting the entity during a period, except those that result from revenues (expenses) or investments (withdrawals) by owners.

   a. **OPERATING GAINS AND LOSSES** Gains and losses related to the business enterprise's central operations (e.g., write-down of inventory to LCM) are classified as operating.

   b. **NONOPERATING GAINS AND LOSSES** Gains and loses not attributable to operations are classified as nonoperating.

D. **STATEMENT OF RETAINED EARNINGS**
This statement is presented as a supplement to the income statement and serves as a link between beginning and ending retained earnings. The format of the Statement of Retained Earnings is illustrated in Exhibit 3.

EXHIBIT 3 ♦ STATEMENT OF RETAINED EARNINGS

Beginning balance, as reported	$ XXX
+/– Prior period adjustments, net of $_____ tax	XXX
Beginning balance, as adjusted	XXX
+ Net income (– Net loss)	XXX
– Dividends	(XXX)
Ending balance	$ XXX

IV. STATEMENT OF CASH FLOWS

A. DESCRIPTION

SFAS 95, *Statement of Cash Flows*, requires that a statement of cash flows be issued whenever a balance sheet and an income statement are issued. This statement provides relevant information about the cash receipts and cash payments of an enterprise during a period.

B. FORMAT

Net cash from operating activities can be determined under either the direct or indirect method. Under the direct approach, operating cash payments are deducted from operating cash receipts, effectively resulting in a cash basis income statement. The indirect approach converts net income to net cash flow from operating activities by adding back noncash charges in the income statement to net income and subtracting noncash credits from net income.

C. CLASSIFICATION

The statement of cash flows classifies cash receipts and cash payments resulting from operating, investing, and financing activities.

1. **OPERATING ACTIVITIES** All transactions and other events that are not investing or financing activities. Cash flows from operating activities are generally the cash effects of transactions and other events that enter into the determination of net income.

2. **INVESTING ACTIVITIES** Cash flows resulting from making and collecting loans, acquiring and disposing of debt or equity instruments, and acquiring and disposing of property, plant, and equipment.

3. **FINANCING ACTIVITIES** Cash flows resulting from the issuance and repayment of debt, the issuance and repurchase of capital stock, and the payment of dividends.

D. NONCASH INVESTING AND FINANCING TRANSACTIONS

Noncash investing and financing transactions are not reported in the statement of cash flows because the statement reports only the effects of operating, investing, and financing activities that directly affect cash flows. If significant, noncash investing and financing transactions are reported in related disclosures.

V. COMPREHENSIVE INCOME REPORTING

A. DEFINITIONS

1. **COMPREHENSIVE INCOME** SFAC 6 defines comprehensive income as "the change in equity of a business enterprise during a period from transactions and other events and circumstances from nonowner sources."

   a. Comprehensive income includes all changes in equity during a period except those resulting from investments by owners and distributions to owners.

    b. Over the life of the business, comprehensive income equals the net difference between cash receipts and outlays, excluding cash investments by owners and cash distributions to owners, regardless of whether cash or accrual accounting is used.

    c. SFAS 130 divides comprehensive income into the components of net income and other comprehensive income.

  2. **OTHER COMPREHENSIVE INCOME** SFAS 130 uses this term to refer to revenues, expenses, gains, and losses that under generally accepted accounting principles are included in comprehensive income but excluded from net income.

B. **REQUIREMENTS**

  1. **COMPREHENSIVE INCOME** SFAS 130, *Reporting Comprehensive Income,* requires that comprehensive income be displayed prominently within a financial statement in a full set of general-purpose financial statements. Comprehensive income must be shown on the face of one of the statements, not just in the notes to the financial statements.

  2. **CLASSIFICATION** Comprehensive income is comprised of two components, net income and other comprehensive income. An entity must classify items of other comprehensive income by their nature: foreign currency items, minimum pension liability adjustments, unrealized gains and losses on certain investments in debt and equity securities, and certain gains and losses on hedging activities.

EXHIBIT 4 ♦ COMPREHENSIVE INCOME REPORTING

Net Income		$ XXX
Other Comprehensive Income:		
Foreign currency adjustments, net of tax of $XXX	$XXX	
Unrealized Gain/Loss on Marketable Securities:		
Unrealized holding gain/loss arising during period,		
net of tax of $XXX	$XXX	
Reclassification adjustment,		
net of tax of $XXX, for gain/loss included in net income	<u>XXX</u> XXX	
Minimum pension liability adjustment, net of tax of $XXX	XXX	<u>XXX</u>
Comprehensive Income		<u>$ XXX</u>

  3. **ACCUMULATED BALANCE OF OCI** An entity must also display the accumulated balance of other comprehensive income separately from retained earnings and additional paid-in capital in the equity section of a statement of financial position. An entity must disclose accumulated balances for each classification in that separate component of equity on the face of the statement of financial position, in the statement of changes in equity, or in the notes to the financial statements.

VI. STATEMENTS OF FINANCIAL ACCOUNTING CONCEPTS

A. **OBJECTIVES**
Statements of Financial Accounting Concepts (SFACs) are intended by the FASB to set forth objectives and fundamentals that will be the basis for future development of financial accounting and reporting standards. The idea is to create a conceptual framework consisting of coherent inter-related objectives and principles that will lead to consistent standards of accounting and reporting.

B. **AUTHORITY**
SFACs, however, do **not** establish standards prescribing accounting procedures or disclosures, nor supersede, amend, or otherwise modify present GAAP. Therefore, Statements of Concepts are **not** considered authoritative pronouncements in the context of Rule 203 of the AICPA Code of

Professional Conduct. Since their promulgation, SFACs have been a constant, although limited, source of CPA Exam questions.

C. **OBJECTIVES OF FINANCIAL REPORTING BY BUSINESS ENTERPRISES (SFAC 1)**

1. **FINANCIAL STATEMENTS** Financial statements are most significant in the scheme of financial reporting. Although financial reporting may consist entirely of financial statements, a financial report may or may not include financial statements.

2. **LIMITATIONS** Financial reports are based on information that is expressed in units of money and often are based on approximations or estimations. These expressions document transactions that have already occurred. Given these limitations, financial reporting is simply one element to be considered in a total understanding of a business enterprise.

3. **BENEFITS VS. COSTS** The benefits accruing to the users of financial reports must outweigh the production costs of the reports.

4. **NEEDS OF USERS** The objectives of SFAC 1 stem primarily from the needs of external users (e.g., investors and creditors) who lack the authority to prescribe the information they desire. The kind and quality of information needed by investors and creditors is indicative of the kind and quality of information that should generally be helpful to the broad economic community.

5. **AID IN DECISION MAKING** The objectives focus on establishing goals for financial reporting that will enable financial reports to aid investors, creditors, and others in making sound economic decisions. The objectives are not meant to directly determine the resolution of those decisions. Users must be willing to expend a reasonable amount of time in order to understand the information and use it properly.

6. **SCOPE OF INFORMATION** Financial reports should provide information about an enterprise's economic resources, obligations, and owners' equity. In addition, they should provide information concerning financial performance and earnings. Finally, financial reports should indicate how an enterprise obtains and spends cash, how it borrows, and how it distributes dividends. The majority of the wide variety of users of financial information are interested in the capacity of an enterprise to generate favorable cash flow.

7. **MANAGEMENT PERFORMANCE** Information concerning the performance of management in guiding the enterprise should also be included in financial reporting. Management is responsible for the earnings of an enterprise. Consequently, management's performance can be closely correlated to increases or decreases in earnings. Financial reports in and of themselves are limited in their capacity to precisely measure the effect of management policy on the health of the enterprise. Therefore, management is in a unique position to fairly explain and interpret financial reports.

D. **QUALITATIVE CHARACTERISTICS OF ACCOUNTING INFORMATION (SFAC 2)**
The purpose of this Statement is to examine the characteristics that make accounting information useful for decision making. Once these desired characteristics have been isolated, accountants can choose among alternate accounting methods the one that maximizes these qualitative criteria, subject to cost-benefit and materiality constraints.

1. **USEFULNESS OF ACCOUNTING INFORMATION** Information useful for decision making should be both relevant and reliable.

   a. **RELEVANCE** Information is relevant if it is capable of making a difference in a decision by helping users to form predictions about the outcomes of past, present, and future events or to confirm or correct prior expectations. In other words, relevant information must be timely and must have either predictive or feedback value.

(1) TIMELINESS Information is timely if it is available to a decision maker before it loses its capacity to influence decisions.

(2) PREDICTIVE VALUE Information has predictive value if it helps users increase the likelihood of correctly forecasting the outcome of past or present events.

(3) FEEDBACK VALUE Information has feedback value if it enables users to confirm or correct prior expectations.

b. RELIABILITY Information is reliable when it represents what it purports to represent, coupled with an assurance for the user that it has that representational quality. Reliability must often be measured by degrees; information is rarely either absolutely reliable or unreliable. Reliability is increased when—in addition to being representationally faithful—the information is both verifiable and neutral.

(1) REPRESENTATIONAL FAITHFULNESS Correspondence or agreement between a measure or description and the phenomenon that it purports to represent.

(2) VERIFIABILITY Information can be said to be verifiable when a large number of independent observers derive similar results using the same measurement methods.

(3) NEUTRALITY Neutrality means that the information is free from bias towards a predetermined result.

EXHIBIT 5 ◆ A HIERARCHY OF ACCOUNTING QUALITIES

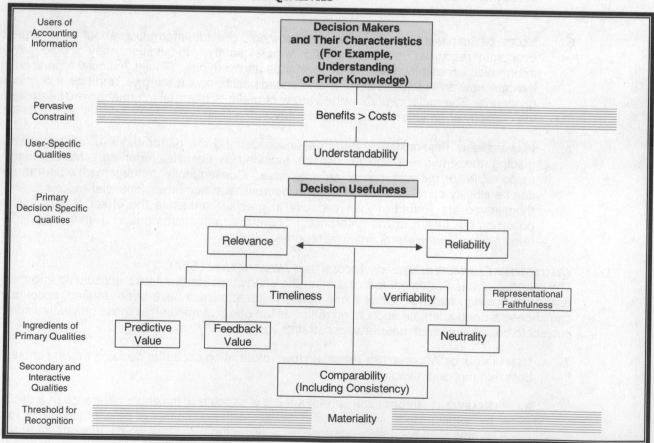

2. USER-SPECIFIC FACTORS The degree of usefulness of information to individual users—particularly the relevancy of information—may vary according to the specific needs of the user. It is virtually impossible to provide information that will completely satisfy the needs of all users; thus, the information provided usually represents a compromise among the perceived needs of the various users (i.e., general purpose financial statements).

3. **CONSTRAINTS**

    a. **COST** In determining the kind and amount of information to be provided, the cost of obtaining the information must be considered. Information is valuable only to the extent that the cost of procuring and analyzing it is less than the benefits derived from its use.

    b. **MATERIALITY** The kind and amount of information to be provided is also restricted by materiality considerations. Information is immaterial if the amounts involved are too small to make a difference in the decision. The concept of materiality applies to both relevance and reliability.

E. *RECOGNITION AND MEASUREMENT IN FINANCIAL STATEMENTS OF BUSINESS ENTERPRISES* (SFAC 5)

    1. **SCOPE** Some useful information is better provided by financial statements, and some is better provided or can only be disclosed in notes to financial statements, parenthetically, or by supplementary information or other means of financial reporting. The scope of this Concepts Statement is limited to recognition and measurement in financial statements.

    2. **COMPLETENESS** A full set of financial statements provides information that is necessary to satisfy the broad purposes of financial reporting, as described in SFAC 1. A full set of financial statements includes information (some of which may be combined in a single statement) showing the financial position at the end of the period, earnings (net income) for the period, comprehensive income (total nonowner changes in equity) for the period, cash flows during the period, and investments by and distributions to owners during the period.

    3. **MAINTENANCE CONCEPTS** The full set of articulated financial statements discussed in this Statement is based on the concept of financial capital maintenance.

        a. **FINANCIAL CAPITAL MAINTENANCE CONCEPT** Under this concept, a return on financial capital results only if the financial (money) amount of an enterprise's net assets at the end of a period exceeds the corresponding amount at the beginning of the period, after excluding the effects of transactions with owners. The financial capital concept is the traditional view and is the capital maintenance concept in present financial statements and comprehensive income.

EXHIBIT 6 ♦ TYPES OF INFORMATION USED IN INVESTMENT, CREDIT, AND SIMILAR DECISIONS

<————— **All information useful for investment, credit, and similar decisions** —————>
(Concepts Statement 1, paragraph 22)

<————— **Financial reporting** —————>
(Concepts Statement 1, paragraphs 5-8)

<——— Area directly affected by existing FASB standards ———>

<——— Basic financial statements ———>
(in AICPA auditing standards literature)

Scope of recognition and
<—measurement—>
Concepts Statement

Financial Statements	Notes to Financial Statements (& parenthetical disclosures)	Supplementary Information	Other Means of Financial Reporting	Other Information
Examples: ❑ Statement of financial position ❑ Statements of earnings and comprehensive income ❑ Statement of cash flows ❑ Statement of investments by and distributions to owners	Examples: ❑ Accounting policies ❑ Contingencies ❑ Inventory methods ❑ Number of shares of stock outstanding ❑ Alternative measures (market values of items carried at historical cost)	Examples: ❑ Changing prices disclosures (FASB Statement 89) ❑ Oil and gas reserves information (FASB Statement 69)	Examples: ❑ Management discussion and analysis ❑ Letters to stockholders	Examples: ❑ Discussion of competition and order backlog in SEC form 10-K (under SEC Reg. ¶S-K) ❑ Analysts' reports ❑ Economic statistics ❑ News articles about company

b. **PHYSICAL CAPITAL MAINTENANCE CONCEPT** In contrast, under this concept, a return on physical capital results only if the physical productive capacity of the enterprise at the end of the period exceeds its capacity at the beginning. Thus, the physical capital concept can be implemented only if the enterprise's productive assets, inventory, etc., are measured by their current cost.

c. **CONCEPT DIFFERENCES** The main difference between the two concepts involves the effect of price changes during the period. Under the financial capital concept, if the effects of price changes are recognized, they are reported as holding gains or losses, (i.e., included in income). Under the physical capital concept, such changes are considered adjustments to equity.

4. **RECOGNITION** The process of formally recording or incorporating an item into the financial statements of an entity as an asset, liability, revenue, expense, or the like.

5. **RECOGNITION CRITERIA** An item and information about it must meet four fundamental recognition criteria to be recognized, subject to cost-benefit and materiality considerations.

a. **DEFINITION** The item meets the definition of an element of financial statements.

b. **MEASURABILITY** The item has a relevant attribute measurable with sufficient reliability.

c. **RELEVANCE** The information may make a difference in user decisions.

d. **RELIABILITY** The information is representationally faithful, verifiable, and neutral.

6. **REVENUES AND GAINS** Guidance for recognizing revenues and gains is as follows:

   a. **REALIZED** Revenues and gains generally are not recognized until realized or realizable.

   b. **EARNED** Revenues are not recognized until earned. For gains, being earned is generally less significant than being realized or realizable, since gains commonly involve no "earning process."

7. **EXPENSES AND LOSSES** Guidance for recognizing expenses and losses is based on the following:

   a. **CONSUMPTION OF ECONOMIC BENEFITS** May be recognized either directly or by relating them to revenues recognized during the period.

   b. **LOSS OR LACK OF BENEFIT** Expenses or losses are recognized if it becomes evident that previously recognized future economic benefits of assets have been reduced or eliminated, or that liabilities have been incurred or increased, without associated economic benefits.

F. **ELEMENTS OF FINANCIAL STATEMENTS (SFAC 6)**

   1. **TEN ELEMENTS** SFAC 6 identifies ten elements of financial statements.

      a. Seven elements of financial statements of both business enterprises and not-for-profit organizations—assets, liabilities, equity (business enterprises) or net assets (not-for-profit organizations), revenues, expenses, gains, and losses.

      b. Three elements of business enterprises only—investment by owners, distributions to owners, and comprehensive income.

   2. **ACCRUAL ACCOUNTING** Accrual accounting attempts to record the financial effects on an entity of transactions and other events and circumstances that have cash consequences for the entity in the periods in which those transactions, events, and circumstances occur, rather than only in the periods in which cash is received or paid by the entity. Accrual accounting is characterized by the use of accruals, deferrals, allocations, and amortizations.

      a. **ACCRUAL** Accrual is the accounting process of recognizing assets or liabilities and the related liabilities, assets, revenues, expenses, gains, or losses for amounts expected to be received or paid, usually in cash, in the future.

      b. **DEFERRAL** Deferral is the accounting process of recognizing a liability resulting from a current cash receipt or an asset resulting from a current cash payment with deferred recognition of revenues, expenses, gains, or losses.

      c. **ALLOCATION** Allocation is the accounting process of assigning or distributing an amount according to a plan or a formula.

      d. **AMORTIZATION** Amortization is the accounting process of reducing an amount by periodic payments or write-downs. It is an allocation process for accounting for prepayments and deferrals by reducing a liability or an asset and recognizing a revenue or an expense.

   3. **REALIZATION AND RECOGNITION**

      a. **REALIZATION** Realization is the process of converting noncash resources and rights into money. This term is most precisely used in accounting and financial reporting to refer to sales of assets for cash or claims to cash. The related terms realized and unrealized, therefore, identify revenues or gains or losses on assets sold and unsold, respectively.

b. **RECOGNITION** Recognition is the process of formally recording or incorporating an item in the financial statements of an entity. Thus, an asset, liability, revenue, expense, gain, or loss may be recognized (recorded) or unrecognized (unrecorded).

4. **MATCHING** Combined or simultaneous recognition of the revenues and expenses that result directly and jointly from the same transactions and other events.

a. **PERIOD COSTS** Some costs cannot be directly related to particular revenues, yet result in benefits that are exhausted in the same period in which the cost was incurred. These costs are usually recognized as expenses in the period in which incurred. Examples: administrative salaries, store utilities, etc.

b. **COST ALLOCATION** Other costs yield their benefits over two or more periods of time. These costs are usually allocated to the periods benefited through a systematic and rational cost allocation method (e.g., depreciation and amortization).

G. **USING CASH FLOW INFORMATION AND PRESENT VALUE IN ACCOUNTING MEASUREMENTS (SFAC 7)**

1. **BACKGROUND** This statement was issued by the FASB in 2000 and presents the FASB's conclusions about the use and approach to making interest computations in financial reporting. It is limited to measurement issues and does not address recognition. It is intended to be a general guide, primarily for the FASB, which can be used in subsequent deliberations involving interest computations. A key point to bear in mind is that this statement does not alter any existing authoritative standard.

2. **PRESENT VALUE MEASUREMENT OF ASSETS AND LIABILITIES** Most accounting measurements use an observable marketplace-determined amount, such as cash exchanged, current cost, or current market value. However, in other instances, estimates of future cash flows must be used as the basis for measuring an asset or a liability. SFAC 7 provides a framework for using future cash flows as the basis for accounting measurements at initial recognition or fresh-start measurements as well as for the interest method of amortization. Additionally, it provides general principles that govern the use of present value computations, particularly when the amount and/or timing of future cash flows are uncertain.

3. **PRESENT VALUE AS SURROGATE FOR MARKET VALUE** In order to provide more relevant information (a primary qualitative characteristic of financial reporting), present value must represent some observable measurement attribute of assets or liabilities. In the absence of observed transaction prices, accounting measurements at initial recognition and fresh-start measurements should attempt to capture the elements that taken together would comprise a market price if one existed (fair value). While the expectations of management are often useful and informative, ultimately, it is the market that dictates market price when exchanges occur. However, for certain assets or liabilities, management's estimates may be the only information available on which to value the asset or liability. In that case, the use of present value can be seen as a surrogate for market value.

4. **UNCERTAINTIES** An accounting measurement that uses present value should reflect the uncertainties inherent in the estimated cash flows. This means that risk should be specifically incorporated into the computation. SFAC 7 provides guidance on how to incorporate risk into the analysis, including its effect on both the timing and amount of future cash flows.

5. **PROJECTION OF FUTURE CASH FLOWS** In the past, present value computations have relied on a single estimate of cash flows and a single interest rate. SFAC 7 calls for the use of expected cash flows, which incorporates uncertainty, use of ranges, and probabilistic computations in the projection of future cash flows.

6. **MEASURING LIABILITIES** In measuring liabilities, the SFAC 7 indicates that there are different issues at hand. Nonetheless, the ultimate objective remains the same—to reflect fair value. SFAC 7 provides additional guidance for measuring liabilities.

7. **CREDIT RISK** Credit risk can affect a variety of components in the present value computation and should be incorporated in the present value computation. Additionally, in measuring liabilities, the entity's credit standing should always be incorporated into that measurement.

VII. AUTHORITY OF PRONOUNCEMENTS

A. ACCOUNTING STANDARD-SETTING BODIES AND THEIR PRONOUNCEMENTS

1. **COMMITTEE ON COOPERATION WITH STOCK EXCHANGES (1932-1934)** The American Institute of Accountants (known today as the American Institute of Certified Public Accountants, or AICPA) created in 1932 a Committee on Cooperation With Stock Exchanges. The Committee made a series of recommendations, which later were adopted by the AICPA.

2. **COMMITTEE ON ACCOUNTING PROCEDURE AND ACCOUNTING RESEARCH BULLETINS (1939-1959)** In 1939, the Institute formed a second committee, the Committee on Accounting Procedures (CAP), with the objective of narrowing the areas of differences and inconsistencies in the practice of accounting. During its existence, CAP issued 51 pronouncements, known as Accounting Research Bulletins (ARBs). ARB No. 43 consisted of a rewrite of the prior 42 pronouncements.

3. **ACCOUNTING PRINCIPLES BOARD AND OPINIONS AND STATEMENTS (1959-1973)** CAP was replaced in 1959 by the Accounting Principles Board (APB). From 1959 through 1973, the APB promulgated 31 pronouncements known as Opinions. In addition, the Board issued four Statements. Unlike Opinions, APB Statements were simply recommendations, not requirements.

4. **FINANCIAL ACCOUNTING STANDARDS BOARD AND STATEMENTS, INTERPRETATIONS, CONCEPTS, TECHNICAL BULLETINS, AND EMERGING ISSUES TASK FORCE STATEMENTS (1973-PRESENT)** The APB was substituted in 1973 by the Financial Accounting Standards Board (FASB), an independent private-sector body composed of seven full-time members and a 35 member Advisory Council. The promulgations issued by the FASB have the same authority as the prior APB Opinions, but are known as Statements of Financial Accounting Standards. In addition, the FASB also issues Interpretations of prior pronouncements. FASB Interpretations have as much force as ARBs, Opinions, and FASB Statements. Beginning in 1978, the FASB started a new series, Statements of Financial Accounting Concepts, with the purpose of setting forth fundamental concepts upon which financial accounting and reporting standards would be based. Unlike a Statement of Financial Accounting Standards or Interpretation, a Statement of Financial Accounting Concepts does not establish generally accepted accounting principles. In addition, the FASB issues Emerging Issues Task Force Consensus and FASB Technical Bulletins that are less authoritative than FASB Statements of Financial Accounting Standards and Interpretations.

B. GAAP HIERARCHY
SAS 69 establishes a hierarchy for applying accounting principles to financial statements in conformity with GAAP. The hierarchy is presented in Exhibit 7.

EXHIBIT 7 ◆ GAAP HIERARCHY

1. FASB Statements and Interpretations, APB Opinions, and AICPA Accounting Research Bulletins

2. FASB Technical Bulletins, AICPA Industry Audit and Accounting Guides, and AICPA Statements of Position cleared by the FASB

3. Consensus positions of the FASB's EITF, and AcSEC Practice Bulletins cleared by the FASB

4. AICPA accounting interpretations, "Qs&As" published by the FASB staff, as well as industry practices widely recognized and prevalent

5. Other accounting literature, including FASB Concepts Statements; APB Statements; AICPA Issues Papers; AcSEC Practice Bulletins; minutes of FASB EITF; International Accounting Standards Committee statements; pronouncements of other professional associations or regulatory agencies; and accounting articles and textbooks

CHAPTER 1—AN OVERVIEW OF FINANCIAL ACCOUNTING & REPORTING

PROBLEM 1-1 MULTIPLE CHOICE QUESTIONS (50 to 63 minutes)

1. Reporting inventory at the lower of cost or market is a departure from the accounting principle of
a. Historical cost.
b. Consistency.
c. Conservatism.
d. Full disclosure. (5/94, FAR, #3, 4818)

2. Which of the following disclosures should prospective financial statements include?

	Summary of significant accounting policies	Summary of significant assumptions
a.	Yes	Yes
b.	Yes	No
c.	No	Yes
d.	No	No

(R/99, FAR, #3, 6772)

3. What is the purpose of information presented in notes to the financial statements?
a. To provide disclosures required by generally accepted accounting principles.
b. To correct improper presentation in the financial statements.
c. To provide recognition of amounts **not** included in the totals of the financial statements.
d. To present management's responses to auditor comments. (5/94, FAR, #6, 4821)

4. What is the underlying concept that supports the immediate recognition of a contingent loss?
a. Substance over form
b. Consistency
c. Matching
d. Conservatism (11/94, FAR, #3, 5268)

5. According to the FASB conceptual framework, which of the following is an essential characteristic of an asset?
a. The claims to an asset's benefit are legally enforceable.
b. An asset is tangible.
c. An asset is obtained at a cost.
d. An asset provides future benefits. (5/92, Theory, #2, 2694)

6. According to the FASB's conceptual framework, asset valuation accounts are
a. Assets.
b. Neither assets **nor** liabilities.
c. Part of stockholders' equity.
d. Liabilities. (11/88, Theory, #1, 9001)

7. One of the elements of a financial statement is comprehensive income. Comprehensive income excludes changes in equity resulting from which of the following?
a. Loss from discontinued operations
b. Prior period error correction
c. Dividends paid to stockholders
d. Unrealized loss on investments in noncurrent marketable equity securities
(5/95, FAR, #2, 5538)

8. According to the FASB conceptual framework, which of the following statements conforms to the realization concept?
a. Equipment depreciation was assigned to a production department and then to product unit costs.
b. Depreciated equipment was sold in exchange for a note receivable.
c. Cash was collected on accounts receivable.
d. Product unit costs were assigned to cost of goods sold when the units were sold.
(11/93, Theory, #6, 4511)

9. According to the FASB conceptual framework, an entity's revenue may result from
a. A decrease in an asset from primary operations.
b. An increase in an asset from incidental transactions.
c. An increase in a liability from incidental transactions.
d. A decrease in a liability from primary operations.
(11/92, Theory, #3, 3436)

10. The primary purpose of a statement of cash flows is to provide relevant information about
a. Differences between net income and associated cash receipts and disbursements.
b. An enterprise's ability to generate future positive net cash flows.
c. The cash receipts and cash disbursements of an enterprise during a period.
d. An enterprise's ability to meet cash operating needs. (5/94, FAR, #5, 4820)

11. What are the Statements of Financial Accounting Concepts intended to establish?
a. Generally accepted accounting principles in financial reporting by business enterprises.
b. The meaning of "Present fairly in accordance with generally accepted accounting principles."
c. The objectives and concepts for use in developing standards of financial accounting and reporting.
d. The hierarchy of sources of generally accepted accounting principles. (5/94, FAR, #2, 4817)

12. During a period when an enterprise is under the direction of a particular management, its financial statements will directly provide information about
a. Both enterprise performance and management performance.
b. Management performance but **not** directly provide information about enterprise performance.
c. Enterprise performance but **not** directly provide information about management performance.
d. Neither enterprise performance nor management performance. (5/94, FAR, #4, 4819)

13. According to the FASB conceptual framework, the objectives of financial reporting for business enterprises are based on
a. Generally accepted accounting principles.
b. Reporting on management's stewardship.
c. The need for conservatism.
d. The needs of the users of the information.
(11/95, FAR, #1, 6083)

14. According to the FASB conceptual framework, which of the following situations violates the concept of reliability?
a. Data on segments having the same expected risks and growth rates are reported to analysts estimating future profits.
b. Financial statements are issued nine months late.
c. Management reports to stockholders regularly refer to new projects undertaken, but the financial statements never report project results.
d. Financial statements include property with a carrying amount increased to management's estimate of market value. (5/95, FAR, #1, 5537)

15. According to Statements of Financial Accounting Concepts, neutrality is an ingredient of

	Reliability	Relevance
a.	Yes	Yes
b.	Yes	No
c.	No	Yes
d.	No	No (11/94, FAR, #1, 5266)

16. According to the FASB conceptual framework, predictive value is an ingredient of

	Reliability	Relevance
a.	Yes	Yes
b.	No	Yes
c.	No	No
d.	Yes	No (5/92, Theory, #3, 2695)

17. According to the FASB conceptual framework, which of the following relates to both relevance and reliability?
a. Comparability
b. Feedback value
c. Verifiability
d. Timeliness (11/92, Theory, #2, 3435)

18. According to the FASB conceptual framework, the usefulness of providing information in financial statements is subject to the constraint of
a. Consistency.
b. Cost-benefit.
c. Reliability.
d. Representational faithfulness.
(11/95, FAR, #2, 6084)

19. According to the FASB conceptual framework, comprehensive income includes which of the following?

	Loss on discontinued operations	Investments by owners
a.	Yes	Yes
b.	Yes	No
c.	No	Yes
d.	No	No
		(5/98, FAR, #1, 6604)

20. Under Statement of Financial Accounting Concepts No. 5, which of the following items would cause earnings to differ from comprehensive income for an enterprise in an industry **not** having specialized accounting principles?
a. Unrealized loss on investments in available-for-sale marketable equity securities
b. Unrealized loss on investments in trading marketable equity securities
c. Loss on exchange of similar assets
d. Loss on exchange of dissimilar assets
(5/91, Theory, #1, amended, 1750)

21. FASB's conceptual framework explains both financial and physical capital maintenance concepts. Which capital maintenance concept is applied to currently reported net income, and which is applied to comprehensive income?

	Currently reported net income	Comprehensive income
a.	Financial capital	Physical capital
b.	Physical capital	Physical capital
c.	Financial capital	Financial capital
d.	Physical capital	Financial capital

(11/91, Theory, #1, 2509)

22. Some costs cannot be directly related to particular revenues but are incurred to obtain benefits that are exhausted in the period in which the costs are incurred. An example of such a cost is
a. Salespersons' monthly salaries.
b. Salespersons' commissions.
c. Transportation to customers.
d. Prepaid insurance. (5/85, Theory, #2, 1775)

23. According to the FASB conceptual framework, the process of reporting an item in the financial statements of an entity is
a. Allocation.
b. Matching.
c. Realization.
d. Recognition. (5/94, FAR, #1, 4816)

24. In the hierarchy of generally accepted accounting principles, APB Opinions have the same authority as AICPA
a. Statements of Position.
b. Industry Audit and Accounting Guides.
c. Issues Papers.
d. Accounting Research Bulletins.

(11/94, FAR, #2, 5267)

25. Which of the following accounting pronouncements is the most authoritative?
a. FASB Statement of Financial Accounting Concepts
b. FASB Technical Bulletin
c. AICPA Accounting Principles Board Opinion
d. AICPA Statement of Position

(11/92, Theory, #1, 3434)

ESSAY QUESTION

ESSAY 1-2 (15 to 25 minutes)

Mono Tech Co. began operations in 1995 and confined its activities to one project. It purchased equipment to be used exclusively for research and development on the project, and other equipment that is to be used initially for research and development and subsequently for production. In 1996, Mono constructed and paid for a pilot plant that was used until December 1997 to determine the best manufacturing process for the project's product. In December 1997, Mono obtained a patent and received cash from the sale of the pilot plant. In 1998, a factory was constructed and commercial manufacture of the product began.

REQUIRED:

a. 1. According to the FASB conceptual framework, what are the three essential characteristics of an asset?

2. How do Mono's project expenditures through 1997 meet the FASB conceptual framework's three essential characteristics of an asset? Do **not** discuss why the expenditures may **not** meet the characteristics of an asset.

3. Why is it difficult to justify the classification of research and development expenditures as assets?

b. How should Mono report:

1. The effects of equipment expenditures in its income statements and balance sheets from 1995 through 1998?

2. Pilot plant construction costs and sale proceeds in its 1996 and 1997 statements of cash flows using the direct method?

(11/93, Theory, #5 amended, 6186)

SOLUTION 1-1 MULTIPLE CHOICE ANSWERS

ENVIRONMENT OF ACCOUNTING

1. (a) The accounting principle of historical cost requires assets as well as liabilities to be recorded and carried on the books at cost. Therefore, reporting inventory at the lower of cost or market is a departure from this principle.

2. (a) To assist in understanding prospective financial statements, summaries of both significant accounting policies and significant assumptions should be included in the disclosures.

3. (a) The notes to the financial statements provide disclosures required by generally accepted accounting principles. The notes may be used to amplify or explain items presented in the main body of the financial statements but not to correct errors or omissions in the statements. Management's responses to auditor comments would normally be reported in a separate letter to the auditors and not as part of the financial statements.

4. (d) While a contingent loss may be recognized *before* it is realized, a contingent gain cannot be recognized *until* it is realized. Therefore, the underlying concept that supports the immediate recognition of a contingent loss is conservatism. The convention of conservatism urges the accountant to refrain from overstatement of net income or net assets.

FINANCIAL STATEMENT ELEMENTS

5. (d) SFAC 6, par. 26, states, "An asset has three essential characteristics: (1) it embodies a probable future benefit that involves a capacity, singly or in combination with other assets, to contribute directly or indirectly to future net cash inflows, (2) a particular entity can obtain the benefit and control others' access to it, and (3) the transaction or other event giving rise to the entity's right to or control of the benefit has already occurred." The legal enforceability of a claim to a benefit is not a prerequisite for a benefit to qualify as an asset if the entity has the ability to obtain and control the benefit in other ways (par. 26). Assets may be intangible and they may be acquired without cost (par. 26).

6. (b) Per SFAC 6, par. 34, "A separate item that reduces or increases the carrying amount of an asset is sometimes found in financial statements. For example, an estimate of uncollectible amounts reduces receivables to the amount expected to be collected, or a premium on a bond receivable increases the receivable to its cost or present value. Those 'valuation accounts' are part of the related assets and are *neither assets in their own right nor liabilities*."

7. (c) Comprehensive income includes all changes in equity during a period except those resulting from investments by owners and distributions to owners.

8. (b) Per SFAC 6, par. 143, "Realization in the most precise sense means the process of converting noncash resources and rights into money and is most precisely used in accounting and financial reporting to refer to sales of assets for cash or *claims to cash*." Thus, the sale of the depreciated equipment for a note (i.e., a claim to cash) conforms to the realization concept. None of the transactions in the other choices involve the conversion of a noncash resource or right into cash or claims to cash.

9. (d) Revenues are inflows or other enhancements of assets or settlements of liabilities from activities that constitute the entity's major or central operations (SFAC 6, par. 78). An expense would result from an outflow or other using up of assets from activities that constitute the entity's major or central operations (par. 78). Gains and losses result from changes in net assets from an entity's peripheral or incidental transactions (par. 84).

10. (c) The primary purpose of a statement of cash flows is to provide relevant information about the cash receipts and cash disbursements of an enterprise during a period.

OBJECTIVES OF SFAC'S

11. (c) The Statements of Financial Accounting Concepts are intended by the FASB to set forth objectives and fundamentals that will be the basis for future development of financial accounting and reporting standards. SFACs do not establish standards prescribing accounting procedures or disclosures, nor supersede, amend, or otherwise modify present GAAP.

OBJECTIVES OF FINANCIAL REPORTING

12. (c) Financial statements provide information about an enterprise's economic resources, obligations, and owner's equity. In addition, they should provide information concerning financial performance, earnings, how the entity spends and receives cash, and how it distributes dividends.

The objective of financial reporting is to aid investors, creditors, and others in making sound economic decisions. Information regarding management performance is also part of financial reporting. Since management is responsible for the earnings of an enterprise, management performance can be closely correlated to increases or decreases in earnings. However, this information is not *directly* provided for, but rather inferred from the financial data contained in the financial statements.

13. (d) According to SFAC 1, "Objectives of Financial Reporting by Business Enterprises," the need for information on which to base investment, credit, and similar decisions underlies the objectives of financial reporting. The objectives of financial reporting are not based upon the need for conservatism, reporting on management's stewardship, or GAAP.

QUALITATIVE CHARACTERISTICS

14. (d) Reliability is increased when, in addition to being representationally faithful, the information is both verifiable and neutral. Increasing the carrying amount of property to management's estimate of market value is not verifiable or neutral. Answer (a) relates to comparability; answers (b) and (c) relate to relevance.

15. (b) Information is reliable if it is reasonably free from error and bias, and faithfully represents what it purports to represent. Reliable information has the ingredients of verifiability, *neutrality*, and representational faithfulness. Information is relevant if it has the capacity to make a difference in a decision by helping users form predictions about the outcomes of past, present, and future events or confirm or correct prior expectations. For information to be relevant, it must be timely and have either predictive or feedback value.

16. (b) Per SFAC 2, relevance and reliability are the two primary qualities of information. The "ingredients" of relevance are predictive value, feedback value, and timeliness. The "ingredients" of reliability are verifiability, neutrality, and representational faithfulness.

17. (a) Comparability is a secondary quality of information that interacts with both relevance and reliability to contribute to the usefulness of the information (SFAC 2, par. 33). Feedback value and timeliness are ingredients of relevance and not of reliability. To be relevant, information must be timely and it must have predictive value, feedback value, or both. Verifiability is an ingredient of reliability and not of relevance. To be reliable, information must have representational faithfulness and it must be verifiable and neutral.

18. (b) A specific constraint in terms of the usefulness of information in financial statements pertains to the cost-benefit relationship. In determining the kind and amount of information to be provided, the cost of obtaining the information must be considered. Information is valuable only to the extent that the cost of procuring and analyzing it is less than the benefits derived from its use. While consistency, reliability, and representational faithfulness are important aspects of financial information, they are not associated with constraints.

COMPREHENSIVE INCOME

19. (b) Comprehensive income includes all changes in equity during a period except those resulting from investments by owners and distributions to owners. Loss on discontinued operations is part of comprehensive income.

20. (a) Under SFAC 5, unrealized loss on investments in available-for-sale marketable equity securities is a component of comprehensive income but is *not* a component of earnings. Unrealized loss on investment in trading marketable equity securities, loss on exchange of similar assets, and loss on exchange of dissimilar assets are all items that are included in earnings (and therefore are *also* components of comprehensive income).

21. (c) The financial capital maintenance concept defines income as the change in net resources other than from owner transactions. The financial capital maintenance concept is the capital maintenance concept used in present financial statements and comprehensive income. In contrast, under the physical capital maintenance concept, a return on physical capital results only if the physical productive capacity of the enterprise at the end of the period exceeds its capacity at the beginning of the period, also after excluding the effects of transactions with owners. The physical capital maintenance concept can be implemented only if inventories and property, plant, and equipment are measured by their current costs.

ACCRUAL ACCOUNTING CONCEPTS

22. (a) SFAC 6, par. 148, specifically mentions *salesmen's monthly salaries* as an example that fits the description of a cost that cannot be directly related to particular revenues, but rather it is incurred in order to obtain benefits that are exhausted during the period. Salespersons' commissions and transportation to customers are

mentioned as examples of items that are *directly* related to sales revenues. Prepaid insurance is mentioned as an asset yielding benefits over several periods.

23. (d) Recognition is the process of formally recording or incorporating an item in the financial statements of an entity.

AUTHORITY OF PRONOUNCEMENTS

24. (d) The AICPA Code of Professional Conduct requires that members prepare financial statements in accordance with generally accepted accounting principles (Rule 203). Pronouncements of an authoritative body designated by the AICPA Council to establish accounting principles have greater authority than pronouncements of bodies composed of expert accountants that follow a due process procedure for the intended purpose of establishing accounting principles or describing existing practices that are generally accepted (SAS 69). Therefore, FASB Statements

on Financial Accounting Standards and Interpretations, APB Opinions and Interpretations, and CAP (Committee on Accounting Procedure) Accounting Research Bulletins have greater authority than AICPA Statements of Position, AICPA Industry Audit and Accounting Guides, and AICPA Issue Papers.

25. (c) Rule 203 of the AICPA Code of Professional Conduct requires that members prepare financial statements in accordance with generally accepted accounting principles. Generally accepted accounting principles are construed to be FASB Statements of Financial Accounting Standards and FASB Interpretations, AICPA Accounting Principles Board (APB) Opinions and Interpretations, and CAP (Committee on Accounting Procedure) Accounting Research Bulletins. FASB Statements of Financial Accounting Concepts, FASB Technical Bulletins, and AICPA Statements of Position are less authoritative than APB Opinions because they do not establish GAAP.

PERFORMANCE BY SUBTOPICS

Each category below parallels a subtopic covered in Chapter 1. Record the number and percentage of questions you correctly answered in each subtopic area.

Environment of Accounting

Question #	Correct √
1	
2	
3	
4	
# Questions	4

Correct _____
% Correct _____

Financial Statement Elements

Question #	Correct √
5	
6	
7	
8	
9	
10	
# Questions	6

Correct _____
% Correct _____

Objectives of SFAC's

Question #	Correct √
11	
# Questions	1

Correct _____
% Correct _____

Objectives of Financial Reporting

Question #	Correct √
12	
13	
# Questions	2

Correct _____
% Correct _____

Qualitative Characteristics

Question #	Correct √
14	
15	
16	
17	
18	
# Questions	5

Correct _____
% Correct _____

Comprehensive Income

Question #	Correct √
19	
20	
21	
# Questions	3

Correct _____
% Correct _____

Accrual Accounting Concepts

Question #	Correct √
22	
23	
# Questions	2

Correct _____
% Correct _____

Authority of Pronouncements

Question #	Correct √
24	
25	
# Questions	2

Correct _____
% Correct _____

ESSAY SOLUTION

SOLUTION 1-2 CHARACTERISTICS OF AN ASSET

a. 1. According to the FASB conceptual framework, the three essential characteristics of an asset are:

- It embodies a **probable future benefit** that involves a capacity to contribute to future net cash inflows.
- A particular entity can obtain the benefit and control others' access to it.
- The **transaction or other event** giving rise to the entity's right to or control of the benefit has **already occurred**.

2. Mono's project expenditures through 1997 meet the FASB conceptual framework's three essential characteristics of an asset as follows:

- Since Mono intends to produce the product, it presumably **anticipates future net cash inflows**.
- Mono has obtained a patent that will enable it to **control the benefits** arising from the product.
- The control is a consequence of past events.

3. It is difficult to justify the classification of research and development expenditures as assets because at the time expenditures are made the **future benefits are uncertain**, and **difficult to measure**.

b. 1. Expenditures for equipment to be used exclusively for research and development should be reported as research and development expense in the period incurred. Expenditures for equipment to be used both for research and development and for production should be capitalized and reported as fixed assets, less accumulated depreciation, on Mono's balance sheets from 1995 through 1998. An appropriate depreciation method should be used, with depreciation from 1995 through 1997 reported as research and development expense. Depreciation for 1998 should be added to cost of inventory, via factory overhead, and expensed as cost of goods sold.

2. **Cash payments** for the pilot plant construction should be reported as **cash outflows from operating activities** on Mono's 1996 statement of cash flows. **Cash received from the sale** of the pilot plant should be reported as a **cash inflow from operating activities** on Mono's 1997 statement of cash flows.

CHANGE ALERT

SFAS 138: *ACCOUNTING FOR CERTAIN DERIVATIVE INSTRUMENTS AND CERTAIN HEDGING ACTIVITIES*

SFAS 138 addresses a limited number of issues that caused implementation problems for numerous companies in the application of SFAS 133.

There are four basic things that are amended by this new standard: (1) the normal purchases and sales exceptions have been extended to certain contracts; (2) the specific risks identified as the hedged risk have been redefined; (3) certain recognized foreign-currency denominated assets and liabilities may be the hedged item in fair value or cash flow hedges; and (4) certain intercompany derivatives may be designated as the hedging instruments in certain cash flow hedges.

These issues are highly technical and not likely to be tested, but will allow companies to more easily implement SFAS 133. However, the following additional terminology was defined in this statement and candidates should be familiar with these terms for the exam.

Benchmark Interest Rate The benchmark interest rate is a widely recognized and quoted rate in an active financial market as a rate associated with no risk of default. It is widely used as an underlying basis for determining the interest rates of individual financial instruments and commonly referenced in interest-rate-related transactions. In some markets, government borrowing rates may be used. In other markets, an interbank offered rate may be used. Currently in the US, only the interest rates on direct Treasury obligations of the US government and, for practical reasons, the LIBOR swap rate are considered to be benchmark interest rates.

LIBOR Swap Rate LIBOR (London Interbank Offered Rate) swap rate is the fixed rate on a single-currency, constant-notional interest rate swap that has its floating-rate leg referenced to the LIBOR. The fixed rate is derived as the rate that would result in the swap having a zero fair value at inception; the rate at which the present value of the fixed cash flows are equal to the present value of the floating cash flows.

SFAS 140: **ACCOUNTING FOR TRANSFERS AND SERVICING OF FINANCIAL ASSETS AND EXTINGUISHMENTS OF LIABILITIES**

SFAS 140 replaces SFAS 125, revising the standards for accounting for securitizations and other transfers of financial assets and collateral and requires certain disclosures. It carries over most of the provisions of SFAS 125.

CHAPTER 2

CASH, SHORT-TERM INVESTMENTS & RECEIVABLES

CHAPTER 2

CASH, SHORT-TERM INVESTMENTS & RECEIVABLES

I. CURRENT ASSETS

A. DEFINITION
Current assets are economic benefits owned by a firm that are reasonably expected to be converted into cash or consumed during the entity's operating cycle or one year, whichever is longer.

B. EXAMPLES
Include cash, temporary investments in marketable securities, accounts and notes receivable, inventories, and most prepaid expenses (ARB 43).

II. CASH AND CASH EQUIVALENTS

A. PRESENTATION
Cash is by definition the most liquid asset of an enterprise; thus, it is usually the first item presented in the current assets section of the balance sheet.

B. COMPONENTS OF CASH

1. Coin and currency on hand, including petty cash funds

2. Negotiable paper (i.e., transferable by endorsement). Examples include claims to cash such as bank checks, money orders, traveler's checks, bank drafts, and cashier's checks

3. Money market funds

4. Passbook savings accounts (although banks have the legal right to demand notice before withdrawal, they seldom exercise this right)

5. Deposits held as compensating balances against borrowing arrangements with a lending institution that are **not** legally restricted

6. Checks written by the enterprise, but not mailed until **after** the financial statement date, should be *added back* to the cash balance

7. Time certificates of deposit with original maturities of three months or less

C. ITEMS EXCLUDED FROM CASH

1. **CERTAIN TIME CERTIFICATES OF DEPOSIT** Time certificates of deposit with original maturities of longer than three months are classified as either temporary or long-term investments depending upon maturity dates and managerial intent.

2. **COMPENSATING BALANCES** Legally restricted deposits held as compensating balances against borrowing arrangements with a lending institution are classified as follows:

   a. If held as a compensating balance against a *short*-term borrowing arrangement, the restricted deposit is classified as a *current* asset but segregated from unrestricted cash.

   b. If held as a compensating balance against a *long*-term borrowing arrangement, the restricted deposit is classified as a *noncurrent* asset in either the investments or other assets section.

3. **RESTRICTED CASH** Restricted cash is classified based upon the date of availability or disbursement.

   a. **CURRENT** If restricted for a current asset or current liability, the restricted cash is classified as a current asset but segregate from unrestricted cash.

   b. **NONCURRENT** If restricted for a noncurrent asset or noncurrent liability (e.g., cash to be used for plant expansion or the retirement of long-term debt), the restricted cash is classified as a noncurrent asset in either the investments or other assets section regardless of whether the cash is expected to be disbursed within one year of the financial statement date.

4. **OVERDRAFTS** Overdrafts in accounts with no available cash in another account at the same bank to offset are classified as current liabilities.

5. **CERTAIN DEPOSITS** Deposits in banks under receivership or in foreign banks that are restricted as to conversion into dollars and/or transfer are segregated from unrestricted cash and are classified as current or noncurrent assets depending upon expected dates of availability.

6. **POSTDATED CHECKS** Postdated checks received from customers are classified as receivables.

7. **IOUs** IOUs from officers or employees are classified as receivables.

8. **POSTAGE** Postage stamps are classified as supplies or prepaid expenses.

D. **RECONCILIATION OF BANK BALANCES**

1. **NEED FOR PERIODIC RECONCILIATION OF BANK STATEMENTS**

   a. **CONTROL** Errors can be uncovered and corrected on a timely basis.

   b. **INFORMATION** Appropriate amounts are provided for entries in books.

2. **REASONS FOR DIFFERENCES**

   a. **ITEMS RECORDED IN BOOKS AND NOT REPORTED IN BANK STATEMENT** Deposits in transit and cash on hand should be added to the bank balance. Outstanding checks should be subtracted from the bank balance.

   b. **ITEMS REPORTED IN BANK STATEMENT AND NOT RECORDED IN BOOKS** Interest earned and collections by the bank should be added to the book balance. Bank service charges, returned checks (i.e., NSF checks), and payments by the bank should be subtracted from the book balance.

   c. **ERRORS** Differences may also result from errors in books or bank statement.

   d. **CERTIFIED AND CASHIER'S CHECKS** As both the bank and the enterprise have deducted the amounts of these checks from the enterprise's account, they do **not** represent reconciling items.

3. **FORMAT** A common format of the bank reconciliation statement is to reconcile both book and bank balances to a common amount known as the "true balance." This approach has the advantage of providing the cash figure to be reported in the balance sheet. Furthermore, journal entries necessary to adjust the books can be taken directly from the "book balance" section of the reconciliation.

EXAMPLE 1 ♦ BANK RECONCILIATION

On July 31, 20X1, The Company's bank statement showed a balance of $4,056, whereas the book balance was $4,706. Deposits in transit and cash on hand amounted to $588 and $456, respectively. During July, the bank collected a $215 note for The Company and charged the account $15 for service fees; neither of these transactions had been recorded by The Company. In addition, a check for $110 received from a customer and deposited by The Company was returned on July 31 for lack of funds. The following checks were outstanding at the end of July:

#320	$ 24.00
#321	$235.00
#325	$ 45.00

REQUIRED: Reconcile the bank and book balances to the true cash amount at July 31, 20X1.

SOLUTION:

BANK			BOOKS		
7/31 balance per bank		$4,056	7/31 balance per books		$4,706
Add			*Add*		
Deposit in transit	$588		Note collected by bank		215
Cash on hand	456	1,044			4,921
		5,100			
Less			*Less*		
Outstanding checks:			Bank service charge	$ 15	
#320	$ 24		Returned NSF check	110	(125)
#321	235				
#325	45	(304)			
True cash		$4,796	True cash		$4,796

Entries to adjust the books are taken directly from the reconciliation:

Cash	215	
Notes Receivable		215
Bank Service Charge Expense	15	
Cash		15
Special Receivable—NSF Check	110	
Cash		110

III. INVESTMENTS IN SECURITIES

A. USES

Funds not needed for the daily operations of the business are usually invested in short-term marketable securities to generate additional income. Some funds may be committed for longer periods by investing in securities to be held long term.

B. ACQUISITION COST

All debt and equity securities are recorded at cost, which includes broker's fees, taxes, and any other direct costs of acquisition. In the case of debt securities purchased between interest dates, accrued interest is **not** part of the cost of the securities.

C.   DEBT SECURITIES
Generally, the discount or premium on temporary investments in debt securities is not recorded separately in the accounts and not amortized because the investment is ordinarily held for only a short time and hence any amortized amount would be immaterial.

IV.   INVESTMENTS IN MARKETABLE DEBT AND EQUITY SECURITIES (SFAS 115)

A.   APPLICABILITY
SFAS 115 applies to investments in equity securities that have a readily determinable fair value and to all investments in debt securities. SFAS 115 does **not** apply to investments accounted for under the equity method nor to investments in consolidated subsidiaries.

B.   CLASSIFICATION
SFAS 115, *Accounting for Certain Investments in Debt and Equity Securities*, classifies securities in one of three categories: trading securities, available-for-sale (AFS) securities, or held-to-maturity (HTM) securities.

1.   **TRADING SECURITIES** Debt and equity securities that are bought and held principally for the purpose of selling them in the near term. Generally used with the objective of generating profits on short-term differences in price.

   a.   They are reported at fair value (market value).

   b.   Unrealized holding gains and losses are included in current earnings.

2.   **AVAILABLE-FOR-SALE SECURITIES** Debt and equity securities not classified as either held-to-maturity or trading securities.

   a.   They are reported at fair value (market value).

   b.   Unrealized holding gains and losses are excluded from current earnings and are instead reported in other comprehensive income.

3.   **HELD-TO-MATURITY SECURITIES** Debt securities that the enterprise has the positive intent and the ability to hold to maturity.

   a.   They are reported at amortized cost.

   b.   They are not adjusted for unrealized holding gains and losses, although fair value must be disclosed.

C.   ACQUISITION COST
Marketable debt and equity securities are recorded at cost, which includes the purchase price and other direct costs of acquisition, such as broker's fees and taxes.

D.   END-OF-YEAR VALUATION
HTM securities are reported at amortized cost. Trading securities and AFS securities are accounted for at fair value, determined at the balance sheet date. The excess of cost over fair value or fair value over cost is recorded as a credit or debit in a "Market Adjustment" account. The offsetting entry goes to an income statement account for trading securities, and to an Other Comprehensive Income account for available-for-sale securities.

EXAMPLE 2 ◆ MARKETABLE SECURITIES

On November 1, securities are purchased for $500. At year end, the fair value is $400. The entries are as follows:

	Trading Securities			Available-for-Sale Securities (AFS)	
11/1	Investment in Securities	500		Investment in Securities	500
	Cash		500	Cash	500
12/31	Unrealized Holding Gain or Loss on Securities (Income)	100		Unrealized Holding Gain or Loss on Securities (Other Comprehensive Income)	100
	Market Adjustment—Trading		100	Market Adjustment—AFS	100

E. **OTHER THAN TEMPORARY DECLINE IN FAIR VALUE**
If the decline in fair value for AFS or HTM securities is determined to be other than temporary, the cost basis of the individual security is written down to fair value that becomes the new cost basis and a realized loss is recognized in current earnings.

1. **SUBSEQUENT INCREASES** The new cost basis is not changed for subsequent recoveries in fair value. Subsequent increases in fair value of AFS securities are accounted for as unrealized gains by debiting the Market Adjustment account and crediting the Unrealized Holding Gain or Loss (Other Comprehensive Income) account.

2. **SUBSEQUENT DECREASES** Subsequent decreases in fair value of AFS securities, if not other-than-temporary, are accounted for as unrealized losses by debiting the Unrealized Holding Gain or Loss (Other Comprehensive Income) account and crediting the Market Adjustment account.

EXHIBIT 1 ◆ SUMMARY OF SFAS 115

	TRADING	AVAILABLE-FOR-SALE	HELD-TO-MATURITY
Type of security	Debt or Equity	Debt or Equity	Debt
Accounting at acquisition	Cost (purchase price plus other direct costs of acquisition)	Cost (purchase price plus other direct costs of acquisition)	Cost (purchase price plus other direct costs of acquisition)
End-of-year valuation	Fair value	Fair value	Amortized cost
Valuation adjustments	Market Adjustment account	Market Adjustment account	Not adjusted for fair value
Change in fair value	Reported in income	Reported in other comprehensive income	Not applicable
Other than temporary declines in fair value below cost	Reported in income	Reported in income	Reported in income
Balance Sheet classification	Current asset	Either current or non-current asset	Noncurrent asset (Unless maturing within one year)
Dividends and interest earned	Reported in income using interest method to amortize associated premium or discount*	Reported in income using interest method to amortize associated premium or discount	Reported in income using interest method to amortize associated premium or discount

* Generally, the amount of amortization for short-term investments is immaterial and therefore not recorded.

EXAMPLE 3 ◆ AVAILABLE-FOR-SALE PORTFOLIO, UNREALIZED GAIN

The aggregate cost and fair value (FV) of Zeta Corp.'s investments in marketable securities at 12/31/X1 and 12/31/X2 are given below.

	Marketable Securities - 12/31/X1		Marketable Securities - 12/31/X2	
	Cost	FV	Cost	FV
Security W	$ 800	$1,300	$ 800	$1,100
Security X	800	1,000	800	700
Security Y	900	600	1,000*	900
Security Z	900	600	1,000*	1,400
	$3,400	$3,500	$3,600	$4,100

* Increases reflect net acquisitions during the period.

Assume that the securities are classified as available-for-sale.

REQUIRED:

Determine the following:

a. Amount to report for these investments on the 12/31/X1 balance sheet.

b. Amount of unrealized gain or loss to be recognized in 20X2.

c. Amount to report for these investments on the 12/31/X2 balance sheet.

SOLUTION:

a. The fair value of the securities at 12/31/X1 ($3,500) is *greater* than its aggregate cost ($3,400). Therefore, the Market Adjustment—AFS account would have a $100 debit balance at 12/31/X1 and the Unrealized Holding Gain or Loss (Other Comprehensive Income) account would have a $100 credit balance at 12/31/X1.

The securities portfolio is presented in the asset section of the 12/31/X1 balance sheet as follows:

Investment in securities at fair value $3,500

b. At the end of 20X2, the fair value of the portfolio ($4,100) is $500 greater than its aggregate cost ($3,600). An additional $400 debit is required to bring the year-end balance in the valuation account to $500, resulting in the following journal entry:

Market Adjustment—AFS   400
　　Unrealized Holding Gain or Loss (OCI)   400

This brings the Market Adjustment—AFS account balance up to the $500 ($4,100 – $3,600) difference between cost and fair value at year end. Since it pertains to the AFS portfolio, the net unrealized holding gain of $500 is reported in Accumulated Other Comprehensive Income in the equity section.

c. The securities portfolio is presented in the asset section of the 12/31/X2 balance sheet as follows:

Investment in securities at fair value $4,100

NOTE: If the securities are classified as current, they would appear in the current asset section of the balance sheet. If they are classified as noncurrent, they would appear in the long-term investment section.

EXAMPLE 4 ♦ AVAILABLE-FOR-SALE PORTFOLIO, UNREALIZED LOSS

Assume the fair value of the portfolio at 12/31/X1 in Example 3 was $3,100 rather than $3,500 ($300 less than its aggregate cost). Therefore, the Market Adjustment—AFS account would have a $300 credit balance at 12/31/X1 and the Unrealized Holding Gain or Loss (Other Comprehensive Income) account would have a $300 debit balance at 12/31/X1.

At 12/31/X2, assume the fair value of the portfolio was $3,500 (only $100 *less* than its $3,600 aggregate cost). Therefore, the Market Adjustment—AFS account must be reduced by $200 with a corresponding reduction of the balance in the Unrealized Holding Gain or Loss (Other Comprehensive Income) account. The journal entry is as follows:

Market Adjustment—AFS	200	
Unrealized Holding Gain or Loss (OCI)		200

This brings the Market Adjustment—AFS account balance down to the $100 ($3,600 – $3,500) difference between cost and fair value at year end. Because it applies to the AFS category, the net unrealized loss of $100 is reported in Other Comprehensive Income.

The security portfolio is presented in the asset section of the 12/31/X2 balance sheet as follows:

Investment in securities at fair value	$3,500

EXAMPLE 5 ♦ TRADING SECURITIES PORTFOLIO

Assuming the same facts as the above two examples, the solutions for the trading securities category are the same, except that the changes in the Market Adjustment—Trading account flow through the current income statement, rather than through Other Comprehensive Income.

Thus, in Example 3, the journal entry would appear as follows:

Market Adjustment—Trading	400	
Unrealized Holding Gain or Loss (Income)		400

The unrealized holding gain of $400 would appear in the Other Revenues & Gains section of the 20X2 income statement.

In Example 4, the journal entry for the trading category would appear as follows:

Market Adjustment—Trading	200	
Unrealized Holding Gain or Loss (Income)		200

The $200 credit to the Unrealized Holding Gain or Loss (Income) account would appear in the Other Revenues & Gains section of the 20X2 income statement.

F. TRANSFERS BETWEEN CATEGORIES
Securities may be transferred among the three classifications: trading, AFS, and HTM; although such reclassification should be rare under the guidelines of SFAS 115.

1. TRANSFERS FROM TRADING If a security is transferred from the trading category, any previously recognized unrealized holding gain or loss should not be reversed. Additionally, the security should be transferred at fair value with a gain or loss recognized upon transfer.

2. TRANSFERS TO TRADING If a security is transferred into the trading category, any unrealized holding gain or loss related to this security should be recognized in earnings immediately.

3. **TRANSFERS FROM HTM TO AFS** If a debt security is transferred from the HTM category to the AFS category, any unrealized holding gain or loss related to this security should be recognized in an Other Comprehensive Income account consistent with the treatment for available-for-sale securities.

4. **TRANSFERS FROM AFS TO HTM** If a debt security is transferred from the AFS category to the HTM category, any unrealized holding gain or loss related to this security should still be reported in an Other Comprehensive Income account and amortized over the remaining life of the security.

G. SALE OF SECURITIES

1. **REALIZED GAIN OR LOSS** The realized gain or loss from the sale of a debt or equity security is the difference between the net proceeds received from the sale (i.e., the gross selling price of the security less brokerage commissions and taxes) and the cost or unamortized cost of the security (not its fair value at the most recent balance sheet date).

2. **PREVIOUSLY RECOGNIZED LOSSES OR RECOVERIES** In determining the realized gain or loss on the sale, no regard is given to previously recognized unrealized losses or recoveries or to the amount accumulated in the Market Adjustment account.

3. **RECLASSIFICATION ADJUSTMENTS**

a. Reclassification adjustments, required by SFAS 130, are made to avoid double counting in comprehensive income gains or losses realized and included in net income of the current period that were previously included in other comprehensive income as unrealized gains or losses.

b. Reclassification adjustments for unrealized gains and losses on certain investments in debt and equity securities may be summarized on the face of the financial statement in which comprehensive income is reported or disclosed in the notes to the financial statements.

V. FINANCIAL INSTRUMENTS AND DERIVATIVES

A. DEFINITIONS

1. **FINANCIAL INSTRUMENT** A financial instrument is cash, evidence of an ownership interest in an entity, or a contract that does both of the following:

a. **CONTRACTUAL OBLIGATION** Imposes on one entity a contractual obligation (1) to deliver cash or another financial instrument to a second entity or (2) to exchange other financial instruments on potentially unfavorable terms with the second entity.

b. **CONTRACTUAL RIGHT** Conveys to that second entity a contractual right (1) to receive cash or another financial instrument from the first entity or (2) to exchange other financial instruments on potentially favorable terms with the first entity.

2. **DERIVATIVE INSTRUMENT** A derivative instrument is an instrument or other contract that has the following three characteristics:

a. **UNDERLYING AND NOTIONAL AMOUNT OR PAYMENT PROVISION** A derivative instrument has at least one underlying and at least one notional amount or payment provision or both.

b. **ZERO OR SMALL INVESTMENT** A derivative instrument either requires no initial net investment, or one that is smaller than would be required for other types of contracts expected to have a similar response to market factor changes.

    c.   **NET SETTLEMENT** A derivative instrument requires or permits net settlement, can be readily settled net by a means outside the contract, or provides for delivery of an asset that puts the recipient in a position not substantially different from net settlement.

3.   **UNDERLYING** An underlying is a specified interest rate, security price, commodity price, foreign exchange rate, index of prices or rates, or other variable. An underlying may be a price or rate of an asset or liability, but it is not the asset or the liability.

4.   **NOTIONAL AMOUNT** A notional amount is a number of currency units, shares, bushels, pounds, or other units specified in a derivative instrument. The notional amount is called a face amount in some contracts.

5.   **FAIR VALUE** Fair value is the amount at which an asset (liability) could be bought (incurred) or sold (settled) in a current transaction between willing parties other than in a forced or liquidation sale. Generally, quoted market prices, if available, are the best evidence of fair value. If quoted market prices are unavailable, the estimate of fair value should be based on the best information available in the circumstances.

6.   **HEDGING** Hedging is a risk management strategy to protect against the possibility of loss, such as from price fluctuations. Generally, the strategy involves counterbalancing transactions in which a loss on one financial instrument or cash flow stream would be offset by a gain on the related derivative.

7.   **FIRM COMMITMENT** A firm commitment is an agreement with an unrelated party, binding on both parties and usually legally enforceable, with the following characteristics:

    a.   **SIGNIFICANT TERMS** The agreement specifies all significant terms, including the quantity to be exchanged, the fixed price, and the timing of the transaction. The fixed price may be expressed as a specified amount of an entity's functional currency or of a foreign currency, or as a specified interest rate or specified effective yield.

    b.   **NONPERFORMANCE** The agreement includes a disincentive for nonperformance that is sufficient to make performance probable.

8.   **FORECASTED TRANSACTION** A forecasted transaction is a transaction that is expected to occur for which there is no firm commitment, and does not give an entity any present rights to future benefits or a present obligation for future sacrifices.

B.   **DERIVATIVE INSTRUMENTS AND HEDGING ACTIVITIES (SFAS 133 & 138)**

1.   **BACKGROUND**

    a.   **ESTABLISHING ACCOUNTING AND REPORTING STANDARDS** SFAS 133, *Accounting for Derivative Instruments and Hedging Activities,* was issued by the Financial Accounting Standards Board in 1998 and was amended by SFAS 138 in 2000. These pronouncements establish accounting and reporting standards for derivative instruments and for hedging activities. Previous disclosure standards applicable to financial instruments and derivatives did not address the fundamental accounting issues. While these disclosures improved investors' understanding of the derivatives held by companies, the FASB did not consider disclosure a satisfactory substitute for recognition and measurement. As a consequence, the FASB issued SFAS 133, which goes beyond disclosures of derivatives and requires that companies include their derivatives in the financial statements. This greatly reduces off-balance-sheet-risk.

    b.   **SUPERSEDED AND AMENDED LITERATURE** SFAS 133 superseded SFAS 80, *Accounting for Futures Contracts*, SFAS 105, *Disclosure of Information about Financial Instruments with Off-Balance-Sheet Risk and Financial Instruments with Concentrations of Credit Risk,* and SFAS 119, *Disclosure about Derivative Financial Instruments and*

Fair Value of Financial Instruments. It amended SFAS 107, *Disclosures about Fair Value of Financial Instruments* and SFAS 52, *Foreign Currency Translation.*

EXHIBIT 2 ♦ HIGHLIGHTS OF ACCOUNTING FOR DERIVATIVE INSTRUMENTS AND HEDGING ACTIVITIES

- Derivatives are recognized as **assets or liabilities** on the financial statements.

- **Fair value** is used to measure derivatives.

- Changes in fair value of **non-hedge derivatives** are reported as **gains or losses in earnings**.

- Accounting for the unrealized gains or losses from the changes in fair value of **hedge derivatives** depends on the intended use of the derivative.

  1. **Fair Value Hedge**—Reported in **earnings**.

  2. **Cash Flow Hedge**—Effective portion reported in **other comprehensive income**; ineffective portions reported in earnings.

  3. **Hedge of a Net Investment in a Foreign Operation**—Effective portion reported in **other comprehensive income**; ineffective portion reported in earnings.

2. **RECOGNITION AS ASSETS AND LIABILITIES AT FAIR VALUE** An entity must recognize in the statement of financial position all derivatives as either assets or liabilities and measure them at fair value.

   a. **RIGHTS AND OBLIGATIONS** Derivatives are assets and liabilities because they are rights and obligations. Many can be settled for cash simply by making a phone call. The ability to settle a derivative in a gain position by receiving cash is evidence of the right to a future economic benefit and indicates the instrument is an asset. Similarly, the fact that a cash payment is required to settle a derivative in a loss position is evidence of the duty to sacrifice assets in the future and indicates the instrument is a liability.

   b. **RECOGNITION** Recognizing those assets and liabilities will make the financial statements more complete and more informative.

   c. **EMBEDDED DERIVATIVES** Some contracts may not meet the definition of a derivative instrument in their entirety, but may contain "embedded" derivative instruments. Embedded derivatives must be separately valued if their economic characteristics and risks are not clearly and closely related to the economic characteristics and risks of the host contract.

3. **HEDGING DERIVATIVES**

   a. **TYPES OF HEDGES** If certain conditions are met, the derivative may be designated as one of three categories of hedges, depending on its intended use: fair value hedge, cash flow hedge, or foreign currency hedge.

      (1) **FAIR VALUE HEDGE** A hedge of the exposure to changes in the fair value of an asset or liability, or an unrecognized firm commitment.

      (2) **CASH FLOW HEDGE** A hedge of the exposure to variable cash flows on an existing, recognized asset or liability (such as all or certain future interest payments on variable-rate debt) or a forecasted transaction (such as a forecasted purchase or sale).

(3) **FOREIGN CURRENCY HEDGE** A hedge of the foreign currency exposure of a net investment in a foreign operation, an unrecognized firm commitment, an available-for-sale security, or a foreign-currency-denominated forecasted transaction.

b. **HEDGE CRITERIA** For derivatives that are intended to be fair value or cash flow hedges and are effective as fair value or cash flow hedges, all of the following criteria must be met:

(1) **FORMAL DOCUMENTATION** At the inception of the hedge, there must be formal documentation of the hedging relationship and the entity's risk management objective and strategy for undertaking the hedge, including identification of the hedging instrument, the related hedged item, the nature of the risk being hedged, and how the hedging instrument's effectiveness in offsetting the hedged item's exposure attributable to the hedged risk will be assessed. There must be a reasonable basis for how the entity plans to assess the hedging instrument's effectiveness.

(2) **EXPECTATION OF EFFECTIVENESS** Both at the inception of the hedge and on an ongoing basis, the hedging relationship must be expected to be highly effective in achieving offsetting changes in fair value or cash flows attributable to the hedged risk, consistent with the originally documented risk management strategy for that particular hedging relationship, during the period that the hedge is designated. An assessment of effectiveness is required whenever financial statements or earnings are reported, and at least every three months.

(3) **POTENTIAL FOR GAIN** If a net written option is designated as hedging a recognized asset or liability, the combination of the hedged item and the written option must provide at least as much potential, for a fair value hedge, for gains as a result of a favorable change in the fair value of the combined instruments as exposure to losses from an unfavorable change in their combined fair value; or for a cash flow hedge, favorable cash flows as exposure to unfavorable cash flows.

c. **CRITERIA FOR A HEDGED ITEM IN A FAIR VALUE HEDGE** The following are the primary criteria; there are other specific exclusions provided for in SFAS 133.

(1) The hedged item is specifically identified as either all or a specific portion of a recognized asset or liability or of a firm commitment.

(2) The hedged item is a single asset or liability, or is a portfolio of similar assets or a portfolio of similar liabilities. If similar assets or similar liabilities are aggregated and hedged as a portfolio, the individual assets or individual liabilities must share the risk exposure for which they are designated as being hedged.

(3) The hedged item presents an exposure to changes in fair value for the hedged risk that could affect reported earnings.

d. **CRITERIA FOR A FORECASTED TRANSACTION AS A HEDGED TRANSACTION IN A CASH FLOW HEDGE** A forecasted transaction is eligible for designation as a hedged transaction in a cash flow hedge if all of the following primary criteria are met:

(1) The forecasted transaction is a single transaction or a series of individual transactions. If individual forecasted transactions are aggregated and hedged as a group, either (a) the individual transactions must be projected to occur within a short period of time from a single identified date for the group or (b) the date at which the variability of the cash flows of each of the individual transactions is projected to cease must be within a short period of time from a single identified date for the group. Additionally, the individual transactions must share the same risk exposure for which they are designated as being hedged.

(2) The forecasted transaction is probable and there is a positive expectation that the forecasted transaction, or group of similar forecasted transactions, will occur within an insignificant variance from the initially projected date of the forecasted transaction relative to the original length of time from the inception of the hedge to that projected date.

(3) The forecasted transaction is a transaction with a third party external to the reporting entity and presents an exposure to variations in cash flows for the hedged risk that could affect reported earnings.

4. **UNREALIZED GAINS AND LOSSES** Unrealized gains and losses resulting from changes in the fair value of a derivative will be accounted for in either current earnings or in other comprehensive income, depending on the intended use of the derivative.

a. **NON-HEDGING DERIVATIVE** The gain or loss is *recognized in earnings* in the period of change for derivatives not held for hedging purposes.

b. **FAIR VALUE HEDGE** The gain or loss is *recognized in earnings* in the period of change, together with the offsetting loss or gain in the hedged item. Net losses or gains in the hedging activity indicates the effectiveness of the hedge; i.e. if the net loss or gain is zero, then the hedge was highly effective. The effect of that accounting is to reflect in earnings the extent to which the hedge is not effective in achieving offsetting changes in fair value. Thus both overhedged and underhedged positions will be included in income.

c. **CASH FLOW HEDGE** The effective portion of the gain or loss is initially reported as a component of *other comprehensive income* and subsequently reclassified into earnings when the forecasted transaction affects earnings. The overhedged ineffective portion of the gain or loss is reported in earnings immediately. For example, if the derivative is a hedge of anticipated cash flows associated with the acquisition of inventory, the gain or loss on the derivative would be included in income when the cost of sales is recognized. If, however, the forecasted cash flow were the acquisition of property and equipment, the gain or loss on the derivative would be recognized based on the depreciation of the property and equipment.

d. **FOREIGN CURRENCY HEDGES**

(1) **FOREIGN CURRENCY FAIR VALUE HEDGE** The gain or loss on an unrecognized firm commitment or an available-for-sale security designated as a fair value foreign currency hedge is recognized currently in *earnings*. The gain or loss on the hedged item adjusts the carrying amount of the hedged item and is also recognized currently in earnings. (Note that this is the same treatment as for a fair value hedge.) If the hedged item is an available-for-sale security, the recognition of gain or loss in earnings rather than in other comprehensive income is an exception to the normal accounting treatment of gains and losses on available-for-sale securities, in order to offset the gain or loss on the hedging instrument that is reported in current earnings.

(2) **FOREIGN CURRENCY CASH FLOW HEDGE** The *effective portion* of the gain or loss on a forecasted foreign-currency-denominated transaction or a forecasted intercompany foreign-currency-denominated transaction designated as a cash flow hedge is reported in *other comprehensive income*, and the ineffective portion is reported in earnings. Effectiveness is defined as the degree that the gain (loss) for the hedging instrument offsets the loss (gain) on the hedged item.

(3) **HEDGE OF A NET INVESTMENT IN A FOREIGN OPERATION** The gain or loss on a hedging derivative instrument, or the foreign currency transaction gain or loss on a nonderivative hedging instrument, that is designated as an economic hedge, and is effective as an economic hedge, of the net investment in a foreign operation is reported in *other comprehensive income*, as part of the cumulative translation adjustment, to the extent it is effective as a hedge.

5. **DISCLOSURE REQUIREMENTS**

a. **OBJECTIVES** An entity that holds or issues hedging instruments must disclose its objectives for holding or issuing those instruments, the context needed to understand those objectives, and its strategies for achieving those objectives.

b. **TYPE** The description must distinguish between instruments designated for fair value hedges, cash flow hedges, foreign currency hedges, and all other derivatives.

c. **RISK POLICY** The description must indicate the entity's risk management policy for each type of hedge, including a description of the items or transactions for which risks are hedged.

d. **PURPOSE** For non-hedge derivatives, the description must indicate the purpose of the derivative activity.

e. **ADDITIONAL DISCLOSURES ENCOURAGED** The entity is encouraged, but not required, to provide additional qualitative disclosures, including the entity's objectives and strategies within the context of an entity's overall risk management profile.

f. **EFFECTIVENESS** For fair value hedges, the net gain or loss recognized in earnings during the reporting period representing the amount of the hedges' ineffectiveness and the component of the derivative instruments' gain or loss, if any, excluded from the assessment of hedge effectiveness and a description of where the net gain or loss is reported in the financial statements must be disclosed.

g. **RECOGNIZED GAINS AND LOSSES** When a hedged firm commitment no longer qualifies as a fair value hedge, the amount of net gain or loss recognized in earnings must be disclosed.

h. **CASH FLOW HEDGES** For cash flow hedges, disclosure must include:

(1) The net gain or loss recognized in earnings during the reporting period representing the amount of the hedges' ineffectiveness and the component of the derivative instruments' gain or loss, if any, excluded from the assessment of hedge effectiveness and a description of where the net gain or loss is reported in the financial statements.

(2) A description of the transactions or other events that will result in the reclassification into earnings of gains and losses reported in accumulated other comprehensive income, and the estimated net amount of the existing gains or losses at the reporting date expected to be reclassified into earnings within the next 12 months.

(3) The maximum length of time over which the entity is hedging its exposure to the variability in future cash flows for forecasted transactions excluding those forecasted transactions related to the payment of variable interest on existing financial instruments.

(4) The amount of gains and losses reclassified into earnings as a result of the discontinuance of cash flow hedges because it is probable that the original forecasted transactions will not occur.

i. **FOREIGN CURRENCY HEDGES** For foreign currency hedge instruments, the net amount of gains or losses included in the cumulative translation adjustment during the reporting period must be disclosed.

j. **OTHER COMPREHENSIVE INCOME** An entity must display as a separate classification within other comprehensive income the net gain or loss on derivative instruments designated and qualifying as cash flow hedging instruments that are reported in comprehensive income.

k. **ACCUMULATED OTHER COMPREHENSIVE INCOME** An entity must separately disclose, as part of the accumulated other comprehensive income disclosures, the beginning and ending accumulated derivative gain or loss, the related net change associated with current period hedging transactions, and the net amount of any reclassification into earnings.

EXAMPLE 6 ♦ HEDGE OF COMMODITY PRICE RISK ON PURCHASE OF INVENTORIES

Cereal Co. manufactures breakfast cereals and is concerned about the volatility of grain prices, since such volatility will significantly impact its profit margins on sales of cereal products. Cereal Co. anticipates acquiring 10 million bushels of grain in six months at the then current spot rate. To protect against future price changes in the commodity, on the current date, Cereal Co. acquires grain futures for 10 million bushels at the current spot rate for delivery in six months. Assume the current price is $.40 per bushel, and the price in six months when grain is acquired is $.45 per bushel.

Assume that the entity acquires the 10 million bushels of grain in six months at $.45 per bushel. It then sells the finished products over the following three months. Assume all of the hedging criteria are met.

REQUIRED: Give the journal entries to record the commodity futures on the current date, prior to the settlement of the contract and a summary entry for the realization of the gain over the three following months as the inventory is sold. The entries to record actual settlement of the contract and acquisition of inventory are not required.

SOLUTION:

Current date:

Investment in Grain Futures	4,000,000	
Due to Broker		4,000,000

6 months, prior to settlement of contract:

Investment in Grain Futures	500,000	
Unrealized Gain on Derivative—		
Accumulated Other Comprehensive Income		500,000

Settlement of contract and acquisition of inventory:
Cereal Co. would settle the contract and purchase inventory at the current market price. This results in inventory of $4,500,000.

3 months following, in proportion to sales of inventory:

Unrealized Gain on Derivative—		
Accumulated Other Comprehensive Income	500,000	
Gain on Derivatives		500,000

EXAMPLE 7 ♦ HEDGE OF FOREIGN CURRENCY EXCHANGE RATE RISK ON AN ACQUISITION OF EQUIPMENT

Assume that an entity anticipates acquiring equipment from a foreign manufacturer. The equipment is expected to be delivered in three months and will cost 1,200,000 FCU (Foreign Currency Units). The equipment will have a 5-year useful life and straight-line depreciation will be used. To hedge the foreign currency exchange rate exposure, the entity acquires forward contracts on the currency for delivery in three months. The current forward rate is $1 = .5 FCU. The spot (forward) rate in three months (at settlement) is $1 = .3 FCU. Assume all of the hedging criteria are met.

REQUIRED: Give the journal entries to record the acquisition of the foreign currency derivative, unrealized gain, realization of gain, and depreciation expense.

SOLUTION:

Current date:

Due from Broker (1,200,000/.5)	2,400,000	
Foreign Currency Derivative		2,400,000

3 Months, prior to settlement of contract:

Due from Broker ($4,000,000* − $2,400,000)	1,600,000	
Unrealized Gain on Derivative—		
Accumulated Other Comprehensive Income		1,600,000

*1,200,000/.3

Settlement of contract and acquisition of equipment:
The entity would settle the contract and purchase the equipment, resulting in equipment recorded at $4,000,000.

Recorded each year for five years:

Unrealized Gain on Derivative—		
Accumulated OCI ($1,600,000/5)	320,000	
Gain on Derivatives		320,000
Depreciation Expense ($4,000,000/5)	800,000	
Accumulated Depreciation		800,000

6. **TERMINOLOGY** This list is not intended to be all inclusive. It includes a sample of derivatives and instruments that contain embedded derivatives.

NOTE: Candidates studying for the CPA Exam do not need to memorize the following list. It is included so that candidates may become familiar with terminology that could be used in questions regarding derivative instruments.

a. **BENCHMARK INTEREST RATE** The benchmark interest rate is a widely recognized and quoted rate in an active financial market as a rate associated with no risk of default. It is widely used as an underlying basis for determining the interest rates of individual financial instruments and commonly referenced in interest-rate-related transactions. In some markets, government borrowing rates may be used. In other markets, an interbank offered rate may be used. Currently in the US, only the interest rates on direct Treasury obligations of the US government and, for practical reasons, the LIBOR swap rate are considered to be benchmark interest rates.

b. **LIBOR SWAP RATE** LIBOR (London Interbank Offered Rate) swap rate is the fixed rate on a single-currency, constant-notional interest rate swap that has its floating-rate leg referenced to the LIBOR. The fixed rate is derived as the rate that would result in the swap having a zero fair value at inception; the rate at which the present value of the fixed cash flows are equal to the present value of the floating cash flows.

c.   **INTEREST RATE SWAP AGREEMENT**   An interest rate swap agreement is an arrangement used to limit interest rate risk. Two companies swap interest payments, but not the principal, in an interest rate swap agreement. A company with a substantial amount of variable rate debt may wish to swap into fixed-rate debt to limit its exposure to rising interest rates. A company with a high fixed rate may wish to swap to a floating rate in anticipation of falling interest rates. Companies with lower credit ratings often cannot borrow in the fixed-rate market but can swap into it. Such transactions were previously considered off-balance sheet financing because only the original borrowings were reported on the balance sheet and the rights and obligations related to the interest payments per the swap agreement were not reported on the balance sheet, but only in the disclosures. Under SFAS 133, this is an example of a derivative required to be reported on the balance sheet.

d.   **SWAPTION**   A swaption is an option to require delivery of a swap contract, which is a derivative.

e.   **EMBEDDED DERIVATIVE**   A derivative embedded in a host contract in a hybrid instrument.

f.   **HOST CONTRACT**   A hybrid contract that contains an embedded derivative.

g.   **INVERSE FLOATER**   A bond with a coupon rate of interest that varies inversely with changes in specified general interest rate levels or indexes (such as LIBOR).

h.   **LEVERED INVERSE FLOATER**   A bond with a coupon that varies indirectly with changes in general interest rate levels and applies a multiplier (greater than 1.00) to the specified index in its calculation of interest.

i.   **DELIVERED FLOATER**   A bond with a coupon rate of interest that lags overall movements in specified general interest rate levels or indices.

j.   **RANGE FLOATER**   A bond with a coupon that depends on the number of days that a reference rate stays within a preestablished collar; otherwise, the bond pays either zero percent interest or a below-market rate.

k.   **RATCHET FLOATER**   A bond that pays a floating rate of interest and has an adjustable cap, adjustable floor, or both that move in sync with each new reset rate.

l.   **FIXED-TO-FLOATING NOTE**   A bond that pays a varying coupon (first-year coupon is fixed; second- and third-year coupons are based on LIBOR, Treasury bills, or prime rate).

m.   **INDEXED AMORTIZING NOTE**   A bond that repays principal based on a predetermined amortization schedule or target value. The amortization is linked to changes in a specific mortgage-backed security index or interest rate index. The maturity of the bond changes as the related index changes. This instrument includes a varying maturity.

n.   **EQUITY-INDEXED NOTE**   A bond for which the return of interest, principal, or both is tied to a specified equity security or index (such as the Standard and Poor's 500 index).

o.   **VARIABLE PRINCIPAL REDEMPTION BOND**   A bond whose principal redemption value at maturity depends on the change in an underlying index over a predetermined observation period. A typical example would be a bond that guarantees a minimum par redemption value of 100% and provides the potential for a supplemental principal payment at maturity as compensation for the below market rate of interest offered with the instrument.

p. **CRUDE OIL KNOCK-IN NOTE** A bond that has a 1% coupon and guarantees repayment of principal with upside potential based on the strength of the oil market.

q. **GOLD-LINKED BULL NOTE** A bond that has a fixed 3% coupon and guarantees repayment of principal with upside potential if the price of gold increases.

r. **STEP-UP BOND** A bond that provides an introductory above-market yield and steps up to a new coupon, which will be below then-current market rates or alternatively, the bond may be called in lieu of the step-up in the coupon rate.

s. **CREDIT-SENSITIVE BOND** A bond that has a coupon rate of interest that resets based on changes in the issuer's credit rating.

t. **INFLATION BOND** A bond with a contractual principal amount that is indexed to the inflation rate but cannot decrease below par; the coupon rate is typically below that of traditional bonds of similar maturity.

u. **DISASTER BOND** A bond that pays a coupon above that of an otherwise comparable traditional bond; however, all or a substantial portion of the principal amount is subject to loss if a specified disaster experience occurs.

v. **CERTAIN PURCHASES IN A FOREIGN CURRENCY** A U.S. company enters into a contract to purchase corn from a local American supplier in six months for yen; the yen is the functional currency of neither party to the transaction. The corn is expected to be delivered and used over a reasonable period in the normal course of business.

w. **PARTICIPATING MORTGAGE** A mortgage in which the investor receives a below-market interest rate and is entitled to participate in the appreciation in the market value of the project that is financed by the mortgage upon sale of the project.

x. **CONVERTIBLE DEBT** An investor receives a below-market interest rate and receives the option to convert its debt instrument into the equity of the issuer at an established conversion rate. The terms of the conversion require that the issuer deliver shares of stock to the investor. Generally, the written option is not considered to be a derivative instrument for the issuer. However, the investor generally should separate the embedded option contract from the host contract and account for the embedded option contract as a derivative instrument, unless the stock is privately held and not readily convertible to cash.

7. **EXCEPTIONS** The following contracts are not subject to the requirements of SFAS 133:

a. **REGULAR-WAY SECURITY TRADES** Regular-way security trades are contracts with no net settlement provision and no market mechanism to facilitate net settlement. They provide for delivery of a security within the time generally established by regulations or conventions in the marketplace or exchange in which the transaction is being executed.

b. **NORMAL PURCHASES AND NORMAL SALES** Normal purchases and normal sales are contracts with no net settlement provision and no market mechanism to facilitate net settlement. They provide for the purchase or sale of something other than a financial instrument or derivative instrument that will be delivered in quantities expected to be used or sold by the reporting entity over a reasonable period in the normal course of business.

c. **CERTAIN INSURANCE CONTRACTS** An insurance contract that entitles the holder to be compensated only if, as a result of an identifiable insurable event (other than a change in price), the holder incurs a liability or there is an adverse change in the value of a specific asset or liability for which the holder is at risk. Examples include traditional life insurance contracts, traditional property and casualty contracts.

C. *DISCLOSURES ABOUT FAIR VALUE OF FINANCIAL INSTRUMENTS* (SFAS 107)

1. **REQUIRED DISCLOSURES** An entity must disclose the following, either in the body of the financial statements or in the accompanying notes.

   a. **FAIR VALUE** The fair value of financial instruments for which it is practicable to estimate that value

   b. **ESTIMATION METHODS** The method(s) and significant assumptions used to estimate the fair value of financial instruments

2. **EVIDENCE OF FAIR VALUE** Quoted market prices, if available, are the best evidence of the fair value of financial instruments. If quoted market prices are not available, management's best estimate of fair value may be based on the quoted market price of a financial instrument with similar characteristics or on valuation techniques.

3. **TRADE RECEIVABLES AND PAYABLES** For trade receivables and payables, no disclosure is required under SFAS 107 when the carrying amount approximates fair value.

4. **PRACTICABLE/NOT PRACTICABLE** In the context of SFAS 107, practicable means that an estimate of fair value can be made without incurring excessive costs. If it is not practicable to estimate the fair value of a financial instrument or a class of financial instruments, the following should be disclosed.

   a. **PERTINENT INFORMATION** Information pertinent to estimating the fair value of that financial instrument or class of financial instruments, such as the carrying amount, effective interest rate, and maturity

   b. **REASONS** The reasons why it is not practicable to estimate fair value

5. **CONCENTRATION OF CREDIT RISK** An entity must disclose all significant concentrations of *credit risk* arising from **all** financial instruments, whether from an individual counterparty or groups of counterparties.

   a. **CREDIT RISK** *Credit* risk is the possibility that a loss may occur from the failure of another party to perform according to the terms of a contract.

   b. **GROUP CONCENTRATIONS** Group concentrations of credit risk exist if a number of counterparties are engaged in similar activities and have similar economic characteristics that would cause their ability to meet contractual obligations to be similarly affected by changes in economic or other conditions.

   c. **DISCLOSURE REQUIREMENTS** For each significant concentration, disclosure must be made as follows:

      (1) Information about the (shared) activity, region, or economic characteristic that identifies the concentration.

      (2) The maximum amount of loss exposure due to credit risk if all parties to the financial instruments failed completely to perform and the amounts due proved to be of no value to the entity.

      (3) The entity's policy of requiring collateral or other security to support financial instruments subject to credit risk, information about the entity's access to that

collateral or security, and the nature and a brief description of the collateral or other security.

(4) The entity's policy of entering into master netting arrangements to mitigate the credit risk and information about such arrangements and the extent the arrangements reduce the credit risk.

6. **MARKET RISK** An entity is encouraged, but not required to disclose quantitative information about the market risks of financial instruments that is consistent with the way it manages or adjusts those risks. *Market* risk is the possibility that future changes in market prices may make a financial instrument less valuable or more onerous.

7. **EXCLUDED ENTITIES** The disclosures about fair value prescribed by SFAS 107 are not required for employers' and plans' obligations for pension benefits, other postretirement benefits, and employee stock option and stock purchase plans, substantially extinguished debt subject to the disclosure requirements of SFAS 125, lease contracts, warranty obligations and rights, unconditional purchase obligations, investments accounted for under the equity method, minority interests in consolidated subsidiaries, equity investments in consolidated subsidiaries, and equity instruments issued by the entity and classified in stockholders' equity in the statement of financial position.

D. **TRANSFERS & SERVICING OF FINANCIAL ASSETS & EXTINGUISHMENTS OF LIABILITIES (SFAS 140)**

1. **PURPOSE AND SCOPE** This statement establishes accounting and reporting standards for transfers and servicing of financial assets and extinguishments of liabilities. The standards focus on control; an entity must recognize the financial and servicing assets it controls and the liabilities it has incurred, derecognize financial assets when control has been surrendered, and derecognize liabilities when extinguished. The standards establish guidelines to determine transfers of financial assets that are sales and transfers that are secured borrowing.

a. **ACCOUNTING FOR TRANSFERS AND SERVICING OF FINANCIAL ASSETS** A transfer in which control is surrendered by the transferor shall be accounted for as a sale to the extent that consideration other than beneficial interests in the transferred assets is received in exchange. For control to be surrendered, all of the following conditions must be met.

(1) The transferred assets must be isolated from the transferor and must be beyond the reach of the transferor and its creditors, even in bankruptcy.

(2) Either the transferee obtains the rights to pledge or exchange the transferred assets, or the transferee is a qualified special purpose entity and the holders of the beneficial interest of that special purpose entity can pledge or exchange the interest. The transferor cannot place restrictions or conditions on what the transferee does with the transferred assets.

(3) The transferor does not maintain effective control over the transferred assets through repurchase or redemption agreements.

b. **SALE VS. COLLATERALIZED BORROWING** If the above conditions are met, the transfer is accounted for as a sale and the assets received and liabilities incurred in the exchange are measured at fair value. If not all of the above conditions are met, the exchange would be accounted for as collateralized borrowing.

EXAMPLE 8 ◆ TRANSFER AND SERVICING OF FINANCIAL ASSETS

Assume that ABC Company originates $50,000 of loans that can be prepaid. These loans yield 10% interest income over their expected lives. ABC transfers 80% of the principal plus interest of 8.5% to another entity. ABC will continue to service the loans and will receive the interest income not sold. Additionally, ABC has an option to purchase the loans, and there is a recourse obligation requiring ABC to repurchase delinquent loans.

ABC receives the following in the transfer (each amount represents fair value):

Cash	$40,000
Call option (to repurchase loans)	3,500
Recourse obligation	2,500
Servicing asset	3,000
20% interest retained	10,000

The fair value of the net proceeds received in the transfer is:

Cash	$40,000
Call option	3,500
Recourse obligation	(2,500)
Net proceeds	$41,000

REQUIRED:

a. Allocate the carrying amount of the loan ($50,000) between the portion sold and the portion retained based upon the relative fair values.

b. Calculate the gain or loss on the sale.

c. Show the journal entries required for ABC to record the transfer and to recognize the servicing asset.

d. Show how the amounts would appear on ABC's balance sheet after the transfer.

SOLUTION:

a. Allocation of the carrying amount of the loan, based upon relative fair values, is calculated as follows:

Interest	Fair Value	% Allocation of Total Fair Value	Carrying Amount
Interest sold	$41,000	75.9%	$37,950
Servicing asset	3,000	5.6%	2,800
20% interest retained	10,000	18.5%	9,250
Total	$54,000	100.0%	$50,000

b. The gain/loss on the sale is calculated as follows:

Net proceeds	$41,000
Carrying amount of loans sold	37,950
Gain on sale	$ 3,050

c. ABC would record the transfer and the servicing asset as follows:

Cash	40,000	
Call option	3,500	
Loans		37,950
Recourse obligation		2,500
Gain on sale		3,050
Servicing asset	2,800	
Loans		2,800

(continued on next page)

d. Since the loans retained have an assigned carrying amount of $9,250, the following amounts appear on ABC's balance sheet after the transfer:

ASSETS:		LIABILITIES:	
Cash	$40,000	Recourse obligation	$2,500
Loans	9,250		
Call option	3,500		
Servicing asset	2,800		

2. **FINANCIAL-COMPONENTS APPROACH** This statement is based on a financial-components approach, which is the recognition that financial assets and liabilities can be divided into a variety of components. A transaction may be treated partially as a sale and partially as collateralized borrowing.

3. **TERMINOLOGY**

   a. **INTEREST-ONLY STRIP** A contractual right to receive some or all of the interest due on a bond, mortgage loan, collateralized mortgage obligation, or other interest-bearing financial asset.

   b. **CLEANUP CALL** An option held by the servicer, which may be the transferor, to purchase transferred financial assets when the amount of outstanding assets falls to a level at which the cost of servicing those assets becomes burdensome.

   c. **SECURITIZATION** The process by which financial assets are transformed into securities.

   d. **WASH SALES** A situation where the same financial asset is purchased soon before or after the sale of the financial asset. Wash sales were previously not recognized, however, under SFAS 125, wash sales are accounted for as sales, unless there is a concurrent contract to repurchase in which the entity retains control of the asset.

   e. **FACTORING** Arrangements to discount accounts receivable on a nonrecourse, notification basis. If the arrangements meet the criteria for surrendering control (*see* D.1.a. above), the transactions are accounted for as sales.

VI. ACCOUNTS RECEIVABLE

A. DEFINITION
The term "accounts receivable" is generally used to designate claims arising from the sale of goods or the performance of services. Receivables not arising from normal operations, such as amounts due from stockholders, officers, or employees, should be reported separately from trade accounts receivable.

B. VALUATION
Accounts receivable should be reported at their *net realizable value*—the net amount expected to be received in cash. This raises two major problems: (1) determining the amount due, and (2) estimating the extent to which receivables will not be collected.

1. **DETERMINING THE AMOUNT DUE**

   a. **DISCOUNTS FOR PROMPT PAYMENT** Conceptually, sales and receivables should be recorded net of any discounts for prompt payment. Failure by the purchaser to take advantage of the discount offered should not be regarded as additional consideration received for the goods or services provided. These additional amounts should instead be considered as interest revenue. If receivables have been recorded at gross, such discounts should be anticipated at year-end and deducted from the accounts receivable.

b. **TRADE AND QUANTITY DISCOUNTS** Sales and accounts receivable should be recorded net of any trade or quantity discounts. The actual consideration agreed upon should be the amount recorded for the transaction. Sometimes the list price of a product is subject to several trade discounts. When more than one discount is given, each discount is applied to the declining balance successively. If a product has a list price of $100 and is subject to trade discounts of 20% and 10%, the actual amount recorded for the sale would be: $100 – 20%($100) = $80; $80 – 10%($80) = $72.

c. **SALES RETURNS AND ALLOWANCES** Future returns and allowances associated with accounts receivable outstanding at the balance sheet date should be anticipated. An allowance account should be credited for the estimated amount. The offsetting debit is to a special inventory account to reflect the expected net realizable value of returned items and the balance is charged to the sales return expense account (a "plug" amount).

d. **FREIGHT CHARGES** The treatment of freight charges depends on the terms of the sale. If they are to be borne by the seller, an expense account is charged; however, if the seller pays the freight but the amount is ultimately charged to the customer, the freight charges are included in the receivable.

   (1) **FOB SHIPPING POINT** When goods are shipped FOB shipping point, the buyer is responsible for paying the freight charges.

   (2) **FOB DESTINATION** When goods are shipped FOB destination, the seller is responsible for paying the freight charges.

2. **ESTIMATING THE EXTENT TO WHICH RECEIVABLES WILL NOT BE COLLECTED** There are basically two generally accepted allowance methods of recognizing the amount of uncollectible receivables and the related bad debt expense. These are the percentage-of-sales and percentage-of-outstanding-receivables methods.

   a. **PERCENTAGE-OF-SALES METHOD** Under this approach, bad debt expense is calculated as a percentage of credit sales for a period. This percentage is determined on the basis of the company's overall experience with credit sales over a period of time and is then adjusted for any relevant conditions. The amount thus estimated is charged to Bad Debt Expense and credited to the Allowance for Uncollectible Accounts, a contra-account to Accounts Receivable. Any previous balance in the allowance account is **not** considered in determining the amount of bad debt expense recognized for the period. The percentage-of-sales method is income statement oriented because it attempts to match bad debt expense with the revenues generated by the credit sales in the same period.

   b. **PERCENTAGE-OF-OUTSTANDING-RECEIVABLES METHOD** This approach is based on the balance in the trade receivables accounts and attempts to value the accounts receivable at their future collectible amounts. A percentage of uncollectible accounts in the gross accounts receivable is determined based on the company's overall experience with uncollectible accounts over a period of time, and is then adjusted for any relevant conditions. This percentage is applied to the ending balance of the gross accounts receivable to obtain the desired ending balance of the allowance for uncollectible accounts. The amount of bad debt expense recognized is the difference between the *existing* balance in the allowance account and the *desired* ending balance. A more refined version of this method entails the *aging* of the gross accounts receivable. Under this approach, gross accounts receivable are classified by age intervals and a different percentage is applied to each age group. After the desired ending balance of the allowance group is determined, the amount of bad debt expense recognized is determined in exactly the same manner as when only one percentage is used—the amount of bad debt expense recognized is the difference between the *existing* balance in the allowance account and the *desired* ending balance. The percentage-of-outstanding-receivables method is balance sheet oriented because it attempts to achieve a proper carrying amount for the accounts receivable at the end of a period because they are reported at their net realizable value.

- Some companies estimate bad debt expense during the year using the percentage-of-sales method and then age their accounts receivable at the end of the year to determine the desired ending balance of the allowance for uncollectible accounts. In this situation, the total amount of bad debt expense recognized for the year is the amount of bad debt expense recognized during the year **plus** the amount recognized at the end of the year to adjust the existing balance in the allowance account to its desired ending balance.

EXAMPLE 9 ♦ ESTIMATING UNCOLLECTIBLE RECEIVABLES

Beginning balances:

Accounts receivable	$10,000
Allowance for uncollectible accounts	(750)
Accounts receivable, net	$ 9,250

Transactions during the period:	
Credit sales	$60,000
Collections on credit sales	55,000

During the period, accounts receivable amounting to $1,000 were written off as uncollectible, bringing the allowance for uncollectible accounts to a $250 debit balance.

TABLE 1—AGING OF ACCOUNTS RECEIVABLE, YEAR-END

		Days Outstanding			
	Total	0-30	31-60	61-90	Over 90
Accounts receivable*	$14,000	$9,000	$3,000	$1,000	$1,000
Est. % uncollectible		x 2%	x 6%	x 20%	x 50%
Est. amount uncollectible	$ 1,060	$ 180	$ 180	$ 200	$ 500

* [$10,000 + ($60,000 − $55,000 − $1,000) = $14,000]

REQUIRED: Estimate uncollectible receivables using the following methods.

a. Percentage-of-Sales: Assume 3% of credit sales is the estimated bad debt expense.

b. Simple Percentage-of-Outstanding-Receivables: Assume 6% of outstanding accounts receivable is estimated to be uncollectible.

c. Aged Percentage-of-Outstanding-Receivables

SOLUTION:

a. Percentage-of-Sales Method

Bad Debt Expense (3% x $60,000)	1,800	
Allowance for Uncollectible Accounts		1,800

The balance of the allowance for uncollectible accounts would be $1,550 ($1,800 − $250) at the end of the period.

b. Percentage-of-Outstanding-Receivables Method—Simple Percentage

Bad Debt Expense	1,090	
Allowance for Uncollectible Accounts		1,090

COMPUTATION

Desired balance in allowance, Cr (6% x $14,000)	$ 840
Present balance, Dr	250
Bad debt expense to be recognized	$1,090

If there was a $250 credit balance in the allowance for uncollectible accounts, bad debt expense of $590 ($840 − $250) would be recognized.

(continued on next page)

---

c. Percentage-of-Outstanding-Receivables Method—Aged Accounts Receivable

Bad Debt Expense	1,310	
Allowance for Uncollectible Accounts		1,310

COMPUTATION

Desired balance (Cr)	$1,060*
Present balance (Dr)	250
Bad debt expense to be recognized	$1,310

* Obtained from the "total" column of Table 1.

---

c. **RECORDING BAD DEBT EXPENSE** Regardless of the allowance method used, the following entry is used to record bad debt expense:

Bad Debt Expense	XX	
Allowance for Uncollectible Accounts		XX

NOTE: This entry decreases net income, net accounts receivable, current assets, and working capital.

d. **RECORDING ACCOUNTS WRITTEN OFF** Regardless of the allowance method used to estimate uncollectible receivables, the following journal entry should be made to record accounts written off during the period:

Allowance for Uncollectible Accounts	XX	
Accounts Receivable—Joe Doe		XX

NOTE: This entry has no effect on net income, net accounts receivable, current assets, or working capital.

e. **RECORDING SUBSEQUENT COLLECTIONS** Journal entries to record the collection of an account previously written off as uncollectible are as follows:

(1)

Accounts Receivable—Joe Doe	XX	
Allowance for Uncollectible Accounts		XX

To reopen the individual account to the balance it had when written off.

(2)

Cash	XX	
Accounts Receivable—Joe Doe		XX

To record the receipt of cash in partial payment of the receivable.

NOTE: These entries have no net effect on net income, current assets, or working capital.

f. **DIRECT WRITE-OFF METHOD** The direct write-off method of recognizing bad debt expense requires the identification of specific balances that are deemed to be uncollectible before any bad debt expense is recognized. At the time that a specific account is deemed uncollectible, the account is removed from accounts receivable and a corresponding amount of bad debt expense is recognized. Since the direct write-off method does not recognize bad debt expense until a specific amount is deemed uncollectible, it does not match the cost of making a credit sale with the revenues generated by the sale, and it does not achieve a proper carrying amount for the accounts receivable at the end of a period because they are reported at more than their net realizable value.

VII. NOTES RECEIVABLE

A. DEFINITION

Notes receivable are claims usually **not** arising from sales in the ordinary course of business. Legally, the claim is evidenced by a note representing an unconditional promise to pay. Typically, notes receivable result from the following transactions.

1. Sale of property other than in the ordinary course of business—for instance, disposition of operating assets

2. Special arrangements concerning overdue accounts receivable

3. Loans to stockholders, employees, and affiliates

B. TYPES OF NOTES

Notes can be classified as either *interest-bearing*, in which case the maker of the note pays an interest amount in addition to the face amount of the note, or *noninterest-bearing*, in which case the interest is included in the face amount.

C. RECORDING OF NOTES RECEIVABLE

APB 21 generally requires the recording of notes receivable at their present value.

1. **INTEREST-BEARING NOTES** For interest-bearing notes calling for the prevailing rate of interest at the time of issuance, the present value of the note is the same as the face amount of the note.

2. **EXCHANGED FOR CASH** Where a note is exchanged *solely* for cash and no other rights or privileges are exchanged, it is presumed to have a present value at issuance equal to the cash proceeds exchanged (APB 21, par. 10).

3. **NONINTEREST-BEARING OR OTHER NOTES** For noninterest-bearing notes and those with an unrealistic stated rate of interest, the receivable must be reported at its present value or the fair value of the property, good, or service exchanged, whichever is more clearly determinable. If material, the resultant discount or premium should be amortized over the life of the note by use of the *interest method*. Under this method, interest is calculated by applying the prevailing rate at the time of issuance to the carrying amount of the note at the beginning of the period. The prevailing rate of interest is usually defined as the cost of borrowing for a specific debtor (APB 21).

4. **LOAN ORIGINATION FEES** Loan origination fees are deferred and amortized over the life of the loan as an adjustment to interest income. Such amounts, if material, are amortized using the interest method.

EXAMPLE 10 ♦ RECORDING NOTES RECEIVABLE, INTEREST METHOD

On January 1, 20X0, Company X received a $10,000 note in exchange for equipment sold. The stated rate of interest was 5%, payable yearly on December 31. The prevailing interest rate at the time of the exchange was determined to be 8%. The note matures on December 31, 20X4.

REQUIRED: Compute the discount and interest income. Prepare the journal entries required to record the sale, the discount amortization, and the collection of the note, assuming no gain or loss on the sale of equipment.

(continued on next page)

SOLUTION:

a. Computation of Discount and Interest Income—Determine the present value (PV) of the note at the time of acquisition.

Obtaining the interest factors from the tables in Appendix D, the calculation is:

PV = $10,000 (.681)* + $500 (3.993)** = <u>$8,807</u>

---
* The present value of $1 for 5 periods at 8%.
** The present value of an annuity of $1 in arrears for 5 periods at 8%.

NOTE: Interest factors are provided in the CPA Examination. Memorizing the present value interest factor formula and annuity interest factor formula is not necessary. The ability to select the correct interest factor is necessary.

b. The next step is to construct a discount amortization table.

1 Date	2 Interest Income (8% x Col. 5)	3 Interest Payment (5% x $10,000)	4 Discount Amortiz. (2 – 3)	5 Present Value (PV + 4)
1/1/X0	--	--	--	$8,807
12/31/X0	$705	$500	$205	9,012
12/31/X1	721	500	221	9,233
12/31/X2	739	500	239	9,472
12/31/X3	758	500	258	9,730
12/31/X4	770*	500	270	$10,000

---
* $8 difference due to rounding.

c. The entries required to record the sale of the equipment, the discount amortization, and the collection of the note:

1/1/X0	Notes Receivable	10,000	
	Discount on Note Receivable		1,193
	Equipment		8,807

To record the exchange of the equipment for the note receivable.

12/31/X0	Cash	500	
	Discount on Note Receivable	205	
	Interest Income		705

To record the receipt of a $500 nominal interest payment and amortize the discount on the note. This entry would be repeated at the end of each year until maturity, the yearly amounts being taken directly from the amortization table.

12/31/X4	Cash	500	
	Discount on Note Receivable	270	
	Interest Income		770

To record receipt of interest and amortization (as before).

12/31/X4	Cash	10,000	
	Notes Receivable		10,000

To record the receipt of the $10,000 principal.

D. **IMPAIRMENT OF NOTES RECEIVABLE**

1. **INITIAL RECOGNITION OF IMPAIRMENT**

a. **IMPAIRMENT DEFINED** A creditor should consider a loan to be impaired when, "based on current information and events, it is probable that the creditor will be unable to collect all amounts due according to the contractual terms of the loan agreement." The accounting rules for creditors when loans are impaired is covered by SFAS 114.

b. **MEASUREMENT** The creditor measures the impaired loan at

(1) **PRESENT VALUE METHOD** The present value of future principal and interest cash inflows, net of discounted disposal costs, all discounted at the loan's effective interest rate;

(2) **MARKET PRICE METHOD** The loan's observable market price; or

(3) **FAIR VALUE OF COLLATERAL METHOD** The fair value of collateral pledged, if the loan is collateral-dependent. If foreclosure is probable, this method is to be used.

c. **VALUATION ALLOWANCE ACCOUNT** If the measure of the impaired loan is **less** than the recorded investment in the loan (excluding any existing valuation allowance, but including accrued interest and net deferred loan fees/costs and unamortized premium or discount), the creditor creates or adjusts an existing valuation allowance account (Allowance for Impaired Loan) with a corresponding charge or debit to the bad debt expense account.

d. **NET CARRYING AMOUNT** The loan's net carrying amount shall not exceed the loan's recorded investment at any time.

EXAMPLE 11 ♦ INITIAL RECOGNITION OF IMPAIRMENT

On January 1, 20X1, Risky Developers Inc. borrowed $100,000 from Easymoney Corp. The promissory note called for 10% interest, payable annually on Dec. 31, with a maturity date of December 31, 20X3. Risky made the first interest payment on time but, due to financial difficulties, defaulted on the payment due Dec. 31, 20X2. On July 1, 20X3, Risky and Easymoney reached an agreement to reduce the principal amount to $60,000, and the interest rate to 6%, with the payment of principal and interest due December 31, 20X5. The discounted present value of the principal and interest is $55,000, net of discounted related costs, and discounted at the loan's effective interest rate.

REQUIRED: Provide the journal entry to record the initial recognition of impairment on the creditor's (Easymoney's) books.

SOLUTION:

7/1/X3 Bad Debt Expense	60,500	
Allowance for Impaired Loan		60,500

Computation:

Principal		$100,000
Accrued Interest:		
12/31/X2 ($100,000 x 10%)	$10,000	
6/30/X3 ($100,000 + $10,000)(10%)(1/2)	5,500	15,500
Investment in Loan		$115,500
PV of P & I		(55,000)
Allowance for Impaired Loan		$ 60,500

2. SUBSEQUENT RECOGNITION OF INCOME OR EXPENSE

a. PRESENT VALUE METHOD If the initial impairment was measured by the discounted future cash flows (1.b.(1), above), use any of the following three methods:

(1) An *increase* in present value attributable to *time passage* is reported as interest income accrued on the net carrying amount of the loan, using the same effective interest rate used in discounting the future cash flows.

(2) The entire change in the present value in amounts or timing of future cash flows is reported as an increase or reduction in bad debt expense.

(3) A cost recovery basis of accounting may be used for income recognition purposes. Thus, an impaired loan on which no amounts of cash are collected would result in no income recognition. Use of the cost recovery method does not, of course, alter the total income recognized on the loan; it merely delays the timing of the income recognition.

b. OTHER METHODS If the initial impairment was measured by the observable market price of the impaired loan [1.b.(2), above], or by the fair value of the collateral [1.b.(3), above]:

(1) A decrease in the measure of the impaired loan is an addition to the bad debt expense.

(2) An increase in the measure of the impaired loan is a reduction of the bad debt expense.

EXAMPLE 12 ♦ SUBSEQUENT RECOGNITION OF INCOME OR EXPENSE

Refer to Example 11, and add the following information: At December 31, 20X3, based upon the effective rate of interest, income to be recognized on creditor's books is $2,750.

REQUIRED: Provide the journal entry to record the recognition of income at December 31, 20X3.

SOLUTION:

Allowance for Impaired Loan	2,750	
Interest Income		2,750

Alternatively, the entry on the creditor's books could be:

Allowance for Impaired Loan	2,750	
Bad Debt Expense		2,750

c. SUBSEQUENT CHANGE If there is a subsequent material change in the future cash flows' amounts or timing, or in the loan's market price or the collateral's fair value, the creditor should remeasure the impairment amount, and adjust accordingly the valuation allowance and the bad debt expense accounts.

EXAMPLE 13 ♦ SUBSEQUENT MATERIAL CHANGE IN CASH FLOWS

> Refer to Examples 11 and 12, and add the following information: At July 1, 20X4, there is a further change to extend the term to June 30, 20X6. The new discounted future cash flows is $53,000.
>
> **REQUIRED:** Provide the journal entry to record the revised recognition of impairment on creditor's books.
>
> **SOLUTION:**
>
> | | | |
> |---|---|---|
> | Bad Debt Expense | 4,750 | |
> | Allowance for Impaired Loan | | |
> | [($115,500 − $60,500 + $2,750) − $53,000] | | 4,750 |

3. **REQUIRED DISCLOSURES**

    a. **RECEIVABLES INFORMATION** The total receivable, differentiating between the receivables with related allowances and receivables without allowances, must be disclosed. The amounts of the related allowances must also be disclosed.

    b. **INTEREST INCOME INFORMATION** How the interest income was recognized must be disclosed; whether all in bad debt or broken into an interest income component and a bad debt component. The company's policy for recognizing income on impaired loans must also be disclosed.

    c. **ALLOWANCE RECONCILIATION** The reconciliation of the allowance must be disclosed, because of the possibility of additional changes from cash flows charged against the allowance or direct write-offs.

    d. **CASH RECEIVED INFORMATION** The amount of cash received for the period and how the cash was recognized must be disclosed. This is necessary because under SFAS 114, income may be recognized without cash receipt.

VIII. **ACCOUNTS AND NOTES RECEIVABLE AS IMMEDIATE SOURCES OF CASH**

   A. **OVERVIEW**
   It may become desirable for the holder of receivables to immediately convert them into cash. This can be accomplished by any of four methods discussed below: discounting, assignment, factoring, and pledging. If the conversion into cash meets the criteria in V.D.1.a., the transaction is accounted for as a sale. If the criteria are not met, the transfer is accounted for as a secured borrowing.

   B. **DISCOUNTING**
   Discounting refers to the sale of a note to a third party, usually a bank or other financial institution. These sales are usually on a "with recourse" basis, which means that upon default of the debtor, the seller of the note becomes liable for its maturity value. Two calculations are necessary prior to discounting.

   1. **INTEREST** Interest accrued prior to discounting must be determined

   2. **PROCEEDS** The proceeds to be received from discounting must be calculated

EXAMPLE 14 ♦ DISCOUNTING

Assume Y Company has a $4,000, 90-day, 8% interest-bearing note; 30 days after acquiring the note, Y Company decides to discount it at a bank that charges a 10% discount rate.

REQUIRED:

a. Determine the accrued interest income for the 30 days that Y Company held the note.

b. Determine the proceeds Y Company received from the bank.

SOLUTIONS:

a. Accrued interest income: $4,000 x 8% x 1/12 = $26.67

b. Proceeds from discounting the note receivable:

Proceeds = Maturity value – Discount charged by bank

Face amount	$4,000
Interest ($4,000 x 8% x 3/12)	80
Maturity value	4,080
Interest cost ($4,080 x 10% x 2/12)	(68)
Proceeds from discounting	$4,012

3. **CONTINGENT LIABILITY** The contingent liability assumed by the seller of a note "with recourse" must be disclosed. Two approaches are used.

a. Footnote disclosure

b. "Contra asset" to Notes Receivable

EXAMPLE 15 ♦ CONTINGENT LIABILITY

Assume that the note in the last example was discounted with recourse. The entries to record the discounting, and the repayment or default, for each of the two approaches are:

	Footnote disclosure		Contra asset	
	Dr.	Cr.	Dr.	Cr.
a. *Discounting of N/R*				
Cash	4,012.00		4,012.00	
Interest Expense*	14.67		14.67	
Interest Income*		26.67		26.67
N/R		4,000.00		--
N/R Discounted		--		4,000.00
b. *Repayment of note by maker*				
N/R Discounted	(no entry)		4,000	
N/R				4,000
c. *Default by maker on note discounted "with recourse"*				
N/R Overdue	4,080		4,080	
Cash		4,080		4,080
N/R Discounted	(no entry)		4,000	
N/R				4,000

* For greater disclosure, interest income and expense are recorded separately, rather than as a net amount.

C. **ASSIGNMENT OF ACCOUNTS RECEIVABLE**

The assignment of accounts receivable represents a formal arrangement whereby the rights to accounts receivable are assigned to a financial institution in exchange for cash. Recording of the transaction involves the transfer of the receivables to a special account, Accounts Receivable Assigned. At the same time, a liability is entered for the amount of cash received from the financial institution. Assignment usually includes "with recourse" and "non-notification" clauses. "With recourse" means that the assignor remains liable for the collection of the receivables. "Non-notification" means that the debtors are not notified of the assignment, and therefore continue making their payments to the seller. These payments are forwarded by the seller to the financial institution, thus reducing the original liability. At any point, the seller's equity in the receivables is represented as the difference between the accounts assigned and the related liability.

EXAMPLE 16 ♦ ASSIGNMENT OF ACCOUNTS RECEIVABLE

Receivables Co. assigns accounts receivable having a net carrying amount of $10,000 to Financing Inc. in exchange for $7,000 cash. Interest of 1% per month is charged on the outstanding balance of the obligation. Collections on accounts receivable are to be remitted to Financing Inc. on a monthly basis; $2,000 is collected during the first month.

REQUIRED: Record these transactions in Receivables Co.'s books.

SOLUTION:

Accounts Receivable Assigned	10,000	
Accounts Receivable		10,000
Cash	7,000	
Note Payable—Financing Inc.		7,000
Cash	2,000	
Accounts Receivable Assigned		2,000
Note Payable—Financing Inc.	1,930	
Interest Expense	70	
Cash		2,000

Following these transactions, Receivables Company would present the accounts receivable in its balance sheet as follows:

A/R assigned (net) ($10,000 – $2,000)	$ 8,000
Less: N/P on A/R assigned ($7,000 – $1,930)	(5,070)
Equity in A/R assigned	$ 2,930

D. **FACTORING**

Factoring is similar to a sale of receivables because it is generally without recourse (i.e., the financing institution or "factor" assumes the risk of collectivity) and the factor generally handles the billing and collection function. A transfer of receivables to a factor without recourse is accounted for as any other sale of an asset: debit cash, credit the receivables, and record a gain or loss for the difference. If the factoring is *with recourse*, it may be accounted for as a sale of the receivables or as secured borrowing, depending on whether certain criteria are met.

E. **PLEDGING**

Receivables may be pledged as security for loans. Collections on the receivables are usually required to be applied to a reduction of the loan. Where receivables are pledged, adequate disclosure must be made in the financial statements.

EXHIBIT 3 ♦ SALE OF RECEIVABLES

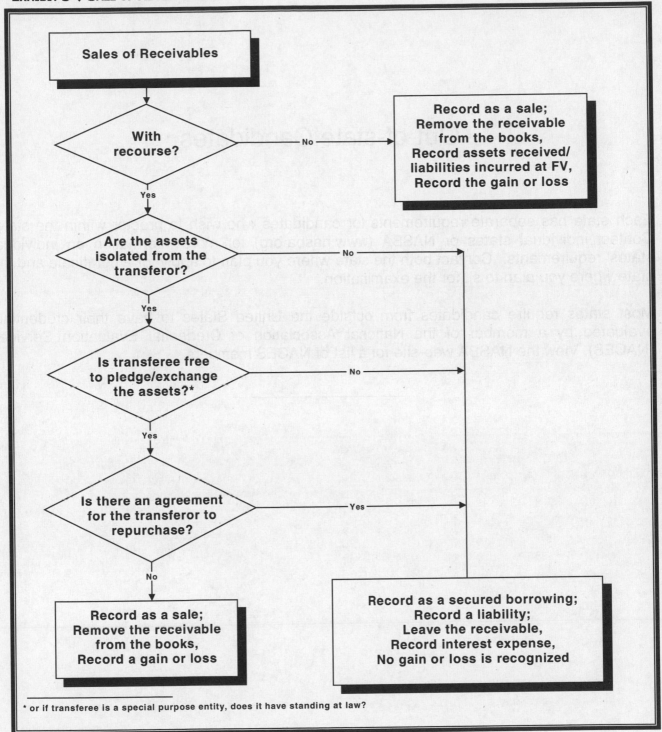

* or if transferee is a special purpose entity, does it have standing at law?

Out-of-state Candidates

Each state has separate requirements for candidates who wish to proctor within the state. Contact individual states or NASBA (www.nasba.org) for more information on individual states' requirements. Contact both the state where you plan to apply for a certificate and the state where you plan to sit for the examination.

Most states require candidates from outside the United States to have their credentials evaluated by a member of the National Association of Credential Evaluation Services (NACES). View the NASBA web-site for a list of NACES members.

CHAPTER 2—CASH, SHORT-TERM INVESTMENTS & RECEIVABLES

PROBLEM 2-1 MULTIPLE CHOICE QUESTIONS (122 to 153 minutes)

1. The following trial balance of Trey Co. at December 31, 1993, has been adjusted except for income tax expense.

	Dr.	Cr.
Cash	$ 550,000	
Accounts receivable, net	1,650,000	
Prepaid taxes	300,000	
Accounts payable		$ 120,000
Common stock		500,000
Additional paid-in capital		680,000
Retained earnings		630,000
Foreign currency translation adjustment	430,000	
Revenues		3,600,000
Expenses	2,600,000	
	$5,530,000	$5,530,000

- During 1993, estimated tax payments of $300,000 were charged to prepaid taxes. Trey has not yet recorded income tax expense. There were no differences between financial statement and income tax income, and Trey's tax rate is 30%.

- Included in accounts receivable is $500,000 due from a customer. Special terms granted to this customer require payment in equal semi-annual installments of $125,000 every April 1 and October 1.

In Trey's December 31, 1993 balance sheet, what amount should be reported as total current assets?
a. $1,950,000
b. $2,200,000
c. $2,250,000
d. $2,500,000   (11/94, FAR, #8, 5273)

2. Mare Co.'s December 31, 1993 balance sheet reported the following current assets:

Cash	$ 70,000
Accounts receivable	120,000
Inventories	60,000
Total	$250,000

An analysis of the accounts disclosed that accounts receivable consisted of the following:

Trade accounts	$ 96,000
Allowance for uncollectible accounts	(2,000)
Selling price of Mare's unsold goods out on consignment, at 130% of cost, **not** included in Mare's ending inventory	26,000
Total	$120,000

At December 31, 1993, the total of Mare's current assets is
a. $224,000.
b. $230,000.
c. $244,000.
d. $270,000.   (11/94, FAR, #11, 5276)

3. Burr Company had the following account balances at December 31, 1997:

Cash in banks	$2,250,000
Cash on hand	125,000
Cash legally restricted for additions to plant (expected to be disbursed in 1998)	1,600,000

Cash in banks includes $600,000 of compensating balances against short-term borrowing arrangements. The compensating balances are not legally restricted as to withdrawal by Burr. In the current assets section of Burr's December 31, 1997 balance sheet, total cash should be reported at
a. $1,775,000.
b. $2,250,000.
c. $2,375,000.
d. $3,975,000.   (11/88, PI, #1, amended, 9002)

4. The following information pertains to Grey Co. at December 31, 1993:

Checkbook balance	$12,000
Bank statement balance	16,000
Check drawn on Grey's account, payable to a vendor, dated and recorded 12/31/93 but not mailed until 1/10/94	1,800

On Grey's December 31, 1993 balance sheet, what amount should be reported as cash?
a. $12,000
b. $13,800
c. $14,200
d. $16,000   (5/94, FAR, #12, 4827)

5. Inch Co. had the following balances at December 31, 1999:

Cash in checking account	$ 35,000
Cash in money market account	75,000
U.S. Treasury bill, purchased 12/1/99, maturing 2/28/00	200,000
U.S. Treasury bill, purchased 12/1/98, maturing 5/31/00	150,000

Inch's policy is to treat as cash equivalents all highly-liquid investments with a maturity of three months or less when purchased. What amount should Inch report as cash and cash equivalents in its December 31, 1999, balance sheet?
a. $110,000
b. $235,000
c. $310,000
d. $460,000   (R/00, FAR, #1, 6896)

6. At December 31, 1993, Kale Co. had the following balances in the accounts it maintains at First State Bank:

Checking account #101	$175,000
Checking account #201	(10,000)
Money market account	25,000
90-day certificate of deposit, due 2/28/94	50,000
180-day certificate of deposit, due 3/15/94	80,000

Kale classifies investments with original maturities of three months or less as cash equivalents. In its December 31, 1993 balance sheet, what amount should Kale report as cash and cash equivalents?
a. $190,000
b. $200,000
c. $240,000
d. $320,000   (5/94, FAR, #13, 4828)

ITEMS 7 AND 8 are based on the following data:

Poe Inc. had the following bank reconciliation at March 31, 1997:

Balance per bank statement, 3/31/97	$ 46,500
Add: Deposit in transit	10,300
	56,800
Less: Outstanding checks	(12,600)
Balance per books, 3/31/97	$ 44,200

Data per bank for the month of April 1997 follow:

Deposits	$58,400
Disbursements	49,700

All reconciling items at March 31, 1997, cleared the bank in April. Outstanding checks at April 30, 1997, totaled $7,000. There were no deposits in transit at April 30, 1997.

7. What is the cash balance per books at April 30, 1997?
a. $48,200
b. $52,900
c. $55,200
d. $58,500   (5/90, PI, #1, amended, 0875)

8. What is the amount of cash disbursements per books in April 1997?
a. $44,100
b. $49,200
c. $54,300
d. $56,700   (Editors, 9003)

9. When the fair value of an investment in debt securities exceeds its amortized cost, how should each of the following debt securities be reported at the end of the year?

	Debt securities classified as	
	Held-to-maturity	Available-for-sale
a.	Amortized cost	Amortized cost
b.	Amortized cost	Fair value
c.	Fair value	Fair value
d.	Fair value	Amortized cost

(11/96, FAR, #6, 6452)

10. Nola has a portfolio of marketable equity securities which it does not intend to sell in the near term. How should Nola classify these securities, and how should it report unrealized gains and losses from these securities?

	Classify as	Report as a
a.	Trading securities	Component of income from continuing operations
b.	Available-for-sale securities	Component of other comprehensive income
c.	Trading securities	Component of other comprehensive income
d.	Available-for-sale securities	Component of income from continuing operations

(5/94, FAR, #14, amended, 4829)

11. A marketable debt security was purchased on September 1, 1994, between interest dates, and classified as an available-for-sale security. The next interest payment date was February 1, 1995. Because of a permanent decline in market value, the cost of the debt security substantially exceeded its market value at December 31, 1994. On the balance sheet at December 31, 1994, the debt security should be carried at
a. Market value plus the accrued interest paid.
b. Market value.
c. Cost plus the accrued interest paid.
d. Cost.   (11/88, Theory, #3, amended, 4575)

12. A marketable equity security is transferred from the trading category to the available-for-sale category. At the transfer date, the security's cost exceeds its market value. What amount is used at the transfer date to record the security in the available-for-sale category?
a. Market value, regardless of whether the decline in market value below cost is considered permanent or temporary.
b. Market value, only if the decline in market value below cost is considered permanent.
c. Cost, if the decline in market value below cost is considered temporary.
d. Cost, regardless of whether the decline in market value below cost is considered permanent or temporary. (5/92, Theory, #42, amended, 4581)

13. The following information pertains to Smoke Inc.'s investments in marketable equity securities, classified as available-for-sale:

• On December 31, 1994, Smoke has a security with a $70,000 cost and a $50,000 fair value. (No Market Adjustment account exists.)

• A marketable equity security costing $50,000, has a $60,000 fair value on December 31, 1994. Smoke believes the recovery from an earlier lower fair value is permanent.

What is the net effect of the above two items on the balances of Smoke's Market Adjustment account for available-for-sale marketable equity securities as of December 31, 1994?
a. No effect
b. Creates a $10,000 debit balance
c. Creates a $20,000 credit balance
d. Creates a $10,000 credit balance
              (5/92, PI, #14, amended, 4578)

14. For a marketable trading securities portfolio, which of the following amounts should be included in the period's net income?

I. Unrealized losses during the period
II. Realized gains during the period
III. Changes in the Market Adjustment account during the period

a. III only
b. II only
c. I and II
d. I, II, and III   (5/91, Theory, #22, amended, 4573)

15. The following information was extracted from Gil Co.'s December 31, 1993 balance sheet:

Noncurrent assets:
    Investments in available-for-sale
      marketable equity securities
      (carried at market) $ 96,450

Accumulated other comprehensive income:
    Net unrealized loss on investments
    in marketable equity securities   (19,800)

Historical cost of the long-term Investments in marketable equity securities was
a. $ 63,595.
b. $ 76,650.
c. $ 96,450.
d. $116,250.   (5/91, PII, #18, amended, 4566)

16. On December 29, 1993, BJ Co. sold a marketable equity security that had been purchased on January 4, 1992. BJ owned no other marketable equity security. An unrealized loss was reported in the 1992 income statement. A realized gain was reported in the 1993 income statement. How was the marketable equity security classified, and did its 1992 market price decline exceed its 1993 market price recovery?

	Classification	1992 market price decline exceeded 1993 market price recovery
a.	Trading	Yes
b.	Available-for-sale	No
c.	Held-to-maturity	Yes
d.	Trading	No

(11/90, Theory, #6, amended, 4574)

17. During 1994, Scott Corp. purchased marketable equity securities and classified them as available-for-sale. Pertinent data follow:

Security	Cost	Fair value at 12/31/94
D	$ 36,000	$ 40,000
E	80,000	60,000
F	180,000	186,000
	$296,000	$286,000

Scott appropriately carries these securities at fair value. The amount of unrealized loss on these securities in Scott's 1994 income statement should be
a. $20,000.
b. $14,000.
c. $10,000.
d. $0.   (5/90, PI, #2, amended, 4568)

18. During 1997, Wall Co. purchased 2,000 shares of Hemp Corp. common stock for $31,500 as an available-for-sale investment. The market value of this investment was $29,500 at December 31, 1997. Wall sold all of the Hemp common stock for $14 per share on December 15, 1998, incurring $1,400 in brokerage commissions and taxes. On the sale, Wall should report a realized loss of
a. $4,900.
b. $3,500.
c. $2,900.
d. $1,500.   (5/90, PI, #57, amended, 0978)

19. Lee Corp. reported the following marketable equity security on its December 31, 1994 balance sheet, classified as an available-for-sale security:

Neu Corp. common stock, at cost	$100,000
Market adjustment to reflect decline in fair value	(20,000)
Balance	$ 80,000

At December 31, 1995, the fair value of Lee's investment in the Neu Corp. stock was $85,000. As a result of the 1995 increase in this stock's fair value, Lee's 1995 income statement should report
a. An unrealized gain of $5,000.
b. A realized gain of $5,000.
c. An unrealized loss of $15,000.
d. No gain or loss. (11/89, PII, #3, amended, 9004)

20. A company should report the marketable equity securities that it has classified as trading at
a. Lower of cost or market, with holding gains and losses included in earnings.
b. Lower of cost or market, with holding gains included in earnings only to the extent of previously recognized holding losses.
c. Fair value, with holding gains included in earnings only to the extent of previously recognized holding losses.
d. Fair value, with holding gains and losses included in earnings.
          (5/95, FAR, #6, amended, 5442)

ITEMS 21 AND 22 are based on the following:

Sun Corp. had investments in equity securities classified as trading costing $650,000. On June 30, 1995, Sun decided to hold the investments indefinitely and accordingly reclassified them from trading to available-for-sale on that date. The investment's fair value was $575,000 at December 31, 1994; $530,000 at June 30, 1995; and $490,000 at December 31, 1995.

21. What amount of loss from investments should Sun report in its 1995 income statement?
a. $ 45,000
b. $ 85,000
c. $120,000
d. $160,000   (5/93, PI, #3, amended, 4045)

22. What amount should Sun report as net unrealized loss on investments in equity securities in other comprehensive income at the end of 1995?
a. $ 40,000
b. $ 45,000
c. $ 85,000
d. $160,000   (5/93, PI, #4, amended, 4046)

23. Which of the following risks are inherent in an interest rate swap agreement?

I. The risk of exchanging a lower interest rate for a higher interest rate
II. The risk of nonperformance by the counterparty to the agreement

a. I only
b. II only
c. Both I and II
d. Neither I nor II   (11/96, FAR, #8, 6454)

24. Disclosure of information about significant concentrations of credit risk is required for
a. All financial instruments.
b. Financial instruments with credit risk only.
c. Financial instruments with market risk only.
d. Financial instruments with risk of accounting loss only. (5/95, FAR, #4, amended, 5540)

25. Whether recognized or unrecognized in an entity's financial statements, disclosure of the fair values of the entity's financial instruments is required when
a. It is practicable to estimate those values.
b. The entity maintains accurate cost records.
c. Aggregated fair values are material to the entity.
d. Individual fair values are material to the entity.
(R/99, FAR, #15, 6784)

26. If it is not practicable for an entity to estimate the fair value of a financial instrument, which of the following should be disclosed?

I. Information pertinent to estimating the fair value of the financial instrument
II. The reasons it is not practicable to estimate fair value

a. I only
b. II only
c. Both I and II
d. Neither I nor II (11/96, FAR, #9, 6455)

27. Delta Inc. sells to wholesalers on terms of 2/15, net 30. Delta has no cash sales but 50% of Delta's customers take advantage of the discount. Delta uses the gross method of recording sales and trade receivables. An analysis of Delta's trade receivables balances at December 31, 1993, revealed the following:

Age	Amount	Collectible
0-15 days	$100,000	100%
16-30 days	60,000	95%
31-60 days	5,000	90%
Over 60 days	2,500	$500
	$167,500	

In its December 31, 1993 balance sheet, what amount should Delta report for allowance for discounts?
a. $1,000
b. $1,620
c. $1,675
d. $2,000 (5/94, FAR, #15, 4830)

28. On June 1, 1998, Pitt Corp. sold merchandise with a list price of $5,000 to Burr on account. Pitt allowed trade discounts of 30% and 20%. Credit terms were 2/15, n/40 and the sale was made F.O.B. shipping point. Pitt prepaid $200 of delivery costs for Burr as an accommodation. On June 12, 1998, Pitt received from Burr a remittance in full payment amounting to
a. $2,744.
b. $2,940.
c. $2,944.
d. $3,140. (5/90, PI, #10, amended, 0895)

29. The following information relates to Jay Co.'s accounts receivable for 1992:

Accounts receivable, 1/1/92	$ 650,000
Credit sales for 1992	2,700,000
Sales returns for 1992	75,000
Accounts written off during 1992	40,000
Collections from customers during 1992	2,150,000
Estimated future sales returns at 12/31/92	50,000
Estimated uncollectible accounts at 12/31/92	110,000

What amount should Jay report for accounts receivable, before allowances for sales returns and uncollectible accounts, at December 31, 1992?
a. $1,200,000
b. $1,125,000
c. $1,085,000
d. $ 925,000 (5/93, PI, #12, 4054)

30. In its December 31, 1999 balance sheet, Fleet Co. reported accounts receivable of $100,000 before allowance for uncollectible accounts of $10,000. Credit sales during 2000 were $611,000, and collections from customers, excluding recoveries, totaled $591,000. During 2000, accounts receivable of $45,000 were written off and $17,000 were recovered. Fleet estimated that $15,000 of the accounts receivable at December 31, 2000, were uncollectible. In its December 31, 2000 balance sheet, what amount should Fleet report as accounts receivable before allowance for uncollectible accounts?
a. $58,000
b. $67,000
c. $75,000
d. $82,000 (R/00, FAR, #2, 6897)

31. Which method of recording uncollectible accounts expense is consistent with accrual accounting?

	Allowance	Direct write-off
a.	Yes	Yes
b.	Yes	No
c.	No	Yes
d.	No	No (5/95, FAR, #35, 5571)

32. On March 31, 1993, Vale Co. had an unadjusted credit balance of $1,000 in its allowance for uncollectible accounts. An analysis of Vale's trade accounts receivable at that date revealed the following:

Age	Amount	Estimated uncollectible
0-30 days	$60,000	5%
31-60 days	4,000	10%
Over 60 days	2,000	$1,400

What amount should Vale report as allowance for uncollectible accounts in its March 31, 1993 balance sheet?
a. $4,800
b. $4,000
c. $3,800
d. $3,000   (11/93, PI, #18, 4387)

33. Hall Co.'s allowance for uncollectible accounts had a credit balance of $24,000 at December 31, 1991. During 1992, Hall wrote off uncollectible accounts of $96,000. The aging of accounts receivable indicated that a $100,000 allowance for doubtful accounts was required at December 31, 1992. What amount of uncollectible accounts expense should Hall report for 1992?
a. $172,000
b. $120,000
c. $100,000
d. $ 96,000   (5/93, PI, #47, 4088)

34. When the allowance method of recognizing uncollectible accounts is used, the entry to record the write-off of a specific account
a. Decreases both accounts receivable and the allowance for uncollectible accounts.
b. Decreases accounts receivable and increases the allowance for uncollectible accounts.
c. Increases the allowance for uncollectible accounts and decreases net income.
d. Decreases both accounts receivable and net income.   (11/94, FAR, #12, 5277)

35. Bee Co. uses the direct write-off method to account for uncollectible accounts receivable. During an accounting period, Bee's cash collections from customers equal sales adjusted for the addition or deduction of the following amounts:

	Accounts written-off	Increase in accounts receivable balance
a.	Deduction	Deduction
b.	Addition	Deduction
c.	Deduction	Addition
d.	Addition	Addition

(5/91, Theory, #9, 1784)

36. On the December 31, 1997 balance sheet of Mann Co., the current receivables consisted of the following:

Trade accounts receivable	$ 93,000
Allowance for uncollectible accounts	(2,000)
Claim against shipper for goods lost in transit (November 1997)	3,000
Selling price of unsold goods sent by Mann on consignment at 130% of cost (**not** included in Mann's ending inventory)	26,000
Security deposit on lease of warehouse used for storing some inventories	30,000
Total	$150,000

At December 31, 1997, the correct total of Mann's current net receivables was
a. $ 94,000.
b. $120,000.
c. $124,000.
d. $150,000.   (11/90, PI, #5, amended, 0887)

37. Inge Co. determined that the net value of its accounts receivable at December 31, 1993, based on an aging of the receivables, was $325,000. Additional information is as follows:

Allowance for uncollectible accounts—1/1/93	$ 30,000
Uncollectible accounts written-off during 1993	18,000
Uncollectible accounts recovered during 1993	2,000
Accounts receivable at 12/31/93	350,000

For 1993, what would be Inge's uncollectible accounts expense?
a. $ 5,000
b. $11,000
c. $15,000
d. $21,000   (11/94, FAR, #45, 9005)

38. The following accounts were abstracted from Roxy Co.'s unadjusted trial balance at December 31, 1997:

	Debit	Credit
Accounts receivable	$1,000,000	
Allowance for uncollectible accounts		8,000
Net credit sales		$3,000,000

Roxy estimates that 3% of the gross accounts receivable will become uncollectible. After adjustment at December 31, 1997, the allowance for uncollectible accounts should have a credit balance of

a. $90,000.
b. $82,000.
c. $38,000.
d. $30,000.   (5/90, PI, #9, amended, 0894)

39. For the year ended December 31, 1997, Beal Co. estimated its allowance for uncollectible accounts using the year-end aging of accounts receivable. The following data are available:

Allowance for uncollectible accounts, 1/1/97	$42,000
Provision for uncollectible accounts during 1997 (2% on credit sales of $2,000,000)	40,000
Uncollectible accounts written-off, 11/30/97	46,000
Estimated uncollectible accounts per aging, 12/31/97	52,000

After year-end adjustment, the uncollectible accounts expense for 1997 should be

a. $46,000.
b. $48,000.
c. $52,000.
d. $56,000.   (5/90, PI, #54, amended, 0897)

40. A method of estimating uncollectible accounts that emphasizes asset valuation rather than income measurement is the allowance method based on

a. Aging the receivables.
b. Direct write-off.
c. Gross sales.
d. Credit sales less returns and allowances.
          (11/89, Theory, #7, 1816)

41. At January 1, 1994, Jamin Co. had a credit balance of $260,000 in its allowance for uncollectible accounts. Based on past experience, 2% of Jamin's credit sales have been uncollectible. During 1994, Jamin wrote off $325,000 of uncollectible accounts. Credit sales for 1994 were $9,000,000. In its December 31, 1994 balance sheet, what amount should Jamin report as allowance for uncollectible accounts?

a. $115,000
b. $180,000
c. $245,000
d. $440,000   (5/95, FAR, #9, 5545)

42. In its December 31 balance sheet, Butler Co. reported trade accounts receivable of $250,000 and related allowance for uncollectible accounts of $20,000. What is the total amount of risk of accounting loss related to Butler's trade accounts receivable, and what amount of that risk is off-balance sheet risk?

	Risk of accounting loss	Off-balance sheet risk
a.	$0	$0
b.	$230,000	$0
c.	$230,000	$20,000
d.	$250,000	$20,000

          (R/99, FAR, #6, 6775)

43. Leaf Co. purchased from Oak Co. a $20,000, 8%, 5-year note that required five equal annual year-end payments of $5,009. The note was discounted to yield a 9% rate to Leaf. At the date of purchase, Leaf recorded the note at its present value of $19,485. What should be the total interest revenue earned by Leaf over the life of this note?

a. $5,045
b. $5,560
c. $8,000
d. $9,000   (11/94, FAR, #38, 5300)

44. On August 15, 1991, Benet Co. sold goods for which it received a note bearing the market rate of interest on that date. The four-month note was dated July 15, 1991. Note principal, together with all interest, is due November 15, 1991. When the note was recorded on August 15, which of the following accounts increased?

a. Unearned discount
b. Interest receivable
c. Prepaid interest
d. Interest revenue   (5/92, Theory, #21, 2714)

ITEMS 45 AND 46 are based on the following:

On December 1, 1995, Money Co. gave Home Co. a $200,000, 11% loan. Money paid proceeds of $194,000 after the deduction of a $6,000 nonrefundable loan origination fee. Principal and interest are due in 60 monthly installments of $4,310, beginning January 1, 1996. The repayments yield an effective interest rate of 11% at a present value of $200,000 and 12.4% at a present value of $194,000.

45. What amount of income from this loan should Money report in its 1995 income statement?
a. $0
b. $1,833
c. $2,005
d. $7,833   (5/96, FAR, #5, 6278)

46. What amount of accrued interest receivable should Money report in its 1995 balance sheet?
a. $0
b. $1,833
c. $2,005
d. $7,833   (Editorial Board)

47. On May 1, 1997, Lane Corp. bought a parcel of land for $100,000. Seven months later, Lane sold this land to a triple-A rated company for $150,000, under the following terms: 25% at closing, and a first mortgage note (at the market rate of interest) for the balance. The first payment on the note, plus accrued interest, is due December 1, 1998. Lane reported this sale on the installment basis in its 1997 tax return. In its 1997 income statement, how much gain should Lane report from the sale of this land?
a. $0
b. $12,500
c. $37,500
d. $50,000   (5/87, PII, #13, amended, 0902)

48. Frame Co. has an 8% note receivable dated June 30, 1991, in the original amount of $150,000. Payments of $50,000 in principal plus accrued interest are due annually on July 1, 1992, 1993, and 1994. In its June 30, 1993, balance sheet, what amount should Frame report as a current asset for interest on the note receivable?
a. $0
b. $ 4,000
c. $ 8,000
d. $12,000   (11/93, PI, #17, 4386)

ITEMS 49 AND 50 are based on the following:

On January 2, 1992, Emme Co. sold equipment with a carrying amount of $480,000 in exchange for a $600,000 noninterest-bearing note due January 2, 1995. There was no established exchange price for the equipment. The prevailing rate of interest for a note of this type at January 2, 1992, was 10%. The present value of 1 at 10% for three periods is 0.75.

49. In Emme's 1992 income statement, what amount should be reported as interest income?
a. $ 9,000
b. $45,000
c. $50,000
d. $60,000   (11/93, PI, #46, 4415)

50. In Emme's 1992 income statement, what amount should be reported as gain (loss) on sale of machinery?
a. ($ 30,000) loss
b. $ 30,000 gain
c. $120,000 gain
d. $270,000 gain   (11/93, PI, #47, 4416)

51. On December 31, 1991, Jet Co. received two $10,000 notes receivable from customers in exchange for services rendered. On both notes, interest is calculated on the outstanding principal balance at the annual rate of 3% and payable at maturity. The note from Hart Corp., made under customary trade terms, is due in nine months and the note from Maxx Inc. is due in five years. The market interest rate for similar notes on December 31, 1991, was 8%. The compound interest factors to convert future values into present values at 8% follow:

Present value of $1 due in nine months: .944
Present value of $1 due in five years: .680

At what amounts should these two notes receivable be reported in Jet's December 31, 1991 balance sheet?

	Hart	Maxx
a.	$ 9,440	$6,800
b.	$ 9,652	$7,820
c.	$10,000	$6,800
d.	$10,000	$7,820

                                        (5/92, PI, #15, 2582)

52. On December 30, 1994, Chang Co. sold a machine to Door Co. in exchange for a noninterest-bearing note requiring ten annual payments of $10,000. Door made the first payment on December 30, 1994. The market interest rate for similar notes at date of issuance was 8%. Information on present value factors is as follows:

Period	Present value of $1 at 8%	Present value of ordinary annuity of $1 at 8%
9	0.50	6.25
10	0.46	6.71

In its December 31, 1994 balance sheet, what amount should Chang report as note receivable?
a. $45,000
b. $46,000
c. $62,500
d. $67,100   (5/95, FAR, #8, 5544)

53. When a loan receivable is impaired but foreclosure is **not** probable, which of the following may the creditor use to measure the impairment?

I. The loan's observable market price
II. The fair value of the collateral if the loan is collateral dependent

a. I only
b. II only
c. Either I or II
d. Neither I nor II   (11/96, FAR, #7, 6453)

54. Ace Co. sold to King Co. a $20,000, 8%, 5-year note that required five equal annual year-end payments. This note was discounted to yield a 9% rate to King. The present value factors of an ordinary annuity of $1 for five periods are as follows:

8%   3.992
9%   3.890

What should be the total interest revenue earned by King on this note?
a. $9,000
b. $8,000
c. $5,560
d. $5,050   (5/92, PI, #41, 2612)

55. Roth Inc. received from a customer a one-year, $500,000 note bearing annual interest of 8%. After holding the note for six months, Roth discounted the note at Regional Bank at an effective interest rate of 10%. What amount of cash did Roth receive from the bank?

a. $540,000
b. $523,810
c. $513,000
d. $495,238   (11/93, PI, #15, 4384)

56. On November 1, 1992, Davis Co. discounted with recourse at 10% a one-year, noninterest-bearing, $20,500 note receivable maturing on January 31, 1993. What amount of contingent liability for this note must Davis disclose in its financial statements for the year ended December 31, 1992?
a. $0
b. $20,000
c. $20,333
d. $20,500   (11/93, PI, #41, 4410)

57. After being held for 40 days, a 120-day, 12% interest-bearing note receivable was discounted at a bank at 15%. The proceeds received from the bank equal
a. Maturity value less the discount at 12%.
b. Maturity value less the discount at 15%.
c. Face value less the discount at 12%.
d. Face value less the discount at 15%.
          (11/92, Theory, #4, 3437)

58. On July 1, 1997, Kay Corp. sold equipment to Mando Co. for $100,000. Kay accepted a 10% note receivable for the entire sales price. This note is payable in two equal installments of $50,000 plus accrued interest on December 31, 1997, and December 31, 1998. On July 1, 1998, Kay discounted the note at a bank at an interest rate of 12%. Kay's proceeds from the discounted note were
a. $48,400.
b. $49,350.
c. $50,350.
d. $51,700.   (11/90, PII, #1, amended, 0890)

59. Rand Inc. accepted from a customer a $40,000, 90-day, 12% interest-bearing note dated August 31, 1997. On September 30, 1997, Rand discounted the note at the Apex State Bank at 15%. However, the proceeds were not received until October 1, 1997. In Rand's September 30, 1997 balance sheet, the amount receivable from the bank, based on a 360-day year, includes accrued interest revenue of
a. $170.
b. $200.
c. $300.
d. $400.   (5/90, PI, #12, amended, 0896)

60. A note receivable bearing a reasonable interest rate is sold to a bank with recourse. At the date of the discounting transaction, the notes receivable discounted account should be
a. Decreased by the proceeds from the discounting transaction.
b. Increased by the proceeds from the discounting transaction.
c. Increased by the face amount of the note.
d. Decreased by the face amount of the note.

(5/89, Theory, #3, 1823)

61. Gar Co. factored its receivables without recourse with Ross Bank. Gar received cash as a result of this transaction, which is best described as a
a. Loan from Ross collateralized by Gar's accounts receivable.
b. Loan from Ross to be repaid by the proceeds from Gar's accounts receivable.
c. Sale of Gar's accounts receivable to Ross, with the risk of uncollectible accounts retained by Gar.
d. Sale of Gar's accounts receivable to Ross, with the risk of uncollectible accounts transferred to Ross.

(5/95, FAR, #7, 5543)

OTHER OBJECTIVE FORMAT QUESTION

NUMBER 2-2 (15 to 25 minutes)

ITEMS 1 THROUGH 4 are based on the following:

Camp Co. purchased various securities during 1994 to be classified as held-to-maturity securities, trading securities, or available-for-sale securities.

ITEMS 1 THROUGH 4 describe various securities purchased by Camp. For each item, select the appropriate category for each security. A category may be used once, more than once, or not at all.

Categories
(H) Held-to-maturity
(T) Trading
(A) Available-for-sale

1. Debt securities bought and held for the purpose of selling in the near term.

2. U.S. Treasury bonds that Camp has both the positive intent and the ability to hold to maturity.

3. $3 million debt security bought and held for the purpose of selling in three years to finance payment of Camp's $2 million long-term note payable when it matures.

4. Convertible preferred stock that Camp does not intend to sell in the near term.

ITEMS 5 THROUGH 10 are based on the following:

The following information pertains to Dayle Inc.'s portfolio of marketable investments for the year ended December 31, 1994:

	Cost	Fair value, 12/31/93	1994 activity Purchases	1994 activity Sales	Fair value, 12/31/94
Held-to-maturity securities					
Security ABC			$100,000		$ 95,000
Trading securities					
Security DEF	$150,000	$160,000			155,000
Available-for-sale securities					
Security GHI	190,000	165,000		$175,000	
Security JKL	170,000	175,000			160,000

Security ABC was purchased at par. All declines in fair value are considered to be temporary.

ITEMS 5 THROUGH 10 describe amounts to be reported in Dayle's 1994 financial statements. For each item, select the correct numerical response.

An amount may be selected once, more than once, or not at all. Ignore income tax considerations.

5. Carrying amount of security ABC at 12/31/94.

6. Carrying amount of security DEF at 12/31/94.

7. Carrying amount of security JKL at 12/31/94.

ITEMS 8 THROUGH 10 require a second response. For each item, indicate whether a gain (G) or a loss (L) is to be reported.

8. Recognized gain or loss on sale of security GHI.

9. Unrealized gain or loss to be reported in 1994 income statement.

10. Unrealized gain or loss to be reported at December 31, 1994, in accumulated other comprehensive income.

Answer List	
(A)	$0
(B)	$ 5,000
(C)	$ 10,000
(D)	$ 15,000
(E)	$ 25,000
(F)	$ 95,000
(G)	$100,000
(H)	$150,000
(I)	$155,000
(J)	$160,000
(K)	$170,000

(11/95, FAR, amended, #61-70)

PROBLEMS/ESSAY QUESTIONS

ESSAY 2-3 (15 to 25 minutes)

REQUIRED:

a. What is a financial instrument? Define and give an example of derivative financial instruments.

b. Define *off-balance-sheet risk of accounting loss.*

c. Define both *market risk* and *credit risk.* What is meant by the term *concentration of credit risk?*

d. Define *fair value.* Discuss the methods management might use to estimate the fair values of various financial instruments.
(5/97, FAR, #1, amended, 6614-6617)

ESSAY 2-4 (15 to 25 minutes)

Gregor Wholesalers Co. sells industrial equipment for a standard three-year note receivable. Revenue is recognized at time of sale. Each note is secured by a lien on the equipment and has a face amount equal to the equipment's list price. Each note's stated interest rate is below the customers' market rate at date of sale. All notes are to be collected in three equal annual installments beginning one year after sale. Some of the notes are subsequently discounted at a bank with recourse, some are subsequently discounted without recourse, and some are retained by Gregor. At year-end, Gregor evaluates all outstanding notes receivable and provides for estimated losses arising from defaults.

REQUIRED:

a. What is the appropriate valuation basis for Gregor's notes receivable at the date it sells equipment?

b. How should Gregor account for the discounting, without recourse, of a February 1, 1992 note receivable discounted on May 1, 1992? Why is it appropriate to account for it in this way?

c. At December 31, 1992, how should Gregor measure and account for the impact of estimated losses resulting from notes receivable that it

1. Retained and did **not** discount?
2. Discounted at a bank with recourse?
(11/93, Theory, amended, #3, 6187)

ESSAY 2-5 (15 to 25 minutes)

Magrath Company has an operating cycle of less than one year and provides credit terms for all of its customers. On April 1, 1989, the company factored, without recourse, some of its accounts receivable.

On July 1, 1997, Magrath sold special order merchandise and received a noninterest-bearing note due June 30, 1999. The market rate of interest for this note is determinable.

Magrath uses the allowance method to account for uncollectible accounts. During 1997, some accounts were written off as uncollectible and other accounts previously written off as uncollectible were collected.

REQUIRED:

a. How should Magrath account for and report the accounts receivable factored on April 1, 1997? Why is this accounting treatment appropriate?

b. How should Magrath report the effects of the noninterest-bearing note on its income statement for the year ended December 31, 1997, and its December 31, 1997 balance sheet?

c. How should Magrath account for the collection of the accounts previously written off as uncollectible?

d. What are the two basic approaches to estimating uncollectible accounts under the allowance method? What is the rationale for each approach?

(5/90, Theory, amended, #2)

PROBLEM 2-6 (20 to 25 minutes)

Sigma Co. began operations on January 1, 1990. On December 31, 1990, Sigma provided for uncollectible accounts based on 1% of annual credit sales. On January 1, 1991, Sigma changed its method of determining its allowance for uncollectible accounts by applying certain percentages to the accounts receivable aging as follows:

Days past invoice date	Percent deemed to be uncollectible
0-30	1
31-90	5
91-180	20
Over 180	80

In addition, Sigma wrote off all accounts receivable that were over one year old. The following additional information relates to the years ended December 31, 1991, and 1990:

	1991	1990
Credit sales	$3,000,000	$2,800,000
Collections	2,915,000	2,400,000
Accounts written-off	27,000	None
Recovery of accounts previously written-off	7,000	None

Days past invoice date		
0-30	300,000	250,000
31-90	80,000	90,000
91-180	60,000	45,000
Over 180	25,000	15,000

REQUIRED:

a. Prepare a schedule showing the calculation of the allowance for uncollectible accounts at December 31, 1991.

b. Prepare a schedule showing the computation of the provision for uncollectible accounts for the year ended December 31, 1991.

(5/92, PI, #4)

PROBLEM 2-7 (45 to 55 minutes)

Kern Inc. had the following long-term receivable account balances at December 31, 1996:

Note receivable from the sale of an idle building	$750,000
Note receivable from an officer	200,000

Transactions during 1997 and other information relating to Kern's long-term receivables follows:

- The $750,000 note receivable is dated May 1, 1996, bears interest at 9%, and represents the balance of the consideration Kern received from the sale of its idle building to Able Co. Principal payments of $250,000 plus interest are due annually beginning May 1, 1997. Able made its first principal and interest payment on May 1, 1997. Collection of the remaining note installments is reasonably assured.

- The $200,000 note receivable is dated December 31, 1994, bears interest at 8%, and is due on December 31, 1999. The note is due from Frank Black, president of Kern Inc., and is collateralized by 5,000 shares of Kern's common stock. Interest is payable annually on December 31, and all interest payments were made through December 31, 1997. The quoted market price of Kern's common stock was $45 per share on December 31, 1997.

- On April 1, 1997, Kern sold a patent to Frey Corp. in exchange for a $100,000 noninterest-bearing note due on April 1, 1999. There was no established exchange price for the patent, and the note had no ready market. The prevailing interest rate for this type of note was 10% at April 1, 1997. The present value of $1 for two periods at 10% is 0.826. The patent had a carrying amount of $40,000 at January 1, 1997, and the amortization for the year ended December 31, 1997 would have been $8,000. Kern is reasonably assured of collecting the note receivable from Frey.

- On July 1, 1997, Kern sold a parcel of land to Barr Co. for $400,000 under an installment sale contract. Barr made a $120,000 cash down payment on July 1, 1997, and signed a four-year 10% note for the $280,000 balance. The equal annual payments of principal and interest on the note will be $88,332, payable on July 1 of each year from 1998 through 2001. The fair value of the land at the date of sale was $400,000. The cost of the land to Kern was $300,000. Collection of the remaining note installments is reasonably assured.

REQUIRED:

Prepare the following and show supporting computations:

a. Long-term receivables section of Kern's December 31, 1997 balance sheet.

b. Schedule showing current portion of long-term receivables and accrued interest receivable to be reported in Kern's December 31, 1997 balance sheet.

c. Schedule showing interest revenue from long-term receivables and gains recognized on sale of assets to be reported in Kern's 1997 income statement.　　　　(5/91, PI, amended, #4)

SOLUTION 2-1 MULTIPLE CHOICE ANSWERS

CURRENT ASSETS

1. **(a)** The operating cycle of an enterprise is the *average* period of time between expenditures for goods and services and the date those expenditures are converted into cash. Since there is no indication that Trey's operating cycle is greater than one year, a twelve month time period should be used as the basis for determining the amount to be reported as total current assets. Included in Trey's accounts receivable is $500,000 due from a customer. *Special terms* granted to this customer require payment in equal semiannual installments of $125,000 every April 1 and October 1. Therefore, $250,000 (i.e., $125,000 semiannual payments to be received on 4/1/95 and 10/1/95) of this receivable should be excluded from current assets at 12/31/93 because this amount would be received after 12/31/94. During 1993, estimated tax payments of $300,000 were charged to prepaid taxes. Since Trey's income tax expense for 1993 is also $300,000 [i.e., ($3,600,000 − $2,600,000) x 30%], there are, in fact, no net prepaid taxes at 12/31/93. The amount Trey should report as total current assets at 12/31/93 is determined as follows:

Cash	$ 550,000
Accounts receivable, net ($1,650,000 − $250,000)	1,400,000
Current assets, 12/31/93	$1,950,000

2. **(c)** Since the goods out on consignment have not yet been sold, two adjustments are required. Accounts receivable decreases by the $26,000 selling price of the unsold goods that was included in its balance. Inventories increases by the $20,000 (i.e., $26,000 ÷ 130%) cost of the unsold goods which was not included in its balance. Total current assets at 12/31/93 is determined as follows:

Cash	$ 70,000
Accounts receivable ($120,000 − $26,000)	94,000
Inventories ($60,000 + $20,000)	80,000
Current assets, 12/31/93	$244,000

CASH

3. **(c)** The $600,000 of compensating balances against short-term borrowing arrangements is properly includible in unrestricted cash in current assets because the compensating balances are not legally restricted as to withdrawal by Burr. The $1,600,000 of cash legally restricted for additions to plant should *not* be included in cash in current assets because it is not readily available to meet current obligations. Cash that is restricted as to withdrawal or use for other than current operations, designated for expenditure in the acquisition or construction of noncurrent assets, or segregated for the liquidation of long-term debts should be excluded from current assets (ARB 43). The total cash that Burr should report in the current assets section of its balance sheet is computed as follows:

Cash in banks	$2,250,000
Cash on hand	125,000
Cash reported in current assets	$2,375,000

4. **(b)** The $1,800 check was not mailed as of 12/31/93 and needs to be added back to the checkbook balance to arrive at the true cash balance as of 12/31/93. The starting point is the checkbook, not the bank statement, because the bank statement does not include checks in transit.

5. **(c)** Cash is by definition the most liquid asset of an enterprise; thus, it is usually the first item presented in the current assets section of the balance sheet. In this question, cash and cash equivalents are calculated as follows:

Cash in checking account	$ 35,000
Cash in money market account	75,000
U.S. Treasury Bill purchased 12/1/99	200,000
Total cash and cash equivalents on 12/31/99	$310,000

The U.S. Treasury bill purchased on 12/1/98 is not a cash equivalent because the maturity of the instrument was more than three months from the purchase date.

6. (c)

Checking account #101	$175,000
Checking account #201	(10,000)
Money market account	25,000
90-day certificate of deposit	50,000
Cash and cash equivalents	$240,000

7. (a)   The cash balance per books at April 30, is computed by subtracting the outstanding checks at April 30, from the balance per bank. First, adjust the bank balance from March to the end of April.

Cash balance per bank statement, 3/31	$ 46,500
Add: Deposits per bank, April	58,400
Less: Disbursements per bank, April	(49,700)
Cash balance per bank, 4/30 (all reconciling items at 3/31 cleared the bank in April)	55,200
Less: Outstanding checks, 4/30	(7,000)
Cash balance per books, 4/30	$ 48,200

8. (a)

Total disbursements per bank statement, April	$ 49,700
Less: Outstanding checks at 3/31	(12,600)
Add: Outstanding checks at 4/30	7,000
Cash disbursement per books, April	$ 44,100

INVESTMENTS IN MARKETABLE SECURITIES

9. (b)   In accordance with SFAS 115, at the end of the year, held-to-maturity securities are reported at amortized cost. Trading securities and available-for-sale securities are accounted for at fair value. The unrealized holding gains and losses are included in current earnings for trading securities, and in other comprehensive income for available-for-sale securities.

10. (b)   Marketable securities which an entity does not intend to sell in the near future are classified as available-for-sale (AFS) securities. Unrealized gains and losses for AFS securities are reported in other comprehensive income. If the entity did intend to sell the securities in the near future, then they would be classified as trading securities and any unrealized gains or losses would be reported as a component of income from continuing operations.

11. (b)   Subsequent to purchase, debt securities classified as available-for-sale are carried in the investment account at cost, net of premium or discount amortization to date, with a separate valuation account for any difference between unamortized cost and fair value. If there is a decline in market value which is deemed *permanent*, then the security should be written down to *fair value* by a credit to the investment account and a realized loss is recognized.

Debt securities purchased between interest dates should be recorded separately from the accrued interest, as follows:

Investment in Marketable Debt Securities	XX
Accrued Interest Receivable	XX
Cash (cost of security plus accrued interest)	XX

12. (a)   If there is a change in the classification of a marketable equity security between trading and available-for-sale, the security is transferred between the corresponding portfolios at the fair value at the date of transfer. If fair value is less than cost, the fair value becomes the new cost basis, and the difference is accounted for as if it were a realized loss and included in the determination of net income.

13. (d)   The securities are measured at their fair value, with a Market Adjustment account established for the difference from cost. A $20,000 loss difference is offset by a $10,000 gain difference; the net is a $10,000 credit balance needed in the Market Adjustment account.

14. (d)   Realized gains and losses related to marketable equity securities should always be included in net income. In addition, with trading marketable securities, unrealized losses and other changes in the Market Adjustment account flow through the income statement.

15. (d)   The carrying amount of an available-for-sale marketable equity securities portfolio should be its market value. The amount by which aggregate cost of the portfolio exceeds market value should be accounted for as a valuation allowance. An amount equal to the valuation allowance is reported in accumulated other comprehensive income within owners' equity. Since the portfolio in question has a valuation allowance, its market value is less than cost. Thus, the historical cost of the portfolio is the sum of the amount of the valuation allowance of the portfolio and the market value of the portfolio ($19,800 + $96,450 = $116,250).

16. (d)   An unrealized loss was reported in the 1992 income statement for a temporary decline in the market value of an investment in a marketable equity security; hence, the investment must have been classified as a trading security. (An unrealized loss on an investment in marketable securities classified as available-for-sale would be shown in other comprehensive income rather than as an income statement item.) The market price decline in 1992 was *less* than the increase in market price during 1993 because there was a realized gain reported on the 1993 income statement which means that the security was sold for a price exceeding its cost.

Thus, in 1993, the market price increased enough to recover the unrealized loss experienced in 1992 and to produce a gain on the sale of the investment.

17. (d) Marketable securities classified as available-for-sale (AFS) are to be reported at fair value. The amount by which aggregate cost of an AFS portfolio exceeds its fair value should be accounted for as a credit to the Market Adjustment—AFS account. In addition, an amount equal to the balance of the Market Adjustment—AFS account should be reported separately within equity in accumulated other comprehensive income. The balance in the Market Adjustment—AFS account at year-end is a $10,000 credit ($296,000 − $286,000). An increase in the Market Adjustment—AFS account is recognized in other comprehensive income, not in net income; only changes in the Market Adjustment—Trading account are recognized in income.

18. (a) The realized loss reported from the sale of the marketable securities is determined as the difference between the proceeds received (i.e., the gross selling price of the shares less any brokerage commissions and taxes incurred in the sale) and the cost of the securities.

Gross selling price of 2,000 share @ $14	$ 28,000
Less: Brokerage commissions and taxes incurred	(1,400)
Proceeds received from sale of securities	26,600
Cost of securities sold	(31,500)
Recognized loss on sale	$ (4,900)

19. (d) At 12/31/94, the required balance of the Market Adjustment—AFS account was a $20,000 credit ($100,000 − $80,000). At 12/31/95, the required balance of the Market Adjustment—AFS account is a $15,000 credit ($100,000 − $85,000). Thus, in 1995, the required balance of the Market Adjustment—AFS account decreased by $5,000. Although changes in the Market Adjustment account related to a trading category of marketable securities are included in the determination of net income in the period in which they occur, changes in the Market Adjustment account related to the available-for-sale category are included in other comprehensive income. Thus, Lee does not recognize any gain or loss from a change in the Market Adjustment—AFS account on its income statement.

20. (d) According to SFAS 115, trading securities are reported at fair value and unrealized holding gains and losses are included in current earnings.

21. (a) Per SFAS 115, the transfer of a security from the trading category of investments shall be accounted for at fair value. The unrealized holding loss resulting from the decrease in market value while classified as trading securities shall be included in earnings. As of the date of transfer, June 30, 1995, the securities had experienced a decline in fair value of $45,000 ($575,000 − $530,000) from the end of the prior year. Upon transfer to a different category of investment, this unrealized loss is required to be included in earnings. (The decline from $650,000 to $575,000 would have been included as an unrealized loss on the 1994 income statement.)

22. (a) Unrealized holding losses for available-for-sale (AFS) securities shall be excluded from earnings and reported in other comprehensive income until realized. The decrease in fair value over the time period in which the securities were classified as trading securities would have been reported in earnings. However, the decrease occurring after the transfer to the AFS category, $40,000 ($530,000 − $490,000), would be reflected in other comprehensive income.

FINANCIAL INSTRUMENT DISCLOSURE

23. (c) An interest rate swap agreement is an arrangement used to limit interest rate risk. Two companies swap interest payments, but not the principal, in an agreement, such as an exchange of a variable interest rate for a fixed rate. The risk of accounting loss from an interest rate swap includes both (1) the risk of exchanging a lower interest rate for a higher rate and (2) the risk of nonperformance by the other party.

24. (a) SFAS 107 requires an entity to disclose all significant concentrations of credit risk arising from *all* financial instruments.

25. (a) According to SFAS 107, an entity must disclose the fair value of financial instruments for which it is practicable to estimate that value. The entity should, of course, maintain accurate cost records, and materiality is a factor, but if it would be excessively costly to estimate fair values, an entity is not required to disclose the fair values. Note, however, that if the entity does not disclose fair value, it must disclose information relating to the financial instruments, including the reasons why it is not practicable to estimate fair value.

26. (c) According to SFAS 107, if it is not practicable to estimate the fair value of a financial instrument, the following should be disclosed: (1) the information pertinent to estimating the fair value of that financial instrument, such as the carrying amount, effective interest rate, and maturity; and (2) the reasons why it is not practicable to estimate fair value.

DETERMINING THE AMOUNT DUE

27. (a) Only the receivables which have aged 0-15 days are eligible for the discount. The discount is computed using 50% of the dollar amount eligible, not 50% of the discount. Only 50% of the customers take advantage of the discount.

Amount eligible for discount	$100,000
% of customers that take the discount	x 50%
Amount of eligible amount taken	50,000
Discount allowed	x 2%
Allowance for discount	$ 1,000

28. (c) The amount of the remittance is computed as follows. First, subtract the amount of the trade discounts from the list price of the goods. Second, subtract the amount of the cash discount. Finally, add the amount of Pitt's prepayment of delivery costs made as an accommodation for Burr.

List price of merchandise	$ 5,000
Less: Trade discount—30%	(1,500)
Balance	3,500
Less: Trade discount—20%	(700)
Balance	2,800
Less: 2% cash discount, remittance received within 15 days of sale—credit terms, 2/15, n/40 ($2,800 x 2%)	(56)
Amount received for merchandise	2,744
Add: Reimbursement of Pitt's prepayment of delivery costs for Burr made as an accommodation	200
Remittance received from Burr in full payment	$ 2,944

ALLOWANCE FOR UNCOLLECTIBLE ACCOUNTS

29. (c) Credit sales increase accounts receivable. Collections from customers, accounts written-off, and sales returns decrease accounts receivable. Since the estimated future sales returns and the estimated uncollectible accounts are recorded in allowance accounts to the accounts receivable, they do not directly decrease the balance of the Accounts Receivable account. The amount to be reported for accounts receivable, before allowances for sales returns and uncollectible accounts at 12/31/92, can be determined by the following analysis of the Accounts Receivable account for 1992:

Accounts Receivable			
Balance, 1/1/92	650,000		
Credit sales, 1992	2,700,000	2,150,000	Collections from customers during 1992
		40,000	Accounts written-off, 1992
		75,000	Sales returns, 1992
Balance, 12/31/92	1,085,000		

30. (c) During 2000, accounts receivable was increased by credit sales. The A/R balance was decreased by collections from customers and by accounts written off. Accounts recovered resulted in an increase and a decrease of equal amount to the

A/R balance. The amount to be reported for accounts receivable at 12/31/00, before allowance for uncollectible accounts, is detailed in the following analysis:

Accounts Receivable			
Balance, 1/1/00	100,000	591,000	Customer collections, 2000
Credit sales, 2000	611,000	45,000	Accounts written-off, 2000
Accounts reinstated, 2000	17,000	17,000	Accounts recovered, 2000
Balance, 12/31/00	75,000		

31. (b) The allowance method of recording uncollectible account expense matches uncollectible account expense with the revenues generated by credit sales in the same period. Therefore, the allowance method of recording uncollectible account expense is consistent with accrual accounting. Since the write-off of an account receivable often occurs in a period after the revenues were generated, the direct write-off method of recording uncollectible account expense does not necessarily match uncollectible account expense with the revenues generated by credit sales in the same period. Therefore, the direct write-off method is not consistent with accrual accounting.

32. (a) While the unadjusted credit balance in the allowance accounts would be used to compute the uncollectible account expense for the period ending 3/31/93, the amount is not used to compute the balance of the allowance for uncollectible accounts at 3/31/93. The amount to be reported as the allowance for uncollectible accounts at 3/31/93 is computed as follows:

Age	Accounts receivable	Estimated % uncollectible	Allowance for uncollectible accounts
0-30 days	$60,000	5%	$3,000
31-60 days	4,000	10%	400
Over 60 days	2,000	*	1,400
			$4,800

* The dollar amount is given in the data.

33. (a) The Allowance for Uncollectible Accounts had a credit balance of $24,000 at 12/31/91. During 1992, $96,000 of uncollectible accounts were written-off. Therefore, the allowance account had a debit balance of $72,000 (i.e., $96,000 − $24,000) before recognition of uncollectible account expense for 1992. Since the aging of accounts receivable indicated that a credit balance of $100,000 was required at 12/31/92, for the Allowance Account, Hall should recognize uncollectible account expense of $172,000 (i.e., $72,000 + $100,000) in 1992.

34. (a) The entry to record the write-off of a specific account receivable using the allowance method involves a debit to Allowance for Uncollectible Accounts and a credit to Accounts Receivable. This affects each of the accounts in the entry, but not net income.

35. (a) An increase in accounts receivable indicates that there was an excess of sales over cash collections during the period. A write-off of receivables will offset the gross increase in accounts receivable without affecting cash. Regardless of the method used to account for uncollectible accounts, the cash collections from customers equal sales adjusted for a deduction for an increase in accounts receivable balance and a deduction for accounts written-off during the period.

36. (a) The goods out on consignment have not yet been sold and, thus, must be included in Mann's *inventory* at their *cost* of $20,000 ($26,000 ÷ 130%). The security deposit on lease of the warehouse should be classified as a noncurrent asset. The total current net receivables at 12/31/97 is determined as follows:

Trade accounts receivable	$ 93,000
Less: Allowance for uncollectible accounts	(2,000)
Plus: Claim against shipper for goods lost in transit	3,000
Current net receivables	$ 94,000

37. (b) To determine the uncollectible accounts expense for 1993, the allowance for uncollectible accounts at 12/31/93 must first be determined as follows:

Accounts receivable, 12/31/93	$ 350,000
Net realizable value of the receivables	(325,000)
Allowance for uncollectible accounts, 12/31/93	$ 25,000

Uncollectible accounts expense for 1993 can now be determined by the following analysis of the allowance for uncollectible accounts:

Allowance for Uncollectible Accounts			
1993 Write-offs	$18,000	$30,000	Balance, 1/1/93
		2,000	Uncollectible accounts recovered, 1993
		14,000	Balance before recognition of 1993 uncollectible accounts expense
		11,000	Uncollectible accounts expense, 1993 (forced)
		$25,000	Balance, 12/31/93

38. (d) Under the percentage-of-receivables method, the allowance for uncollectible accounts is determined at the end of the period by multiplying the ending accounts receivable balance by an estimate of the percentage of gross accounts receivable that will become uncollectible.

Accounts receivable, 12/31/97	$ 1,000,000
Estimated percentage of uncollectible accounts	x 3%
Allowance for uncollectible accounts, 12/31/97	$ 30,000

39. (d) The uncollectible accounts expense for 1997 is $56,000 ($40,000 + $16,000). The uncollectible accounts expense for the year can be determined by the following analysis of the allowance for uncollectible accounts:

Allowance for Uncollectible Accounts			
		42,000	Balance, 1/1/97 (given)
1997 Write-offs (given)	46,000	40,000	Uncollectible accounts expense recorded during year ($2,000,000 x 2%)
		36,000	Balance before adjustment
		16,000	Adjustment to increase allowance account to desired ending balance
		52,000	Desired ending balance per aging (given)

40. (a) The allowance method based on aging the receivables attempts to value the receivables at their future collectible amounts. Thus, it emphasizes asset valuation rather than income measurement. Allowance methods based on sales attempt to match bad debts with the revenues generated by the sales in the same period. Therefore, they emphasize income measurement rather than asset valuation. The direct write-off method is not an allowance method. The direct write-off method does not recognize bad debt expense until a specific amount is deemed uncollectible and, therefore, does not report the receivables at their net realizable value.

41. (a) Based on the information given, Jamin Co. uses the percentage-of-sales method, under which bad debt expense is calculated as a percentage of credit sales for a period. This amount is charged to Bad Debt Expense and credited to the Allowance for Uncollectible Accounts. Any previous balance in the allowance account is not considered in determining the amount of bad debt expense.

Allowance for Uncollectible Accounts			
		260,000	Beg. bal. 1/1/94
Write-offs in 1994	325,000	180,000	Bad debt expense 1994*
		115,000	12/31/94 balance

* Credit sales of $9,000,000 x 2% = $180,000

42. (b) The total risk of accounting loss is the amount of potential loss the entity would suffer if all parties to the financial instruments failed completely to perform and the amounts due proved to be of no value to the entity. Butler Co. had already recorded

an allowance for uncollectible accounts of $20,000 on its trade accounts receivable of $250,000, so the net of $230,000 is the risk of accounting loss. The entire amount is shown on the balance sheet, thus there is no off-balance sheet risk involved.

NOTES RECEIVABLE

43. (b) Total interest revenue earned over the life of the note is determined as the excess of the summation of the required annual year-end payments over the present value of the note.

Summation of required annual year-end payments ($5,009 x 5)	$ 25,045
Less: Present value of note	(19,485)
Interest revenue earned over life of note	$ 5,560

44. (b) When an interest-bearing instrument is sold between interest payment dates, the seller collects accrued interest from the buyer. The buyer will later collect interest for a full interest period at the next interest payment date. In the case at hand, inventory is being exchanged for the note. Because the market rate of interest is equal to the note's stated rate, the note's present value is equal to the face amount of the note plus the one month's accrued interest. The journal entry to record the exchange involves a debit to Note Receivable for its face amount, a debit to Interest Receivable for the one month of accrued interest, and a credit to Sales Revenue for the sum of the note's face amount and the one month of accrued interest.

45. (c) Where a note is exchanged solely for cash and no other rights or privileges are exchanged, it is presumed to have a present value at issuance equal to the cash proceeds exchanged (APB 21). The note receivable is recorded at its present value, which in the case of Money Co. is $194,000. Income on this loan for December 1995 is calculated based on the effective rate of interest on the present value of the loan; $194,000 x 12.4% = $24,056 x 1/12 = $2,005.

46. (c) Accrued interest receivable is calculated by multiplying the face amount of the note by the stated rate for the applicable period of time; $200,000 x 11% x 1/12 = $1,833. A helpful way of clearly seeing the difference between accrued interest receivable (balance sheet account) and interest income (income statement account) is by preparing the journal entries at December 1 and December 31.

12/1/95

Notes Receivable	200,000	
Loan Origination Fee		6,000
Cash		194,000

12/31/95

Accrued Interest Receivable (face value x stated rate x time)	1,833
Amortization of Loan Origination Fees (plug)	172
Interest Income (PV x effective rate x time)	2,005

47. (d) ARB 43 states that profit is deemed to be realized when a sale in the ordinary course of business is effected, unless the circumstances are such that the collection of the sale price is not reasonably assured. APB 10 states, "in absence of these circumstances, the installment method of recognizing revenue is not acceptable." Because the company purchasing the land has a triple-A credit rating, the gain realized on the sale should be recognized in full in the period of sale. In addition, since the mortgage note bears interest at the market rate, it is recorded at its face amount. The gain reported from the sale of the land is determined as follows:

Cash ($150,000 x 25%)	$ 37,500
Mortgage note ($150,000 x 75%)	112,500
Fair value of proceeds received	150,000
Carrying amount of land	(100,000)
Gain realized and recognized in 1997	$ 50,000

48. (c) The note can be recorded at its face amount of $150,000 because there is no indication that the rate of interest (8%) stipulated by the parties to the transaction does not represent fair and adequate compensation for the use of the funds. Payments of $50,000 in principal plus accrued interest are due annually on July 1, 1992, 1993, and 1994. Therefore, the amount that should be reported as accrued interest receivable at 6/30/93 is computed as follows:

Carrying amount of note, 6/30/91	$150,000
Less: Principal payment, 7/1/92	(50,000)
Carrying amount of note, 7/1/92	100,000
Times: Stated interest rate	x 8%
Interest receivable, 6/30/93	$ 8,000

Frame should report the interest receivable as a current asset in its 6/30/93 balance sheet, because the amount is to be received within one year of the balance sheet date (i.e., it is to be received 7/1/93).

49. (b) A noninterest-bearing note exchanged for property, goods, or services should not be recorded at its face amount. Since there is not an established exchange price for the equipment and the question does not indicate the fair value of the note, the note should be recorded at its present value, which is computed by discounting all future

payments of the note at the prevailing rate of interest for a note of this type. The amount that should be reported as interest income in 1992 is computed as follows:

Face amount of note	$ 600,000
Less: Imputed interest	
[$600,000 x (1 – .75)	(150,000)
Carrying amount of note, 1/2/92	450,000
Times: Effective interest rate	x 10%
Interest income, 1992	$ 45,000

50.   (a)   A noninterest-bearing note exchanged for property, goods, or services should not be recorded at its face amount. Since there is not an established exchange price for the equipment and the question does not indicate the fair value of the note, the note should be recorded at its present value, which is computed by discounting all future payments of the note at the prevailing rate of interest for a note of this type. The loss that should be reported on the sale of the machinery is computed as follows:

Present value of note ($600,000 x .75)	$ 450,000
Carrying amount of machinery	(480,000)
Loss on sale of machinery	$ (30,000)

51.   (d)   Both notes were received on the balance sheet date. Since the note receivable from Hart arose from a transaction with a customer in the normal course of business and is due in customary trade terms not exceeding one year, it can be reported at its face amount of $10,000 despite the fact that the 3% stated interest rate of the note differs from the prevailing market interest rate of 8% for similar notes at the date of the transaction [APB 21, par 3(a)]. On the other hand, the note receivable from Maxx, which also arose from a transaction with a customer in the normal course of business, is due in five years (i.e., more than one year). Therefore, the note from Maxx cannot be reported at its face amount because the 3% stated interest rate of the note differs from the prevailing market interest rate of 8% for similar notes at the date of the transaction. Because neither the fair value of the services performed by Jet nor the fair value of the note received from Maxx is indicated, the note should be reported at its present value, determined by discounting all future cash payments of the note at the prevailing (i.e., market) rate of interest for a note of this type. Therefore, the note receivable from Maxx should be reported at $7,820, determined as follows:

Principal amount	$10,000
Interest on outstanding principal balance	
due on maturity date	
[($10,000 x 3%) x 5]	1,500
Amount due on maturity date	11,500
Present value factor of $1 at 8%	
for 5 periods	x .680
Present value of note received from Maxx	$ 7,820

52.   (c)   APB 21 generally requires the recording of notes receivable at their present value. At December 31, 1994, Chang is owed 9 more annual payments of $10,000. The appropriate factor to apply is the present value of ordinary annuity of $1 at 8% for 9 periods, which is given as 6.25. $10,000 x 6.25 = $62,500.

53.   (c)   According to SFAS 114, a creditor should consider a loan to be impaired when, "based on current information and events, it is probable that the creditor will be unable to collect all amounts due according to the contractual terms of the loan agreement." If foreclosure is not probable, the creditor measures the impaired loan at one of the following: (1) the loan's observable market price, (2) the fair value of collateral pledged, or (3) the present value of future principal and interest cash inflows, net of discounted disposal costs all discounted at the loan's effective interest rate. If foreclosure is probable, the second method is to be used to value a collateral dependent impaired loan.

DISCOUNTING OF RECEIVABLES

54.   (c)   The total amount of interest revenue to be earned by King over the life of the note is determined as the excess of the summation of the required annual year-end payments over the present value of the note discounted to yield a 9% rate to King, determined as follows:

Summation of required annual year-end payments		
[5 x $5,010 (as determined below)]		$ 25,050
Less: Present value of note:		
Face amount of note	20,000	
Divide by: PV factor of an ordinary		
annuity of $1 for 5 periods at 8%	÷ 3.992	
Required equal annual year-end		
payments under note	5,010	
Times: PV factor of an ordinary annuity of		
$1 for 5 periods at the yield rate of 9%	x 3.890	(19,490)
Interest revenue to be earned over the life of		
the note		$ 5,560

55. (c) The amount of cash received from the bank is computed as follows:

Face amount of note	$500,000
Add: Interest to maturity ($500,000 x 8%)	40,000
Maturity value of note	540,000
Less: Bank discount ($540,000 x 10% x 6/12)	(27,000)
Proceeds from discounted note	$513,000

56. (d) Davis discounted the note receivable with recourse. If the maker fails to pay at maturity, the note is presented to Davis, who is then liable for $20,500, the amount due at maturity. Davis should disclose this contingent liability in its 12/31/92 financial statements.

57. (b) Determining the proceeds received from discounting a note receivable consists of three steps, as follows:

(1) Determine the maturity value of the note. This amount is based on the face amount, the stated rate of interest, and the time of maturity of the note.

(2) Apply the bank's discount rate to the maturity value of the note to obtain the amount of the discount charged by the bank.

(3) Subtract the discount charged by the bank from the maturity value of the note to obtain the proceeds received from the bank.

58. (d) The cash received from the discounted note is determined as follows:

Face amount of note, 7/1/97	$100,000
Less: Payment of first installment, 12/31/97	(50,000)
Face amount of note, 12/31/97 (due 12/31/98)	50,000
Add: Interest to maturity ($50,000 x 10% x 12/12)	5,000
Maturity value of remaining portion of note	55,000
Less: Bank discount ($55,000 x 12% x 6/12)	(3,300)
Proceeds from discounted note	$ 51,700

59. (a) The amount of accrued interest revenue is determined by subtracting the face amount of the note from the proceeds to be received from the bank.

Face amount of note	$ 40,000
Add: Interest to maturity ($40,000 x 12% x 90/360)	1,200
Maturity value of note	41,200
Less: Bank discount ($41,200 x 15% x 60/360)	(1,030)
Proceeds from discounted note	40,170
Less: Face amount of note	(40,000)
Accrued interest revenue, 9/30/97	$ 170

60. (c) A company which discounts a note receivable with recourse is contingently liable to the lender. It must pay the lender the amount due at maturity if the maker of the note fails to pay the obligation. The contingent liability is usually shown in the accounts by recording the note discounted in a Notes Receivable Discounted account at the face amount of the note. The Notes Receivable Discounted account is reported as a contra asset and is deducted from Notes Receivable in the balance sheet as follows:

Notes receivable	$ XXX	
Less: Notes receivable discounted	(XXX)	$XXX

FACTORING OF RECEIVABLES

61. (d) Factoring of receivables is in substance a sale of receivables when the transfer is without recourse (i.e., the financing institution or "factor" assumes the risk of collection).

PERFORMANCE BY SUBTOPICS

Each category below parallels a subtopic covered in Chapter 2. Record the number and percentage of questions you correctly answered in each subtopic area.

Current Assets

Question#	Correct √
1	
2	
# Questions 2	

Correct ____
% Correct ____

Cash

Question #	Correct √
3	
4	
5	
6	
7	
8	
# Questions 6	

Correct ____
% Correct ____

Investments in Marketable Securities

Question #	Correct √
9	
10	
11	
12	
13	
14	
15	
16	
17	
18	
19	
20	
21	
22	
# Questions 14	

Correct ____
% Correct ____

Financial Instrument Disclosure

Question #	Correct √
23	
24	
25	
26	
# Questions 4	

Correct ____
% Correct ____

Determining the Amount Due

Question #	Correct √
27	
28	
# Questions 2	

Correct ____
% Correct ____

Allowance for Uncollectible Accounts

Question #	Correct √
29	
30	
31	
32	
33	
34	
35	
36	
37	
38	
39	
40	
41	
42	
# Questions 14	

Correct ____
% Correct ____

Notes Receivable

Question #	Correct √
43	
44	
45	
46	
47	
48	
49	
50	
51	
52	
53	
# Questions 11	

Correct ____
% Correct ____

Discounting of Receivables

Question #	Correct √
54	
55	
56	
57	
58	
59	
60	
# Questions 7	

Correct ____
% Correct ____

Factoring of Receivables

Question #	Correct √
61	
# Questions 1	

Correct ____
% Correct ____

OTHER OBJECTIVE FORMAT SOLUTION

SOLUTION 2-2 MARKETABLE SECURITIES

1. (T) Trading securities are debt and equity securities that are bought and held principally for the purpose of selling them in the near term.

2. (H) Held-to-maturity (HTM) securities are debt securities that the enterprise has the positive intent and the ability to hold to maturity.

3. (A) Available-for-sale (AFS) securities are debt and equity securities not classified as either HTM or trading securities.

4. (A) AFS securities are debt and equity securities not classified as either HTM or trading securities.

5. (G) $100,000. HTM securities are reported at amortized cost and are not adjusted for unrealized holding gains and losses, although fair value must be disclosed.

6. (I) $155,000. Trading securities are reported at fair market value.

7. (J) $160,000. AFS securities are reported at fair market value.

8. (D,L) The recognized gain or loss from the sale of a debt or equity security is the difference between the net proceeds received from the sale and the cost or amortized cost of the security. $175,000 – $190,000 = $15,000 loss.

9. (B,L) The $5,000 unrealized loss pertains to the trading securities, as these are the only securities for which unrealized holding gains and losses are included in current earnings. $155,000 fair value at 12/31/94 – $160,000 fair value at 12/31/93 = $5,000 unrealized loss.

10. (C,L) The $10,000 loss pertains to security JKL as AFS securities are the only securities for which net unrealized holding gains or losses are reported in accumulated other comprehensive income. $160,000 fair value at 12/31/94 – $170,000 cost = $10,000 net unrealized loss.

PROBLEMS/ESSAY SOLUTIONS

Solution 2-3 (10 points)

Financial Instruments

a. A **financial instrument** is **cash, evidence of an ownership interest in an entity, or a contractual right to receive or deliver cash or another financial instrument**. A **derivative financial instrument** is a product whose **value is derived, at least in part, from the value and characteristics of one or more underlying assets**. Examples of derivative financial instruments include: futures; forward, swap, or options contracts; interest-rate caps; and fixed-rate loan commitments.

b. **Off-balance-sheet risk** of accounting loss is the **risk of accounting loss from a financial instrument that exceeds the amount recognized for the financial instrument in the balance sheet.**

c. **Market risk** is the **possibility that future changes in market prices may make a financial instrument less valuable or more burdensome**. **Credit risk** is the **possibility that a loss may occur from the failure of the other party to perform** according to the terms of a contract. **Concentrations of credit risk** exist when receivables have **common characteristics that may affect their collection**. One common characteristic might be that the receivables are due from companies in the same industry or in the same region of the country.

d. The **fair value** of a financial instrument is the amount at which the instrument could be exchanged in a current transaction between **willing parties, other than in a forced or liquidation sale**. **Quoted market price**, if available, is the best evidence of the fair value of a financial instrument. If quoted prices are not available, the best estimate of fair value might be based on **valuation techniques** or on the quoted market price of a financial instrument with similar characteristics.

Solution 2-4 Valuation of Notes Receivable

a. The appropriate valuation basis of a note receivable at the date of sale is its **discounted present value** of the future amounts receivable for **principal and interest** using the **customers' market rate of interest**, if known or determinable, at the date of the equipment's sale.

b. Gregor should **increase** the **carrying amount** of the note receivable by the **effective interest revenue earned** for the period February 1 to May 1, 1992. Gregor should account for the discounting of the note receivable without recourse by **increasing cash** for the **proceeds received, eliminating the carrying amount of the note receivable**, and **recognizing a loss (gain)** for the resulting difference.

This reporting is appropriate since the note's carrying amount is correctly recorded at the date it was discounted and the discounting of a note receivable without recourse is equivalent to a sale of that note. Thus the difference between the cash received and the carrying amount of the note at the date it is discounted is reported as a loss (gain).

c. 1. For notes receivable not discounted, Gregor should **recognize an uncollectible notes expense**. The expense **equals the adjustment** required to bring the balance of the allowance for uncollectible notes receivable **equal to the estimated uncollectible amounts less the fair values of recoverable equipment**.

2. For notes receivable discounted with recourse, Gregor should **recognize an uncollectible notes expense**. The expense **equals** the **estimated amounts payable for customers' defaults less the fair values of recoverable equipment**.

SOLUTION 2-5 ACCOUNTS AND NOTES RECEIVABLE

a. To account for the accounts receivable factored on April 1, 1997, Magrath should **decrease accounts receivable by the amount** of accounts receivable **factored**, **increase cash** by the **amount received** from the factor, and **record a loss equal to the difference**. The **loss** should be **reported in the income statement**. Factoring of accounts receivable on a without recourse basis is **equivalent to a sale**.

b. The **carrying amount** of the note at July 1, 1997, is the **maturity amount discounted for two years at the market interest rate**. For the noninterest-bearing note receivable, the **interest revenue** for 1997 should be determined by multiplying the **carrying amount** of the note at July 1, 1997, **times the market rate of interest at the date of the note times one-half**.

The noninterest-bearing note receivable should be reported in the December 31, 1997 balance sheet, as a **noncurrent asset** at its **face amount less** the **unamortized discount**.

c. Magrath should account for the collection of the accounts previously written off as uncollectible as follows:

- **Increase** both **accounts receivable** and the **allowance for uncollectible accounts**.
- **Increase cash** and **decrease accounts receivable**.

d. One approach estimates uncollectible accounts based on **credit sales**. This approach focuses on **income determination** by attempting to **match uncollectible accounts expense** with the **revenues generated**.

The other allowance approach estimates uncollectible accounts based on the balance in or **aging of receivables**. The approach focuses on **asset valuation** by attempting to **report receivables at net realizable value**.

SOLUTION 2-6 COMPUTATION OF ALLOWANCE FOR DOUBTFUL ACCOUNTS

a.

Sigma Co.
SCHEDULE OF CALCULATION OF
ALLOWANCE FOR UNCOLLECTIBLE ACCOUNTS
December 31, 1991

0 to 30 days	$300,000 x 1%	$ 3,000
31 to 90 days	80,000 x 5%	4,000
91 to 180 days	60,000 x 20%	12,000
Over 180 days	25,000 x 80%	20,000
Accounts receivable	$465,000	
Allowance for uncollectible accounts		$39,000

b.	**Balance December 31, 1990**	$ 28,000
	Write-offs during 1991	(27,000)
	Recoveries during 1991	7,000
	Balance before 1991 provision	8,000
	Required allowance at December 31, 1991	39,000
	1991 provision	$ 31,000

SOLUTION 2-7 NONINTEREST-BEARING NOTE RECEIVABLE

a.

Kern Inc.
LONG-TERM RECEIVABLES SECTION OF BALANCE SHEET
December 31, 1997

9% note receivable from sale of idle building, due in annual installments of $250,000 to May 1, 1999, less current installment	**$250,000**	[1]
8% note receivable from officer, due December 31, 1999, collateralized by 5,000 shares of Kern Inc. common stock with a fair value of $225,000	200,000	
Noninterest-bearing note from sale of patent, net of 10% imputed interest, due April 1, 1999	**88,795**	[2]
Installment contract receivable, due in annual installments of $88,332 to July 1, 2001, less current installment	219,668	[3]
Total long-term receivables	$758,463	

b.

Kern Inc.
SELECTED BALANCE SHEET ACCOUNTS
December 31, 1997

Current portion of long-term receivables:		
Note receivable from sale of idle building	**$250,000**	[1]
Installment contract receivable	60,332	[3]
Total	$310,332	
Accrued interest receivable:		
Note receivable from sale of idle building	$ 30,000	[4]
Installment contract receivable	14,000	[5]
Total	$ 44,000	

c.

Kern Inc.
INTEREST REVENUE FROM LONG-TERM RECEIVABLES
AND GAINS RECOGNIZED ON SALE OF ASSETS
For the year ended December 31, 1997

Interest revenue:		
Note receivable from sale of idle building	$ 52,500	[6]
Note receivable from sale of patent	6,195	[2]
Note receivable from officer	16,000	[7]
Installment contract receivable from sale of land	14,000	[5]
Total interest revenue	$ 88,695	
Gains recognized on sale of assets:		
Patent	$ 44,600	[8]
Land	100,000	[9]
Total gains recognized	$144,600	

Explanation of Amounts:

[1] **Long-term portion of 9% note receivable at 12/31/97**

Face amount, 5/1/96	$ 750,000
Less: Installment received 5/1/97	(250,000)
Balance, 12/31/97	500,000
Less: Installment due 5/1/98	(250,000)
Long-term portion, 12/31/97	$ 250,000

[2] **Noninterest-bearing note, net of imputed interest at 12/31/97**

Face amount, 4/1/97	$ 100,000
Less: Imputed interest [$100,000 − $82,600 ($100,000 x 0.826)]	(17,400)
Balance, 4/1/97	82,600
Add: Interest earned to 12/31/97 [$82,600 x 10% x 9/12]	6,195
Balance, 12/31/97	$ 88,795

(continued on next page)

Explanation of Amounts (cont):

[3] Long-term portion of installment contract receivable at 12/31/97

Contract selling price, 7/1/97	$ 400,000
Less: Cash down payment	(120,000)
Balance, 12/31/97	280,000
Less: Installment due 7/1/98 [$88,332 – $28,000 ($280,000 x 10%)]	(60,332)
Long-term portion, 12/31/97	**$ 219,668**

[4] Accrued interest--note receivable, sale of idle building at 12/31/97
Interest accrued from 5/1 to 12/31/97 [$500,000 x 9% x 8/12]   **$ 30,000**

[5] Accrued interest--installment contract at 12/31/97
Interest accrued from 7/1 to 12/31/97 [$280,000 x 10% x 1/2]   **$ 14,000**

[6] Interest revenue--note receivable, sale of idle building, for 1997

Interest earned from 1/1 to 5/1/97 [$750,000 x 9% x 4/12]	$ 22,500
Interest earned from 5/1 to 12/31/97 [$500,000 x 9% x 8/12]	30,000
Interest revenue	**$ 52,500**

[7] Interest revenue--note receivable, officer, for 1997
Interest earned 1/1 to 12/31/97 [$200,000 x 8%]   **$ 16,000**

[8] Gain recognized on sale of patent

Stated selling price		$ 100,000
Less: Imputed interest		(17,400) [2]
Actual selling price		82,600
Less: Cost of patent (net)		
Carrying amount 1/1/97	$40,000	
Less amortization 1/1 to 4/1/97 [$8,000 x 1/4]	(2,000)	(38,000)
Gain recognized		**$ 44,600**

[9] Gain recognized on sale of land

Selling price	$ 400,000
Less: Cost	(300,000)
Gain recognized	**$ 100,000**

Wondering how you can prepare for essay questions?

Some candidates who are otherwise confident about the exam are overwhelmed by essay questions. The following tips are designed to help you increase your confidence when presented with questions requiring free-form answers.

Review the **Accounting for 5%** appendix. This appendix has an example of what the AICPA labels as "ideal" and "good" solutions. Notice that the gap between "ideal" and "good" is larger than the gap between "good" and "poor." This works to your benefit.

As you progress through your study plan, answer an essay from each major topic; waiting until the last month leaves you little time to prepare for essays. The more uncomfortable that you are with essays, the more important this becomes. Bear in mind, you might not realize that you are uncomfortable with essays, if you don't try answering some of them.

Once you grade your essay in comparison to the unofficial solution, reflect on the question. Assigning a point value is probably the least important part of answering the question. Any mistakes or omissions are solid learning opportunities. Additional information about essay techniques is in the **Practical Advice** appendix. Also, some Hot*Spot videos spend time on essay-answering techniques explicitly.

Read through the essay questions (with their related unofficial solutions) of essay questions you will not be answering within the next few days. This provides a good review of the material you have just covered, as well as acquainting you with the types of questions and the length of the expected responses.

Once you know the content, you will be able to prepare a response regardless of the question format. However, exam time is limited, and you don't want the pressure of time considerations to distract you from providing your best answer to a question. To reduce the pressure, remember that you must earn 75 points to pass—it doesn't matter which format that you use to earn those 75 points. Practice more essay questions that cover topics that have high point value; be prepared to answer an essay question in any topic area.

Remember, with the techniques and information in your material,

A passing score is well within reach!

CHAPTER 3

INVENTORY

CHAPTER 3

INVENTORY

I. OVERVIEW

A. DEFINITION
The term inventory is defined by ARB 43, Chapter 4, *Inventory Pricing*, as items of tangible personal property that are held for sale in the ordinary course of business, in the process of production for such sale, or which are to be currently consumed in the production of goods or services to be available for sale. The measuring of inventories involves two distinct problems: (1) determining *physical quantities* and (2) determining an appropriate *dollar valuation.*

B. OWNERSHIP CRITERIA
Only items that are *owned* by the enterprise should be included in inventory. Ownership is determined by possession of title, rather than mere physical possession of the goods.

1. **GOODS IN TRANSIT FROM VENDOR** If shipped "F.O.B. destination," the goods are **not** inventoriable until *received*. However, if shipped "F.O.B. shipping point," the goods should be inventoried when *shipped* by the vendor.

2. **GOODS IN TRANSIT TO CUSTOMER** The cost of inventory items sold "F.O.B. destination" should remain in inventory until the goods are *received* by the purchaser, while the cost of inventory items sold "F.O.B. shipping point" should be removed from inventory when the goods are *shipped*.

3. **GOODS ON CONSIGNMENT** Goods *out* on consignment should be included in inventory at cost because title to the goods has not changed. Conversely, goods *held* on consignment should **not** be included in inventory. Costs incurred by a consignor on a transfer of goods to a consignee (e.g., shipping costs, warehousing costs, and in-transit insurance premiums) should be considered as inventory cost to the consignor.

4. **TRANSPORTATION CHARGES** F.O.B. means "free on board" and requires the seller, at his or her expense, to deliver the goods to the destination indicated as F.O.B. Therefore, if goods are shipped F.O.B. *shipping point*, transportation charges are buyer's responsibility; if F.O.B. *destination*, they are seller's responsibility.

II. MEASURING INVENTORIES

A. PHYSICAL QUANTITIES
Determination of physical inventory quantities is accomplished by the use of one or both of the following systems:

1. **PERIODIC INVENTORY SYSTEM** This system is characterized by no entries being made to the inventory account during the period. Acquisitions of inventory goods are debited to "Purchases" while issuances are not recorded, so that at any point in time the balance in the inventory account reflects the amount at the *beginning* of the period. The inventory on hand is *periodically* determined by physical count. Cost of goods sold (CGS) is a residual amount obtained by subtracting the ending inventory from the sum of beginning inventory and net purchases.

2. **PERPETUAL INVENTORY SYSTEM** A continuous record is maintained of items entering into and issued from inventory. The balance in the inventory account at any time reveals the inventory that should be on hand.

B. **ACQUISITION COST**

1. **COST METHOD** The *primary* basis of accounting for inventories is cost. The *cost* of an inventory item is the cash price or fair value of other consideration given in exchange for it.

   a. **MERCHANDISE INVENTORY** With respect to merchandise inventory, this cost figure is net of trade and/or cash discounts, if any, but should include freight-in, taxes, insurance while in transit, warehousing costs, and similar charges paid by the purchaser to bring the article to its existing condition and location.

   b. **FINISHED GOODS INVENTORY** The finished goods inventory of a manufacturer must include the cost of direct materials, direct labor and *both* variable and fixed manufacturing overhead. Interest cost should **not** be capitalized for inventories that are routinely manufactured or otherwise produced in large quantities on a repetitive basis.

   c. **FREIGHT-OUT** Freight-out is a selling expense and, thus, should **not** be included in the cost of inventory.

   d. **DISCOUNTS** A *trade discount* is a deduction from the list or catalog price of merchandise to arrive at the gross selling price. Trade discounts are not recorded in the seller's or purchaser's accounting records. A *chain discount* occurs when a list price is subject to several trade discounts. In this situation, the amount of each trade discount is determined by multiplying (1) the list price of the merchandise **less** the amount of prior trade discounts by (2) the trade discount percentage.

   EXAMPLE 1 ♦ CHAIN DISCOUNT

   > Cairns Corp. purchased merchandise with a list price of $20,000, subject to trade discounts of 10% and 5%. Cairns should record the cost of this merchandise as $17,100, computed as follows:
   >
   > | | |
   > |---|---:|
   > | List price | $20,000 |
   > | Less: Trade discount—10% | (2,000) |
   > | Balance | 18,000 |
   > | Less: Trade discount—5% | (900) |
   > | Cost of the merchandise | $17,100 |

2. **RELATIVE SALES VALUE METHOD** When a group of varying units are purchased at a single lump-sum price (sometimes called a "basket purchase"), the total cost of the units should be allocated to the various units on the basis of their relative sales value.

   EXAMPLE 2 ♦ RELATIVE SALES VALUE METHOD

   > On May 1, 20X1, Brevard Development Company purchased a tract of land for $600,000. Additional costs of $100,000 were incurred in subdividing the land during May through December 20X1. Of the tract acreage, 80% was subdivided into residential lots as shown below and 20% was conveyed to the city for roads and a park.
   >
   > | Lot class | Number of lots | Sales price per lot |
   > |:---:|:---:|:---:|
   > | A | 100 | $2,000 |
   > | B | 200 | 4,000 |
   > | C | 200 | 5,000 |
   >
   > (continued on next page)

Under the relative sales value method, the cost allocated to each lot is determined as follows:

(A) Lot class	(B) Number of lots	(C) Sales price per lot	(D) (B × C) Total Sales price	(E) Relative sales price	(F) Total cost	(G) (E × F) Cost allocated to lots	(H) (G ÷ B) Cost per lot
A	100	$2,000	$ 200,000	10.0%	$700,000	$ 70,000	$ 700
B	200	4,000	800,000	40.0%	700,000	280,000	1,400
C	200	5,000	1,000,000	50.0%	700,000	350,000	1,750
			$2,000,000			$700,000	

3. EXCEPTIONS TO THE COST RULE

a. DECLINE IN MARKET VALUE When the utility of an inventory item is impaired, the pricing of the item is at cost or market, whichever is lower (*see* D., below).

b. REPLACEMENT COST This departure from the cost basis is justified for used, damaged, or repossessed inventory items. The valuation of these goods is based upon the hypothetical replacement cost of similar items in similar conditions of use.

c. VALUATION AT SALE PRICE Specific guidelines for valuation of inventories at sale price are provided by ARB 43. This method of valuation is justifiable only by inability to determine appropriate approximate costs, immediate marketability at quoted market price, and the characteristic of units' interchangeability. Examples commonly given include precious metals and agricultural products with assured sales prices. When inventories are stated above cost, this fact should be disclosed in the financial statements.

d. LOSSES ON PURCHASE COMMITMENTS When there is a firm commitment to purchase goods in a future period at a set price (i.e., an enforceable contract exists), any loss resulting from a drop in the market value of such goods should be recognized in the current period.

EXHIBIT 1 ♦ JOURNAL ENTRIES FOR A LOSS ON PURCHASE COMMITMENTS

Loss on Purchase Commitment   (Contract price – FV)
    Allowance for Loss on PC   (Contract price – FV)
To record estimated loss at the end of the period.

Inventory (or purchases)   (Current FV)
Allowance for Loss on PC   (Allowance account balance)
    Cash   (Contract price)
To record purchase in subsequent period. Had there been a further change in FV, it would be recorded by crediting or debiting an unrealized income (or loss) account, as appropriate.

C. COST FLOW ASSUMPTIONS

The per-unit cost of inventory items purchased at different times will often vary. In order to allocate the total cost of goods available for sale (i.e., beginning inventory plus net purchases) between cost of goods sold and ending inventory, a *cost flow* method must be adopted. The following cost flow methods are commonly used:

1. SPECIFIC IDENTIFICATION This costing method requires the ability to identify each unit sold or in inventory. The cost of goods sold is the cost of the specific items sold, and the ending inventory is the cost of the specific items still on hand. It is used when inventory goods are few in number, have individually high costs, and can be clearly identified.

2. **FIRST-IN, FIRST-OUT (FIFO)** This method assumes that the goods first acquired are the first sold. Hence, the earliest costs are charged to CGS and the ending inventories are stated in terms of the most recent costs. FIFO is balance sheet-oriented, since it tends to report ending inventories at their approximate replacement cost. Income, however, may be misstated because old costs are matched to current revenues. Use of FIFO necessitates maintaining records of separate lot prices (layers). The easiest way to determine the cost of ending inventory under FIFO involves 4 simple steps: (a) determine the number of units in ending inventory; (b) segregate ending inventory into price layers, beginning with the most recent purchase prices; (c) determine the cost of each layer (i.e., unit cost multiplied by number of units); and (d) add up the cost of all the layers.

EXAMPLE 3 ♦ FIFO

During 20X1, ABC Inc. determined ending inventory and cost of goods sold under the FIFO cost flow assumption as follows:

	Units	Unit cost	Total
Beginning inventory	100	$5	$ 500
Purchase, 1/12/X1	200	6	1,200
Purchase, 8/25/X1	150	7	1,050
Goods available for sale	450		2,750
Ending inventory	200*		1,350**
Cost of goods sold	250		$1,400

*   Determined by physical count of inventory
**   Determined by applying the most recent prices to the ending inventory quantity, as below:

8/25/X1 layer	150	@ $7	$1,050
1/12/X1 layer	50	@ $6	300
EI, 20X1	200		$1,350

3. **LAST-IN, FIRST-OUT (LIFO)** This method charges CGS with the *latest* acquisition costs, while ending inventories are reported at the *older* costs of the earliest units. The objective of LIFO is to charge against current revenues the cost of the goods acquired to replace those sold, rather than the original cost of the goods actually sold. Therefore, LIFO provides a better measure of earnings, particularly during periods of rising prices. However, balance sheet presentation may suffer because the inventory is presented at the oldest unit costs that may substantially differ from current replacement cost.

a. **EFFECT OF CHANGING PRICES** During periods of *rising* prices, the LIFO inventory cost-flow method reports a *higher* cost of sales and a *lower* amount for ending inventory than FIFO. During periods of *falling* prices, the reverse is true; the LIFO inventory cost flow method would report a *lower* cost of sales and a *higher* amount for ending inventory.

b. **PERPETUAL VS. PERIODIC** Under the FIFO cost-flow method, a perpetual system would result in the same dollar amount of ending inventory as a periodic inventory system. Under the LIFO cost-flow method, however, a perpetual system would generally **not** result in the same dollar amount of ending inventory as a periodic inventory system.

c. **LIFO METHODS** LIFO is generally applied by one of two different methods.

(1) **QUANTITY LIFO** This classical application of LIFO is generally limited to use in small businesses or where there is a small number of different inventory items. Application of quantity LIFO requires that records of separate lot prices be kept for each inventory item. At the end of the period, inventory items are valued at

the oldest costs. Note that the same 4 steps used to value ending inventory under FIFO can be used for LIFO, except that step (2) now involves the *oldest* inventory layers. An application of quantity LIFO is illustrated by Example 4.

EXAMPLE 4 ♦ QUANTITY LIFO

Consider this data at the end of 20X2:

	Quantity		Amount	
Beginning inventory (@ unit price):				
20X0, base layer (@ $2.00)	120		$240	
20X1 layer (@ $2.10)	40	160	84	$ 324
20X2 Purchases:				
Jan. (@ $2.15)	100		215	
Apr. (@ $2.20)	200		440	
Aug. (@ $2.30)	250		575	
Nov. (@ $2.30)	300	850	690	1,920
Goods available for sale		1,010		2,244
Ending inventory, 20X2		290		605*
Cost of goods sold		720		$1,639

* Computed as follows:

Base layer	120	@	$2.00 =	$240
20X1 layer	40	@	2.10 =	84
Jan. purchase	100	@	2.15 =	215
Apr. purchase	30	@	2.20 =	66
EI 20X2	290			$605

(2) **DOLLAR-VALUE LIFO** Widely used in practice, this is a procedure designed to reduce the inventory clerical costs usually associated with LIFO and to minimize the probability of reporting the liquidation of the LIFO inventory layers. The application of dollar-value LIFO is based on the use of the dollar value of inventory pools of similar items, rather than physical units, as a basis for allocating inventory costs. A *base year dollar cost* is determined in the year of adoption by dividing total inventory cost by number of units. The ending inventory in each subsequent period is costed at both the base year dollar amount and current year dollar costs. The ratio obtained by dividing these two amounts (Ending Inventory (EI) valued at *current year costs* over EI at *base year cost*), is the *price index* for the current period. A layer of inventory is added every time the ending inventory stated at base year dollars exceeds the beginning inventory (also stated at base year dollars). This new layer is costed by multiplying it by the specific price index for the current period. If an inventory liquidation has occurred, the reductions are taken from the most recent layers acquired. The application of dollar-value LIFO is illustrated by Example 5.

EXAMPLE 5 ♦ DOLLAR-VALUE LIFO

On the basis of the quantity and price information in Table 1, columns 1 and 2, a price index is computed (columns 3, 4, and 5). This price index is used to value each inventory layer in Table 2. The price indices in Table 1 are figured by comparing current year prices to the base year prices.

Table 1—Price Indices

	1		2	3	4	5
				Base	Current	
				Year Amount	Year	Price
	Ending Inventory			(1A x $2.50)	Amount	Index
Year	Item	Quantity	@*	(1B x $4.00)	(1 x 2)	(4 ÷ 3)
20X0 (base)	A	10,000	$2.50	$25,000	$25,000	--
	B	6,000	4.00	24,000	24,000	--
20X0 Total				$49,000	$49,000	1.00
20X1	A	11,600	2.60	$29,000	$30,160	--
	B	6,100	4.25	24,400	25,925	--
20X1 Total				$53,400	$56,085	1.05
20X2	A	12,200	2.95	$30,500	$35,990	--
	B	6,200	4.45	24,800	27,590	--
20X2 Total				$55,300	$63,580	1.15
20X3	A	10,600	**	$26,500	**	--
	B	5,800	**	23,200	**	--
20X3 Total				$49,700		**

* These unit prices may represent the weighted average of all purchase prices paid during the year or the latest price paid.

** No price indices are computed nor new layers added due to inventory liquidation.

Table 2—Valuation of the Ending Inventory, 20X1-20X3:

	12/31/X1	Layers	Index	Valuation
Total	$ 53,400			
20X0 layer	(49,000)	$49,000	1.00	$49,000
20X1 layer	$ 4,400	4,400	1.05	4,620
Total 12/31/X1		$53,400		$53,620

	12/31/X2	Layers	Index	Valuation
Total	$ 55,300			
20X0 layer	(49,000)	$49,000	1.00	$49,000
20X1 layer	(4,400)	4,400	1.05	4,620
20X2 layer	$ 1,900	1,900	1.15	2,185
Total 12/31/X2		$55,300		$55,805

	12/31/X2	Reduction	12/31/X3	Index	Valuation
20X0 layer	$49,000		$49,000	1.00	$49,000
20X1 layer	4,400	$ 3,700	700	1.05	735
20X2 layer	1,900	1,900	0	1.15	0
Total 12/31/X3	$55,300	$ 5,600	$49,700		$49,735

CHAIN-LINK (OR LINK-CHAIN) METHOD The chain-link method may also be used. In the chain-link method, a price change index is figured from year-beginning to year-end each year. To arrive at the price index for a current layer of inventory, the indices for all the intervening years from the current to the base year are multiplied together.

4. **THE AVERAGE INVENTORY METHODS** These assume that cost of goods sold and ending inventory should be based on the average cost of the inventories available for sale during the period. A *weighted average* is generally used with a *periodic* inventory system while a *moving average* requires the use of a *perpetual* system. The weighted-average method costs inventory items on the basis of average prices paid, weighted according to the quantity purchased at each price. The moving average requires computation of a new average after each purchase. Issues are priced at the latest average unit cost.

EXAMPLE 6 ♦ AVERAGE INVENTORY METHODS

During 20X1 ABC Inc. purchased and sold several lots of inventory item X, as follows:

Purchases:	Units	Unit Cost	Extended Cost
2/15/X1	10,000	$3.00	$30,000
6/1/X1	5,000	$3.30	16,500
8/10/X1	6,000	$3.38	20,280
Goods available	21,000		$66,780

Sales:			
7/1/X1	7,000		
9/10/X1	9,000		
Goods sold	16,000		
Ending inventory	5,000		

The cost of the ending inventory of item X using the *weighted-average* method is $15,900 determined as follows:

Ending inventory in units	5,000
Weighted average cost per unit ($66,780 ÷ 21000)	x $3.18
Ending inventory	$15,900

The cost of the ending inventory of item X using the *moving-average* method is $16,100, determined as follows:

	1	2	3	4
Date	Units	@	Extended	Moving Avg. (3 ÷ 1)
2/15/X1	10,000	$3.00	$30,000	$3.00
6/1/X1	5,000	3.30	16,500	--
	15,000		46,500	3.10
7/1/X1	(7,000)	3.10	(21,700)	--
	8,000		24,800	3.10
8/10/X1	6,000	3.38	20,280	--
	14,000		45,080	3.22
9/10/X1	(9,000)	3.22	(28,980)	--
End inventory	5,000		$16,100	3.22

D. **LOWER-OF-COST-OR-MARKET (LCM)**
The cost basis (specific identification or cost flow assumption) ordinarily achieves the objective of properly matching inventory costs and revenue. This is only satisfactory, however, as long as the utility of the inventory equals or exceeds its cost. When the utility of inventory is impaired or otherwise reduced by damage, deterioration or any other cause, the decline in value should be charged against revenue in the period in which the decline occurred. The measurement of this decline is accomplished by pricing the inventory at cost or market, whichever is lower (ARB 43).

1. **DEFINITION OF MARKET** As used in the phrase lower-of-cost-or-market, market means current replacement cost (by purchase or reproduction) except for the following:

a. Market should not exceed the net realizable value (estimated selling price in the ordinary course of business less reasonably predictable costs of completion and disposal). This would be the *maximum*, or *ceiling*, amount at which market could be valued.

b. Market should not be less than the net realizable value minus normal profit. This would be the *minimum*, or *floor*, amount at which market could be valued.

Exhibit 2 ♦ Market Under Lower-of-Cost-or-Market Rule

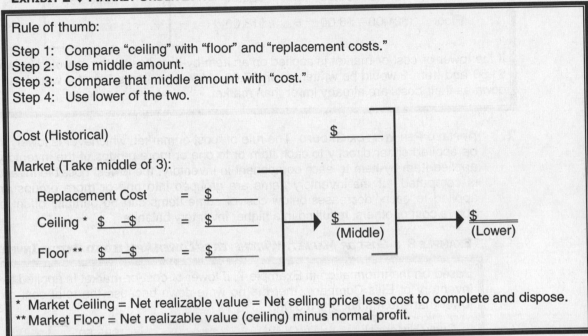

Rule of thumb:

Step 1: Compare "ceiling" with "floor" and "replacement costs."
Step 2: Use middle amount.
Step 3: Compare that middle amount with "cost."
Step 4: Use lower of the two.

Cost (Historical) $_____

Market (Take middle of 3):

    Replacement Cost   = $_____

    Ceiling * $_____ −$_____ = $_____ → $_____ (Middle) → $_____ (Lower)

    Floor ** $_____ −$_____ = $_____

* Market Ceiling = Net realizable value = Net selling price less cost to complete and dispose.
** Market Floor = Net realizable value (ceiling) minus normal profit.

Example 7 ♦ Cost or Market, Whichever Is Lower Computation

Information related to Ellis Company's inventory at December 31, 20X6 is given in columns 1 through 6. Lower-of-cost-or-market inventory calculations are illustrated in columns 7 through 10. The format shown in Exhibit 2 is also shown for inventory Item 1.

(1) Item	(2) Cost	(3) Replacement Cost (Market)	(4) Selling Price	(5) Cost of Completion	(6) Normal Profit	(7) Ceiling Maximum (4) - (5)	(8) Floor Minimum (7) - (6)	(9) Market: Limited by Floor and Ceiling	(10) Lower-of-Cost-or-Market
1	$20.50	$ 19.00	$ 25.00	$ 1.00	$ 6.00	$ 24.00	$ 18.00	$ 19.00	$19.00
2	25.00	17.00	30.00	2.00	10.00	28.00	18.00	18.00	18.00
3	10.00	12.00	15.00	1.00	3.00	14.00	11.00	12.00	10.00
4	40.00	55.00	60.00	6.00	4.00	54.00	50.00	54.00	40.00
	$95.50	$103.00	$130.00	$10.00	$23.00	$120.00	$ 97.00	$103.00	$87.00

(continued on next page)

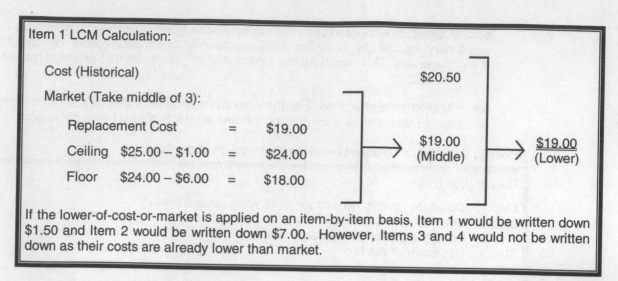

Item 1 LCM Calculation:

Cost (Historical)

Market (Take middle of 3):

Replacement Cost	=	$19.00	
Ceiling	$25.00 – $1.00	=	$24.00
Floor	$24.00 – $6.00	=	$18.00

$20.50

$19.00 (Middle)

$19.00 (Lower)

If the lower-of-cost-or-market is applied on an item-by-item basis, Item 1 would be written down $1.50 and Item 2 would be written down $7.00. However, Items 3 and 4 would not be written down as their costs are already lower than market.

2. **APPLIED PER ITEM OR GROUPS** The rule of "cost or market, whichever is lower" may properly be applied either directly to each item or to one or more groups of the inventory. If LCM is applied item by item to each component in inventory, the lowest possible inventory balance is computed. If the inventory items are grouped into one or more groups and the LCM applied to each, decreases below cost of some items can be partially offset by increases above cost of others, resulting in a higher inventory balance.

EXAMPLE 8 ♦ *COST OR MARKET, WHICHEVER IS LOWER* APPLIED TO ENTIRE INVENTORY

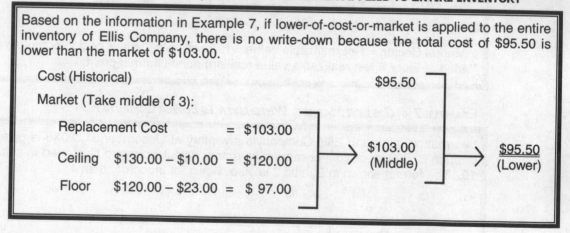

Based on the information in Example 7, if lower-of-cost-or-market is applied to the entire inventory of Ellis Company, there is no write-down because the total cost of $95.50 is lower than the market of $103.00.

Cost (Historical)

Market (Take middle of 3):

Replacement Cost	=	$103.00	
Ceiling	$130.00 – $10.00	=	$120.00
Floor	$120.00 – $23.00	=	$97.00

$95.50

$103.00 (Middle)

$95.50 (Lower)

3. **CONSERVATISM AND MATCHING CONCEPTS** The lower-of-cost-or-market produces a realistic estimate of future cash flows to be realized from the sale of inventories. This is consistent with the principle of conservatism, and recognizes (matches) the anticipated loss in the income statement in the period in which the price decline occurs.

III. INVENTORY ESTIMATION METHODS

A. GROSS MARGIN METHOD

This method rests on the assumption that the gross margin (GM) percentage is relatively stable. Cost of goods sold (CGS) is determined by applying the gross margin ratio to sales and subtracting this amount from the sales figure. Ending inventory is computed by subtracting the estimated CGS from the actual goods available for sale (GAFS), obtained from the beginning inventory and purchases accounts.

1. **NOT GAAP** The gross margin method is **not** generally accepted for annual financial reporting purposes.

2. **USE OF GROSS MARGIN METHOD** This method is used to (a) verify the accuracy of the year-end physical count, (b) estimate ending inventory and cost of goods sold for interim financial reporting, and (c) estimate inventory losses from theft and casualties (fires, floods).

EXAMPLE 9 ♦ GROSS MARGIN (PROFIT) METHOD

Maggie Company has a recent gross profit history of 40% of net sales. The following data are available from Maggie's accounting records for the three months ended March 31, 20X6:

Inventory at 1/1/X6	$ 650,000
Purchases	3,200,000
Net sales	4,500,000
Purchase returns	25,000

REQUIRED: Using the gross profit method, estimate the cost of the inventory at March 31, 20X6.

SOLUTION:

Beginning inventory		$ 650,000
Purchases		3,200,000
Purchase returns		(25,000)
Goods available for sale		3,825,000
Less: Estimated cost of goods sold:		
Net sales	$ 4,500,000	
Less: Gross margin (40% x $4,500,000)	(1,800,000)	(2,700,000)
Estimated ending inventory		$ 1,125,000

B. RETAIL METHOD

This method of inventory estimation is often used by department stores and other retailers whose inventory goods are usually labeled upon receipt at their retail sales prices. Application of this method requires that records be kept of beginning inventory and purchases for the period, both at cost and retail, additional markups and markdowns, and sales for the period. The ending inventory at cost is estimated by converting the ending inventory expressed in retail dollars to cost dollars, through the use of a cost/retail ratio. The retail method is generally applied under one of three following methods:

1. **WEIGHTED AVERAGE, LCM** The weighted average is accomplished by combining beginning inventory and net purchases to determine a single cost/retail ratio. The LCM effect is achieved by including net markups, but **not** net markdowns, in the denominator of the ratio. This results in a larger denominator for the ratio and, thus, a lower ratio is obtained. Applying this lower ratio to ending inventory at retail, the inventory is reported at an amount below cost. This amount is intended to approximate lower of average cost or market.

2. **LIFO RETAIL** As a LIFO cost flow is assumed, (a) separate cost/retail ratios must be computed for beginning inventory and net purchases, and (b) LCM need not be used. Therefore, both net markups and net markdowns are included in the denominator of the purchases' cost/retail ratio. This results in a smaller denominator for the ratio and, thus, a higher ratio is obtained.

3. **DOLLAR-VALUE LIFO RETAIL** Combines retail and dollar-value LIFO methods. Under this method

   a. Ending inventory at retail is determined in the same manner as LIFO retail.

   b. Ending inventory at retail is then divided by the current price index to determine ending inventory at retail at base year dollars.

c. Ending inventory at retail at base year dollars is then compared to beginning inventory at base year dollars. If the ending inventory at retail at base year dollars is larger, a new layer has been added; this layer is converted to current dollars by applying the current price index. If ending inventory at retail at base year dollars is smaller, liquidation takes place by layers, in LIFO order.

d. Any incremental layer for the year, as determined in c., above, is then converted to cost by multiplying it by the cost/retail for purchases for the period. This layer is then added to the previous LIFO ending inventory at cost.

EXAMPLE 10 ◆ RETAIL METHODS

The LFGW Company commenced operations on January 1, 20X0. An external price index is used for dollar-value LIFO computations. This index was 125 at January 1, 20X0, and 150 at December 31, 20X0. The following data was available from the records of the Company for the year ended December 31, 20X0:

	Cost	Retail
Merchandise inventory January 1, 20X0	$120,000	$200,000
Purchases, net	720,000	990,000
Markups, net		10,000
Markdowns, net		40,000
Sales, net		860,000

REQUIRED: Using the retail method, estimate merchandise inventory at December 31, 20X0, under the following methods:

a. Weighted average, LCM
b. LIFO retail
c. Dollar-value LIFO retail

SOLUTION:

a. Weighted Average, LCM:

	Cost	Retail		
Beginning inventory	$120,000	$ 200,000		
Purchases, net	720,000	990,000		
Markups, net	--	10,000		
WA/LCM cost/retail ratio	$840,000 ÷	$1,200,000	=	70%
Less: Sales, net		(860,000)		
Markdowns, net		(40,000)		
Ending inventory at retail		$ 300,000		
Ending inventory at cost ($300,000 x 70%)	$210,000			

b. LIFO Retail:

	Cost	Retail		
Beginning inventory	$120,000 ÷	$ 200,000	=	60%
Purchases, net	720,000	990,000		
Markups, net		10,000		
Markdowns, net		(40,000)		
Purchases cost/retail ratio	$720,000 ÷	$ 960,000	=	75%
Goods available for sale		$1,160,000		
Less: Sales, net		(860,000)		
Ending inventory at retail		$ 300,000		

(continued on next page)

Inventory layer	EI at retail		Cost/Retail ratio		EI at retail cost
Beginning	$200,000	x	60%	=	$120,000
Purchases	100,000	x	75%	=	75,000
	$300,000				$195,000

NOTE: Under a LIFO cost-flow assumption, the sum of ending inventory in retail dollars is composed of beginning inventory retail dollars (to the extent available) and a layer of purchase retail dollars for any increase in retail dollars for the period. The beginning inventory retail dollars and the purchase layer retail dollars are then converted to cost dollars by their separate cost/retail ratios.

c. Dollar-Value LIFO Retail:

	Cost	Retail
Ending inventory at retail at base year dollars ($300,000 ÷ 1.20*)		$ 250,000
Base layer, January 1, 20X0	$120,000	(200,000)
Incremental 20X0 layer at base year dollars		$ 50,000
Incremental 20X0 layer at current year dollars ($50,000 x 1.20)		$ 60,000
Incremental 20X0 layer at cost ($60,000 x 75%)	45,000	
Ending inventory, dollar-value LIFO	$165,000	

* Current year external price index (150 ÷ 125 = 1.20)

State Boards of Accountancy

Certified Public Accountants are licensed to practice by individual State Boards of Accountancy. Application forms and requirements to sit for the CPA exam should be requested from your individual State Board. IT IS EXTREMELY IMPORTANT THAT YOU COMPLETE THE APPLICATION FORM CORRECTLY AND RETURN IT TO YOUR STATE BOARD BEFORE THE SPECIFIED DEADLINE. Errors and/or delays may result in the rejection of your application. Be extremely careful in filling out the application and be sure to enclose all required materials. In many states, applications must be received by the State Board at least **ninety** days before the examination date. Requirements as to education, experience, internship, and other matters vary. If you have not already done so, take a moment to call the appropriate state board for specific and current requirements. Complete the application in a timely manner.

It may be possible to sit for the exam in another state as an out-of-state candidate. Candidates wishing to do so should contact the State Board of Accountancy in their home state. Addresses of State Boards of Accountancy are provided in the **Practical Advice** section of this volume.

Approximately one month before the exam, check to see that your application to sit for the exam has been processed. DON'T ASSUME THAT YOU ARE PROPERLY REGISTERED UNLESS YOU HAVE RECEIVED YOUR CANDIDATE ID NUMBER.

The AICPA publishes a booklet entitled *Information for Uniform CPA Examination Candidates*, usually distributed by State Boards of Accountancy to candidates upon receipt of their applications. To request a complimentary copy, write your State Board or the AICPA, Examination Division, 1211 Avenue of the Americas, New York, NY 10036. The addresses of State Boards are in the **Practical Advice** section of this volume. The information contained in this booklet is also available on the AICPA's website: www.aicpa.org.

CHAPTER 3—INVENTORY

PROBLEM 3-1 MULTIPLE CHOICE QUESTIONS (80 to 100 minutes)

1. On December 30, 1992, Astor Corp. sold merchandise for $75,000 to Day Co. The terms of the sale were net 30, F.O.B. shipping point. The merchandise was shipped on December 31, 1992, and arrived at Day on January 5, 1993. Due to a clerical error, the sale was not recorded until January 1993 and the merchandise, sold at a 25% markup, was included in Astor's inventory at December 31, 1992. As a result, Astor's cost of goods sold for the year ended December 31, 1992, was
a. Understated by $75,000.
b. Understated by $60,000.
c. Understated by $15,000.
d. Correctly stated. (11/93, PI, #51, 4420)

2. The following items were included in Opal Co.'s inventory account at December 31, 1992:

Merchandise out on consignment, at sales price, including 40% markup on selling price	$40,000
Goods purchased, in transit, shipped F.O.B. shipping point	36,000
Goods held on consignment by Opal	27,000

By what amount should Opal's inventory account at December 31, 1992, be reduced?
a. $103,000
b. $ 67,000
c. $ 51,000
d. $ 43,000 (5/93, PI, #20, 4062)

3. Herc Co.'s inventory at December 31, 1993, was $1,500,000, based on a physical count priced at cost, and before any necessary adjustment for the following:

- Merchandise costing $90,000, shipped F.O.B. shipping point from a vendor on December 30, 1993, was received and recorded on January 5, 1994.
- Goods in the shipping area were excluded from inventory although shipment was not made until January 4, 1994. The goods, billed to the customer F.O.B. shipping point on December 30, 1993, had a cost of $120,000.

What amount should Herc report as inventory in its December 31, 1993 balance sheet?
a. $1,500,000
b. $1,590,000
c. $1,620,000
d. $1,710,000 (11/94, FAR, #13, 5278)

4. On December 1, 1992, Alt Department Store received 505 sweaters on consignment from Todd. Todd's cost for the sweaters was $80 each, and they were priced to sell at $100. Alt's commission on consigned goods is 10%. At December 31, 1992, 5 sweaters remained. In its December 31, 1992 balance sheet, what amount should Alt report as payable for consigned goods?
a. $49,000
b. $45,400
c. $45,000
d. $40,400 (5/93, PI, #29, 4071)

5. During 1994, Kam Co. began offering its goods to selected retailers on a consignment basis. The following information was derived from Kam's 1994 accounting records:

Beginning inventory	$122,000
Purchases	540,000
Freight in	10,000
Transportation to consignees	5,000
Freight out	35,000
Ending inventory—held by Kam	145,000
—held by consignees	20,000

In its 1994 income statement, what amount should Kam report as cost of goods sold?
a. $507,000
b. $512,000
c. $527,000
d. $547,000 (5/95, FAR, #33, 5569)

6. On December 28, 1990, Kerr Manufacturing Co. purchased goods costing $50,000. The terms were F.O.B. destination. Some of the costs incurred in connection with the sale and delivery of the goods were as follows:

Packaging for shipment	$1,000
Shipping	1,500
Special handling charges	2,000

These goods were received on December 31, 1990. In Kerr's December 31, 1990 balance sheet, what amount of cost for these goods should be included in inventory?
a. $54,500
b. $53,500
c. $52,000
d. $50,000 (11/91, PI, #12, 2400)

7. Southgate Co. paid the in-transit insurance premium for consignment goods shipped to Hendon Co., the consignee. In addition, Southgate advanced part of the commissions that will be due when Hendon sells the goods. Should Southgate include the in-transit insurance premium and the advanced commissions in inventory costs?

	Insurance premium	Advanced commissions
a.	Yes	Yes
b.	No	No
c.	Yes	No
d.	No	Yes

(5/92, Theory, #23, 2716)

8. Town Inc. is preparing its financial statements for the year ended December 31, 1994. At December 31, 1994, Town had outstanding purchase orders in the ordinary course of business for purchase of a raw material to be used in its manufacturing process. The market price is currently higher than the purchase price and is not anticipated to change within the next year. What is the reporting requirement?
a. Disclosure only
b. Accrual only
c. Both accrual and disclosure
d. Neither accrual nor disclosure

(11/95, FAR, #80, amended, 6154)

9. On July 1, 1994, Casa Development Co. purchased a tract of land for $1,200,000. Casa incurred additional costs of $300,000 during the remainder of 1994 in preparing the land for sale. The tract was subdivided into residential lots as follows:

Lot Class	Number of lots	Sales price per lot
A	100	$24,000
B	100	16,000
C	200	10,000

Using the relative sales value method, what amount of costs should be allocated to the Class A lots?
a. $300,000
b. $375,000
c. $600,000
d. $720,000

(5/95, FAR, #10, 5546)

10. Bren Co.'s beginning inventory at January 1, 1993, was understated by $26,000, and its ending inventory was overstated by $52,000. As a result, Bren's cost of goods sold for 1993 was
a. Understated by $26,000.
b. Overstated by $26,000.
c. Understated by $78,000.
d. Overstated by $78,000. (11/94, FAR, #43, 5305)

11. A company records inventory at the gross invoice price. Theoretically, how should the following affect the costs in inventory?

	Warehousing costs	Cash discounts available
a.	Increase	Decrease
b.	No effect	Decrease
c.	No effect	No effect
d.	Increase	No effect

(11/87, Theory, #1, 1844)

12. According to the FASB conceptual framework, which of the following attributes would **not** be used to measure inventory?
a. Historical cost
b. Replacement cost
c. Net realizable value
d. Present value of future cash flows

(11/95, FAR, #5, 6087)

13. A company decided to change its inventory valuation method from FIFO to LIFO in a period of rising prices. What was the result of the change on ending inventory and net income in the year of the change?

	Ending inventory	Net income
a.	Increase	Increase
b.	Increase	Decrease
c.	Decrease	Decrease
d.	Decrease	Increase

(11/95, FAR, #9, 6091)

14. Estimates of price-level changes for specific inventories are required for which of the following inventory methods?
a. Conventional retail
b. Dollar-value LIFO
c. Weighted average cost
d. Average cost retail   (11/93, Theory, #3, 4508)

15. Drew Co. uses the average cost inventory method for internal reporting purposes and LIFO for financial statement and income tax reporting. At December 31, 1992, the inventory was $375,000 using average cost and $320,000 using LIFO. The unadjusted credit balance in the LIFO Reserve account on December 31, 1992, was $35,000. What adjusting entry should Drew record to adjust from average cost to LIFO at December 31, 1992?

	Debit	Credit
a. Cost of Goods Sold	$55,000	
Inventory		$55,000
b. Cost of Goods Sold	$55,000	
LIFO Reserve		$55,000
c. Cost of Goods Sold	$20,000	
Inventory		$20,000
d. Cost of Goods Sold	$20,000	
LIFO Reserve		$20,000

(11/93, PI, #19, 4388)

16. Generally, which inventory costing method approximates most closely the current cost for each of the following?

	Cost of goods sold	Ending inventory
a.	LIFO	FIFO
b.	LIFO	LIFO
c.	FIFO	FIFO
d.	FIFO	LIFO

(11/91, Theory, #7, 2515)

ITEMS 17 AND 18 are based on the following:

During January 1993, Metro Co., which maintains a perpetual inventory system, recorded the following information pertaining to its inventory:

	Units	Unit cost	Total cost	Units on hand
Balance on 1/1/93	1,000	$1	$1,000	1,000
Purchased on 1/7/93	600	3	1,800	1,600
Sold on 1/20/93	900			700
Purchased on 1/25/93	400	5	2,000	1,100

17. Under the moving-average method, what amount should Metro report as inventory at January 31, 1993?
a. $2,640
b. $3,225
c. $3,300
d. $3,900   (5/93, PI, #18, 4060)

18. Under the LIFO method, what amount should Metro report as inventory at January 31, 1993?
a. $1,300
b. $2,700
c. $3,900
d. $4,100   (5/93, PI, #19, 4061)

19. Walt Co. adopted the dollar-value LIFO inventory method as of January 1, 1994, when its inventory was valued at $500,000. Walt's entire inventory constitutes a single pool. Using a relevant price index of 1.10, Walt determined that its December 31, 1994, inventory was $577,500 at current year cost, and $525,000 at base year cost. What was Walt's dollar-value LIFO inventory at December 31, 1994?
a. $525,000
b. $527,500
c. $552,500
d. $577,500   (5/95, FAR, #11, 5547)

20. Brock Co. adopted the dollar-value LIFO inventory method as of January 1, 1991. A single inventory pool and an internally computed price index are used to compute Brock's LIFO inventory layers. Information about Brock's dollar value inventory follows:

	Inventory		
Date	At base year cost	At current year cost	At dollar-value LIFO
1/1/91	$40,000	$40,000	$40,000
1991 layer	5,000	14,000	6,000
12/31/91	45,000	54,000	46,000
1992 layer	15,000	26,000	?
12/31/92	$60,000	$80,000	$?

What was Brock's dollar-value LIFO inventory at December 31, 1992?
a. $80,000
b. $74,000
c. $66,000
d. $60,000   (11/93, PI, #20, 4389)

21. The UNO Company was formed on January 2, 1997, to sell a single product. Over a two-year period, UNO's acquisition costs have increased steadily. Physical quantities held in inventory were equal to three months' sales at December 31, 1997, and zero at December 31, 1998. Assuming the periodic inventory system, the inventory cost method which reports the highest amount for each of the following is

	Inventory December 31, 1997	Cost of sales 1998
a.	LIFO	FIFO
b.	LIFO	LIFO
c.	FIFO	FIFO
d.	FIFO	LIFO

(11/89, Theory, #9, amended, 9006)

22. The dollar-value LIFO inventory cost flow method involves computations based on

	Inventory pools of similar items	A specific price index for each year
a.	No	Yes
b.	No	No
c.	Yes	No
d.	Yes	Yes

(11/86, Theory, #6, 1865)

23. When the double-extension approach to the dollar-value LIFO inventory method is used, the inventory layer added in the current year is multiplied by an index number. Which of the following correctly states how components are used in the calculation of this index number?

a. In the numerator, the average of the ending inventory at base year cost and at current year cost.
b. In the numerator, the ending inventory at current year cost, and, in the denominator, the ending inventory at base year cost.
c. In the numerator, the ending inventory at base year cost, and, in the denominator, the ending inventory at current year cost.
d. In the denominator, the average of the ending inventory at base year cost and at current year cost.　　　(11/91, Theory, #28, 2536)

24. Ashe Co. recorded the following data pertaining to raw material X during January 1990:

	Units			
Date	Received	Cost	Issued	On hand
1/01 Inventory		$8.00		3,200
1/11 Issue			1,600	1,600
1/22 Purchase	4,800	$9.60		6,400

The moving-average unit cost of X inventory at January 31, 1990, is
a. $8.80.
b. $8.96.
c. $9.20.
d. $9.60.　　　(11/90, PI, #8, 9007)

25. On January 1, 1996, Poe Company adopted the dollar-value LIFO inventory method. Poe's entire inventory constitutes a single pool. Inventory data for 1996 and 1997 are as follows:

Date	Inventory at current year cost	Inventory at base year cost	Relevant price index
01/01/96	$150,000	$150,000	1.00
12/31/96	220,000	200,000	1.10
12/31/97	276,000	230,000	1.20

Poe's LIFO inventory value at December 31, 1997, is
a. $230,000.
b. $236,000.
c. $241,000.
d. $246,000.　　　(5/88, PI, #22, amended, 0916)

26. Jones Wholesalers stocks a changing variety of products. Which inventory costing method will be most likely to give Jones the lowest ending inventory when its product lines are subject to specific price increases?
a. Specific identification
b. Weighted average
c. Dollar-value LIFO
d. FIFO periodic　　　(11/92, Theory, #15, 3448)

27. The original cost of an inventory item is below the net realizable value and above the net realizable value less a normal profit margin. The inventory item's replacement cost is below the net realizable value less a normal profit margin. Under the lower of cost or market method, the inventory item should be valued at
a. Original cost.
b. Replacement cost.
c. Net realizable value.
d. Net realizable value less normal profit margin.　　　(5/97, FAR, #1, 6473)

28. Kahn Co., in applying the lower-of-cost-or-market method, reports its inventory at replacement cost. Which of the following statements are correct?

	The original cost is greater than replacement cost	The net realizable value, less a normal profit margin, is greater than replacement cost
a.	Yes	Yes
b.	Yes	No
c.	No	Yes
d.	No	No

(5/92, Theory, #25, 2718)

29. The original cost of an inventory item is below both replacement cost and net realizable value. The net realizable value less normal profit margin is below the original cost. Under the lower-of-cost-or-market method, the inventory item should be valued at
a. Replacement cost.
b. Net realizable value.
c. Net realizable value less normal profit margin.
d. Original cost.　　　(11/92, Theory, #14, 3447)

30. The lower-of-cost-or-market rule for inventories may be applied to total inventory, to groups of similar items, or to each item. Which application generally results in the lowest inventory amount?
a. All applications result in the same amount
b. Total inventory
c. Groups of similar items
d. Separately to each item

(11/93, Theory, #4, 4509)

31. Based on a physical inventory taken on December 31, 1992, Chewy Co. determined its chocolate inventory on a FIFO basis at $26,000 with a replacement cost of $20,000. Chewy estimated that, after further processing costs of $12,000, the chocolate could be sold as finished candy bars for $40,000. Chewy's normal profit margin is 10% of sales. Under the lower-of-cost-or-market rule, what amount should Chewy report as chocolate inventory in its December 31, 1992 balance sheet?
a. $28,000
b. $26,000
c. $24,000
d. $20,000

(11/93, PI, #21, 4390)

32. The following information pertains to an inventory item:

Cost	$12.00
Estimated selling price	13.60
Estimated disposal cost	.20
Normal gross margin	2.20
Replacement cost	10.90

Under the lower-of-cost-or-market rule, this inventory item should be valued at
a. $10.70.
b. $10.90.
c. $11.20.
d. $12.00.

(11/89, PII, #10, 0913)

33. Due to a decline in market price in the second quarter, Petal Co. incurred an inventory loss. The market price is expected to return to previous levels by the end of the year. At the end of the year the decline had not reversed. When should the loss be reported in Petal's interim income statements?
a. Ratably over the second, third, and fourth quarters
b. Ratably over the third and fourth quarters
c. In the second quarter only
d. In the fourth quarter only

(5/93, Theory, #21, 9008)

34. Which of the following statements are correct when a company applying the lower-of-cost-or-market method reports its inventory at replacement cost?

I. The original cost is less than replacement cost.
II. The net realizable value is greater than replacement cost.

a. I only
b. II only
c. Both I and II
d. Neither I nor II

(11/94, FAR, #14, 5279)

35. Dart Company's accounting records indicated the following information:

Inventory, 1/1/97	$ 500,000
Purchases during 1997	2,500,000
Sales during 1997	3,200,000

A physical inventory taken on December 31, 1997, resulted in an ending inventory of $575,000. Dart's gross profit on sales has remained constant at 25% in recent years. Dart suspects some inventory may have been taken by a new employee. At December 31, 1997, what is the estimated cost of missing inventory?
a. $ 25,000
b. $100,000
c. $175,000
d. $225,000

(11/87, PI, #9, amended, 9009)

36. The retail Inventory method includes which of the following in the calculation of both cost and retail amounts of goods available for sale?
a. Purchase returns
b. Sales returns
c. Net markups
d. Freight in

(11/90, Theory, #16, 1796)

37. Hutch Inc. uses the conventional retail inventory method to account for inventory. The following information relates to 1991 operations:

	Average	
	Cost	Retail
Beginning inventory and purchases	$600,000	$920,000
Net markups		40,000
Net markdowns		60,000
Sales		780,000

What amount should be reported as cost of sales for 1991?
a. $480,000
b. $487,500
c. $520,000
d. $525,000

(5/92, PI, #49, 2620)

38. Dean Company uses the retail inventory method to estimate its inventory for interim statement purposes. Data relating to the computation of the inventory at July 31, 1997, are as follows:

	Cost	Retail
Inventory, 2/1/97	$ 180,000	$ 250,000
Purchases	1,020,000	1,575,000
Markups, net		175,000
Sales		1,705,000
Estimated normal shoplifting losses		20,000
Markdowns, net		125,000

Under the approximate lower-of-average-cost-or-market retail method, Dean's estimated inventory at July 31, 1997 is
a. $ 90,000.
b. $ 96,000.
c. $102,000.
d. $150,000.   (11/87, PI, #53, amended, 0919)

39. On December 31, 1996, Jason Company adopted the dollar-value LIFO retail inventory method. Inventory data for 1997 are as follows:

	LIFO cost	Retail
Inventory, 12/31/96	$360,000	$500,000
Inventory, 12/31/97	--	660,000
Increase in price level for 1997		10%
Cost to retail ratio for 1997		70%

Under the LIFO retail method, Jason's inventory at December 31, 1997, should be
a. $437,000.
b. $462,000.
c. $472,000.
d. $483,200.   (5/86, PI, #12, amended, 0927)

40. Union Corp. uses the first-in, first-out retail method of inventory valuation. The following information is available:

	Cost	Retail
Beginning inventory	$12,000	$ 30,000
Purchases	60,000	110,000
Net additional markups		10,000
Net markdowns		20,000
Sales revenue		90,000

If the lower-of-cost-or-market rule is disregarded, what would be the estimated cost of the ending inventory?
a. $24,000
b. $20,800
c. $20,000
d. $19,200   (5/90, PI, #13, 0910)

PROBLEMS/ESSAY QUESTIONS

ESSAY 3-2 (15 to 25 minutes)

Huddell Company, which is both a wholesaler and retailer, purchases merchandise from various suppliers FOB destination, and incurs substantial warehousing costs. The dollar-value LIFO method is used for the wholesale inventories. Huddell determines the estimated cost of its retail ending inventories using the conventional retail inventory method, which approximates lower of average cost or market.

REQUIRED:

a. When should the purchases from various shippers generally be included in Huddell's inventory? Why?

b. How should Huddell account for the warehousing costs? Why?

c. 1. What are the advantages of using the dollar-value LIFO method as opposed to the traditional LIFO method?
2. How does the application of the dollar-value LIFO method differ from the application of the traditional LIFO method?

d. 1. In the calculation of the cost to retail percentage used to determine the estimated cost of its ending retail inventories, how should Huddell use
• Net markups?
• Net markdowns?
2. Why does Huddell's retail-inventory method approximate lower of average cost or market?   (5/90, Theory, #4)

PROBLEM 3-3 (23 to 28 minutes)

On January 1, 1995, Silver Industries Inc. adopted the dollar-value LIFO method of determining inventory costs for financial and income tax reporting. The following information relates to this change:

- Silver has continued to use the FIFO method, which approximates current costs, for internal reporting purposes. Silver's FIFO inventories at December 31, 1995, 1996, and 1997 were $100,000, $137,500, and $195,000, respectively.
- The FIFO inventory amounts are converted to dollar-value LIFO amounts using a single inventory pool and cost indices developed using the link-chain method. Silver estimated that the current year cost change indices, which measure year-to-year cost changes, were 1.25 for 1996 and 1.20 for 1997.

REQUIRED:

Prepare a schedule showing the computation of Silver's dollar-value LIFO inventory at December 31, 1996 and 1997. Show all calculations.

(11/92, PI, #4(b), amended, 6188)

ESSAY 3-4 (15 to 25 minutes)

Happlia Co. imports expensive household appliances. Each model has many variations and each unit has an identification number. Happlia pays all costs for getting the goods from the port to its central warehouse in Des Moines. After repackaging, the goods are consigned to retailers. A retailer makes a sale, simultaneously buys the appliance from Happlia, and pays the balance due within one week. To alleviate the overstocking of refrigerators at a Minneapolis retailer, some were reshipped to a Kansas City retailer where they were still held in inventory at December 31, 1990. Happlia paid the costs of this reshipment. Happlia uses the specific identification inventory costing method.

REQUIRED:

a.   In regard to the specific identification inventory costing method
   1.   Describe its key elements.
   2.   Discuss why it is appropriate for Happlia to use this method.

b.   1.   What general criteria should Happlia use to determine inventory carrying amounts at December 31, 1990? Ignore lower-of-cost-or-market considerations.
   2.   Give four examples of costs included in these inventory carrying costs.

c.   What costs should be reported in Happlia's 1990 income statement? Ignore lower-of-cost-or-market considerations.

(5/91, Theory, #3)

PROBLEM 3-5 (30 to 40 minutes)

York Co. sells one product, which it purchases from various suppliers. York's trial balance at December 31, 1993, included the following accounts:

Sales (33,000 units @ $16)	$528,000
Sales discounts	7,500
Purchases	368,900
Purchase discounts	18,000
Freight-in	5,000
Freight-out	11,000

York Co.'s inventory purchases during 1993 were as follows:

	Units	Cost per unit	Total cost
Beg. inventory, Jan. 1	8,000	$8.20	$ 65,600
Purchases, quarters ended:			
March 31	12,000	8.25	99,000
June 30	15,000	7.90	118,500
September 30	13,000	7.50	97,500
December 31	7,000	7.70	53,900
	55,000		$434,500

Additional information:

York's accounting policy is to report inventory in its financial statements at the lower of cost or market, applied to total inventory. Cost is determined under the last-in, first-out (LIFO) method.

York has determined that, at December 31, 1993, the replacement cost of its inventory was $8 per unit and the net realizable value was $8.80 per unit. York's normal profit margin is $1.05 per unit.

REQUIRED:

a.   Prepare York's schedule of cost of goods sold, with a supporting schedule of ending inventory. York uses the direct method of reporting losses from market decline of inventory.

b.   Explain the rule of lower of cost or market and its application in this situation. (5/94, FAR, #4, 4974)

Solution 3-1 MULTIPLE CHOICE ANSWERS

OWNERSHIP CRITERIA

1. **(b)** Goods should be removed from the seller's inventory when legal title passes to the purchaser. Therefore, Astor should exclude the cost of the goods shipped F.O.B. shipping from inventory at 12/31/92 because title of these goods passed to Day when the goods were picked up by the common carrier on 12/31/92. Since the goods were erroneously in Astor's inventory at 12/31/92, Astor's 1992 ending inventory and cost of goods sold were overstated and understated, respectively, by the $60,000 (i.e., $75,000 ÷ 125% cost of the goods).

2. **(d)** Opal's inventory account should be reduced by $43,000 (i.e., $16,000 + $27,000) at 12/31/92. The merchandise out on consignment should be included in Opal's inventory at cost. Therefore, Opal's inventory must be reduced by the amount of the markup. Note that the question states that the merchandise out on consignment includes 40% *markup on selling price*, not a 40% markup on cost. The markup is easily calculated because the selling price is given. Selling price of $40,000 times 40% equals a markup of $16,000. Since Opal does not have title to the $27,000 of goods held on consignment, the cost of these goods should also be excluded from Opal's inventory. The cost of the $36,000 of goods in transit at 12/31/92, purchased F.O.B. shipping point, are properly included in Opal's inventory because title of the goods passed to Opal when the goods were shipped.

3. **(d)** Goods should be included in the purchaser's inventory when legal title passes to the purchaser. Therefore, Herc should include the $90,000 cost of goods shipped to it F.O.B. shipping point in inventory at 12/31/93 because title of these goods passed to Herc when the goods were picked up by the common carrier on 12/30/93. Herc should also include the $120,000 cost of goods in its shipping area in inventory at 12/31/93. These goods should be included in inventory because shipment of these goods to the customer was not made until 1994.

4. **(c)** Goods held on consignment remain the property of the consignor. The consignee does not incur a liability for consigned goods until the goods are sold to a third party. The amount that Alt should report as payable for consigned goods at 12/31/92 is determined as follows:

Consignment sales (500 x $100)	$50,000
Less: Alt's commission on consignment sales ($50,000 x 10%)	(5,000)
Alt's payable for consigned goods, 12/31/92	$45,000

5. **(b)** Goods out on consignment remain the property of the consignor and must be included in the consignor's inventory at purchase price or production cost, including freight and other costs incurred to process the goods up to the time of sale. Kam's 1994 cost of goods sold is determined as follows:

Beginning inventory		$122,000
Add: Inventoriable costs		
Purchases	$540,000	
Freight in	10,000	
Transportation to consignees	5,000	555,000
Goods available for sale		$677,000
Less: EI ($145,000 + $20,000)		(165,000)
Cost of goods sold, 1994		$512,000

6. **(d)** The term *F.O.B. destination* means free on board at destination; that is, the goods are shipped to their destination without charge to the buyer. Thus, the costs incurred in connection with the sale and delivery of the goods (i.e., packaging for shipment, shipping, and special handling charges) are borne by the seller. Thus, Kerr's cost of the goods purchased is $50,000.

7. **(c)** The goods shipped to the consignee remain the property of the consignor. The consignor should include the in-transit insurance premium for the goods out on consignment in inventory costs because it is a cost necessary to get the goods in the place and condition for their intended sale. The consignor should charge the advanced commissions to a prepaid commissions expense account. The commissions should not be included in inventory costs because they were not necessary to get the merchandise ready for sale. When the goods are sold by the consignee, the consignor should report the commissions as a selling expense.

LOSSES ON PURCHASE COMMITMENTS

8. **(d)** Because the outstanding purchase orders occurred in the ordinary course of business and the raw materials have not yet been received, the purchase is not required to be accrued. Because the price difference is only a market price difference occurring in the ordinary course of business, disclosure it not required.

MEASURING INVENTORIES

9. **(c)** Under the relative sales value method, the total cost of the individual units purchased at a single lump-sum price should be allocated to the

various units on the basis of their relative sales value. The total cost includes the purchase price of $1,200,000 plus the additional costs of $300,000 to prepare the land for sale.

Lot Class	Number of lots	Sales price per lot	Total sales for class
A	100	$24,000	$2,400,000
B	100	16,000	1,600,000
C	200	10,000	2,000,000
Total			$6,000,000

Class A lots ($2,400,000) ÷ Total sales value ($6,000,000) = 40%.

Purchase price of entire tract	$1,200,000
Additional costs of preparing land for sale	300,000
Total cost	$1,500,000
Class A lots relative value percentage	x 40%
Costs allocated to Class A lots	$ 600,000

10. (c) An understatement of beginning inventory understates the cost of goods available for sale, thereby understating cost of goods sold. An overstatement of ending inventory also understates cost of goods sold. Therefore, cost of goods sold for 1993 is understated by the sum of the understatement of beginning inventory and the overstatement of ending inventory.

11. (a) Warehousing costs are usually treated as an expense in the period in which they are incurred, although conceptually they comprise part of the total cost of merchandise made ready for sale. Conceptually, the cost of inventory should be reduced for cash discounts available, because the acquisition cost of an asset should not exceed its cash equivalent price.

12. (d) The primary basis for accounting for inventories is cost. The cost of an inventory item is the cash price or fair value of other consideration given in exchange for it. Historical cost, replacement cost, and net realizable value are all appropriate methods for measuring inventory. The present value of future cash flows (which would include profits not yet earned) pertains to the time value of money and is not appropriate for measuring inventory.

COST FLOW ASSUMPTIONS

13. (c) During periods of rising prices, the LIFO inventory cost flow method reports a higher cost of sales and a lower amount for ending inventory than FIFO. Therefore, a change from FIFO to LIFO during this period would result in a decrease in net income and a decrease in ending inventory.

14. (b) As a general rule, dollar-value LIFO uses a "double-extension method" to compute:

(1) the value of the ending inventory in terms of base year prices, and (2) the value of ending inventory at current prices. The ratio of (2) over (1), above, provides the specific price index for valuing any layers of inventory added in the period. None of the other inventory methods require estimates of price-level changes for specific inventories.

15. (d) Some companies use LIFO for tax and external reporting purposes, but they maintain a FIFO, average cost, or standard cost system for internal reporting purposes. The difference between the inventory method used for internal reporting purposes and LIFO is often referred to as the LIFO reserve. The LIFO reserve is a contra-inventory account that must be adjusted to its required balance at the financial statement date. At 12/31/92, Drew's inventory was $375,000 using average cost and $320,000 using LIFO. Therefore, the required balance in the LIFO reserve at 12/31/92 is $55,000 (i.e., $375,000 − $320,000). Since the unadjusted balance of the LIFO reserve at 12/31/92 was $35,000, the reserve must be increased by $20,000 (i.e., $55,000 − $35,000). The following entry to record this adjustment increases both cost of goods sold and the LIFO reserve by the amount of the adjustment.

Cost of Goods Sold	20,000	
LIFO Reserve		20,000

16. (a) In using LIFO, the cost of the last goods in are used in pricing the cost of goods sold. In using FIFO, the cost of the last goods in are used in pricing the ending inventory. Therefore, the LIFO method will result in having cost of goods sold most closely approximate current cost and the FIFO method will result in having ending inventory most closely approximate current cost.

17. (b) Under the moving-average method, a new average unit price is computed every time a purchase is made. The inventory is then priced on the basis of this "moving average." Thus, the amount that Metro should report as inventory at 1/31/93 under the moving-average method is computed as follows:

	Units	Unit cost	Total cost
Balance on 1/1/93	1,000	$1.00	$1,000
Purchased on 1/7/93	600	3.00	1,800
Balance after purchase	1,600	1.75*	$2,800
Sold on 1/20/93	900	1.75	1,575
Balance after sale	700	1.75	$1,225
Purchased on 1/25/93	400	5.00	2,000
Balance after purchase	1,100		$3,225

* $2,800 ÷ 1,600 units

18. (b)   Where the LIFO cost flow method is used in conjunction with a perpetual inventory system, the cost of the last goods purchased are matched against revenue every time a sale is made. Therefore, Metro's 1/31/93 inventory is priced at $2,700 (i.e., $700 + $2,000), computed as follows:

Date	Purchased	Sold	Balance
1/1			(1,000 @ $1) $1,000
1/7	(600 @ $3) $1,800		(1,000 @ $1) $1,000
			(600 @ $3) $1,800
1/20		(600 @ $3) $1,800	(700 @ $1) $ 700
		(300 @ $1) $ 300	
1/25	(400 @ $5) $2,000		(700 @ $1) $ 700
			(400 @ $5) $2,000

19. (b)   The 1994 layer is determined by the difference of the ending inventory at base year cost and the beginning inventory (which is the base year in this case) at base year cost and applying the relevant price index to the difference.

Ending inventory at base year cost	$ 525,000
Less: Beginning inventory at base year cost	(500,000)
1994 layer at base year cost	$ 25,000
Relevant price index	1.10
1994 layer at 1994 prices	$ 27,500
Beginning inventory (1/1/94) at DV LIFO	500,000
Dollar-value LIFO inventory, 12/31/94	$ 527,500

20. (c)   The inventory amount reported at 12/31/92 under the dollar-value LIFO method is computed as follows:

Date	Layers at base year cost	Price index	Ending inventory at LIFO cost
01/01/91	$40,000	1.0000 [1]	$40,000
12/31/91	5,000	1.2000 [2]	6,000
12/31/92	15,000	1.3333 [3]	20,000
	$60,000		$66,000

[1] $40,000 ÷ $40,000. [2] $54,000 ÷ $45,000. [3] $80,000 ÷ $60,000.

The price index is computed by dividing the ending inventory at current year cost by its base year cost.

21. (c)   Under the last-in, first-out (LIFO) method of inventory valuation, the units remaining in ending inventory are costed at the oldest unit costs available. On the other hand, under the first-in, first-out (FIFO) method of inventory valuation, the units remaining in ending inventory are costed at the most recent unit costs available. Therefore, because inventory acquisition costs increased steadily during 1997, the FIFO method of inventory valuation would report a higher amount for ending inventory than the LIFO method. The question indicates that there were no goods in inventory at 12/31/98. Therefore, cost of goods sold for 1998 is comprised of the cost of inventory purchases made in 1998 and the cost of ending inventory at 12/31/97. Because the cost of the ending inventory at 12/31/97 is higher under FIFO, cost of goods sold for 1998 would also be higher under FIFO.

22. (d)   The dollar-value LIFO method, by definition, is based on the aggregation of similar inventory items into pools. Acquisitions and issuances of similar materials are recorded in the same pool, even if the substitute items are not exactly the same as the replaced items. As a general rule, dollar-value LIFO uses a "double-extension method" to determine: (1) the value of the ending inventory in terms of base year prices, and (2) the value of the ending inventory at current prices. The ratio of (2) over (1), above, provides the specific price index for valuing any layers of inventory added in the period.

23. (b)   The inventory layer added in the current year is computed in terms of base year prices. It then must be converted to current year cost because the layer was added during the current year. Because we are converting to current year cost from base year cost, the index is computed by dividing the ending inventory at current year cost by the ending inventory at base year cost.

24. (c)   The moving-average cost of the inventory is determined as follows:

$$\frac{\$12,800^* + \$46,080^{**}}{1,600 + 4,800} = \$9.20$$

*   Cost of 1,600 (3,200 − 1,600) units of 1/1/90 inventory on hand at date of last purchase (1,600 units x $8.00 = $12,800).
**   Cost of latest purchase (4,800 units x $9.60 = $46,080).

25. (c)   The inventory amount reported under the dollar-value LIFO method is determined as follows:

Date	Layers at base year cost	Price index	Ending inventory at LIFO cost
01/01/96	$150,000	1.00	$150,000
12/31/96	50,000 [1]	1.10	55,000
12/31/97	30,000 [2]	1.20	36,000
	$230,000		$241,000

[1] $200,000 − $150,000. [2] $230,000 − $200,000.

26. (c)   The last-in, first-out (LIFO) methods of inventory valuation assign the oldest costs available to ending inventory. Therefore, when inventory is subject to specific price increases, the dollar-value LIFO method would report the lowest ending inventory of the inventory methods listed.

LOWER OF COST OR MARKET

27. (d) Under the lower-of-cost-or-market method, market means current replacement cost with the exception that market value should not exceed the net realizable value (ceiling) and should not be less than the net realizable value minus normal profit (floor). Because in this question replacement cost is below the floor, this would be the minimum amount at which market could be valued. This market value is then compared to the original cost and the lower amount is used for the value of the inventory item. The question states that the original cost is above the net realizable value less a normal profit margin, thus, the market value is the lower amount.

28. (b) ARB 43, Chapter 4, requires valuation of inventory items at the lower of cost or market. As used in this context, market means current replacement cost. Since the goods in question are reported at replacement cost, original cost is greater than replacement cost. Replacement cost cannot exceed the net realizable value of the goods (ceiling) and cannot be less than the net realizable value reduced by an allowance for a normal profit margin (floor). Therefore, the net realizable value of the goods, less a normal profit margin, must be less than replacement cost.

29. (d) According to the lower-of-cost-or-market rule, market is defined as replacement cost. Market cannot exceed net realizable value and cannot be less than net realizable value less normal profit margin. In this instance, original cost is between net realizable value and net realizable value less normal profit margin. Since original cost is within the parameters for replacement cost and is less than replacement cost, the inventory should be reported at original cost.

30. (d) The application of the lower-of-cost-or-market rule directly to each inventory item generally results in the lowest inventory amount because unrealized losses on inventory items cannot be off-set by unrealized gains on other inventory items. Generally, a different inventory amount would be reported when the lower-of-cost-or-market rule is applied to (1) total inventory, (2) groups of similar inventory items, or (3) each inventory item. Answers (b) and (c) are incorrect. These methods of applying the lower-of-cost-or-market rule for inventories would allow unrealized losses on some inventory items to be offset by unrealized gains on others. This would result in a higher inventory amount than if the lower-of-cost-or-market rule for inventories were applied to each inventory item.

31. (c) Under the lower-of-cost-or-market rule, replacement cost cannot exceed a "ceiling" of net realizable value (estimated selling price less estimated cost of completion and disposal) and cannot be below a "floor" of net realizable value reduced by a normal profit margin.

	Replacement Cost Parameters		
Cost	Replacement cost	Ceiling (NRV)	Floor (NRV – NP)
$26,000	$20,000	$28,000 [1]	$24,000 [2]

[1] $40,000 – $12,000. [2] $28,000 – ($40,000 x 10%).

The replacement cost is below the prescribed range [i.e., $20,000 < ($24,000 to $28,000)]. Therefore, the "floor" of $24,000 is the assigned market value. Because the assigned market value of $24,000 is below the historical cost of $26,000, the inventory should be valued at $24,000.

32. (c) Under the lower-of-cost-or-market rule, replacement cost cannot exceed a "ceiling" of net realizable value (estimated selling price less estimated cost of disposal) and cannot be below a "floor" of net realizable value reduced by a normal profit margin.

	Replacement Cost Parameters		
Cost	Replacement cost	Ceiling (NRV)	Floor (NRV – NP)
$12.00	$10.90	$13.40 [1]	$11.20 [2]

[1] $13.60 – $.20. [2] $13.40 – $2.20.

The replacement cost is below the prescribed range; therefore, the "floor" of $11.20 is the assigned market value. Because the assigned market value of $11.20 is below the historical cost of $12.00, the inventory item should be valued at $11.20.

33. (d) Petal incurred an inventory loss from a decline in market price in the second quarter which it expected to be restored by the end of the fiscal year. Per APB 28, par. 14(c), inventory losses from market declines, which can reasonably be expected to be restored in the fiscal year, need not be recognized at the interim date since no loss is expected to be incurred in the fiscal year. Therefore, since Petal expected the market price to return to previous levels by the end of the year, Petal would not have recognized the inventory loss until the fourth quarter, when the decline had not reversed.

34. (b) The answer to this question assumes that the original cost, replacement cost, and net realizable value of the inventory *differ* in amount. Statement II is correct. Under lower-of-cost-or-market procedures for inventory valuation, market value cannot exceed a "ceiling" of net realizable value and cannot be below a "floor" of net realizable value reduced by a normal profit margin. Since the inventory is reported at its replacement cost, the net realizable of the inventory exceeds its replacement cost. Statement I is incorrect. Under lower-of-cost-or-market procedures, inventory is reported at the lower of original cost or market value (which is replacement cost in this case). Since the inventory is reported at replacement cost, the original cost of the inventory is *greater* than its replacement cost.

GROSS MARGIN METHOD

35. (a) The missing inventory is estimated by determining the difference between the estimated ending inventory using the gross margin method and the actual physical inventory on hand at year-end.

Beginning inventory		$ 500,000
Purchases		2,500,000
Goods available for sales		$ 3,000,000
Less: Estimated CGS		
Sales	$ 3,200,000	
Less gross margin		
(25% x $3,200,000)	800,000	(2,400,000)
Estimated ending inventory		$ 600,000
Less: Actual physical inventory		(575,000)
Estimated cost of missing inventory		$ 25,000

RETAIL METHOD

36. (a) When the retail method is employed, purchase returns is included in the calculation of both cost and retail amounts of goods available for sale (AFS). Sales returns does not appear in the computation of the cost amount of goods AFS. Net markups appears in the retail amount of goods AFS (assuming the retail method is used to approximate a lower-of-average-cost-or-market figure) but not in the cost amount of goods AFS. Freight in appears in the cost amount of goods available for sale but not in the retail amount of goods AFS.

37. (d) Cost of sales is determined by subtracting the estimated ending inventory at cost from the cost of the beginning inventory and purchases (i.e., $600,000 – $75,000 = $525,000). Under the conventional retail inventory method (i.e., lower of average cost or market), the amount to be reported as cost of sales is determined as follows:

	Cost	Retail
Beg. inventory and purchases	$600,000	$ 920,000
Net markups		40,000
Close-to-retail amounts	$600,000	$ 960,000
Less: Sales		(780,000)
Net Markdowns		(60,000)
Estimated EI at retail		$ 120,000
Cost-to-retail ratio ($600,000 ÷ $960,000)		x 62.5%
Estimated ending inventory at cost		$ 75,000

38. (a) Under the approximate lower-of-average-cost-or-market retail method, the estimated inventory is computed as follows:

	Cost	Retail
Inventory, 2/1/97	$ 180,000	$ 250,000
Purchases	1,020,000	1,575,000
Markups, net		175,000
Cost ratio	$1,200,000	$ 2,000,000
Less: Sales		(1,705,000)
Markdowns, net		(125,000)
Est. normal shoplifting losses		(20,000)
Estimated ending inventory at retail		$ 150,000
Cost-to-retail ratio ($1,200,000 ÷ $2,000,000)		x 60%
Estimated ending inventory at cost		$ 90,000

39. (a) Under the LIFO retail method, Jason's inventory at 12/31/97 is determined as follows:

Inventory at retail, 12/31/97 adjusted for price level increase ($660,000 ÷ 1.1)	$ 600,000
Beginning inventory at retail, base year price	(500,000)
New layer added in 1997	$ 100,000
Times: Price level adjustment	x 1.1
1997 layer, at LIFO retail	$ 110,000
Times: Cost to retail ratio	x .70
1997 layer, at LIFO cost	$ 77,000
Add: Beg. inventory, at LIFO cost	360,000
Ending inventory	$ 437,000

40. (a) Under the first-in, first-out (FIFO) retail method of inventory valuation, the goods in beginning inventory are charged to cost of goods sold during the period; therefore, the cost/retail ratio is based only on the purchases for the period. If the lower-of-cost-or-market rule is disregarded, both net additional markups and net markdowns are included in the purchases cost-to-retail ratio. The estimated cost of Union's ending inventory is computed as follows:

	Cost	Retail
Purchases	$ 60,000	$110,000
Net additional markups	--	10,000
Net markdowns	--	(20,000)
Purchases cost-to-retail ratio amts.	$ 60,000	$100,000
Beginning inventory	12,000	30,000
Goods available for sale	$72,000	$130,000
Less: Sales		(90,000)
Estimated ending inventory at retail		$ 40,000
Times: Purchases cost-to-retail ratio		
($60,000 ÷ $100,000)		x 60%
Estimated ending inventory at cost		$ 24,000

PERFORMANCE BY SUBTOPICS

Each category below parallels a subtopic covered in Chapter 3. Record the number and percentage of questions you correctly answered in each subtopic area.

Ownership Criteria

Question #	Correct √
1	
2	
3	
4	
5	
6	
7	
# Questions	7

Correct _____
% Correct _____

Losses on Purchase Commitments

Question #	Correct √
8	
# Questions	1

Correct _____
% Correct _____

Measuring Inventories

Question #	Correct √
9	
10	
11	
12	
# Questions	4

Correct _____
% Correct _____

Cost Flow Assumptions

Question #	Correct √
13	
14	
15	
16	
17	
18	
19	
20	
21	
22	
23	
24	
25	
26	
# Questions	14

Correct _____
% Correct _____

Lower of Cost or Market

Question #	Correct √
27	
28	
29	
30	
31	
32	
33	
34	
# Questions	8

Correct _____
% Correct _____

Gross Margin Method

Question #	Correct √
35	
# Questions	1

Correct _____
% Correct _____

Retail Method

Question #	Correct √
36	
37	
38	
39	
40	
# Questions	5

Correct _____
% Correct _____

PROBLEMS/ESSAY SOLUTIONS

SOLUTION 3-2 VARIOUS ASPECTS OF ACCOUNTING FOR INVENTORIES

a. Purchases from various suppliers generally should be included in Huddell's inventory when Huddell **receives the goods**. Title to goods purchased F.O.B. destination is assumed to pass when the goods are received.

b. Huddell should account for the warehousing costs as **additional cost of inventory**. All necessary and reasonable costs of readying goods for sale should be included in inventory.

c. 1. The advantages of using the dollar-value LIFO method are to **reduce the cost of accounting** for inventory and to **minimize** the **probability of reporting** the **liquidation** of LIFO inventory layers.

2. The application of dollar-value LIFO is based on **dollars of inventory**, an inventory **cost index for each year**, and **broad inventory pools**. The **inventory layers are identified** with the inventory cost index for the year in which the layer was added. In contrast, traditional LIFO is applied to individual units at their cost.

d. 1. Huddell's **net markups** should be included only in the **retail amounts (denominator)** to determine the **cost to retail percentage**.

Huddell's net markdowns should be **ignored** in the calculation of the cost to retail percentage.

2. By **not deducting net markdowns** from the retail amounts to determine the cost to retail percentage, Huddell produces a **lower cost to retail percentage** than would result if net markdowns were deducted. Applying this lower percentage to ending inventory at retail, the inventory is **reported at an amount below cost**. This amount is intended to approximate lower of average cost or market.

SOLUTION 3-3 DOLLAR-VALUE LIFO

Silver Inc.
COMPUTATION OF DOLLAR-VALUE LIFO INVENTORY
December 31, 1996 and 1997

Year	FIFO inventory	Current year cost change Index	Link-chain cost index	Inventory at base year costs
1995	$100,000	1.00	1.00	$100,000
1996	137,500	1.25	1.25	110,000
1997	195,000	1.20	1.50	130,000

Year	LIFO inventory layers at base year costs	Link-chain cost index	1996 dollar-value LIFO inventory	1997 dollar-value LIFO inventory
1995	$100,000	1.00	$100,000	**$100,000**
1996	10,000	1.25	12,500	**12,500**
1997	20,000	1.50		**30,000**
	$130,000		$112,500	**$142,500**

SOLUTION 3-4 VARIOUS ASPECTS OF ACCOUNTING FOR INVENTORIES

a. **1.** The specific identification method requires **each unit to be clearly distinguished** from similar units either by description, identification number, location, or other characteristic. **Costs are accumulated for specific units** and **expensed as the units are sold**. Thus, the specific identification method results in recognized cost flows being identical to actual physical flows. Ideally, **each unit is relatively expensive** and the number of such units **relatively few** so that recording of costs is not burdensome. Under the specific identification method, if similar items have different costs, cost of goods sold is influenced by the specific units sold.

2. It is appropriate for Happlia to use the specific identification method because **each appliance is expensive**, and **easily identified** by number and description. The specific identification method is feasible because Happlia **already maintains records** of its units held by individual retails. Management's ability to manipulate cost of goods sold is minimized because once the inventory is in retailer's hands Happlia's management cannot influence the units selected for sales.

b. **1.** Happlia should include in inventory carrying amounts **all necessary and reasonable costs** to get an appliance into a useful condition and place for sale. **Common (or joint) costs** should be **allocated** to individual units. Such costs **exclude** the **excess costs** incurred in transporting refrigerators to Minneapolis and their reshipment to Kansas City. These unit costs should only **include normal freight** costs from Des Moines to Kansas City. In addition, **costs incurred to provide time utility** to the goods, i.e., ensuring that they are available when required, will also be **included in inventory** carrying amounts.

2. Examples of inventoriable costs include the **unit invoice price**, plus an allocated proportion of the **port handling fees**, **import duties**, **freight costs** to Des Moines and to retailers, **insurance costs**, **repackaging**, and **warehousing costs**.

c. The 1990 income statement should report in **cost of goods sold** all inventory costs related to units **sold in 1990**, regardless of when cash is received from retailers. **Excess freight costs** incurred for shipping the refrigerators from Minneapolis to Kansas City should be included in determining operating income.

SOLUTION 3-5

a.

York Co.
Schedule of Cost of Goods Sold
For the Year Ended December 31, 1993

Beginning inventory		$ 65,600
Add: Purchases		368,900
Less: Purchase discounts		(18,000)
Add: Freight-in		5,000
Goods available for sale		$ 421,500
Less: Ending inventory		(176,000) [1]
Cost of Goods Sold		$ 245,500

[1] Inventory at market:
 22,000 units @ $8 = $176,000

York Co.
Supporting Schedule of Ending Inventory
December 31, 1993

Inventory at cost (LIFO):

	Units	Cost per unit	Total cost
Beg. inventory, Jan. 1	8,000	$8.20	$ 65,600
Purchases, quarters ended:			
March 31	12,000	8.25	99,000
June 30	2,000	7.90	15,800
	22,000		$180,400

b. Inventory should be valued at the **lower of cost or market**. Market means **current replacement cost**, except that:

(1) Market should **not exceed the net realizable value**; and

(2) Market should **not be less than net realizable value reduced by** an allowance for an approximately **normal profit margin**.

In this situation, because replacement cost ($8 per unit) is less than net realizable value, but greater than net realizable value reduced by a normal profit margin, replacement cost is used as market. **Because inventory valued at market ($176,000) is lower than** inventory valued **at cost** ($180,400), inventory **should be reported in the financial statements at market**.

WEB SITES

(Each address has www. as a prefix, except WY.)

AK	dced.state.ak.us/occ/pcpa.htm	MT	discoveringmontana.com/dli/bsd
AL	asbpa.state.al.us	NE	nol.org/home/BPA
AZ	accountancy.state.az.us	NV	accountancy/state.nv.us
AR	state.ar.us/asbpa	NH	state.nh.us/accountancy
CA	dca.ca.gov/cba	NC	state.nc.us/cpabd
DC	dcra.org/acct/newboa.shtm	ND	state.nd.us/ndsba
FL	myflorida.com	OK	sta.ok.us/~oab
GU	guam.net/gov/gba	OR	boa.state.or.us/boa.html
ID	state.id.us/boa	SD	state.sd.us/dcr/accountancy
IL	illinois-cpa-exam.com/cpa.htm	TX	tsbpa.state.tx.us
KY	state.ky.us/agencies/boa	UT	commerce.state.ut.us
MD	dllr.state.md.us/license/occprof/account.html	VI	usvi.org/dlca/liscensing/cpa.html
MN	boa.state.mn.us	WV	state.wv.us/wvboa
MS	msbpa.state.ms.us	WY	cpaboard.state.wy.us

These sites are subject to change without notice. Bisk Education assumes no responsibility with regard to address accuracy. The Bisk Education web site **(www.cpaexam.com)** has several links to state boards and NASBA.

EXAMINATION SERVICES

CPA Examination Services, a division of the National Association of State Boards of Accountancy (NASBA) administers the examination for 25 states. Contact CPA Examination Services at (800) CPA-EXAM (272-3926), (615) 880-4250, or www.nasba.org.

CO	CT	DE	GA	HI	IA	IN	KS	LA	MA	ME	MI	
MO	NJ	NM	NY	OH	PA	PR	RI	SC	TN	VA	VT	WA

Continental Testing Services at (800) 717-1201 administers the examination for WI.

See the **Practical Advice** appendix for more information.

CHAPTER 4

PROPERTY, PLANT & EQUIPMENT

CHANGE ALERT

SFAS 144, *Accounting for the Impairment or Disposal of Long-Lived Assets*

In October 2001, the FASB issued SFAS 144, *Accounting for the Impairment or Disposal of Long-Lived Assets*. This statement amends APB Opinion 30, *Reporting the Results of Operations—Reporting the Effects of Disposal of a Segment of a Business, and Extraordinary, Unusual and Infrequently Occurring Events and Transactions,* and ARB 51, *Consolidated Financial Statements*. SFAS 144 supercedes SFAS 121, *Accounting for the Impairment of Long-Lived Assets and for Long-Lived Assets to Be Disposed of* and EITF Issue No. 95-18, *Accounting and Reporting for a Discontinued Business Segment When the Measurement Date Occurs after the Balance Sheet Date but Before the Issuance of Financial Statements*. As this guidance is effective for fiscal periods beginning after December 15, 2001, with early application encouraged, SFAS 144 is eligible to be tested starting with the **May 2002** exam. Superceded guidance is also eligible to be tested on the May 2002 exam.

SFAS 144 establishes a single accounting model for long-lived assets to be disposed of by sale. Previously, assets of a segment of a business accounted for as a discontinued operation under Opinion 30 used a different model.

CHAPTER 4

PROPERTY, PLANT & EQUIPMENT

I. INTRODUCTION

A. EXPENSING VS. CAPITALIZING

Property, plant, and equipment are tangible assets acquired for long-term use in the normal operations of a business. If an outlay will provide a service benefit beyond the current period, it is a capital expenditure and is recorded as an asset. Expenditures that benefit only the current period are charged to expense as incurred and are referred to as revenue expenditures. The concept of materiality influences the decision whether to capitalize expenditures. Most companies expense all items costing less than a certain amount, regardless of their estimated useful lives. This is permissible as long as the total effect is immaterial, **and** this policy is consistently applied.

B. CLASSIFICATION

Productive assets are classified according to their characteristics, as follows:

1. **LIMITED LIVES** Plant and equipment have limited service lives; thus, their costs must be allocated to the periods benefited by the application of depreciation charges.

2. **INDEFINITE LIFE** Land is deemed to have an indefinite life and, therefore, is not depreciated.

3. **NATURAL RESOURCES** Wasting assets are natural resources such as mineral, gas, and oil deposits, and standing timber. Their costs must be allocated to inventory by the application of depletion charges because these resources are subject to exhaustion through extraction.

II. RECORDING THE ACQUISITION

A. ACQUISITION COST

Assets are to be recorded at their acquisition cost. Acquisition cost is defined as the cash price, or its equivalent, plus all other costs reasonably necessary to bring it to the location and to make it ready for its intended use. Examples of these additional costs include transportation, insurance while in-transit, special foundations, installation, test runs, and the demolition of an old building, less any scrap proceeds received. Property, plant, and equipment may be acquired in various ways.

1. **PURCHASE FOR CASH** Record the asset net of any trade or quantity discounts available.

2. **PURCHASE ON DEFERRED PAYMENT PLAN** The asset should be recorded at its cash equivalent price. If the cash equivalent price is unavailable, an imputed interest rate should be used to record the asset at the present value of the payments to be made.

3. **PURCHASE BY ISSUANCE OF SECURITIES** The asset should be recorded at its fair value or the fair value of the securities issued, whichever is more clearly determinable. If there is an active market for the security and the additional securities issued can be reasonably expected to be absorbed without a decline in their value, the fair value of the securities should be used. If the securities exchanged are bonds and no established market exists, the asset should be recorded at the present value of the interest and principal payments to be made, discounted by use of an implicit or "imputed" rate. If equity securities are issued and no fair value is determinable, the appraisal value of the asset acquired should be used for the recording of the transaction.

4. **SELF-CONSTRUCTION** The cost of assets constructed for the use of the business should include all directly related costs, such as direct materials, direct labor, and additional overhead incurred.

5. **INTEREST COSTS** SFAS 34, *Capitalization of Interest Cost*, requires the capitalization of interest costs incurred during the construction period. The interest cost capitalized is a part of the cost of acquiring the asset and is written off over the estimated useful life of the asset.

   a. Assets qualifying for interest capitalization include assets constructed or produced for self-use on a repetitive basis, assets acquired for self-use through arrangements requiring down payments or progress payments, and assets constructed or produced as discrete projects for sale or lease (e.g., ships or real estate developments). Assets **not** qualifying for interest capitalization include inventories that are routinely manufactured on a repetitive basis, assets in use or ready for use, and assets not in use and not being prepared for use.

   b. The amount of interest cost to be capitalized is the interest cost incurred during the acquisition period that could have been avoided if expenditures for the asset had not been made. If a specific interest rate is associated with the asset, that rate should be used to the extent that the average accumulated expenditures on the asset do not exceed the amount borrowed at the specific rate. If the average accumulated expenditures on an asset exceed the amount of specific new borrowings associated with the asset, the excess should be capitalized at the weighted average of the rates applicable to other borrowings of the enterprise.

   c. The interest rate determined above is applied to the *average* amount of accumulated expenditures for the asset during the period. For example, if construction of a qualifying asset begins in January and the accumulated expenditures at year-end amount to $400,000, the interest rate is applied to the $200,000 average accumulated expenditure [($0 + $400,000) / 2]. (**NOTE**: The preceding assumes that construction expenditures take place *evenly* throughout the period. If expenditures fluctuate widely, the average accumulated expenditure should be computed monthly.)

   d. The total interest cost capitalized in a period may **not** exceed the total interest cost incurred during that period.

   e. Interest *earned* by the enterprise during the period is **not** offset to interest costs incurred in determining the amount of interest to be capitalized.

6. **GIFTS** Donated assets should be recorded at their fair value along with any incidental costs incurred. When the asset is received from a governmental entity, no income is recognized, and the offsetting credit is to an owners' equity account, Additional Paid-In Capital—Donated Assets. Assets donated by entities other than governmental units are included in revenue in the period of receipt (SFAS 116).

7. **GROUP PURCHASES** If several dissimilar assets are purchased for a lump sum, the total amount paid should be allocated to each individual asset on the basis of its relative fair value. This is accomplished by the use of the following equation:

   Asset Y = Total cost of assets x FV of Y / Total FV

8. **ACQUISITION BY EXCHANGE** APB 29, *Accounting for Nonmonetary Transactions*, provides the standards for the accounting of nonmonetary transactions and nonreciprocal transfers. APB 29 applies to exchanges of inventories and productive assets for *similar* assets and to exchanges of *dissimilar* assets. Similar assets are assets that are of the same general type, perform the same function, or are employed in the same line of business. If the cash received is 25 percent or more of the fair value in the exchange, the transaction is treated as monetary (EITF 86-29).

EXAMPLE 1 ♦ CAPITALIZING INTEREST ON ASSETS CONSTRUCTED FOR SELF-USE

On January 1, 20X1, Expansions Inc. borrowed $1,000,000 to finance the construction of a warehouse for its own use. The loan was to be repaid in 10 equal payments of $199,250, including interest of 15%, beginning on January 1, 20X2. No other loans are presently outstanding. The total cost of labor, materials, and overhead assigned to the warehouse was $1,000,000. Construction was completed on December 30, 20X1. The warehouse is depreciated using the straight-line method over an estimated useful life of 20 years, with no salvage value. The proceeds borrowed were invested in short-term liquid assets until needed to pay construction expenditures, yielding $24,000 interest income.

REQUIRED: Determine the capitalized cost of the asset, as of December 30, 20X1, the interest expense for 20X1 (assume no other debt outstanding), and the depreciation expense for 20X2.

SOLUTION:

Cost of completed asset:	
Materials, labor, overhead, etc.	$1,000,000
Capitalized interest cost, [($0 + $1,000,000) ÷ 2] x .15	75,000
Capitalized cost of asset	$1,075,000
Interest expense, 20X1:	
Total interest cost incurred, 20X1 ($1,000,000 x .15)	$ 150,000
Less capitalized interest cost	(75,000)
Interest expense, 20X1	$ 75,000
Depreciation expense, 20X2:	
Capitalized cost of asset	$1,075,000
Estimated useful life	÷ 20
Depreciation expense, 20X2	$ 53,750

EXAMPLE 2 ♦ LESS THAN ENTIRE AMOUNT BORROWED

The facts are the same as in *Example 1*, except that Expansions Inc., needed to borrow only $300,000 (at 15%) to finance construction of the $1,000,000 warehouse. The remaining cash was provided from operations and from the sale of miscellaneous investments. During all of 20X1, Expansions' only other long-term liabilities consisted of $2,000,000, 10%, 20-year bonds (sold at par in 20X0) and a $500,000, 14%, interest-bearing note payable due in 20X4.

REQUIRED: Determine the amount of interest that should be capitalized in 20X1.

SOLUTION:

Accumulated average expenditures ($0 + $1,000,000) ÷ 2	$500,000
Interest on new borrowings specifically associated with asset, ($300,000 x .15)	$ 45,000
Weighted average rate on other borrowings, applied to accumulated	
average expenditures in excess of $300,000, ($200,000 x .108*)	21,600
Total interest cost capitalized during 20X1**	$ 66,600

---

*Computation of weighted average rate:

$$\frac{\text{Total interest}}{\text{Total principle}} = \frac{(\$2,000,000 \times 10\%) + (\$500,000 \times 14\%)}{\$2,000,000 + \$500,000} = .108$$

**Does not exceed the total interest cost incurred during the year ($300,000 x 15%) + ($2,000,000 x 10%) + ($500,000 x 14%) = $315,000.

a. **DISSIMILAR ASSETS** In general, accounting for nonmonetary transactions should be based on the fair values of the assets involved. The acquisition is recorded at the fair value of the asset surrendered or the FV of the asset received, whichever is more clearly determinable. Gains or losses should be recognized as the earnings process has culminated for the asset exchanged.

EXAMPLE 3 ♦ NONMONETARY EXCHANGE OF DISSIMILAR ASSETS

Asset A, with a book value of $15,000, is exchanged for dissimilar Asset B, valued at $18,000.

REQUIRED: Prepare the journal entry to record this exchange.

SOLUTION:

Asset B	18,000	
Asset A		15,000
Gain on Exchange		3,000

(1) If monetary consideration (boot) is paid and an asset surrendered, the asset acquired is recorded at the FV of the asset given up plus the boot paid.

(2) If cash (a form of boot) is received in the transaction, the asset acquired is recorded at the FV of the asset surrendered **less** the amount of cash received.

b. **SIMILAR ASSETS** Exchanges not resulting in a culmination of the earnings process are recorded on the basis of the *book value* of the assets involved, not to exceed their FV. Where similar assets are exchanged and no additional monetary consideration is involved, the accounting for the asset acquired should be based on the book value of the nonmonetary asset surrendered. No *gains* are recognized. However, a *loss* is recognized to the extent that the book value of the asset given up exceeds the FV of the asset received.

EXAMPLE 4 ♦ NONMONETARY EXCHANGE OF SIMILAR ASSETS

Asset A, with a book value of $15,000, is exchanged for similar Asset C.

REQUIRED:

(a) Prepare the journal entry for the exchange if Asset C is valued at $14,000.
(b) Prepare the journal entry for the exchange if Asset C is valued at $18,000.
(c) Explain the difference in the entries required in (a) and (b).

SOLUTIONS:

(a) Asset C	14,000	
Loss on Exchange	1,000	
Asset A		15,000
(b) Asset C	15,000	
Asset A		15,000

(c) When a loss is indicated in a nonmonetary exchange of similar assets, the loss is recognized and the new asset is recorded at fair value. If a gain is indicated, it is not recognized and the new asset is recorded at the book value of the old asset.

(1) If one of the parties to the exchange *pays* boot, the asset received is recorded at the book value of the asset surrendered plus the boot paid, not to exceed the FV of the asset received.

(2) The party receiving the boot accounts for the transaction as part sale and part exchange. The sale portion is determined by the proportion of the boot received to the fair value of the total consideration received.

   (a) A gain is recorded on the sale portion, if applicable, because the earnings process is deemed to have culminated for a portion of the asset sold.

   (b) In the case of a loss, the full amount of the loss is recognized.

EXAMPLE 5 ♦ EXCHANGE OF SIMILAR ASSETS, CASH RECEIVED

Asset A is exchanged for similar Asset D, valued at $12,000

REQUIRED: Prepare the journal entry to record this exchange assuming

(a) Asset A has a book value of $11,000 and $3,000 cash is paid.
(b) Asset A has a book value of $16,000 and $3,000 cash is paid.
(c) Asset A has a book value of $16,000 and $6,000 cash is received.

SOLUTIONS:

(a)			
	Cash	3,000	
	Asset D [1]	8,800	
	Asset A		11,000
	Gain on Exchange [2]		800

COMPUTATIONS:

[1]	BV of Asset A	$11,000
	BV, old asset x Cash boot / (Cash + FV, new asset)	
	$11,000 x 3,000 / ($3,000 + $12,000) =	(2,200)
	Carrying amount of new Asset D	$ 8,800

[2]	Cash received	$ 3,000
	Portion of BV sold, per above	(2,200)
	Gain on sale of Asset A	$ 800

(b)			
	Cash	3,000	
	Asset D	12,000	
	Loss on Exchange	1,000	
	Asset A		16,000

(c)			
	Cash	6,000	
	Asset D	12,000	
	Asset A		16,000
	Gain on Exchange		2,000

Transaction (c) is treated as monetary—the cash received is 25% or more of the fair value in the exchange; $6,000/($6,000 + $12,000) = 33.3%

c. **NONRECIPROCAL TRANSFERS** A transfer of a nonmonetary asset to a stockholder or to another entity, such as in charitable contributions, in a **nonreciprocal** transfer should be recorded at the fair value of the asset transferred, and a gain or loss should be recognized on the disposition of the asset.

EXHIBIT 1 ♦ ACCOUNTING FOR NONMONETARY EXCHANGES

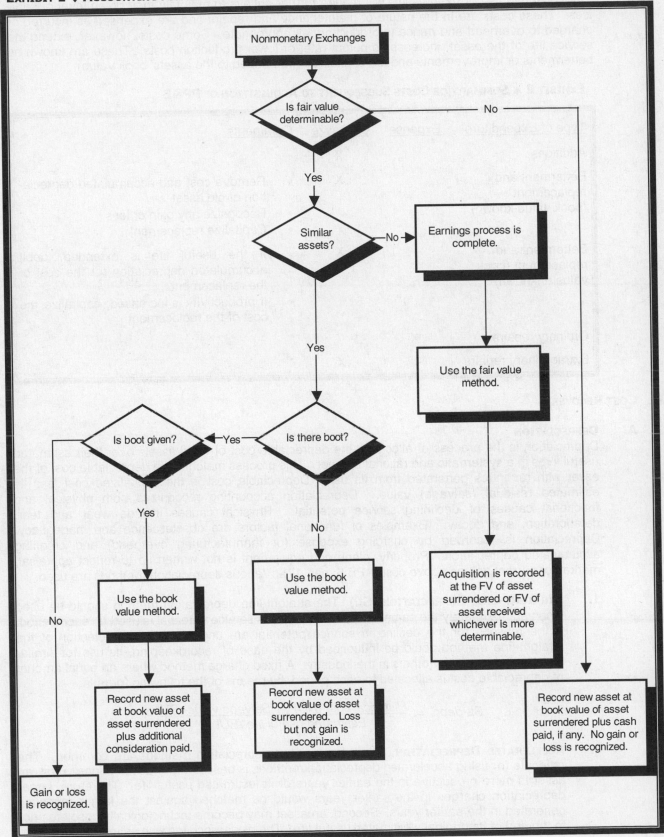

B.   COSTS INCURRED SUBSEQUENT TO ACQUISITION

The continued use of fixed assets will require further outlays to maintain their given level of services. These costs are in the nature of maintenance and repairs and are expensed as incurred or charged to overhead and hence to production, as appropriate. Some costs, however, extend the service life of the asset, increase its output rate, or lower production costs. These are known as betterments or improvements and are *capitalized* (i.e., added to the assets' book value).

EXHIBIT 2 ◆ SUMMARY OF COSTS SUBSEQUENT TO ACQUISITION OF PP&E

Type of Expenditure	Expense	Capitalize	Comments
Additions		X	
Betterment and replacement (book value known)		X	• Remove cost and accumulated depreciation of old asset • Recognize any gain or loss • Capitalize replacement
Betterment and replacement (book value unknown)		X	• If the useful life is extended, debit accumulated depreciation for the cost of the replacement • If productivity is increased, capitalize the cost of the replacement
Ordinary repairs	X		
Extraordinary repairs		X	

III. COST RECOVERY

A.   DEPRECIATION

Depreciation is the process of allocating the depreciable cost of fixed assets over their estimated useful lives in a systematic and rational manner. This process matches the depreciable cost of the asset with revenues generated from its use. Depreciable cost is the capitalized cost less its estimated residual (salvage) value. Depreciation accounting recognizes both physical and functional causes of declining service potential. Physical causes include wear and tear, deterioration, and decay. Examples of functional factors are obsolescence and inadequacy. Depreciation is recorded by charging expense (or manufacturing overhead) and crediting accumulated depreciation. Property, plant, and equipment is not written up to reflect appraisal, market, or current values above cost (APB 6, par. 17). Various depreciation methods are used.

1.   STRAIGHT-LINE DEPRECIATION (SL) The straight-line depreciation method should be used when approximately the same amount of an asset's service potential is used up each period. If the reasons for the decline in service potential are unclear, then the selection of the straight-line method could be influenced by the ease of recordkeeping, its use for similar assets, and its use by others in the industry. A fixed charge method where an equal amount of depreciable cost is allocated to each period, by means of the following formula:

$$SL\ depr. = \frac{Historical\ cost\ (HC) - Salvage\ value\ (SV)}{Estimated\ useful\ life\ (EUL)}$$

2.   ACCELERATED DEPRECIATION Three accelerated depreciation methods are common. The rationale for using accelerated depreciation methods is based on two assumptions. First, an asset is more productive in the earlier years of its estimated useful life. Therefore, larger depreciation charges in the earlier years would be matched against the larger revenues generated in the earlier years. Second, an asset may become technologically obsolete prior to the end of its originally estimated useful life. The risk associated with estimated long-term cash flows is greater than the risk associated with near-term cash flows. Accelerated depreciation recognizes this condition.

a. **SUM-OF-THE-YEARS'-DIGITS (SYD)** A decreasing fraction is applied each year to the depreciable base (i.e., HC − SV). The denominator of the fraction is obtained by adding the number of years of EUL at the *beginning* of the asset's life. For instance, the denominator for an asset with n years would be computed as $[n + (n − 1) + (n − 2) + \ldots + 1]$. The use of the equation $[n(n+1)/2]$ provides the same result and may be more practical when n is a large number. Once determined, the denominator remains unchanged for all future computations. The numerator of the fraction is given by the remaining years of EUL, including the current year, and thus it decreases with time.

EXAMPLE 6 ♦ SUM-OF-THE-YEARS' DIGITS DEPRECIATION

Historical Cost (HC) $1,000
Salvage Value (SV) $ 100
Estimated Useful Life (EUL)   3 years

REQUIRED: Calculate the depreciation using the syd method.

SOLUTION:

Depreciable base (HC − SV): $1,000 − 100 = $900

Denominator of fraction (remains unchanged): 3 + 2 + 1 = 6, or 3(3 + 1) / 2 = 6

Numerator of fraction: Remaining years of life at the beginning of each period: 3, 2, 1

	Fraction	x	Depreciable base	=	Depreciation charge
Year 1	3/6		$900		$450
Year 2	2/6		900		300
Year 3	1/6		900		150

---

b. **DOUBLE-DECLINING-BALANCE (DDB)** A rate of depreciation twice the SL rate is applied to the *book value* (i.e., declining balance) of the asset to obtain the depreciation expense for the period. (Note that the SV is not used in the calculation of depreciation expense under DDB except as a lower bound for the asset's BV.)

$$Depreciation \ for \ current \ period \ = \ \frac{2}{EUL} \ x \ (HC - AD)$$

Where: AD = Accumulated depreciation

EXAMPLE 7 ♦ DOUBLE-DECLINING-BALANCE DEPRECIATION

Historical Cost (HC)	$1,200		
Salvage Value (SV)	$ 100		
Estimated Useful Life (EUL)	3 years		

REQUIRED: Calculate the depreciation using the DDB method.

SOLUTION:

Depreciable base $1,200
Lower bound $100

	Fraction	Depreciable base	Depreciation
Year 1	2/3	$1,200	$800
Year 2	2/3	$1,200 − 800 = $400	$267
Year 3	2/3	$1,200 − 1,067 = $133	$ 33*

* May not depreciate below the lower bound ($133 x 2/3 = $89)

c. **FIXED-PERCENTAGE-OF-DECLINING-BALANCE** A fixed percentage (usually 125 percent to 175 percent of the SL rate) is applied to the decreasing book value of the asset. It is similar to the DDB method in c., above, except that instead of double (i.e., 200 percent) the SL rate, a lower percentage is used.

3. **VARIABLE CHARGE METHODS** Depreciation is based upon the actual *usage* of the asset. Both of the two commonly used methods are represented by the formula below:

$$\frac{\text{Depreciation}}{\text{expense}} = \frac{HC - SV}{\text{Total expected output or usage}} \times \text{Current output or use}$$

a. **SERVICE HOURS** The expected useful life (EUL) of the asset is determined on the basis of service hours, rather than years. Depreciation expense for the current period is a proportion of current hours of service to EUL (in service hours).

b. **UNITS-OF-OUTPUT** The EUL is stated in units of output, rather than years.

4. **MULTIPLE-ASSET DEPRECIATION** In order to reduce the number of computations needed, assets are sometimes depreciated in groups, rather than individually. Two types are used.

a. **GROUP DEPRECIATION** Homogeneous assets having similar service lives are lumped together and one depreciation rate is applied to the entire group. Retirements are recorded by a credit to the asset for the amount of cost and a debit to accumulated depreciation for the same amount less any proceeds received in disposition. Note that **no** gains or losses are recognized.

b. **COMPOSITE DEPRECIATION** Similar to the group system but applied to groups of assets having a wider range of service lives. The composite rate is determined by calculating the annual depreciation expense for each asset, adding up these amounts, and expressing this as a percentage of the total cost of all the assets.

EXAMPLE 8 ♦ COMPOSITE DEPRECIATION

Asset class	Asset cost	–	Salvage value	=	Depr'n. base	÷	EUL (yrs.)	=	SL Depr'n.
A	$ 120,000		$20,000		$100,000		10		$10,000
B	60,000		10,000		50,000		5		10,000
C	30,000		5,000		25,000		5		5,000
	$210,000		$35,000		$175,000				$25,000

Composite depreciation rate: ($25,000 ÷ $210,000) = 11.905%
Composite life: ($175,000 ÷ $25,000) = 7 years

The annual composite depreciation charge for the group of assets above would be $25,000 ($210,000 x 11.905%) and, assuming no additions or retirements, the group would be depreciated to the salvage value of its assets at the end of their seven-year average life. Additions are debited to the group at cost. Retirements are recorded by a credit to the asset account, a debit to cash or receivable for the consideration received, and the balance is debited to accumulated depreciation. No gains or losses are recognized.

5. **FRACTIONAL-YEAR DEPRECIATION** Assets are seldom acquired or disposed of at the exact date of the beginning or the end of the entity's accounting period. Fractional-year depreciation is generally accounted for under one of three different approaches.

a. Depreciation for one entire year in the year of acquisition and none in the year of disposal.

b. Half-year's depreciation in the year of acquisition and the year of disposal.

c. Proportional depreciation based on the number of months the asset was used, both for the year of acquisition and disposal. When assets are acquired or retired during the year, the amount of depreciation for a given period is determined by allocating the annual depreciation based on the number of months (weeks, days) that the asset was held during the period.

B. **DEPLETION**
Depletion refers to periodic allocation of acquisition costs of natural resources. A per-unit depletion rate is computed by dividing the depletable base of the natural resource (i.e., purchase price, exploring, drilling, and other development costs), less any estimated residual value, by the estimated number of units of the resource available for extraction. This unit rate is applied to the number of units extracted during the period to obtain the total amount of depletion for the period (i.e., inventoried and expensed). The unit rate is applied to the number of units *sold* during the period to determine the amount of depletion to be recognized as an *expense*.

IV. **IMPAIRMENT OR DISPOSAL OF LONG-LIVED ASSETS (SFAS 121, 144)**

A. **SFAS 121 GUIDANCE**
SFAS 121 establishes accounting standards for the impairment of (1) long-lived assets, specific identifiable intangibles, and related goodwill to be held and used; (2) long-lived assets and specific identifiable intangibles slated for disposal; and (3) certain assets of a rate-regulated entity. SFAS 121 does not apply to financial instruments, long-term customer relationships of a financial institution, mortgage and other servicing rights, deferred policy acquisition costs, or deferred tax assets or to assets whose accounting is prescribed by SFAS 50, SFAS 53, SFAS 63, SFAS 86, and SFAS 90.

1. **IMPAIRMENT LOSS RECOGNITION** Long-lived assets, specific identifiable intangibles, and related goodwill *to be held and used* must be reviewed for impairment as events or changes in situations indicate that the carrying amount of an asset may not be recoverable. When the carrying amount of the asset under review exceeds the expected future cash flows resulting from the use and eventual disposition of the asset (without consideration of interest charges or time value of money), an impairment loss is recognized.

   a. **IMPAIRMENT LOSS CALCULATION** The impairment loss is the amount by which the carrying amount of the asset exceeds the fair value of the asset.

   b. **NEW COST BASIS** The fair value then becomes the asset's new cost basis. For a depreciable asset, the new cost is depreciated over the asset's remaining useful life.

   c. **RESTORATION PROHIBITED** Restoration of previously recognized impairment losses is prohibited.

EXAMPLE 9 ♦ IMPAIRMENT OF LONG-LIVED ASSET

In Joan Co.'s review of long-lived assets to be held and used, an asset with a cost of $10,000 and accumulated depreciation of $5,500 was determined to have a fair value of $3,500.

REQUIRED: Determine the amount of impairment loss to be recognized if the expected future cash flows is (a) $5,000, and (b) $3,000.

SOLUTION a:

The carrying value of $4,500 is less than the future cash flows of $5,000, so no loss is recognized even though the carrying value is greater than the fair value.

SOLUTION b:

The carrying value of $4,500 is greater than the future cash flows of $3,000. Thus, impairment loss is recognized. The amount of impairment loss to be recognized is determined by calculating the difference between the carrying amount and the fair value.

Carrying Amount	$ 4,500
Fair Value	(3,500)
Impairment Loss	$ 1,000

2. **DISPOSAL PLANS** Long-lived assets and specific identifiable intangibles *slated for disposal* are reported at the lower of carrying amount or fair value less disposal costs, unless the assets are covered by APB 30, *Reporting the Results of Operations*. To qualify for treatment under SFAS 121, management must have committed to a plan for disposition of the long-lived assets, which can be by sale or abandonment.

3. **RATE-REGULATED ENTITY** A rate-regulated entity must recognize an impairment for the amount of excluded costs when a regulator excludes a cost, totally or partially, from the entity's rate base.

B. **SFAS 144 GUIDANCE**
   SFAS 144, *Accounting for the Impairment or Disposal of Long-Lived Assets*, divides assets into three categories of impaired assets: held for use, held for disposal by sale, and held for disposal other than by sale. An asset group is a group of assets and liabilities that represents the unit of accounting for a long-lived asset to be held for use. SFAS 144 is effective for periods beginning after December 15, 2001, with early adoption encouraged.

1. **CRITERIA** Criteria to determine when long-lived assets are held for sale, include requirements that (a) the asset is available for prompt sale as is, subject only to customary and

usual sales terms for such assets; and (b) the asset sale is probable, and generally, to be completed within 12 months.

2. **RETRO-ACTIVE CLASSIFICATION** SFAS 144 prohibits retroactive classification of the asset when the criteria for classification as held for sale are met before financial statement issuance, but after the balance sheet date.

3. **RECLASSIFICATION** If a long-lived asset classified as held for sale is reclassified as held and used, the reclassified asset is valued at the lower of (a) fair value at the date that the asset is reclassified as held and used; or (b) book value before being classified as held for sale, adjusted for any depreciation (or amortization) that would have been recognized had the asset classification continuously been held and used.

4. **ASSETS HELD FOR USE** SFAS 144 requires recognition of an impairment loss only if a long-lived asset's, or asset group's, undiscounted cash flows are less than the book value. The amount of an impairment loss is the difference between an asset's book and fair value. The new book value is used as a basis for depreciation. Goodwill need not be allocated to long-lived assets to be tested for impairment.

5. **DISPOSALS OTHER THAN BY SALE** SFAS 144 provides guidance for long-lived assets that will be abandoned, exchanged for a similar productive asset (exchanged), or distributed to owners in a spin-off (distributed). SFAS 144 requires that these long-lived assets be considered held and used until disposal, plus:

   a. Revision in the depreciable life of a long-lived asset to be abandoned.

   b. Recognition of an impairment loss when a long-lived asset is exchanged or distributed if book value exceeds fair value (amending APB Opinion No. 29, *Accounting for Nonmonetary Transactions*).

6. **DISPOSALS BY SALE** The same accounting model is used for all long-lived assets to be sold, whether previously held and used or newly acquired. A long-lived asset to be sold is measured at the lower of its book or fair value less cost to sell and its depreciation (or amortization) discontinues. Therefore, discontinued operations are no longer valued at net realizable value (NRV), and future operating losses are no longer recognized before they occur.

V. DISPOSAL OF FIXED ASSETS

A. VOLUNTARY
Accounting for the voluntary disposal of an operational asset usually involves crediting the asset account for the cost of the asset, removing the accumulated depreciation by a debit to that account, debiting the appropriate account for any proceeds received, and recognizing a gain or loss on disposal (balancing figure). (Exceptions to this treatment are when multiple-asset depreciation methods are used. If the disposal qualifies as an exchange of nonmonetary assets, accounting should follow the guidelines of an acquisition by exchange.)

B. INVOLUNTARY
Property, plant, and equipment may be totally or partially destroyed by storm, fire, flood, or other similar causes. Damaged assets should be written down to their remaining value in use, if any, and a loss recognized in the current period. This loss would be reported as prescribed by SFAS 121 and APB 30 or SFAS 144.

1. **CASUALTY LOSSES** Property, plant, and equipment are usually insured against casualty losses. A gain or loss should be recognized depending on whether the amount due from the insurer exceeds the *carrying amount* of the loss.

2. **RECOGNITION OF GAIN OR LOSS REGARDLESS OF REPLACEMENT** Per FASB Interp. 30, *Accounting for Involuntary Conversions of Nonmonetary Assets to Monetary Assets*, an interpretation of APB 29, a gain or loss on the involuntary conversion (e.g., due to casualty, condemnation, theft, etc.) of a nonmonetary asset should be recognized even if the proceeds received as a result of the involuntary conversion (e.g., insurance settlement, condemnation award, etc.) are reinvested in a replacement nonmonetary asset. Removal and clean-up costs are used to determine the gain or loss recognized on the involuntary conversion. Incidental costs incurred in the acquisition of replacement property are capitalized as costs of acquiring the replacement property (i.e., they do not affect the gain or loss recognized on the involuntary conversion).

CHAPTER 4—PROPERTY, PLANT & EQUIPMENT

PROBLEM 4-1 MULTIPLE CHOICE QUESTIONS (114 to 143 minutes)

1. Samm Corp. purchased a plot of land for $100,000. The cost to raze a building on the property amounted to $50,000 and Samm received $10,000 from the sale of scrap materials. Samm built a new plant on the site at a total cost of $800,000 including excavation costs of $30,000. What amount should Samm capitalize in its land account?
a. $150,000
b. $140,000
c. $130,000
d. $100,000   (R/00, FAR, #3, 6898)

2. Cole Co. began constructing a building for its own use in January 1993. During 1993, Cole incurred interest of $50,000 on specific construction debt, and $20,000 on other borrowings. Interest computed on the weighted-average amount of accumulated expenditures for the building during 1993 was $40,000. What amount of interest cost should Cole capitalize?
a. $20,000
b. $40,000
c. $50,000
d. $70,000   (5/94, FAR, #17, 4832)

3. Theoretically, which of the following costs Incurred in connection with a machine purchased for use in a company's manufacturing operations would be capitalized?

	Insurance on machine while in transit	Testing and preparation of machine for use
a.	Yes	Yes
b.	Yes	No
c.	No	Yes
d.	No	No

(5/95, FAR, #12, 5548)

4. Slate Co. and Talse Co. exchanged similar plots of land with fair values in excess of carrying amounts. In addition, Slate received cash from Talse to compensate for the difference in land values. As a result of the exchange, Slate should recognize
a. A gain equal to the difference between the fair value and the carrying amount of the land given up.
b. A gain in an amount determined by the ratio of cash received to total consideration.
c. A loss in an amount determined by the ratio of cash received to total consideration.
d. **Neither** a gain **nor** a loss.
(5/95, FAR, #30, 5566)

5. During 1990, Burr Co. had the following transactions pertaining to its new office building:

Purchase price of land	$ 60,000
Legal fees for contracts to purchase land	2,000
Architects' fees	8,000
Demolition of old building on site	5,000
Sale of scrap from old building	3,000
Construction cost of new building (fully completed)	350,000

In Burr's December 31, 1990 balance sheet, what amounts should be reported as the cost of land and cost of building?

	Land	Building
a.	$60,000	$360,000
b.	$62,000	$360,000
c.	$64,000	$358,000
d.	$65,000	$362,000 (5/91, PI, #24, 0931)

6. Amble Inc. exchanged a truck with a carrying amount of $12,000 and a fair value of $20,000 for a truck and $4,000 cash. The fair value of the truck received was $16,000. At what amount should Amble record the truck received in the exchange?
a. $ 8,000
b. $ 9,600
c. $12,000
d. $16,000   (5/93, PII, #10, amended, 4119)

7. An asset is being constructed for an enterprise's own use. The asset has been financed with a specific new borrowing. The interest cost incurred during the construction period as a result of expenditures for the asset is
a. Interest expense in the construction period.
b. A prepaid asset to be written off over the estimated useful life of the asset.
c. A part of the historical cost of acquiring the asset to be written off over the estimated useful life of the asset.
d. A part of the historical cost of acquiring the asset to be written off over the term of the borrowing used to finance the construction of the asset.
(5/86, Theory, #17, 1878)

8. A company is constructing an asset for its own use. Construction began in 1996. The asset is being financed entirely with a specific new borrowing. Construction expenditures were made in 1996 and 1997 at the end of each quarter. The total amount of interest cost capitalized in 1997 should be determined by applying the interest rate on the specific new borrowing to the
a. Total accumulated expenditures for the asset in 1996 and 1997.
b. Average accumulated expenditures for the asset in 1996 and 1997.
c. Average expenditures for the asset in 1997.
d. Total expenditures for the asset in 1997.
                (11/87, Theory, #4, amended, 1847)

9. Herr Inc. has a fiscal year ending April 30. On May 1, 1997, Herr borrowed $10,000,000 at 15% to finance construction of its own building. Repayments of the loan are to commence the month following completion of the building. During the year ended April 30, 1998, expenditures for the partially completed structure totaled $6,000,000. These expenditures were incurred evenly throughout the year. Interest earned on the unexpended portion of the loan amounted to $400,000 for the year. How much should be shown as capitalized interest on Herr's financial statements at April 30, 1998?
a. $0
b. $ 50,000
c. $ 450,000
d. $1,100,000   (5/83, PII, #14, amended, 0966)

10. Pine City owned a vacant plot of land zoned for industrial use. Pine gave this land to Medi Corp. solely as an incentive for Medi to build a factory on the site. The land had a fair value of $300,000 at the date of the gift. This nonmonetary transaction should be reported by Medi as
a. Extraordinary income.
b. Additional paid-in capital.
c. A credit to retained earnings.
d. A memorandum entry.   (11/91, PII, #9, 2457)

11. On July 1, 1997, Town Company purchased for $540,000 a warehouse building and the land on which it is located. The following data were available concerning the property:

	Current appraised value	Seller's original cost
Land	$200,000	$140,000
Warehouse building	300,000	280,000
	$500,000	$420,000

Town should record the land at
a. $140,000.
b. $180,000.
c. $200,000.
d. $216,000.   (11/85, PI, #12, amended, 0959)

12. During 1992, Beam Co. paid $1,000 cash and traded inventory, which had a carrying amount of $20,000 and a fair value of $21,000, for other inventory in the same line of business with a fair value of $22,000. What amount of gain (loss) should Beam record related to the inventory exchange?
a. $ 2,000
b. $ 1,000
c. $0
d. $(1,000)   (5/93, PII, #9, 4118)

13. On October 1, 1990, Shaw Corp. purchased a machine for $126,000 that was placed in service on November 30, 1990. Shaw incurred additional costs for this machine as follows:

Shipping	$3,000
Installation	4,000
Testing	5,000

In Shaw's December 31, 1990 balance sheet, the machine's cost should be reported as
a. $126,000.
b. $129,000.
c. $133,000.
d. $138,000.   (5/91, PI, #23, 0930)

14. During 1990, Bay Co. constructed machinery for its own use and for sale to customers. Bank loans financed these assets both during construction and after construction was complete. How much of the interest incurred should be reported as interest expense in the 1990 income statement?

	Interest incurred for machinery for own use	Interest incurred for machinery held for sale
a.	All interest incurred	All interest incurred
b.	All interest incurred	Interest incurred after completion
c.	Interest incurred after completion	Interest incurred after completion
d.	Interest incurred after completion	All interest incurred

                (5/91, Theory, #23, 1788)

15. Pine Football Company had a player contract with Duff that is recorded in its books at $500,000 on July 1, 1997. Ace Football Company had a player contract with Terry that is recorded in its books at $600,000 on July 1, 1997. On this date, Pine traded Duff to Ace for Terry and paid a cash difference of $50,000. The fair value of the Terry contract was $700,000 on the exchange date. After the exchange, the Terry contract should be recorded in Pine's book as

a. $550,000.
b. $600,000.
c. $650,000.
d. $700,000.   (5/89, PI, #28, amended, 0945)

16. May Co. and Sty Co. exchanged nonmonetary assets. The exchange did not culminate an earning process for either May or Sty. May paid cash to Sty in connection with the exchange. To the extent that the amount of cash exceeds a proportionate share of the carrying amount of the asset surrendered, a realized gain on the exchange should be recognized by

	May	Sty
a.	Yes	Yes
b.	Yes	No
c.	No	Yes
d.	No	No

(5/91, Theory, #35, 1791)

17. Madden Company owns a tract of land which it purchased in 1994 for $100,000. The land is held as a future plant site and has a fair market value of $140,000 on July 1, 1997. Hall Company also owns a tract of land held as a future plant site. Hall paid $180,000 for the land in 1996 and the land has a fair market value of $200,000 on July 1, 1997. On this date, Madden exchanged its land and paid $50,000 cash for the land owned by Hall. At what amount should Madden record the land acquired in the exchange?

a. $150,000
b. $160,000
c. $190,000
d. $200,000   (11/83, PI, #16, amended, 9010)

18. Dahl Co. traded a delivery van and $5,000 cash for a newer van owned by West Corp. The following information relates to the values of the vans on the exchange date:

	Carrying value	Fair value
Old van	$30,000	$45,000
New van	40,000	50,000

Dahl's income tax rate is 30%. What amounts should Dahl report as gain on exchange of the vans?

a. $15,000
b. $ 1,000
c. $ 700
d. $0   (11/92, PI, #46, 3279)

19. On December 31, 2003, Vey Co. traded equipment with an original cost of $100,000 and accumulated depreciation of $40,000 for similar productive equipment with a fair value of $120,000. In addition, Vey received $30,000 cash in connection with this exchange. What should be Vey's carrying amount for the equipment received at December 31, 2003?

a. $ 90,000
b. $ 60,000
c. $ 48,000
d. $120,000   (5/92, PI, #19, amended, 2586)

20. Yola Co. and Zaro Co. are fuel oil distributors. To facilitate the delivery of oil to their customers, Yola and Zaro exchanged ownership of 1,200 barrels of oil without physically moving the oil. Yola paid Zaro $30,000 to compensate for a difference in the grade of oil. On the date of the exchange, cost and market values of the oil were as follows:

	Yola Co.	Zaro Co.
Cost	$100,000	$126,000
Market values	120,000	150,000

In Zaro's income statement, what amount of gain should be reported from the exchange of the oil?

a. $0
b. $ 4,800
c. $24,000
d. $30,000   (5/92, PII, #11, 2643)

21. On July 1, 1991, Balt Co. exchanged a truck for 25 shares of Ace Corp.'s common stock. On that date, the truck's carrying amount was $2,500, and its fair value was $3,000. Also, the book value of Ace's stock was $60 per share. On December 31, 1991, Ace had 250 shares of common stock outstanding and its book value per share was $50. What amount should Balt report in its December 31, 1991 balance sheet as investment in Ace?

a. $3,000
b. $2,500
c. $1,500
d. $1,250   (11/92, PI, #20, 3253)

22.   Vik Auto and King Clothier exchanged goods, held for resale, with equal fair values. Each will use the other's goods to promote their own products. The retail price of the car that Vik gave up is less than the retail price of the clothes received. What profit should Vik recognize for the nonmonetary exchange?
a.   A profit is **not** recognized.
b.   A profit equal to the difference between the retail prices of the clothes received and the car.
c.   A profit equal to the difference between the retail price and the cost of the car.
d.   A profit equal to the difference between the fair value and the cost of the car.

(11/92, Theory, #24, 3457)

23.   An entity disposes of a nonmonetary asset in a nonreciprocal transfer. A gain or loss should be recognized on the disposition of the asset when the fair value of the asset transferred is determinable and the nonreciprocal transfer is to

	Another entity	A stockholder of the entity
a.	No	Yes
b.	No	No
c.	Yes	No
d.	Yes	Yes

(11/88, Theory, #36, 9011)

24.   Derby Co. incurred costs to modify its building and to rearrange its production line. As a result, an overall reduction in production costs is expected. However, the modifications did not increase the building's market value, and the rearrangement did not extend the production line's life. Should the building modification costs be capitalized?

	Building modification costs	Production line rearrangement costs
a.	Yes	No
b.	Yes	Yes
c.	No	No
d.	No	Yes

(5/92, Theory, #11, 2704)

25.   During 1996, Yvo Corp. installed a production assembly line to manufacture furniture. In 1997, Yvo purchased a new machine and rearranged the assembly line to install this machine. The rearrangement did not increase the estimated useful life of the assembly line, but it did result in significantly more efficient production. The following expenditures were incurred in connection with this project:

Machine	$75,000
Labor to install machine	14,000
Parts added in rearranging the assembly line to provide future benefits	40,000
Labor and overhead to rearrange the assembly line	18,000

What amount of the above expenditures should be capitalized in 1997?
a. $147,000
b. $107,000
c. $ 89,000
d. $ 75,000   (11/90, PII, #4, amended, 0934)

26.   On June 18, 1997, Dell Printing Co. incurred the following costs for one of its printing presses:

Purchase of collating and stapling attachment	$84,000
Installation of attachment	36,000
Replacement parts for overhaul of press	26,000
Labor and overhead in connection with overhaul	14,000

The overhaul resulted in a significant increase in production. Neither the attachment nor the overhaul increased the estimated useful life of the press. What amount of the above costs should be capitalized?
a. $0
b. $ 84,000
c. $120,000
d. $160,000   (5/90, PI, #16, amended, 0940)

27.   A building suffered uninsured water and related damage. The damaged portion of the building was refurbished with upgraded materials. The cost and related accumulated depreciation of the damaged portion are identifiable. To account for these events, the owner should
a.   Capitalize the cost of refurbishing and record a loss in the current period equal to the carrying amount of the damaged portion of the building.
b.   Capitalize the cost of refurbishing by adding the cost to the carrying amount of the building.
c.   Record a loss in the current period equal to the cost of refurbishing and continue to depreciate the original cost of the building.
d.   Record a loss in the current period equal to the sum of the cost of refurbishing and the carrying amount of the damaged portion of the building.

(11/90, Theory, #13, 1794)

28. On January 2, 1998, Parke Corp. replaced its boiler with a more efficient one. The following information was available on that date:

Purchase price of new boiler	$60,000
Carrying amount of old boiler	5,000
Fair value of old boiler	2,000
Installation cost of new boiler	8,000

The old boiler was sold for $2,000. What amount should Parke capitalize as the cost of the new boiler?
a. $68,000
b. $66,000
c. $63,000
d. $60,000   (5/89, PI, #25, amended, 0943)

29. An expenditure to install an improved electrical system is a

	Capital expenditure	Revenue expenditure
a.	No	Yes
b.	No	No
c.	Yes	No
d.	Yes	Yes

(5/88, Theory, #8, 1832)

30. On January 2, 1993, Lem Corp. bought machinery under a contract that required a down payment of $10,000, plus 24 monthly payments of $5,000 each, for total cash payments of $130,000. The cash equivalent price of the machinery was $110,000. The machinery has an estimated useful life of 10 years and estimated salvage value of $5,000. Lem uses straight-line depreciation. In its 1993 income statement, what amount should Lem report as depreciation for this machinery?
a. $10,500
b. $11,000
c. $12,500
d. $13,000   (5/94, FAR, #45, 4860)

31. On January 1, 1993, Crater Inc. purchased equipment having an estimated salvage value equal to 20% of its original cost at the end of a 10-year life. The equipment was sold December 31, 1997, for 50% of its original cost. If the equipment's disposition resulted in a reported loss, which of the following depreciation methods did Crater use?
a. Double-declining-balance
b. Sum-of-the-years'-digits
c. Straight-line
d. Composite (5/93, Theory, #27, amended, 4215)

32. Which of the following uses the straight-line depreciation method?

	Group depreciation	Composite depreciation
a.	No	No
b.	Yes	No
c.	Yes	Yes
d.	No	Yes

(5/93, Theory, #28, 4216)

33. A depreciable asset has an estimated 15% salvage value. At the end of its estimated useful life, the accumulated depreciation would equal the original cost of the asset under which of the following depreciation methods?

	Straight-line	Productive output
a.	Yes	No
b.	Yes	Yes
c.	No	Yes
d.	No	No

(5/89, Theory, #4, 9012)

34. Spiro Corp. uses the sum-of-the-years'-digits method to depreciate equipment purchased in January 1996 for $20,000. The estimated salvage value of the equipment is $2,000 and the estimated useful life is four years. What should Spiro report as the asset's carrying amount as of December 31, 1998?
a. $1,800
b. $2,000
c. $3,800
d. $4,500   (1999, FAR, #7, 6776)

35. On April 1, 1995, Kew Co. purchased new machinery for $300,000. The machinery has an estimated useful life of five years, and depreciation is computed by the sum-of-the-years'-digits method. The accumulated depreciation on this machinery at March 31, 1997 should be
a. $192,000.
b. $180,000.
c. $120,000.
d. $100,000.   (5/90, PI, #17, amended, 0941)

36. A machine with a 5-year estimated useful life and an estimated 10% salvage value was acquired on January 1, 1994. On December 31, 1997, accumulated depreciation, using the sum-of-the-years'-digits method, would be
a. (Original cost less salvage value) multiplied by 1/15.
b. (Original cost less salvage value) multiplied by 14/15.
c. Original cost multiplied by 14/15.
d. Original cost multiplied by 1/15.
(5/92, Theory, #16, amended, 2709)

37. The graph below depicts three depreciation expense patterns over time.

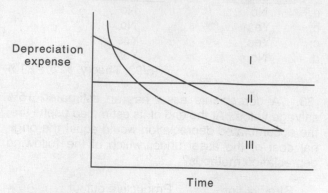

Which depreciation expense pattern corresponds to the sum-of-the-years'-digits method and which corresponds to the double-declining-balance method?

	Sum-of-the-years'-digits	Double-declining-balance
a.	III	II
b.	II	I
c.	I	III
d.	II	III

(11/90, Theory, #14, 9013)

38. Turtle Co. purchased equipment on January 2, 1991, for $50,000. The equipment had an estimated five-year service life. Turtle's policy for five-year assets is to use the 200% double-declining depreciation method for the first two years of the asset's life, and then switch to the straight-line depreciation method. In its December 31, 1993 balance sheet, what amount should Turtle report as accumulated depreciation for equipment?
a. $30,000
b. $38,000
c. $39,200
d. $42,000   (5/94, FAR, #18, 4833)

39. South Co. purchased a machine that was installed and placed in service on January 1, 1990, at a cost of $240,000. Salvage value was estimated at $40,000. The machine is being depreciated over 10 years by the double-declining-balance method. For the year ended December 31, 1991, what amount should South report as depreciation expense?
a. $48,000
b. $38,400
c. $32,000
d. $21,600   (5/92, PI, #50, 2621)

40. Rye Co. purchased a machine with a four-year estimated useful life and an estimated 10% salvage value for $80,000 on January 1, 1992. In its income statement, what would Rye report as the depreciation expense for 1994 using the double-declining-balance method?
a. $ 9,000
b. $10,000
c. $18,000
d. $20,000   (5/95, FAR, #37, 5573)

41. A fixed asset with a five-year estimated useful life and no residual value is sold at the end of the second year of its useful life. How would using the sum-of-the-years'-digits method of depreciation instead of the double-declining-balance method of depreciation affect a gain or loss on the sale of the fixed asset?

	Gain	Loss
a.	Decrease	Decrease
b.	Decrease	Increase
c.	Increase	Decrease
d.	Increase	Increase

(5/90, Theory, #20, 1808)

42. A machine with a four-year estimated useful life and an estimated 15 percent salvage value was acquired on January 1. Would depreciation expense using the sum-of-the-years'-digits method of depreciation be higher or lower than depreciation expense using the double-declining-balance method of depreciation in the first and second years?

	First year	Second year
a.	Higher	Higher
b.	Higher	Lower
c.	Lower	Higher
d.	Lower	Lower

(5/84, Theory, #10, 9014)

43. Depreciation is computed on the original cost less estimated salvage value under which of the following depreciation methods?

	Double-declining-balance	Productive output
a.	No	No
b.	No	Yes
c.	Yes	Yes
d.	Yes	No

(5/88, Theory, #25, 1842)

44. What factor must be present to use the units-of-production (activity) method of depreciation?
a. Total units to be produced can be estimated.
b. Production is constant over the life of the asset.
c. Repair costs increase with use.
d. Obsolescence is expected.

(5/92, Theory, #15, 2708)

45. Which of the following utilizes the straight-line depreciation method?

	Composite depreciation	Group depreciation
a.	Yes	Yes
b.	Yes	No
c.	No	Yes
d.	No	No

(11/86, Theory, #27, 1872)

46. When equipment is retired, accumulated depreciation is debited for the original cost less any residual recovery under which of the following depreciation methods?

	Composite depreciation	Group depreciation
a.	No	No
b.	No	Yes
c.	Yes	No
d.	Yes	Yes

(11/84, Theory, #15, 1888)

47. A company using the composite depreciation method for its fleet of trucks, cars, and campers retired one of its trucks and received cash from a salvage company. The net carrying amount of these composite asset accounts would be decreased by the
a. Cash proceeds received and original cost of the truck.
b. Cash proceeds received.
c. Original cost of the truck less the cash proceeds.
d. Original cost of the truck. (5/88, Theory, #9, 1833)

48. In January 1994, Vorst Co. purchased a mineral mine for $2,640,000 with removable ore estimated at 1,200,000 tons. After it has extracted all the ore, Vorst will be required by law to restore the land to its original condition at an estimated cost of $180,000. Vorst believes it will be able to sell the property afterwards for $300,000. During 1994, Vorst incurred $360,000 of development costs preparing the mine for production and removed and sold 60,000 tons of ore. In its 1994 income statement, what amount should Vorst report as depletion?
a. $135,000
b. $144,000
c. $150,000
d. $159,000   (5/95, FAR, #36, 5572)

49. Land was purchased to be used as the site for the construction of a plant. A building on the property was sold and removed by the buyer so that construction on the plant could begin. The proceeds from the sale of the building should be

a. Netted against the costs to clear the land and expensed as incurred.
b. Netted against the costs to clear the land and amortized over the life of the plant.
c. Deducted from the cost of the land.
d. Classified as other income.

(5/92, Theory, #12, 2705)

50. Weir Co. uses straight-line depreciation for its property, plant, and equipment, which, stated at cost, consisted of the following:

	12/31/92	12/31/91
Land	$ 25,000	$ 25,000
Buildings	195,000	195,000
Machinery and equipment	695,000	650,000
	915,000	870,000
Less: Accumulated depreciation	(400,000)	(370,000)
	$ 515,000	$ 500,000

Weir's depreciation expense for 1992 and 1991 was $55,000 and $50,000, respectively. What amount was debited to accumulated depreciation during 1992 because of property, plant, and equipment retirements?
a. $40,000
b. $25,000
c. $20,000
d. $10,000   (11/93, PI, #23, 4392)

51. On December 31, 1990, a building owned by Carr Inc. was destroyed by fire. Carr paid $12,000 for removal and clean-up costs. The building had a book value of $250,000 and a fair value of $280,000 on December 31, 1990. What amount should Carr use to determine the gain or loss on this involuntary conversion?
a. $250,000
b. $262,000
c. $280,000
d. $292,000   (5/91, PI, #27, 0933)

52. On July 1, 1991, one of Rudd Co.'s delivery vans was destroyed in an accident. On that date, the van's carrying amount was $2,500. On July 15, 1991, Rudd received and recorded a $700 invoice for a new engine installed in the van in May 1991, and another $500 invoice for various repairs. In August, Rudd received $3,500 under its insurance policy on the van, which it plans to use to replace the van. What amount should Rudd report as gain (loss) on disposal of the van in its 1991 income statement?
a. $1,000
b. $ 300
c. $0
d. $ (200)   (5/92, PI, #45, 2616)

53. Ocean Corp.'s comprehensive insurance policy allows its assets to be replaced at current value. The policy has a $50,000 deductible clause. One of Ocean's waterfront warehouses was destroyed in a winter storm. Such storms occur approximately every four years. Ocean incurred $20,000 of costs in dismantling the warehouse and plans to replace it. The following data relate to the warehouse:

Current carrying amount	$ 300,000
Replacement cost	1,100,000

What amount of gain should Ocean report as a separate component of income before extraordinary items?
a. $1,030,000
b. $ 780,000
c. $ 730,000
d. $0

(5/92, PI, #46, 2617)

54. In January 1995, Winn Corp. purchased equipment at a cost of $500,000. The equipment had an estimated salvage value of $100,000, an estimated 8-year useful life, and was being depreciated by the straight-line method. Two years later, it became apparent to Winn that this equipment suffered a permanent impairment of value. In January 1997, management determined the carrying amount should be only $175,000, with a 2-year remaining useful life, and the salvage value should be reduced to $25,000. In Winn's December 31, 1997 balance sheet, the equipment should be reported at a carrying amount of
a. $350,000.
b. $175,000.
c. $150,000.
d. $100,000.

(5/91, PI, #26, amended, 0932)

55. A state government condemned Cory Co.'s parcel of real estate. Cory will receive $750,000 for this property, which has a carrying amount of $575,000. Cory incurred the following costs as a result of the condemnation:

Appraisal fees to support a $750,000 value	$2,500
Attorney fees for the closing with the state	3,500
Attorney fees to review contract to acquire replacement property	3,000
Title insurance on replacement property	4,000

What amount of cost should Cory use to determine the gain on the condemnation?
a. $581,000
b. $582,000
c. $584,000
d. $588,000

(11/91, PI, #19, 2407)

56. Lano Corp.'s forest land was condemned for use as a national park. Compensation for the condemnation exceeded the forest land's carrying amount. Lano purchased similar, but larger, replacement forest land for an amount greater than the condemnation award. As a result of the condemnation and replacement, what is the net effect on the carrying amount of forest land reported in Lano's balance sheet?
a. The amount is increased by the excess of the replacement forest land's cost over the condemned forest land's carrying amount.
b. The amount is increased by the excess of the replacement forest land's cost over the condemnation award.
c. The amount is increased by the excess of the condemnation award over the condemned forest land's carrying amount.
d. No effect, because the condemned forest land's carrying amount is used as the replacement forest land's carrying amount.

(5/92, Theory, #13, 2706)

57. On January 2, 1994, Reed Co. purchased a machine for $800,000 and established an annual depreciation charge of $100,000 over an eight-year life. During 1996, after issuing its 1995 financial statements, Reed concluded that: (1) the machine suffered permanent impairment of its operational value, and (2) $200,000 is a reasonable estimate of the amount expected to be recovered through use of the machine for the period January 1, 1997 through December 31, 2001. In Reed's December 31, 1997 balance sheet, the machine should be reported at a carrying amount of
a. $0.
b. $100,000.
c. $160,000.
d. $400,000.

(5/93, PI, #24, amended, 4066)

OTHER OBJECTIVE FORMAT QUESTIONS

PROBLEM 4-2 (15 to 20 minutes)

During 1992, Sloan Inc. began a project to construct new corporate headquarters. Sloan purchased land with an existing building for $750,000. The land was valued at $700,000 and the building at $50,000.

Sloan planned to demolish the building and construct a new office building on the site. **ITEMS 1 THROUGH 8** represent various expenditures by Sloan for this project.

REQUIRED:

For each expenditure in items **1 THROUGH 8**, select from the list below the appropriate accounting treatment.

L. Classify as land and do not depreciate.
B. Classify as building and depreciate.
E. Expense.

ITEMS TO BE ANSWERED:

1. Purchase of land for $700,000.
2. Interest of $147,000 on construction financing incurred after completion of construction.
3. Interest of $186,000 on construction financing paid during construction.
4. Purchase of building for $50,000.
5. $18,500 payment of delinquent real estate taxes assumed by Sloan on purchase.
6. $12,000 liability insurance premium during the construction period.
7. $65,000 cost of razing existing building.
8. Moving costs of $136,000.

(11/92, PI, #4(a), 3292-3299)

PROBLEM 4-3 (15 to 25 minutes)

This questions consists of 14 items. Select the **best** answer for each item.

ITEMS 1 THROUGH 6 represent expenditures for goods held for resale and equipment.

REQUIRED:

FOR ITEMS 1 THROUGH 6, determine for each item whether the expenditure should be capitalized (C) or expensed as a period cost (E).

1. Freight charges paid for goods held for resale.
2. In-transit insurance on goods held for resale purchased F.O.B. shipping point.
3. Interest on note payable for goods held for resale.
4. Installation of equipment.
5. Testing of newly-purchased equipment.
6. Cost of current year service contract on equipment.

ITEMS 7 THROUGH 10 are based on the following 1993 transactions:

- Link Co. purchased an office building and the land on which it is located by paying $800,000 cash and assuming an existing mortgage of

$200,000. The property is assessed at $960,000 for realty tax purposes, of which 60% is allocated to the building.

- Link leased construction equipment under a 7-year capital lease requiring annual year-end payments of $100,000. Link's incremental borrowing rate is 9%, while the lessor's implicit rate, which is not known to Link, is 8%. Present value factors for an ordinary annuity for seven periods are 5.21 at 8% and 5.03 at 9%. Fair value of the equipment is $515,000.

- Link paid $50,000 and gave a plot of undeveloped land with a carrying amount of $320,000 and a fair value of $450,000 to Club Co. in exchange for a plot of undeveloped land with a fair value of $500,000. The land was carried on Club's books at $350,000.

REQUIRED:

FOR ITEMS 7 THROUGH 10, calculate the amount to be recorded for each item.

7. Building
8. Leased equipment
9. Land received from Club on Link's books
10. Land received from Link on Club's books

ITEMS 11 THROUGH 14 are based on the following information:

On January 2, 1992, Half Inc. purchased a manufacturing machine for $864,000. The machine has an eight-year estimated life and a $144,000 estimated salvage value. Half expects to manufacture 1,800,000 units over the life of the machine. During 1993, Half manufactured 300,000 units.

REQUIRED:

ITEMS 11 THROUGH 14 represent various depreciation methods. For each item, calculate depreciation expense for 1993 (the second year of ownership) for the machine described above under the method listed.

11. Straight-line
12. Double-declining-balance
13. Sum-of-the-years'-digits
14. Units of production   (11/94, FAR #2, 5321-5334)

ESSAY QUESTION

ESSAY 4-4 (15 to 25 minutes)

Portland Co. uses the straight-line depreciation method for depreciable assets. All assets are depreciated individually except manufacturing machinery, which is depreciated by the composite method.

During the year, Portland exchanged a delivery truck with Maine Co. for a larger delivery truck. It paid cash equal to 10% of the larger truck's value.

REQUIRED:

a. What factors should have influenced Portland's selection of the straight-line depreciation method?

b. How should Portland account for and report the truck exchange transaction?

c. 1. What benefits should Portland derive from using the composite method rather than the individual basis for manufacturing machinery?

2. How should Portland have calculated the manufacturing machinery's annual depreciation expense in its first year of operation?

(11/91, Theory, #3, 6189)

SOLUTION 4-1 MULTIPLE CHOICE ANSWERS

ACQUISITION COST

1. (b) Land must be recorded at its acquisition cost. Generally, acquisition cost is defined as the cash price, or its equivalent, plus all other costs reasonably necessary to make it ready for its intended use. Such additional costs include demolition of an old building, less any scrap proceeds received. Land is capitalized as follows:

Purchase price of land	$ 100,000
Add: Cost to raze old building	50,000
Less: Proceeds from sale of scrap	(10,000)
Capitalized value of land	$ 140,000

2. (b) The amount of interest that may be capitalized is based on the weighted-average amount of accumulated expenditures. The weighted-average amount of accumulated expenditures applies the avoidable interest concept. This concept limits the amount of interest to be capitalized to the lower of the actual interest cost incurred during the period or avoidable interest. Avoidable interest is the amount of interest cost incurred during the period that theoretically could have been avoided if expenditures for the asset had not been made.

3. (a) The acquisition cost of a machine for use in a company's manufacturing operations includes all costs reasonably necessary to bring the asset to the location where it is to be used and to make it ready for its intended use, including insurance while in-transit and test runs.

4. (b) The party receiving monetary consideration in an exchange of similar nonmonetary assets accounts for the transaction as a part sale-part exchange. The sale portion of the book value of the asset surrendered is determined by the proportion of the monetary consideration received to the fair value of the total consideration received. A gain should be recorded on this portion, if applicable, because the earnings process is deemed to have culminated for this portion of the asset sold. The remainder of any gain experienced is deferred. In the case of a loss, the full amount of the loss is recognized.

5. (c) The cost of demolishing the old building (net of any scrap proceeds) is a reasonable and necessary cost to get the land ready for its intended use. The amounts to be reported as the cost of land and cost of building are determined as follows:

Demolition of old building on site	$ 5,000
Purchase price of land	60,000
Legal fees for contracts to purchase land	2,000
Sale of scrap from old building	(3,000)
Cost of land	$ 64,000
Architect's fees	$ 8,000
Construction cost of new building	350,000
Cost of building	$ 358,000

6. (b) The exchange of similar productive assets does not result in the culmination of an earnings process (APB 29, par. 21). The extent of cash received signifies the portion of the exchanged asset that has been sold and thus the amount of gain that can be recognized. The gain Amble recognizes on the exchange is computed as follows:

Cash received	$ 4,000
Fair value of truck received	16,000
Total fair value received	20,000
Carrying amount of truck exchanged	(12,000)
Gain realized on exchange	8,000
Extent earnings process culminated:	
Cash/Total fair value received ($4,000/$20,000)	x 20%
Gain recognized on exchange	$ 1,600

The recorded cost of the truck acquired in the exchange is computed as follows:

Fair value of truck received	$ 16,000
Unrecognized gain on exchange ($8,000 – $1,600)	(6,400)
Recorded cost of truck acquired	$ 9,600

7. (c) SFAS 34 requires the capitalization of interest cost incurred during the construction of most assets having an extended construction period. Capitalized interest is included in the cost of the asset in the same manner as any other construction cost; it is then written off over the life of the asset as part of the periodic depreciation charges.

8. (b) The amount of interest cost to be capitalized is that portion of interest cost incurred during the asset's acquisition period that theoretically could have been avoided if expenditures for the asset had not been made. In this question, the amount of interest cost to be capitalized in 1997 is determined by applying the interest rate on the specific new borrowing to the average accumulated expenditures for the asset in 1996 and 1997 (SFAS 34).

9. (c) The amount of interest to be capitalized in accordance with SFAS 34 is determined by applying an interest rate to the average amount of accumulated expenditures for the asset during the period. The interest rate to be used is the rate on new borrowings which are specifically associated with the acquisition of the new asset, or a weighted average of the interest rates on all debt outstanding during the period (SFAS 34, par. 13). The amount of interest thus determined is *not* reduced or in any way offset by interest income earned during the construction period (*FASB Technical Bulletin 81-5*).

Average expenditure during year ($6,000,000 ÷ 2)	$3,000,000
Interest (capitalization) rate	x .15
Capitalized interest	$ 450,000

10. (b) The contribution of land by a governmental unit to an enterprise for industrial use is an example of a nonreciprocal transfer. A nonmonetary asset received in a nonreciprocal transfer should be recorded at the fair value of the asset received (APB 29, par. 18). The corresponding credit for a corporation is "Additional Paid-In Capital—Donated Assets." Donated assets should *not* be recorded as income or gain or added to retained earnings when received from governmental entities. Assets donated by entities other than governmental units should be included in revenue in the period of receipt (SFAS 116).

11. (d) When several dissimilar assets are purchased for a lump sum, the amount paid should be allocated to each asset on the basis of its relative fair value.

$$\text{Land} = (\text{Total cost of assets}) \times \frac{\text{FMV of land}}{\text{Total FMV}}$$

$$\text{Land} = (\$540,000) \times \frac{\$200,000}{\$500,000} = \$216,000$$

12. (c) This transaction is an exchange of similar productive assets. Beam has a $1,000 gain on the exchange because the inventory it surrendered has a fair value in excess of its carrying amount (i.e., $21,000 – $20,000). However, a gain on the exchange of similar productive assets by a party paying monetary consideration cannot be recognized. Rather, Beam would record the inventory received at the amount of boot paid, plus the carrying amount of the inventory surrendered (i.e., $1,000 + $20,000). It is important to note that any loss realized in a similar exchange would be recognized.

13. (d) The acquisition cost of the machine includes all of the costs incurred to get it ready for its intended use. Thus, the costs incurred in shipping, installing, and testing the machine are capitalized and added to its purchase price, resulting in an acquisition cost for the machine of $138,000 ($126,000 + $3,000 + $4,000 + $5,000).

14. (d) According to SFAS 34, interest cost during construction is to be capitalized on assets that are constructed for an enterprise's own use or assets intended for sale or lease that are constructed as discrete projects. However, interest cost shall not be capitalized for inventories that are routinely manufactured or otherwise produced in large quantities on a repetitive basis. Once the constructed assets are completed, all interest should be expensed as incurred. In the question at hand, it is not clear, but it is assumed that the machinery constructed for sale is routinely manufactured in large quantities on a repetitive basis. Therefore, the interest during construction should be capitalized only for the equipment constructed for Bay's own use. The interest incurred during construction of the inventory items should be expensed. The interest incurred after completion should be expensed on both groups of equipment.

15. (a) The exchange of similar assets should be accounted for under APB 29, *Accounting for Nonmonetary Transactions*. The player contract acquired should be recorded at $550,000, the carrying amount of the player contract exchanged ($500,000) plus the cash paid ($50,000). The $700,000 fair value of the contract received is

greater than the contract plus the cash given up ($550,000), indicating a gain; however, the party paying additional monetary consideration does not record a gain and records the asset received at the monetary consideration paid plus the book value of the asset surrendered.

16. (c)   An exchange of similar productive assets is described in APB 29 as an exchange that does not culminate an earning process. No gain is to be recognized by the party who gives boot (May) in an exchange of similar productive assets. The recipient of boot in an exchange of similar productive assets (Sty) should recognize a realized gain only to the extent that the amount of cash exceeds a proportionate share of the carrying amount of the asset surrendered.

17. (a)   In the exchange of similar assets when additional monetary consideration is paid, the asset received is recorded at the carrying amount of the asset surrendered plus the additional monetary consideration paid, not to exceed the fair value of the asset received.

Carrying amount of asset surrendered	$100,000
Additional consideration (cash)	50,000
Amount to record acquired land	$150,000

18. (d)   Dahl is giving boot in an exchange of similar productive assets. Although Dahl has a realized gain on its old van of $15,000 (i.e., $45,000 – 30,000), no portion of a realized gain on the exchange of similar productive assets by a party *paying* monetary consideration is recognized. Dahl should record the new van at the amount of the boot paid plus the carrying amount of the old van given in the exchange (i.e., $5,000 + $30,000 = $35,000).

19. (c)   In the exchange of similar assets, the party receiving additional monetary consideration accounts for the transaction as a part sale-part exchange, recognizing only a portion of the gain and recording the cost of the new equipment at its fair value less the unrecognized portion of the gain, as follows:

Cash received		$ 30,000
Fair value of equipment received		120,000
Total fair value received		150,000
Carrying amount of equipment exchanged:		
Cost	$100,000	
Accumulated depreciation	(40,000)	(60,000)
Gain realized on exchange		90,000
Extent earnings process culminated:		
Cash	$ 30,000	
Total fair value received	$150,000 x	20%
Gain recognized on exchange		$ 18,000

Fair value of equipment acquired	$120,000
Unrecognized gain ($90,000 – $18,000)	(72,000)
Recorded cost of equipment acquired	$ 48,000

The exchange would be recorded as follows:

Cash	30,000	
New Equipment	48,000	
Accumulated Depreciation	40,000	
Old Equipment		100,000
Gain on Exchange		18,000

20. (b)   The exchange of a product held for sale in the ordinary course of business for a product to be sold in the same line of business to facilitate sales to customers other than parties to the exchange does not result in the culmination of an earnings process (APB 29, par. 21). Only to the extent cash has been received has a portion of the asset exchanged been sold and a gain can be recognized. The fair value of the asset acquired is reduced by the portion of the gain realized which is not recognized. The gain recognized on the exchange is determined, then the recorded cost of the inventory acquired can be determined.

Cash received		$ 30,000
Fair value of inventory received		120,000
Total fair value received		150,000
Carrying amount of inventory exchanged		(126,000)
Gain realized on exchange		24,000
Extent earnings process culminated:		
Cash	$ 30,000	
Total fair value received	$150,000 x	20%
Gain recognized on exchange		$ 4,800

Fair value of inventory acquired	$ 120,000
Unrecognized gain ($24,000 – $4,800)	(19,200)
Recorded cost of inventory acquired	$ 100,800

21. (a)   Balt's exchange of its truck for the shares of Ace's common stock is a dissimilar nonmonetary exchange. Therefore, Balt should record its investment in Ace at the fair value of the truck given or the fair value of the shares acquired, whichever is more clearly evident. The fair value of the truck given should be used because the fair value of the shares acquired is not given.

22. (d)   This transaction is a dissimilar nonmonetary exchange because it is an exchange of goods held for resale (a car) for dissimilar property (clothing) as a means of selling the goods to customers. Therefore, accounting for the exchange should be based on the fair values of the assets involved, which is the same basis as that used in monetary exchanges, and a gain or loss should be recognized equal to the difference between the fair value and carrying amount of the asset relinquished (APB 29, par. 18). Vik should record the clothes received at their fair value and recognize a gain

equal to the difference between the fair value and the cost of the relinquished car.

23. (d) Per APB 29, par. 18, "In general, accounting for nonmonetary transactions should be based on the fair values of the assets (or services) involved which is the same basis as that used in monetary transactions. A transfer of a nonmonetary

asset to a stockholder or to another entity in a non-reciprocal transfer should be recorded at the fair value of the asset transferred, and a gain or loss should be recognized on the disposition of the asset."

Cost Incurred Subsequent to Acquisition

24. (b) Both the building modification costs and the production line rearrangement costs should be capitalized because they have resulted in an overall reduction of production costs, the benefits of which extend beyond the current period.

25. (a) All of the expenditures related to the purchase of the new machine ($75,000 + $14,000) and the rearrangement of the assembly line to install this machine ($40,000 + $18,000) should be capitalized. The costs associated with the rearrangement of the assembly line are capitalized because the rearrangement has resulted in significantly more efficient production, the benefits of which extend beyond the current period.

26. (d) The collating and stapling attachment is an addition to the printing press and so its cost (including installation cost) should be capitalized. The overhaul resulted in a significant increase in the productivity of the printing press; therefore, its cost (replacement parts, labor and overhead) should also be capitalized. The total cost capitalized is $160,000 (i.e., $84,000 + $36,000 + $26,000 + $14,000).

27. (a) The damaged portion of the building was refurbished with upgraded materials which indicates that a "betterment" is involved. There are future benefits due to the refurbishing expenditures; thus, they should be capitalized. The cost and related accumulated depreciation of the damaged portion of the building are identifiable so they should be removed from the books (with a resulting debit to "loss" for the difference) because this portion of the building has been replaced and upgraded.

28. (a) The replacement of the boiler with a more efficient boiler is a betterment (or improvement) as it is the substitution of a better asset for an existing asset. The amounts associated with the old boiler do *not* affect the acquisition cost of the new boiler:

Purchase price	$60,000
Plus: Installation cost	8,000
Acquisition cost	$68,000

29. (c) The expenditure to install an improved electrical system represents a betterment (or improvement); that is, the substitution of a better asset for an existing asset. The expenditure increases the service potential of the electrical system. Because this increased service potential is a benefit that will be enjoyed throughout the life of the electrical system, the expenditure should be capitalized and depreciated over the life of the system. Revenue expenditures, on the other hand, are recurring expenditures that do not add to the service potential of a plant asset; they serve merely to maintain a given level of services. Revenue expenditures should be expensed when incurred.

Straight-Line Depreciation

30. (a) Assets are to be recorded at their acquisition cost. Acquisition cost is the cash price, or its equivalent. Therefore, the yearly depreciation of the machinery is computed as follows:

$$\frac{\$110,000 - 5,000}{10 \text{ years}} = \$10,500/\text{year}$$

31. (c) The carrying amount of the equipment at the date of sale is computed by subtracting the accumulated depreciation on the equipment from the cost of the equipment. Under the straight-line method, the accumulated depreciation on the equipment at the date of sale is equal to 40% of the original cost of the equipment [i.e., (100% − 20%) x 1/10 x 5]. Thus, under the straight-line method, the carrying amount of the equipment at the date of sale is 60% (i.e., 100% − 40%) of the original cost of the equipment. Since the equipment was sold for only 50% of its original cost, use of the straight-line depreciation method would have resulted in a loss being recognized on the sale equal to 10% (i.e., 60% − 50%) of the original cost of the equipment.

32. (c) The composite depreciation method refers to the depreciation of a collection of assets that are dissimilar. The group depreciation method refers to the depreciation of a collection of assets that are similar in nature. From an accounting standpoint, there is no distinction between the two methods. The same procedures are followed for both, and both utilize the straight-line depreciation method.

33. **(d)** At the end of the estimated useful life of a depreciable plant asset, the amount of accumulated depreciation would equal the depreciable base of the plant asset (i.e., its acquisition cost less any estimated salvage value), regardless of the depreciation method used.

SUM-OF-THE-YEARS'-DIGITS

34. **(c)** The asset's carrying amount is calculated as follows:

Cost		$ 20,000
Depreciation:		
1996 [(4/10)($20,000 – 2,000)]	$7,200	
1997 [(3/10)($20,000 – 2,000)]	5,400	
1998 [(2/10)($20,000 – 2,000)]	3,600	(16,200)
Carrying amount 12/31/98		$ 3,800

35. **(b)** The accumulated depreciation on the machinery at 3/31/90 is computed below:

Depreciation recognized through 3/31/97:	
Year 1: 4/1/95-3/31/96 [5/15 x ($300,000 – $0)]	$ 100,000
Year 2: 4/1/96-3/31/97 [4/15 x ($300,000 – $0)]	80,000
Accumulated depreciation, 3/31/97	$ 180,000

36. **(b)** Since the machine has a five-year estimated useful life, the amount to be depreciated each year would be computed as follows:

Year	Depreciation fraction	x	Depreciable base
1—1994	5/15		Cost less salvage value
2—1995	4/15		Cost less salvage value
3—1996	3/15		Cost less salvage value
4—1997	2/15		Cost less salvage value
5—1998	1/15		Cost less salvage value
15			

On December 31, 1997, four years of depreciation would have been recorded. The accumulated depreciation would be 14/15 (i.e., 5/15 + 4/15 + 3/15 + 2/15) multiplied by the machine's depreciable base (i.e., cost less salvage value).

37. **(d)** The depreciation pattern corresponding to the sum-of-the-years'-digits (SYD) method is the straight sloping line (II) and the pattern corresponding to the double-declining-balance (DDB) method is the curved line (III). The straight line parallel with the horizontal axis describes the pattern of the straight-line (SL) method of depreciation because the SL method results in a constant amount of depreciation each period. The line for the pattern of the SYD method is a straight sloping line because the method results in a decreasing depreciation charge based on a decreasing fraction of depreciable cost where each fraction has the same denominator (sum of the years). The line for the pattern of the DDB method will be a curved sloping line because that type of method employs a constant percentage multiplied by a decreasing balance to obtain a decreasing charge for depreciation.

DOUBLE-DECLINING-BALANCE

38. **(b)** In its December 31, 1993 balance sheet, Turtle should report $32,000 + $6,000 = $38,000 as accumulated depreciation. Double-declining-balance is computed using twice the straight-line rate, which in this case is 40% (1/5 = .20 x 2 = .40). Depreciation for the first two years is computed as follows:

	Book value beginning of year	Rate	Depreciation expense	Accumulated depreciation	Book value end of year
1991	$50,000	40%	$20,000	$20,000	$30,000
1992	30,000	40%	12,000	32,000	18,000

In 1993, depreciation is computed by dividing the remaining book value of $18,000 by the remaining life of 3 years = $6,000.

39. **(b)** Under the double-declining-balance method of depreciation, a rate equal to twice the straight-line rate (e.g., 2 x 10%) is applied against the remaining carrying amount of the plant asset (i.e., Cost – Accumulated depreciation). Salvage value is ignored, except that the plant asset cannot be depreciated below this amount.

1990 Depreciation expense [($240,000 – $0) x 20%]	$48,000
1991 Depreciation expense [($240,000 – $48,000) x 20%]	$38,400

40. **(b)** Under the double-declining-balance method of depreciation, the annual depreciation charge is computed by multiplying the carrying amount of the plant asset (i.e., Cost minus Accumulated depreciation) by a rate equal to 200% of the straight-line rate (e.g., 200% x 25% = 50%). Salvage value is not used in the depreciation formula, but the plant asset cannot be depreciated below its salvage value.

1992 Depreciation expense [50% x ($80,000 – $0)]	$40,000
1993 Depreciation expense [50% x ($80,000 – $40,000)]	$20,000
1994 Depreciation expense [50% x ($80,000 – $60,000*)]	$10,000

41. **(b)** This question requires the determination of how using the sum-of-the-years'-digits (SYD) method of depreciation, instead of the double-declining-balance (DDB) method of depreciation, affects the gain or loss on the sale of a fixed asset with a five-year estimated useful life and no residual value that is sold at the end of the second year of its useful life. A gain or loss on the sale of a fixed asset is computed by comparing the proceeds received from its sale to its carrying amount at the date of sale. To determine the carrying amount of the fixed asset in question at the date of sale, two years of depreciation must be subtracted from its cost.

Because the cost of the fixed asset is not given, there are two options: (1) determine depreciation as a percent or fraction of the unknown cost of the fixed asset, "x," or (2) plug in any value for the cost of the machine and simply compute depreciation under both methods based on this amount. We chose the latter approach, assigning to the machine a cost of $300. Now we can compare the carrying amount of the fixed asset at the date of sale under both methods, as follows:

Cost of fixed asset	$ 300
Depreciation to date of sale:	
Yr. 1: 5/15 x ($300 − $0)	(100)
Yr. 2: 4/15 x ($300 − $0)	(80)
Carrying amount, date of sale, SYD	$ 120

Cost of fixed asset	$ 300
Depreciation to date of sale:	
Yr. 1: 2/5 x ($300 − $0)	(120)
Yr. 2: 2/5 x ($300 − $120)	(72)
Carrying amount, date of sale, DDB	$ 108

The fixed asset has a greater carrying amount at the date of sale under the SYD method. Therefore, using the SYD method of depreciation, instead of the DDB method of depreciation, decreases any gain and increases any loss recognized on the sale of the fixed asset.

42. (c) This question requires you to compare the depreciation expense for a machine during the first two years of its life, using the SYD and the DDB methods. Because the purchase price of the machine is not given, you have two options: (1) determine depreciation as a percent or fraction of the unknown cost of the machine "x," or (2) plug in any value for the cost of the machine, and then simply compute depreciation under both methods based on this amount. We chose the latter approach, assigning to the machine a cost of $200 and a salvage value of $30 (i.e., 15%). Now the problem can be solved as follows:

SYD Yr. 1: 4/10 x ($200 − $30)	=	$ 68
SYD Yr. 2: 3/10 x ($200 − $30)	=	$ 51
DDB Yr. 1: 2/4 x ($200 − $0)	=	$100
DDB Yr. 2: 2/4 x ($200 − $100)	=	$ 50

VARIABLE CHARGE METHODS

43. (b) It is important to note that although an estimated salvage value is not directly incorporated into the formula for computing annual depreciation expense under the double-declining-balance (DDB) method, total depreciation expense over the life of the plant asset under this method cannot exceed the depreciable base (i.e., Historical cost minus Salvage value) of the plant asset. An estimated salvage value is directly incorporated into the formula for computing annual depreciation expense under the productive output method:

$$\text{Depreciation expense} = \frac{\text{Historical cost} - \text{Estimated salvage value}}{\text{Estimated productive output}} \times \text{Productive output current period}$$

An estimated salvage value is not directly incorporated into the formula for computing annual depreciation expense under the DDB method:

$$\text{Depreciation expense} = \frac{2}{\text{Estimated useful life}} \times \text{Historical cost} - \text{Accumulated depreciation}$$

44. (a) The units-of-production depreciation method allocates the cost of plant assets on the basis of units produced (i.e., activity). Depreciation for a period is computed by multiplying the number of units produced during the period by the amount of depreciation per unit. The amount of depreciation per unit is determined by dividing the depreciable base of the plant asset (i.e., cost minus estimated salvage value) by the estimated number of total units to be produced. Thus, an estimate of total units to be produced must be available to use this method. Production does not have to be at a constant level over the life of the asset in order to use this method. Expected repair costs do not affect this method. Obsolescence does not have to be expected to use this method.

MULTIPLE ASSET DEPRECIATION METHOD

45. (a) The composite depreciation method refers to the depreciation of a collection of assets that are dissimilar. The group depreciation method refers to the depreciation of a collection of assets that are similar in nature. From an accounting standpoint, there is no distinction between the two methods. The same procedures are followed for both, and both can utilize the straight-line depreciation method.

46. (d) Under both the group depreciation and the composite depreciation methods, assets are depreciated on the basis of their average lives. New assets are recorded at cost, and retirements are accounted for by crediting Assets for the original cost of the equipment and debiting Accumulated Depreciation for the original cost less proceeds received; thus, no gain or loss is recognized on disposal. The theoretical justification for this is that some assets will be retired early, while some will be used longer than originally estimated. The same approach is used under both group and composite

depreciation—the only difference is that "group depreciation" refers to pools of assets that are similar in nature, whereas "composite" refers to essentially dissimilar assets.

47.   (b)   Under the composite or group method of depreciation, no gain or loss is recognized upon the retirement of a plant asset. This practice is justified because some assets will be retired before the average service life and others after the average service life. Accumulated depreciation is debited for the difference between original cost and the cash received; no gain or loss is recorded on the disposition. The sale of a truck costing $18,000 for $3,000 cash would be recorded as follows:

Cash	3,000	
Accumulated Depreciation	15,000	
Truck		18,000

The net carrying amount of these composite asset accounts is decreased by the cash proceeds received of $3,000 (cost removed of $18,000 minus accumulated depreciation removed of $15,000).

DEPLETION

48.   (b)   The amount to be reported as depletion in the 1994 income statement is determined as follows:

Purchase price of mine	$2,640,000
Development costs to prepare for production	360,000
Estimated restoration costs	180,000
Estimated residual value	(300,000)
Depletion base of mine	$2,880,000
Estimated tons of removable ore	÷1,200,000
Depletion charge per ton	$ 2.40
Tons sold in 1994	x 60,000
Depletion reported in 1994 income statement	$ 144,000

VOLUNTARY DISPOSALS

49.   (c)   Sometimes a structure is constructed on a newly acquired site with an existing building on it. If the existing building is sold and the buyer assumes the costs for its removal, the entire amount of the proceeds from the sale of the building should be deducted from the cost of the land.

50.   (b)   Weir's Accumulated Depreciation account increased by $30,000 ($400,000 – $370,000) during 1992, despite the fact that $55,000 of depreciation expense was recorded during 1992. Therefore, the debit to accumulated depreciation during 1992 because of plant and equipment retirements was $25,000 (i.e., $55,000 – $30,000).

CASUALTY DISPOSALS

51.   (b)   The amount upon which the gain or loss is based is determined as follows:

Building carrying amount, 12/31/90	$250,000
Removal and clean-up costs	12,000
Amount to determine gain or loss on involuntary conversion	$262,000

52.   (b)   FASB Interpretation 30 provides that a gain or loss on the involuntary conversion (e.g., casualty, condemnation, theft) of a nonmonetary asset should be recognized in income even if the proceeds received as a result of the involuntary conversion are reinvested in a replacement nonmonetary asset. The normal maintenance performed on the van (i.e., the various repairs) should not be capitalized. Normal maintenance does not enhance the service potential of the van, it serves only to maintain a given level of services from the van. On the other hand, the cost of the new engine should be capitalized because the expenditure for the new engine is nonrecurring in nature, enhances the service potential of the van, and is expected to yield benefits over a number of accounting periods. The amount of the gain that Rudd should recognize as a result of the involuntary conversion is determined as follows:

Insurance proceeds		$ 3,500
Carrying amount of van:		
Carrying amount, 7/1/91	$ 2,500	
Cost of new engine installed prior to involuntary conversion	700	(3,200)
Gain recognized on involuntary conversion		$ 300

53.   (c)   FASB Interpretation 30 provides that a gain or loss on the involuntary conversion (e.g., casualty, condemnation, theft) of a nonmonetary asset should be recognized in income even if the proceeds received as a result of the involuntary conversion are reinvested in a replacement nonmonetary asset. The amount of the gain that Ocean should recognize as a result of the involuntary conversion is determined as follows:

Insurance proceeds ($1,100,000 – $50,000)		$1,050,000
Amount to determine gain:		
Carrying amount of warehouse on date of conversion	$300,000	
Add: Cost of dismantling warehouse	20,000	(320,000)
Gain recognized on involuntary conversion		$ 730,000

The warehouse was destroyed in a severe winter storm, which occur approximately every four years. Since the occurrence of such storms is not infrequent, the gain on the involuntary conversion is reported as a separate component of income before extraordinary items.

54. (d)   In January 1997, the equipment was written down to a new cost basis of $175,000 due to a permanent impairment of its operational value. Since the estimated salvage value of the equipment on the date of the write-down is $25,000, the $150,000 ($175,000 − $25,000) depreciable base of the equipment should be allocated over the equipment's remaining estimated useful life of 2 years. At 12/31/97, the carrying amount of the equipment is $100,000 [$175,000 − ($150,000 ÷ 2)].

55. (a)   The amount of cost that should be used to determine the gain on condemnation is $581,000 (i.e., the property's carrying amount of $575,000 plus the $2,500 appraisal fee plus the $3,500 attorney fees for the closing with the state). The attorney fees to review the contract to acquire replacement property and the title insurance on the replacement property are costs of acquiring the replacement property.

56. (a)   The condemnation of the forest land represents an example of an involuntary conversion of a nonmonetary asset to a monetary asset. FASB Interpretation 30 requires that any gain or loss realized on the property converted be recognized in income even though the enterprise reinvests or is obligated to reinvest the monetary assets in replacement nonmonetary assets. Since any gain or loss realized on the property converted is recognized in income, the replacement nonmonetary asset is recorded at cost. Because the cost of the replacement forest land exceeds the condemnation award which exceeds the condemned forest land's carrying amount, the debit to Forest Land to record the cost of the replacement property exceeds the credit to Forest Land to remove the carrying amount of the condemned property, and, thus, the carrying amount of Forest Land in the balance sheet increases by the amount of this excess.

IMPAIRMENT

57. (c)   During 1997 the machine was written down to $200,000 due to a permanent impairment of its operational value. Thus, $200,000 is the new cost basis of the machine, which is to be depreciated over the machine's remaining estimated useful life of five years. At 12/31/97 the carrying amount of the machine is $160,000, i.e., ($200,000 − $0) x 4/5.

PERFORMANCE BY SUBTOPICS

Each category below parallels a subtopic covered in Chapter 4. Record the number and percentage of questions you correctly answered in each subtopic area.

Acquisition Cost

Question #	Correct √
1	
2	
3	
4	
5	
6	
7	
8	
9	
10	
11	
12	
13	
14	
15	
16	
17	
18	
19	
20	
21	
22	
23	
# Questions	23

Correct _____
% Correct _____

Cost Incurred Subsequent to Acquisition

Question #	Correct √
24	
25	
26	
27	
28	
29	
# Questions	6

Correct _____
% Correct _____

Straight-Line Depreciation

Question #	Correct √
30	
31	
32	
33	
# Questions	4

Correct _____
% Correct _____

Sum-of-the-Years'-Digits

Question #	Correct √
34	
35	
36	
37	
# Questions	4

Correct _____
% Correct _____

Double-Declining-Balance

Question #	Correct √
38	
39	
40	
41	
42	
# Questions	5

Correct _____
% Correct _____

Variable Charge Methods

Question #	Correct √
43	
44	
# Questions	2

Correct _____
% Correct _____

Multiple Asset Depreciation Method

Question #	Correct √
45	
46	
47	
# Questions	3

Correct _____
% Correct _____

Depletion

Question #	Correct √
48	
# Questions	1

Correct _____
% Correct _____

Voluntary Disposals			Casualty Disposals			Impairment		
Question #	Correct √		Question #	Correct √		Question #	Correct √	
49			51			57		
50			52			# Questions	1	
# Questions	2		53					
			54			# Correct	_____	
# Correct	_____		55			% Correct	_____	
% Correct	_____		56					
			# Questions	6				
			# Correct	_____				
			% Correct	_____				

OTHER OBJECTIVE FORMAT SOLUTIONS

SOLUTION 4-2 ACQUISITION COSTS OF PLANT ASSETS

1. (L) The purchase price of the land should be capitalized in the Land account.

2. (E) The interest cost on the construction financing incurred *after* completion of the construction should be expensed. Interest capitalization ceases when the asset is substantially complete and ready for its intended use (SFAS 34, par. 18).

3. (B) The new office building requires a period of time to get it ready for its intended use. Therefore, the interest cost on the construction financing incurred during the construction period should be capitalized as part of the historical cost of constructing the building.

4. (L) Where a building is to be constructed on a newly acquired site with an existing building on it, the amount paid for the existing building should be capitalized in the Land account.

5. (L) The payment of accrued or delinquent property taxes on the land at the time of purchase should be capitalized in the Land account.

6. (B) The liability insurance premium incurred during the construction period should be capitalized in the Building account because it was a reasonable and necessary cost of constructing the building.

7. (L) Since the existing building was torn down to prepare the site for the new building, the cost of demolition of the existing building, less any salvage proceeds, is a cost of getting the land ready for its intended use and should be included in the cost of the land.

8. (E) The moving costs should be expensed as incurred; they should not be included in the cost of the land or building.

SOLUTION 4-3 ACQUISITION COSTS/DEPRECIATION METHODS

1. (C) The freight charges should be capitalized as an inventory cost because all reasonable and necessary costs of bringing goods for sale to their existing condition and location should be included in inventory.

2. (C) Since title to goods purchased F.O.B. shipping point passes when the goods are shipped, the purchaser incurs any in-transit insurance charges on the goods. In-transit insurance charges should be capitalized as an inventory cost because all reasonable and necessary costs of bringing goods for sale to their existing condition and location should be included in inventory.

3. (E) Interest cost should not be capitalized for inventories routinely manufactured or otherwise produced on a repetitive basis (SFAS 34, par. 10). Therefore, interest cost on the note payable for goods held for resale should be expensed as a period cost.

4. (C) Expenditures to install equipment should be capitalized because the capitalized cost of equipment includes all reasonable and necessary costs of preparing the equipment for its intended use.

5. (C) Expenditures to test newly-purchased equipment should be capitalized because the capitalized cost of equipment includes all reasonable and necessary costs of preparing the equipment for its intended use.

6. (E) The cost of the current year service contract on the equipment should be expensed as a period cost. Expenditures to maintain plant assets in operating condition should be charged to repair and maintenance expense.

7. $600,000. The cost of the office building and land on which it is located is $1,000,000, the sum of

the $800,000 cash payment made and the $200,000 existing mortgage assumed by Link. Since 60% of the property tax assessment on the building and land is allocated to the building, it can be inferred that the fair value of the building is 60% of the sum of the fair values of the building and the land. Thus, Link should record the building at $600,000, 60% of the $1,000,000 cost of the building and land.

8. $503,000. At the inception of a capital lease, the lessee records an asset and the corresponding lease liability at the lesser of the present value of the minimum lease payments or the fair value of the leased property. Although the lessor's implicit rate in the lease of 8% is lower than the lessee's incremental borrowing rate of 9%, it is not known to the lessee. Therefore, the present value of the minimum lease payments should be computed using the lessee's incremental borrowing rate of 9%. The leased equipment is recorded at the present value of the minimum lease payments of $503,000 (i.e., $100,000 x 5.03) because this amount is less than the $515,000 fair value of the equipment.

9. $370,000. The exchange of a plot of undeveloped land for another plot of undeveloped land does not result in the culmination of an earnings process, because it is a nonmonetary exchange of similar assets. No gain is recognized by a party (Link) who gives boot in an exchange of similar nonmonetary assets. Link records the plot of land received at $370,000 (i.e., $320,000 + $50,000), the sum of the carrying amounts of the assets surrendered because this amount does not exceed the $500,000 fair value of the plot of land received.

10. $315,000. The exchange of a plot of undeveloped land for another plot of undeveloped land does not result in the culmination of an earnings process because it is a nonmonetary exchange of similar assets. The extent of boot (e.g. cash) received signifies the portion of the exchanged asset that has been sold, and thus the amount of gain that can be recognized. The nonmonetary asset acquired in the exchange is recorded at its fair value less the amount of gain on the surrendered asset not recognized on the exchange. The gain Club recognizes on the exchange is computed, then the recorded cost of the land acquired in the exchange can be computed.

Cash received	$ 50,000
Plus: FV of land received	450,000
Total FV received	500,000
Less: Carrying amount of land exchanged	(350,000)
Gain on exchange	150,000
Extent earnings process culminated:	
Cash/total FV rec'd. ($50,000/$500,000)	× 10%
Gain recognized on exchange	$ 15,000
FV of land received	$ 450,000
Gain not recognized on the exchange ($150,000 − $15,000)	(135,000)
Recorded cost of land acquired	$ 315,000

11. $90,000. Under the straight-line method, the depreciation charge for 1993 is computed as follows:

Cost of machine	$ 864,000
Less: Estimated salvage value	(144,000)
Depreciable base of machine	720,000
Divide by: Estimated useful life in years	÷ 8
Annual depreciation charge	$ 90,000

12. $162,000. Under the double-declining-balance method (DDB), the depreciation charge for the first year of ownership must be computed before the depreciation charge for the second year of ownership can be computed.

The depreciation charge for 1992 (the first year of ownership) under DDB is computed as follows:

Cost of machine, 1/2/92	$ 864,000
Less: Accumulated depreciation, 1/2/92	(0)
Carrying amount of machine, 1/2/92	864,000
Times: Twice the SL rate [(100% ÷ 8) X 2]	× 25%
Depreciation charge for 1992	$ 216,000

The depreciation charge for 1993 (the second year of ownership) under DDB is computed as follows:

Cost of machine, 1/2/92	$ 864,000
Less: Accumulated depreciation, 1/1/93	(216,000)
Carrying amount of machine, 1/1/93	648,000
Times: Twice the straight-line rate	× 25%
Depreciation charge for 1993	$ 162,000

13. $140,000. Under the sum-of-the-years'-digits method, the depreciation charge for 1993 is computed as follows:

Cost of machine, 1/2/92	$ 864,000
Less: Estimated salvage value	(144,000)
Depreciable base of machine	720,000
Times: Fraction for second year of 8 year life*	× 7/36
Depreciation charge for 1993	$ 140,000

---

* The numerator of the fraction is the number of years of useful life remaining at 1/1/93 (i.e., 8 − 1). The denominator is the sum of the years of the estimated useful life of the machine.

14. $120,000.   Under the units of production method, the depreciation charge for 1993 is computed as follows:

Cost of machine	$ 864,000
Less: Estimated salvage value	(144,000)
Depreciable base of machine	720,000
Divide by: Estimated useful life in units	÷ 1,800,000
Depreciation charge per unit of output	$ .40
Times: Units produced in 1993	x 300,000
Depreciation charge recorded for 1993	$ 120,000

ESSAY SOLUTION

SOLUTION 4-4   DEPRECIATION AND NONMONETARY EXCHANGES

a.   Portland should have selected the straight-line depreciation method when approximately the **same amount of an asset's service potential is used up each period**. If the reasons for the decline in service potential are unclear, then the selection of the straight-line method could be influenced by the **ease of recordkeeping**, its use for **similar assets**, and its use by **others in the industry**.

b.   Portland should record **depreciation expense to the date** of the exchange. If the **original** truck's **carrying amount is greater than its fair value**, a **loss** results.   The truck's **capitalized cost** and **accumulated depreciation** are **eliminated**, and the loss on the trade-in is reported as part of **income from continuing operations**. The newly acquired truck is recorded at fair value. If the original truck's **carrying amount is less than its fair value** at trade-in, then there is an **unrecognized gain**. The newly acquired truck is recorded at **fair value less** the **unrecognized gain. Cash** is **decreased** by the **amount paid**.

c.   1.   By associating depreciation with a group of machines instead of each individual machine, Portland's **bookkeeping** process is greatly **simplified**. Also, since actual **machine lives vary** from the average depreciable life, **unrecognized net losses** on **early dispositions** are expected to be **offset** by **continuing depreciation** on machines **usable beyond** the **average** depreciable life. Periodic income does not fluctuate as a result of recognizing gains and losses on manufacturing machine dispositions.

2.   Portland should **divide the depreciable cost** (capitalized cost less residual value) of each machine by its **estimated life** to obtain its annual depreciation.   The **sum** of the individual annual depreciation amounts should then be **divided by** the **sum of the individual capitalized costs** to obtain the annual composite depreciation rate.

Wondering how to allocate your study time?

In your excitement to answer multiple choice questions, don't forget that the examiners ask questions in other formats!

The first pass through a chapter:

1.   Strive to answer **all** the multiple choice questions.

2.   Choose one or more of the essay and other objective format questions to answer.

When you review the chapter later:

1.   Answer **at least** those objective questions that you did not understand the first time. (If you had a lucky guess, did you really understand?)

2.   Select a new essay question to answer.

When you review the chapter for the final time (for some chapters, the second time may **be** the final time):

1.   Only review the notes you would review just before the exam. For a whole exam section, this should take less than five minutes. Answer the questions "cold turkey" (without reviewing the text materials just before answering questions).

2.   Answer **at least** those objective questions that you did not understand the first time.

3.   Select a new essay question to answer.

Remember, with the techniques and information in your material,

A passing score is well within reach!

CHANGE ALERT

In June 2001, the FASB released SFAS 142, *Goodwill and Other Intangible Assets,* changing the accounting for goodwill from an amortization method to an impairment-only approach. Amortization of goodwill, including goodwill recorded in past business combinations, ceases upon adoption of SFAS 142, which for companies with calendar year ends, is January 1, 2002. This statement supersedes APB Opinion No. 17, *Intangible Assets.*

This statement changes the unit of accounting for goodwill and other intangible assets subsequent to their initial recognition in the following significant respects:

- This statement bases the accounting for goodwill on the reporting units, the units of the combined entity into which the acquired entity is integrated, as a more aggregate view of goodwill. Previously, accounting for goodwill was based on a transaction approach and treated the entity as if it remained a stand-alone entity rather than being integrated with the acquiring entity.

- Previously, goodwill and other intangible assets were treated as wasting assets, with finite lives, and thus were amortized, reducing net income each year. Amortization also had an arbitrary maximum of 40 years. This new statement does not presume that the assets are wasting assets. Goodwill and intangible assets with indefinite useful lives will not be amortized, but rather will be tested at least annually for impairment. Intangible assets with finite useful lives will continue to be amortized over their useful lives, but without the constraint of an arbitrary ceiling.

- This statement provides specific guidance for testing goodwill for impairment. Goodwill is to be tested for impairment at least annually, using a two-step process, beginning with an estimation of the fair value of a reporting unit. The first step is a screen for potential impairment, and the second step measures the amount of impairment, if any. If certain criteria are met, the annual requirement can be satisfied without a remeasurement of the fair value of a reporting unit.

- The statement also provides specific guidance on testing for impairment intangible assets that will not be amortized. The testing will be done at least annually by comparing the fair values of those intangible assets with their recorded amounts.

- The statement requires disclosure of information about goodwill and other intangible assets in the years subsequent to their acquisition not previously required. Disclosures shall include information about the changes in the carrying amount of goodwill from period to period (in the aggregate and by reportable segment), the carrying amount of intangible assets by major intangible asset class for those assets subject to amortization and for those not subject to amortization, and the estimated intangible asset amortization expense for the next five years.

CHAPTER 5

INTANGIBLE ASSETS, R&D COSTS & OTHER ASSETS

CHAPTER 5

INTANGIBLE ASSETS, R&D COSTS
& OTHER ASSETS

I. INTANGIBLE ASSETS

A. DEFINITIONS

1. **INTANGIBLE ASSETS** Intangibles are assets without physical substance that provide economic benefits through the rights and privileges associated with their possession. Intangibles may be classified as identifiable or unidentifiable and externally acquired or internally developed. Examples of identifiable intangible assets include patents, franchises, licenses, leaseholds, leasehold improvements, copyrights, and trademarks.

2. **PATENT** A patent represents a special right to a particular product or process that has value to the holder of the right. Only the external acquisition costs of a patent should be capitalized; research and development costs incurred to internally develop a patent should be expensed as incurred. In addition, the cost of a competing patent acquired to protect an existing patent and the cost of a successful legal defense of an existing patent should also be capitalized. On the other hand, the cost of an unsuccessful defense, along with any amounts previously capitalized for the patent, should be expensed in the period in which the court decision is rendered.

3. **FRANCHISE** A franchise represents a special right to operate under the name and guidance of another enterprise over a limited geographic area. A franchise is always externally purchased; it cannot be internally developed. Capitalize all significant costs incurred to acquire the franchise (*e.g.,* purchase price, legal fees, etc.). If the acquisition cost of the franchise requires future cash payments, these payments should be capitalized at their present value using an appropriate interest rate. On the other hand, periodic service fees charged as a percentage of revenues are not capitalized; these costs represent a current operating expense of the franchisee.

4. **LICENSE** A license is a permit issued by a governmental agency allowing an entity to conduct business in a certain specified geographical area. Capitalize significant costs incurred to acquire the license and amortize the cost over the lesser of its useful or legal life, not to exceed 40 years.

5. **LEASEHOLD** A leasehold is a right to use rented properties, usually for a number of years. In some situations, for example, a ten-year lease may require the immediate cash payment of the annual rent for the first and tenth years. The prepayment of the rent for the tenth year would be recorded as a leasehold and would be classified as an intangible asset until the tenth year, when it would be charged to rent expense.

6. **LEASEHOLD IMPROVEMENT** A leasehold improvement is an improvement made by the lessee to leased property for which benefits are expected beyond the current accounting period. Leasehold improvements are not separable from the leased property and revert to the lessor at the end of the lease term. The cost of leasehold improvements should be capitalized and amortized over the lesser of their estimated useful life or the remaining term of the lease. If a lease has a renewal option, which the lessee intends to exercise, the leasehold improvement should be amortized over the *lesser* of its estimated useful life or the sum of the remaining term of the lease **and** the period covered by the renewal option.

7. **COPYRIGHT** A copyright is an exclusive right granted by the Federal government giving the owner protection against the illegal reproduction by others of the owner's written works, designs, and literary productions. Although the copyright period is for the life of the creator plus 70 years, the cost of a copyright should be amortized over the useful life of the copyright, not to exceed 40 years.

8. **TRADEMARK** A trademark is a symbol, design, or logo that is used in conjunction with a particular product, service, or enterprise. Generally, only the external acquisition costs of trademarks are capitalized; internal acquisition costs are usually expensed when incurred. Amortize any costs capitalized over the lesser of the useful life of the trademark or 40 years.

B. *GOODWILL AND OTHER INTANGIBLE ASSETS* **(SFAS 142)**

SFAS 142, *Goodwill and Other Intangible Assets,* changes the accounting for goodwill from an amortization method to an impairment-only approach. Amortization of goodwill, including goodwill recorded in past business combinations, ceases upon adoption of SFAS 142. SFAS 142 supersedes APB Opinion No. 17, *Intangible Assets.* SFAS 142 changes the unit of accounting for goodwill and other intangible assets subsequent to their initial recognition in the following significant respects:

1. SFAS 142 bases the accounting for goodwill on the reporting units, the units of the combined entity into which the acquired entity is integrated, as a more aggregate view of goodwill. Previously, accounting for goodwill was based on a transaction approach and treated the acquired entity as if it remained a stand-alone entity rather than being integrated with the acquiring entity.

2. SFAS 142 does not presume that the assets are wasting assets. Goodwill and intangible assets with indefinite useful lives are not amortized, but rather are tested at least annually for impairment. Intangible assets with finite useful lives continue to be amortized over their useful lives, but without the constraint of an arbitrary ceiling. Previously, goodwill and other intangible assets were treated as wasting assets, with finite lives, and thus were amortized, reducing net income each year. Amortization also had an arbitrary maximum of 40 years.

3. SFAS 142 provides specific guidance for testing goodwill for impairment. Goodwill is tested for impairment at least annually, using a two-step process, beginning with an estimation of the fair value of a reporting unit. The first step is a screen for potential impairment, and the second step measures the amount of impairment, if any. If certain criteria are met, the annual requirement can be satisfied without a remeasurement of the fair value of a reporting unit.

4. SFAS 142 also provides specific guidance on testing for impairment intangible assets that will not be amortized. The testing is done at least annually by comparing the fair values of those intangible assets with their recorded amounts.

5. SFAS 142 requires disclosure of information about goodwill and other intangible assets in the years subsequent to their acquisition not previously required. Disclosures include information about the changes in the carrying amount of goodwill from period to period (in the aggregate and by reportable segment), the carrying amount of intangible assets by major intangible asset class for those assets subject to amortization and for those not subject to amortization, and the estimated intangible asset amortization expense for the next five years.

C. **INITIAL RECOGNITION AND MEASUREMENT OF INTANGIBLE ASSETS**

1. **FAIR VALUE** Intangible assets acquired shall be initially recognized and measured based on fair value, except those acquired in a business combination. If acquired as a group of assets, the cost shall be allocated to the individual assets acquired based on their relative fair values. No goodwill will be recognized. Intangible assets acquired in a business

combination are subject to accounting treatment covered in the chapter on consolidated financial statements.

2. **INTERNALLY DEVELOPED INTANGIBLE ASSETS** The costs of internally developing, maintaining, or restoring intangible assets, including goodwill, that are not specifically identifiable, that have indeterminate lives, are recognized as expense when incurred.

D. ACCOUNTING FOR INTANGIBLE ASSETS AFTER ACQUISITION

1. **FINITE USEFUL LIFE** An intangible asset with a finite useful life is amortized.

2. **INDEFINITE USEFUL LIFE** An intangible asset with an indefinite useful life is not amortized. If no legal, regulatory, contractual, competitive, economic, or other factors limit the useful life, it is considered to be indefinite. The term indefinite does not mean infinite.

3. **DETERMINING THE USEFUL LIFE** The useful life is the period over which the asset is expected to contribute directly or indirectly to future cash flows. The estimate of the useful life should take into consideration all pertinent factors, including the expected use of the asset by the entity; any legal, regulatory, or contractual provisions that may limit the useful life and such provisions that might result in renewal or extension of the useful life without substantial cost; the effects of obsolescence, demand, competition, and other economic factors; and the expected maintenance expenditures required.

4. **AMORTIZABLE INTANGIBLE ASSETS**

   a. **PERIOD OF AMORTIZATION** An intangible asset shall be amortized over the best estimate of its useful life.

   b. **METHOD OF AMORTIZATION** The method of amortization should reflect the pattern in which the economic benefits are consumed or used up. If that pattern cannot be reliably determined, a straight-line amortization shall be used.

   c. **RESIDUAL VALUE** The amount of an intangible asset to be amortized shall be the amount initially assigned to the asset less any residual value.

   d. **REEVALUATION** Each reporting period the remaining useful life should be evaluated to determine whether events and circumstances warrant a revision to the remaining period of amortization.

      (1) If determined that the remaining useful life is changed, the remaining amount of the intangible asset should be amortized prospectively over the revised remaining useful life

      (2) If determined that the remaining useful life is indefinite, the asset should be tested for impairment and no longer amortized

5. **IMPAIRMENT LOSS**

   a. **ANNUALLY** At least annually, all intangible assets should be tested for impairment.

   b. **RECOGNITION OF IMPAIRMENT** An impairment loss should be recognized if the carrying amount of an intangible asset is not recoverable and its carrying amount exceeds its fair value. After an impairment loss is recognized, the adjusted carrying amount of the asset shall be its new accounting basis. Subsequent reversal of a previously recognized impairment loss is prohibited.

6. **GOODWILL IMPAIRMENT TESTING** Goodwill is not amortized, but is tested for impairment at least annually. The goodwill impairment test may be performed any time during the fiscal year provided the test is performed at the same time every year.

a. **REPORTING UNIT** Goodwill is tested for impairment at a reporting unit level. A reporting unit is an operating segment or one level below an operating segment, referred to as a component. A component of an operating segment is a reporting unit if the component constitutes a business for which discrete financial information is available and segment management regularly reviews the operating results of that component.

b. **TWO-STEP IMPAIRMENT TEST**

(1) **STEP ONE** The first step used to identify potential impairment compares the fair value of a reporting unit with its carrying amount, including goodwill. If the fair value exceeds its carrying amount, goodwill of the reporting unit is considered not impaired and the second step is unnecessary. If, on the contrary, the carrying amount exceeds its fair value, the second step should be performed.

- **FAIR VALUE MEASUREMENTS** The fair value is the amount at which the asset could be bought or sold in a current transaction between willing parties. Quoted market prices are the best evidence of fair value and should be used if available. Otherwise, the best information available should be used, including prices for similar assets and results of using other valuation techniques, such as present value. The estimates should be based on reasonable and supportable assumptions and consider all available evidence. If a range is estimated, the likelihood of possible outcomes shall be considered. Other techniques include multiples of earnings or revenue or similar performance measurements.

(2) **STEP TWO** The second step compares the implied fair value of reporting unit goodwill with the carrying amount of that goodwill. If the carrying amount exceeds the implied fair value of that goodwill, an impairment loss shall be recognized in an amount equal to that excess. The loss recognized cannot exceed the carrying amount of goodwill. After a goodwill impairment loss is recognized, the adjusted carrying amount of goodwill shall be its new accounting basis. Subsequent reversal of a previously recognized goodwill impairment loss is prohibited.

E. **FINANCIAL STATEMENT PRESENTATION**

1. **INTANGIBLE ASSETS** At a minimum, all intangible assets shall be aggregated and presented as a separate line item in the statement of financial position. This does not preclude presentation of more detailed information. Goodwill should be presented as a separate line item.

2. **AMORTIZATION EXPENSE AND IMPAIRMENT LOSSES** The amortization expense and impairment losses for intangible assets are presented in income statement line items within continuing operations. Goodwill impairment losses are presented as a separate line item in the income statement before the subtotal of income from continuing operations unless the impairment is associated with a discontinued operation. An impairment loss resulting from impairment testing is **not** recognized as a change in accounting principle.

3. **DISCLOSURES**

a. **IN PERIOD OF ACQUISITION** In the notes to the financial statements, the following disclosures should be made in the period of acquisition:

(1) **INTANGIBLE ASSETS SUBJECT TO AMORTIZATION** The total amount assigned and the amount assigned to any major intangible asset class, the amount of any significant residual value and the weighted-average amortization period, in total and by major intangible asset class.

(2) **INTANGIBLE ASSETS NOT SUBJECT TO AMORTIZATION** The total amount assigned and the amount assigned to any major intangible asset class

(3) **OTHER INFORMATION** The amount of research and development assets acquired and written off in the period and the line item in the income statement in which the amounts written off are aggregated.

b. **ALL OTHER PERIODS** In the financial statements or in the notes to the financial statement, the following disclosures should be made.

(1) **INTANGIBLE ASSETS SUBJECT TO AMORTIZATION** The gross carrying amount and accumulated amortization, in total and by major intangible asset class, the aggregate amortization expense for the period, and the estimated aggregate amortization expense for each of the five succeeding fiscal years.

(2) **INTANGIBLE ASSETS NOT SUBJECT TO AMORTIZATION** The total carrying amount and the carrying amount for each major intangible asset class.

(3) **GOODWILL** The changes in the carrying amount of goodwill during the period including the aggregate amount of goodwill acquired, the aggregate amount of impairment losses recognized, and the amount of goodwill included in the gain or loss on disposal of all or a portion of a reporting unit.

c. **PERIODS WHEN IMPAIRMENT LOSS IS RECOGNIZED** The notes to the financial statements for periods that impairment loss is recognized should include descriptions of the impaired asset and the facts and circumstances leading to the impairment, the amount of the impairment loss and the method for determining fair value, the caption in the income statement that includes the impairment loss, and any other information that might be significant.

II. RESEARCH AND DEVELOPMENT (SFAS 2)

A. DEFINITIONS

Research activities are those aimed at the discovery of knowledge that will be useful in developing or significantly improving products or processes. *Development* activities are those concerned with translating research findings and other knowledge into plans or designs for new or significantly improved products or processes.

1. **EXAMPLES OF R&D** Examples of activities that are typically *included* in R&D

a. Laboratory research aimed at discovery of new knowledge

b. Searching for applications of new research findings or other knowledge

c. Conceptual formulation and design of product or process alternatives

d. Testing in search for or evaluation of product or process alternatives

e. Modification of the formulation or design of a product or process

f. Design, construction, and testing of pre-production prototypes and models

g. Design of tools, jigs, molds, and dies involving new technology

    h.   Pilot plant costs if **not** of a scale economically feasible for commercial production

    i.   Engineering activities until product meets specific functional and economic requirements and is ready for manufacture

2.   **EXAMPLES OF NON-R&D ITEMS** Examples of activities that are *excluded* from R&D

    a.   Engineering follow-through in early stages of *commercial* production

    b.   Quality control during *commercial* production including *routine* testing of products

    c.   Troubleshooting in connection with breakdowns during *commercial* production

    d.   *Routine*, ongoing efforts to improve existing products

    e.   Adaptation of *existing* capability to meet particular requirements or customer's needs as part of continuing *commercial* activity

    f.   *Seasonal* or other periodic design changes to *existing* products

    g.   *Routine* design of tools, jigs, molds, and dies

    h.   Construction, relocation, rearrangement, or start-up activities (including design and construction engineering) of facilities or equipment other than the following:

        (1)   Pilot plants

        (2)   Facilities or equipment whose only use Is for a particular R&D project

    i.   Legal work to secure, sell, or license *patents*

B.   **ACCOUNTING FOR R&D COSTS**

1.   **EXPENSE R&D COSTS** Future economic benefits deriving from R&D activities, if any, are uncertain in their amount and timing. Due to these uncertainties, SFAS 2, *Accounting for Research and Development Costs*, requires that most R&D costs be charged to expense the year in which incurred. Capitalization of R&D costs, except as indicated below, is not acceptable.

2.   **ASSETS ONLY IF HAVE ALTERNATIVE FUTURE USES** Materials, equipment, facilities, or intangibles purchased from others that are acquired for a particular R&D project and have *no alternative use* in other R&D projects or in normal operations should be *expensed* in the period in which acquired. However, these items should be recorded as *assets* if *alternative future uses* are expected, whether in other R&D activities or in normal operations. Assets recorded for R&D costs with alternative future uses should be amortized over their useful lives by periodic charges to R&D expense. If, at any point, these assets are no longer deemed to have alternative future uses, the remaining unamortized cost is charged to R&D expense for the period.

EXAMPLE 1 ♦ RESEARCH AND DEVELOPMENT

In 20X7 Futura Inc. began an extensive research and development program. The following R&D related costs were incurred during 20X7:

Jan. 2:	Purchase of general purpose lab building (10-year life)	$150,000
Jan. 5:	Purchase of general purpose lab equipment (5-year life)	25,000
Jan. 7:	Purchase of a machine to be used exclusively on Project X (4-year life)	8,000
Jan. 30:	Acquired materials and supplies, as follows:	
	Materials to be used in Project X	10,000
	Miscellaneous lab supplies for several projects	12,000

In addition, $40,000 of direct labor costs was incurred on various R&D projects and $3,000 of overhead costs was appropriately allocated to R&D activities during 20X7. All but $4,000 of the materials purchased for Project X and $5,000 of the general purpose supplies were consumed during 20X7.

REQUIRED: Determine Futura's R&D expense for 20X7.

SOLUTION:

Depreciation on lab building ($150,000 ÷ 10)	$ 15,000
Depreciation on general purpose lab equipment ($25,000 ÷ 5)	5,000
Machine to be used exclusively on Project X*	8,000
Materials for Project X*	10,000
Miscellaneous lab supplies ($12,000 – $5,000)	7,000
Direct labor	40,000
Appropriately allocated overhead	3,000
Total R&D expense, 20X7	$ 88,000

*The cost of equipment and materials to be used on a single R&D project (i.e., having no alternative future uses) should be expensed as R&D when incurred.

3. **OTHER ISSUES** R&D costs conducted for others under the provisions of a contract may be carried as assets. Contractually reimbursable R&D costs should not be expensed as R&D per SFAS 2.

C. REQUIRED DISCLOSURES

Total R&D costs expensed in each period for which an income statement is presented must be clearly disclosed.

III. COMPUTER SOFTWARE TO BE SOLD, LEASED, OR OTHERWISE MARKETED (SFAS 86)

A. RESEARCH AND DEVELOPMENT COSTS

Costs incurred internally in creating a computer software product are charged to expense when incurred as research and development until technological feasibility has been established for the product.

1. **TECHNOLOGICAL FEASIBILITY** Technological feasibility is established only upon completion of a detailed program design or, in its absence, completion of a working model.

2. **COSTS TO ESTABLISH TECHNOLOGICAL FEASIBILITY** All costs of planning, designing, coding, and testing activities that are necessary to establish technological feasibility are expensed as research and development when incurred.

B. PRODUCTION COSTS

The costs of producing product masters incurred subsequent to establishing technological feasibility are capitalized.

1. CODING AND TESTING These costs include coding and testing performed subsequent to establishing technological feasibility.

2. COMPUTER SOFTWARE COSTS Capitalization of computer software costs ceases when the product is available for general release to customers.

C. AMORTIZATION

Capitalized software costs are amortized on a product-by-product basis.

1. AMOUNT TO AMORTIZE The annual amortization is the *greater* of the amount computed using the following.

a. PERCENT OF REVENUE APPROACH The ratio that current gross revenues for a software product bear to the total of current and anticipated future gross revenue for that software product

b. STRAIGHT-LINE METHOD The straight-line method over the remaining estimated economic life of the product including the period being reported on

EXAMPLE 2 ♦ AMORTIZATION EXPENSE

On December 31, 20X7, the Clone Company had $200,000 of capitalized costs for a new computer software product with an economic useful life of five years. Sales for 20X8 were thirty percent of expected total sales of the software.

REQUIRED: Determine the amortization expense for 20X8.

SOLUTION: Under the percent of revenue approach, the amortization expense for 20X8 would be $60,000 ($200,000 x 30%). Under the straight-line approach, the amortization would be $40,000 ($200,000 ÷ 5 years). The amortization for 20X8 is $60,000, determined under the percent of revenue approach, because it results in a *greater* amortization charge.

2. WHEN TO BEGIN AMORTIZATION Amortization starts when the product is available for release to customers.

D. INVENTORY COSTS

Costs incurred for (1) duplicating the computer software and training materials from product masters and (2) physically packaging the product for distribution are capitalized as inventory. Capitalized inventory costs are expensed when the inventory is sold.

E. VALUATION

Capitalized software production costs are reported at the lower of unamortized cost or net realizable value.

IV. COMPUTER SOFTWARE DEVELOPED OR OBTAINED FOR INTERNAL USE (SOP 98-1)

A. PRELIMINARY PROJECT STAGE

Computer software costs that are incurred in the preliminary project stage should be expensed as incurred. Activities in this stage include conceptual formulation and evaluation of alternatives, determination of existence of needed technology, and final selection of alternatives.

B.   APPLICATION DEVELOPMENT STAGE

1.   CAPITALIZED COSTS Most costs in this stage are capitalized, including external direct costs, payroll and payroll-related costs for those who are directly involved with the project, and interest costs. Activities in this stage include design of the chosen path, design of the software configuration, coding, installation to hardware, and testing. Capitalization of the costs should cease when the software project is substantially complete and ready for its intended use, which generally is after all substantial testing is completed.

2.   EXPENSED COSTS Training costs and data conversion costs are generally expensed.

C.   POST-IMPLEMENTATION/OPERATION STAGE

1.   EXPENSED COSTS Internal and external training and maintenance costs should be expensed as incurred.

2.   AMORTIZATION Capitalized costs are amortized over the estimated useful life, and adjusted periodically with changes in the estimates of the useful life or when the value of the asset is impaired.

3.   CAPITALIZED COSTS The costs of upgrades are capitalized.

4.   OTHER CONSIDERATIONS If, after the development of internal-use software is completed, the entity decides to market the software, net proceeds received from the license of the computer should be applied against the carrying amount of the software.

V.   OTHER ASSETS

A.   PREPAID EXPENSES
Under accrual accounting, revenues and expenses are recognized when earned or incurred, respectively. Thus when a firm pays in advance for a good or service such as insurance, rent, interest, etc., the cost of the item is first recorded as an asset—Prepaid Expense.

1.   CURRENT VS. NONCURRENT In a classified balance sheet, a prepaid expense should be separated into a current and a noncurrent portion. In general, the current portion of the prepaid expense is the amount that expires within the next 12 months.

2.   REALIZED EXPENSE As the benefits from the prepayment are realized (i.e., the costs expire), the prepaid expenses are reduced and charged to an appropriate expense account, such as insurance expense, rent expense, interest expense, etc.

EXAMPLE 3 ♦ PREPAID INSURANCE

On April 1, 20X7, Denso Co. purchased for $120,000 a 4-year blanket casualty insurance policy covering all its buildings, equipment, and inventory. Denso is a calendar year corporation that issues a classified balance sheet.

REQUIRED: Provide the journal entries if Denso Co. initially records this policy as an asset and as an expense; and show the proper balance sheet presentation at December 31, 20X7.

(continued on next page)

SOLUTION:

1. Journal entries if initially recorded as an asset

   April 1, 20X7
   Prepaid Insurance   120,000
       Cash   120,000

   December 31, 20X7
   Insurance Expense*   22,500
       Prepaid Insurance   22,500

*Premium paid	$120,000
Number of months	÷ 48
Monthly insurance expense	2,500
Months policy in force, 20X7	x 9
Insurance expense, 20X7	$ 22,500

2. Journal entries if initially recorded as an expense

   April 1, 20X7
   Insurance Expense   120,000
       Cash   120,000

   December 31, 20X7
   Prepaid Insurance**   97,500
       Insurance Expense   97,500

**Premium paid	$120,000
Insurance expense, 20X7 (see 1., above)	22,500
Prepaid insurance, 12/31/X7	$ 97,500

3. Balance sheet presentation, December 31, 20X7
   Current Assets
       Prepaid insurance (12 mos. x $2,500) $ 30,000

   Noncurrent Assets
   Prepaid insurance (27 mos. x $2,500) $ 67,500

B.   **CASH SURRENDER VALUE OF LIFE INSURANCE POLICIES**

    1.   **IN GENERAL** Companies frequently insure the lives of key executives. Insurance premiums paid on many such life insurance policies consist of an amount for life insurance and a balance that constitutes a form of savings. The savings portion is manifested in the growing *cash surrender value* or amount realizable by the owner of the policy should the policy be canceled. Cash surrender value of life insurance policies are usually classified as noncurrent assets, among Investments and Funds.

    2.   **EXPENSE REPORTED** The amount to be reported as life insurance expense for a year is the annual premium paid, less (a) the increase in cash surrender value and (b) any dividends received.

C.   **SPECIAL PURPOSE FUNDS**

    1.   **DEFINITION** These funds result from the setting aside of specific assets, usually under the custody of a trustee for a particular purpose. Some funds may be voluntarily created, such

as preferred stock acquisition funds and plant expansion funds. Other funds result from contractual obligations, such as debt retirement funds. The funds may or may not be under the custody of a separate trustee.

2. **ACCOUNTING** The accounting depends on the specific nature of the fund, legal requirements, etc. The fund is initially established by crediting cash or other assets and debiting the fund account. The fund is affected by (a) additions or withdrawals to the fund, (b) earnings on the fund, (c) gains or losses on the disposal of assets in the fund, and (d) expenses of operating the fund. The exchange of one asset for another within the fund (such as the exchange of cash for an investment) will not have any net effect on the balance of the fund. The fund accounts for its own investments and generally records its own revenues and expenses. The fund balance at the end of the period is presented as a net amount, as a separate line item generally under Investments and Funds.

CHAPTER 5—INTANGIBLE ASSETS, R&D COSTS & OTHER ASSETS

PROBLEM 5-1 MULTIPLE CHOICE QUESTIONS (84 to 105 minutes)

1. Gray Co. was granted a patent on January 2, 1991, and appropriately capitalized $45,000 of related costs. Gray was amortizing the patent over its estimated useful life of fifteen years. During 1994, Gray paid $15,000 in legal costs in successfully defending an attempted infringement of the patent. After the legal action was completed, Gray sold the patent to the plaintiff for $75,000. Gray's policy is to take no amortization in the year of disposal. In its 1994 income statement, what amount should Gray report as gain from sale of patent?
a. $15,000
b. $24,000
c. $27,000
d. $39,000   (11/95, FAR, #33, 6115)

2. During 1999, Jase Co. incurred research and development costs of $136,000 in its laboratories relating to a patent that was granted on July 1, 1999. Costs of registering the patent equaled $34,000. The patent's legal life is 20 years, and its estimated economic life is 10 years. In its December 31, 1999 balance sheet, what amount should Jase report as patent, net of accumulated amortization?
a. $ 32,300
b. $ 33,000
c. $161,500
d. $165,000   (5/95, FAR, #13, amended, 5549)

3. On January 2, 1989, Lava Inc. purchased a patent for a new consumer product for $90,000. At the time of purchase, the patent was valid for 15 years; however, the patent's useful life was estimated to be only 10 years due to the competitive nature of the product. On December 31, 1992, the product was permanently withdrawn from sale under governmental order because of a potential health hazard in the product. What amount should Lava charge against income during 1992, assuming amortization is recorded at the end of each year?
a. $ 9,000
b. $54,000
c. $63,000
d. $72,000   (11/93, PI, #54, 4423)

4. Which of the following statements concerning patents is correct?
a. Legal costs incurred to successfully defend an internally developed patent should be capitalized and amortized over the patent's remaining economic life.
b. Legal fees and other direct costs incurred in registering a patent should be capitalized and amortized on a straight-line basis over a five-year period.
c. Research and development contract services purchased from others and used to develop a patented manufacturing process should be capitalized and amortized over the patent's economic life.
d. Research and development costs incurred to develop a patented item should be capitalized and amortized on a straight-line basis over 17 years.   (5/93, Theory, #25, 4213)

5. Malden Inc. has two patents that have allegedly been infringed by competitors. After investigation, legal counsel informed Malden that it had a weak case on patent A34 and a strong case in regard to patent B19. Malden incurred additional legal fees to stop infringement on B19. Both patents have a remaining legal life of 8 years. How should Malden account for these legal costs incurred relating to the two patents?
a. Expense costs for A34 and capitalize costs for B19.
b. Expense costs for both A34 and B19.
c. Capitalize costs for both A34 and B19.
d. Capitalize costs for A34 and expense costs for B19.   (11/92, Theory, #29, 3462)

6. On January 2, 2002, Judd Co. bought a trademark from Krug Co. for $500,000. Judd retained an independent consultant, who estimated the trademark's remaining life to be 50 years. Its unamortized cost on Krug's accounting records was $380,000. In Judd's December 31, 2002 balance sheet, what amount should be reported as accumulated amortization?
a. $ 7,600
b. $ 9,500
c. $10,000
d. $12,500   (11/93, PI, #25, amended, 4394)

7. Hull Co. bought a trademark from Roe Corp. on January 1, 2000, for $224,000. Hull retained an independent consultant who estimated the trademark's remaining useful life to be 50 years. Its unamortized cost on Roe's accounting records was $112,000. In Hull's December 31, 2000 balance sheet, what amount should be reported as accumulated amortization?

a. $5,600
b. $4,480
c. $2,800
d. $2,240   (11/91, PI, #4, amended, 2392)

8. On January 2, 1993, Rafa Co. purchased a franchise with a useful life of ten years for $50,000. An additional franchise fee of 3% of franchise operation revenues must be paid each year to the franchisor. Revenues from franchise operations amounted to $400,000 during 1993. In its December 31, 1993 balance sheet, what amount should Rafa report as an intangible asset-franchise?

a. $33,000
b. $43,800
c. $45,000
d. $50,000   (5/94, FAR, #20, 4835)

9. During January 1995, Yana Co. incurred landscaping costs of $120,000 to improve leased property. The estimated useful life of the landscaping is fifteen years. The remaining term of the lease is eight years, with an option to renew for an additional four years. However, Yana has not reached a decision with regard to the renewal option. In Yana's December 31, 1995, balance sheet, what should be the net carrying amount of landscaping costs?

a. $0
b. $105,000
c. $110,000
d. $112,000   (11/97, FAR, #8, 6488)

10. Star Co. leases a building for its product showroom. The ten-year non-renewable lease will expire on December 31, 1997. In January 1992, Star redecorated its showroom and made leasehold improvements of $48,000. The estimated useful life of the improvements is 8 years. Star uses the straight-line method of amortization. What amount of leasehold improvements, net of amortization, should Star report in its June 30, 1992 balance sheet?

a. $45,600
b. $45,000
c. $44,000
d. $43,200   (5/93, PI, #22, 4064)

11. On January 1, 1995, Nobb Corp. signed a 12-year lease for warehouse space. Nobb has an option to renew the lease for an additional 8-year period on or before January 1, 1999. During January 1997, Nobb made substantial improvements to the warehouse. The cost of these improvements was $540,000, with an estimated useful life of 15 years. At December 31, 1997, Nobb intended to exercise the renewal option. Nobb has taken a full year's amortization on this leasehold. In Nobb's December 31, 1997 balance sheet, the carrying amount of this leasehold improvement should be

a. $486,000.
b. $504,000.
c. $510,000.
d. $513,000.   (5/91, PI, #25, amended, 0997)

12. On January 1, 1996, Bay Co. acquired a land lease for a 21-year period with no option to renew. The lease required Bay to construct a building in lieu of rent. The building, completed on January 1, 1997, at a cost of $840,000, will be depreciated using the straight-line method. At the end of the lease, the building's estimated market value will be $420,000. What is the building's carrying amount in Bay's December 31, 1997 balance sheet?

a. $798,000
b. $800,000
c. $819,000
d. $820,000   (11/91, PI, #16, amended, 2404)

13. On December 1, 1991, Clark Co. leased office space for five years at a monthly rental of $60,000. On the same date, Clark paid the lessor the following amounts:

First months' rent	$ 60,000
Last months' rent	60,000
Security deposit (refundable at lease expiration)	80,000
Installation of new walls and offices	360,000

What should be Clark's 1991 expense relating to utilization of the office space?

a. $ 60,000
b. $ 66,000
c. $120,000
d. $140,000   (11/92, PI, #56, 3288)

14. On January 2, 1997, Ames Corp. signed an eight-year lease for office space. Ames has the option to renew the lease for an additional four-year period on or before January 2, 2004. During January 1997, Ames incurred the following costs:

- $120,000 for general improvements to the leased premises with an estimated useful life of ten years.
- $50,000 for office furniture and equipment with an estimated useful life of ten years.

At December 31, 1997, Ames' intentions as to exercise of the renewal option are uncertain. A full year's amortization of leasehold improvements is taken for calendar year 1997. In Ames' December 31, 1997 balance sheet, accumulated amortization should be
a. $10,000.
b. $15,000.
c. $17,000.
d. $21,250.   (5/90, PI, #18, amended, 1003)

15. On September 29, 1995, Wall Co. paid $860,000 for all the issued and outstanding common stock of Hart Corp. On that date, the carrying amounts of Hart's recorded assets and liabilities were $800,000 and $180,000, respectively. Hart's recorded assets and liabilities had fair values of $840,000 and $140,000, respectively. In Wall's September 30, 1995 balance sheet, what amount should be reported as goodwill?
a. $ 20,000
b. $160,000
c. $180,000
d. $240,000   (R/00, FAR, #5, 6900)

16. On January 2, 2003, Paye Co. purchased Shef Co. at a cost that resulted in recognition of goodwill of $200,000. During the first quarter of 2003, Paye spent an additional $80,000 on expenditures designed to maintain goodwill. In its December 31, 2003 balance sheet, what amount should Paye report as goodwill?
a. $ 80,000
b. $195,000
c. $200,000
d. $280,000   (11/94, FAR, #17, amended, 9015)

17. On June 30, 2000, Union Inc. purchased goodwill of $125,000 when it acquired the net assets of Apex Corp. During 2000, Union incurred additional costs of developing goodwill, by training Apex employees ($50,000) and hiring additional Apex employees ($25,000). Union's December 31, 2000 balance sheet should report goodwill of
a. $200,000.
b. $175,000.
c. $150,000.
d. $125,000.   (5/91, PI, #28, amended, 0998)

18. During 1993, Orr Co. incurred the following costs:

Research and development services performed by Key Corp. for Orr	$150,000
Design, construction, and testing of preproduction prototypes and models	200,000
Testing in search for new products or process alternatives	175,000

In its 1993 income statement, what should Orr report as research and development expense?
a. $150,000
b. $200,000
c. $350,000
d. $525,000   (11/94, FAR, #44, 5306)

19. Brill Co. made the following expenditures during 1992:

Costs to develop computer software for internal use in Brill's general management information system	$100,000
Costs of market research activities	75,000

What amount of these expenditures should Brill report in its 1992 income statement as research and development expenses?
a. $175,000
b. $100,000
c. $ 75,000
d. $0   (11/93, PI, #56, 4425)

20. Wizard Co. purchased two machines for $250,000 each on January 2, 1997. The machines were put into use immediately. Machine A has a useful life of five years and can only be used in one research project. Machine B will be used for two years on a research and development project and then used by the production division for an additional eight years. Wizard uses the straightline method of depreciation. What amount should Wizard include in 1997 research and development expense?
a. $ 75,000
b. $275,000
c. $375,000
d. $500,000   (11/98, FAR, #11, 6738)

21. West Inc. made the following expenditures relating to Product Y:

- Legal costs to file a patent on Product Y—$10,000. Production of the finished product would not have been undertaken without the patent.
- Special equipment to be used solely for development of Product Y—$60,000. The equipment has no other use and has an estimated useful life of four years.
- Labor and material costs incurred in producing a prototype model—$200,000.
- Cost of testing the prototype—$80,000.

What is the total amount of costs that will be expensed when incurred?
a. $280,000
b. $295,000
c. $340,000
d. $350,000   (5/92, PI, #52, 2622)

22. On January 1, 1990, Jambon purchased equipment for use in developing a new product. Jambon uses the straight-line depreciation method. The equipment could provide benefits over a 10-year period. However, the new product development is expected to take five years, and the equipment can be used only for this project. Jambon's 1990 expense equals
a. The total cost of the equipment.
b. One-fifth of the cost of the equipment.
c. One-tenth of the cost of the equipment.
d. Zero.   (11/91, Theory, #32, 2540)

23. Cody Corp. incurred the following costs during 1997:

Design of tools, jigs, molds, and dies involving new technology	$125,000
Modification of the formulation of a process	160,000
Troubleshooting in connection with breakdowns during commercial production	100,000
Adaptation of an existing capability to a particular customer's need as part of a continuing commercial activity	110,000

In its 1997 income statement, Cody should report research and development expense of
a. $125,000.
b. $160,000.
c. $235,000.
d. $285,000.   (11/90, PI, #42, amended, 1000)

ITEMS 24 AND 25 are based on the following:

During 1990, Pitt Corp. incurred costs to develop and produce a routine, low-risk computer software product, as follows:

Completion of detail program design	$13,000
Costs incurred for coding and testing to establish technological feasibility	10,000
Other coding costs after establishment of technological feasibility	24,000
Other testing costs after establishment of technological feasibility	20,000
Costs of producing product masters for training materials	15,000
Duplication of computer software and training materials from product masters (1,000 units)	25,000
Packaging product (500 units)	9,000

24. In Pitt's December 31, 1990 balance sheet, what amount should be reported in inventory?
a. $25,000
b. $34,000
c. $40,000
d. $49,000   (5/91, PI, #21, 0995)

25. In Pitt's December 31, 1990 balance sheet, what amount should be capitalized as software cost, subject to amortization?
a. $54,000
b. $57,000
c. $59,000
d. $69,000   (5/91, PI, #22, 0996)

26. On December 31, 1990, Bit Co. had capitalized costs for a new computer software product with an economic life of five years. Sales for 1991 were 30 percent of expected total sales of the software. At December 31, 1991, the software had a net realizable value equal to 90 percent of the capitalized cost. What percentage of the original capitalized cost should be reported as the net amount on Bit's December 31, 1991 balance sheet?
a. 70%
b. 72%
c. 80%
d. 90%   (5/92, Theory, #14, 2707)

27. On December 31, 1997, the New Bite Company had capitalized costs for a new computer software product with an economic life of four years. Sales for 1998 were ten percent of expected total sales of the software. At December 31, 1998, the software had a net realizable value equal to eighty percent of the capitalized cost. The unamortized cost reported on the December 31, 1998 balance sheet should be

a. Net realizable value.
b. Ninety percent of net realizable value.
c. Seventy-five percent of capitalized cost.
d. Ninety percent of capitalized cost.

(11/89, Theory, #12, amended, 9016)

28. An analysis of Thrift Corp.'s unadjusted prepaid expense account at December 31, 1992, revealed the following:

- An opening balance of $1,500 for Thrift's comprehensive insurance policy. Thrift had paid an annual premium of $3,000 on July 1, 1991.

- A $3,200 annual insurance premium payment made July 1, 1992.

- A $2,000 advance rental payment for a warehouse Thrift leased for one year beginning January 1, 1993.

In its December 31, 1992 balance sheet, what amount should Thrift report as prepaid expenses?

a. $5,200
b. $3,600
c. $2,000
d. $1,600

(5/93, PI, #27, 4069)

29. Roro Inc. paid $7,200 to renew its only insurance policy for three years on March 1, 1995, the effective date of the policy. At March 31, 1995, Roro's unadjusted trial balance showed a balance of $300 for prepaid insurance and $7,200 for insurance expense. What amounts should be reported for prepaid insurance and insurance expense in Roro's financial statements for the three months ended March 31, 1995?

	Prepaid insurance	Insurance expense
a.	$7,000	$300
b.	$7,000	$500
c.	$7,200	$300
d.	$7,300	$200

(5/95, FAR, #14, 5550)

30. Under East Co.'s accounting system, all insurance premiums paid are debited to prepaid insurance. For interim financial reports, East makes monthly estimated charges to insurance expense with credits to prepaid insurance. Additional information for the year ended December 31, 1990, is as follows:

Prepaid insurance at December 31, 1989	$105,000
Charges to insurance expense during 1990 (including a year-end adjustment of $17,500)	437,500
Prepaid insurance at December 31, 1990	122,500

What was the total amount of insurance premiums paid by East during 1990?

a. $332,500
b. $420,000
c. $437,500
d. $455,000

(5/91, PI, #30, 9017)

31. The premium on a three-year insurance policy expiring on December 31, 1991, was paid in total on January 2, 1989. If the company has a 6-month operating cycle, then on December 31, 1989, the prepaid insurance reported as a current asset would be for

a. 6 months.
b. 12 months.
c. 18 months.
d. 24 months.

(5/90, Theory, #6, 1758)

32. On January 1, 1991, Sip Co. signed a 5-year contract enabling it to use a patented manufacturing process beginning in 1991. A royalty is payable for each product produced, subject to a minimum annual fee. Any royalties in excess of the minimum will be paid annually. On the contract date, Sip prepaid a sum equal to two years' minimum annual fees. In 1991, only minimum fees were incurred. The royalty prepayment should be reported in Sip's December 31, 1991 financial statements as

a. An expense only.
b. A current asset and an expense.
c. A current asset and noncurrent asset.
d. A noncurrent asset. (11/92, Theory, #28, 3461)

33. Ott Company acquired rights to a patent from Grey under a licensing agreement that required an advance royalty payment when the agreement was signed. Ott remits royalties earned and due, under the agreement, on October 31 each year. Additionally, on the same date, Ott pays, in advance, estimated royalties for the next year. Ott adjusts prepaid royalties at year-end. Information for the year ended December 31, 1997, is as follows:

Date		Amount
01/01	Prepaid royalties	$ 65,000
10/31	Royalty payment (charged to royalty expense)	110,000
12/31	Year-end credit adjustment to royalty expense	25,000

In its December 31, 1997 balance sheet, Ott should report prepaid royalties of

a. $25,000.
b. $40,000.
c. $85,000.
d. $90,000. (11/86, PI, #1, amended, 0986)

34. On May 1, 1990, Marno County issued property tax assessments for the fiscal year ended June 30, 1991. The first of two equal installments was due on November 1, 1990. On September 1, 1990, Dyur Co. purchased a 4-year old factory in Marno subject to an allowance for accrued taxes. Dyur did not record the entire year's property tax obligation, but instead records tax expenses at the end of each month by adjusting prepaid property taxes or property taxes payable, as appropriate. The recording of the November 1, 1990 payment by Dyur should have been allocated between an increase in prepaid property taxes and a decrease in property taxes payable in which of the following percentages?

	Percentage Allocated to	
	Increase in prepaid property taxes	Decrease in property taxes payable
a.	66-2/3%	33-1/3%
b.	0%	100%
c.	50%	50%
d.	33-1/3%	66-2/3%

(5/91, Theory, #13, 2045)

35. On January 2, 1993, Jann Co. purchased a $150,000 whole-life insurance policy on its president. The annual premium is $4,000. The company is both the owner and the beneficiary. Jann charged officers' life insurance expense as follows:

1993	$ 4,000
1994	3,600
1995	3,000
1996	2,200
Total	$12,800

In its December 31, 1996, balance sheet, what amount should Jann report as investment in cash surrender value of officers' life insurance?
a. $0
b. $ 3,200
c. $12,800
d. $16,000

(5/97, FAR, #2, 6474)

36. Upon the death of an officer, Jung Co. received the proceeds of a life insurance policy held by Jung on the officer. The proceeds were not taxable. The policy's cash surrender value had been recorded on Jung's books at the time of payment. What amount of revenue should Jung report in its statements?
a. Proceeds received.
b. Proceeds received less cash surrender value.
c. Proceeds received plus cash surrender value.
d. None.

(11/95, FAR, #35, 6117)

37. An increase in the cash surrender value of a life insurance policy owned by a company would be recorded by
a. Decreasing annual insurance expense.
b. Increasing investment income.
c. Recording a memorandum entry only.
d. Decreasing a deferred charge.

(11/94, FAR, #46, 5307)

38. In 1992, Chain Inc. purchased a $1,000,000 life insurance policy on its president, of which Chain is the beneficiary. Information regarding the policy for the year ended December 31, 1997, follows:

Cash surrender value, 1/1/97	$ 87,000
Cash surrender value, 12/31/97	108,000
Annual advance premium paid 1/1/97	40,000

During 1997, dividends of $6,000 were applied to increase the cash surrender value of the policy. What amount should Chain report as life insurance expense for 1997?
a. $40,000
b. $25,000
c. $19,000
d. $13,000

(11/92, PI, #51, amended, 3284)

39. On March 1, 1993, a company established a sinking fund in connection with an issue of bonds due in 2000. At December 31, 1997, the independent trustee held cash in the sinking fund account representing the annual deposits to the fund and the interest earned on those deposits. How should the sinking fund be reported in the company's balance sheet at December 31, 1997?
a. The cash in the sinking fund should appear as a current asset.
b. Only the accumulated deposits should appear as a noncurrent asset.
c. The entire balance in the sinking fund account should appear as a current asset.
d. The entire balance in the sinking fund account should appear as a noncurrent asset.

(11/93, Theory, #43, amended, 4548)

40. The following information relates to noncurrent investments that Fall Corp. placed in trust as required by the underwriter of its bonds:

Bond sinking fund balance, 12/31/91	$ 450,000
1992 additional investment	90,000
Dividends on investments	15,000
Interest revenue	30,000
Administration costs	5,000
Carrying amount of bonds payable	1,025,000

What amount should Fall report in its December 31, 1992 balance sheet related to its noncurrent investment for bond sinking fund requirements?

a. $585,000
b. $580,000
c. $575,000
d. $540,000

(5/93, PI, #16, 4058)

41. At October 31, 1992, Dingo Inc. had cash accounts at three different banks. One account balance is segregated solely for a November 15, 1992, payment into a bond sinking fund. A second account, used for branch operations, is overdrawn. The third account, used for regular corporate operations, has a positive balance. How should these accounts be reported in Dingo's October 31, 1992 classified balance sheet?

a. The segregated account should be reported as a noncurrent asset, the regular account should be reported as a current asset and the overdraft should be reported as a current liability.
b. The segregated and regular accounts should be reported as current assets, and the overdraft should be reported as a current liability.
c. The segregated account should be reported as a noncurrent asset, and the regular account should be reported as a current asset net of the overdraft.
d. The segregated and regular accounts should be reported as current assets net of the overdraft.

(11/92, Theory, #13, 3446)

42. An issuer of bonds uses a sinking fund for the retirement of the bonds. Cash was transferred to the sinking fund and subsequently used to purchase investments. The sinking fund

I. Increases by revenue earned on the investments.
II. Is **not** affected by revenue earned on the investments.
III. Decreases when the investments are purchased.

a. I only
b. I and III
c. II and III
d. III only

(11/91, Theory, #36, 2544)

ESSAY QUESTION

ESSAY 5-2 (15 to 25 minutes)

Clonal Inc., a biotechnology company, developed and patented a diagnostic product called Trouver. Clonal purchased some research equipment to be used exclusively for Trouver and other research equipment to be used on Trouver and subsequent research projects. Clonal defeated a legal challenge to its Trouver patent, and began production and marketing operations for the product.

Corporate headquarters' costs were allocated to Clonal's research division as a percentage of the division's salaries.

REQUIRED:

a. How should the equipment purchased for Trouver be reported in Clonal's income statements and balance sheets?

b. 1. Describe the matching principle.
2. Describe the accounting treatment of research and development costs and consider whether this is consistent with the matching principle. What is the justification for the accounting treatment of research and development costs?

c. How should corporate headquarters' costs allocated to the research division be classified in Clonal's income statement? Why?

d. How should the legal expenses incurred in defending Trouver's patent be reported in Clonal's statement of cash flows (direct method)?

(11/90, Theory, #4, 6190)

SOLUTION 5-1 MULTIPLE CHOICE ANSWERS

INTANGIBLE ASSETS WITH FINITE USEFUL LIVES

1. **(b)** The cost of a successful legal defense of an existing patent should be capitalized because it offers probable future benefits.

Cost of patent (1991)	$ 45,000
Amortization (3 yrs. x $45,000/15)	(9,000)
Carrying value 12/31/93	36,000
Capitalization of legal costs	15,000
Carrying value of patent (1994)	$ 51,000
Proceeds from sale	$ 75,000
Carrying value of patent	(51,000)
Gain from sale	$ 24,000

2. **(a)** Research and development costs incurred to develop a product should be expensed as incurred. Only the costs of acquiring a patent should be capitalized. Thus, only the cost of registering the patent, $34,000, is capitalized. The capitalized cost of an intangible asset, such as a patent, should be amortized over the asset's economic life. For 1999, 1/2 year of amortization is $1,700 ($34,000 ÷ 10 years × 1/2 year). The value reported on the balance sheet, net of amortization, is $32,300 ($34,000 – $1,700).

3. **(c)** On 12/31/92, the patented product was permanently withdrawn from sale under governmental order. Therefore, the unamortized cost of the patent at 12/31/92 should be charged to income.

Purchase price of patent	$ 90,000
Less: Amortization prior to 1992 ($90,000 x 3/10)	(27,000)
Unamortized cost of patent 1992	$ 63,000

4. **(a)** Legal costs incurred to successfully defend a patent should be capitalized, regardless of whether the patent was externally acquired or internally developed. While legal fees and other direct costs of registering a patent should be capitalized, the capitalized cost of the patent should be amortized over the lesser of the economic useful life or legal life of the patent. Research and development costs incurred to develop a patent should be expensed when incurred per SFAS 2.

5. **(a)** While the cost of a successful defense of a patent should be capitalized because it establishes the legal rights of the owner, other legal costs incurred for an existing patent should be expensed as incurred. Therefore, Malden should capitalize the cost of the successful defense of patent B19 and expense the legal costs incurred to determine that it had a weak case of patent infringement for patent A34.

6. **(c)** The $500,000 acquisition cost of the trademark acquired is amortized over the useful life, resulting in accumulated amortization of $10,000 at 12/31/02. The unamortized cost of the trademark on Krug's accounting records is irrelevant in determining Judd's acquisition cost.

7. **(b)** The $224,000 acquisition cost of the trademark is amortized over the useful life, resulting in amortization expense of $4,480 for 2000. The unamortized cost of the trademark on Roe's accounting records is irrelevant in determining the amount of Hull's acquisition cost.

8. **(c)** The 3% of revenues fee is expensed in the period incurred, not capitalized and amortized. The franchise has a useful life of 10 years and must be amortized over its determinable useful life of 10 years.

Franchise	$50,000
Amortization ($50,000 x 10%)	(5,000)
Intangible asset, 12/31/93	$45,000

9. **(b)** The landscaping costs are leasehold improvements and should be capitalized and amortized over the lesser of the estimated useful life or the remaining term of the lease, including renewal options. The remaining term of the lease, with or without the renewal option, is less than the estimated useful life of 15 years. Because Yana Co. has not reached a decision to exercise the option to renew for the additional four years, the landscaping costs should be amortized over the 8-year remaining term of the lease. At December 31, 1995, one year of amortization, $15,000 ($120,000 ÷ 8 years) should be expensed. Cost of $120,000 less amortization of $15,000 equals a net carrying amount of $105,000.

10. **(c)** Leasehold improvements are improvements made by the lessee to leased property which are not separable from the leased property and revert to the lessor at the end of the lease term. Since the lease is nonrenewable, the leasehold improvements made 1/1/92 should be amortized over the *lesser* of the remaining term of the lease (i.e., 6 years) or the estimated useful life of the leasehold improvements (i.e., 8 years). Thus, at 06/30/92, the carrying amount of the leasehold improvements made on 1/1/92 is $44,000 (i.e., $48,000 – [($48,000 ÷ 6) x 6 months/12 months]).

11. **(b)** Leasehold improvements are improvements made by the lessee to leased property which are not separable from the leased property and

revert to the lessor at the end of the lease term. Since Nobb intends to exercise the renewal option, the leasehold improvement should be amortized over the *lesser* of the sum of the remaining term of the lease *and* the period covered by the renewal option [i.e., (12 – 2) + 8 = 18 years] or the estimated useful life of the leasehold improvement (i.e., 15 years). Thus, at 12/31/97, the carrying amount of the leasehold improvement is $504,000 [$540,000 – ($540,000 ÷ 15)].

12. (a) The building constructed on the leased property in lieu of rent represents a leasehold improvement because the building will revert to the lessor at the end of the lease term. The $840,000 cost of the building is allocated equally over the *remaining* 20-year period of the lease, resulting in annual amortization of $42,000. Thus, the building's carrying amount at 12/31/97 is $798,000 ($840,000 cost minus $42,000 amortization to date).

13. (b) The installation of the new walls and offices represent leasehold improvements since they are not separable from the leased property and revert to the lessor at the end of the lease term. The leasehold improvements should be amortized over the lease term. The prepayment of the last month's rent was made to secure the lease and should be reported as a leasehold within intangible assets at December 31, 1991. The 1991 expense relating to the use of the office space is determined as follows:

Rent for December 1991	$60,000
Amortization of leasehold improvements for December 1991 ($360,000 ÷ 60)	6,000
Total expense relating to use of office space	$66,000

14. (b) Leasehold improvements are improvements made by the lessee to leased property. The improvements are not separable from the leased property and revert to the lessor at the end of the lease term. Of the items listed, only the general improvements made to the leased premises represent a leasehold improvement. As such, it should be amortized over the *lesser* of the lease term (i.e., 8 years) or the estimated useful life of the leasehold improvement (i.e., 10 years). The likelihood of lease renewal is too uncertain to warrant apportioning the cost over the sum of the remaining term of the lease and the period covered by the renewal option (i.e., 12 years). Therefore, the accumulated amortization to be reported in the 12/31/97 balance sheet is $15,000 ($120,000 ÷ 8 years). The office furniture and equipment are not leasehold improvements since they are separable from the leased premises and do not revert to the lessor at the end of the lease term.

GOODWILL

15. (b) Purchased goodwill is recognized and recorded at an amount equal to the excess of the cost of the enterprise acquired over the fair value of the identifiable net assets. Purchased goodwill is calculated as follows:

Purchase price of 100% of Hart Corp's O/S common stock		$ 860,000
Less: Fair value of identifiable net assets of Hart Corp.	$700,000	
Times percentage acquired by Wall Co.	x 100%	(700,000)
Goodwill attributable to the acquisition		$ 160,000

16. (c) The $200,000 of goodwill acquired in connection with the purchase of Shef should be capitalized. The $80,000 of expenditures to maintain the goodwill should be expensed when incurred because costs of developing, maintaining, or restoring goodwill should not be capitalized.

17. (d) Costs of goodwill from a business combination accounted for as a purchase should be capitalized. However, costs of developing, maintaining, or restoring goodwill should be expensed when incurred. Thus, the *purchased goodwill* of $125,000 from the acquisition of the net assets of Apex should be capitalized, while the $75,000 ($50,000 + $25,000) of additional cost of *developing goodwill* should be expensed as incurred.

RESEARCH & DEVELOPMENT

18. (d) SFAS 2, par. 9 and 10, provides examples of activities that are typically included in, and those excluded from, research and development. All three of the activities identified in the question are examples of activities that typically would be included in research and development.

19. (d) Neither of the two activities identified is an example of an activity that typically would be considered a research and development activity (SFAS 2, par. 9). Most costs in the application development stage of developing software for internal use are capitalized and not expensed as incurred. Market research activities are not included in R&D because these activities relate to the selling and marketing operations of a company.

20. (b) Materials, equipment, facilities, or intangibles purchased for a particular R&D project and have no alternative use in other R&D projects or in normal operations should be expensed in the period in which acquired. However, if alternative future uses are expected, these items should be

recorded as assets and amortized over their useful lives. Machine A can only be used in one research project and should be expensed in the current year. Machine B has alternative future uses and a 10 year life; thus, the current research and development expense should include depreciation for one year.

Machine A	$250,000
Machine B ($250,000/10 years)	25,000
R&D expense, 1997	$275,000

21. (c) The cost of equipment is expensed as research and development costs when incurred when the equipment can be used only in *one* particular research and development project (i.e., the equipment has no alternative future uses in other research and development projects or otherwise). In addition, costs incurred in the design, construction, and testing of preproduction prototypes and models are also expensed as research and development costs when incurred. Thus, the total amount of costs that will be expensed as research and development costs when incurred is $340,000 (i.e., $60,000 + $200,000 + $80,000). The cost of the legal work in connection with patent application would be capitalized as part of the cost of the patent (see SFAS 2, par. 9 - 11).

22. (a) Per SFAS 2, par. 11, the costs of equipment or facilities that are acquired or constructed for research and development activities and have alternative future uses (in research and development or otherwise) should be capitalized when acquired or constructed. However, the cost of equipment or facilities that are acquired or constructed for a particular research and development project and have no alternative future uses (in other research and development projects or otherwise) are expensed as research and development costs at the time the costs are incurred.

23. (d) Research and development expense for 1997 is $285,000. The design of tools, jigs, molds, and dies involving new technology ($125,000) and the modification of the formulation of a process ($160,000) are activities that typically would be *included* in research and development (SFAS 2, par. 9). Troubleshooting in connection with breakdowns during commercial production and the adaptation of an existing capability to a particular customer's need as part of a continuing commercial activity are activities that would typically be *excluded* from research and development (par. 10).

COMPUTER SOFTWARE

24. (b) All costs incurred to establish the technological feasibility of a computer software product should be charged to expense as research and development when incurred (SFAS 86, par. 3). The technological feasibility of a computer software product is established only when the enterprise has completed all planning, designing, coding, and testing activities that are necessary to establish that the product can be produced (par. 4). Thus, the cost of completion of the detail program design ($13,000) and the costs incurred for coding and testing to establish technological feasibility of the product ($10,000) should be expensed as research and development. The costs incurred for duplicating the computer software document and training materials from the product masters ($25,000) and for physically packaging the product for distribution ($9,000) should be capitalized as inventory for $34,000 (par. 9).

25. (c) Costs of producing product masters incurred *subsequent* to establishing technological feasibility should be capitalized. These costs include coding and testing performed subsequent to establishing technological feasibility (SFAS 86, par. 3). Thus, the costs of producing product masters for training materials ($15,000) and the coding costs ($24,000) and testing costs ($20,000) incurred *after* establishment of technological feasibility should be capitalized (i.e., $59,000).

26. (a) The annual amortization of the capitalized software cost is the greater of: (1) the ratio of current revenues to current and future revenues (e.g., 30%) or (2) the straight-line method over the remaining useful life of the software including the period to be reported upon (e.g., 1 ÷ 5 = 20%). Because the software has a net realizable value of 90% of the capitalized cost, it can be reported on the balance sheet at 70% (i.e., 1 − 30%) of its capitalized cost (see SFAS 86, par. 8).

27. (c) The annual amortization of the capitalized software cost is the greater of (1) the ratio of current revenues to current and future revenues (e.g., 10%) or (2) the straight-line method over the remaining estimated useful life of the software including the period reported upon (e.g., 1 ÷ 4 = 25%). Because the software has a net realizable value of 80% of the capitalized cost, it can properly be reported on the balance sheet at 75% (i.e., 1 − 25%) of the capitalized cost.

PREPAID EXPENSES

28. (b) The amount to be reported as prepaid expenses at 12/31/92 is $3,600. This amount is comprised of (1) the $1,600 (i.e., $3,200 x 6/12) portion of the annual insurance premium payment made 7/1/92 that pertains to 1993 and (2) the $2,000

advance one-year rental payment for the lease which begins in 1993. The $1,500 opening balance of the prepaid expense account pertains to insurance coverage that expired during 1992; therefore, it is not used to determine the 12/31/92 prepaid expense account balance.

29. (b) The correct amount to be shown in the Prepaid Insurance account at March 31, 1995, is 35 months of premiums:

$7,200 \div 36$ months = $200 per month
$200 per month x 35 months = $7,000

Prepaid Insurance

Unadjusted balance (given)	300	
Adjustment (forced)	6,700	
Ending bal. 3/31/95	7,000	

Insurance Expense

Unadjusted balance (given)	7,200	
		6,700 Adjustment
Ending bal. 3/31/95	500	

30. (d) The insurance premiums paid can be most easily determined by the following analysis of the Prepaid Insurance account (work backwards through the account):

Prepaid Insurance

Balance, 12/31/89 (given)	105,000		
Premiums paid (forced)	455,000		
Balance before charges to expense (subtotal)	560,000	437,500	Charge to expense in 1990 (given)
Balance, 12/31/90 (given)	122,500		

31. (b) The operating cycle of an enterprise is the average period of time between the expenditure of cash for goods and services and the date those goods and services are converted into cash. Thus, it is the average length of time from cash expenditure, to inventory, to sale, to accounts receivable, and back to cash. A 1-year time period is to be used as a basis for the segregation of current assets in cases where there are several operating cycles occurring within a year (ARB 43, Ch. 3, par. 5). Since the company in question has a six-month operating cycle, it has two operating cycles within a year. Thus, the 1-year (i.e., twelve month) time period should be used as the basis for determining the amount of prepaid insurance to be reported as a current asset.

32. (b) Royalties were prepaid equal to the sum of two year's minimum annual fees on the contract date. Only the minimum annual fees were incurred in the first year of the contract. Since the second year's minimum annual fees will be consumed in the upcoming year, half of the royalty prepayment should be reported as an expense and half should be reported as a current asset at the end of the first contract year.

33. (d) The answer is determined as follows:

Prepaid royalties, 1/1	$ 65,000
Royalty payment, 10/31	110,000
Less: 1997 royalty exp. ($110,000 − $25,000)	(85,000)
Prepaid royalties, 12/31	$ 90,000

34. (d) On September 1, 1990, Dyur Co. would have credited two months of taxes from the seller to Property Taxes Payable. At the end of September and October, Dyur would have recorded one month of property taxes each month by a credit to Property Taxes Payable. When the payment was made for six months of taxes on November 1, 1990, the payment would be for the four months prior to that date that have already been accrued and for the two months that follow the payment date which should be recorded as Prepaid Property Taxes. Therefore, 2/3 of the payment should be allocated to a decrease in property taxes payable and 1/3 of the payment should be recorded as an increase in prepaid property taxes.

CASH SURRENDER VALUE OF LIFE INSURANCE

35. (b) The annual premium on a whole-life insurance policy includes a portion to cash surrender value. The balance is reported as life insurance expense. Jann Co. paid a total of $16,000 in premiums from 1993 to 1996 ($4,000 x 4 years). Of this amount, $12,800 was charged to life insurance expense, and the balance of $3,200 ($16,000 − $12,800) is reported as an investment in cash surrender value.

36. (b) The cash surrender value has been accounted for as an asset and has reduced insurance expense over the years the premium payments have been made. The receipt of life insurance proceeds is first applied to the cash surrender value to remove the asset and the balance is recorded as revenue.

37. (a) The amount that a company should recognize as insurance expense for a life insurance policy that it owns is the annual premium less (1) the increase in cash surrender value and (2) any dividends received.

38. (c) Premiums paid on this policy consist of an amount for life insurance and a balance which constitutes a form of savings. In this question, the cash surrender value of the policy increased by $21,000 (i.e., $108,000 − $87,000) in 1997. This amount, which *includes* the dividends of $6,000

applied to increase the cash surrender value of the policy, is subtracted from the premium paid to determine the life insurance expense for the year (i.e., $40,000 – $21,000 = $19,000).

SPECIAL PURPOSE FUNDS

39. **(d)** Because the bond sinking fund is earmarked for the retirement of long-term debt, its entire balance (i.e., all contributions to the fund plus all interest accumulations added to the fund balance to date) should be reported as a noncurrent asset in the Investments section of the balance sheet.

40. **(b)** The bond sinking fund balance increases as a result of the additional investment and the income on the investments in the fund (i.e., the dividend and interest revenue). It decreases due to the expenses of the fund (i.e., the administrative costs incurred). The carrying amount of the bonds payable does not affect the bond sinking fund balance. The amount to be reported for the bond sinking fund in the noncurrent investments section of the balance sheet is computed as follows:

Bond sinking fund balance, 12/31/91	$450,000
Add: Additional investment, 1992	90,000
Dividends on investments	15,000
Interest revenue	30,000
Less: Administrative costs	(5,000)
Bond sinking fund balance, 12/31/92	$580,000

41. **(a)** Cash that is segregated for the liquidation of long-term debts should be excluded from current assets (ARB 43, Ch. 43A, par. 6). Hence, the account balance which is segregated solely for payment into the bond sinking fund should be reported as a noncurrent asset. The bank overdraft should be reported as a current liability because there is no available cash in another account at that bank to offset the overdrawn account (i.e., the bank overdraft should not be netted against the account used for regular operations held at the third bank). The cash in the regular account at the third bank is to be used for current operations, hence it should be reported as a current asset.

42. **(a)** The sinking fund is affected by (1) additions or withdrawals to the fund, (2) earnings on the fund, (3) gains or losses on the disposal of assets in the fund, (4) expenses of operating the fund. The exchange of one asset for another within the fund (such as the exchange of cash for an investment) will not have any net effect on the balance of the fund.

PERFORMANCE BY SUBTOPIC

Each category below parallels a subtopic covered in Chapter 5. Record the number and percentage of questions you correctly answered in each subtopic area.

Intangible Assets With Finite Useful Lives

Question #	Correct √
1	
2	
3	
4	
5	
6	
7	
8	
9	
10	
11	
12	
13	
14	
# Questions	14

Correct _____
% Correct _____

Goodwill

Question #	Correct √
15	
16	
17	
# Questions	3

Correct _____
% Correct _____

Research & Development

Question #	Correct √
18	
19	
20	
21	
22	
23	
# Questions	6

Correct _____
% Correct _____

Computer Software

Question #	Correct √
24	
25	
26	
27	
# Questions	4

Correct _____
% Correct _____

Prepaid Expenses

Question #	Correct √
28	
29	
30	
31	
32	
33	
34	
# Questions	7

Correct _____
% Correct _____

Cash Surrender Value of Life Insurance

Question #	Correct √
35	
36	
37	
38	
# Questions	4

Correct _____
% Correct _____

Special Purpose Funds

Question #	Correct √
39	
40	
41	
42	
# Questions	4

Correct _____
% Correct _____

ESSAY SOLUTIONS

SOLUTION 5-2   RESEARCH AND DEVELOPMENT COSTS/PATENT

a.   The costs of research equipment used exclusively for Trouver would be reported as research and development **expenses in the period incurred.**

The costs of research equipment used on **both Trouver and future** research projects would be **capitalized** and shown as **equipment (less accumulated depreciation)** on the **balance sheet.** An appropriate method of depreciation should be used. **Depreciation** on capitalized research equipment should be reported as a **research and development expense.**

b.   1.   Matching refers to the process of expense recognition by associating costs with revenues on a cause and effect basis.

2.   Research and development costs are usually **expensed** in the **period incurred** and may **not** be matched with revenues. This accounting treatment is justified by the **high degree** of **uncertainty** regarding the **amount and timing of future benefits.** A **direct relationship** between research and development costs and future revenues generally **cannot be demonstrated.**

c.   Corporate headquarters' costs allocated to research and development would be classified as **general and administrative expenses** in the **period incurred,** because they are **not clearly related** to research and development activities.

d.   On Clonal's statement of cash flows, the legal expenses incurred in defending the patent should be reported under **investing activities** in the **period paid.**

SELECT HOT•SPOTS™ VIDEO DESCRIPTIONS

CPA 3210 Assets

Bob Monette provides comprehensive coverage of accounts receivable, cash, investments in marketable debt and equity securities, off-balance sheet risk, fair value disclosure of financial instruments, derivative financial instruments, transfers of assets, notes receivable, expensing vs capitalizing of fixed assets, depreciation, exchange of similar and dissimilar assets, research and development costs, intangible assets, computer software costs…and more!

CPA 3250 Inventory

Provides comprehensive coverage of accounting for inventory, including measurement and ownership criteria and cost flow assumptions. Inventory methods are explained and illustrated in detail and include dollar value LIFO, link chain method and double extension method, lower of cost or market, and methods of estimation, including gross margin and retail methods. The effect of inventory errors is examined.

CPA 2090 Bonds & Other Liabilities

Provides comprehensive coverage of bonds from both the issuer's and investor's perspectives. Learn about bond discounts and premiums, both the straight-line and effective interest methods of amortizing the discounts and premiums, and term, serial, convertible, and debenture bonds. Also covered are current and accrued liabilities, estimated liabilities, and contingent liabilities.

Call our customer representatives toll-free at 1 (800) 874-7877 for more details about videos.

CHAPTER 6

BONDS

CHAPTER 6

BONDS

I. LONG-TERM INVESTMENTS

A. DEFINITIONS

1. **BONDS** Bonds are contractual agreements wherein the issuer (borrower) promises to pay the purchaser (lender) a principal amount at a designated future date. In addition, the borrower makes periodic interest payments based on the *face* amount of the bond and the stated rate of interest.

2. **HELD-TO-MATURITY SECURITIES** Under SFAS 115, held-to-maturity securities are defined as debt securities that the enterprise has the intent and the ability to hold to maturity. Securities classified as held-to-maturity are accounted for under the amortized cost method discussed in this section.

3. **SERIAL AND TERM BONDS** Bonds providing for repayment of principal in a series of installments are called *serial* bonds, whereas bonds maturing at a specified date are called *term* bonds.

4. **DEBENTURE BONDS** Debenture bonds are unsecured bonds; they are not supported by a lien or mortgage on specific assets.

5. **CALLABLE BONDS** Callable bonds may be retired at the issuer's option.

6. **CONVERTIBLE BONDS** Convertible bonds may be converted to stock at the bondholder's option.

B. ACQUISITION

Initial recording will be at an amount equal to the purchase price of the bond plus other direct costs of acquisition (e.g., broker's fees). The market price of a bond is determined based on the "market interest rate" that takes into consideration the stated (face) interest rate of the bonds, the credit worthiness of the debtor, the maturity date of the bonds, and other factors. The market price of the bond is equal to the present value of the bond's interest and principal payments, discounted using the market interest rate for that type of bond. If bonds are bought between interest dates, the purchaser will have to pay an additional amount for the interest accrued on the bond since the last interest date (or the bond date, if before the first interest date). This additional amount is **not** part of the cost of the bond investment, but must be recorded separately as purchased interest (i.e., interest receivable).

EXAMPLE 1 ♦ ACQUISITION OF BOND AND INTEREST PAYMENT

X buys at par on September 1, 20X1, a 10%, $1,000 bond issued on June 1, 20X1. Interest dates are June 1 and December 1.

Investment in Bonds	1,000	
Interest Receivable (10% x $1,000 x 3 months/12 months)	25	
Cash		1,025
To record the purchase of bonds on September 1.		
Cash (10% x $1,000 x 6/12)	50	
Interest Receivable		25
Interest Income		25
To record receipt of the interest proceeds on December 1.		

C. PREMIUM OR DISCOUNT

A premium or discount on bonds arises when the stated interest rate of the bonds is higher or lower, respectively, than the current market interest rate for similar securities. Bond premium or discount generally is **not** separately recorded (i.e., the bond investment is recorded at a net amount). Premiums or discounts on bonds held as a long-term investment must be amortized from date of acquisition to maturity date. APB 21, specifies that the interest method should be used to amortize these differences. Other methods of amortization (straight-line), may be used if the effects are not material. The amortization of a premium decreases both the bond investment and investment income, while the amortization of a discount increases these accounts.

EXAMPLE 2 ♦ BONDS ACQUIRED AT A DISCOUNT

On June 30, 20X1, ABC Corp. purchased 100 new bonds issued by XYZ Inc., with a total face amount of $100,000 and a 10% stated interest rate. The bonds mature in ten years and pay interest semiannually, on June 30 and December 31 (20 semiannual payments). The effective yield for similar securities is 12% annually and is reflected in the $88,530 purchase price paid by ABC Corp.

REQUIRED: Show how the appropriate purchase price of $88,530 for the $100,000 face amount of bonds is determined using the present value (PV) tables in Appendix D. In addition, prepare the journal entry to record the acquisition of the bonds.

SOLUTION:

Maturity (face) amount to be received	$ 100,000	
PV factor for a single amount (6%, 20 periods)—Table 2	x .311805	
Present value of the maturity amount		$31,180.50
Semiannual interest payment to be received ($100,000 x 10% x 6/12)	5,000	
PV factor for an ordinary annuity (6%, 20 periods)—Table 4	x11.469921	
Present value of future interest payments		57,349.60
Present value of the bonds		$88,530.10
Bond Investment	88,530	
Cash		88,530

EXAMPLE 3 ♦ INTEREST INCOME AND DISCOUNT AMORTIZATION

REQUIRED: Refer to the facts of Example 2. Provide ABC Corporation's entries to record interest income and discount amortization for the year ending December 31, 20X1, assuming (1) straight-line and (2) interest methods of discount amortization.

SOLUTION:

(1) *Straight-Line Method*:

Cash ($100,000 x .05)	5,000	
Bond Investment [($100,000 – $88,530) ÷ 20]	574*	
Interest Income		5,574

(2) *Interest Method*:

Cash ($100,000 x .05)	5,000	
Bond Investment (balancing amount)	312*	
Interest Income ($88,530 x .06)		5,312

* **NOTE:** The total amortization of the bond investment discount will be the same over the 10-year life of the bonds under either the straight-line or the interest method. As noted earlier, the amortization of the bond investment discount increases the Bond investment and Interest Income accounts. The amortization of a bond investment premium would decrease these accounts.

EXHIBIT 1 ♦ BOND PREMIUMS AND DISCOUNTS

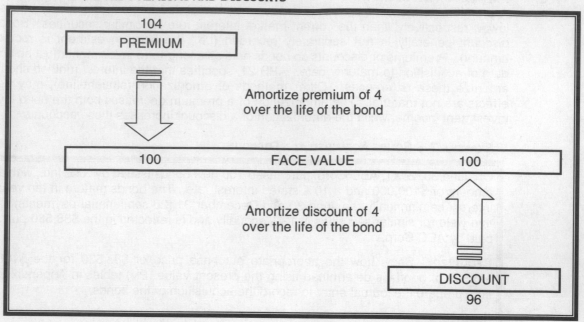

EXHIBIT 2 ♦ EFFECTIVE INTEREST METHOD

Bond issued at:	Effective interest rate	X	Carrying value	=	Amount of interest income/expense
Discount	Constant		Increasing		Increasing
Premium	Constant		Decreasing		Decreasing

D.   INTEREST ACCRUAL

The bond interest payment date and the investor's year-end may not coincide. In this case, the investor must accrue the interest income earned through year-end, including the required amortization of premium or discount.

EXAMPLE 4 ♦ DIFFERENT YEAR-END AND PAYMENT DATES

Refer to the facts of <u>Example 2</u>, but assume that ABC's year-end is March 31.

REQUIRED: Provide ABC's journal entries on March 31, 20X2 to record interest and discount amortization under both the straight-line and the interest methods.

SOLUTION:

(1)   *Straight-Line Method:*

Accrued Interest Receivable ($100,000 x .05 x 3/6)	2,500	
Bond Investment ($574 x 3/6)*	287	
Interest Income		2,787

(2)   *Interest Method:*

Accrued Interest Receivable	2,500	
Bond Investment (balancing amount)	165	
Interest Income [($88,530 + $312) x .06 x 3/6]		2,665

---

* On March 31, 20X2, ABC records interest income for 3 months of the six month payment. The 10% rate is an annual rate.

E.   SALE OF BOND INVESTMENTS
The sale of bonds held for investment will result in a gain or loss equal to the difference between the carrying amount of the bonds and the proceeds received on their disposal. This gain or loss is **not** an extraordinary item.

1.   **CARRYING AMOUNT** In determining the carrying amount of the bonds, adjustment must be made for premium or discount amortization to date of sale.

2.   **BONDS SOLD BETWEEN INTEREST DATES** If the bonds are sold between interest dates, part of the proceeds must be assigned to the interest accrued since the last interest date.

EXAMPLE 5 ♦ SALE OF BOND INVESTMENT

Refer to the facts of <u>Example 2</u>. On August 31, 20X5, ABC sold the 100 bonds to LMN Inc. for $92,000, which included interest accrued on the bonds. ABC amortized the original discount on the bonds under the straight-line method.

REQUIRED: Determine the gain (or loss) to be recognized by ABC on the sale of the bonds.

SOLUTION:

Proceeds received	$92,000
Less: Amount attributable to accrued interest, $100,000 x .05 x 2/6	(1,667)
Sale price of bonds	90,333
Carrying amount*	93,313
Gain (loss) on sale of bonds	$ (2,980)

COMPUTATIONS:

*Original purchase price, June 30, 20X1	$88,530
Plus discount amortization:	
Through June 30, 20X5 ($574 x 8)	4,592
July 1 to August 31, 20X5 ($574 ÷ 3)	191
Carrying amount of the bonds	$93,313

F.   CHANGES IN MARKET VALUE
Temporary fluctuations in the market value of bonds classified as held-to-maturity are not recognized in the accounts. Other than temporary market value declines are discussed in Chapter 2.

II. BONDS PAYABLE

A.   OVERVIEW
Bonds payable represent a contractual obligation to make periodic interest payments on the amount borrowed and to repay the principal upon maturity. Therefore, when a company sells a bond issue it is in effect selling two cash flows.

1.   **PRINCIPAL** The receipt of the bond principal at its maturity

2.   **INTEREST** The receipt of the periodic interest payments

B.   PRESENT VALUE
To estimate the proceeds to be received from the issuance of bonds payable (ignoring bond issue costs), the present values of the bond principal and interest payments must be determined. The stated interest rate of the bonds is used to determine the periodic interest payments. The prevailing market (yield) rate is used to discount the cash flows to arrive at their present value.

C.   *DISCLOSURE*
SFAS 47 requires that the combined aggregate amount of maturities and sinking fund requirements for all long-term borrowings be disclosed for each of the five years following the date of the latest balance sheet presented.

III. RECORDING THE BOND ISSUE BY DEBTOR

A. BOND ISSUANCE

When bonds are issued, only the face amount of the bonds is recorded in the Bonds Payable account. The bond discount or premium, if any, is recorded in a separate account and reported in the balance sheet as a direct deduction from or addition to the face amount of the bond.

EXAMPLE 6 ♦ BOND ISSUANCE

On January 1, 20X1, Maple Company issued five-year bonds with a face amount of $200,000 and a stated interest rate of 8%, payable semiannually on June 30 and December 31. The bonds were priced to yield 6%. The present value factor for the present value of $1 for 10 periods at 3% is .74409; the factor for the present value of an ordinary annuity of $1 for 10 periods at 3% is 8.53020.

REQUIRED: Determine the total issue price of the bonds. Record their issuance.

SOLUTION:

Present value of principal payment	
[$200,000 x .74409 (PV of $1 for 10 periods at 3%)]	$148,818
Present value of periodic interest payments [($200,000 x 8% ÷ 2) x 8.53020]	68,242
Amount received from the issuance of the bonds	$217,060

The stated rate of interest (8%) is above the market rate (6%). Therefore, these bonds were sold at a premium. The following entry is made to record the issuance of the bonds:

Cash	217,060	
Bonds Payable		200,000
Bond Premium (difference)		17,060

B. BOND SELLING PRICE

1. **PREMIUM** A bond will sell at a **premium** (more than par) when the stated interest rate is *greater* than the market rate for similar debt.

2. **DISCOUNT** A bond will sell at a **discount** (less than par) when the stated interest rate is *less* than the market rate.

3. **PAR** A bond will sell at **par** when the stated interest rate *equals* the market rate.

C. BOND ISSUE COSTS

1. **COSTS INCLUDED** Bond issue costs include legal fees, accounting fees, underwriting commissions, registration, printing and engraving, and other such costs incurred in preparing and selling a bond issue.

2. **CLASSIFICATION** According to APB 21, *Interest on Receivables and Payables*, bond issue costs should be classified as a *deferred charge* (i.e., asset) and amortized over the life of the bonds as an increase to interest expense. (Alternately, under the Statements of Financial Accounting Concepts, issuance costs could be accounted for either as an expense in the period incurred or as a reduction of the noncurrent debt liability, and accounted for the same as debt discount.)

3. **AMORTIZATION** The amortization of bond issue costs is affected when a bond issue is sold between interest dates because the issue costs should be amortized over the period from the date of sale (not the date of the bond) to the maturity date.

IV. PREMIUM AND DISCOUNT AMORTIZATION BY DEBTOR

A. STRAIGHT-LINE METHOD

Straight-line amortization calls for the amortization of an equal amount of premium or discount each period over the life of the bonds. The straight-line method is acceptable only when the premium or discount is immaterial, because it fails to determine the periodic interest expense in terms of the effective rate of interest.

EXAMPLE 7 ♦ STRAIGHT-LINE AMORTIZATION

To amortize the premium in Example 6 using the straight-line method, divide the premium by the number of interest periods: $17,060 ÷ 10 = $1,706.

B. INTEREST METHOD

The interest method of amortization calls for recognizing interest expense at the effective interest rate at which the bonds were sold. Thus, the interest method overcomes the criticism of the straight-line method because it offers a more accurate measurement of interest expense.

EXAMPLE 8 ♦ INTEREST METHOD AMORTIZATION

To amortize the premium in Example 6 using the interest method, multiply the carrying amount of the bond issue ($217,060) by the effective yield (3%). This equals interest expense for the period ($6,512). The difference between the cash interest payment and the interest expense equals the amount of premium amortization for the period ($8,000 − $6,512 = $1,488). This procedure is followed each period until the maturity date when the premium (or discount) will be fully amortized.

EXAMPLE 9 ♦ INTEREST PAYMENTS

REQUIRED: Record the first four interest payments for the bonds illustrated in Example 6, rounding amounts to the nearest dollar.

SOLUTION:

6/30/X1:	Interest Expense [($200,000 + 17,060) x .03]	6,512	
	Bond Premium (to balance)	1,488	
	Cash ($200,000 x .04)		8,000
12/31/X1:	Interest Expense [($200,000 + 15,572*) x .03]	6,467	
	Bond Premium (to balance)	1,533	
	Cash ($200,000 x .04)		8,000
	* $17,060 − $1,488		
6/30/X2:	Interest Expense [($200,000 + $14,039*) x .03]	6,421	
	Bond Premium (to balance)	1,579	
	Cash ($200,000 x .04)		8,000
	* $15,572 − $1,533		
12/31/X2:	Interest Expense [($200,000 + 12,460*) x .03]	6,374	
	Bond Premium (to balance)	1,626	
	Cash ($200,000 x .04)		8,000
	* $14,039 − $1,579		

EXHIBIT 3 ♦ BOND PREMIUM AMORTIZATION TABLE

(1) Period	(2) Cash interest payments	(3) 3% x Prior (6) interest expense	(4) (2) – (3) Premium amortization	(5) Prior (5) – (4) unamortized premium	(6) $200,000 + (5) Carrying amount
0	--	--	--	$17,060.00	$217,060.00
1	$8,000	$6,511.80	$1,488.20	15,571.80	215,571.80
2	8,000	6,467.15	1,532.85	14,038.95	214,038.95
3	8,000	6,421.17	1,578.83	12,460.12	212,460.12
4	8,000	6,373.80	1,626.20	10,833.93	210,833.93
5	8,000	6,325.02	1,674.98	9,158.94	209,158.94
6	8,000	6,274.77	1,725.23	7,433.71	207,433.71
7	8,000	6,223.01	1,776.99	5,656.72	205,656.72
8	8,000	6,169.70	1,830.30	3,826.43	203,826.43
9	8,000	6,114.79	1,885.21	1,941.22	201,941.22
10	8,000	6,058.79*	1,941.21	0	200,000.00

* $.55 difference due to rounding

C. AMORTIZATION EFFECTS

Amortization of a bond *premium* will *decrease* interest expense and the carrying amount of the bond for the issuer, while the amortization of a bond *discount* will *increase* the issuer's interest expense and the carrying amount of the bond.

D. INTEREST AND YEAR-END DATES DIFFER

An adjusting entry is required when interest dates do not coincide with the end of the accounting period, to record accrued interest expense and bond premium or discount amortization.

EXAMPLE 10 ♦ INTEREST AND YEAR-END DATES DIFFER

In Example 6, assume the end of the accounting period comes 3 months after the bonds are issued. The required entry at 3/31/X1 would be the following:

Interest Expense ($6,512 x 3/6)	3,256	
Bond Premium ($1,488 x 3/6)	744	
Accrued Interest Payable ($8,000 x 3/6)		4,000

E. ISSUANCE BETWEEN INTEREST DATES

Bonds payable are often sold between interest dates. If bond issue costs or a bond premium or discount is involved, it must be amortized over the period the bonds are outstanding.

EXAMPLE 11 ♦ ISSUANCE BETWEEN INTEREST DATES

On March 1, 20X1, Trisha Company issued 12% ten-year bonds with a face amount of $1,000. The bonds are dated January 1, 20X1, and interest is payable semiannually on January 1 and July 1. The bonds were sold at par and accrued interest.

REQUIRED: Present the journal entries required to record the issuance of the bonds and the first interest payment.

(continued on next page)

SOLUTION:

The issuance of the bonds would be recorded as follows:

Cash	1,020	
Bonds Payable (face amount)		1,000
Accrued Interest Payable ($1,000 x .12 x 2/12)		20

The payment of interest on July 1 would be recorded as follows:

Interest Expense (to balance)	40	
Accrued Interest Payable (from above)	20	
Cash ($1,000 x .12 x 6/12)		60

F.   USE OF OTHER AMORTIZATION

Use of the effective interest method results in a constant *rate* of interest when applied to the carrying amount of the bonds at the beginning of the period. As with long-term notes payable, other amortization methods may be used when the results do *not differ materially* from those obtained with the *effective interest method*.

V.   RETIREMENT OF BONDS

A.   EXTINGUISHMENT OF DEBT

1.   CIRCUMSTANCES FOR AN EXTINGUISHMENT OF DEBT   A debtor will consider debt to be extinguished for financial reporting purposes in the following situations:

    a.   PAYMENT   The debtor pays the creditor and is relieved of all its obligations with respect to the debt, including the debtor's reacquisition of its outstanding debt securities through cancellation or holding as treasury bonds.

    b.   LEGAL RELEASE   The debtor is legally released from being the primary obligor under the debt, either judicially or by the creditor.

2.   EXTINGUISHMENT VS. REFUNDING   Extinguishment includes the reacquisition of debt securities regardless of whether the securities are canceled or held as so-called treasury bonds. Refunding refers to achieving the reacquisition by the use of proceeds from issuing other securities.

3.   GAIN OR LOSS RECOGNITION   The extinguishment of debt, irrespective of the method used (except certain conversions of convertible bonds into stock or extinguishment through a troubled debt restructuring) involves recognition of a gain or loss in the period in which the extinguishment took place. The gain or loss is reported as an extraordinary item, net of related income tax effects.

B.   WRITE-OFF PRINCIPAL AND PREMIUM/DISCOUNT

When all or part of a bond issue is retired before maturity, it is necessary to write off both the principal and the pro rata portion of the unamortized premium or discount on the bonds retired.

C.   EXTRAORDINARY GAIN OR LOSS

The difference between carrying amount of the bonds retired before maturity and the redemption price should be recorded as an *extraordinary* gain or loss, net of the related income tax effect.

EXAMPLE 12 ♦ EXTRAORDINARY ITEM

On January 1, 20X1, Ben Corporation issued $600,000 of 5% ten-year bonds at 103. Ben records amortization using the straight-line method (i.e., the amount is considered immaterial). On December 31, 20X5, when the fair value of the bonds was 97, Ben repurchased $300,000 of the bonds in the open market at 97. Ben has recorded interest and amortization for 20X5. Ben should record this retirement as follows:

Bonds Payable ($600,000 x .50)	300,000	
Bond Premium ($9,000 x .50)	4,500	
Cash ($300,000 x .97)		291,000
Extraordinary Gain on Bond Retirement		13,500*

*COMPUTATIONS:

Original carrying amount ($600,000 x 103%)		$618,000
Premium to be amortized ($618,000 – $600,000)	$18,000	
Amortization [($18,000 ÷ 10) x 5 yrs.]	9,000	9,000
Carrying amount of bonds, 12/31/X5		609,000
Portion of bonds retired		x 50%
Carrying amount of bonds retired		304,500
Purchase price ($300,000 x 97%)		291,000
Gain on bond retirement, before income taxes		$ 13,500

NOTE: If Ben has an effective income tax rate of 30% and income taxes are considered, the extraordinary gain, net of the related income tax effects, would be $9,450 [$13,500 x (1 – 30%)].

D.   **WRITE-OFF OF BOND ISSUE COSTS**
If bond issue costs have been incurred and recorded as an asset (i.e., as a deferred charge), when a bond issue is retired before maturity it is also necessary to write off a pro rata portion of the bond issue costs. The amount of such write-off increases any loss or reduces any gain recognized on the retirement.

EXAMPLE 13 ♦ WRITE-OFF OF BOND ISSUE COSTS

If bond issue costs of $10,000 were recorded as an asset in the issuance of the bonds in Example 12, above, the gain on retirement before income taxes would be $11,000 [$13,500 – ($10,000 x 5/10 x 50%)].

VI. **BONDS WITH ADDITIONAL FEATURES**

A.   **SERIAL BONDS**
Bonds providing for a series of installments for repayment of principal.

1.   **PRESENT VALUES** To determine the selling price of serial bonds, compute the present value of the principal and interest payments for each series separately, then total the present value of each series.

2.   **DECLINING PRINCIPAL** The amortization of bond premium or discount on serial bonds requires the recognition of a declining debt principal. Successive bond years cannot be charged with equal amounts of premium or discount because of a shrinking debt and successively smaller interest payments.

3.   **AMORTIZATION OF PREMIUM/DISCOUNT** Bond premium or discount, if material, should be amortized using the effective interest method prescribed by APB 21.

B.   **CONVERTIBLE BONDS**
Convertible bonds provide the bond holder the option of converting the bond to capital stock, typically common stock. According to APB 14, *Accounting for Convertible Debt and Debt Issued With*

Stock Purchase Warrants, no proceeds from the debt issue are to be assigned to the conversion feature (even though the convertible bonds may sell for substantially more than similar nonconvertible bonds). The reason for no allocation to *equity* is that the debt cannot be separated from the conversion feature, as would be the case with detachable stock warrants.

1. **BOOK VALUE METHOD** The conversion of the bonds into common stock is generally recorded by crediting the paid-in capital accounts for the carrying amount of the debt at the date of the conversion; thus, no gain or loss is recognized upon conversion. Costs associated with the conversion are **not** recognized as an expense. The paid-in capital accounts are credited for the carrying amount of the debt converted, **less** any costs associated with the conversion.

2. **MARKET VALUE METHOD** Alternately, the market value method recognizes a gain or loss on retirement equal to the difference between the carrying amount of the debt at the date of the conversion and the fair value of the shares issued upon conversion.

EXAMPLE 14 ♦ BOND CONVERSION

Bonds with a face amount of $10,000 and a carrying amount of $10,400 are converted into 100 shares of $50 par common stock with $90 fair value.

REQUIRED: Record the conversion of the bonds in the books of the issuer under the following:

(1) The book value method
(2) The market value method

SOLUTION:

(1) *Book Value Method*:

Bonds Payable	10,000	
Bond Premium	400	
Common Stock (100 x $50 PV)		5,000
Add'l. Paid-In Capital (to balance)		5,400

(2) *Market Value Method*:

Bonds Payable	10,000	
Bond Premium	400	
Common Stock (100 x $50 PV)		5,000
Add'l. Paid-In Capital [100 x ($90 FV – $50 PV)]		4,000
Gain on Conversion ($10,400 – $9,000)		1,400

3. **INDUCED CONVERSIONS OF CONVERTIBLE DEBT (SFAS 84)** APB 26 generally requires gain or loss recognition on the *retirement* of debt, including certain convertible debt. Opinion 26, however, does not apply to debt that is *converted* to equity securities of the debtor pursuant to conversion privileges provided in the terms of the debt at issuance. As illustrated in Example 10, the conversion of convertible debt securities to stock may or may not result in gain recognition, depending on whether the book value or the market value method is used. (However, the same method must be consistently applied.)

   a. **APPLICABILITY** SFAS 84, *Induced Conversions of Convertible Debt*, applies to a specific situation in which a debtor attempts to induce prompt conversion of convertible debt to equity securities.

      (1) To achieve this, the debtor may offer debt holders a higher conversion ratio, payment of additional consideration, or other favorable changes to the original terms of conversion. Under SFAS 84, induced conversions that meet certain specified criteria will be excluded from the scope of APB 26 and will be accounted for instead as indicated in b., below. These criteria are as follows:

(a) The conversion occurs pursuant to changed conversion privileges that are exercisable only for a limited period of time.

(b) The changed terms are applicable to the issuance of all of the equity securities issuable pursuant to the original conversion privileges for each debt instrument that is converted.

(2) The changed terms may involve reduction of the original conversion price, thereby resulting in the issuance of additional shares of stock, issuance of warrants or other securities not provided for in the original conversion terms, or payment of cash or other consideration to those debt holders who convert during the specified time period.

b. **EXPENSE RECOGNITION** When convertible debt is converted to equity securities of the debtor pursuant to an inducement offer described in a., above, the debtor enterprise should recognize an expense equal to the fair value of all securities and other consideration transferred in excess of the fair value of securities issuable pursuant to the original conversion terms.

(1) This expense should **not** be reported as an extraordinary item.

(2) The fair value of the securities or other consideration should be measured as of the date the inducement offer is accepted by the convertible debt holder. Normally this will be the date the debt holder converts the convertible debt into equity securities or enters into a binding agreement to do so.

c. **EXCLUSIONS** This Statement does not apply to conversions pursuant to other changes in conversion privileges or to changes in terms of convertible debt instruments that are different from those described above.

C. **DEBT ISSUED WITH DETACHABLE STOCK WARRANTS**
When bonds are issued with detachable stock warrants, APB 14, *Accounting for Convertible Debt and Debt Issued With Stock Purchase Warrants*, requires allocation of the proceeds between the warrants and the debt security based on relative fair values. If the FV of one security is not determinable, the proceeds are assigned based on the FV of the other security. The rationale behind this allocation is that, even if the warrants are exercised, the debt will still remain. There are two separate elements, the debt and the warrants. The warrants are accounted for as paid-in capital.

EXAMPLE 15 ♦ DETACHABLE STOCK WARRANTS

On November 1, 20X3, two hundred $1,000, 8% bonds due October 31, 20X7, were sold at 103 with one detachable stock purchase warrant attached to each bond. The fair value of the bonds without the stock warrants is 98. The fair value of the warrants has not been determined. Each warrant entitles the holder to purchase ten shares of common stock (par $10) at $30 per share.

Borrower			Investor (net)		
Cash	206,000		Bond Investment	196,000	
Bond Discount	4,000		Stock Warrants	10,000	
Bond Payable		200,000	Cash		206,000
APIC-Stock Warrants		10,000			

(continued on next page)

COMPUTATIONS:

Cash proceeds [(200 x $1,000) x 103%]	$206,000
Proceeds allocated to bonds (200 x $1,000 x 98%)	196,000
Proceeds allocated to warrants (remainder)	$ 10,000
Bond discount ($200,000 – $196,000)	$ 4,000

If 100 of the 200 stock purchase warrants are exercised:

Borrower		Investor (net)	
Cash (100 x 10 x $30)	30,000	Inv. in Common Stock	
APIC-Stock Warrants		(1,000 x $35)	35,000
($10,000 x 100/200)	5,000	Stock Warrants	
Common Stock		($10,000 x 100/200)	5,000
(1,000 x $10 PV)	10,000	Cash (100 x 10 x $30)	30,000
APIC-Common St. (to bal.)	25,000		

VII. COMPARISON OF BORROWER AND INVESTOR JOURNAL ENTRIES

A. PREMIUMS & DISCOUNTS

EXAMPLE 16 ♦ STRAIGHT-LINE PREMIUM AMORTIZATION

On January 1, 20X1, a $1,000 face value, two-year bond, with a 10% coupon rate of interest is sold for 104. The effective yield is 7.8%. Interest is paid semi-annually on June 30 and December 31. Use the straight-line method to amortize the premium.

Borrower			Investor		
January 1, 20X1					
Cash	1,040		Invest. in Bond	1,040	
Bond Payable		1,000	Cash		1,040
Premium		40			
June 30, 20X1					
Interest Expense	40		Cash	50	
Premium	10		Invest. in Bond		10
Cash		50	Interest Income		40
Same journal entries for next 3 periods.			Same journal entries for next 3 periods.		
December 31, 20X2					
Bond Payable	1,000		Cash	1,000	
Cash		1,000	Invest. in Bond		1,000

EXAMPLE 17 ♦ STRAIGHT-LINE DISCOUNT AMORTIZATION

Same facts as Example 16, except that the bond is sold for 96 and the effective interest rate is 12.3%.

Borrower			Investor		
January 1, 20X1					
Cash	960		Invest. in Bond	960	
Discount	40		Cash		960
Bond Payable		1,000			
June 30, 20X1					
Interest Expense	60		Cash	50	
Cash		50	Invest. in Bond	10	
Discount		10	Interest Income		60
Same journal entries for next 3 periods.			Same journal entries for next 3 periods.		
December 31, 20X2					
Bond Payable	1,000		Cash	1,000	
Cash		1,000	Invest. in Bond		1,000

EXAMPLE 18 ♦ INTEREST METHOD OF PREMIUM AMORTIZATION

Same facts as Example 16, except use the interest method to amortize the premium.

Borrower			Investor		
January 1, 20X1					
Cash	1,040.00				
Bond Payable		1,000.00	Invest. in Bond	1,040.00	
Premium		40.00	Cash		1,040.00
June 30, 20X1					
Interest Expense			Cash	50.00	
[$1,000 + $40) × 3.9%]	40.56		Invest. in Bond		9.44
Premium	9.44		Interest Income		40.56
Cash		50.00			
December 31, 20X1					
Interest Expense			Cash	50.00	
[($1,000 + 30.56) × 3.9%]	40.19		Invest. in Bond		9.81
Premium	9.81		Interest Income		40.19
Cash		50.00			
June 30, 20X2					
Interest Expense			Cash	50.00	
[(1,000 + 20.75) × 3.9%]	39.81		Invest. in Bond		10.19
Premium	10.19		Interest Income		39.81
Cash		50.00			
December 31, 20X2					
Interest Expense			Cash	50.00	
(1,000 + 10.56) × 3.9%]	39.41		Invest. in Bond		10.59
Premium	10.59		Interest Income		39.41
Cash		50.00			
Bond Payable	1,000.00		Cash	1,000.00	
Cash		1,000.00	Invest. in Bond		1,000.00

(Amortization of Premium: 9.44 + 9.81 + 10.19 + 10.59 = 40.03 **NOTE**: Difference due to rounding.)

EXAMPLE 19 ♦ INTEREST METHOD OF DISCOUNT AMORTIZATION

Same facts as Example 17, except use the interest method to amortize the discount.

Borrower			Investor		
January 1, 20X1					
Cash	960.00		Invest. in Bond	960.00	
Discount	40.00		Cash		960.00
Bond Payable		1,000.00			
June 30, 20X1					
Interest Expense			Cash	50.00	
[(1,000 − 40) × 6.15%]	59.04		Invest. in Bond	9.04	
Cash		50.00	Interest Income		59.04
Discount		9.04			
December 31, 20X1					
Interest Expense			Cash	50.00	
[($1,000 − 30.96) × 6.15%]	59.60		Invest. in Bond	9.60	
Cash		50.00	Interest Income		59.60
Discount		9.60			
June 30, 20X2					
Interest Expense			Cash	50.00	
[(1,000 − 21.36) × 6.15%]	60.19		Invest. in Bond	10.19	
Cash		50.00	Interest Income		60.19
Discount		10.19			
December 31, 20X2					
Interest Expense			Cash	50.00	
[(1,000 − 11.18) × 6.15%]	60.81		Invest. in Bond	10.81	
Cash		50.00	Interest Income		60.81
Discount		10.81			

(Amortization of discount: 9.04 + 9.60 + 10.19 + 10.81 = 39.63 **NOTE:** Difference due to rounding.)

B. MIDPERIOD ISSUE

EXAMPLE 20 ♦ ISSUANCE BETWEEN INTEREST DATES

$1,000 face value, 2-year bond with a 10% coupon rate of interest is sold on April 1, 20X1, at par. Interest is paid semi-annually on June 30 and December 31.

Borrower			Investor		
April 1, 20X1					
Cash	1,025		Invest. in Bond	1,000	
Bond Payable		1,000	Interest Receivable	25	
			Cash		1,025
Interest Payable		25			
June 30, 20X1					
Interest Expense	25		Cash	50	
Interest Payable	25		Interest Income		25
Cash		50	Interest Receivable		25

C. CONVERTIBLE BONDS

EXAMPLE 21 ♦ CONVERTIBLE BONDS, BOOK VALUE METHOD

On January 1, 20X1, 100 bonds with $1,000 face values and each with 20 nondetachable stock warrants (100 × 20 = 2,000) are sold at 105. Twenty warrants, one bond, and $800 may be converted into one share of $200 par value common stock. 50% of the bonds are converted on June 30, and the book value method is used to record the conversion.

Borrower			Investor		
January 1, 20X1					
Cash	105,000		Invest. in Bond	105,000	
Bond Payable		100,000	Cash		105,000
Premium		5,000			
June 30, 20X1					
Cash	40,000		Invest. in Stock	92,500	
Bond Payable	50,000		Cash		40,000
Premium	2,500		Invest. in Bond		52,500
Common Stock		10,000			
APIC		82,500			

COMPUTATIONS:

Bond	$1,000	x 50	=	$ 50,000
Premium	$5,000	x 50%	=	2,500
Cash	$ 800	x 50	=	40,000
				$ 92,500
Common stock	$200 par	x 50	=	(10,000)
APIC				$ 82,500

EXAMPLE 22 ♦ CONVERTIBLE BONDS, MARKET VALUE METHOD

On January 1, 20X1, 100 bonds with $1,000 face values and each with 20 nondetachable stock warrants (100 × 20 = 2,000) are sold at 105. Twenty warrants, one bond, and $800 may be converted into one share of $200 par value common stock. All of the bonds are converted on June 30, 20X1. The market value method is used to record the conversion and the fair value of the stock on the date of conversion is $2,000.

Borrower			Investor		
January 1, 20X1					
Cash	105,000		Invest. in Bond	105,000	
Bond Payable		100,000	Cash		105,000
Premium		5,000			
June 30, 20X1					
Cash	80,000		Invest. in Stock	200,000	
Bond Payable	100,000		Cash		80,000
Premium	5,000		Invest. in Bond		105,000
Loss on Conversion	15,000		Gain on Conversion		15,000
Common Stock		20,000			
APIC		180,000			

COMPUTATIONS:

Bond	$1,000 x 100	=	$100,000
Cash	$ 800 x 100	=	80,000
Common stock	$200 par x 100	=	20,000
APIC	($2,000 – 200) x 100	=	180,000

Common stock	$ 20,000	
APIC	180,000	
		$ 200,000
Bond	$100,000	
Premium	5,000	
Cash	80,000	
		(185,000)
Loss		$ 15,000

D. WARRANTS

EXAMPLE 23 ♦ DETACHABLE WARRANTS

On January 1, 20X1, 100 bonds with $1,000 face values and each with 20 detachable stock warrants (100 × 20 = 2,000) are sold at 105. Twenty warrants and $800 may be converted into one share of $200 par value common stock. The warrants have a fair value of $12,000 and expire on July 1, 20X1. One half of the warrants are exercised on June 30 and the other half expire on July 1.

Borrower			Investor		
January 1, 20X1					
Cash	105,000		Invest. in Bond	93,000	
Discount	7,000		Warrants	12,000	
Bond Payable		100,000	Cash		105,000
APIC—Warrants		12,000			
June 30, 20X1					
Cash	40,000		Invest. in Stock	46,000	
APIC—Warrant	6,000		Cash		40,000
Common Stock		10,000	Warrants		6,000
APIC		36,000			
July 1, 20X1					
APIC—Warrant	6,000		Loss on Investment	6,000	
APIC		6,000	Warrants		6,000

COMPUTATIONS:

Warrant	$12,000	x 50%	=	$ 6,000
Cash	$ 800	x 50	=	40,000
				$ 46,000
Common stock	$200 par	x 50	=	(10,000)
APIC				$ 36,000

Don't forget the helpful hints in the material at the front and back of this text!

Now that you have had a chance to become familiar with the text format, you may want to skim the **Getting Started, Practical Advice,** and **Accounting for 5%** sections of the book again. These provide:

- information on how to integrate materials so they work best for you

- helpful information on answering all question types

- information on the heavily tested topics on exams

- information on how to use your time wisely

- exam taking techniques that will earn extra points on the exam

Remember, with the techniques and information in your material,

A passing score is well within reach!

CHAPTER 6—BONDS

PROBLEM 6-1 MULTIPLE CHOICE QUESTIONS (96 to 120 minutes)

1. Kale purchased bonds at a discount on the open market as an investment and intends to hold these bonds to maturity. Kale should account for these bonds at
a. Cost.
b. Amortized cost.
c. Fair value.
d. Lower of cost or market.
(11/94, FAR, #10, amended, 5275)

2. An investor purchased a bond classified as a long-term investment between interest dates at a discount. At the purchase date, the carrying amount of the bond is more than the

	Cash paid to seller	Face amount of bond
a.	No	Yes
b.	No	No
c.	Yes	No
d.	Yes	Yes

(5/91, Theory, #4, 1781)

3. In 1991, Lee Co. acquired, at a premium, Enfield Inc. 10-year bonds as a long-term investment. At December 31, 1992, Enfield's bonds were quoted at a small discount. Which of the following situations is the most likely cause of the decline in the bonds' market value?
a. Enfield issued a stock dividend.
b. Enfield is expected to call the bonds at a premium, which is less than Lee's carrying amount.
c. Interest rates have declined since Lee purchased the bonds.
d. Interest rates have increased since Lee purchased the bonds. (5/93, Theory, #11, 4199)

4. On July 1, 1992, York Co. purchased as a long-term investment $1,000,000 of Park Inc.'s 8% bonds for $946,000, including accrued interest of $40,000. The bonds were purchased to yield 10% interest. The bonds mature on January 1, 1999, and pay interest annually on January 1. York uses the effective interest method of amortization. In its December 31, 1992 balance sheet, what amount should York report as investment in bonds?
a. $911,300
b. $916,600
c. $953,300
d. $960,600
(5/93, PI, #15, 4057)

5. On July 1, 1991, Cody Co. paid $1,198,000 for 10%, 20-year bonds with a face amount of $1,000,000. Interest is paid on December 31 and June 30. The bonds were purchased to yield 8%. Cody uses the effective interest rate method to recognize interest income from this investment. What should be reported as the carrying amount of the bonds in Cody's December 31, 1991 balance sheet?
a. $1,207,900
b. $1,198,000
c. $1,195,920
d. $1,193,050
(5/92, PI, #12, 2579)

6. On October 1, 1996, Park Co. purchased 200 of the $1,000 face amount, 10% bonds of Ott, Inc., for $220,000, including accrued interest of $5,000. The bonds, which mature on January 1, 2003, pay interest semiannually on January 1 and July 1. Park used the straight-line method of amortization and appropriately recorded the bonds as a long-term investment. On Park's December 31, 1997 balance sheet, the bonds should be reported at
a. $215,000.
b. $214,400.
c. $214,200.
d. $212,000.
(11/90, PI, #4, amended, 0971)

7. On July 1, 1997, Pell Co. purchased Green Corp. ten-year, 8% bonds with a face amount of $500,000 for $420,000. The bonds mature on June 30, 2005 and pay interest semiannually on June 30 and December 31. Using the interest method, Pell recorded bond discount amortization of $1,800 for the six months ended December 31, 1997. From this long-term investment, Pell should report 1997 revenue of
a. $16,800.
b. $18,200.
c. $20,000.
d. $21,800.
(5/90, PI, #46, amended, 0976)

8. On July 1, 1997, East Co. purchased as a long-term investment $500,000 face amount, 8% bonds of Rand Corp. for $461,500 to yield 10% per year. The bonds pay interest semiannually on January 1 and July 1. In its December 31, 1997 balance sheet, East should report interest receivable of
a. $18,460.
b. $20,000.
c. $23,075.
d. $25,000.
(11/88, PI, #18, amended, 9018)

9. Jent Corp. purchased bonds at a discount of $10,000. Subsequently, Jent sold these bonds at a premium of $14,000. During the period that Jent held this investment, amortization of the discount amounted to $2,000. What amount should Jent report as gain on the sale of bonds?
a. $12,000
b. $22,000
c. $24,000
d. $26,000   (5/94, FAR, #43, 4858)

10. The market price of a bond issued at a premium is equal to the present value of its principal amount
a. Only, at the stated interest rate.
b. And the present value of all future interest payments, at the stated interest rate.
c. Only, at the market (effective) interest rate.
d. And the present value of all future interest payments, at the market (effective) interest rate.
                                    (11/97, FAR, #9, 6489)

11. On January 1, 1994, Oak Co. issued 400 of its 8%, $1,000 bonds at 97 plus accrued interest. The bonds are dated October 1, 1993, and mature on October 1, 2003. Interest is payable semiannually on April 1 and October 1. Accrued interest for the period October 1, 1993, to January 1, 1994, amounted to $8,000. On January 1, 1994, what amount should Oak report as bonds payable, net of discount?
a. $380,300
b. $388,000
c. $388,300
d. $392,000   (5/94, FAR, #29, 4844)

12. Perk, Inc. issued $500,000, 10% bonds to yield 8%. Bond issuance costs were $10,000. How should Perk calculate the net proceeds to be received from the issuance?
a. Discount the bonds at the stated rate of interest.
b. Discount the bonds at the market rate of interest.
c. Discount the bonds at the stated rate of interest and deduct bond issuance costs.
d. Discount the bonds at the market rate of interest and deduct bond issuance costs.
                                    (R/99, FAR, #9, 6778)

13. On June 30, 1990, Huff Corp. issued at 99, one thousand of its 8%, $1,000 bonds. The bonds were issued through an underwriter to whom Huff paid bond issue costs of $35,000. On June 30, 1990, Huff should report the bond liability at
a. $ 955,000.
b. $ 990,000.
c. $1,000,000.
d. $1,025,000.   (11/90, PI, #24, 1031)

14. On January 2, 1992, Gill Co. issued $2,000,000 of 10-year, 8% bonds at par. The bonds, dated January 1, 1992, pay interest semiannually on January 1 and July 1. Bond issue costs were $250,000. What amount of bond issue costs are unamortized at June 30, 1993?
a. $237,500
b. $225,000
c. $220,800
d. $212,500   (11/93, PI, #34, 4403)

15. During 1992, Lake Co. issued 3,000 of its 9%, $1,000 face value bonds at 101½. In connection with the sale of these bonds, Lake paid the following expenses:

Promotion costs $20,000
Engraving and printing   25,000
Underwriters' commissions   200,000

What amount should Lake record as bond issue costs to be amortized over the term of the bonds?
a. $0
b. $220,000
c. $225,000
d. $245,000   (11/92, PI, #37, 3270)

16. Dixon Co. incurred costs of $3,300 when it issued, on August 31, 1991, 5-year debenture bonds dated April 1, 1991. What amount of bond issue expense should Dixon report in its income statement for the year ended December 31, 1991?
a. $ 220
b. $ 240
c. $ 495
d. $3,300   (5/92, PI, #29, 2598)

17. A company issued ten-year term bonds at a discount in 1996. Bond issue costs were incurred at that time. The company uses the effective interest method to amortize bond issue costs. Reporting the bond issue costs as a deferred charge would result in
a. More of a reduction in net income in 1997 than reporting the bond issue costs as a reduction of the related debt liability.
b. The same reduction in net income in 1997 as reporting the bond issue costs as a reduction of the related debt liability.
c. Less of a reduction in net income in 1997 than reporting the bond issue costs as a reduction of the related debt liability.
d. No reduction in net income in 1997.
                                    (11/88, Theory, #15, amended, 9019)

18. For a bond issue which sells for less than its face amount, the market rate of interest is
a. Dependent on rate stated on the bond.
b. Equal to rate stated on the bond.
c. Less than rate stated on the bond.
d. Higher than rate stated on the bond.
(11/86, Theory, #17, 1870)

19. Theoretically, which of the following could be accounted for as a deferred charge, a reduction of the related debt liability, or an expense of the period of borrowing?
a. Discount on bonds payable
b. Premium on bonds payable
c. Bond issue costs
d. Loss on extinguishment of debt
(11/84, Theory, #24, 1889)

20. On January 2, 1994, Nast Co. issued 8% bonds with a face amount of $1,000,000 that mature on January 2, 2000. The bonds were issued to yield 12%, resulting in a discount of $150,000. Nast incorrectly used the straight-line method instead of the effective interest method to amortize the discount. How is the carrying amount of the bonds affected by the error?

	At December 31, 1994	At January 2, 2000
a.	Overstated	Understated
b.	Overstated	No effect
c.	Understated	Overstated
d.	Understated	No effect

(5/95, FAR, #20, 5556)

21. Webb Co. has outstanding a 7%, 10-year $100,000 face-value bond. The bond was originally sold to yield 6% annual interest. Webb uses the effective interest rate method to amortize bond premium. On June 30, 1992, the carrying amount of the outstanding bond was $105,000. What amount of unamortized premium on bond should Webb report in its June 30, 1993 balance sheet?
a. $1,050
b. $3,950
c. $4,300
d. $4,500
(11/93, PI, #36, 4405)

22. On May 1, 1992, Bolt Corp. issued 11% bonds in the face amount of $1,000,000 that mature on May 1, 2002. The bonds were issued to yield 10%, resulting in bond premium of $62,000. Bolt uses the effective interest method of amortizing bond premium. Interest is payable semiannually on November 1 and May 1. In its October 31, 1992 balance sheet, what amount should Bolt report as unamortized bond premium?

a. $62,000
b. $60,100
c. $58,900
d. $58,590
(11/92, PI, #38, 3271)

23. On July 1, 1995, Cobb Inc. issued 9% bonds in the face amount of $1,000,000, which mature on July 1, 2005. The bonds were issued for $939,000 to yield 10%, resulting in a bond discount of $61,000. Cobb uses the interest method of amortizing bond discount. Interest is payable annually on June 30. At June 30, 1997, Cobb's unamortized bond discount should be
a. $52,810.
b. $51,000.
c. $48,800.
d. $43,000.
(5/89, PI, #46, amended, 1064)

24. On January 2, 1994, West Co. issued 9% bonds in the amount of $500,000, which mature on January 2, 2004. The bonds were issued for $469,500 to yield 10%. Interest is payable annually on December 31. West uses the interest method of amortizing bond discount. In its June 30, 1994 balance sheet, what amount should West report as bonds payable?
a. $469,500
b. $470,475
c. $471,025
d. $500,000
(11/94, FAR, #24, 5288)

25. A five-year term bond was issued by a company on January 1, 1996, at a premium. The carrying amount of the bond at December 31, 1997, would be
a. The same as the carrying amount at January 1, 1996.
b. Higher than the carrying amount at December 31, 1996.
c. Lower than the carrying amount at December 31, 1998.
d. Lower than the carrying amount at December 31, 1996.
(5/87, Theory, #17, amended, 1861)

26. How would the amortization of discount on bonds payable affect each of the following?

	Carrying amount of bond	Net income
a.	Increase	Decrease
b.	Increase	Increase
c.	Decrease	Decrease
d.	Decrease	Increase

(11/84, Theory, #25, 1890)

27. How would the amortization of premium on bonds payable affect each of the following?

	Carrying amount of bond	Net income
a.	Increase	Decrease
b.	Increase	Increase
c.	Decrease	Decrease
d.	Decrease	Increase

(11/83, Theory, #15, 9020)

28. A bond issued on June 1, 1993, has interest payment dates of April 1 and October 1. Bond interest expense for the year ended December 31, 1993, is for a period of
a. Three months.
b. Four months.
c. Six months.
d. Seven months. (5/94, FAR, #46, 4861)

29. On July 1, 1994, Eagle Corp. issued 600 of its 10%, $1,000 bonds at 99 plus accrued interest. The bonds are dated April 1, 1994 and mature on April 1, 2004. Interest is payable semiannually on April 1 and October 1. What amount did Eagle receive from the bond issuance?
a. $579,000
b. $594,000
c. $600,000
d. $609,000 (5/95, FAR, #19, 5555)

30. On November 1, 1991, Mason Corp. issued $800,000 of its 10-year, 8% term bonds dated October 1, 1991. The bonds were sold to yield 10%, with total proceeds of $700,000 plus accrued interest. Interest is paid every April 1 and October 1. What amount should Mason report for interest payable in its December 31, 1991 balance sheet?
a. $17,500
b. $16,000
c. $11,667
d. $10,667 (11/92, PI, #23, 3256)

31. A 15-year bond was issued in 1987 at a discount. During 1997, a 10-year bond was issued at face amount with the proceeds used to retire the 15-year bond at its face amount. The net effect of the 1997 bond transactions was to increase long-term liabilities by the excess of the 10-year bond's face amount over the 15-year bond's
a. Face amount.
b. Carrying amount.
c. Face amount less the deferred loss on bond retirement.
d. Carrying amount less the deferred loss on bond retirement. (5/91, Theory, #5, amended, 1782)

32. On July 31, 1993, Dome Co. issued $1,000,000 of 10%, 15-year bonds at par and used a portion of the proceeds to call its 600 outstanding 11%, $1,000 face value bonds, due on July 31, 2003, at 102. On that date, unamortized bond premium relating to the 11% bonds was $65,000. In its 1993 income statement, what amount should Dome report as gain or loss, before income taxes, from retirement of bonds?
a. $ 53,000 gain
b. $0
c. $(65,000) loss
d. $(77,000) loss (11/94, FAR, #42, 5304)

33. Weald Co. took advantage of market conditions to refund debt. This was the fifth refunding operation carried out by Weald within the last four years. The excess of the carrying amount of the old debt over the amount paid to extinguish it should be reported as a(an)
a. Deferred credit to be amortized over life of new debt.
b. Part of continuing operations.
c. Extraordinary gain, net of income taxes.
d. Extraordinary loss, net of income taxes.
(5/93, Theory, #18, 9023)

34. On June 30, 1992, King Co. had outstanding 9%, $5,000,000 face value bonds maturing on June 30, 1997. Interest was payable semiannually every June 30 and December 31. On June 30, 1992, after amortization was recorded for the period, the unamortized bond premium and bond issue costs were $30,000 and $50,000, respectively. On that date, King acquired all its outstanding bonds on the open market at 98 and retired them. At June 30, 1992, what amount should King recognize as gain before income taxes on redemption of bonds?
a. $ 20,000
b. $ 80,000
c. $120,000
d. $180,000 (11/92, PI, #47, 3280)

35. On January 1, 1990, Hart Inc., redeemed its 15-year bonds of $500,000 face amount for 102. They were originally issued on January 1, 1978 at 98 with a maturity date of January 1, 1993. The bond issue costs relating to this transaction were $20,000. Hart amortizes discounts, premiums, and bond issue costs using the straight-line method. What amount of extraordinary loss should Hart recognize on the redemption of these bonds?
a. $16,000
b. $12,000
c. $10,000
d. $0 (11/90, PI, #50, 1040)

36. On January 1, 1992, Fox Corp. issued 1,000 of its 10%, $1,000 bonds for $1,040,000. These bonds were to mature on January 1, 2002 but were callable at 101 any time after December 31, 1995. Interest was payable semiannually on July 1 and January 1. On July 1, 1997, Fox called all of the bonds and retired them. Bond premium was amortized on a straight-line basis. Before income taxes, Fox's gain or loss in 1997 on this early extinguishment of debt was
a. $30,000 gain.
b. $12,000 gain.
c. $10,000 loss.
d. $ 8,000 gain.   (5/90, PI, #40, amended, 9022)

37. Blue Corp.'s December 31, 1991 balance sheet contained the following items in the long-term liabilities section:

9-3/4% registered debentures, callable
  in 2002, due in 2007 $700,000
9-1/2% collateral trust bonds,
  convertible into common stock
  beginning in 2000, due in 2010   600,000
10% subordinated debentures ($30,000
  maturing annually beginning in 1997)   300,000

What is the total amount of Blue's term bonds?
a. $ 600,000
b. $ 700,000
c. $1,000,000
d. $1,300,000   (11/92, PI, #39, 3272)

38. Hancock Co.'s December 31, 1990 balance sheet contained the following items in the long-term liabilities section:

Unsecured
9.375% registered bonds ($25,000
  maturing annually beginning in 1994) $275,000
11.5% convertible bonds, callable
  beginning in 1999, due 2010   125,000

Secured
9.875% guaranty security bonds, due
  2010 $250,000
10.0% commodity backed bonds
  ($50,000 maturing annually beginning
  in 1995)   200,000

What are the total amounts of serial bonds and debenture bonds?

	Serial bonds	Debenture bonds
a.	$475,000	$400,000
b	$475,000	$125,000
c.	$450,000	$400,000
d.	$200,000	$650,000

(5/91, PI, #47, 9024)

39. On March 31, 1992, Ashley Inc.'s bondholders exchanged their convertible bonds for common stock. The carrying amount of these bonds on Ashley's books was less than the market value but greater than the par value of the common stock issued. If Ashley used the book value method of accounting for the conversion, which of the following statements correctly states an effect of this conversion?
a. Stockholders' equity is increased.
b. Additional paid-in capital is decreased.
c. Retained earnings is increased.
d. An extraordinary loss is recognized.
(5/93, Theory, #12, 4200)

40. Clay Corp. had $600,000 convertible 8% bonds outstanding at June 30, 1990. Each $1,000 bond was convertible into 10 shares of Clay's $50 par value common stock. On July 1, 1990, the interest was paid to bondholders, and the bonds were converted into common stock, which had a fair market value of $75 per share. The unamortized premium on these bonds was $12,000 at the date of conversion. Under the book value method, this conversion increased the following elements of the stockholders' equity section by

	Common stock	Additional paid-in capital
a.	$300,000	$312,000
b.	$306,000	$306,000
c.	$450,000	$162,000
d.	$600,000	$ 12,000

(11/91, PI, #37, 2425)

ITEMS 41 AND 42 are based on the following:

On January 2, 1994, Chard Co. issued 10-year convertible bonds at 105. During 1997, these bonds were converted into common stock having an aggregate par value equal to the total face amount of the bonds. At conversion, the market price of Chard's common stock was 50 percent above its par value.

41. On January 2, 1994, cash proceeds from the issuance of the convertible bonds should be reported as
a. Contributed capital for the entire proceeds.
b. Contributed capital for the portion of the proceeds attributable to the conversion feature and as a liability for the balance.
c. A liability for the face amount of the bonds and contributed capital for the premium over the face amount.
d. A liability for the entire proceeds.
(11/90, Theory, #29, amended, 1799)

42. Depending on whether the book value method or the market value method was used, Chard would recognize gains or losses on conversion when using the

	Book value method	Market value method
a.	Either gain or loss	Gain
b.	Either gain or loss	Loss
c.	Neither gain nor loss	Loss
d.	Neither gain nor loss	Gain

(11/90, Theory, #30, 9025)

43. On December 31, 1993, Moss Co. issued $1,000,000 of 11% bonds at 109. Each $1,000 bond was issued with 50 detachable stock warrants, each of which entitled the bondholder to purchase one share of $5 par common stock for $25. Immediately after issuance, the market value of each warrant was $4. On December 31, 1993, what amount should Moss record as discount or premium on issuance of bonds?
a. $ 40,000 premium
b. $ 90,000 premium
c. $110,000 discount
d. $200,000 discount   (5/94, FAR, #34, 4849)

44. On December 30, 1992, Fort Inc. issued 1,000 of its 8%, 10-year, $1,000 face value bonds with detachable stock warrants at par. Each bond carried a detachable warrant for one share of Fort's common stock at a specified option price of $25 per share. Immediately after issuance, the market value of the bonds without the warrants was $1,080,000 and the market value of the warrants was $120,000. In its December 31, 1992 balance sheet, what amount should Fort report as bonds payable?
a. $1,000,000
b. $ 975,000
c. $ 900,000
d. $ 880,000   (11/93, PI, #33, 4402)

45. On March 1, 1992, Evan Corp. issued $500,000 of 10% nonconvertible bonds at 103, due on February 28, 2002. Each $1,000 bond was issued with 30 detachable stock warrants, each of which entitled the holder to purchase, for $50, one share of Evan's $25 par common stock. On March 1, 1992, the market price of each warrant was $4. By what amount should the bond issue proceeds increase stockholders' equity?
a. $0
b. $15,000
c. $45, 000
d. $60,000   (5/93, PI, #32, 4073)

46. Bonds with detachable stock warrants were issued by Flack Co. Immediately after issue, the aggregate market value of the bonds and the warrants exceeds the proceeds. Is the portion of the proceeds allocated to the warrants less than their market value, and is that amount recorded as contributed capital?

	Less than Warrants' market value	Contributed capital
a.	No	Yes
b.	Yes	No
c.	Yes	Yes
d.	No	No

(11/91, Theory, #37, 2545)

47. Ray Corp. issued bonds with a face amount of $200,000. Each $1,000 bond contained 100 detachable stock warrants for shares of Ray's common stock. Total proceeds from the issue amounted to $240,000. The market value of each warrant was $2, and the market value of the bonds without the warrants was $196,000. The bonds were issued at a discount of
a. $0
b. $ 678.
c. $ 4,000.
d. $33,898.   (5/91, PI, #5, amended, 1023)

48. Main Co. issued bonds with detachable common stock warrants. Only the warrants had a known market value. The sum of the fair value of the warrants and the face amount of the bonds exceeds the cash proceeds. This excess is reported as
a. Discount on bonds payable.
b. Premium on bonds payable.
c. Common stock subscribed.
d. Contributed capital in excess of par-stock warrants.   (11/90, Theory, #31, 1800)

OTHER OBJECTIVE FORMAT QUESTIONS

PROBLEM 6-2 (15 to 25 minutes)

PROBLEM NUMBER 6-2 consists of 7 items. Select the **best** answer for each item.

On July 1, 1997, Ring Co. issued $250,000, 14% bonds payable at a premium. The bonds are due in ten years. Interest is payable semiannually every June 30 and December 31. On December 31, 1997 and June 30, 1998, Ring made the semiannual interest payments due and recorded interest expense and amortization of bond premium.

With the proceeds of the bond issuance, Ring retired other debt. Ring recorded a gain on the early extinguishment of the other debt.

REQUIRED:

ITEMS 1 THROUGH 7, contained in the partially-completed amortization table below, represent formulas used to calculate information needed to complete the table. Select your answers from the following list of formulas. Each formula may be selected once, more than once, or not at all. "Stated interest rate" and "effective interest rate" are stated on an annual basis.

	Cash paid	Interest expense	Amortization	Carrying amount	Unamortized premium
7/1/97				(1)	
12/31/97	(2)	$14,100	(3)	$349,100	(4)
6/30/98	$17,500	(5)	$3,536	(6)	

Effective Annual Interest Rate: (7)

Formulas	
A. Face amount x stated interest rate	J. (Face amount x stated interest rate) x ½
B. Face amount x effective interest rate	K. (Face amount x effective interest rate) x ½
C. Carrying amount x stated interest rate	L. (Carrying amount at the beginning of the period x stated interest rate) x ½
D. Carrying amount x effective interest rate	
E. Present value of face amount + present value of all future payments at date of issuance	M. (Carrying amount at the beginning of the period x effective interest rate) x ½
	N. Carrying amount – face amount
F. Carrying amount of bonds in the previous period – amortization for the current period	O. (Interest expense/carrying amount at the beginning of the period) x 2
G. Carrying amount of bonds in the previous period + amortization for the current period	P. (Cash paid/carrying amount) x 2
H. Cash paid – interest expense	Q. Face amount – unamortized premium
I. Cash paid + interest expense	

(11/98, FAR, #1-7, 6739-6745)

PROBLEM 6-3 (45 to 55 minutes)

ITEMS a THROUGH e are based on the following:

Hamnoff Inc.'s $50 par value common stock has always traded above par. During 1992, Hamnoff had several transactions that affected the following balance sheet accounts:

I. Bond discount
II. Bond premium
III. Bond payable
IV. Common stock
V. Additional paid-in capital
VI. Retained earnings

REQUIRED:

FOR ITEMS a THROUGH e determine whether the transaction increased (I), decreased (D), or had no effect (N) on each of the balances in the above accounts.

a. Hamnoff issued bonds payable with a nominal rate of interest that was less than the market rate of interest.

b. Hamnoff issued convertible bonds, which are common stock equivalents, for an amount in excess of the bonds' face amount.

c. Hamnoff issued common stock when the convertible bonds described in item 62 were submitted for conversion. Each $1,000 bond was converted into 20 common shares. The book value method was used for the early conversion.

d. Hamnoff issued bonds, with detachable stock warrants, for an amount equal to the face amount of the bonds. The stock warrants have a determinable value.

e. Hamnoff declared and issued a 2% stock dividend.
(11/93, Theory, #61-65)

PROBLEM 6-4 (15 to 25 minutes)

ITEMS 1 THROUGH 7 are based on the following:

On January 2, 1994, North Co. issued bonds payable with a face value of $480,000 at a discount. The bonds are due in 10 years and interest is payable semiannually every June 30 and December 31. On June 30, 1994, and on December 31, 1994, North made the semiannual interest payments due and recorded interest expense and amortization of bond discount.

ITEMS 1 THROUGH 7, contained in the partially-completed amortization table below, represent information needed to complete the table. For each item, select from the following lists the correct numerical response. A response may be selected once, more than once, or not at all.

	Cash	Interest Expense	Amortization	Discount	Carrying Amount
1/2/94					(3)
6/30/94	(2)	18,000	3,600	(1)	363,600
12/31/94	$14,400	(6)	(7)		

Annual Interest Rates: Stated (4)
Effective (5)

Rates			
(A)	3.0%	(D)	6.0%
(B)	4.5%	(E)	9.0%
(C)	5.0%	(F)	10.0%

Amounts			
(G)	$ 3,420	(P)	$ 21,600
(H)	$ 3,600	(Q)	$116,400
(I)	$ 3,780	(R)	$120,000
(J)	$ 3,960	(S)	$123,600
(K)	$14,400	(T)	$360,000
(L)	$17,820	(U)	$363,600
(M)	$18,000	(V)	$367,200
(N)	$18,180	(W)	$467,400
(O)	$18,360	(X)	$480,000

(11/95, FAR, #71-77)

ESSAY QUESTION

ESSAY 6-5 (15 to 25 minutes)

On January 2, 1995, Drew Company issued 9% term bonds dated January 2, 1995, at an effective annual interest rate (yield) of 10%. Drew uses the effective interest method of amortization. On July 1, 1997, the bonds were extinguished early when Drew acquired them in the open market for a price greater than face amount.

On September 1, 1997, Drew issued for cash 7% nonconvertible bonds dated September 1, 1997, with detachable stock purchase warrants. Immediately after issuance, both the bonds and the warrants had separately determined market values.

REQUIRED:

a. 1. Were the 9% term bonds issued at face amount, at a discount, or at a premium? Why?

2. Would the amount of interest expense for the 9% term bonds using the effective interest method of amortization be higher in the first or second year of the life of the bond issue? Why?

b. 1. How should gain or loss on early extinguishment of debt be determined? Does the early extinguishment of the 9% term bonds result in a gain or loss? Why?

2. How should Drew report the early extinguishment of the 9% term bonds on the 1997 income statement?

c. How should Drew account for the issuance of the 7% nonconvertible bonds with detachable stock purchase warrants?

(5/90, Theory, #3, amended, 6191)

SOLUTION 6-1 MULTIPLE CHOICE ANSWERS

INVESTMENTS IN BONDS

1. **(b)** Debt securities that the enterprise has the positive intent and ability to hold to maturity are classified as held-to-maturity securities and reported at amortized cost (SFAS 115, par. 7). Only securities classified as either trading securities or available-for-sale securities are reported at fair value (par. 12). Debt and equity securities should not be reported at cost or lower-of-cost-or-market if they are accounted for under SFAS 115.

2. **(b)** A bond issued between interest payment dates requires the investor to pay the seller for accrued interest in addition to the price of the bond. A bond issued at a discount is a bond issued at a price below the bond's face amount. Hence, at the date of purchase, the carrying amount of a bond purchased at a discount between interest payment dates is less than the cash paid to the seller and is also less than the face amount of the bond.

3. **(d)** The purchaser of a bond acquires the right to receive two cash flows: a lump sum paid at maturity for the face amount of the bond, and an annuity consisting of periodic interest payments over the life of the bond. The price the market is willing to pay for the bond is equal to the present value of these two cash flows, discounted at the prevailing market interest rate for bonds having the same maturity and perceived degree of risk. When interest rates increase, the present value of the two cash flows decreases, causing the market value of the bonds to decline. Answer (a) is incorrect because the issuance of a stock dividend should not cause a decline in the market value of the bonds. Answer (b) is incorrect because the bonds are currently quoted at a small discount, and the bonds are expected to be called at a premium (i.e., above face amount),

this situation would most likely have the effect of causing a rise in the market value of the bonds. Answer (c) is incorrect because a decline in interest rates would cause a rise in the bond's market value.

4. **(a)** The carrying amount of the bond investment at 12/31/92 is determined by adding the amortization of the bond discount from the date of purchase to the cost of the bond investment, as follows:

Bond investment cost, 7/1/92		
($946,000 – $40,000)		$906,000
Plus amortization of bond discount		
to 12/31/92:		
Bond investment cost, 7/1/92	$906,000	
Times: Effective interest rate		
(10% ÷ 2)	x 5%	
Interest income, 7/1/92 - 12/31/92	45,300	
Portion of annual interest payment		
applicable to 7/1/92 - 12/31/92		
[($1,000,000 x 8%) ÷ 2]	(40,000)	5,300
Bond investment carrying amount, 12/31/92		$911,300

5. **(c)** The amount at which the bonds should be reported at 12/31/91 is determined as follows:

Bond investment carrying amount, 7/1/91		$1,198,000
Less amortization of bond premium		
to 12/31/91:		
Bond investment carrying amount,		
7/1/91	$1,198,000	
Times: Effective interest rate		
(8% ÷ 2)	x 4%	
Interest income, 7/1/91 - 12/31/91	47,920	
Semiannual interest payment		
[$1,000,000 x (10% ÷ 2)]	(50,000)	(2,080)
Bond investment carrying amount,		
12/31/91		$1,195,920

6. **(d)** The carrying amount of the bonds at 12/31/97 is determined by subtracting the amortization of the bond premium from the date of purchase from the cost of the bond investment, as follows:

Bond cost, 10/1/96 ($220,000 – $5,000)	$215,000
Less amortization of bond premium to 12/31/97:	

Bond investment cost, 10/1/96	$ 215,000	
Less: Face amount of bonds (200 x $1,000)	(200,000)	
Bond premium	$ 15,000	
Divided by: Months to maturity (10/1/96 to 1/1/2003)	÷ 75	
Monthly premium amortization	$ 200	
Times: Months from 10/1/96 to 12/31/97	x 15	(3,000)
Bond carrying amount, 12/31/97		$212,000

7. (d) Bonds purchased at a discount are purchased at less than their face amount. The subsequent amortization of the discount increases the carrying amount of the bond investment and the amount of interest income recognized.

Simple interest, 7/1/97 - 12/31/97 [$500,000 x (8% ÷ 2)]	$ 20,000
Amortization of discount on bond investment (given)	1,800
Interest revenue recognized in 1997	$21,800

8. (b) The bonds pay interest semiannually on January 1 and July 1. The interest to be received on 1/1/98 should be reported as bond interest receivable at 12/31/97. The bond interest receivable at 12/31/97 is determined as follows:

Face amount of bond investment	$ 500,000
Times: Semiannual stated interest rate (8% ÷ 2)	x 4%
Semiannual interest payment	$ 20,000

9. (b) Since the bond was purchased at a discount, the initial carrying value of the bond investment is $10,000 less than the face amount. The amortization of the discount increases the bond investment and so, on the date of sale the bond investment is carried on Jent Corp.'s books at $8,000 less (i.e., $10,000 – 2,000) than the face amount. Therefore, the sale of the bond at a premium (i.e., at $14,000 more than the face amount of the bond) results in recognition of a gain (i.e., $8,000 + $14,000).

ISSUANCE OF BONDS

10. (d) The market price of a bond is equal to the present value of the bond's interest and principal payments, discounted using the market interest rate for that type of bond.

11. (b) 400 bonds x (1,000 x 97%) = $388,000 bonds payable.

12. (d) The net proceeds of a bond issuance is determined by calculating the present value of the projected cash flows of the bonds at the yield rate (market rate) of interest and then deducting bond issuance costs. The stated rate of interest is used to determine the amount of cash to be paid at each payment date, but the market rate is the rate used to discount the cash flows to present values.

13. (b) The $35,000 of bond issue costs should be reported as a deferred charge (i.e., an asset) and amortized over the term of the bonds (APB 21, par. 16). The bond liability should be reported at the sum of the face amount of the bonds less the related discount.

Face amount of bonds ($1,000 x 1,000)	$ 1,000,000
Discount on bonds [$1,000,000 – ($1,000,000 x 99%)]	(10,000)
Amount to be reported as bond liability, 6/30/90	$ 990,000

14. (d) The amount of the unamortized bond issue costs at 6/30/93 is computed as follows:

Bond issue costs, 1/2/92		$ 250,000
Less amortization, 1/2/92 to 6/30/93:		
Bond issue costs	$ 250,000	
Divide by: Number of semi-annual interest dates (10 x 2)	÷ 20	
Semiannual amortization of bond issue costs	12,500	
Times: Number of interest dates from 1/2/92 to 6/30/93	x 3	(37,500)
Unamortized bond issue costs, 6/30/93		$212,500

15. (d) Engraving and printing costs, accounting and legal fees, commissions paid to underwriters, promotion costs, and other similar charges are incurred when bonds are issued. According to generally accepted accounting principles (i.e., APB 21, *Interest on Receivables and Payables*), bond issue costs should be recorded as a deferred charge and amortized over the life of the debt, in a manner similar to that used for discount on bonds. Therefore, $245,000 (i.e., $20,000 + $25,000 + $200,000) should be recorded as bond issue costs to be amortized over the term of the bonds.

16. (b) The bond issue was sold between interest dates (i.e., the bonds are dated April 1, 1991 but were issued five months later on August 31, 1991). The amortization of bond issue costs is affected when a bond issue is sold between interest dates because the issue costs should be amortized over the period from the date of sale (not the date of the bond) to the maturity date. Therefore, the amount of bond issue costs that Dixon should expense for 1991 is determined as follows:

Bond issue costs	$3,300
Months from date of sale to maturity date [(5 x 12) – 5]	÷ 55
Monthly bond issue cost amortization	60
Months bonds were outstanding during 1991	x 4
Bond issue cost amortization for 1991	$ 240

17. (b) The reporting of the bond issue costs as a deferred charge or as a reduction of the related debt liability does not affect the amortization of the

bond issue costs. Interest expense is increased by an identical amount of bond issue cost amortization under both reporting alternatives.

18. (d)   A bond issue will sell for less than its face amount (i.e., at a discount) when the nominal or stated interest rate is less than the market rate [or, as indicated in answer (d), when the market rate of interest is higher than the nominal rate].

19. (c)   Bond issue costs is the only item that could theoretically be accounted for in any of the three manners listed. Because the borrower obtains the use of the proceeds received over the life of the bonds, it is argued that the bond issue costs benefit the borrower over this entire period and thus should be recorded as a deferred charge and amortized over the life of the bonds (APB 21, par. 16). Alternatively, the issue costs could be considered a reduction of the related debt liability, since these costs reduce the amount actually received by the borrower (and thus it also increases the effective interest rate on the obligation). This is the position taken by SFAC 3. Finally, it can be argued that since the expenditure for bond issue costs is not an asset, it should not be capitalized at all, but rather fully expensed in the year incurred.

PREMIUM AND DISCOUNT AMORTIZATION

20. (b)   Using the straight-line method instead of the effective interest method to amortize the discount for 1994 results in larger amortization of the discount as shown below, thus understating the discount and overstating the carrying amount of the bonds. The discount will be fully amortized by the maturity date using either method so there would be no effect on the carrying amount of the bonds at January 2, 2000, for using the incorrect method.

Straight-line method:
Bonds payable		$1,000,000
Less: Discount:		
Original discount	$150,000	
Amortization ($150,000 ÷ 6 years)	(25,000)	(125,000)
Carrying value, 12/31/94		$ 875,000

Effective interest method:
Bonds payable		$1,000,000
Less: Discount:		
Original discount	$150,000	
Amortization *	(22,000)	(128,000)
Carrying value, 12/31/94		$ 872,000

*Amortization as of 12/31/94 using effective interest method:

Face amount of bonds	$1,000,000
Less: Discount on sale	(150,000)
Net cash realized	$ 850,000
Effective interest rate	x 12%
Interest expense, 12/31/94	$ 102,000
Less: Interest payment ($1,000,000) x (8%)	(80,000)
Amortization of discount, 12/31/94	$ 22,000

21. (c)   The amount of the unamortized bond premium at 6/30/93 is computed as follows:

Unamortized bond premium, 6/30/92 ($105,000 – $100,000)		$5,000
Bond premium amortization, 6/30/92 - 6/30/93:		
Bonds payable carrying amount, 6/30/92	$105,000	
Times: Annual effective interest rate	x 6%	
Interest expense, 6/30/92 - 6/30/93	6,300	
Annual interest payment ($100,000 x 7%)	(7,000)	(700)
Unamortized bond premium, 6/30/93		$4,300

22. (b)   The amount of the unamortized bond premium at 10/31/92 is determined as follows:

Unamortized bond premium, 5/1/92		$62,000
Bond premium amortization, 5/1/92 - 10/31/92:		
Bonds payable carrying amount, 5/1/92 ($1,000,000 + $62,000)	$1,062,000	
Semiannual effective interest rate (10% ÷ 2)	x 5%	
Interest expense, 5/1/92 - 10/31/92	53,100	
Semiannual interest payment due 11/1/92 [$1,000,000 x (11% ÷ 2)]	(55,000)	(1,900)
Unamortized bond premium, 10/31/92		$60,100

23. (a)   The unamortized bond discount at June 30, 1997 is determined as follows:

Unamortized bond discount, 7/1/95		$61,000
Bond discount amortization, 7/1/95 - 6/30/97:		
Amortization for 7/1/95 - 6/30/96:		
Bonds payable carrying amount, 7/1/95	$939,000	
Effective interest rate	x 10%	
Interest expense, 7/1/95 - 6/30/96	93,900	
Interest payment ($1,000,000 x 9%)	(90,000)	(3,900)
Amortization for 7/1/96 - 6/30/97:		
Bonds payable carrying amount, 7/1/96 ($939,000 + $3,900)	$942,900	
Effective interest rate	x 10%	
Interest expense, 7/1/96 - 6/30/97	94,290	
Interest payment ($1,000,000 x 9%)	(90,000)	(4,290)
Unamortized bond discount, 6/30/97		$52,810

24. (b)   The amount that should be reported as bonds payable at 6/30/94 is computed as follows:

Bonds payable carrying amount, 1/2/94		$469,500
Add amortization of bond discount, 1/2/94 - 6/30/94:		
Bonds carrying amount, 1/2/94	$469,500	
Effective interest rate (10% x 6/12)	x 5%	
Interest expense, 1/2/94 - 6/30/94	23,475	
Interest payment [$500,000 x (9% x 6/12)]	(22,500)	975
Bonds payable carrying amount, 6/30/94		$470,475

25. (d) When bonds are issued at a premium, the Premium on Bonds Payable account is added to the Bonds Payable account to determine the initial carrying amount of the bonds. As the bond premium is amortized, the carrying amount of the bond decreases.

26. (a) When bonds are issued at a discount, the Discount on Bonds Payable account is a contra-liability account to Bonds Payable, i.e., it reduces the carrying amount of the bonds. Thus, as the bond discount is amortized, the carrying amount of the bonds increases. The bond discount amortization increases the interest expense on the bonds, and so net income decreases.

27. (d) The carrying amount of the bonds is the sum of their face amount and the unamortized premium. Therefore, premium amortization will reduce the carrying amount of the bonds. Bond premium amortization will increase income because it will reduce the interest expense associated with the bonds.

28. (d) When the interest date does not coincide with the end of the accounting period, the issuer must accrue interest expense through year-end. Therefore, bond interest expense for the year ended December 31, 1993, is for a period of seven months—from the date of issuance of June 1 to year-end of December 31.

29. (d)

Bond Price:	
$1,000 x 99% x 600 bonds	$ 594,000
Plus: Accrued interest at stated interest rate	
(10% x $1,000 x 600 bonds x 3/12)	15,000
Proceeds from bond issuance	$609,000

30. (b) Interest payable is the cash interest accumulated that is not yet paid at the balance sheet date. The bonds have a semiannual interest payment of $32,000 [i.e., $800,000 x (8% ÷ 2)]. Since the bonds are dated 10/1/91, Mason should report three months of interest payable, or $16,000 (i.e., $32,000 x 3/6), at 12/31/91.

REDEMPTION OF BONDS PAYABLE

31. (b) The new 10-year bond was issued at its face amount which, from the facts, either equals or exceeds the face amount of the 15-year bond which exceeds the carrying amount of the 15-year bond because the 15-year bond was issued at a discount (a price less than the face amount). The excess of the retirement price (face amount) of the 15-year bond over its carrying amount will be recorded as a loss at retirement. Therefore, the issuance of the new bond and the retirement of the old bond will have the net effect of increasing the total of long-term liabilities by the excess of the new bond's face amount over the old bond's carrying amount.

32. (a) A gain is recognized because the cost to redeem the bonds is less than the carrying amount of the bonds. The pretax gain from retirement of bonds is determined as follows:

Face amount of bonds retired (600 x $1,000)	$ 600,000
Add: Unamortized bond premium	65,000
Bond carrying amount at retirement date	665,000
Less: Cost to retire ($600,000 x 102%)	(612,000)
Pretax gain on retirement of bonds	$ 53,000

33. (c) Normally, to be classified as an extraordinary item, a transaction or event must be unusual in nature and infrequent in occurrence, given the environment in which the entity operates. However, even though refunding operations are not infrequent for Weald, the resulting gains and losses should be classified as extraordinary because SFAS 4, par. 8, requires that gains and losses on extinguishment of debt be reported as extraordinary items, net of their related income tax effect. Since the carrying amount of the old debt is greater than the amount paid to extinguish the old debt, the transaction results in a gain.

34. (b) The pretax gain on the redemption of the bonds is determined as follows:

Face amount of bonds	$ 5,000,000
Add: Unamortized bond premium	30,000
Less: Unamortized bond issue costs	(50,000)
Bond carrying amount at redemption date	4,980,000
Cost to redeem ($5,000,000 x 98%)	(4,900,000)
Pretax gain on redemption of bonds	$ 80,000

A gain is recognized because the cost to redeem the bonds is less than the carrying amount of the bonds.

35. (a) The pretax extraordinary loss on the redemption is computed as follows:

Face amount of bonds		$ 500,000
Less unamortized discount at extinguishment:		
Discount at issuance [$500,000– ($500,000 x 98%)]	$ 10,000	
Amortization to date of extinguishment ($10,000 x 12/15*)	(8,000)	(2,000)
Less unamortized bond issue costs at extinguishment:		
Bond issue costs incurred	$ 20,000	
Amortization to date of extinguishment ($20,000 x 12/15*)	(16,000)	(4,000)
Bond carrying amount at extinguishment		494,000
Cost to redeem ($500,000 x 102%)		(510,000)
Pretax loss on early extinguishment of debt		$ (16,000)

A loss is recognized on the redemption because the cost to redeem the bonds exceeds the carrying amount of the bonds. Gains or losses from the early extinguinary of debt, if material, are reported as an extraordinary item (SFAS 4).

---

* The interest on the 15-year (i.e., 1/1/78 to 1/1/93) bonds was payable annually. Thus, there were 15 interest dates over the life of the bonds. The discount and bond issue costs must be amortized up to the extinguishment date (i.e., 1/1/90—the twelfth interest date).

36. (d) The pretax gain on the early extinguishment of debt is computed as follows:

Face amount of bonds (1,000 x $1,000)		$ 1,000,000
Add unamortized premium at extinguishment:		
Premium at issuance		
($1,040,000 – $1,000,000)	$ 40,000	
Amortized to date of extinguishment:		
($40,000 x 11/20*)	(22,000)	18,000
Bond carrying amount at extinguishment		1,018,000
Cost to reacquire ($1,000,000 x 101%)		(1,010,000)
Pretax gain on early extinguishment of debt		$ 8,000

---

* The interest on the 10-year (i.e., 1/1/92 - 1/1/2002) bonds was payable semiannually. Therefore, there were 20 (i.e., 10 x 2) interest dates over the life of the bonds. The premium must be amortized up to the date of retirement (i.e., 7/1/97—the eleventh interest date).

SERIAL BONDS

37. (d) Bond issues maturing on a single date are called term bonds. Bond issues maturing in installments are called serial bonds. Since the 9-3/4% registered debentures due in 2007 and the 9-1/2% collateral trust bonds due in 2010 each mature on a single date, the total amount of term bonds is $1,300,000 (i.e., $700,000 + $600,000). Since the 10% subordinated debentures mature annually beginning in 1997, the total amount of serial bonds is $300,000.

38. (a) Bond issues maturing on a single date are called term bonds, whereas bond issues maturing in installments are called serial bonds. Since the 9.375% registered bonds and the 10.0% commodity back bonds both mature in installments, the total amount of serial bonds is $475,000 (i.e., $275,000 + $200,000). Debenture bonds are unsecured bonds; they are not supported by a lien or mortgage on specific assets. Since the 9.375% registered bonds and the 11.5% convertible bonds are unsecured, the total amount of debenture bonds is $400,000 (i.e., $275,000 + $125,000).

CONVERTIBLE BONDS

39. (a) Ashley used the book value method to account for the conversion of the bonds to common stock. Under this method, paid-in capital accounts are credited for the carrying amount of the debt and no gain or loss is recognized on the conversion. Therefore, Ashley's stockholders' equity is increased as a result of the conversion. Additional paid-in capital will be increased because the carrying amount of these bonds exceeds the par value of the common stock issued. Paid-in capital accounts are credited for the carrying amount of the debt under the book value method, retained earnings is unaffected. Under the book value method, no gain or loss is recognized on the conversion.

40. (a) Under the book value method, the paid-in capital accounts are credited for the carrying amount of the debt; no gain or loss is recognized on the conversion. The market price per common share is irrelevant under this method. The conversion of the bonds under the book value method is recorded as follows:

Bonds Payable	600,000	
Bond Premium	12,000	
Common Stock [($600,000 ÷ 1,000)		
x 10 shs. x $50 PV]		300,000
Additional Paid-In Capital (to balance)		312,000

41. (d) In APB 14, par. 12, the Board specified that no portion of the proceeds from the issuance of convertible debt should be accounted for as attributable to the conversion feature; all of the proceeds should be recorded in debt accounts. The justification for this rule is that the conversion feature and the debt instrument are inseparable.

42. (c) A major characteristic of the book value method is that neither a gain nor a loss is recognized on the conversion of bonds to stock; the carrying amount of debt is taken out of the debt accounts and recorded in stockholders' equity accounts. The market value method may result in a gain or loss because the stock is to be recorded at the market value of the stock (or bonds) and the carrying amount of the debt is to be removed from liability accounts. A difference between the market value of the stock and the carrying amount of the debt is to be recorded as a gain or loss, whichever is appropriate. Because of the relationships of amounts involved, it is evident that the market value of the stock exceeds the carrying amount of the debt; therefore, a loss will be recorded on the conversion. Those relationships are as follows: (1) the aggregate par value of the stock was equal to the total face amount (par value) of the bonds, (2) the market value of the stock is 50% above its par, and (3) the carrying amount of the debt is less than 5% above its par (the bonds were issued in a prior year at a 5% premium and at least 30% of that premium had been amortized prior to 1997). **NOTE**: Also see the Owners' Equity chapter.

BONDS WITH DETACHABLE STOCK WARRANTS

43. (c) Since the fair market value of the bonds is not determinable, the incremental method is used to determine the value of the bonds and the warrants. That is, the market value is used for the warrants and the remainder of the purchase price is allocated to the bonds. The market value of the warrants is known and, therefore, be used to determine the portion of the total purchase price that is allocated to the warrants. The computation is as follows:

Purchase price (1,000 bonds x $1,000 x 109%)	$1,090,000
Fair value of the warrants (1,000 x 50 x $4)	(200,000)
Portion allocated to bonds	$ 890,000
Face value of bonds	$1,000,000
Portion allocated to bonds	(890,000)
Discount on bonds	$ 110,000

44. (c) To compute the amount at which the bonds payable should be reported, the proceeds from the bonds and the detachable stock warrants must be allocated between the two securities based on their aggregate relative fair values at the date of issue.

	Relative aggregate fair value	FMV%	Proceeds to be allocated	Proceeds allocated to each
Bonds payable	$1,080,000	90%	$1,000,000	$ 900,000
Stock warrants	120,000	10%	1,000,000	100,000
	$1,200,000	100%		$1,000,000

Since the bonds are allocated $900,000 of the proceeds received, they were issued at a discount of $100,000 (i.e., $1,000,000 − $900,000). Therefore, the bonds should be reported in the balance sheet at $900,000 (i.e., $1,000,000 face amount less $100,000 unamortized discount).

45. (d) APB 14 requires allocation of the proceeds between the bonds and the detachable stock purchase warrants based on their relative fair values at the date of issue. If both fair values are not known, then the fair value of either security is used. The question provides the fair value of the warrants, but not the fair value of the bonds without the warrants; therefore, the fair value of the warrants is used to allocate the proceeds for the two securities. A stockholders' equity account, Paid-In Capital— Stock Purchase Warrants, is increased by the $60,000 [i.e., ($500,000 ÷ 1,000) x 30 x $4] fair value of the warrants. The remaining proceeds of $455,000 [i.e., ($500,000 x 103%) − $60,000] would be allocated to the bonds, which would result in the

recording of a $45,000 (i.e., $500,000 − $455,000) discount on the bonds.

46. (c) The proceeds from the issuance of bonds with detachable stock purchase warrants should be allocated to the two securities based on the relative market values of the securities involved. The amount allocated to the warrants is reported as paid-in capital (i.e., contributed capital). Since the aggregate market value of the bonds and the warrants exceeds the proceeds, the amount of proceeds allocated to the bonds and the amount of proceeds allocated to the warrants will be less than the market values of the respective securities.

47. (b) To determine the amount of the discount to be recorded for the bonds issued, the proceeds from the bonds and the detachable stock purchase warrants must be allocated between the securities based on their relative fair market values at the date of issue, as follows:

	Relative aggregate fair value	FMV%	Proceeds to be allocated	Proceeds allocated to each
Bonds payable	$196,000	83.051%	$240,000	$ 199,322
Stock warrants	40,000*	16.949%	240,000	40,678
	$236,000	100.000%		$240,000

* [($200,000 ÷ $1,000) x 100 x $2]

Since the bonds are allocated $199,322 of the proceeds received, they were issued at a discount of $678 ($200,000 − $199,322).

48. (a) The proceeds from the issuance of debt with detachable warrants is to be allocated to paid-in capital (the warrants) and to debt (the bonds) based on the relative fair values of the two securities at the time of issuance (APB 14, par. 16). When only the market value of the warrants is known, it is used to record the paid-in capital attributable to the issuance of the warrants. The remainder of the proceeds is recorded in debt accounts. A journal entry approach will be helpful in thinking through the rest of the question. Paid-In Capital is to be credited for the market value of the warrants. Bonds Payable is to be credited for the face amount of the bonds. Cash is to be debited for the cash proceeds. Because the question says that the fair value of the warrants and the face amount of the bonds exceed the cash proceeds, the entry needs a debit to balance. That debit has to relate to the bonds, so it must be to Discount on Bonds Payable. Thus, the amount of proceeds allocated to debt is less than the face amount of the bonds so the bonds were issued at a discount.

PERFORMANCE BY SUBTOPICS

Each category below parallels a subtopic covered in Chapter 6. Record the number and percentage of questions you correctly answered in each subtopic area.

Investments in Bonds

Question #	Correct √
1	
2	
3	
4	
5	
6	
7	
8	
9	
# Questions	9

Correct _____
% Correct _____

Issuance of Bonds

Question #	Correct √
10	
11	
12	
13	
14	
15	
16	
17	
18	
19	
# Questions	10

Correct _____
% Correct _____

Premium and Discount Amortization

Question #	Correct √
20	
21	
22	
23	
24	
25	
26	
27	
28	
29	
30	
# Questions	11

Correct _____
% Correct _____

Redemption of Bonds Payable

Question #	Correct √
31	
32	
33	
34	
35	
36	
# Questions	6

Correct _____
% Correct _____

Serial Bonds

Question #	Correct √
37	
38	
# Questions	2

Correct _____
% Correct _____

Convertible Bonds

Question #	Correct √
39	
40	
41	
42	
# Questions	4

Correct _____
% Correct _____

Bonds With Detachable Stock Warrants

Question #	Correct √
43	
44	
45	
46	
47	
48	
# Questions	6

Correct _____
% Correct _____

OTHER OBJECTIVE FORMAT SOLUTIONS

SOLUTION 6-2

1. (E) The market price, or carrying value, of a bond is equal to the present value of the interest and principal (face) payments. In this problem, the original carrying amount can easily be calculated once the first period's premium amortization is calculated, by adding the premium amortization to the carrying amount at the end of the payment period. ($349,100 + $3,400 = $352,500)

2. (J) The cash paid on each interest date is the face amount times the stated rate times the portion of the year included in the payment period. ($250,000 x 14% x ½ year = $17,500)

3. (H) Amortization of the bond premium is the amount of cash paid less the interest expense for the payment period. ($17,500 – $14,100 = $3,400)

4. (N) The unamortized premium is the current carrying amount less the face amount. ($349,100 – $250,000 = $99,100)

5. (M) The interest expense is the carrying amount at the beginning of the period times the effective interest rate times the portion of the year in the payment period. ($349,100 x 8% x ½ = $13,964) In this problem, the interest expense can easily be derived by subtracting the premium amortization amount for the payment period from the cash paid. ($17,500 – $3,536 = $13,964)

6. (F) The carrying amount at the end of the period is the carrying amount at the beginning of the period less the premium amortization for the current period. ($349,100 – $3,536 = $345,564)

7. (O) The effective annual interest rate is the interest expense for the year divided by the carrying amount at the beginning of the period. Because the interest expense amount on the table is only for

½ year, it must be doubled. ($14,100/$352,500 x 2 = 8%); ($13,964/$349,100 x 2 = 8%)

SOLUTION 6-3 ISSUANCE OF BONDS

a. (I, N, I, N, N, N) A bond issue with a nominal rate of interest that is less than the market rate of interest will sell for less than its face amount (i.e., the bond will be sold at a discount). The following entry to record bonds payable sold at a discount increases the Bond Discount and Bonds Payable accounts but has no effect on the Bond Premium, Common Stock, Additional Paid-In Capital, and Retained Earnings accounts:

Cash	XX	
Bond Discount	XX	
Bonds Payable		XX

b. (N, I, I, N, N, N) APB 14, par. 12, specifies that no portion of proceeds from convertible debt should be accounted for as attributed to the conversion feature; all of the proceeds should be recorded in debt accounts. The justification for this rule is that the conversion feature and the debt feature are inseparable. The following entry to record convertible bonds sold for an amount in excess of the bond's face amount (i.e., at a premium) increases the Bond Premium and Bonds Payable accounts but has no effect on the Bond Discount, Common Stock, Additional Paid-In Capital, and Retained Earnings accounts:

Cash	XX	
Bond Premium		XX
Bonds Payable		XX

c. (N, D, D, I, I, N) Under the book value method, no gain or loss is recognized on the conversion of bonds payable to common stock. To record the conversion, paid-in capital accounts are credited for the carrying amount of the debt converted. The entry to record the conversion decreases the Bond Payable account and increases the Common Stock account by equal amounts because each bond has a $1,000 face amount and is convertible into 20 shares of $50 par value common stock (i.e., 20 x $50 = $1,000). Since the convertible bonds were issued at a premium, and the conversion entry decreases the Bonds Payable account and increases the Common Stock account by equal amounts, the conversion entry also decreases the Bond Premium account and increases the Additional Paid-In Capital accounts by the unamortized amount of the Bond Premium. The conversion entry has no effect on the Bond Discount or Retained Earnings accounts.

Bonds Payable	XX	
Bond Premium	XX	
Common Stock		XX
Additional Paid-In Capital		XX

d. (I, N, I, N, I, N) Proceeds from the issuance of bonds with detachable stock warrants should be allocated between the bonds and warrants on the basis of their relative market values at time of issuance. The amount of proceeds allocable to the warrants increases Additional Paid-In Capital. Bonds Payable increases by the face amount of the bonds issued. The question states that the bonds and warrants are issued for an amount equal to the face amount of the bonds. Since a portion of the proceeds is allocable to the warrants, the amount of proceeds allocable to the bonds is less than the face at a discount, thereby increasing the Bond Discount account. The issuance of the bonds with detachable stock purchase warrants has no effect on the Bond Premium and Retained Earnings accounts.

e. (N, N, N, I, I, D) Since the 2% stock dividend is less than 20 to 25% of the number of shares outstanding, it is considered to be a "small" stock dividend. Therefore, it should be recorded by capitalizing a portion of Retained Earnings equal to the fair value of the shares issued. Thus, as a result of the "small" stock dividend, Retained Earnings will decrease by the fair value of the shares issued, Common stock will increase by the par value of the shares issued, and Additional Paid-In Capital will increase by the excess of the fair value over the par value of the shares issued. Bond Discount, Bond Premium, and Bonds Payable are not affected by the issuance of a stock dividend.

SOLUTION 6-4 BONDS PAYABLE

1. (Q) The amount of the unamortized discount on 6/30/94 is the difference between the face value and the carrying amount on 6/30/94. ($480,000 – $363,600 = $116,400.)

2. (K) The cash paid to bondholders is the same each semiannual payment; thus, the 6/30/94 cash paid is the same amount as the 12/31/94 cash paid, which is given in the problem, of $14,400. (The cash paid to bondholders is the stated rate applied to the face amount of $480,000, for 1/2 year.) In addition, the cash paid to bondholders when the bonds are issued at a discount is the difference between the interest expense and the amortization for the interest period. ($18,000 – $3,600 = $14,400).

3. (T) The difference between the face value of $480,000 and the discount at issuance equals the carrying amount at 1/2/94. Adding back the amortization at 6/3/94 of $3,600 to the discount at 6/30/94 of $116,400, calculated in #71, the discount at issuance is equal to $120,000. Thus, $480,000 – $120,000 = $360,000. Another way to calculate the carrying amount at issuance from the information given is to subtract the 6/30/94 amortization of $3,600 from the carrying amount at 6/30/94 of $363,600.

4. (D) The stated interest rate is equal to double the semi-annual interest paid divided by the face value of the bonds. ($14,400 X 2) / $480,000 = .06.

5. (F) The effective interest rate is double the interest expense for the first six months divided by the actual cash received for the bond issue. ($18,000 x 2) / $360,000 = .10.

6. (N) The interest expense for the second six month period is the carrying amount as of 6/30/94 times half (6 months / 12 months) of the effective interest rate. $363,600 x .10 x 6/12 = $18,180.

7. (I) The amortization for the second six month period is the interest expense for that period minus the cash paid. $18,180 – $14,400 = $3,780.

ESSAY SOLUTION

SOLUTION 6-5 ACCOUNTING FOR BONDS PAYABLE

a. 1. The 9% bonds were issued at a **discount** (less than face amount). Although the bonds provide for payment of interest of 9% of face amount, this rate was **less than** the **prevailing or market rate** for bonds of similar quality at the time the bonds were issued. Thus, the issue price of the bonds, which is the present value of the principal and interest payments discounted at 10%, is less than the face amount.

2. The amount of interest expense would be **higher in the second year** of the life of the bond issue than in the first year of the life of the bond issue. According to the effective interest method of amortization, the 10% effective interest rate is applied to the bond carrying amount. In a discount situation, the **bond carrying amount increases each year,** and this results in a greater interest expense in each successive year.

b. 1. Gain or loss on early extinguishment of debt should be determined by **comparing the carrying amount** of the bonds at the **date of extinguishment** with the **acquisition price.** If the carrying amount **exceeds** the acquisition price, a **gain** results. If the carrying amount is **less** than the acquisition price, a **loss** results.

In this case, a **loss** results. The term bonds were **issued at a discount**. Therefore, the **carrying amount** of the bonds at the date of extinguishment must be **less than** the **face amount**, which is **less than** the **acquisition price**.

2. Drew should report the loss from early extinguishment of debt in its 1997 income statement as an **extraordinary item, net of income taxes**.

c. The proceeds from the issuance of the 7% nonconvertible bonds with detachable stock purchase warrants should be recorded as an **increase in cash**. These proceeds should be **allocated between** the **bonds and the warrants** on the **basis of their relative market values**. The portion of the proceeds allocable to the bonds should be accounted for as **long-term debt**, while the portion allocable to the warrants should be accounted for as **paid-in capital**.

CHANGE ALERT

SFAS No. 143, *ACCOUNTING FOR ASSET RETIREMENT OBLIGATIONS*

In June 2001, the FASB issued SFAS 143, *Accounting for Asset Retirement Obligations.* SFAS 143 is first eligible to be tested on the May 2002 exam; however, due to the specialized nature of its content, SFAS 143 is beyond the likely scope of future exams. SFAS 143 addresses accounting for costs and liabilities related to tangible long-term asset retirement. While it applies to all entities, the statement was developed to address oil and gas producing companies in particular. SFAS 143 is effective for fiscal years beginning after June 15, 2002, with earlier application encouraged.

CHAPTER 7

LIABILITIES

CHAPTER 7

LIABILITIES

I. CURRENT LIABILITIES

A. DEFINITION

Liabilities are obligations, based on past transactions, to convey assets or perform services in the future. The definition of *current* liabilities is logically correlated with the definition of current assets. The term current liabilities is used principally to designate obligations whose liquidation is reasonably expected to require the use of existing resources properly classifiable as current assets, or the creation of other current liabilities (ARB 43). Accounting for, and classification of, current liabilities is affected by the degree of certainty attached to the future payments.

B. VALUATION

Ideally, liabilities should be recorded based on the present value of the future outlays involved. In the case of current liabilities, the difference between the present value and the amount to be paid is not likely to be material; therefore, APB 21, *Interest on Receivables and Payables*, sanctions the reporting of current liabilities at their face amount.

C. DEFINITELY DETERMINABLE LIABILITIES

The *amounts* and *due dates* of definitely determinable liabilities are established with considerable certainty. This certainty may be established by statutory law, contractual provision, or trade custom.

1. **ACCOUNTS PAYABLE** Liabilities incurred in obtaining goods and services from vendors in the entity's ordinary course of business.

   a. **UNSECURED** Generally, accounts payable are not secured by collateral and do not require the periodic payment of interest.

   b. **PROPER CUTOFF** Accounts payable should reflect the cost of those goods and services that have been appropriately included in inventory (or other asset account) or expensed.

      (1) **FOB SHIPPING POINT** Raw materials purchased on account, F.O.B. shipping point, are inventoriable when *shipped*; thus, a liability should be recorded at that time.

      (2) **FOB DESTINATION** Under an F.O.B. destination point contract, the goods and the related liability should not be recorded until the goods are *received*.

2. **NOTES PAYABLE** Loans obtained from banks and other lending institutions represent current liabilities if they are due in the succeeding operating period. These notes may be either *interest-bearing* or *noninterest-bearing*.

EXAMPLE 1 ♦ INTEREST-BEARING NOTE PAYABLE

ABC Inc. borrows $5,000 from a local bank at the market rate of interest of 8% on June 30, 20X0. The principal plus the interest is due June 30, 20X1.

REQUIRED: Provide the journal entries to record this interest-bearing note on the books of ABC Inc.

SOLUTION:

June 30, 20X0		
Cash	5,000	
Notes Payable, Short-Term		5,000
December 31, 20X0		
Interest Expense ($5,000 x .08 x 6/12)	200	
Accrued Interest Payable		200
June 30, 20X1		
Notes Payable, Short-Term	5,000	
Accrued Interest Payable	200	
Interest Expense	200	
Cash		5,400

EXAMPLE 2 ♦ NONINTEREST-BEARING NOTE PAYABLE

Assume that ABC borrowed $5,000 on June 30, 20X0 and signed an 8% noninterest-bearing note due in one year.

REQUIRED: Provide ABC's journal entries.

SOLUTION:

June 30, 20X0		
Cash (face amount less discount)	4,600	
Discount on Notes Payable ($5,000 x .08)	400	
Notes Payable, Short-Term		5,000
Dec. 31, 20X0		
Interest Expense ($400 x 6/12)	200	
Discount on Notes Payable		200
June 30, 20X1		
Notes Payable, Short-Term	5,000	
Interest Expense ($400 x 6/12)	200	
Discount on Notes Payable		200
Cash		5,000

NOTE: The effective interest rate on the discounted note is approximately 8.7% ($400 ÷ $4,600) since less cash is received than the amount on which the interest rate is computed.

3. **DIVIDENDS PAYABLE** When declared, cash and property dividends represent legal obligations due within one year and, therefore, are reported as current liabilities. Stock dividends and undeclared dividends on cumulative preferred stock are not reported as liabilities. Cumulative preferred stock dividends in arrears, however, must be disclosed in the notes to the statements.

4. **ADVANCES AND RETURNABLE DEPOSITS** Advanced payments received from customers and others are liabilities until the transaction is completed; returnable deposits are liabilities until the relationship with the third party is terminated.

5. ACCRUED LIABILITIES (EXPENSES) An accrued expense is an expense incurred but not yet paid in cash. Accrued expenses are recorded as follows:

Expense	XX	
Payable or Accrued Liability		XX

a. An example of an accrued expense is salaries incurred for the last week of the accounting period that are not payable until the subsequent accounting period. Accrued payroll liabilities include social security taxes and federal unemployment taxes borne by the employer.

b. Federal income taxes withheld from employees and the employees' share of social security taxes should **not** be classified as accrued payroll expenses by the employer.

6. DEFERRED REVENUES Deferred revenue is revenue collected in cash but not yet earned.

a. An example of deferred revenue is rent collected in advance by a lessor in the last month of the accounting period, which represents the rent for the first month of the subsequent accounting period.

b. Other examples include subscriptions collected in advance and gift certificates issued but not yet redeemed. When gift certificates are issued, a deferred revenue account should be increased by the face amount of the gift certificates. This deferred revenue account is decreased when the gift certificates are redeemed or lapse.

c. Deferred revenues are recorded as follows:

Cash	XX	
Unearned Revenues (a liability account)		XX

d. When the revenues are earned, the following entry is made:

Unearned Revenues	XX	
Revenue		XX

7. CURRENT MATURITIES OF LONG-TERM DEBT The portion of long-term debt due within the next fiscal period should be classified as a current liability if payment is expected to require the use of current assets or the creation of other current liabilities. The liability should not be classified as current if the maturing portion will be paid from the proceeds of a new bond issue or other noncurrent assets (e.g., a bond sinking fund).

D. LIABILITIES DEPENDENT ON OPERATING RESULTS

1. INCOME TAX LIABILITY In accordance with federal and state tax laws, a corporation computes income taxes payable based on operating results for the period.

a. PAYABLE Income taxes payable within the next period or operating cycle, whichever is longer, are classified as current liabilities.

b. DEFERRED Taxable income and pretax accounting income may differ and, therefore, income tax *payable* (based on taxable income) and income tax *expense* (based on pretax accounting income) may differ substantially. This gives rise to *deferred taxes*. Deferred taxes should be netted out in their current and noncurrent portions for balance sheet presentation.

2. BONUSES TO EMPLOYEES Bonus agreements based on profits usually fall into one of two classes: (1) the bonus is based on net income after income taxes, but before deducting the bonus, **or** (2) the bonus is based on net income after deducting both income taxes and the bonus. The amount of the bonus is determined by solving simultaneous equations that describe the terms of the bonus agreement.

EXHIBIT 1 ♦ COMPUTATIONS OF BONUSES BASED ON PROFITS

B =	Bonus	T_r =	Tax rate
B_r =	Bonus rate	I =	Income before income taxes and bonus
T =	Tax		

1. Bonus computed on net income after income taxes but before deducting the bonus; solve these simultaneous equations:

   a. $B = B_r(I - T)$
   b. $T = T_r(I - B)$

2. Bonus computed on net income after deducting both income taxes and the bonus; solve these simultaneous equations:

   a. $B = B_r(I - T - B)$
   b. $T = T_r(I - B)$

EXAMPLE 3 ♦ EMPLOYEE BONUS

Generous Corp. provides a bonus to its employees equal to 10% of net income (i.e., after deducting taxes and bonus). Income from operations for 20X1 was $90,000. Assume a 40% tax rate.

REQUIRED: Compute the employee bonus liability for Generous Corp.

SOLUTION:

Step 1: Substitute the value of T, as given in Exhibit 1, equation 2.b., into equation 2.a.

   $B = B_r(I - T - B)$
   $B = B_r[I - T_r(I - B) - B]$

Step 2: Substitute the known values and solve for B.

   $B = .10[\$90{,}000 - .40(\$90{,}000 - B) - B]$
   $B = .10[\$90{,}000 - \$36{,}000 + .4B - B]$
   $B = .10[\$54{,}000 - .6B]$
   $B = \$5{,}400 - .06B$
 $1.06B = \$5{,}400$
     $B = \underline{\$5{,}094}$

E. **ESTIMATED LIABILITIES**
Estimated liabilities are known liabilities whose *amount* is uncertain at the end of the accounting period. Examples include product warranties and guarantees, promotional premiums, and compensated absences. Derivative instruments that represent obligations that meet the definition of liabilities are measured at fair value and reported as liabilities in the financial statements, in accordance with SFAS 133.

1. **PRODUCT WARRANTIES AND GUARANTEES** A warranty or guarantee is a promise made by the seller to the buyer to make good certain deficiencies in the product during a specified period of time after the sale. Product guarantees and warranties create a liability for the seller from the date of the sale to the end of the warranty period. In accounting for guarantees and warranties, recording of the liability may take place either at the point of sale or at the end of the accounting period.

    a. **RECORDING**

       (1) Journal entries when the liability is recorded at the point of sale:

Warranty Expense	XX	
Estimated Warranty Liability		XX
To record estimated warranty expense.		

Estimated Warranty Liability	XX	
Cash or Other Assets		XX
To record actual warranty expenditures.		

(2) When the liability is recorded at the end of the accounting period no entry is made at the date of sale.

b. **DIRECT COSTS** Any *direct costs* for servicing customer claims are debited to warranty expense and credited to cash or other assets.

c. **YEAR-END ADJUSTMENT** At the end of the accounting period, an estimate of the year's warranty liability is made based on past experience and current estimates. Any difference between the estimate and the actual amounts already charged to warranty expense is recorded as follows (assuming the estimated liability exceeds the amounts actually charged):

Warranty Expense	XX	
Warranty Liability		XX

EXAMPLE 4 ♦ PRODUCT WARRANTY

A new product introduced by Shoddy Corporation carries a two-year warranty against defects. The estimated warranty costs related to dollar sales are as follows:

Year of sale	3%
Year after sale	5%

Sales and actual warranty expenditures for the years ended December 31, 20X8 and 20X9 are as follows:

	Sales	Actual Warranty Expenditures
20X8	$400,000	$10,000
20X9	500,000	35,000

REQUIRED:

Determine Shoddy's estimated warranty liability as of December 31, 20X9 and its warranty expense for the year ended December 31, 20X9.

SOLUTION:

Sales (20X8 and 20X9)	$900,000
Estimated warranty cost percentage (3% and 5%)	x 8%
Estimated warranty costs for 20X8 and 20X9 sales	72,000
Warranty expenditures to date ($10,000 + $35,000)	(45,000)
Warranty liability, 12/31/X9	$ 27,000

The warranty expense recognized in 20X9 is <u>$40,000</u> [$500,000 x (3% + 5%)].

2. **PREMIUMS** In order to increase sales and promote certain products, companies may offer premiums to those customers who return boxtops, coupons, labels, wrappers, etc., as proof of purchase. The cost of these premiums represents an expense that should be matched against revenue from the sales benefited. At the end of the accounting period, an expense account should be debited and a liability account credited for the cost of outstanding premiums *expected* to be redeemed in subsequent periods.

EXAMPLE 5 ◆ PREMIUMS

> The Whole Grain Cereal Company offers a T-shirt to those customers who present 10 cereal boxtops. Whole Grain purchases 2,000 T-shirts at a unit cost of $2.50. Between the time the premiums were offered and the end of the accounting period, 25,000 boxes of cereal were sold. Whole Grain expects that 80% of the boxtops will be returned. A total of 2,000 boxtops had been received as of the end of the accounting period.
>
> **REQUIRED:** Provide the journal entries for Whole Grain to properly account for the premiums.
>
> **SOLUTION:**
>
> | | | |
> |---|---|---|
> | Premium Merchandise Inventory | 5,000 | |
> | Cash (2,000 x $2.50) | | 5,000 |
> | To record the purchase of 2,000 T-shirts | | |
> | | | |
> | Premium Expense [(2000 ÷ 10) x $2.50] | 500 | |
> | Premium Merchandise Inventory | | 500 |
> | To record the redemption of 2,000 boxtops | | |
> | | | |
> | Premium Expense | 4,500 | |
> | Estimated Premium Liability | | 4,500 |
> | To record the estimated premium liability at year-end | | |
>
> **COMPUTATIONS:**
>
> | | |
> |---|---|
> | Expected number of premiums to be issued [(25,000 x .80) ÷ 10] | 2,000 |
> | Premiums issued to date (2,000 ÷ 10) | (200) |
> | Premiums expected to be issued | 1,800 |
> | Unit cost | x $2.50 |
> | Estimated premium liability | $ 4,500 |
>
> | | | |
> |---|---|---|
> | Estimated Premium Liability [(4,000 ÷ 10) x $2.50] | 1,000 | |
> | Premium Merchandise Inventory | | 1,000 |
> | To record the redemption of 4,000 boxtops in the subsequent period | | |

3. **COMPENSATED ABSENCES (SFAS 43) AND POSTEMPLOYMENT BENEFITS (SFAS 112)**

    a. **ACCRUE LIABILITY** If material, a liability should be accrued at year-end for the estimated cost of compensated absences and postemployment benefits.

        (1) **COMPENSATED ABSENCES** Compensated absences include vacation, occasional sick days, and holidays. The substance of the employer's sick leave policy takes precedence over its form. An employer is generally not required to accrue a liability for nonvesting accumulating rights to receive sick pay benefits. However, future compensation for sick leave should be accrued if the employees customarily are paid or allowed compensated absences for accumulated, nonvesting sick leave days, even though the employees are not actually absent as a result of illness.

        (2) **POSTEMPLOYMENT BENEFITS** Postemployment benefits to be provided to former or inactive employees prior to retirement include salary continuation, severance benefits, continuation of other fringe benefits such as insurance, job training, and disability related benefits such as workers' compensation.

    b. **CONDITIONS** A liability for employees' compensation for future absences and postemployment benefits should be accrued if **all** the following conditions are met:

        (1) The obligation to pay future compensation is for employee services already rendered.

(2) The obligation relates to employee rights that vest or accumulate. *Vested rights* are those for which the employer is obligated to pay to the employee, regardless of termination of employment. *Accumulated rights* are those that may be carried forward to one or more future periods, even though there might be a limitation on the amounts carried forward.

(3) Payment of the compensation is *probable*.

(4) The amount can be reasonably *estimated*.

c. **INABILITY TO ESTIMATE** If the first three conditions are met but no amount is accrued due to inability to estimate future payments for compensated absences or postemployment benefits, this fact must be disclosed.

EXHIBIT 2 ♦ COMPENSATED ABSENCES

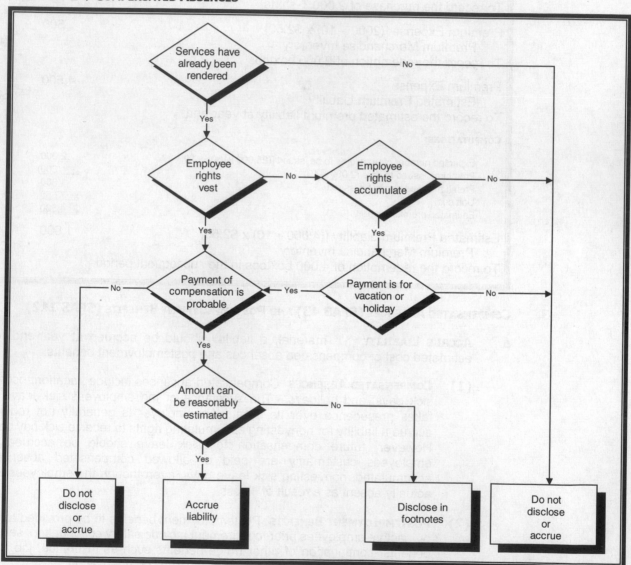

d. **CONDITIONS NOT MET** Postemployment benefits that do not meet the conditions above, shall be accounted for in accordance with SFAS 5, *Accounting for Contingencies* (see F., below).

e. **APPLICABILITY** SFAS 43 and 112 do not apply to postemployment benefits provided through a pension or postretirement benefit plan, individual deferred compensation arrangements, or special or contractual termination benefits covered in SFAS 88 and 106.

F.   **CONTINGENT LIABILITIES (SFAS 5)**

1.   **LIABILITY AND AMOUNT UNCERTAIN** Contingent liabilities arise from events or circumstances occurring before the balance sheet date, the resolution of which is contingent upon a *future* event or circumstance. The distinction between contingencies and other liabilities hinges on the uncertainty as to the *existence* of the liability and **not** on the uncertainty as to the *amount* of the liability. Examples of contingent liabilities include (a) obligations related to product warranties, (b) obligations related to product coupons and premiums, (c) obligations related to product defects, (d) pending or threatened litigation, and (e) actual or possible claims and assessments.

2.   **CLASSIFICATION OF CONTINGENCIES** Accounting treatment depends on the likelihood that future events will confirm the contingent loss **and** whether the amount can be reasonably estimated.

   a.   **PROBABLE** Likely to occur. Where the likelihood of confirmation of a loss is considered *probable* and the loss can be *reasonably estimated*, the estimated loss should be accrued by a charge to income and the nature of the contingency should be disclosed. If, however, only a *range* of possible loss can be estimated—and no amount in the range is a better estimate than the others—the *minimum* amount in the range should be accrued. In addition, the nature of the contingency and the additional exposure to loss should be disclosed (FASB Interp. 14).

   b.   **REASONABLY POSSIBLE** More than remote, but less than probable. Where the loss is considered *reasonably possible*, no charge should be made to income **but** the nature of the contingency should be disclosed. This treatment also applies to probable losses that cannot be reasonably estimated.

   c.   **REMOTE** Slight chance of occurring. Where likelihood of loss is considered *remote*, disclosure is normally **not** required. *Exceptions include* guarantees of indebtedness of others, banks' standby letters of credit, and guarantees to repurchase receivables.

3.   **NO DISCLOSURE**

   a.   **CERTAIN UNASSERTED CLAIMS** No disclosure is required for a loss contingency concerning an unasserted claim or assessment when no claimant has shown an awareness of such unless it is considered probable that the claim will be asserted, **and** there is a reasonable possibility of an unfavorable result.

   b.   **UNSPECIFIED BUSINESS RISKS** General, unspecified business risks are not loss contingencies; no accrual or disclosure is required.

4.   **GAIN CONTINGENCIES** Gain Contingencies should be disclosed but not recognized as income. Care should be taken to avoid misleading implications as to the likelihood of realization.

5.   **POSTEMPLOYMENT BENEFITS** Postemployment Benefits that do not meet the conditions for accrual stated in SFAS 43, *Accounting for Compensated Absences*, should be accounted for as a probable or reasonably possible contingency.

6.   **ENVIRONMENTAL REMEDIATION LIABILITIES (SOP 96-1)** The accrual of an environmental liability is required if information available prior to issuance of the financial statements indicates that it is *probable* that a liability has been incurred at the date of the financial statements and the amount of the loss can be *reasonably estimated*.

   a.   **CONDITION PROBABLE** If a claim has been asserted and an entity can be held responsible for it, then condition probable is met. If an entity has been notified by the EPA or a relevant state agency, for example, that the entity is a potentially responsible party (PRP) and the entity had some involvement, then it is probable that the entity will incur some costs.

b. **ESTIMATE OF LIABILITY AND LOSS** A variety of factors should be considered in making the estimate, including pre-cleanup activities, such as testing, engineering studies, and feasibility studies, conducted to define the extent of the damage; remedial activities to clean up the environmental damage; government oversight and enforcement costs, which includes fines and penalties; and operation and maintenance activities, including post-remediation monitoring.

c. **RELATED ASSETS** An entity's balance sheet may include several assets that relate to an environmental remediation obligation, including receivables from other PRPs that are not providing initial funding, anticipated recoveries from insurers, and anticipated recoveries from prior owners.

EXHIBIT 3 ♦ CONTINGENCIES

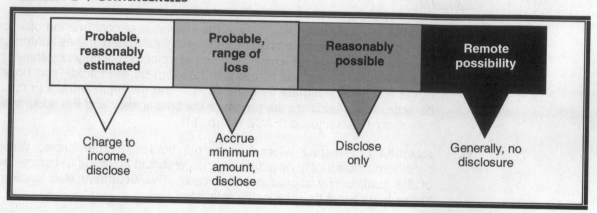

II. LONG-TERM LIABILITIES

A. DEFINITION

Long-term liabilities are all obligations not expected to be liquidated by the use of existing current assets or by the creation of current liabilities. Examples include (1) long-term notes payable, (2) refinancing of short-term obligations, and (3) bonds payable. As bonds payable are discussed in a separate chapter, they will not be discussed here.

B. DISCLOSURES

SFAS 47 requires that the combined aggregate amount of maturities and sinking fund requirements for all long-term borrowings be disclosed for each of the five years following the date of the latest balance sheet period.

C. NOTES PAYABLE

1. **NOTE ISSUED FOR CASH** APB 21, *Interest on Receivables and Payables*, specifies, when a note is issued solely for cash, it is generally presumed to have a present value at issuance equal to the cash proceeds exchanged. If special rights or privileges are included in the transaction, they must be measured separately.

2. **NOTE EXCHANGED FOR PROPERTY, GOODS, OR SERVICES** When a note is exchanged for property, goods, or services, it is assumed that the rate of interest stipulated by the note is fair and adequate compensation. Therefore, unless the interest rate is not stated or is unreasonable, the note should be recorded at its face amount because this amount would approximate the note's present value.

3. **INTEREST RATE NOT STATED OR UNREASONABLE** When the interest rate applicable to a note payable is not stated or is unreasonable,

a. **FAIR VALUE** Record the note at the fair value of the property, goods, or services exchanged or at the amount that approximates the market value of the note, whichever is more clearly determinable. The difference between that amount and the face amount of the note is recorded as a discount or premium.

b. **PRESENT VALUE** In the absence of established exchange prices for the related property, goods, or services or evidence of the market value of the note, the note is recorded at its present value by discounting all future payments on the note using an imputed interest rate—the market rate of interest for the level of risk involved. The difference between the present value and the face amount of the note is recorded as a discount or premium.

c. **IMPUTED INTEREST RATE** The imputed interest rate is determined by considering the credit standing of the debtor, prevailing rates for similar debt, and rates at which the debtor can obtain funds.

d. **DISCOUNT OR PREMIUM AMORTIZATION** The discount or premium should be amortized as interest expense over the life of the note in such a way as to result in a constant rate of interest when applied to the carrying amount of the note at the beginning of any given period. APB 21 allows the use of amortization methods other than the interest method (e.g., straight-line) if the results do not differ materially from those obtained with the interest method.

EXAMPLE 6 ♦ INTEREST RATE NOT STATED

XYZ Company acquires a patent on January 1, 20X1, in exchange for a three-year noninterest-bearing note of $100,000. There was no established exchange price for the patent, and the note has no ready market. The prevailing rate of interest for a note of this type is 8% at the date of the exchange. (The imputed interest rate is the prevailing interest rate of 8%.) The PV interest factor for an amount in three years discounted at 8% is .79383 (see Appendix D, Table 2).

REQUIRED: Provide the journal entries to record the patent and the note, the interest expense at year-ends, and the payment of the note.

SOLUTION:

To record the patent and the note:

1/1/X1 Patent ($100,000 x .79383)	79,383	
Discount on Note Payable ($100,000 – $79,383)	20,617	
Note Payable		100,000

To record interest expense at year-ends:

20X1: Interest Expense [($100,000 – $20,617) x .08]	6,351	
Discount on Note Payable		6,351
20X2: Interest Expense [($100,000 – $14,266*) x .08]	6,859	
Discount on Note Payable		6,859
20X3: Interest Expense [($100,000 – $7,407**) x .08]	7,407	
Discount on Note Payable		7,407

To record the payment of the note:

Note Payable	100,000	
Cash		100,000

* $20,617 – $6,351.
** $14,266 – $6,859.

EXAMPLE 7 ♦ UNREASONABLE INTEREST RATE STATED

Assume the same data as in Example 6, except that the note specifies annual interest payments of 5% on December 31. This rate is considered unreasonably low based on the current market rate of 8%. (The imputed interest rate is the current market rate of 8%.) The interest factor for a three-year annuity at 8% is 2.57710 (see Appendix D, Table 4).

REQUIRED: Provide the related journal entries.

SOLUTION:

To record the asset and the note:

Patent	92,268	
Discount on Note Payable ($100,000 – $92,268)	7,732	
Note Payable		100,000

COMPUTATIONS:

Present value of principal ($100,000 x .79383)	$79,383
Present value of interest payments ($5,000 x 2.57710)	12,885
Present value of note	$92,268

To record interest expense at year-ends:

20X1:	Interest Expense [($100,000 – $7,732) x .08]	7,381	
	Cash ($100,000 x .05)		5,000
	Discount on Note Payable (to balance)		2,381
20X2:	Interest Expense [($100,000 – $5,351*) x .08]	7,572	
	Cash ($100,000 x .05)		5,000
	Discount on Note Payable (to balance)		2,572
20X3:	Interest Expense [($100,000 – $2,779**) x .08]	7,778	
	Cash ($100,000 x .05)		5,000
	Discount on Note Payable (to balance)		2,778

To record the payment of the note:

Note Payable	100,000	
Cash		100,000

---

* $7,732 – $2,381.
** $5,351 – $2,572.

D. REFINANCING OF SHORT-TERM OBLIGATIONS (SFAS 6)

SFAS 6 provides guidelines for the classification of short-term obligations that are expected to be refinanced on a long-term basis.

1. **RECLASSIFICATION TO NONCURRENT LIABILITIES** Short-term obligations are those scheduled to mature within one year or operating cycle, whichever is longer. Generally, short-term obligations are classified as current liabilities, since they will require the use of working capital during the ensuing period. However, if they are to be refinanced on a long-term basis, they will not require the use of working capital; in this case, short-term obligations will be appropriately classified as noncurrent liabilities.

2. **REFINANCING DEFINED** Refinancing a short-term obligation on a long-term basis means either of the following:

   a.   Replacing it with long-term obligations or equity securities.

    b. Renewing, extending, or replacing it with short-term obligations for an uninterrupted period greater than one year (or operating cycle) from the balance sheet date.

3. RECLASSIFICATION REQUIREMENTS Exclusion from current liabilities requires that two conditions be met:

    a. INTENTION The enterprise must intend to refinance the obligation on a long-term basis.

    b. ABILITY The enterprise must have the ability to consummate the refinancing. Evidence of the ability to consummate the refinancing is provided by either of the following:

        (1) A refinancing that occurs after the balance sheet date but before the balance sheet is issued.

        (2) A *financing agreement* before the balance sheet is issued that permits the refinancing and extends beyond one year or operating cycle. If any violation of the agreement has occurred, a waiver from the lender must be obtained. Further, the lender must be expected to be financially capable of honoring the agreement.

4. PORTIONS OF PAST OBLIGATIONS NOT REFINANCED If post-balance sheet refinancing of a short-term obligation has taken place, any portion **not** refinanced must be shown as a current liability.

5. LIMITATIONS ON THE AMOUNT EXCLUDED FROM CURRENT LIABILITIES If a financing agreement provides evidence of the ability to refinance, the amount excluded from current liabilities is limited to the amount available for refinancing under the agreement. Limitations on the amount excluded arise from the following:

    a. Obligations in excess of the amount available for refinancing under the agreement.

    b. Restrictions imposed by other agreements on the use of funds obtained under the refinancing arrangement.

    c. Agreements that do not specify that a fixed amount of funds will be available. In this case, only an amount equal to the minimum sum expected to be available at any date during the period can be excluded. If the minimum sum cannot be reasonably estimated, the obligation must be shown as a current liability.

EXAMPLE 8 ♦ EXCLUSIONS FROM CURRENT LIABILITIES

> The First National Bank agrees to lend ABC Corporation, on a revolving credit basis, an amount equal to 75% of the Company's receivables. During the year the receivables are expected to range between a low of $500,000 in the first quarter to a high of $2,000,000 in the fourth quarter. The minimum amount available for refinancing of short-term liabilities is $375,000 based on the expected low for trade receivables of $500,000. For balance sheet presentation, the maximum amount that can be excluded from current liabilities is $375,000.

6. REPAID FROM CURRENT ASSETS FASB Interp. 8, *Classification of a Short-Term Obligation Repaid Prior to Being Replaced by a Long-Term Security*, indicates that short-term obligations repaid after the balance sheet date and subsequently refinanced before the issuance of the balance sheet must be classified as current liabilities as of the balance sheet date because current assets were used for the repayment.

E. **ASSET RETIREMENT OBLIGATIONS (SFAS 143)**

SFAS 143 addresses accounting for costs and liabilities related to tangible long-term asset retirement. Asset retirement obligation must be recognized as a liability (not a contra-asset) at fair value in the period in which it is incurred if subject to reasonable estimation. The liability is discounted and accretion expense is recognized using the credit-adjusted risk-free interest rate in effect at initial recognition. **Note**: The editors expect exam coverage on this to be light.

III. EXTINGUISHMENT OF DEBT (SFAS 125)

A. **CONDITIONS**

A liability should not be removed from the financial statements until it has been extinguished, which occurs if either of the following conditions are met:

1. **PAYMENT** The debtor pays the creditor and is relieved of its obligation for the liability. This may include delivering cash, other financial assets, goods, or services, or reacquiring outstanding debt securities; or

2. **RELEASE** The debtor is legally released from being the primary obligor on the liability, either by the creditor or the courts, such as in the case of bankruptcy.

B. **IN-SUBSTANCE DEFEASANCE NOT EXTINGUISHMENT**

In-substance defeasance is no longer accounted for as an extinguishment of debt. In-substance defeasance is a situation where a debt remains outstanding, but the debtor places risk-free monetary assets, such as U.S. government securities, in a trust that restricts the use of the assets to meeting all of the cash flow requirements on the debt. Previously, this was allowed to be accounted for as an extinguishment of debt; the liability was derecognized (removed from the balance sheet) and the trust was not recognized as an asset on the balance sheet. SFAS 125 requires that this type of transaction be accounted for as a separate asset and liability.

C. **EXTINGUISHMENT VS. REFUNDING**

Extinguishment includes the reacquisition of debt securities regardless of whether the securities are canceled or held as so-called treasury bonds. Refunding refers to achieving the reacquisition by the use of proceeds from issuing other securities.

D. **GAIN OR LOSS RECOGNITION**

APB 26, *Early Extinguishment of Debt*, as amended by SFAS 125, indicates that all extinguishments are fundamentally alike. Therefore, the extinguishment of debt, irrespective of the method used (except certain conversions of convertible bonds into stock or extinguishment through a troubled debt restructuring) should involve recognition of a gain or loss in the period in which the extinguishment took place. The gain or loss is the difference between the reacquisition price and the net carrying amount of the extinguished debt, and is reported as an extraordinary item, net of related income tax effects.

IV. TROUBLED DEBT RESTRUCTURINGS (SFAS 15, 114, 118)

A. **DEFINITION**

A troubled debt restructuring occurs when a creditor, for economic or legal reasons related to the debtor's financial difficulties, grants a concession to the debtor that the creditor would not otherwise consider. This concession may take either of two forms: (1) *transfer of assets or an equity interest* in the debtor in satisfaction of the debt (C., below), or (2) a *modification of the terms* of the obligation, including a reduction of the interest rate, extension of the maturity date, or reduction of the face amount of the debt and accrued interest (D., below). Troubled Debt Restructurings are covered in SFAS 15 and amended by SFAS 114 and SFAS 118.

B. **DEBT RESTRUCTURING VS. TROUBLED DEBT RESTRUCTURING**

Generally, a debtor who can obtain funds from other than the existing creditor at an interest rate near the current rate for nontroubled debt is **not** involved with a troubled debt restructuring, even though the debtor may be experiencing difficulty. In a troubled debt restructuring, the creditor is granting the concession in order to protect as much of the investment as possible.

C.   **TYPES OF TROUBLED DEBT RESTRUCTURINGS**
A troubled debt restructuring may involve the transfer of assets by the debtor to the creditor in partial or full settlement of the obligation. Alternatively, the agreement may call for the granting of an equity interest in the debtor to the creditor, or a combination of both. In either case, in a *troubled* debt restructuring the total fair value of the consideration given to discharge the obligation will be **less** than the recorded amount (i.e., principal and accrued interest) of the debt. (If the fair value of the consideration received by the creditor equals or exceeds the amount of the debt, the transaction will not be classified as a *troubled* debt restructuring, by definition.)

1.   **ACCOUNTING BY DEBTORS** The debtor will recognize a gain on the retirement of debt, equal to the difference between the carrying amount of the obligation settled and the fair value of the assets and/or equity interest transferred to the creditor.

a.   **EXTRAORDINARY GAIN** This gain will be classified as an *extraordinary item*, per SFAS 4 (i.e., the same as a gain on any extinguishment of debt).

b.   **ORDINARY GAIN OR LOSS** To the extent *assets* are transferred pursuant to the restructuring, the debtor will recognize an *ordinary* gain or loss equal to the difference between the fair value and the carrying amount of the assets transferred (i.e., the same as if the assets had been sold at their fair value for cash).

2.   **ACCOUNTING BY CREDITORS** The creditor will recognize a loss equal to the difference between the fair value of the assets and/or equity interest received and the recorded amount of the receivable (including accrued interest). This loss, to the extent not offset against an allowance for uncollectibles or other valuation account, will be recognized in full in the period the restructuring takes place.

a.   **ORDINARY LOSS** Generally, the loss recognized by the creditor will be *ordinary*.

b.   **RECORD AT FAIR VALUE** The creditor will record the assets and/or equity securities received at their fair value.

EXAMPLE 9 ♦ TROUBLED DEBT RESTRUCTURING

On January 1, 20X1, Risky Developers Inc. borrowed $100,000 from Easymoney Corp. The promissory note calls for 10% interest, payable annually on Dec. 31, and matures on Dec. 31, 20X3. Risky made the first interest payment on time but, due to financial difficulties, defaulted on the payment due Dec. 31, 20X2. On July 1, 20X3, Risky and Easymoney reached an agreement whereby the entire obligation would be discharged by the transfer of a parcel of land valued at $40,000 and Risky preferred stock with a par and fair value of $35,000. The land had been purchased by Risky in 20X0 for $50,000.

REQUIRED: Provide the journal entries to record the troubled debt restructuring in the books of both the debtor and creditor.

(continued on next page)

SOLUTION:

Debtor:

Note Payable, Including Accrued Interest [$100,000 + 10% ($100,000) + 10% ($110,000) (6/12)]	115,500	
Loss on Disposal of Land, Ordinary	10,000	
Land		50,000
Preferred Stock		35,000
Extraordinary Gain on Debt Restructuring [$115,500 − ($40,000 + $35,000)]		40,500

Creditor:

Land	40,000	
Investment in Risky Preferred Stock	35,000	
Loss on Settlement of Receivable (ordinary)	40,500	
Notes Receivable, Incl. Accrued Interest		115,500

D. MODIFICATION OF TERMS—DEBTOR ACCOUNTING

A troubled debt restructuring may involve a reduction of interest rate, a partial forgiveness of principal and interest payments, and/or extension of maturity date. Accounting for debtors is determined by whether the sum of the cash payments under the new terms (not discounted to present value) equal or exceed the amount of the obligation.

1. PAYMENTS LESS THAN OBLIGATION When the aggregate payments under new terms are **less** than the amount of the obligation, the debtor reduces the carrying amount of the payable to the aggregate future cash payments.

    a. EXTRAORDINARY GAIN The debtor records an extraordinary gain equal to the difference between the carrying amount of the payable (including accrued interest) and the aggregate future payments required under the new terms.

    b. PAYMENTS REDUCE PRINCIPAL Future payments are recorded as a reduction of principal, and no interest expenses are recognized.

2. PAYMENTS EQUAL TO OR MORE THAN OBLIGATION When the aggregate payments under new terms are equal to or more than the amount of the obligation, the debtor

    a. NO GAIN OR LOSS Does not change the amount of the obligation, nor is any gain or loss recorded.

    b. PAYMENTS TO PRINCIPAL AND INTEREST Allocates subsequent payments between interest and principal on the basis of a constant rate of interest (i.e., the interest method of APB 21).

3. DEBTOR AND CREDITOR ACCOUNTING DIFFER Note that the debtor and the creditor account for the modification in different manners. The debtor uses the *aggregate* of the future cash payments and the creditor uses the present value of the future cash payments. Creditor accounting of impaired loans is detailed in Chapter 2.

V. HIGHLIGHTS OF FEDERAL BANKRUPTCY LAW

The law of bankruptcy is primarily tested in the Business Law & Professional Responsibilities portion of the CPA Exam. However, Exams have frequently included a multiple choice question on this topic, generally concerning the rules of priority and distribution. These rules are summarized below for straight bankruptcies or liquidations.

A. CHAPTER 7 BANKRUPTCY

Chapter 7 of the *Federal Bankruptcy Code* covers straight bankruptcies or liquidations. It involves the collection of the debtor's nonexempt property, the liquidation or sale of such property, and the distribution of the proceeds to the creditors by the trustee in the manner provided by the Federal Bankruptcy Code. After the distribution of the proceeds, the debtor is *discharged* from having to satisfy any personal liability of his or hers concerning any of the discharged debts.

B.   PRIORITY OF CLAIMS
The claims filed by the creditors against the bankrupt debtor are classified according to their *priority*, that is, the order in which they will receive any of the liquidation proceeds that are ultimately distributed.

C.   ORDER OF PRIORITY

1.   SECURED CLAIMS Claims secured by a lien on property are entitled to first priority, but only on the distribution of the proceeds from the liquidation of their collateral, and only to the extent the loan is secured. If the value of the collateral is **less** than the amount of the claim, the excess amount of the claim is unsecured.

2.   UNSECURED CLAIMS Claims not secured by a lien on any property of the debtor. There are many different classes of unsecured claims and their priority depends upon the nature of the claim.

D.   DISTRIBUTION RULES

1.   PRIORITY Under a Chapter 7 case, claims of a higher priority are satisfied before those of a next priority class. If the assets are insufficient to satisfy all the claims within a particular class, they will be satisfied pro rata for that class.

2.   EXCESS PROCEEDS Any liquidation proceeds and/or other assets remaining after satisfying **all** claims are returned to the debtor.

EXAMPLE 10 ♦ DISTRIBUTION IN BANKRUPTCY

ABC Company filed a petition for a bankruptcy under Chapter 7. Creditors have secured claims of $300,000 and unsecured claims of $625,000. The following list of assets has been obtained:

	Amount secured	Amount received upon liquidation
Asset #1	$100,000	$100,000
Asset #2	75,000	50,000
Asset #3	125,000	150,000
Free Assets	--	300,000
	$300,000	$600,000

REQUIRED: Determine the distribution of the proceeds received from liquidation.

SOLUTION: Claims secured by Asset #1 and Asset #3 are fully secured and will be satisfied in full ($100,000 and $125,000, respectively). The excess $25,000 of proceeds received over the amount of the secured claim for Asset #3 will go towards satisfying unsecured claims. As for Asset #2, its secured creditor is only <u>partially</u> secured, since the amount received for the asset is less than the amount of the claim; therefore, this creditor is now an unsecured creditor in the amount of $25,000. There is ultimately $325,000 [$600,000 − ($100,000 + $50,000 + $125,000)] left to be distributed to the unsecured claims. Since the unsecured claims total $650,000 ($625,000 of original unsecured claims plus $25,000 unsecured claim from creditor of Asset #2), the unsecured creditors will each receive one-half of their claims. Therefore, Asset #2's secured creditor will receive <u>$62,500</u> [$50,000 + ($25,000 x 50%)].

Examination Format

The examination consists of the following sections and formats:

Section	Format 4-Option Multiple Choice	Other Objective Answer Formats	Essays or Problems
Financial Accounting & Reporting	50-60%	20-30%	20-30%
Accounting & Reporting--Taxation, Managerial, and Governmental and Not-for-Profit Organizations	50-60%	40-50%	---
Auditing	50-60%	20-30%	20-30%
Business Law & Professional Responsibilities	50-60%	20-30%	20-30%

CHAPTER 7—LIABILITIES

Problem 7-1 MULTIPLE CHOICE QUESTIONS (130 to 163 minutes)

1. Mill Co.'s trial balance included the following account balances at December 31, 1992:

Accounts payable	$15,000
Bonds payable, due 1993	25,000
Discount on bonds payable, due 1993	3,000
Dividends payable 1/31/93	8,000
Notes payable, due 1994	20,000

What amount should be included in the current liability section of Mill's December 31, 1992 balance sheet?
a. $45,000
b. $51,000
c. $65,000
d. $78,000 (11/93, PI, #1, 4370)

2. Lyle Inc. is preparing its financial statements for the year ended December 31, 1992. Accounts payable amounted to $360,000 before any necessary year-end adjustment related to the following:

- At December 31, 1992, Lyle has a $50,000 debit balance in its accounts payable to Ross, a supplier, resulting from a $50,000 advance payment for goods to be manufactured to Lyle's specifications.
- Checks in the amount of $100,000 were written to vendors and recorded on December 29, 1992. The checks were mailed on January 5, 1993.

What amount should Lyle report as accounts payable in its December 31, 1992 balance sheet?
a. $510,000
b. $410,000
c. $310,000
d. $210,000 (11/93, PI, #30, 4399)

3. Rabb Co. records its purchases at gross amounts but wishes to change to recording purchases net of purchase discounts. Discounts available on purchases recorded from October 1, 1991, to September 30, 1992, totaled $2,000. Of this amount, $200 is still available in the accounts payable balance. The balances in Rabb's accounts as of and for the year ended September 30, 1992, before conversion are:

Purchases	$100,000
Purchase discounts taken	800
Accounts payable	30,000

What is Rabb's accounts payable balance as of September 30, 1992, after the conversion?
a. $29,800
b. $29,200
c. $28,800
d. $28,200 (11/92, PI, #21, 3254)

4. Kew Co.'s accounts payable balance at December 31, 1990, was $2,200,000 before considering the following data:

- Goods shipped to Kew F.O.B. shipping point on December 22, 1990, were lost in transit. The invoice cost of $40,000 was not recorded by Kew. On January 7, 1991, Kew filed a $40,000 claim against the common carrier.
- On December 27, 1990, a vendor authorized Kew to return, for full credit, goods shipped and billed at $70,000 on December 3, 1990. The returned goods were shipped by Kew on December 28, 1990. A $70,000 credit memo was received and recorded by Kew on January 5, 1991.
- Goods shipped to Kew F.O.B. destination on December 20, 1990, were received on January 6, 1991. The invoice cost was $50,000.

What amount should Kew report as accounts payable in its December 31, 1990 balance sheet?
a. $2,170,000
b. $2,180,000
c. $2,230,000
d. $2,280,000 (5/91, PI, #34, 1015)

5. Ivy Co. operates a retail store. All items are sold subject to a 6% state sales tax, which Ivy collects and records as sales revenue. Ivy files quarterly sales tax returns when due, by the 20th day following the end of the sales quarter. However, in accordance with state requirements, Ivy remits sales tax collected by the 20th day of the month following any month such collections exceed $500. Ivy takes these payments as credits on the quarterly sales tax return. The sales taxes paid by Ivy are charged against sales revenue. Following is a monthly summary appearing in Ivy's first quarter 1995 sales revenue account:

	Debit	Credit
January	$ --	$10,600
February	600	7,420
March	--	8,480
	$ 600	$26,500

In its March 31, 1995 balance sheet, what amount should Ivy report as sales taxes payable?
a. $ 600
b. $ 900
c. $1,500
d. $1,590 (5/95, FAR, #15, 5551)

6. House Publishers offered a contest in which the winner would receive $1,000,000, payable over 20 years. On December 31, 1993, House announced the winner of the contest and signed a note payable to the winner for $1,000,000, payable in $50,000 installments every January 2. Also on December 31, 1993, House purchased an annuity for $418,250 to provide the $950,000 prize monies remaining after the first $50,000 installment, which was paid on January 2, 1994. In its December 31, 1993 balance sheet, what amount should House report as note payable-contest winner, net of current portion?

a. $368,250
b. $418,250
c. $900,000
d. $950,000

(11/94, FAR, #22, 5286)

7. On March 1, 1993, Fine Co. borrowed $10,000 and signed a two-year note bearing interest at 12% per annum compounded annually. Interest is payable in full at maturity on February 28, 1995. What amount should Fine report as a liability for accrued interest at December 31, 1994?

a. $0
b. $1,000
c. $1,200
d. $2,320

(11/95, FAR, #16, 6098)

8. Cali Inc. had a $4,000,000 note payable due on March 15, 1995. On January 28, 1995, before the issuance of its 1994 financial statements, Cali issued long-term bonds in the amount of $4,500,000. Proceeds from the bonds were used to repay the note when it came due. How should Cali classify the note in its December 31, 1994 financial statements?

a. As a current liability, with separate disclosure of the note refinancing.
b. As a current liability, with no separate disclosure required.
c. As a noncurrent liability, with separate disclosure of the note refinancing.
d. As a noncurrent liability, with no separate disclosure required.

(5/95, FAR, #5, 5541)

9. On December 31, 1992, Roth Co. issued a $10,000 face value note payable to Wake Co. in exchange for services rendered to Roth. The note, made at usual trade terms, is due in nine months and bears interest, payable at maturity, at the annual rate of 3%. The market interest rate is 8%. The compound interest factor of $1 due in nine months at 8% is .944. At what amount should the note payable be reported in Roth's December 31, 1992 balance sheet?

a. $10,300
b. $10,000
c. $ 9,652
d. $ 9,440

(11/93, PI, #27, 4396)

10. On August 1, 1991, Vann Corp.'s $500,000, one-year, noninterest-bearing note due July 31, 1992, was discounted at Homestead Bank at 10.8%. Vann uses the straight-line method of amortizing bond discount. What amount should Vann report for notes payable in its December 31, 1991 balance sheet?

a. $500,000
b. $477,500
c. $468,500
d. $446,000

(11/92, PI, #22, 3255)

11. Which of the following is reported as interest expense?

a. Pension cost interest
b. Postretirement healthcare benefits interest
c. Imputed interest on noninterest bearing note
d. Interest incurred to finance construction of machinery for own use

(11/93, Theory, #33, 4538)

12. A company issued a short-term note payable with a stated 12 percent rate of interest to a bank. The bank charged a .5% loan origination fee and remitted the balance to the company. The effective interest rate paid by the company in this transaction would be

a. Equal to 12.5%.
b. More than 12.5%.
c. Less than 12.5%.
d. Independent of 12.5%. (5/90, Theory, #8, 9026)

13. Black Co. requires advance payments with special orders for machinery constructed to customer specifications. These advances are nonrefundable. Information for 1993 is as follows:

Customer advances—balance 12/31/92	$118,000
Advances received with orders in 1993	184,000
Advances applied to orders shipped in 1993	164,000
Advances applicable to orders canceled in 1993	50,000

In Black's December 31, 1993 balance sheet, what amount should be reported as a current liability for advances from customer?

a. $0
b. $ 88,000
c. $138,000
d. $148,000

(11/94, FAR, #25, 9027)

14. Kent Co., a division of National Realty Inc., maintains escrow accounts and pays real estate taxes for National's mortgage customers. Escrow funds are kept in interest-bearing accounts. Interest, less a 10% service fee, is credited to the mortgagee's account and used to reduce future escrow payments. Additional information follows:

Escrow accounts liability, 1/1/92 $ 700,000
Escrow payments received during 1992   1,580,000
Real estate taxes paid during 1992   1,720,000
Interest on escrow funds during 1992   50,000

What amount should Kent report as escrow accounts liability in its December 31, 1992 balance sheet?
a. $510,000
b. $515,000
c. $605,000
d. $610,000   (11/93, PI, #32, 4401)

15.   Barnel Corp. owns and manages 19 apartment complexes. On signing a lease, each tenant must pay the first and last months' rent and a $500 refundable security deposit. The security deposits are rarely refunded in total, because cleaning costs of $150 per apartment are almost always deducted. About 30% of the time, the tenants are also charged for damages to the apartment, which typically cost $100 to repair. If a one-year lease is signed on a $900 per month apartment, what amount would Barnel report as refundable security deposit?
a. $1,400
b. $ 500
c. $ 350
d. $ 320   (11/92, PI, #26, 3259)

16.   Under state law, Acme may pay 3% of eligible gross wages or it may reimburse the state directly for actual unemployment claims. Acme believes that actual unemployment claims will be 2% of eligible gross wages and has chosen to reimburse the state. Eligible gross wages are defined as the first $10,000 of gross wages paid to each employee. Acme had five employees, each of whom earned $20,000 during 1993. In its December 31, 1993 balance sheet, what amount should Acme report as accrued liability for unemployment claims?

a. $1,000
b. $1,500
c. $2,000
d. $3,000   (5/94, FAR, #22, 4837)

17.   Lime Co.'s payroll for the month ended January 31, 1995, is summarized as follows:

Total wages $10,000
Federal income tax withheld   1,200

All wages paid were subject to FICA. FICA tax rates were 7% each for employee and employer. Lime remits payroll taxes on the 15th of the following month. In its financial statements for the month ended January 31, 1995, what amounts should Lime report as total payroll tax liability and as payroll tax expense?

	Liability	Expense
a.	$1,200	$1,400
b.	$1,900	$1,400
c.	$1,900	$ 700
d.	$2,600	$ 700

                 (11/95, FAR, #13, 6095)

18.   For the week ended June 30, 1995, Free Co. paid gross wages of $20,000, from which federal income taxes of $2,500 and FICA were withheld. All wages paid were subject to FICA tax rates of 7% each for employer and employee. Free makes all payroll-related disbursements from a special payroll checking account. What amount should Free have deposited in the payroll checking account to cover net payroll and related payroll taxes for the week ended June 30, 1995?
a. $21,400
b. $22,800
c. $23,900
d. $25,300   (R/00, FAR, #6, 6901)

19.   Ross Co. pays all salaried employees on a Monday for the five-day workweek ended the previous Friday. The last payroll recorded for the year ended December 31, 1992, was for the week ended December 25, 1992. The payroll for the week ended January 1, 1993, included regular weekly salaries of $80,000 and vacation pay of $25,000 for vacation time earned in 1992 not taken by December 31, 1992. Ross had accrued a liability of $20,000 for vacation pay at December 31, 1991. In its December 31, 1992 balance sheet, what amount should Ross report as accrued salary and vacation pay?
a. $64,000
b. $68,000
c. $69,000
d. $89,000   (11/93, PI, #28, 4397)

20.   In its 1993 financial statements, Cris Co. reported interest expense of $85,000 in its income statement and cash paid for interest of $68,000 in its cash flow statement. There was no prepaid interest or interest capitalization either at the beginning or end of 1993. Accrued interest at December 31, 1992, was $15,000. What amount should Cris report as accrued interest payable in its December 31, 1993 balance sheet?
a. $ 2,000
b. $15,000
c. $17,000
d. $32,000   (11/94, FAR, #18, 5282)

21. On July 1, 1993, Ran County issued realty tax assessments for its fiscal year ended June 30, 1994. On September 1, 1993, Day Co. purchased a warehouse in Ran County. The purchase price was reduced by a credit for accrued realty taxes. Day did not record the entire year's real estate tax obligation, but instead records tax expenses at the end of each month by adjusting prepaid real estate taxes or real estate taxes payable, as appropriate. On November 1, 1993, Day paid the first of two equal installments of $12,000 for realty taxes. What amount of this payment should Day record as a debit to real estate taxes payable?

a. $ 4,000
b. $ 8,000
c. $10,000
d. $12,000

(11/94, FAR, #19, 5283)

22. Dunne Co. sells equipment service contracts that cover a two-year period. The sale price of each contract is $600. Dunne's past experience is that, of the total dollars spent for repairs on service contracts, 40% is incurred evenly during the first contract year and 60% evenly during the second contract year. Dunne sold 1,000 contracts evenly throughout 1992. In its December 31, 1992 balance sheet, what amount should Dunne report as deferred service contract revenue?

a. $540,000
b. $480,000
c. $360,000
d. $300,000

(11/93, PI, #38, 4407)

23. Winn Co. sells subscriptions to a specialized directory that is published semiannually and shipped to subscribers on April 15 and October 15. Subscriptions received after the March 31 and September 30 cutoff dates are held for the next publication. Cash from subscribers is received evenly during the year and is credited to deferred subscription revenue. Data relating to 1990 are as follows:

Deferred subscription revenue 1/1/90 $ 750,000
Cash receipts from subscribers   3,600,000

In its December 31, 1990 balance sheet, Winn should report deferred subscription revenue of

a. $2,700,000.
b. $1,800,000.
c. $1,650,000.
d. $ 900,000.

(11/91, PI, #29, 2417)

24. For $50 a month, Rawl Co. visits its customers' premises and performs insect control services. If customers experience problems between regularly scheduled visits, Rawl makes service calls at no additional charge. Instead of paying monthly, customers may pay an annual fee of $540 in advance. For a customer who pays the annual fee in advance, Rawl should recognize the related revenue

a. When the cash is collected.
b. At the end of the fiscal year.
c. At the end of the contract year after all of the services have been performed.
d. Evenly over the contract year as the services are performed.

(11/94, FAR, #21, 5285)

25. Regal Department Store sells gift certificates, redeemable for store merchandise, that expire one year after their issuance. Regal has the following information pertaining to its gift certificates sales and redemptions:

Unredeemed at 12/31/90	$ 75,000
1991 sales	250,000
1991 redemptions of prior year sales	25,000
1991 redemptions of current year sales	175,000

Regal's experience indicates that 10% of gift certificates sold will not be redeemed. In its December 31, 1991 balance sheet, what amount should Regal report as unearned revenue?

a. $125,000
b. $112,500
c. $100,000
d. $ 50,000

(11/92, PI, #30, 3263)

26. Todd Care Co. offers three payment plans on its 12-month contracts. Information on the three plans and the number of children enrolled in each plan for the September 1, 1991, through August 31, 1992, contract year follows:

Plan	Initial payment per child	Monthly fees per child	Number of children
#1	$500	$ --	15
#2	200	30	12
#3	--	50	9
			36

Todd received $9,900 of initial payments on September 1, 1991, and $3,240 of monthly fees during the period September 1 through December 31, 1991. In its December 31, 1991 balance sheet, what amount should Todd report as deferred revenues?

a. $3,300
b. $4,380
c. $6,600
d. $9,900

(11/92, PI, #29, amended, 3262)

27. In June 1992, Northan Retailers sold refundable merchandise coupons. Northan received $10 for each coupon redeemable from July 1 to December 31, 1992, for merchandise with a retail price of $11. At June 30, 1992, how should Northan report these coupon transactions?

a. Unearned revenues at the merchandise's retail price
b. Unearned revenues at the cash received amount
c. Revenues at the merchandise's retail price
d. Revenues at the cash received amount

(11/92, Theory, #7, 3440)

28. Able Inc. had the following amounts of long-term debt outstanding at December 31, 1991:

14-1/2% term note, due 1992	$ 3,000
11-1/8% term note, due 1995	107,000
8% note, due in 11 equal annual principal payments, plus interest beginning December 31, 1992	110,000
7% guaranteed debentures, due 1996	100,000
Total	$320,000

Able's annual sinking-fund requirement on the guaranteed debentures is $4,000 per year. What amount should Able report as current maturities of long-term debt in its December 31, 1991 balance sheet?

a. $ 4,000
b. $ 7,000
c. $10,000
d. $13,000

(11/92, PI, #5, 3238)

29. Vadis Co. sells appliances that include a three-year warranty. Service calls under the warranty are performed by an independent mechanic under a contract with Vadis. Based on experience, warranty costs are estimated at $30 for each machine sold. When should Vadis recognize these warranty costs?

a. Evenly over the life of the warranty
b. When the service calls are performed
c. When payments are made to the mechanic
d. When the machines are sold

(11/94, FAR, #27, 5290)

30. During 1990, Gum Co. introduced a new product carrying a two-year warranty against defects. The estimated warranty costs related to dollar sales are 2% within 12 months following the sale and 4% in the second 12 months following the sale. Sales and actual warranty expenditures for the years ended December 31, 1990 and 1991, are as follows:

	Sales	Actual warranty expenditures
1990	$150,000	$2,250
1991	250,000	7,500
	$400,000	$9,750

What amount should Gum report as estimated warranty liability in its December 31, 1991 balance sheet?

a. $ 2,500
b. $ 4,250
c. $11,250
d. $14,250

(5/92, PI, #35, 2606)

31. Oak Co. offers a three-year warranty on its products. Oak previously estimated warranty costs to be 2% of sales. Due to a technological advance in production at the beginning of 1994, Oak now believes 1% of sales to be a better estimate of warranty costs. Warranty costs of $80,000 and $96,000 were reported in 1992 and 1993, respectively. Sales for 1994 were $5,000,000. What amount should be disclosed in Oak's 1994 financial statements as warranty expense?

a. $ 50,000
b. $ 88,000
c. $100,000
d. $138,000

(11/95, FAR, #44, 6126)

32. Dunn Trading Stamp Co. records stamp service revenue and provides for the cost of redemptions in the year stamps are sold to licensees. Dunn's past experience indicates that only 80% of the stamps sold to licensees will be redeemed. Dunn's liability for stamp redemptions was $6,000,000 at December 31, 1996. Additional information for 1997 is as follows:

Stamp service revenue from stamps sold to licensees	$4,000,000
Cost of redemptions (stamps sold prior to 1/1/97)	2,750,000

If all the stamps sold in 1997 were presented for redemption in 1998, the redemption cost would be $2,250,000. What amount should Dunn report as a liability for stamp redemptions at December 31, 1997?

a. $7,250,000
b. $5,500,000
c. $5,050,000
d. $3,250,000

(11/90, PI, #28, amended, 1035)

33. Case Cereal Co. frequently distributes coupons to promote new products. On October 1, 1991, Case mailed 1,000,000 coupons for $.45 off each box of cereal purchased. Case expects 120,000 of these coupons to be redeemed before the December 31, 1991, expiration date. It takes 30 days from the redemption date for Case to receive the coupons from the retailers. Case reimburses the retailers an additional $.05 for each coupon redeemed. As of December 31, 1991, Case had paid retailers $25,000 related to these coupons and had 50,000 coupons on hand that had not been processed for payment. What amount should Case report as a liability for coupons in its December 31, 1991 balance sheet?

a. $35,000
b. $29,000
c. $25,000
d. $22,500

(11/92, PI, #24, 3257)

34. In December 1994, Mill Co. began including one coupon in each package of candy that it sells and offering a toy in exchange for 50 cents and five coupons. The toys cost Mill 80 cents each. Eventually 60% of the coupons will be redeemed. During December, Mill sold 110,000 packages of candy and no coupons were redeemed. In its December 31, 1994 balance sheet, what amount should Mill report as estimated liability for coupons?

a. $ 3,960
b. $10,560
c. $19,800
d. $52,800

(5/95, FAR, #21, 5557)

35. Pine Corp. is required to contribute, to an employee stock ownership plan (ESOP), 10% of its income after deduction for this contribution but before income tax. Pine's income before charges for the contribution and income tax was $75,000. The income tax rate is 30%. What amount should be accrued as a contribution to the ESOP?

a. $7,500
b. $6,818
c. $5,250
d. $4,773

(5/91, PI, #36, 1016)

36. At December 31, 1991, Taos Co. estimates that its employees have earned vacation pay of $100,000. Employees will receive their vacation pay in 1992. Should Taos accrue a liability at December 31, 1991, if the rights to this compensation accumulated over time or if the rights are vested?

	Accumulated	Vested
a.	Yes	No
b.	No	No
c.	Yes	Yes
d.	No	Yes

(11/92, Theory, #25, 3458)

37. The following information pertains to Rik Co.'s two employees:

Name	Weekly salary	Number of weeks worked in 1991	Vacation rights vest or accumulate
Ryan	$800	52	Yes
Todd	600	52	No

Neither Ryan nor Todd took the usual two-week vacation in 1991. In Rik's December 31, 1991 financial statements, what amount of vacation expense and liability should be reported?

a. $2,800
b. $1,600
c. $1,400
d. $0

(5/92, PII, #15, 2647)

38. Gavin Co. grants all employees two weeks of paid vacation for each full year of employment. Unused vacation time can be accumulated and carried forward to succeeding years and will be paid at the salaries in effect when vacations are taken or when employment is terminated. There was no employee turnover in 1997. Additional information relating to the year ended December 31, 1997 is as follows:

Liability for accumulated vacations at 12/31/96	$35,000
Pre-1997 accrued vacations taken from 1/1/97 to 9/30/97 (the authorized period for vacations)	20,000
Vacations earned for work in 1997 (adjusted to current rates)	30,000

Gavin granted a 10% salary increase to all employees on October 1, 1997, its annual salary increase date. For the year ended December 31, 1997, Gavin should report vacation pay increase of

a. $45,000.
b. $33,500.
c. $31,500.
d. $30,000.

(5/90, PII, #53, amended, 9028)

39. Eagle Co. has cosigned the mortgage note on the home of its president, guaranteeing the indebtedness in the event that the president should default. Eagle considers the likelihood of default to be remote. How should the guarantee be treated in Eagle's financial statements?

a. Disclosed only
b. Accrued only
c. Accrued and disclosed
d. Neither accrued nor disclosed

(11/95, FAR, #17, 6099)

40. Brite Corp. had the following liabilities at December 31, 1993:

Accounts payable	$ 55,000
Unsecured notes, 8%, due 7/1/94	400,000
Accrued expenses	35,000
Contingent liability	450,000
Deferred income tax liability	25,000
Senior bonds, 7%, due 3/31/94	1,000,000

The contingent liability is an accrual for possible losses on a $1,000,000 lawsuit filed against Brite. Brite's legal counsel expects the suit to be settled in 1995, and has estimated that Brite will be liable for damages in the range of $450,000 to $750,000.

The deferred income tax liability is not related to an asset for financial reporting and is expected to reverse in 1995.

What amount should Brite report in its December 31, 1993 balance sheet for current liabilities?
a. $ 515,000
b. $ 940,000
c. $1,490,000
d. $1,515,000   (5/94, FAR, #11, 4826)

41. Invern Inc. has a self-insurance plan. Each year, retained earnings is appropriated for contingencies in an amount equal to insurance premiums saved less recognized losses from lawsuits and other claims. As a result of a 1991 accident, Invern is a defendant in a lawsuit in which it will probably have to pay damages of $190,000.

What are the effects of this lawsuit's probable outcome on Invern's 1991 financial statements?
a. An increase in expenses and no effect on liabilities.
b. An increase in both expenses and liabilities.
c. No effect on expenses and an increase in liabilities.
d. No effect on either expenses or liabilities.
(11/92, Theory, #17, 3450)

42. Wyatt Co. has a probable loss that can only be reasonably estimated within a range of outcomes. No single amount within the range is a better estimate than any other amount. The loss accrual should be
a. Zero.
b. The maximum of the range.
c. The mean of the range.
d. The minimum of the range.
(11/90, Theory, #35, 1801)

43. During 1990, Manfred Corp. guaranteed a supplier's $500,000 loan from a bank. On October 1, 1991, Manfred was notified that the supplier had defaulted on the loan and filed for bankruptcy protection. Counsel believes Manfred will probably have to pay between $250,000 and $450,000 under its guarantee. As a result of the supplier's bankruptcy, Manfred entered into a contract in December 1991 to retool its machines so that Manfred could accept parts from other suppliers. Retooling costs are estimated to be $300,000. What amount should Manfred report as a liability in its December 31, 1991 balance sheet?
a. $250,000
b. $450,000
c. $550,000
d. $750,000   (11/92, PI, #31, 3264)

44. During 1994, Haft Co. became involved in a tax dispute with the IRS. At December 31, 1994, Haft's tax advisor believed that an unfavorable outcome was probable. A reasonable estimate of additional taxes was $200,000, but could be as much as $300,000. After the 1994 financial statements were issued, Haft received and accepted an IRS settlement offer of $275,000. What amount of accrued liability should Haft have reported in its December 31, 1994 balance sheet?
a. $200,000
b. $250,000
c. $275,000
d. $300,000   (5/95, FAR, #22, 5558)

45. Management can estimate the amount of loss that will occur if a foreign government expropriates some company assets. If expropriation is reasonably possible, a loss contingency should be
a. Disclosed but not accrued as a liability.
b. Disclosed and accrued as a liability.
c. Accrued as a liability but not disclosed.
d. Neither accrued as a liability nor disclosed.
(11/94, FAR, #26, 5289)

46. On January 17, 1991, an explosion occurred at a Sims Co. plant causing extensive property damage to area buildings. Although no claims had yet been asserted against Sims by March 10, 1991, Sims' management and counsel concluded that it is likely that claims will be asserted and that it is reasonably possible Sims will be responsible for damages. Sims' management believed that $1,250,000 would be a reasonable estimate of its liability. Sims' $5,000,000 comprehensive public liability policy has a $250,000 deductible clause. In Sims' December 31, 1990 financial statements, which were issued on March 25, 1991, how should this item be reported?
a. As an accrued liability of $250,000
b. As a footnote disclosure indicating the possible loss of $250,000
c. As a footnote disclosure indicating the possible loss of $1,250,000
d. No footnote disclosure or accrual is necessary
(5/92, PI, #36, 2607)

47. What is the underlying concept governing the generally accepted accounting principles pertaining to recording gain contingencies?
a. Conservatism
b. Relevance
c. Consistency
d. Reliability   (11/95, FAR, #3, 6085)

48. At December 31, 1992, Date Co. awaits judgment on a lawsuit for a competitor's infringement of Date's patent. Legal counsel believes it is probable that Date will win the suit and indicated the most likely award together with a range of possible awards. How should the lawsuit be reported in Date's 1992 financial statements?
a. In note disclosure only
b. By accrual for the most likely award
c. By accrual for the lowest amount of the range of possible awards
d. Neither in note disclosure nor by accrual
                    (11/93, Theory, #21, 4526)

49. During January 1992, Haze Corp. won a litigation award for $15,000 which was tripled to $45,000 to include punitive damages. The defendant, who is financially stable, has appealed only the $30,000 punitive damages. Haze was awarded $50,000 in an unrelated suit it filed, which is being appealed by the defendant. Counsel is unable to estimate the outcome of these appeals. In its 1992 financial statements, Haze should report what amount of pretax gain?
a. $15,000
b. $45,000
c. $50,000
d. $95,000   (11/92, PII, #53, 3387)

50. During 1993, Smith Co. filed suit against West Inc. seeking damages for patent infringement. At December 31, 1993, Smith's legal counsel believed that it was probable that Smith would be successful against West for an estimated amount in the range of $75,000 to $150,000, with all amounts in the range considered equally likely. In March 1994, Smith was awarded $100,000 and received full payment thereof. In its 1993 financial statements, issued in February 1994, how should this award be reported?
a. As a receivable and revenue of $100,000
b. As a receivable and deferred revenue of $100,000
c. As a disclosure of a contingent gain of $100,000
d. As a disclosure of a contingent gain of an undetermined amount in the range of $75,000 to $150,000   (5/94, FAR, #57, 4872)

51. On December 30, 1997, Bart Inc. purchased a machine from Fell Corp. in exchange for a noninterest bearing note requiring eight payments of $20,000. The first payment was made on December 30, 1997, and the others are due annually on December 30. At date of issuance, the prevailing rate of interest for this type of note was 11%. Present value factors are as follows:

Period	Present value of ordinary annuity of 1 at 11%	Present value of annuity in advance of 1 at 11%
7	4.712	5.231
8	5.146	5.712

On Bart's December 31, 1997 balance sheet, the note payable to Fell was
a. $ 94,240.
b. $102,920.
c. $104,620.
d. $114,240.   (5/90, PI, #29, amended, 1045)

ITEMS 52 AND 53 are based on the following:

On October 1, 1991, Fleur Retailers signed a 4-month, 16% note payable to finance the purchase of holiday merchandise. At that date, there was no direct method of pricing the merchandise, and the note's market rate of interest was 11%. Fleur recorded the purchase at the note's face amount. All of the merchandise was sold by December 1, 1991. Fleur's 1991 financial statements reported interest payable and interest expense on the note for three months at 16%. All amounts due on the note were paid February 1, 1992.

52. Fleur's 1991 cost of goods sold for the holiday merchandise was
a. Overstated by the difference between the note's face amount and the note's October 1, 1991, present value.
b. Overstated by the difference between the note's face amount and the note's October 1, 1991, present value plus 11% interest for two months.
c. Understated by the difference between the note's face amount and the note's October 1, 1991, present value.
d. Understated by the difference between the note's face amount and the note's October 1, 1991, present value plus 16% interest for two months.
                    (5/92, Theory, #18, 2711)

53. As a result of Fleur's accounting treatment of the note, interest, and merchandise, which of the following items was reported correctly?

	12/31/91 retained earnings	12/31/91 interest payable
a.	Yes	Yes
b.	No	No
c.	Yes	No
d.	No	Yes

                    (5/92, Theory, #19, 2712)

54. Ames Inc. has $500,000 of notes payable due June 15, 1991. Ames signed an agreement on December 1, 1990, to borrow up to $500,000 to refinance the notes payable on a long-term basis with no payments due until 1992. The financing agreement stipulated that borrowings may not exceed 80% of the value of the collateral Ames was providing. At the date of issuance of the December 31, 1990 financial statements, the value of the collateral was $600,000 and is not expected to fall below this amount during 1991. In Ames' December 31, 1990 balance sheet, the obligation for these notes payable should be classified as

	Short-term	Long-term
a.	$500,000	$0
b.	$100,000	$400,000
c.	$20,000	$480,000
d.	$0	$500,000

(5/91, PI, #35, 9029)

55. Included in Lee Corp.'s liability account balances at December 31, 1997, were the following:

14% note payable issued October 1, 1997, maturing September 30, 1998 $125,000

16% note payable issued April 1, 1995, payable in six equal annual installments of $50,000 beginning April 1, 1996 200,000

Lee's December 31, 1997 financial statements were issued on March 31, 1998. On January 15, 1998, the entire $200,000 balance of the 16% note was refinanced by issuance of a long-term obligation payable in a lump sum. In addition, on March 10, 1998, Lee consummated a noncancelable agreement with the lender to refinance the 14%, $125,000 note on a long-term basis, on readily determinable terms that have not yet been implemented. Both parties are financially capable of honoring the agreement, and there have been no violations of the agreement's provisions. On the December 31, 1997 balance sheet, the amount of the notes payable that Lee should classify as short-term obligations is
a. $175,000.
b. $125,000.
c. $50,000.
d. $0.

(11/90, PI, #11, amended, 1026)

56. At December 31, 1990, Cain Inc. owed notes payable of $1,750,000, due on May 15, 1991. Cain expects to retire this debt with proceeds from the sale of 100,000 shares of its common stock. The stock was sold for $15 per share on March 10, 1991, prior to the issuance of the year-end financial statements. In Cain's December 31, 1990 balance sheet, what amount of the notes payable should be excluded from current liabilities?

a. $0
b. $250,000
c. $1,500,000
d. $1,750,000

(11/91, PI, #21, 2409)

57. Nu Corp. agreed to give Rand Co. a machine in full settlement of a note payable to Rand. The machine's original cost was $140,000. The note's face amount was $110,000. On the date of the agreement:

- The note's carrying amount was $105,000, and its present value was $96,000.
- The machine's carrying amount was $109,000, and its fair value was $96,000.

What amount of gains (losses) should Nu recognize, and how should these be classified in its income statement?

	Extraordinary	Other
a.	$(4,000)	$0
b.	$0	$(4,000)
c.	$5,000	$(4,000)
d.	$9,000	$(13,000)

(5/92, PI, #53, 2624)

58. Ace Corp. entered into a troubled debt restructuring agreement with National Bank. National agreed to accept land with a carrying amount of $75,000 and a fair value of $100,000 in exchange for a note with a carrying amount of $150,000. Disregarding income taxes, what amount should Ace report as extraordinary gain in its income statement?
a. $0
b. $25,000
c. $50,000
d. $75,000

(R/00, FAR, #10, 6905)

ITEMS 59 AND 60 are based on the following:

The following information pertains to the transfer of real estate pursuant to a troubled debt restructuring by Knob Co. to Mene Corp. in full liquidation of Knob's liability to Mene:

Carrying amount of liability liquidated	$150,000
Carrying amount of real estate transferred	100,000
Fair value of real estate transferred	90,000

59. What amount should Knob report as a pretax extraordinary gain (loss) on restructuring of payables?
a. $(10,000)
b. $0
c. $50,000
d. $60,000

(11/93, PI, #57, 4426)

60.   What amount should Knob report as ordinary gain (loss) on transfer of real estate?
a. $ (10,000)
b. $0
c. $ 50,000
d. $ 60,000

(11/93, PI, #58, 4427)

61.   On October 15, 1991, Kam Corp. informed Finn Co. that Kam would be unable to repay its $100,000 note due on October 31 to Finn. Finn agreed to accept title to Kam's computer equipment in full settlement of the note. The equipment's carrying value was $80,000 and its fair value was $75,000. Kam's tax rate is 30%. What amounts should Kam report as ordinary gain (loss) and extraordinary gain for the year ended September 30, 1992?

	Ordinary gain (loss)	Extraordinary gain
a.	$ (5,000)	$17,500
b.	$0	$20,000
c.	$0	$14,000
d.	$20,000	$0

(11/92, PI, #59, 3290)

62.   In 1992, May Corp. acquired land by paying $75,000 down and signing a note with a maturity value of $1,000,000. On the note's due date, December 31, 1997, May owed $40,000 of accrued interest and $1,000,000 principal on the note. May was in financial difficulty and was unable to make any payments. May and the bank agreed to amend the note as follows:

•   The $40,000 of interest due on December 31, 1997, was forgiven.

•   The principal of the note was reduced from $1,000,000 to $950,000 and the maturity date extended 1 year to December 31, 1998.

•   May would be required to make one interest payment totaling $30,000 on December 31, 1998.

As a result of the troubled debt restructuring, May should report a gain, before taxes, in its 1997 income statement of
a. $40,000
b. $50,000
c. $60,000
d. $90,000

(11/91, PI, #52, amended, 9030)

63.   Seco Corp. was forced into bankruptcy and is in the process of liquidating assets and paying claims. Unsecured claims will be paid at the rate of forty cents on the dollar. Hale holds a $30,000 noninterest-bearing note receivable from Seco collateralized by an asset with a book value of

$35,000 and a liquidation value of $5,000. The amount to be realized by Hale on this note is
a. $ 5,000.
b. $12,000.
c. $15,000.
d. $17,000.

(5/91, PII, #14, 1024)

64.   Kent Co. filed a voluntary bankruptcy petition, and the statement of affairs reflected the following amounts:

	Book value	Estimated current value
Assets:		
Assets pledged with fully secured creditors	$ 300,000	$370,000
Assets pledged with partially secured creditors	180,000	120,000
Free assets	420,000	320,000
	$ 900,000	$810,000
Liabilities:		
Liabilities with priority	$ 70,000	
Fully secured creditors	260,000	
Partially secured creditors	200,000	
Unsecured creditors	540,000	
	$1,070,000	

Assume that the assets are converted to cash at the estimated current values and the business is liquidated. What amount of cash will be available to pay unsecured nonpriority claims?
a. $240,000
b. $280,000
c. $320,000
d. $360,000

(11/90, PI, #31, amended, 1037)

65.   Kamy Corp. is in liquidation under Chapter 7 of the Federal Bankruptcy Code. The bankruptcy trustee has established a new set of books for the bankruptcy estate. After assuming custody of the estate, the trustee discovered an unrecorded invoice of $1,000 for machinery repairs performed before the bankruptcy filing. In addition, a truck with a carrying amount of $20,000 was sold for $12,000 cash. This truck was bought and paid for in the year before the bankruptcy. What amount should be debited to estate equity as a result of these transactions?
a. $0
b. $1,000
c. $8,000
d. $9,000

(5/92, PII, #10, 2642)

OTHER OBJECTIVE FORMAT QUESTIONS

Problem 7-2 (15 to 25 minutes)

ITEMS 1 THROUGH 12 are based on the following:

Edge Co., a toy manufacturer, is in the process of preparing its financial statements for the year ended December 31, 1993. Edge expects to issue its 1993 financial statements on March 1, 1994.

REQUIRED:

ITEMS 1 THROUGH 12 represent various information that has not been reflected in the financial statements. For each item, the following two responses are required:

a. Determine if an adjustment is required and select the appropriate amount, if any, from the list below.

b. Determine (Yes/No) if additional disclosure is required, either on the face of the financial statements or in the notes to the financial statements.

   Adjustment amounts
A. No adjustment is required.
B. $100,000
C. $150,000
D. $250,000
E. $400,000
F. $500,000

ITEMS TO BE ANSWERED:

1. Edge owns a small warehouse located on the banks of a river in which it stores inventory worth approximately $500,000. Edge is not insured against flood losses. The river last overflowed its banks twenty years ago.

2. During 1993, Edge began offering certain health care benefits to its eligible retired employees. Edge's actuaries have determined that the discounted expected cost of these benefits for current employees is $150,000.

3. Edge offers an unconditional warranty on its toys. Based on past experience, Edge estimates its warranty expense to be 1% of sales. Sales during 1993 were $10,000,000.

4. On October 30, 1993, a safety hazard related to one of Edge's toy products was discovered. It is considered probable that Edge will be liable for an amount in the range of $100,000 to $500,000.

5. On November 22, 1993, Edge initiated a lawsuit seeking $250,000 in damages from patent infringement.

6. On December 17, 1993, a former employee filed a lawsuit seeking $100,000 for unlawful dismissal. Edge's attorneys believe the suit is without merit. No court date has been set.

7. On December 15, 1993, Edge guaranteed a bank loan of $100,000 for its president's personal use.

8. On December 31, 1993, Edge's board of directors voted to discontinue the operations of its computer games division and sell all the assets of the division. The division was sold on February 15, 1994. On December 31, 1993, Edge estimated that losses from operations, net of tax, for the period January 1, 1994, through February 15, 1994, would be $400,000 and that the gain from the sale of the division's assets, net of tax, would be $250,000. These estimates were materially correct.

9. On January 5, 1994, a warehouse containing a substantial portion of Edge's inventory was destroyed by fire. Edge expects to recover the entire loss, except for a $250,000 deductible, from insurance.

10. On January 24, 1994, inventory purchased F.O.B. shipping point from a foreign country was detained at that country's border because of political unrest. The shipment is valued at $150,000. Edge's attorneys have stated that it is probable that Edge will be able to obtain the shipment.

11. On January 30, 1994, Edge issued $10,000,000 bonds at a premium of $500,000.

12. On February 4, 1994, the IRS assessed Edge an additional $400,000 for the 1992 tax year. Edge's tax attorneys and tax accountants have stated that it is likely that the IRS will agree to a $100,000 settlement. (5/94, FAR, #3, 4948-71)

PROBLEM 7-3 (7 to 13 minutes)

Items 1 through 6 are based on the following:

Town Inc. is preparing its financial statements for the year ended December 31, 1994.

ITEMS 1 THROUGH 6 represent various commitments and contingencies of Town at December 31, 1994, and events subsequent to December 31, 1994, but prior to the issuance of the 1994 financial statements. For each item, select from the following list the reporting requirement. A response may be selected once, more than once, or not at all.

Reporting Requirement
(D) Disclosure only.
(A) Accrual only.
(B) Both accrual and disclosure.
(N) Neither accrual nor disclosure.

1. On December 1, 1994, Town was awarded damages of $75,000 in a patent infringement suit it brought against a competitor. The defendant did not appeal the verdict, and payment was received in January 1995.

2. A former employee of Town has brought a wrongful-dismissal suit against Town. Town's lawyers believe the suit to be without merit.

3. At December 31, 1994, Town had outstanding purchase orders in the ordinary course of business for purchase of a raw material to be used in its manufacturing process. The market price is currently higher than the purchase price and is not anticipated to change within the next year.

4. A government contract completed during 1994 is subject to renegotiation. Although Town estimates that it is reasonably possible that a refund of approximately $200,000-$300,000 may be required by the government, it does not wish to publicize this possibility.

5. Town has been notified by a governmental agency that it will be held responsible for the cleanup of toxic materials at a site where Town formerly conducted operations. Town estimates that it is probable that its share of remedial action will be approximately $500,000.

6. On January 5, 1995, Town redeemed its outstanding bonds and issued new bonds with a lower rate of interest. The reacquisition price was in excess of the carrying amount of the bonds.   (11/95, FAR, #78-83, 6152-6157)

PROBLEM/ESSAY QUESTIONS

PROBLEM 7-4 (30 to 40 minutes)

Deck Co. has just hired a new president, Palmer, and is reviewing its employee benefit plans with the new employee. For current employees, Deck offers a compensation plan for future vacations. Deck also provides post-employment benefits to former or inactive employees.

On the date of Palmer's hire, Palmer entered into a deferred compensation contract with Deck. Palmer is expected to retire in ten years. The contract calls for a payment of $150,000 upon termination of employment following a minimum three-year service period. The contract also provides that interest of 10% compounded annually, be credited on the amount due each year after the third year.

REQUIRED:

a. Give an example of post-employment benefits. State the conditions under which Deck is required to accrue liabilities for compensated absences and post-employment benefits. State Deck's disclosure requirements if these conditions, in full or in part, are not met.

b. Describe the general accrual period for amounts to be paid under a deferred compensation contract. State the theoretical rationale for requiring accrual of these liabilities and related expenses.

c. Prepare a schedule of the expense and accrued liability related to Palmer's deferred compensation agreement to be reported in Deck's financial statements for the first four years of the contract.   (5/96, FAR, #16, 6289)

PROBLEM 7-5 (40 to 50 minutes)

The following is the long-term liabilities section of Tempo Co.'s December 31, 1990 balance sheet:

Long-term liabilities:		
Note payable—bank; 15 principal payments of $5,000, plus 10% interest due annually on September 30	$75,000	
Less: Current portion	(5,000)	$ 70,000
Capital lease obligation—16 payments of $9,000 due annually on January 1	76,600	
Less: Current portion	(1,340)	75,260
Deferred income tax liability		15,750
Total long-term liabilities		$161,010

- Tempo's incremental borrowing rate on the date of the lease was 11% and the lessor's implicit rate, which was known by Tempo, was 10%.

- The only difference between Tempo's taxable income and pretax accounting income is depreciation on a machine acquired on January 1, 1990, for $250,000. The machine's estimated useful life is five years, with no salvage value. Depreciation is computed using the straight-line method for financial reporting purposes and the MACRS method for tax purposes. Depreciation expense for tax and financial reporting purposes for 1991 through 1994 is as follows:

Year	Tax depreciation	Financial depreciation	Tax depr'n over (under) financial depr'n
1991	$80,000	$50,000	$ 30,000
1992	40,000	50,000	(10,000)
1993	35,000	50,000	(15,000)
1994	30,000	50,000	(20,000)

The enacted federal income tax rates are 30% for 1990 and 1991, and 35% for 1992 through 1994.

- Included in Tempo's December 1990 balance sheet was a deferred tax asset of $9,000.
- For the year ended December 31, 1991, Tempo's income before income taxes was $430,000.
- On July 1, 1991, Tempo received proceeds of $459,725 from a $500,000 bond issuance. The bonds mature in 30 years and interest of 11% is payable each January 1 through July 1. The bonds were issued at a price to yield the investors 12%. Tempo uses the effective interest method to amortize the bond discount.

REQUIRED:

a. Prepare a schedule showing Tempo's income before income taxes, current income tax expense, deferred income tax expense, and net income. Show supporting calculations for current and deferred income tax amounts.

b. Prepare a schedule showing the calculation of Tempo's interest expense for the year ended December 31, 1991.

c. Prepare the long-term liabilities section of Tempo's December 31, 1991 balance sheet. Show supporting calculations. (5/92, PI, #5, amended, 6192)

Essay 7-6 (15 to 25 minutes)

Supey Chemical Co. encountered the following two situations in 1990:

- Supey must pay an indeterminate amount for toxic waste cleanup on its land. An adjoining land owner, Gap Toothpaste, sold its property because of possible toxic contamination by Supey of the water supply and resulting potential adverse public reaction towards its product. Gap sued Supey for damages. There is a reasonable possibility that Gap will prevail in the suit.

- At December 31, 1990, Supey has a noncancelable purchase contract for 10,000 pounds of Chemical XZ, for delivery in June 1991. Supey does not hedge its contracts. Supey uses this chemical to make Product 2-Y. In December 1990, the U.S. Food and Drug Administration banned the sale of Product 2-Y in concentrated form. Supey will be allowed to sell Product 2-Y in a diluted form; however, it will take at least five years to use the 10,000 pounds of Chemical XZ. Supey believes the sales price of the diluted product will not be sufficient to recover the contract price of Chemical XZ.

REQUIRED:

a. **1.** In its 1990 financial statements, how should Supey report the toxic waste cleanup? Why is this reporting appropriate?

2. In its 1990 financial statements, how should Supey report Gap's claim against it? Why is this reporting appropriate?

b. In its 1990 financial statements, how should Supey report the effects of the contract to purchase Chemical XZ? Why is this reporting appropriate?
(11/91, Theory, #4)

Essay 7-7 (5 to 8 minutes)

Essex Company has a compensation plan for future vacations for its employees.

REQUIRED:

What conditions must be met for Essex to accrue compensation for future vacations? What is the theoretical rationale for accruing compensation for future vacations? (11/89, Theory, #4c, 3527)

Solution 7-1 MULTIPLE CHOICE ANSWERS

CURRENT LIABILITIES

1. (a) Current liabilities are obligations which are due within one year of the balance sheet date. The notes payable are due in 1994; therefore, they are reported in the long-term liabilities section of the balance sheet at 12/31/92. Therefore, the amount that should be included in the current liability section of Mill's 12/31/92 balance sheet is computed as follows:

Accounts payable		$15,000
Bonds payable, due 1993	$25,000	
Discount on bonds payable	3,000	22,000
Dividends payable in 1993		8,000
Current liabilities, 12/31/92		$45,000

2. (a) The $360,000 accounts payable balance at 12/31/92 should be increased for (1) the $50,000 debit balance for the advance to the supplier because Lyle should report this amount as an asset and (2) the $100,000 of checks written to vendors recorded in 1992 but not mailed until after the financial statement date (i.e., the checks were mailed 1/5/93). Thus, in its 12/31/92 balance sheet, Lyle should report accounts payable of $510,000 (i.e., $360,000 + $50,000 + $100,000).

3. (a) After the conversion, the accounts payable balance will be reported net of purchase discounts. The gross balance of the accounts payable of $30,000 is reduced by the $200 of discounts still available in the accounts payable balance to arrive at the net amount of $29,800.

4. (a) The cost of goods should be included in accounts payable when legal title passes from the seller to the purchaser. Kew should include the $40,000 cost of the goods lost in transit in accounts payable at 12/31/90. The goods were shipped F.O.B. *shipping point*, and the title of these goods passed to Kew when the vendor delivered the goods to the common carrier on 12/22/90. Since the vendor authorized Kew to return goods for full credit before year-end, and Kew shipped the goods before year-end, the 12/31/90 accounts payable balance should be reduced by $70,000, the cost of the goods returned. The $50,000 cost of the goods that were shipped from a vendor F.O.B. *destination* on 12/20/90 should not be included in accounts payable at 12/31/90. Title of these goods did not pass to Kew until Kew received the goods on 1/6/91. Thus, accounts payable should be reported at $2,170,000 ($2,200,000 + $40,000 − $70,000) at 12/31/90.

5. (b) Ivy Co. should report sales taxes based on February and March sales as sales taxes payable in its March 31, 1995 balance sheet. The taxes based on January sales were paid in February because they exceeded $500 ($10,600 sales ÷ 1.06 = sales of $10,000; $10,600 − $10,000 = $600 in sales taxes). This is the $600 debit in February. February and March sales taxes are calculated as follows:

	Total credits to sales revenue account (a)	Sales without sales taxes (a÷1.06) (b)	Sales taxes (a–b)
February	$7,420	$7,000	$420
March	$8,480	$8,000	$480
Total sales taxes payable, 3/31/95			$900

NOTES PAYABLE

6. (b) The amount that should be reported as the noncurrent portion of Note Payable to Contest Winner at 12/31/93 is $418,250, the cost of the annuity purchased to provide for the $950,000 of prize monies to be paid after 12/31/94. This is the most objective available evidence of the present value of the prize money due.

7. (d) Fine's liability for accrued interest at December 31, 1994:

March 1, 1993 to Feb. 28, 1994	
($10,000 @ 12% X 12/12)	$1,200
March 1, 1994 to Dec. 31, 1994	
[12% ($10,000 + $1,200) X 10/12]	1,120
Total accrued interest	$2,320

8. (c) The portion of long-term debt due within the next fiscal period is classified as a current liability if payment is expected to require the use of current assets or the creation of other current liabilities. According to SFAS 6, short-term debt expected to be refinanced on a long-term basis is to be excluded from current liabilities when the enterprise has the intent and ability to refinance the obligation on a long-term basis. One way intent and ability are demonstrated is by post-balance-sheet-date issuance of a long-term obligation or equity securities. Separate disclosure of such refinancing is required.

9. (b) The note payable arose from a transaction with a vendor in the normal course of business and is due in customary trade terms not exceeding one year; therefore, the note can be reported at its face amount of $10,000, despite the fact that the 3% stated interest rate of the note does not approximate the prevailing market interest rate of 8% for similar notes at the date of the transaction.

10. (c) The amount that should be reported for the noninterest-bearing note payable at 12/31/91 is determined as follows:

Face amount of note		$500,000
Less: Unamortized discount, 12/31/91:		
Maturity value of note	$500,000	
Times: Discount rate	x 10.8%	
Bank discount	54,000	
Less: Amortization, 8/1/91-12/31/91		
($54,000 x 5/12)	(22,500)	(31,500)
Carrying amount of note, 12/31/91		$468,500

11. (c) The note should not be recorded at its face amount because it is noninterest-bearing. APB 21 requires that noninterest-bearing notes be recorded at the fair value of the property, goods, or services exchanged, or at an amount which approximates the market value of the note, whichever is the more clearly determinable. If neither of these amounts can be determined, the note should be recorded at its present value, computed by discounting all future payments of the note at the prevailing rate of interest for similar notes. The difference between the face amount of the noninterest-bearing note payable and the amount at which it is recorded is amortized as interest expense over the life of the note by the effective interest method.

Pension cost interest is a component of net periodic pension cost (SFAS 87, par. 20). Postretirement healthcare benefits interest is a component of net periodic postretirement healthcare benefits cost (SFAS 106, par. 46). Interest cost incurred to finance construction of machinery for a company's own use is capitalized as part of the cost of the machinery (SFAS 34, par. 9).

12. (b) The note's 12 percent rate of interest and the bank's .5% loan origination fee are based upon the face amount of the note. The cash received by the note holder is the face amount of the note *less* the loan origination fee. Since less cash is received than the amount on which the interest rate and loan origination fee is computed, the effective interest rate is more than 12.5%.

ADVANCES AND RETURNABLE DEPOSITS

13. (b) The amount to be reported as a current liability for customer deposits can be determined by using a T-account approach as follows:

		Customer Deposits	
		$118,000	Balance, 12/31/92
Advances applied to orders shipped in 1993	$164,000	184,000	Advances received with orders in 1993
Advances applicable to orders canceled in 1993	50,000		
		$ 88,000	Balance, 12/31/93

14. (c) The amount to be reported as escrow accounts liability at 12/31/92 is computed as follows:

Escrow liability, 1/1/92		$ 700,000
Add: Escrow payments received during 1992	$1,580,000	
Interest on escrow funds during 1992, less 10% service fee		
[$50,000 – ($50,000 x 10%)]	45,000	1,625,000
		2,325,000
Less: Real estate taxes paid during 1992		(1,720,000)
Escrow liability, 12/31/92		$ 605,000

15. (b) The lessor should report the full amount of the $500 refundable security deposit as a liability until the lessor has earned a portion of it by cleaning or repairing vacated apartments. Revenue is not recognized until it has been earned. Deferred revenue is reported as a liability.

ACCRUED LIABILITIES

16. (a) 2% of $10,000 = $200 x 5 employees = $1,000. Acme has chosen to reimburse the state for actual claims instead of using the 3% of eligible gross wages rate. The liability is computed using eligible gross wages, not total wages, for each

employee. The actual unemployment claim is accrued, not the state rate times actual wages.

17. (d) The liability and expense are calculated as follows:

	Liability	Expense
FIT withheld	$1,200	
FICA employee portion ($10,000 @ 7%)	700	
FICA employer portion ($10,000 @ 7%)	700	$700
Totals	$2,600	$700

18. (a) Free Co. has total wages expense of $21,400 for the week ended June 30, 1995. This amounts to $20,000 plus $1,400 (7% x $20,000) for the employer's share of FICA. The total deposit will be distributed as follows:

Net pay to employees	$16,100
Federal income taxes	2,500
FICA (employer's and employees' shares)	2,800
Total deposit to payroll checking account	$21,400

19. (d) The amount that should be reported as accrued salary and vacation pay at 12/31/92 is computed as follows:

Accrued salary at 12/31/92 ($80,000 x 4/5*)	$64,000
Accrued vacation time earned in 1992	25,000
Accrued salary and vacation time at 12/31/92	$89,000

---

* Four days of the 5-day workweek ended 1/1 pertain to 1992.

20. (d) The amount to be reported as accrued interest payable at 12/31/93 is determined as follows:

Interest expense for 1993	$85,000
Cash paid for interest during 1993	(68,000)
Increase in accrued interest payable during 1993	17,000
Accrued interest payable, 12/31/92	15,000
Accrued interest payable, 12/31/93	$32,000

21. (b) On September 1, 1993, Day would have collected two months of real estate taxes from the seller and credited the amount to Real Estate Taxes Payable. At the end of September and October, Day would have recorded one month of real estate taxes each month by a credit to Real Estate Taxes Payable. When the payment was made for six months of real estate taxes, on November 1, 1993, the $12,000 payment would be for the four months prior to that date that would have already been accrued and for the two months that follow the payment date. Therefore, $8,000 (i.e., $12,000 x 4/6) of the payment should be recorded as a *decrease* in Real Estate Taxes Payable and $4,000 (i.e., $12,000 x 2/6) of the payment should be recorded as an *increase* in Prepaid Real Estate Taxes.

DEFERRED REVENUE

22. (b) Sales of service contracts in 1992 are $600 x 1,000 contracts, for a total of $600,000. A portion of this revenue is earned and recognized in 1992 and the rest is deferred. The 60% earned evenly during the second contract year is all deferred at the end of 1992. The portion of the 40% that is earned in the first year is recognized as revenue and the balance is deferred. Because both the contract sales and the repairs expense are made evenly throughout the year, an average can be used; i.e. half of the 40% is recognized as revenue and half is deferred. The total deferred service contract revenue is calculated as follows:

Second contract year ($600,000 x 60%)	$360,000
First contract year [($0 + $600,000)/2 x 40%]	120,000
Total deferred service contract revenue 12/31/92	$480,000

23. (d) Because the deferred subscription revenues at 12/31/89 were earned in 1990, they do not affect the computation of deferred subscription revenue at 12/31/90. The amount to be reported as deferred subscription revenue at 12/31/90 is determined as follows:

Cash receipts from customers during 1990	$3,600,000
Portion received after 9/30/90 cutoff date to be earned in 1991	x 3/12
Deferred subscription revenue at 12/31/90	$ 900,000

24. (d) Accrual accounting recognizes revenue in the period(s) it is earned. Therefore, the revenue should be recognized evenly over the contract year as the services are performed.

25. (d) Of the $250,000 of gift certificates sold in 1991, only $225,000 [i.e., $250,000 x (100% − 10%)] are expected to be redeemed. Since $175,000 of the gift certificates sold in 1991 were redeemed in 1991, $50,000 should be reported as unearned revenue at 12/31/91. (At 12/31/91, there is no liability for unredeemed gift certificates sold in 1990 because the certificates expire one year after their issuance.)

26. (c) Todd received $9,900 [i.e., ($500 x 15) + ($200 x 12)] of initial payments on its 12-month contracts for the 9/1/91 through 8/31/92 contract year. Since four months of the initial payments on the contracts have been earned as of 12/31/91, eight months of the initial payments on the contracts should be reported as deferred revenue at that date (i.e., $9,900 x 8/12 = $6,600).

27. (b) When the refundable merchandise coupons are sold, the sales price collected represents

unearned revenue. Earned revenue will be recognized later when the coupons are redeemed.

CURRENT MATURITIES OF LONG-TERM DEBT

28. **(d)** The amount of the principal payments on the long-term debt that are due in 1992 should be reported as the amount of current maturities of long-term debt at 12/31/91.

14½% term note, due 1992	$ 3,000
8% note, principal payment due 12/31/92 ($110,000 ÷ 11)	10,000
Current maturities of long-term debt, 12/31/91	$13,000

WARRANTIES

29. **(d)** If it is probable that customers will make claims under warranties relating to goods or services that have been sold, and a reasonable estimate of the costs involved can be made, the warranty costs should be charged to operating expense in the year of sale.

30. **(d)** The estimated warranty liability should be determined as follows:

Sales (1990 and 1991)	$400,000
Estimated warranty cost percentage (2% + 4%)	x 6%
Estimated warranty cost for 1990 and 1991 sales	24,000
Warranty expenditures to date	(9,750)
Estimated warranty liability, 12/31/91	$ 14,250

31. **(a)** As Oak believes 1% of sales to be the best estimate of warranty costs, the warranty expense should be accrued accordingly. ($5,000,000 x 1% = $50,000). The technological advance applied only to 1994 sales; thus, in this case, the estimates of warranty costs reported in 1992 and 1993 are not changed.

PREMIUMS

32. **(c)** The liability for stamp redemptions is determined as follows:

Liability for stamp redemptions, 12/31/96	$ 6,000,000
Less: Cost of redeemed stamps sold before 1/1/97	(2,750,000)
Add: Expected redemption cost of stamps sold in 1997 ($2,250,000 x 80%)	1,800,000
Liability for stamp redemptions, 12/31/97	$ 5,050,000

COUPONS

33. **(a)** The coupon liability at 12/31/91 is not reduced by the 50,000 coupons on hand because the coupons had not been processed for payment at 12/31/91. The liability for unredeemed coupons is determined as follows:

Coupons expected to be redeemed	120,000
Times: Payment for each coupon redeemed ($.45 + $.05)	x $.50
Estimated total coupon liability	$ 60,000
Less: Payments to retailers as of 12/31/91	(25,000)
Remaining coupon liability, 12/31/91	$ 35,000

34. **(a)** Coupon liability is estimated as follows:

Cost of toys to Mill Co., each	$ 0.80
Less: Cash to be received with redemption	(0.50)
Net cost to Mill Co. for each toy	$ 0.30
Total packages of candy sold in December	110,000
Times: Anticipated redemption rate	x 60%
Total coupons anticipated to be redeemed	66,000
Divided by: Number of coupons required for each toy	÷ 5
Anticipated number of toys needed	13,200
Times: Net cost to Mill Co. for each toy (above)	x $0.30
Total estimated liability for coupons, 12/31/94	$ 3,960

BONUSES

35. **(b)** The amount of the contribution can be determined algebraically, as follows, where C = contribution:

$$
\begin{aligned}
C &= .10\,(\$75,000 - C) \\
C &= \$7,500 - .10C \\
1.10C &= \$7,500 \\
C &= \underline{\$6,818}
\end{aligned}
$$

COMPENSATED ABSENCES

36. **(c)** An employer must accrue a liability for employees' rights to receive vacation pay benefits if the four conditions identified in SFAS 43, par. 6, are met. Three of these conditions are met in the question data. These are: (1) the obligation is attributable to employees' services already rendered, (2) payment of the compensation is probable, and (3) the amount can be reasonably estimated (i.e., the employees have earned vacation pay of $100,000 that they will receive in 1992). The fourth condition necessary for accrual is that the employees' rights to receive the vacation pay benefits vest or accumulate.

37. **(b)** The employer should accrue a liability of $1,600 (i.e., $800 x 2) for Ryan's two weeks of vacation pay because the four conditions for accrual are met: (1) the obligation is attributable to employees' services already rendered, (2) the obligation relates to rights that vest or accumulate, (3) payment of the compensation is probable, and (4) the amount can be reasonably estimated (SFAS 43, par. 6). The employer should not accrue a liability for Todd's two weeks of vacation pay because Todd's vacation rights do not vest or accumulate.

38. (c)   The amount of expense recognized is the increase in the cost of the pre-1997 accrued vacations and the cost of vacations earned for work performed in 1997. The amount is determined as follows:

Liability for accrued vacations, 12/31/96	$35,000
Less: Pre-1997 accrued vacations taken 1/1/97 to 9/30/97	(20,000)
Liability for pre-1997 vacations at time of 10% salary increase, 10/1/97	15,000
Times: 10% salary increase to reflect salaries in effect when vacations may be taken	x 10%
Additional cost of pre-1997 vacations	1,500
Cost of vacations earned for work performed in 1997	30,000
Vacation pay expense recognized in 1997	$31,500

CONTINGENCIES

39. (a)   Contingent liabilities that are considered to have a remote possibility of loss normally do not require disclosure. Exceptions include the guarantees of indebtedness of others, in which case disclosure, but not accrual, is required.

40. (c)

Accounts payable	$ 55,000
Unsecured notes	400,000
Accrued expenses	35,000
Senior bonds	1,000,000
	$1,490,000

41. (b)   The potential loss for damages that may be paid should be reported by accruing a loss in the income statement and a liability in the balance sheet. Accrual is required because both of the following conditions are met: (1) it is considered probable that a liability has been incurred, and (2) the amount of the loss can be reasonably estimated (SFAS 5, par. 8). In addition, the nature of the lawsuit should be separately disclosed in the notes to the financial statements (par. 9). The loss should not be charged to the appropriation of retained earnings for contingencies (par. 15).

42. (d)   SFAS 5, par. 8, provides that an estimated loss from a loss contingency shall be accrued by a charge to income if both of the following conditions are met: (1) it is probable that an asset has been impaired or a liability has been incurred, and (2) the amount of the loss can be reasonably estimated. Par. 3 of FIN 14 states that when the reasonable estimate of loss is a range and some amount within the range appears at the time to be a better estimate than any other amount within the range, that amount shall be accrued. "When no amount within the range is a better estimate than any other amount, however, the minimum amount in the range shall be accrued."

43. (a)   To accrue a contingent liability, SFAS 5 requires that the likelihood of the loss be probable and the amount be reasonably estimable. It is probable that Manfred will have to pay between $250,000 to $450,000 under its guarantee of the supplier's loan. Since no indication is given that any amount in the range is a better estimate than the others, the lower limit of the range, $250,000, is accrued as a contingent liability. On the other hand, the contract Manfred entered into to retool its machines involves a commitment but not a liability because no performance has been made by the other party to the contract. Thus, there is no asset or liability to be reported for the contract.

44. (a)   According to SFAS 5, a loss from a contingent liability, arising from events or circumstances occurring before the balance sheet date and the resolution of which is contingent upon a future event or circumstance, of which an unfavorable outcome is probable, should be accrued. The amount should be estimated and the minimum amount in the range of estimates, unless one amount is a better estimate than the others, should be accrued.

45. (a)   Since the contingent loss from the expropriation of assets is judged to be reasonably possible, it should be disclosed in the footnotes, but not accrued. A contingent loss is accrued only in situations where the loss is probable and estimable.

46. (b)   To accrue a contingent liability, SFAS 5 requires that the likelihood of the loss be probable and the amount be reasonably subject to estimation. Since the likelihood of the loss contingency in question is only *reasonably possible*, the loss contingency should not be accrued; it should only be disclosed. The disclosure should indicate the nature of the contingency and the amount of the possible loss of $250,000, the deductible clause of the policy.

GAIN CONTINGENCIES

47. (a)   Gain contingencies should be disclosed in the financial statements in a footnote rather than being reflected in income because doing so could result in recognizing income prior to its realization. This treatment reflects the principle of conservatism which means that accountants who are selecting between two possible alternatives should choose the accounting alternative which is least likely to overstate assets and income.

48. (a)   SFAS 5 provides that gain contingencies are not accrued before realization. Thus, no gain contingency can be accrued until the lawsuit is settled. However, the gain contingency should be

disclosed in the footnotes to the financial statements.

49. (a) In its 1992 financial statements, Haze should report a pretax gain of $15,000 (i.e., $45,000 – $30,000) for the amount of litigation award from the financially stable defendant that is not being appealed. The portion of the litigation awards that are being appealed (i.e., $30,000 and $50,000) represent gain contingencies and, thus, should not be accrued before realization. The gain contingencies should, however, be disclosed in the footnotes in the financial statements.

50. (d) Per SFAS 5, contingencies that might result in gains usually are not reflected in the accounts since to do so might be to recognize revenue prior to its realization. Adequate disclosure shall be made of contingencies that might result in gains, but care shall be exercised to avoid misleading implications as to the likelihood of realization. Thus, Smith Co. may disclose the range of the future gain only in the footnotes to the financial statements.

LONG-TERM NOTES PAYABLE

51. (a) The factor for the present value of an *annuity in advance* is used because the first payment of the note was made *immediately* (i.e., 12/30/97). The carrying amount of the note is determined as follows:

Periodic annual payments	$ 20,000
Times: Present value of an annuity in advance of $1 at 11% for 8 periods	x 5.712
Present value of all cash flows	114,240
Less: Payment, 12/30/97	(20,000)
Carrying amount of note, 12/31/97	$ 94,240

52. (c) The note should not be recorded at its face amount because its stated interest rate of 16% does not approximate the market rate of interest of 11% for similar notes. APB 21 requires that when a note which does not bear the market rate of interest is exchanged for property, goods, or services, the note is to be recorded at the fair value of the property, goods, or services or the fair value of the note, whichever is more clearly determinable. Since neither of these amounts are determinable for the note in question, the note should be recorded at its present value. The interest rate to be used in the discounting process is the borrower's incremental borrowing rate (market rate) at the date the note is issued (11% in this case). Because the market rate of 11% is less than the stated rate of the note of 16%, the present value of the note is greater than the face amount of the note. Therefore, the correct journal entry at the date the note was issued would

involve a debit to Purchases for the present value of the note, a credit to Note Payable for the face amount of the note, and a credit to Premium on Note Payable for the excess of the note's present value over its face amount. Fleur recorded the purchase at the note's face amount which understated the cost of the merchandise which was subsequently sold in 1991. Therefore, 1991 cost of goods sold is understated by the amount of the unrecorded premium on the note (i.e., the excess of the note's present value over its face amount).

53. (d) The four-month note was issued on October 1, 1991. Fleur reported three months of interest payable at December 31, 1991, computed using the stated rate of the note. Therefore, interest payable is correctly reported at December 31, 1991. On the other hand, retained earnings is overstated at December 31, 1991, because (1) 1991 cost of goods sold was understated by the full amount of the unrecorded note premium and (2) interest expense reported for the note for 1991 was overstated by 3/4 of the amount of the note premium (i.e., the amount of the note premium that should have been amortized for the three months the note was outstanding during 1991).

54. (c) SFAS 6 provides that short-term obligations refinanced on a long-term basis should be reported as long-term obligations. The amount that may be classified as long-term obligations is limited to the amount available under the refinancing agreement. According to the facts of the question, the refinancing agreement limited the amount available to the lesser of $500,000 or 80% of the value of the collateral provided. Thus, $480,000 [($600,000 x 80%) < $500,000] should be classified as long-term obligations and the remaining $20,000 should be classified as short-term obligations.

55. (d) The entire $200,000 balance of the 16% note is properly excluded from short-term obligations because before the balance sheet was issued, Lee refinanced the note by issuance of a long-term obligation. The $125,000, 14% note is also properly excluded from short-term obligations because before the balance sheet was issued, Lee entered into a financing agreement that clearly permits Lee to refinance the short-term obligation on a long-term basis on terms that are readily determinable, and all of the following conditions are met: (1) the agreement is noncancelable as to all parties and extends beyond one year; (2) at the balance sheet date, and at the date of its issuance, Witt is not in violation of the agreement; and (3) the lender is financially capable of honoring the agreement.

56. **(c)** Since after the date of the enterprise's balance sheet but before the balance sheet was issued, $1,500,000 (100,000 x $15) of common stock was issued for the purpose of refinancing the note payable on a long-term basis, $1,500,000 of the note payable should be excluded from current liabilities at the balance sheet date.

57. **(d)** Nu Corp. recognizes an extraordinary gain on the early extinguishment of the debt equal to the excess of the carrying amount of the obligation settled over the fair value of the asset transferred. Nu Corp. also recognizes an ordinary loss equal to the excess of the carrying amount over the fair value of the asset transferred, which is reported in income from continuing operations.

Carrying amount of obligation at date of extinguishment	$105,000
Fair value of asset transferred	(96,000)
Extraordinary gain on early extinguishment	$ 9,000

Carrying amount of asset transferred	$109,000
Fair value of asset transferred	(96,000)
Loss on transfer of asset	$ 13,000

TROUBLED DEBT RESTRUCTURINGS

58. **(c)** The debtor (Ace) will recognize an extraordinary gain on the retirement of debt, equal to the difference between the carrying amount of the obligation settled and the fair value of the assets and/or equity interest transferred to the creditor.

Carrying amount of Ace Corp.'s note to National Bank	$ 150,000
Less: Fair value of land transferred to National Bank	(100,000)
Extraordinary gain reported on Ace Corp.'s income statement	$ 50,000

The question does not ask for the ordinary gain (loss), but it would be calculated as follows:

Fair value of land transferred to National Bank	$100,000
Less: Carrying value of land transferred	(75,000)
Ordinary gain reported on Ace Corp.'s income statement	$ 25,000

59. **(d)** The debtor recognizes a pretax extraordinary gain on troubled debt restructuring equal to the excess of the carrying amount of the obligation over the fair value of the asset transferred at the date of the restructuring.

Carrying amount of liability liquidated	$150,000
Less: Fair value of real estate transferred	(90,000)
Pretax extraordinary gain recognized on restructure	$ 60,000

60. **(a)** The debtor reports a $10,000 (i.e., $100,000 – $90,000) ordinary loss equal to the excess of the carrying amount over the fair value of the real estate transferred. The loss is reported in income from continuing operations.

61. **(a)** The debtor recognizes an ordinary loss equal to the excess of the carrying amount over the fair value of the computer equipment transferred (i.e., $80,000 – $75,000 = $5,000). The loss is reported in income from continuing operations. The debtor recognizes an extraordinary gain on troubled debt restructuring equal to the difference between the carrying amount of the obligation settled and the fair value of the asset transferred.

Carrying amount of obligation at restructure date	$100,000
Less: Fair value of computer equipment transferred	(75,000)
Pretax extraordinary gain recognized on restructure	25,000
Less: Applicable income taxes ($25,000 x 30%)	(7,500)
Extraordinary gain recognized on restructure	$ 17,500

62. **(c)** When the aggregate payments under new terms of an impaired loan are less than the amount of the obligation, the *debtor* records an extraordinary gain equal to the difference between the carrying amount of the payable, including accrued interest, and the aggregate future cash payments required under the new terms. May Corp. is the debtor and owes $1,000,000 principal plus $40,000 of accrued interest. Under the new terms, May is required to pay future cash payments of $950,000 plus $30,000. The extraordinary gain, before taxes, is $1,040,000 – $980,000 = $60,000. Note that the *creditor* (in this case, the bank) would use the present value, not the aggregate, of the future cash payments in its accounting for this loan.

BANKRUPTCY

63. **(c)** The amount realized on the note receivable is computed as follows:

Liquidation value of asset		$ 5,000
Amount realized on unsecured portion of note:		
Face amount of note	$30,000	
Less: Liquidation value of asset	(5,000)	
Unsecured portion of note	25,000	
Times: Percentage for unsecured claims	x 40%	10,000
Amount realized on note receivable		$15,000

64. **(d)** Secured creditors are paid first with the proceeds from the sale of specific assets upon which they have liens. Any excess proceeds from such sales are first applied against the liabilities with priority, and then to the unsecured creditors. If the claims of partially secured creditors exceed the proceeds from the sale of the assets pledged with such creditors, such excess constitutes an unsecured claim. The amount available for unsecured nonpriority claims is $360,000, as follows:

Total cash available		$ 810,000
Less: Payments to fully secured creditors	$ 260,000	
Payments to partially secured creditors	120,000	
Payments to creditors with priority	70,000	(450,000)
Cash avail. for unsecured nonpriority claims		$ 360,000

65. (d) A trustee in a bankruptcy case takes over the assets of the debtor corporation and is accountable for those assets until released by the bankruptcy court. In liquidation (Chapter 7) cases, the trustee often establishes a new set of books for the bankruptcy estate. The assets are recorded at carrying amounts rather than at expected realizable values because of subjectivity in estimating realizable amounts at the time of filing. The trustee records gains and losses and liquidation expenses directly in the Estate Equity account. Any unrecorded assets or liabilities that are discovered by the trustee are also entered in the Estate Equity account. Therefore, $9,000 [i.e., $1,000 + ($20,000 − $12,000)] should be debited to Estate Equity as a result of the discovery of the unrecorded invoice and the sale of the truck.

PERFORMANCE BY SUBTOPICS

Each category below parallels a subtopic covered in Chapter 7. Record the number and percentage of questions you correctly answered in each subtopic area.

Current Liabilities

Question #	Correct √
1	
2	
3	
4	
5	
# Questions	5
# Correct	
% Correct	

Notes Payable

Question #	Correct √
6	
7	
8	
9	
10	
11	
12	
# Questions	7
# Correct	
% Correct	

Advances and Returnable Deposits

Question #	Correct √
13	
14	
15	
# Questions	3
# Correct	
% Correct	

Accrued Liabilities

Question #	Correct √
16	
17	
18	
19	
20	
21	
# Questions	6
# Correct	
% Correct	

Deferred Revenue

Question #	Correct √
22	
23	
24	
25	
26	
27	
# Questions	6
# Correct	
% Correct	

Current Maturities of Long-Term Debt

Question #	Correct √
28	
# Questions	1
# Correct	
% Correct	

Warranties

Question #	Correct √
29	
30	
31	
# Questions	3
# Correct	
% Correct	

Premiums

Question #	Correct √
32	
# Questions	1
# Correct	
% Correct	

Coupons

Question #	Correct √
33	
34	
# Questions	2
# Correct	
% Correct	

Bonuses

Question #	Correct √
35	
# Questions	1
# Correct	
% Correct	

Compensated Absences

Question #	Correct √
36	
37	
38	
# Questions	3
# Correct	
% Correct	

Contingencies

Question #	Correct √
39	
40	
41	
42	
43	
44	
45	
46	
# Questions	8
# Correct	
% Correct	

Gain Contingencies

Question #	Correct √
47	
48	
49	
50	
# Questions	4
# Correct	
% Correct	

Long-Term Notes Payable

Question #	Correct √
51	
52	
53	
54	
55	
56	
57	
# Questions	7
# Correct	
% Correct	

OTHER OBJECTIVE FORMAT SOLUTIONS

SOLUTION 7-2 ESTIMATED AND CONTINGENT LIABILITIES

1. (A,N) General, unspecified business risks, including the practice of self-insurance of catastrophes, are not considered loss contingencies. Therefore, no accrual or disclosure is required.

2. (C,Y) SFAS 112, *Employers' Accounting for Postemployment Benefits*, requires accrual of the liability for postemployment benefits to be provided to former or inactive employees prior to retirement. Therefore, the $150,000 of expected costs to Edge for benefits for current employees must be accrued in the financial statements. Additional information relating to the postemployment benefit plan, including a description of the plan, must be disclosed in the notes to the financial statements.

3. (B,N) Based on past experience, it is probable that customers will make claims under Edge's unconditional warranty and a reasonable estimate of the costs can be made. Therefore, an accrual of the warranty expense and the related liability must be made for $100,000 (i.e., $10,000,000 x 1%). No additional disclosures are required for the warranty.

4. (B,Y) Where the likelihood of confirmation of a loss is considered probable and the loss can be reasonably estimated, the estimated loss should be accrued by a charge to income. If only a range of possible loss can be estimated, the minimum amount in the range should be accrued. In addition, the nature of the contingency and the additional exposure to loss should be disclosed. Therefore, Edge should accrue the $100,000 minimum loss with an additional disclosure describing the contingency and the potential additional $400,000 loss.

5. (A,Y) The lawsuit initiated by Edge represents a gain contingency. Gain contingencies should be disclosed but not recognized as income. In addition, care should be taken to avoid misleading implications as to the likelihood of realization. **NOTE:**

In the "AICPA Unofficial Answers to Exam Questions," the answer is listed as (A,N). The Editors believe this is erroneous, as it contradicts FASB No. 5.

6. (A,N) Where the likelihood of loss is considered remote (i.e., the suit is believed to be without Merit by Edge's attorneys), no accrual or disclosure is normally required.

7. (A,Y) Certain types of loss contingencies must be disclosed regardless of the probability of loss. These exceptions include guarantees of indebtedness of others, banks' standby letters of credit, and guarantees to repurchase receivables. Therefore, the guarantee of the president's loan must be disclosed by Edge in the financial statements.

8. (C,Y) The gain or loss on the disposal of a segment includes both the estimated income from segment operations until disposal and the estimated gain or loss on the sale of the segment assets. If the disposal of the segment is expected to result in a loss, the total loss must be recognized in the current period's financial statements. Therefore, Edge will report a $150,000 loss (i.e., $400,000 loss + $250,000 gain) from discontinued operations in its December 31, 1993 financial statements. In addition, the notes to the financial statements must disclose the following information: (1) the identity of the segment of the business that has been or will be discontinued; (2) the expected disposal date; (3) the expected manner of disposal; (4) a description of the remaining assets and liabilities of the segment at the financial statement date; and (5) the income or loss from operations and any proceeds from disposal of the segment during the period from the measurement date to the financial-statement date.

9. (A,Y) Subsequent events that arose after the balance sheet date do not result in adjustments to the account balances of the previous period. However, some events, including the purchase of a business, the loss of inventories or plant assets due

to a casualty, and the sale of a bond or capital stock issue, must be disclosed in order to prevent the financial statements from being misleading. Thus, the loss must be disclosed by Edge in the financial statements.

10. (A,N) Subsequent events that arose after the balance sheet date do not result in adjustments to the account balances of the previous period. In addition, these events do not normally require disclosure in the financial statements.

11. (A,Y) Subsequent events that arose after the balance sheet date do not result in adjustments to the account balances of the previous period. However, some events, including the purchase of a business, the loss of inventories or plant assets due to a casualty, and the sale of a bond or capital stock issue, must be disclosed in order to prevent the financial statements from being misleading. Thus, the bond issue must be disclosed by Edge in the financial statements.

12. (B,Y) Where the likelihood of confirmation of a loss is considered probable and the loss can be reasonably estimated, the estimated loss should be accrued by a charge to income and the nature of the contingency should be disclosed. Since Edge's lawyers believe it is likely (i.e., probable) that the IRS will agree to a $100,000 settlement, an estimated loss of $100,000 should be accrued in Edge's December 31, 1993 financial statements with an additional disclosure describing the nature of the contingency.

SOLUTION 7-3 CONTINGENCIES

1. (B) Because the damages were awarded prior to the balance sheet date and were received prior to issuance of the financial statements, the award should be both accrued and disclosed in the financial statements.

2. (N) Two conditions must be met for a loss contingency to be accrued as a charge to income as of the date of the financial statements. It must be probable that as of the date of the financial statements an asset has been impaired or a liability incurred, and the amount of the loss must be reasonably estimated. In this case the loss would not be accrued as the possibility of loss has been judged remote by Town's lawyers. If one or both of the conditions for loss accrual are not met and the loss contingency is classified as probable or reasonably possible, financial statement disclosure is required. In this case, the loss contingency is remote, therefore disclosure is not required.

3. (N) Because the outstanding purchase orders occurred in the ordinary course of business and the raw materials have not yet been received, the purchase is not required to be accrued. Because the price difference is only a market price difference occurring in the ordinary course of business, disclosure it not required.

4. (D) Two conditions must be met for a loss contingency to be accrued as a charge to income as of the date of the financial statements. It must be probable that as of the date of the financial statements an asset has been impaired or a liability incurred, and the amount of the loss must be reasonably estimated. In this case, an asset has not been impaired, nor a liability incurred, so no accrual is required. If one or both of the conditions for loss accrual are not met and the loss contingency is classified as probable or reasonably possible, financial statement disclosure is required, therefore disclosure is required in this case.

5. (B) Two conditions must be met for a loss contingency to be accrued as a charge to income as of the date of the financial statements. It must be probable that as of the date of the financial statements an asset has been impaired or a liability incurred, and the amount of the loss must be reasonably estimated. In this case, a liability has been incurred and the amount is reasonably estimated, so accrual is required. If the loss contingency is classified as probable or reasonably possible, financial statement disclosure is required, therefore disclosure is required in this case.

6. (D) Events that did not exist at the balance sheet date but arose subsequent to that date should not result in adjustment to the financial statements. Some of these events, however, may require disclosure in order to prevent the financial statements from being misleading. Examples of events that require disclosure include sale of bonds or capital stock and the redemption of outstanding bonds.

PROBLEM/ESSAY SOLUTIONS

SOLUTION 7-4 EMPLOYEE BENEFITS

a. An example of post-employment benefits offered by employers is continuation of health care benefits. Deck is required to accrue liabilities for compensated absences and post-employment benefits if all of the following conditions are met:

- The obligation is attributable to employees' services already rendered,
- The employees' rights accumulate or vest,
- Payment is probable, and
- The amount of the benefits can be reasonably estimated.

If an obligation cannot be accrued solely because the amount cannot be reasonably estimated, the financial statements should disclose that fact.

b. Estimated amounts to be paid under a deferred compensation contract should be accrued over the period of an employee's active employment from the time the contract is signed to the employee's full eligibility date. The theoretical rationale for accrual of these obligations to be paid in the future is that accrual matches the cost of the benefits to the period in which services are rendered, and results in recognition of a measurable liability.

c.

Deck Co.
SCHEDULE OF DEFERRED
COMPENSATION AMOUNTS
For the Years 1995 through 1998

For the year ended	Accrued liability	Deferred compensation expense
12/31/95	$ 50,000	$50,000 [a]
12/31/96	$100,000	$50,000
12/31/97	$150,000	$50,000
12/31/98	$165,000	$15,000 [b]

[a] $150,000 ÷ 3 (straight-line method)
[b] $150,000 x 10%

SOLUTION 7-5 NOTES AND BONDS PAYABLE/CAPITAL LEASE/DEFERRED TAX LIABILITY

a.

Tempo Co.
INCOME TAX EXPENSE AND NET INCOME
For the Year Ended December 31, 1991

Income before income taxes		$ 430,000
Income tax expense:		
Current [30% x (430,000 – 30,000)]	$120,000	
Deferred [see computation below]	9,000	(129,000)
Net income		$ 301,000

Computation:

Deferred income tax expense		
Temporary difference—depreciation		
1992	$ 10,000	
1993	15,000	
1994	20,000	$ 45,000
Effective tax rate for years		
1992 through 1994		35%
Deferred tax liability, 12/31/91		$ 15,750
Less: 12/31/90 deferred tax asset	9,000	
12/31/90 deferred tax liability	(15,750)	(6,750)
1991 deferred income tax expense		$ 9,000

b.

Tempo Co.
CALCULATION OF INTEREST EXPENSE
For the Year Ended December 31, 1991

Note payable—bank		
1/1/91 to 9/30/91		
—$75,000 x 10% x 9/12	$5,625	
10/1/91 to 12/31/91		
—$70,000 x 10% x 3/12	1,750	$ 7,375
Capital lease obligation		
1/1/91 to 12/31/91		
—$75,260 x 10%		7,526
Bonds payable		
7/1/91 to 12/31/91		
—$459,725 x 12% x 6/12		27,584
		$42,485

c.

Tempo Co.
LONG-TERM LIABILITIES SECTION OF
BALANCE SHEET
December 31, 1991

Long-term liabilities:		
Note payable—bank; 14 principal payments of $5,000 plus 10% interest due annually on September 30	$70,000	
Less current portion	(5,000)	$ 65,000
Capital lease obligation—15 payments of $9,000 due annually on January 1	75,260	
Less current portion	(1,474)	73,786
11% bonds payable due June 30, 2021, less unamortized discount of $40,191		459,809
Deferred income tax liability [($15,000 + $20,000) x .35]		12,250
Total long-term liabilities		$610,845

SOLUTION 7-6   ACCOUNTING FOR CONTINGENCIES (SFAS 5)

a.   1.   Notes to Supey's 1990 **financial statements** should **disclose** the **nature** of the loss on cleanup and indicate that an **estimate** of the loss, or **range** of the loss, **cannot be made.   No accrual** should be made because the loss **cannot be reasonably estimated** and **accrual** of an **uncertain amount** would **impair the integrity** of the financial statements.

      2.   Supey should **disclose the **nature** of Gap's claim in the **notes** to the 1990 **financial statements.** Disclosure should include an **estimate** of the **potential loss.** Supey should **not accrue** the loss because it is **only reasonably possible** that it will have to pay for Gap's losses.

b.   An **estimated loss on the purchase commitment, **equal to** the **unrecoverable amount** of the contract price, should be reported as part of 1990 **income from continuing operations** and as a **current liability** at December 31, 1990. The **net loss** on the **purchase commitment** should be **measured and recognized** in the **period** in which it **occurs.**

Since Supey did not hedge this contract, reporting this loss recognizes the commitment's impact on future cash flows.

SOLUTION 7-7   ACCOUNTING FOR COMPENSATED ABSENCES (SFAS 43)

Essex must accrue compensation for future vacations if **all** of the following conditions are met:

- Essex's obligation relating to employees' rights to receive compensation for future vacations is attributable to employees' **services already rendered.**
- The obligation relates to **rights** that **vest or accumulate.**
- **Payment** of the vacation benefits is **probable.**
- The amount can be reasonably estimated.

The theoretical rationale is that accruing compensation **matches** the cost of vacation benefits to the period in which services are rendered, and results in **recognition** of a **measurable liability**.

Post-Exam Diagnostics

The AICPA Board of Examiners' Advisory Grading Service will provide boards of accountancy with individual diagnostic reports for all candidates along with the candidates' grades. The diagnostic reports show the candidate's level of proficiency on each examination section. The boards of accountancy <u>may</u> mail the diagnostic reports to candidates along with their grades: candidates should contact the state board in their jurisdiction to find out its policy on this.

Remember that candidates are required to sign a statement of confidentiality in which they promise not to reveal questions or answers. Due to the nondisclosure requirements, Totaltape's editors are no longer able to address questions about specific examination questions, although we continue to supply help with similar study problems and questions in our texts.

Grades will be mailed approximately 90 days after the examination.

CHAPTER 8

LEASES

CHAPTER 8

LEASES

I. OVERVIEW

A. GAAP

SFAS 13, *Accounting for Leases*, as amended and clarified by subsequent pronouncements, is the primary source of promulgated GAAP concerning leases.

B. DEFINITIONS

1. **LEASE** A lease is an agreement conveying the right to use property, plant or equipment (land and/or depreciable assets) usually for a stated period of time. A lease that transfers substantially all of the benefits and risks incidental to the ownership of property should be accounted for as an acquisition of an asset and the incurrence of a liability by the lessee, and as a sale or financing agreement by the lessor. All other leases should be accounted for as operating leases.

2. **LEASE TERM** The fixed noncancelable term of the lease **plus** the following:

   a. All periods, if any, covered by bargain renewal options.

   b. All periods for which failure to renew the lease imposes a penalty on the lessee in an amount such as to make renewal reasonably assured.

   c. All periods preceding the date that a bargain purchase option becomes exercisable.

   d. All periods representing renewals or extensions of the lease term at the lessor's option.

   e. In no case, however, should the lease term extend beyond the date at which a bargain purchase option becomes exercisable.

3. **MINIMUM LEASE PAYMENTS** The definition of minimum lease payments (MLP) parallels that of the lease term, above. If the lease contains a bargain purchase option, **only** the minimum rental payments over the lease term up to the date at which the bargain purchase option becomes exercisable **and** the payment called for by the bargain purchase option are included in the MLP. Otherwise, MLP includes the following:

   a. Minimum rental payments called for by the lease over the lease term.

   b. Any guarantee by the lessee, or a third party related to the lessee, of a residual value of the leased asset at the end of the lease.

   c. Any penalty that the lessee may be required to pay upon failure to renew the lease. However, if the penalty is such that renewal has been assumed and the lease term accordingly extended (see 2.b., above), the amount of the penalty should **not** be included in the MLP.

   d. For lessors, in addition to the above amounts, minimum lease payments also include any guarantee of the residual value by a third party unrelated to either the lessor or lessee if the third party is financially capable of discharging its obligations.

e. Minimum lease payments do **not** include executory costs paid by either the lessor or the lessee, nor do they include any contingent rentals.

4. **EXECUTORY COSTS**

a. Executory costs are expenditures such as insurance, maintenance and taxes required to be paid on the asset during the asset's economic life. They are considered **period costs** which should be expensed when paid or accrued by either the lessor or lessee.

b. If the **lessor** retains the responsibility to pay, the portion of the minimum lease payments representing these executory costs should be removed from the lessee's minimum lease payments (if the portion is unknown, it should be estimated).

c. If the **lessee** retains the responsibility to pay, executory costs are **not** included in minimum lease payments. Rather they are charged to an appropriate expense account (e.g., insurance expense, property taxes, repairs and maintenance, etc.).

5. **PRESENT VALUE DISCOUNT RATES USED BY LESSEES AND LESSORS**

a. The **lessee** uses the **incremental borrowing rate** (discount rate lessee would pay in the lending market to purchase the asset leased) in computing the present value of the minimum lease payments, **unless both** of the following requirements are satisfied:

(1) The lessee knows or can practicably discover the **lessor's implicit interest rate** used in the lease.

(2) That implicit interest rate is **lower** than the lessee's incremental borrowing rate.

If both requirements are satisfied, the lessor's interest rate implicit in the lease is used in computing the present value of the minimum lease payments for asset and liability recording, instead of the lessee's incremental borrowing rate.

b. The **lessor's** interest rate implicit in the lease is the interest rate that will discount the minimum lease payments **plus** unguaranteed residual value to the fair value of the leased property at the lease inception date.

6. **RESIDUAL VALUE** The estimated fair value of the leased property at the end of the lease term.

a. **GUARANTEED RESIDUAL VALUE**

(1) The guaranteed residual value is a specifically determinable amount payable at termination of the lease. The payment may constitute a purchase payment for the leased property, or it may be made to satisfy a deficiency below a "stated amount" which the lessee guarantees the lessor on realization of the property. The "stated amount" would be the guaranteed residual value.

(2) The guaranteed residual value is **included** in the minimum lease payments for both lessors and lessees.

b. **UNGUARANTEED RESIDUAL VALUE**

(1) The unguaranteed residual value is not guaranteed by the lessee or by a third party related to the lessee.

(2) The unguaranteed residual value is **not** included in MLP by either lessor or lessee.

(3) The lessor's gross investment in the lease is equal to the sum of MLP plus the unguaranteed residual value of the leased property.

7. **LESSOR/LESSEE** The lessor leases the asset to the lessee. Lease payments are made by the lessee to the lessor.

II. CRITERIA FOR CLASSIFYING LEASES

A. LESSEE

1. **CAPITAL LEASE** Classify and account for the lease as a capital lease if at the date of the lease agreement (date of lease inception), the lease satisfies **at least one** of the following four criteria. However, if the beginning of the lease term falls within the last 25% of the total estimated economic life of the leased asset, then criteria c. and d. are inapplicable. The lease should then be classified as a capital lease **only** if it meets a. or b.

   a. The lease transfers ownership of the property to the lessee by the end of the lease.

   b. The lease contains a bargain purchase option.

   c. The lease term is equal to 75% or more of the estimated economic life of the leased property (as determined at the inception of the lease).

   d. The present value of the minimum lease payments (excluding executory costs) **equals or exceeds** 90% of the fair value of the leased property at lease inception.

2. **OPERATING LEASE** If a lease does **not** satisfy at least one of the four criteria for a capital lease, then the lessee must classify and account for the lease as an operating lease.

Lessee must meet just <u>ONE</u> condition to capitalize.

TO Transfers of Ownership at end of lease (upon final payment or required buyout)

BOP Bargain Purchase Option

75 75% of asset economic life is committed in lease term

90 90% of leased property FMV < PV of future lease payments

B. LESSOR

1. **TYPES OF LEASES** Lessor classifies as either **sales-type** or **direct financing type** leases meeting all the following criteria:

   a. The lease is a capital lease for the lessee. It is important to note that the lessor always uses the interest rate implicit in the lease in calculating the present value of the minimum lease payments.

   b. Collectibility of the minimum lease payments is reasonably predictable.

   c. No important uncertainties exist regarding the unreimbursable costs yet to be incurred by the lessor under the lease.

EXHIBIT 1 ♦ CAPITAL LEASE CRITERIA

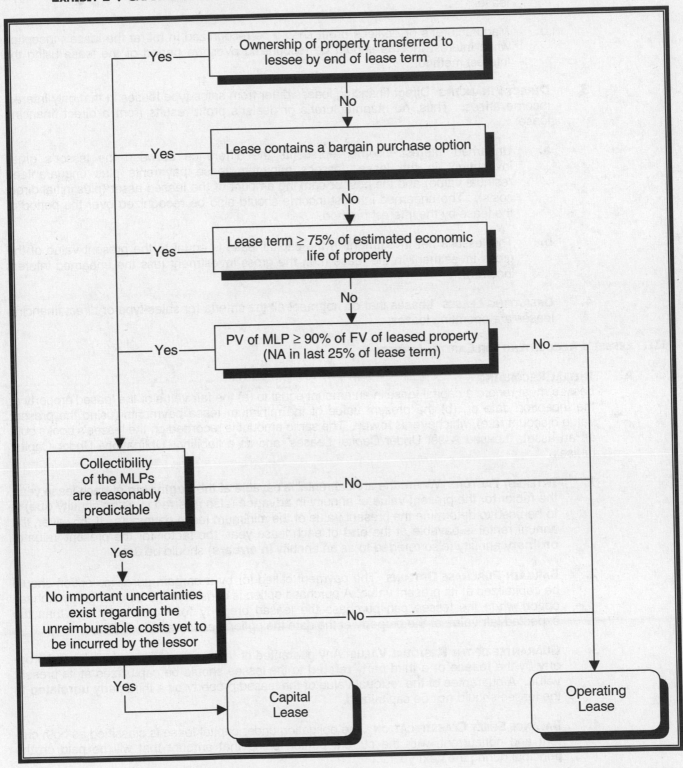

2. **SALES-TYPE LEASES** Sales-type leases are, in substance, sales of assets on an installment basis.

    a. Sales-type leases contain a manufacturer's or dealer's profit (or loss). This profit (or loss) is the difference between the cost or carrying amount of the asset and its fair value. A second type of profit, interest income, is also recognized in a sales-type lease.

b. Manufacturer's or dealer's profit should be recognized in full at the lease's inception while interest income should be recognized over the period of the lease using the interest method.

3. **DIRECT FINANCING** Direct financing leases differ from sales-type leases in that only interest income arises. Thus, no manufacturer's or dealer's profit results from a direct financing lease.

a. Unearned interest income represents the difference between the lessor's gross investment in the lease (lessor's minimum lease payments plus unguaranteed residual value) and the cost or carrying amount of the leased asset (plus initial direct costs). The unearned interest income should also be recognized over the period of the lease by the interest method.

b. The lessor's net investment in the capital lease is equal to the present value of the gross investment in the lease (i.e., the gross investment less the unearned interest income).

4. **OPERATING LEASES** Leases that do not meet all the criteria for sales-type or direct financing leases are operating leases.

III. LESSEE'S ACCOUNTING FOR CAPITAL LEASES

A. INITIAL RECORDING
Lessee must record a capital lease in an amount equal to (a) the fair value of the leased property at the inception date or, (b) the present value of the minimum lease payments (using the present value discount rate), whichever is **lower**. The same amount is recorded on the lessee's books both as an asset, "Leased Asset Under Capital Leases" and as a liability, "Obligations Under Capital Leases."

1. **INTEREST FACTORS** Where the annual rental is payable at the **beginning** of each lease year, the factor for the present value of annuity in **advance** (also referred to as an annuity **due**) is to be used to determine the present value of the minimum lease payments. If, however, the annual rental is payable at the **end** of each lease year, the factor for the present value of **ordinary** annuity (also referred to as an annuity **in arrears**) should be used.

2. **BARGAIN PURCHASE OPTIONS** The payment called for by a bargain purchase option should be capitalized at its present value. A purchase option is considered to be a bargain purchase option when the lessee can purchase the leased property for significantly less than the expected fair value of the property at the date the option becomes exercisable.

3. **GUARANTEE OF THE RESIDUAL VALUE** Any guarantee of the residual value of the leased property by the **lessee** or a third party **related** to the lessee should be capitalized at its present value. A guarantee of the residual value of the leased property by a third party **unrelated** to the lessee should **not** be capitalized.

4. **BALANCE SHEET CLASSIFICATION** The obligation under capital lease is classified as both current and noncurrent, with the current portion being that amount that will be paid on the principal during the next year.

B. AMORTIZATION

1. **AMORTIZATION OF THE LEASED ASSET** Amortization should be consistent with the lessee's normal depreciation policy for similar owned assets.

a. **AMORTIZE OVER REMAINING ESTIMATED ECONOMIC LIFE** If the lease qualifies as a capital lease because it satisfies **either** the first two lease classification criteria (i.e., the lease agreement transfers ownership of the asset by the end of the lease term **or** contains a bargain purchase option), the lessee must amortize the leased asset over the remaining **estimated economic life of the asset**.

b. **AMORTIZE OVER LEASE TERM** If the lease is classified as a capital lease because it satisfies criteria other than the first two lease classification criteria, the lessee will amortize the leased asset over the **lease term** (rather than the life of the asset).

c. **AMORTIZE TO EXPECTED RESIDUAL VALUE** For capital leases where there is a transfer of ownership (i.e., there is a title transfer or the lease contains a bargain purchase option), the leased asset is amortized to its expected residual value, if any, to the lessee at the end of the lease term.

2. **AMORTIZATION OF THE LEASE LIABILITY**

a. **EFFECTIVE INTEREST METHOD** The effective interest method is used to amortize the lease liability.

b. **ALLOCATION OF LEASE PAYMENTS** Each lease payment made by the lessee is allocated between interest expense and the reduction of the lease obligation; it is **not** recorded as rent expense. Under this method, each successive uniform payment is comprised of a **decreasing** amount of interest expense and an **increasing** amount of reduction of the lease obligation.

c. **AMORTIZATION RATE** Although the asset and liability balances at the inception of the lease are the same present value amount (or fair value if lower at lease inception), each balance will be amortized at different rates during the asset life or lease term.

EXAMPLE 1 ♦ LESSEE'S ACCOUNTING FOR CAPITAL LEASES

Lessor and Lessee enter into a lease for a computer on January 1, 20X0. The lease terms are as follows:

The lease duration is 3 years, noncancelable, with 2 renewal options of 1 year each. The lease provides for a termination penalty assuring renewal of the lease for 2 years after the 3-year regular term ends. The leased equipment consists of a computer which has a cost and fair value to lessor at lease inception of $100,000. The estimated economic life of the asset is 6 years. The asset has no residual value. The lease rental is $27,991/year, which includes executory costs, payable at the beginning of each year. Lessor pays executory costs of $4,800/year, at beginning of each year.

Lessee's incremental rate: 10%

Lessor's implicit rate: 8% (known to the lessee)

REQUIRED: Record in lessee's books all entries related to the lease during the first year. Show supporting computations.

ANALYSIS: The lease is a capital lease because its term (5 years) exceeds 75% of the computer's estimated economic life (6 years). Additionally, the present value of the minimum lease payments ($100,000) exceeds 90% of the fair value of the computer ($100,000). See Schedule 3, below, for computation of PV of MLP.

(continued on next page)

SOLUTION:

01/01/X0	Leased Equipment Under Capital Leases	100,000	
	Obligation Under Capital Leases		100,000
	To record capitalized lease. See Schedule 3.		

	Executory Expenses (detailed)	4,800	
	Obligation Under Capital Leases	23,191	
	Cash		27,991
	To record first year's minimum lease payment and executory costs. See Schedule 2.		

| 12/31/X0 | Amortization Expense on Leased Equipment | 20,000 | |
| | Accumulated Amortization of Leased Equipment Under Capital Leases | | 20,000 |

To record the amortization of the asset based on the straight-line depreciation method (method normally used by lessee for other owned assets) over the lease term (no transfer of ownership; no bargain purchase option). Computation: $100,000 ÷ 5 = $20,000. See Schedule 1 for lease term determination.

12/31/X0	Interest Expense	6,145	
	Accrued Interest Payable		6,145
	To record interest expense on lease obligation. See Schedule 4.		

01/01/X1	Executory Expenses (detailed)	4,800	
	Accrued Interest Payable	6,145	
	Obligation Under Capital Leases	17,046	
	Cash		27,991
	To record second-year's minimum lease payment and executory costs. See Schedule 4.		

12/31/X1: The entries to record depreciation and interest expense would be similar to the prior year's. The depreciation amount remains constant; the interest amount is from Schedule 4.

Schedule 1—Lease Term

Noncancelable term	3 years
Additional period for which termination penalty assures renewal	2 years
Total lease term	5 years

Schedule 2—Minimum Lease Payments

Yearly lease payments including yearly executory costs	$ 27,991
Yearly executory costs	(4,800)
Net yearly lease payments	$ 23,191
Lease term (years)	x 5
Total lessee MLP	$115,955

Schedule 3—Present Value of Minimum Lease Payments

Since the lease payments are payable in advance, the present value factor is derived as follows: Choose from Appendix D the appropriate factor for the present value of an ordinary annuity of $1 per period for 4 periods at 8% (3.3121). To this 4-period factor add 1.000 (3.3121 + 1.000 = 4.3121) in order to find the present value of an annuity in advance payable in 5 years at 8%.

Minimum lease payments net of executory costs	$ 23,191	
Factor for annuity in advance at 8%	x 4.3121	
	$100,000	($1.91 difference due to rounding)

(continued on next page)

Since the lessor's implicit interest rate was known <u>and</u> was lower than the lessee's incremental borrowing rate of 10%, the lessor's implicit rate of 8% was used to calculate the present value of the asset and the liability on the lessee's books.

<u>Schedule 4</u>—Lease Payments and Interest Accruals (Lessee)

Date	Description	8% Interest expense	Lease payment amount	Interest	Amortization of principal	Balance of lease obligation
01/01/X0	Initial bal.					$100,000
01/01/X0	Payment		$23,191		$23,191	76,809
12/31/X0	Int. accr.	$6,145				76,809
01/01/X1	Payment		23,191	$6,145	17,046	59,763
12/31/X1	Int. accr.	4,781				59,763
01/01/X2	Payment		23,191	4,781	18,410	41,353
12/31/X2	Int. accr.	3,308				41,353
01/01/X3	Payment		23,191	3,308	19,883	21,470
12/31/X3	Int. accr.	1,718				21,470
01/01/X4	Payment		23,191	1,718	21,470	0*

* All calculations and balances rounded to achieve table balance.

C.   RECOGNITION OF IMPAIRMENT LOSS

In accordance with SFAS 121 and 144, assets subject to capital leases should be reviewed by the lessee whenever circumstances indicate that the carrying amount of the asset may not be recoverable. The review consists of estimating the future net cash flows; and, without discounting or considering interest charges, if the future cash flows is less than the carrying amount of the asset, impairment loss is recognized. Impairment loss recognized is the amount by which the carrying amount of the asset exceeds the **fair value** of the asset.

IV. LESSOR'S ACCOUNTING

A.   SALES-TYPE LEASES

The lessor accounts for a sales-type lease by recording the following:

1. **GROSS INVESTMENT IN THE LEASE** The lessor's gross investment in the lease is equal to the sum of the following:

    a. **LESSOR'S MINIMUM LEASE PAYMENTS (MLP)**

        (1) **Guaranteed** residual value is included in the minimum lease payments of **both parties**.

        (2) Residual value or rental payments beyond the lease, guaranteed by a financially capable third party **unrelated** to either lessee or lessor, are also included in the **lessor's minimum lease payments.**

    b. **UNGUARANTEED RESIDUAL VALUE ACCRUING TO LESSOR**

2. **NET INVESTMENT IN THE LEASE** Present value of lessor's gross investment in the lease. In equation form

    Net investment in lease = PV of (MLP + Unguaranteed residual value)

3. **UNEARNED INTEREST INCOME** Difference between the gross investment in the lease and the present value of its two components (i.e., the MLP and the unguaranteed residual value).

Unearned interest income is reported as a contra-asset to gross investment in the lease. It is amortized as interest income by the "interest method" over the lease term.

4. **SALES PRICE IN THE LEASE** Equal to the present value of the lessor's minimum lease payments (MLP)

    a. Present value computed using the lessor's implicit interest rate.

    b. Unguaranteed residual value is **not** included in the lessor's minimum lease payments.

    c. Since the lessor's implicit interest rate is used, the present value of the lessor's minimum lease payments will equal the fair value of the leased asset less the present value of any unguaranteed residual value accruing to the lessor.

5. **COST OF SALES** Book value or carrying amount of asset leased out reduced by the present value of the unguaranteed residual value accruing to the lessor. In equation form

    Cost of sales = Book value − PV of unguaranteed residual value

6. **INITIAL DIRECT COSTS** Costs incurred by the lessor that are directly associated with negotiating and consummating **completed** leasing transactions. Examples include commissions, legal fees, cost of preparing documents and the applicable portion of the compensation of employees directly involved with completed leasing transactions.

    a. Does **not** include administrative expenses or expenses of negotiating leases that are not consummated.

    b. Does **not** include **executory costs.**

7. **MANUFACTURER'S OR DEALER'S PROFIT** Equal to the present value of the minimum lease payments reduced by the cost of sales and by the initial direct costs. In equation form

    Manufacturer's or dealer's profit = PV of MLP − (Cost of sales + Initial direct costs)

EXAMPLE 2 ♦ LESSOR'S CLASSIFICATION AND ACCOUNTING FOR SALES-TYPE LEASES

Lessor and lessee sign a lease on January 1, 20X0 containing the following terms:
Lease duration: 5 years beginning January 1, 20X0.
Leased asset's estimated economic life: 6 years
Estimated residual value: $14,000, unguaranteed.
Lease payments: $50,000/year, payable at year-end.
Leased asset's manufacturing cost: $150,000
Lease closing costs: $2,000 (initial direct costs)
Lease provisions: Lease does not contain a bargain renewal or a bargain purchase option.
Implicit lease interest rate: 10%

Lessor has determined that the collectibility of lease payments is reasonably predictable and there are no important uncertainties regarding costs yet to be incurred by the lessor.

REQUIRED:

(a) Is this an operating, sales-type, or direct financing lease? Support your answer.

(b) Record <u>lessor's</u> journal entries during the first year of the lease.

(c) Record lessor's journal entry at the end of the lease.

(continued on next page)

SOLUTION:

(a) Lease Classification—The lease satisfies the tests for classification as a <u>sales-type</u> lease.

<u>Test 1</u>: The lease term exceeds 75% of the estimated economic life of the leased property. Furthermore, the lease does not begin during the last 25% of the asset's total economic life. (5 *year lease* ÷ 6 *year economic life* = 83%)

<u>Test 2</u>: Collectibility of lease rentals is reasonably assured, <u>and</u> there are no important uncertainties regarding lessor costs yet to be incurred.

<u>Test 3</u>: Sales-Type Test—The present value of the minimum lease payments (as determined in Schedule 1, below) exceeds the cost of the asset to the lessor, less the present value of the unguaranteed residual value accruing to the lessor, resulting in a manufacturer's or dealer's profit.

(b) Journal entries to record lease during first year (lessor)

01/01/X0	Gross Investment in Lease (Schedule 1)	264,000	
	Cost of Goods Leased (Schedule 2)	141,307	
	Selling Expenses (Schedule 2)	2,000	
	Sales Revenue (Schedule 2)		189,540
	Equipment		150,000
	Unearned Interest Income (Schedule 1)		65,767
	Cash		2,000

To record sale of property under lease to lessee.

(c) Journal entry at end of the lease (lessor)

12/31/X0	Cash	50,000	
	Gross Investment in Lease		50,000
	Unearned Interest Income	19,823	
	Interest Income (Schedule 3)		19,823

To record first year's lease payment and interest income earned.

12/31/X4	Equipment	14,000	
	Gross Investment in Lease		14,000

To record receipt of the leased asset by lessor at the end of lease term and removal of lease receivable from books.

Schedule 1—Lessor's Gross Investment in the Lease, PV, and Unearned Interest Income

Gross investment in lease:		
Annual lease payment	$ 50,000	
Lease term (years)	x 5	
Summation of MLP	250,000	
Add: Unguaranteed residual value	14,000	$264,000
PV of investment in lease:		
PV of MLP, $50,000 x PVA(n=5, i=10%); $50,000 x 3.7908	$189,540	
PV of unguaranteed residual value,		
$14,000 x PV (n=5, i=10%); $14,000 x .6209	8,693	(198,233)
Unearned interest income		$ 65,767

(continued on next page)

Schedule 2—Lessor's Cost of Sales and Manufacturer's or Dealer's Profit

Sales price (i.e., PV of MLP)		$189,540
Cost of goods leased:		
Manufacturing cost of asset	$150,000	
Less: PV of unguaranteed residual accruing to lessor	(8,693)	(141,307)
Gross margin		48,233*
Less: Initial direct costs		(2,000)
Manufacturer's or dealer's profit		$ 46,233*

* Not required for this problem, shown for illustrative purposes.

Schedule 3—Lease Payments and Interest Accruals

Date	Lease payment	Interest income on net investment in lease (10%)	Reduction of investment in lease	Net investment in lease
01/01/X0				$198,233
12/31/X0	$50,000	$19,823	$30,177	168,056
12/31/X1	50,000	16,806	33,194	134,862
12/31/X2	50,000	13,486	36,514	98,348
12/31/X3	50,000	9,835	40,165	58,183
12/31/X4	50,000	5,818	44,182	14,000*

* This balance remaining in the net investment account represents the estimated residual value of the leased asset at the end of the term ($1 difference due to rounding).

B. DIRECT FINANCING LEASES

1. **DEFINITION** A direct financing lease is a lease that meets the same criteria as a sales-type lease **except** it does **not** give rise to a manufacturer's or dealer's profit (i.e., the cost or carrying amount of the asset is equal to its fair value). The only income that arises from this type of lease is interest income.

2. **GROSS INVESTMENT IN LEASE** The sum of MLP (net of lessor-paid executory costs) and unguaranteed residual value should be recorded as gross investment in the lease.

3. **UNEARNED INCOME** The difference between gross investment in the lease and cost or carrying amount of the leased property should be recorded as unearned income.

4. **INITIAL DIRECT COSTS** Initial direct costs should be added to the net investment in a direct financing lease and amortized over the life of the lease. It is not acceptable to recognize a portion of the unearned income at inception of the lease to offset initial direct costs.

5. **NET INVESTMENT IN LEASE** The net investment in the lease is the gross investment in the lease plus any unamortized initial direct costs less the unearned income.

6. **AMORTIZATION** The unearned income and any initial direct costs should be amortized over the lease term using the "interest" method.

EXAMPLE 3 ♦ LESSOR'S CLASSIFICATION AND ACCOUNTING FOR DIRECT FINANCING LEASES

Lessor and lessee sign a lease on January 1, 20X0. The lease contains the following terms:

Lease duration: 3 years beginning January 1, 20X0
Estimated economic life: 4 years
Unguaranteed residual value: $5,200 at the end of Year 3
Annual lease payments: (payable at year-end) $19,277
Leased asset cost (same as FV): $50,000
Lessor implicit rate: 12%
Lessee incremental borrowing rate: 12.5%
Present value of minimum lease payments: $50,000 [($19,277 x 2.4018) + ($5,200 x .7117)]

REQUIRED:

(a) Classify the lease from the viewpoint of the <u>lessor</u>. Support your answer.

(b) Provide lessor's entries to account for the lease during the lease term. Show supporting computations.

SOLUTION:

(a) <u>Lease Classification:</u> The lease meets the description and classification tests for direct financing leases. The cost and fair value of the property are identical; therefore, no manufacturer's or dealer's profit exists. One or more of the various criteria for classification as a direct financing lease are met because the lease term equals 75% of the equipment's estimated economic life and the present value of the minimum lease payments exceeds 90% of the fair value of the leased property at lease inception date. The second test for direct financing lease classification is also satisfied because the lease in this example is assumed to be one in which (a) the collectibility of the minimum lease payments is reasonably assured <u>and</u> (b) there are no further unreimbursable costs yet to be incurred by the lessor.

(b) Journal entries to record the lease during each of the three years of the lease term.

01/01/X0	Gross Investment in Lease (Schedule 1)	63,031	
	Equipment		50,000
	Unearned Interest Income		13,031
	To record the lease at inception.		
12/31/X0	Cash (Schedule 2)	19,277	
	Gross Investment in Lease		19,277
	Unearned Interest Income (Schedule 2)	6,000	
	Interest Income		6,000
	To record receipt of MLP and recognition of interest income.		
12/31/X1	Cash (Schedule 2)	19,277	
	Gross Investment in Lease		19,277
	Unearned Interest Income (Schedule 2)	4,407	
	Interest Income		4,407
	To record the second year's receipt of MLP and recognition of interest income.		
12/31/X2	Cash (Schedule 2)	19,277	
	Gross Investment in Lease		19,277
	Unearned Interest Income (Schedule 2)	2,622	
	Interest Income		2,622
	To record the third year's receipt of MLP and recognition of interest income.		
12/31/X3	Equipment (Schedule 2)	5,200	
	Gross Investment in Lease		5,200
	To record the return of the equipment.		

(continued on next page)

Schedule 1—Lessor's Gross Investment in the Lease, Book Value, and Unearned Interest Income

Gross investment in lease:

Annual lease payment	$19,277	
Lease term (years)	x 3	
Summation of MLP	57,831	
Add: Unguaranteed residual value	5,200	$ 63,031
Book value of the equipment (equal to its FV)		(50,000)
Unearned interest income		$ 13,031

Schedule 2—Lease Payments and Interest Income Recognized

Date	Lease Payment	Interest on Net Investment (12%)	Reduction of Net Investment in Lease	Balance of Net Investment
01/01/X0				$50,000
12/31/X0	$19,277	$6,000	$13,277	36,723
12/31/X1	19,277	4,407	14,870	21,853
12/31/X2	19,277	2,622	16,655	5,200*

* Balance remaining in the net investment account represents the estimated residual value of the leased asset (rounded).

V. OPERATING LEASES

A. DEFINITION

All leases that do not meet the four criteria for capital leases are operating leases. Operating leases do not involve a transfer of the risks and benefits of ownership (as do capital leases). Further, leases must meet **additional** criteria to be classified as capital leases by **lessors**.

B. PAYMENTS

Under operating leases, lessees/lessors recognize rent as expense/revenue over the lease term as it becomes payable/receivable according to the provisions of the lease. If the rentals vary from a straight-line basis (e.g., the lessee pays a "lease bonus" at the inception of the lease or the lease agreement specifies scheduled rent increases over the lease term), the expense/revenue should continue to be recognized on a straight-line basis unless another systematic and rational basis is more representative of the time pattern in which the benefit from the leased property is diminished.

C. LESSOR

The lessor depreciates the leased property using its normal depreciation policy. Any initial direct costs (e.g., commissions, legal fees, etc.) incurred by the lessor in negotiating and consummating the operating lease are amortized over the lease term in a straight-line manner. The lessor recognizes executory costs as expenses when they are incurred. Rent received in advance by the lessor for an operating lease is a deferred revenue which should be recognized as revenue in the period specified by the lease. The lessor includes a leased asset subject to an operating lease in testing for impairment of long-lived assets, in accordance with SFAS 121.

D. LESSEE

The rental expense recognized by the lessee for an operating lease is comprised of (a) the periodic rental payments as they become payable if equal in amount (or on a straight-line basis if not equal in amount) and (b) the amortization of any lease bonus. The net rental income recognized by the lessor for an operating lease is comprised of (a) the periodic rental payments as they become receivable if equal in amount (or on a straight-line basis if not equal in amount), (b) the amortization of any lease bonus, (c) depreciation, (d) the amortization of any initial direct costs incurred, and (e) executory costs incurred.

E. ASSET

The leased property is not transferred from the books of the lessor to the lessee; it is included with or near the property, plant, and equipment in the balance sheet of the lessor.

EXAMPLE 4 ◆ ACCOUNTING FOR OPERATING LEASES

On January 1, 20X0, Montalba Company, a lessor of office machines, purchased for $700,000 a new machine, which is expected to have a ten-year life, and will be depreciated at a rate of $70,000 per year. The same day the machine was leased to Norton Company for a four-year period expiring January 1, 20X4, at an annual rental of $120,000. Norton also paid $72,000 to Montalba on January 1, 20X0, as a lease bonus. Montalba paid $16,000 of commissions associated with negotiating the lease in January 20X0. During 20X0, Montalba incurred insurance and other related costs of $18,000 under the lease. There is no provision for the renewal of the lease or purchase of the machine by Norton at the expiration of the lease term.

REQUIRED:

(a) Compute the amount of rental expense that Norton Company should recognize for the year ended December 31, 20X0.

(b) Compute the amount of operating profit that Montalba Company should report for this leased asset for the year ended December 31, 20X0.

SOLUTION:

(a)
Equal annual rental payment	$120,000
Amortization of lease bonus ($72,000 ÷ 4 years)	18,000
Rental expense, 20X0	$138,000

(b)
Equal annual rental payment		$120,000
Amortization of lease bonus ($72,000 ÷ 4 years)		18,000
Rental revenue		138,000
Less: Depreciation	$70,000	
Amortization of initial direct costs ($16,000 ÷ 4 years)	4,000	
Executory costs	18,000	(92,000)
Operating profit on leased asset, 20X0		$ 46,000

NOTE: Both Norton and Montalba account for the lease as an operating lease because it failed to meet capital lease criteria.

VI. SALE-LEASEBACK TRANSACTIONS

A. DEFINITION

Sale-leaseback transactions involve the sale of property to a purchaser-lessor and a lease of the same property back to the seller-lessee. The economic purpose of this type of transaction is that the seller-lessee obtains financing for the use of the property and the purchaser-lessor (usually a financial institution or investor) obtains interest income. Tax considerations may also play an important role in sale-leaseback transactions.

B. SELLER-LESSEE

1. **OPERATING VS CAPITAL LEASE** If the lease meets any of the four criteria for classification as a capital lease, the lessee will account for it as a capital lease. Otherwise, the lease will be treated as an operating lease.

2. **ACCOUNTING FOR GAINS AND LOSSES** In either case, a gain or loss on the sale of the asset will generally be deferred and amortized.

   a. **CAPITAL LEASE** If a Capital Lease, the gain or loss will be deferred and amortized in proportion to the amortization of the leased asset. For instance, in a capital lease where there is no ownership transfer and the asset is amortized in a straight-line manner, the deferred gain or loss will be amortized in a straight-line manner over the term of the lease. If ownership transfers, the gain or loss will be amortized over the estimated life of the asset. If the leased asset is amortized under another method, such as DDB or SYD, the same method should be used to amortize the deferred gain or loss. At the time of sale, the deferred gain or loss should be reported as an asset valuation allowance.

b. **OPERATING LEASE** If an Operating Lease, the gain or loss will be deferred and amortized in proportion to the related gross rentals charged to expense during the period. This will usually result in straight-line amortization. At the time of sale, a deferred gain should be reported as a deferred credit.

EXAMPLE 5 ♦ SALE AND LEASEBACK CAPITAL LEASE

On January 1, 20X1, ABC Co. sold equipment to XYZ Inc., having a $100,000 BV and $130,000 FV. Simultaneously, ABC agreed to lease back the equipment for five years, at an annual rental of $34,295, due at year-end (implicit interest rate of 10%). The estimated useful life of the equipment was 5 years, with no residual value. ABC Co. depreciates similar assets on a straight-line basis. Assuming this lease qualified as a capital lease, ABC Co. would record the first year's entries as follows:

01/01/X1	Cash	130,000	
	Equipment (net)		100,000
	Deferred Gain		30,000
	Leased Equipment Under Capital Lease	130,000	
	Obligation Under Capital Lease		130,000
12/31/X1	Interest Expense (10% x 130,000)	13,000	
	Obligation Under Capital Lease ($34,295 – $13,000)	21,295	
	Cash		34,295
	Amortization Expense on Leased Equipment	26,000	
	Accumulated Amortization ($130,000 ÷ 5)		26,000
	Deferred Gain ($30,000 ÷ 5)	6,000	
	Amortization Expense on Leased Equipment		6,000

3. EXCEPTIONS TO THE DEFERMENT REQUIREMENTS

a. **MINOR PORTION RETAINED** If the seller-lessee retains only a **minor** portion of the remaining use of the property sold, the sale and leaseback are recorded as two separate transactions (i.e., the **entire** gain or loss is **recognized at the point of sale**). Professional judgment is required for determining whether the portion of remaining use retained by the seller-lessee is "minor." In general, if the PV of the rental payments under the leaseback agreement is **less than 10%** of the FV of the property sold, the seller-lessee will be deemed to retain a "minor" portion.

b. **EXCESS GAINS** If the seller-lessee retains more than a minor portion of the leased asset but **less** than substantially all of its remaining use **and** realizes a gain on the sale, the excess gain (if any) is recognized at the date of sale, as follows:

(1) **IF AN OPERATING LEASE** Gain in excess of the PV of MLP should be recognized at the date of sale. The remaining portion of the gain should be deferred and amortized as indicated in 2., above. PV of MLP is determined using the smaller of lessee's incremental borrowing rate or interest rate implicit in the lease.

(2) **IF A CAPITAL LEASE** The excess gain over the recorded amount of the leased asset should be recognized at the date of sale. The remaining portion of the gain should be deferred and amortized as indicated in 2., above.

C. **ECONOMIC LOSSES** If the fair value of the property at the time of the transaction is less than its undepreciated cost, a **loss** should be recognized immediately up to the amount of the difference between undepreciated cost and fair value.

C. PURCHASER-LESSOR

A lessor will account for a sale-leaseback transaction in the same manner as for other leases, that is, as if the property had been purchased from and leased to two separate parties.

EXAMPLE 6 ♦ LOSS ON SALE-LEASEBACK

Equipment with a book value of $15,000 is sold for $10,000 and simultaneously leased back by the seller. The fair market value and the present value of the lease payments is $13,000.

REQUIRED: Determine the amount of loss to be recognized at the date of sale and the amount to be deferred.

SOLUTION:

Equipment book value	$ 15,000
Sales price	(10,000)
Total loss	$ 5,000
Equipment book value	$ 15,000
Fair value	(13,000)
Loss recognized at date of sale	$ 2,000
Total loss	$ 5,000
Loss recognized at date of sale	(2,000)
Loss deferred	$ 3,000

EXPLANATION: Of the loss of $5,000, the $2,000 difference between book value and fair value is a real (economic) loss and should be recognized immediately. The remaining amount of $3,000 is deferred and amortized.

VII. DISCLOSURE REQUIREMENTS

A. LESSEE

1. **CAPITAL LEASES** The lessee is required to disclose the gross amount of assets recorded under capital leases, and the future MLP in the aggregate and for each of the succeeding 5 years.

2. **OPERATING LEASES WITH INITIAL OR REMAINING NONCANCELABLE TERM IN EXCESS OF 1 YEAR** The lessee is required to disclose the future minimum rental payments required, in aggregate, and for each of next 5 years and a general description of leasing arrangements.

B. LESSOR

1. **SALES-TYPE AND DIRECT FINANCING LEASES** The lessor must disclose the net investment components, including future MLP, unguaranteed residual value, unearned income, and the future MLP to be received in each of the succeeding 5 years.

2. **OPERATING LEASES** The lessor must disclose the cost and carrying amount, if different, of property leased or held for leasing, by major class and total accumulated depreciation; the minimum future rentals on noncancelable leases, in aggregate, for each of the next 5 years; and a general description of leasing arrangements.

Problems and Essay Question Grading

Problems and essay questions are graded by CPAs and AICPA staff members, using the following procedures:

First grading

The first grading is done by graders assigned to individual questions. For example, each problem in the Financial Accounting & Reporting section will be graded by a different grader. A grader assigned to a single question, which will be graded during the full grading session of six or seven weeks, becomes an expert in the subject matter of the question and in the evaluation of the candidates' answers. Thus, grading is objective and uniform.

The purpose of the first grading is to separate the candidates' papers into three groups: obvious passes, marginal, and obvious failures.

Second grading

Upon completion of the first grading, a second grading is made by reviewers. Obvious passes and failures are subjected to cursory reviews as part of the grading controls. Marginal papers (papers with grades of 70 to 74), however, receive an extensive review. These papers are regraded to grades of 69 or 75.

The graders who make the extensive reviews have had years of experience grading the CPA Examination. They have also participated in the development of the grading bases and have access to item analysis for objective questions, identifying concepts as discriminating (those included by most candidates passing the exam) or as rudimentary (those included by candidates both passing and failing the exam). An important indicator of the competence of the candidate is whether grade points were earned chiefly from discriminating concepts or from rudimentary concepts.

Additional grading

Further information regarding the grading procedures is included in the **Practical Advice** section of this volume.

CHAPTER 8—LEASES

PROBLEM 8-1 MULTIPLE CHOICE QUESTIONS (98 to 123 minutes)

1. Lease M does not contain a bargain purchase option, but the lease term is equal to 90% of the estimated economic life of the leased property. Lease P does not transfer ownership of the property to the lessee at the end of the lease term, but the lease term is equal to 75% of the estimated economic life of the leased property. How should the lessee classify these leases?

	Lease M	Lease P
a.	Capital lease	Operating lease
b.	Capital lease	Capital lease
c.	Operating lease	Capital lease
d.	Operating lease	Operating lease

(11/92, Theory, #27, 3460)

2. One criterion for a capital lease is that the term of the lease must equal a minimum percentage of the leased property's estimated economic life at the inception of the lease. What is this minimum percentage?
a. 51%
b. 75%
c. 80%
d. 90%   (5/94, FAR, #26, 4841)

3. In the long-term liabilities section of its balance sheet at December 31, 1992, Mene Co. reported a capital lease obligation of $75,000, net of current portion of $1,364. Payments of $9,000 were made on both January 2, 1993, and January 2, 1994. Mene's incremental borrowing rate on the date of the lease was 11% and the lessor's implicit rate, which was known to Mene, was 10%. In its December 31, 1993 balance sheet, what amount should Mene report as capital lease obligation, net of current portion?
a. $66,000
b. $73,500
c. $73,636
d. $74,250   (5/94, FAR, #25, 4840)

4. On January 1, 1991, Mollat Co. signed a 7-year lease for equipment having a 10-year economic life. The present value of the monthly lease payments equaled 80% of the equipment's fair value.

The lease agreement provides for neither a transfer of title to Mollat, nor a bargain purchase option. In its 1991 income statement, Mollat should report
a. Rent expense equal to the 1991 lease payments.
b. Rent expense equal to the 1991 lease payments less interest expense.
c. Lease amortization equal to one-tenth of the equipment's fair value.
d. Lease amortization equal to one-seventh of 80% of the equipment's fair value.

(5/92, Theory, #34, 2727)

5. On January 1, 1990, JCK Co. signed a contract for an 8-year lease of its equipment with a 10-year life. The present value of the 16 equal semiannual payments in advance equaled 85% of the equipment's fair value. The contract had no provision for JCK, the lessor, to give up legal ownership of the equipment. Should JCK recognize rent or interest revenue in 1992, and should the revenue recognized in 1992 be the same or smaller than the revenue recognized in 1991?

	1992 revenues recognized	1992 amount recognized compared to 1991
a.	Rent	The same
b.	Rent	Smaller
c.	Interest	The same
d.	Interest	Smaller

(5/93, Theory, #38, 4226)

6. On December 30, 1991, Rafferty Corp. leased equipment under a capital lease. Annual lease payments of $20,000 are due December 31 for 10 years. The equipment's estimated life is 10 years, and the interest rate implicit in the lease is 10%. The capital lease obligation was recorded on December 30, 1991, at $135,000, and the first lease payment was made on that date. What amount should Rafferty include in current liabilities for this capital lease in its December 31, 1991 balance sheet?
a. $ 6,500
b. $ 8,500
c. $11,500
d. $20,000   (11/92, PI, #4, amended, 3237)

7. On December 30, 1997, Haber Co. leased a new machine from Gregg Corp. The following data relate to the lease transaction at the inception of the lease:

Lease term	10 years
Annual rental payable at the end of each lease year	$100,000
Estimated life of machine	12 years
Implicit interest rate	10%
Present value of an annuity of $1 in advance for 10 periods at 10%	6.76
Present value of an annuity of $1 in arrears for 10 periods at 10%	6.15
Fair value of the machine	$700,000

The lease has no renewal option, and the possession of the machine reverts to Gregg when the lease terminates. At the inception of the lease, Haber should record a lease liability of
a. $0.
b. $615,000.
c. $630,000.
d. $676,000.   (11/89, PI, #27, amended, 1203)

8. For a capital lease, the amount recorded initially by the lessee as a liability should
a. Equal the total of the minimum lease payments during the lease term.
b. Exceed the total of the minimum lease payments during the lease term.
c. Not exceed the fair value of the leased property at the inception of the lease.
d. Exceed the present value at the beginning of the lease term of minimum lease payments during the lease term.   (11/87, Theory, #11, 2073)

9. Cott, Inc. prepared an interest amortization table for a five-year lease payable with a bargain purchase option of $2,000, exercisable at the end of the lease. At the end of the five years, the balance in the leases payable column of the spreadsheet was zero. Cott has asked Grant, CPA, to review the spreadsheet to determine the error. Only one error was made on the spreadsheet. Which of the following statements represents the best explanation for this error?
a. The beginning present value of the lease did **not** include the present value of the bargain purchase option.
b. Cott subtracted the annual interest amount from the lease payable balance instead of adding it.
c. The present value of the bargain purchase option was subtracted from the present value of the annual payments.
d. Cott discounted the annual payments as an ordinary annuity, when the payments actually occurred at the beginning of each period.
      (1999, FAR, #19, 6788)

10. On December 29, 1991, Action Corp. signed a 7-year capital lease for an airplane to transport its sports team around the country. The airplane's fair value was $841,500. Action made the first annual lease payment of $153,000 on December 31, 1991. Action's incremental borrowing rate was 12%, and the interest rate implicit in the lease, which was known by Action, was 9%. The following are the rounded present value factors for an annuity due:

9%   for 7 years 5.5
12% for 7 years 5.1

What amount should Action report as capital lease liability in its December 31, 1991 balance sheet?
a. $841,500
b. $780,300
c. $688,500
d. $627,300   (11/92, PI, #33, 3266)

11. Neal Corp. entered into a 9-year capital lease on a warehouse on December 31, 1992. Lease payments of $52,000, which include real estate taxes of $2,000, are due annually, beginning on December 31, 1993, and every December 31 thereafter. Neal does not know the interest rate implicit in the lease; Neal's incremental borrowing rate is 9%. The rounded present value of an ordinary annuity for nine years at 9% is 5.6. What amount should Neal report as capitalized lease liability at December 31, 1992?
a. $280,000
b. $291,200
c. $450,000
d. $468,000   (11/93, PI, #39, 4408)

12. East Company leased a new machine from North Company on May 1, 1997, under a lease with the following information:

Lease term	10 years
Annual rental payable at beginning of each lease year	$40,000
Estimated life of machine	12 years
Implicit interest rate	14%
Present value of an annuity of $1 in advance for 10 periods at 14%	5.95
Present value of $1 for 10 periods at 14%	0.27

East has the option to purchase the machine on May 1, 2006, by paying $50,000, which approximates the expected fair value of the machine on the option exercise date. On May 1, 1997, East should record a capitalized leased asset of
a. $251,500.
b. $238,000.
c. $224,500.
d. $198,000.   (5/86, PI, #20, amended, 1216)

13. Robbins Inc. leased a machine from Ready Leasing Co. The lease qualifies as a capital lease and requires 10 annual payments of $10,000 beginning immediately. The lease specifies an interest rate of 12% and a purchase option of $10,000 at the end of the tenth year, even though the machine's estimated value on that date is $20,000. Robbins' incremental borrowing rate is 14%.

The present value of an annuity due of $1 at:
    12% for 10 years is 6.328
    14% for 10 years is 5.946
The present value of $1 at:
    12% for 10 years is .322
    14% for 10 years is .270

What amount should Robbins record as lease liability at the beginning of the lease term?
a. $62,160
b. $64,860
c. $66,500
d. $69,720   (5/92, PI, #34, 2605)

14. At the inception of a capital lease, the guaranteed residual value should be
a. Included as part of minimum lease payments at present value.
b. Included as part of minimum lease payments at future value.
c. Included as part of minimum lease payments only to the extent that guaranteed residual value is expected to exceed estimated residual value.
d. Excluded from minimum lease payments.
       (11/94, FAR, #20, 5284)

15. On January 31, 1997, Clay Company leased a new machine from Saxe Corp. The following data relate to the lease transaction at the inception of the lease:

Lease term	10 years
Annual rental payable at beginning of each lease year	$50,000
Estimated life of machine	15 years
Implicit interest rate	10%
Present value of an annuity of $1 in advance for 10 periods at 10%	6.76
Present value of annuity of $1 in arrears for 10 periods at 10%	6.15
Fair value of the machine	$400,000

The lease has no renewal option, and the possession of the machine reverts to Saxe when the lease terminates. At the inception of the lease, Clay should record a lease liability of

a. $400,000.
b. $338,000.
c. $307,500.
d. $0.   (5/88, PI, #35, amended, 1207)

16. During January, 1990, Vail Co. made long-term improvements to a recently leased building. The lease agreement provides for neither a transfer of title to Vail nor a bargain purchase option. The present value of the minimum lease payments equals 85% of the building's market value, and the lease term equals 70% of the building's economic life. Should assets be recognized for the building and the leasehold improvements?

	Building	Leasehold improvements
a.	Yes	Yes
b.	No	Yes
c.	Yes	No
d.	No	No

       (11/91, Theory, #33, 2541)

17. On January 2, 1991, Cole Co. signed an 8-year noncancelable lease for a new machine, requiring $15,000 annual payments at the beginning of each year. The machine has an estimated life of 12 years, with no salvage value. Title passes to Cole at the lease expiration date. Cole used straight-line depreciation for all of its plant assets. Aggregate lease payments have a present value on January 2, 1991, of $108,000, based on an appropriate rate of interest. For 1991, Cole should record depreciation (amortization) expense for the leased machine at
a. $0.
b. $ 9,000.
c. $13,500.
d. $15,000.   (11/92, PI, #55, amended, 3287)

18. On January 2, 1992, Nori Mining Co. (lessee) entered into a 5-year lease for drilling equipment. Nori accounted for the acquisition as a capital lease for $240,000, which includes a $10,000 bargain purchase option. At the end of the lease, Nori expects to exercise the bargain purchase option. Nori estimates that the equipment's fair value will be $20,000 at the end of its 8-year life. Nori regularly uses straight-line depreciation on similar equipment. For the year ended December 31, 1992, what amount should Nori recognize as depreciation expense on the leased asset?
a. $48,000
b. $46,000
c. $30,000
d. $27,500   (11/93, PI, #55, 4424)

19. On January 1, 1997, Day Corp. entered into a 10-year lease agreement with Ward Inc. for industrial equipment. Annual lease payments of $10,000 are payable at the end of each year. Day knows that the lessor expects a 10% return on the lease. Day has a 12% incremental borrowing rate. The equipment is expected to have an estimated life of 10 years. In addition, a third party has guaranteed to pay Ward a residual value of $5,000 at the end of the lease.

The present value of an ordinary annuity of $1 at:
    12% for 10 years is 5.6502
    10% for 10 years is 6.1446
The present value of $1 at:
    12% for 10 years is .3220
    10% for 10 years is .3855

In Day's October 31, 1997 balance sheet, the principal amount of the lease obligation was
a. $63,374.
b. $61,446.
c. $58,112.
d. $56,502.　　　　(5/90, PI, #35, amended, 1198)

20. Oak Co. leased equipment for its entire 9-year estimated life, agreeing to pay $50,000 at the start of the lease term on December 31, 1991, and $50,000 annually on each December 31 for the next eight years. The present value on December 31, 1991, of the nine lease payments over the lease term, using the rate implicit in the lease which Oak knows to be 10%, was $316,500. The December 31, 1991 present value of the lease payments using Oak's incremental borrowing rate of 12% was $298,500. Oak made a timely second lease payment. What amount should Oak report as capital lease liability in its December 31, 1992 balance sheet?
a. $350,000
b. $243,150
c. $228,320
d. $0　　　　(11/93, PI, #35, amended, 4404)

21. On January 2, 1995, Marx Co. as lessee signed a 5-year noncancelable equipment lease with annual payments of $200,000 beginning December 31, 1995. Marx treated this transaction as a capital lease. The five lease payments have a present value of $758,000 at January 2, 1995, based on interest of 10%. What amount should Marx report as interest expense for the year ended December 31, 1995?
a. $0
b. $48,400
c. $55,800
d. $75,800　　　　(5/96, FAR, #4, 6277)

22. A 6-year capital lease entered into on December 31, 1994, specified equal minimum annual lease payments due on December 31 of each year. The first minimum annual lease payment, paid on December 31, 1994, consists of which of the following?

	Interest expense	Lease liability
a.	Yes	Yes
b.	Yes	No
c.	No	Yes
d.	No	No

(11/95, FAR, #12, 6094)

23. On January 1, 1997, Vick Company as lessee signed a 10-year noncancelable lease for a machine stipulating annual payments of $20,000. The first payment was made on January 1, 1997. Vick appropriately treated this transaction as a capital lease. The ten lease payments have a present value of $135,000 at January 1, 1997, based on implicit interest of 10%. For the year ended December 31, 1997, Vick should record interest expense of
a. $0.
b. $ 6,500.
c. $11,500.
d. $13,500.　　　　(11/86, PI, #45, amended, 1215)

24. On December 31, 1996, Roe Co. leased a machine from Colt for a 5-year period. Equal annual payments under the lease are $105,000 (including $5,000 annual executory costs) and are due on December 31 of each year. The first payment was made on December 31, 1996, and the second payment was made on December 31, 1997. The five lease payments are discounted at 10% over the lease term. The present value of minimum lease payments at the inception of the lease and before the first annual payment was $417,000. The lease is appropriately accounted for as a capital lease by Roe. In its December 31, 1997 balance sheet, Roe should report a lease liability of
a. $317,000.
b. $315,000.
c. $285,300.
d. $248,700.　　　　(11/90, PI, #22, amended, 1192)

25. A 6-year capital lease specifies equal minimum annual lease payments. Part of this payment represents interest and part represents a reduction in the net lease liability. The portion of the minimum lease payment in the fourth year applicable to the reduction of the net lease liability should be
a. The same as in the third year.
b. Less than in the third year.
c. Less than in the fifth year.
d. More than in the fifth year.

(5/87, Theory, #13, 9032)

26. A lessee had a 10-year capital lease requiring equal annual payments. The reduction of the lease liability in year 2 should equal
a. The current liability shown for the lease at the end of year 1.
b. The current liability shown for the lease at the end of year 2.
c. The reduction of the lease obligation in year 1.
d. One-tenth of the original lease liability.

(5/90, Theory, #11, 2063)

27. Howe Co. leased equipment to Kew Corp. on January 2, 1992, for an 8-year period expiring December 31, 1999. Equal payments under the lease are $600,000 and are due on January 2 of each year. The first payment was made on January 2, 1992. The list selling price of the equipment is $3,520,000 and its carrying cost on Howe's books is $2,800,000. The lease is appropriately accounted for as a sales-type lease. The present value of the lease payments at an imputed interest rate of 12% (Howe's incremental borrowing rate) is $3,300,000. What amount of profit on the sale should Howe report for the year ended December 31, 1992?
a. $720,000
b. $500,000
c. $ 90,000
d. $0

(11/93, PI, #44, 4413)

28. Winn Co. manufactures equipment that is sold or leased. On December 31, 1997, Winn leased equipment to Bart for a 5-year period ending December 31, 2002, at which date ownership of the leased asset will be transferred to Bart. Equal payments under the lease are $22,000 (including $2,000 executory costs) and are due on December 31 of each year. The first payment was made on December 31, 1997. Collectibility of the remaining lease payments is reasonably assured, and Winn has no material cost uncertainties. The normal sales price of the equipment is $77,000, and cost is $60,000. For the year ended December 31, 1997, what amount of income should Winn realize from the lease transaction?
a. $17,000
b. $22,000
c. $23,000
d. $33,000

(11/90, PI, #33, amended, 1193)

29. Peg Co. leased equipment from Howe Corp. on July 1, 1997 for an 8-year period expiring June 30, 2005. Equal payments under the lease are $600,000 and are due on July 1 of each year. The first payment was made on July 1, 1997. The rate of interest contemplated by Peg and Howe is 10%. The cash selling price of the equipment is $3,520,000, and the cost of the equipment on Howe's accounting records is $2,800,000. The lease is appropriately recorded as a sales-type lease. What is the amount of profit

on the sale and interest revenue that Howe should record for the year ended December 31, 1997?

	Profit on sale	Interest revenue
a.	$720,000	$176,000
b.	$720,000	$146,000
c.	$ 45,000	$176,000
d.	$ 45,000	$146,000

(11/89, PI, #34, amended, 1204)

30. Farm Co. leased equipment to Union Co. on July 1, 1994, and properly recorded the sales-type lease at $135,000, the present value of the lease payments discounted at 10%. The first of eight annual lease payments of $20,000 due at the beginning of each year was received and recorded on July 3, 1994. Farm had purchased the equipment for $110,000. What amount of interest revenue from the lease should Farm report in its 1994 income statement?
a. $0
b. $5,500
c. $5,750
d. $6,750

(5/95, FAR, #28, 5564)

31. A lease is recorded as a sales-type lease by the lessor. The difference between the gross investment in the lease and the sum of the present values of the two components of the gross investment (the net receivable) should be
a. Amortized over the period of the lease as interest revenue using the interest method.
b. Amortized over the period of the lease as interest revenue using the straight-line method.
c. Recognized in full as interest revenue at the lease's inception.
d. Recognized in full as manufacturer's or dealer's profit at the lease's inception.

(5/87, Theory, #27, 9033)

32. On August 1, 1997, Kern Company leased a machine to Day Company for a 6-year period requiring payments of $10,000 at the beginning of each year. The machine cost $48,000, which is the fair value at the lease date, and has an estimated life of eight years with no residual value. Kern's implicit interest rate is 10% and present value factors are as follows:

Present value of an annuity due of $1
   at 10% for 6 periods   4.791
Present value of an annuity due of $1
   at 10% for 8 periods   5.868

Kern appropriately recorded the lease as a direct financing lease. At the inception of the lease, the gross lease receivables account balance should be
a. $60,000.
b. $58,680.
c. $48,000.
d. $47,910.

(5/85, PI, #6, amended, 9034)

33. Glade Co. leases computer equipment to customers under direct-financing leases. The equipment has no residual value at the end of the lease, and the leases do not contain bargain purchase options. Glade wishes to earn 8% interest on a 5-year lease of equipment with a fair value of $323,400. The present value of an annuity due of $1 at 8% for five years is 4.312. What is the total amount of interest revenue that Glade will earn over the life of the lease?

a. $ 51,600
b. $ 75,000
c. $129,360
d. $139,450   (11/95, FAR, #29, 6111)

34. On January 1, 1997, Park Co. signed a 10-year operating lease for office space at $96,000 per year. The lease included a provision for additional rent of 5% of annual company sales in excess of $500,000. Park's sales for the year ended December 31, 1997 were $600,000. Upon execution of the lease, Park paid $24,000 as a bonus for the lease. Park's rent expense for the year ended December 31, 1997 is

a. $ 98,400.
b. $101,000.
c. $103,400.
d. $125,000.   (5/90, PI, #56, amended, 1200)

35. Wall Co. leased office premises to Fox Inc. for a 5-year term beginning January 2, 1992. Under the terms of the operating lease, rent for the first year is $8,000 and rent for years 2 through 5 is $12,500 per annum. However, as an inducement to enter the lease, Wall granted Fox the first six months of the lease rent-free. In its December 31, 1992 income statement, what amount should Wall report as rental income?

a. $12,000
b. $11,600
c. $10,800
d. $ 8,000   (11/93, PI, #50, 4419)

36. A 20-year property lease, classified as an operating lease, provides for a 10% increase in annual payments every five years. In the sixth year compared to the fifth year, the lease will cause the following expenses to increase

	Rent	Interest
a.	No	Yes
b.	Yes	No
c.	Yes	Yes
d.	No	No

(5/90, Theory, #24, 2065)

37. Conn Corp. owns an office building and normally charges tenants $30 per square foot per year for office space. Because the occupancy rate is low,

Conn agreed to lease 10,000 square feet to Hanson Co. at $12 per square foot for the first year of a 3-year operating lease. Rent for remaining years will be at the $30 rate. Hanson moved into the building on January 1, 1992, and paid the first year's rent in advance. What amount of rental revenue should Conn report from Hanson in its income statement for the year ended September 30, 1992?

a. $ 90,000
b. $120,000
c. $180,000
d. $240,000   (11/92, PI, #45, 3278)

38. As an inducement to enter a lease, Graf Co., a lessor, granted Zep Inc., a lessee, twelve months of free rent under a 5-year operating lease. The lease was effective on January 1, 1993, and provides for monthly rental payments to begin January 1, 1994. Zep made the first rental payment on December 30, 1993. In its 1993 income statement, Graf should report rental revenue in an amount equal to

a. Zero.
b. Cash received during 1993.
c. One-fourth of the total cash to be received over the life of the lease.
d. One-fifth of the total cash to be received over the life of the lease.   (11/94, FAR, #41, 5303)

39. On January 1, 1997, Wren Co. leased a building to Brill under an operating lease for ten years at $50,000 per year, payable the first day of each lease year. Wren paid $15,000 to a real estate broker as a finder's fee. The building is depreciated $12,000 per year. For 1997, Wren incurred insurance and property tax expense totaling $9,000. Wren's net rental income for 1997 should be

a. $27,500.
b. $29,000.
c. $35,000.
d. $36,500.   (11/90, PI, #37, amended, 1194)

40. When should a lessor recognize in income a nonrefundable lease bonus paid by a lessee on signing an operating lease?

a. When received
b. At the inception of the lease
c. At the expiration of the lease
d. Over the life of the lease

(11/95, FAR, #34, 6116)

41. In a sale-leaseback transaction, the seller-lessee retains the right to substantially all of the remaining use of the equipment sold. The profit on the sale should be deferred and subsequently amortized by the lessee when the lease is classified as a(an)

	Capital lease	Operating lease
a.	No	Yes
b.	No	No
c.	Yes	No
d.	Yes	Yes

(11/87, Theory, #10, 2072)

42. In a sale-leaseback transaction, a gain resulting from the sale should be deferred at the time of the sale-leaseback and subsequently amortized when

I. The seller-lessee has transferred substantially all the risks of ownership.
II. The seller-lessee retains the right to substantially all of the remaining use of the property.

a. I only
b. II only
c. Both I and II
d. Neither I nor II   (11/95, FAR, #11, 6093)

43. Able sold its headquarters building at a gain, and simultaneously leased back the building. The lease was reported as a capital lease. At the time of sale, the gain should be reported as
a. Operating income.
b. An extraordinary item, net of income tax.
c. An item of other comprehensive income.
d. An asset valuation allowance.
(11/90, Theory, #24, amended, 2060)

44. Rig Co. sold its factory at a gain, and simultaneously leased it back for 10 years. The factory's remaining economic life is 20 years. The lease was reported as an operating lease. At the time of sale, Rig should report the gain as
a. An extraordinary item, net of income tax.
b. An asset valuation allowance.
c. An item of other comprehensive income.
d. A deferred credit.
(5/92, Theory, #32, amended, 2725)

45. On June 30, 1992, Lang Co. sold equipment with an estimated useful life of eleven years and immediately leased it back for ten years. The equipment's carrying amount was $450,000; the sales price was $430,000; and the present value of the lease payments, which is equal to the fair value of the equipment, was $465,000. In its June 30, 1992 balance sheet, what amount should Lang report as deferred loss?
a. $35,000
b. $20,000
c. $15,000
d. $0   (11/92, PI, #35, 3268)

46. The following information pertains to a sale and leaseback of equipment by Mega Co. on December 31, 1991:

Sales price	$400,000
Carrying amount	$300,000
Monthly lease payment	$ 3,250
Present value of lease payments	$ 36,900
Estimated remaining life	25 years
Lease term	1 year
Implicit rate	12%

What amount of deferred gain on the sale should Mega report at December 31, 1991?
a. $0
b. $ 36,900
c. $ 63,100
d. $100,000   (5/92, PI, #31, 2600)

47. On December 31, 1997, Parke Corp. sold Edlow Corp. an airplane with an estimated remaining life of ten years. At the same time, Parke leased back the airplane for three years. Additional information is as follows:

Sales price	$600,000
Carrying amount of airplane at date of sale	$100,000
Monthly rental under lease	$ 6,330
Interest rate implicit in the lease as computed by Edlow and known by Parke (this rate is lower than the lessee's incremental borrowing rate)	12%
Present value of operating lease rentals ($6,330 for 36 months @ 12%)	$190,581

The leaseback is considered an operating lease.

In Parke's December 31, 1997 balance sheet, what amount should be included as deferred revenue on this transaction?

a. $0
b. $190,581
c. $309,419
d. $500,000   (11/88, PI, #21, amended, 9035)

48. On January 1, 1997, West Co. entered into a 10-year lease for a manufacturing plant. The annual minimum lease payments are $100,000. In the notes to the December 31, 1998 financial statements, what amounts of subsequent years' lease payments should be disclosed?

	Amount for appropriate required period	Aggregate amount for the period thereafter
a.	$100,000	$0
b.	$300,000	$500,000
c.	$500,000	$300,000
d.	$500,000	$0

(11/89, PI, #53, amended, 9038)

49. On July 1, 1992, South Co. entered into a 10-year operating lease for a warehouse facility. The annual minimum lease payments are $100,000. In addition to the base rent, South pays a monthly allocation of the building's operating expenses, which amounted to $20,000 for the year ended June 30, 1993. In the notes to South's June 30, 1993 financial statements, what amounts of subsequent years' lease payments should be disclosed?

a. $100,000 per annum for each of the next five years and $500,000 in the aggregate.
b. $120,000 per annum for each of the next five years and $600,000 in the aggregate.
c. $100,000 per annum for each of the next five years and $900,000 in the aggregate.
d. $120,000 per annum for each of the next five years and $1,080,000 in the aggregate.

(11/93, PI, #42, 4411)

PROBLEM/ESSAY QUESTIONS

PROBLEM 8-2 (40 to 50 minutes)

Problem 8-2 consists of two unrelated parts.

a. On February 20, 1997, Riley Inc. purchased a machine for $1,200,000 for the purpose of leasing it. The machine is expected to have a 10-year life, no residual value, and will be depreciated on the straight-line basis. The machine was leased to Sutter Company on March 1, 1997, for a 4-year period at a monthly rental of $18,000. There is no provision for the renewal of the lease or purchase of the machine by the lessee at the expiration of the lease term. Riley paid $60,000 of commissions associated with negotiating the lease in February 1997.

REQUIRED:

1. What expense should Sutter record as a result of the above facts for the year ended December 31, 1997? Show supporting computations in good form.

2. What income or loss before income taxes should Riley record as a result of the above facts for the year ended December 31, 1997? Show supporting computations in good form.

b. Dumont Corporation, a lessor of office machines, purchased a new machine for $500,000 on December 31, 1996, which was delivered the same day (by prior arrangement) to Finley Company, the lessee. The following information relating to the lease transaction is available:

- The leased asset has an estimated useful life of seven years which coincides with the lease term.
- At the end of the lease term, the machine will revert to Dumont, at which time it is expected to have a residual value of $60,000 (none of which is guaranteed by Finley).
- Dumont's implicit interest rate is 12%, which is known by Finley.
- Finley's incremental borrowing rate is 14% at December 31, 1996.

- Lease rentals consist of seven equal annual payments, the first of which was paid on December 31, 1996.
- The lease is appropriately accounted for as a direct financing lease by Dumont and as a capital lease by Finley. Both lessor and lessee are calendar year corporations and depreciate all fixed assets on the straight-line basis.

Information of present value factors is as follows:

Present value of $1 for seven periods at 12%	0.452
Present value of $1 for seven periods at 14%	0.400
Present value of an annuity of $1 in advance for seven periods at 12%	5.111
Present value of an annuity of $1 in advance for seven periods at 14%	4.889

REQUIRED (round all amounts to the nearest dollar):

1. Compute the annual rental under the lease. Show all computations in good form.

2. Compute the amounts of the gross lease rentals receivable and the unearned interest revenue that Dumont should disclose at the inception of the lease on December 31, 1996. Show computations in good form.

3. What expense should Finley record for the year ended December 31, 1997? Show supporting computations in good form.

(5/81, PI, #5, amended)

ESSAY 8-3 (15 to 25 minutes)

On January 1, 1997, Hendrick Company entered into two noncancelable leases for machines to be used in its manufacturing operations. The first lease transfers ownership of the machine to the lessee by the end of the lease term. The second lease contains a bargain purchase option. Payments have been made on both leases during 1997.

REQUIRED:

a. How should Hendrick classify each of the two leases? Why?

b. How should a lessee report a capital lease on its balance sheet and income statement?

c. How should a lessee report an operating lease on its balance sheet and income statement?

(11/86, Theory, #3, amended)

ESSAY 8-4 (12 to 18 minutes)

On December 31, 1996, Port Co. sold 6-month old equipment at fair value and leased it back. There was a loss on the sale. Port pays all insurance, maintenance, and taxes on the equipment. The lease provides for eight equal annual payments, beginning December 31, 1997, with a present value equal to 85% of the equipment's fair value and sales price. The lease's term is equal to 80% of the equipment's estimated life. There is no provision for Port to reac-

quire ownership of the equipment at the end of the lease term.

REQUIRED:

a. **1.** Why is it important to compare an equipment's fair value to its lease payments' present value and its estimated life to the lease term?

2. Evaluate Port's leaseback of the equipment in terms of each of the four criteria for determination of a capital lease.

b. How should Port account for the sale portion of the sale-leaseback transaction at December 31, 1996?

c. How should Port report the leaseback portion of the sale-leaseback transaction on its December 31, 1997 balance sheet?

(5/91, Theory, #4b, c, amended, 6193)

SOLUTION 8-1 MULTIPLE CHOICE ANSWERS

CLASSIFICATION

1. (b) Per SFAS 13, par. 7, a lease shall be classified as a capital lease by the lessee if at its inception the lease meets one or more of the following criteria: (1) the lease transfers ownership of the property to the lessee by the end of the lease term, (2) the lease contains a bargain purchase option, (3) the lease term is equal to 75 percent or more of the estimated economic life of the leased property, (4) the present value of the minimum lease payment (excluding executory costs) equals or exceeds 90 percent of the fair value of the leased property. Since leases M and P both meet the third item in the list above, both leases should be classified as capital leases.

2. (b) The lease term must be equal to 75% or more of the estimated economic life of the leased property for a capital lease.

CAPITAL LEASES—LESSEE

3. (b) The capital lease obligation must be reduced by only the principal portion of the $9,000 payment. The $75,000 is already net of the $1,364 payment made on January 2, 1993, and must be further reduced by the amount of amortization of the lease obligation for 1993. The lessor's implicit rate of interest is known to the lessee and it is less than the lessee's incremental borrowing rate, thus the lessee must use the lessor's implicit rate. The

amount of capital lease obligation, net of current portion is calculated as follows:

Capital lease obligation, 12/31/92	$75,000
Less: Current portion [$9,000 – ($75,000 x 10%)]	(1,500)
Capital lease obligation, 12/31/93	$73,500

4. (a) The lessee has entered into an operating lease because none of the criteria of a capital lease are met. The lease does not transfer ownership of the equipment to the lessee by the end of the lease term nor does it contain a bargain purchase option. The lease term is *less than* 75% (i.e., 7 ÷ 10 = 70%) of the estimated economic life of the equipment and the present value of the minimum lease payments at the beginning of the lease term is *less than* 90% (i.e., 80% < 90%) of the fair value of the equipment. The lessee records neither an asset nor an obligation for an operating lease; instead, the lessee records its lease payments as rent expense.

5. (d) The lease meets one of the criteria of a capital lease since the lease term is equal to 75 percent or more (i.e., 8 ÷ 10 = 80%) of the estimated economic life of the leased equipment. Therefore, since there is no indication that the collectibility of the minimum lease payments is not reasonably assured or that important uncertainties surround the amount of unreimbursable costs yet to be incurred, the lessor has apparently entered into a sales-type or direct financing lease. Therefore, the lessor would recognize interest revenue—not rent revenue—in

1992, the third year of the lease. In the lessor's balance sheet, an asset entitled "net investment in sales-type (or direct financing) lease" would be reported, the balance of which decreases over the lease term. The amount of interest revenue the lessor recognizes in a period is calculated by multiplying the net investment in the lease by the interest rate implicit in the lease. Since the balance of the net investment in the lease decreases over the lease term and the interest rate implicit in the lease is constant over the lease term, the amount of interest revenue recognized each period decreases over the lease term. Therefore, the lessor would recognize a smaller amount of interest revenue in 1992 (the third year of the lease) compared to 1991 (the second year of the lease).

6. (b) At the inception of a capital lease, the lessee records an asset and a liability (i.e., obligation under capital lease). This liability is classified as both current and noncurrent, with the current portion being the amount that will be paid on the principal during the next year. Therefore, the amount that Rafferty should include in current liabilities for the capital lease at 12/31/91 is determined as follows:

Minimum lease payment (MLP), 12/31/92		$ 20,000
Less portion of 12/31/92 MLP allocable to interest:		
Balance of capital lease obligation before payment, 12/30/91	$135,000	
Less: MLP, 12/31/91	(20,000)	
Balance of capital lease obligation, 12/31/91	115,000	
Times: Implicit interest rate of lease	x 10%	(11,500)
Portion of 12/31/92 MLP allocable to principal reduction (and reported as a current liability at 12/31/91)		$ 8,500

INITIAL RECORDING BY LESSEE

7. (b) The lease is a capital lease because the lease term is equal to 75% or more (10 ÷ 12 = 83.3%) of the estimated life of the leased property. Therefore, the lessee, at the inception of the lease, records the asset and the corresponding lease liability at the lesser of the present value of the minimum lease payments or the fair value of the lease property. Because the annual rental is payable at the *end* of each lease year, the present value factor for an annuity in *arrears* is to be used (i.e., the present value factor for an annuity in *advance* can only be used when the first annual rental payment is made *immediately*). The capital lease obligation is recorded at the present value of the minimum lease payments of $615,000 (i.e., $100,000 x 6.15) because this amount is less than the $700,000 fair value of the machine.

8. (c) SFAS 13, par. 10, states, "The lessee shall record a capital lease as an asset and an obligation at an amount equal to the present value at the beginning of the lease term of minimum lease payments during the lease term, excluding that portion of payments representing executory costs such as insurance, maintenance, and taxes to be paid by the lessor, together with any profit thereon. However, if the amount so determined exceeds the fair value of the leased property at the inception of the lease, the amount recorded as the asset and obligation shall be the fair value."

9. (a) If the bargain purchase option had been included in the capitalized lease amount, the final balance would have equaled the amount of the bargain purchase option. Since the balance was zero, the bargain purchase option must have been excluded. Subtracting the annual interest amount from the lease payable balance would have resulted in a negative lease payable balance, rather than zero. Subtracting the present value of the bargain purchase option from the present value of the annual payments would have caused the beginning lease payable balance to be understated and thus result in a negative lease payable balance before the end of the lease. Discounting the annual payments as an ordinary annuity, paid in arrears, rather than in advance would have resulted in an understated beginning lease payable balance and would also have resulted in a negative lease payable balance before the end of the lease.

10. (c) The lessee records a capital lease as an asset and an obligation at an amount equal to the lesser of the present value of the minimum lease payments or the fair value of the leased property. The present value of the minimum lease payments should be computed using the lessor's implicit rate in the lease of 9%, since it is known to the lessee and lower than the lessee's incremental borrowing rate of 12%. Since the annual rental payment is payable at the *beginning* of each lease year, the present value factor for an *annuity due* is used. The capital lease obligation is recorded at the present value of the minimum lease payments of $841,500 (i.e., $153,000 x 5.5) on 12/29/91 because this amount does not exceed the fair value of the leased property (i.e., $841,500). The capital lease liability is reported in the 12/31/91 balance sheet at $688,500 (i.e., $841,500 – $153,000) to reflect the first annual rental payment made 12/29/91.

11. (a) At the inception of a capital lease, the lessee records an asset and the corresponding lease liability at the lesser of the fair value of the leased property (not provided in this problem) or the present value of the minimum lease payments. The

lessee's incremental borrowing rate of 9% is used to capitalize the lease liability because the lessee does not know the interest rate implicit in the lease. The lessee's obligation to pay executory costs such as insurance, maintenance, and taxes in connection with the leased property should be excluded from the amount of the annual minimum lease payments, thus the amount of Neal's minimum lease payments is $50,000 (i.e., $52,000 − $2,000). Neal's first minimum lease payment is not due until 12/31/93. Thus, in its 12/31/92 balance sheet, Neal should report a capitalized lease liability of $280,000 (i.e., $50,000 x 5.6).

12. (b) The lease qualifies as a capital lease because the lease term (10 years) equals or exceeds 75% of the estimated life of the machine (12 years). The amount to be capitalized is the present value of the minimum lease payments (MLP), which does *not* include the $50,000 purchase option (only *bargain* purchase options are included in MLP).

Annual lease payment	$ 40,000
PV annuity in advance factor, i=14%, n=10	x 5.95
Capitalized lease amount	$238,000

13. (c) The lessee records a capital lease as an asset and an obligation at an amount equal to the lesser of the fair value of the leased property (not provided in this question) or the present value of the minimum lease payments. The minimum lease payments include the minimum rental payments called for by the lease over the lease term (i.e., ten payments of $10,000) and payment called for by the bargain purchase option (i.e., $10,000). The purchase option qualifies as a bargain purchase option because the lessee is permitted to purchase the leased property for a price which is significantly lower than the expected fair value of the property at the date the option becomes exercisable (i.e., $10,000 < $20,000). Since the annual rental payment is payable at the *beginning* of each lease year, the present value factor for an *annuity due* is used. The present value of the minimum lease payments should be computed using the lessor's implicit interest rate of 12%, since it is both known to the lessee (i.e., it was specified in the lease) and lower than the lessee's incremental borrowing rate of 14%. The recorded capital lease liability at the beginning of the lease term is determined as follows:

Present value of minimum rental payments called for over the lease term ($10,000 x 6.328)	$ 63,280
PV of bargain purchase option ($10,000 x .322)	3,220
Capital lease liability at beginning of lease term	$ 66,500

14. (a) A capital lease refers to a capitalized lease from a lessee's viewpoint. Any guarantee by the lessee of the residual value at the expiration of the lease term is included in minimum lease payments. When the lessee agrees to make up any deficiency below a stated amount in the lessor's realization of the residual value, the guarantee to be included in the minimum lease payments shall be the stated amount, rather than an estimate of the deficiency to be made up. The lessee records the minimum lease payments at present value [SFAS 13].

15. (d) Clay should not record a lease liability at the inception of the lease as none of the following criteria of a capital lease are met: (1) The lease does *not* transfer ownership of the property to the lessee by the end of the lease term. (The possession of the machine reverts to the lessor when the lease terminates.) (2) The lease does *not* contain a bargain purchase option. (3) The lease term is *less than* 75 percent (10 ÷ 15 = 66.7%) of the estimated economic life of the leased property. (4) The present value of the minimum lease payments at the beginning of the lease term is *less than* 90% [($50,000 x 6.76) ÷ $400,000 = 84.5%] of the fair value of the leased property at the inception of the lease. (The present value of the minimum lease payments in question Is computed using the present value of annuity of $1 in advance because the rental payments are to be made at the *beginning* of each lease year.)

LEASED ASSET

16. (b) The building lease does not meet any of the four criteria of a capital lease; therefore, no asset should be recognized for the building. [The lease agreement provides for neither a transfer of title by the end of the lease term nor a bargain purchase option. The lease term is less than 75% (i.e., 70% < 75%) of the building's estimated economic life, and the present value of the minimum lease payments is less than 90% (i.e., 80% < 90%) of the fair value of the building at the inception of the lease.] The long-term improvements benefit more than one period so they should be expensed over the periods benefited; therefore, an asset should be recognized at the date the leasehold improvement costs are incurred.

17. (b) Under SFAS 13, if a lease qualifies as a capital lease because it (1) transfers ownership of the leased asset by the end of the lease term or (2) contains a bargain purchase option, then the lessee depreciates the leased asset over its estimated economic life. Therefore, the leased asset in question is recorded at $108,000 (given) and is depreciated over its estimated economic life of 12 years since

title passes to the lessee at the expiration of the lease. Depreciation (amortization) expense for 1991 under the straight-line method is $9,000 [i.e., ($108,000 – $0) ÷ 12].

18. **(d)** Under SFAS 13, if a lease qualifies as a capital lease because it (1) transfers ownership of the leased asset by the end of the lease term or (2) contains a bargain purchase option, then the lessee depreciates the leased asset over its estimated economic life. The leased asset is recorded on the books at $240,000 and is depreciated over its estimated economic life of 8 years, since the lessee expects to exercise the bargain purchase option. The lessee amortizes the leased asset in the same manner as other owned assets. Thus, the equipment's estimated fair value at the end of its estimated life is used to compute the depreciable base of the leased property. Under the straight-line method, the amount of annual depreciation expense Nori should recognize on the leased asset is $27,500 [i.e., ($240,000 – $20,000) ÷ 8].

LEASE LIABILITY

19. **(b)** The lease is a capital lease because the lease term is equal to 75% or more (10 ÷ 10 = 100%) of the estimated economic life of the leased property. Therefore, the lessee, at the inception of the lease, records the asset and the corresponding lease liability at the lesser of the fair value of the leased property (not provided in this problem) or the present value of the minimum lease payments. The implicit interest rate of the lease of 10% is used to capitalize the lease liability because it is known by the lessee, and it is lower than the lessee's incremental borrowing rate of 12%. The principal amount of the lease obligation at October 31, 1997 is determined as follows:

Annual minimum lease payments	$10,000
Appropriate factor for lessor's implicit interest rate of 10%	x6.1446
Balance of capitalized lease liability, 1/1/97 - 12/30/97 (first lease payment to be made 12/31/97)	$61,446

A guarantee by a third party *related* to the lessee of the residual value at the expiration of the lease term is considered to be a minimum lease payment. However, there is *no* indication that the third party that has guaranteed to pay Ward a residual value of $5,000 is related to the lessee. Therefore, the guarantee of the residual value by the apparently *unrelated* third party is not used to determine the capitalized lease liability.

20. **(b)** The amount to be reported as the capital lease liability at 12/31/92 is computed as follows:

Balance before payment, 12/31/91		$316,500
Less: Minimum lease payment, 12/31/91		(50,000)
Balance after MLP, 12/31/91		266,500
Less principal reduction from 12/31/92 MLP:		
MLP, 12/31/92	$50,000	
Less: Portion allocable to interest ($266,500 x 10%)	(26,650)	(23,350)
Balance after MLP, 12/31/92		$243,150

21. **(d)** Lessee's accounting for a capital lease requires the use of the effective interest method. The present value of the lease payments is recorded as the lease liability, and interest expense is based upon this amount. The amount reported as interest expense for the first year of this lease is calculated as follows:

Lease liability	$758,000
Interest rate	x 10%
Interest expense	$ 75,800

The balance of the $200,000 lease payment is applied to principal, reducing the lease liability. Interest expense in each subsequent year is based upon the lease liability as reduced by previous reductions in principal.

22. **(c)** When the first annual lease payment is paid at the inception of a capital lease, the first payment applies in its entirety to reduce the lease liability because no time has yet passed during which interest would accrue. Subsequent payments are allocated between interest expense and the reduction of the lease obligation.

23. **(c)** Vick should record interest expense based on the lease obligation outstanding during 1997 (i.e., after subtracting the first lease payment, which was made at the beginning of the lease period).

PV of lease obligation, January 1, 1997	$135,000
January 1, 1997 payment	(20,000)
Lease obligation outstanding, 1997	115,000
Implicit interest rate	x 10%
Interest expense, 1997	$ 11,500

24. **(d)** The balance of the capitalized lease liability is computed as follows:

Balance before payment, 12/31/96	$ 417,000
Less: MLP, 12/31/96	(100,000)*
Balance after MLP, 12/31/96	317,000
Less principal reduction from 12/31/97 MLP:	
MLP, 12/31/97	$100,000
Interest expense ($317,000 x 10%)	(31,700) (68,300)
Balance after MLP, 12/31/97	$ 248,700

---

* The amount of Roe's annual MLP is $100,000 (i.e., $105,000 – $5,000). The lessor's obligation to pay executory costs such as insurance, maintenance, and taxes in connection with leased property should be excluded from the amount of the annual MLP.

25. (c) Obligations under capital leases are amortized using the interest method. Under this method, the uniform payments are comprised of (1) interest expense, and (2) a reduction of principal. Since a portion of each payment reduces the principal balance, the interest expense portion of the next payment is based on a smaller principal balance, and less interest expense is recognized. Each successive uniform payment is comprised of a decreasing amount of interest expense and an increasing amount of principal reduction.

26. (a) At the inception of a capital lease, the lessee records an asset and a liability (i.e., obligation under capital lease). This liability is classified as both current and noncurrent, with the current portion being that amount that will be paid on the principal during the next year. Therefore, for the lease in question, the reduction of the lease liability in year 2 should equal the current liability shown for the lease at the end of year 1.

SALES-TYPE LEASES

27. (b) The fair value of the leased property at the inception of the lease is $3,300,000, which is the present value of the minimum lease payments at the lessor's incremental borrowing rate. The excess of the fair value of leased property at the inception of the lease over its cost or carrying amount should be classified by the lessor as manufacturer's or dealer's profit from a sales-type lease and recognized in full at the inception of the lease.

FV of leased property at inception of lease (PV of MLP)	$ 3,300,000
Less: Carrying amount of equipment	(2,800,000)
Manufacturer's or dealer's profit recognized on sale	$ 500,000

28. (a) The lease qualifies as a sales-type lease because (1) the lease transfers ownership of the property to the lessee by the end of the lease term, (2) collectibility of the minimum lease payments is reasonably assured, and (3) no important uncertainties surround the amount of

unreimbursable costs yet to be incurred by the lessor under the lease. In 1997, the lessor should recognize a manufacturer's profit of $17,000, which is the excess of the normal sales price of the equipment over its cost ($77,000 – $60,000). The lessor should not recognize any interest income from this lease in 1997 because the lease term began on December 31, 1997.

29. (b) The amount of interest revenue to be recorded is determined by applying the interest rate implicit in the lease to the lessor's net receivable at 7/1/97. The excess of the fair value of leased property at the inception of the lease over its cost or carrying amount should be classified by the lessor as manufacturer's or dealer's profit from a sales-type lease and recognized in full at the inception of the lease.

Cash selling price of equipment	$ 3,520,000
Cost of the equipment	(2,800,000)
Profit on sale	$ 720,000
Gross investment in lease before receipt, 7/1/97 ($600,000 x 8)	$ 4,800,000
Less: Receipt, 7/1/97	(600,000)
Gross investment in lease after receipt, 7/1/97	4,200,000
Less: Unearned interest revenue ($4,800,000 – $3,520,000)	(1,280,000)
Net receivable, 7/1/97	2,920,000
Times: Interest rate implicit in lease (10% ÷ 2)	x 5%
Interest revenue to be recognized for 1997	$ 146,000

30. (c) Interest revenue is calculated as follows:

Net investment in lease (PV), 7/1/94	$135,000
Less: Payment received, 7/3/94	(20,000)
Net investment in lease after 7/3/94 payment	115,000
Interest rate	10%
First year interest revenue	11,500
July through December, 1994, 1/2 year	.5
Interest revenue for 1994	$ 5,750

31. (a) In a sales-type lease, the lessor recognizes two types of income: (1) manufacturer's or dealer's profit, and (2) interest income. The manufacturer's or dealer's profit is the excess of the fair value of the leased property over the cost at the inception of the lease, and it is recognized in full at the inception of the lease. The difference between the gross investment, in the lease and the sum of the present values of the two components of the gross investment is recorded as unearned income. The unearned income is amortized over the lease term as interest revenue using the interest method.

DIRECT FINANCING LEASES

32. (a) According to SFAS 13, the gross lease receivable under a direct financing lease is the sum of the minimum lease payments (net of executory costs) plus the unguaranteed residual value accruing to the lessor. In this question, there is no unguaranteed residual involved; therefore, the receivable is calculated as 6 annual payments of $10,000, or $60,000.

33. (a) The unearned interest income is the difference between the lessor's gross investment in the lease and the fair value of the leased asset. The fair value of the equipment is divided by the present value of an annuity due at 8% to arrive at the annual payment. The annual payment times the number of payments is the gross investment. $323,400 ÷ 4.312 = $75,000; $75,000 X 5 = $375,000; $375,000 - $323,400 = $51,600.

OPERATING LEASES

34. (c) Accrual accounting recognizes expenses in the periods they are incurred, rather than only when the related cash is paid. Therefore, the lease bonus should be allocated ratably over the lease term as an increase to rent expense. Park's rent expense for 1997 is determined as follows:

Equal annual rental payment	$ 96,000
Amortization of lease bonus ($24,000 ÷ 10)	2,400
Additional rent due to sales exceeding $500,000 [($600,000 – $500,000) x 5%]	5,000
Rental expense for 1997	$103,400

35. (c) Accrual accounting recognizes revenue in the period(s) it is earned, rather than only when the related cash is received. Thus, the total amount of rental revenue to be received should be allocated ratably over the lease term.

Rental receipts during first year of lease ($8,000 x 6/12)	$ 4,000
Rental receipts during years 2 through 5 ($12,500 x 4)	50,000
Rental receipts over lease term	54,000
Divide by: Years in lease term	÷ 5
Annual rental revenue recognized	$ 10,800

36. (d) Certain operating lease agreements specify scheduled rent increases over the lease term. The effects of those scheduled rent increases, which are included in minimum lease payments under SFAS 13, should be recognized by lessors and lessees on a straight-line basis over the lease term, unless another systematic and rational allocation basis is more representative of the time pattern in which the leased property is physically employed. Using factors such as the time value of money, anticipated inflation, or expected future revenues is inappropriate, because these factors do not relate to the time pattern of the physical usage of the leased property. Therefore, the annual rent expense reported by the lessee for the lease in question should be constant over the 20-year term of the lease. Since the lease in question is an operating lease, the lessee should not report any interest expense as a result of the lease.

37. (c) Accrual accounting recognizes revenues in the periods earned, rather than only when the related cash is received. Therefore, the total amount of rental revenue to be received should be allocated ratably over the 36 months in the lease term.

Rental receipts during first year of lease (10,000 x $12)	$120,000
Rental receipts during second and third years of lease (10,000 x $30 x 2)	600,000
Total rental revenue over lease term	720,000
Divide by: Months in lease term (3 x 12)	÷ 36
Monthly rental revenue	20,000
Times: Months rented during period	x 9
Rental revenue for year ended 9/30/92	$180,000

38. (d) Revenue from an operating lease should be recognized on a straight-line basis, even if the rentals vary from a straight-line basis. Therefore, the total amount of rental revenue from the operating lease should be allocated ratably over the 5-year lease term (SFAS 13).

39. (a) The net rental income for 1997 is computed as follows:

Equal annual rental payment		$ 50,000
Less: Depreciation	$12,000	
Executory costs (insurance and property taxes)	9,000	
Amortization of initial direct costs ($15,000 ÷ 10 years)	1,500	(22,500)
Net rental income from operating lease		$ 27,500

40. (d) If rental payments vary from a straight-line basis (e.g., the lessee pays a "lease bonus" at the inception of the lease, or the lease agreement specifies scheduled rent increases over the lease term), the expense for the lessee and the revenue for the lessor should continue to be recognized on a straight-line basis unless another systematic and rational basis is more representative of the time pattern in which the benefit from the leased property is derived.

SALE-LEASEBACK

41. (d) In this sale-leaseback transaction, the seller-lessee retains the right to substantially all of the remaining life of the equipment. If the lease meets one of the criteria for a capital lease, any profit on the sale is deferred and amortized in proportion to the amortization of the leased asset. If the seller-lessee accounts for the lease as an operating lease, any profit on the sale is deferred and amortized in proportion to the related gross rental charged to expense over the lease term.

42. (b) A sale-leaseback transaction in which the seller-lessee has transferred substantially all the risks of ownership is in substance a sale and, according to SFAS 28, should be accounted for on the separate terms of the sale and of the leaseback, unless the rentals called for by the leaseback are unreasonable in relation to current market conditions. Thus, a gain on the sale is recognized at the point of sale and is not deferred. A sale-leaseback transaction in which the seller-lessee retains the right to substantially all of the remaining use of the property is in substance a financing transaction and, according to SFAS 28, the gain should be deferred and amortized.

43. (d) The gain on the sale of an asset in a sale-leaseback should be deferred and amortized in proportion to the amortization of the leased asset, if the lease is a capital lease (SFAS 28, par. 3). The building under a capital lease is reported net of the unamortized deferred profit on the seller-lessee's balance sheet.

44. (d) The situation described is one of a sale-leaseback transaction. According to SFAS 28, par. 3, any profit or loss on the sale should be deferred and amortized in proportion to the related gross rental charged to expense over the lease term, if an operating lease (or in proportion to the amortization of the leased asset, if a capital lease). Thus, at the time of sale, the gain on the sale of the factory should be reported as a deferred credit. Gains or losses on sale-leaseback transactions should not be reported as extraordinary items or as items of other comprehensive income. Since the seller-lessee does not report an asset for the leased property acquired under the operating lease, the gain on the sale-leaseback cannot be reported as an asset valuation allowance. The gain on the sale-leaseback should be reported as a deferred credit in the liabilities section of the balance sheet.

45. (b) Since the fair value of the asset sold is more than its carrying amount (i.e., $465,000 > $450,000), the $20,000 (i.e., $450,000 − $430,000) indicated loss on the sale is in substance a prepayment of rent. Thus, the $20,000 indicated loss should be deferred and amortized as prepaid rent.

46. (a) Gains and losses on sale-leaseback transactions are generally deferred and amortized over the term of the lease. There are two exceptions to this general rule: (1) where the seller-lessee retains only a *minor* portion of the use of the property, or (2) where the seller-lessee retains more than a minor portion but less than substantially all of the use of the property. The seller-lessee is deemed to have retained a *minor* portion of the use of the

property if the present value of the minimum lease payments is less than 10% of the fair value of the property. In this case, the sale and leaseback are accounted for as two separate transactions and the full amount of the gain or loss realized on the sale of the property is recognized at the date of sale. In this question, the present value of the minimum lease payments is less than 10% of the fair value of the property [i.e., $36,900 < ($400,000 x 10%)]. Therefore, the seller-lessee recognizes the full amount of the $100,000 (i.e., $400,000 sales price − $300,000 carrying amount) profit from the sale of the equipment at the date of sale. No portion of the profit from the sale would be reported as deferred revenue.

47. (b) This question pertains to a sale and leaseback transaction. SFAS 28, *Accounting for Sales With Leasebacks*, requires that when the seller-lessee retains *more than a minor part but less than substantially all* of the use of the property through the leaseback, any gain is immediately recognized to the extent that it exceeds the present value of the minimum lease payments. The remainder of the gain is deferred and recognized over the lease term as a reduction of reported rent expense. The seller-lessee is deemed to have retained a *minor* part of the use of the property if the present value of the lease payments is less than 10% of the fair value of the property. On the other hand, *substantially all* means that the present value of the lease payments exceeds 90% of the fair value of the property. In this question, the present value of the lease payments is more than 10%, but less than 90%, of the fair value of the property ($190,581 ÷ $600,000 = 31.8%). Therefore, of the $500,000 ($600,000 − $100,000) gain realized on the sale of the airplane, $190,581 (the present value of the lease rentals) should be reported as deferred revenue.

DISCLOSURE REQUIREMENTS

48. (c) In the notes to the 12/31/98 financial statements, West should disclose the $500,000 ($100,000 x 5) of minimum lease payments pertaining to the next five succeeding fiscal years *and* the $300,000 [$100,000 x (10 − 2 − 5)] of minimum lease payments pertaining to the fiscal years after this 5-year period.

49. (c) For operating leases having initial or remaining noncancelable lease terms in excess of one year, the lessee should disclose future minimum lease payments required as of the latest balance sheet date for *each of the five succeeding fiscal years and in the aggregate*. Since South is required to make annual minimum lease payments of $100,000 over the remaining noncancelable 9-year

(i.e., 10 − 1) lease term, then in the notes to its 6/30/93 financial statements, South should disclose $100,000 per annum for each of the next five years and $900,000 (i.e., $100,000 x 9) in the aggregate for the subsequent years' lease payments.

PERFORMANCE BY SUBTOPICS

Each category below parallels a subtopic covered in Chapter 8. Record the number and percentage of questions you correctly answered in each subtopic area.

Classification

Question #	Correct √
1	
2	
# Questions	2

\# Correct _____
% Correct _____

Capital Leases—Lessee

Question #	Correct √
3	
4	
5	
6	
# Questions	4

\# Correct _____
% Correct _____

Initial Recording by Lessee

Question #	Correct √
7	
8	
9	
10	
11	
12	
13	
14	
15	
# Questions	9

\# Correct _____
% Correct _____

Leased Asset

Question #	Correct √
16	
17	
18	
# Questions	3

\# Correct _____
% Correct _____

Lease Liability

Question #	Correct √
19	
20	
21	
22	
23	
24	
25	
26	
# Questions	8

\# Correct _____
% Correct _____

Operating Leases

Question #	Correct √
34	
35	
36	
37	
38	
39	
40	
# Questions	7

\# Correct _____
% Correct _____

Sales-Type Leases

Question #	Correct √
27	
28	
29	
30	
31	
# Questions	5

\# Correct _____
% Correct _____

Direct Financing Leases

Question #	Correct √
32	
33	
# Questions	2

\# Correct _____
% Correct _____

Sale-Leaseback

Question #	Correct √
41	
42	
43	
44	
45	
46	
47	
# Questions	7

\# Correct _____
% Correct _____

Disclosure Requirements

Question #	Correct √
48	
49	
# Questions	2

\# Correct _____
% Correct _____

PROBLEM/ESSAY SOLUTIONS

SOLUTION 8-2 OPERATING/DIRECT FINANCING/ CAPITAL LEASES

a. 1.
Sutter Company
COMPUTATION OF EXPENSE ON OPERATING LEASE
For the Year Ended December 31, 1997

Rental expense ($18,000 x 10 months)	**$ 180,000**

a. 2.
Riley Inc.
COMPUTATION OF INCOME BEFORE INCOME TAXES ON OPERATING LEASE
For the Year Ended December 31, 1997

Rental income ($18,000 x 10 months)		**$ 180,000**
Deduct:		
Depreciation		
[($1,200,000 ÷ 10) x 10/12]	$100,000	
Amortization of commission for negotiating lease		
($60,000 x 10/48)	12,500	(112,500)
Income from operating lease		**$ 67,500**

b. 1.
Dumont Corporation
COMPUTATION OF ANNUAL RENTAL UNDER DIRECT FINANCING LEASE
Dated December 31, 1996

Cost of leased machine	$ 500,000
Deduct present value of estimated residual value [$60,000 x 0.452 (present value of $1 at 12% for 7 periods)]	(27,120)
Net investment to be recovered	472,880
Present value of an annuity of $1 in advance for 7 periods at 12%	÷ 5.111
Annual rental	**$ 92,522**

b. 2.
Dumont Corporation
COMPUTATION OF GROSS LEASE RENTALS RECEIVABLE AND UNEARNED INTEREST REVENUE AT INCEPTION OF DIRECT FINANCING LEASE
Dated December 31, 1996

Gross lease rentals receivable ($92,522 x 7)		$ 647,654
Deduct recovery of net investment in machine on capital lease		
Cost of machine	$500,000	
Residual value of machine	(60,000)	(440,000)
Unearned interest revenue		**$ 207,654**

b. 3.
Finley Company
COMPUTATION OF EXPENSE ON LEASE RECORDED AS A CAPITAL LEASE
For the Year Ended December 31, 1997

Depreciation [$472,880 (Schedule 1) ÷ 7]	$ 67,554
Interest expense (Schedule 1)	45,643
Total expense on lease	**$ 113,197**

SCHEDULE 1
INTEREST EXPENSE
Year Ended December 31, 1997

Liability under capital lease (initial value) [$92,522 x 5.111 (present value of an annuity of $1 in advance for 7 periods at 12%*)]	$ 472,880
Deduct lease payment on December 31, 1996	(92,522)
Balance December 31, 1996 (after initial payment)	380,358
Interest rate	x 12%*
Interest expense year ended December 31, 1997	**$ 45,643**

* Finley Company must use Dumont Corporation's (Lessor's) implicit rate of 12% (which is known to it), since it is lower than Finley's incremental borrowing rate of 14%.

SOLUTION 8-3 LESSEE ACCOUNTING FOR CAPITAL AND OPERATING LEASES

a. Hendrick should classify each lease as a **capital lease**. A capital lease **transfers substantially all** of the **benefits and risks** inherent to the **ownership of property**. In order for a lease to qualify as a capital lease for a lessee, it must meet at its inception one or more of the four criteria established by the Financial Accounting Standards Board.

The first lease is a capital lease because it **transfers ownership of the machine** to the lessee, Hendrick, by the **end of the lease term**.

The second lease is also a capital lease because it contains a **bargain purchase option**.

b. A lessee should report a capital lease on its balance sheet as a **noncurrent asset** and **related liability** under **lease obligations**. The noncurrent asset should be reported at its **capitalized cost less accumulated amortization**. The liability would be reported at an amount **equal to the capitalized cost** of the asset **reduced by** the **principal portion** of **minimum lease payments** made by the lessee. In addition, the liability would be appropriately classified as **current and long-term debt**.

A lessee should report on its income statement **amortization** which has been determined in a manner consistent with the lessee's **normal**

depreciation policy for owned assets. A lessee should also report as an **expense** on its income statement the **interest portion** of the **minimum lease payment**.

The minimum lease payment should be allocated between a reduction of the liability on the balance sheet and interest expense on the income statement, in a manner which produces a **constant periodic rate of interest** on the remaining balance of the liability.

c. Normally, operating lease payments should be charged to **expense** on the income statement over the **lease term** on a **straight-line basis**.

Therefore, a leased asset and its related obligation should **not be reported** on the **lessee's balance sheet**.

SOLUTION 8-4 SALE-LEASEBACK TRANSACTIONS

a. **1.** Comparisons of an equipment's fair value to its lease payments' present value, and of its estimated life to the lease term, are used to determine whether the lease is equivalent to an **installment sale**, and therefore is a **capital lease**.

2. A lease is categorized as a capital lease, if, at the date of the lease agreement, it meets any one of four criteria. As the lease has no provision for Port to reacquire ownership of the equipment, it **fails** the two criteria of **transfer of ownership at the end of the lease** and a **bargain purchase** option. Port's lease payments, with a present value equaling 85% of the equipment's fair value, **fail** the criterion for a **present value equaling or exceeding 90% of the equipment's fair value**. However, the lease would be **classified as** a **capital lease**, because its term of 80% of the equipment's estimated life **exceeds the criterion** of being **at least 75% of the equipment's estimated life**.

b. Port should account for the sale portion of the sale-leaseback transaction at December 31, 1996, by **increasing cash** for the **sale price**, **decreasing equipment** by the **carrying amount**, and **recognizing a loss** for the excess of the equipment's carrying amount over its sale price.

c. On the December 31, 1997 balance sheet, the equipment should be included as a **fixed asset**, at the **lease payment's present value** at **December 31, 1996, less 1997 amortization**.

On the December 31, 1997 balance sheet, the **lease obligation** will equal the **lease payments' present value** at December 31, 1996, **less principal repaid** December 31, 1997. This amount will be reported in **current liabilities** for the principal to be **repaid in 1998**, and the balance in **noncurrent liabilities**.

CHAPTER 9

PENSIONS & OTHER POSTRETIREMENT BENEFITS

CHAPTER 9

PENSIONS & OTHER POSTRETIREMENT BENEFITS

I. INTRODUCTION

There are many similarities in accounting for pensions and accounting for other postretirement benefits. This chapter will illustrate accounting for pensions in detail and then highlight the differences in accounting for postretirement benefits.

A. BACKGROUND

1. **SFAS 87** SFAS 87, *Employers' Accounting for Pensions*, establishes standards of financial reporting and accounting for an employer who offers pension benefits to employees. The most significant part of SFAS 87 involves an employer's accounting for a *single-employer*, defined *benefit* pension plan. In addition, provisions apply to an employer that sponsors a defined *contribution* plan.

2. **SFAS 88** SFAS 88, *Employers' Accounting for Settlements and Curtailments of Defined Benefit Pension Plans and for Termination Benefits*, expands the accounting standards for pensions.

3. **SFAS 106** SFAS 106, *Employers' Accounting for Postretirement Benefits Other Than Pensions*, essentially represents an extension of the measurement principles related to defined benefit pension plans (modified for different fact circumstances) to postretirement benefits other than pensions. While SFAS 106 is applicable to all forms of postretirement benefits other than pensions (e.g., health care, life insurance, and welfare benefits), the Statement is written to focus primarily on postretirement health care benefits.

4. **SFAS 132** SFAS 132, *Employers' Disclosures About Pensions and Other Postretirement Benefits*, modifies the disclosures required by companies about their pension and nonpension benefit plans to make the disclosures more uniform and to provide better information to investors about the economics of the benefit plans sponsored by employers.

B. FUNDAMENTALS

Three fundamental aspects shape financial reporting in the application of accrual accounting to pensions.

1. **DELAYING RECOGNITION OF CERTAIN EVENTS** Changes in the pension obligation and changes in the value of assets set aside to meet those obligations are not recognized as they occur. They are systematically and gradually recognized over subsequent periods.

2. **REPORTING NET COST** A single net cost amount is reported in the employer's financial statements. This net cost aggregates at least three items that might be reported separately for any other part of an entity's operations, including the compensation cost of the benefits promised, the interest cost resulting from deferring the payment of those benefits, and the return from investing in the assets related to those benefits.

3. **OFFSETTING LIABILITIES AND ASSETS** The employer's balance sheet reflects as a net amount the recognized values of assets contributed to a plan and the liabilities for pensions recognized as net pension cost of past periods. These assets and liabilities are netted, even though the liabilities have not been satisfied, the assets may still be controlled, and the employer is still subject to both the risks and rewards involved.

II. **SINGLE-EMPLOYER DEFINED BENEFIT PENSION PLANS**

    A. **DEFINITIONS**

        The following definitions apply specifically to accounting for pensions. Most of these terms apply also to accounting for postretirement benefits, with minor modification.

        1. **ACCUMULATED BENEFIT OBLIGATION** The actuarial present value of benefits (whether vested or nonvested) attributed by the pension benefit formula to employee services rendered before a specified date and based on employee services and compensation (if applicable) prior to that date.

        2. **ACTUARIAL PRESENT VALUE** The value, as of a specified date, of an amount or series of amounts payable or receivable thereafter, with each amount adjusted to reflect (a) the time value of money (through discounts for interest) and (b) the probability of payment (by means of decrements for events such as death, disability, withdrawal, or retirement) between the specified date and the expected date of payment.

        3. **ANNUITY CONTRACT** A contract in which an insurance company unconditionally undertakes a legal obligation to provide specified pension benefits to specific individuals in return for a fixed consideration or premium.

        4. **ATTRIBUTION** The process of assigning benefits or costs to periods of employee service.

        5. **CONTRIBUTORY PLAN** A pension plan under which employees contribute part of the cost. In some contributory plans, employees wishing to be covered must contribute; in other contributory plans, participants' contributions result in increased benefits.

        6. **DEFINED BENEFIT PENSION PLAN** A pension plan that defines an amount of pension *benefit* to be provided, usually as a function of one or more factors such as age, years of service, or compensation.

        7. **DEFINED CONTRIBUTION PENSION PLAN** A plan that provides pension benefits in return for services rendered, provides an individual account for each participant, and specifies how *contributions* to the individual's account are to be determined (instead of specifying the amount the individual is to receive).

        8. **EXPECTED RETURN ON PLAN ASSETS** An amount calculated as a basis for determining the extent of delayed recognition of the effects of changes in the fair value of assets. The expected return on plan assets is determined based on the expected long-term rate of return on plan assets and the market-related value of plan assets.

        9. **GAIN OR LOSS** A change in the value of either the projected benefit obligation or the plan assets resulting from **experience** different from that assumed or from a change in an actuarial assumption.

        10. **FUNDING POLICY** The program regarding the amounts and timing of contributions by the employer(s), participants, and any other sources.

        11. **MARKET-RELATED VALUE OF PLAN ASSETS** A balance used to calculate the expected return on plan assets. Market-related value can be either fair value or a calculated value that recognizes changes in fair value in a systematic and rational manner over not more than five years.

        12. **NET PERIODIC PENSION COST** The amount recognized in an employer's financial statements as the cost of a pension plan for a period. Components of net periodic pension cost are service cost, interest cost, actual return on plan assets, gain or loss, amortization of unrecognized prior service cost, and amortization of the unrecognized net obligation or asset existing at the date of initial application of Statement 87.

13. **PENSION BENEFIT FORMULA** The basis for determining payments to which participants may be entitled under a pension plan. Pension benefit formulas usually refer to the employee's service or compensation or both.

14. **PLAN ASSETS** Assets (usually stocks, bonds, and other investments) that have been segregated and restricted (usually in a trust) to provide benefits. Plan assets include amounts contributed by the employer (and by employees for a contributory plan) and amounts earned from investing the contributions, less benefits paid.

15. **PRIOR SERVICE COST** The cost of retroactive benefits granted in a plan amendment (or initiation of a new plan).

16. **PROJECTED BENEFIT OBLIGATION** The actuarial present value as of a date of all benefits attributed by the pension benefit formula to employee service rendered prior to that date. The projected benefit obligation is measured using assumptions as to future compensation levels if the pension benefit formula is based on those future compensation levels (pay-related, final-pay, final-average-pay, or career-average-pay plans).

17. **RETROACTIVE BENEFITS** Benefits granted in a plan amendment (or initiation) that are attributed by the pension benefit formula to employee services rendered in periods prior to the amendment. The cost of the retroactive benefits is referred to as prior service cost.

18. **UNFUNDED ACCUMULATED BENEFIT OBLIGATION** The excess of the accumulated benefit obligation over the fair value of plan assets.

19. **UNRECOGNIZED NET GAIN OR LOSS** The cumulative net gain or loss that has not been recognized as a part of net periodic pension cost.

20. **VESTED BENEFIT OBLIGATION** The actuarial present value of vested benefits (benefits for which the employee's right to receive a present or future pension benefit is no longer contingent on remaining in the service of the employer).

B. **OVERVIEW**

The fundamental objective in accounting and reporting of defined benefit plans is to provide a measure of pension cost that reflects the terms of the underlying plan and recognizes the compensation cost of an employee's pension benefits over the employee's approximate service period. This objective can be accomplished by dividing the discussion into three sections:

1. Recognition of net periodic pension cost.

2. Recognition of liabilities and assets.

3. Disclosure requirements.

C. **NET PERIODIC PENSION COST**

Net Periodic Pension Cost is the recognized cost of the plan for the period. Note that pension cost may be an expense for the period (e.g., pension cost related to administrative or marketing personnel) or it may be inventoriable as manufacturing overhead (e.g., pension cost related to factory personnel). Pension cost consists of six components.

1. **SERVICE COST** The service cost component is the actuarial present value of benefits attributed by the pension benefit formula to the employee's service during the period (i.e., the benefits earned during the period).

   a. **ACTUARIAL ASSUMPTIONS** Service costs are based on actuarial assumptions (reflecting time value of money, mortality, turnover, early retirement, etc.).

b. **FUTURE COMPENSATION** Service costs reflect future compensation levels to the extent that the pension benefit formula defines pension benefits as a function of future compensation levels.

2. **INTEREST ON PBO** This component is the increase in the projected benefit obligation due to the passage of time. The interest rate to be used in the calculation is the rate at which the pension benefit could be effectively settled (i.e., the assumed discount rate). This same assumed discount rate is used in the measurement of the projected, accumulated, and vested benefit obligations, and the service cost component of net periodic pension cost.

COMPONENTS OF THE EMPLOYER'S NET PERIODIC PENSION COST

S SERVICE COST (+)

I INTEREST ON PBO (+)

P PLAN ASSET RETURN (−)

P PRIOR SVC COST AMORTZ (+)

A ACTUARIAL GAINS (−)
LOSSES (+)

FASB ADJUSTMENT ASSET (−)
OBLIGATION (+)

NET PENSION EXPENSE

---

3. **PLAN ASSET ACTUAL RETURN** This component of net periodic pension cost reduces the pension cost for the period. It is based on the fair value of plan assets at the beginning and end of the period, adjusted for contributions and benefit payments. Algebraically,

ARPA = End FV − Beg. FV − C + B

Where: ARPA = Actual return on plan assets
End FV = FV of plan assets at end of period
Beg. FV = FV of plan assets at beginning of period
C = Contributions to the plan during the period
B = Benefits paid during the period

NOTE: For purposes of presenting the net periodic pension cost, SFAS 87 requires the disclosure of the actual return on plan assets, as indicated in this paragraph. However, net periodic pension cost is subsequently adjusted for the difference between actual return and expected return. The net effect of this is that net pension cost for any given period reflects the expected return for that period. The difference between the expected and actual return is deferred and subject to amortization in future periods.

EXAMPLE 1 ♦ PLAN ASSET ACTUAL RETURN

The following facts pertain to the ABC Co. pension plan for 20X7.

Expected return on plan assets	15%
FV of plan assets, on 1/1/X7	$100,000
on 12/31/X7	$130,000
Contributions to pension plan	$ 14,000
Benefits paid to retired employees	$ 8,000

REQUIRED: Determine the actual return on plan assets (ARPA) component of net pension cost for 20X7. Assume contribution and benefit payments were made at year-end.

SOLUTION: ARPA = $130,000 − $100,000 − $14,000 + $8,000 = $24,000

4. **PRIOR SERVICE COST AMORTIZATION** This is the spreading of the cost of retroactive benefits generated by a plan amendment (including initiation of a plan) that granted increased benefits based on service rendered in prior periods.

a. **COST OF RETROACTIVE BENEFITS** The cost of these retroactive benefits is the increase in the projected benefit obligation at the date of the amendment. These costs are to be amortized by assigning an equal amount to *each* year of future service of *each* employee active at the date of the amendment who is expected to receive benefits under the plan. Prior service cost is incurred with the expectation that the employer will realize economic benefits in future periods. Plan amendments can reduce projected benefit obligations. These reductions reduce any other prior service costs and any excess is amortized.

b. **ALTERNATIVE APPROACHES** Since the amortization of prior service costs, under the method described in a., above, can be quite complex, SFAS 87 permits the use of alternative approaches that would amortize the cost over a shorter period of time. For example, a straight-line method that amortizes the cost over the average remaining service life of the active participants would be acceptable.

EXHIBIT 1 ♦ PRIOR SERVICE COST

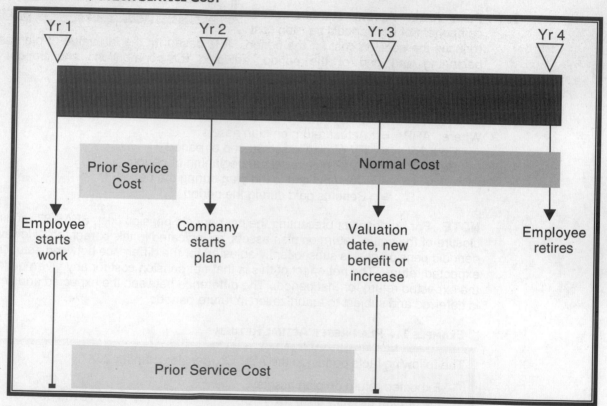

5. **ACTUARIAL GAINS AND LOSSES TO THE EXTENT RECOGNIZED** This refers to changes in the amount of either the projected benefit obligation or plan assets resulting from experience different from that assumed, and also changes in assumptions. It includes both realized and unrealized gains and losses. The gain or loss component of net periodic pension cost consists of (1) the difference between the actual return on plan assets and the expected return on plan assets, and (2) the amortization of the unrecognized net gain or loss from previous periods.

a. **GAIN OR LOSS ON PLAN ASSETS** As far as plan assets are concerned, the gain or loss is the difference between the *actual* return on assets during the period and the *expected* return on assets for the period. The expected return is determined by using the expected long-term rate of return and the market-related value of plan assets.

(1) The *expected long-term rate of return* is the average rate of earnings expected on the funds invested and includes the return expected to be available for reinvestment.

(2) *The market-related value* of plan assets can be either the fair value of the assets or a calculated value that recognizes changes in fair value in a systematic and rational manner over not more than five years (e.g., a moving average of plan asset values over the last five years).

b. **AMORTIZATION OF UNRECOGNIZED GAINS OR LOSSES** *Statement 87* does **not** require the recognition of gains or losses as a component of net periodic pension cost in the period in which they arise. However, in some cases it does require, as a minimum, amortization of any unrecognized net gain or loss to be included as a component of net periodic pension cost.

(1) This will be required if, as of the *beginning* of the year, the unrecognized net gain or loss exceeds *10 percent* of the *greater* of the projected benefit obligation or the market-related value of plan assets.

(2) The excess must be amortized, at a minimum, over the average remaining service period of the active employees expected to receive benefits under the plan. Other methods of amortization may be used, but the amortization amount computed under such methods cannot be **less** than the minimum amortization described above. In addition, the method used should be applied consistently, applied similarly to both gains and losses, and disclosed.

EXAMPLE 2 ♦ ACTUARIAL GAINS AND LOSSES TO THE EXTENT RECOGNIZED

Refer to the facts of Example 1. In addition, assume the following information as of the beginning of 20X7:

Projected benefit obligation	$135,000
Unrecognized gain (loss) from previous periods	$ 20,000
Average remaining service period of active employees	20 years

REQUIRED:

(a) Determine the difference between the actual return on plan assets and the expected return on plan assets for 20X7.

(b) Determine the amortization of the unrecognized net gain or loss from previous periods.

(c) Determine the gain or loss pension cost component recognized in 20X7.

(d) Determine the unrecognized gain(loss) carried forward to 20X8.

SOLUTION:

(a) Difference between actual and expected returns on plan assets, 20X7:

Actual return on plan assets (determined in Example 1)	$ 24,000
Expected return on plan assets ($100,000 FV on 1/1/X7 x 15%)	(15,000)
Difference between the actual and expected returns on assets	$ 9,000

(continued on next page)

9-7

(b) Amortization of the unrecognized net gain(loss) from previous periods:

Unrecognized gain (loss)	$ 20,000
10% of the greater of projected benefit obligation ($135,000) or market-related value of assets on January 1 ($100,000)	(13,500)
Unrecognized net gain(loss) subject to amortization	6,500
Divided by average remaining service period of employees	÷ 20
Amortization	$ 325

(c) Gains and losses to the extent recognized, 20X7:

Excess actual return on plan assets over expected return, deferred (determined in a)	$ 9,000
Less: Amortization of unrecognized gain (loss) from previous periods (determined in b)	(325)
Gain recognized	$ 8,675

(d) Unrecognized gain (loss) carried forward to 20X8:

Unrecognized gain (loss), 1/1/X7	$ 20,000
Less amortization to date	(325)
Plus deferred gain (loss) from difference between actual and expected returns on plan assets during 20X7	9,000
Unrecognized gain	$ 28,675

NOTE: The actual return ($24,000) is a reduction in net pension expense and the gain ($8,675) increases net pension expense. The net amount ($15,325) represents the expected return ($15,000) and the amortization of unrecognized gains ($325).

6. **FASB ADJUSTMENT: AMORTIZATION OF THE UNRECOGNIZED NET OBLIGATION (AND LOSS OR COST) OR UNRECOGNIZED NET ASSET (AND GAIN) EXISTING AT THE DATE OF THE INITIAL APPLICATION OF SFAS 87** The plan sponsor must determine, as of the measurement date for the beginning of the fiscal year in which the Statement is first applied, the amount of (a) the projected benefit obligation and (b) the fair value of plan assets plus previously recognized unfunded accrued pension cost, or less previously recognized prepaid pension cost. The difference between these two amounts, whether it represents an unrecognized net obligation (and loss or cost) or an unrecognized net asset (and gain), should be amortized on a *straight-line* basis over the *average remaining service period* of employees expected to receive benefits under the plan. However, if the average remaining service period is *less than* 15 years, the employer may elect to use a 15-year period.

EXHIBIT 2 ♦ ELEMENTS OF PENSION COST

Decreases Pension Cost	Increases Pension Cost
Plan Asset Actual Return	Service Cost
Actuarial Gain Amortized	Interest Cost
Actuarial Loss Deferred	Prior Service Cost Amortization
FASB Adjustment: Amortization of Unrecognized Net Asset	Actuarial Loss Amortized
	Actuarial Gain Deferred
	FASB Adjustment: Amortization of Unrecognized Net Obligation

D.   RECOGNITION OF LIABILITIES AND ASSETS

1.   **ACCRUED/PREPAID PENSION COST** The recognition of a liability (unfunded accrued pension cost) is required when the net periodic pension cost exceeds the amount the employer has contributed to the plan. An asset (prepaid pension cost) must be recognized when the amount contributed to the plan by the employer exceeds the net periodic pension cost recognized.

EXAMPLE 3 ◆ ACCRUED/PREPAID PENSION COST

Taylor Co. implemented a defined-benefit pension plan for its employees on January 2, 20X7 and contributed $185,000 to the plan during 20X7. The net periodic pension cost for the year was determined to be $200,000.

REQUIRED: Determine the amount of Taylor Co.'s accrued/prepaid pension cost, as of 12/31/X7.

SOLUTION:

Net periodic pension cost, 20X7	$ 200,000
Less: Contributions, 20X7	(185,000)
Accrued pension cost, 12/31/X7	$ 15,000

---

2.   **MINIMUM LIABILITY** In addition to the accrued or prepaid pension cost, if the accumulated benefit obligation exceeds the fair value of plan assets, a minimum liability must be recognized for the difference (i.e., the unfunded accumulated benefit obligation).

a.   **ADJUSTMENT** The amount of the adjustment (i.e., the additional liability) considers any existing balance of accrued or prepaid pension cost. An existing balance in the Accrued Pension Cost account *reduces* the amount of the adjustment. An existing balance in the Prepaid Pension Cost account *increases* the amount of the adjustment.

b.   **INTANGIBLE ASSET RECOGNITION** If an additional liability is recognized because of unfunded accumulated benefit obligations, an equal amount will be recognized as an intangible asset. However, this asset may not exceed the amount of unrecognized prior service cost.

c.   **RECOGNITION OF EXCESS IN OTHER COMPREHENSIVE INCOME** If any excess does occur, it must be reported, net of any related income tax effect, in other comprehensive income.

EXAMPLE 4 ◆ MINIMUM LIABILITY

Refer to the facts of Example 3. In addition, as of 12/31/X7, Taylor Co.'s accumulated benefit obligation was $225,000, the fair value of plan assets was $190,000, and the unrecognized prior service cost was $15,000.

REQUIRED: Determine as of 12/31/X7, Taylor Co.'s 20X7 (a) minimum liability required, (b) the additional liability, if any, required, (c) the amount, if any, of intangible asset to be recognized, and (d) the amount, if any, of minimum liability adjustments to be reported in other comprehensive income (ignore income taxes).

(continued on next page)

SOLUTIONS:

(a) Minimum liability:

Accumulated benefit obligation	$ 225,000
Less: FV of plan assets	(190,000)
Unfunded accumulated benefit obligation (minimum liability)	$ 35,000

(b) Additional liability:

Minimum liability required (determined in a)	$ 35,000
Less: Accrued pension cost (determined in Example 3)	(15,000)
Additional liability required	$ 20,000

(c) Intangible asset:

As determined in (b) above, additional liability of $20,000 is greater than the unrecognized prior service costs of $15,000; thus the intangible asset recognized is limited to $15,000.

(d) Minimum liability adjustment to be reported in other comprehensive income:

Additional liability required (determined in b)	$ 20,000
Less: Unrecognized prior service costs	(15,000)
Adjustment to other comprehensive income	$ 5,000

EXAMPLE 5 ♦ COMPREHENSIVE DEFINED BENEFIT PENSION PLAN

XYZ Corp. has an employee who is estimated to be retiring in 4 years (on 12/31/X4). This employee is entered into a defined benefit pension plan at 1/1/X1. The plan pays a lump sum upon retirement of $1,000 for each year of service after the date of entry into the plan. Assume an appropriate discount rate (from an actuary) of 10%, and an expected and actual return on plan assets of 10%. Additionally, assume funding by XYZ Corp. of $800 at 12/31/X1 and $800 at 12/31/X2. On 1/1/X3 XYZ Corp. amended the plan to pay $1,500 for each year of service upon retirement, retroactive for one year of prior service. Funding at 12/31/X3 was $1,800 and at 12/31/X4 was $1,487.20.

NOTE: This example accounts for one employee enrolled in a pension plan. The example could easily be extended to combined groups of similar employees to account for all participants of a plan. Additionally, although pensions would usually pay participants on a periodic basis after retirement, these payments could be transformed into an equivalent lump-sum distribution at the date of retirement.

REQUIRED: Show the calculation of the projected benefit obligation and the net periodic pension cost and the necessary journal entries at 12/31/X1, 12/31/X2, 12/31/X3, and 12/31/X4.

SOLUTION:

12/31/X1	Projected benefit obligation	
	(P.V. at 10% of $1,000 in 3 years = .751315 x $1,000)	$ 751.31
	Service cost (.751315 x $1,000)	$ 751.31
	Interest on projected benefit obligation	0
	Expected return on plan assets	0
	Prior service cost	0
	Gains and losses	0
	Net periodic pension cost calculation	$ 751.31

(continued on next page)

12/31/X1	Pension Expense (or manufacturing overhead) Prepaid/Accrued Pension Cost Cash To record 20X1 pension expense and funding.	751.31 48.69 	 800.00

12/31/X2	Projected benefit obligation (P.V. at 10% of $2,000 in 2 years = .826446 x $2,000)		$1,652.89
	Service cost (.826446 x $1,000)		$ 826.45
	Interest on (beginning) projected benefit obligation (10% x $751.31)		75.13
	Actual return on plan assets (10% x $800)		(80.00)
	Prior service costs		0
	Gains and losses		0
	Net periodic pension cost calculation		$ 821.58

12/31/X2	Pension Expense (or manufacturing overhead)
	    Prepaid/Accrued Pension Cost
	    Cash
	To record 20X2 pension expense and funding.
		821.58
		
			21.58
			800.00

12/31/X3	Projected benefit obligation [P.V. at 10% in 1 year = .909091 x ($1,000 + $1,500 + $1,500)]		$3,636.36
	Service cost (.909091 x $1,500)		$1,363.64
	Interest on projected benefit obligation (10% x 2,066.11*)		206.61
	Actual return on plan assets [10% x ($800 + $800 + 80)]		(168.00)
	Amortization of prior service costs ($413.22** ÷ 2)		206.61
	Gains and losses		0
	Net periodic pension cost calculation		$1,608.86

*   Prior year's adjusted projected benefit obligation (.826446 x $2,500 = $2,066.11)
**   Prior service costs = P.V. of $500 = .826446 x $500 = $413.22

12/31/X3	Pension Expense (or manufacturing overhead) Prepaid/Accrued Pension Cost Cash To record 20X3 pension expense and funding.	1,608.86 191.14 	 1,800.00

12/31/X4	Projected benefit obligation (P.V. at 10% of $5,500 in 0 years)		$5,500.00
	Service cost		$1,500.00
	Interest on projected benefit obligation (10% x $3,636.36)		363.64
	ARPA [10% ($800 + $800 + $80 + $1,800 + $168)]		(364.80)
	Amortization of prior service costs ($413.22 ÷ 2)		206.61
	Gains and losses		0
	Net periodic pension cost calculation		$1,705.45

12/31/X4	Pension Expense (or manufacturing overhead) Accrued/Prepaid Pension Cost Cash To record 20X4 pension expense and funding.	1,705.45 	 218.25 1,487.20

SUMMARY:	Total pension expense ($751.31 + $821.58 + $1,608.86 + $1,705.45)		$4,887.20
	Total return on plan assets ($0 + $80 + $168 + $364.80)		$ 612.80
	Total funding (cash) payments ($800 + $800 + $1,800 + $1,487.20)		4,887.20
	Amount due to retiring employee		$5,500.00

III. DEFINED CONTRIBUTION PLANS

A. DEFINITION
Defined contribution plans are plans in which the terms specify how *contributions* to the individual participants' accounts are to be determined (**not** the benefits to be received).

B. BENEFITS
The following determines benefits of participants:

1. The *amounts contributed* to the participants' account(s)

2. *Returns* earned on investments of contributions

3. *Allocations* of forfeitures of other participants' benefits

C. NET PENSION COST
The net pension cost should be the following:

1. The contribution called for by the plan for the period in which the individual renders services.

2. If the plan calls for contributions for periods after the individual has rendered services (e.g., after retirement), the cost should be accrued during the employee's service period.

IV. SETTLEMENTS AND CURTAILMENTS OF DEFINED BENEFIT PENSION PLANS AND TERMINATION BENEFITS (SFAS 88)

A. DEFINITIONS

1. **SETTLEMENT**

   a. Is an irrevocable action

   b. Relieves the employer or plan of primary responsibility for a benefit obligation

   c. Eliminates significant risks related to the obligation and the assets used to effect the settlement

2. **CURTAILMENT** Curtailment is an event that significantly reduces the expected years of future service of present employees or eliminates for a significant number of employees the accrual of defined benefits for some or all of their future services.

3. **RELATIONSHIP BETWEEN SETTLEMENTS AND CURTAILMENTS**

   a. **PURCHASE ANNUITY CONTRACTS** If an employer purchases nonparticipating annuity contracts for vested benefits and continues to provide defined benefits for future service, either in the same plan or in a successor plan, a settlement has occurred but **not** a curtailment.

   b. **BENEFITS REDUCED** If benefits to be accumulated in future periods are reduced (for example, because half of a work force is dismissed or a plant is closed), but the plan remains in existence and continues to pay benefits, to invest assets, and to receive contributions, a curtailment has occurred but **not** a settlement.

   c. **PLAN TERMINATED** If a plan is terminated (that is, the obligation is settled and the plan ceases to exist) and not replaced by a successor defined benefit plan, *both* a settlement and a curtailment have occurred (whether or not the employees continue to work for the employer).

B.   SETTLEMENTS

A gain or loss must be recognized in earnings when a pension obligation is settled. The amount of the gain or loss is limited to the unrecognized net gain or loss from realized or unrealized changes in the amount of either projected benefit obligation or plan assets resulting from experience different from that assumed or from changes in assumptions. In simple language, either all or a pro rata share of the unrecognized gain or loss is recognized when a plan is settled. If full settlement takes place, all unrecognized net gains or losses are recognized. If only a portion of the plan is settled, a pro rata share of the unrecognized net gains or losses is recognized.

C.   CURTAILMENTS

The unrecognized prior service cost associated with years of service no longer expected to be rendered as the result of the curtailment is a *loss*. Unrecognized prior service cost includes any remaining unrecognized net obligation existing at the date of initial application of SFAS 87, *Employers' Accounting for Pensions*. Note, in the case of a curtailment, the projected benefit obligation may also be decreased or increased.

D.   TERMINATION BENEFITS

Termination benefits may be either special termination benefits offered only for a short period of time or contractual termination benefits required by the terms of a plan only if a specific event, such as a plant closing, occurs. When an employer offers special termination benefits to an employee, the employer must recognize a liability and a loss when the employee accepts the offer and the amount can be reasonably estimated. If the employer offers a contractual termination benefit, the employer must recognize a liability and a loss when it is probable that employees will be entitled to benefits and the amount can reasonably be estimated. The cost of termination benefits recognized as a liability and a loss includes the amount of any lump-sum payments and the present value of any expected future payments.

E.   DISPOSAL OF A SEGMENT

If the gain or loss from a settlement or curtailment is directly related to a disposal of a segment of a business, it should be included in determining the gain or loss associated with that event and recognized pursuant to APB 30.

V.   POSTRETIREMENT BENEFITS OTHER THAN PENSIONS (SFAS 106)

A.   OVERVIEW

The fundamental objective in accounting for and reporting of postretirement benefits other than pensions is basically the same as for accounting and reporting of pension benefits; that is, to provide a measure of the costs that reflects the terms of the underlying agreement.

B.   ATTRIBUTION METHOD

Both accounting for pensions under SFAS 87 and accounting for postretirement benefits other than pensions under SFAS 106 assign benefit costs on a years-of-service approach. These costs should be allocated over the approximate service years of employees.

C.   NET POSTRETIREMENT BENEFIT COST

The components of the calculation of net benefit cost for postretirement benefits are essentially the same as the components for the calculation of net period pension cost, with some differences. Exhibit 3 summarizes the components of net benefit cost, emphasizing the differences in terminology and the differences in the treatment of transition amounts.

1.   TERMINOLOGY There are some modifications in terminology due to the different benefit agreements being measured.

2.   TRANSITION AMOUNTS There are differences in the treatment of transition amounts.

a.   AMORTIZATION OVER 20 INSTEAD OF 15 YEARS In accounting for pension costs as described earlier in this chapter, the unrecognized net obligation (and loss or cost) or unrecognized net asset (and gain) existing at the date of the initial application of

SFAS 87 is amortized on a straight-line basis over the employees' average remaining service period. If the average remaining service period is less than 15 years, the employer may elect to use a 15-year period. In accounting for postretirement benefits other than pensions, amortization of the unrecognized net obligation (and loss or cost) or unrecognized net asset (and gain) existing at the date of the initial application of SFAS 106 is amortized on a straight-line basis over the employees' average remaining service period. However, if the average remaining service period is less than 20 years, the employer may elect to use a 20-year period.

b. **OPTION OF IMMEDIATE RECOGNITION** The transition amounts for postretirement benefits other than pensions may be recognized immediately in net income as a change in accounting principle, as an alternative to amortization. This option is not available in accounting for pension costs.

EXHIBIT 3 ♦ COMPONENTS OF BENEFIT COST UNDER SFAS 87 AND SFAS 106, WITH EMPHASIS ON DIFFERENCES

	POSTRETIREMENT BENEFITS OTHER THAN PENSIONS	NON-PAY-RELATED PENSION PLANS*
	SFAS 106	**SFAS 87**
1. Service Cost	Actuarial present value of **postretirement** benefit obligation attributed to current period.	Actuarial present value of **pension** benefit obligation attributed to current period.
2. Interest Cost	Accumulated Benefit Obligation multiplied by settlement rate.	Accumulated Benefit Obligation multiplied by settlement rate.
3. Actual Return on Plan Assets	Change in fair value of plan assets during the period after adjusting for contributions and benefit payments.	Change in fair value of plan assets during the period after adjusting for contributions and benefit payments.
4. Prior Service Cost	Change in Accumulated Benefit Obligation for new or amended benefits granted to plan participants.	Change in Accumulated Benefit Obligation for new or amended benefits granted to plan participants.
5. Gains and Losses	Change in Accumulated Benefit Obligation and plan assets from experience different from that assumed or from changes in assumptions. May be recognized immediately or delayed with minimum amortization required.	Change in Accumulated Benefit Obligation and plan assets from experience different from that assumed or from changes in assumptions. May be recognized immediately or delayed with minimum amortization required.
6. Transition Amounts	Overfunded or underfunded Accumulated Benefit Obligation at transition to implementing SFAS 106. **May delay or immediately recognize** amounts. If delay, amortize over service lives with option for **20-year amortization** period when service lives are less than 20 years. **If immediate, recognize in net income as a change in accounting principle.**	Overfunded or underfunded Accumulated Benefit Obligation at transition to implementing SFAS 87. **Must delay recognition** and amortize over service lives with option for **15-year amortization** period when service lives are less than 15 years.
= Net Cost	Net **Postretirement Benefit** Cost	Net **Period Pension** Cost

* Do not be confused about the use of the Accumulated Benefit Obligation in this comparison table. When pension plans are pay related, the Projected Benefit Obligation would be used for interest calculations, transition amounts, etc.

D.   RECOGNITION OF LIABILITIES AND ASSETS
A liability or an asset is recognized for a postretirement benefit plan in the same manner as for a pension plan, with the exception that there is *no minimum liability* requirement in SFAS 106 and thus no intangible asset requirement.

EXHIBIT 4 ♦ LIABILITY/ASSET RECOGNITION UNDER SFAS 87 AND SFAS 106, WITH EMPHASIS ON DIFFERENCES

	POSTRETIREMENT BENEFITS OTHER THAN PENSIONS SFAS 106	NON-PAY-RELATED PENSION PLANS* SFAS 87
Accrued/Prepaid Cost	Accrued postretirement benefit cost (liability) recognized when net cost exceeds the amount contributed. Prepaid postretirement benefit cost (asset) recognized when amount contributed exceeds net cost.	Unfunded accrued pension cost (liability) recognized when net periodic pension cost exceeds amount contributed. Prepaid pension cost (asset) recognized when amount contributed exceeds net periodic pension cost.
Minimum Liability	***No minimum liability required.***	Minimum liability is excess of Accumulated Benefit Obligation over fair value of plan assets at financial statement date.
Intangible Asset	***No intangible asset required.***	Intangible asset is the amount of additional liability needed to equal the minimum liability. Intangible asset may not exceed the amount of unrecognized prior service cost; if excess exists, it is reported net of income tax effect in other comprehensive income.

* Do not be confused about the use of the Accumulated Benefit Obligation in this comparison table. When pension plans are pay related, the Projected Benefit Obligation would be used for interest calculations, transition amounts, etc.

VI.   DISCLOSURES (SFAS 132)

A.   PURPOSE
The disclosures required by SFAS 132 are designed to make the disclosures that companies make about their pension and nonpension benefit plans more uniform and to provide better information to investors about the economics of the plans.

B.   REQUIRED DISCLOSURES
The following disclosures are required by SFAS 132.

1.   A reconciliation of beginning and ending balances of the benefit obligation showing separately the effects during the period of the following components: service cost, interest cost, contributions by plan participants, actuarial gains and losses, foreign currency exchange rate changes, benefits paid, plan amendments, business combinations, divestitures, curtailments, settlements, and special termination benefits.

2.   A reconciliation of beginning and ending balances of the fair value of plan assets showing separately the effects during the period attributable to the following: actual return on plan assets, foreign currency exchange rate changes, contributions by the employer, contributions by employees or retirees, benefits paid, business combinations, divestitures, curtailments, and settlements.

3.   The funded status of the plans, the amounts not recognized in the balance sheet, and the amounts recognized in the balance sheet including:

a. The amount of any unamortized prior service cost.

b. The amount of any unrecognized net gain or loss including asset gains and losses not yet reflected in the market-related value.

c. The amount of any remaining unamortized transition amount from initially applying SFAS 87 or SFAS 106.

d. The net pension and other postretirement benefit prepaid assets or accrued liabilities.

e. Any intangible asset or accumulated element of other comprehensive income recognized under SFAS 87 because of an underfunded pension obligation (the minimum liability computation of SFAS 87).

4. The amount of net periodic benefit cost recognized showing separately the following components: service cost, interest cost, expected return on plan assets, amount of gains and losses recognized, amortization of prior service cost, and amount of gain or loss recognized because of a settlement or curtailment.

5. Amount included in other comprehensive income for the period because of a change in the additional minimum pension liability.

6. Key assumptions used in the computations including the weighed-average discount rate, the weighted-average rate of compensation increase, the weighted-average expected long-term rate of return on plan assets.

7. Assumed heath care cost trend rate(s) for the next year and a general description of the direction and pattern of change as well as the ultimate trend rate(s) and when the rate is expected to occur.

8. The effect of a one-percentage-point increase and the effect of a one-percentage-point decrease in the assumed health care costs trend rates on:

a. The aggregate of the service and interest cost; and

b. The accumulated postretirement benefit obligations for health care benefits.

9. The amounts and types of securities of the employer and related parties included in plan assets, the approximate amount of future annual benefits of plan participants covered by insurance contracts issued by the employer or related parties and the plan during the period.

10. Any alternative amortization method used to amortize prior service amounts or unrecognized actuarial gains and losses.

11. Any substantive commitment, such as a past practice or history of regular benefit increases, used as the basis for accounting for the benefit obligation.

12. The cost of providing special or contractual termination benefits recognized during the period and a description of the nature of the event.

13. An explanation of any significant change in the benefit obligation or plan assets not readily apparent from the other disclosures.

CHAPTER 9—PENSIONS & OTHER POSTRETIREMENT BENEFITS

PROBLEM 9-1 MULTIPLE CHOICE QUESTIONS (68 to 85 minutes)

1. The following information pertains to Lee Corp.'s defined benefit pension plan for 1997:

Service cost	$160,000
Actual and expected gain on plan assets	35,000
Unexpected loss on plan assets related to a 1997 disposal of a subsidiary	40,000
Amortization of unrecognized prior service cost	5,000
Annual interest on pension obligation	50,000

What amount should Lee report as pension expense in its 1997 income statement?
a. $250,000
b. $220,000
c. $210,000
d. $180,000   (5/92, PII, #14, amended, 2646)

2. The following information pertains to the 1997 activity of Ral Corp.'s defined benefit pension plan:

Service cost	$300,000
Return on plan assets	80,000
Interest cost on pension benefit obligation	164,000
Amortization of actuarial loss	30,000
Amortization of unrecognized net obligation	70,000

Ral's 1997 pension cost was
a. $316,000.
b. $484,000.
c. $574,000.
d. $644,000.   (5/91, PII, #17, amended, 1221)

3. Visor Co. maintains a defined benefit pension plan for its employees. The service cost component of Visor's net periodic pension cost is measured using the
a. Unfunded accumulated benefit obligation.
b. Unfunded vested benefit obligation.
c. Projected benefit obligation.
d. Expected return on plan assets.
     (11/93, Theory, #30, 4535)

4. Effective January 1, 1997, Flood Co. established a defined benefit pension plan with no retroactive benefits. The first of the required equal annual contributions was paid on December 31, 1997. A 10% discount rate was used to calculate service cost and a 10% rate of return was assumed for plan assets. All information on covered employees for 1997 and 1998 is the same. How should the service cost for 1998 compare with 1997, and should the 1997 balance sheet report an accrued or a prepaid pension cost?

	Service cost for 1998 compared to 1997	Pension cost reported on the 1997 balance sheet
a.	Equal to	Accrued
b.	Equal to	Prepaid
c.	Greater than	Accrued
d.	Greater than	Prepaid

     (11/90, Theory, #21, amended, 2059)

5. Interest cost included in the net pension cost recognized by an employer sponsoring a defined benefit pension plan represents the
a. Amortization of the discount on unrecognized prior service costs.
b. Increase in the fair value of plan assets due to the passage of time.
c. Increase in the projected benefit obligation due to the passage of time.
d. Shortage between the expected and actual returns on plan assets. (5/92, Theory, #20, 2713)

6. For a defined benefit pension plan, the discount rate used to calculate the projected benefit obligation is determined by the

	Expected return on plan assets	Actual return on plan assets
a.	Yes	Yes
b.	No	No
c.	Yes	No
d.	No	Yes

     (5/91, Theory, #37, 2057)

7. The following information pertains to Gali Co.'s defined benefit pension plan for 1994:

Fair value of plan assets, beginning of year	$350,000
Fair value of plan assets, end of year	525,000
Employer contributions	110,000
Benefits paid	85,000

In computing pension expense, what amount should Gali use as actual return on plan assets?
a. $ 65,000
b. $150,000
c. $175,000
d. $260,000   (5/95, FAR, #39, 5575)

8. On July 31, 1997, Tern Co. amended its single employee defined benefit pension plan by granting increased benefits for services provided prior to 1997. This prior service cost will be reflected in the financial statement(s) for
a. Years before 1997 only.
b. Year 1997 only.
c. Year 1997, and years before and following 1997.
d. Year 1997, and following years only.
(11/92, Theory, #26, amended, 3459)

9. Jan Corp. amended its defined benefit pension plan, granting a total credit of $100,000 to four employees for services rendered prior to the plan's adoption. The employees, A, B, C, and D, are expected to retire from the company as follows:

"A" will retire after three years.
"B" and "C" will retire after five years.
"D" will retire after seven years.

What is the amount of prior service cost amortization in the first year?
a. $0
b. $ 5,000
c. $20,000
d. $25,000   (R/99, FAR, #13, 6782)

10. Which of the following components should be included in net pension cost by an employer sponsoring a defined benefit pension plan?

	Amortization of unrecognized prior service cost	Fair value of plan assets
a.	Yes	No
b.	Yes	Yes
c.	No	Yes
d.	No	No

(5/89, Theory, #20, 2069)

11. As of December 31, 1987, the projected benefit obligation and plan assets of a noncontributory defined benefit plan sponsored by Reed Inc., were:

Projected benefit obligation	$ 780,000
Plan assets at fair value	(600,000)
Initial unfunded obligation	$ 180,000

At December 31, 1987, all amounts accrued as net periodic pension cost had been contributed to the plan. The average remaining service period of active plan participants expected to receive benefits was estimated to be 10 years at the date of transition. Some participants' estimated service periods are 20

and 25 years. To minimize an accrual for pension cost, what amount of unrecognized net obligation should Reed amortize?
a. $ 7,200
b. $ 9,000
c. $12,000
d. $18,000   (5/89, PI, #35, amended, 1226)

12. The following information pertains to Kane Co.'s defined benefit pension plan:

Prepaid pension cost, January 1, 1994	$ 2,000
Service cost	19,000
Interest cost	38,000
Actual return on plan assets	22,000
Amortization of unrecognized prior service cost	52,000
Employer contributions	40,000

The fair value of plan assets exceeds the accumulated benefit obligation. In its December 31, 1994 balance sheet, what amount should Kane report as unfunded accrued pension cost?
a. $45,000
b. $49,000
c. $67,000
d. $87,000   (5/95, FAR, #18, 5554)

13. On January 2, 1995, Loch Co. established a noncontributory defined-benefit pension plan covering all employees and contributed $400,000 to the plan. At December 31, 1995, Loch determined that the 1995 service and interest costs on the plan were $720,000. The expected and the actual rate of return on plan assets for 1995 was 10%. There are no other components of Loch's pension expense. What amount should Loch report as accrued pension cost in its December 31, 1995 balance sheet?
a. $280,000
b. $320,000
c. $360,000
d. $720,000   (R/00, FAR, #7, 6902)

14. A company that maintains a defined benefit pension plan for its employees reports an unfunded accrued pension cost. This cost represents the amount that the
a. Cumulative net pension cost accrued exceeds contributions to the plan.
b. Cumulative net pension cost accrued exceeds the vested benefit obligation.
c. Vested benefit obligation exceeds plan assets.
d. Vested benefit obligation exceeds contributions to the plan.   (11/93, Theory, #29, 4534)

15. Webb Co. implemented a defined benefit pension plan for its employees on January 1, 1995. During 1995 and 1996, Webb's contributions fully funded the plan. The following data are provided for 1998 and 1997:

	1998 Estimated	1997 Actual
Projected benefit obligation, December 31	$750,000	$700,000
Accumulated benefit obligation, December 31	520,000	500,000
Plan assets at fair value, December 31	675,000	600,000
Projected benefit obligation in excess of plan assets	75,000	100,000
Pension expense	90,000	75,000
Employer's contribution	?	50,000

What amount should Webb contribute in order to report an accrued pension liability of $15,000 in its December 31, 1998 balance sheet?

a. $ 50,000
b. $ 60,000
c. $ 75,000
d. $100,000   (5/92, PI, #25, amended, 2593)

16. Cey Company has a defined benefit pension plan. Cey's policy is to fund net periodic pension cost annually, payment to an independent trustee being made two months after the end of each year. Data relating to the pension plan for 1996 are as follows:

Net pension cost for 1996	$190,000
Unrecognized prior service cost, 12/31/96	150,000
Accumulated benefit obligation, 12/31/96	480,000
Fair value of plan assets, 12/31/96	500,000

How much should appear on Cey's balance sheet at December 31, 1996, for pension liability?

	Current	Noncurrent
a.	$0	$480,000
b.	$0	$330,000
c.	$190,000	$150,000
d.	$190,000	$0

(5/87, PI, #15, amended, 1228)

17. At December 31, 1997, the following information was provided by the Kerr Corp. pension plan administrator:

Fair value of plan assets	$3,450,000
Accumulated benefit obligation	4,300,000
Projected benefit obligation	5,700,000

What is the amount of the pension liability that should be shown on Kerr's December 31, 1997 balance sheet?

a. $5,700,000
b. $2,250,000
c. $1,400,000
d. $ 850,000   (11/90, PI, #15, amended, 1222)

18. On January 2, 1992, Loch Co. established a noncontributory defined benefit plan covering all employees and contributed $1,000,000 to the plan. At December 31, 1992, Loch determined that the 1992 service and interest costs on the plan were $620,000. The expected and the actual rate of return on plan assets for 1992 was 10%. There are no other components of Loch's pension expense. What amount should Loch report in its December 31, 1992 balance sheet as prepaid pension cost?

a. $280,000
b. $380,000
c. $480,000
d. $620,000   (11/93, PI, #26, 4395)

19. On January 2, 1992, East Corp. adopted a defined benefit pension plan. The plan's service cost of $150,000 was fully funded at the end of 1992. Prior service cost was funded by a contribution of $60,000 in 1992. Amortization of prior service cost was $24,000 for 1992. At December 31, 1992, what amount should East report as prepaid pension cost?

a. $90,000
b. $84,000
c. $60,000
d. $36,000   (5/93, PI, #28, 4070)

20. Dell Co. adopted a defined benefit pension plan on January 1, 1997. Dell amortizes the prior service cost over 16 years and funds prior service cost by making equal payments to the fund trustee at the end of each of the first ten years. The service (normal) cost is fully funded at the end of each year. The following data are available for 1997:

Service (normal) cost for 1997	$220,000
Prior service cost:	
Amortized	83,400
Funded	114,400

Dell's prepaid pension cost at December 31, 1997, is

a. $114,400.
b. $ 83,400.
c. $ 31,000.
d. $0.   (5/91, PI, #32, amended, 1220)

21. Payne Inc., implemented a defined-benefit pension plan for its employees on January 2, 1993. The following data are provided for 1993, as of December 31, 1993:

Accumulated benefit obligation	$103,000
Plan assets at fair value	78,000
Net periodic pension cost	90,000
Employer's contribution	70,000

What amount should Payne record as additional minimum pension liability at December 31, 1993?
a. $0
b. $ 5,000
c. $20,000
d. $45,000   (5/94, FAR, #28, 4843)

22. An employer sponsoring a defined benefit pension plan is subject to the minimum pension liability recognition requirement. An additional liability must be recorded equal to the unfunded
a. Accumulated benefit obligation plus the previously recognized accrued pension cost.
b. Accumulated benefit obligation less the previously recognized accrued pension cost.
c. Projected benefit obligation plus the previously recognized accrued pension cost.
d. Projected benefit obligation less the previously recognized accrued pension cost.
          (11/91, Theory, #31, 2539)

23. Mercer Inc., maintains a defined benefit pension plan for its employees. As of December 31, 1997, the market value of the plan assets is less than the accumulated benefit obligation, and less than the projected benefit obligation. The projected benefit obligation exceeds the accumulated benefit obligation. In its balance sheet as of December 31, 1997, Mercer should report a minimum liability in the amount of the
a. Excess of the projected benefit obligation over the fair value of the plan assets.
b. Excess of the accumulated benefit obligation over the fair value of the plan assets.
c. Projected benefit obligation.
d. Accumulated benefit obligation.
          (11/90, Theory, #20, amended, 2058)

24. Barrett Co. maintains a defined benefit pension plan for its employees. At each balance sheet date, Barrett should report a minimum liability at least equal to the
a. Accumulated benefit obligation.
b. Projected benefit obligation.
c. Unfunded accumulated benefit obligation.
d. Unfunded projected benefit obligation.
          (5/90, Theory, #37, 2066)

ITEMS 25 AND 26 are based on the following:

The following information pertains to Hall Co.'s defined-benefit pension plan at December 31, 1994:

Unfunded accumulated benefit obligation	$25,000
Unrecognized prior service cost	12,000
Net periodic pension cost	8,000

Hall made no contributions to the pension plan during 1994.

25. At December 31, 1994, what amount should Hall record as additional pension liability?
a. $ 5,000
b. $13,000
c. $17,000
d. $25,000   (11/95, FAR, #14, 6096)

26. In its December 31, 1994, other comprehensive income, what amount should Hall report as excess of additional pension liability over unrecognized prior service cost?
a. $ 5,000
b. $13,000
c. $17,000
d. $25,000   (11/95, FAR, #15, amended, 6097)

27. The following data relates to Nola Co.'s defined benefit pension plan as of December 31, 1993:

Unfunded accumulated benefit obligation	$140,000
Unrecognized prior service cost	45,000
Accrued pension cost	80,000

What amount should Nola report as excess of additional pension liability over unrecognized prior service cost in other comprehensive income?
a. $15,000
b. $35,000
c. $95,000
d. $175,000   (11/94, FAR, #34, amended, 5296)

28. Nome Co. sponsors a defined benefit plan covering all employees. Benefits are based on years of service and compensation levels at the time of retirement. Nome determined that, as of September 30, 1992, its accumulated benefit obligation was $380,000, and its plan assets had a $290,000 fair value. Nome's September 30, 1992, trial balance showed prepaid pension cost of $20,000. In its September 30, 1992, balance sheet, what amount should Nome report as additional pension liability?
a. $110,000
b. $360,000
c. $380,000
d. $400,000   (11/92, PI, #25, 3258)

29. On June 1, 1995, Ward Corp. established a defined benefit pension plan for its employees. The following information was available at May 31, 1997:

Projected benefit obligation	$14,500,000
Accumulated benefit obligation	12,000,000
Unfunded accrued pension cost	200,000
Plan assets at fair market value	7,000,000
Unrecognized prior service cost	2,550,000

To report the proper pension liability in Ward's May 31, 1997 balance sheet, what is the amount of the adjustment required?
a. $2,250,000
b. $4,750,000
c. $4,800,000
d. $7,300,000   (11/91, PI, #23, amended, 2411)

30. An employer's obligation for postretirement health benefits that are expected to be provided to or for an employee must be fully accrued by the date the
a. Employee is fully eligible for benefits.
b. Employee retires.
c. Benefits are utilized.
d. Benefits are paid.   (5/94, FAR, #27, 4842)

31. Bounty Co. provides postretirement health care benefits to employees who have completed at least 10 years service and are aged 55 years or older when retiring. Employees retiring from Bounty have a median age of 62, and no one has worked beyond age 65. Fletcher is hired at 48 years old. The attribution period for accruing Bounty's expected postretirement health care benefit obligation to Fletcher is during the period when Fletcher is age
a. 48 to 65.
b. 48 to 58.
c. 55 to 65.
d. 55 to 62.   (11/93, Theory, #27, 4532)

32. A company with a defined benefit pension plan must disclose in the notes to its financial statements a reconciliation of

a. The vested and nonvested benefit obligation of its pension plan with the accumulated benefit obligation.
b. The accrued or prepaid pension cost reported in its balance sheet with the pension expense reported in its income statement.
c. The accumulated benefit obligation of its pension plan with its projected benefit obligation.
d. The funded status of its pension plan with the accrued or prepaid pension cost reported in its balance sheet.   (5/95, FAR, #57, 5593)

33. The following information pertains to Seda Co.'s pension plan:

Actuarial estimate of projected benefit obligation at 1/1/97	$72,000
Assumed discount rate	10%
Service costs for 1997	18,000
Pension benefits paid during 1997	15,000

If no change in actuarial estimates occurred during 1997, Seda's projected benefit obligation at December 31, 1997 was
a. $64,200.
b. $75,000.
c. $79,200.
d. $82,200.   (11/90, FAR, #16, amended, 1223)

34. Which of the following information should be included in disclosures by a company providing health care benefits to its retirees?

I. The assumed health care cost trend rate used to measure the expected cost of benefits covered by the plan
II. The accumulated post-retirement benefit obligation

a. I and II
b. I only
c. II only
d. Neither I nor II
        (5/93, Theory, #30, amended, 4218)

OTHER OBJECTIVE FORMAT QUESTION

PROBLEM 9-2 (40 to 50 minutes)

The following information pertains to Sparta Co.'s defined benefit pension plan.

Discount rate	8%
Expected rate of return	10%
Average service life	12 years

At January 1, 1992:

Projected benefit obligation	600,000
Fair value of pension plan assets	720,000
Unrecognized prior service cost	240,000
Unamortized prior pension gain	96,000

At December 31, 1992:

Projected benefit obligation	910,000
Fair value of pension plan assets	825,000

Service cost for 1992 was $90,000. There were no contributions made or benefits paid during the year. Sparta's unfunded accrued pension liability was $8,000 at January 1, 1992. Sparta uses the straight-line method of amortization over the maximum period permitted.

REQUIRED:

a. FOR ITEMS 1 THROUGH 5, calculate the amounts to be recognized as components of Sparta's unfunded accrued pension liability at December 31, 1992.

1. Interest cost.
2. Expected return on plan assets.
3. Actual return on plan assets.
4. Amortization of prior service costs.
5. Minimum amortization of unrecognized pension gain.

b. FOR ITEMS 6 THROUGH 10, determine whether the component increases (I) or decreases (D) Sparta's unfunded accrued pension liability.

6. Service cost.
7. Deferral of gain on pension plan assets.
8. Actual return on plan assets.
9. Amortization of prior service costs.
10. Amortization of unrecognized pension gain.

(5/93, PI, #4 (61-70), 4100-4109)

ESSAY QUESTIONS

ESSAY 9-3 (15 to 20 minutes)

Wyatt, CPA, is meeting with Brown, the controller of Emco, a wholesaler, to discuss the accounting issues relating to pensions. Brown is aware of Statement of Financial Accounting Standards (FAS) No. 106, *Employers' Accounting for Postretirement Benefits Other Than Pensions*, but is uncertain about the benefits and beneficiaries covered by this Statement. Brown believes that, regardless of FAS 106, no estimate of postretirement obligation can be reasonable because it would be based on too many assumptions. For this reason, Brown wishes to continue to account for the postretirement benefits that Emco pays to its retirees on the pay-as-you-go (cash) basis. Brown has asked Wyatt to write a brief memo to Brown that Brown can use to explain these issues to Emco's president.

REQUIRED:

Write a brief advisory memo from Wyatt to Brown to state the principal benefit covered by FAS 106 and give an example of other benefits covered by FAS 106. Explain the reasoning given in FAS 106 for requiring accruals based on estimates. Indicate the primary recipients of postretirement benefits other than pensions. (11/94, FAR, #5, amended, 5740)

ESSAY 9-4 (15 to 25 minutes)

At December 31, 1991, as a result of its single employer-defined benefit pension plan, Bighorn Co. had an unrecognized net loss and an unfunded accrued pension cost. Bighorn's pension plan and its actuarial assumptions have not changed since it

began operations in 1987. Bighorn has made annual contributions to the plan.

REQUIRED:

a. Identify the components of net pension cost that should be recognized in Bighorn's 1991 financial statements.

b. What circumstances caused Bighorn's

1. Unrecognized net loss?
2. Ununded accrued pension cost?

c. How should Bighorn compute its minimum pension liability and any additional pension liability? (5/92, Theory, #5)

ESSAY 9-5 (10 to 17 minutes)

Essex Company has a single-employer defined benefit pension plan for its employees.

REQUIRED:

a. Define the interest cost component of net pension cost for a period. How should Essex determine its interest cost component of net pension cost for a period?

b. Define prior service cost. How should Essex account for prior service cost? Why? (11/89, Theory, #4a, b, 3572)

SOLUTION 9-1 MULTIPLE CHOICE ANSWERS

NET PERIODIC PENSION COST

1. (d) The unexpected loss on plan assets related to the disposal of a subsidiary should not be included in the determination of net pension cost. Per APB 30, a gain or loss that is directly related to a disposal of a segment should be recognized as a part of the gain or loss associated with that event. The amount of net pension cost to be recognized is determined as follows:

Service cost	$160,000
Annual interest on pension obligation	50,000
Actual and expected gain on plan assets	(35,000)
Amortization of unrecognized prior service cost	5,000
Net pension cost	$180,000

2. (b) Ral's 1997 pension cost is determined as follows:

Service cost	$300,000
Return on plan assets	(80,000)
Interest cost on projected benefit obligation	164,000
Amortization of actuarial loss	30,000
Amortization of unrecognized net obligation	70,000
Pension cost, 1997	$484,000

3. (c) The service cost component of net periodic pension cost is a portion of the projected benefit obligation. Therefore, it is measured using the projected benefit obligation.

4. (d) Service cost for a period is the increase in the projected benefit obligation due to services rendered by employees during that period. All information on covered employees for 1997 and 1998 is the same, and 1998 is one year closer to the payment of retirement benefits. Therefore, service cost will be greater in 1998 as compared to 1997 because the present value computation will be greater due to one less year of discounting. The plan requires equal annual contributions, but service costs are less in the beginning and more later. Therefore, the contribution in 1997 will exceed 1997 service costs, resulting in prepaid pension cost to be reported on the 1997 balance sheet.

5. (c) Interest cost included in net pension cost is determined as the increase in the projected benefit obligation due to the passage of time (SFAS 87, par. 22).

6. (b) According to SFAS 87, par. 44, the projected benefit obligation is determined by use of the settlement rate and *not* by the expected return on plan assets or by the actual return on plan assets. These latter two rates, however, do have an impact on the determination of the net periodic pension cost.

7. (b) In computing pension expense, the amount Gali should use as actual return on plan assets is determined as follows:

Increase in fair value of plan assets ($525,000 − $350,000)	$175,000
Less: Increase in fair value of plan assets due to employer contributions	(110,000)
Add: Decrease in fair value of plan assets due to benefit payments	85,000
Actual return on plan assets, 1994	$150,000

8. (d) The plan amendment granted increased benefits for services provided prior to 1997. Because the plan amendment was granted with the expectation that Tern will realize economic benefits in future periods, the cost of providing the retroactive benefits should not be included in pension cost entirely in the year of amendment. Instead, the prior service cost should be recognized during the future service periods of those employees active at the date of the amendment who are expected to receive benefits under the plan (i.e., in 1997 and following years).

9. (c) The cost of retroactive benefits generated by a plan amendment is amortized by assigning an equal amount to each year of future service for each employee active at the date of the amendment expected to receive benefits under the plan. SFAS 87 permits the use of simplified methods, including the use of the straight-line method that amortizes the cost over the average remaining service life of the active participants. The average remaining service life is 5 years, calculated by adding the expected remaining years of service of the participants (3 + 5 + 5 + 7 = 20 years) and dividing by the number of participants (4). The total credit of $100,000 would thus be amortized over 5 years, at $20,000 per year. If instead the amortization is calculated by prorating for each year over the next 7 years, during the first year 4 participants remain in active service; 4/20($100,000) = $20,000. In this problem, during each of the first three years the amortization is the same under either method.

10. (a) Per SFAS 87, par. 20, the following components should be included in the net pension cost recognized for an employer sponsoring a defined benefit pension plan: (1) service cost, (2) interest cost, (3) actual return on plan assets, (4) amortization of unrecognized prior service cost, (5) gain or loss (including the effects of changes in

assumptions) to the extent recognized, and (6) amortization of the unrecognized net obligation (and loss or cost) or unrecognized net asset (and gain) existing at the date of initial application of SFAS 87. The fair value of plan assets should *not* be included in net pension cost.

11. (c) The $180,000 of unrecognized net obligation at the beginning of 1988, is computed as the excess at that date of the projected benefit obligation over the fair value of plan assets ($780,000 – $600,000 = $180,000), since at that date all amounts accrued as net periodic pension cost had been contributed to the plan. Typically, the unrecognized net obligation should be amortized on a straight-line basis over the average remaining service period of employees expected to receive benefits under the plan. However, because the average remaining service period is less than 15 years (10 < 15), Reed may elect to use a 15-year period. Therefore, the amount of unrecognized net obligation that Reed should amortize to minimize its accrual for pension cost is $12,000 ($180,000 ÷ 15).

ACCRUED / PREPAID PENSION LIABILITY

12. (a) Unfunded accrued pension costs consists of the net periodic pension cost adjusted for employer contributions and previous prepaid costs or accrued costs:

Service cost	$19,000
Interest cost	38,000
Amortization of unrecognized prior service cost	52,000
Actual return on plan assets	(22,000)
Net periodic pension cost	$87,000

Net periodic pension cost for 1994		$87,000
Less: Prepaid pension cost, 1/1/94	$ 2,000	
Employer contributions	40,000	(42,000)
Unfunded accrued pension cost 12/31/94		$45,000

13. (a) Loch Co.'s 12/31/95 accrued pension cost is determined as follows:

Service and interest costs for 1995	$720,000
Less: Contributions for 1995	(400,000)
Less: Actual return on plan assets (10% of $400,000)	(40,000)
Accrued pension cost, 12/31/95	$280,000

14. (a) A liability (unfunded accrued pension cost) is recognized for the amount that cumulative net periodic pension cost exceeds contributions to the plan (SFAS 87, par. 35).

15. (d) During 1997 and 1998, Webb expects to accrue pension cost of $165,000 (i.e., $75,000 +

$90,000). In order to report an accrued pension liability of $15,000 in its 12/31/98 balance sheet, Webb must make funding payments of $150,000 (i.e., $165,000 – $15,000) during 1997 and 1998. Since Webb made a funding payment of $50,000 in 1997, it will have to make a funding payment of $100,000 (i.e., $150,000 – $50,000) in 1998. Since the fair value of plan assets exceeds the accumulated benefit obligation at 12/31/97 (i.e., $600,000 > $500,000) and 12/31/98 (i.e., $675,000 > $520,000), no additional pension liability need be reported in the balance sheet at either date.

16. (d) The $190,000 net pension cost for 1996 is to be funded two months after the financial statement date, and thus is reported as a current liability at December 31, 1996. A liability is reported when the accumulated benefit obligation exceeds the fair value of plan assets. Since the fair value of plan assets ($500,000) exceeds the accumulated benefit obligation ($480,000) at December 31, 1996, no additional pension liability is reported.

17. (d) The amount of the pension liability that should be reported is the amount of the unfunded accumulated benefit obligation (i.e., the excess of the accumulated benefit obligation over the fair value of plan assets).

Accumulated benefit obligation	$ 4,300,000
Fair value of plan assets	(3,450,000)
Unfunded accumulated benefit obligation	$ 850,000

18. (c) Loch contributed $1,000,000 to the plan. Therefore, in its 12/31/92 balance sheet, Loch should report prepaid pension cost of $480,000 (i.e., $1,000,000 – $520,000). Loch's 1992 pension cost is computed as follows:

Service and interest cost	$ 620,000
Return on plan assets ($1,000,000 x 10%)	(100,000)
Pension cost, 1992	$ 520,000

19. (d) In 1992, East accrued pension cost of $174,000 (i.e., $150,000 service cost + $24,000 prior service cost amortization) and made funding payments of $210,000 (i.e., $150,000 payment for service cost + $60,000 payment for prior service cost). Therefore, the amount of East's prepaid pension cost at 12/31/92 is $36,000 (i.e., $210,000 funding payments – $174,000 accrued pension cost).

20. (c) During 1997, Dell accrued pension cost of $303,400 ($220,000 + $83,400) and made funding payments of $334,400 ($220,000 + $114,400). At 12/31/97, Dell's prepaid pension cost is $31,000 ($334,400 – $303,400).

MINIMUM LIABILITY

21.   (b)   The additional minimum pension liability is calculated as follows:

Accumulated benefit obligation	$103,000
Plan assets at fair value	(78,000)
Unfunded accumulated benefit obligation	$ 25,000
Net periodic pension cost	$ 90,000
Employer's contribution	(70,000)
Accrued pension cost	$ 20,000
Unfunded accumulated benefit obligation	$ 25,000
Accrued pension cost	(20,000)
Additional liability required	$ 5,000

22.   (b)   Per SFAS 87, par. 36, "If the accumulated benefit obligation exceeds the fair value of plan assets, the employer shall recognize in the statement of financial position a liability (including unfunded accrued pension cost) that is at least equal to the unfunded accumulated benefit obligation." Thus, if a liability for accrued pension cost is already reported, the additional liability to be recorded is the amount by which the minimum liability (unfunded accumulated benefit) exceeds the accrued pension cost.

23.   (b)   SFAS 87, par. 36, states, "If the accumulated benefit obligation exceeds the fair value of the plan assets, the employer shall recognize in the statement of financial position a liability (including unfunded accrued pension cost) that is at least equal to the *unfunded accumulated benefit obligation.*"

24.   (c)   The amount to be reported as the minimum liability relating to the pension plan is the amount of the unfunded accumulated benefit obligation (i.e., the excess of the accumulated benefit obligation over the fair value of the plan assets). (SFAS 87, par 36.)

25.   (c)   The net periodic pension cost of $8,000 for 1994 exceeded the $0 cash contributions to the pension plan during 1994 by $8,000. At December 31, 1994, Hall should record an additional pension liability as follows:

Unfunded accumulated benefit obligation	$25,000
Accrued pension liability	(8,000)
Additional pension liability	$17,000

26.   (a)   At December 31, 1994, Hall should report as excess of additional pension liability over unrecognized prior service cost as follows:

Additional pension liability	$ 17,000
Unrecognized prior service cost	(12,000)
Excess of additional pension liability 12/31/94	$ 5,000

27.   (a)   Nola has an unfunded accumulated benefit obligation of $140,000. Therefore, Nola should report a minimum pension liability in the balance sheet for this amount. Because Nola has $80,000 of accrued pension cost, an additional pension liability should be recognized for $60,000 (i.e., $140,000 − $80,000). In recording the additional pension liability, an intangible asset (i.e., deferred pension cost) can only be recorded for $45,000 because the recognition of the intangible asset is limited to the amount of unrecognized prior service cost. The $15,000 ($60,000 − $45,000) excess of the additional pension liability required to be recognized over the unrecognized prior service cost represents a net loss not yet recognized as net periodic pension cost and should be reported in other comprehensive income (per SFAS 130).

28.   (a)   This is a poorly worded question. The amount of the adjustment to record the minimum pension liability to be reported in the 9/30/92 balance sheet is determined as follows:

Accumulated benefit obligation	$ 380,000
Fair value of plan assets	(290,000)
Unfunded accumulated benefit obligation	90,000
Add prepaid pension cost	20,000
Additional liability to be recorded	$ 110,000

The excess of the accumulated benefit obligation over the fair value of plan assets (i.e., $90,000) is the amount of the pension liability to be reported in the 9/30/92 balance sheet. Because there is prepaid pension cost of $20,000, recognition of an additional pension liability of $110,000 is required. The prepaid pension cost of $20,000 and the additional liability of $110,000 are netted into one amount and reported as pension liability in the amount of $90,000.

29.   (c)   The excess of the accumulated benefit obligation over the fair value of the plan assets is the amount of the pension liability to be reported in the balance sheet. Because there is accrued pension cost of $200,000, recognition of an additional pension liability of $4,800,000 is required. The accrued pension cost of $200,000 and the additional liability required of $4,800,000 are combined into one amount and reported as accrued pension cost or pension liability in the amount of $5,000,000. The amount of the adjustment required to reflect the minimum pension liability is determined as follows:

Accumulated benefit obligation	$12,000,000
Less: Fair value of plan assets	(7,000,000)
Unfunded accumulated benefit obligation	5,000,000
Less: Accrued pension cost	(200,000)
Additional liability required	$ 4,800,000

POSTRETIREMENT BENEFITS

30. (a) The postretirement benefit cost is accrued over the attribution period, which is defined as the period of service during which the employee earns the benefits under the terms of the plan. Generally, the attribution begins when an employee is hired and ends on the date the employee is eligible to receive the benefits and ceases to earn additional benefits.

31. (b) The attribution period for accruing the expected postretirement health care benefit obligation begins with the date of hire and ends at the full eligibility date (SFAS 106, par. 44). Bounty provides postretirement health care benefits to employees who have completed at least 10 years of service and are aged 55 years or older when retiring. Fletcher is hired at 48 years old. Therefore, the attribution period for accruing Bounty's expected postretirement health care benefit obligation to Fletcher is during the period when Fletcher is aged 48 to 58, because at age 58, Fletcher will have completed 10 years of service and be 55 years or older.

DISCLOSURE REQUIREMENTS

32. (d) SFAS 132 requires disclosures including a schedule reconciling the funded status of the plan with the amount of net pension asset or liability recognized in the statement of financial position.

33. (d) The projected benefit obligation at 12/31/97 is determined as follows:

Projected benefit obligation at 1/1/97	$ 72,000
Interest cost for 1997 ($72,000 x 10%)	7,200
Service costs for 1997	18,000
Pension benefits paid during 1997	(15,000)
Projected benefit obligation at 12/31/97	$ 82,200

Interest cost represents the increase in the projected benefit obligation due to the passage of time, and is computed by multiplying the projected benefit obligation at 1/1/97 by the assumed discount (settlement) rate. The projected benefit obligation is increased by the service costs incurred in 1997 and reduced by the pension benefits paid during 1997.

34. (a) Per SFAS 132, an employer sponsoring a benefit plan should disclose, among other things, the assumed health care cost trend rate(s) for the next year and a general description of the direction and pattern of change as well as the ultimate trend rate(s) and when the rate is expected to occur. The employer must also disclose the accumulated post-retirement benefit obligation.

PERFORMANCE BY SUBTOPICS

Each category below parallels a subtopic covered in Chapter 9. Record the number and percentage of questions you correctly answered in each subtopic area.

Net Periodic Pension Cost

Question #	Correct √
1	
2	
2	
4	
5	
6	
7	
8	
9	
10	
11	
# Questions	11
# Correct	
% Correct	

Accrued/Prepaid Pension Liability

Question #	Correct √
12	
13	
14	
15	
16	
17	
18	
19	
20	
# Questions	9
# Correct	
% Correct	

Minimum Liability

Question #	Correct √
21	
22	
23	
24	
25	
26	
27	
28	
29	
# Questions	9
# Correct	
% Correct	

Postretirement Benefits

Question #	Correct √
30	
31	
# Questions	2
# Correct	
% Correct	

Disclosure Requirements

Question #	Correct √
32	
33	
34	
# Questions	3
# Correct	
% Correct	

OTHER OBJECTIVE FORMAT SOLUTION

SOLUTION 9-2 UNFUNDED ACCRUED PENSION LIABILITY

1. **$48,000.** Interest cost included in net pension cost is determined as the increase in the projected benefit obligation due to the passage of time (SFAS 87, par. 22). Thus, the amount of interest cost that Sparta should include in the calculation of 1992 net pension cost is computed as follows:

Projected benefit obligation, 1/1/92	$600,000
Times: Discount rate at which pension benefits could be effectively settled	x 8%
Interest cost for 1992	$ 48,000

2. **$72,000.** The expected return on plan assets is determined based on the expected long-term rate of return on plan assets and the market-related value of plan assets. The market-related value of plan assets is either fair value or a calculated value that recognizes changes in fair value in a systematic and rational manner over not more than five years (SFAS 87, par. 30). Therefore, Sparta's expected return on plan assets for 1992 is computed as follows:

Fair value of plan assets, 1/1/92	$720,000
Times: Expected rate of return	x 10%
Expected return on plan assets for 1992	$ 72,000

3. **$105,000.** For a funded plan, the actual return on plan assets is determined based on the fair value of plan assets at the beginning and the end of the period, adjusted for contributions and benefit payments (SFAS 87, par. 23). Therefore, since there were no contributions made or benefits paid during 1992, the actual return on Sparta's plan assets is $105,000 (i.e., $825,000 − $720,000), the increase in the fair value of plan assets in 1992.

4. **$20,000.** Prior service cost is the increase in the projected benefit obligation at the date of a plan amendment (or initiation of a plan). Prior service cost is amortized during the future service periods of those employees active at the date of the amendment (or initiation) who are expected to receive benefits under the plan. Since the amortization of prior service cost can be quite complex, a straight-line method that amortizes the cost over the average remaining service life of the active participants is acceptable. Therefore, the amount of prior service cost that

Sparta should include in the calculation of 1992 net pension cost is $20,000 (i.e., $240,000 ÷ 12).

5. **$2,000.** The minimum amortization of unrecognized pension gain that Sparta should include in the calculation of net pension cost is determined, as of the beginning of the year, as the amount by which the unrecognized pension gain exceeds 10% of the greater of the projected benefit obligation or the market-related value of plan assets, divided by the average remaining service period of active employees expected to receive benefits under the plan.

Unrecognized pension gain, 1/1/92	$96,000
Less: 10% of fair value of plan assets (i.e., the market-related value of plan assets), 1/1/92 ($720,000* x 10%)	(72,000)
Excess of unrecognized pension gain over 10% of the greater of the projected benefit obligation or the market-related value of plan assets at 1/1/92	24,000
Divide by: Average service life	÷12
Minimum amortization of unrecognized pension gain,	$ 2,000

---

* At 1/1/92, the fair value of plan assets exceeds the projected benefit obligation (i.e., $720,000 > $600,000).

6. **(I)** Service cost is the actuarial present value of benefits attributed by the pension benefit formula to employee service during that period (SFAS 87, par. 21). Since service cost increases net pension cost, it also increases the unfunded accrued pension liability.

7. **(I)** Since the deferral of the gain on pension plan assets increases net pension cost, it also increases the unfunded pension liability.

8. **(D)** Since the actual return on plan assets decreases net pension cost, it also decreases the unfunded accrued pension liability.

9. **(I)** Since the amortization of prior service costs increases net pension cost, it also increases the unfunded accrued pension liability.

10. **(D)** Since the amortization of unrecognized pension gain decreases net pension cost, it also decreases the unfunded accrued pension liability.

ESSAY SOLUTIONS

SOLUTION 9-3

To: Brown

From: Wyatt

As we discussed, here is a brief overview of Statement of Financial Accounting Standards No. 106. *Employers' Accounting for Postretirement Benefits Other Than Pensions*

The **primary recipients** of postretirement benefits other than pensions are **retired employees**, their **beneficiaries**, and covered **dependents**. The principle benefit covered by FAS 106 is **postretirement health care** benefits. Examples of other benefits include **tuition assistance**, **legal services**, **life insurance benefits**, **day care**, and **housing subsidies**.

The reasoning given in FAS 106 is that accrual of the obligation based on **best estimates** is **superior to implying**, by a failure to accrue, that **no obligation exists prior to the payment** of benefits.

SOLUTION 9-4 PENSIONS: VARIOUS ASPECTS OF ACCOUNTING FOR PENSIONS

a. The components of Bighorn's 1991 net pension cost calculation are:

- **Service cost.**
- **Interest cost.**
- **Actual return on plan assets.**
- **Gain or loss.**
- **The difference between the actual and expected return on plan assets.**
- **Any amortization of the unrecognized gain or loss from previous periods.**

---

b. **1.** Bighorn's unrecognized net loss results from **differences** between **actuarial assumptions** and **experiences** for both its **projected benefit obligation and returns on plan assets**.

2. Bighorn's unfunded accrued pension cost occurs because **cumulative net pension cost exceeds cash contributed** to the pension fund.

c. Bighorn's minimum pension liability equals the **excess** of the **accumulated benefit obligation** over the **fair value of plan assets**. Bighorn's additional pension liability would equal any **excess** of this **minimum pension liability** over the **unfunded accrued pension cost**.

SOLUTION 9-5 PENSIONS: INTEREST COST/PRIOR SERVICE COST

a. The interest cost component of the net pension cost for a period is the **increase** in the **projected benefit obligation** due to the **passage of time**. Essex would determine its interest cost component by applying an **assumed discount rate** to the **beginning** projected benefit obligation.

b. Prior service cost is the cost of **retroactive benefits** (increased benefits based on services rendered in prior periods) granted at the **date of adoption or amendment** of a pension plan. Prior service cost should be included in **net pension cost** during the **future service periods** of those **employees active** at the date of the pension plan adoption or amendment, as appropriate, who are expected to **receive benefits** under the pension plan. Prior service cost is incurred with the expectation that the **employer** will **realize economic benefits** in **future periods**.

WHAT IS ELIGIBLE TO BE TESTED?

From the AICPA's *Information for CPA Candidates*:

"Candidates are responsible for knowing accounting and auditing pronouncements, including the governmental and not-for-profit organizations areas, six months after a pronouncement's *effective* date, unless early application is permitted. When early application is permitted, candidates are responsible for knowing the new pronouncement six months after the *issuance* date. In this case, candidates are responsible for knowing both the old and new pronouncements until the old pronouncement is superseded. For the federal taxation area, candidates are responsible for knowing the Internal Revenue Code and Federal Tax Regulations in effect six months before the Examination date. For the business law & professional responsibilities section, candidates are responsible for knowing federal laws six months after their *effective* date and for uniform acts one year after their adoption by a simple majority of the jurisdictions."

See the **Practical Advice** section of this volume for additional information.

CHANGE ALERT

INTERPRETATION NO. 44, *ACCOUNTING FOR CERTAIN TRANSACTIONS INVOLVING STOCK COMPENSATION*

Interpretation No. 44 is intended to provide interpretive guidance on several implementation issues related to APB Opinion 25 on accounting for stock issued to employees. The two most significant issues clarified are as follows:

DEFINITION OF EMPLOYEE An individual would be considered an employee if the company granting the options has sufficient control over the individual as to establish an employer-employee relationship. The relationship is based on case law and IRS regulations. The FASB granted an exception to this definition for elected outside members of the company's board of directors, because directors serve the company in a unique capacity and should be granted employee status when determining the accounting for options.

Grants to employees may be accounted for according to APB Opinion No. 25. Under Opinion No. 25, fixed option plans for employees have no compensation expense associated with the options when the employee's exercise price is equal to the fair value of the stock at the grant date. Fixed option plans are those plans whose terms, including price, number of shares granted, and time-certain vesting, remain the same throughout the duration of the plan.

Grants to nonemployees must be accounted for (rather than just disclosed) using the fair value model of SFAS 123.

ACCOUNTING FOR OPTIONS THAT HAVE BEEN REPRICED When a company directly or indirectly reprices options, it has changed the terms of the plan, which would convert the award from a fixed to a variable award as of the date of the repricing. Accounting for variable awards under APB Opinion No. 25 includes an element of compensation expense.

CHAPTER 10

OWNERS' EQUITY

CHAPTER 10

OWNERS' EQUITY

I. DEFINITIONS

A. OWNERS' EQUITY

SFAC 6 defines owners' equity as the residual interest in the assets of an entity after deducting its liabilities. In a business enterprise, the equity is the ownership interest. In other words, it is the combined total of contributed capital and all other increments in capital from profitable operations or other sources.

1. **TYPES OF OWNERSHIP** Owners' equity may take several forms, depending on the type of ownership involved.

   a. A *sole proprietorship's* equity consists of a single proprietor's equity account, Owners' Equity or Net Worth. This is the sum of the beginning capital balance, plus additional investments during the period, plus net income (or minus net loss) minus withdrawals. Because of the simplicity of this concept, we will not review it any further.

   b. A *partnership's* equity consists of one capital account for each partner. A partner's investments and allocations of income and withdrawals are recorded in his or her individual capital account.

   c. A *corporation's* equity consists of two main components: (a) contributed capital, which includes capital stock and additional paid-in capital, and (b) retained earnings.

2. **ACCUMULATED BALANCE OF OTHER COMPREHENSIVE INCOME** In addition to capital and retained earnings, owners' equity includes the accumulated balance of other comprehensive income, in accordance with SFAS 130, which is reported separately from the capital and retained earnings accounts, in the following classifications:

   a. Foreign currency items

   b. Minimum pension liability adjustments

   c. Unrealized gains and losses on certain investments in debt and equity securities

   d. Gains and losses on certain hedging activities

B. TYPES OF CAPITAL STOCK

1. **PAR VALUE** Stock with a specified par value per share printed on the certificate. Generally, the stockholder's maximum liability to creditors in the case of insolvency is par value. The par value of all shares issued and subscribed will normally represent the legal or stated capital.

2. **NO-PAR VALUE** Stock with no specific par value assigned to it. No-par stock avoids the contingent liability involved with the issuance of par value stock at a price below par (discount). Additionally, the stated or assigned consideration received for all no-par value shares generally represents the legal or stated capital of the corporation.

3. **NO-PAR WITH A STATED VALUE** Essentially treated in the same manner as par value stock.

C.   LEGAL CAPITAL

The portion of contributed capital required by statute to be retained in the business for the protection of creditors is called legal capital.

1.   Legal or stated capital is usually valued as the total par or stated value of all shares issued. If stock is issued without a par or stated value, the total amount received for the stock is used.

2.   The following limitations are placed upon the corporation by law to safeguard its legal capital:

a.   Legal capital may not be used as a basis for dividends.

b.   Acquisition of treasury stock is limited to the amount of retained earnings.

c.   The amount of legal capital cannot be reduced arbitrarily by the corporation.

D.   CONTRIBUTED CAPITAL

Contributed capital represents injections of capital by stockholders.

1.   **CAPITAL STOCK** The par or stated value of the stock purchased by owners, plus

2.   **ADDITIONAL PAID-IN CAPITAL** Paid-in capital in excess of par or stated value.

E.   COMMON STOCK

Common stock represents the residual ownership interest in the corporation. Distributions on common stock are generally subordinate to the rights of other securities. Thus, holders of common stock usually bear the greatest financial risks, but may also enjoy the greatest potential rewards. The four basic rights of a common stockholder are as follows:

1.   Voting Rights

2.   Dividend Rights

3.   Preemptive Rights to Purchase Stock Issued by the Corporation

4.   Rights to Share in the Distribution of Assets if the Corporation Is Liquidated

F.   PREFERRED STOCK

1.   Preferred stock is a security that has certain preferences or priorities not found in common stock.

a.   Preference as to dividends at a stated percentage of par or, if no-par, at a stated dollar amount and must be paid before dividends on common stock.

b.   Preference as to assets in the event of a liquidating distribution.

c.   Absence of voting rights (must be specifically prohibited in the charter).

2.   **FEATURES**

a.   **REDEEMABLE** Shareholders may redeem shares, at their option, at a specified price per share.

b.   **CONVERTIBLE** Shareholders may exchange shares, at their option, for common stock. The journal entry to record a conversion is as follows:

Preferred Stock	(shs. x par)	
Add'l. PIC—Preferred	(if any)	
Common Stock		(shs. x par)
Add'l. PIC—Common		(to balance)

c. **CALLABLE** The corporation may, at its option, purchase preferred stock for the purpose of canceling it. The journal entry to record a cancellation is as follows:

Preferred Stock	(par)	
Add'l. PIC—Preferred	(if any)	
Retained Earnings	("loss")	
Cash		(call price)
Add'l. PIC—Retirement of PS		("gain")

3. PREFERRED STOCK DIVIDENDS

a. CUMULATIVE OR NONCUMULATIVE

(1) **CUMULATIVE** If all or part of the stated dividend on cumulative preferred stock is not paid in a given year, the unpaid portion accumulates (i.e., dividends in arrears). No dividends can be paid on common stock until the accumulated dividends are paid on the preferred stock. Dividends in arrears are not a liability; however, they should be disclosed parenthetically or in the footnotes to the financial statements.

(2) **NONCUMULATIVE** If a dividend on noncumulative preferred stock is not paid in a given year, the dividend is lost forever.

b. PARTICIPATING, PARTIALLY PARTICIPATING, NONPARTICIPATING

(1) **FULLY PARTICIPATING** preferred stock is entitled to share excess dividends on a pro rata basis (based on par or stated value) with common stock. For instance, 4% fully participating preferred stock will earn not only a 4% return, but also, if amounts paid on common stock exceed 4%, then dividends will be shared ratably with the common stockholders.

(2) **PARTIALLY PARTICIPATING** preferred stock is limited in its participation with common stock to some additional percentage of par or stated value or a specified dollar amount per share as stated on the stock certificate. For instance, the stock certificate may specify that 6% preferred will participate up to a maximum of 9% of par value, or 6% preferred will participate only in distributions in excess of a 10% rate on common stock.

(3) **NONPARTICIPATING** is limited to receiving dividends at the preferential rate.

G. SECURITIES
Securities are the evidence of debt or ownership or a related right. The term securities generally includes options and warrants as well as debt and stock.

H. PARTICIPATION RIGHTS
Participation rights are contractual rights of security holders to receive dividends or returns from the security issuer's profits, cash flows, or returns on investments.

II. ISSUES OF CAPITAL STOCK

A. CASH CONSIDERATION

The issuance of stock is generally recorded by debiting cash or the appropriate asset accounts for the FV of the consideration received. Capital Stock is credited for the par or stated value of the shares issued, and the balancing figure is credited to Additional Paid-In Capital.

1. Assume 500 shares of $10 par value common stock are sold for $30 per share. The journal entry to record the stock issue is as follows:

Cash (500 shs. x $30)	15,000	
Common Stock (500 shs. x $10 P.V.)		5,000
Add'l. PIC—Common (to balance)		10,000

2. A shareholder who acquires stock from the corporation at less than par value incurs a contingent liability to the corporation's creditors for the difference between the par value and the issue price. The issuance of stock at a discount is illegal in most states today.

B. PURSUANT TO SUBSCRIPTION

1. A subscription is a contract to purchase one or more shares of stock in the future. Subscriptions Receivable is debited for the balance due from the purchasers, Common Stock Subscribed is credited for the par or stated value of the shares to be issued, and any premium is credited to Additional Paid-In Capital. Usually, shares of stock are not issued until the full subscription price is paid.

EXAMPLE 1 ♦ SUBSCRIPTION ISSUE

ABC Corp. received subscriptions for 20,000 shares of $50 par value common stock at $75 per share. ABC required an initial payment of 25% of the subscription price. ABC would record the following journal entries:

Date of subscription contract		
Cash (20,000 x $75 x 25%)	375,000	
Subscriptions Receivable (20,000 x $75 x 75%)	1,125,000	
Common Stock Subscribed (20,000 x $50)		1,000,000
Add'l. PIC—Common Stock (20,000 x $25)		500,000
Cash receipt and issuance of stock		
Cash	1,125,000	
Subscriptions Receivable		1,125,000
Common Stock Subscribed	1,000,000	
Common Stock		1,000,000

2. When a subscriber defaults on a subscription contract, amounts paid to the corporation may be

    a. Returned in full.

    b. Retained by the corporation, and an equivalent number of shares issued.

    c. Retained to cover any losses on resale and the balance, if any, returned.

C. PROPERTY OTHER THAN CASH

1. Where stock is issued for noncash consideration, the property received and the amount of contributed capital should be recorded at the fair value of the property received or the market value of the stock, whichever is more objectively determinable. If fair values are not determinable, then appraised values or values set by the board of directors may be used.

2. Journal entry illustrating exchange

Assets	(FV)	
Common Stock		(par or stated value)
Add'l. PIC—Common Stock		(to balance)

D. INCORPORATION OF A GOING CONCERN

1. An unincorporated firm (i.e., a sole proprietorship or a partnership) may decide to adopt the corporate form. To achieve this, the new corporation will issue stock (and possibly debt securities) in exchange for the assets of the going concern.

2. The newly created corporation will **not** recognize gain or loss on the issuance of its stock and securities in exchange for the business' assets.

    a. The assets acquired will be recorded at their FVs. Current liabilities assumed generally are recorded at face amount and long-term liabilities at their present value.

    b. The stock issued will be recorded at par or stated value. Any excess FV of the net assets acquired over par or stated value of the capital stock is credited to additional paid-in capital.

EXAMPLE 2 ♦ INCORPORATION OF A GOING CONCERN

On January 1, 20X4, Kyle Fleming decided to incorporate his automobile repair and restoration business, Fleming Automotive. To this effect, he transferred the assets and liabilities of his business to a new corporation, Auto Concepts, Inc., receiving in exchange all 1,000 shares of its $10 par value stock. Fleming Automotive's balance sheet prior to the incorporation is reproduced below. The FV of the current assets was $25,000; the equipment was appraised at $130,000.

Fleming Automotive
Balance Sheet, as of December 31, 20X3

Current assets	$ 20,000
Equipment	150,000
Less, accumulated depreciation	(60,000)
Total assets	$110,000
Liabilities	$ 30,000
Kyle Fleming, Capital	80,000
Total liabilities and equity	$110,000

REQUIRED: Provide the journal entry necessary to incorporate the new business.

SOLUTION:

Current Assets	25,000	
Equipment	130,000	
Liabilities		30,000
Common Stock, $10 Par		10,000
Add'l. Paid-In Capital (balancing figure)		115,000

E. DIFFERENT CLASS OF SECURITIES IN CONSIDERATION OF A LUMP-SUM PURCHASE PRICE

When a corporation sells two or more classes of stock for a lump sum, the problem is to allocate the proceeds between several classes of stock. There are two methods of allocating the lump sum.

1. THE PROPORTIONAL METHOD Allocation of the lump sum between the classes of stock in accordance with their relative fair values.

2. THE INCREMENTAL METHOD Allocation of the lump sum based on the known fair value of one security with the remainder of the lump sum being allocated to the other security.

III. RETAINED EARNINGS

A. DEFINITION

The retained earnings account is the final terminus for all profit and loss accounts. The balance represents the accumulated income of the corporation, less dividends declared and amounts transferred to paid-in capital accounts.

B. CLASSIFICATION

Retained earnings is divided into the following:

1. APPROPRIATED RETAINED EARNINGS The portion unavailable for dividends. Some reasons for appropriation are to create a reserve for plant expansion, to satisfy legal requirements of a bond indenture, or to provide a cushion for expected future losses. A journal entry illustrating the appropriation of retained earnings for plant construction may be as follows:

Retained Earnings	XX	
Appropriated RE—Plant Construction		XX

Any costs or losses associated with the actual construction of the plant should not be charged to the appropriation. When the appropriation is no longer needed, the entry is reversed.

- Owing to the application of most state corporate laws, retained earnings is often appropriated in the amount of the cost of treasury stock acquired under both the cost and par value methods.

2. UNAPPROPRIATED RETAINED EARNINGS That portion of retained earnings available for dividend distribution.

C. STATEMENT OF CHANGES IN RETAINED EARNINGS

APB 12 states, "disclosure of changes in the separate accounts comprising stockholders' equity (in addition to retained earnings) is required to make the financial statements sufficiently informative. Disclosure...may take the form of separate statements or may be made in the basic financial statements or notes thereto." Frequently, the statement of changes in retained earnings is presented in the following form:

Retained earnings, Jan. 1, 20X1, as reported	XXX
+/– Cumulative effect of retroactive changes in accounting principles	XXX
+/– Prior period adjustments	XXX
Retained earnings, Jan. 1, 20X1, as adjusted	XXX
+ Net income (– Net loss)	XXX
– Dividends declared	(XXX)
Retained earnings, Dec. 31, 20X1	XXX

D. **EXCLUSIONS**
Retained earnings should not include the following:

1. *Gains* from treasury stock transactions

2. *Gifts* of property

3. Additions to owners' equity attributable to *reappraisals* of property

E. **QUASI-REORGANIZATION**
A reorganization or revision of the capital structure, which is permitted in some states. This procedure eliminates an accumulated deficit as if the company had been legally reorganized without much of the cost and difficulty of a legal reorganization. Thus, the corporation will be able to pay dividends again. It involves the following steps:

1. Assets are revalued at net realizable value, but there is no net asset increase. (Any loss on revaluation increases the deficit.)

2. A minimum of the amount of the adjusted deficit must be available in paid-in capital (PIC). This might be created by donation of stock from shareholders or reduction of the par value.

3. The deficit is charged against PIC and thus is eliminated.

IV. DIVIDENDS

A. **DEFINITION**
Dividends represent the distribution to stockholders of a proportionate share of retained earnings or, as in the case of liquidating dividends, a return of capital. Dividends (except stock dividends) reduce stockholders' equity through the distribution of assets or the incurrence of a liability.

EXHIBIT 1 ♦ CASH DIVIDENDS

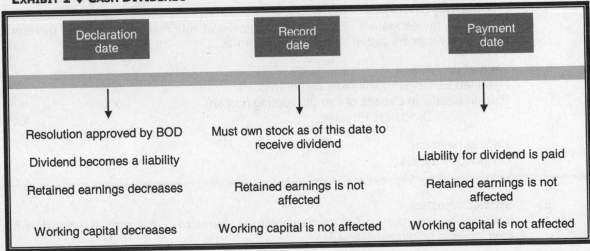

B. **SIGNIFICANT DATES**

1. **DATE OF DECLARATION** The date on which dividends are formally declared by the board of directors and the declared dividends (except stock dividends) become a liability. The journal entry usually recorded on this date is

Retained Earnings   XX
    Dividends Payable   XX

2. **DATE OF RECORD** The date used to establish those stockholders who will receive the declared dividends. No journal entry is required unless the number of shares outstanding have changed from the date of declaration.

3. **DATE OF PAYMENT** The distribution of assets on this date would be recorded as follows (assuming the entry in 1., above):

Dividends Payable	XX	
Cash or Other Property		XX

C. **PROPERTY DIVIDENDS**

At the date of declaration, property dividends are recorded at the fair value of assets given up, and any difference between fair value and carrying amount of the asset is recorded as a gain or loss as a component of income from continuing operations. For example, assume ABC Company transfers to shareholders marketable debt securities that cost $1,500 by declaring a property dividend. The fair value of the securities was $2,000 at the date of declaration.

Date of declaration

Retained Earnings	2,000	
Property Dividends Payable		2,000

Investment in Marketable Securities	500	
Gain on Investment in Marketable Securities		500

Date of payment

Property Dividends Payable	2,000	
Investment in Marketable Securities		2,000

NOTE: Any change in the fair value of the asset to be distributed between the date of declaration and date of payment is ignored.

D. **LIQUIDATING DIVIDENDS**

Liquidating dividends are distributions in excess of retained earnings and, therefore, represent a return of investment rather than a share in profits.

Date of declaration

Retained Earnings (nonliquidating portion)	XX	
Paid-In Capital in Excess of Par (liquidating portion)	XX	
Dividends Payable		XX

Date of payment

Dividends Payable	XX	
Cash		XX

E. **STOCK DIVIDENDS**

Issuance by a corporation of its own common shares to its common shareholders in proportion to their existing holdings (ARB 43).

1. **EFFECT ON INCOME OF SHAREHOLDER** The shareholder has no income as a result of the stock dividend because the stock dividend (or stock split) is not a distribution division or severance of the corporate assets. The cost of the shares held *before* the stock dividend should be allocated to all of the shares held *after* the receipt of the dividend (or split).

2. **RECORDING A STOCK DIVIDEND** Stock dividends operate to transfer a part of the retained earnings to contributed capital (capitalization of retained earnings). In recording the stock dividend, a charge is made to retained earnings (thereby making a portion of retained earnings no longer available for distribution) and credits are made to paid-in capital accounts. Because the declaration and issuance of a stock dividend decreases retained

earnings and increases paid-in capital by equal amounts, total stockholders' equity is **not** affected. The amount of retained earnings capitalized depends on the size of the stock dividend and the apparent effect which the dividend has on the market value of the shares.

a. **SMALL STOCK DIVIDENDS** When the stock dividend is relatively small (not in excess of 20 to 25 percent of outstanding stock) the fair value (at the date of declaration) of the additional shares should be transferred from retained earnings to paid-in capital. The entry to record the declaration and issuance of a small stock dividend is as follows:

Retained Earnings	(FV)	
Common Stock		(Par)
Add'l. PIC—CS		(Balance)

b. **LARGE STOCK DIVIDENDS** When the stock dividend is large (greater than 25% of the outstanding shares) only the *par or stated value* of the additional shares is to be capitalized. The journal entry to record the declaration and issuance of a large stock dividend is as follows:

Retained Earnings	(Par)	
Common Stock		(Par)

F. **STOCK SPLITS**

Increase the number of shares outstanding and proportionately decrease the par or stated value of the stock. There is no change in the dollar amount of capital stock, additional paid-in capital, retained earnings, or total stockholders' equity. Stock splits are issued mainly to reduce the unit market price per share of the stock, in order to obtain a wider distribution. *Reverse stock splits* simply decrease shares outstanding and proportionately increase the par or stated value of the stock (ARB 43).

EXAMPLE 3 ♦ STOCK SPLIT

ABC Corp. declares a 3-for-1 stock split on common stock in order to increase trading of the stock on the open market. Prior to the split, the corporation had 300,000 shares of $12 par value common stock issued and outstanding. The journal entry to record the stock split would be the following:

Common Stock (par $12; 300,000 shares outstanding)	3,600,000	
Common Stock (par $4; 900,000 shares outstanding)		3,600,000

NOTE: The corporation may elect to record the stock split in a memorandum entry.

EXHIBIT 2 ♦ TOTAL STOCKHOLDERS' EQUITY

	RETAINED EARNINGS	PAR VALUE PER SHARE	TOTAL PAR VALUE	ADD'L. PAID-IN CAPITAL	# OF SHARES OUTST.	TOTAL S.H. EQUITY
Small stock dividend	⇓ by FV of shares issued	x	⇑	⇑	⇑	x
Large stock dividend	⇓ by par value of shares issued	x	⇑	x	⇑	x
Stock split	x	⇓	x	x	⇑	x

⇑ = increase
⇓ = decrease
x = no change

V. TREASURY STOCK

A. DEFINITION

Treasury stock is the corporation's common or preferred stock that has been reacquired by purchase, by settlement of an obligation to the corporation, or through donation. Acquisition of treasury stock reduces assets and total stockholders' equity (unless donated) while the reissuance of treasury stock increases assets and total stockholders' equity. Treasury stock is **not** an asset. There are two basic methods to account for treasury stock: the cost method, and the par value method (ARB 43). The cost method is more commonly used in practice.

B. COST METHOD

The cost method views the purchase and subsequent disposition of stock as one transaction. The treasury stock is recorded (debited), carried, and reissued at the acquisition cost.

1. **REISSUED IN EXCESS OF ACQUISITION COST** If the stock is reissued at a price in *excess* of the acquisition cost, the excess is credited to an appropriately titled Paid-In Capital account (e.g., Additional Paid-In Capital From Treasury Stock Transactions).

2. **REISSUED AT LESS THAN ACQUISITION COST** If the stock is reissued at **less** than the acquisition cost, the deficit is first charged against any existing balance in the Additional Paid-In Capital From Treasury Stock Transactions account. The excess, if any, is then charged against Retained Earnings.

3. **BALANCE SHEET PRESENTATION** Under the cost method, treasury stock is presented on the balance sheet as an unallocated reduction of total stockholders' equity (i.e., contributed capital *and* retained earnings).

C. PAR VALUE METHOD

The par value method views the purchase and subsequent disposition of stock as two distinct transactions. Under this method, the acquisition of the treasury shares is viewed as a constructive retirement of the stock. Since capital stock is carried on the balance sheet at par (or stated value), the acquisition of treasury stock is also recorded at *par* (or stated value), by debiting Treasury Stock. Likewise, we charge Additional Paid-In Capital—Common Stock with a pro rata amount of any excess over par or stated value recorded on the original issuance of the stock. Note that the effect of these two entries is to remove the treasury stock from the accounts, i.e., as if it had been retired.

1. If the acquisition cost of the treasury stock is *less* than the price at which the stock was *originally issued*, the difference is credited to APIC From Treasury Stock.

2. On the other hand, if the acquisition price exceeds the stock's original issue price, then the excess is *debited* to APIC From Treasury Stock, but only to the extent of any existing balance (i.e., from prior treasury stock transactions). The excess, if any, is debited to Retained Earnings.

3. The reissuance of treasury stock under the par value method is accounted for in the same manner as an original stock issuance. However, any reissuances of treasury stock at less than par value will reduce (debit) Additional Paid-In Capital From Treasury Stock until that balance is exhausted, then debit Retained Earnings for any excess.

EXAMPLE 4 ♦ TREASURY STOCK TRANSACTIONS COMPARISON

Cost Method			Par Value Method		
ORIGINAL ISSUE of 1,000 shares of $10 par value common stock at $15 per share:					
Cash (1,000 shares @ $15)	15,000		Cash	15,000	
Common Stock (1,000 sh. @ $10)		10,000	Common Stock		10,000
APIC—CS (1,000 sh. @ $5)		5,000	APIC—CS		5,000
ACQUISITION of 100 shares at $18 per share:					
Treasury Stock	1,800		Treasury Stock (100 sh. @ $10)	1,000	
Cash (100 sh. @ $18)		1,800	APIC—CS (100 sh. @ $5)	500	
			Retained Earnings (to balance)	300	
			Cash		1,800
ACQUISITION of 50 shares at $9 per share:					
Treasury Stock	450		Treasury Stock (50 sh. @ $10)	500	
Cash (50 sh. @ $9)		450	APIC—CS (50 sh. @ $5)	250	
			Cash (50 sh. @ $9)		450
			APIC—TS (to balance)		300
REISSUANCE of 50 shares at $20 per share (FIFO):					
Cash (50 sh. @ $20)	1,000		Cash (50 sh. @ $20)	1,000	
Treasury Stock (50 sh. @ $18)		900	Treasury Stock (50 sh. @ $10)		500
APIC—TS (to balance)		100	APIC—TS (to balance)		500
REISSUANCE of 50 shares at $9 per share (FIFO):					
Cash (50 sh. @ $9)	450		Cash (50 sh. @ $9)	450	
APIC—TS (up to existing bal.)	100		APIC—TS (to balance)	50	
Retained Earnings (to balance)	350		Treasury Stock (50 sh. @ $10)		500
Treasury Stock (50 sh. @ $18)		900			

D.   SIMILARITIES BETWEEN METHODS

Regardless of the accounting method used, the following are true:

1. Treasury stock is not an asset.

2. No gains or losses are recognized on treasury stock transactions.

3. Retained earnings may be *decreased* but never *increased* by treasury stock transactions.

4. Total stockholders' equity is the same under both the cost and par value methods. Total stockholders' equity *decreases* by the cost of treasury shares acquired and *increases* by the proceeds received from the reissuance of treasury stock, regardless of whether the treasury stock is accounted for by the cost or the par value method.

5. In many states, retained earnings is restricted in the amount of the cost of treasury stock under both the cost and the par value methods.

E. RETIREMENT OF TREASURY STOCK

A corporation may decide to retire some or all of its treasury stock. Retired stock is classified as authorized and unissued (i.e., as if it had never been issued). Accounting for the retirement of treasury stock depends on the method used initially to record it, i.e., cost or par value method. Assume retirement of 20 shares of $100 par value stock originally issued at $105 per share.

EXAMPLE 5 ♦ RETIREMENT OF TREASURY STOCK

Cost Method			Par Value Method		
REACQUISITION of 20 shares at $110 per share:					
Common Stock (20 sh. @ $100)	2,000		Common Stock (20 sh. @ $100)	2,000	
APIC—CS (20 sh. @ $5)	100		Treasury Stock		2,000
Retained Earnings (to balance)	100				
Treasury Stock (20 sh. @ $110)		2,200			
REACQUISITION of 20 shares at $98 per share:					
Common Stock	2,000		Common Stock	2,000	
APIC—CS	100		Treasury Stock		2,000
APIC—Retirement of CS (to bal.)		140			
Treasury Stock (20 sh. @ $98)		1,960			

VI. SUMMARY: EFFECT OF VARIOUS TRANSACTIONS ON RETAINED EARNINGS

Quite often, CPA Exam questions require you to determine the effect of certain transactions on Retained Earnings. These are summarized below and in Exhibit 3.

A. INCREASES

In general, retained earnings (RE) is increased only as a result of net income generated by the firm. In addition, retained earnings may increase as a result of a prior period adjustment (e.g., the correction of an error) or certain special changes in accounting principle (e.g., change from the completed-contract to the percentage-of-completion method of accounting for long-term construction contracts).

B. DECREASES

Retained earnings decreases as a result of dividends (cash, property, or stock) and net losses suffered by the firm. In addition, treasury stock transactions, certain stock splits, prior period adjustments, and certain special changes in accounting principle may also reduce retained earnings.

EXHIBIT 3 ♦ TRANSACTIONS AFFECTING RETAINED EARNINGS

Transactions	Effect on RE	Amount
Operations—gains, and losses	Increase or decrease	Net income or net loss
Dividends—cash, or property	Decrease	Amount of cash or FV of property distributed (Note that gain or loss is also recognized on declaration of property dividends.)
Stock dividends:		
1. Small (≤ 20 to 25%)	Decrease	FV of stock distributed
2. Large (> 25%)	Decrease	Par value of stock distributed
Stock splits:		
1. Par reduced proportionally	No change	-0-
2. Par not reduced	Decrease	Par value of new shares
Acquisition of treasury stock:		
1. Cost method	No change	-0-
2. Par value method	No change or decrease	-0- [if cost ≤ (par + APIC)] Purchase price in excess of par and pro rata APIC
Sale of treasury stock:		
1. Cost method	No change or decrease	-0- (if sale price > cost) Excess of cost over sale price, but offset first to APIC on TS transactions
2. Par value method	No change	-0-
Prior period adjustments	Increase or decrease	Amount of adjustment, net of income tax
Certain special changes in accounting principle	Increase or decrease	Amount of adjustment, net of income tax

VII. STOCK RIGHTS AND STOCK WARRANTS

A. STOCK RIGHTS
Represents privileges extended by corporations to acquire additional shares of capital stock under prescribed conditions within a stated time period. Corporations often issue stock rights to existing common stockholders if additional common shares are to be issued to give them the opportunity to purchase a proportionate number of shares of the new offering.

B. STOCK WARRANTS
Physical evidence of stock rights. The warrants specify the number of rights conveyed, the number of shares to which the rightholders are entitled, the price at which the rightholders may purchase the additional shares, and the life of the rights (i.e., the time period over which the rights may be exercised).

C. **ACCOUNTING FOR STOCK RIGHTS**

1. **ISSUANCE OF RIGHTS** No entry is required when stock rights are issued to existing stockholders (other than a memorandum entry); therefore, common stock, additional paid-in capital, and retained earnings are **not** affected when stock rights are issued.

2. **EXERCISE OF RIGHTS** An entry is required only when stock rights are exercised. Cash is debited for the number of common shares acquired times the exercise price of the shares. Common stock is credited for the par or stated value of the shares issued. Additional paid-in capital is credited for the excess of the cash received over the par or stated value of the shares.

Cash (shares x exercise price)	XX	
Common Stock (shares x par/stated value)		XX
Additional Paid-In Capital (to balance)		XX

With respect to stock rights, common stock and additional paid-in capital can be increased only when the rights are exercised. Retained earnings is not affected when stock rights are exercised.

3. **LAPSE OF RIGHTS** No entry is required when stock rights are issued to existing stockholders (other than a memorandum entry); therefore, no entry is required when stock rights expire. Common stock, additional paid-in capital, and retained earnings are **not** affected when stock rights lapse.

VIII. **EMPLOYEES AND STOCK**

A. **OVERVIEW**

1. **STOCK OPTION AND STOCK PURCHASE PLANS** Corporations often adopt plans whereby employees may obtain shares of stock under specified conditions. The *reasons* for establishing such plans include to raise additional equity capital, to enhance employees' loyalty to the company through widespread ownership of the stock by the employees, and to provide additional compensation to key personnel.

2. **GAAP** Accounting for stock options is covered extensively in Chapter 13B of ARB 43, *Compensation Involved in Stock Option and Stock Purchase Plans*, in APB 25, *Accounting for Stock Issued to Employees*, and in SFAS 123, *Accounting for Stock-Based Compensation*. Basically, the appropriate accounting treatment for stock option plans is determined by whether the plan is *compensatory* or *noncompensatory*.

B. **NONCOMPENSATORY PLANS**
Noncompensatory plans pose no unique accounting problems. These plans are adopted primarily for the purpose of raising capital and inducing widespread ownership among a company's employees. Noncompensatory plans do not involve compensation expense and when the stock is issued, it is accounted for as an ordinary issue of stock. The following four characteristics are essential in a noncompensatory plan:

1. Substantially all full-time employees may participate.

2. Stock is offered to employees equally or based on a uniform percentage of salary.

3. The time permitted for exercise is limited to a reasonable period.

4. The discount from market price of the stock is no greater than would be reasonable in an offer to stockholders or others.

C.   COMPENSATORY PLANS
Compensatory plans are those that do not meet the four criteria for noncompensatory plans.

1.   Classification as a compensatory plan does not necessarily require that compensation cost be recognized.

2.   If the employee pays less than the quoted market price of the stock at the measurement date, compensation expense must be measured and allocated to the appropriate periods of the employee's services.

3.   The definition of an employee includes elected outside members of the company's board of directors. An individual is considered an employee if the company granting the options has sufficient control over the individual as to establish an employer-employee relationship.

D.   COMPENSATION MEASUREMENT

1.   MEASUREMENT DATE   The measurement date is *usually* the date of the grant. APB 25 specifies the measurement date as the first date on which both the following facts are known:

  a.   The number of shares that an individual employee is entitled to receive; and

  b.   The option or purchase price, if any.

2.   INTRINSIC VALUE METHOD (APB 25)   *Compensation cost* is the difference between the quoted market price of the stock at the measurement date and the amount, if any, to be paid by the employee.

3.   FAIR VALUE BASED METHOD (SFAS 123)   SFAS 123 encourages (but does not require) entities to adopt a *fair value based* method of accounting for stock-based compensation plans, rather than using the *intrinsic value based* method called for in APB 25.

  a.   FAIR VALUE   Fair value is defined as the amount at which willing parties in a current transaction would buy or sell an asset, other than in a forced or liquidation sale. The fair value based method calls for recognizing compensation cost of stock-based compensation by determining a fair value for the compensation, without limiting the valuation to quoted market prices. The intrinsic value based method of APB 25, uses the quoted market price of the stock at the grant or the measurement date in the computation of compensation cost. Fixed stock option plans, which are the most common type of stock compensation plans, often have no quoted market price at grant date, and thus, by definition, have no intrinsic value, which results in no recognition of compensation cost under APB 25.

  b.   VALUATION MODELS   SFAS 123 requires the use of a valuation model to estimate the value of the stock-based compensation granted. SFAS 123 suggests the use of the Black-Scholes, binomial or similar pricing model which takes into account the following information as of the grant date: (1) the exercise price, (2) the expected life of the option, (3) the current price of the stock, (4) the expected volatility of the stock, (5) the expected dividends on the stock, and (6) the risk-free interest rate for the expected term of the option.

  c.   EXCHANGES WITH NONEMPLOYEES   When options or other equity instruments are exchanged for goods or services with a nonemployee, the transaction will need to be reflected at fair value. In such a case, the value received may be more readily determinable than the value of the options given.

  d.   DISCLOSURE   Entities electing to continue measuring compensation cost under the intrinsic value based method prescribed in APB 25 must provide pro forma disclosures of the impact on earnings using a valuation model as called for in SFAS 123.

4. **GRANTED FOR FUTURE SERVICES** If the stock or options are granted as compensation for future services, deferred compensation cost is debited and the amount is recognized as compensation expense in the appropriate period. Deferred compensation expense is a contra-equity account.

EXAMPLE 6 ♦ COMPENSATORY PLAN

Assume an option is granted on January 1, 20X5 to a key executive to purchase 200 shares of $20 par common stock at $25 per share when the market price is $30 per share. The key executive is awarded the option based on services to be rendered equally in 20X5 and 20X6.

REQUIRED:

Make journal entries to record: (1) compensation cost on the measurement date, (2) yearly compensation expense, and (3) issuance of the stock if the option is exercised at the end of 20X6.

SOLUTION:

(1) *January 1, 20X5*

Deferred Comp. Cost [($30 − $25) x 200]	1,000	
Paid-In Capital—Stock Options Outstanding		1,000

(2) *December 31, 20X5 and 20X6*

Compensation Expense ($1,000 ÷ 2)	500	
Deferred Compensation Cost		500

(3) *December 31, 20X6*

Cash (200 x $25)	5,000	
Paid-In Capital—Stock Options Outstanding	1,000	
Common Stock (200 x $20)		4,000
Add'l. Paid-In Cap., Common (to balance)		2,000

NOTE: On the balance sheet, deferred compensation cost is recorded as a deduction from stock options outstanding; it is not an asset. The "net" of these two accounts represents the compensation that the employee has earned to date.

5. **MEASUREMENT AND GRANT DATES DIFFERENT** When the measurement date occurs subsequent to the grant date, compensation expense is recorded and accrued at the end of each period based on the quoted market price at the end of the period, the estimated number of shares earned, and the option price.

6. **ACCRUING FOR SERVICE PREVIOUSLY RENDERED** Where the employee works for several periods *before* the stock is issued, the employer should accrue a portion of the compensation expense from the stock issuance.

7. **UNEARNED STOCK COMPENSATION** Where the stock is issued before some or all of the services are performed, the compensation that is unearned is shown as a separate reduction to shareholder equity, and is recognized as an expense over the years in which services are performed.

8. **UNEXERCISED STOCK OPTIONS FOR NONVESTED EMPLOYEES** If a stock option is *not exercised* because an employee fails to fulfill an obligation under the option agreement, the estimate of compensation expense recorded in previous periods should be adjusted by decreasing compensation expense in the year of forfeiture.

9. **EXPIRED STOCK OPTIONS OF VESTED EMPLOYEES** Previously recognized compensation cost is not reversed if a vested employee's stock option expires unexercised.

10. **ADJUSTMENTS TO COMPENSATION EXPENSE** Adjustments to compensation expense in subsequent periods may be necessary as new estimates are determined.

11. **REPRICED OPTIONS** When a company directly or indirectly reprices options, it has changed the terms of the plan, which would convert the award from a fixed to a variable award as of the date of the repricing. Accounting for variable awards under APB 25 includes an element of compensation expense.

12. **STOCK APPRECIATION RIGHTS** Stock Appreciation Rights entitle employees to receive cash or stock in an amount equal to the excess of the market value of a stated number of shares over a stated price.

    a. In contrast to stock option plans, stock appreciation plans permit employees to share in stock appreciation without making a cash outlay.

    b. Compensation should be measured at the end of each period as the amount by which the quoted market value of the shares exceeds the predetermined price specified by the plan, and should be accrued as a charge to expense over the period the employee performs the related services.

    c. Changes in the quoted market value should be reflected as an adjustment (increase or decrease) of compensation expense and the related liability in the periods in which the changes occur until the date the number of shares and purchase price, if any, are both known. Thus, compensation expense increases (decreases) if the market value of the stock increases (decreases) from one period to another.

EXAMPLE 7 ♦ STOCK APPRECIATION RIGHTS

On January 1, 20X1, for past services, Rollins Company granted Sharon Carrier, its president, 2,000 stock appreciation rights that are exercisable immediately and expire five years after date of grant. On exercise, Carrier is entitled to receive cash for the excess of the market value of the stock on the exercise date over the market value on the date of grant. Carrier exercised all of the rights on December 31, 20X3. The per share market prices of Rollins' stock were as follows:

January 1, 20X1	$35
December 31, 20X1	40
December 31, 20X2	38
December 31, 20X3	50

The increase (decrease) in compensation expense that Rollins should recognize as a result of the stock appreciation rights in 20X1, 20X2, and 20X3 is determined as follows:

	20X1	20X2	20X3
Market price of stock, December 31	$ 40	$ 38	$ 50
Market price of stock, January 1	35	40	38
Increase (decrease) in market price	5	(2)	12
Stock appreciation rights	x 2,000	x 2,000	x 2,000
Increase (decrease) in compensation expense	$10,000	$ (4,000)	$24,000

The compensation expense required over the three-year period is $30,000 [2,000 x ($50 – $35)].

(continued on next page)

> The journal entries required for each of the three years are as follows:
>
> | 20X1 | Compensation Expense | 10,000 | |
> |------|----------------------|--------|--------|
> | | Stock Appreciation Plan Liability | | 10,000 |
> | 20X2 | Stock Appreciation Plan Liability | 4,000 | |
> | | Compensation Expense | | 4,000 |
> | 20X3 | Compensation Expense | 24,000 | |
> | | Stock Appreciation Plan Liability | | 24,000 |

13. EMPLOYEE STOCK OWNERSHIP PLANS (ESOP)

a. The compensation expense that an entity should recognize for an employee stock ownership plan is the amount contributed or committed to be contributed for the period. When a noncash asset or the entity's stock is contributed to the plan, the fair value of the noncash asset and the fair value of the entity's stock is used to measure compensation expense.

EXAMPLE 8 ♦ ESOP

> On May 1, 20X1, Harrell Corporation established an employee stock ownership plan. On May 1, 20X1, Harrell contributed $20,000 cash and 1,000 shares of its $10 par value common stock to the ESOP. On this date the market price of the stock was $23 a share.
>
> **REQUIRED:**
>
> Determine the amount of compensation expense that Harrell should report in its 20X1 income statement.
>
> **SOLUTION:**
>
> | | |
> |---|---|
> | Cash contributed | $20,000 |
> | Fair value of common stock contributed (1,000 shares x $23) | 23,000 |
> | Compensation expense recognized in 20X1 | $43,000 |

b. When an obligation of an employee stock ownership plan is covered by a guarantee of the employer or a commitment by the employer to make future contributions to the plan sufficient to meet debt service requirements, the obligation should be presented as a liability in the balance sheet of the employer. When the employer's liability is recorded, an offsetting debit is recorded that is reported as a reduction of stockholders' equity. Therefore, an employer reports a reduction of stockholders' equity equal to the obligation reported for the plan.

14. EMPLOYEE STOCK PURCHASE PLANS

a. **NONCOMPENSATORY** The following conditions must be met for an employee stock purchase plan to be considered noncompensatory, per SFAS 123, and are more restrictive than the criteria listed under APB 25.

(1) The plan contains no options features except that employees may be permitted to enroll in the plan during a short period, not more than 31 days, after the purchase price has been established. The purchase price may be based on the market price at the purchase date. The employees may be permitted to cancel participation before the purchase date and obtain a refund of amounts previously paid.

    (2)   The discount from the market price does not exceed the greater of (1) a per-share discount that would be reasonable in a recurring offer of stock to shareholders or others or (2) the per-share amount of stock issue costs avoided by not having to raise capital through a public offering. A 5% or smaller discount will automatically meet this condition. Larger discounts will require justification by the company.

    (3)   Substantially all full-time employees that meet limited employment qualifications may participate on an equitable basis.

  b.   **COMPENSATORY** If the plan is deemed to be compensatory, then compensation cost will need to be recognized using either the option pricing approach of SFAS 123 or the intrinsic value approach (i.e., the difference between the exercise and market price) of APB 25.

E. **DISCLOSURE**
The following information must be disclosed by all companies regardless of the accounting approach taken.

  1.   The number and weighted-average exercise prices of options: (a) for those outstanding at the beginning of the year, (b) for those outstanding at the end of the year, (c) for those exercisable at the end of the year, (d) for those granted during the year, (e) for those exercised during the year, (f) for those forfeited during the year, and (g) for those expired during the year.

  2.   The weighted-average grant-date fair value of options granted during the year.

  3.   The number and weighted-average grant-date fair value of equity instruments other than options.

  4.   A description of the method and significant assumptions used during the year to estimate the fair values of options.

  5.   Total compensation cost recognized in income for stock-based employee compensation awards.

  6.   The terms of significant modifications of outstanding awards.

IX. **DISCLOSURE REQUIREMENTS**

  A. **APPLICABILITY**
All entities, public and nonpublic, that have issued securities are required to make certain disclosures about their capital structures. These disclosure requirements, previously covered in various pronouncements, were recently consolidated into one pronouncement, SFAS 129, *Disclosure of Information about Capital Structure*.

  B. **RIGHTS AND PRIVILEGES OF SECURITIES OUTSTANDING**
An entity is required to disclose in the financial statements, in summary form, the pertinent rights and privileges of the various securities outstanding. Examples include, dividend and liquidation preferences, participation rights, call prices and dates, conversion or exercise prices or rates and pertinent dates, sinking-fund requirements, unusual voting rights, and significant terms of contracts to issue additional shares.

  C. **NUMBER OF SHARES ISSUED**
An entity is required to disclose the number of shares issued upon conversion, exercise, or satisfaction of required conditions during at least the most recent annual fiscal period and any subsequent interim period presented.

D. **LIQUIDATION PREFERENCE OF PREFERRED STOCK**

1. If an entity issues preferred stock or other senior stock that has a preference in involuntary liquidation considerably in excess of the par or stated value of the shares, the entity is required to disclose this information in the equity section of the statement of financial position. The disclosure may be made parenthetically or "in short", but not on a per-share basis or in the notes.

2. In addition, the entity is required to disclose, either on the statement of financial position or in the notes, the aggregate or per-share amounts at which preferred stock may be called or is subject to redemption through sinking-fund operations, and the aggregate or per share amounts of arrearages in cumulative preferred dividends.

E. **REDEEMABLE STOCK**
The amount of redemption requirements related to redeemable stock must be disclosed for all issues of capital stock that are redeemable at fixed or determinable prices on fixed or determinable dates in each of the five years following the date of the latest statement of financial position presented.

CHAPTER 10—OWNERS' EQUITY

PROBLEM 10-1 MULTIPLE CHOICE QUESTIONS (144 to 180 minutes)

1. Rice Co. was incorporated on January 1, 1991, with $500,000 from the issuance of stock and borrowed funds of $75,000. During the first year of operations, net income was $25,000. On December 15, Rice paid a $2,000 cash dividend. No additional activities affected owners' equity in 1991. At December 31, 1991, Rice's liabilities had increased to $94,000. In Rice's December 31, 1991, balance sheet, total assets should be reported at
a. $598,000.
b. $600,000.
c. $617,000.
d. $692,000.   (11/92, PI, #6, 3239)

2. Zinc Co.'s adjusted trial balance at December 31, 1991, includes the following account balances:

Common stock, $3 par	$600,000
Additional paid-in capital	800,000
Treasury stock, at cost	50,000
Net unrealized loss on AFS marketable equity securities	20,000
Retained earnings: Appropriated for uninsured earthquake losses	150,000
Retained earnings: Unappropriated	200,000

What amount should Zinc report as total stockholders' equity in its December 31, 1991 balance sheet?
a. $1,680,000
b. $1,720,000
c. $1,780,000
d. $1,820,000   (5/92, PI, #5, amended, 2572)

3. On January 2, 1993, Smith purchased the net assets of Jones' Cleaning, a sole proprietorship, for $350,000, and commenced operations of Spiffy Cleaning, a sole proprietorship. The assets had a carrying amount of $375,000 and a market value of $360,000. In Spiffy's cash-basis financial statements for the year ended December 31, 1993, Spiffy reported revenues in excess of expenses of $60,000. Smith's drawings during 1993 were $20,000. In Spiffy's financial statements, what amount should be reported as Capital—Smith?
a. $390,000
b. $400,000
c. $410,000
d. $415,000   (11/94, FAR, #36, 5298)

4. At December 31, 1991 and 1992, Carr Corp. had outstanding 4,000 shares of $100 par value 6% cumulative preferred stock and 20,000 shares of $10 par value common stock. At December 31, 1991, dividends in arrears on the preferred stock were $12,000. Cash dividends declared in 1992 totaled $44,000. Of the $44,000, what amounts were payable on each class of stock?

	Preferred stock	Common stock
a.	$44,000	$0
b.	$36,000	$ 8,000
c.	$32,000	$12,000
d.	$24,000	$20,000

(5/93, PII, #4, 4113)

5. At December 31, 1992 and 1993, Apex Co. had 3,000 shares of $100 par, 5% cumulative preferred stock outstanding. No dividends were in arrears as of December 31, 1991. Apex did not declare a dividend during 1992. During 1993, Apex paid a cash dividend of $10,000 on its preferred stock. Apex should report dividends in arrears in its 1993 financial statements as a (an)

a. Accrued liability of $15,000.
b. Disclosure of $15,000.
c. Accrued liability of $20,000.
d. Disclosure of $20,000.   (5/94, FAR, #8, 4823)

6. On April 1, 1993, Hyde Corp., a newly formed company, had the following stock issued and outstanding:

- Common stock, no par, $1 stated value, 20,000 shares originally issued for $30 per share.
- Preferred stock, $10 par value, 6,000 shares originally issued for $50 per share.

Hyde's April 1, 1993, statement of stockholders' equity should report

	Common stock	Preferred stock	Additional paid-in capital
a.	$ 20,000	$ 60,000	$820,000
b.	$ 20,000	$300,000	$580,000
c.	$600,000	$300,000	$0
d.	$600,000	$ 60,000	$240,000

(5/93, PI, #6, 4048)

7. Beck Corp. issued 200,000 shares of common stock when it began operations in 1990 and issued an additional 100,000 shares in 1991. Beck also issued preferred stock convertible to 100,000 shares of common stock. In 1992, Beck purchased 75,000 shares of its common stock and held it in Treasury. At December 31, 1992, how many shares of Beck's common stock were outstanding?

a. 400,000
b. 325,000
c. 300,000
d. 225,000   (5/93, PII, #2, 4111)

8. The condensed balance sheet of Adams & Gray, a partnership, at December 31, 1992, follows:

Current assets	$250,000
Equipment (net)	30,000
Total assets	$280,000
Liabilities	$ 20,000
Adams, capital	160,000
Gray, capital	100,000
Total liabilities and capital	$280,000

On December 31, 1992, the fair values of the assets and liabilities were appraised at $240,000 and $20,000, respectively, by an independent appraiser. On January 2, 1993, the partnership was incorporated and 1,000 shares of $5 par value common stock were issued. Immediately after the incorporation, what amount should the new corporation report as additional paid-in capital?

a. $275,000
b. $260,000
c. $215,000
d. $0   (5/93, PII, #6, 4115)

9. On December 1, 1997, shares of authorized common stock were issued on a subscription basis at a price in excess of par value. A total of 20% of the subscription price of each share was collected as a down payment on December 1, 1997, with the remaining 80% of the subscription price of each share due in 1998. Collectibility was reasonably assured. At December 31, 1997, the stockholders' equity section of the balance sheet would report additional paid-in capital for the excess of the subscription price over the par value of the shares of common stock subscribed and
a. Common stock issued for 20% of the par value of the shares of common stock subscribed.
b. Common stock issued for the par value of the shares of common stock subscribed.

c. Common stock subscribed for 80% of the par value of the shares of common stock subscribed.
d. Common stock subscribed for the par value of the shares of common stock subscribed.
                          (11/88, Theory, #17, amended, 1996)

10. East Co. issued 1,000 shares of its $5 par common stock to Howe as compensation for 1,000 hours of legal services performed. Howe usually bills $160 per hour for legal services. On the date of issuance, the stock was trading on a public exchange at $140 per share. By what amount should the additional paid-in capital account increase as a result of this transaction?
a. $135,000
b. $140,000
c. $155,000
d. $160,000   (11/94, FAR, #28, 5291)

11. Jay & Kay partnership's balance sheet at December 31, 1990, reported the following:

Total assets	$100,000
Total liabilities	20,000
Jay, capital	40,000
Kay, capital	40,000

On January 2, 1991, Jay and Kay dissolved their partnership and transferred all assets and liabilities to a newly formed corporation. At the date of incorporation, the fair value of the net assets was $12,000 more than the carrying amount on the partnership's books, of which $7,000 was assigned to tangible assets and $5,000 was assigned to goodwill. Jay and Kay were each issued 5,000 shares of the corporation's $1 par value common stock. Immediately following incorporation, additional paid-in capital in excess of par should be credited for
a. $68,000.
b. $70,000.
c. $77,000.
d. $82,000.   (11/91, PII, #8, 2456)

12. On July 1, 1992, Cove Corp., a closely held corporation, issued 6% bonds with a maturity value of $60,000, together with 1,000 shares of its $5 par value common stock, for a combined cash amount of $110,000. The market value of Cove's stock cannot be ascertained. If the bonds were issued separately, they would have sold for $40,000 on an 8% yield to maturity basis. What amount should Cove report for additional paid-in capital on the issuance of the stock?
a. $75,000
b. $65,000
c. $55,000
d. $45,000   (11/92, PII, #44, 3378)

13. On March 1, 1992, Rya Corp. issued 1,000 shares of its $20 par value common stock and 2,000 shares of its $20 par value convertible preferred stock for a total of $80,000. At this date, Rya's common stock was selling for $36 per share, and the convertible preferred stock was selling for $27 per share. What amount of the proceeds should be allocated to Rya's convertible preferred stock?

a. $60,000
b. $54,000
c. $48,000
d. $44,000   (5/92, PII, #1, 2633)

14. During 1992, Brad Co. issued 5,000 shares of $100 par convertible preferred stock for $110 per share. One share of preferred stock can be converted into three shares of Brad's $25 par common stock at the option of the preferred shareholder. On December 31, 1993, when the market value of the common stock was $40 per share, all of the preferred stock was converted. What amount should Brad credit to Common Stock and to Additional Paid-In Capital—Common Stock as a result of the conversion?

	Common stock	Additional paid-in capital
a.	$375,000	$175,000
b.	$375,000	$225,000
c.	$500,000	$ 50,000
d.	$600,000	$0

(11/94, FAR, #29, 5292)

15. The following changes in Vel Corp.'s account balances occurred during 1992:

	Increase
Assets	$89,000
Liabilities	27,000
Capital stock	60,000
Additional paid-in capital	6,000

Except for a $13,000 dividend payment and the year's earnings, there were no changes in retained earnings for 1992. What was Vel's net income for 1992?

a. $ 4,000
b. $ 9,000
c. $13,000
d. $17,000   (5/93, PII, #3, 4112)

16. At December 31, 1991, Eagle Corp. reported $1,750,000 of appropriated retained earnings for the construction of a new office building, which was completed in 1992 at a total cost of $1,500,000. In 1992, Eagle appropriated $1,200,000 of retained earnings for the construction of a new plant. Also, $2,000,000 of cash was restricted for the retirement of bonds due in 1993. In its 1992 balance sheet, Eagle should report what amount of appropriated retained earnings?

a. $1,200,000
b. $1,450,000
c. $2,950,000
d. $3,200,000   (5/93, PII, #5, 4114)

17. A retained earnings appropriation can be used to

a. Absorb a fire loss when a company is self-insured.
b. Provide for a contingent loss that is probable and reasonable.
c. Smooth periodic income.
d. Restrict earnings available for dividends.
                    (5/92, Theory, #37, 2730)

18. The following information pertains to Meg Corp.:

• Dividends on its 1,000 shares of 6%, $10 par value cumulative preferred stock have not been declared or paid for 3 years.
• Treasury stock that cost $15,000 was reissued for $8,000.

What amount of retained earnings should be appropriated as a result of these items?

a. $0
b. $1,800
c. $7,000
d. $8,800   (5/92, PII, #6, 2638)

19. The primary purpose of a quasi-reorganization is to give a corporation the opportunity to

a. Obtain relief from its creditors.
b. Revalue understated assets to their fair values.
c. Eliminate a deficit in retained earnings.
d. Distribute the stock of a newly-created subsidiary to its stockholders in exchange for part of their stock in the corporation.
                    (11/94, FAR, #37, 5299)

20. The stockholders' equity section of Brown Co.'s December 31, 1994, balance sheet consisted of the following:

Common stock, $30 par, 10,000 shares authorized and outstanding	$ 300,000
Additional paid-in capital	150,000
Retained earnings (deficit)	(210,000)

On January 2, 1995, Brown put into effect a stock-holder-approved quasi-reorganization by reducing the par value of the stock to $5 and eliminating the deficit against additional paid-in capital. Immediately after the quasi-reorganization, what amount should Brown report as additional paid-in capital?
a. $ (60,000)
b. $150,000
c. $190,000
d. $400,000   (11/95, FAR, #25, 6107)

21. Rudd Corp. had 700,000 shares of common stock authorized and 300,000 shares outstanding at December 31, 1991. The following events occurred during 1992:

January 31	Declared 10% stock dividend
June 30	Purchased 100,000 shares
August 1	Reissued 50,000 shares
November 30	Declared 2-for-1 stock split

At December 31, 1992, how many shares of common stock did Rudd have outstanding?
a. 560,000
b. 600,000
c. 630,000
d. 660,000   (5/93, PII, #1, 4110)

22. On January 15, 2000, Rico Co. declared its annual cash dividend on common stock for the year ended January 31, 2000. The dividend was paid on February 9, 2000, to stockholders of record as of January 28, 2000. On what date should Rico decrease retained earnings by the amount of the dividend?
a. January 15, 2000
b. January 31, 2000
c. January 28, 2000
d. February 9, 2000   (1999, FAR, #10, 6779)

23. Bal Corp. declared a $25,000 cash dividend on May 8, 1991, to stockholders of record on May 23, 1991, payable on June 3, 1991. As a result of this cash dividend, working capital
a. Was **not** affected.
b. Decreased on June 3.
c. Decreased on May 23.
d. Decreased on May 8.   (5/92, PII, #3, 2635)

24. A company declared a cash dividend on its common stock on December 15, 1990, payable on January 12, 1991. How would this dividend affect stockholders' equity on the following dates?

	December 15, 1990	December 31, 1990	January 12, 1991
a.	Decrease	No effect	Decrease
b.	Decrease	No effect	No effect
c.	No effect	Decrease	No effect
d.	No effect	No effect	Decrease

(5/91, Theory, #17, 1971)

25. On June 27, 1992, Brite Co. distributed to its common stockholders 100,000 outstanding common shares of its investment in Quik Inc., an unrelated party. The carrying amount on Brite's books of Quik's $1 par common stock was $2 per share. Immediately after the distribution, the market price of Quik's stock was $2.50 per share. In its income statement for the year ended June 30, 1992, what amount should Brite report as gain before income taxes on disposal of the stock?
a. $250,000
b. $200,000
c. $ 50,000
d. $0   (5/93, PI, #45, 4086)

26. Bain Corp. owned 20,000 common shares of Tell Corp. purchased in 1993 for $180,000. On December 15, 1997, Bain declared a property dividend of all of its Tell Corp. shares on the basis of one share of Tell for every 10 shares of Bain common stock held by its stockholders. The property dividend was distributed on January 15, 1998. On the declaration date, the aggregate market price of the Tell shares held by Bain was $300,000. The entry to record the declaration of the dividend would include a debit to retained earnings (or property dividends declared) of
a. $0.
b. $120,000.
c. $180,000.
d. $300,000.   (11/88, PI, #60, amended, 9040)

27. Instead of the usual cash dividend, Evie Corp. declared and distributed a property dividend from its overstocked merchandise. The excess of the merchandise's carrying amount over its market value should be
a. Ignored.
b. Reported as a separately disclosed reduction of retained earnings.
c. Reported as an extraordinary loss, net of income taxes.
d. Reported as a reduction in income before extraordinary items.   (5/92, Theory, #36, 2729)

28. On December 1, 1991, Nilo Corp. declared a property dividend of marketable securities to be distributed on December 31, 1991, to stockholders of record on December 15, 1991. On December 1, 1991, the marketable securities had a carrying amount of $60,000 and a fair value of $78,000. What is the effect of this property dividend on Nilo's 1991 retained earnings, after all nominal accounts are closed?
a. $0
b. $18,000 increase
c. $60,000 decrease
d. $78,000 decrease   (5/92, PII, #4, 2636)

29. East Corp., a calendar-year company, had sufficient retained earnings in 1993 as a basis for dividends, but was temporarily short of cash. East declared a dividend of $100,000 on April 1, 1993, and issued promissory notes to its stockholders in lieu of cash. The notes, which were dated April 1, 1993, had a maturity date of March 31, 1994, and a 10% interest rate. How should East account for the scrip dividend and related interest?
a. Debit retained earnings for $110,000 on April 1, 1993.
b. Debit retained earnings for $110,000 on March 31, 1994.
c. Debit retained earnings for $100,000 on April 1, 1993, and debit interest expense for $10,000 on March 31, 1994.
d. Debit retained earnings for $100,000 on April 1, 1993, and debit interest expense for $7,500 on December 31, 1993.   (5/94, FAR, #31, 4846)

30. On January 2, 1994, Lake Mining Co.'s board of directors declared a cash dividend of $400,000 to stockholders of record on January 18, 1994, payable on February 10, 1994. The dividend is permissible under law in Lake's state of incorporation. Selected data from Lake's December 31, 1993 balance sheet are as follows:

Accumulated depletion	$100,000
Capital stock	500,000
Additional paid-in capital	150,000
Retained earnings	300,000

The $400,000 dividend includes a liquidating dividend of
a. $0.
b. $100,000.
c. $150,000.
d. $300,000.   (5/94, FAR, #32, 4847)

31. Ole Corp. declared and paid a liquidating dividend of $100,000. This distribution resulted in a decrease in Ole's

	Paid-in capital	Retained earnings
a.	No	No
b.	Yes	Yes
c.	No	Yes
d.	Yes	No

(11/91, PII, #6, 2454)

32. A corporation declared a dividend, a portion of which was liquidating. How would this declaration affect each of the following?

	Additional paid-in capital	Retained earnings
a.	Decrease	No effect
b.	Decrease	Decrease
c.	No effect	Decrease
d.	No effect	No effect

(11/89, Theory, #21, 1987)

ITEMS 33 AND 34 are based on the following:

The following format was used by Gee Inc. for its 1991 statement of owners' equity:

	Common stock, $1 par	Additional paid-in capital	Retained earnings
Balance at 1/1/91	$90,000	$800,000	$175,000
Additions and deductions:			
100% stock dividend			
5% stock dividend			
Balance at 12/31/91			

When both the 100% and the 5% stock dividends were declared, Gee's common stock was selling for more than its $1 par value.

33. How would the 100% stock dividend affect the additional paid-in capital and retained earnings amounts reported in Gee's 1991 statement of owners' equity?

	Additional paid-in capital	Retained earnings
a.	Increase	Increase
b.	Increase	Decrease
c.	No change	Increase
d.	No change	Decrease

(5/92, PI, #2, 2569)

34. How would the 5% stock dividend affect the additional paid-in capital and retained earnings amounts reported in Gee's 1991 statement of owners' equity?

	Additional paid-in capital	Retained earnings
a.	Increase	Decrease
b.	Increase	Increase
c.	No change	Decrease
d.	No change	Increase

(5/92, PI, #3, 2570)

35. The following stock dividends were declared and distributed by Sol Corp.:

Percentage of common shares outstanding at declaration date	Fair value	Par value
10	$15,000	$10,000
28	40,000	30,800

What aggregate amounts should be debited to retained earnings for these stock dividends?
a. $40,800
b. $45,800
c. $50,000
d. $55,000

(5/91, PII, #12, 1093)

36. On May 18, 1992, Sol Corp.'s board of directors declared a 10% stock dividend. The market price of Sol's 3,000 outstanding shares of $2 par value common stock was $9 per share on that date. The stock dividend was distributed on July 21, 1992, when the stock's market price was $10 per share. What amount should Sol credit to additional paid-in capital for this stock dividend?
a. $2,100
b. $2,400
c. $2,700
d. $3,000

(11/92, PII, #41, 3375)

37. Long Co. had 100,000 shares of common stock issued and outstanding at January 1, 1993. During 1993, Long took the following actions:

March 15 — Declared a 2-for-1 stock split, when the fair value of the stock was $80 per share.

December 15 — Declared a $.50 per share cash dividend.

In Long's statement of stockholders' equity for 1993, what amount should Long report as dividends?
a. $ 50,000
b. $100,000
c. $850,000
d. $950,000

(11/94, FAR, #31, 5294)

38. Stock dividends on common stock should be recorded at their fair market value by the investor when the related investment is accounted for under which of the following methods?

	Cost	Equity
a.	Yes	Yes
b.	Yes	No
c.	No	Yes
d.	No	No

(11/94, FAR, #39, 5301)

39. How would a stock split affect each of the following?

	Assets	Total stock-holders' equity	Additional paid-in capital
a.	Increase	Increase	No effect
b.	No effect	No effect	No effect
c.	No effect	No effect	Increase
d.	Decrease	Decrease	Decrease

(5/85, Theory, #17, 2012)

40. On December 1, 1992, Line Corp. received a donation of 2,000 shares of its $5 par value common stock from a stockholder. On that date, the stock's market value was $35 per share. The stock was originally issued for $25 per share. By what amount would this donation cause total stockholders' equity to decrease?
a. $70,000
b. $50,000
c. $20,000
d. $0

(5/93, PI, #11, 4053)

41. Grid Corp. acquired some of its own common shares at a price greater than both their par value and original issue price but less than their book value. Grid uses the cost method of accounting for treasury stock. What is the impact of this acquisition on total stockholders' equity and the book value per common share?

	Total stockholders' equity	Book value per share
a.	Increase	Increase
b.	Increase	Decrease
c.	Decrease	Increase
d.	Decrease	Decrease

(11/91, Theory, #40, 2548)

42. Nest Co. issued 100,000 shares of common stock. Of these, 5,000 were held as treasury stock at December 31, 1993. During 1994, transactions involving Nest's common stock were as follows:

May 3 — 1,000 shares of treasury stock were sold.

August 6 — 10,000 shares of previously unissued stock were sold.

November 18 — A 2-for-1 stock split took effect.

Laws in Nest's state of incorporation protect treasury stock from dilution. At December 31, 1994, how many shares of Nest's common stock were issued and outstanding?

	Shares	
	Issued	Outstanding
a.	220,000	212,000
b.	220,000	216,000
c.	222,000	214,000
d.	222,000	218,000

(11/95, FAR, #18, 6100)

43. Selected information from the accounts of Row Co. at December 31, 1995, follows:

Total income since incorporation	$420,000
Total cash dividends paid	130,000
Total value of property dividends distributed	30,000
Excess of proceeds over cost of treasury stock sold, accounted for using the cost method	110,000

In its December 31, 1995, financial statements, what amount should Row report as retained earnings?
a. $260,000
b. $290,000
c. $370,000
d. $400,000

(5/96, FAR, #1, 6274)

44. If a corporation sells some of its treasury stock at a price that exceeds its cost, this excess should be
a. Reported as a gain in the income statement.
b. Treated as a reduction in the carrying amount of remaining treasury stock.
c. Credited to additional paid-in capital.
d. Credited to retained earnings.

(11/94, FAR, #32, 5295)

45. In 1989, Seda Corp. acquired 6,000 shares of its $1 par value common stock at $36 per share. During 1990, Seda issued 3,000 of these shares at $50 per share. Seda uses the cost method to account for its treasury stock transactions. What accounts and amounts should Seda credit in 1990 to record the issuance of the 3,000 shares?

	Treasury stock	Additional paid-in capital	Retained earnings	Common stock
a.		$102,000	$42,000	$6,000
b.		$144,000		$6,000
c.	$108,000	$ 42,000		
d.	$108,000		$42,000	

(11/91, PII, #7, 2455)

46. Cyan Corp. issued 20,000 shares of $5 par common stock at $10 per share. On December 31, 1993, Cyan's retained earnings were $300,000. In March 1994, Cyan reacquired 5,000 shares of its common stock at $20 per share. In June 1994, Cyan sold 1,000 of these shares to its corporate officers for $25 per share. Cyan uses the cost method to record treasury stock. Net income for the year ended December 31, 1994, was $60,000. At December 31, 1994, what amount should Cyan report as retained earnings?
a. $360,000
b. $365,000
c. $375,000
d. $380,000

(11/95, FAR, #19, 6101)

47. Treasury stock was acquired for cash at a price in excess of its original issue price. The treasury stock was subsequently reissued for cash at a price in excess of its acquisition price. Assuming that the par value method of accounting for treasury stock transactions is used, what is the effect on total stockholders' equity of each of the following events?

	Acquisition of treasury stock	Reissuance of treasury stock
a.	Decrease	No effect
b.	Decrease	Increase
c.	Increase	Decrease
d.	No effect	No effect

(5/90, Theory, #15, 1982)

48. The par-value method of accounting for treasury stock differs from the cost method in that
a. Any gain is recognized upon repurchase of stock but a loss is treated as an adjustment to retained earnings.
b. No gains or losses are recognized on the issuance of treasury stock using the par-value method.
c. It reverses the original entry to issue the common stock with any difference between carrying amount and purchase price adjusted through paid-in capital and/or retained earnings and treats a subsequent reissuance like a new issuance of common stock.
d. It reverses the original entry to issue the common stock with any difference between carrying amount and purchase price being shown as an ordinary gain or loss and does **not** recognize any gain or loss on a subsequent resale of the stock. (5/89, Theory, #10, 1993)

49. On incorporation, Dee Inc., issued common stock at a price in excess of its par value. No other stock transactions occurred except treasury stock was acquired for an amount exceeding this issue price. If Dee uses the par value method of accounting for treasury stock appropriate for retired stock, what is the effect of the acquisition on the following?

	Net common stock	Additional paid-in capital	Retained earnings
a.	No effect	Decrease	No effect
b.	Decrease	Decrease	Decrease
c.	Decrease	No effect	Decrease
d.	No effect	Decrease	Decrease

(5/91, Theory, #18, 1972)

50. Asp Co. was organized on January 2, 1994, with 30,000 authorized shares of $10 par common stock. During 1994 the corporation had the following capital transactions:

January 5 — issued 20,000 shares at $15 per share.
July 14 — purchased 5,000 shares at $17 per share.
December 27 — reissued the 5,000 shares held in treasury at $20 per share.

Asp used the par value method to record the purchase and reissuance of the treasury shares. In its December 31, 1994, balance sheet, what amount should Asp report as additional paid-in capital in excess of par?

a. $100,000
b. $125,000
c. $140,000
d. $150,000 (11/95, FAR, #20, 6102)

51. Posy Corp. acquired treasury shares at an amount greater than their par value, but less than their original issue price. Compared to the cost method of accounting for treasury stock, does the par value method report a greater amount for additional paid-in capital and a greater amount for retained earnings?

	Additional paid-in capital	Retained earnings
a.	Yes	Yes
b.	Yes	No
c.	No	No
d.	No	Yes

(11/91, Theory, #39, 2547)

52. When preparing a draft of its 1990 balance sheet, Mont Inc., reported net assets totaling $875,000. Included in the asset section of the balance sheet were the following:

Treasury stock of Mont Inc., at cost, which approximates market value on December 31	$24,000
Idle machinery	11,200
Cash surrender value of life insurance on corporate executives	13,700
Allowance for decline in market value of available-for-sale equity investments	8,400

At what amount should Mont's net assets be reported in the December 31, 1990, balance sheet?
a. $851,000
b. $850,100
c. $842,600
d. $834,500 (5/91, PI, #1, amended, 1084)

53. At December 31, 1997, Rama Corp. had 20,000 shares of $1 par value treasury stock that had been acquired in 1997 at $12 per share. In May 1998, Rama issued 15,000 of these treasury shares at $10 per share. The cost method is used to record treasury stock transactions. Rama is located in a state where laws relating to acquisition of treasury stock restrict the availability of retained earnings for declaration of dividends. At December 31, 1998, what amount should Rama show in notes to financial statements as a restriction of retained earnings as a result of its treasury stock transactions?
a. $ 5,000
b. $10,000
c. $60,000
d. $90,000 (5/89, PII, #6, amended, 1103)

54. In 1990, Fogg Inc. issued $10 par value common stock for $25 per share. No other common stock transactions occurred until March 31, 1992, when Fogg acquired some of the issued shares for $20 per share and retired them. Which of the following statements correctly states an effect of this acquisition and retirement?
a. 1992 net income is decreased.
b. 1992 net income is increased.
c. Additional paid-in capital is decreased.
d. Retained earnings is increased.

(5/93, Theory, #10, 4198)

55. In 1990 Rona Corp. issued 5,000 shares of $10 par value common stock for $100 per share. In 1998, Rona reacquired 2,000 of its shares at $150 per share from the estate of one of its deceased officers and immediately canceled these 2,000 shares. Rona uses the cost method in accounting for its treasury stock transactions. In connection with the retirement of these 2,000 shares, Rona should debit

	Additional paid-in capital	Retained earnings
a.	$ 20,000	$280,000
b.	$100,000	$180,000
c.	$180,000	$100,000
d.	$280,000	$0

(11/89, PII, #12, amended, 1096)

56. Park Corp.'s stockholders' equity accounts at December 31, 1997 were as follows:

Common stock, $20 par	$8,000,000
Additional paid-in capital	2,550,000
Retained earnings	1,275,000

All shares of common stock outstanding at December 31, 1997, were issued in 1984 for $26 a share. On January 4, 1998, Park reacquired 20,000 shares of its common stock at $24 a share and retired them. Immediately after the shares were retired, the balance in additional paid-in capital would be
a. $2,430,000.
b. $2,470,000.
c. $2,510,000.
d. $2,590,000.   (5/88, PI, #42, amended, 1106)

57. On December 31, 1991, Pack Corp.'s board of directors canceled 50,000 shares of $2.50 par value common stock held in treasury at an average cost of $13 per share. Before recording the cancellation of the treasury stock, Pack had the following balances in its stockholder's equity accounts:

Common Stock	$540,000
Additional paid-in capital	750,000
Retained earnings	900,000
Treasury stock, at cost	650,000

In its balance sheet at December 31, 1991, Pack should report common stock outstanding of
a. $0.
b. $250,000.
c. $415,000.
d. $540,000.   (11/92, PII, #50, 3384)

58. Quoit Inc. issued preferred stock with detachable common stock warrants. The issue price exceeded the sum of the warrants' fair value and the preferred stocks' par value. The preferred stocks' fair value was not determinable. What amount should be assigned to the warrants outstanding?
a. Total proceeds.
b. Excess of proceeds over the par value of the preferred stock.
c. The proportion of the proceeds that the warrants' fair value bears to the preferred stocks' par value.
d. The fair value of the warrants.

(5/93, Theory, #13, 4201)

59. On November 2, 1992, Finsbury Inc. issued warrants to its stockholders giving them the right to purchase additional $20 par value common shares at a price of $30. The stockholders exercised all warrants on March 1, 1993. The shares had market prices of $33, $35, and $40 on November 2, 1992, December 31, 1992, and March 1, 1993, respectively. What were the effects of the warrants on Finsbury's additional paid-in capital and net income?

	Add'l paid-in capital	Net income
a.	Increased in 1993	No effect
b.	Increased in 1992	No effect
c.	Increased in 1993	Decreased in 1992 and 1993
d.	Increased in 1992	Decreased in 1992 and 1993

(11/93, Theory, #15, 4520)

60. Cricket Corp. issued, without consideration, rights allowing stockholders to subscribe for additional shares at an amount greater than par value but less than both market and book values. When the rights are exercised, how are the following accounts affected?

	Retained earnings	Additional paid-in capital
a.	Decreased	Not affected
b.	Not affected	Not affected
c.	Decreased	Increased
d.	Not affected	Increased

(5/91, Theory, #19, 1973)

61. A company issued rights to its existing shareholders to purchase for $15 per share, 5,000 unissued shares of common stock with a par value of $10 per share. Common stock will be credited at
a. $15 per share when the rights are exercised.
b. $15 per share when the rights are issued.
c. $10 per share when the rights are exercised.
d. $10 per share when the rights are issued.
(5/84, Theory, #24, 9041)

62. A company issued rights to its existing shareholders without consideration. The rights allowed the recipients to purchase unissued common stock for an amount in excess of par value. When the rights are issued, which of the following accounts will be increased?

	Common stock	Additional paid-in capital
a.	Yes	Yes
b.	Yes	No
c.	No	No
d.	No	Yes

(11/95, FAR, #21, 6103)

63. In September 1989, West Corp. made a dividend distribution of one right for each of its 120,000 shares of outstanding common stock. Each right was exercisable for the purchase of 1/100 of a share of West's $50 variable rate preferred stock at an exercise price of $80 per share. On March 20, 1993, none of the rights had been exercised, and West redeemed them by paying each stockholder $0.10 per right. As a result of this redemption, West's stockholders' equity was reduced by
a. $ 120.
b. $ 2,400.
c. $12,000.
d. $36,000.
(11/95, FAR, #22, 6104)

64. On January 2, 1993, Kine Co. granted Morgan, its president, compensatory stock options to buy 1,000 shares of Kine's $10 par common stock. The options call for a price of $20 per share and are exercisable for 3 years following the grant date. Morgan exercised the options on December 31, 1993. The market price of the stock was $50 on January 2, 1993, and $70 on December 31, 1993. By what net amount should stockholders' equity increase as a result of the grant and exercise of the options?
a. $20,000
b. $30,000
c. $50,000
d. $70,000
(5/94, FAR, #33, 4848)

65. In a compensatory stock option plan for which the grant, measurement, and exercise date are all different, the stock options outstanding account should be reduced at the
a. Date of grant.
b. Measurement date.
c. Beginning of the service period.
d. Exercise date.
(5/93, Theory, #14, 4202)

66. On January 2, 1993, Farm Co. granted an employee an option to purchase 1,000 shares of Farm's common stock at $40 per share. The option became exercisable on December 31, 1993, after the employee had completed one year of service, and was exercised on that date. The market prices of Farm's stock were as follows:

| January 2, 1993 | $50 |
| December 31, 1993 | 65 |

What amount should Farm recognize as compensation expense for 1993?
a. $0
b. $10,000
c. $15,000
d. $25,000
(11/94, FAR, #33, 9042)

67. On June 1, 1991, Oak Corp. granted stock options to certain key employees as additional compensation. The options were for 1,000 shares of Oak's $2 par value common stock at an option price of $15 per share. Market price of this stock on June 1, 1991, was $20 per share. The options were exercisable beginning January 2, 1992, and expire on December 31, 1993. On April 1, 1992, when Oak's stock was trading at $21 per share, all the options were exercised. What amount of pretax compensation should Oak report in 1991 in connection with the options?
a. $6,000
b. $5,000
c. $2,500
d. $2,000
(11/92, PII, #56, 3390)

68. For a compensatory stock option plan for which the date of grant and the measurement date are different, compensation cost should be recognized in the income statement
a. At the later of grant or measurement date.
b. At the exercise date.
c. At the adoption date of the plan.
d. Of each period in which the services are rendered.
(11/84, Theory, #35, 9043)

69. Wolf Co.'s grant of 30,000 stock appreciation rights enables key employees to receive cash equal to the difference between $20 and the market price of the stock on the date each right is exercised. The service period is 1996 through 1998, and the rights are exercisable in 1999 and 2000. The market price of the stock was $25 and $28 at December 31, 1996 and 1997, respectively. What amount should Wolf report as the liability under the stock appreciation rights plan in its December 31, 1997 balance sheet?

a. $0
b. $130,000
c. $160,000
d. $240,000   (11/91, PI, #22, amended, 2410)

70. On January 2, 1997, Morey Corp. granted Dean, its president, 20,000 stock appreciation rights for past services. Those rights are exercisable immediately and expire on January 1, 2000. On exercise, Dean is entitled to receive cash for the excess of the stock's market price on the exercise date over the market price on the grant date. Dean did not exercise any of the rights during 1997. The market price of Morey's stock was $30 on January 2, 1997 and $45 on December 31, 1997. As a result of the stock appreciation rights, Morey should recognize compensation expense for 1997 of

a. $0.
b. $100,000.
c. $300,000.
d. $600,000.   (5/90, PI, #55, amended, 1094)

ITEMS 71 AND 72 are based on the following data:

On April 1, 1997, Fay Corporation established an employee stock ownership plan (ESOP). Selected transactions relating to the ESOP during 1997 were as follows:

- On April 1, 1997, Fay contributed $30,000 cash and 3,000 shares of its $10 par common stock to the ESOP. On this date, the market price of the stock was $18 a share.

- On October 1, 1997, the ESOP borrowed $100,000 from Union National Bank and acquired 5,000 shares of Fay's common stock in the open market at $17 a share. The note is for one year, bears interest at 10%, and is guaranteed by Fay.

- On December 15, 1997, the ESOP distributed 6,000 shares of Fay common stock to employees of Fay in accordance with the plan formula.

71. In its 1997 income statement, how much should Fay report as compensation expense relating to the ESOP?

a. $184,000
b. $120,000
c. $ 84,000
d. $ 60,000   (11/87, PI, #56, amended, 1108)

72. In Fay's December 31, 1997 balance sheet, how much should be reported as a reduction of shareholders' equity and as an endorsed note payable in respect of the ESOP?

	Reduction of shareholders' equity	Endorsed note payable
a.	$0	$0
b.	$0	$100,000
c.	$100,000	$0
d.	$100,000	$100,000

(11/87, PI, #57, amended, 1109)

OTHER OBJECTIVE FORMAT QUESTION

PROBLEM 10-2 (15 to 25 minutes)

Min Co. is a publicly held company whose shares are traded in the over-the-counter market. The stockholders' equity accounts at December 31, 1993, had the following balances:

Preferred stock, $100 par value, 6% cumulative; 5,000 shares authorized; 2,000 issued and outstanding	$ 200,000
Common stock, $1 par value, 150,000 shares authorized; 100,000 issued and outstanding	100,000
Additional paid-in capital	800,000
Retained earnings	1,586,000
Total stockholders' equity	$2,686,000

Transactions during 1994 and other information relating to the stockholders' equity accounts were as follows:

- February 1, 1994—Issued 13,000 shares of common stock to Ram Co. in exchange for land. On the date issued, the stock had a market price of $11 per share. The land had a carrying value on Ram's books of $135,000, and an assessed value for property taxes of $90,000.

- March 1, 1994—Purchased 5,000 shares of its own common stock to be held as treasury stock for $14 per share. Min uses the cost method to account for treasury stock. Transactions in treasury stock are legal in Min's state of incorporation.

- May 10, 1994—Declared a property dividend of marketable securities held by Min to common shareholders. The securities had a carrying value of $600,000; fair value on relevant dates were:

Date of declaration 5/10	$720,000
Date of record 5/25	758,000
Date of distribution 6/1	736,000

- October 1, 1994—Reissued 2,000 shares of treasury stock for $16 per share.

- November 4, 1994—Declared a cash dividend of $1.50 per share to all common shareholders of record November 15, 1994. The dividend was paid on November 25, 1994.

- December 20, 1994—Declared the required annual cash dividend on preferred stock for 1994. The dividend was paid on January 5, 1995.

- January 16, 1995—Before closing the accounting records for 1994, Min became aware that no amortization had been recorded for 1993 for a patent purchased on July 1, 1993. The patent was properly capitalized at $320,000 and had an estimated useful life of eight years when purchased. Min's income tax rate is 30%. The appropriate correcting entry was recorded on the same day.

- Adjusted net income for 1994 was $838,000.

REQUIRED:

For all items, calculate the amounts requested.

ITEMS 1 THROUGH 4 represent amounts to be reported on Min's 1994 statement of retained earnings.

1. Prior period adjustment.

2. Preferred dividends.

3. Common dividends—cash.

4. Common dividends—property.

ITEMS 5 THROUGH 8 represent amounts to be reported on Min's statement of stockholders' equity at December 31, 1994.

5. Number of common shares issued at December 31, 1994.

6. Amount of common stock issued.

7. Additional paid-in capital, including treasury stock transactions.

8. Treasury stock.

ITEMS 9 AND 10 represent other financial information for 1993 and 1994.

9. Book value per share at December 31, 1993, before prior period adjustment.

10. Numerator used in calculation of 1994 earnings per share for the year.

(5/95, FAR, #2, 5597-5606)

PROBLEM/ESSAY QUESTIONS

PROBLEM 10-3 (No time estimation given)

Field Co.'s stockholders' equity account balances at December 31, 1995, were as follows:

Common stock	$ 800,000
Additional paid-in capital	1,600,000
Retained earnings	1,845,000

The following 1996 transactions and other information relate to the stockholders' equity accounts:

- Field had 400,000 authorized shares of $5 par common stock, of which 160,000 shares were issued and outstanding.

- On March 5, 1996, Field acquired 5,000 shares of its common stock for $10 per share to hold as treasury stock. The shares were originally issued at $15 per share. Field uses the cost method to account for treasury stock. Treasury stock is permitted in Field's state of incorporation.

- On July 15, 1996, Field declared and distributed a property dividend of inventory. The inventory had a $75,000 carrying value and a $60,000 fair market value.

- On January 2, 1994, Field granted stock options to employees to purchase 20,000 shares of Field's common stock at $18 per share, which was the market price on that date. The options may be exercised within a three-year period beginning January 2, 1996. The measurement date is the same as the grant date. On October 1, 1996, employees exercised all 20,000 options when the market value of the stock was $25 per share. Field issued new shares to settle the transaction.

- Field's net income for 1996 was $240,000.
- Field intends to issue new stock options to key employees in 1997. Field's management is aware that Statement of Financial Accounting Standards No. 123, *Accounting for Stock-Based Compensation*, which was issued in 1995, discusses both the "intrinsic value" method and the "fair value" method of accounting for stock options. Field's management is unsure of the difference between the two methods.

REQUIRED:

a. Prepare the stockholders' equity section of Field's December 31, 1996, balance sheet. Support all computations.

b. In a brief memo to Field's management, explain how compensation cost is measured under both the "fair value" method and the "intrinsic value" method of accounting for stock options, and when the measured cost is recognized.

(11/97, FAR, Essay #2, 6502-6503)

PROBLEM 10-4 (45 to 55 minutes)

Trask Corp., a public company whose shares are traded in the over-the-counter market, had the following stockholders' equity account balances at December 31, 1991:

Common stock	$ 7,875,000
Additional paid-in capital	15,750,000
Retained earnings	16,445,000
Treasury common stock	750,000

Transactions during 1992, and other information relating to the stockholders' equity accounts, were as follows:

- Trask had 4,000,000 authorized shares of $5 par value common stock; 1,575,000 shares were issued, of which 75,000 were held in treasury.
- On January 21, 1992, Trask issued 50,000 shares of $100 par value, 6% cumulative preferred stock in exchange for all of Rover Co.'s assets and liabilities. On that date, the net carrying amount of Rover's assets and liabilities was $5,000,000. The carrying amounts of Rover's assets and liabilities equaled their fair values. On January 22, 1992, Rover distributed the Trask shares to its stockholders in complete

liquidation and dissolution of Rover. Trask had 150,000 authorized shares of preferred stock.

- On February 17, 1992, Trask formally retired 25,000 of its 75,000 treasury common stock shares. The shares were originally issued at $15 per share and had been acquired on September 25, 1991, for $10 per share. Trask uses the cost method to account for treasury stock.
- Trask owned 15,000 shares of Harbor Inc. common stock purchased in 1989 for $600,000. The Harbor stock was included in Trask's short-term marketable securities portfolio. On March 5, 1992, Trask declared a property dividend of one share of Harbor common stock for every 100 shares of Trask common stock held by a stockholder of record on April 16, 1992. The market price of Harbor stock on March 5, 1992, was $60 per share. The property dividend was distributed on April 29, 1992.
- On January 2, 1990, Trask granted stock options to employees to purchase 200,000 shares of the company's common stock at $12 per share, which was also the market price on that date. The options are exercisable within a three-year period beginning January 2, 1992. The measurement date is the same as the grant date. On June 1, 1992, employees exercised 150,000 options when the market value of the stock was $25 per share. Trask issued new shares to settle the transaction.
- On October 27, 1992, Trask declared a 2-for-1 stock split on its common stock and reduced the per share par value accordingly. Trask stockholders of record on August 2, 1992, received one additional share of Trask common stock for each share of Trask common stock held. The laws in Trask's state of incorporation protect treasury stock from dilution.
- On December 12, 1992, Trask declared the yearly cash dividend on preferred stock, payable on January 11, 1993, to stockholders of record on December 31, 1992.
- On January 16, 1993, before the accounting records were closed for 1992, Trask became aware that depreciation expense was understated by $350,000 for the year ended December 31, 1991. The after-tax effect on 1991 net income was $245,000. The appropriate correcting entry was recorded on the same day.
- Net income for 1992 was $2,400,000.

REQUIRED:

a. Prepare Trask's statement of retained earnings for the year ended December 31, 1992. Assume that Trask prepares only single-period financial statements for 1992.

b. Prepare the stockholders' equity section of Trask's balance sheet at December 31, 1992.

c. Compute the book value per share of common stock at December 31, 1992.

Show all supporting calculations in good form.

(11/93, PI, #4)

ESSAY 10-5 (15 to 25 minutes)

Brady Company has 30,000 shares of $10 par value common stock authorized and 20,000 shares issued and outstanding. On August 15, 1997, Brady purchased 1,000 shares of treasury stock for $12 per share. Brady uses the cost method to account for treasury stock. On September 19, 1997, Brady sold 500 shares of the treasury stock for $14 per share. In October 1997, Brady declared and distributed 2,000 shares as a stock dividend from unissued shares when the market value of the common stock was $16 per share.

On December 20, 1997, Brady declared a $1 per share cash dividend, payable on January 10, 1998, to shareholders of record on December 31, 1997.

REQUIRED:

a. How should Brady account for the purchase and sale of the treasury stock, and how should the treasury stock be presented in Brady's balance sheet at December 31, 1997?

b. How should Brady account for the stock dividend, and how would it affect Brady's stockholders' equity at December 31, 1997? Why?

c. How should Brady account for the cash dividend, and how would it affect Brady's balance sheet at December 31, 1997? Why?

(11/85, Theory, #5, amended)

ESSAY 10-6 (15 to 25 minutes)

On November 5, 1994, Gunpowder Corp.'s board of directors approved a stock option plan for key executives. On January 2, 1995, a specific number of stock options were granted. These options were exercisable between January 2, 1997, and December 31, 1999, at 90% of the quoted market price on January 2, 1995. The service period is for 1995 and 1996. Some options were forfeited when an executive resigned in 1996. All other options were exercised during 1997.

REQUIRED:

a. When is Gunpowder's stock option measurement date? Why?

b. How should Gunpowder determine the compensation expense, if any, for the stock option plan in 1995?

c. What is the effect of forfeiture of the stock options on Gunpowder's financial statements for 1996? Why?

d. What is the effect of the stock option plan on the balance sheet at December 31, 1997? Be specific as to the changes in balance sheet accounts between November 5, 1994, and December 31, 1997. (11/90, Theory, #5, amended, 3539)

SOLUTION 10-1 MULTIPLE CHOICE ANSWERS

OWNERS' EQUITY

1. **(c)** Rice's total assets will equal the sum of its liabilities and stockholders' equity at 12/31/91.

Total liabilities, 12/31/91 (given)		$ 94,000
Total stockholders' equity, 12/31/91:		
Proceeds from stock issue	$ 500,000	
Net income for 1991	25,000	
Cash dividend declared in 1991	(2,000)	523,000
Total liabilities and stockholders' equity		
(and thus total assets) at 12/31/91		$617,000

2. **(a)** The amount that should be reported as total stockholder's equity is determined as follows:

Common stock, $3 par	$ 600,000	
Additional paid-in capital	800,000	
Total paid-in capital		$1,400,000
Retained earnings appropriated		
for uninsured earthquake loss	150,000	
Retained earnings unappropriated	200,000	
Total retained earnings		350,000
		1,750,000
Less: Treasury stock, at cost	50,000	
Net unrealized loss on AFS		
marketable equity securities	20,000	(70,000)
Total stockholders' equity		$1,680,000

3. (a) In the financial statements of the sole proprietorship, the amount that should be reported as Smith's capital balance is determined as follows:

Capital—Smith, 1/2/93 (i.e., cost of net assets contributed by owner at 1/2/93)	$ 350,000
Add: Income of sole proprietorship for 1993	60,000
Less: Smith's drawings during 1993	(20,000)
Capital—Smith, 12/31/93	$ 390,000

PREFERRED STOCK DIVIDENDS

4. (b) The amounts payable to each class of stock are computed as follows:

Cash dividends declared in 1992		$ 44,000
Cash dividends payable to preferred stock:		
Dividends in arrears at 12/31/91	$12,000	
Dividend for 1992 (4,000 x $100 x 6%)	24,000	(36,000)
Cash dividends payable to common stock		$ 8,000

5. (d) The preferred stock is cumulative. Therefore, if a dividend is not paid in any given year, it becomes a dividend in arrears. No liability exists until the board of directors declares a dividend, therefore a dividend in arrears is not accrued, but is disclosed in the notes to the financial statements. No dividend was declared in 1992, resulting in a dividend in arrears of $15,000 ($100 x 5% x 3,000 shares). Therefore, in its 1993 financial statements, Apex should report dividends in arrears as a $20,000 ($15,000 from 1992 + $5,000 from 1993) disclosure. In 1993, the dividend in arrears is $5,000.

Dividend ($100 x 5% x 3,000 shares)	$ 15,000
Less: Amount paid	(10,000)
Dividend in arrears	$ 5,000

ISSUE OF CAPITAL STOCK

6. (a) The following balances should be reported in Hyde's 4/1/93, statement of stockholders' equity: Common Stock, $20,000; Preferred Stock, $60,000; and APIC, $820,000 (i.e., $580,000 + $240,000). Assuming that Hyde has only one APIC account, the issuance of the common and preferred stock would be recorded as follows:

Cash (20,000 x $30)	600,000	
Common Stock (20,000 x $1)		20,000
Additional Paid-In Capital (to balance)		580,000
Cash (6,000 x $50)	300,000	
Preferred Stock (6,000 x $10)		60,000
Additional Paid-In Capital (to balance)		240,000

7. (d) The 225,000 common shares outstanding at 12/31/92 are computed by subtracting the 75,000 common shares held in Treasury at that date from the 300,000 (i.e., 200,000 + 100,000) common shares issued in 1990 and 1991. The number of common shares outstanding at 12/31/92 is not affected by the convertible preferred stock because there is no indication that any of the preferred stock had been converted into common stock at 12/31/92.

8. (c) In the journal entry to record the incorporation of the partnership, Additional Paid-In Capital is credited for the difference between the fair value of the net assets contributed and the par value of the stock issued.

Assets (at fair value)	240,000	
Liabilities (at fair value)		20,000
Common Stock (1,000 x $5)		5,000
Additional Paid-In Capital (to balance)		215,000

9. (d) When the subscription is recorded the par value of the common stock subscribed is recorded as common stock subscribed and the excess of the subscription price over the par value of the common stock subscribed is recorded as APIC.

Cash (20% down payment)	XX	
Subscriptions Receivable (balance due)	XX	
Common Stock Subscribed (shares x par value)		XX
Additional Paid-In Capital (to balance)		XX

10. (a) The acquisition of services by issuance of common stock is a nonmonetary exchange that should be recorded at the fair value of the stock issued or the services performed, whichever is more clearly evident. The fair value of the stock issued should be used to record this transaction because (1) on the date of issuance, the stock was trading on a public exchange and thus had the more clearly evident fair value and (2) the fair value of the stock issued is less than the amount usually billed for the services received. Thus, the increase in additional paid-in capital as a result of the transaction is the excess of the fair value over the par value of the common stock multiplied by the number of shares issued. ($140 – $5 = $135 x 1,000 = $135,000)

11. (d) To record the incorporation of the partnership, APIC is credited for the difference between the fair value of the net assets contributed and the par value of the common stock issued.

Assets ($100,000 + $12,000)	112,000	
Liabilities (carrying amount = fair value)		20,000
Common Stock (5,000 x $1 x 2)		10,000
Additional Paid-In Capital (to balance)		82,000

12. (b) Since the market value of both securities is not determinable, the incremental method should be used to allocate the cash proceeds between the two securities. Since the market value of the bonds is known, the cash proceeds in excess

of this amount are allocated to the common stock. The excess of the proceeds allocated to the common stock over the par value is recorded as APIC.

Lump sum cash proceeds	$ 110,000
Less: Market value of bonds	(40,000)
Cash proceeds allocated to common stock	70,000
Less: Par value of common stock (1,000 x $5)	(5,000)
APIC on issuance of common stock	$ 65,000

13. (c)   The amount of the proceeds received that should be allocated to the preferred stock is $48,000 [i.e., ($54,000 ÷ $90,000) x $80,000]. Since the fair value is available for each class of security, the lump sum received should be allocated to the two classes of securities by their relative fair value.

Fair value of common stock (1,000 x $36)	$36,000
Fair value of preferred stock (2,000 x $27)	54,000
	$90,000

14. (a)   Common Stock should be credited for $375,000 [i.e., (5,000 x 3) x $25], the par value of the common shares issued to effect the conversion. Additional Paid-In Capital—Common Stock should be credited for $175,000, the excess of the carrying amount of the preferred stock converted over the par value of common shares issued to effect the conversion [i.e., (5,000 x $110) – $375,000].

RETAINED EARNINGS

15. (b)   During 1992, stockholders' equity increased by $62,000 (i.e., $89,000 – $27,000). Since paid-in capital increased by $66,000 (i.e., $60,000 + $6,000), retained earnings must have decreased by $4,000 (i.e., $66,000 – $62,000). Since the only charge to retained earnings was for a dividend payment of $13,000, net income for 1992 must have been $9,000.

16. (a)   In its 1992 balance sheet, Eagle should report $1,200,000 of appropriated retained earnings for the construction of a new plant. Since the new office building was completed in 1992, the $1,750,000 of retained earnings reported appropriated for that purpose at 12/31/91 should have been returned to unappropriated retained earnings in 1992. The cash restricted for the retirement of bonds due in 1993 (i.e., within one year of the balance sheet date) should be reported as a current asset separate from unrestricted cash. The $2,000,000 of restricted cash does not affect the amount of appropriated retained earnings.

17. (d)   The purpose of a retained earnings appropriation is to restrict a portion of retained earnings as to availability for dividends. A retained earnings appropriation cannot be used to absorb a fire loss when a company is self-insured, provide for a contingent loss that is probable and reasonably estimable, or to smooth periodic income.

18. (a)   No amount of retained earnings should be appropriated as a result of the cumulative preferred stock dividends in arrears or the reissued treasury stock. Cumulative preferred stock dividends in arrears should be disclosed either on the face of the balance sheet or in a footnote to the financial statements (APB 15, par. 50, fn. 16). Owing to the application of most state corporate laws, retained earnings is often appropriated in the amount of the cost of treasury stock acquired under both the cost and par value methods; however, the treasury stock in question has been *reissued* by the corporation.

19. (c)   The primary purpose of a quasi-reorganization is to eliminate an accumulated deficit (negative retained earnings balance) so that the corporation has a "fresh start" with a zero balance in retained earnings. Although the accounting procedures for a quasi-reorganization involve restating assets of the enterprise to their fair values, this is not the primary purpose. There should be no net asset write-up.

20. (c)   The balance in the APIC account after the quasi-reorganization is the beginning balance, plus the difference in the old and new par values, times the number of issued shares [($30 – $5) x 10,000 = $250,000], less the retained earnings deficit. $150,000 + $250,000 – $210,000 = $190,000.

SIGNIFICANT DATES

21. (a)   The common shares outstanding at 12/31/92 are computed as follows:

Common shares outstanding, 12/31/91	300,000
Common shares issued for 10% stock dividend, 1/31/92 (300,000 x 10%)	30,000
Treasury shares purchased, 6/30/92	(100,000)
Treasury shares reissued, 8/1/92	50,000
Common shares issued for 2-for-1 stock split, 11/30/92 (300,000 + 30,000 – 100,000 + 50,000)	280,000
Common shares outstanding, 12/31/92	560,000

22. (a)   The date of declaration is the date on which dividends are formally declared by the board of directors and declared cash dividends become a liability. The journal entry required at the date of declaration includes a debit (decrease) to retained earnings. No journal entry is required at the date of record. The journal entry on the payment date reduces cash and the liability, but has no effect on retained earnings.

23. (d) On May 8, the date of declaration, the liability for dividends payable is recorded by a debit to Retained Earnings and a credit to Cash Dividends Payable. Since the declaration of the cash dividend increases current liabilities without affecting current assets, working capital is decreased on this date. On May 23, the date of record, which stockholders will receive the cash dividend is determined. Assuming that the common shares outstanding did not change between the date of declaration and the date of record, no journal entry is made on the date of record and, thus, working capital is not affected on this date. On June 3, the date of payment, the cash dividend is paid and is recorded by a debit to Cash Dividends Payable and a credit to Cash. Since current assets and current liabilities decrease by the same amount, working capital is not affected on this date.

24. (b) A cash dividend is recorded when it is declared by a debit to Retained Earnings and a credit to Cash Dividends Payable. There is no adjusting entry at the end of the period. The entry at the payment date will include a debit to Cash Dividends Payable and a credit to Cash. Therefore, the cash dividend reduces stockholders' equity only at the date of declaration.

PROPERTY DIVIDENDS

25. (c) Property dividends are recorded at the property's fair value at the date of declaration. The excess of the fair value over the carrying amount of the property distributed is recognized as a gain by the distributing corporation at the date of declaration. The gain before income taxes that Brite recognizes on the disposal of the investment shares distributed as a property dividend is computed as follows:

Fair value of shares distributed (100,000 x $2.50)	$ 250,000
Less: Carrying amount of shares distributed (100,000 x $2.00)	(200,000)
Pretax gain on the shares distributed	$ 50,000

26. (d) A transfer of a nonmonetary asset to a stockholder in a nonreciprocal transfer should be recorded at the fair value of the asset transferred, and a gain or loss should be recognized on the disposition of the asset (APB 29, par. 18). Thus, Bain should record the following entries at the declaration date:

Investment in Stock of Tell Corp. ($300,000 – $180,000)	120,000	
Gain on Disposal of Investment		120,000
Retained Earnings	300,000	
Property Dividend Payable		300,000

27. (d) Evie should record the property dividend at the fair value of the merchandise at the date of declaration. Since the carrying amount of the merchandise exceeds its fair value at the date of declaration, Evie should recognize the excess as a loss in income from continuing operations.

28. (c) A transfer of a nonmonetary asset to a stockholder in a nonreciprocal transfer should be recorded at the fair value of the asset transferred, and a gain or loss should be recognized on the disposition of the asset equal to the difference between the fair value and carrying amount of the asset (APB 29, par. 18). After all nominal accounts (e.g., Gain on Disposition of Investment) are closed, the effect of this property dividend is to decrease Retained Earnings by $60,000 (i.e., $78,000 – $18,000). Thus, Nilo should record the following entries at the declaration date:

Marketable Securities ($78,000 – $60,000)	18,000	
Gain on Disposition of Investment		18,000
Retained Earnings	78,000	
Property Dividend Payable		78,000

29. (d) At the date of declaration, April 1, 1993, the journal entry is as follows:

Retained Earnings	100,000	
Notes Payable to Stockholders		100,000

At the end of the year, interest should be accrued.

Interest Expense ($100,000 x 10% x 9/12)	7,500	
Interest Payable		7,500

The interest portion of the payment is not treated as part of the dividend. When the dividend is declared, it becomes a liability and needs to be reported on the Balance Sheet at that time. In addition, once again, the interest portion is not part of the dividend. If the entry to accrue the interest expense is made on December 31, 1993, and is reversed on January 1, 1994, then interest expense would be debited for $10,000 on March 31, 1994. However, since answer (c) does not state this, you should not assume that the reversing entries were made.

LIQUIDATING DIVIDENDS

30. (b) Any dividend that does not come out of retained earnings is a reduction of corporate paid-in capital and, to that extent, is a liquidating dividend. Therefore, the liquidating dividend is determined as follows:

Dividend	$ 400,000
Retained earnings	(300,000)
Liquidating dividend	$ 100,000

31. (d) Any dividend not based on earnings must be a reduction of corporate paid-in capital and, to that extent, it is a liquidating dividend. Since no portion of the dividend is based on accumulated past earnings, paid-in capital decreases by the full amount of the dividend, while retained earnings is unaffected. The following journal entry illustrates the effects of the declaration and payment of a $100,000 liquidating cash dividend:

Additional Paid-In Capital   100,000
    Cash Dividends Payable   100,000

32. (b) Any dividend not based on earnings must be a reduction of additional paid-in capital and, to that extent, it is a liquidating dividend. The following journal entry illustrates the effects of the declaration of a partially liquidating cash dividend:

Retained Earnings   XX
Additional Paid-In Capital   XX
    Cash Dividends Payable   XX

STOCK DIVIDENDS AND STOCK SPLITS

33. (d) Since the 100% stock dividend exceeds 25% of the number of shares outstanding, it is considered a "large" stock dividend. Therefore, it should be recorded by capitalizing a portion of Retained Earnings equal to the par value of the shares issued. As a result of the stock dividend, Retained Earnings will decrease and Common Stock will increase by the par value of the shares issued. APIC will not change as a result of the "large" stock dividend.

34. (a) Since the 5% stock dividend is less than 20 to 25% of the number of shares outstanding, it is considered to be a "small" stock dividend. Therefore, it should be recorded by capitalizing a portion of Retained Earnings equal to the fair value of the shares issued. As a result of the "small" stock dividend, Retained Earnings will decrease by the fair value of the shares issued, Common Stock will increase by the par value of the shares issued, and APIC will increase by the excess of the fair value over the par value of the shares issued.

35. (b) The issuance of a "small" stock dividend (i.e., less than 20 to 25% of the number of shares outstanding) should be recorded by capitalizing a portion of retained earnings equal to the fair value of the shares issued. On the other hand, the issuance of a "large" stock dividend (i.e., more than 20 to 25% of the number of shares outstanding) should be recorded by capitalizing a portion of retained earnings equal to the par value of the shares issued. Thus, retained earnings should be debited for (1) the fair value of the 10% stock dividend

($15,000) and (2) the par value of the 28% stock dividend ($30,800).

36. (a) The declaration of a "small" stock dividend (i.e., < 20-25% of the number of common shares outstanding) should be recorded by capitalizing a portion of retained earnings equal to the fair value of the shares to be issued. Fluctuations in the fair value of the shares between the date of declaration and the date of issuance are not recorded. Thus, the declaration of the 10% stock dividend in question would be recorded as follows:

Retained Earnings [(3,000 x 10%) x $9 FMV] 2,700
  Common Stock Dividend Distributable
    [(3,000 x 10%) x $2 PV]   600
  Additional Paid-In Capital (to balance) 2,100

37. (b) The amount to be reported as dividends is determined as follows:

Common shares outstanding, 1/1/93	100,000
Adjustment for 2-for-1 stock split, 3/15/93	x 2
Common shares outstanding, 3/15/93 - 12/31/93	200,000
Times: Cash dividend per common share, 12/15/93	x $.50
Cash dividends declared during 1993	$100,000

38. (d) Stock dividends received on common stock may be recorded only by memorandum entry, regardless of the method of accounting for the investment. Under the cost method, a new cost basis per share would be computed. Under the equity method, a new carrying amount per share would be computed.

39. (b) A stock split consists of a reduction in the par value per share, together with a proportional increase in the number of shares outstanding. For instance, in a 2-for-1 split, the par value per share is halved, while the number of shares outstanding is doubled. *Total* par value, additional paid-in capital, stockholders' equity, and total assets remain unchanged.

TREASURY STOCK

40. (d) The question does not indicate whether the donated shares are accounted for as treasury stock under the cost method or the par value method, or whether the donated shares were canceled and retired. Therefore, this question cannot be answered by constructing a journal entry to record the donation of the shares. Instead, the question can be answered by knowing that the donation of the common stock would be accounted for entirely within stockholders' equity accounts. Therefore, the amount reported for total stockholders' equity would be unchanged as a result of the donation of the stock.

41. (c) When treasury stock is acquired, total stockholders' equity decreases by the cost of the treasury shares, regardless of the method used to account for the treasury stock. The book value per common share is computed by dividing total stockholders' equity applicable to common stock by the number of common stock shares outstanding. The acquisition of treasury shares at a price less than their book value will reduce both the numerator and denominator of the book value ratio; however, the reduction of the numerator is less than the amount that was in there for these shares. The excess book value for those shares would now be spread over the remaining shares outstanding, resulting in an increase in the book value per common share.

42. (a) The calculation for the number of shares of Nest's common stock issued and outstanding as of December 31, 1994, is as follows:

	Issued	Outstanding
Previously issued	100,000	95,000
May 3, 1994 sale of treasury stock		1,000
Aug. 6, 1994 additional stock sold	10,000	10,000
Subtotal prior to stock split	110,000	106,000
Nov. 18, 1994 2-for-1 stock split	x 2	x 2
Dec. 31, 1994 balance	220,000	212,000

COST METHOD

43. (a) The calculation for Row's retained earnings is as follows:

Income since incorporation	$ 420,000
Less: Cash dividends paid	(130,000)
Less: Property dividends	(30,000)
Retained earnings 12/31/95	$ 260,000

The excess of proceeds over cost of treasury stock sold, accounted for using the cost method, is credited to an appropriately titled Paid-In Capital account, such as Additional Paid-In Capital From Treasury Stock Transactions.

44. (c) The answer to this question *assumes that the cost method is used to account for the treasury stock.* Under the cost method, if treasury stock is sold at a price that exceeds its cost, the excess should be credited to Additional Paid-In Capital. The excess should not be reported as a gain in the income statement or as a credit to Retained Earnings. Retained Earnings may be decreased, but never increased, by treasury stock transactions.

45. (c) Under the cost method, the acquisition of the 6,000 shares of treasury stock is recorded as follows:

Treasury Stock (6,000 shares x $36)	216,000	
Cash		216,000

Under the cost method, the issuance of 3,000 shares of the treasury stock is recorded as follows:

Cash (3,000 shares x $50)	150,000	
Treasury Stock (3,000 shares x $36)		108,000
Additional Paid-In Capital (to balance)		42,000

46. (a) Under the cost method, treasury stock is recorded and carried at the acquisition cost ($20 per share). Cyan sold some of the shares for $5 per share more than the acquisition cost. This excess is credited to a Paid-In Capital From Treasury Stock account and Retained Earnings is not affected. If Cyan sold any of the shares for less than the acquisition cost, the deficit would first be charged to any existing balance in the Paid-In Capital From Treasury Stock account, and the excess, if any, would be charged against Retained Earnings. The amount that Cyan should report as retained earnings at December 31, 1994, is calculated as follows:

Retained earnings, Dec. 31, 1993	$300,000
Net income for 1994	60,000
Retained earnings, Dec. 31, 1994	$360,000

PAR VALUE METHOD

47. (b) The effect on total stockholders' equity from either the acquisition or the reissuance of treasury stock is the same regardless of whether the shares are accounted for under the cost method or the par value method. Under both methods, the acquisition of treasury stock decreases assets and stockholders' equity by the acquisition cost of the shares. Under both methods, the reissuance of the treasury stock increases assets and stockholders' equity by the proceeds received for the shares. These answers are not affected by the relationships among the original issuance price of the stock, the cost of the treasury stock, and the reissuance price of the treasury stock.

48. (c) Answer (c) states the primary distinction between the two methods. The theoretical justification for the par value method is that the purchase of treasury stock is in fact a constructive retirement of those shares; therefore, reacquired stock is recorded essentially by reversing the amounts at which the stock was originally issued and adjusting any difference to APIC or Retained Earnings. Reissuance of the stock is treated as if it were a new issue, i.e., the excess purchase price received over par is credited to APIC.

49. (b) The entry to record the acquisition of the treasury stock in excess of its original issue price using the par value method will involve a debit to Treasury Stock for the par value of the stock, a debit to APIC for the amount of the premium on the

original issuance, a debit to Retained Earnings for the excess of the cost of the treasury stock over the original issuance price, and a credit to Cash for the cost of the treasury shares. When the par value method is used, the balance of the Treasury Stock account is contra to the Common Stock account. Therefore, the use of the par value method will result in a decrease in net common stock, a decrease in APIC and a decrease in retained earnings.

50. (b) Under the par value method, the recording of the acquisition of treasury stock effectively removes the treasury stock from the accounts. The excess in acquisition price over the original issuance price ($17 – $15 = $2/share) is debited to Additional Paid-In Capital From Treasury Stock, but only to the extent of any existing balance from prior treasury stock transactions. The difference, if any, is debited to Retained Earnings. The amount that Asp would report as APIC in its December 31, 1994 balance sheet is calculated as follows:

1/5/94	20,000 shares @ $5/share over par	$100,000
7/14/94	5,000 shares @ $5/share treasury stock	(25,000)
12/27/94	5,000 shares @ $20 – $10 par = $10/per share	50,000
12/31/94	APIC balance	$125,000

SIMILARITIES BETWEEN METHODS

51. (c) The best way to analyze this question is by an example. Assume one share of stock was issued for $13 and purchased for the treasury at $12. The journal entry to record the acquisition of the treasury share under the cost method is as follows:

Treasury Stock	12	
Cash		12

The journal entry to record the acquisition of the treasury stock using the par value method is as follows:

Treasury Stock	10	
Premium on Common Stock	3	
Cash		12
Paid-In Capital From Treasury Stock Transactions		1

Both the Premium on Common Stock and Paid-In Capital From Treasury Stock Transactions accounts are additional paid-in capital accounts. Because the par value method removes the effect of the original issuance price on APIC (the premium amount) from APIC and records the "gain" (excess of original issuance price over cost of treasury stock) as APIC, total additional paid-in capital is reduced when the par value method is used in this scenario. Additional paid-in capital is not affected by the acquisition of treasury stock when the cost method is used. Retained earnings is not affected by either the cost method or the par value method in this situation.

(Retained earnings would have been reduced in using the par value method if the cost of the treasury share had exceeded the original issuance price.)

52. (a) The idle machinery, the cash surrender value of the life insurance on the corporate executives, and the contra account, Allowance for Decline in Market Value of Noncurrent Equity Securities, are all properly included in computing net assets. The amount that should be reported for net assets is computed as follows:

Net assets, before adjustments	$875,000
Less: Cost of treasury stock	(24,000)
Net assets, 12/31/90	$851,000

53. (c) Rama is located in a state which restricts retained earnings for an amount equal to the cost of any treasury stock acquired. Thus, the amount that Rama should disclose as a restriction of retained earnings as a result of the treasury stock transactions is $60,000 [(20,000 – 15,000) x $12 cost per share].

RETIREMENT

54. (c) The effect of the acquisition and retirement of each common share is to decrease APIC by $10 (i.e., $15 – $5). A corporation cannot record a gain or loss on the acquisition and retirement of its own common stock. Retained earnings can be decreased but never increased as a result of the acquisition and retirement of a corporation's own common stock. The following entry would be used to record the acquisition and retirement of one share of Fogg's own common stock:

Common Stock	10	
APIC—Common Stock	15	
Cash		20
APIC—Retirement of Stock		5

55. (c) The Common Stock account decreases by the par value of the shares retired. The APIC account decreases by the original increase to the APIC account when the 2,000 shares were issued. The Retained Earnings account decreases by the amount by which the cost of the 2,000 shares exceeds the proceeds from their issuance. The retirement of the common shares would be recorded as follows:

Common Stock (2,000 x $10 PV)	20,000	
Additional Paid-In Capital [2,000 x ($100 – $10 PV)]	180,000	
Retained Earnings [2,000 x ($150 – $100)]	100,000	
Cash (2,000 x $150)		300,000

56. (b) Immediately after the shares were retired, the balance in the APIC account would be $2,470,000 ($2,550,000 – $80,000). Assuming that

Park has only one APIC account, the retirement of the common stock would be recorded as follows:

Common Stock (20,000 x $20 PV)	400,000	
Additional Paid-In Capital (to balance)	80,000	
Cash (20,000 x $24)		480,000

57. (c) When treasury stock is accounted for under the cost method, the cost of the treasury stock is reported as an unallocated reduction of the stockholders' equity. Under this method, the treasury stock did not reduce the Common Stock account prior to their cancellation. The amount that Pack should report as common stock outstanding is determined as follows:

Par value of common stock before recording cancellation of treasury stock	$ 540,000
Less: Par value of treasury stock canceled (50,000 shares x $2.50 par value)	(125,000)
Par value of common stock outstanding after cancellation of treasury stock	$ 415,000

STOCK WARRANTS

58. (d) The proceeds should be allocated between the preferred stock and the detachable stock purchase warrants based on their relative fair market values at date of issue. If the relative fair values are not known, then the fair value of either security is used. In this question, the fair value of the warrants is known, but the fair value of the preferred stock without the warrants is not. Therefore, the amount assigned to the warrants is the fair value of the warrants. The remaining amount of the proceeds is assigned to the preferred stock.

STOCK RIGHTS

59. (a) No entry is required when stock rights are issued to existing stockholders (other than a memorandum entry). Therefore, APIC and net income were not affected in 1992 when the stock rights were issued. Stock issued upon the exercise of stock rights is recorded the same as any other issuance. Therefore, when the stock rights were exercised in 1993, APIC increased by the excess of the $30 exercise price over the $20 par value of the common stock, and net income was not affected.

60. (d) Stock issued upon the exercise of stock rights is recorded the same as any other issuance. Therefore, additional paid-in capital will increase by the excess of the exercise price over par value and retained earnings will not be affected.

61. (c) The issuance of stock rights is generally recorded by memorandum entry only (but must be disclosed in the notes to the financial statements). When the rights are exercised, common stock will be credited at its par value of $10 per share, regardless of the option price or the FMV of the stock. The difference between the option price and the par value of the stock (i.e., $15 − $10 = $5) will be credited to Additional Paid-In Capital when the stock is issued.

62. (c) No entry (other than a memorandum entry) is made when stock rights are issued to existing stockholders without consideration.

63. (c) No entry (other than a memorandum entry) is made when stock rights are issued to existing stockholders. However, the redemption of the rights resulted in an outflow of cash. As this did not increase a noncash asset or reduce liabilities, it must affect an equity account. 120,000 x $0.10 = $12,000.

COMPENSATORY PLANS

64. (a) To record the journal entry at the grant date, the total compensation expense is determined as follows:

Market value of 1,000 shares at date of grant ($50/share)	$ 50,000
Option price of 1,000 shares at date of grant ($20/share)	(20,000)
Total compensation expense	$ 30,000

The resulting entry is:

Deferred Compensation Expense	30,000	
Paid-In Capital—Stock Options		30,000

Deferred compensation expense is a contra stockholders' equity account. Therefore, the net effect on stockholders' equity when the options are granted is zero. The following journal entry is recorded when the options are exercised:

Cash (1,000 x $20)	20,000	
Paid-In Capital—Stock Options	30,000	
Common Stock (1,000 x $10)		10,000
Paid-In Capital in Excess of Par		40,000

Stockholders' equity is increased $40,000 + $10,000 − $30,000 = $20,000.

65. (d) Although periodic compensation expense is recognized from the date of grant to the measurement date, deferred compensation cost and stock options outstanding can only be recorded on the measurement date (the date on which both the number of optioned shares and the option price are known). The account Stock Options Outstanding is increased on the measurement date. The subsequent exercising, forfeiture, or lapsing of the stock options reduces this account.

66. (b) Under APB 25, compensation expense is the difference between the quoted market price of the stock at the measurement date and the amount, if any, to be paid by the employee. The measurement date is usually the grant date. The amount of compensation expense to be recognized is determined as follows:

Market price of stock, 1/2/93	$ 50
Less: Option price	(40)
Excess of market price over option price	10
Shares under option	x 1,000
Compensation expense recognized in 1993	$10,000

67. (b) The amount of pretax compensation to be recognized in 1991 in connection with the options is determined as follows:

Market price of stock, 6/1/91*	$ 20
Option price	(15)
Excess of market price over option price	5
Shares under option	x 1,000
Pretax compensation recognized in 1991**	$ 5,000

---

* This is the measurement date because the number of shares the employee is entitled to receive (1,000) and the option price ($20) are both known at this date.

** The options become exercisable January 2, 1992; therefore, all of the pretax compensation cost should be recognized in 1991.

68. (d) Compensation costs of a stock option plan should be recognized (i.e., expensed) in the period(s) in which the employee performs the services. If the measurement date is later than the date of grant, compensation cost is estimated by comparing the year-end market price of the stock to the option price.

69. (c) The amount that should be reported as the liability under the stock appreciation rights plan at 12/31/97 is two-thirds of the estimated compensation cost of the rights.

Market price of stock, 12/31/97	$ 28
Predetermined price specified by the plan	(20)
Increase in market price, 12/31/97	$ 8
Stock appreciation rights	x 30,000
Liability for stock appreciation rights, 12/31/97	$240,000
Times: Portion accrued as of 12/31/97	x 2/3
Accrued compensation cost, 12/31/97	$160,000

70. (c) *FASB Interpretation 28* specifies that compensation expense arising from stock appreciation rights should be measured at the end of each period as the amount by which the quoted market value of the shares of the enterprise's stock covered by a grant exceeds the option price or value specified under the plan. Changes, either increases or decreases, in the quoted market value of those shares should be reflected as an adjustment of compensation expense in the periods in which the changes occur until the date the number of shares and purchase price, if any, are known. Therefore, the amount of compensation expense that Morey should recognize for 1997 as a result of the stock appreciation rights is determined as follows:

Market price of stock, 12/31/97	$ 45
Market price of stock, 1/2/97	(30)
Increase in market price	$ 15
Stock appreciation rights	x 20,000
Additional compensation expense, 1997	$300,000

71. (c) The compensation expense to be reported in the 1997 income statement relating to the ESOP is determined as follows:

Cash contributed	$30,000
Common stock contributed (3,000 shares x $18 fair value)	54,000
Compensation expense	$84,000

72. (d) The $100,000 endorsed note payable pertaining to the ESOP appears both as a liability and a reduction of stockholders' equity.

PERFORMANCE BY SUBTOPICS

Each category below parallels a subtopic covered in Chapter 10. Record the number and percentage of questions you correctly answered in each subtopic area.

Owners' Equity

Question #	Correct √
1	
2	
3	

Questions   3
Correct _____
% Correct _____

Preferred Stock Dividends

Question #	Correct √
4	
5	

Questions   2

Correct _____
% Correct _____

Issue of Capital Stock

Question #	Correct √
6	
7	
8	
9	
10	
11	
12	
13	
14	

Questions   9

Correct _____
% Correct _____

Retained Earnings

Question #	Correct √
15	
16	
17	
18	
19	
20	

Questions   6

Correct _____
% Correct _____

Significant Dates

Question #	Correct √
21	
22	
23	
24	

Questions   4

Correct _____
% Correct _____

Property Dividends

Question #	Correct √
25	
26	
27	
28	
29	

Questions   5

Correct _____
% Correct _____

Liquidating Dividends

Question #	Correct √
30	
31	
32	

Questions   3

Correct _____
% Correct _____

Stock Dividends and Stock Splits

Question #	Correct √
33	
34	
35	
36	
37	
38	
39	

Questions   7

Correct _____
% Correct _____

Treasury Stock

Question #	Correct √
40	
41	
42	

Questions   3

Correct _____
% Correct _____

Cost Method

Question #	Correct √
43	
44	
45	
46	

Questions   4

Correct _____
% Correct _____

Par Value Method

Question #	Correct √
47	
48	
49	
50	

Questions   4

Correct _____
% Correct _____

Similarities Between Methods

Question #	Correct √
51	
52	
53	

Questions   3

Correct _____
% Correct _____

Retirement

Question #	Correct √
54	
55	
56	
57	

Questions   4

Correct _____
% Correct _____

Stock Warrants

Question #	Correct √
58	

Questions   1

Correct _____
% Correct _____

Stock Rights

Question #	Correct √
59	
60	
61	
62	
63	

Questions   5

Correct _____
% Correct _____

Compensatory Plans

Question #	Correct √
64	
65	
66	
67	
68	
69	
70	
71	
72	

Questions   9

Correct _____
% Correct _____

OTHER OBJECTIVE FORMAT SOLUTION

SOLUTION 10-2 CALCULATIONS

1. $14,000. The correction of an error in financial statements of a prior period is a "prior period adjustment." Prior period adjustments should be reported in the current retained earnings statement as an adjustment of the opening balance, net of related income taxes (APB 9). The patent cost is properly amortized over its estimated useful life of 8 years and was owned for 6 months during 1993. Hake has a 30% tax rate. [($320,000 ÷ 8) x 6/12 x (1–.30) = $14,000.]

2. $12,000. The required cash dividend on preferred stock is calculated by multiplying the outstanding preferred stock by the par value and the earnings rate (2,000 shares x $100 par value x 6%). As there are no unpaid amounts from prior years, this is the only amount required to be paid this year.

3. $165,000. Cash dividends on common stock are calculated by multiplying the declared cash dividends per share times the number of outstanding common shares at the time of declaration (110,000 x $1.50). The outstanding shares on 11/4/94 are the original 100,000 shares + the 13,000 2/1/94 issue – the 5,000 treasury shares purchased 3/1/94 + 2,000 treasury shares reissued 10/1/94.

4. $720,000. Property dividends are recorded at the fair value of assets given up, and any difference between fair value and carrying amount of the asset is recorded as a gain or loss as a component of income from continuing operations. Any change in the fair value of the asset to be distributed between the date of declaration and date of payment is ignored.

5. 113,000. The number of common shares issued at 12/31/94 are the original 100,000 shares + the 13,000 2/1/94 issue. The treasury stock activity is irrelevant as none of these shares were retired. (Treasury stock is issued but not outstanding.)

6. $113,000. The number of common shares issued at 12/31/94 are the original 100,000 shares + the 13,000 2/1/94 issue. The treasury stock activity is irrelevant as none of these shares were retired. (Treasury stock is issued but not outstanding.) The par value of the stock is $1 per share (113,000 x $1 = $113,000).

7. $934,000. The additional paid-in capital (APIC) balance is the beginning balance of $800,000 adjusted for 1994 transactions. In issues of stock for property other than cash, the property received and the amount of contributed capital should be recorded at the fair value of the property received or the market value of the stock, whichever is more objectively determinable. The value of the land purchased on 2/1/94 is best determinable by the value of stock traded in the over-the-counter market. As the stock has a $1 par value, the remaining $10 per share goes to APIC ($10 x 13,000 = $130,000). Under the cost method of accounting for treasury stock, any reissuance at a price in excess of the acquisition cost, the excess is credited to an appropriate APIC account. [($16 – $14) x 2,000 shares = $4,000]; ($800,000 + $130,000 + $4,000 = $934,000).

8. $42,000. The treasury stock is recorded at cost under the cost method, so the Treasury Stock account is debited for $70,000 (5,000 x $14/shares) when the 5,000 treasury shares are purchased. Since 2,000 shares or 40% of the treasury shares are then resold, the Treasury Stock account is only credited for 40% of the $70,000, or $28,000. This leaves a balance of $42,000 in the Treasury Stock account at year end.

9. $24.86. The book value per share is computed by dividing the number of common shares outstanding at December 31, 1993 (100,000) into total stockholders' equity less the amount related to the preferred stock. In this problem ($2,686,000 – $200,000) ÷ 100,000 = $24.86.

10. $826,000. The numerator to be used in calculating 1994 earnings per share is the adjusted net income for 1994 of $838,000 less the preferred dividends of $12,000, or $826,000.

PROBLEM/ESSAY SOLUTIONS

SOLUTION 10-3 STOCKHOLDERS' EQUITY SECTION OF THE BALANCE SHEET/FAIR VALUE AND INTRINSIC VALUE METHODS

a.

Field Co.
STOCKHOLDERS' EQUITY SECTION OF BALANCE SHEET
December 31, 1996

Common stock, $5 par value, 400,000 shares authorized, 180,000 shares issued, 175,000 shares outstanding		$ 900,000 [1]
Additional paid-in capital		1,860,000 [2]
Retained earnings:		
Beginning balance	$1,845,000	
Add: Net income	240,000	
Less: Property dividend distributed	(60,000)	2,025,000
		$4,785,000
Less common stock in treasury, 5,000 shares at cost		(50,000)
Total stockholders' equity		$4,735,000

[1] Shares issued: 160,000 + 20,000 = 180,000 x $5 = $900,000

[2] Additional paid-in capital: 1,600,000 + [20,000 x ($18 – 5)] = 1,600,000 + 260,000

b.
To: Management, Field Co.
Re: Accounting for Stock-Based Compensation

As you are aware, Statement of Financial Accounting Standards No. 123 discusses both the "intrinsic value" method and the "fair value" method of accounting for stock options. The purpose of this memo is to inform you of the difference between the two methods and of when the company should record compensation cost associated with 1997 stock option issuances.

Under the **"fair value" method** of accounting for stock options, compensation cost **is measured at the grant date** based on the **value of the award**. This value is computed using an **option-pricing model**. Under the **"intrinsic value" method**, compensation cost is the **excess, if any, of the quoted market price of the stock at the grant date** (or other measurement date) **over the amount an employee must pay** to acquire the stock.

Under both methods, compensation cost, if any, is **recognized over the service period**, which is usually the vesting period.

SOLUTION 10-4 STATEMENT OF RETAINED EARNINGS/ STOCKHOLDERS' EQUITY SECTION OF THE BALANCE SHEET

a.

Trask Corp.
STATEMENT OF RETAINED EARNINGS
For the Year Ended December 31, 1992

Balance, December 31, 1991		
As originally reported		$ 16,445,000
Less: Prior period adjustment from error understating depreciation	$350,000	
Less: Income tax effect	105,000	(245,000)
As restated		16,200,000
Net income		2,400,000
		18,600,000
Deduct dividends		
Cash dividend on preferred stock	300,000 [1]	
Dividend in kind on common stock	900,000 [2]	(1,200,000)
Balance, December 31, 1992		$ 17,400,000

Explanation of Amounts:

[1]	Preferred stock dividend	
	Par value of outstanding preferred shares	$ 5,000,000
	Multiplied by: Dividend rate	x .06
	Dividends paid on preferred stock	$ 300,000

[2]	Dividend in kind on common stock	
	Fair market value of Harbor stock distributed [15,000 shares @ $60]	$ 900,000

b.

Trask Corp.
STOCKHOLDERS' EQUITY SECTION OF BALANCE SHEET
December 31, 1992

Preferred stock, $100 par value, 6% cumulative; 150,000 shares authorized; 50,000 shares issued and outstanding	$ 5,000,000
Common stock, $2.50 par value; 4,000,000 shares authorized; 3,400,000 shares issued	8,500,000 [3]
Additional paid-in capital	16,675,000 [4]
Retained earnings	17,400,000
	47,575,000
Less: Common stock in treasury, 100,000 shares at cost	(500,000)
Total stockholders' equity	$47,075,000

Explanation of Amounts:

[3]	Number of common shares issued and outstanding	
	Number of common shares issued, 12/31/91	1,575,000
	Less: Common shares retired	(25,000)
	Number of common shares issued, 6/1/92	150,000
		1,700,000
	Two-for-one stock split, 10/27/92	x 2
	Number of common shares issued after stock split	3,400,000
	Less: Common shares held in treasury	(100,000)
	Total number of common shares outstanding	3,300,000

Amount of common shares issued

Amount of common shares issued, 12/31/91	$ 7,875,000
Less: Common shares retired at par value	(125,000)
Number of common shares issued, 6/1/92	750,000
Total amount of common shares issued	**$ 8,500,000**

[4] Amount of additional paid-in capital

Amount at 12/31/91 (1,575,000 @ $10)	$15,750,000
Less: Treasury stock retired [25,000 shares @ $5 ($10 cost – $5 par value)]	(125,000)
Amount received upon issuance of common shares, 6/1/92 (150,000 shares @ $7)	1,050,000
	$16,675,000

c.

Trask Corp.
COMPUTATION OF BOOK VALUE PER SHARE OF COMMON STOCK
December 31, 1992

Total stockholders' equity	$47,075,000
Deduct allocation to preferred stock	(5,000,000)
Allocation to common stock	$42,075,000
Divided by number of common shares outstanding [3,400,000 – 100,000]	÷ 3,300,000
Book value per share of common stock	**$ 12.75**

SOLUTION 10-5 TREASURY STOCK/STOCK AND CASH DIVIDENDS

a. Brady should account for the purchase of the treasury stock on August 15, 1997, by **debiting treasury stock** and **crediting cash** for the **cost** of the purchase (1,000 shares x $12 per share). Brady should account for the sale of the treasury stock on September 19, 1997, by **debiting cash** for the **selling price** (500 shares x $14 per share), **crediting treasury stock for cost** (500 shares x $12 per share), and **crediting additional paid-in capital from treasury stock** transactions for the excess of the selling price over the cost (500 shares x $2 per share). The remaining treasury stock (500 shares x $12 per share) should be **presented separately in the stockholders' equity** section of Brady's December 31, 1997, balance sheet as an **unallocated reduction of stockholders' equity**. These shares are considered issued but not part of common stock outstanding.

b. Brady should account for the stock dividend by **debiting retained earnings** for $16 per share (the **market value** of the stock in October 1997, the date of the stock dividend) multiplied by the 2,000 shares distributed. Brady should then **credit common stock** for the **par value** of the common stock ($10 per share) multiplied by the 2,000 shares distributed, and **credit additional paid-in capital** for the **excess** of the **market value** ($16 per share) **over** the **par**

value ($10 per share) multiplied by the 2,000 shares distributed. **Total** stockholders' equity **does not change**, but, because this is considered a **small stock dividend**, recognition has been made of a capitalization of retained earnings equivalent to the market value of the additional shares resulting from the stock dividend.

c. Brady should account for the cash dividend on December 20, 1997, the **declaration date**, by **debiting retained earnings** and **crediting cash dividends payable** for $1 per share multiplied by the number of shares outstanding. A cash dividend is a **distribution** to the **corporation's stockholders**. The **liability** for this distribution is incurred on the **declaration date**, and it is a **current** liability because it is payable within one year (January 10, 1997). The effect of the cash dividend on Brady's balance sheet at December 31, 1997, is an **increase in current liabilities** and a **decrease in retained earnings**.

SOLUTION 10-6 COMPENSATORY STOCK OPTION PLANS

a. Gunpowder's stock option measurement date is **January 2, 1995**. The stock option measurement date is the **first date** on which the employer knows **both**:

- The **number of shares** that an individual is **entitled to receive** and
- The **option or purchase price**.

b. The compensation expense for 1995 is **equal to** the **market price** of Gunpowder's stock on **January 2, 1995, less** the **option price, times** the **number** of **options outstanding times one-half**.

c. When options are forfeited, **compensation expense, contributed capital-stock options**, and **deferred compensation** (if used) are all **decreased**. This is necessary because the **total compensation expense** is **less** than that **estimated** in 1995.

d. Cash was **increased** by the **stock option price** [90% of the quoted market price on January 2, 1995] **multiplied** by the **number of shares issued**. **Retained earnings** was **reduced** by the **compensation expense** recorded in **1995** and **1996**. **Contributed capital** was **increased** by the **balancing** amount for the above entries.

CHAPTER 11

REPORTING THE RESULTS OF OPERATIONS

CHAPTER 11

REPORTING THE RESULTS OF OPERATIONS

I. OVERVIEW

A. CONCEPTS OF INCOME

The determination and presentation of various items on the income statement are influenced by two alternative concepts, the *current operating concept* and the *all-inclusive concept*. Proponents of the all-inclusive approach insist that the income statement should include unusual and nonrecurring items in order to measure the long-range operating performance of the enterprise. Proponents of the current operating concept emphasize the importance of normal recurring operations in evaluating the performance of the entity. They contend that the inclusion of unusual and nonrecurring items in the income statement distorts net income. The method required by APB 9, *Reporting the Results of Operations*, reflects a compromise between the all-inclusive and current-operating concepts.

1. All regular items of income and expense, including unusual and infrequently occurring items, are included in the determination of net income.

2. Income from discontinued operations and extraordinary items are reported separately from the results of continuing operations.

3. Prior period adjustments are presented as adjustments to the beginning balance of retained earnings.

B. INCOME STATEMENT FORMAT

1. **SINGLE-YEAR PRESENTATION** APB 30, *Reporting the Results of Operations*, indicates the following format in Exhibit 1 for the presentation of the income statement for a single year.

EXHIBIT 1 ♦ PRESENTATION OF THE INCOME STATEMENT (SFAS 144)

Income from continuing operations before income taxes		$ XXX
Provision for income taxes		XXX
Income (loss) from continuing operations		XXX
Income from continuing operations (after income taxes)		$ XXX
Discontinued operations (Note X):		
Income (loss) from operations of discontinued		
Division A (including loss on disposal of $XXX)	$XXX	
Income taxes	XXX	
Income from discontinued operations		XXX
Income before extraordinary items		$ XXX
Extraordinary items (less applicable income taxes of $XXX)		XXX
Cumulative effect on prior years of a change in accounting		
principle (less applicable income taxes of $XXX)		XXX
Net income		$ XXX

2. **COMPARATIVE STATEMENTS** The presentation of comparative financial statements enhances the usefulness of annual and other reports. Comparative statements project more relevant and meaningful information than do noncomparative statements. Moreover, comparative statements prepared on a consistent basis from one period to the next are especially valuable because they measure difference in operating results based on the same measurement criteria (ARB 43).

3. **MULTIPLE-STEP FORMAT** The presentation of income from continuing operations in a *multiple step format* emphasizes a functional or object classification of each statement item, and sets forth various intermediate levels of income.

EXHIBIT 2 ♦ MULTIPLE-STEP FORMAT

Sales			$950,000
Less sales returns and allowances			(16,500)
Net sales			933,500
Cost of goods sold:			
Beginning inventory		$ 230,000	
Purchases	$590,000		
Less purchase returns			
and allowances	(19,300)		
Net purchases		570,700	
Freight-in		2,000	
Goods available for sale		802,700	
Less ending inventory		(220,000)	(582,700)
Gross margin			350,800
Operating expenses:			
Selling		150,000	
General & administrative		72,000	(222,000)
Income from operations			128,800
Other revenues:			
Rent	$ 2,500		
Interest and dividends	6,700		
Gain on sale of machinery	8,000	$ 17,200	
Other expenses:			
Interest	$ 5,200		
Loss on sale of investments	6,000	(11,200)	6,000
Income before income taxes and			
extraordinary items*			134,800
Provision for income taxes			(60,660)
Income before extraordinary items			74,140
Extraordinary item:			
Loss due to earthquake, less			
tax saving of $3,150			(3,850)
Net income			$ 70,290

* This line would be "Income from continuing operations before income taxes" if there were discontinued operations reported during the period.

4. **SINGLE-STEP FORMAT** Income from continuing operations may be presented in a *multiple step format* or a *single step format*. Presentation of income from continuing operations in a *single step format* is often used for publicly issued statements. Revenues are grouped under one classification while expenses are grouped under another classification.

EXHIBIT 3 ♦ SINGLE-STEP FORMAT

Revenues:		
Sales (less returns and allowances of $16,500)		$ 933,500
Rent		2,500
Interest and dividends		6,700
Gain on sale of machinery		8,000
Total revenues		950,700
Expenses:		
Cost of goods sold	$582,700	
Selling	150,000	
General & administrative	72,000	
Interest	5,200	
Loss on sale of investments	6,000	(815,900)
Income before income taxes and extraordinary items*		134,800
Provision for income taxes		(60,660)
Income before extraordinary items		74,140
Extraordinary item: Loss due to earthquake,		
less tax saving of $3,150		(3,850)
Net income		$ 70,290

* This line would be "Income from continuing operations before income taxes" <u>if</u> there were discontinued operations reported during the period.

II. COMPONENTS OF THE INCOME STATEMENT

A. INCOME FROM CONTINUING OPERATIONS

1. REVENUES AND EXPENSES Revenue and expense items (and gains and losses) that are considered to be of a usual and recurring nature are reported in income from continuing operations.

C   Continuing Operations

D   Discontinued Operations

E   Extraordinary Items

F   eFfect of Change in Accounting Principle

---

2. UNUSUAL AND INFREQUENT ITEMS Items that are considered to be *either* unusual in nature *or* infrequent in occurrence are reported as a *separate component* of income from continuing operations. The nature and financial effects of this type of item should be disclosed on the face of the income statement, or alternatively, in the notes to the financial statements. These items should **not** be reported net of income taxes or in any other manner that would imply that they are extraordinary items.

3. TAX PROVISION The provision for income taxes associated with income from continuing operations should be presented as a single line item.

B. DISCONTINUED OPERATIONS: REPORTING UNDER SFAS 144

SFAS 144, *Accounting for Impairment or Disposal of Long-Lived Assets*, is effective for statements issued for fiscal periods beginning after December 15, 2001, with early application encouraged. (Both APB Opinion 30 and SFAS 144 are eligible to be tested on the **May 2002** CPA exam.) The results of discontinued operations are reported separately from continuing operations. *Discontinued operations* refers to the operations of a component of an entity that has been disposed of or is still operating, but is the subject of a formal plan for disposal. SFAS 144 defines *component of an entity* as a segment, reporting unit, or asset group whose operations and cash flows are clearly distinguished from the rest of the entity, operationally as well as for financial reporting purposes. See Exhibit 12 on page 11-32 for examples of discontinued operations.

1. INCOME STATEMENT SFAS 144 provides an illustration (incorporated into Exhibit 1) of the income statement presentation for reporting the results of discontinued operations. The results of operations of a component of an entity are reported as part of discontinued operations, for current and prior periods (in the periods in which they occur), provided that:

a.   **OPERATIONS** Operations and cash flows have been (or will be) removed from the entity's ongoing operations due to the disposal transaction.

b.   **CONTINUING INVOLVEMENT** The entity ceases any significant continuing involvement in the component's operations after the disposal transaction.

2.   **BALANCE SHEET** The component is valued at current fair value less cost to sell. Asset(s) that are classified as held for sale, and their related liabilities, are presented separately in the asset and liability sections of the balance sheet (not offset and presented as a single item).

a.   **FUTURE OPERATING LOSSES** No liability for future operating losses is recognized. Expected future operating losses that other buyers and sellers would not recognize as part of the fair value less cost to sell are **not** indirectly recognized as part of an expected loss on the sale by reducing the book value of the asset (or asset group) to an amount less than its current fair value less cost to sell. This provision is designed to limit *big bath* accounting (the inclusion of losses with a questionable relation to the disposal, in order that profits in future periods appear more favorable).

b.   **EXPENSES** While classified as held for sale, the asset is not depreciated or amortized, although accrual of other related expenses, such as interest or rent, continue.

3.   **NON-COMPONENT ASSETS** Income from **continuing** operations includes gains or losses from an asset (or asset group) that is classified as held for sale, but that is below the level of a *component of the entity*. If disposal will not occur for more than 12 months, costs to sell are discounted to present value.

4.   **CONTINGENCIES** Changes to the previously reported discontinued operations amounts are reported in current period statements as discontinued operations. Such adjustments may occur due to the resolution of contingencies regarding purchase price, purchaser indemnification, environmental warranty obligations, product warranty obligations, and directly-related employee benefit plan obligations.

C.   **DISCONTINUED OPERATIONS: REPORTING UNDER APB 30**
The results of *continuing* operations are reported separately from *discontinued* operations and any gain or loss from the disposal of a segment should be reported in conjunction with the related results of discontinued operations. Under APB 30, *Reporting the Results of Operations*, the measurement and disposal dates are essential for determining the amounts to be reported for discontinued segments. APB 30 is superceded by SFAS 144 for financial statements for periods beginning after December 15, 2001.

1.   **DISCONTINUED OPERATIONS DEFINED** Discontinued operations refers to the operations of a segment of a business that has been sold, abandoned, spun-off, or otherwise disposed of, or is still operating but is the subject of a formal plan for disposal. The term "segment of a business" refers to a component of an entity whose activities represent a separate major *line of business* or *class of customer*. The segment's assets, results of operations, and activities must be clearly distinguished, physically, operationally, and for financial reporting purposes, from the other assets, results of operations, and activities of the entity.

2.   **DISPOSAL OF A BUSINESS SEGMENT** APB 30 has a more narrow scope than SFAS 144. The disposal of a segment of a business is distinguished from other disposals of assets incident to the evolution of the entity's business. Other disposals would include the disposal of a part of a line of business, the shifting of production or marketing activities for a particular line of business from one location to another, the phasing out of a product line, or other changes occasioned by technological improvements.

3. **MEASUREMENT DATE** The date on which management commits itself to a formal plan to dispose of a segment of the business whether by sale or abandonment.

4. **DISPOSAL DATE** The date of closing the sale if the disposal is by sale, **or** the date that operations cease if the disposal is by abandonment.

EXHIBIT 4 ♦ DISCONTINUED OPERATIONS

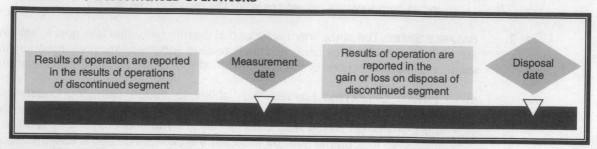

5. **RESTATEMENT OF PRIOR PERIODS** Financial statements of current and prior periods that include the results of operations of a disposed segment *prior to the measurement date* should be restated to present the results of operations of the disposed segment as a separate component of income before extraordinary items.

6. **DETERMINING SEGMENT GAINS AND LOSSES**

    a. **MEASUREMENT AND DISPOSAL DATES IN SAME PERIOD** When the measurement date and the disposal date fall within the same fiscal period, the gain or loss on the disposed segment should include the following:

        (1) The income (loss) from disposed segment operations *between* the measurement date and the disposal date (i.e., the phase-out period).

        (2) Any gain or loss on the disposal of the discontinued segment's assets. Adjustments, costs, and expenses that (a) are clearly a *direct* result of the decision to dispose of the segment and (b) are clearly not the adjustments of carrying amounts or costs, or expenses that should have been recognized on a going-concern basis prior to the measurement date should be included in determining the gain or loss on disposal. Costs and expenses *directly* associated with the decision to dispose include items such as severance pay, additional pension costs, and employee relocation costs.

    b. **MEASUREMENT AND DISPOSAL DATES IN DIFFERENT PERIODS** When the measurement date and the disposal date occur in *different accounting periods*, the gain or loss on the disposed segment is calculated by separating (1) realized gain or loss items between the measurement date and the end of the fiscal period and (2) *estimated* gain or loss items between the end of the fiscal period and the disposal date.

    c. **REALIZED ITEMS** Realized items include the following:

        (1) The income (loss) on segment operations, net of income tax, between the measurement date and the end of the fiscal period.

        (2) The gain (loss) on the sale of segment assets.

    d. **ESTIMATED ITEMS** Estimated items include the following:

        (1) The estimated income (loss) from segment operations between the end of the fiscal period and the disposal date.

        (2) The estimated gain (loss) on the sale of segment assets.

e. **EXPECTED GAINS AND LOSSES** If the total of the *estimated* items is a net *expected gain*, it is recognized only to the extent that it offsets *realized losses*. If there is an expected *realized* gain, any *expected* gain is not recognized until it is realized in a subsequent period. If the total of the *estimated* items is a net expected loss, then the expected loss is recognized in total, regardless of whether the realized portion is a gain or loss.

7. **INCOME STATEMENT PRESENTATION** APB 30 requires an income statement presentation for reporting the results of discontinued operations of a business as illustrated in Exhibit 5. Note that operating losses up to the measurement date are the first component under discontinued operations.

EXHIBIT 5 ♦ DISCONTINUED OPERATIONS (APB 30)

Income from continuing operations (after income taxes)	$XXX
Discontinued operations:	
Income (loss) from operations of discontinued	
Division X (net of income taxes)	$XXX
Gain (loss) on disposal of Division X,	
including provisions for operating losses	
during phase-out period (net of income taxes)	XXX XXX
Net income	$XXX

EXAMPLE 1 ♦ DISCONTINUED OPERATIONS (APB 30)

On April 30, 20X1, Empire Corporation, whose fiscal year-end is September 30, adopted a plan to discontinue the operations of Bello Division on November 30, 20X1. Bello contributed a major portion of Empire's sales volume. Empire estimated that Bello would sustain a loss of $460,000 from May 1, 20X1, through September 30, 20X1, and would sustain an additional loss of $220,000 from October 1, 20X1, to November 30, 20X1. Empire also estimated that it would realize a gain of $600,000 on the sale of Bello's assets. At September 30, 20X1, Empire determined that Bello had actually lost $1,120,000 for the fiscal year, of which $420,000 represented the loss from May 1 to September 30, 20X1.

REQUIRED: Ignoring income tax effects, determine the amounts that should be reported in the discontinued operations section of Empire's income statement for the year ended September 30, 20X1, for income from operations of the discontinued segment, and the gain or loss on disposal of the discontinued segment.

SOLUTION:

Loss from operations of discontinued segment:	
Operating loss for fiscal year ended 9/30/X1	$1,120,000
Operating loss from measurement date to end	
of fiscal year (5/1/X1 to 9/30/X1)	(420,000)
Operating loss from beginning of fiscal year	
to measurement date (10/1/X0 to 4/30/X1)	$ 700,000
Loss on disposal of discontinued segment:	
Operating loss from measurement date to end	
of fiscal year (5/1/X1 to 9/30/X1)	$ 420,000
Estimated operating loss from end of fiscal	
year to disposal date (10/1/X1 to 11/30/X1)	220,000
Realized and expected losses occurring after	
measurement date	640,000
Expected gain from sale of Bello's assets	(600,000)
Loss on disposal of discontinued segment	$ 40,000

EXAMPLE 2 ♦ DISCONTINUED OPERATIONS (APB 30)

On July 1, 20X3, Tyler Corporation approved a formal plan to sell its plastics division, considered a segment of the business. The sale will occur in the first three months of 20X4. The division had an operating loss of $400,000 for the six months ended December 31, 20X3, and expects to incur a loss of $200,000 for the first quarter of 20X4. The sales price is $22,000,000 and the carrying amount at the date of sale should be $20,000,000. Tyler's effective tax rate for 20X3 is 30%.

REQUIRED: For the year ended December 31, 20X3, determine the amount of the gain Tyler should report on the disposal of the plastics division.

SOLUTION: Tyler does <u>not</u> report a gain on the disposal of the plastics division for the year ended 12/31/X3; the net expected gain on disposal <u>cannot</u> be recognized until it is <u>realized</u> in a subsequent period.

Expected gain from sale of segment's assets:		
Estimated sales price		$ 22,000,000
Expected carrying amount at disposal date		(20,000,000)
Expected (unrealized) gain from sale of segment's assets		2,000,000
Realized and expected losses after measurement date:		
Operating loss from measurement date to end of fiscal year (7/1/X3 to 12/31/X3)	$400,000	
Estimated operating loss from end of fiscal year to disposal date (12/31/X3 to 3/31/X4)	200,000	(600,000)
Net expected gain on disposal that cannot be recognized until realized in a subsequent period		$ 1,400,000

D. EXTRAORDINARY ITEMS

An extraordinary item should be classified separately in the income statement if it is material in relation to income before extraordinary items or to the trend of annual earnings before extraordinary items, or is material by other appropriate criteria. Items should be considered individually and not in the aggregate in determining whether an extraordinary event or transaction is material. If the item is determined to be extraordinary, it should be presented separately on the income statement net of related income tax after discontinued operations of a segment of a business and before cumulative effect of accounting changes (see Exhibit 1).

1. **CRITERIA** Most events and transactions affecting the operations of an enterprise are of a normal, recurring nature. For an occurrence to be classified as "extraordinary" it must meet both of the following criteria (APB 30):

   a. **UNUSUAL NATURE** The underlying event or transaction should possess a high degree of abnormality and be of a type clearly unrelated to, or incidentally related to, the ordinary and typical activities of the entity, taking into account the environment in which the entity operates.

   b. **INFREQUENCY OF OCCURRENCE** The underlying event or transaction should be of a type that would not reasonably be expected to recur in the foreseeable future, taking into account the environment in which the entity operates.

2. **EXTINGUISHMENT OF DEBT** SFAS 4, *Reporting Gains and Losses From Extinguishment of Debt*, specifies that gains and losses from extinguishment of debt that are included in the determination of net income should be aggregated and, *if material,* classified as an extraordinary item, net of related income tax effect.

3. **NON-EXTRAORDINARY GAINS/LOSSES** The following gains and losses should **not** be reported as extraordinary items because they are *usual* in nature **or** may be expected to recur as a consequence of customary and continuing business activities. In certain circumstances, gains or losses such as a. and d., below, should be included in extraordinary items if they are the direct result of an event that meets the criteria for an extraordinary item.

   a. Write-down or write-off of receivables, inventories, equipment leased to others, and intangible assets

   b. Gains or losses from exchange or translation of foreign currencies, including those relating to major devaluations and revaluations

   c. Gains or losses on disposal of a segment of a business

   d. Other gains or losses from sale or abandonment of property, plant, or equipment used in the business

   e. Effects of a strike, including strikes against competitors and major suppliers

   f. Adjustments of accruals on long-term contracts

E. **CHANGES IN ACCOUNTING PRINCIPLES**
   A change in accounting principle results from the adoption of a generally accepted accounting principle (GAAP) different from the GAAP previously used for reporting purposes. The term "accounting principle" includes not only accounting principles but also the methods of applying them. Adoption of a principle to record transactions for the first time or to record the effects of transactions that were previously immaterial is **not** considered to be a change in accounting principle.

   1. **EXAMPLES** Changes in accounting principle include the following:

      a. A change in the method of inventory pricing, such as from LIFO to FIFO

      b. A change in depreciation method, such as from the double-declining-balance method to the straight-line method

      c. A change in the method of accounting for long-term construction contracts, such as from the completed-contract method to the percentage-of-completion method

   2. **APB 20** APB 20, *Accounting Changes*, requires justification for a change in accounting principle. Promulgation of a new accounting principle by the FASB is considered sufficient justification for a change in accounting principle.

   3. **RECOGNITION** Most changes in accounting principle should be recognized by including the cumulative effect of the change in the net income of *the period of the change*.

      a. **CUMULATIVE EFFECT** The cumulative effect is the difference *between* the amount of retained earnings at the beginning of the period of a change *and* the amount of retained earnings that would have been reported at that date if the new accounting principle had been applied retroactively for all prior periods that would have been affected.

      b. **INCOME STATEMENT PRESENTATION** The amount of the cumulative effect should be shown in the income statement between the captions *extraordinary items* and *net income*. The cumulative effect is **not** an extraordinary item, but should be reported in a manner similar to an extraordinary item.

c. **PER SHARE INFORMATION** The per share information shown on the face of the income statement should include the per share amount of the cumulative effect of the accounting change.

d. **PRO FORMA EFFECTS OF RETROACTIVE APPLICATION** APB 20 also requires that the *pro forma* effects of retroactive application on income before extraordinary items and net income, as well as the earnings per share amounts for these items, be shown on the face of the income statement.

EXAMPLE 3 ◆ CHANGE IN ACCOUNTING PRINCIPLE

In 20X6, XYZ Corporation purchased machinery for $150,000. The machinery had an estimated useful life of 10 years and no salvage value. Early in 20X8, the decision was made to change the depreciation method on plant and equipment from the double-declining-balance method to the straight-line method.

REQUIRED: Calculate the cumulative effect for the change.

SOLUTION:

Double-declining-balance method:		
20X6: ($150,000 – $0) x .20	$30,000	
20X7: ($150,000 – $30,000) x .20	24,000	$ 54,000
Straight-line method:		
20X6: $150,000 x .10	$15,000	
20X7: $150,000 x .10	15,000	(30,000)
Cumulative effect on prior years of the accounting change*		$ 24,000

Accumulated Depreciation   24,000
   Cumulative Effect of Accounting Change   24,000
To record cumulative effect of a change in depreciation method.

---

* Income tax effects were ignored in order to simplify the illustration. If an income tax rate of 30% were assumed, the cumulative effect of the accounting change would be $16,800 [i.e., $24,000 x (1–30%)].

NOTE: The depreciation expense for 20X8 is determined under the newly adopted straight-line method. Therefore, 20X8 depreciation expense is $15,000.

4. **RETROACTIVE TREATMENT REQUIRED** For certain changes in accounting principle, *retroactive* treatment is required (i.e., the financial statements of all prior periods presented should be restated).

a. **ADJUSTMENT TO BEGINNING RETAINED EARNINGS** The cumulative effect of the change in accounting principle should be reported as an adjustment to the beginning balance of retained earnings, net of the related income tax effect. These changes include the following:

(1) **CHANGE FROM LIFO** A change from the LIFO method of inventory pricing to another inventory pricing method (but **not** a change **to** LIFO)

(2) **CHANGE IN LONG-TERM CONSTRUCTION CONTRACTS** A change in the method of accounting for long-term construction-type contracts

b. **DISCLOSURE REQUIRED**

(1) The nature and justification for the change in accounting principle.

(2) The effect of the change on income before extraordinary items, net income, and the related per share amounts should be disclosed for all periods presented, either on the face of the income statement or in the notes thereto.

(3) Since the financial statements of all prior periods presented are restated, pro forma effects of retroactive application should not be reported.

EXHIBIT 6 ♦ SUMMARY OF THE PRESENTATION OF AN INCOME STATEMENT

Item	Criteria	Examples	Placement
Unusual or infrequent gains or losses	Unusual or infrequent but not both	Write-down or write-off of receivables, inventories, equipment leased to others, other gains or losses from the sale or abandonment or impairment of property, plant, or equipment used in the business	**C** D E F
Changes in estimate	A revision of an accounting measurement	Changing the useful life of a depreciable asset from 5 to 7 years	**C** D E F
Discontinued operations	The disposal of a component of the entity which represents separate operations and cash flows.	A component that has been sold, abandoned, or spun-off. The component's operations and cash flows must be clearly distinguished.	C **D** E F
Extraordinary items	Both unusual and infrequent in nature	Casualty gains and losses	C D **E** F
Changes in principle	Change from one generally accepted accounting principle to another one (GAAP → GAAP)	Change from the straight-line method of depreciation to the sum-of-the-years'-digits method	C D E **F**

III. REPORTING COMPREHENSIVE INCOME (SFAS 130)

A. SCOPE

SFAS 130 applies to all entities that report financial position, results of operations, and cash flows in a full set of financial statements. It does not apply to an entity that has no items of other comprehensive income in any period presented. It also does not apply to not-for-profit organizations. This statement establishes standards on how to report and display comprehensive income and its components. It does not, however, specify when to recognize or how to measure the items that are included in comprehensive income. The recognition and measurement of comprehensive income is based upon current accounting standards (GAAP).

B. COMPREHENSIVE INCOME

1. **ITEMS TO INCLUDE** Comprehensive income includes all changes in equity during a period except those resulting from investments by owners and distributions to owners. SFAS 130 divides comprehensive income into net income and other comprehensive income.

2. PRESENTATION Comprehensive income must be displayed prominently within a financial statement in a full set of general-purpose financial statements. Comprehensive income must be shown on the face of one of the statements, not just in the notes to the financial statements.

3. COMPONENTS AND TOTAL REPORTED All components of comprehensive income must be reported in the financial statements in the period in which they are recognized. A total amount for comprehensive income must be displayed in the financial statement where the components of other comprehensive income are reported.

C. OTHER COMPREHENSIVE INCOME

1. ITEMS TO INCLUDE Items that previously were included in the equity section as a separate component of owners' equity are required by SFAS 130 to be reported in other comprehensive income. These items continue to be determined in the same manner; GAAP has not changed regarding the nature of these items and how and when they are measured and reported. Other comprehensive income has no effect on direct adjustments to equity accounts, such as capital stock transactions and transactions related to retained earnings.

2. CLASSIFICATION An entity must classify items of other comprehensive income by their nature, in one of these classifications: foreign currency items, minimum pension liability adjustments, unrealized gains and losses on certain investments in debt and equity securities, and gains and losses on cash flow hedging derivative instruments. Additional classifications or additional items within current classifications may result from future accounting standards.

a. FOREIGN CURRENCY ITEMS Included in this classification are foreign currency translation adjustments and gains and losses on foreign currency transactions that are designated as, and are effective as, economic hedges of a net investment in a foreign entity. Also included is the effective portion of gains and losses on hedging derivative instruments in a hedge of a forecasted foreign-currency-denominated transaction, and the effective portion of the gain or loss in the hedging derivative or nonderivative instrument in a hedge of a net investment in a foreign operation, in accordance with SFAS 133.

b. MINIMUM PENSION LIABILITY ADJUSTMENTS Where additional liability exceeds unamortized prior service cost, the excess is reported in other comprehensive income.

c. UNREALIZED GAINS AND LOSSES ON CERTAIN INVESTMENTS Unrealized Gains and Losses on Certain Investments in Debt and Equity Securities, accounted for in accordance with SFAS 115, including

(1) Unrealized holding gains and losses on available for sale securities

(2) Unrealized holding gains and losses that result from a debt security being transferred into the available-for-sale category from the held-to-maturity category

(3) Subsequent decreases or increases in the fair value of available-for-sale securities previously written down as impaired

(4) A change in the market value of a futures contract that qualifies as a hedge of an asset reported at fair value

d. GAINS AND LOSSES ON CASH FLOW HEDGING DERIVATIVE INSTRUMENTS The effective portion of these gains and losses are reported as a component of other comprehensive income and reclassified into earnings when the hedged forecasted transaction affects earnings, in accordance with SFAS 133.

D.   ACCUMULATED BALANCE OF OTHER COMPREHENSIVE INCOME
An entity is required to display the accumulated balance of other comprehensive income separately from retained earnings, capital stock, and additional paid-in capital in the equity section of a statement of financial position.   A descriptive title such as *accumulated other comprehensive income* must be used.   An entity must disclose accumulated balances for each classification in that separate component of equity on the face of the statement of financial position, in the statement of changes in equity, or in the notes to the financial statements.   The classifications must correspond to classifications used elsewhere in the same set of statements for components of other comprehensive income.

E.   RECLASSIFICATION ADJUSTMENTS

1.   TO AVOID DOUBLE COUNTING Adjustments must be made to avoid double counting in comprehensive income items that are displayed as part of net income for a period that also had been included as part of other comprehensive income in that period or earlier periods.

2.   FOR EACH CLASSIFICATION Reclassification adjustments must be determined for each classification of other comprehensive income, except minimum pension liability adjustments. Minimum pension liability adjustments must be shown net.

3.   DISPLAY IN FINANCIAL STATEMENTS Reclassification adjustments may be displayed on the face of the financial statement in which comprehensive income is reported.   Alternatively, reclassification adjustments may be shown net on the face of the financial statement and the gross changes be disclosed in the notes to the financial statements.

F.   REPORTING RELATED INCOME TAX
An entity may display components of other comprehensive income in two alternative ways.

1.   NET-OF-TAX BASIS Each of the components of comprehensive income may be reported on a net-of-tax basis.

2.   SUMMARY NET-OF-TAX BASIS Each of the other comprehensive income items may be reported before tax, with one line reporting the tax provision of all of those elements.   If this alternative is used, the tax provision for each individual item must be shown within the notes to the financial statements.

G.   INTERIM-PERIOD REPORTING
An entity must report a total for comprehensive income in condensed financial statements of interim periods.

H.   FORMAT OPTIONS
An entity may choose from several possible formats to report comprehensive income.

1.   ONE-STATEMENT APPROACH Since net income is a significant part of comprehensive income, the one-statement approach combines the statement of income and comprehensive income. The statement presents the various components of net income and then reports the elements of other comprehensive income.   Although earnings per share may be shown for various income statement items, it is not required to be reported for comprehensive income.

2.   TWO-STATEMENT APPROACH The income statement and the statement of comprehensive income are separate statements in the two-statement format.   The statement of comprehensive income begins with net income and then includes the other items of comprehensive income.

3.   STATEMENT-OF-CHANGES-IN-EQUITY APPROACH Comprehensive income may be reported on the statement of changes in equity.

EXHIBIT 7 ♦ ONE-STATEMENT APPROACH, WITH TAX EFFECT SHOWN PARENTHETICALLY (SFAS 144)

ABC Company
Statement of Income and Comprehensive Income
For the year ended December 31, 20X1

Revenues		$ 450,000
Expenses		(300,000)
Loss on sale of securities		(20,000)
Income from Continuing Operations, before taxes		$ 130,000
Provision for taxes		(54,000)
Income from Continuing Operations		76,000
Discontinued Operations:		
Loss on operations of discontinued component	$(33,000)	
Income taxes	(22,000)	
Loss on Discontinued Operations		$ (55,000)
Income before Extraordinary Items		$ 21,000
Extraordinary Gain, net of tax		18,000
Income before cumulative effect of accounting change		$ 39,000
Cumulative effect of accounting change, net of tax		(10,000)
Net Income		$ 29,000
Other Comprehensive Income:		
Foreign currency adjustments, net of tax of $6,000	$ 9,000	
Unrealized Loss on Marketable Securities:		
Unrealized holding loss arising during period, net of tax of $18,000	$ (42,000)	
Less: reclassification adjustment, net of tax of $6,000, for loss included in net income	14,000	(28,000)
Minimum pension liability adjustment, net of tax of $4,000		(6,000)
Other Comprehensive Income		$ (25,000)
Comprehensive Income		$ 4,000

EXHIBIT 8 ♦ TWO-STATEMENT APPROACH, WITH TAX EFFECT SHOWN AS A SINGLE AMOUNT* (APB 30)

ABC Company
Statement of Income
For the year ended December 31, 20X1

Revenues		$ 450,000
Expenses		(300,000)
Loss on sale of securities		(20,000)
Income from Continuing Operations, before taxes		$ 130,000
Provision for taxes		(54,000)
Income from Continuing Operations		$ 76,000
Discontinued Operations:		
Loss on operations of discontinued segment, net of tax	$(30,000)	
Loss on disposal of discontinued segment, net of tax	(25,000)	
Loss on Discontinued Operations		$ (55,000)
Income before Extraordinary Items		$ 21,000
Extraordinary Gain, net of tax		18,000
Income before cumulative effect of accounting change		$ 39,000
Cumulative effect of accounting change, net of tax		(10,000)
Net Income		$ 29,000

* A footnote must provide the details of the tax effect

(continued on next page)

ABC Company
Statement of Comprehensive Income
For the year ended December 31, 20X1

Net Income			$ 29,000
Other Comprehensive Income:			
Foreign currency adjustments		$ 15,000	
Unrealized Loss on Marketable Securities:			
Unrealized holding loss arising during period	$(60,000)		
Less: reclassification adjustment for loss included in net income	20,000	(40,000)	
Minimum pension liability adjustment		(10,000)	
Other Comprehensive Income, before tax		$(35,000)	
Income tax expense		10,000	
Other Comprehensive Income			$ (25,000)
Comprehensive Income			$ 4,000

EXHIBIT 9 ♦ STATEMENT-OF-CHANGES-IN-EQUITY APPROACH*

ABC Company
Statement of Changes in Equity
For the year ended December 31, 20X1

	Total	Comprehensive Income	Retained Earnings	Accumulated Other Comprehensive Income	Common Stock	Paid-in Capital
Beginning balance	$ 600,000		$ 200,000	$ 165,000	$ 50,000	$ 185,000
Comprehensive income						
Net income	29,000	$ 29,000	29,000			
Other comprehensive income, net of tax:						
Unrealized loss on marketable securities net of reclassification adjustment	(28,000)	(28,000)				
Foreign currency adjustment	9,000	9,000				
Minimum pension liability adjustment	(6,000)	(6,000)				
Other comprehensive income		(25,000)		(25,000)		
Comprehensive income		$ 4,000				
Common stock issued	50,000				20,000	30,000
Dividends declared on common stock	(20,000)		(20,000)			
Ending balance	$ 634,000		$ 209,000	$ 140,000	$ 70,000	$ 215,000

* Net-of-tax presentation with tax amounts reflected in notes

IV. ADDITIONAL REPORTING CONSIDERATIONS

A. CHANGES IN ACCOUNTING ESTIMATES

Changes in estimates used in accounting are necessary consequences of periodic presentations of financial statements. Preparing financial statements requires estimating the effects of future events. Future events and their effects cannot be perceived with certainty. Therefore, estimating requires the exercise of judgment. Accounting estimates change as new events occur, as more experience is acquired, or as additional information is obtained.

1. CHANGE IN ESTIMATE INSEPARABLE FROM A CHANGE IN PRINCIPLE In some cases, a change in accounting *estimate* and a change in accounting principle are inseparable. When the effects of the two changes cannot be separated, the change should be accounted for as a *change in estimate*.

2. **EXAMPLES OF CHANGES IN ESTIMATES** Changes in the following items would usually require a change in accounting estimate.

   a. Useful lives and salvage values of depreciable assets

   b. Recovery periods benefited by a deferred cost

   c. Expected losses on receivables

   d. Warranty costs

3. **PERIOD OF RECOGNITION** A change in accounting estimate should be accounted for in the period of change if the change only affects that period, or in the current and subsequent periods, if the change affects both, as a component of income from continuing operations. A change in estimate does **not** require the presentation of pro forma effects of retroactive application or restatement of prior period financial statements. The effects of the change in estimate on income *before* extraordinary items, *net income*, and related *per share* amounts should be disclosed in the period of the change or in future periods if the change affects those periods.

4. **DISCLOSURE** No disclosure is required for estimates made in the ordinary course of accounting if the effects are not material. An example is the bad debt estimate.

EXAMPLE 4 ♦ CHANGE IN ESTIMATE

Assume machinery with a cost of $450,000 is being depreciated over a 15-year life. After 10 years, information becomes available that indicates a useful life of 20 years for the machinery. Accounting for the change in depreciation estimate in the eleventh year would be as follows:

Historical cost	$450,000
Depreciation to date ($30,000 x 10)	(300,000)
Remaining balance	$150,000
Balance to be depreciated over	
remaining useful life ($150,000 ÷ 10)	$ 15,000

To record depreciation expense in the year of the change:

Depreciation Expense	15,000	
Accumulated Depreciation		15,000

The notes to the income statement would include the following disclosure:

Note A: *During the year 20XX, the estimated useful life of certain machinery was changed from 15 years to 20 years. The effect of the change was to increase net income by $15,000 (ignoring taxes). Earnings per share amounts increased $1.50.*

The financial statements of prior periods presented would <u>not</u> be restated, nor would the pro forma effects of retroactive application be reported.

B. CHANGES IN REPORTING ENTITY
A special type of change in accounting principle that results in financial statements of a different reporting entity (i.e., a different group of companies comprise the reporting entity after the change).

1. **REPORTING THE CHANGE** Report by *restating* the financial statements of all prior periods presented to reflect the new reporting entity. Do **not** report (1) the cumulative effect of the change on the amount of retained earnings at the beginning of the period in which the change is made or (2) pro forma effects on net income and earnings per share of retroactive application.

2. **EXAMPLES** Examples include (a) presenting consolidated or combined statements in place of statements of individual companies, (b) changing specific subsidiaries comprising the group of companies for which consolidated financial statements are presented, and (c) changing the companies included in combined financial statements.

C. CORRECTION OF ERRORS (APB 20)

1. **OVERVIEW** Errors in financial statements result from mathematical mistakes, mistakes in the application of accounting principles, or the oversight or misuse of facts that existed at the time the financial statements were prepared. Errors commonly found in financial statements include the following:

   a. Estimates based on *unreasonable assumptions*; for example, the use of an unrealistic depreciation rate.

   b. Recording *erroneous amounts* for assets and equities. For example, incorrect footing of inventory totals would cause inventories to be misstated on the balance sheet.

   c. *Failure to record* prepaid and accrued expenses.

   d. The *improper classification* of assets as expenses and vice versa. The purchase price of a plant asset may be incorrectly charged to expense rather than an asset account.

   e. In addition, the change from an accounting principle that is **not** generally accepted to one that **is** generally accepted is treated as the correction of an error; for example, a change from the direct write-off method to the allowance method of accounting for uncollectible accounts.

2. **REPORTED AS PRIOR PERIOD ADJUSTMENTS**

   a. **PRIOR PERIOD ADJUSTMENTS** *Prior Period Adjustments* (SFAS 16) specifies that for an item to be classified as a prior period adjustment, it must be an item of profit or loss related to the correction of an error in the financial statements of a prior period. Prior period adjustments bypass the income statement. They are instead reported net of their income tax effect in the statement of retained earnings as an adjustment to the beginning balance of retained earnings.

   b. **REPORTING CORRECTED ERRORS** APB 20, *Accounting Changes*, states, "the nature of an error in previously issued financial statements and the effect of its correction on income before extraordinary items, net income, and the related per share amounts should be *disclosed in the period in which the error was discovered and corrected*. Financial statements of subsequent periods need not repeat the disclosures."

   c. **RESTATING PRIOR PERIODS** APB 9, *Reporting the Results of Operation*, requires that statements of prior periods presented for comparative purposes be restated to reflect the retroactive application of the prior period adjustments.

d. **STATEMENT OF RETAINED EARNINGS** A prior period adjustment would be reported in the statement of retained earnings as follows:

Retained earnings, beginning balance	$XXX
Prior period adjustment (+/–)	XX
Retained earnings, beginning balance, adjusted	XXX
Add net income (or less net loss)	XXX
Less dividends	(XX)
Retained earnings, ending balance	$XXX

3. **CLASSIFICATION OF ERRORS** Accounting errors may be classified by time of discovery or according to their effect on the balance sheet, income statement, or both.

a. **OCCURRENCE AND DISCOVERY IN SAME PERIOD** Errors that occur and are discovered in the same accounting period may be corrected by reversing the incorrect entry and recording the correct one or by directly correcting the account balances with a single entry.

b. **OCCURRENCE AND DISCOVERY IN DIFFERENT PERIODS** Errors that occur in one accounting period and are discovered in a subsequent accounting period are more involved: the cumulative effect of each error on periods prior to the period of discovery is calculated and recorded as a direct adjustment to the beginning balance of retained earnings.

c. **EFFECT ON BALANCE SHEET** Only balance sheet accounts are affected, for instance, if the inventory account is debited instead of the equipment account or if notes payable is credited instead of accounts payable. When the error is discovered, an entry is recorded to correct the account balances.

d. **EFFECT ON INCOME STATEMENT** Revenue or expense classification errors will affect only the income statement for the period. If Sales Revenue is credited instead of Rent Revenue or Interest Expense is debited instead of Wage Expense, the amounts presented on the income statement for these accounts will be misstated. Net income for the period, however, will not be affected. If the error is discovered *prior to the year-end closings*, an entry can be recorded to correct the account balances. If the error is discovered *in a subsequent period*, no correction is necessary. However, the restatement of comparative financial statements is required.

e. **EFFECT ON BOTH STATEMENTS** Some errors affect both the balance sheet and the income statement, and may be classified in the following two ways:

(1) **COUNTERBALANCING ERRORS** Counterbalancing errors will "correct" themselves over two consecutive accounting periods. Generally, a counterbalancing error will cause a misstatement of net income and balance sheet accounts in one period that will be offset by an equal misstatement in the following period. Balance sheet accounts and combined net income for both periods will be stated correctly at the end of the second period (ignoring tax effects).

EXAMPLE 5 ♦ COUNTERBALANCING ERRORS

Assume that a company neglects to record accrued wage expense at the end of a fiscal period. In the <u>first year</u>, the error would have the following effects:

<u>Income Statement</u>
Wage expense understated
Net income overstated

<u>Balance Sheet</u>
Liabilities understated
Retained earnings overstated

In the <u>second year</u>, the payment of accrued wage expense will be charged to wage expense of the current year causing the following effects:

<u>Income Statement</u>
Wage expense overstated
Net income understated

<u>Balance Sheet</u>
Accounts are correctly stated due
   to the counterbalancing effect
   on error.

(2) **NON-COUNTERBALANCING ERRORS** Errors that are **not** counterbalancing cause successive balance sheet amounts and net income to be incorrectly stated until the errors are discovered and corrected. For example, suppose that instead of capitalizing the cost of an asset, the cost is charged to expense. In the year the error occurs, expenses will be *overstated* and net income *understated*. During the life of the asset, net income will be overstated by the amount of *unrecorded* depreciation. Additionally, assets on the balance sheet will be understated throughout the service life of the unrecorded asset.

D. **_DISCLOSURE OF ACCOUNTING POLICIES_ (APB 22)**
All significant accounting policies followed by an enterprise should be disclosed in its financial statements. No specific disclosure format is required. APB 22 prefers a *separate* note, or a summary preceding the notes entitled *Summary of Significant Accounting Policies*. The accounting policy disclosures should identify and describe the principles and methods that materially affect the financial position and operations.

1. **POLICY CHOICES** Disclosure should include policies involving a choice of alternative acceptable policies, policies peculiar to that particular industry, and unusual applications of acceptable principles.

2. **EXAMPLES** Examples of disclosure requirements include depreciation methods, methods of pricing inventory, methods of recognizing profit on long-term construction contracts, and basis of consolidation.

3. **NO DUPLICATION OF INFORMATION** Financial statement disclosure of accounting policies should **not** duplicate details presented elsewhere as part of the financial statements, such as composition of inventories or plant assets, depreciation expense, and maturity dates of long-term debt.

E. **_RELATED PARTY DISCLOSURES_ (SFAS 57)**

1. **DEFINITION** Transactions between related parties include transactions between the following:

    a. A parent company and its subsidiaries

    b. Subsidiaries of a common parent

    c. An enterprise and its principal owners, management, or members of their immediate families

      d.   Affiliates

  2.   **EXAMPLES** Examples of related party transactions include:

      a.   Sales, purchases, and transfers of realty and personal property

      b.   Services received or furnished (e.g., accounting, management, engineering, and legal services)

      c.   Use of property and equipment by lease or otherwise

      d.   Borrowings, lendings, and guarantees

      e.   Intercompany billings based on allocations of common costs

      f.   Filings of consolidated tax returns

  3.   **DISCLOSURES** Financial statements should include disclosures of material related party transactions, other than compensation arrangements, expense allowances, and other similar items in the ordinary course of business. However, disclosure of transactions that are *eliminated* in the preparation of *consolidated or combined financial statements* (e.g., intercompany sales) is not required. The disclosures should include the following:

      a.   The nature of the relationship(s) involved.

      b.   A description of the transactions, including transactions to which no amounts or nominal amounts were ascribed, for each of the periods for which income statements are presented, and such other information necessary to an understanding of the effects of the transactions on the financial statements.

      c.   The dollar amounts of transactions for each of the periods for which income statements are presented and the effects of any change in the method of establishing the terms from that used in the preceding period.

      d.   Amounts due from or to related parties as of the date of each balance sheet presented and, if not otherwise apparent, the terms and manner of settlement.

  4.   **REPRESENTATIONS** Transactions involving related parties cannot be presumed to be carried out on an arm's-length basis, as the requisite conditions of competitive, free-market dealings may not exist. Representations about transactions with related parties, if made, should not imply that the related party transactions were consummated on terms equivalent to those that prevail in arm's length transactions unless such representations can be substantiated.

  5.   **CONTROL RELATIONSHIPS** If the reporting enterprise and one or more other enterprises are under common ownership or management control and the existence of that control could result in operating results or financial position of the reporting enterprise significantly different from those that would have been obtained if the enterprises were autonomous, the nature of the control relationship should be disclosed even though there are no transactions between the enterprises.

F.   **DEVELOPMENT STAGE ENTERPRISES (SFAS 7)**

  1.   **CRITERIA** An enterprise is in the development stage if "substantially all" of its efforts are devoted to establishing a new business and *either* of the following is present:

      a.   Principal operations have not begun.

      b.   Principal operations have begun, but revenue produced is insignificant.

2. **PRESENTATION OF FINANCIAL STATEMENTS**

    a. **GAAP** Financial statements issued by a development stage enterprise should be presented in conformity with generally accepted accounting principles applicable to *established operating enterprises*.

        (1) Special accounting practices that are based on a distinctive accounting for development stage enterprises are **not** acceptable.

        (2) Generally accepted accounting principles that apply to established operating enterprises govern the recognition of revenue by a development stage enterprise and determine whether a cost incurred by a development stage enterprise is to be charged to expense when incurred or is to be capitalized or deferred. Accordingly, capitalization or deferral of costs shall be subject to the same assessment of recoverability that would be applicable in an established operating enterprise.

        (3) Financial reporting by a development stage enterprise differs from financial reporting for an established operating enterprise in regard only to the *additional information*.

    b. **STATEMENTS REQUIRED** The financial statements to be issued by a development stage enterprise and the additional information to be included are as follows:

        (1) **BALANCE SHEET** Cumulative net losses are reported as part of stockholders' equity using terms such as "deficit accumulated during the development stage."

        (2) **INCOME STATEMENT** Includes cumulative expenses and revenues from the inception of the development stage.

        (3) **STATEMENT OF CASH FLOWS** Includes cumulative amounts from date of inception.

        (4) **STATEMENT OF STOCKHOLDERS' EQUITY** Includes the following from the date of inception:

            (a) *Number of shares, warrants, etc.,* issued and date of issuance.

            (b) *Dollar amounts* received for shares, etc., of each issuance. Noncash consideration received must be assigned a dollar value and must indicate the nature of the consideration and the valuation basis used.

    c. **DISCLOSURE** Financial statements of a development stage enterprise should be identified as such and the nature of activities disclosed.

G. **ACCRUAL ACCOUNTING**

    1. **DEFINITION** Accrual accounting recognizes and reports the effects of transactions and other events on the assets and liabilities of a business enterprise in the time periods to which they relate rather than only when cash is received or paid. Accrual accounting attempts to match revenues and the expenses associated with those revenues in order to determine net income for an accounting period.

    2. **REVENUE RECOGNITION** *Revenues* are recognized when earned.

    3. **EXPENSE RECOGNITION** *Expenses* are recognized and recorded as follows:

        a. **ASSOCIATING CAUSE AND EFFECT** Some expenses are recognized and recorded on a presumed direct association with specific revenue.

b. **SYSTEMATIC AND RATIONAL ALLOCATION** In the absence of a direct association with specific revenue, some expenses are recognized and recorded by attempting to allocate expenses in a systematic and rational manner among the periods in which benefits are provided.

c. **IMMEDIATE RECOGNITION** Some costs are associated with the current accounting period as expenses because (1) costs incurred during the period provide no discernible future benefits, (2) costs recorded as assets in prior periods no longer provide discernible benefits, or (3) allocating costs either on the basis of association with revenues or among several accounting periods is considered to serve no useful purpose.

4. **ACCRUALS** An accrual represents a transaction that affects the determination of income for the period but has not yet been reflected in the cash accounts of that period.

a. **ACCRUED REVENUE** Accrued revenue is revenue earned but not yet collected in cash. An example of accrued revenue is accrued interest revenue earned on bonds from the last interest payment date to the end of the accounting period.

b. **ACCRUED EXPENSE** An accrued expense is an expense incurred but not yet paid in cash. An example of an accrued expense is salaries incurred for the last week of the accounting period that are not payable until the subsequent accounting period.

5. **DEFERRALS** A deferral represents a transaction that has been reflected in the cash accounts of the period but has not yet affected the determination of income for that period.

a. **DEFERRED REVENUE** Deferred revenue is revenue collected or collectible in cash but not yet earned. An example of deferred revenue is rent collected in advance by a lessor in the last month of the accounting period, which represents the rent for the first month of the subsequent accounting period.

b. **DEFERRED/PREPAID EXPENSE** A deferred (prepaid) expense is an expense paid or payable in cash but not yet incurred. An example of a deferred (prepaid) expense is an insurance premium paid in advance in the current accounting period, which represents insurance coverage for the subsequent accounting period.

EXHIBIT 10 ♦ REVENUE AND EXPENSE ITEM EFFECTS

Revenue or Expense Item	Plus or Minus Adjustments to Derive Accrual Basis	Illustrative Amounts
Collections from sales		$190
Adjustments:		
1. Increase in accounts receivable	+	7
2. Decrease in accounts receivable	−	
3. Uncollectible accounts written off	+	5
Sales revenue		$202
Collections from other revenues		$184
Adjustments:		
1. Increase in revenue receivable	+	
2. Decrease in revenue receivable	−	(4)
3. Increase in unearned revenue	−	(10)
4. Decrease in unearned revenue	+	
Revenue recognized		$170

(continued on next page)

Payments for purchases	$ 91
Adjustments:	
1. Increase in inventory −	(7)
2. Decrease in inventory +	
3. Increase in accounts payable +	9
4. Decrease in accounts payable −	
Cost of goods sold	$ 93
Payment for Expenses	$ 92
Adjustments:	
1. Increase in prepaid expenses −	(9)
2. Decrease in prepaid expenses +	
3. Increase in accrued expenses payable +	8
4. Decrease in accrued expenses payable −	
Expenses recognized	$ 91

NOTE: This exhibit is for revenue or expense item effects, *not* the effects to income.

V.   *INTERIM FINANCIAL REPORTING* (APB 28)

A.   CONCEPTS

In APB 28, the Board concluded that each interim period should be viewed as an *integral part of an annual period* and not as a separate, independent period. In order to maintain comparability between interim and annual financial statements, the Opinion states that the principles and practices used to prepare the latest annual financial statements should also be used to prepare the interim statements. However, certain procedures applied to the annual statements may require modification at the interim reporting dates so that the results for the interim period may better relate to the results of operations for the annual period.

B.   ORDINARY REVENUES AND EXPENSES

1.   **REVENUES** *Revenues* should be recognized as earned during an interim period on the same basis as followed for recognition of income for the full year. For example, revenues from long-term construction-type contracts accounted for under the percentage-of-completion method should be recognized in interim periods on the same basis as is followed for the full year. Losses from such contracts should be recognized in full during the interim period in which the existence of the losses becomes evident.

2.   **PRODUCT COSTS** *Costs* and *expenses* associated directly with products sold or services rendered for annual reporting purposes should be similarly treated for interim reporting purposes. Some exceptions are appropriate for valuing inventory at interim reporting dates.

     a.   **INVENTORY ESTIMATION** Some companies use *estimated gross profit* rates to estimate ending inventory and cost of goods sold during interim periods or use other methods different from those used at annual inventory dates. These companies should disclose the methods used at the interim date and any significant adjustments that result from reconciliation with the annual physical inventory.

     b.   **LIFO AND LIQUIDATION OF BASE PERIOD INVENTORIES** Companies that use the *LIFO method* may encounter a liquidation of base period inventories at an interim date that is expected to be replaced by the end of the annual period. The inventory at the interim date should not give effect to the LIFO liquidation, and cost of sales for the interim reporting period should include the replacement cost of the liquidated LIFO base.

     c.   **LOWER OF COST OR MARKET** The use of *lower of cost or market* may result in inventory losses that should not be deferred beyond the interim period in which the decline occurs. Recoveries of these losses in subsequent periods should be recognized as gains, *but only to the extent* of losses recognized in previous interim periods of the same fiscal year. *Temporary* market declines need not be recognized at the interim date since no loss is expected to be incurred in the fiscal year.

d. **STANDARD COSTS** Companies that use *standard costs* for valuing inventory at year-end should use the same procedures for valuing inventory at interim dates. Material and volume variances that are *planned* and expected to be absorbed by year-end should be deferred until the end of the year. *Unplanned* variances should be reported in the interim period in the same manner as year-end variances.

3. **COSTS OTHER THAN PRODUCT COSTS** *Costs and expenses other than product costs* should be charged to income in interim periods as incurred, or be allocated among interim periods based on an estimate of time expired, benefit received, or activity associated with the periods. Procedures adopted for assigning specific cost and expense items to an interim period should be consistent with the bases followed by the company in reporting results of operations at annual reporting dates. However, when a specific cost or expense item charged to expense for annual reporting purposes benefits *more than one interim period*, the cost or expense item may be allocated to those interim periods.

a. **NOT IDENTIFIABLE TO SPECIFIC PERIOD** Some *costs and expenses* incurred in an interim period, however, cannot be readily identified with the activities or benefits of other interim periods and should be charged to the interim period in which incurred.

b. **NO ARBITRARY ASSIGNMENT** *Arbitrary assignment* of the amount of such costs to an interim period should not be made.

c. **GAIN & LOSS DEFERRALS** *Gains and losses* that arise in any interim period similar to those that would not be deferred at year-end should not be deferred to later interim periods within the same fiscal year.

4. **ALLOCATION OF INDIRECT COSTS EXAMPLES** The following examples from APB 28 may be helpful in applying the standards for allocation of costs and expenses not directly associated with revenues in interim financial statements.

a. When a cost that is expensed for annual reporting purposes clearly benefits two or more interim periods (e.g., annual major repairs), each interim period should be charged for an appropriate portion of the annual cost by the use of accruals or deferrals.

b. Property taxes (and similar costs such as insurance, interest, and rent) may be accrued or deferred at an annual reporting date to achieve a full year's charge of taxes to costs and expenses. Similar procedures should be adopted at each interim reporting date to provide an appropriate cost in each period.

c. Advertising costs may be deferred within a fiscal year if the benefits of an expenditure clearly extend beyond the interim period in which the expenditure is made.

5. **INTERIM PERIOD FINANCIAL STATEMENTS** Interim period financial statements should bear a reasonable portion of such year-end adjustments as inventory shrinkage, allowance for uncollectible accounts, and discretionary year-end bonuses.

6. **SEASONAL VARIATIONS** Companies whose revenues and expenses are subject to material *seasonal variations* should disclose the seasonal nature of their activities, and consider supplementing their interim reports with information for twelve-month periods ended at the interim date for the current and preceding years.

C. **INTERIM PERIOD INCOME TAX PROVISIONS**
(FASB Interp. 18)

1.   **ESTIMATED EFFECTIVE TAX RATE**   At the end of each interim period, the company should make its best estimate of the effective tax rate expected to be applicable for the full fiscal year. This estimated effective tax rate should be used to provide for income taxes on a current year-to-date basis. The effective tax rate should reflect foreign tax rates, percentage depletion, and other available tax planning alternatives. However, in arriving at the esti-mated full year tax rate, no effect should be included for the income tax related to significant unusual or extraordinary items that will be separately reported or reported net of their related income tax effects for the interim period or for the fiscal year.

2.   **NONORDINARY ITEMS**   *Unusual* or *infrequently occurring* items (nonordinary items) should be included in determining interim period income, but should be excluded in determining the full year effective income tax rate.

D. **DISCONTINUED SEGMENTS AND EXTRAORDINARY ITEMS**
Extraordinary items and the *gain or loss from disposal of a component of an entity* and their related income tax effects should be included in the determination of net income for the interim period in which they occur. An item should be classified as extraordinary in the interim period if it is material in relation to annual net income. Extraordinary items and the gain or loss from disposal of a component of an entity should **not** be prorated among interim periods.

E. **ACCOUNTING CHANGES**
APB 28 recommends that, whenever possible, companies adopt any accounting changes during the first interim period of a fiscal year. In practice, however, accounting changes are made throughout the fiscal year. Recognizing this fact, SFAS 3, *Reporting Accounting Changes in Interim Financial Statements*, amended APB 28 and prescribed special procedures for reporting the cumulative effect of an accounting change when adoption of the new accounting principle occurs in other than the first interim period.

1.   **CUMULATIVE EFFECT CHANGE IN FIRST INTERIM PERIOD**   If a *cumulative effect* type account-ing change is made during the **first** interim period of the fiscal year, the cumulative effect of the change on retained earnings at the beginning of that fiscal year should be included in the net income of the first interim period.

2.   **CUMULATIVE EFFECT CHANGE IN OTHER THAN FIRST INTERIM PERIOD**   If a *cumulative effect* type accounting change is made in *other* than the first interim period, the change is accounted for *as if it occurred in the first interim period*. Financial information for prechange interim periods should be restated by applying the newly adopted accounting principle to those prechange interim periods. The restated net income of the first interim period of the fiscal year in which the change takes place should include the cumulative effect of the change on retained earnings at the beginning of that fiscal year. Whenever financial information that includes the prechange interim periods is presented, it should be presented separately on the restated basis.

3.   **SPECIAL CHANGES REQUIRING RETROACTIVE RESTATEMENT**   The following *special changes* in accounting principles, set forth in APB 20, *Accounting Changes*, require *retroactive restatement of prior period financial statements*. Restatement of previously issued *interim financial information* will be required if a "special change" occurs in other than the first interim period. The estimated effective tax rate will also require restatement in order to properly reflect the effect of the newly adopted accounting principles on annual ordinary income (or loss).

a.   A change from the LIFO method of inventory pricing to another method.

b.   A change in the method of accounting for long-term construction-type contracts.

4.   CHANGE IN ACCOUNTING ESTIMATE The effect of a *change in accounting estimate*, including a change in the estimated effective annual tax rate, should be accounted for in the period in which the change in estimate is made. No restatement of previously reported interim information should be made for changes in estimates. The effect on earnings of a change in estimate made in a current interim period should be reported in the current and subsequent interim periods if material in relation to any period presented.

F.   MINIMUM DISCLOSURE REQUIREMENTS

Minimum disclosure requirements for reporting summarized financial data to security holders of publicly traded companies are listed below. When summarized financial data are regularly reported on a quarterly basis, information with respect to the current quarter and the current year-to-date or the last-twelve-months-to-date should be furnished together with comparable data for the preceding year.

1.   Sales or gross revenues, provision for income taxes, extraordinary items, cumulative effect of a change in accounting principles, net income, and comprehensive income

2.   Primary and fully diluted earnings per share data for each period presented

3.   Seasonal revenue, costs or expenses

4.   Significant changes in estimates or provisions for income taxes

5.   Disposal of a segment of a business and extraordinary, unusual, or infrequently occurring items

6.   Contingent items

7.   Changes in accounting principles or estimates

8.   Significant changes in financial position

9.   Information about reportable operating segments, including revenues from external customers, intersegment revenues, a measure of segment profit or loss, material changes in total assets, a description of differences in segments or measurement of segment profit or loss, and a reconciliation of the total of segment profit or loss to consolidated income.

VI.   *DISCLOSURES ABOUT SEGMENTS OF AN ENTERPRISE AND RELATED INFORMATION* (SFAS 131)

A.   OVERVIEW

1.   **MANAGEMENT APPROACH METHOD** SFAS 131, *Disclosure about Segments of an Enterprise and Related Information,* requires that general-purpose financial statements include selected information reported on a single basis of segmentation using the management approach method. The management approach is based on the way that management organizes the segments within the enterprise for making operating decisions and assessing performance. The components are called *operating segments.* Consequently, the segments are evident from the structure of the enterprise's internal organization, and financial statement preparers should be able to provide the required information in a cost-effective and timely manner.

2.   **OBJECTIVES** The objective of SFAS 131 is to provide information about an enterprise to help users of financial statements better understand the enterprise's performance, better assess its prospects for future net cash flows, and make more informed judgments about the enterprise as a whole.

3.   **REPORTING REQUIREMENTS** An enterprise is required to report a measure of segment profit or loss, segment assets and certain related items, but not segment cash flow, or segment liabilities.

4. **APPLICABILITY** SFAS 131 applies to *public* business enterprises. It does not apply to non-public enterprises or not-for-profit organizations.

B. DEFINITIONS

1. **OPERATING SEGMENTS** Operating segments have three characteristics. Not every part of an entity is necessarily part of an operating segment.

   a. **REVENUE PRODUCING** An operating segment is a component of an enterprise with revenue producing (even if no revenue is yet earned) and expense incurring activities.

   b. **REVIEW BY DECISION MAKER** The operating results of an operating segment are regularly reviewed by the entity's chief operating decision maker.

   c. **AVAILABILITY OF FINANCIAL INFORMATION** Discrete financial information is available for an operating segment.

2. **CHIEF OPERATING DECISION MAKER** The chief operating decision maker is identified by the function of allocating resources and assessing the performance of a segment, not necessarily by title. The chief operating decision maker may be, for example, the chief executive officer, the president, or the chief operating officer. It may be one person or it may be a group, such as the Chairman and the Board of Directors.

3. **SEGMENT MANAGER** Generally, an operating segment has a segment manager directly accountable to the chief operating decision maker. The term segment manager is also identified by function, not necessarily by a specific title. The chief operating decision maker in some cases may also be the segment manager for an operating segment. The same person may be a segment manager for more than one operating segment.

4. **REPORTABLE SEGMENTS** Reportable segments include operating segments that exceed the quantitative thresholds. A reportable segment may also result from aggregating two or more segments in accordance with the aggregation criteria. The quantitative thresholds and the aggregation criteria are outlined in the text that follows. Exhibit 11 summarizes identifying reportable operating segments.

C. AGGREGATION CRITERIA
Operating segments often exhibit similar long-term financial performance if they have similar economic characteristics. Two or more operating segments may be aggregated into a single operating segment if aggregation is consistent with the objective and basic principles of SFAS 131, if the segments have similar economic characteristics, and if the segments are similar in each of the following areas:

1. The nature of the products and services

2. The nature of the production processes

3. The type or class of customer for their products and services

4. The methods used to distribute their products or provide their services

5. The nature of the regulatory environment, if applicable; for example, banking, insurance, or public utilities

EXHIBIT 11 ♦ DIAGRAM FOR IDENTIFYING REPORTABLE OPERATING SEGMENTS

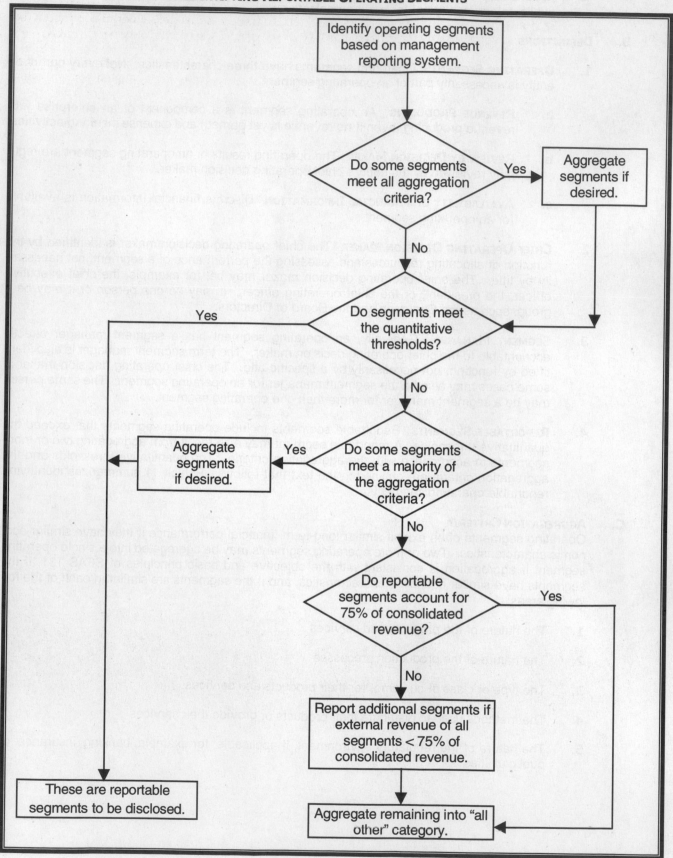

D. **QUANTITATIVE THRESHOLDS**

1. **SEGMENT TESTS** An enterprise is required to report separately information about an operating segment that meets any of the following quantitative thresholds:

a. **REVENUE TEST** Its reported revenue is 10% or more of the combined revenue of all operating segments. Revenue includes both sales to external customers and inter-segment sales or transfers.

b. **PROFIT(LOSS) TEST** The absolute amount of its reported profit or loss is *10% or more* of the *greater*, in *absolute amount*, of

(1) The combined reported profit of all operating segments that did not report a loss, or

(2) The combined reported loss of all operating segments that did report a loss.

c. **ASSETS TEST** Its assets are 10% or more of the combined assets of all operating segments.

EXAMPLE 6 ♦ QUANTITATIVE THRESHOLDS

A, B, and C are operating segments of a public corporation. Pertinent information regarding sales, profit and loss, and assets of the three segments are given below.

	A	B	C	Combined	Elimination	Consolidated
Sales:						
Unaffiliated	$ 800	$ 20	$ 40	$ 860		$ 860
Intersegment	40	500		540	$(540)	
Total sales	$ 840	$ 520	$ 40	$1,400	$(540)	$ 860
Profit(loss)	$ 200	$(300)	$ 25	$ (75)		$ (75)
Assets	$1,200	$ 150	$400	$1,750		$1,750

REQUIRED: Determine which segments should be reported separately, based on the quantitative thresholds requirements.

SOLUTION: Revenue Test—10% of combined segment revenues equals $140 [10% X ($840 + $520 + $40)]; therefore, segments A and B meet the revenue requirement for segmental disclosure.

Profit(loss) Test—The absolute amount of combined reported losses of all segments having losses exceed the combined profits of the profitable segments (i.e., $300 exceeds $225). The reported profit of segment A ($200), and the absolute amount of loss of segment B ($300) is 10% or more of the absolute amount of combined reported loss of all operating segments ($300); therefore, segments A and B meet this test.

Assets Test—10% of combined assets equals $175 [10% X ($1,200 + $150 + $400]; therefore, segments A and C meet this test.

All three segments meet at least one of the quantitative thresholds criteria for reportable segments; consequently, segmental disclosure should be reported for three segments.

2. **EXCEPTIONS** Exceptions to the quantitative thresholds are as follows:

a. **COMBINING OPERATING SEGMENTS** An entity may combine information about operating segments not meeting the quantitative thresholds to produce a reportable segment only if the operating segments share a majority of the aggregation criteria listed in C. above.

b. **MINIMUM REPORTABLE SEGMENTS** If the total of external revenue reported by operating segments is less than 75% of total consolidated revenue, additional operating segments must be identified as reportable segments until at least 75% of total consolidated revenue is included in reportable segments.

c. **"ALL OTHER" CATEGORY** Non-reportable business activities and operating segments are required to be combined and disclosed in an "all other" category separate from other reconciling items in the reconciliations. The sources of the revenue must be described.

d. **MANAGEMENT JUDGMENT** If management judges an operating segment to be of continuing significance even though it no longer meets the criteria for reportability, information about that segment should continue to be reported separately in the current period.

e. **RESTATEMENT OF PRIOR-PERIOD INFORMATION** Information from prior periods presented for comparative purposes must be restated to reflect the newly reportable segment as a separate segment, unless it is impracticable to do so, such as when the information is not available and the cost to develop the information would be excessive.

f. **PRACTICAL LIMIT REACHED** There may be a practical limit to the number of reportable segments beyond which segment information may become overly detailed. No precise limit has been determined, but generally an enterprise should consider whether this limit has been reached as the number of reportable segments increases above 10.

E. REQUIRED DISCLOSURES

1. **GENERAL INFORMATION** An enterprise is required to disclose the following general information:

   a. **IDENTIFICATION FACTORS** Factors used to identify reportable segments, such as differences in products and services, geographic areas, or regulatory environments.

   b. **REVENUE SOURCES** Types of products and services from which each reportable segment derives its revenues.

2. **SEGMENT PROFIT OR LOSS AND ASSETS AND BASIS OF MEASUREMENT**

   a. **PROFIT/LOSS AND TOTAL ASSETS** An enterprise shall report a measure of profit or loss and total assets for each reportable segment. These measures are generally based upon the measures as reported to and used by the chief operating decision maker, and may include revenues from external customers; revenues from transactions with other operating segments of the same enterprise; interest revenue; interest expense; depreciation, depletion, and amortization expense; unusual items; equity in the net income of investees accounted for by the equity method; income tax expense or benefit; extraordinary items; and significant other noncash items.

   b. **INTEREST REVENUE AND INTEREST EXPENSE** An enterprise must report interest revenue separately from interest expense for each reportable segment unless a majority of the segment's revenues are from interest.

   c. **INVESTMENT IN EQUITY INVESTEES AND ADDITIONS TO LONG-LIVED ASSETS** If the specified amounts are included in the determination of segment assets reviewed by the chief operating decision maker, the enterprise is required to disclose the amount of investment in equity method investees, and total expenditures for additions to long-lived assets other than financial instruments, long-term customer relationships of a financial institution, mortgage and other servicing rights, deferred policy acquisition costs, and deferred tax assets.

    d.   **EXPLANATION OF MEASUREMENTS** An enterprise must provide an explanation of the measurements used, at a minimum:

        (1)   The basis of accounting for any transactions between reportable segments

        (2)   The nature of any differences between the measurements applied to the reportable segments and the consolidated statements

        (3)   The nature of any changes from prior periods in the measurement methods used

        (4)   The nature and effect of any asymmetrical allocations to segments. For example, an enterprise might allocate depreciation expense to a segment without allocating the related depreciable assets to that segment.

  3.   **RECONCILIATIONS** An enterprise is required to report reconciliations of the totals of segment revenues, reported profit or loss, assets, and other significant items to corresponding enterprise amounts. All significant reconciling items must be separately identified and described.

  4.   **INTERIM PERIOD REPORTING** An enterprise is required to disclose information about each reportable segment in condensed financial statements of interim periods, including revenues from external customers, intersegment revenues, measures of segment profit or loss, material changes in total assets, descriptions of differences in measurement or segmentation, and a reconciliation of segments profit or loss to consolidated income.

  5.   **ENTERPRISE-WIDE DISCLOSURES** If the following information is not provided as part of the segment information disclosed, it must also be disclosed:

    a.   Revenues from external customers for each product and service or group of similar products and services unless it is impracticable to do.

    b.   Revenues from external customers based on geographic area, including domestic revenues and foreign revenue.

    c.   Long-lived assets located in the enterprise's country of domicile, and located in foreign countries.

    d.   Information about major customers. Enterprises must disclose the total amount of revenues from each single customer that amounts to 10% or more of the enterprise's revenues and identify the segment(s) reporting the revenues. The identity of the customer need not be disclosed.

VII. OTHER COMPREHENSIVE BASIS OF ACCOUNTING

  A.   **OVERVIEW**
    Other Comprehensive Basis of Accounting (OCBOA) is a basis of accounting not in conformity with generally accepted accounting principles, as follows:

    1.   A basis of accounting used to comply with regulatory requirements.

    2.   A basis of accounting used by an entity to file its tax return.

    3.   The cash receipts and disbursements basis of accounting.

4. A definite set of criteria having substantial support, such as the price-level basis of accounting.

B. CASH BASIS

In cash basis accounting, the effects of transactions and other events on the assets and liabilities of a business enterprise are recognized and reported only when cash is received or paid; while in accrual accounting, these effects are recognized and reported in the time periods to which they relate. Cash accounting does not attempt to match revenues and the expenses associated with those revenues. The conversion of various income statement amounts from the cash basis to the accrual basis is summarized in Exhibit 10.

C. INCOME-TAX BASIS

In income-tax basis accounting, the effects of events on a business enterprise are recognized when taxable income or deductible expense is recognized on the tax return. Nontaxable income and nondeductible expenses are still included in the determination of income.

EXHIBIT 12 ♦ DISCONTINUED OPERATIONS: COMPONENT VS. NON-COMPONENT DISPOSALS (SFAS 144)

Component Disposals	Non-Component Disposals
Two companies manufacture and sell consumer products with several product groups, with different product lines and brands. For both companies, a product group is the lowest level at which operations and cash flows can be distinguished.	
Caring Pharmaceuticals plans to sell the beauty product group and its operations.	Nesbit Household Products discontinues cosmetic brands associated with losses.
Two companies operate nationwide restaurant chains, each with numerous company-owned sites. For both companies, a single restaurant is the lowest level at which operations and cash flows can be distinguished.	
Cluck-to-Go decides to exit its northeast region. It removes its name from the northeast restaurants and sells the buildings.	New Wave Coffee sells all restaurants in its west coast region to franchisees. New Wave will receive franchise fees, provide advertising, and supply select ingredients.
Two companies operate retail home appliance chains, each with numerous company-owned sites. For both companies, a single store is the lowest level at which operations and cash flows can be distinguished.	
Cheap Freddie's closes stores in areas with declining populations, selling the buildings and moving remaining inventory to stores in other regions.	Never-a-care, Inc., closes pairs of Never-a-care Appliances stores and opens Never-a-cloud Superstores, central to former locations, with an expanded range of products.
Two sporting goods producers have golf club divisions that design, manufacture, market, and distribute golf clubs. For both companies, a division is the lowest level at which operations and cash flows can be distinguished.	
Committed Sports, Inc., agrees to a plan to sell the golf club division to an independent conglomerate.	Never Say Die Manufacturers sells its golf club manufacturing plants. Never Say Die plans to outsource its golf club manufacturing.

CHAPTER—11 REPORTING THE RESULTS OF OPERATIONS

PROBLEM 11-1 MULTIPLE CHOICE QUESTIONS (208 to 260 minutes)

1. On October 1, 1991, Acme Fuel Co. sold 100,000 gallons of heating oil to Karn Co. at $3 per gallon. Fifty thousand gallons were delivered on December 15, 1991, and the remaining 50,000 gallons were delivered on January 15, 1992. Payment terms were: 50% due on October 1, 1991, 25% due on first delivery, and the remaining 25% due on second delivery. What amount of revenue should Acme recognize from this sale during 1991?
a. $ 75,000
b. $150,000
c. $225,000
d. $300,000   (5/92, PI, #37, 2608)

2. The following costs were incurred by Griff Co., a manufacturer, during 1992:

Accounting and legal fees	$ 25,000
Freight-in	175,000
Freight-out	160,000
Officers' salaries	150,000
Insurance	85,000
Sales representatives' salaries	215,000

What amount of these costs should be reported as general and administrative expenses for 1992?
a. $260,000
b. $550,000
c. $635,000
d. $810,000   (11/93, PI, #52, 4421)

3. Which of the following should be included in general and administrative expenses?

	Interest	Advertising
a.	Yes	Yes
b.	Yes	No
c.	No	Yes
d.	No	No (5/95, FAR, #34, 5570)

4. The following information pertained to Azur Co. for the year:

Purchases	$102,800
Purchase discounts	10,280
Freight-in	15,420
Freight-out	5,140
Beginning inventory	30,840
Ending inventory	20,560

What amount should Azur report as cost of goods sold for the year?
a. $102,800
b. $118,220

c. $123,360
d. $128,500   (R/99, FAR, #11, 6780)

ITEMS 5 AND 6 are based on the following:

Vane Co.'s trial balance of income statement accounts for the year ended December 31, 1993, included the following:

	Debit	Credit
Sales		$575,000
Cost of sales	$240,000	
Administrative expenses	70,000	
Loss on sale of equipment	10,000	
Sales commissions	50,000	
Interest revenue		25,000
Freight out	15,000	
Loss on early retirement of LT debt	20,000	
Uncollectible accounts expense	15,000	
Totals	$420,000	$600,000

Other information:
Finished goods inventory:

January 1, 1993	$400,000
December 31, 1993	360,000

Vane's income tax rate is 30%. In Vane's 1993 multiple-step income statement,

5. What amount should Vane report as the cost of goods manufactured?
a. $200,000
b. $215,000
c. $280,000
d. $295,000   (5/94, FAR, #9, 4824)

6. What amount should Vane report as income after income taxes from continuing operations?
a. $126,000
b. $129,500
c. $140,000
d. $147,000   (5/94, FAR, #10, 4825)

7. On January 1, 1991, Brecon Co. installed cabinets to display its merchandise in customers' stores. Brecon expects to use these cabinets for five years. Brecon's 1991 multi-step income statement should include
a. One-fifth of the cabinet costs in cost of goods sold.
b. One-fifth of the cabinet costs in selling, general, and administrative expenses.
c. All of the cabinet costs in cost of goods sold.
d. All of the cabinet costs in selling, general, and administrative expenses.
          (5/92, Theory, #17, 9044)

8. The following information pertains to Deal Corp.'s 1992 cost of goods sold:

Inventory, 12/31/91	$ 90,000
1992 purchases	124,000
1992 write-off of obsolete inventory	34,000
Inventory, 12/31/92	30,000

The inventory written off became obsolete due to an unexpected and unusual technological advance by a competitor. In its 1992 income statement, what amount should Deal report as cost of goods sold?
a. $218,000
b. $184,000
c. $150,000
d. $124,000 (5/93, PI, #48, 4089)

9. In Baer Food Co.'s 1997 single-step income statement, the section titled "Revenues" consisted of the following:

Net sales revenue		$187,000
Results from discontinued operations:		
Loss from operations of segment		
(net of $1,200 tax effect)	$(2,400)	
Gain on disposal of segment		
(net of $7,200 tax effect)	14,400	12,000
Interest revenue		10,200
Gain on sale of equipment		4,700
Cumulative change in 1995 and 1996		
income due to change in depreciation		
method (net of $750 tax effect)		1,500
Total revenues		$215,400

In the revenues section of the 1997 income statement, Baer Food should have reported total revenues of
a. $216,300.
b. $215,400.
c. $203,700.
d. $201,900. (5/91, PI, #3, amended, 1115)

10. During 1997, Kerr Company sold a parcel of land used as a plant site. The amount Kerr received was $100,000 in excess of the land's carrying amount. Kerr's income tax rate for 1997 was 30%. In its 1997 income statement, Kerr should report a gain on sale of land of
a. $0.
b. $ 30,000.
c. $ 70,000.
d. $100,000. (11/88, PI, #42, amended, 9045)

11. A material loss should be presented separately as a component of income from continuing operations when it is
a. An extraordinary item.
b. A cumulative-effect-type change in accounting principle.

c. Unusual in nature and infrequent in occurrence.
d. Not unusual in nature but infrequent in occurrence. (5/95, FAR, #40, 5576)

12. The effect of a material transaction that is infrequent in occurrence but **not** unusual in nature should be presented separately as a component of income from continuing operations when the transaction results in a

	Gain	Loss
a.	Yes	Yes
b.	Yes	No
c.	No	No
d.	No	Yes

(5/94, FAR, #40, 4855)

13. Flint Corporation elected early adoption of SFAS No. 144, *Accounting for the Impairment or Disposal of Long-Lived Assets*. On February 2, Flint Corp.'s board of directors voted to discontinue operations of its frozen food division and to sell the division's assets on the open market as soon as possible. The division reported net operating losses of $20,000 in January and $30,000 in February. On February 26, sale of the division's assets resulted in a gain of $90,000. What amount of gain from disposal of a business segment should Flint recognize in its income statement for the three months ended March 31?
a. $0
b. $40,000
c. $60,000
d. $90,000 (R/00, FAR, #8, amended, 6903)

14. Ace, Inc., has adopted SFAS No. 144, *Accounting for the Impairment or Disposal of Long-Lived Assets*. A segment of Ace, Inc., was discontinued during 2003. In comparative financial statements for 2002, Ace's loss on disposal should
a. Exclude comparative financial statements for contingent product warranty obligation costs.
b. Include operating losses during fiscal year 2003.
c. Exclude additional pension costs associated with the decision to dispose.
d. Include operating losses of fiscal year 2002 up to the date a disposal plan was adopted. (5/93, Theory, #37, amended, 4225)

15. Wand, Inc., has adopted FASB Statement No. 144, *Accounting for the Impairment or Disposal of Long-Lived Assets.* On October 1, 2003, Wand Inc. committed itself to a formal plan to sell its Kam division's assets. Wand estimated that the loss from the disposal of assets in February 2004 would be $25,000. Wand also estimated that Kam would incur operating losses of $100,000 for the period of October 1, through December 31, 2003, and $50,000 for the period January 1, 2004, through

February 28, 2004. These estimates were materially correct. Disregarding income taxes, what should Wand report as loss from discontinued operations in its comparative 2003 and 2004 income statements?

	2003	2004
a.	$175,000	$0
b	$125,000	$ 50,000
c.	$100,000	$ 75,000
d.	$0	$175,000

(11/94, Theory, #52, amended, 5313)

16. Host, Co. has adopted FASB Statement No. 144, *Accounting for the Impairment or Disposal of Long-Lived Assets.* On October 1, 2004, Host Co. approved a plan to dispose of a segment of its business. Host expected that the sale would occur on April 1, 2005, at an estimated gain of $350,000. The segment had actual and estimated operating losses as follows:

1/1/04 to 9/30/04	($300,000)
10/1/04 to 12/31/04	(200,000)
1/1/05 to 3/31/05	(400,000)

In its December 31, 2004, income statement, what should Host report as a loss on disposal of the segment before income taxes?
a. $200,000
b. $250,000
c. $500,000
d. $600,000   (5/95, FAR, #44, amended, 5580)

ITEMS 17 AND 18 are based on the following:

On December 31, 1999, the Board of Directors of Maxx Manufacturing Inc. committed to a plan to discontinue the operations of its Alpha division in 2000. Maxx estimated that Alpha's 2000 operating loss would be $500,000 and that Alpha's facilities would be sold for $300,000 less than their carrying amounts. Alpha's 1999 operating loss was $1,400,000. Maxx's effective tax rate is 30%. Maxx has not yet adopted SFAS No. 144, *Accounting for the Impairment or Disposal of Long-Lived Assets.*

17. In its 1999 income statement, what amount should Maxx report as loss from discontinued operations?
a. $ 980,000
b. $1,330,000
c. $1,400,000
d. $1,900,000   (5/93, PI, #57, amended, 4096)

18. In its 1999 income statement, what amount should Maxx report as loss on disposal of discontinued operations?

a. $210,000
b. $300,000
c. $560,000
d. $800,000   (5/93, PI, #58, amended, 4097)

19. Doe Corp. has **not** yet adopted FASB Statement No. 144, *Accounting for the Impairment or Disposal of Long-Lived Assets.* During January 2000, Doe Corp. agreed to sell the assets and product line of its Hart division. The sale on January 15, 2001, resulted in a gain on disposal of $900,000. Hart's operating losses were $600,000 for 2000 and $50,000 for the period January 1 through January 15, 2001. Disregarding income taxes, what amount of net gain(loss) should be reported in Doe's comparative 2001 and 2000 income statements?

	2001	2000
a.	$0	$ 250,000
b.	$250,000	$0
c.	$850,000	$(600,000)
d.	$900,000	$(650,000)

(11/95, FAR, #39, amended, 6121)

20. Deer Corp. has **not** yet adopted SFAS No. 144, *Accounting for the Impairment or Disposal of Long-Lived Assets.* On April 30, Deer approved a plan to dispose of a segment of its business. For the period January 1 through April 30, the segment had revenues of $500,000 and expenses of $800,000. The assets of the segment were sold on October 15, at a loss for which no tax benefit is available. In its income statement for the calendar year how should Deer report the segment's operations from January 1 to April 30?
a. $500,000 and $800,000 included with revenues and expenses, respectively, as part of continuing operations.
b. $300,000 reported as part of the loss on disposal of a segment.
c. $300,000 reported as an extraordinary loss.
d. $300,000 reported as a loss from operations of a discontinued segment.

(11/95, FAR, #40, amended, 6122)

21. In September 1996, Koff Co.'s operating plant was destroyed by an earthquake. Earthquakes are rare in the area in which the plant was located. The portion of the resultant loss not covered by insurance was $700,000. Koff's income tax rate for 1996 is 40%. In its 1996 income statement, what amount should Koff report as extraordinary loss?
a. $0
b. $280,000
c. $420,000
d. $700,000   (5/97, FAR, #5, 6477)

22. Midway Co. had the following transactions during 1992:

- $1,200,000 pretax loss on foreign currency exchange due to a major unexpected devaluation by the foreign government.
- $500,000 pretax loss from discontinued operations of a division.
- $800,000 pretax loss on equipment damaged by a hurricane. This was the first hurricane ever to strike in Midway's area. Midway also received $1,000,000 from its insurance company to replace a building, with a carrying value of $300,000, that had been destroyed by the hurricane.

What amount should Midway report in its 1992 income statement as extraordinary loss before income taxes?
a. $ 100,000
b. $1,300,000
c. $1,800,000
d. $2,500,000   (5/93, PI, #59, 4098)

23. In 1992, hail damaged several of Toncan Co.'s vans. Hailstorms had frequently inflicted similar damage to Toncan's vans. Over the years, Toncan had saved money by not buying hail insurance and either paying for repairs, or selling damaged vans and then replacing them. In 1992, the damaged vans were sold for less than their carrying amount. How should the hail damage cost be reported in Toncan's 1992 financial statements?
a. The actual 1992 hail damage loss as an extraordinary loss, net of income taxes.
b. The actual 1992 hail damage loss in continuing operations, with no separate disclosure.
c. The expected average hail damage loss in continuing operations, with no separate disclosure.
d. The expected average hail damage loss in continuing operations, with separate disclosure.
(5/93, Theory, #35, 4223)

24. A transaction that is unusual in nature and infrequent in occurrence should be reported separately as a component of income
a. After cumulative effect of accounting changes and before discontinued operations of a segment of a business.
b. After cumulative effect of accounting changes and after discontinued operations of a segment of a business.

c. Before cumulative effect of accounting changes and before discontinued operations of a segment of a business.
d. Before cumulative effect of accounting changes and after discontinued operations of a segment of a business.   (11/94, Theory, #53, 5314)

25. Kent Co. incurred the following infrequent losses during 1991:

- A $300,000 loss was incurred on disposal of one of four dissimilar factories.
- A major currency devaluation caused a $120,000 exchange loss on an amount remitted by a foreign customer.
- Inventory valued at $190,000 was made worthless by a competitor's unexpected product innovation.

In its 1991 income statement, what amount should Kent report as losses that are not considered extraordinary?
a. $610,000
b. $490,000
c. $420,000
d. $310,000   (5/92, PI, #54, 2625)

26. In open market transactions, Gold Corp. simultaneously sold its long-term investment in Iron Corp. bonds and purchased its own outstanding bonds. The broker remitted the net cash from the two transactions. Gold's gain on the purchase of its own bonds exceeded its loss on the sale of the Iron bonds. Gold should report the
a. Net effect of the two transactions as an extraordinary gain.
b. Net effect of the two transactions in income before extraordinary items.
c. Effect of its own bond transaction gain in income before extraordinary items, and report the Iron bond transaction as an extraordinary loss.
d. Effect of its own bond transaction as an extraordinary gain, and report the Iron bond transaction loss in income before extraordinary items.
(11/95, FAR, #41, 6123)

27. During 1994 both Raim Co. and Cane Co. suffered losses due to the flooding of the Mississippi River. Raim is located two miles from the river and sustains flood losses every two to three years. Cane, which has been located fifty miles from the river for the past twenty years, has never before had flood losses. How should the flood losses be reported in each company's 1994 income statement?

	Raim	*Cane*
a.	As a component of income from continuing operations	As an extraordinary item
b.	As a component of income from continuing operations	As a component of income from continuing operations
c.	As an extraordinary item	As a component of income from continuing operation
d.	As an extraordinary item	As an extraordinary item

(11/95, FAR, #42, 6124)

28. At December 31, 1998, Off-Line Co. changed its method of accounting for demo costs from writing off the costs over two years to expensing the costs immediately. Off-Line made the change in recognition of an increasing number of demos placed with customers that did not result in sales. Off-Line had deferred demo costs of $500,000 at December 31, 1997, $300,000 of which were to be written off in 1998 and the remainder in 1999. Off-Line's income tax rate is 30%. In its 1998 income statement, what amount should Off-Line report as cumulative effect of change in accounting principle?
a. $140,000
b. $200,000
c. $350,000
d. $500,000   (R/99, FAR, #12, 6781)

29. On August 31, 1992, Harvey Co. decided to change from the FIFO periodic inventory system to the weighted average periodic inventory system. Harvey is on a calendar year basis. The cumulative effect of the change is determined
a. As of January 1, 1992.
b. As of August 31, 1992.
c. During the eight months ending August 31, 1992, by a weighted average of the purchases.
d. During 1992 by a weighted average of the purchases.   (5/93, Theory, #20, 4208)

30. The cumulative effect of a change in accounting principle should be recorded separately as a component of income after continuing operations, when the change is from the
a. Cash basis of accounting for vacation pay to the accrual basis.
b. Straight-line method of depreciation for previously recorded assets to the double declining balance method.

c. Presentation of statements of individual companies to their inclusion in consolidated statements.
d. Completed-contract method of accounting for long-term construction-type contracts to the percentage-of-completion method.

(11/93, Theory, #26, 4531)

31. On January 2, 1992, to better reflect the variable use of its only machine, Holly Inc. elected to change its method of depreciation from the straight-line method to the units of production method. The original cost of the machine on January 2, 1990, was $50,000, and its estimated life was 10 years. Holly estimates that the machine's total life is 50,000 machine hours. Machine hours usage was 8,500 during 1991 and 3,500 during 1990. Holly's income tax rate is 30%. Holly should report the accounting change in its 1992 financial statements as a (an)
a. Cumulative effect of a change in accounting principle of $2,000 in its income statement.
b. Adjustment to beginning retained earnings of $2,000.
c. Cumulative effect of a change in accounting principle of $1,400 in its income statement.
d. Adjustment to beginning retained earnings of $1,400.   (11/93, PI, #4, 4373)

ITEMS 32 AND 33 are based on the following:

On January 1, 1990, Warren Co. purchased a $600,000 machine, with a five-year useful life and no salvage value. The machine was depreciated by an accelerated method for book and tax purposes. The machine's carrying amount was $240,000 on December 31, 1991. On January 1, 1992, Warren changed retroactively to the straight-line method for financial statement purposes. Warren can justify the change. Warren's income tax rate is 30%.

32. In its 1992 income statement, what amount should Warren report as the cumulative effect of this change?
a. $120,000
b. $ 84,000
c. $ 36,000
d. $0   (5/93, PI, #53, 4094)

33. On January 1, 1992, what amount should Warren report as deferred income tax liability as a result of the change?
a. $120,000
b. $ 72,000
c. $ 36,000
d. $0   (5/93, PI, #54, 4095)

34. In 1990, Brighton Co. changed from the individual item approach to the aggregate approach in applying the lower of FIFO cost or market to inventories. The cumulative effect of this change should be reported in Brighton's financial statements as a
a. Prior period adjustment, with separate disclosure.
b. Component of income from continuing operations, with separate disclosure.
c. Component of income from continuing operations, without separate disclosure.
d. Component of income after continuing operations, with separate disclosure.

(11/91, Theory, #26, 1943)

ITEMS 35 AND 36 are based on the following:

During 1994, Orca Corp. decided to change from the FIFO method of inventory valuation to the weighted-average method. Inventory balances under each method were as follows:

	FIFO	Weighted-average
January 1, 1994	$71,000	$77,000
December 31, 1994	79,000	83,000

Orca's income tax rate is 30%.

35. In its 1994 financial statements, what amount should Orca report as the cumulative effect of this accounting change?
a. $2,800
b. $4,000
c. $4,200
d. $6,000

(5/95, FAR, #45, 5581)

36. Orca should report the cumulative effect of this accounting change as a(an)
a. Prior period adjustment.
b. Component of income from continuing operations.
c. Extraordinary item.
d. Component of income after extraordinary items.

5/95, FAR, #46, 5582)

37. Milton Co. began operations on January 1, 1989. On January 1, 1991, Milton changed its inventory method from LIFO to FIFO for both financial and income tax reporting. If FIFO had been used in prior years, Milton's inventories would have been higher by $60,000 and $40,000 at December 31, 1991 and 1990, respectively. Milton has a 30% income tax rate. What amount should Milton report as the cumulative effect of this accounting change in its income statement for the year ended December 31, 1991?
a. $0
b. $14,000
c. $28,000
d. $42,000

(11/92, PI, #60, 3291)

38. On January 1, 1997, Poe Construction Inc., changed to the percentage-of-completion method of income recognition for financial statement reporting. Poe can justify this change in accounting principle. As of December 31, 1996, Poe compiled data showing that income under the completed-contract method aggregated $700,000. If the percentage-of-completion method had been used, the accumulated income through December 31, 1996, would have been $880,000. Assuming an income tax rate of 40% for all years, the cumulative effect of this accounting change should be reported by Poe in the 1997
a. Retained earnings statement as a $180,000 credit adjustment to the beginning balance.
b. Income statement as a $180,000 credit.
c. Retained earnings statement as a $108,000 credit adjustment to the beginning balance.
d. Income statement as a $108,000 credit.

(5/86, PI, #58, amended, 1160)

39. When a full set of general-purpose financial statements are presented, comprehensive income and its components should
a. Appear as a part of discontinued operations, extraordinary items, and cumulative effect of a change in accounting principle.
b. Be reported net of related income tax effect, in total and individually.
c. Appear in a supplemental schedule in the notes to the financial statements.
d. Be displayed in a financial statement that has the same prominence as other financial statements.

(R/99, FAR, #1, 6770)

40. How should the effect of a change in accounting principle that is inseparable from the effect of a change in accounting estimate be reported?
a. As a component of income from continuing operations
b. By restating the financial statements of all prior periods presented
c. As a correction of an error
d. By footnote disclosure only

(5/97, FAR, #4, 6476)

41. For 1991, Pac Co. estimated its two-year equipment warranty costs based on $100 per unit sold in 1991. Experience during 1992 indicated that the estimate should have been based on $110 per unit. The effect of this $10 difference from the estimate is reported
a. In 1992 income from continuing operations.
b. As an accounting change, net of tax, below 1992 income from continuing operations.
c. As an accounting change requiring 1991 financial statements to be restated.
d. As a correction of an error requiring 1991 financial statements to be restated.

(11/93, Theory, #23, 4528)

42. When a company changes the expected service life of an asset because additional information has been obtained, which of the following should be reported?

	Pro forma effects of retroactive application	Cumulative effect of a change in accounting principle
a.	Yes	Yes
b.	No	Yes
c.	Yes	No
d.	No	No

(5/91, Theory, #27, 1901)

43. How should the effect of a change in accounting estimate be accounted for?
a. By restating amounts reported in financial statements of prior periods.
b. By reporting pro forma amounts for prior periods.
c. As a prior period adjustment to beginning retained earnings.
d. In the period of change and future periods if the change affects both. (11/94, Theory, #54, 5315)

44. On January 2, 1989, Union Co. purchased a machine for $264,000 and depreciated it by the straight-line method using an estimated useful life of eight years with no salvage value. On January 2, 1992, Union determined that the machine had a useful life of six years from the date of acquisition and will have a salvage value of $24,000. An accounting change was made in 1992 to reflect the additional data. The accumulated depreciation for this machine should have a balance at December 31, 1992, of
a. $176,000.
b. $160,000.
c. $154,000.
d. $146,000. (11/93, PI, #60, 4429)

45. Matt Co. included a foreign subsidiary in its 1991 consolidated financial statements. The subsidiary was acquired in 1985 and was excluded from previous consolidations. The change was caused by the elimination of foreign exchange controls. Including the subsidiary in the 1991 consolidated financial statements results in accounting change that should be reported
a. By footnote disclosure only.
b. Currently and prospectively.
c. Currently with footnote disclosure of pro forma effects of retroactive application.
d. By restating the financial statements of all prior periods presented. (5/92, Theory, #40, 2733)

46. Which of the following statements is correct regarding accounting changes that result in financial statements that are, in effect, the statements of a different reporting entity?
a. Cumulative-effect adjustments should be reported as separate items on the financial statements pertaining to the year of change.
b. No restatements or adjustments are required if the changes involve consolidated methods of accounting for subsidiaries.
c. No restatements or adjustments are required if the changes involve the cost or equity methods of accounting for investments.
d. The financial statements of all prior periods presented should be restated.

(5/94, FAR, #39, 4854)

47. The cumulative effect of an accounting change on the amount of retained earnings at the beginning of the period in which the change is made should generally be included in net income for the period of the change for a

	Change in accounting principle	Change in accounting entity
a.	Yes	Yes
b.	Yes	No
c.	No	Yes
d.	No	No

(5/84, Theory, #32, 1959)

48. The correction of an error in the financial statements of a prior period should be reported, net of applicable income taxes, in the current
a. Retained earnings statement after net income but before dividends.
b. Retained earnings statement as an adjustment of the opening balance.
c. Income statement after income from continuing operations and before extraordinary items.
d. Income statement after income from continuing operations and after extraordinary items.

(11/93, Theory, #22, 4527)

49. Conn Co. reported a retained earnings balance of $400,000 at December 31, 1991. In August 1992, Conn determined that insurance premiums of $60,000 for the three-year period beginning January 1, 1991, had been paid and fully expensed in 1991. Conn has a 30% income tax rate. What amount should Conn report as adjusted beginning retained earnings in its 1992 statement of retained earnings?
a. $420,000
b. $428,000
c. $440,000
d. $442,000 (11/93, PI, #10, 4379)

50. Which of the following errors could result in an overstatement of both current assets and stockholders' equity?
a. An understatement of accrued sales expenses.
b. Noncurrent note receivable principal is misclassified as a current asset.
c. Annual depreciation on manufacturing machinery is understated.
d. Holiday pay expense for administrative employees is misclassified as manufacturing overhead.
(5/93, Theory, #17, 4205)

51. In single period statements, which of the following should be reflected as an adjustment to the opening balance of retained earnings?
a. Effect of a failure to provide for uncollectible accounts in the previous period.
b. Effect of a decrease in the estimated useful life of depreciable equipment.
c. Cumulative effect of a change of income recognition from the installment sale method to recognition at point of sale.
d. Cumulative effect of a change from an accelerated method to straight-line depreciation.
(11/91, Theory, #25, 2533)

52. Pear Co.'s income statement for the year ended December 31, 1992, as prepared by Pear's controller, reported income before taxes of $125,000. The auditor questioned the following amounts that had been included in income before taxes:

Equity in earnings of Cinn Co.	$ 40,000
Dividends received from Cinn	8,000
Adjustments to profits of prior years for arithmetical errors in depreciation	(35,000)

Pear owns 40% of Cinn's common stock. Pear's December 31, 1992 income statement should report income before taxes of
a. $ 85,000.
b. $117,000.
c. $120,000.
d. $152,000.
(5/93, PI, #5, 4047)

53. Foy Corp. failed to accrue warranty costs of $50,000 in its December 31, 1992 financial statements. In addition, a change from straight-line to accelerated depreciation made at the beginning of 1993 resulted in a cumulative effect of $30,000 on Foy's retained earnings. Both the $50,000 and the $30,000 are net of related income taxes. What amount should Foy report as prior period adjustments in 1993?
a. $0
b. $30,000
c. $50,000
d. $80,000
(11/94, Theory, #55, 5316)

54. Lore Co. changed from the cash basis of accounting to the accrual basis of accounting during 1994. The cumulative effect of this change should be reported in Lore's 1994 financial statements as a
a. Prior period adjustment resulting from the correction of an error.
b. Prior period adjustment resulting from the change in accounting principle.
c. Component of income before extraordinary item.
d. Component of income after extraordinary item.
(11/95, FAR, #43, 6125)

55. While preparing its 1991 financial statements, Dek Corp. discovered computational errors in its 1990 and 1989 depreciation expense. These errors resulted in overstatement of each year's income by $25,000, net of income taxes. The following amounts were reported in the previously issued financial statements:

	1990	1989
Retained earnings, 1/1	$700,000	$500,000
Net income	150,000	200,000
Retained earnings, 12/31	$850,000	$700,000

Dek's 1991 net income is correctly reported at $180,000. Which of the following amounts should be reported as prior period adjustments and net income in Dek's 1991 and 1990 comparative financial statements?

	Year	Prior period adjustment	Net income
a.	1990	--	$150,000
	1991	($50,000)	180,000
b.	1990	($50,000)	$150,000
	1991	--	180,000
c.	1990	($25,000)	$125,000
	1991	--	180,000
d.	1990	--	$125,000
	1991	--	180,000

(5/92, PII, #2, 2634)

56. On December 31, 1991, Deal Inc. failed to accrue the December 1991 sales salaries that were payable on January 6, 1992. What is the effect of the failure to accrue sales salaries on working capital and cash flows from operating activities in Deal's 1991 financial statements?

	Working capital	Cash flows from operating activities
a.	Overstated	No effect
b.	Overstated	Overstated
c.	No effect	Overstated
d.	No effect	No effect

(11/92, Theory, #5, 3438)

57. Which of the following should be disclosed in a summary of significant accounting policies?

I. Management's intention to maintain or vary the dividend payout ratio
II. Criteria for determining which investments are treated as cash equivalents
III. Composition of the sales order backlog by segment

a. I only
b. I and III
c. II only
d. II and III   (11/92, Theory, #37, 3470)

58. The summary of significant accounting policies should disclose the
a. Pro forma effect of retroactive application of an accounting change.
b. Basis of profit recognition on long-term construction contracts.
c. Adequacy of pension plan assets in relation to vested benefits.
d. Future minimum lease payments in the aggregate and for each of the five succeeding fiscal years.   (5/91, Theory, #32, 1903)

59. Which of the following information should be included in Melay Inc.'s 1997 summary of significant accounting policies?
a. Property, plant, and equipment is recorded at cost with depreciation computed principally by the straight-line method.
b. During 1997, the Delay Segment was sold.
c. Operating segment 1997 sales are Alay $1M, Belay $2M, and Celay $3M.
d. Future common share dividends are expected to approximate 60% of earnings.
          (11/93, Theory, #19, amended, 4524)

60. Which of the following information should be disclosed in the summary of significant accounting policies?
a. Refinancing of debt subsequent to the balance sheet date.
b. Guarantees of indebtedness of others.
c. Criteria for determining which investments are treated as cash equivalents.
d. Adequacy of pension plan assets relative to vested benefits.   (11/94, Theory, #59, 5319)

61. Dex Co. has entered into a joint venture with an affiliate to secure access to additional inventory. Under the joint venture agreement, Dex will purchase the output of the venture at prices negotiated on an arms'-length basis. Which of the following is(are) required to be disclosed about the related party transaction?

I. The amount due to the affiliate at the balance sheet date.
II. The dollar amount of the purchases during the year.

a. I only
b. II only
c. Both I and II
d. Neither I nor II   (R/99, FAR, #20, 6789)

62. Lemu Co. and Young Co. are under the common management of Ego Co. Ego can significantly influence the operating results of both Lemu and Young. While Lemu had no transactions with Ego during the year, Young sold merchandise to Ego under the same terms given to unrelated parties. In the notes to their respective financial statements, should Lemu and Young disclose their relationship with Ego?

	Lemu	Young
a.	Yes	Yes
b.	Yes	No
c.	No	Yes
d.	No	No

          (5/98, FAR, #6, 6609)

63. Which of the following related party transactions by a company should be disclosed in the notes to the financial statements?

I. Payment of per diem expenses to members of the board of directors
II. Consulting fees paid to a marketing research firm, one of whose partners is also a director of the company

a. I only
b. II only
c. Both I and II
d. Neither I nor II   (11/96, FAR, #10, 6456)

64. Dean Co. acquired 100% of Morey Corp. prior to 1989. During 1989, the individual companies included in their financial statements the following:

	Dean	Morey
Officers' salaries	$ 75,000	$50,000
Officers' expenses	20,000	10,000
Loans to officers	125,000	50,000
Intercompany sales	150,000	--

What amount should be reported as related party disclosures in the notes to Dean's 1989 consolidated financial statements?
a. $150,000
b. $155,000
c. $175,000
d. $330,000   (11/90, PI, #53, 1129)

65. For which type of material related-party transactions does Statement of Financial Accounting Standard No. 57, *Related-Party Disclosures*, require disclosure?
a. Only those not reported in the body of the financial statements.
b. Only those that receive accounting recognition.
c. Those that contain possible illegal acts.
d. All those other than compensation arrangements, expense allowances, and other similar items in the ordinary course of business.

(11/95, FAR, #7, 6089)

66. ABC Co. was organized on July 15, 1995, and earned no significant revenues until the first quarter of 1998. During the period 1995-97, ABC acquired plant and equipment, raised capital, obtained financing, trained employees, and developed markets. In its financial statements as of December 31, 1997, ABC should defer all costs incurred during 1995-97,
a. Net of revenues earned, which are recoverable in future periods.
b. Net of revenues earned.
c. Which are recoverable in future periods.
d. Without regard to net revenues earned or recoverability in future periods.

(5/90, Theory, #39, amended, 1918)

67. Tanker Oil Co., a developmental stage enterprise, incurred the following costs during its first year of operations:

Legal fees for incorporation and other
  related matters $55,000
Underwriters' fees for initial stock
  offering   40,000
Exploration costs and purchases of
  mineral rights   60,000

Tanker had no revenue during its first year of operation. What amount may Tanker capitalize as organizational costs?
a. $155,000
b. $115,000
c. $ 95,000
d. $ 55,000

(5/93, PII, #14, 9049)

68. Financial reporting by a development stage enterprise differs from financial reporting for an established operating enterprise in regard to footnote disclosures
a. Only.
b. And expense recognition principles only.
c. And revenue recognition principles only.
d. And revenue and expense recognition principles.

(5/92, Theory, #49, 2742)

69. A development stage enterprise should use the same generally accepted accounting principles that apply to established operating enterprises for

	Revenue recognition	*Deferral of expenses*
a.	Yes	Yes
b.	Yes	No
c.	No	No
d.	No	Yes

(11/95, FAR, #4, 6086)

70. Lex Corp. was a development stage enterprise from October 10, 1995 (inception), to December 31, 1996. The year ended December 31, 1997, is the first year in which Lex is an established operating enterprise. The following are among the costs incurred by Lex:

	For the period 10/10/95 to 12/31/96	For the year ended 12/31/97
Leasehold improvements, equipment, and furniture	$1,000,000	$ 300,000
Security deposits	60,000	30,000
Research and development	750,000	900,000
Laboratory operations	175,000	550,000
General and administrative	225,000	685,000
Depreciation	25,000	115,000
	$2,235,000	$2,580,000

From its inception through the period ended December 31, 1997, what is the total amount of costs incurred by Lex that should be charged to operations?
a. $3,425,000
b. $2,250,000
c. $1,775,000
d. $1,350,000

(11/90, PI, #58, amended, 1131)

71. Lind Corp. was a development stage enterprise from its inception on October 10, 1995 to December 31, 1996. The following were among Lind's expenditures for this period:

Leasehold improvements, equipment,
  and furniture $1,200,000
Research and development   850,000
Laboratory operations   175,000
General and administrative   275,000

The year ended December 31, 1997 was the first year in which Lind was an established operating enterprise. For the period ended December 31, 1996, what total amount of expenditures should Lind have capitalized?
a. $2,500,000
b. $2,225,000
c. $2,050,000
d. $1,200,000

(5/90, PII, #52, amended, 1139)

72. Deficits accumulated during the development stage of a company should be
a. Reported as organization costs.
b. Reported as a part of stockholders' equity.
c. Capitalized and written off in the first year of principal operations.
d. Capitalized and amortized over a five-year period beginning when principal operations commence.
(11/90, Theory, #8, 1908)

73. Fenn Stores Inc. had sales of $1,000,000 during December, 1992. Experience has shown that merchandise equaling 7% of sales will be returned within 30 days and an additional 3% will be returned within 90 days. Returned merchandise is readily resalable. In addition, merchandise equaling 15% of sales will be exchanged for merchandise of equal or greater value. What amount should Fenn report for net sales in its income statement for the month of December 1992?
a. $900,000
b. $850,000
c. $780,000
d. $750,000
(5/93, PI, #37, 4078)

74. In 1990, Super Comics Corp. sold a comic strip to Fantasy Inc. and will receive royalties of 20% of future revenues associated with the comic strip. At December 31, 1991, Super reported royalties receivable of $75,000 from Fantasy. During 1992, Super received royalty payments of $200,000. Fantasy reported revenues of $1,500,000 in 1992 from the comic strip. In its 1992 income statement, what amount should Super report as royalty revenue?
a. $125,000
b. $175,000
c. $200,000
d $300,000
(5/93, PI, #44, 4085)

75. Tara Co. owns an office building and leases the offices under a variety of rental agreements involving rent paid in advance monthly or annually. Not all tenants make timely payments of their rent. Tara's balance sheets contained the following data:

	1989	1990
Rentals receivable	$ 9,600	$12,400
Unearned rentals	32,000	24,000

During 1990, Tara received $80,000 cash from tenants. What amount of rental revenue should Tara record for 1990?
a. $90,800
b. $85,200
c. $74,800
d. $69,200
(5/91, PI, #53, 1117)

76. Ichor Co. reported equipment with an original cost of $379,000 and $344,000, and accumulated depreciation of $153,000 and $128,000, respectively, in its comparative financial statements for the years ended December 31, 1995, and 1994. During 1995, Ichor purchased equipment costing $50,000, and sold equipment with a carrying value of $9,000. What amount should Ichor report as depreciation expense for 1995?
a. $19,000
b. $25,000
c. $31,000
d. $34,000
(11/97, FAR, #10, 6490)

77. Troop Co. frequently borrows from the bank to maintain sufficient operating cash. The following loans were at 12% interest rate, with interest payable at maturity. Troop repaid each loan on its scheduled maturity date.

Date of Loan	Amount	Maturity date	Term of loan
11/1/95	$10,000	10/31/96	1 year
2/1/96	30,000	7/31/96	6 months
5/1/96	16,000	1/31/97	9 months

Troop records interest expense when the loans are repaid. Accordingly, interest expense of $3,000 was recorded in 1996. If **no** correction is made, by what amount would 1996 interest expense be understated?
a. $1,080
b. $1,240
c. $1,280
d. $1,440
(5/97, FAR, #6, 6478)

78. Zach Corp. pays commissions to its sales staff at the rate of 3% of net sales. Sales staff are not paid salaries but are given monthly advances of $15,000. Advances are charged to commission expense, and reconciliations against commissions are prepared quarterly. Net sales for the year ended March 31, 1992, were $15,000,000. The unadjusted balance in the commissions expense account on March 31, 1992, was $400,000. March advances were paid on April 3, 1992. In its income statement for the year ended March 31, 1992, what amount should Zach report as commission expense?
a. $465,000
b. $450,000
c. $415,000
d. $400,000
(5/93, PI, #49, 4090)

79. House Publishers offered a contest in which the winner would receive $1,000,000, payable over 20 years. On December 31, 1993, House announced the winner of the contest and signed a note payable to the winner for $1,000,000, payable in $50,000 installments every January 2. Also on December 31, 1993, House purchased an annuity for $418,250 to provide the $950,000 prize monies remaining after the first $50,000 installment, which was paid on January 2, 1994. In its 1993 income statement, what should House report as contest prize expense?
a. $0
b. $ 418,250
c. $ 468,250
d. $1,000,000   (11/94, FAR, #23, 5287)

80. Able Co. provides an incentive compensation plan under which its president receives a bonus equal to 10% of the corporation's income before income tax but after deduction of the bonus. If the tax rate is 40% and net income after bonus and income tax was $360,000, what was the amount of the bonus?
a. $36,000
b. $60,000
c. $66,000
d. $90,000   (11/94, Theory, #48, 5309)

81. Clark Co.'s advertising expense account had a balance of $146,000 at December 31, 1993, before any necessary year-end adjustment relating to the following:

- Included in the $146,000 is the $15,000 cost of printing catalogs for a sales promotional campaign in January 1994.
- Radio advertisements broadcast during December 1993 were billed to Clark on January 2, 1994. Clark paid the $9,000 invoice on January 11, 1994.

What amount should Clark report as advertising expense in its income statement for the year ended December 31, 1993?
a. $122,000
b. $131,000
c. $140,000
d. $155,000   (11/94, Theory, #47, 5308)

82. Pak Co.'s professional fees expense account had a balance of $82,000 at December 31, 1991, before considering year-end adjustments relating to the following:

- Consultants were hired for a special project at a total fee not to exceed $65,000. Pak has recorded $55,000 of this fee based on billings for work performed in 1991.

- The attorney's letter requested by the auditors dated January 28, 1992, indicated that legal fees of $6,000 were billed on January 15, 1992, for work performed in November 1991, and unbilled fees for December 1991 were $7,000.

What amount should Pak report for professional fees expense for the year ended December 31, 1991?
a. $105,000
b. $ 95,000
c. $ 88,000
d. $ 82,000   (5/92, PI, #48, 2619)

83. Ward, a consultant, keeps her accounting records on a cash basis. During 1994, Ward collected $200,000 in fees from clients. At December 31, 1993, Ward had accounts receivable of $40,000. At December 31, 1994, Ward had accounts receivable of $60,000, and unearned fees of $5,000. On an accrual basis, what was Ward's service revenue for 1994?
a. $175,000
b. $180,000
c. $215,000
d. $225,000   (5/95, FAR, #25, 5561)

84. On April 1, 1993, Ivy began operating a service proprietorship with an initial cash investment of $1,000. The proprietorship provided $3,200 of services in April and received full payment in May. The proprietorship incurred expenses of $1,500 in April which were paid in June. During May, Ivy drew $500 against her capital account. What was the proprietorship's income for the two months ended May 31, 1993, under the following methods of accounting?

	Cash basis	Accrual basis
a.	$1,200	$1,200
b.	$1,700	$1,700
c.	$2,700	$1,200
d.	$3,200	$1,700 (11/93, PI, #43, 4412)

85. Compared to its 1992 cash basis net income, Potoma Co.'s 1992 accrual basis net income increased when it
a. Declared a cash dividend in 1991 that it paid in 1992.
b. Wrote off more accounts receivable balances than it reported as uncollectible accounts expense in 1992.
c. Had lower accrued expenses on December 31, 1992, than on January 1, 1992.
d. Sold used equipment for cash at a gain in 1992.
    (11/93, Theory, #40, 4545)

86. Compared to the accrual basis of accounting, the cash basis of accounting understates income by the net decrease during the accounting period of

	Accounts receivable	Accrued expenses
a.	Yes	Yes
b.	Yes	No
c.	No	No
d.	No	Yes

(5/94, FAR, #42, 4857)

87. Class Corp. maintains its accounting records on the cash basis but restates its financial statements to the accrual method of accounting. Class had $60,000 in cash-basis pretax income for 1992. The following information pertains to Class's operations for the years ended December 31, 1992 and 1991:

	1992	1991
Accounts receivable	$40,000	$20,000
Accounts payable	15,000	30,000

Under the accrual method, what amount of income before taxes should Class report in its December 31, 1992 income statement?
a. $25,000
b. $55,000
c. $65,000
d. $95,000   (5/93, PI, #40, 4081)

88. Conceptually, interim financial statements can be described as emphasizing
a. Timeliness over reliability.
b. Reliability over relevance.
c. Relevance over comparability.
d. Comparability over neutrality.
(11/95, FAR, #6, 6088)

89. APB Opinion No. 28, *Interim Financial Reporting*, concluded that interim financial reporting should be viewed primarily in which of the following ways?
a. As useful only if activity is spread evenly throughout the year.
b. As if the interim period were an annual accounting period.
c. As reporting for an integral part of an annual period.
d. As reporting under a comprehensive basis of accounting other than GAAP.
(5/95, FAR, #3, 5539)

90. For external reporting purposes, it is appropriate to use estimated gross profit rates to determine the cost of goods sold for

	Interim financial reporting	Year-end financial reporting
a.	Yes	Yes
b.	Yes	No
c.	No	Yes
d.	No	No

(11/83, Theory, #35, 1961)

91. An inventory loss from a permanent market decline of $360,000 occurred in May 1997. Cox Co. appropriately recorded this loss in May 1997 after its March 31, 1997 quarterly report was issued. What amount of inventory loss should be reported in Cox's quarterly income statement for the three months ended June 30, 1997?
a. $0
b. $ 90,000
c. $180,000
d. $360,000   (5/90, PII, #43, amended, 1134)

92. Wilson Corp. experienced a $50,000 decline in the market value of its inventory in the first quarter of its fiscal year. Wilson had expected this decline to reverse in the third quarter, and in fact, the third quarter recovery exceeded the previous decline by $10,000. Wilson's inventory did not experience any other declines in market value during the fiscal year. What amounts of loss and/or gain should Wilson report in its interim financial statements for the first and third quarters?

	First quarter	Third quarter
a.	$0	$0
b.	$0	$10,000 gain
c.	$50,000 loss	$50,000 gain
d.	$50,000 loss	$60,000 gain

(R/99, FAR, #18, 6787)

93. On March 15, 1992, Krol Co. paid property taxes of $90,000 on its office building for the calendar year 1992. On April 1, 1992, Krol paid $150,000 for unanticipated repairs to its office equipment. The repairs will benefit operations for the remainder of 1992. What is the total amount of these expenses that Krol should include in its quarterly income statement for the three months ended June 30, 1992?
a. $172,500
b. $ 97,500
c. $ 72,500
d. $ 37,500   (11/92, PII, #52, 3386)

94. For interim financial reporting, a company's income tax provision for the second quarter of 1992 should be determined using the
a. Effective tax rate expected to be applicable for the full year of 1992 as estimated at the end of the first quarter of 1992.
b. Effective tax rate expected to be applicable for the full year of 1992 as estimated at the end of the second quarter of 1992.
c. Effective tax rate expected to be applicable for the second quarter of 1992.
d. Statutory tax rate for 1992.
(11/93, Theory, #31, 4536)

95. During the first quarter of 1993, Tech Co. had income before taxes of $200,000, and its effective income tax rate was 15%. Tech's 1992 effective annual income tax rate was 30%, but Tech expects its 1993 effective annual income tax rate to be 25%. In its first quarter interim income statement, what amount of income tax expense should Tech report?
a. $0
b. $30,000
c. $50,000
d. $60,000   (5/93, PII, #17, 4125)

96. On June 30, 1991, Mill Corp. incurred a $100,000 net loss from disposal of a business segment. Also, on June 30, 1991, Mill paid $40,000 for property taxes assessed for the calendar year 1991. What amount of the foregoing items should be included in the determination of Mill's net income or loss for the six-month interim period ended June 30, 1991?
a. $140,000
b. $120,000
c. $ 90,000
d. $ 70,000   (5/92, PII, #12, 2644)

97. Kell Corp.'s $95,000 net income for the quarter ended September 30, 1990, included the following after-tax items:

- A $60,000 extraordinary gain, realized on April 30, 1990, was allocated equally to the second, third, and fourth quarters of 1990.

- A $16,000 cumulative-effect loss resulting from a change in inventory valuation method was recognized on August 2, 1990.

In addition, Kell paid $48,000 on February 1, 1990, for 1990 calendar-year property taxes. Of this amount, $12,000 was allocated to the third quarter of 1990.

For the quarter ended September 30, 1990, Kell should report net income of
a. $ 91,000.
b. $103,000.
c. $111,000.
d. $115,000.   (11/91, PII, #13, 2461)

98. Terra Co.'s total revenues from its three operating segments were as follows:

Segment	Sales to external customers	Intersegment sales	Total revenues
Lion	$ 70,000	$ 30,000	$100,000
Monk	22,000	4,000	26,000
Nevi	8,000	16,000	24,000
Combined	100,000	50,000	150,000
Elimination	—	(50,000)	(50,000)
Consolidated	$100,000	$ —	$100,000

Which operating segment(s) is(are) deemed to be reportable segments?
a. None.
b. Lion only.
c. Lion and Monk only.
d. Lion, Monk, and Nevi.   (11/95, FAR, #8, amended, 6090)

99. Correy Corp. and its divisions are engaged solely in manufacturing operations. The following data (consistent with prior years' data) pertain to Correy's operating segments for the year ended December 31, 1997:

Operating Segment	Total revenue	Operating profit	Identifiable assets at 12/31/97
A	$10,000,000	$1,750,000	$20,000,000
B	8,000,000	1,400,000	17,500,000
C	6,000,000	1,200,000	12,500,000
D	3,000,000	550,000	7,500,000
E	4,250,000	675,000	7,000,000
F	1,500,000	225,000	3,000,000
	$32,750,000	$5,800,000	$67,500,000

In its segment information for 1997, how many reportable segments does Correy have?
a. Three
b. Four
c. Five
d. Six   (5/90, PII, #56, amended, 1141)

100. Which of the following is **not** a comprehensive basis of accounting other than generally accepted accounting principles?
a. Cash receipts and disbursements basis of accounting
b. Basis of accounting used by an entity to file its income tax return
c. Basis of accounting used by an entity to comply with the financial reporting requirements of a government regulatory agency
d. Basis of accounting used by an entity to comply with the financial reporting requirements of a lending institution.   (11/98, FAR, #7, 6734)

101. On February 1, 1995, Tory began a service proprietorship with an initial cash investment of $2,000. The proprietorship provided $5,000 of services in February and received full payment in March. The proprietorship incurred expenses of $3,000 in February, which were paid in April. During March, Tory drew $1,000 against the capital account. In the proprietorship's financial statements for the two months ended March 31, 1995, prepared under the cash basis method of accounting, what amount should be reported as capital?

a. $1,000
b. $3,000
c. $6,000
d. $7,000   (11/95, FAR, #24, 6106)

102. The following information pertains to Eagle Co.'s 1993 sales:

Cash sales
| Gross | $ 80,000 |
| Returns and allowance | 4,000 |

Credit sales
| Gross | 120,000 |
| Discounts | 6,000 |

On January 1, 1993, customers owed Eagle $40,000. On December 31, 1993, customers owed Eagle $30,000. Eagle uses the direct write-off method for bad debts. No bad debts were recorded in 1993. Under the cash basis of accounting, what amount of net revenue should Eagle report for 1993?
a. $ 76,000
b. $170,000
c. $190,000
d. $200,000   (11/94, Theory, #58, 5318)

103. Income tax-basis financial statements differ from those prepared under GAAP in that income tax-basis financial statements
a. Do **not** include nontaxable revenues and non-deductible expenses in determining income.
b. Include detailed information about current and deferred income tax liabilities.
c. Contain **no** disclosures about capital and operating lease transactions.
d. Recognize certain revenues and expenses in different reporting periods.
       (R/99, FAR, #2, 6771)

104. In financial statements prepared on the income-tax basis, how should the nondeductible portion of expenses, such as meals and entertainment, be reported?
a. Included in the expense category in the determination of income.
b. Included in a separate category in the determination of income.
c. Excluded from the determination of income but included in the determination of retained earnings.
d. Excluded from the financial statements.
       (11/95, FAR, #56, 6138)

OTHER OBJECTIVE FORMAT QUESTIONS

PROBLEM 11-2 (15 to 20 minutes)

Problem Number 2 consists of 4 items. Select the best answer for each item.

On January 2, 1996, Falk Co. hired a new controller. During the year, the controller, working closely with Falk's president and outside accountants, made changes in existing accounting policies, instituted new accounting policies, and corrected several errors dating from prior to 1996.

Falk's financial statements for the year ended December 31, 1996, will not be presented in comparative form with its 1995 financial statements.

REQUIRED:

ITEMS 1 THROUGH 4 represent Falk's transactions.

List A represents possible classifications of these transactions as a change in accounting principle, a change in accounting estimate, correction of an error in previously presented financial statements, or neither an accounting change nor an error correction.

List B represents the general accounting treatment required for these transactions. These treatments are:

- Cumulative effect approach—Include the cumulative effect of the adjustment resulting from the accounting change or error correction in the 1996 financial statements.
- Retroactive restatement approach—Adjust 1996 beginning retained earnings if the error or change affects a period prior to 1996.
- Prospective approach—Report 1996 and future financial statements on the new basis, but do not adjust beginning retained earnings or include the cumulative effect of the change in the 1996 income statements.

List A (Select one)
Type of Change
A. Change in accounting principle.
B. Change in accounting estimate.
C. Correction of an error in previously presented financial statements.
D. Neither an accounting change nor an error correction.

List B (Select one)
General Accounting Treatment
X.   Cumulative effect approach.
Y.   Retroactive restatement approach.
Z.   Prospective approach.

For **ITEMS 1 AND 2**, select a classification for each transaction from List A and the general accounting treatment required to report the change from List B.

1.   Falk manufactures customized equipment to customer specifications on a contract basis. Falk changed its method of accounting for these long-term contracts from the completed-contract method to the percentage-of-completion method because Falk is now able to make reasonable estimates of future construction costs.

2.   Based on improved collection procedures, Falk changed the percentage of credit sales used to determine the allowance for uncollectible accounts from 2% to 1%.

For **ITEMS 3 AND 4**, in addition to selecting a classification for each transaction from List A **and** the general accounting treatment required to report the change from List B, a third response is required. For these items, determine the amount, if any, of the cumulative change or prior period adjustment, ignoring income tax effects.

3.   Effective January 1, 1996, Falk changed from average cost to FIFO to account for its inventory. Cost of goods sold under each method was as follows:

Year	Average cost	FIFO
Years prior to 1995	$71,000	$77,000
1995	79,000	82,000

4.   In January 1995, Falk purchased a machine with a five-year life and no salvage value for $40,000. The machine was depreciated using the straight-line method. On December 30, 1996, Falk discovered that depreciation on the machine had been calculated using a 25% rate.

(11/97, FAR, #2, 6492-6501)

PROBLEM 11-3 (15 to 25 minutes)

On January 2, 1993, Quo Inc., hired Reed to be its controller. During the year, Reed, working closely with Quo's president and outside accountants, made changes in accounting policies, corrected several errors dating from 1992 and before, and instituted new accounting policies.

Quo's 1993 financial statements will be presented in comparative form with its 1992 financial statements.

REQUIRED:

ITEMS 1 THROUGH 10 represent Quo's transactions. List A represents possible classifications of these transactions as: a change in accounting principle, a change in accounting estimate, a correction of an error in previously presented financial statements, or neither an accounting change nor an accounting error.

List B represents the general accounting treatment required for these transactions. These treatments are:

• Cumulative effect approach—Include the cumulative effect of the adjustment resulting from the accounting change or error correction in the 1993 financial statements, and do **not** restate the 1992 financial statements.

• Retroactive restatement approach—Restate the 1992 financial statements and adjust 1992 beginning retained earnings if the error or change affects a period prior to 1992.

• Prospective approach—Report 1993 and future financial statements on the new basis, but do **not** restate 1992 financial statements.

For each item, select one from List A and one from List B.

List A (Select one)
A.   Change in accounting principle.
B.   Change in accounting estimate.
C.   Correction of an error in previously presented financial statements.
D.   Neither an accounting change nor an accounting error.

List B (Select one)
X.   Cumulative effect approach.
Y.   Retroactive restatement approach.
Z.   Prospective approach.

ITEMS TO BE ANSWERED:

1.   Quo manufactures heavy equipment to customer specifications on a contract basis. On the basis that it is preferable, accounting for these long-term contracts was switched from the completed-contract method to the percentage-of-completion method.

2.   As a result of a production breakthrough, Quo determined that manufacturing equipment previously depreciated over 15 years should be depreciated over 20 years.

3.   The equipment that Quo manufactures is sold with a five-year warranty. Because of a production

breakthrough, Quo reduced its computation of warranty costs from 3% of sales to 1% of sales.

4. Quo changed from LIFO to FIFO to account for its finished goods inventory.

5. Quo changed from FIFO to average cost to account for its raw materials and work in process inventories.

6. Quo sells extended service contracts on its products. Because related services are performed over several years, in 1993 Quo changed from the cash method to the accrual method of recognizing income from these service contracts.

7. During 1993, Quo determined that an insurance premium paid and entirely expensed in 1992 was for the period January 1, 1992, through January 1, 1994.

8. Quo changed its method of depreciating office equipment from an accelerated method to the straight-line method to more closely reflect costs in later years.

9. Quo instituted a pension plan for all employees in 1993 and adopted Statement of Financial Accounting Standards No. 87, Employers' Accounting for Pensions. Quo had not previously had a pension plan.

10. During 1993, Quo increased its investment in Worth Inc. from a 10% interest, purchased in 1992, to 30%, and acquired a seat on Worth's board of directors. As a result of its increased investment, Quo changed its method of accounting for investment in subsidiary from the cost method to the equity method. (5/94, FAR, #61-70 4938-4947)

PROBLEM 11-4 (15 to 25 minutes)

Hake Co. is in the process of preparing its financial statements for the year ended December 31, 1994.

REQUIRED:

ITEMS 1 THROUGH 6 represent various transactions that occurred during 1994. The following **two** responses are required for each item:

- Compute the amount of gain, loss, or adjustment to be reported in Hake's 1994 financial statements. Disregard income taxes.
- Select from the list below the financial statement category in which the gain, loss, or adjustment should be presented. A category may be used once, more than once, or not at all.

Financial Statement Categories

A. Income from continuing operations
B. Extraordinary item
C. Cumulative effect of change in accounting principle
D. Prior period adjustment to beginning retained earnings
E. Other comprehensive income

ITEMS TO BE ANSWERED:

1. On June 30, 1994, after paying the semiannual interest due and recording amortization of bond discount, Hake redeemed its 15-year, 8%, $1,000,000 par bonds at 102. The bonds, which had a carrying amount of $940,000 on January 1, 1994, had originally been issued to yield 10%. Hake uses the effective interest method of amortization, and had paid interest and recorded amortization on June 30. Compute the amount of gain or loss on redemption of the bonds and select the proper financial statement category.

2. As of January 1, 1994, Hake decided to change the method of computing depreciation on its sole piece of equipment from the sum-of-the-years'-digits method to the straight-line method. The equipment, acquired in January 1991 for $520,000, had an estimated life of five years and a salvage value of $20,000. Compute the amount of the accounting change and select the proper financial statement category.

3. In October 1994, Hake paid $375,000 to a former employee to settle a lawsuit out of court. The lawsuit had been filed in 1993, and at December 31, 1993, Hake had recorded a liability from lawsuit based on legal counsel's estimate that the loss from the lawsuit would be between $250,000 and $750,000. Compute the amount of gain or loss from settlement of the lawsuit and select the proper financial statement category.

4. In November 1994, Hake purchased two marketable equity securities, I and II, which it bought and held principally to sell in the near term, and in fact sold on February 28, 1995. Relevant data is as follows:

		Fair Value	
	Cost	12/31/94	2/28/95
I.	$125,000	$145,000	$155,000
II.	235,000	205,000	230,000

Compute the amount of holding gain or loss at December 31, 1994, and select the proper financial statement category.

5.   During 1994, Hake received $1,000,000 from its insurance company to cover losses suffered during a hurricane. This was the first hurricane ever to strike in Hake's area. The hurricane destroyed a warehouse with a carrying amount of $470,000, containing equipment with a carrying amount of $250,000 and inventory with a carrying amount of $535,000 and a fair value of $600,000. Compute the amount of gain or loss from the hurricane and select the proper financial statement category.

6.   At December 31, 1994, Hake prepared the following worksheet summarizing the translation of its wholly owned foreign subsidiary's financial statements into dollars. Hake had purchased the foreign subsidiary for $324,000 on January 2, 1994. On that date, the carrying amounts of the subsidiary's assets and liabilities equaled their fair values.

	Foreign currency amounts	Applicable exchange rates	Dollars
Net assets at January 2, 1994 (date of purchase)	720,000	$.45	$324,000
Net income, 1994	250,000	.42	105,000
Net assets at December 31, 1994	970,000		$429,000
Net assets at December 31, 1994	970,000	.40	$388,000

Compute the amount of the foreign currency translation adjustment and select the proper financial statement category.

(5/95, FAR, #3, amended 5607-5618)

PROBLEM/ESSAY QUESTIONS

Essay 11-5 (30 to 40 minutes)

The following pro forma statement of income and changes in equity accounts was prepared by the newly-hired staff accountant of Topaz, Inc., a non-public company, for the year ended December 31, 1995.

Topaz, Inc.
STATEMENT OF INCOME AND CHANGES IN RETAINED EARNINGS
December 31, 1995

Revenues and gains:
Gross sales
Purchase discounts
Recovery of accounts receivable written off in prior years
Interest revenue
Gain on early extinguishment of debt
    Total revenues and gains

Expenses and losses:
Cost of goods sold
Sales returns and allowances
Selling expenses
General and administrative expenses
Cash dividends declared
    Total expenses and losses
Income before discontinued operations and extraordinary item

Discontinued operations:
Loss on disposal of discontinued styles, net of tax effect

Extraordinary item:
Correction of errors in prior years' statements, net of tax effect
Retained earnings at beginning of year
Income taxes
Net income
Retained earnings at end of year

Additional information:
    Topaz uses the allowance method to account for uncollectible accounts.
    The loss on disposal of discontinued styles resulted from the sale of outdated styles within a product line.
    Topaz had no temporary tax differences at the beginning or the end of the year.

Required:

Identify the weaknesses in classification and presentation in the above Statement of Income and Changes in Retained Earnings. Explain the proper classification and presentation. **Do not prepare a corrected statement.**   (11/96, FAR, #2, 6472)

Essay 11-6 (15 to 25 minutes)

Hillside Company has not yet adopted SFAS No. 144, *Accounting for Impairment or Disposal of Long-Lived Assets*. Hillside Company had a loss during the year ended December 31, 2001, that is properly reported as an extraordinary item.

On July 1, 2001, Hillside committed itself to a formal plan for sale of a business segment. A loss is expected from the proposed sale. Segment operating losses were incurred continuously throughout 2001, and were expected to continue until final disposition in 2002. Costs were incurred in 2001 to relocate segment employees.

Required:

a. How should Hillside report the extraordinary item in its income statement? Why?

b. How should Hillside report the effect of the discontinued operations in its 2001 income statement?

c. How should Hillside report the costs that were incurred to relocate employees of the discontinued segment? Why?

Do not discuss earnings per share requirements.
(11/89, Theory, #5, amended, 3615)

ESSAY 11-7 (10 to 15 minutes)

Barnet Co. is determining reporting of segments for operations. The company has separate financial information for several components of its operations and uses the information in various forms for decision making purposes. The components of operations are at sales and profitability levels ranging from 1%-35%.

REQUIRED:

a. What is the purpose of segment disclosures?

b. How should Barnet decide what segments to report? (Editorial Board)

PROBLEM 11-8 (30 to 40 minutes)

The following information pertains to Baron Flowers, a calendar-year sole proprietorship, which maintained its books on the cash basis during the year.

Baron Flowers
TRIAL BALANCE
December 31, 1994

	Dr.	Cr.
Cash	$ 25,600	
Accounts receivable, 12/31/93	16,200	
Inventory, 12/31/93	62,000	
Furniture & fixtures	118,200	
Land improvements	45,000	
Accumulated depr., 12/31/93		$ 32,400
Accounts payable, 12/31/93		17,000
Baron, Drawings		
Baron, Capital, 12/31/93		124,600
Sales		653,000
Purchases	305,100	
Salaries	174,000	
Payroll taxes	12,400	
Insurance	8,700	
Rent	34,200	
Utilities	12,600	
Living expenses	13,000	
	$827,000	$827,000

Baron has developed plans to expand into the wholesale flower market and is in the process of negotiating a bank loan to finance the expansion.

The bank is requesting 1994 financial statements prepared on the accrual basis of accounting from Baron. During the course of a review engagement, Muir, Baron's accountant, obtained the following additional information.

1. Amounts due from customers totaled $32,000 at December 31, 1994.

2. An analysis of the above receivables revealed that an allowance for uncollectible accounts of $3,800 should be provided.

3. Unpaid invoices for flower purchases totaled $30,500 and $17,000, at December 31, 1994, and December 31, 1993, respectively.

4. The inventory totaled $72,800 based on a physical count of the goods at December 31, 1994. The inventory was priced at cost, which approximates market value.

5. On May 1, 1994, Baron paid $8,700 to renew its comprehensive insurance coverage for one year. The premium on the previous policy, which expires on April 30, 1994, was $7,800.

6. On January 2, 1994, Baron entered into a twenty-five-year operating lease for the vacant lot adjacent to Baron's retail store for use as a parking lot. As agreed in the lease, Baron paved and fenced in the lot at a cost of $45,000. The improvements were completed on April 1, 1994, and have an estimated useful life of fifteen years. No provision for depreciation or amortization has been recorded. Depreciation on furniture and fixtures was $12,000 for 1994.

7. Accrued expenses at December 31, 1993 and 1994, were as follows:

	1993	1994
Utilities	$ 900	$1,500
Payroll taxes	1,100	1,600
	$2,000	$3,100

8. Baron is being sued for $400,000. The coverage under the comprehensive insurance policy is limited to $250,000. Baron's attorney believes that an unfavorable outcome is probable and that a reasonable estimate of the settlement is $300,000.

9. The salaries account includes $4,000 per month paid to the proprietor. Baron also receives $250 per week for living expenses.

a. Using the worksheet [below] prepare the adjustments necessary to convert the trial balance of Baron Flowers to the accrual basis of accounting for the year ended December 31, 1994. Formal journal entries are not required to support your adjustments. However, use the numbers given with the additional information to cross-reference the postings in the adjustment columns on the worksheet.

b. Write a brief memo to Baron explaining why the bank would require financial statements prepared on the accrual basis instead of the cash basis.

(11/95, FAR, #4)

Baron Flowers
WORKSHEET TO CONVERT TRIAL BALANCE TO ACCRUAL BASIS
December 31, 1994

Account title	Cash basis Dr.	Cash basis Cr.	Adjustments Dr.	Adjustments Cr.	Accrual Basis* Dr.*	Accrual Basis* Cr.*
Cash	25,600					
Accounts rec'ble, 12/31/93	16,200					
Inventory, 12/31/93	62,000					
Furniture & fixtures	118,200					
Land improvements	45,000					
Accumulated depreciation & amortization, 12/31/93		32,400				
Accounts payable, 12/31/93		17,000				
Baron, Drawings						
Baron, Capital, 12/31/93		124,600				
Sales		653,000				
Purchases	305,100					
Salaries	174,000					
Payroll taxes	12,400					
Insurance	8,700					
Rent	34,200					
Utilities	12,600					
Living expenses	13,000					
	827,000	827,000				

* Completion of these columns is not required.

ESSAY 11-9 (15 to 25 minutes)

On January 1, 1991, Windsor Corp. made the following changes in its accounting policies:

- Changed from the LIFO inventory method to the FIFO inventory method.
- Adopted the straight-line depreciation method for all future machinery acquisitions, but continued to use sum-of-the-years'-digits depreciation method for all machinery purchased before 1991.
- Changed from the cash to the accrual basis of accounting for accumulated vacation pay.

Windsor prepares two-year comparative financial statements.

REQUIRED:

a. What type of accounting change is the change from the LIFO to the FIFO inventory costing method? How should Windsor report this change in its 1991 comparative financial statements?

b. What type of accounting change is Windsor's change from the sum-of-the-years'-digits to the straight-line depreciation method for all machinery purchased after 1990? How should Windsor report this change?

c. What type of change occurs when recognition of vacation pay expense is changed from the cash basis to the accrual basis? How should Windsor report this change? (11/92, Theory, #4 6194)

PROBLEM 11-10 (30 to 40 minutes)

The following condensed trial balance of Probe Co., a publicly held company, has been adjusted except for income tax expense.

Probe Co.
CONDENSED TRIAL BALANCE

	12/31/93 Balances Dr. (Cr.)	12/31/92 Balances Dr. (Cr.)	Net change Dr. (Cr.)
Cash	$ 473,000	$ 817,000	$(344,000)
Accounts receivable, net	670,000	610,000	60,000
Property, plant, and equipment	1,070,000	995,000	75,000
Accumulated depreciation	(345,000)	(280,000)	(65,000)
Dividends payable	(25,000)	(10,000)	(15,000)
Income taxes payable	35,000	(150,000)	185,000
Deferred income tax liability	(42,000)	(42,000)	---
Bonds Payable	(500,000)	(1,000,000)	500,000
Unamortized premium on bonds	(71,000)	(150,000)	79,000
Common stock	(350,000)	(150,000)	(200,000)
Additional paid-in capital	(430,000)	(375,000)	(55,000)
Retained earnings	(185,000)	(265,000)	80,000
Sales	(2,420,000)		
Cost of sales	1,863,000		
Selling and administrative expenses	220,000		
Interest income	(14,000)		
Interest expense	46,000		
Depreciation	88,000		
Loss on sale of equipment	7,000		
Gain on extinguishment of bonds	(90,000)		
	$ 0	$ 0	$ 300,000

Additional information:
- During 1993 equipment with an original cost of $50,000 was sold for cash, and equipment costing $125,000 was purchased.
- On January 1, 1993, bonds with a par value of $500,000 and related premium of $75,000 were redeemed. The $1,000 face value, 10% par bonds had been issued on January 1, 1984, to yield 8%. Interest is payable annually every December 31 through 2003.
- Probe's tax payments during 1993 were debited to Income Taxes Payable. For the year ended December 31, 1992, Probe recorded a deferred income tax liability of $42,000 based on temporary differences of $120,000 and an enacted tax rate of 35%. Probe's 1993 financial statement income before income taxes was greater than its 1993 taxable income, due entirely to temporary differences, by $60,000. Probe's cumulative net taxable temporary differences at December 31, 1993, were $180,000. Probe's enacted tax rate for the current and future years is 30%.
- 60,000 shares of common stock, $2.50 par, were outstanding on December 31, 1992. Probe issued an additional 80,000 shares on April 1, 1993.
- There were no changes to retained earnings other than dividends declared.

REQUIRED:

Prepare Probe Co.'s multiple-step income statement for the year ended December 31, 1993, with earnings per share information and supporting computations for current and deferred income tax expense.

(11/94, amended, FAR, #4)

SOLUTION 11-1 MULTIPLE CHOICE ANSWERS

INCOME FROM CONTINUING OPERATIONS

1. (b) Revenues are only considered to be earned when the entity has substantially accomplished what it must do to be entitled to the benefits represented by the revenues (SFAC 5, par. 83). Although Acme has sold 100,000 gallons of heating oil to Karn during 1991, Acme has only delivered 50,000 of these gallons to Karn during 1991. Therefore, Acme should only recognize revenue of $150,000 (i.e., 50,000 gallons x $3) during 1991 from this sale.

2. (a) The freight-in cost is an inventoriable cost. The freight-out cost and the sales representatives' salaries should both be reported as selling expenses in 1992. The amount of the costs that should be reported as general and administrative expenses for 1992 is computed as follows:

Accounting and legal fees	$ 25,000
Officers' salaries	150,000
Insurance	85,000
General and administrative expenses, 1992	$260,000

3. (d) Neither expense should be included in general and administrative expenses. The advertising expense is a selling expense because it results from the company's efforts to make sales. The interest expense is a nonoperating expense because it results from secondary or auxiliary activities of the company. General and administrative expenses are expenses of general administration.

4. (b) Freight-out is not included as part of cost of goods sold. Cost of goods sold for the year is calculated as follows:

Beginning inventory		$ 30,840
Purchases	$ 102,800	
Purchase discount	(10,280)	
Freight-in	15,420	107,940
Available		138,780
Ending Inventory		(20,560)
Cost of Goods Sold		$118,220

5. (a) Freight out is classified as an operating expense, not as part of cost of goods sold.

Inventory, December 31, 1993	$ 360,000
Cost of sales	240,000
	600,000
Less: Inventory, January 1, 1993	(400,000)
Cost of goods manufactured	$ 200,000

6. (c)

Sales		$ 575,000
Interest revenue		25,000
Cost of sales	$240,000	
Administrative expenses	70,000	
Sales commissions	50,000	
Freight out	15,000	
Uncollectible accounts expense	15,000	
Loss on sale of equipment	10,000	(400,000)
Income from continuing operations before taxes		200,000
Income taxes		(60,000)
Income from continuing op.		$ 140,000

7. (b) The cabinets are expected to provide benefits over five years; hence, they meet the definition of an asset (probable future economic benefits). The cabinets are used in the selling function; therefore, the expired portion of the cabinet costs should be classified as a selling expense and not as part of cost of goods sold.

8. (c) Because the amount of the write-off of obsolete inventory is material, it should be reported separately from cost of goods sold in income from continuing operations. The amount that Deal should report as cost of goods sold is determined as follows:

Inventory, 12/31/91		$ 90,000
Add: 1992 purchases		124,000
Goods available for sale		$214,000
Less: Inventory, 12/31/92	$ 30,000	
Write-off of obsolete inventory	34,000	(64,000)
Cost of goods sold, 1992		$150,000

9. (d) The results from discontinued operations and the cumulative effect of the change in depreciation method cannot be included in the revenues section of the single-step income statement since these amounts must be reported in the statement *below* income from continuing operations.

Net sales revenue	$187,000
Interest revenue	10,200
Gain on sale of equipment	4,700
Total revenues reported in single-step income statement	$201,900

10. **(d)** APB 30 provides that gains and losses from sale or abandonment of property, plant, or equipment used in the business should **not** be reported as extraordinary items. APB 30 goes on to provide that a material event or transaction that is unusual in nature or occurs infrequently but not both and, therefore, does not meet the criteria for classification as an extraordinary item, should be reported as a separate component of income from continuing operations. Such an item should **not** be reported on the face of the income statement net of income taxes or in any other manner that may imply that it is extraordinary. Therefore, the gain on the sale of the parcel of land used as a plant site is reported at $100,000; it is **not** reported net of its related income tax effect.

11. **(d)** A transaction that is unusual in nature or infrequent in occurrence, but not both, is reported as a component of income from continuing operations (APB 30). A transaction must be *both* unusual in nature and infrequent in occurrence to be classified as an extraordinary item.

12. **(a)** When a transaction is either infrequent or unusual, but not both, it is presented separately as a component of income from continuing operations. This is true regardless of whether the transaction results in a gain or loss.

DISCONTINUED OPERATIONS (SFAS 144)

13. **(b)** SFAS 144, para. 43 states, "In the period in which a component of an entity either has been disposed of or is classified as held for sale, the income statement of a business enterprise for current and prior periods shall report the results of operations of the component...in discontinued operations...in the periods(s) in which they occur." Flint Corp.'s gain from disposal of its frozen food division is computed as follows:

Gain from sale of division assets on Feb 26	$ 90,000
Less: Operating loss during the fiscal year	(50,000)
Gain on disposal of segment, before income taxes	$ 40,000

The operating loss of $20,000 in January would not have been included in the calculation under APB Opinion No. 30, because it was before the measurement date. APB 30 was superceded by SFAS 144.

14. **(d)** SFAS 144, para. 43 states, "In the period in which a component of an entity either has been disposed of or is classified as held for sale, the income statement of a business enterprise for current and prior periods shall report the results of operations of the component...in discontinued operations...in the periods(s) in which they occur." SFAS 144, para. 44 lists amounts reported in discontinued operations, including, "the resolution of contingencies that arise from...product warranty obligations...the settlement of employee benefit plan obligations (pension...and other post-employment benefits) provided that the settlement is directly related to the disposal transaction."

15. **(c)** SFAS 144, para. 43 states, "The income statement of a business enterprise for current and prior periods shall report the results of operations of the component...in discontinued operations...in the period(s) in which they occur."

16. **(c)** See the explanation to #15.

DISCONTINUED OPERATIONS (APB 30)

17. **(a)** December 31, 1999, is the measurement date—the date the plan to dispose of the segment was approved. The $980,000 [i.e., $1,400,000 x (1 – 30%)] net-of-tax effect of the 1999 operating loss is the first component under discontinued operations. APB 30, par. 8, requires an income statement presentation for reporting the results of discontinued operations as follows:

Income from continuing operations (after income taxes)		$XXX
Discontinued operations:		
Income (loss) from operations of discontinued segment (net of income taxes)		$XXX
Gain (loss) on disposal of segment, including provisions for operating losses during phase-out period (net of income taxes)	XXX	XXX
Net income		$XXX

18. **(c)** The loss on the disposal of the discontinued segment is computed as follows:

Estimated loss on sale of segment's facilities	$ 500,000
Operating loss from measurement date to expected date of disposal	300,000
Loss on disposal of segment, before income taxes	800,000
Applicable income tax benefit ($800,000 x 30%)	(240,000)
Loss on disposal, net of applicable income taxes	$ 560,000

19. **(b)** When the measurement date and the disposal date occur in different accounting periods, the gain or loss on the disposal of the discontinued segment is calculated by combining realized gain or loss items between the measurement date and the end of the fiscal period and estimated gain or loss items between the end of the fiscal period and the

disposal date. Estimated gains can only be included to the extent of realized losses. Thus, the 2000 operating loss of $600,000 is reduced to zero in the 2000 income statement by a portion of the gain on disposal. For 2001, the gain on disposal of $900,000 is reduced by the $600,000 loss in 2000 and further reduced by the January 1 through 15, 2001, loss of $50,000, for a reported gain of $250,000.

20. **(d)** The operating results of a discontinued segment are reported separately from results of continuing operations. Results of the discontinued operations prior to the measurement date (April 30) are reported under the caption "Loss from Operations of Discontinued Segment." Results of the discontinued operations after the measurement date are included with the loss on sale of the segment assets under the caption "Loss on Disposal of Discontinued Segment."

EXTRAORDINARY ITEMS

21. **(c)** The loss due to the earthquake qualifies as an extraordinary item because it is **both** unusual in nature and infrequent in occurrence. An extraordinary item should be presented separately on the income statement, net of related income tax.

Loss not covered by insurance	$ 700,000
Less: Tax benefit ($700,000 X .40)	(280,000)
Extraordinary item, net of tax	$ 420,000

22. **(a)** APB 30 provides that (1) gains or losses on disposal of a segment of a business and (2) gains or losses from exchange or translation of foreign currencies, including those relating to major devaluations and revaluations should not be reported as extraordinary items. To be classified as an extraordinary item, APB 30 requires that the item must be both unusual in nature and infrequent in occurrence, taking into account the environment in which the entity operates. The loss due to hurricane damage should be reported as an extraordinary item since the hurricane was the first ever to strike in Midway's area. Since the loss realized on the damage to the equipment and the gain realized on the destruction of the building are a direct result of the hurricane, they are considered to be extraordinary. Therefore, the amount Maxx should report as the extraordinary loss before income taxes in 1992 is computed as follows:

Pretax loss on equipment damaged by hurricane		$ 800,000
Less: Pretax gain on building destroyed by hurricane:		
Proceeds from insurance co.	$ 1,000,000	
Carrying amount of building	(300,000)	(700,000)
Extraordinary loss before income taxes		$ 100,000

23. **(b)** To be classified as an extraordinary item, APB 30 requires that an event must be both unusual in nature and infrequent in occurrence, taking into account the environment in which the entity operates. The loss due to hailstorms is stated to occur frequently; therefore it should be reported in income from continuing operations. The loss should be reported at its actual amount because the full amount of a realized loss must be recognized in income when it occurs.

24. **(d)** A gain or loss from a transaction that is unusual in nature and infrequent in occurrence should be reported as an extraordinary item (APB 30, par. 20). Extraordinary items should be reported separately as a component of income *before* the cumulative effect of accounting changes and *after* discontinued operations of a segment of a business.

25. **(a)** APB 30, par. 23, provides that (1) gains or losses from the sale of property, plant, or equipment used in the business; (2) gains or losses from exchange or translation of foreign currencies, including those relating to major devaluations and revaluations; and (3) the write-down or write-off of receivables, inventories, and intangible assets should not be reported as extraordinary items. Thus, the amount of loss not considered extraordinary is $610,000 (i.e., $300,000 + $120,000 + $190,000).

26. **(d)** SFAS 4 specifies that material aggregate gains and losses from extinguishment of debt are classified as extraordinary items. Any gain or loss from the sale of long-term investments is reported as income from continuing operations.

27. **(a)** Generally, for an event to be classified as extraordinary, it must be both unusual in nature and infrequent of occurrence. As Raim sustains flood losses every two to three years, neither of these conditions is met. For Cane, the flood loss is both unusual and infrequent.

CHANGES IN ACCOUNTING PRINCIPLES

28. **(c)** The cumulative effect of the change in accounting principle is calculated as follows:

Deferred demo costs, 12/31/97		$ 500,000
Less income tax @ 30%		(150,000)
Cumulative effect to report 12/31/98		$ 350,000

29. (a) A change from the FIFO periodic inventory system to the weighted average periodic inventory system is a change in accounting principle. The cumulative effect of the change is the difference between the amount of retained earnings at the beginning of the period of change and the amount of retained earnings that would have been reported at that date if the new accounting principle had been retroactively applied for all affected periods (APB 20, par. 20). Therefore, since Harvey is on a calendar year basis, the cumulative effect of the change in accounting principle should be determined as of January 1, 1992.

30. (b) The change in depreciation methods for previously recorded assets is a cumulative-effect-type change in accounting principle. The cumulative effect of the change should be reported separately as a component of income after continuing operations. A change from the cash basis of vacation pay expense recognition to the accrual basis is a change from an accounting principle that is not generally accepted to one that is generally accepted. Such a change is considered an error correction. The financial statements of prior periods presented should be restated, and the beginning balance of retained earnings should be adjusted to correct prior errors. The change from the presentation of statements of individual companies to their inclusion in consolidated statements is a change in reporting entity. The cumulative effect of a change in reporting entity should not be reported. However, financial statements of prior periods presented should be restated. A change in method of accounting for long-term construction-type contracts is a retroactive-effect-type change in accounting principle. The cumulative effect of the change should be reported as an adjustment to the beginning balance of retained earnings.

31. (c) The cumulative effect of a change in accounting principle is the difference between the retained earnings at the beginning of the period of change and the amount that would have been reported at that date if the new accounting principle had been applied retroactively for all affected periods. A change from the straight-line method of depreciation to the units-of-production method of depreciation is a cumulative-effect-type change in accounting principle. Therefore, the accounting change is reported in the income statement of the period of change between the captions "extraordinary items" and "net income." The cumulative effect of the change in accounting principle at 1/1/92 is computed by Holly as follows:

Accumulated depreciation under units of production method, 1/1/92 [($50,000 ÷ 50,000) x (8,500 + 3,500)]	$ 12,000
Accumulated depreciation under straight-line method, 1/1/92 [($50,000 ÷ 10) x 2]	(10,000)
Cumulative effect of change in accounting principle, before income taxes, 1/1/92	2,000
Less income taxes ($2,000 x 30%)	(600)
Cumulative effect of change in accounting principle	$ 1,400

32. (b) The old (accelerated) depreciation method resulted in a $360,000 (i.e., $600,000 cost − $240,000 carrying amount) balance for Accumulated Depreciation at 1/1/92. Retroactively applying the new (SL) depreciation method results in a $240,000 (i.e., [($600,000 − 0) ÷ 5] x 2) balance for accumulated depreciation at 1/1/92. Thus, the new method results in a $120,000 (i.e., $360,000 − $240,000) lower balance for accumulated depreciation at 1/1/92 for financial reporting purposes. The $120,000 cumulative effect on income resulting from the difference between the old (accelerated) depreciation method and the new SL method is reduced by the $36,000 tax effect (i.e., $120,000 x 30%) on that difference. In its 1992 income statement, Warren should report $84,000 (i.e., $120,000 − $36,000) as the cumulative effect of the change in accounting principle, net of related income tax.

33. (c) Changing from an accelerated method to straight line for financial statement purposes results in a temporary difference of $120,000 in future taxable amounts (accumulated depreciation using the accelerated method of $360,000 less $240,000 using the straight-line method). The amount of tax effect for the taxable amounts is calculated by applying the enacted tax rate for future years of 30%, resulting in a $36,000 (i.e., $120,000 x 30%) deferred tax liability to be recorded as a result of the change.

34. (d) Both the individual item approach and the aggregate approach are generally accepted methods of applying the lower-of-cost-or-market to inventory items. When an entity changes from one generally accepted method to another acceptable method, it has a change in accounting principle. This particular change does not appear on the list of special cases of a change in principle, so, in the period of change, the cumulative effect of the change on prior periods is reported separately as a component of income after income from continuing operations, not as a correction of an error. A change in principle is reported separately, *after* extraordinary items on the income statement. A change in accounting principle is reported separately *after* continuing operations.

35. (c) A change from the FIFO method of inventory valuation to the weighted-average method is a change in accounting principle. The cumulative effect of the change in accounting principle is the difference between the amount of retained earnings at the beginning of the period of change and the amount of retained earnings that would have been reported at that date if the new accounting principle had been applied retroactively for all affected periods. Since the new (weighted-average) method results in a $6,000 higher inventory valuation than the old (FIFO) method at the beginning of the period of change, the amount of expense recognized as cost of goods sold in prior periods is reduced by $6,000. This has the effect of increasing the beginning balance of retained earnings. The beginning balance of retained earnings is not increased by the full $6,000, because the reduction in cost of goods sold would have increased the amount of income tax expense by $1,800 (i.e., $6,000 x 30%).

36. (d) A change in inventory valuation method is a change in accounting principle. Since the change in inventory method is other than a change from the LIFO method to another method of inventory valuation (e.g., FIFO to the weighted-average method); the cumulative effect of the change in accounting principle should be reported as a component of income after extraordinary items in the period of change.

37. (a) A change from LIFO to another inventory method is a change in accounting principle that should be reported retroactively by applying the new method in restatement of prior periods and adjusting the beginning balance of *retained earnings* (APB 20, par. 27). The cumulative effect of the accounting change is the difference between the amount of retained earnings at the beginning of the period of change and the amount of retained earnings that would have been reported at that date if the new accounting principle had been applied retroactively for all affected periods. Since the new (FIFO) method results in a $40,000 higher inventory valuation than the old (LIFO) method at the beginning of the period of change, the amount of expense recognized as cost of goods sold in prior periods is reduced by $40,000. This has the effect of increasing the beginning balance of retained earnings. However, the beginning balance of retained earnings cannot be increased by the full $40,000, because the reduction in the cost of goods sold would have increased the amount of income tax expense previously recognized by $12,000 (i.e., $40,000 x 30%). Thus, the cumulative effect of the accounting change is reported as a $28,000 (i.e.,

$40,000 − $12,000) addition to the beginning balance of *retained earnings*.

38. (c) Changes in accounting principle are generally reported net of tax on the income statement, following extraordinary items but before net income. APB 20, *Accounting Changes*, provides several exceptions to this rule, including changes in the method of accounting for long-term construction contracts (par. 27). This type of change in accounting principle is accounted for as an adjustment to the beginning balance of retained earnings, net of its income tax effect.

Income under percentage-of-completion method	$ 880,000
Income under completed-contract method	(700,000)
Increase in income under percentage-of-completion	180,000
Less: Income tax effect ($180,000 x 40%)	(72,000)
Credit to 1/1/97 retained earnings	$ 108,000

COMPREHENSIVE INCOME

39. (d) According to SFAS 130, comprehensive income and all items that are required to be recognized as components of comprehensive income should be reported in a financial statement that is displayed with the same prominence as other financial statements. Discontinued operations, extraordinary items, and the cumulative effect of a change in accounting principle (other than the changes that require retroactive treatment) are components of the income statement, reported after income from continuing operations and before net income. If comprehensive income is reported in the same statement as net income, other comprehensive income and comprehensive income are reported after net income. An entity may display components of other comprehensive income in either net-of-tax basis or summary net-of-tax basis. Comprehensive income must be shown on the face of one of the statements, not just in the notes to the financial statements.

CHANGES IN ACCOUNTING ESTIMATES

40. (a) When a change in accounting estimate and a change in accounting principle are inseparable, the change should be accounted for as a change in estimate, which is a component of income from continuing operations. A change in estimate does not require the restatement of prior period financial statements. Corrections of errors are considered prior period adjustments and are not reported on the income statement but are reported as adjustments to beginning retained earnings. Material effects of a change in estimate on income before extraordinary items, net income, and related per share amounts should be disclosed. Footnote

disclosure only is not proper accounting treatment of a change in estimate.

41. (a)   Per APB 20, *Accounting Changes*, a change in estimated warranty costs is an example of a change in accounting estimate. The effect of a change in accounting estimate should be accounted for as a component of income from continuing operations entirely in the period of change if it affects that period only. Therefore, the effect of the additional $10 of estimated warranty costs for 1991 and 1992 should be reported in 1992 income from continuing operations since the change in accounting estimate affected only 1992.

42. (d)   A change in the expected service life of an asset because additional information has been obtained is an example of a change in an accounting estimate. According to APB 20, a change in estimate should be accounted for prospectively. Therefore, no cumulative effect of the change is reported and no pro forma effects of retroactive application are disclosed.

43. (d)   APB 20, par. 31, states, "The effect of a change in accounting estimate should be accounted for In (1) the period of change if the change affects that period only, or (2) the period of change and future periods if the change affects both. A change in accounting estimate should not be accounted for by restaring amounts reported in financial statements of prior periods or by reporting pro forma amounts for prior periods."

44. (d)   The change in the estimated useful life of the machine is a change in accounting estimate. APB 20 requires that the effect of the change in accounting estimate be accounted for prospectively in the period of change and future periods, because both are affected. Therefore, the accumulated depreciation for the machine at 12/31/92 is computed as follows:

Accumulated depreciation, 1/1/92		
[($264,000 – $0) ÷ 8] x 3 years		$ 99,000
Depreciation for 1992:		
Cost of machine	$264,000	
Accumulated depreciation, 1/1/92	(99,000)	
Carrying amount of machine, 1/1/92	165,000	
Less: Estimated salvage value	(24,000)	
Depreciable base of machine, 1/1/92	141,000	
Divide by: Estimated remaining		
useful life (6 – 3)	÷ 3	47,000
Accumulated depreciation, 12/31/92		$146,000

CHANGES IN REPORTING ENTITIES

45. (d)   Since the subsidiary was excluded from previous consolidations, its inclusion in the current year's consolidated financial statements results in a special type of change in accounting principle that results in financial statements which, in effect, are those of a different reporting entity. The change in the reporting entity should be reported by restating the financial statements of all prior periods presented to reflect the new reporting entity. (see APB 20, par. 12, 34 and 35).

46. (d)   An accounting change that results in a change of entity should be reported by restating the financial statements of all prior periods presented to show the financial information for the new reporting entity for all periods.

47. (b)   Changes in accounting principle generally are accounted for by presenting the cumulative effect of the change net of income tax, as a separate component of net income. A change in the accounting entity, on the other hand, is presented by restating the financial statements for all periods presented.

CORRECTION OF ERRORS

48. (b)   The correction of an error in financial statements of a prior period is a "prior period adjustment." Prior period adjustments should be reported in the current retained earnings statement as an adjustment of the opening balance, net of related income taxes (APB 9, par. 18).

49. (b)   The recognition of the effect of fully expensing the premiums for the three-year insurance policy represents the correction of an error of a prior period. The correction of the error should be reported as an adjustment to the beginning balance of retained earnings, net of its related income tax effect. The correction results in $40,000 (i.e., $60,000 x 2/3) less insurance expense recognized in 1991. This increases the beginning balance of retained earnings. However, the beginning balance of retained earnings cannot be increased by the full $40,000, because the reduction in insurance expense would have increased the amount of income tax expense previously recognized by $12,000 (i.e., $40,000 x 30%). Thus, the beginning balance of retained earnings is increased by $28,000 (i.e., $40,000 – $12,000) due to the correction of the error. Therefore, the amount to be reported as the adjusted beginning balance of retained earnings is $428,000 (i.e., $400,000 + $28,000).

50. (d)   Since holiday pay for administrative employees is a period cost, it should have been expensed when incurred. Instead, it was misclassified and inventoried as manufacturing overhead. This error overstates both inventory and net income,

thus overstating both current assets and stockholders' equity. The understatement of an accrued expense overstates net income and stockholders' equity and understates current liabilities. Misclassifying noncurrent note receivable principal as a current asset overstates current assets and understates noncurrent assets but does not affect stockholders' equity. The understatement of depreciation expense overstates noncurrent assets, net income, and stockholders' equity.

51. (a) The recognition of the effect of the failure to provide for uncollectible accounts in the previous period represents the correction of an error of a prior period. The correction of the error should be reported as an adjustment to the opening balance of retained earnings, net of its related income tax effects. A decrease in the estimated life of depreciable assets represents a change in accounting estimate which is to be accounted for prospectively (in the period of change and future periods) as a component of income from continuing operations. A change from the installment sale method to the point of sale method of income recognition represents a change in accounting principle (this assumes that the installment sale method was appropriately being used because of not being able to reasonably estimate the collectibility of the related receivables). The cumulative effect of changing to the new accounting principle should be reported separately in the income statement after income from continuing operations. A change from an accelerated method to the straight-line method of depreciation represents a change in accounting principle. The cumulative effect of changing to the new accounting principle should be reported separately in the income statement after income from continuing operations.

52. (d) Since Pear owns 40% of Cinn's common stock, Pear has the ability to exercise significant influence over Cinn by virtue of its investment and should account for its investment in Cinn by the equity method. Therefore, Pear's $40,000 equity in Cinn's earnings is properly included in Pear's 1992 income before taxes. Under the equity method, the dividends received from Cinn reduce the carrying amount of the investment; they do not affect the amount of investment income that Pear recognizes. Therefore, the $8,000 of dividends received from Cinn erroneously included in 1992 income before taxes are subtracted to correct that figure. The arithmetical errors in depreciation of prior years represents a correction of errors of prior periods. The correction of the errors should be reported as an adjustment to the opening balance of retained earnings, net of the related income tax

effect. Therefore, the $35,000 of arithmetical errors in depreciation of prior years that Pear had inadvertently subtracted from 1992 income before taxes are added back to correct that figure. The amount that Pear should report for income before taxes is determined as follows:

Income before taxes 1992, before adjustment	$125,000
Less: Dividends received from equity method investee	(8,000)
Add: Arithmetical errors in depreciation of prior years	35,000
Corrected income before taxes, 1992	$152,000

53. (c) Frey should report $50,000 as a prior period adjustment in 1993. The recognition of the effect in 1993 of the failure to accrue $50,000 of warranty costs in 1992 is the correction of an error of a prior period. The correction of the error should be reported in the 1993 financial statements as an adjustment to the beginning balance of retained earnings, net of its related income tax effect. The change from straight-line to accelerated depreciation represents a change in accounting principle. The $30,000 cumulative effect (on prior periods) of changing to the new accounting principle should be reported separately in the income statement after income from continuing operations.

54. (a) The change from the cash basis of accounting (not GAAP) to the accrual basis of accounting (GAAP) is a correction of an error. The correction of an error in prior period income is a prior period adjustment.

55. (c) The understatement of 1989 and 1990 depreciation expense discovered in preparing the 1991 financial statements represents the correction of an error in previously issued financial statements (i.e., a prior period adjustment). Prior period adjustments are reported retroactively by (1) correcting all prior period statements presented and (2) restating the beginning balance of retained earnings for the first period presented when the error effects extend to a period prior to that one. Therefore, since 1991 and 1990 comparative financial statements are presented, the understatement of 1989 depreciation expense should be reported as a prior period adjustment in the 1990 financial statements as a $25,000 decrease in the beginning balance of retained earnings. In addition, 1990 net income should be reported at $125,000 (i.e., $150,000 – $25,000) in order to reflect the correct amount of 1990 depreciation expense. Since the understatement of depreciation expense pertains to 1989 and 1990 and is reported retroactively, the reported amount of 1991 net income of $180,000 is not affected by the errors.

56. (a) The company failed to record an accrued expense at the end of 1991. This error

would understate current liabilities at the end of 1991, thus overstating working capital as of the balance sheet date. The failure to accrue the expense has no effect on the cash account, and therefore no effect on cash flows from operating activities for 1991.

DISCLOSURE OF ACCOUNTING POLICY

57. (c) The Summary of Significant Accounting Policies should identify and describe the accounting principles followed by the reporting entity and the methods of applying those principles (APB 22, par. 12). Examples of disclosures by a business enterprise commonly required with respect to accounting policies include those relating to basis of consolidation, depreciation methods, amortization of intangibles, inventory pricing, recognition of profit on long-term construction type contracts, and criteria for determining which investments are treated as cash equivalents. Items (I) and (III) are examples of financial statement disclosures which are not related to accounting policies.

58. (b) The Summary of Significant Accounting Policies should identify and describe the accounting principles followed by the reporting entity and the methods of applying those principles (APB 22, par. 12). Examples of disclosures by a business enterprise commonly required with respect to accounting policies include those relating to basis of consolidation, depreciation methods, amortization of intangibles, inventory pricing, and recognition of profit on long-term construction-type contracts (par. 13). Financial statement disclosure of accounting policies should not duplicate details (for example, composition of inventories or of plant assets) presented elsewhere as part of the financial statements (par. 14). Answers (a), (c), and (d) are examples of financial statement disclosures which are not related to accounting policies.

59. (a) The Summary of Significant Accounting Policies should identify and describe the accounting policies followed by the reporting entity and the methods of applying those principles (APB 22, par. 12). Examples of disclosures by a business enterprise commonly required with respect to accounting policies include those relating to basis of consolidation, depreciation methods, amortization of intangibles, inventory pricing, recognition of profit on long-term construction-type contracts, and criteria for determining which investments are treated as cash equivalents. Answers (b), (c), and (d) are examples of financial statement disclosures which are not related to accounting policies.

60. (c) The Summary of Significant Accounting Policies should identify and describe the accounting principles, followed by the reporting entity and the methods of applying those principles (APB 22, par. 12). Examples of disclosures by a business enterprise commonly required with respect to accounting policies include those relating to the basis of consolidation, depreciation methods, amortization of intangibles, inventory pricing, recognition of profit on long-term construction-type contracts, and criteria for determining which investments are treated as cash equivalents. Answers (a), (b), and (d) are examples of financial statement disclosures which are **not** related to accounting policies.

RELATED PARTY DISCLOSURES

61. (c) Financial statements should include disclosures of material related party transactions, including the nature of the relationships involved, a description of the transactions, the dollar amounts of transactions for each of the periods for which income statements are presented, and the amounts due from or to related parties as of the date of each balance sheet presented.

62. (a) If the reporting enterprise and one or more other enterprises are under common ownership or management control and the existence of that control could result in operating results or financial position of the reporting enterprise significantly different from those that would have been obtained if the enterprises were autonomous, the nature of the control relationship should be disclosed even though there are no transactions between the enterprises. Therefore, both Lemo and Young should disclose their relationship with Ego.

63. (b) Financial statements should include disclosures of material related party transactions, other than compensation arrangements, expense allowances, and other similar items in the ordinary course of business. Therefore, the consulting fees paid to a director must be disclosed in the notes to the financial statements. The per diem expenses would be included in expense allowances and would not need to be disclosed.

64. (c) Financial statements should include disclosures of material-related party transactions other than (1) compensation arrangements, (2) expense allowances, (3) other similar items in the ordinary course of business, and (4) transactions that are eliminated in the preparation of consolidated or combined financial statements. Thus, Dean should report related party disclosures totaling $175,000 ($125,000 + $50,000), the amount of the loans to officers. The amounts for officers' salaries, officers'

expenses, and intercompany sales should not be disclosed as related party transactions.

65. (d) SFAS 57 requires that all material related-party transactions that are not eliminated in consolidated or combined financial statements be disclosed. However, according to SFAS 57, the following related-party transactions do not have to be disclosed: compensation arrangements, expense allowances, and similar items incurred in the ordinary course of business.

DEVELOPMENTAL STAGE ENTERPRISES

66. (c) ABC should be considered to be a development stage enterprise during the period 1995-1997 because (1) it was devoting substantially all of its efforts to establishing a new business (i.e., it acquired plant and equipment, raised capital, obtained financing, trained employees, and developed markets) and (2) it earned no significant revenues. Generally accepted accounting principles that apply to established operating enterprises determine whether a cost incurred by a development stage enterprise should be charged to expense when incurred or should be capitalized or deferred. Capitalization or deferral of costs is subject to the same assessment of recoverability that is applicable to an established operating enterprise. Thus, in its December 31, 1997 financial statements, ABC should defer all costs incurred during its development stage which it believes are recoverable in future periods.

67. (d) Financial statements issued by a development stage enterprise should be presented in conformity with generally accepted accounting principles that apply to established operating enterprises. These accounting principles determine whether a cost incurred by a development stage enterprise should be charged to expense when incurred or should be capitalized or deferred. Organization costs include (1) accounting services incidental to organization, (2) legal services for drafting the corporate charter and bylaws, (3) state incorporation filing fees, and (4) costs of temporary directors and of organizational meetings. Under generally accepted accounting principles, there are two primary methods of accounting for initial stock issue costs. The first method records initial stock issue costs as a reduction of additional paid-in capital. The second method capitalizes initial stock issue costs as organization costs. The first method of charging initial stock issue costs to additional paid-in capital predominates in practice. Therefore, Tanker should capitalize as organization costs the $55,000 legal fees for incorporation and other related matters and may capitalize as organization

costs the $40,000 of underwriters' fees for the initial stock offering.

68. (a) Financial reporting by a development stage enterprise differs from financial reporting for an established operating enterprise in regard to footnote disclosures only (e.g., a development stage enterprise should disclose, from the date of its inception, cumulative revenues and expenses in regards to the income statement and cumulative amounts with respect to the statement of cash flows as certain additional information). Otherwise, no special accounting standards apply to development stage enterprises. Generally accepted accounting principles that apply to established operating enterprises govern the recognition of revenue by a development stage enterprise and determine whether a cost incurred by such an enterprise should be charged to expense when incurred or should be capitalized or deferred (SFAS 7, par. 10 - 12).

69. (a) Financial statements issued by a development stage enterprise should be presented in conformity with GAAP applicable to established operating enterprises. Special accounting practices that are based on a distinctive accounting for development stage enterprises are not acceptable. Financial reporting by a development stage enterprise differs from financial reporting for an established operating enterprise in regard only to required additional information.

70. (a) Financial statements issued by a development stage enterprise should be presented in conformity with GAAP that apply to established operating enterprises. These accounting principles determine whether a cost incurred by a development stage enterprise should be charged to expense when incurred or should be capitalized or deferred. Lex should capitalize both the cost of the leasehold improvements, equipment, and furniture, and the cost of the security deposits. Thus, the total amount of costs incurred by Lex that should be charged to operations from its inception through the period ended 12/31/97 is $3,425,000, determined as follows:

Research and development ($750,000 + $900,000)	$ 1,650,000
Laboratory operations ($175,000 + $550,000)	725,000
General and administrative ($225,000 + $685,000)	910,000
Depreciation ($25,000 + $115,000)	140,000
Total amount of costs charged to operations	$3,425,000

71. (d) Generally accepted accounting principles that apply to established operating enterprises determine whether a cost incurred by a development stage enterprise should be charged to expense when incurred or should be capitalized or deferred. Therefore, only the $1,200,000 cost of the leasehold

improvements, equipment, and furniture should have been capitalized by Lind. The research and development costs, laboratory operations costs, and the general and administrative costs should have been expensed when incurred.

72. (b)   The balance sheet of a development stage enterprise should include any cumulative net losses reported with a caption such as "deficit accumulated during the development stage" in the stockholders' equity section [SFAS 7, par. 11(a)]. It is never acceptable to capitalize a deficit. A deficit is a debit item that belongs in the stockholders' equity section of the balance sheet, not in the asset section.

REVENUE RECOGNITION

73. (a)   The amount reported for net sales should not be reduced for the portion of the sales equaling merchandise that is estimated to be exchanged for merchandise of equal or greater value. The amount that Fenn should report for net sales for December 1992 is determined as follows:

Sales, December 1992	$1,000,000
Less: Estimated sales that will be returned	
[$1,000,000 x (7% + 3%)]	(100,000)
Net sales, December 1992	$ 900,000

74. (d)   Accrual accounting recognizes revenue in the period it is earned rather than when the related cash is received. Under the royalty agreement, Super earns 20% of revenues associated with the comic strip. Therefore, in 1992, Super should recognize royalty revenue of $300,000 (i.e., $1,500,000 x 20%).

75. (a)   The $2,800 increase in rentals receivable represents rental revenue earned but not yet received in cash. The $8,000 decrease in unearned rentals represents rental revenue earned that had been received in cash in a prior period. The rental revenue to be reported in 1990 can most easily be determined by the preparation of the following journal entry:

Cash (given)	80,000	
Rentals Receivable ($12,400 – $9,600)	2,800	
Unearned Rentals ($32,000 – $24,000)	8,000	
Rental Revenue (to balance)		90,800

EXPENSE RECOGNITION

76. (c)   Depreciation expense for 1995 may be derived as follows:

Equipment cost, 12/31/94	$ 344,000
Cost of 1995 purchase	50,000
Equipment cost without sale	394,000
Equipment cost, 12/31/95	(379,000)
Cost of equipment sold	15,000
Carrying value of equipment sold	(9,000)
Accumulated depreciation of equipment sold	$ 6,000
Accumulated depreciation, 12/31/94	$ 128,000
Accumulated depreciation of equipment sold (from above)	(6,000)
Balance without 1995 depreciation	122,000
Accumulated depreciation, 12/31/95	(153,000)
Depreciation expense 1995	$ 31,000

77. (a)   Interest expense should be accrued in the period in which it is earned, rather than the period in which it is paid. In 1996, total interest expense of $4,080 should be reported, as shown below. If only $3,000 interest expense is recorded, the understatement is $1,080.

Dates of Loan	Amount	Monthly Interest	Months in 1996	1996 Interest
11/01/95-10/31/96	$10,000	$100	10	$ 1,000
02/01/96-07/31/96	30,000	300	6	1,800
05/01/96-01/31/97	16,000	160	8	1,280
Total interest				$ 4,080
Less interest expense recorded				(3,000)
Understated interest				$ 1,080

78. (b)   Accrual accounting recognizes expenses in the period they are incurred rather than when the related cash is paid. Zach pays commissions to its sales staff at the rate of 3% of net sales. For the year ended 3/31/93, Zach should report commission expense of $450,000 ($15,000,000 x 3%).

79. (c)   On 12/31/93, House announced the winner of the contest and signed a note payable to the winner. The amount to be reported as contest prize expense for 1993 is determined as follows:

First installment of note payable due 1/2/94	$ 50,000
Cost of annuity purchased on 12/31/93 to provide prize monies remaining after first installment	418,250
Contest prize expense for 1993	$468,250

80. (b)   Net income after bonus and income taxes is $360,000. The income tax rate is 40%. Therefore, income after bonus but before income taxes is $600,000 [i.e., $360,000 ÷ (100% – 40%)]. The bonus is equal to 10% of the corporation's income after bonus but before income taxes. Therefore, the amount of the bonus is $60,000 (i.e., $600,000 x 10%).

81. (c) Clark's advertising expense for 1993 is computed as follows:

Advertising expense, before year-end adjustment	$ 146,000
Add: Advertising costs incurred during December 1993, paid in January 1994	9,000
Less: Prepayment for January 1994 advertising campaign	(15,000)
Advertising expense for 1993	$ 140,000

82. (b) The $55,000 consultants' fee for work performed in 1991 had already been recorded by Pak; therefore, no adjustment is necessary for this item. Pak's professional fee expense for 1991 is determined as follows:

Professional fee expense, before year-end adjustment	$ 82,000
Legal fees for work performed in 1991, unbilled as of 12/31/91	13,000
Professional fee expense, 1991	$ 95,000

CASH VS. ACCRUAL

83. (c)

Collection of fees in 1994	$200,000
Less: Accounts receivable, Jan. 1, 1994	(40,000)
Plus: Accounts receivable, Dec. 31, 1994	60,000
Less: Unearned revenue, Dec. 31, 1994	(5,000)
Service revenue for 1994	$215,000

84. (d) The sole proprietor's drawing of $500 is recorded as a reduction of her capital account under both the cash-basis and accrual-basis methods of accounting. The proprietorship's income under the cash-basis and accrual-basis for the two months ended 5/31/93 is computed as follows:

	Cash-Basis	Accrual-Basis
Revenue for services provided April 1993, payment received May 1993	$3,200	$3,200
Expenses incurred April 1993, paid June 1993	--	(1,500)
Proprietorship's income for two months ended May 31, 1993	$3,200	$1,700

85. (c) Potoma's accrued expenses decreased during 1992. Hence, Potoma's 1992 payments for expenses exceeded the amount of expense recognized on the accrual basis in 1992. The increased amount of expenses recognized in 1992 under the cash basis increases Potoma's 1992 accrual basis net income as compared to its 1992 cash basis net income. The declaration or payment of a cash dividend does not affect net income computed under either the cash or accrual basis. Compared to its 1992 cash basis net income, Potoma's 1992 accrual basis net income decreased when it recognized uncollectible accounts expense in 1992. Potoma's

1992 cash basis net income is not affected by either the accounts receivable balances written off in 1992 or the uncollectible account expense recognized in 1992. The sale of the used equipment at a gain increases net income under both the cash and accrual basis by equal amounts.

86. (d) When accounts receivable decrease during a period, revenues on a cash basis are more than revenues on an accrual basis because cash collections are more than revenues reported on an accrual basis. Thus, compared to the accrual basis of accounting, the cash basis of accounting *over-states* income by the net decrease in the accounts receivable. When accrued expenses decrease during a period, expenses on a cash basis are more than expenses on an accrual basis because cash payments are more than expenses reported on an accrual basis. Thus, compared to the accrual basis of accounting, the cash basis of accounting *understates* income by the net decrease in the accrued expenses.

87. (d) Accrual accounting (1) recognizes revenue in the period it is earned rather than when the related cash is received and (2) recognizes expenses in the period incurred rather than when the related cash is paid. The accrual basis pretax income that Class should report in its 1992 income statement is determined as follows:

Cash basis pretax income, 1992	$ 60,000
Add: Increase in accounts receivable—revenues earned but not yet collected in cash ($40,000 – $20,000)	20,000
Decrease in accounts payable—payments made not representing current year expenses ($30,000 – $15,000)	15,000
Accrual basis pretax income, 1992	$ 95,000

INTERIM REPORTING

88. (a) Interim reporting requirements arose because annual financial statements are frequently not timely enough for decision makers. Because interim financial statements are annualized based on estimates, they may not be as reliable as annual financial statements.

89. (c) In APB 28, the Board concluded that each interim period should be viewed as an integral part of an annual period. In order to maintain comparability, the principles and practices used to prepare the latest annual statements should also be used to prepare the interim statements.

90. (b) APB 28 generally requires a company to use for interim financial reporting purposes the same principles and practices used for annual reporting. For the sake of expediency, however, certain practical deviations are permitted where the results of using a different practice are likely to be immaterial. Thus, the Opinion allows the use of gross profit rates for determining the cost of goods sold for interim period statements. The use of gross profit rates for estimating ending inventory is not acceptable for annual financial statements.

91. (d) APB 28, par. 14.(b), states, "Inventory losses from market declines should not be deferred beyond the interim period in which the decline occurs." Therefore, Cox should recognize the full amount of the inventory loss from the permanent market decline that occurred in May 1997 in the quarterly income statement for the three months ended June 30, 1997.

92. (a) The use of lower of cost or market may result in inventory losses that should not be deferred beyond the interim period in which the decline occurs. Recoveries of these losses in subsequent periods should be recognized as gains, but only to the extent of losses recognized in previous interim periods of the same fiscal year. Temporary market declines, however, need not be recognized at the interim dates since no loss is expected to be incurred in the fiscal year. Because Wilson expected the decline to reverse within the fiscal year, no loss should be recorded for the first quarter. Even though the recovery exceeded the previous decline by $10,000, gains are recognized only to the extent of losses recognized in previous interim periods of the same fiscal year.

93. (c) Annual property taxes should be accrued or deferred at each interim reporting date to provide an appropriate cost in each period and allocated ratably to each interim period of the year [APB 28, par. 16(c)]. Because the unanticipated repairs to the office equipment benefit the last three quarters of the year, each of these periods should be charged with an appropriate portion of the cost by the use of accruals or deferrals [par 16(a)].

Annual property taxes ($90,000 ÷ 4)	$22,500
Unanticipated repairs incurred in April ($150,000 ÷ 3)	50,000
Expense reported in 6/30/92 income statement	$72,500

INTERIM PERIOD INCOME TAX PROVISIONS

94. (b) Per APB 28, par. 23, "At the end of each interim period, a company should make its best estimate of the effective tax rate expected to be applicable for the full fiscal year. The rate so determined should be used in providing for income taxes on a current year-to-date basis."

95. (c) Per APB 28, par. 23, "At the end of each interim period, a company should make its best estimate of the effective tax rate expected to be applicable for the full fiscal year. The rate so determined should be used in providing for income taxes on a current year-to-date basis." Therefore, the amount of income tax expense that Tech should report in its 1993 first quarter interim income statement is $50,000—Tech's 1993 first quarter's income before taxes of $200,000 multiplied by the 25% effective annual income tax rate Tech expects for 1993.

96. (b) The effects of disposals of a segment should be included in the determination of net income for the interim period in which they occur (APB 28, par. 21). Annual property taxes may be accrued or deferred at each interim reporting date to provide an appropriate cost in each period and thus are allocated ratably to each interim period of the year [par. 16(c)]. The amount to be reported in income for the six-month interim period ended 6/30/91 for the disposal of the business segment and the property taxes is determined as follows:

Net loss incurred 6/30/91 on disposal of business segment	$100,000
Annual property taxes ($40,000 ÷ 2)	20,000
	$120,000

97. (a) Kell should report all of the extraordinary gain realized in the second quarter in the second quarter's income statement. Extraordinary items should not be prorated over the balance of the fiscal year (APB 28, par. 22). The cumulative-effect-type accounting change made in the third quarter should be accounted for as if it occurred in the first quarter; no cumulative effect of the change should be included in net income of the third quarter (SFAS 3, par. 10). The $12,000 of calendar-year property taxes are properly allocated to the third quarter; annual property taxes should be accrued or deferred at each interim reporting date to provide an appropriate cost in each period and thus are allocated ratably to each interim period of the year [APB 28, par. 16(c)]. Thus, the net income that Kell should report for the quarter ended 9/30/90 is determined as follows:

Net income for the quarter ended 9/30/90, as reported	$ 95,000
Less: Portion of extraordinary gain realized in second quarter allocated to third quarter ($60,000 ÷ 3)	(20,000)
Add: Cumulative-effect loss resulting from change in accounting principle included in third quarter net income	16,000
Corrected net income for the quarter ended 9/30/90	$ 91,000

SEGMENT REPORTING

98. (d) An operating segment is deemed to be a reportable segment if it meets one or more of the revenue, profit(loss), and assets tests. If an operating segment's revenue, including both sales to external customers and intersegment sales and transfers, is 10% or more of the combined revenue of all operating segments, it meets the revenue test. Lion, Monk, and Nevi each have more than 10% of combined revenues and are deemed to be reportable segments.

99. (c) An operating segment is identified as a reportable segment if it meets one or more of the three tests: revenue, profit(loss), and assets. (1) Revenue test—Its revenue (including both sales to external customers and intersegment sales and transfers) is 10% or more of the combined revenue of all operating segments. (2) Profit(loss) test—Its profit or loss is 10% or more of the greater of the following two absolute amounts: Combined profits of all segments that did not report losses, or the sum of all losses for all segments reporting losses. (3) Assets test—Its assets are 10% or more of the combined assets of all operating segments. Segments A, B, C, and E have revenue greater than $3,275,000, which is 10% of the combined revenue. They also have profits greater than $580,000, which is 10% of the combined profits (no segments reported losses). Segments A, B, C, D, and E all have assets greater than $6,750,000, which is 10% of the combined assets. Only segment F does not meet at least one of the three tests. Therefore, Correy has five reportable segments for 1997.

OCBOA

100. (d) According to SAS 62, a comprehensive basis of accounting other than generally accepted accounting principles is one of the following:

- A basis of accounting used to comply with regulatory requirements;
- A basis used for tax purposes;
- A cash basis;
- A definite set of criteria having substantial support, such as the price-level basis of accounting.

A basis of accounting used by an entity to comply with the financial reporting requirements of a lending institution does not fit any of the categories.

101. (c) The balance in the capital account at March 31, 1995, is the beginning balance plus the service revenues received less the owner's draw. The expenses incurred in February and paid in April are not included in the calculation, as Tory has a cash basis of accounting. $2,000 + $5,000 − $1,000 = $6,000.

102. (d) The decrease in accounts receivable represents collections in the current period of credit sales of a prior period. The amount of net revenue that should be recognized under the cash basis of accounting is determined as follows:

Gross cash sales	$ 80,000	
Less: Returns and allowances	(4,000)	
Receipts from cash sales		$ 76,000
Gross credit sales	$120,000	
Less: Discounts	(6,000)	
Net credit sales	114,000	
Add: Decrease in accounts receivable ($40,000 − $30,000)	10,000	
Receipts from credit sales		124,000
Receipts from cash and credit sales		$ 200,000

103. (d) Tax-basis financial statements recognize certain revenues and expenses in different reporting periods than GAAP financial statements. Nontaxable income and nondeductible expenses are still included in the determination of income in tax-basis statements. Detailed information about current and deferred income tax liabilities is included in GAAP financial statements. Income tax-basis financial statements may include disclosures about capital and operating lease transactions.

104. (a) In financial statements prepared on the income-tax basis, the nondeductible portion of expenses is included in the expense category in the determination of income, according to the AICPA Technical Information for Practitioners Series #1, entitled, "Other Comprehensive Basis of Accounting," Section 11,500, Par. 4. (Editorial note: This is an infrequently tested topic.)

PERFORMANCE BY SUBTOPICS

Each category below parallels a subtopic covered in Chapter 11. Record the number and percentage of questions you correctly answered in each subtopic area.

Income From Continuing Operations

Question #	Correct √
1	
2	
3	
4	
5	
6	
7	
8	
9	
10	
11	
12	
# Questions	12

Correct _____
% Correct _____

Discontinued Operations (SFAS 144)

Question #	Correct √
13	
14	
15	
16	
# Questions	4

Correct _____
% Correct _____

Discontinued Operations (APB 30)

Question #	Correct √
17	
18	
19	
20	
# Questions	4

Correct _____
% Correct _____

Extraordinary Items

Question #	Correct √
21	
22	
23	
24	
25	
26	
27	
# Questions	7

Correct _____
% Correct _____

Changes in Accounting Principles

Question #	Correct √
28	
29	
30	
31	
32	
33	
34	
35	
36	
37	
38	
# Questions	11

Correct _____
% Correct _____

Comprehensive Income

Question #	Correct √
39	
# Questions	1

Correct _____
% Correct _____

Changes in Accounting Estimates

Question #	Correct √
40	
41	
42	
43	
44	
# Questions	5

Correct _____
% Correct _____

Changes in Reporting Entities

Question #	Correct √
45	
46	
47	
# Questions	3

Correct _____
% Correct _____

Correction of Errors

Question #	Correct √
48	
49	
50	
51	
52	
53	
54	
55	
56	
# Questions	9

Correct _____
% Correct _____

Disclosure of Accounting Policy

Question #	Correct √
57	
58	
59	
60	
# Questions	4

Correct _____
% Correct _____

Related Party Disclosures

Question #	Correct √
61	
62	
63	
64	
65	
# Questions	5

Correct _____
% Correct _____

Developmental Stage Enterprises

Question #	Correct √
66	
67	
68	
69	
70	
71	
72	
# Questions	7

Correct _____
% Correct _____

Revenue Recognition

Question #	Correct √
73	
74	
75	
# Questions	3

Correct _____
% Correct _____

Expense Recognition

Question #	Correct √
76	
77	
78	
79	
80	
81	
82	
# Questions	7

Correct _____
% Correct _____

Cash vs Accrual

Question #	Correct √
83	
84	
85	
86	
87	
# Questions	5

Correct _____
% Correct _____

Interim Reporting

Question #	Correct √
88	
89	
90	
91	
92	
93	
# Questions	6

Correct _____
% Correct _____

Interim Period Income Tax Provisions

Question #	Correct √
94	
95	
96	
97	
# Questions	4

Correct _____
% Correct _____

Segment Reporting			OCBOA		
Question #	Correct √		Question #	Correct √	
98			100		
99			101		
# Questions	2		102		
			103		
# Correct	_____		104		
% Correct	_____		# Questions	5	
			# Correct	_____	
			% Correct	_____	

OTHER OBJECTIVE FORMAT SOLUTIONS

SOLUTION 11-2 FINANCIAL ACCOUNTING CONCEPTS (1 point) AND ACCOUNTING CHANGES AND CORRECTIONS (4 points)

1. (A,Y) Changing from the completed-contract method to the percentage-of-completion method of accounting for long term contracts is a change in accounting principle that requires retroactive treatment. The cumulative effect of the change in accounting principle should be reported as an adjustment to the beginning balance of retained earnings, net of the related income tax effect, and the financial statements of all prior periods presented should be restated.

2. (B,Z) Changing the percentage of credit sales used to determine the allowance for uncollectible accounts from 2% to 1% is a change in accounting estimate and requires using the prospective approach. The allowance for uncollectible accounts and the related expense for current and future financial statements should be reported on the new basis, and beginning retained earnings should not be adjusted.

3. (A,X, $9,000) Changing from the average cost to FIFO methods of inventory is a change in accounting principle requiring the cumulative effect approach. The cumulative effect of the change should be reflected in the net income of the period of the change, between extraordinary items and net income.

The cumulative effect is the difference between the amount of retained earnings at the beginning of the period of a change and the amount of retained earnings that would have been reported at that date if the new accounting principle had been applied retroactively for all prior periods that would have been affected. The cumulative effect in this case is the difference between the cost of goods sold for the years prior to January 1, 1996, as follows:

	FIFO	Average Cost	Difference
Prior to 1995	$77,000	$71,000	$6,000
1995	82,000	79,000	3,000
Cumulative effect prior to 1/1/96			$9,000

4. (C,Y, $2,000) The error in the calculation of depreciation resulted in the need for a correction of the error in previously presented financial statements, requiring the retroactive restatement approach. Beginning retained earnings of the current year should be adjusted, as follows:

Incorrect depreciation calculation ($40,000 x 25%)	$10,000
Less: Correct depreciation calculation ($40,000 x 20%)	(8,000)
Adjustment to beginning retained earnings	$ 2,000

SOLUTION 11-3 PRESENTATION OF FINANCIAL STATEMENTS

1. (A,Y) APB 20, para. 8, indicates that a "characteristic of a change in accounting principle is that it concerns a choice from among two or more generally accepted principles." Both completed contracts and percentage-of-completion are generally accepted principles and so A is the correct answer from list A. Paragraph 27 indicates that "a change in the method of accounting for long-term construction-type contracts" should be accounted for by retroactive restatement. While this question does not use the term "construction," presumably heavy equipment being manufactured to customer specifications would fall in this category.

2. (B,Z) Service lives of depreciable assets are specifically mentioned in APB 20 as being among the types of changes in estimate. Changes in estimate are to be reflected prospectively.

3. (B,Z) Warranty costs are also mentioned as examples of changes in estimate which are to be handled prospectively.

4. (A,Y) A change in the method of inventory pricing is a change in principle and Paragraph 27 of APB 20 indicates that a change from LIFO to

another method of inventory pricing should be accounted for by retroactive restatement.

5. (A,X) While a change from LIFO to another method should be accounted for by retroactive restatement, other changes in inventory pricing are accounted for in the regular manner, that is, by showing the "cumulative effect" (net of tax) as of the beginning of the year of change in the income statement.

6. (C,Y) APB 20, para. 13, indicates that a change from an accounting principle that is not generally accepted (e.g., the cash method) to one that is generally accepted (the accrual method) is a correction of an error. Per APB 9, these require retroactive restatement.

7. (C,Y) See solution to previous question.

8. (A,X) A change in the method of depreciation constitutes a change in accounting principle. Normally, changes in accounting principle must be recognized using the cumulative effect approach.

9. (D,Z) APB 20, para. 6, indicates that initial adoption of an accounting principle in recognition of events or transactions occurring for the first time is not a change in principle.

10. (D,Y) APB 20, para. 8, indicates that a characteristic of a change in accounting principle "is that it concerns a choice from among two or more generally accepted accounting principles" and that "modification of an accounting principle necessitated by transactions or events that are clearly different in substance from those previously occurring" is not a change in accounting principles. With a 30% interest in Worth, Inc., and a member on Worth's board of directors, Quo is in a different position than it was before. The cost method (assuming that was appropriate in the past and that there are no problems with SFAS 115 relating to "marketable securities") may have been appropriate then but would not be acceptable, now assuming Quo has considerable influence over the investee. Therefore, there is no change in accounting principle from one that is acceptable to one that is also acceptable. Only the equity method would be acceptable. Hence D., APB 18, para. 19(m), indicates that when "an investment qualifies for the use of the equity method, the investment, results of operations (current and prior periods presented)...should be adjusted retroactively."

SOLUTION 11-4 FINANCIAL STATEMENT CATEGORIES

1. $73,000 (B) Gains or losses on the extinguishment of debt are generally reported as extraordinary items. The bonds are redeemed for $1,020,000 ($1,000,000 x 1.02). The amortization of the bond discount at June 30, 1994 must be added to the carrying amount of the bonds on January 1, 1995 before the gain or loss on extinguishment may be computed. The amortization of the discount is computed as follows:

$ 940,000 x .10 x 6/12	$ 47,000
$1,000,000 x .08 x 6/12	(40,000)
Amortization of discount	$ 7,000

The carrying value at the time of redemption was $947,000 ($940,000 + $7,000). The excess of the price paid to redeem the bonds ($1,020,000) over the carrying value ($947,000) is the loss on the bond redemption of $73,000.

2. $100,000 (C)

	Straight-line	Sum-of-the years'-digits
1991	$100,000	$166,667
1992	100,000	133,333
1993	100,000	100,000
Total	$300,000	$400,000

The straight-line depreciation is computed for each year as follows: ($520,000–$20,000)/5 = $100,000. The sum-of-the-years'-digits depreciation is computed as follows:

1991	($520,000 – $20,000)	x	5/15	$166,667
1992	($520,000 – $20,000)	x	4/15	$133,333
1993	($520,000 – $20,000)	x	3/15	$100,000

The difference between the two totals ($100,000) is the cumulative effect of the change in accounting principle on retained earnings at the beginning of the period of change.

3. $125,000 loss (A) In 1993, the loss was probable according to the attorney with an estimated loss between $250,000 and $750,000. Since the scenario given does not state that any amount within the range is more probable than any other amount, under FIN 14 the lowest amount of the loss in the estimated range should be recorded. Therefore, $250,000 would have been accrued in the 1993 financial statements. When the actual loss realized was $375,000 in 1994, the accrued liability of $250,000 would be debited, a current period loss (reported in income from continuing operations) for $125,000 would be debited, and a credit would be made to cash for $375,000.

4. $10,000 loss (A) The holding loss to be reported in income from continuing operations at December 31, 1994 is $10,000. The cost of

securities I and II is $360,000 ($125,000 + $235,000), while the fair value at December 31, 1994 is $350,000 ($145,000 + $205,000). The difference between the two is the holding loss. The securities are classified as trading because they were bought and held to sell in the near term. Since the securities are trading securities, the holding loss is reported in income from continuing operations.

5. $255,000 loss (B)

Book value of the warehouse	$ 470,000
Book value of the equipment	250,000
Book value of the inventory	535,000
Total loss	1,255,000
Less: Insurance proceeds	(1,000,000)
Extraordinary loss	$ 255,000

The loss is extraordinary because of the unusual and infrequent (this is the first hurricane ever to hit this area) nature of the event causing the loss. The book value of the inventory is used in the computation of the loss.

6. $41,000 loss (E)   The adjustment due to translation is the difference between the net assets at December 31, 1994 after the remeasurement ($429,000) and the net assets at December 31, 1994 translated for the exchange rate at the balance sheet date ($388,000), or $41,000. The foreign currency translation adjustment should be reported in other comprehensive income. Any gain or loss on the *remeasurement* of the financial statements should be reflected in the income statement. (See Ch. 17)

PROBLEM/ESSAY SOLUTIONS

SOLUTION 11-5 STATEMENT OF INCOME AND CHANGES IN EQUITY ACCOUNTS (10 points)

There are a number of weaknesses noted in the Statement of Income and Changes in Retained Earnings.

The first weakness noted is the **heading**. An income statement reports the results of an entity's earning activities for an accounting period. Accordingly, the statement should be titled **"For the Year Ended December 31, 1995."**

The **Revenues and gains** section improperly includes several items. **"Purchase discounts"** should reduce the cost of purchases or cost of goods sold. It is not theoretically sound to consider as revenue savings on purchases. Also, under the allowance method of accounting for uncollectible accounts, **recovery of accounts receivable written off in previous years** should be credited to the allowance for uncollectible accounts.

The **Expenses and losses** section also contains errors. **Sales returns and allowances** should be offset against or deducted from gross sales. **Cash dividends** are not an expense, but should be shown as a reduction of retained earnings.

Discontinued operations includes a loss that does not meet the criteria for discontinued operations. The **loss on disposal of discontinued styles** should be classified as **ordinary and usual** and be reported in the Expenses and losses section of the income statement. An **ordinary loss should not be shown net of tax effect**.

Income before extraordinary item should be shown before the extraordinary item. The caption for the extraordinary item is properly positioned on the income statement, but contains two errors. First, **early extinguishment of debt**, incorrectly reported under "Revenues and gains," is always reported as an extraordinary item, net of tax effect.

Second, the **error** discovered from the previous year is not an extraordinary item, but should be treated as a **prior period adjustment**. Accordingly, the **retained earnings balance** at the beginning of the year should be **adjusted by the amount of the error correction, net of tax effect**, and the income statement should include a subtotal titled **"Retained earnings at beginning of year as restated."** **Cash dividends declared** should be deducted from this subtotal.

Income taxes and net income should be shown elsewhere on the Statement. **Income taxes** should be deducted in arriving at income before extraordinary item, either included as the last item in the expenses section or shown as a separate line item before income before extraordinary item. **Net income** should be reported immediately before beginning retained earnings.

Note: This essay would not differ appreciably depending on use of APB 30 or SFAS 144.

SOLUTION 11-6 EXTRAORDINARY ITEMS/ DISCONTINUED OPERATIONS (APB 30)

a. Hillside should report the extraordinary item **separately, net of applicable income taxes, below**

the **continuing operations** section in the income statement. Exclusion of extraordinary items from the results of continuing operations is intended to produce a measure of income from continuing operations that is useful in **projecting future operating cash flows**.

b. Hillside should report the discontinued operations **separately** in the 1997 income statement immediately **below income from continuing operations**. Discontinued operations should be comprised of **two categories**, with each category reported **net of income taxes**:

- Loss from operations of the discontinued segment from the beginning of the year to the measurement date.
- **Loss on disposal** of the discontinued segment, including the **provision** for **operating losses** during the **phase-out period**.

c. Hillside should include the costs incurred to relocate employees in the **loss on disposal** of discontinued segment in its 1997 income statement. These costs are a **direct result** of the **commitment to dispose of its segment**.

SOLUTION 11-7 SEGMENTAL REPORTING

a. The objective of disclosures about segments of an enterprise is to provide information about the different types of business activities in which the enterprise engages and the different economic environments in which it operates. These objectives include helping stakeholders better understand the enterprise's performance, better assess it prospects for future net cash flows, and make more informed judgments about the enterprise as a whole.

b. Barnet should use the management approach in determining what segments to report. This approach is based on the way that management organizes the segments within the enterprise for making operating decisions and assessing performance.

The structure of the enterprise, within materiality limits, should be considered. Operating segments that provide 10% or more of combined revenue, internal and external, or 10% or more of combined operating profits for segments not reporting a loss, or 10% or more of combined reported losses for segments that reported a loss should be included.

SOLUTION 11-8 CASH BASIS TO ACCRUAL BASIS

a.

Baron Flowers
WORKSHEET TO CONVERT TRIAL BALANCE TO ACCRUAL BASIS
December 31, 1994

Account title	Cash basis Dr.	Cash basis Cr.	Adjustments Dr.		Adjustments Cr.		Accrual Basis* Dr.*	Accrual Basis* Cr.*
Cash	25,600						25,600	
Accounts rec'ble, 12/31/93	16,200		(1)	15,800			32,000	
Inventory, 12/31/93	62,000		(4)	10,800			72,800	
Furniture & fixtures	118,200						118,200	
Land improvements	45,000						45,000	
Accumulated depreciation & amortization, 12/31/93		32,400			(6)	14,250		46,650
Accounts payable, 12/31/93		17,000			(3)	13,500		30,500
Baron, Drawings			(9)	61,000			61,000	
Baron, Capital, 12/31/93		124,600	(7)	2,000	(5)	2,600		125,200
Allowance for uncoll accounts					(2)	3,800		3,800
Prepaid insurance			(5)	2,900			2,900	
Accrued expenses					(7)	3,100		3,100
Est liability from lawsuit					(8)	50,000		50,000
Sales		653,000			(1)	15,800		668,800
Purchases	305,100		(3)	13,500			318,600	
Salaries	174,000				(9)	48,000	126,000	
Payroll taxes	12,400		(7)	500			12,900	
Insurance	8,700				(5)	300	8,400	
Rent	34,200						34,200	
Utilities	12,600		(7)	600			13,200	
Living expenses	13,000				(9)	13,000		
Income summary—inventory			(4)	62,000	(4)	72,800		10,800
Uncollectible accounts			(2)	3,800			3,800	
Depreciation & amortization			(6)	14,250			14,250	
Estimated loss from lawsuit			(8)	50,000			50,000	
	827,000	827,000	237,150		237,150		938,850	938,850

* Completion of these columns is not required.

Explanations of Adjustments

[1] To convert 1994 sales to accrual basis.
Accounts receivable balances:

December 31, 1994	$32,000
December 31, 1993	(16,200)
Increase in sales	**$15,800**

[2] To record provision for uncollectible accounts.

[3] To convert 1994 purchases to accrual basis.
Accounts payable balances:

December 31, 1994	$30,500
December 31, 1993	(17,000)
Increase in purchases	**$13,500**

[4] To record increase in inventory from 12/31/93 to 12/31/94.
Inventory balances:

December 31, 1994	$72,800
December 31, 1993	(62,000)
Increase in inventory	**$10,800**

[5] To adjust prepaid insurance.
Prepaid balances:

December 31, 1994 ($8,700 x 4/12)	$2,900
December 31, 1993 ($7,800 x 4/12)	(2,600)
Decrease in insurance expense	**$ 300**

[6] To record 1994 depreciation and amortization expense.

Cost of leasehold improvement	$45,000
Estimated life	15 years
Amortization ($45,000 x 1/15 x 9/12)	2,250
Depreciation expense on fixtures and equipment	12,000
	$14,250

[7] To convert expenses to accrual basis.

	Balances December 31,		Increase in expenses
	1994	1993	
Utilities	$1,500	$ 900	$ 600
Payroll taxes	1,600	1,100	500
	$3,100	$2,000	$ 1,100

[8] To record lawsuit liability at 12/31/94.

Attorney's estimate of probable loss	$ 300,000
Amount covered by insurance	(250,000)
Baron's estimated liability	$ 50,000

[9] To record Baron's drawings for 1994.

Salary ($4,000 x 12)	$ 48,000
Living expenses	13,000
	$ 61,000

b.

To: Baron Flowers
From: Muir
Re: Accrual basis financial statements

You have asked me to explain why the bank would require financial statements prepared on the accrual basis instead of the cash basis. The bank is concerned about your **ability to repay the loan**. To **assess** that ability, it wants information about your earnings for the period, total assets, and all claims on those assets. This information about your enterprise's performance and financial position is provided **more completely** by accrual basis financial statements than by cash-basis financial statements.

Under the cash basis, **revenues are recognized when received** and **expenses when paid**. Earnings can be manipulated by the timing of cash receipts and disbursements. Accrual basis accounting, while grounded in cash flows, reports transactions and other events with cash consequences at the time the transactions and events occur. Revenues and expenses are reported in the **accounting period benefited** and reflect receivables and payables, not just what the enterprise was able to collect or chose to pay.

SOLUTION 11-9 ACCOUNTING CHANGES

a. A change from the LIFO inventory method to the FIFO inventory method is a **change in accounting principle**. Windsor should **restate the 1990 financial statements**, including adjustment for the **effect on January 1, 1990, retained earnings**, as if the **FIFO** method had been **adopted** at the **beginning of 1990**. The **nature and justification** for the change in inventory method should be **disclosed** in the **notes to** the **1991 financial statements**. The **effects** of the change on **income statement components** should be **disclosed for all periods presented**.

b. Windsor's change from sum-of-the-years'-digits depreciation method for all future machinery acquisitions is a **change in accounting principle**. The **nature and justification** for the change in depreciation methods should be **disclosed in the notes** to the **1991 comparative financial statements**. The **1990** financial statements are **unaffected** by the change, but the effects of the change on 1991 income components should be disclosed.

c. A change from the cash basis of vacation pay expense recognition to the accrual basis is a **change** from an **accounting principle** that is **not generally accepted** to **one** that is **generally accepted**. Such a change is considered an **error correction**. Windsor should **restate** the **1990 financial statements**, including adjustment for the **effect on January 1, 1990, retained earnings**, to correct prior errors. Windsor should **disclose** the **nature and details** of the corrections in **notes to the 1991 financial statements**.

SOLUTION 11-10 MULTIPLE-STEP INCOME STATEMENT

Probe Co.
INCOME STATEMENT
For the Year Ended December 31, 1993

Sales		$2,420,000
Cost of sales		1,863,000
Gross profit		557,000
Selling and administrative expenses	$220,000	
Depreciation	88,000	308,000
Operating income		249,000
Other income (expenses):		
Interest income	14,000	
Interest expense	(46,000)	
Loss on sale of equipment	(7,000)	(39,000)
Income before income tax and extraordinary item		210,000
Income tax:		
Current	45,000 [1]	
Deferred	12,000 [2]	57,000
Income before extraordinary item		153,000
Extraordinary item:		
Gain on extinguishment of debt, net of income taxes of $27,000		63,000
Net income		$ 216,000
Earnings per share:		
Earnings before extraordinary item		$ 1.275 [3]
Extraordinary item		.525
Net income		$ 1.800

Explanation of Amounts:

[1]	Current income tax expense:	
	Income before income tax and extraordinary item	$ 210,000
	Differences between financial statement and taxable income	(60,000)
	Income subject to tax	150,000
	Income tax rate	x 30%
	Income tax excluding extraordinary item	$ 45,000
[2]	Deferred income tax expense:	
	Cumulative temporary differences—12/31/93	$ 180,000
	Income tax rate	x 30%
	Deferred tax liability—12/31/93	54,000
	Deferred tax liability—12/31/92	(42,000)
	Deferred tax expense for 1993	$ 12,000
[3]	Earnings per share:	
	Weighted average number of shares outstanding for 1993:	
	January thru March 60,000 x 3	180,000
	April thru December 140,000 x 9	1,260,000
	Total	1,440,000
		÷ 12
		120,000
	Income before extraordinary item	$ 153,000
	Earnings per share ($153,000 ÷ 120,000)	$ 1.275

SELECT HOT•SPOTS™ VIDEO DESCRIPTIONS

CPA 2080 Leases & Pensions

Provides comprehensive coverage of operating and capital leases, sales type and direct financing capital leases, and sale/leaseback transactions. Employers' accounting for pensions, settlements, curtailments, and termination benefits, postretirement benefits, and postemployment benefits are thoroughly explained. Learn how to calculate the net periodic costs and the assets and liabilities related to pensions and other benefits, as well as the disclosures required.

CPA 3265 Owners' Equity

Provides comprehensive coverage of the elements of stockholder's equity, the effect of other comprehensive income on stockholders' equity, stockholders' rights, issuance and retirement of capital stock, treasury stock—both the cost and par value methods, retained earnings, dividends, stock rights, stock as employee compensation, ESOPs, disclosure requirements...and more!

CPA 3220 Revenue Recognition & Income Statement Presentation

Learn about comprehensive income, what is included, and how it is presented. Bob Monette provides comprehensive coverage of the components of the income statement, what is included in each, and how they are presented in the financial statements. In-depth coverage includes accounting for long-term contracts, installment sales, discontinued operations, extraordinary items, prior period adjustments, changes in accounting principles, changes in estimates, changes in entities...and more!

Call our customer representatives toll-free at 1 (800) 874-7877 for more details about videos.

Grade Review & Appeal

Fee-based grade review and grade appeal services are available. Through them, candidates may request a review and appeal their grades. Although the probability that a candidate's grade will change significantly because of a review or an appeal is extremely low, candidates may decide to review or appeal their grades. Contact your jurisdiction's board of accountancy or NASBA (www.nasba.org) for more information on either service.

_____

CHAPTER 12

REVENUE & EXPENSE RECOGNITION: SPECIAL AREAS

CHAPTER 12

REVENUE & EXPENSE RECOGNITION: SPECIAL AREAS

I. INSTALLMENT METHOD

A. APPLICABILITY

Under GAAP, revenues are usually recognized when two conditions are met: (a) the earnings process is complete or virtually complete, and (b) an exchange has taken place. Thus, revenues are generally recognized at the point of sale. There are several exceptions to this rule. The installment method is an exception to this because it allows revenue to be deferred and recognized each year in proportion to the receivables collected during that year. APB 10, par. 12, states that the installment method of accounting for sales is **not** acceptable unless circumstances exist such that collection of the sales price is "not reasonably assured." APB 10 also permits use of the installment method when receivables are collected over an extended period of time and when there is no reasonable basis for estimating the degree of collectibility.

B. COMPUTATION

Income recognized using the installment method of accounting generally equals cash collected multiplied by the gross profit percentage applicable to those sales. Selling and administrative expenses are not used to compute the gross profit rate. Receivable accounts and deferred profit accounts must be kept separately for each year because the gross profit rate will often vary from year to year. Where an installment receivable extends beyond one year, it should be recorded at the present value of the payments discounted at the market interest rate. At any time after the sale, the installment receivables' balance will be the present value of the remaining monthly payments discounted at the market interest rate at the time of the exchange. The installment method of accounting can be easily understood by working through Example 1.

EXAMPLE 1 ♦ INSTALLMENT METHOD

The Thomas Equipment Company reports income using the installment method of accounting and uses a perpetual inventory system. Installment sales during 20X8 amounted to $400,000 ($120,000 + $280,000). The following information is available:

Year of sale	Gross profit percentage	Installment receivables on Jan. 1, 20X8	Collected during 20X8	Installment receivables on Dec. 31, 20X8
20X6	46%	$ 60,000	$ 60,000	--
20X7	42%	100,000	68,000	$ 32,000
20X8	40%	--	120,000	280,000

REQUIRED: Determine

1. The realized gross profit on installment sales during 20X8 from all sales.

2. The balance in the deferred gross profit account at December 31, 20X8.

SOLUTION:

1. The realized gross profit on installment sales is computed as follows:

Year of sale	Gross profit percentage		Collected during 20X8		Realized gross profit
20X6	46%	x	$ 60,000	=	$ 27,600
20X7	42%	x	68,000	=	28,560
20X8	40%	x	120,000	=	48,000
					$104,160

(continued on next page)

2. The balance in the deferred gross profit account is computed as follows:

Year of sale	Installment receivables on Dec. 31, 20X8		Gross profit percentage		Deferred gross profit
20X7	$ 32,000	x	42%	=	$ 13,440
20X8	280,000	x	40%	=	112,000
					$125,440

II. COST RECOVERY METHOD

A. APPLICABILITY

Like the installment method, the cost recovery method of revenue recognition is **not** generally accepted. Under exceptional circumstances, however, the cost recovery method may be used. The cost recovery method may be used where collectibility of proceeds is doubtful, where an investment is very speculative in nature, and/or where the final sale price is to be determined by future events.

B. COMPUTATION

Under the cost recovery method, all amounts collected are treated as a recoupment of the cost of the item sold, until the entire cost associated with the transaction has been recovered. Only at this point is profit recognized. The cost recovery method is the most conservative method of revenue recognition. This method is used when the uncertainty of collection is so great that use of the installment method is precluded.

EXAMPLE 2 ♦ COST RECOVERY METHOD

On January 2, 20X1, Old Mine Co. sold a gold mine that had become unprofitable to Golddiggers, Inc., a newly incorporated venture that hoped to wring additional profits from the mine by use of a revolutionary—but yet unproven—method of extraction. At the time of the sale, the gold mine had a carrying amount of $450,000 in Old Mine's books. The sales agreement called for a $100,000 down payment and two notes of $200,000 bearing interest of 10% with one note payable, including accrued interest, due on January 2, 20X2 and one note payable, including accrued interest, due on January 2, 20X3. Because of the extreme uncertainty concerning the eventual collection of the notes' proceeds, Old Mine appropriately accounted for this transaction under the cost recovery method.

REQUIRED: Assuming the notes were paid when due, including interest and principal, determine Old Mine's income from this transaction for the years ending December 31, 20X1, 20X2, and 20X3. Provide appropriate journal entries.

SOLUTION:

Year	Amount collected	Unrecovered cost (20X0: $450,000)	Deferred profit Dr. (Cr.)	Recognized profit (Cr.)
20X1	$100,000	$350,000	($50,000)	$ 0
20X2	220,000	130,000	(20,000)	0
20X3	242,000	0	70,000	(112,000)

Journal Entries:

20X1:	Cash	100,000	
	Notes Receivable	400,000	
	Gold Mine (net)		450,000
	Deferred Profit		50,000

(continued on next page)

20X2:	Cash [$200,000 + ($200,000 x 10%)]	220,000	
	Notes Receivable		200,000
	Deferred Profit		20,000
20X3:	Cash [$200,000 + ($220,000 x 10%)]	242,000	
	Deferred Profit	70,000	
	Recognized Profit		112,000
	Notes Receivable		200,000

III. COMPLETION OF PRODUCTION METHOD

A. APPLICABILITY

Revenue is sometimes recognized at completion of the production activity. The recognition of revenue at completion of production is justified *only* if certain conditions are present. The necessary conditions are:

1. There must be a relatively stable market for the product;

2. Marketing costs must be nominal; and

3. The units must be homogeneous.

B. EXAMPLES

The *three* necessary conditions are rarely present except in the case of certain precious metals and agricultural products.

IV. REVENUE RECOGNITION WHEN RIGHT OF RETURN EXISTS (SFAS 48)

A. TIME OF SALE

Revenue from sales when the buyer has the right to return the product should be recognized at the *time of sale* only if *all* the following conditions are met:

1. The seller's price to the buyer is substantially fixed or determinable at the date of sale;

2. The buyer has paid the seller, or the buyer is obligated to pay the seller, and the obligation is *not contingent on resale of the product;*

3. The buyer's obligation to the seller would not be changed in the event of theft, physical destruction, or damage of the product;

4. The buyer acquiring the product for resale has economic substance apart from that provided by the seller;

5. The seller does not have significant obligations for future performance to directly bring about resale of the product by the buyer; and

6. The amount of future returns can be reasonably estimated.

B. DEFERRAL

If these conditions are **not** met, revenue (and cost of sales) must be recognized when the return privilege has substantially expired or when these conditions are subsequently met, whichever occurs first.

C. COSTS OR LOSSES

Any *costs or losses* that may be expected in connection with sales revenue recognized at the time of sale, must be accrued (see also SFAS 5, *Accounting for Contingencies*).

V. LONG-TERM CONSTRUCTION CONTRACTS (ARB 45)

A. RECOMMENDATION

Due to the length of time implicit in long-term construction contracts, significant problems often arise concerning the measurement and timing of income recognition. The two methods most commonly used in these types of contracts are the completed-contract method and the percentage-of-completion method. The use of the percentage-of-completion method is recommended when costs to complete and extent of progress can be reasonably estimated. If no dependable estimates can be made or inherent hazards are present, the completed-contract method is preferable.

B. COMPLETED-CONTRACT METHOD

No income is recognized on the contract until it is completed or substantially completed and the work accepted. However, if at any point expected contract costs exceed the contract price, losses are recognized immediately and in full in the current period.

1. **BALANCE SHEET PRESENTATION** Excess of accumulated costs over related progress billings should be shown as a current asset on the balance sheet, while an excess of accumulated progress billings over related costs should be shown as a current liability. Contracts should be separated to accurately segregate asset and liability contracts.

2. **ADVANTAGE** The principal advantage of the completed-contract method is that it is based on results as finally determined rather than on estimates for unperformed work which may involve unforeseen costs and possible losses.

3. **DISADVANTAGE** The principal disadvantage is it does not reflect current performance when the life of the contract extends over several periods and thus diminishes the interperiod comparability of the financial statements.

C. PERCENTAGE-OF-COMPLETION METHOD

Income may be recognized as work on the contract progresses. The amount of income recognized in the period is added to Construction in Progress.

1. **INCOME RECOGNITION** Income should be recognized on the basis of either of the following:

    a. The percentage derived from incurred costs to date over total expected costs; or

$$\left[\frac{Actual\ cost\ to\ date}{Estimated\ total\ cost} \times \begin{array}{c} Total\ estimated \\ contract\ income \end{array} \right] - \begin{array}{c} Income \\ previously \\ recognized \end{array} = \begin{array}{c} Income \\ to\ be \\ recognized \end{array}$$

    b. Some other measure of progress toward completion as may be appropriate under the circumstances. Thus, the percentage-of-completion method may be based on estimates of completion to date developed by architects or engineers.

2. **PROGRESS BILLINGS** *Progress billings* and *collections on progress billings* are **not** generally accepted as a method of recognizing income because they often do not bear a meaningful relationship to the work performed on the contract. Typically, billings may be accelerated in the early stages of the contract to provide the contractor with the working capital needed to begin performance. If income were recognized on progress billings, it would be possible for a contractor to materially distort the contractor's income merely by rendering progress billings without regard to any degree of progress on the contract. Progress Billings is a contra account to Construction in Progress.

3. **LOSS RECOGNITION** When current estimates of total contract costs indicate a loss, the loss should be recognized immediately and in full in the current period.

4. **CURRENT ASSETS/LIABILITIES** Each contract may give rise to a current asset or liability.

    a. An excess of costs incurred and income recognized over progress billings should be reported as a *current asset.*

    b. An excess of progress billings over related costs and income recognized constitutes a *current liability.*

    c. Current assets and current liabilities pertaining to two or more contracts should not be netted out for financial statement presentation.

5. **ADVANTAGES** The principal advantages of the percentage-of-completion method are the following:

    a. Periodic recognition of income as work is performed thus enhancing the interperiod comparability of the financial statements; and

    b. Reflection of the status of uncompleted contracts provided through current estimates of completion costs.

6. **DISADVANTAGE** The principal disadvantage is the necessity of relying on estimates of ultimate contract costs and of consequently accruing income based upon those estimates.

EXAMPLE 3 ♦ PERCENTAGE-OF-COMPLETION VS. COMPLETED-CONTRACT

On January 1, 20X1, Estimator, Inc. entered into two $1,800,000 fixed-price contracts to construct office buildings. The estimated time for both projects was three years.

	20X1	20X2	20X3
Contract A			
Incurred costs to date	$ 250,000	$ 320,000	$1,530,000
Est. costs to complete	1,250,000	1,280,000	0
Total estimated costs	1,500,000	1,600,000	1,530,000
Billed during year	220,000	1,130,000	450,000
Collected during year	180,000	1,040,000	580,000
Contract B			
Incurred costs to date	$ 250,000	$ 320,000	$1,810,000
Est. costs to complete	1,250,000	1,490,000	0
Total estimated costs	1,500,000	1,810,000	1,810,000
Billed during year	220,000	1,130,000	450,000
Collected during year	180,000	1,040,000	580,000

REQUIRED: Prepare the journal entries and determine income (loss) recognized in all three years for both contracts under the percentage-of-completion method and the completed-contract method (in 1,000s).

SOLUTION:

Percentage-of-Completion Entries
1. To record the costs of construction.
2. To record progress billings.
3. To record collections.
4. To recognize revenue and gross profit.
5. To record the completion of the contract.

(continued on next page)

Contract A		20X1		20X2		20X3	
1.	Construction in Progress	250		70		1,210	
	Cash (or Accounts Payable)		250		70		1,210
2.	Accounts Receivable	220		1,130		450	
	Progress Billings		220		1,130		450
3.	Cash	180		1,040		580	
	Accounts Receivable		180		1,040		580
4.(X1)	Construction Expenses	250					
	Construction in Progress	50 [1]					
	Revenue from LT Contracts		300				
4.(X2)	Construction Expenses			70			
	Construction in Progress			10 [2]			
	Revenue from LT Contracts			60			
4.(X3)	Construction Expenses					1,210	
	Construction in Progress					230 [3]	
	Revenue from LT Contracts						1,440
5.	Progress Billings					1,800	
	Construction in Progress						1,800 [4]

[1] (250 / 1,500) x [1,800 - (250 + 1,250)] - 0 = 50
[2] (320 / 1,600) x [1,800 - (320 + 1,280)] - 50 = -10
[3] (1,530 / 1,530) x [1,800 - 1,530] - (50-10) = 230
[4] 250 + 50 + 70 - 10 + 230 + 1,210 = 1,800

Contract B		20X1		20X2		20X3	
1.	Construction in Progress	250		70		1,490	
	Cash (or Accounts Payable)		250		70		1,490
2.	Accounts Receivable	220		1,130		450	
	Progress Billings		220		1,130		450
3.	Cash	180		1,040		580	
	Accounts Receivable		180		1,040		580
4.(X1)	Construction Expenses	250					
	Construction in Progress	50 [1]					
	Revenue from LT Contracts		300				
4.(X2)	Construction Expenses			70			
	Construction in Progress			60 [2]			
	Revenue from LT Contracts			10			
4.(X3)	Construction Expenses					1,490	
	Revenue from LT Contracts						1,490
5.	Progress Billings					1,800	
	Construction in Progress						1,800 [3]

[1] (250 / 1,500) x [1,800 – (250 + 1,250)] – 0 = 50
[2] Reverse recognized profit and recognize estimated loss in full. –50 + (1,800 – 1,810) = –60
[3] 250 + 50 + 70 – 60 + 1,490 = 1,800

(continued on next page)

Completed-Contract Entries

1, 2, and 3. The entries to record the costs of construction, progress billings, and collections are the same as entries 1, 2, and 3 for the percentage-of-completion method for both contracts.

4. To record the contract loss first evident in 20X2 on Contract B.

5. To recognize revenue and gross profit and record the completion of the contract.

		20X1	20X2	20X3
Contract A				
5.	Construction Expenses			1,530
	Construction in Progress			1,530
	Progress Billings			1,800
	Revenue from LT Contracts			1,800
Contract B				
4.	Loss From LT Contracts		10	
	Construction in Progress		10	
5.	Construction Expenses			1,800
	Construction in Progress			1,800
	Progress Billings			1,800
	Revenue from LT Contracts			1,800

Income (Loss) Recognized

Contract A	20X1	20X2	20X3	Total
% of Completion	$50	<$10>	$230	$270
Completed Contract	0	0	270	270

Contract B				
% of Completion	50	<60>	0	<10>
Completed Contract	0	<10>	0	<10>

NOTE: Contract A has a loss in year 20X2, but overall the contract is profitable. Contract B has an overall loss, which is recognized in 20X2, the year the loss is evident.

VI. CONSIGNMENTS

A. DEFINITION

A consignment is a transfer of goods from the owner (consignor) to another person (consignee) who acts as a sales agent for the owner in a principal-agent relationship. The transfer is **not** a sale and the consignee never has title to the goods. When the consignee sells the goods, title passes directly from the consignor to the third party buyer.

B. REVENUE RECOGNITION

Consignment sales revenue is recognized at the time of the sale at the sales price. The commission paid to the consignee is reported as a selling expense; it is **not** netted against sales revenue.

EXAMPLE 4 ♦ CONSIGNMENT SALE

On October 10, 20X7, Dunn Co. consigned 50 freezers to Taylor Co. for sale at $1,000 each and paid $800 in transportation costs. On December 30, 20X7, Taylor reported the sale of 20 freezers and remitted $18,000. The remittance was net of the agreed 10% commission.

REQUIRED: Determine the amount Dunn should recognize as consignment sales revenue for 20X7.

(continued on next page)

SOLUTION: Consignment sales revenue is recognized at the time of the sale at the sales price. Thus, consignment sales revenue of $20,000 (20 freezers x $1,000 sales price) should be reported in 20X7. The 10% commission should be reported as a selling expense; it should <u>not</u> be netted against sales revenue. The following journal entry would be used to record the consignment sale:

Cash	18,000	
Consignment Sales Commissions	2,000	
Consignment Sales Revenues		20,000

VII. FRANCHISE FEE REVENUE (SFAS 45)

A. INITIAL FEES

1. **INCOME RECOGNITION** Initial franchise fees from franchise sales ordinarily must be recognized (with provision for estimated uncollectible amounts) when all material services or conditions relating to the sale have been substantially performed or satisfied by the franchisor. Services are considered to be substantially performed when

    a. The franchisor has no remaining obligation or intent to refund any cash received or forgive any unpaid notes or receivables.

    b. Substantially all *initial* services of the franchisor required by the franchise agreement have been performed.

    c. No other material conditions or obligations related to the determination of substantial performance exist.

2. **INSTALLMENT AND COST RECOVERY METHODS** Installment or cost recovery accounting methods may be used to account for franchise fee revenue *only* when revenue is collectible over an extended period and no reasonable basis exists for estimating collectibility.

3. **DEFERRED INCOME** If it is probable that *continuing franchise fees* will not cover the cost of the continuing services to be provided by the franchisor and also allow reasonable profit, then a portion of the *original franchise fee* should be deferred and amortized over the life of the franchise. The deferred amount should be enough to cover future costs and provide a reasonable profit on the continuing services.

B. CONTINUING FEES

1. **REVENUE RECOGNITION** Report as revenue when the fees are earned and become receivable from the franchisee.

2. **EXPENSE RECOGNITION** Costs related to continuing franchise fees should be expensed as incurred.

C. COSTS

1. **DIRECT COSTS** Direct incremental costs relating to franchise sales ordinarily should be deferred until the related revenue is recognized; however, the deferred costs must not exceed anticipated revenue less estimated additional related costs.

2. **INDIRECT COSTS** Indirect costs of a regular and recurring nature irrespective of the level of sales should be expensed as incurred.

3. **MATCH COSTS WITH RELATED REVENUE** Costs yet to be incurred should be accrued and charged against income no later than the period in which the related revenue is recognized.

EXAMPLE 5 ◆ FRANCHISE FEE REVENUE

Bigger Burger, Inc., sold a fast food restaurant franchise to Ronald M. Donald. The sale agreement, signed on January 2, 20X4, called for a $30,000 down payment plus two $10,000 annual payments, due January 2, 20X5 and January 2, 20X6, representing the value of initial franchise services rendered by Bigger Burger. The agreement required the franchisee to pay 5% of its gross revenues to the franchisor; deemed sufficient to cover the cost and a reasonable profit margin on continuing franchise services to be performed by Bigger Burger. The restaurant opened early in 20X4, and its sales for the year amounted to $500,000.

REQUIRED: Assuming a 10% interest rate, determine Bigger Burger's 20X4 total revenue from the Donald franchise.

Solution:

Initial franchise fee:		
Down payment	$30,000	
P.V. of installments ($10,000 x 1.7355)	17,355	$47,355
5% of gross sales (.05 x $500,000)		25,000
Interest income ($17,355 x .10)		1,735
20X4 Total Revenue		$74,090

VIII. ROYALTIES

A. ACCRUAL BASIS

Royalty revenue and royalty expense are recognized under the rules of accrual accounting.

1. REVENUE RECOGNITION Royalty revenue is recognized in the period(s) the royalties are earned. Royalties received in advance are not recognized as revenue at the date of the royalty agreement.

2. EXPENSE RECOGNITION Royalty expense is recognized in the period the royalties are incurred. Royalties paid in advance are not recognized as an expense at the date of the royalty agreement.

B. COMPUTATION

In general, the amount of royalty revenue or expense to recognize during a period is computed by multiplying the period's sales applicable to the royalty agreement by the royalty percentage.

EXAMPLE 6 ◆ ROYALTIES

On January 2, 20X7, Shaw Company sold the copyright to a book to Poe Publishers, Inc. for royalties of 20% of future sales. On the same date, Poe paid Shaw a royalty advance of $100,000 to be applied against royalties for 20X8 sales. On September 30, 20X7, Poe made a $42,000 royalty remittance to Shaw for sales in the six-month period ended June 30, 20X7. In January 20X8, before issuance of its 20X7 financial statements, Shaw learned that Poe's sales of the book totaled $250,000 for the last half of 20X7.

REQUIRED: Determine how much royalty revenue Shaw should report in 20X7.

SOLUTION: The $100,000 advance to be applied against royalties for 20X8 sales is <u>not</u> used to compute royalty revenue. Neither royalty revenue nor royalty expense is recognized on the cash basis.

Royalties for Jan. 1 - June 30, 20X7 (paid Sept. 30, 20X7)	$42,000
Royalties for July 1 - Dec. 31, 20X7 ($250,000 x 20%)	50,000
Royalty revenue for 20X7	$92,000

CHAPTER 12—REVENUE & EXPENSE RECOGNITION: SPECIAL AREAS

PROBLEM 12-1 MULTIPLE CHOICE QUESTIONS (80 to 100 minutes)

1. Bear Co., which began operations on January 2, 1997, appropriately uses the installment sales method of accounting. The following information is available for 1997:

Installment sales	$1,400,000
Realized gross profit on installment sales	240,000
Gross profit percentage on sales	40%

For the year ended December 31, 1997, what amounts should Bear report as accounts receivable and deferred gross profit?

	Accounts receivable	Deferred gross profit
a.	$600,000	$320,000
b.	$600,000	$360,000
c.	$800,000	$320,000
d.	$800,000	$560,000

(11/98, FAR, #8, 6735)

2. Since there is no reasonable basis for estimating the degree of collectibility, Astor Co. uses the installment method of revenue recognition for the following sales:

	1993	1992
Sales	$900,000	$600,000
Collections from:		
1992 sales	100,000	200,000
1993 sales	300,000	--
Accounts written off:		
1992 sales	150,000	50,000
1993 sales	50,000	--
Gross profit percentage	40%	30%

What amount should Astor report as deferred gross profit in its December 31, 1993 balance sheet for the 1992 and 1993 sales?
a. $150,000
b. $160,000
c. $225,000
d. $250,000

(5/94, FAR, #23, 4838)

3. Luge Co., which began operations on January 2, 1992, appropriately uses the installment sales method of accounting. The following information is available for 1992:

Installment accounts receivable, December 31, 1992	$800,000
Deferred gross profit, December 31, 1992 (before recognition of realized gross profit for 1992)	560,000
Gross profit on sales	40%

For the year ended December 31, 1992, cash collections and realized gross profit on sales should be

	Cash collections	Realized gross profit
a.	$400,000	$320,000
b.	$400,000	$240,000
c.	$600,000	$320,000
d.	$600,000	$240,000

(11/93, PI, #16, 4385)

4. For financial statement purposes, the installment method of accounting may be used if the
a. Collection period extends over more than 12 months.
b. Installments are due in different years.
c. Ultimate amount collectible is indeterminate.
d. Percentage-of-completion method is inappropriate.

(11/91, Theory, #6, 2514)

5. On January 2, 1991, Blake Co. sold a used machine to Cooper Inc. for $900,000, resulting in a gain of $270,000. On that date, Cooper paid $150,000 cash and signed a $750,000 note bearing interest at 10%. The note was payable in three annual installments of $250,000 beginning January 2, 1992. Blake appropriately accounted for the sale under the installment method. Cooper made a timely payment of the first installment on January 2, 1992, of $325,000, which included accrued interest of $75,000. What amount of deferred gross profit should Blake report at December 31, 1992?
a. $150,000
b. $172,500
c. $180,000
d. $225,000

(11/93, PI, #45, 4414)

6. On January 2, 1992, Yardley Co. sold a plant to Ivory Inc. for $1,500,000. On that date, the plant's carrying cost was $1,000,000. Ivory gave Yardley $300,000 cash and a $1,200,000 note, payable in 4 annual installments of $300,000 plus 12% interest. Ivory made the first principal and interest payment of $444,000 on December 31, 1992. Yardley uses the installment method of revenue recognition. In its 1992 income statement, what amount of realized gross profit should Yardley report?
a. $344,000
b. $200,000
c. $148,000
d. $100,000 (5/93, PI, #42, 4083)

7. According to the installment method of accounting, gross profit on an installment sale is recognized in income
a. On the date of sale.
b. On the date the final cash collection is received.
c. In proportion to the cash collection.
d. After cash collections equal to the cost of sales have been received. (5/95, FAR, #27, 5563)

8. Dolce Co., which began operations on January 1, 1990, appropriately uses the installment method of accounting to record revenues. The following information is available for the years ended December 31, 1990 and 1991:

	1990	1991
Sales	$1,000,000	$2,000,000
Gross profit realized on sales made in:		
1990	150,000	90,000
1991	--	200,000
Gross profit percentages	30%	40%

What amount of installment accounts receivable should Dolce report in its December 31, 1991 balance sheet?
a. $1,225,000
b. $1,300,000
c. $1,700,000
d. $1,775,000 (5/92, PI, #21, 2588)

9. Gant Co., which began operations on January 1, 1991, appropriately uses the installment method of accounting. The following information pertains to Gant's operations for the year 1991:

Installment sales	$500,000
Regular sales	300,000
Cost of installment sales	250,000
Cost of regular sales	150,000
General and administrative expenses	50,000
Collections on installment sales	100,000

In its December 31, 1991 balance sheet, what amount should Gant report as deferred gross profit?
a. $250,000
b. $200,000
c. $160,000
d. $ 75,000 (11/92, PI, #28, 3261)

10. Pie Co. uses the installment sales method to recognize revenue. Customers pay the installment notes in 24 equal monthly amounts, which include 12% interest. What is an installment note's receivable balance six months after the sale?
a. 75% of the original sales price.
b. Less than 75% of the original sales price.
c. The present value of the remaining monthly payments discounted at 12%.
d. Less than the present value of the remaining monthly payments discounted at 12%. (11/92, Theory, #9, 3442)

11. Lang Co. uses the installment method of revenue recognition. The following data pertain to Lang's installment sales for the years ended December 31, 1993 and 1994:

	1993	1994
Installment receivables at year-end on 1993 sales	$60,000	$30,000
Installment receivables at year-end on 1994 sales	—	69,000
Installment sales	80,000	90,000
Cost of sales	40,000	60,000

What amount should Lang report as deferred gross profit in its December 31, 1994, balance sheet?
a. $23,000
b. $33,000
c. $38,000
d. $43,000 (11/95, FAR, #10, 6092)

12. Drew Co. produces expensive equipment for sale on installment contracts. When there is doubt about eventual collectibility, the income recognition method **least** likely to overstate income is
a. At the time the equipment is completed.
b. The installment method.
c. The cost-recovery method.
d. At the time of delivery. (5/91, Theory, #8, 1896)

13. Cash collection is a critical event for income recognition in the

	Cost-recovery method	Installment method
a.	No	No
b.	Yes	Yes
c.	No	Yes
d.	Yes	No

(11/93, Theory, #39, 4544)

14. It is proper to recognize revenue prior to the sale of merchandise when

I. The revenue will be reported as an installment sale
II. The revenue will be reported under the cost recovery method

a. I only
b. II only
c. Both I and II
d. Neither I nor II   (11/95, FAR, #31, 6113)

15. Wren Co. sells equipment on installment contracts. Which of the following statements best justifies Wren's use of the cost-recovery method of revenue recognition to account for these installment sales?
a. The sales contract provides that title to the equipment only passes to the purchaser when all payments have been made.
b. No cash payments are due until one year from the date of sale.
c. Sales are subject to a high rate of return.
d. There is **no** reasonable basis for estimating collectibility.   (5/94, FAR, #41, 4856)

16. Several of Fox Inc.'s customers are having cash flow problems. Information pertaining to these customers for the years ended March 31, 1991 and 1992, follows:

	3/31/91	3/31/92
Sales	$10,000	$15,000
Cost of sales	8,000	9,000
Cash collections		
on 1991 sales	7,000	3,000
on 1992 sales	--	12,000

If the cost-recovery method is used, what amount would Fox report as gross profit from sales to these customers for the year ended March 31, 1992?
a. $ 2,000
b. $ 3,000
c. $ 5,000
d. $15,000   (11/92, PI, #43, 3276)

17. The following information pertains to a sale of real estate by Ryan Co. to Sud Co. on December 31, 1996:

Carrying amount		$2,000,000
Sales price:		
Cash	$ 300,000	
Purchase money mortgage	2,700,000	3,000,000

The mortgage is payable in nine annual installments of $300,000 beginning December 31, 1997, plus interest of 10%. The December 31, 1997 installment was paid as scheduled, together with interest of $270,000. Ryan uses the cost-recovery method to account for the sale. What amount of income should Ryan recognize in 1997 from the real estate sale and its financing?
a. $570,000
b. $370,000
c. $270,000
d. $0   (5/91, PI, #50, amended, 1317)

18. Amar Farms produced 300,000 pounds of cotton during the 1997 season. Amar sells all of its cotton to Brye Co., which has agreed to purchase Amar's entire production at the prevailing market price. Recent legislation assures that the market price will not fall below $.70 per pound during the next two years. Amar's costs of selling and distributing the cotton are immaterial and can be reasonably estimated. Amar reports its inventory at expected exit value. During 1997, Amar sold and delivered to Brye 200,000 pounds at the market price of $.70. Amar sold the remaining 100,000 pounds during 1998 at the market price of $.72. What amount of revenue should Amar recognize in 1997?
a. $140,000
b. $144,000
c. $210,000
d. $216,000   (11/90, PII, #6, amended, 1321)

19. On January 1, 1997, Dell Inc. contracted with the city of Little to provide custom built desks for the city schools. The contract made Dell the city's sole supplier and required Dell to supply no less than 4,000 desks and no more than 5,500 desks per year for two years. In turn, Little agreed to pay a fixed price of $110 per desk. During 1997, Dell produced 5,000 desks for Little. At December 31, 1997, 500 of these desks were segregated from the regular inventory and were accepted and awaiting pickup by Little. Little paid Dell $450,000 during 1997. What amount should Dell recognize as contract revenue in 1997?
a. $450,000
b. $495,000
c. $550,000
d. $605,000   (11/91, PI, #31, amended, 2419)

20. During 1988, Mitchell Corp. started a construction job with a total contract price of $600,000. The job was completed on December 15, 1997. Additional data are as follows:

	1996	1997
Actual costs incurred	$225,000	$255,000
Estimated remaining costs	225,000	--
Billed to customer	240,000	360,000
Received from customer	200,000	400,000

Under the completed-contract method, what amount should Mitchell recognize as gross profit for 1997?
a. $ 45,000
b. $ 72,000
c. $ 80,000
d. $120,000   (5/90, PII, #41, amended, 1325)

21. A company uses the completed-contract method to account for a long-term construction contract. Revenue is recognized when recorded progress billings

	Are collected	Exceed recorded costs
a.	Yes	Yes
b.	No	No
c.	Yes	No
d.	No	Yes

(5/92, Theory, #44, 2737)

22. When should an anticipated loss on a long-term contract be recognized under the percentage-of-completion method and the completed-contract method, respectively?

	Percentage-of-completion	Completed-contract
a.	Over life of project	Contract complete
b.	Immediately	Contract complete
c.	Over life of project	Immediately
d.	Immediately	Immediately

(11/87, Theory, #16, 1850)

ITEMS 23 AND 24 are based on the following data pertaining to Pell Co.'s construction jobs, which commenced during 1992:

	Project 1	Project 2
Contract price	$420,000	$300,000
Costs incurred during 1992	240,000	280,000
Estimated costs to complete	120,000	40,000
Billed to customers during 1992	150,000	270,000
Received from customers during 1992	90,000	250,000

23. If Pell used the completed-contract method, what amount of gross profit (loss) would Pell report in its 1992 income statement?
a. $ (20,000)
b. $0
c. $ 340,000
d. $ 420,000   (5/93, PI, #38, 4079)

24. If Pell used the percentage-of-completion method, what amount of gross profit (loss) would Pell report in its 1992 income statement?
a. $ (20,000)
b. $ 20,000
c. $ 22,500
d. $ 40,000   (5/93, PI, #39, 4080)

25. Haft Construction Co. has consistently used the percentage-of-completion method. On January 10, 1991, Haft began work on a $3,000,000 construction contract. At the inception date, the estimated cost of construction was $2,250,000. The following data relate to the progress of the contract:

Income recognized at 12/31/91	$ 300,000
Cost incurred 1/10/91 through 12/31/92	1,800,000
Estimated cost to complete at 12/31/92	600,000

In its income statement for the year ended December 31, 1992, what amount of gross profit should Haft report?
a. $450,000
b. $300,000
c. $262,500
d. $150,000   (5/93, PI, #41, 4082)

26. A company used the percentage-of-completion method of accounting for a 5-year construction contract. Which of the following items will the company use to calculate the income recognized in the third year?

	Progress billings to date	Income previously recognized
a.	Yes	No
b.	No	Yes
c.	No	No
d.	Yes	Yes

(11/92, Theory, #8, 3441)

27. State Co. recognizes construction revenue and expenses using the percentage-of-completion method. During 1996, a single long-term project was begun, which continued through 1997. Information on the project follows:

	1996	1997
Accounts receivable from construction contract	$100,000	$300,000
Construction expenses	105,000	192,000
Construction in progress	122,000	364,000
Partial billings on contract	100,000	420,000

Profit recognized from the long-term construction contract in 1997 should be
a. $ 50,000.
b. $108,000.
c. $128,000.
d. $228,000.   (11/91, PI, #40, amended, 2428)

28. Barr Corp. started a long-term construction project in 1990. The following data relate to this project:

Contract price	$4,200,000
Costs incurred in 1990	1,750,000
Estimated costs to complete	1,750,000
Progress billings	900,000
Collections on progress billings	800,000

The project is accounted for by the percentage-of-completion method of accounting. In Barr's 1990 income statement, what amount of gross profit should be reported for this project?
a. $350,000
b. $150,000
c. $133,333
d. $100,000   (5/91, PI, #49, 1316)

29. Lake Construction Company has consistently used the percentage-of-completion method of recognizing income. During 1996, Lake entered into a fixed-price contract to construct an office building for $10,000,000. Information relating to the contract is as follows:

	At December 31,	
	1996	1997
Percentage-of-completion	20%	60%
Estimated total cost at completion	$7,500,000	$8,000,000
Income recognized (cumulative)	500,000	1,200,000

Contract costs incurred during 1997 were
a. $3,200,000
b. $3,300,000
c. $3,500,000
d. $4,800,000   (11/87, PI, #21, amended, 1329)

30. In accounting for a long-term construction contract using the percentage-of-completion method, the progress billings on contracts account is a
a. Contra current asset account.
b. Contra noncurrent asset account.
c. Noncurrent liability account.
d. Revenue account.   (11/85, Theory, #28, 1882)

31. Which of the following is used in calculating the income recognized in the fourth and final year of a contract accounted for by the percentage-of-completion method?

	Actual total costs	Income previously recognized
a.	Yes	Yes
b.	Yes	No
c.	No	Yes
d.	No	No (5/95, FAR, #26, 5562)

ITEMS 32 AND 33 are based on the following:

The following trial balance of Mint Corp. at December 31, 1991, has been adjusted except for income tax expense.

TRIAL BALANCE
December 31, 1991

	Dr.	Cr.
Cash	$ 600,000	
Accounts receivable, net	3,500,000	
Cost in excess of billings on long-term contracts	1,600,000	
Billings in excess of costs on long-term contracts		$ 700,000
Prepaid taxes	450,000	
Property, plant, and equipment, net	1,480,000	
Note payable—noncurrent		1,620,000
Common stock		750,000
Additional paid-in capital		2,000,000
Retained earnings— unappropriated		900,000
Retained earnings— restricted for note payable		160,000
Earnings from long-term contracts		6,680,000
Costs and expenses	5,180,000	
	$12,810,000	$12,810,000

Other financial data for the year ended December 31, 1991, are:

- Mint uses the percentage-of-completion method to account for long-term construction contracts for financial statement and income tax purposes. All receivables on these contracts are considered to be collectible within 12 months.
- During 1991, estimated tax payments of $450,000 were charged to prepaid taxes. Mint has not recorded income tax expense. There were no temporary or permanent differences, and Mint's tax rate is 30%.

In Mint's December 31, 1991 balance sheet, what amount should be reported as:

32. Total noncurrent liabilities?
a. $1,620,000
b. $1,780,000
c. $2,320,000
d. $2,480,000
(11/92, PI, #2, 3235)

33. Total current assets?
a. $5,000,000
b. $5,450,000
c. $5,700,000
d. $6,150,000
(11/92, PI, #3, 3236)

34. On October 20, 1997, Grimm Co. consigned 40 freezers to Holden Co. for sale at $1,000 each and paid $800 in transportation costs. On December 30, 1997, Holden reported the sale of 10 freezers and remitted $8,500. The remittance was net of the agreed 15% commission. What amount should Grimm recognize as consignment sales revenue for 1997?
a. $ 7,700
b. $ 8,500
c. $ 9,800
d. $10,000
(5/90, PI, #44, amended, 1323)

35. Each of Potter Pie Co.'s 21 new franchisees contracted to pay an initial franchise fee of $30,000. By December 31, 1991, each franchisee had paid a nonrefundable $10,000 fee and signed a note to pay $10,000 principal plus the market rate of interest on December 31, 1992, and December 31, 1993. Experience indicates that one franchisee will default on the additional payments. Services for the initial fee will be performed in 1992. What amount of net unearned franchise fees would Potter report at December 31, 1991?
a. $400,000
b. $600,000
c. $610,000
d. $630,000
(11/91, PI, #27, 2415)

36. On December 31, 1990, Rice Inc., authorized Graf to operate as a franchisee for an initial franchise fee of $150,000. Of this amount, $60,000 was received upon signing the agreement and the balance, represented by a note, is due in three annual payments of $30,000 each beginning December 31, 1991. The present value on December 31, 1990, of the three annual payments appropriately discounted is $72,000. According to the agreement, the non-refundable down payment represents a fair measure of the services already performed by Rice; however, substantial future services are required of Rice. Collectibility of the note is reasonably certain. In Rice's December 31, 1990 balance sheet, unearned franchise fees from Graf's franchise should be reported as
a. $132,000.
b. $100,000.
c. $ 90,000.
d. $ 72,000.
(5/91, PI, #40, 1315)

37. Lin Co., a distributor of machinery, bought a machine from the manufacturer in November 1997 for $10,000. On December 30, 1997, Lin sold this machine to Zee Hardware for $15,000 under the following terms: 2% discount if paid within 30 days, 1% discount if paid after 30 days but within 60 days, or payable in full within 90 days if not paid within the discount periods. However, Zee had the right to return this machine to Lin if Zee was unable to resell the machine before expiration of the 90-day payment period, in which case Zee's obligation to Lin would be canceled. In Lin's net sales for the year ended December 31, 1997, how much should be included for the sale of this machine to Zee?
a. $0
b. $14,700
c. $14,850
d. $15,000
(5/87, PII, #20, amended, 9050)

38. Under a royalty agreement with another company, Wand Co. will pay royalties for the assignment of a patent for three years. The royalties paid should be reported as expense
a. In the period paid.
b. In the period incurred.
c. At the date the royalty agreement began.
d. At the date the royalty agreement expired.
(5/95, FAR, #38, 5574)

39. Rill Co. owns a 20% royalty interest in an oil well. Rill receives royalty payments on January 31 for the oil sold between the previous June 1 and November 30, and on July 31 for oil sold between the previous December 1 and May 31. Production reports show the following oil sales:

June 1, 1993—November 30, 1993	$300,000
December 1, 1993—December 31, 1993	50,000
December 1, 1993—May 31, 1994	400,000
June 1, 1994—November 30, 1994	325,000
December 1, 1994—December 31, 1994	70,000

What amount should Rill report as royalty revenue for 1994?
a. $140,000
b. $144,000
c. $149,000
d. $159,000   (11/95, FAR, #30, 6112)

40.   Wren Corp.'s trademark was licensed to Mont Co. for royalties of 15% of sales of the trademarked items. Royalties are payable semiannually on March 15 for sales in July through December of the prior year, and on September 15 for sales in January through June of the same year. Wren received the following royalties from Mont:

	March 15	September 15
1992	$10,000	$15,000
1993	12,000	17,000

Mont estimated that sales of the trademarked items would total $60,000 for July through December 1993.

In Wren's 1993 income statement, the royalty revenue should be
a. $26,000
b. $29,000
c. $38,000
d. $41,000   (11/94, Theory, #40, 5302)

PROBLEM/ESSAY QUESTIONS

Essay 12-2 (15 to 25 minutes)

At December 31, 1997, Roko Co. has two fixed price construction contracts in progress. Both contracts have monthly billings supported by certified surveys of work completed. The contracts are:

- The Ski Park contract, begun in 1996, is 80% complete, is progressing according to bid estimates, and is expected to be profitable.
- The Nassu Village contract, a project to construct 100 condominium units, was begun in 1997. Thirty-five units have been completed.

Work on the remaining units is delayed by conflicting recommendations on how to overcome unexpected subsoil problems. While the total cost of the project is uncertain, a loss is not anticipated.

Required:

a. Identify the alternatives available to account for long-term construction contracts, and specify the criteria used to determine which method is applicable to a given contract.

b. Identify the appropriate accounting method for each of Roko's two contracts, and describe each contract's effect on net income for 1997.

c. Indicate how the accounts related to the Ski Park contract should be reported on the balance sheet at December 31, 1997.
                    (11/90, Theory, #3, amended, 3529)

Essay 12-3 (15 to 25 minutes)

Village Company is accounting for a long-term construction contract using the percentage-of-completion method. It is a three-year fixed-fee contract that is presently in its first year. The latest reasonable estimates of total contract costs indicate that the contract will be completed at a profit. Village will submit progress billings to the customer and has reasonable assurance that collections on these billings will be received in each year of the contract.

Required:

a. What is the justification for the percentage-of-completion method for long-term construction contracts?

b. How would the income recognized in each year of this long-term construction contract be determined using the cost-to-cost method of determining percentage-of-completion?

c. What is the effect on income, if any, of the progress billings and the collections on these billings?   (5/86, Theory, #2)

Essay 12-4 (30 to 40 minutes)

Wyatt, CPA, is meeting with Brown, the controller of Emco, a wholesaler, to discuss the accounting issues regarding two unrelated items:

- Emco is considering offering its customers the right to return its products for a full refund within one year of purchase. Emco expects its sales to increase as a result, but is unable to estimate the amount of future returns.

• Brown is aware of Statement of Financial Accounting Standards (FAS) No. 106, *Employers' Accounting for Postretirement Benefits Other Than Pensions,* but is uncertain about the benefits and beneficiaries covered by this Statement. Brown believes that, regardless of FAS 106, no estimate of postretirement obligation can be reasonable because it would be based on too many assumptions. For this reason, Brown wishes to account for the postretirement benefits that Emco pays to its retirees on the pay-as-you-go (cash) basis.

Brown has asked Wyatt to write a brief memo to Brown that Brown can use to explain these issues to Emco's president.

REQUIRED:

Write a brief advisory memo from Wyatt to Brown to:

a. Explain the general principle of revenue recognition, the method of revenue recognition when right to return exists, and the impact of offering a right to return on Emco's ability to recognize revenue, if any.

b. State the principal benefit covered by FAS 106 and give an example of other benefits covered by FAS 106. Explain the reasoning given in FAS 106 for requiring accruals based on estimates. Indicate the primary recipients of postretirement benefits other than pensions.

(11/94, FAR, #5, amended, 5739)

PROBLEM 12-5 (40 to 50 minutes)

London Inc. began operation of its construction division on October 1, 1991, and entered into contracts for two separate projects. The Beta project contract price was $600,000 and provided for penalties of $10,000 per week for late completion. Although during 1992 the Beta project had been on schedule for timely completion, it was completed four weeks late in August 1993. The Gamma project's original contract price was $800,000. Change orders during 1993 added $40,000 to the original contract price.

The following data pertains to the separate long-term construction projects in progress:

	Beta	Gamma
As of September 30, 1992:		
Costs incurred to date	$360,000	$410,000
Estimated costs to complete	40,000	410,000
Billings	315,000	440,000
Cash collections	275,000	365,000
As of September 30, 1993:		
Costs incurred to date	450,000	720,000
Estimated costs to complete	--	180,000
Billings	560,000	710,000
Cash collections	560,000	625,000

Additional Information:

• London accounts for its long-term construction contracts using the percentage-of-completion method for financial reporting purposes and the completed-contract method for income tax purposes.

• Enacted tax rates are 25% for 1992 and 30% for future years.

• London's income before income taxes from all divisions, before considering revenues from long-term construction projects, was $300,000 for the year ended September 30, 1992. There were no other temporary or permanent differences.

REQUIRED:

a. Prepare a schedule showing London's balances in the following accounts at September 30, 1992, under the percentage-of-completion method:

• Accounts receivable
• Costs and estimated earnings in excess of billings
• Billings in excess of costs and estimated earnings

b. Prepare a schedule showing London's gross profit (loss) recognized for the years ended September 30, 1992 and 1993, under the percentage-of-completion method.

c. Prepare a schedule reconciling London's financial statement income and taxable income for the year ended September 30, 1992, and showing all components of taxes payable and current and deferred income tax expense for the year then ended. Do not consider estimated tax requirements.

(11/93, PI, #5, amended)

SOLUTION 12-1 MULTIPLE CHOICE ANSWERS

INSTALLMENT METHOD

1. (c) Accounts receivable is calculated as follows:

Installment sales		$1,400,000
Less amount received:		
Realized GP	$240,000	
Divided by GP%	÷ 40%	(600,000)
Accounts receivable		$ 800,000

Deferred gross profit is calculated as follows:

Installment sales	$1,400,000
Times GP%	x 40%
Total gross profit	$ 560,000
Less realized gross profit	(240,000)
Deferred gross profit	$ 320,000

Deferred gross profit could also be calculated by multiplying accounts receivable of $800,000 by the gross profit percentage of 40%.

2. (d) $220,000 deferred gross profit from 1993 sales + $30,000 deferred gross profit from 1992 sales = $250,000 deferred gross profit at December 31, 1993.

	1993	1992
Sales	$ 900,000	$ 600,000
Collections in 1992	--	(200,000)
Collections in 1993	(300,000)	(100,000)
Write-offs in 1992	--	(50,000)
Write-offs in 1993	(50,000)	(150,000)
	550,000	100,000
Gross profit percentage	x 40%	x 30%
Deferred gross profit	$ 220,000	$ 30,000

3. (d) Cash collections and realized gross profit on installment sales for 1992, Luge's first year of operations, are computed as follows:

Deferred gross profit at 12/31/92 before recognition of realized gross profit for 1992	$ 560,000
Divide by: Gross profit rate on 1992 sales	÷ 40%
Installment sales, 1992	1,400,000
Less: Installment accounts receivable, 12/31/92	(800,000)
Cash collections on installment sales, 1992	600,000
Times: Gross profit rate on 1992 sales	x 40%
Realized gross profit, 1992	$ 240,000

4. (c) The installment method of accounting is a cash basis of accounting and, therefore, is usually not a generally accepted method. However, if the ultimate amount collectible is indeterminate, then the installment method is considered to be the appropriate method to apply and its use is acceptable in that circumstance (APB 10, Par. 12).

5. (a) The amount of deferred gross profit at 12/31/92 can be computed as follows:

Gross profit on sale of machine		$270,000
Less gross profit realized:		
In 1991—$150,000 × 30%*	$45,000	
In 1992—$250,000 × 30%*	75,000	(120,000)
Deferred gross profit, 12/31/92		$150,000

* $270,000 ÷ $900,000.

6. (b) The gross profit on the sale of the plant is $500,000 (i.e., the $1,500,000 sales price minus the $1,000,000 cost of the plant). Thus, the gross profit margin ratio on the sale to be applied to the annual installment payments is 1/3 (i.e., $500,000 ÷ $1,500,000). In 1992, Yardley received (1) $300,000 at the time of sale, (2) the first annual installment on the note of $300,000, and (3) interest of $144,000 (i.e., $1,200,000 x 12%). The amount of realized gross profit that Yardley should recognize from the installment sale is $200,000, which is calculated by multiplying the sum of the down payment and first installment on the note received by Yardley in 1992 by the gross profit margin ratio on the sale [i.e., ($300,000 + $300,000) x 1/3]. The $144,000 of interest received in 1992 should be recognized separately as interest income.

7. (c) The installment method of accounting allows revenue to be deferred and recognized each year in proportion to the receivables collected during that year.

8. (c) The installment accounts receivable balance is computed by dividing the deferred gross profit on sales at year-end by the gross profit percentage applicable to those sales, as follows:

Installment A/R from 1990 sales:		
Gross profit on sales ($1,000,000 x 30%)	$ 300,000	
Less: Gross profit realized ($150,000 + $90,000)	(240,000)	
Deferred gross profit, 12/31/91	60,000	
Divide by: 1990 GP %	÷ 30%	$ 200,000
Installment A/R from 1991 sales:		
Gross profit on sales ($2,000,000 x 40%)	$ 800,000	
Less: Gross profit realized	÷(200,000)	
Deferred gross profit, 12/31/91	600,000	
Divide by: 1991 GP %	÷ 40%	1,500,000
Installment A/R, 12/31/91		$1,700,000

9. (b) The general and administrative expenses are not used to compute the deferred gross profit at year-end. Under the installment sales method, selling and administrative expenses are expensed when incurred. The deferred gross profit is computed by multiplying the installment accounts receivable balance at year-end by the gross profit percentage applicable to those sales as follows:

Installment sales, 1991	$ 500,000
Collections on installment sales	(100,000)
Installment accounts receivable, 12/31/91	400,000
Gross profit on 1991 installment sales	
[($500,000 – $250,000) ÷ $500,000]	x 50%
Deferred gross profit, 12/31/91	$ 200,000

10. (c)   Since the installment notes extend beyond one year, they are recorded at the present value of the payments discounted at the market interest rate (assumed here to be 12%). At any time after the sale, the installment note's receivable balance will be the present value of the remaining monthly payments discounted at 12%.

11. (c)   Lang's deferred gross profit at Dec. 31, 1994, is calculated as follows:

Receivable on 1993 sales	$ 30,000	
@ GP% ($80,000 – $40,000)/$80,000	x .50	$15,000
Receivable on 1994 sales	$ 69,000	
@ GP% ($90,000 – $60,000)/$90,000	x .33	23,000
Deferred gross profit		$38,000

COST-RECOVERY METHOD

12. (c)   The cost-recovery method defers the recognition of all gross profit until cash collections of revenue are equal to the cost of the item sold. All remaining cash collections are recorded as profit. The recognition of income at the time the equipment is completed [answer (a)] or at the time of delivery [answer (d)] would provide for the recognition of profits before any or much of the cash is received. These methods are, therefore, not appropriate for situations where there is doubt about the collectibility of the sales price. The use of the installment method [answer (c)] would allow for the recognition of profits in proportion to the amount of the revenue collected in cash. The cost-recovery method is less likely to overstate income than the installment method because it defers the recognition of profits longer than the installment method.

13. (b)   Cash collection is a critical event for income recognition under both the cost-recovery and installment methods of accounting. Under the cost-recovery method, recognition of all gross profit is deferred until cash collections of revenue are equal to the cost of the item sold. All remaining cash collections are recorded as profit. Gross profit recognized using the installment method is generally computed by multiplying cash collected during the period by the gross profit percentage applicable to

those sales. Since both the cost-recovery and installment methods of accounting use the cash basis of accounting, neither is a generally accepted method.

14. (d)   Both the installment and cost recovery methods report revenue based upon cash collections that occur after the point of sale.

15. (d)   The cost-recovery method defers the recognition of all gross profit until cash collections of revenue are equal to the cost of the item sold. All remaining cash collections are recorded as profit. This method of revenue recognition is not generally accepted. However, the cost-recovery method may be used where collectibility of proceeds is doubtful, where an investment is very speculative in nature, and/or where the final sale price is to be determined by future events. Therefore, Wren Co. would be justified in accounting for installment sales for which there is *no* reasonable basis for estimating collectibility under the cost-recovery method of revenue recognition.

16. (c)   The cost-recovery method defers the recognition of all gross profit until cash collections of revenue are equal to the cost of the item sold. All remaining cash collections are recorded as gross profit. No profit was recognized on the 1991 sales for the year ended 3/31/91 because the $7,000 collected in the period did not recover the $8,000 cost of sales. For the year ended 3/31/92: (1) collections to date on the 1991 sales were $10,000 (i.e., $7,000 + $3,000), permitting the recognition of $2,000 profit above the 1991 cost of sales of $8,000 and (2) collections on the 1992 sales were $12,000, permitting the recognition of $3,000 profit above the 1992 cost of sales of $9,000. Therefore, the amount of gross profit that Fox should recognize for the year ended 3/31/92 is $5,000 (i.e., $2,000 + $3,000).

17. (d)   Under the cost-recovery method, no profit is recognized until cash payments by the buyer exceed the seller's cost of sales. Therefore, Ryan should not recognize any income in 1997 from the real estate sale and its financing because the accumulated cash payments from the buyer are less than the carrying amount of the real estate [($300,000 + $270,000) < $2,000,000].

COMPLETION-OF-PRODUCTION METHOD

18. (c)   Amar can recognize revenue of $210,000 (i.e., 300,000 lbs. x $.70/lb.) in 1997 for the cotton produced in 1997. It is considered appropriate for Amar to recognize revenue when the cotton is produced because (1) there is a relatively stable market for the cotton (i.e., recent legislation assures that the market price will not fall below

$.70 per pound during the next two years), (2) Amar's costs of selling and distributing the cotton are immaterial and can be reasonably estimated, and (3) the units of cotton are homogeneous.

19. (c) Dell should recognize contract revenue of $550,000 (5,000 x $110) in 1997. Dell can properly recognize the full amount of the contract revenue pertaining to the 5,000 desks produced in 1997 because (1) the number of desks produced is within the parameters of the contract for 1997 (i.e., it is more 4,000 and less than 5,500 desks) and (2) the earnings process is virtually complete (i.e., the desks have been accepted and are awaiting pickup by the customer).

COMPLETED-CONTRACT METHOD

20. (d) At 12/31/96, the estimated total gross profit of the contract is $150,000, determined as follows:

Contract price		$600,000
Estimated total costs:		
Actual costs incurred	$225,000	
Estimated cost to complete	225,000	(450,000)
Estimated total gross profit		$150,000

Mitchell uses the completed-contract method; thus, no portion of the estimated gross profit can be recognized in 1996. The full amount of the gross profit of the contract should be recognized in 1997, the final year of the contract.

Contract price	$ 600,000
Actual cost Incurred ($225,000 + $255,000)	(480,000)
Total gross profit of contract	$ 120,000

21. (b) Progress billings and collections on progress billings are not generally accepted as a method of recognizing income because they often do not bear a meaningful relationship to the work performed on the contract. If income were recognized on the basis of progress billings, it would be possible for a contractor to materially distort the contractor's income merely by rendering progress billings without regard to any degree of progress on the contract.

22. (d) The full amount of an anticipated loss on a long-term construction contract must be recognized immediately under both the percentage-of-completion and completed-contract methods. The recognition of an anticipated loss cannot be deferred to future periods under either method.

23. (a) If the completed-contract method is used, Pell recognizes a gross loss of $20,000 on the two projects because (1) no portion of the $60,000 estimated gross profit on Project 1 can be recognized

in 1992 since the project is not completed at 12/31/92, and (2) the full amount of the $20,000 anticipated loss on Project 2 must be recognized in 1992 because the anticipated loss cannot be deferred to future periods. The estimated total gross profit of each project at 12/31/92 is computed as follows (in 000's):

	Project 1		Project 2	
Contract price	$420		$ 300	
Estimated total costs:				
Cost incurred to date	$240		$280	
Estimated costs to complete	120	(360)	40	(320)
Estimated total gross profit		$ 60		$ (20)

PERCENTAGE-OF-COMPLETION METHOD

24. (b) If the percentage-of-completion method is used, Pell recognizes a gross profit of $20,000 on the two projects combined because (1) $40,000 of the estimated gross profit on Project 1 is recognized in 1992, and (2) the full amount of the $20,000 anticipated loss on Project 2 is recognized in 1992 because no portion of the anticipated loss can be deferred to future periods. The gross profit (loss) to be recognized for each project in 1992 is computed as follows (in 000's):

	Project 1		Project 2	
Contract price	$ 420		$ 300	
Estimated total costs:				
Cost incurred to date	$240		$280	
Estimated costs to complete	120	(360)	40	(320)
Estimated total gross profit		60		$ (20)
Percentage-of-completion:				
Costs incurred to date	$240			
Estimated total costs	÷360	× 2/3		
Gross profit recognized in 1992		$ 40		

25. (d) Under the percentage-of-completion method, the gross profit recognized in the second year of the contract is determined by multiplying the estimated total gross profit of the contract by the estimated percentage-of-completion and then subtracting the gross profit recognized in the first year.

Contract price		$ 3,000,000
Less estimated total costs:		
Costs incurred to date	$1,800,000	
Estimated costs to complete	600,000	(2,400,000)
Estimated total gross profit		600,000
Times estimated percentage of completion:		
Costs incurred to date	$1,800,000	
Estimated total costs	÷2,400,000	x 75%
Gross profit recognizable to date		450,000
Less: Gross profit previously recognized		(300,000)
Gross profit to be recognized in 1992		$ 150,000

26. (b) Income previously recognized is used in the calculation, but progress billings to date are not. The formula used to determine the income recognized in a period under the percentage-of-completion method is as follows:

$$\text{Current Income} = \left[\frac{\text{Actual cost to date}}{\text{Estimated total cost}} \times \text{Total estimated income} \right] - \text{Income previously recognized}$$

27. (a) Under the percentage-of-completion method, an asset, Construction in Progress, is recorded for the actual costs incurred to date *plus* the profit recognized to date on the contract. Thus, the profit recognized from the contract in 1997 can be computed by subtracting the contract costs incurred in 1997 from the increase in the Construction in Progress account during 1997.

Construction in progress, 12/31/97	$ 364,000
Construction in progress, 12/31/96	(122,000)
Increase during 1997 (comprised of contract costs incurred in 1997 and profit recognized in 1997)	242,000
Contract costs incurred in 1997	(192,000)
Profit recognized in 1997	$ 50,000

28. (a) Progress billings and collections on progress billings do not enter into the computation of the amount of gross profit recognized from the contract. Under the percentage-of-completion method, the gross profit recognized in the first year of the contract is determined by multiplying the estimated total gross profit of the contract by the estimated percentage of completion.

Contract price		$ 4,200,000
Less estimated total costs:		
Costs incurred to date	$ 1,750,000	
Estimated costs to complete	1,750,000	(3,500,000)
Estimated total gross profit		700,000
Times estimated percentage of completion:		
Costs incurred to date	$ 1,750,000	
Estimated total costs	÷ 3,500,000 x	50%
Gross profit recognized in 1990		$ 350,000

29. (b) The contract costs incurred during 1997 are determined as follows (in 000's):

	1996	1997
Contract price	$10,000	$ 10,000
Estimated total cost at completion	(7,500)	(8,000)
Estimated gross profit	$ 2,500	$ 2,000
Estimated total cost at completion	$ 7,500	$ 8,000
Percentage-of-completion:		
GP recognized to date	$ 500	$1,200
Estimated total GP	÷2,500 x 20%	÷2,000 x 60%
Contract costs to date	1,500	4,800
Contract costs prior years	(0)	(1,500)
Contract costs current year	$ 1,500	$ 3,300

30. (a) The percentage-of-completion method requires that revenues and gross profit be recognized each period based upon the progress of completion. Construction costs plus gross profit earned to date are accumulated in an inventory account (Construction in Progress) and progress billings are accumulated in a contra inventory account (ARB 45, par. 12).

31. (a) In the final year of a contract accounted for by the percentage-of-completion method, the final income recognition would take place. The calculation would be the total revenue earned over the entire contract less the actual total costs incurred less the income previously recognized.

CONSIGNMENTS

32. (a) Total noncurrent liabilities at 12/31/91 is comprised of the noncurrent note payable of $1,620,000. (The $700,000 of billings in excess of costs on long-term contracts is reported as a current liability. The $160,000 of retained earnings restricted for the note payable is reported as an element of retained earnings.)

33. (c) Under the completed-contract method, cost in excess of related billings on long-term contracts is reported as a current asset, and billings in excess of related costs on long-term contracts is reported separately as a current liability. Current assets and current liabilities pertaining to two or more contracts should not be netted for financial statement purposes (ARB 45, par. 12). Mint does not report any prepaid taxes at 12/31/91 since the $450,000 of income tax expense recognized for 1991 reduces the prior $450,000 balance in the Prepaid Taxes account to zero. Total current assets at 12/31/91 is determined as follows:

Cash	$ 600,000
Accounts receivable, net	3,500,000
Cost in excess of billings on LT contracts	1,600,000
Total current assets, 12/31/91	$5,700,000

34. (d) Consignment sales revenue is recognized at the time of the sale at the sales price. Thus, consignment sales revenue of $10,000 (10 freezers x $1,000 sales price) should be reported in 1997. The 15% commission should be reported as a selling expense; it should *not* be netted against sales revenue. The following journal entry would be used to record the consignment sale:

Cash	8,500	
Consignment Sales Commissions	1,500	
Consignment Sales Revenues		10,000

FRANCHISE FEES

35. (c)   Services for the initial fee have not yet been performed and are expected to be performed in 1992. None of the initial fee, including the non-refundable portion, should be recognized as revenue until 1992. Unearned franchise fees at 12/31/90 is determined as follows:

Initial franchise fee	$ 30,000
Times: New franchises contracted	x 21
Gross unearned franchise fees, 12/31/90	630,000
Less: Estimated defaults on additional payments	(20,000)
Net unearned franchise fees, 12/31/90	$ 610,000

36. (d)   The $60,000 received in 1990 was for services already performed and is, therefore, recognized as income in 1990. The three payments of $30,000 have not yet been earned as of the signing of the agreement because Rice is required to perform substantial future services. Such payments may not be recognized as revenue until the services are performed. The annual payments should be discounted and reported as unearned franchise fees at their present value of $72,000 at 12/31/90.

RIGHT OF RETURN

37. (a)   Zee has the right to return the machine to Lin if Zee is not able to resell the machine before expiration of the 90-day payment period. Per SFAS 48, if an enterprise sells its product but gives the buyer the right to return the product, revenue from the sales transaction is not recognized at the time of sale if the buyer is obligated to pay the seller and the obligation is contingent upon resale of the product.

ROYALTIES

38. (b)   Accrual accounting recognizes expenses in the period they are incurred, not paid. Royalties paid should not be recognized as an expense at the date the royalty agreement began or the date the royalty agreement expires.

39. (c)   Royalty revenue and expense are recognized in the period in which the royalties are earned. The royalty revenue is computed as follows:

Dec. 1, 1993, to May 31, 1994	$400,000
Less: Month of December 1993	(50,000)
Plus: June 1, 1994, to Nov. 30, 1994	325,000
Plus: Month of December 1994	70,000
Total royalty revenue	$745,000
Percentage of Rill's ownership	20%
Rill's royalty revenue	$149,000

40. (a)   Accrual accounting recognizes revenue in the period(s) it is earned, rather than when the related cash is received. The amount of royalty revenue recognized in 1993 is determined as follows:

Royalties for 1/1/93 to 6/30/93 (received 9/15/93)	$17,000
Royalties for 7/1/93 to 12/31/93 ($60,000 x 15%)	9,000
Royalty revenue, 1993	$26,000

PERFORMANCE BY SUBTOPICS

Each category below parallels a subtopic covered in Chapter 12. Record the number and percentage of questions you correctly answered in each subtopic area.

Installment Method

Question #	Correct √
1	
2	
3	
4	
5	
6	
7	
8	
9	
10	
11	

Questions   11

Correct   _____
% Correct   _____

Cost-Recovery Method

Question #	Correct √
12	
13	
14	
15	
16	
17	

Questions   6

Correct   _____
% Correct   _____

Completion-of-Production Method

Question #	Correct √
18	
19	

Questions   2

Correct   _____
% Correct   _____

Completed-Contract Method

Question #	Correct √
20	
21	
22	
23	

Questions   4

Correct   _____
% Correct   _____

Percentage-of-Completion Method

Question #	Correct √
24	
25	
26	
27	
28	
29	
30	
31	

Questions   8

Correct   _____
% Correct   _____

Consignments

Question #	Correct √
32	
33	
34	

Questions   3

Correct   _____
% Correct   _____

Franchise Fees

Question #	Correct √
35	
36	

Questions   2

Correct   _____
% Correct   _____

Right of Return

Question #	Correct √
37	

Questions   1

Correct   _____
% Correct   _____

Royalties

Question #	Correct √
38	
39	
40	

Questions   3

Correct   _____
% Correct   _____

PROBLEM/ESSAY SOLUTIONS

SOLUTION 12-2 LONG-TERM CONTRACTS

a. The **two** alternative accounting methods to account for long-term construction contracts are the **percentage-of-completion** method and the **completed-contract** method. The **percentage-of-completion method must be used if both** of the following conditions are **met at the statement date**:

• **Reasonable estimates of profitability at completion.**
• **Reliable measures of progress toward completion.**

If one or both of these conditions are **not met** at the statement date, the **completed-contract method must be used**.

b. The **Ski Park** contract must be accounted for by the **percentage-of-completion** method. **Eighty percent** of the **estimated total income** on the contract should be **recognized as of December 31, 1997.** Therefore, the **1997 income** to be **recognized** will equal **80%** of the **estimated total**

income **less** the income reported under the contract **in 1996.**

The **Nassu Village** contract must be accounted for by the **completed-contract method.** Therefore, **no income or loss** is **recognized in 1997** under this contract.

c. The **receivable** on the Ski Park contract should be reported as a **current asset.** If **costs plus gross profit to date exceed billings,** the difference should be reported as a **current asset.** If **billings exceed cost plus gross profit to date,** the difference should be reported as a **current liability.**

SOLUTION 12-3 LONG-TERM CONTRACTS

a. The percentage-of-completion method is justified because revenue is earned **as work is performed** under the long-term construction contract. As a result, it provides **more relevant** information. Revenues represent actual or expected cash inflows (or the equivalent) that have occurred or will eventuate as a result of the enterprise's ongoing major or central operations during the period.

b. The income recognized in each year of this long-term construction contract would be determined using the cost-to-cost method of determining percentage of completion as follows:

- The **contract price** is the first part of the determination of the total estimated income for each year. The total actual costs (the second part of the determination of the total estimated income for each year) represent all **costs incurred from the inception of the project** to the end of the current year.

- The **estimated total costs** (the third part of the determination of the total estimated income for each year) **are subtracted from the contract price** to arrive at the estimated total income. The estimated total costs consist of the actual costs to date and the estimated costs to complete the contract and would generally change each year.

- The income recognized in the first year would be the **percentage of the actual costs to date to the estimated total costs multiplied by the estimated total income**. The income recognized in the second (third) year would be the percentage of the actual costs to date to the estimated total costs multiplied by the estimated total income **less the income already recognized** in the first (first and second) year.

c. **Progress billings** sent and **collections** on these billings would **not affect the income recognized** in each year of this long-term contract.

SOLUTION 12-4 RIGHT OF RETURN

To: Brown

From: Wyatt

As we discussed, here is a brief overview of revenue recognition and Statement of Financial Accounting Standards No. 106.

a. Revenue Recognition

The revenue recognition principle provides that revenue is recognized when it is **realized or realizable** and it is **earned**. Accordingly, revenues from the sale of products ordinarily are recognized at the **time of sale**. Revenue from sales transactions in which the buyer has a right to return the product are recognized at time of sale **only if specified conditions are met**. If all these conditions are not met, revenue recognition is postponed; if they are met, sales revenue and cost of sales should be reported in the income statement, reduced to reflect estimated returns.

One of the specified conditions is that the amount of **future returns can be reasonably estimated**. Since Emco cannot reasonably estimate future returns, Emco should **defer recognition of sales revenue** and cost of sales **until the return privilege has substantially expired** or it can **reasonably estimate returns**, whichever occurs first.

b. Postretirement Benefits Other Than Pensions

The primary recipients of postretirement benefits other than pensions are **retired employees**, their **beneficiaries**, and **covered dependents**. The principle benefit covered by FAS 106 is **postretirement health care benefits**. Examples of other benefits include **tuition** assistance, **legal** services, **life insurance** benefits, **day care**, and housing subsidies.

The reasoning given in FAS 106 is that accrual of the obligation based on best estimates is **superior to implying**, by a failure to accrue, that **no obligation exists** prior to the payment of benefits.

SOLUTION 12-5 PERCENTAGE-OF-COMPLETION METHOD

a.

London Inc.
SCHEDULE OF SELECTED BALANCE SHEET ACCOUNTS
September 30, 1992

Accounts receivable $115,000 [1]

Costs and estimated earnings in excess of billings:

Construction in progress	$ 540,000 [2]	
Less: Billings	(315,000)	
Costs and estimated earnings in excess of billings		225,000

Billings in excess of costs and estimated earnings **50,000** [3]

Editor's footnotes:

[1] (Beta $315,000 - $275,000) + (Gamma $440,000 – $365,000) = $115,000.

[2] [$360,000 ÷ ($360,000 + $40,000)] $600,000 = $540,000. An excess of costs incurred and income recognized over progress billings in the Beta Project gave rise to a current asset.

[3] $410,000 costs incurred to date (Gamma) – $20,000 estimated loss = $390,000. Billings $440,000 – $390,000 = $50,000. An excess of progress billings over related costs and income in the Gamma Project gave rise to a current liability. The current asset and current liability should not be netted.

b.

London Inc.
SCHEDULE OF GROSS PROFIT (LOSS)

For the Year Ended September 30, 1992:

	Beta	Gamma
Estimated gross profit (loss):		
Contract price	$ 600,000	$ 800,000
Less: Total costs	(400,000)	(820,000)
Estimated gross profit (loss)	**$ 200,000**	**$ (20,000)**
Percent complete:		
Costs incurred to date	$ 360,000	$ 410,000
Total costs	÷ 400,000	÷ 820,000
Percent complete	90%	50%
Gross profit (loss) recognized	**$ 180,000**	**$ (20,000)**

For the Year Ended September 30, 1993:

	Beta	Gamma
Estimated gross profit (loss):		
Contract price	$ 560,000	$ 840,000
Less: Total costs	(450,000)	(900,000)
Estimated gross profit (loss)	**$ 110,000**	**$ (60,000)**
Percent complete:		
Costs incurred to date	$ 450,000	$ 720,000
Total costs	÷ 450,000	÷ 900,000
Percent complete	100%	80%
Gross profit (loss)	110,000	(60,000)
Less: Gross (profit) loss recognized in prior year	(180,000)	20,000
Gross profit (loss) recognized	**$ (70,000)**	**$ (40,000)**

c.

London Inc.
SCHEDULE OF INCOME TAXES PAYABLE AND INCOME TAX EXPENSE
September 30, 1992

Financial statement income:		
From other divisions		$ 300,000
From Beta project		180,000
From Gamma project		(20,000)
Total financial statement income		**$ 460,000**
Less temporary differences:		
Beta project income		(180,000)
Gamma project loss		20,000
Total taxable income		**$ 300,000**
Taxes payable ($300,000 × 25%)		$ 75,000
Deferred tax liability ($160,000 × 30%)		48,000
Tax expense:		
Current	$ 75,000	
Deferred	48,000	**$ 123,000**

Wondering how to find 20 hours a week for study time?

In the Bisk Education video, *How to Pass the CPA Exam*, Bob Monette shares the method he used to find 20 hours a week to study while working 40 hours a week. (Ask a customer service representative about a copy of this demo video.) Notice how this plan leaves most of the weekend free, ensuring time for you to take care of yourself, spend time with your family, meet with friends, and in general, take care of your other commitments.

Lunch hours, Monday through Friday	5 hours
Three hours, after work, Monday through Thursday	12 hours
Three hours, Saturday morning	3 hours
Sunday, total break from studying	0 hours
Weekly total	20 hours

This plan may work for you, or it may not. Consider Bob's plan and adapt it to your situation. For example, perhaps you prefer to study an hour before work Tuesday through Thursday, and relax on Saturday as well as Sunday.

Also consider how you use time. Listening to audio tapes could transform a hour of radio listening into an hour of study time. Do you have a 30-minute commute to and from work? That could add up to 5 hours in a work week. Do you jog three times a week? That could be study time as well as exercise time.

Remember, with the techniques and information in your material,

A passing score is well within reach!

CHAPTER 13

ACCOUNTING FOR INCOME TAXES

CHAPTER 13

ACCOUNTING FOR INCOME TAXES

I. BASIC CONCEPTS

A. PRETAX FINANCIAL INCOME

Pretax financial income (often called pretax accounting income, and sometimes called book income, financial income, accounting income, or income for financial accounting purposes) is determined on the accrual basis. That is, expenses incurred for the period are deducted from revenues earned for the period to arrive at pretax financial income. Income tax expense (often called *provision for income taxes*) is then deducted from that subtotal to arrive at net income. An excess of expenses over revenues will cause a pretax financial loss. In situations where a loss situation results in a tax refund or tax savings, the provision is referred to as *income tax benefit*.

B. TAXABLE INCOME

Taxable income is determined by following the rules of the Internal Revenue Code. Deductions (called deductible amounts or tax deductible amounts or tax deductible expenses) allowed for the period and allowable exemptions are subtracted from income items (called taxable amounts or taxable revenues) for the period to arrive at taxable income (loss) for the period.

EXHIBIT 1 ♦ FINANCIAL VS. TAXABLE INCOME

Revenues earned	Taxable amounts
− Expenses incurred	− Deductible amounts
Pretax financial income (loss)	Taxable income (loss)
− Income tax expense (benefit)	
Net income (loss)	

C. INCOME TAXES CURRENTLY PAYABLE (REFUNDABLE)

Income taxes currently payable (refundable) is also called current tax expense (or benefit) and is determined by applying the provisions of the tax law to the taxable income or taxable loss figure for a period. The tax law provides that a net operating loss (NOL) may be carried back 2 years and forward 20 years.

EXAMPLE 1 ♦ INCOME TAXES CURRENTLY PAYABLE

Zanthe Corp. has taxable income for 20X8 of $400,000.
The flat tax rate for 20X8 is 40%.

REQUIRED: Compute the amount of income taxes payable for 20X8.

SOLUTION:

Taxable income for 20X8	$ 400,000
Tax rate for 20X8	x 40%
Income taxes currently payable	$ 160,000

EXAMPLE 2 ◆ INCOME TAXES CURRENTLY REFUNDABLE

The Aspen Company has the following history of taxable income and taxes paid:

Year	Taxable income		Tax rate		Taxes paid
20X4	$ 60,000	x	50%	=	$30,000
20X5	50,000	x	45%	=	22,500
20X6	40,000	x	40%	=	16,000
20X7	80,000	x	35%	=	28,000

The tax rate for 20X8 is 30%, and a 25% rate has already been enacted for 20X9 and subsequent years. In 20X8, Aspen reports a $200,000 excess of tax deductible expenses over taxable revenues on its tax return. This excess is often called a net operating loss (NOL).

REQUIRED: Compute the amount of taxes refundable due to a carryback of the 20X8 NOL.

SOLUTION: The $200,000 NOL in 20X8 is first applied to 20X6, which is the earliest of the two years prior to the loss year. The NOL exceeds the 20X6 taxable income so the remaining NOL is then applied to the $80,000 taxable income of 20X7 (in that order).

	Taxable income		Tax rate		Taxes paid
From 20X6:	$ 40,000	x	40%	=	$16,000
From 20X7:	80,000	x	35%	=	28,000
	$120,000				

Taxes refundable due to 20X8 NOL $44,000

NOTE: Because there was insufficient taxable income in the 2 years prior to 20X8 to fully offset the NOL, there is an NOL carryforward for tax purposes of $80,000 (i.e., $200,000 − $120,000) at the end of 20X8.

D.   INCOME TAX EXPENSE (BENEFIT)

Income tax expense (benefit) is the sum of *current* tax expense (benefit) and *deferred* tax expense (benefit) (to be discussed later in this chapter). In the rare instances where taxable income is the same amount as pretax financial income, total income tax expense will equal income taxes currently payable. Income tax expense is often referred to as the *provision for income taxes.* Hence, there can be both a current portion and a deferred portion of the provision.

EXAMPLE 3 ◆ CURRENT INCOME TAX EXPENSE

Refer to the data in Example 1. Pretax financial income is also $400,000 (because there are differences in the computations of taxable income and pretax financial income).

REQUIRED: Prepare the journal entry to record income taxes for 20X8.

SOLUTION:

Income Tax Expense–current	160,000	
Income Taxes Payable ($400,000 x 40%)		160,000

DISCUSSION: Because there are no temporary differences, there are no deferred income taxes. There is only a current portion for the provision; hence, income tax expense (provision) is the same amount as income tax payable ($160,000).

(continued on next page)

FINANCIAL ACCOUNTING & REPORTING

The balance of the expense account will appear on the income statement, and the balance of the payable account will be reported as a current liability on the balance sheet.

A corporation often makes estimated tax payments during the year and charges them to an account titled "Prepaid income taxes." The balance of this account is used to offset the balance of the "Income taxes payable" account; the net amount is classified as a current asset if the prepaid account has the higher balance or as a current liability if the payable account has the higher balance.

EXAMPLE 4 ♦ DEFERRED INCOME TAX EXPENSE

Refer to the data from Example 2. The pretax financial loss for 20X8 was also $200,000 (there are no differences in the computations of taxable income and pretax financial income in any of the years affected).

REQUIRED: Prepare the journal entry at the end of 20X8 to record the benefits of the operating loss carryback. Also prepare the journal entry at the end of 20X8 to record the expected future benefits of the $80,000 loss carryforward.

SOLUTION:

Income Tax Refund Receivable	44,000	
Benefits of Loss Carryback (from Example 2)		44,000
Deferred Tax Asset ($80,000 x 25%)	20,000	
Benefits of Loss Carryforward		20,000

DISCUSSION: The income tax refund receivable balance of $44,000 would be classified as a current asset on the balance sheet. The deferred tax asset balance of $20,000 would be classified as a current asset or a noncurrent asset, depending on whether the benefits of the NOL carryforward are expected to be realized in the year that immediately follows the balance sheet date (in which case it would be classified as a current asset) or in a later year (in which case it would be classified as a noncurrent asset).

Based on the above assumptions, the income statement for 20X8 would report the following:

Operating loss before income taxes	$(200,000)
Benefits of loss carryback	44,000
Benefits of loss carryforward	20,000
Net loss	$(136,000)

If we assume that Aspen reports pretax financial income and taxable income of $92,000 for 20X9 before consideration of the deduction for the NOL carryforward, the income taxes for 20X9 would be recorded as follows:

Income Tax Expense—current	3,000	
Income Tax Expense—deferred	20,000	
Income Taxes Payable [25% x ($92,000 – $80,000)]		3,000
Deferred Tax Asset (25% x $80,000)		20,000

The income statement for 20X9 would report the following:

Income before income taxes		$92,000
Income tax expense:		
Current tax expense	$ 3,000	
Deferred tax expense	20,000	
Total income tax expense		(23,000)
Net income		$69,000

E. **RECONCILIATION OF PRETAX FINANCIAL INCOME AND TAXABLE INCOME**

Most revenues and most expenses are reported on the tax return in the same period that they are reported on the income statement. However, tax laws often differ from the recognition and measurement requirements of financial accounting standards, and it is common to find differences between the amount of pretax financial income (loss) and the amount of taxable income (loss) for a period. Some of the possible differences between the current period's pretax financial income and the current period's taxable income will not cause a difference between pretax financial income and taxable income in some *other* period (i.e., they will not turn around or reverse in some future year). Such differences were called "*permanent differences*" by APB 11, and many people continue to refer to them as permanent differences even though SFAS 109 does not use the term.

EXHIBIT 2 ♦ INCOME RECONCILIATION

Pretax financial income for the current period can be reconciled with taxable income for the current period by using the following format:

Pretax financial income (loss)	$ X,XXX
Excess of taxable revenues over revenues per books	+ XXX
Excess of deductible amounts over expenses per books	(XXX)
Excess of revenues per books over taxable revenues	(XXX)
Excess of expenses per books over deductible amounts	+ XXX
Taxable income (loss)	$ X,XXX

EXAMPLE 5 ♦ PERMANENT DIFFERENCES

Pretax financial income for 20X8 for the Zippy Corporation is $300,000. Included in the $300,000 are tax-exempt revenues of $40,000 and nondeductible expenses of $14,000. The tax rate for all years is 40%.

REQUIRED:

1. Compute the amount of taxable income for 20X8.
2. Prepare the journal entry to record income taxes for 20X8.
3. Show Zippy's income statement for 20X8.

SOLUTION:

1.	Pretax financial income, 20X8	$ 300,000	
	Tax-exempt revenues	(40,000)	
	Nondeductible expenses	14,000	
	Taxable income, 20X8	$ 274,000	
2.	Income Tax Expense—current	109,600	
	Income Taxes Payable ($274,000 x 40%)		109,600
3.	Income before income taxes	$ 300,000	
	Current income tax expense	(109,600)	
	Net income	$ 190,400	

(continued on next page)

> **DISCUSSION:** Because the differences between pretax financial income and taxable income in the current period do not cause differences between pretax financial income and taxable income in any other period, there are no deferred taxes to compute and record. The amount due to the government is based on the amount of taxable income, as always. Because there are no deferred taxes, the amount of income tax expense recorded must be the same amount as the income taxes payable. The effective tax rate ($109,600 ÷ $300,000 = 36.53%) is less than the statutory rate due to an excess of tax-exempt revenues ($40,000) over nondeductible expenses ($14,000).

EXAMPLE 6 ♦ TEMPORARY DIFFERENCES

Pretax financial income for 20X9 for the Zippy Corporation is $400,000. Included in the $400,000 is revenue of $50,000 which will not be taxable until a future period. Deductible amounts of $30,000 on the 20X9 tax return will be expensed on a future income statement. The tax rate is 40% for all years.

REQUIRED:

1. Compute taxable income for 20X9.
2. Prepare the journal entry to record income taxes for 20X9.

SOLUTION:

1.

Pretax financial income, 20X9	$400,000
Excess of revenues over taxable amounts	(50,000)
Excess of deductible amounts over expenses	(30,000)
Taxable income, 20X9	$320,000

2.

Income Tax Expense—current	128,000	
Income Tax Expense—deferred	32,000	
Income Taxes Payable ($320,000 x 40%)		128,000
Deferred Tax Liability [($50,000 + $30,000) x 40%]		32,000

DISCUSSION: Because the differences between pretax financial income and taxable income in the current period do cause differences between pretax financial income and taxable income in some other period, there are deferred taxes to compute and record in 20X9. The amount due to the government (income taxes payable) is based on the amount of taxable income, as always. The amount of deferred taxes recorded is computed in accordance with the liability method prescribed by SFAS 109.

Under the liability method, the deferred tax consequences of the $80,000 ($50,000 + $30,000) future taxable amounts are calculated using enacted future tax rates (40% in this example). (In the journal entry illustrated in this example, it is assumed that there is no existing balance in any deferred tax account at the beginning of 20X9.) The total income tax expense (provision) figure ($160,000) is the amount needed to balance the entry [current tax expense (provision) of $128,000 plus deferred tax expense (provision) of $32,000].

II. SFAS 109 OVERVIEW

A. ACCOUNTING AND REPORTING FOR TEMPORARY DIFFERENCES
SFAS 109 refers to some differences between (1) the amount of taxable income and pretax financial income for a year and (2) the tax bases of assets or liabilities and their reported amounts in financial statements as *temporary differences*. This Statement requires that the *asset and liability method* be used in accounting and reporting for temporary differences.

1. **RECOGNITION AND MEASUREMENT** Under this method, a current or deferred tax liability or asset is recognized for the current or deferred tax consequences of all events that have been recognized in the financial statements, and the current or deferred tax consequences of an event are measured based on provisions of the enacted tax law to determine the amount of taxes payable or refundable currently or in future years.

2. **COMPREHENSIVE ALLOCATION APPROACH** SFAS 109 also establishes financial accounting and reporting standards for the effects of operating losses and tax credit carrybacks and carryforwards. SFAS 109 requires a *comprehensive* (as opposed to a partial) *allocation* approach.

B. OBJECTIVES AND BASIC PRINCIPLES

1. **OBJECTIVES** The objectives of accounting for income taxes are to recognize (a) the amount of taxes payable or refundable for the current year and (b) deferred tax liabilities and assets for the future tax consequences of events that have been recognized in an enterprise's financial statements or tax returns.

2. **BASIC PRINCIPLES** To implement the objectives, the following basic principles are applied in accounting for income taxes at the date of the financial statements:

   a. A current tax liability or asset is recognized for the estimated taxes payable or refundable on tax returns for the current year.

   b. A deferred tax liability or asset is recognized for the estimated future tax effects attributable to temporary differences and carryforwards.

   c. The measurement of current and deferred tax liabilities and assets is based on provisions of the *enacted tax law*; the effects of future changes in tax laws or rates are not anticipated.

   d. The measurement of deferred tax assets is reduced, if necessary, by the amount of any tax benefits that, based on available evidence, are not expected to be realized.

3. **RECOGNITION OF DEFERRED TAX LIABILITIES AND ASSETS** Deferred tax liabilities or assets are recognized for the future tax consequences of the following:

   a. Revenues, expenses, gains, or losses that are included in taxable income of an earlier or later year than the year in which they are recognized in financial income;

   b. Other events that create differences between the tax bases of assets and liabilities and their amounts for financial reporting; and

   c. Operating loss or tax credit carrybacks for refunds of taxes paid in prior years and carryforwards to reduce taxes payable in future years.

III. TEMPORARY DIFFERENCES AND PERMANENT DIFFERENCES

A. TEMPORARY DIFFERENCES

A *temporary difference* is a difference between the tax basis of an asset or liability and its reported amount in the financial statements that will result in taxable or deductible amounts in future years when the reported amount of the asset is recovered or the liability is settled.

1. **ORIGINATION OF TEMPORARY DIFFERENCES** The tax consequences of most events recognized in the current year's financial statements are included in determining income taxes currently payable. However, because tax laws and financial accounting standards differ in their recognition and measurement of assets, liabilities, equity, revenues, expenses, gains, and losses, differences arise between the following:

a. The amount of taxable income and pretax financial income for a year; and

b. The tax basis of assets or liabilities and their reported amounts in financial statements.

2. **FUTURE EFFECTS** Because it is assumed that the reported amounts of assets and liabilities will be recovered and settled, respectively, a difference between the tax basis of an asset or a liability and its reported amount in the balance sheet will result in a taxable or a deductible amount in some future year(s) when the reported amounts of assets are recovered and the reported amounts of liabilities are settled.

3. **TAXABLE AND DEDUCTIBLE TEMPORARY DIFFERENCES** Temporary differences that will result in taxable amounts in future years when the related assets are recovered are often called *taxable* temporary differences. Likewise, temporary differences that will result in deductible amounts in future years when the related liabilities are settled are often called *deductible* temporary differences.

B. TIMING SOURCES

Differences between taxable income and pretax financial income that result from including revenues, expenses, gains, or losses in taxable income of an earlier or later year than the year in which they are recognized in financial income (referred to as "timing differences" by APB 11) create differences (sometimes accumulating over more than one year) between the tax basis of an asset or liability and its reported amount in the financial statements and, thus, are *temporary differences*. Examples of these are as follows:

1. **REVENUES OR GAINS THAT ARE TAXABLE AFTER THEY ARE INCLUDED IN FINANCIAL INCOME** This situation will result in *future taxable amounts*.

   • An example would be the use of the accrual method for accounting for installment sales for computing financial income and the use of the installment (cash) method for tax purposes. This will cause an excess of the reported amount of an asset (receivable) over its tax basis that will result in a taxable amount in a future year(s) when the asset is recovered (when the cash is collected).

2. **EXPENSES OR LOSSES THAT ARE DEDUCTIBLE AFTER THEY ARE INCLUDED IN FINANCIAL INCOME** This situation will result in *future tax deductible amounts*.

   • Examples would be accruals of items such as warranty expense and loss contingencies in computing financial income. Such items are deductible for tax purposes only when they are realized. This type of situation causes a reported amount of a liability to exceed its tax basis (zero) which will result in deductible amounts in a future year(s) when the liability is settled.

3. **REVENUES OR GAINS THAT ARE TAXABLE BEFORE THEY ARE INCLUDED IN FINANCIAL INCOME** This situation will result in *future tax deductible amounts*.

   • An example would be the accounting for revenue received in advance for rent or subscriptions. For tax purposes, the revenue is taxable in the period the related cash is received. The revenue is not included in the computation of financial income until the period in which it is earned. This situation causes a liability's reported amount on the balance sheet to exceed its tax basis (zero) which will result in future tax deductible amounts when the liability is settled.

   NOTE: This case is said to result in future tax deductible amounts because of the future sacrifices required to provide goods or services or to provide refunds to those who cancel their orders.

4. **EXPENSES OR LOSSES THAT ARE DEDUCTIBLE BEFORE THEY ARE INCLUDED IN FINANCIAL INCOME**

This situation will result in *future taxable amounts.* Typically, temporary differences of this type accumulate over several years and then eliminate over several years. Future temporary differences for *existing* depreciable assets (in use at the balance sheet date) are considered in determining the future years in which existing temporary differences result in *net* taxable or deductible amounts.

a. **PREPAID EXPENSE EXAMPLE** One example is when a prepaid expense is deducted for tax purposes in the period it is paid, but deferred and deducted in the period the expense is incurred for purposes of computing financial income.

b. **DEPRECIATION EXPENSE EXAMPLE** The most commonly cited example is the situation where a *depreciable asset* is depreciated faster for tax purposes than it is depreciated for financial accounting purposes. This will cause the asset's carrying amount to exceed its tax basis. Amounts received upon the future recovery of the asset's carrying amount (through use or sale) will exceed its tax basis and the excess will be a taxable amount when the asset is recovered.

EXHIBIT 3 ♦ TEMPORARY DIFFERENCES

	REVENUES AND GAINS	**EXPENSES AND LOSSES**
INCLUDED FOR TAX FIRST	FUTURE DEDUCTIBLE AMOUNT	FUTURE TAXABLE AMOUNT
INCLUDED IN FINANCIAL STATEMENT FIRST	FUTURE TAXABLE AMOUNT	FUTURE DEDUCTIBLE AMOUNT

EXAMPLE 7 ♦ TEMPORARY DIFFERENCE

An enterprise acquired a depreciable asset at the beginning of 20X1. The asset has a cost of $60,000, no residual value, is being depreciated over six years using the straight-line method for financial reporting purposes, and is being depreciated over three years using the straight-line method and the one-half year convention for tax purposes. The depreciation schedules for both financial accounting purposes and tax purposes are as follows:

Year	Depreciation for financial reporting	Depreciation for tax purposes	Difference
20X1	$10,000	$10,000	$ --
20X2	10,000	20,000	(10,000)
20X3	10,000	20,000	(10,000)
20X4	10,000	10,000	--
20X5	10,000	--	10,000
20X6	10,000	--	10,000
	$60,000	$60,000	$ --

REQUIRED: Determine the cumulative temporary difference at the end of each year and describe its impact on future tax returns.

(continued on next page)

> **SOLUTION:**
>
> 1. At the end of 20X1, there is no temporary difference. The carrying amount of the asset is $50,000 and its tax basis is $50,000 (i.e., $60,000 – $10,000).
>
> 2. At the end of 20X2, the cumulative temporary difference is $10,000 and will result in a net future taxable amount of $10,000. This amount will reverse in 20X5.
>
> 3. At the end of 20X3, the cumulative temporary difference is $20,000 and will result in a net future taxable amount of $20,000. This amount will reverse equally in 20X5 and 20X6.
>
> 4. At the end of 20X4, the cumulative temporary difference is $20,000 and will result in a net future taxable amount of $20,000. This amount will reverse equally in 20X5 and 20X6.
>
> 5. At the end of 20X5, the cumulative temporary difference is $10,000 and will result in a future taxable amount of $10,000. This amount will reverse in 20X6.
>
> 6. At the end of 20X6, there is no more temporary difference because the asset is fully depreciated both for financial statements and tax purposes.

C. OTHER SOURCES

Other situations that may cause temporary differences because of differences between the reported amount and the tax basis of an asset or liability are as follows:

1. **TAX CREDITS** A reduction in the tax basis of depreciable assets because of tax credits

2. **INVESTMENT TAX CREDITS** Investment tax credits accounted for by the deferred method

3. **CURRENCY ISSUES** An increase in the tax basis of assets because of indexing whenever the local currency is the functional currency

4. **BUSINESS COMBINATIONS** Business combinations accounted for by the purchase method

D. NOT LINKED TO A PARTICULAR ITEM

Some temporary differences are deferred taxable income or tax deductions and have balances only on the income tax balance sheet and, therefore, cannot be identified with a particular asset or liability for financial reporting. There is no related, identifiable asset or liability for financial reporting, but there is a temporary difference that results from an event that has been recognized in the financial statements; and, based on provisions in the tax law, the temporary difference will result in taxable or deductible amounts in future years. An example is a long-term contract that is accounted for by the percentage-of-completion method for financial reporting and by the completed-contract method for tax purposes. The temporary difference (income on the contract) is deferred income for tax purposes that becomes taxable when the contract is completed.

E. PERMANENT DIFFERENCES

Some events recognized in financial statements do not have tax consequences under the regular U.S. tax system. Certain revenues are exempt from taxation and certain expenses are not deductible. Events that do not have tax consequences do not give rise to temporary differences and, therefore, do not give rise to deferred tax assets or liabilities. These differences between pretax financial income and taxable income that are due to events that will not have future tax consequences are often referred to as permanent differences.

1. **REVENUE EXAMPLES** Examples of permanent differences resulting from revenues that are included in the computation of financial income but are not included in computing taxable income are:

a.   Interest earned on state and municipal obligations;

b.   Life insurance proceeds received by an enterprise on one of its officers; and

c.   Dividends received by one U.S. corporation from another U.S. corporation that are excluded from taxable income due to the dividends-received deduction (70%, 80%, or 100%).

2.   **EXPENSE EXAMPLES** Examples of permanent differences resulting from expenses that are included in the computation of financial income but are not included in computing taxable income are:

a.   Expenses incurred in generating tax-exempt income;

b.   Premiums paid for life insurance on officers when the enterprise is the beneficiary; and

c.   Fines, penalties, and other costs incurred from activities that are a violation of the law.

3.   **DEDUCTION EXAMPLE** An example of a permanent difference resulting from deductions that are allowed in computing taxable income but are not allowed in computing financial income is excess of percentage depletion (statutory allowance) over cost of natural resources.

EXAMPLE 8 ♦ TEMPORARY AND PERMANENT DIFFERENCES

Tigger Corporation has pretax financial income of $100,000 for 20X1 (first year of operations). The following differences exist between pretax financial income and taxable income:

1.   Interest on investments in tax-exempt securities amounts to $22,000.

2.   Fines and violations of the law amount to $3,000.

3.   An excess of accrued warranty expense over amounts paid to satisfy warranties during the year is $18,000.

4.   An excess of installment sales revenue over the cash received is $31,000 (accrual basis used for financial reporting and cash basis used for tax return).

5.   Premiums paid for life insurance on officers is $6,000. Tigger Corp. is the beneficiary.

6.   Depreciation for books is $70,000, whereas depreciation using an accelerated method for tax purposes is $90,000.

7.   Losses accrued for financial accounting purposes for litigation contingencies amounts to $16,000.

REQUIRED:

a.   Identify each of the differences between pretax financial income and taxable income as being either a permanent difference or a temporary difference and reconcile pretax financial income with taxable income.

b.   Compute the net future taxable (deductible) amounts due to temporary differences existing at the end of 20X1.

c.   Assuming a tax rate for the current and future years of 40%, compute the amount of income taxes currently payable and the amount of deferred income taxes.

d.   Prepare the journal entry to record income taxes for 20X1.

(continued on next page)

SOLUTION a:

Pretax financial income		$100,000
Permanent differences:		
[1]	Tax-exempt revenue	(22,000)
[2]	Nondeductible fines	3,000
[5]	Life insurance premiums	6,000
Temporary differences originating:		
[3]	Excess of warranty expense per books	18,000
[4]	Excess of installment revenue per books	(31,000)
[6]	Excess of depreciation per tax return	(20,000)
[7]	Excess of accrued losses per books	16,000
Taxable income		$ 70,000

SOLUTION b:

[3]	Future warranty deductions	$ (18,000)
[4]	Future installment sale collections	31,000
[6]	Excess of book depreciation over tax depreciation in future	20,000
[7]	Future deductions for litigation	(16,000)
Net future taxable amounts		$ 17,000

SOLUTION c:

Taxable income	$ 70,000
Current tax rate	x 40%
Income taxes currently payable	$ 28,000
Net future taxable amounts	$ 17,000
Enacted future tax rate	x 40%
Deferred tax liability at end of 20X1	$ 6,800

NOTE: Because there is a flat tax rate for all future years, deferred taxes are computed by one aggregate calculation; the future taxable and deductible amounts that will result from the elimination of the existing temporary differences do not have to be scheduled for the individual future years affected.

NOTE: The temporary differences originating in the current period that will cause future deductible amounts (accrual of warranty expense and accrual of loss contingency for financial reporting purposes) are added to pretax financial income to arrive at taxable income; temporary differences originating in the current period that will cause future taxable amounts (installment method for installment sales and an accelerated depreciation method for tax purposes) are deducted from pretax financial income to arrive at taxable income.

SOLUTION d:

Income Tax Expense—current	28,000	
Income Tax Expense—deferred	6,800	
Income Taxes Payable ($70,000 x 40%)		28,000
Deferred Tax Liability ($6,800 – $0)		6,800

NOTE: The change required in the deferred tax balance is equal to its appropriate ending balance because there was a zero beginning balance.

EXHIBIT 4 ♦ SUMMARY OF TEMPORARY AND PERMANENT DIFFERENCES

	GAAP Financial Statements	IRC Tax Return	TEMP	PERM	NONE
GROSS INCOME:					
Gross Sales	Income Now	Income Now			✓
Installment Sales	Income Now	Income (Later) When Rec'd	✓		
Dividends					
Equity Method	Income-Sub Earnings	Income is Dividends	✓		
100/80/70% Exclusion	No Exclusion	Excluded Forever		✓	
Rents & Royalties in Advance	Income When Earned	Income When Received	✓		
State & Muni Bond Interest	Income	Never Income		✓	
Life Insurance Proceeds	Income	Never Income		✓	
Gain/Loss Treasury Stock	Not Reported	Not Reported			✓
ORDINARY EXPENSES:					
Officers Compensation (Top)	Expense	$1,000,000 Limit			✓
Bad Debt	Allowance	Direct Write Off	✓		
Interest Expense					
Business Loan	Expense	Expense			✓
Tax Free Investment	Expense	Non Deductible		✓	
Taxable Investment	Expense	Up to Taxable Income			✓
Contributions	All Expensed	Limit to 10% of Inc.	✓		✓
Loss on Abandonment/Casualty	Expense	Expense			✓
Loss on Worthless Subsidiary	Expense	Expense			✓
Depreciation					
MACRS vs. S.L.	Slow Depreciation	Fast Depreciation	✓		
Bonus Depreciation (179)	Not Allowed, Must Depr.	Varies, $24,000 for 2002	✓		
Diff. Basis of Asset	Use GAAP Basis	Use IRC Basis		✓	
Amortization of Purchased Goodwill	Gain/Loss; Revalued each Year (Amortization no longer allowed)	Amortize S/L 15 Yrs.	✓		✓
Depletion					
% vs. S.L.	Cost Over Years	% of Sales	✓		
% in Excess of Cost	Not Allowed	% of Sales		✓	
Life Insur. Exp. (Corp. Gets)	Expense	No Deduction		✓	
Profit & Pension Expense	Expense Accrued	No Deduction Until Paid	✓		
Accrued Exp. (50% owner/family)	Expense Accrued	No Deduction Until Paid	✓		
Net Capital Gain	Income	Income			✓
Research & Development	Expense	Exp. / Amortize / Capital.	✓	✓	✓
SPECIAL ITEMS:					
Net Capital Loss	Report as Loss	Not Deductible	✓		
Carryover (3 Yrs. & 5 Yrs.)	Not Applicable	Unused Loss Allowed	✓		
Shareholder Dealing	Report as Loss	Not Deductible		✓	
Penalties	Expense	Not Deductible		✓	
Est. Liab. Contingency/Warranty	Expense-Accrued	No Deduction Until Paid	✓		
Federal Income Taxes	Expense	Not Deductible		✓	
Bond Sinking Trust Fund	Inc. / Exp. / Gain / Loss	Inc. / Exp. / Gain / Loss	✓	✓	✓
Lobbying / Political	Expense	No Deduction		✓	

IV. COMPUTATION OF DEFERRED TAX LIABILITIES AND ASSETS

A. RECOGNITION AND MEASUREMENT

An enterprise is to recognize a deferred tax liability or asset for all temporary differences and operating loss and tax credit carryforwards.

1. **DEFERRED TAX EXPENSE OR BENEFIT** Deferred tax expense or benefit is the change during the year in an enterprise's deferred tax liabilities and assets.

2. **TOTAL INCOME TAX EXPENSE OR BENEFIT** Total income tax expense (provision) or benefit for the year is the sum of deferred tax expense or benefit and current tax expense or benefit (income taxes currently payable or refundable).

3. **RECOGNITION AND MEASUREMENT** The recognition and measurement of a deferred tax liability or asset is based on the future effects on income taxes, as measured by the provisions of enacted tax laws, resulting from temporary differences and operating loss and tax credit carryforwards at the end of the current year.

4. **JURISDICTIONS** A deferred tax liability or asset is separately computed for each tax jurisdiction (i.e., for each federal, state, local, and foreign taxing authority) because the tax attributes related to one taxing authority cannot be used to directly offset tax attributes related to a different taxing authority.

B. COMPUTATION

The steps in the annual computation of deferred tax liabilities and assets are as follows:

1. **IDENTIFICATION** Identify (a) the types and amounts of existing temporary differences and (b) the nature and amount of each type of operating loss and tax credit carryforward and the remaining length of the carryforward period;

2. **MEASURING DEFERRED TAX LIABILITY** Measure the total deferred tax liability for taxable temporary differences using the applicable tax rate;

3. **MEASURING DEFERRED TAX ASSET** Measure the total deferred tax asset for deductible temporary differences and operating loss carryforwards using the applicable tax rate;

4. **TAX CREDIT CARRYFORWARDS** Measure deferred tax assets for each type of tax credit carryforward; and

5. **VALUATION ALLOWANCE** Reduce deferred tax assets by a valuation allowance if, based on the weight of available evidence, it is *more likely than not* (a likelihood of more than 50%) that some portion or all of the deferred tax assets will not be realized. The valuation allowance should be sufficient to reduce the deferred tax asset to the amount that is more likely than not to be realized.

C. ENACTED TAX RATE

The tax rate that is used to measure deferred tax liabilities and deferred tax assets is the enacted tax rate(s) expected to apply to taxable income in the years that the liability is expected to be settled or the asset recovered. Measurements are based on elections (for example, an election for loss carryforward instead of carryback) that are expected to be made for tax purposes in future years.

1. **DETERMINING APPLICABLE TAX RATE** Presently enacted changes in tax laws and rates that become effective for a particular future year or years must be considered when determining the tax rate to apply to temporary differences reversing in that year or years. Tax laws and rates for the current year are used if no changes have been enacted for future years.

2. **MEASURING THE ASSET OR LIABILITY** An asset for deductible temporary differences that are expected to be realized in future years through carryback of a future loss to the current or a prior year (or a liability for taxable temporary differences that are expected to reduce the refund claimed for the carryback of a future loss to the current or a prior year) is measured using tax laws and rates for the current or a prior year, that is, the year for which a refund is expected to be realized based on loss carryback provisions of the tax law.

3. **FUTURE YEARS** Therefore, if there are no new tax rates enacted for future years, the current rate(s) is (are) used to compute deferred taxes, and aggregate calculations are acceptable. However, if there are new tax rates enacted for future years, a scheduling of the individual future years affected by existing temporary differences is required.

    a. The schedule will show in which future years existing temporary differences cause taxable or deductible amounts.

    b. The appropriate enacted tax rate is applied to each of these future taxable and deductible amounts.

4. **ASSUMPTIONS ABOUT FUTURE TAXABLE INCOME** In determining the appropriate tax rate, an assumption must be made about whether the entity will report taxable income or loss in the various individual future years expected to be affected by the reversal of existing temporary differences.

    a. If taxable income is expected in the year that a future taxable (or deductible) amount is scheduled, use the enacted rate for that future year to calculate the related deferred tax liability (or asset).

    b. If an NOL is expected in the year that a future taxable (or deductible) amount is scheduled, use the enacted rate of what will be the prior year the NOL will be carried back to or the enacted rate of the future year to which the carryforward will apply, whichever Is appropriate, to calculate the related deferred tax liability (or asset).

D. **APPLICABLE TAX RATE**
The objective is to measure a deferred tax liability or asset using the enacted tax rate(s) expected to apply to taxable income in the periods in which the deferred tax liability or asset is expected to be settled or realized.

1. **FLAT RATE VS GRADUATED RATE** Under current U.S. federal tax law, if taxable income exceeds a specified amount, all taxable income is taxed, in substance, at a single flat tax rate. That tax rate shall be used for measurement of a deferred tax liability or asset by enterprises for which graduated tax rates are not a significant factor. Enterprises for which graduated tax rates are a significant factor shall measure a deferred tax liability or asset using the *average graduated tax rate* applicable to the amount of estimated annual taxable income in the periods in which the deferred tax liability or asset is estimated to be settled or realized.

2. **OTHER TAX PROVISIONS** Other provisions of enacted tax laws should be considered when determining the tax rate to apply to certain types of temporary differences and carryforwards (for example, the tax law may provide for different tax rates on ordinary income and capital gains). If there is a phased-in change in tax rates, determination of the applicable tax rate requires knowledge about when deferred tax liabilities and assets will be settled and realized.

EXAMPLE 9 ◆ ANNUAL COMPUTATION OF DEFERRED TAX LIABILITIES AND ASSETS

Bensen's first year of operations is 20X1. For 20X1, Bensen has pretax financial income of $150,000 and taxable income of $50,000. Taxable income is expected in all future years.

a.   Tax rates enacted by the end of 20X1 are as follows:

20X1	40%
20X2	35%
20X3 through 20X6	30%
20X7	25%

b.   Temporary differences existing at the end of 20X1 are as follows:

Installment sale difference (taxable in 20X2)	$ 30,000
Depreciation difference (see below)	90,000
Estimated expenses (deductible in 20X7)	(20,000)
Net temporary difference	$100,000

c.   The temporary difference related to depreciable assets will result in the following future taxable (deductible) amounts:

20X3	$ 50,000
20X4	40,000
	$ 90,000

STEP 1: Identify the types and amounts of existing temporary differences and the nature and amount of each type of operating loss and tax credit carryforward and the remaining length of the carry-forward period.

The installment sale difference is a taxable temporary difference.

The estimated expenses accrued for accounting purposes and deferred for tax purposes cause a deductible temporary difference.

	Amount
Future taxable (deductible) amounts for temporary differences:	
Installment sale	$ 30,000
Depreciation	90,000
Estimated expense	(20,000)

STEP 2: Measure the total deferred tax liability for taxable temporary differences using the applicable tax rates.

	Amount	Rate	Deferred Tax Liab.
Future taxable amounts for temporary differences:			
Installment sale	$ 30,000	35%	$10,500
Depreciation	90,000	30%	27,000
Total			$37,500

The enacted tax rate used to measure the deferred tax consequences of a future taxable amount should be the rate at which the taxable amount will be taxed. Assuming taxable income is expected in all future years, the amount of temporary difference scheduled to reverse in 20X2 and cause a taxable amount that year is tax effected at the 35% rate enacted for 20X2. Similarly, the amount of temporary difference scheduled to reverse in 20X3 ($50,000) and 20X4 ($40,000) and result in a taxable amount those years is tax effected at the 30% tax rate already enacted for that particular future year.

(continued on next page)

STEP 3: Measure the total deferred tax asset for deductible temporary differences and operating loss carryforwards using the applicable tax rate.

	Amount	Rate	Deferred Tax Asset
Future deductible amounts for temporary differences: Estimated expense	$(20,000)	25%	$ 5,000

The enacted tax rate used to measure the deferred tax consequences of a future deductible amount should be the rate at which the deductible amount will provide tax benefits. Taxable income is expected in all future years. Thus, the deductible amount scheduled for 20X7 will provide tax benefits at a rate of 25%.

There are no operating loss carryforwards in this example.

STEP 4: Measure deferred tax assets for each type of tax credit carryforward.

There are no tax credit carryforwards in this example.

STEP 5: Reduce deferred tax assets by a valuation allowance if, based on the weight of available evidence, it is more likely than not (a likelihood of more than 50%) that some portion or all of the deferred tax assets will not be realized. The valuation allowance should be sufficient to reduce the deferred tax asset to the amount that is more likely than not to be realized.

There is no mention of any uncertainty regarding the future realization of the benefits associated with the deferred tax asset. Therefore, assume no valuation allowance is necessary.

NOTE: Deferred tax liabilities and assets are not reported at discounted values.

EXAMPLE 10 ♦ INCOME TAX EXPENSE AND DEFERRED TAXES

Refer to the data for the Bensen Company that appears in Example 9 and the results of the annual computation of deferred liabilities and assets.

REQUIRED:

a.   Prepare the journal entry to record income tax expense, deferred taxes, and income taxes payable for 20X1.

b.   Compute the total income tax expense for 20X1. Indicate the portion that is current and the portion that is due to deferred tax expense or benefit. Draft the bottom portion of the income statement beginning with "Income before income taxes."

c.   Indicate the proper classification(s) of deferred taxes for the December 31, 20X1, balance sheet.

SOLUTION a:

Income Tax Expense—current	20,000	
Income Tax Expense—deferred	32,500	
Deferred Tax Asset	5,000	
Income Taxes Payable		20,000
Deferred Tax Liability		37,500

To record income taxes for the current period, in one compound entry.

(continued on next page)

COMPUTATIONS:

STEP 1: Record the amount of taxes payable or refundable for the current year.

Taxable income	$50,000
Tax rate for 20X1	40%
Income taxes currently payable	$20,000

STEP 2: Record the change required in the deferred tax accounts.

Balance of deferred tax liability, 12/31/X1	$37,500*
Balance of deferred tax liability, 01/01/X1	0
Increase in deferred tax liability	$37,500
Balance of deferred tax asset, 12/31/X1	$ 5,000*
Balance of deferred tax asset, 01/01/X1	0
Increase in deferred tax asset	$ 5,000

---

* These ending balances are the result of the annual computation of deferred tax liabilities and assets illustrated in Example 9, above. Beginning balances are the result of entries recorded in prior periods. There are no beginning balances in this example because 20X1 is Bensen's first year of operations.

STEP 3: Balance the entry by a debit or credit (whichever is appropriate) to income tax expense—current and income tax expense—deferred. In this situation, the net tax provision is $52,500.

An alternative to the above entry is to record the amount of current income tax expense and the amount of deferred income taxes in separate entries.

SOLUTION b:

The amount of total tax expense (provision) to appear on the income statement for 20X1 is $52,500 (current tax expense of $20,000 plus net deferred tax expense of $32,500). The computations for total tax expense are as follows:

Taxable income	$50,000
Tax rate	x 40%
Current tax expense (income taxes payable)	$20,000
Deferred tax liability, 12/31/X1 (Example 9)	$37,500
Deferred tax liability, 01/01/X1	--
Deferred tax expense, 20X1 (increase required in deferred tax liability account)	$37,500
Deferred tax asset, 12/31/X1 (Example 9)	$ 5,000
Deferred tax asset, 01/01/X1	--
Deferred tax benefit, 20X1 (increase required in deferred tax asset account)	$ 5,000
Deferred tax expense, 20X1	$37,500
Deferred tax benefit, 20X1	(5,000)
Net deferred tax expense, 20X1	32,500
Current tax expense, 20X1	20,000
Total income tax expense, 20X1	$52,500

Income before income taxes		$150,000
Provision for income taxes:		
Current tax expense	$20,000	
Deferred tax expense	32,500	
Total income tax expense		(52,500)
Net income		$ 97,500

NOTE: The effective tax rate is $52,500 ÷ $150,000 = 35%.

(continued on next page)

SOLUTION C:

Deferred income taxes should appear on the balance sheet at the end of 20X1 in the following amounts and classifications:

Current liabilities:		Long-term liabilities:	
Deferred tax liability	$10,500	Deferred tax liability	$22,000

EXPLANATION: In a classified balance sheet, an enterprise shall separate deferred tax liabilities and assets into a current and a noncurrent amount. Deferred tax liabilities and assets shall be classified as current or noncurrent based on the classification of the related asset or liability for financial reporting.

In the situation at hand, the $10,500 deferred tax liability caused by the installment sale is classified as a current liability because the installment receivable is classified as a current asset (the temporary difference is reversing in 20X2, which indicates the receivable will be collected in 20X2). The $27,000 net deferred tax liability related to the depreciation type temporary difference is classified as a noncurrent liability because the related assets (property, plant, and equipment) are classified as a noncurrent asset. The $5,000 deferred tax asset resulting from the expenses accrued for accounting purposes is classified as a noncurrent asset because the related accrued liability is a noncurrent liability (the temporary difference is not expected to reverse until 20X7, which indicates the accrued liability is not expected to be settled until 20X7, which makes the liability a noncurrent one). The computations are summarized as follows:

Type of difference	Temporary difference	Tax rate	Deferred taxes	Current or noncurrent
Installment sale	$ 30,000	35%	$10,500	Current
Depreciation	90,000	30%	27,000	Noncurrent
Accrued expenses	(20,000)	25%	(5,000)	Noncurrent

The net current amount is a liability of $10,500. The net noncurrent amount is a liability of $22,000.

EXAMPLE 11 ♦ DEFERRED TAX LIABILITIES AND ASSETS

The first year of operations for the Pandora Corporation was 20X1. Taxable income for 20X1 was $120,000. Pandora was subject to enacted U.S. tax rates of 40% in 20X1 and 30% in 20X2 and later years. Taxable income is expected in all future years. At the end of 20X1, there was only one future taxable temporary difference of $140,000 related to depreciation.

Based on the above, the computation of deferred taxes at the end of 20X1 (using the liability method) was as follows:

	Amount	Rate	Deferred Tax Liab.
Future taxable amounts for temporary differences:			
Depreciation	$140,000	30%	$42,000

Income taxes for 20X1 were properly recorded as follows:

Income Tax Expense—current	48,000	
Income Tax Expense—deferred	42,000	
Income Taxes Payable ($120,000 x 40%)		48,000
Deferred Tax Liability		42,000

Pandora has taxable income for 20X2 of $110,000. Enacted tax rates have not changed so the rate for 20X2 and future years is 30%. At the end of 20X2, cumulative taxable temporary differences related to depreciation are $180,000.

(continued on next page)

REQUIRED:

1. Compute the amount of deferred taxes to be reported on the balance sheet at the end of 20X2.

2. Prepare the journal entry to record income taxes for 20X2.

3. Draft the section of the income statement for 20X2 that relates to reporting income taxes.

SOLUTION 1:

	Amount	Rate	Deferred Tax Liab.
Future taxable amounts for temporary differences:			
Depreciation	$180,000	30%	$ 54,000

SOLUTION 2:

Income Tax Expense—current	33,000	
Income Tax Expense—deferred	12,000	
Income Taxes Payable ($110,000 x 30%)		33,000
Deferred Tax Liability ($54,000 – 42,000)		12,000

COMPUTATIONS:

Deferred tax liability, end of 20X2	$ 54,000
Deferred tax liability, end of 20X1	(42,000)
Deferred tax expense, 20X2 (increase in deferred tax liability account)	12,000
Current tax expense, 20X2	33,000
Total tax expense (provision), 20X2	$ 45,000

SOLUTION 3:

Income before income taxes		$150,000
Income tax expense:		
Current tax expense	$33,000	
Deferred tax expense	12,000	(45,000)
Net income		$105,000

Income before taxes is verified as follows (assuming there are no permanent differences):

Pretax financial income	$ X
Increase in cumulative taxable temporary differences ($180,000 – $140,000)	(40,000)
Taxable income	$110,000
Solving for X: X = $150,000	

EXAMPLE 12 ♦ DEFERRED TAX LIABILITIES AND ASSETS

Jersey Corporation uses different depreciation methods for accounting and tax purposes which result in a $60,000 cumulative temporary difference at December 31, 20X4. This temporary difference will reverse equally over the next 5 years. Taxable income for 20X4 is $46,000. Jersey's balance sheet at December 31, 20X3, reported a net deferred tax liability of $8,000 (noncurrent deferred tax liability of $28,000 and a noncurrent deferred tax asset of $20,000).

1. At December 31, 20X4, the company has a $17,000 liability reported because of the accrual of estimated litigation claims. The company expects to pay the claims and have tax deductible amounts in the future as follows:

20X8	15,000
20X9	2,000

(continued on next page)

2. The enacted tax rates as of the beginning of 20X3 are as follows:

20X3 - 20X5	50%
20X6 - 20X7	40%
20X8 and later	30%

REQUIRED: Assuming Jersey expects taxable income in all future years:

a. Calculate the amount of net deferred taxes that should be reported on Jersey's balance sheet at December 31, 20X4, and indicate whether that net amount is an asset or a liability.

b. Prepare the journal entry for Jersey to record income taxes for 20X4.

SOLUTION a:

	Amount	Rate	Deferred Tax Liab.
Future taxable amounts for temporary differences:			
Depreciation - 20X5	$12,000	50%	$ 6,000
Depreciation - 20X6-X7	24,000	40%	9,600
Depreciation - 20X8-X9	24,000	30%	7,200
	$60,000		$22,800

NOTE: The $60,000 must be divided into three parts to account for the different tax rates.

	Amount	Rate	Deferred Tax Asset
Future deductible amounts for temporary differences:			
Litigation	$17,000	30%	$ 5,100

$22,800 + $(5,100) = $17,700 net deferred tax liability at December 31, 20X4.

SOLUTION b:

Income Tax Expense—current	23,000	
Income Tax Expense—deferred ($14,900 – $5,200)	9,700	
Deferred Tax Liability ($28,000 – $22,800)	5,200	
Income Tax Payable ($46,000 x 50%)		23,000
Deferred Tax Asset ($20,000 – $5,100)		14,900

COMPUTATIONS:

Taxable income	$46,000
Tax rate	x 50%
Income taxes payable for 20X4	$23,000
Deferred tax liability, 12/31/X4—part (a)	$22,800
Deferred tax liability, 12/31/X3	28,000
Deferred tax benefit, 20X4 (decrease required in deferred tax liability account)	$ (5,200)
Deferred tax asset, 12/31/X4—part (a)	$ 5,100
Deferred tax asset, 12/31/X3	20,000
Deferred tax expense, 20X4 (decrease required in deferred tax asset account)	$14,900
Deferred tax benefit, 20X4	$ (5,200)
Deferred tax expense, 20X4	14,900
Net deferred tax expense, 20X4	$ 9,700
Current tax expense, 20X4	$23,000
Deferred tax expense, 20X4	9,700
Total tax expense (provision) for 20X4	$32,700

EXAMPLE 13 ♦ DEFERRED TAX LIABILITIES AND ASSETS

Jersey Corporation, from Example 12, expects taxable income in 20X5 through 20X8 and an NOL in 20X9, the benefits of which are expected to be realized by carryback.

REQUIRED:

a. Calculate the amount of net deferred taxes that should be reported on Jersey's balance sheet at December 31, 20X4, and indicate whether that net amount is an asset or a liability.

b. Prepare the journal entry for Jersey to record income taxes for 20X4.

SOLUTION a: Because Jersey expects an NOL rather than taxable income in 20X9, the tax rate to be used to tax effect the future taxable and deductible amounts scheduled for 20X9 (due to temporary differences existing at the end of 20X4) is the rate of the year to which the expected NOL of 20X9 is to be carried back or forward. In this case, that would be 20X7 (the data indicated an expected carryback and the provisions of the tax code require carryback to the earliest of two years prior to the loss year). Thus, the taxable amount of $12,000 scheduled for 20X9 will reduce a tax refund computed at the rate of 40% and the deductible amount of $2,000 scheduled for 20X9 will increase a tax refund computed at the rate of 40%.

Deferred taxes would be:

	Amount	Rate	Deferred Tax Liab.
Future taxable amounts for temporary differences:			
Depreciation—20X5	$12,000	50%	$ 6,000
Depreciation—20X6-X7, X9	36,000	40%	14,400
Depreciation—20X8-X9	12,000	30%	3,600
	$60,000		$24,000

NOTE: The $60,000 must be divided into three parts to account for the different tax rates and the years the amounts are carried to.

	Amount	Rate	Deferred Tax Asset
Future deductible amounts for temporary differences:			
Litigation—20X8	$15,000	30%	$ 4,500
Litigation—20X9	2,000	40%	800
	$17,000		$ 5,300

$24,000 + $(5,300) = $18,700 deferred tax liability at December 31, 20X4.

SOLUTION b:

Income Tax Expense—current	23,000	
Income Tax Expense—deferred ($14,700 – $4,000)	10,700	
Deferred Tax Liability ($28,000 – $24,000)	4,000	
Income Tax Payable ($46,000 x 50%)		23,000
Deferred Tax Asset ($20,000 – $5,300)		14,700

E. ATTRIBUTES OF THE ASSET AND LIABILITY METHOD

1. **BALANCE SHEET APPROACH** There is an emphasis on the amount to be reported as deferred taxes on the balance sheet (hence, it is said to be *a balance sheet approach or balance sheet-oriented*).

2. **BALANCE OF DEFERRED TAX ASSET OR LIABILITY** The balance in a deferred tax liability or asset account on a balance sheet is the amount of taxes expected to be paid or refunded (or saved) in the future as a result of the turn-around (reversal) of temporary differences existing at the balance sheet date.

3. **CALCULATION** The amount to be reported for deferred taxes on a balance sheet is calculated by using *future tax rates* (i.e., rates that have already been *enacted* for the future) and applying them to cumulative temporary differences based on when and how the temporary differences are expected to affect the tax return in the future.

4. **EFFECT ON INCOME STATEMENT** A temporary difference originating in the current period that causes an increase in a deferred tax liability will also cause a debit (charge) to the provision for deferred taxes on the income statement; an increase in deferred tax asset will result in a credit to the provision for deferred taxes.

5. **DEFERRED TAX EXPENSE OR BENEFIT** Deferred tax expense (benefit) on the income statement is a "residual" amount because it merely reflects the change in the balance sheet deferred tax account(s) from the prior year. The amount of deferred tax expense (benefit) for a year is a by-product of the year's deferred tax calculation because it is the net change during the year in the net deferred tax liability or asset amount.

6. **INCREASE/DECREASE IN DEFERRED TAX ASSET/LIABILITY** An increase in a deferred tax liability or a decrease in a deferred tax asset on the balance sheet results in a *deferred tax expense* on the income statement; an increase in a deferred tax asset or a decrease in a deferred tax liability on the balance sheet will cause a *deferred tax benefit* on the income statement.

7. **SUBSEQUENT CHANGES** The balance sheet deferred tax account(s) are to be adjusted for any subsequent changes in the tax rates or laws.

8. **SINGLE TAX RATE VS DIFFERENT TAX RATES** If a single tax rate applies to all future years, an aggregate computation is appropriate. However, If different tax rates apply to individual future years, a *scheduling* of future taxable and deductible amounts (due to existing temporary differences) with a separate computation for each future year affected is required.

V. OTHER CONSIDERATIONS

A. VALUATION ALLOWANCE

1. **DEFERRED TAX ASSETS** Deferred tax assets are recorded for the future tax benefits of operating loss carryforwards, tax credit carryforwards, and deductible temporary differences existing at a balance sheet date. Deferred tax assets are to be reduced by a valuation allowance if, based on the weight of available evidence, it is more likely than not (a likelihood of more than 50%) that some portion or all of the deferred tax assets will not be realized. The valuation allowance should be sufficient to reduce the deferred tax asset to the amount that is more likely than not to be realized.

EXAMPLE 14 ♦ VALUATION ALLOWANCE

It is the end of Year 1, XYZ's first year of operations. XYZ reports a net operating loss of $50,000 on its tax return for Year 1. At the end of Year 1, XYZ has a temporary difference that will result in future deductible amounts of $80,000. The enacted tax rate for Year 1 is 50%. The tax rate for Year 2 and subsequent years is 40%.

REQUIRED:

1. Prepare the journal entry(s) to record income taxes for Year 1.

2. Assume that at the end of Year 1, it is estimated that 30% of the company's deferred tax assets will not be realized in the future. Prepare the appropriate journal entry.

(continued on next page)

3. Draft the section of the Year 1 income statement that reports income tax expense, beginning with the line "Income Before Income Taxes." Reflect the results of parts 1. and 2., above.

4. Assume that in Year 2, XYZ reports taxable income of $100,000 (before deduction of the NOL carryover and after deducting the $80,000 future deductible amount) and has no temporary differences at the end of Year 2. Prepare the appropriate journal entries to record income taxes and draft the section of the Year 2 income statement that reports income tax expense.

SOLUTION 1:

Deferred Tax Asset	52,000	
Benefits of Loss Carryforward		20,000
Income Tax Expense—deferred		32,000

COMPUTATIONS:

Taxable loss (NOL), Year 1	$(50,000)
Tax rate of future year (for carryforward)	40%
Tax benefits of NOL carryforward	$(20,000)
Future deductible amounts	$(80,000)
Tax rate of future years	40%
Deferred tax asset at end of Year 1	$(32,000)

SOLUTION 2:

Benefits of Loss Carryforward ($20,000 x 30%)	6,000	
Income Tax Expense—deferred ($32,000 x 30%)	9,600	
Allowance to Reduce Deferred Tax		
Asset to Realizable Value		15,600

SOLUTION 3:

Operating loss before income taxes		$(130,000)***
Income tax benefits:		
Benefits of loss carryforward	$ 14,000*	
Deferred tax benefit	22,400**	36,400
Net loss		$ (93,600)

COMPUTATIONS:

  * $20,000 x 70% = $14,000
 ** $32,000 x 70% = $22,400
*** Pretax financial income

Deductible temporary difference originating in Year 1	$ X
Taxable loss	80,000
Solving for X: X = $(130,000)	$ (50,000)

Solution 4:

Income Tax Expense—current ($100,000 x 40%)	40,000	
Income Tax Expense—deferred	22,400*	
Allowance to Reduce Deferred Tax Asset		
to Realizable Value (balance of account)	15,600	
Income Taxes Payable [($100,000 – $50,000) X 40%]		20,000
Deferred Tax Asset (balance of account)		52,000
Benefits of Loss Carryforward		
(income tax expense) ($20,000 x 30%)		6,000

(continued on next page)

Income Statement:

Income before income taxes		$ 180,000**
Income tax expense:		
Current tax expense	$ 40,000	
Deferred tax expense	22,400	
Benefits of loss carryforward	(6,000)	
Total income tax expense		(56,400)
Net income		$ 123,600

COMPUTATIONS:

*Deferred tax asset related to deductibles		$32,000
Allowance related to deductibles		(9,600)
Income tax expense–deferred		$22,400
**Pretax financial income	$ X	
Reversing temporary difference	(80,000)	
Taxable income	$100,000	
Solving for X: X = $180,000		

The one compound journal entry above could be replaced by the following three journal entries:

Income Tax Expense	40,000	
Income Tax Payable [($100,000 – $50,000) X 40%]		20,000
Benefit of Loss Carryforward		20,000
To record current income taxes.		
Income Tax Expense—deferred	32,000	
Benefit of Loss Carryforward	20,000	
Deferred Tax Asset (balance of account)		52,000
To eliminate the deferred asset balance and to recognize deferred tax expense.		
Allowance to Reduce Deferred Tax Asset		
to Realizable Value (balance of account)	15,600	
Benefits of Loss Carryforward ($20,000 x 30%)		6,000
Income Tax Expense—deferred (to balance)		9,600
To eliminate the allowance balance and to recognize the previously unrecognized benefits of the loss carryforward.		

2. **FUTURE REALIZATION OF TAX BENEFIT** Future realization of the tax benefit of an existing deductible temporary difference or carryforward ultimately depends on the existence of sufficient taxable income of the appropriate character (for example, ordinary income or capital gain) within the carryback, carryforward period available under the tax law. The following four possible sources of taxable income may be available under the tax law to realize a tax benefit for deductible temporary differences and carryforwards:

   a. Future reversals of existing taxable temporary differences

   b. Future taxable income exclusive of reversing temporary differences and carryforwards

   c. Taxable income in prior carryback year(s) if carryback is permitted under the tax law

   d. Tax-planning strategies that would, if necessary, be implemented to the following, for example:

      (1) Accelerate taxable amounts to utilize expiring carryforwards

      (2) Change the character of taxable or deductible amounts from ordinary income or loss to capital gain or loss

      (3) Switch from tax-exempt to taxable investments

3. **TAX-PLANNING STRATEGIES** In some circumstances, there are actions (including elections for tax purposes) that (1) are prudent and feasible, (2) an enterprise ordinarily might not take, but would take to prevent an operating loss or tax credit carryforward from expiring unused, and (3) would result in realization of deferred tax assets. SFAS 109 refers to those actions as *tax-planning strategies*. An enterprise shall consider tax-planning strategies in determining the amount of valuation allowance required. Significant expenses to implement a tax-planning strategy or any significant losses that would be recognized if that strategy were implemented (net of any recognizable tax benefits associated with those expenses or losses) shall be included in the valuation allowance.

4. **EVIDENCE TO DETERMINE NEED FOR VALUATION ALLOWANCE** All available evidence, both positive and negative, should be considered to determine whether, based on the weight of that evidence, a valuation allowance is needed. Information about an enterprise's current financial position and its results of operations for the current and preceding years ordinarily is readily available. That historical information is supplemented by all currently available information about future years. Sometimes, however, historical information may not be available (for example, start-up operations), or it may not be as relevant (for example, if there has been a significant, recent change in circumstances) and special attention is required.

5. **NEGATIVE EVIDENCE** Forming a conclusion that a valuation allowance is not needed is difficult when there is negative evidence such as cumulative losses in recent years. Other examples of negative evidence include (but are not limited to) the following:

   a. A history of operating loss or tax credit carryforwards expiring unused

   b. Losses expected in early future years (by a presently profitable entity)

   c. Unsettled circumstances that, if unfavorably resolved, would adversely affect future operations and profit levels on a continuing basis in future years

   d. A carryback, carryforward period that is so brief that it would limit realization of tax benefits if (a) a significant deductible temporary difference is expected to reverse in a single year or (b) the enterprise operates in a traditionally cyclical business

6. **EXAMPLES OF POSITIVE EVIDENCE** Examples (not prerequisites) of positive evidence that might support a conclusion that a valuation allowance is not needed when there is negative evidence include (but are not limited to) the following:

   a. Existing contracts or firm sales backlog that will produce more than enough taxable income to realize the deferred tax asset based on existing sales prices and cost structures.

   b. An excess of appreciated asset value over the tax basis of the entity's net assets in an amount sufficient to realize the deferred tax asset.

   c. A strong earnings history exclusive of the loss that created the future deductible amount (tax loss carryforward or deductible temporary difference) coupled with evidence indicating that the loss (for example, an unusual, infrequent, or extraordinary item) is an aberration rather than a continuing condition.

7. **WEIGHING THE EVIDENCE** An enterprise must use judgment in considering the relative impact of negative and positive evidence. The weight given to the potential effect of negative and positive evidence should be commensurate with the extent to which it can be objectively verified. The more negative evidence that exists the more positive evidence is necessary and the more difficult it is to support a conclusion that a valuation allowance is not needed for some portion or all of the deferred tax asset.

8. **CHANGE IN VALUATION ALLOWANCE** The effect of a change in the beginning-of-the-year balance of a valuation allowance that results from a change in circumstances that causes a change in judgment about the realizability of the related deferred tax asset in future years ordinarily shall be included in income from continuing operations.

B. **ENACTED CHANGE IN TAX LAWS OR RATES**

1. **ADJUSTMENT OF DEFERRED TAX LIABILITY OR ASSET** A deferred tax liability or asset is adjusted for the effect of a change in tax laws or rates. The deferred tax previously provided on items that will become taxable or deductible in any future year affected by the rate change is to be adjusted downward or upward to reflect the new rate. This cumulative effect is included in income from continuing operations for the period that includes the enactment date. Adjustments of a deferred tax liability or asset for enacted changes in tax laws or rates are a component of income tax expense attributable to continuing operations.

2. **INTERIM PERIOD** If the date of enactment occurs during an interim period, APB 28 (as amended by SFAS 109) requires that the effect of the change on the existing balance of a deferred tax liability or asset be recognized in the interim period that includes the enactment date.

EXAMPLE 15 ♦ ENACTED CHANGE IN TAX LAWS OR RATES

Sean Corporation began operations in 20X1. At December 31, 20X1, the Sean Corporation had the following cumulative temporary differences:

1. The reported amount of installment receivables was in excess of the tax basis of those receivables which will result in future taxable amounts of $12,000 ($6,000 in each of years 20X3 and 20X4).

2. The reported amount of an estimated litigation liability was $2,000. There was no such liability for tax purposes (i.e., its tax basis was zero). The liability was expected to be paid (and then result in a tax deductible amount) in 20X4.

The tax rates enacted as of the beginning of 20X1 were as follows:

20X1	50%
20X2 and later years	40%

The net deferred tax liability of $4,000 at the end of 20X1 was calculated as follows:

	Amount	Rate	Deferred Tax Liability (Asset)
Future taxable amounts	$12,000	40%	$4,800
Future deductible amount	(2,000)	40%	(800)
Net deferred tax liability (asset)			$4,000

Taxable income for 20X1 was $22,000. Pretax financial income for 20X1 was $32,000. The journal entry to record income taxes for 20X1 was as follows:

Income Tax Expense—current	11,000	
Income Tax Expense—deferred	4,000	
Deferred Tax Asset	800	
Income Taxes Payable ($22,000 x 50%)		11,000
Deferred Tax Liability		4,800

During 20X2, a new tax rate of 30% was enacted for 20X4. There were no new temporary differences originating in 20X2, and none of the temporary differences existing at the beginning of 20X2 reversed so the cumulative temporary differences existing at the end of 20X2 were the same as those that existed at the end of 20X1. Taxable income for 20X2 amounted to $25,000. Pretax financial income was also $25,000.

(continued on next page)

REQUIRED: Record all journal entries related to income taxes for 20X2.

SOLUTION:

Income Tax Expense—current	10,000	
Deferred Tax Liability ($4,800 – $4,200)	600	
Income Tax Benefit—change in rates ($4,000 – $3,600)		400
Income Taxes Payable ($25,000 x 40%)		10,000
Deferred Tax Asset ($800 – $600)		200

DISCUSSION: A change in an enacted tax rate will cause an immediate cumulative effect on the income tax provision. The deferred tax previously provided on items that will become taxable or deductible in any future year affected by the rate change is to be adjusted downward or upward to reflect the new rate. To determine the adjustment needed to the existing deferred tax account because of the change in the tax rate for 20X4, we need to prepare the scheduling process as it would have been prepared at the end of 20X1 if the new rate for 20X4 had been known at that point in time. That schedule would look as follows:

	Amount	Rate	Deferred Tax Liability (Asset)
Future taxable amounts			
20X3	$6,000	40%	$2,400
20X4	6,000	30%	1,800
Future deductible amount	(2,000)	30%	(600)
Net deferred tax liability (asset)			$3,600

When we compare the results of this scheduling with the results of the scheduling used at the end of 20X1, we find that the deferred tax liability account needs to be decreased by $600 ($4,800 – $4,200) and the deferred tax asset account needs to be decreased by $200 ($800 – $600).

A comparative income statement would report the following:

	20X1		20X2	
Income before income taxes		$ 32,000		$25,000
Income tax expense:				
Current	$11,000		$10,000	
Deferred	4,000			
Adjustment due				
to rate change		(15,000)	(400)	(9,600)
Net income		$ 17,000		$15,400

Note that the effective tax rate for 20X1 was 46.875% (i.e., $15,000 ÷ $32,000) and the effective tax rate for 20X2 was 38.4% (i.e., $9,600 ÷ $25,000).

C. **CHANGE IN TAX STATUS OF AN ENTERPRISE**

1. **RECOGNITION OR ELIMINATION OF DEFERRED TAX ASSET OR LIABILITY** A deferred tax liability or asset should be recognized for temporary differences at the date that a nontaxable enterprise becomes a taxable enterprise (e.g., partnership to corporation or S corporation to C corporation). A deferred tax liability or asset should be eliminated at the date that an enterprise ceases to be a taxable enterprise (e.g., corporation to partnership or C corporation to S corporation).

2. **EFFECTS ON INCOME STATEMENT** The effect of recognizing or eliminating a deferred tax liability or asset is to be included in income from continuing operations.

VI. FINANCIAL STATEMENT PRESENTATION AND DISCLOSURES

A. BALANCE SHEET

1. **REPORTING** In a classified balance sheet, deferred tax assets and liabilities are to be separated and reported in a net current and a net noncurrent amount.

2. **CLASSIFICATION BASED ON RELATED ASSET** Deferred tax liabilities and assets are to be classified as current or noncurrent based on the classification of the related asset or liability for financial reporting. A deferred tax liability or asset that is not related to an asset or liability for financial reporting, including deferred tax assets related to carryforwards, shall be classified according to the expected reversal date of the temporary difference (SFAS 37). The valuation allowance for a particular tax jurisdiction is to be allocated between current and noncurrent deferred tax assets for that jurisdiction on a pro rata basis.

3. **TAX JURISDICTION ISSUE** Deferred tax liabilities and assets attributable to different tax jurisdictions should not be offset.

EXAMPLE 16 ♦ BALANCE SHEET PRESENTATION OF DEFERRED TAXES

Molly Corporation has a tax rate for all periods at 40% and the following temporary differences at December 31, 20X4:

1. Installment receivables appearing on their GAAP balance sheet have a zero tax basis. These receivables are to be collected equally over the next three years and will result in reporting $20,000 gross profit each year for tax purposes. Only one-third of the receivables are classified as a current asset.

2. An accrued payable of $45,000 appearing in the current liability section of the GAAP balance sheet has a zero tax basis.

3. Depreciable assets have an excess of carrying amount over tax basis of $50,000.

Required: Compute deferred taxes at December 31, 20X4, and indicate how they should be classified on the balance sheet at that date.

SOLUTION:

Temporary difference	Future taxable (deductible) amount	Rate	Deferred tax liability (asset)	Current or noncurrent
Installment sales	$20,000	40%	$ 8,000	Current
Installment sales	40,000	40%	16,000	Noncurrent
Accrued expenses	(45,000)	40%	(18,000)	Current
Depreciation	50,000	40%	20,000	Noncurrent

$ 8,000 + $(18,000) = $(10,000) current
$16,000 + $ 20,000 = $ 36,000 noncurrent

Current assets:		Long-term liabilities:	
Deferred tax asset	$10,000	Deferred tax liability	$36,000

DISCUSSION: The deferred tax liability related to the installment sales is one-third current and two-thirds noncurrent because of the classification of the related receivables. The deferred tax asset stemming from the accrual of expenses for books is a current asset because of the current classification of the related accrued payable. The deferred tax liability resulting from different depreciation policies for financial statements and tax returns is classified as noncurrent because the related plant assets are in a noncurrent balance sheet classification.

(continued on next page)

> The current deferred tax items are netted (liability of $8,000 and asset of $18,000) to arrive at an asset of $10,000; the noncurrent items (liabilities of $16,000 and $20,000) are netted to arrive at a liability of $36,000.
>
> The following are to be disclosed:
>
> 1. Total of all deferred tax liabilities
>
> 2. Total of all deferred tax assets
>
> 3. Total valuation allowance recognized for deferred tax assets
>
> 4. Net change during the year in the total valuation allowance
>
> 5. Approximate tax effect of each type of temporary difference and carryforward that gives rise to a significant portion of deferred tax liabilities and deferred tax assets (before allocation of valuation allowances)

B.   INCOME STATEMENT

1.   **ALLOCATION** Income tax expense or benefit for the year is to be allocated among continuing operations, discontinued operations, extraordinary items, the cumulative effect of accounting changes, and items of other comprehensive income (e.g., foreign currency translation adjustments and market value adjustments attributable to available-for-sale marketable equity securities). The process of allocating income taxes to key components of the financial statements is called *intraperiod tax allocation*. Thus, items such as discontinued operations, extraordinary items, cumulative effect of changes in accounting principles, and prior period adjustments are to be reported *net of the related income tax effects*.

   a.   **CONTINUING OPERATIONS** The amount allocated to continuing operations is the tax effect of the pretax income or loss from continuing operations that occurred during the year, plus or minus income tax effects of (1) changes in circumstances that cause a change in judgment about the realization of deferred tax assets in future years, (2) changes in tax laws or rates, and (3) changes in tax status. The remainder is allocated to items other than continuing operations.

   b.   **OTHER THAN CONTINUING OPERATIONS** If there is only one item other than continuing operations, the portion of income tax expense or benefit for the year that remains after the allocation to continuing operations is allocated to that item. If there are two or more items other than continuing operations, the amount that remains after the allocation to continuing operations shall be allocated among those other items in proportion to their individual effects on income tax expense or benefit for the year.

EXAMPLE 17 ♦ INTRAPERIOD TAX ALLOCATION

> Kelly Corporation's pretax financial income and taxable income are the same. Kelly's ordinary loss from continuing operations is $5,000. Kelly also has an extraordinary gain of $9,000 that is a capital gain for tax purposes. The tax rate is 40% on ordinary income and 30% on capital gains. Income taxes currently payable are $1,200 ($4,000 at 30%).
>
> **REQUIRED:** Determine the amount of income tax expense (benefit) to allocate to continuing operations and the amount to allocate to the extraordinary item.
>
> (continued on next page)

> **SOLUTION:**
>
> | | |
> |---|---:|
> | Total income tax expense | $1,200 |
> | Tax benefit allocated to the loss from operations | 1,500 |
> | Incremental tax expense allocated to the extraordinary gain | $2,700 |
>
> The effect of the $5,000 loss from continuing operations was to offset an equal amount of capital gains that otherwise would be taxed at a 30% tax rate. Thus, $1,500 ($5,000 at 30%) of tax benefit is allocated to continuing operations. The $2,700 incremental effect of the extraordinary gain is the $1,200 of total tax expense and the $1,500 tax benefit from continuing operations.

c. **MANNER OF REPORTING** The manner of reporting the tax benefit of an operating loss carryforward or carryback is determined by the source of income or loss of the current year that enabled its recognition. For example, if income from continuing operations in the current year permits recognition of an operating loss carryforward that arose from a discontinued operation of a prior year, the tax benefit attributable to that operating loss carryforward is allocated to income from continuing operations and not by (1) the source of the operating loss carryforward or taxes paid in a prior year or (2) the source of expected future income that will result in realization of a deferred tax asset for an operating loss carryforward from the current year. Thus, the benefit of an NOL carryback would be classified as a component of continuing operations if the income earned in the current year was due to continuing operations even though the NOL resulted from an extraordinary loss in a prior period. (There are a few exceptions to this guideline, including one that deals with business combinations and another involving quasi-reorganizations.)

d. **STOCKHOLDERS' EQUITY** Stockholders' equity is charged or credited for the income tax effects of the following:

(1) Adjustments of the opening balance of retained earnings for certain changes in accounting principles or a correction of an error

(2) Gains and losses recognized in comprehensive income but excluded from net income (e.g., foreign currency translation adjustments, market value adjustments attributable to certain investments in debt and equity securities, and minimum pension liability adjustments, per SFAS 130)

(3) An increase or decrease in contributed capital (e.g., expenditures reported as a reduction of the proceeds from issuing capital stock)

(4) Expenses for employee stock options recognized differently for financial reporting and tax purposes

2. **COMPONENTS OF INCOME TAX EXPENSE** The significant components of income tax expense attributable to continuing operations for each year presented shall be disclosed in the financial statements or notes thereto. Those components would include the following, for example:

a. Current tax expense or benefit

b. Deferred tax expense or benefit (exclusive of the effects of other components listed below)

c. Investment tax credits

d. Government grants (to the extent recognized as a reduction of income tax expense)

    e.   The benefits of operating loss carryforwards

    f.   Tax expense that results from allocating certain tax benefits either directly to contributed capital or to reduce other noncurrent intangible assets of an acquired entity

    g.   Adjustments of a deferred tax liability or asset for enacted changes in tax laws or rates or a change in the tax status of the enterprise

    h.   Adjustments of the beginning-of-the-year balance of a valuation allowance because of a change in circumstances that causes a change in judgment about the realizability of the related deferred tax asset in future years

3.   **RECONCILIATION** A public enterprise shall disclose a reconciliation using percentages or dollar amounts of a reported amount of income tax expense attributable to continuing operations for the year to an amount of income tax expense that would result from applying domestic federal statutory tax rates to pretax income from continuing operations.

4.   **LOSSES AND CARRYFORWARDS** The amounts and expiration dates of operating loss and tax credit carryforwards for tax purposes must be disclosed.

VII. BUSINESS COMBINATIONS AND INVESTMENTS IN COMMON STOCK

A. CONSOLIDATIONS

1.   **GOODWILL** A deferred tax liability or asset shall be recognized for differences between the assigned values and the tax bases of the assets and liabilities recognized in a business combination.

2.   **APPLICATION OF TAX BENEFITS** If a valuation allowance is recognized for the deferred tax asset for an acquired entity's deductible temporary differences or operating loss or tax credit carryforwards at the acquisition date, the tax benefits for those items that are first recognized (that is, by elimination of that valuation allowance) in financial statements after the acquisition date shall be applied (1) first to reduce to zero any goodwill related to the acquisition, (2) second to reduce to zero other noncurrent intangible assets related to the acquisition, and (3) third to reduce income tax expense.

B. "COST METHOD" INVESTMENTS

1.   **NO TEMPORARY DIFFERENCES** The basis for income recognition on investments accounted for by the cost method (i.e., the investor does not have the ability to exercise significant influence over the investee, less than 20% ownership) is dividends received, both for financial accounting and tax purposes. Thus, no temporary differences result from cost method investments.

2.   **DIVIDENDS RECEIVED DEDUCTION** Tax law has generally allowed corporate shareholders owning less than 20% of the stock of a qualifying domestic corporation to deduct 70% of the dividends received. That portion of the dividends received is an event recognized in the financial statements that does not have a tax consequence because it is exempt from taxation. Therefore, the financial accounting tax expense and the tax liability from cost-method investment income will be the same because no tax deferrals result.

EXAMPLE 18 ♦ "COST METHOD" INVESTMENTS

Investments, Inc., owns a 10% interest in Goodbuy Co. In 20X1, Goodbuy reported net income of $500,000 and declared and paid dividends of $300,000.

REQUIRED: Assuming a 30% effective tax rate, determine Investments' tax expense and liability in connection with its ownership interest in Goodbuy.

SOLUTION:

Dividends paid by Goodbuy	$300,000
Investments, Inc.'s ownership interest	x 10%
Dividends received	30,000
70% dividends received deduction	(21,000)
Taxable dividend income	9,000
Effective tax rate	x 30%
Tax expense <u>and</u> liability (no deferrals)	$ 2,700

C.   **"EQUITY METHOD" INVESTMENTS**

1.   **GAAP BASIS AND TAX BASIS DIFFER** When a company has investments accounted for under the "equity method" set forth in APB 18 (i.e., 20% to 50% ownership, "significant influence") investment income is recognized on a different basis for financial accounting and tax purposes.

2.   **DIVIDENDS RECEIVED DEDUCTION** Tax law has generally allowed corporate shareholders owning 20% or more, but less than 80% of the stock of a qualifying domestic corporation to deduct 80% of the dividends received. That portion of the dividends received that is excluded from taxable income is an event recognized in the financial statements that does not have a tax consequence because it is exempt from taxation.

3.   **INCOME TAXES** Income taxes on income from equity method investments is accounted for under the assumption that the investor will eventually receive his or her share in the undistributed income of the equity-method investee.

   a.   Therefore, an equity-method investee's undistributed income should be treated as a temporary difference.

   b.   The tax effect of this temporary difference depends on whether the investor ultimately expects to receive the undistributed income as *dividends* or as a *realized gain* upon disposal of the investment (or as a combination of both).

      (1)   If the undistributed income is expected to be received as dividends, the computation of temporary differences should allow for the dividends-received deduction.

      (2)   If the undistributed income is expected to be received as a realized gain upon disposal of the investment, the computation of temporary differences should **not** include the dividends-received deduction.

EXAMPLE 19 ♦ "EQUITY METHOD" INVESTMENTS

Investments, Inc., owns 30% of the common stock of the Goodbuy Co. and no preferred stock. During 20X1, Goodbuy reported income of $500,000 and paid $300,000 dividends on common stock and $50,000 on preferred stock. Investments' tax rate is 30%, including federal and state taxes.

REQUIRED: Record Investments, Inc.'s tax expense, liability and related deferrals, assuming no transactions occurred in 20X1 other than those dealing with investments and that undistributed income is expected to be received as dividends.

SOLUTION:

Tax Expense—current	5,400	
Tax Expense—deferred	2,700	
Taxes Payable [1]		5,400
Deferred Tax Liability [2]		2,700

COMPUTATIONS:

[1]	Dividends paid to I.I. ($300,000 x 30%)	$ 90,000
	Less 80% deduction	(72,000)
	Dividends included in taxable income	18,000
	Effective tax rate	x 30%
	Taxes payable	$ 5,400
[2]	I.I.'s equity in G's income	$135,000*
	Dividends paid to I.I. ($300,000 x 30%)	(90,000)
	Undistributed income	45,000
	Less 80% deduction	(36,000)
	Temporary difference	9,000
	Enacted tax rate for future	x 30%
	Deferred tax liability	$ 2,700

*	Income to CS holders ($500,000 − $50,000)	$ 450,000
	Investments, Inc., ownership %	x 30%
	I.I.'s equity in Goodbuy's income	$ 135,000

CHAPTER 13—ACCOUNTING FOR INCOME TAXES

PROBLEM 13-1 MULTIPLE CHOICE QUESTIONS (98 to 123 minutes)

1. On January 2, 1996, Ross Co. purchased a machine for $70,000. This machine has a 5-year useful life, a residual value of $10,000, and is depreciated using the straight-line method for financial statement purposes. For tax purposes, depreciation expense was $25,000 for 1996 and $20,000 for 1997. Ross' 1997 income, before income taxes and depreciation expense, was $100,000 and its tax rate was 30%. If Ross had made **no** estimated tax payments during 1997, what amount of current income tax liability would Ross report in its December 31, 1997 balance sheet?
a. $26,400
b. $25,800
c. $24,000
d. $22,500   (5/92, PI, #26, amended, 2595)

2. Dunn Co.'s 1997 income statement reported $90,000 income before provision for income taxes. To compute the provision for federal income taxes, the following 1997 data are provided:

Rent received in advance	$16,000
Income from exempt municipal bonds	20,000
Depreciation deducted for income tax purposes in excess of depreciation reported for financial statement purposes	10,000
Estimated tax payments	0
Enacted corporate income tax rate	30%

If the alternative minimum tax provisions are ignored, what amount of current federal income tax liability should be reported in Dunn's December 31, 1997 balance sheet?
a. $18,000
b. $22,800
c. $25,800
d. $28,800   (11/91, PI, #25, amended, 3310)

3. Pine Corp.'s books showed pretax income of $800,000 for the year ended December 31, 1997. In the computation of federal income taxes, the following data were considered:

Gain on an involuntary conversion (Pine has elected to replace the property within the statutory period using total proceeds.)	$350,000
Depreciation deducted for tax purposes in excess of depreciation deducted for book purposes	50,000
Federal estimated tax payments, 1997	70,000
Enacted federal tax rates, 1997	30%

What amount should Pine report as its current federal income tax liability on its December 31, 1997 balance sheet?
a. $ 50,000
b. $ 65,000
c. $120,000
d. $135,000   (11/90, PI, #16, amended, 3311)

4. Leer Corp.'s pretax income in 1997 was $100,000. The temporary differences between amounts reported in the financial statements and the tax return are as follows:

- Depreciation in the financial statements was $8,000 more than tax depreciation.
- The equity method of accounting resulted in financial statement income of $35,000. A $25,000 dividend was received during the year, which is eligible for the 80% dividends received deduction.

Leer's effective income tax rate was 30% in 1997. In its 1997 income statement, Leer should report a current provision for income taxes of
a. $26,400.
b. $23,400.
c. $21,900.
d. $18,600.   (11/91, PI, #48, amended, 3312)

5. Busy Corp. prepared the following reconciliation between pretax accounting income and taxable income for the year ended December 31, 1997:

Pretax accounting income	$250,000
Taxable income	(150,000)
Difference	$100,000

Analysis of difference:	
Interest on municipal bonds	$ 25,000
Excess of tax over book depreciation	75,000
	$100,000

Busy's effective income tax rate for 1997 is 30%. The depreciation difference will reverse in equal amounts over the next three years at an enacted tax rate of 40%. In Busy's 1997 income statement, what amount should be reported as the current portion of its provision for income taxes?
a. $45,000
b. $67,500
c. $75,000
d. $82,500   (5/92, PI, #56, amended, 2628)

6. Ram Corp. prepared the following reconciliation of income per books with income per tax return for the year ended December 31, 1997:

Book income before income taxes	$ 750,000
Add temporary difference	
Construction contract revenue which will reverse in 2001	100,000
Deduct temporary difference	
Depreciation expense which will reverse in equal amounts in each of the next four years	(400,000)
Taxable income	$ 450,000

Ram's effective income tax rate is 34% for 1997. What amount should Ram report in its 1997 income statement as the current provision for income taxes?
a. $ 34,000
b. $153,000
c. $255,000
d. $289,000   (1/90, PII, #7, amended, 3432)

7. Under current generally accepted accounting principles, which approach is used to determine income tax expense?
a. Asset and liability approach
b. "With and without" approach
c. Net of tax approach
d. Periodic expense approach
        (R/99, FAR, #17, 6786)

8. Which of the following should be recognized for the amount of deferred tax consequences attributable to temporary differences that will result in taxable amounts in future years?

	Deferred tax asset	Deferred tax liability
a.	Yes	Yes
b.	Yes	No
c.	No	Yes
d.	No	No

        (Editors, 3622)

9. Because Jab Co. uses different methods to depreciate equipment for financial statement and income tax purposes, Jab has temporary differences that will reverse during the next year and add to taxable income. Deferred income taxes that are based on these temporary differences should be classified in Jab's balance sheet as a
a. Contra account to current assets.
b. Contra account to noncurrent assets.
c. Current liability.
d. Noncurrent liability.   (5/94, FAR, #24, 4839)

10. Temporary differences arise when expenses are deductible for tax purposes

	After they are recognized in financial income	Before they are recognized in financial income
a.	No	No
b.	No	Yes
c.	Yes	Yes
d.	Yes	No

        (11/89, Theory, #27, 3620)

11. Orleans Co., a cash basis taxpayer, prepares accrual basis financial statements. In its 1997 balance sheet, Orleans' deferred income tax liabilities increased compared to 1996. Which of the following changes would cause this increase in deferred income tax liabilities?

I. An increase in prepaid insurance
II. An increase in rent receivable
III. An increase in warranty obligations

a. I only
b. I and II
c. II and III
d. III only   (5/92, Theory, #9, amended, 3625)

12. In its 1997 income statement, Cere Co. reported income before income taxes of $300,000. Cere estimated that, because of permanent differences, taxable income for 1997 would be $280,000. During 1997 Cere made estimated tax payments of $50,000, which were debited to income tax expense. Cere is subject to a 30% tax rate. What amount should Cere report as income tax expense?
a. $34,000
b. $50,000
c. $84,000
d. $90,000   (11/94, Theory, #51, amended, 5312)

13. Black Co., organized on January 2, 1997, had pretax financial statement income of $500,000 and taxable income of $800,000 for the year ended December 31, 1997. The only temporary differences are accrued product warranty costs, which Black expects to pay as follows:

1998	$100,000
1999	$ 5,000
2000	$ 50,000
2001	$100,000

The enacted income tax rates are 25% for 1997, 30% for 1998 through 2000, and 35% for 2001. Black believes that future years' operations will produce profits. In its December 31, 1997, balance sheet, what amount should Black report as deferred tax asset?

a. $50,000
b. $75,000
c. $90,000
d. $95,000   (11/98 FAR, #10, 6737)

14. West Corp. leased a building and received the $36,000 annual rental payment on June 15, 1997. The beginning of the lease was July 1, 1997. Rental income is taxable when received. West's tax rates are 30% for 1997 and 40% thereafter. West had no other permanent or temporary differences. West determined that no valuation allowance was needed. What amount of deferred tax asset should West report in its December 31, 1997 balance sheet?

a. $ 5,400
b. $ 7,200
c. $10,800
d. $14,400   (5/93, PI, #26, amended, 4068)

15. Stone Co. began operations in 1997 and reported $225,000 in income before income taxes for the year. Stone's 1997 tax depreciation exceeded its book depreciation by $25,000. Stone also had nondeductible book expenses of $10,000 related to permanent differences. Stone's tax rate for 1997 was 40%, and the enacted rate for years after 1997 is 35%. In its December 31, 1997 balance sheet, what amount of deferred income tax liability should Stone report?

a. $ 8,750
b. $10,000
c. $12,250
d. $14,000   (5/93, PI, #36, amended, 4077)

16. Cory Inc. uses the accrual method of accounting for financial reporting purposes and appropriately uses the installment method of accounting for income tax purposes. Installment income of $250,000 will be collected in the following years when the enacted tax rates are:

	Collection of income	Enacted tax rates
1997	$ 25,000	35%
1998	50,000	30%
1999	75,000	30%
2000	100,000	25%

The installment income is Cory's only temporary difference. Taxable income is expected in all future years. What amount should be included in the deferred income tax liability in Cory's December 31, 1997 balance sheet?

a. $62,500
b. $71,250
c. $78,750
d. $87,500   (11/90, PI, #20, amended, 3301)

ITEMS 17 AND 18 are based on the following:

Zeff Co. prepared the following reconciliation of its pretax financial statement income to taxable income for the year ended December 31, 1994, its first year of operations:

Pretax financial income	$160,000
Nontaxable interest received on municipal securities	(5,000)
Long-term loss accrual in excess of deductible amount	10,000
Depreciation in excess of financial statement amount	(25,000)
Taxable income	$140,000

Zeff's tax rate for 1994 is 40%.

17. In its 1994 income statement, what amount should Zeff report as income tax expense—current portion?

a. $52,000
b. $56,000
c. $62,000
d. $64,000   (11/95, FAR, #37, 6119)

18. In its December 31, 1994, balance sheet, what should Zeff report as deferred income tax liability?

a. $2,000
b. $4,000
c. $6,000
d. $8,000   (11/95, FAR, #38, 6120)

19. Mill, which began operations on January 1, 1995, recognizes income from long-term construction contracts under the percentage-of-completion method in its financial statements and under the completed-contract method for income tax reporting. Income under each method follows:

Year	Completed-contract	Percentage-of-completion
1995	$ --	$300,000
1996	400,000	600,000
1997	700,000	850,000

The income tax rate was 30% for 1995 through 1997. For years after 1997, the enacted tax rate is 25%. There are no other temporary differences. Assuming Mill does not expect any tax losses in the near future, Mill should report in its December 31, 1997 balance sheet, a deferred income tax liability of

a. $ 87,500.
b. $105,000.
c. $162,500.
d. $195,000.   (11/91, PI, #38, amended, 3303)

20. On June 30, 1997, Ank Corp. prepaid a $19,000 premium on an annual insurance policy. The premium payment was a tax deductible expense in Ank's 1997 cash basis tax return. The accrual basis income statement will report a $9,500 insurance expense in 1997 and 1998. Ank's income tax rate is 30% in 1997 and 25% thereafter. Taxable income is expected in all future years. In Ank's December 31, 1997 balance sheet, what amount related to the insurance should be reported as a deferred income tax liability?

a. $5,700
b. $4,750
c. $2,850
d. $2,375   (5/91, PI, #41, amended, 3305)

21. Scott Corp. received cash of $20,000 that was included in revenues in its 1997 financial statements, of which $12,000 will not be taxable until 1998. Scott's enacted tax rate is 30% for 1997, and 25% for 1998. What amount should Scott report in its 1997 balance sheet for deferred income tax liability?

a. $2,000
b. $2,400
c. $3,000
d. $3,600   (5/92, PI, #33, amended, 2604)

22. Black Co., organized on January 2, 1997, had pretax accounting income of $500,000 and taxable income of $800,000 for the year ended December 31, 1997. The only temporary difference is accrued product warranty costs which are expected to be paid as follows:

1998	$100,000
1999	50,000
2000	50,000
2001	100,000

The enacted income tax rates are 35% for 1997, 30% for 1998 through 2000, and 25% for 2001. Taxable income is expected in all future years. In Black's December 31, 1997 balance sheet, the deferred income tax asset should be

a. $ 75,000.
b. $ 85,000.
c. $ 90,000.
d. $105,000.   (5/90, PI, #21, amended, 3306)

23. As a result of differences between depreciation for financial reporting purposes and tax purposes, the financial reporting basis of Noor Co.'s sole depreciable asset, acquired in 1994, exceeded its tax basis by $250,000 at December 31, 1994. This difference will reverse in future years. The enacted tax rate is 30% for 1994, and 40% for future years. Noor has no other temporary differences. In its December 31, 1994 balance sheet, how should Noor report the deferred tax effect of this difference?

a. As an asset of $75,000
b. As an asset of $100,000
c. As a liability of $75,000
d. As a liability of $100,000 (5/95, FAR, #16, 5552)

24. In its 1997 income statement, Tow Inc. reported proceeds from an officer's life insurance policy of $90,000 and depreciation of $250,000. Tow was the owner and beneficiary of the life insurance on its officer. Tow deducted depreciation of $370,000 in its 1997 income tax return when the tax rate was 30%. Data related to the reversal of the excess tax deduction for depreciation follow:

Year	Reversal of excess tax deduction	Enacted tax rates
1998	$50,000	35%
1999	40,000	35%
2000	20,000	25%
2001	10,000	25%

There are no other temporary differences. Tow expects to report profits (rather than losses) for tax purposes for all future years. In its December 31, 1997 balance sheet, what amount should Tow report as a deferred income tax liability?

a. $36,000
b. $39,000
c. $63,000
d. $66,000   (11/91, PI, #35, amended, 3307)

25. In its 1997 income statement, Noll Corp. reported depreciation of $400,000 and interest revenue on municipal obligations of $60,000. Noll reported depreciation of $550,000 on its 1997 income tax return. The difference in depreciation is the only temporary difference, and it will reverse equally over the next three years. Noll's enacted income tax rates are 35% for 1997, 30% for 1998 and 25% for 1999 and 2000. Assuming Noll expects to report taxable income in all future years, what amount should be included in the deferred income tax liability in Noll's December 31, 1997 balance sheet?

a. $40,000
b. $52,500
c. $63,000
d. $73,500   (11/90, PI, #19, amended, 3308)

26. Rein Inc. reported deferred tax assets and deferred tax liabilities at the end of 1996 and at the end of 1997. For the year ended 1997 Rein should report deferred income tax expense or benefit equal to the
a. Decrease in the deferred tax assets.
b. Increase in the deferred tax liabilities.
c. Amount of the current tax liability plus the sum of the net changes in deferred tax assets and deferred tax liabilities.
d. Sum of the net changes in deferred tax assets and deferred tax liabilities.
(11/92, Theory, #41, amended, 3474)

27. At the end of year 1, Cody Co. reported a profit on a partially completed construction contract by applying the percentage-of-completion method. By the end of year 2, the total estimated profit on the contract at completion in year 3 had been drastically reduced from the amount estimated at the end of year 1. Consequently, in year 2, a loss equal to one-half of the year 1 profit was recognized. Cody used the completed-contract method for income tax purposes and had no other contracts. The year 2 balance sheet should include a deferred tax

	Asset	Liability
a.	Yes	Yes
b.	No	Yes
c.	Yes	No
d.	No	No

(11/91, Theory, #4, amended, 9051)

28. Which of the following should be used to measure the deferred tax consequences of temporary differences that will result in taxable amounts in future years?

	Enacted changes in tax laws and rates scheduled for future years	Anticipated change in tax laws and rates for future years
a.	Yes	Yes
b.	Yes	No
c.	No	Yes
d.	No	No

(Editors, 3623)

29. Senlo Co., which uses a one-year operating cycle, recognized profits for both financial statement and tax purposes during its two years of operation. Depreciation for tax purposes exceeded depreciation for financial statement purposes in each year.

These temporary differences are expected to reverse in years 3, 4, and 5. At the end of year 2, the deferred tax liability shown as a noncurrent liability is based on the
a. Enacted tax rates for years 3, 4, and 5.
b. Enacted tax rates for years 4 and 5.
c. Enacted tax rate for year 3.
d. Tax rates for years 1 and 2.
(11/90, Theory, #27, amended, 3633)

30. Quinn Co. reported a net deferred tax asset of $9,000 in its December 31, 1993 balance sheet. For 1994, Quinn reported pretax financial statement income of $300,000. Temporary differences of $100,000 resulted in taxable income of $200,000 for 1994. At December 31, 1994, Quinn had cumulative taxable differences of $70,000. Quinn's effective income tax rate is 30%. In its December 31, 1994 income statement, what should Quinn report as deferred income tax expense?
a. $12,000
b. $21,000
c. $30,000
d. $60,000
(5/95, FAR, #42, 5578)

31. For calendar year 1997, Clark Corp. reported depreciation of $300,000 in its income statement. On its 1997 income tax return, Clark reported depreciation of $500,000. Clark's income statement also included $50,000 accrued warranty expense that will be deducted for tax purposes when paid. Clark's enacted tax rates are 30% for 1997 and 1998, and 25% for 1999 and 2000. Taxable income is expected in all future years. The depreciation difference and warranty expense will reverse over the next three years as follows:

	Depreciation difference	Warranty expense
1998	$ 80,000	$10,000
1999	70,000	15,000
2000	50,000	25,000
	$200,000	$50,000

These were Clark's only temporary differences. In Clark's 1997 income statement, the deferred portion of its provision for income taxes should be
a. $67,000.
b. $45,000.
c. $41,000.
d. $37,500.
(11/90, PI, #48, amended, 3314)

32. In 1997, Lobo Corp. reported for financial statement purposes the following revenue and expenses which were not included in taxable income:

Premiums on officers' life insurance
  under which the corporation is the
  beneficiary $ 5,000
Interest revenue on qualified state or
  municipal bonds 10,000
Estimated future warranty costs to be
  paid in 1998 and 1999 60,000

Lobo's enacted tax rate for the current and future years is 30%. Lobo expects to operate profitably in the future. There were no temporary differences in prior years. The deferred tax benefit is
a. $18,000.
b. $19,500.
c. $21,000.
d. $22,500.   (5/90, PI, #41, amended, 3315)

33. For the year ended December 31, 1994, Tyre Co. reported pretax financial statement income of $750,000. Its taxable income was $650,000. The difference is due to accelerated depreciation for income tax purposes. Tyre's effective income tax rate is 30%, and Tyre made estimated tax payments during 1994 of $90,000. What amount should Tyre report as current income tax expense for 1994?
a. $105,000
b. $135,000
c. $195,000
d. $225,000   (5/95, FAR, #41, 5577)

34. Mobe Co. reported the following operating income (loss) for its first three years of operations:

1992 $ 300,000
1993   (700,000)
1994   1,200,000

For each year, there were no deferred income taxes, and Mobe's effective income tax rate was 30%. In its 1993 income tax return, Mobe elected to carry back the maximum amount of loss possible. In its 1994 income statement, what amount should Mobe report as total income tax expense?
a. $120,000
b. $150,000
c. $240,000
d. $360,000   (5/95, FAR, #43, 5579)

35. On its December 31, 1994, balance sheet, Shin Co. had income taxes payable of $13,000 and a current deferred tax asset of $20,000 before determining the need for a valuation account. Shin had reported a current deferred tax asset of $15,000

at December 31, 1993. No estimated tax payments were made during 1994. At December 31, 1994, Shin determined that it was more likely than not that 10% of the deferred tax asset would not be realized. In its 1994 income statement, what amount should Shin report as total income tax expense?
a. $ 8,000
b. $ 8,500
c. $10,000
d. $13,000   (11/95, FAR, #36, 6118)

36. Dodd Corp. is preparing its December 31, 1997 financial statements and must determine the proper accounting treatment for the following situations:

For the year ended December 31, 1997, Dodd has a loss carryforward of $180,000 available to offset future taxable income. However, there are no temporary differences. Based on an analysis of both positive and negative evidence, Dodd has reason to believe it is more likely than not that the benefits of the entire loss carryforward will be realized within the carryforward period. On 12/31/97, Dodd received a $200,000 offer for its patent. Dodd's management is considering whether to sell the patent. The offer expires on 2/28/98. The patent has a carrying amount of $100,000 at 12/31/97.

Assume a current and future income tax rate of 30%. In its 1997 income statement, Dodd should recognize an increase in net income of
a. $0.
b. $ 54,000.
c. $ 70,000.
d. $124,000.   (5/90, PII, #60, amended, 3433)

37. At December 31, 1997, Dorr Inc. has a net operating loss carryforward of $90,000 available to offset future taxable income. At this date, Dorr has temporary differences that will result in taxable amounts of $60,000 during the operating loss carryforward period. The company has sufficient positive evidence to support an assumption that the benefits of the carryforward will be realized in the near future. Assuming a present and future enacted income tax rate of 30%, what amount of the tax benefit of the operating loss carryforward should be recognized in the income statement for the year ended December 31, 1997?
a. $0
b. $ 9,000
c. $18,000
d. $27,000   (Editors, 3318)

38. A deferred tax liability or asset should be adjusted for the effect of a change in

	Tax laws	Tax rates
a.	No	No
b.	No	Yes
c.	Yes	No
d.	Yes	Yes

(Editors, 3626)

39. Hut Co. has temporary taxable differences that will reverse during the next year and add to taxable income. These differences relate to noncurrent assets. Deferred income taxes based on these temporary differences should be classified in Hut's balance sheet as a

a. Current asset.
b. Noncurrent asset.
c. Current liability.
d. Noncurrent liability (11/97, FAR, #11, 6491)

40. Rom Corp. began business in 1997 and reported taxable income of $50,000 on its 1997 tax return. Rom's enacted tax rate is 30% for 1997 and future years. The following is a schedule of Rom's December 31, 1997, temporary differences in thousands of dollars:

	12/31/97 Book basis over (under) tax basis	Future taxable (deductible) amounts			
		1998	1999	2000	2001
Equipment	10	(5)	5	5	5
Warranty liability	(20)	(10)	(10)		
Deferred compensation liability	(15)		(5)		(10)
Installment receivables	30	10		20	
Totals	5	(5)	(10)	25	(5)

What amount should Rom report as current deferred tax assets in its December 31, 1997 balance sheet?
a. $0
b. $1,500
c. $4,500
d. $6,000 (5/92, PI, #24, amended, 2592)

41. In 1997, Rand Inc. reported for financial statement purposes the following items, which were not included in taxable income:

Installment gain to be collected equally in 1998 through 2000	$1,500,000
Estimated future warranty costs to be paid equally in 1998 through 2000	2,100,000

Rand had the installment gain arise from the sale of an investment. There were no temporary differences in prior years. Rand expects taxable income in all future years. Rand's enacted tax rates are 25% for 1997 and 30% for 1998 through 2000. In Rand's December 31, 1997 balance sheet, what

amounts of the net deferred tax asset should be classified as current and noncurrent?

	Current	Noncurrent
a.	$60,000	$100,000
b.	$60,000	$120,000
c.	$50,000	$100,000
d.	$50,000	$120,000

(5/91, PI, #31, amended, 3319)

42. At December 31, 1994, Bren Co. had the following deferred income tax items:

- A deferred income tax liability of $15,000 related to a noncurrent asset
- A deferred income tax asset of $3,000 related to a noncurrent liability
- A deferred income tax asset of $8,000 related to a current liability

Which of the following should Bren report in the noncurrent section of its December 31, 1994 balance sheet?
a. A noncurrent asset of $3,000 and a noncurrent liability of $15,000.
b. A noncurrent liability of $12,000.
c. A noncurrent asset of $11,000 and a noncurrent liability of $15,000.
d. A noncurrent liability of $4,000.

(5/95, FAR, #17, 5553)

43. At the end of 1997, the tax effects of temporary differences for Thorn Co. were as follows:

	Deferred tax assets (liabilities)	Related asset classification
Accelerated tax depreciation	($75,000)	Noncurrent asset
Additional costs in inventory for tax purposes	25,000	Current asset
	($50,000)	

A valuation allowance was not considered necessary. Thorn anticipates that $10,000 of the deferred tax liability will reverse in 1998. In Thorn's December 31, 1997 balance sheet, what amount should Thorn report as noncurrent deferred tax liability?
a. $40,000
b. $50,000
c. $65,000
d. $75,000 (11/94, Theory, #6, amended, 5271)

44. Generally, the manner of reporting the tax benefit of an operating loss carryforward or carryback is determined by the source of the

	Income or loss in the current year	Operating loss carryforward or taxes paid in a prior year
a.	Yes	Yes
b.	Yes	No
c.	No	Yes
d.	No	No

(Editors, 3631)

45. A deferred tax asset of $100,000 was recognized in the 1996 financial statements by the Chaise Company when a loss from discontinued segments was carried forward for tax purposes. A valuation allowance of $100,000 was also recognized in the 1996 statements because it was considered more likely than not that the deferred tax asset would not be realized. Chaise had no temporary differences. The tax benefit of the loss carried forward reduced current taxes payable on 1998 continuing operations. The 1998 income statement would include the tax benefit from the loss brought forward in
a. Income from continuing operations.
b. Gain or loss from discontinued segments.
c. Extraordinary gains.
d. Cumulative effect of accounting changes.
(5/90, Theory, #25, amended, 3632)

46. Income tax expense or benefit for the year should be allocated among

	Discontinued operations	Prior period adjustments
a.	Yes	Yes
b.	Yes	No
c.	No	Yes
d.	No	No

(Editors, 3636)

47. Purl Corporation's income statement for the year ended December 31, 1997, shows the following:

Income before income tax and extraordinary item	$900,000
Gain on life insurance coverage— included in the above $900,000 income amount	100,000
Extraordinary item—loss due to earthquake damage	300,000

Purl's tax rate for 1997 is 30%. How much should be reported as the provision for income tax in Purl's 1997 income statement?
a. $150,000
b. $180,000
c. $240,000
d. $270,000
(Editors, 3321)

48. Taft Corp. uses the equity method to account for its 25% investment in Flame Inc. During 1997, Taft received dividends of $30,000 from Flame and recorded $180,000 as its equity in the earnings of Flame. Additional information follows:

- All the undistributed earnings of Flame will be distributed as dividends in future periods.
- The dividends received from Flame are eligible for the 80% dividends received deduction.
- There are no other temporary differences.
- Enacted income tax rates are 30% for 1997 and thereafter.

In its December 31, 1997 balance sheet, what amount should Taft report for deferred income tax liability?
a. $ 9,000
b. $10,800
c. $45,000
d. $54,000
(5/93, PI, #35, amended, 4076)

49. On January 1, 1997, Lundy Corp. purchased 40% of the voting common stock of Glen Inc., and appropriately accounts for its investment by the equity method. During 1997, Glen reported earnings of $225,000 and paid dividends of $75,000. Lundy assumes that all of Glen's undistributed earnings will be distributed as dividends in future periods when the enacted tax rate will be 30%. Ignore the dividends-received deduction. Lundy's current enacted income tax rate is 25%. Lundy uses the liability method to account for temporary differences and expects to have taxable income in all future periods. The increase in Lundy's deferred income tax liability for this temporary difference is
a. $45,000.
b. $37,500.
c. $27,000.
d. $18,000.
(5/89, PI, #40, amended, 3323)

OTHER OBJECTIVE FORMAT QUESTION

PROBLEM 13-2 (15 to 25 minutes)

PROBLEM 13-2 consists of 2 parts. Each part consists of 4 items. Select the **best** answer for each item.

REQUIRED:

a. ITEMS 1 THROUGH 4 describe circumstances resulting in differences between financial statement income and taxable income. For each numbered item, determine whether the difference is:

List
(A) A temporary difference resulting in a deferred tax asset
(B) A temporary difference resulting in a deferred tax liability
(C) A permanent difference

An answer may be selected once, more than once, or not at all.

1. For plant assets, the depreciation expense deducted for tax purposes is in excess of the depreciation expense used for financial reporting purposes.

2. A landlord collects some rents in advance. Rents received are taxable in the period in which they are received.

3. Interest is received on an investment in tax-exempt municipal obligations.

4. Costs of guarantees and warranties are estimated.

b. The following partially completed worksheet contains Lane Co.'s reconciliation between financial statement income and taxable income for the three years ended April 30, 1997, and additional information.

Lane Co.
INCOME TAX WORKSHEET
For the Three Years Ended April 30, 1997

	April 30, 1995	April 30, 1996	April 30, 1997
Pretax financial income	$ 900,000	$1,000,000	$1,200,000
Permanent differences	100,000	100,000	100,000
Temporary differences	200,000	100,000	150,000
Taxable income	$ 600,000	$ 800,000	$ 950,000
Cumulative temporary differences (future taxable amounts)	$ 200,000	$ (6)	$ 450,000
Tax rate	20%	25%	30%
Deferred tax liability	$ 40,000	$ 75,000	$ (8)
Deferred tax expense	$ —	$ (7)	$ —
Current tax expense	$ (5)	$ —	$ —

The tax rate changes were enacted at the beginning of each tax year and were not known to Lane at the end of the prior year.

REQUIRED:

ITEMS 5 THROUGH 8 represent amounts omitted from the worksheet. For each item, determine the amount omitted from the worksheet. Select the amount from the following list. An answer may be used once, more than once, or not at all.

5. Current tax expense for the year ended April 30, 1995.

6. Cumulative temporary differences at April 30, 1996.

7. Deferred tax expense for the year ended April 30, 1996

8. Deferred tax liability at April 30, 1997.

(5/97, FAR, #1, 6479-6486)

Amount			
(A)	$ 25,000	(H)	$ 135,000
(B)	$ 35,000	(I)	$ 140,000
(C)	$ 45,000	(J)	$ 160,000
(D)	$ 75,000	(K)	$ 180,000
(E)	$ 100,000	(L)	$ 200,000
(F)	$ 112,500	(M)	$ 300,000
(G)	$ 120,000	(N)	$ 400,000

PROBLEM/ESSAY QUESTIONS

PROBLEM/ESSAY 13-3 (30 to 40 minutes)

Chris Green, CPA, is auditing Rayne Co.'s 1997 financial statements. The controller, Dunn, has provided Green with the following information:

- At December 31, 1996, Rayne had a note payable to Federal Bank with a balance of $90,000. The annual principal payment of $10,000, plus 8% interest on the unpaid balance, was paid when due on March 31, 1997.

- On January 2, 1997, Rayne leased two automobiles for executive use under a capital lease. Five annual lease payments of $15,000 are due beginning January 3, 1997. Rayne's incremental borrowing rate on the date of the lease was 11% and the lessor's implicit rate, which was known by Rayne, was 10%. The lease was properly recorded at $62,500, before the first payment was made.

- On July 1, 1997, Rayne received proceeds of $538,000 from a $500,000 bond issuance. The bonds mature in 15 years and interest of 11% is payable semiannually on June 30 and December 31. The bonds were issued at a price to yield investors 10%. Rayne uses the effective interest method to amortize bond premium.

- Dunn has prepared a schedule of all differences between financial statement and income tax return income. Dunn believes that as a result of pending legislation, the enacted tax rate at December 31, 1997, will be increased for 1998. Dunn is uncertain which differences to include and which rates to apply in computing deferred taxes under FASB 109 *Accounting for Income Taxes.* Dunn has requested an overview of FASB 109 from Green.

REQUIRED:

a. Prepare a schedule of interest expense for the year ended December 31, 1997.

b. Prepare a brief memo to Dunn from Green:

- Identifying the objectives of accounting for income taxes,
- Defining temporary differences,
- Explaining how to measure deferred tax assets and liabilities, and
- Explaining how to measure deferred income tax expense or benefit.

(5/94, FAR, #5, amended, 4975)

PROBLEM/ESSAY 13-4 (40 to 50 minutes)

The following condensed trial balance of Powell Corp., a publicly owned company, has been adjusted except for income tax expense:

Powell Corp.
Condensed Trial Balance
June 30, 1997

	Dr	Cr
Total assets	$25,080,000	
Total liabilities		$ 9,900,000
5% cumulative preferred stock		2,000,000
Common stock		10,000,000
Retained earnings		2,900,000
Machine sales		750,000
Service revenues		250,000
Interest revenues		10,000
Gain on sale of factory		250,000
Cost of sales— machines	425,000	
Cost of services	100,000	
Administrative exp.	300,000	
R & D expenses	110,000	
Interest expense	5,000	
Loss from asset disposal	40,000	
	$26,060,000	$26,060,000

Other information and financial data for the year ended June 30, 1997, follows:

- The weighted average number of common shares outstanding during 1997 was 200,000. The potential dilution from the exercise of stock options held by Powell's officers and directors was not material.

- There were no dividends-in-arrears on Powell's preferred stock at July 1, 1996. On May 1, 1997, Powell's directors declared a 5% preferred stock dividend to be paid in August 1997.

- During 1997, one of Powell's foreign factories was expropriated by the foreign government, and Powell received a $900,000 payment from the foreign government in settlement. The carrying value of the plant was $650,000. Powell has never disposed of a factory.

- Administrative expenses includes a $5,000 premium payment for a $1,000,000 life insurance policy on Powell's president, of which the corporation is the beneficiary.

- Powell depreciates its assets using the straight-line method for financial reporting purposes and an accelerated method for tax purposes. The differences between book and tax depreciation are as follows:

June 30	Financial statements over (under) tax depreciation
1997	$(15,000)
1998	10,000
1999	5,000

There were no other temporary differences.

- Powell's enacted tax rate for the current and future years is 30%.

REQUIRED:

a. Using the single-step format, prepare Powell's income statement for the year ended June 30, 1997.

b. Prepare a schedule reconciling Powell's financial statement net income to taxable income for the year ended June 30, 1997.   (11/92, PI, amended, #5)

SOLUTION 13-1 MULTIPLE CHOICE ANSWERS

RECONCILIATION OF PRETAX FINANCIAL INCOME & TAXABLE INCOME

1. **(c)**   To compute Ross' current income tax liability, Ross' taxable income must be determined; then, taxable income must be multiplied by the year's expected income tax rate, as follows:

Pretax income before depreciation	$100,000
Depreciation for tax purposes	(20,000)
Taxable income	80,000
Tax rate expected	x 30%
Current income tax expense	24,000
Estimated tax payments	(0)
Current income tax liability	$ 24,000

2. **(b)**   To determine Dunn's current federal income tax liability, Dunn's pretax financial income is adjusted to its taxable income; then, taxable income is multiplied by the current year's enacted corporate income tax rate.

Pretax financial income	$90,000
Rent received in advance included in taxable income when received but not recognized in financial income until earned	16,000
Income from municipal bonds recognized for financial accounting purposes that is exempt from taxation	(20,000)
Depreciation deducted for income tax purposes in excess of depreciation reported for financial statement purposes	(10,000)
Taxable income	76,000
Enacted corporate income tax rate	x 30%
Current federal income tax liability (no estimated tax payments were made for the current year)	$22,800

3. **(a)**   To determine Pine's current federal income tax liability, Pine's pretax financial income is adjusted to its taxable income. Next, taxable income is multiplied by the current year's enacted corporate income tax rate. Finally, estimated payments reduce the liability.

Pretax financial income	$ 800,000
Temporary differences:	
Gain on involuntary conversion deferred for tax purposes	(350,000)
Excess depreciation for tax purposes	(50,000)
Taxable income	400,000
Enacted tax rate	x 30%
Taxes payable	120,000
Estimated tax payments	(70,000)
Balance of current tax liability	$ 50,000

4. **(b)**   To determine the current provision for income taxes (i.e., the current income tax expense), the reported pretax financial income must be adjusted to taxable income; then, taxable income must be multiplied by the year's income tax rate, as follows:

Pretax financial income	$100,000
Less: Investment income recognized in the financial statements in excess of dividend income included in taxable income [$35,000 – ($25,000 x 20%)]	(30,000)
Add: Depreciation recorded in the financial statements in excess of depreciation deducted for tax purposes	8,000
Taxable income	78,000
Effective income tax rate	x 30%
Current provision for income taxes	$ 23,400

5. **(a)**

Pretax financial income	$ 250,000
Permanent difference—interest	(25,000)
Temporary difference—excess tax depreciation	(75,000)
Taxable income	$ 150,000
Tax rate	30%
Current provision	$ 45,000

6. **(b)**   The current portion of the provision for income taxes (which is the same as the amount of taxes due to the government for the current period) is computed by multiplying the taxable income figure by the statutory tax rate for the current period. The statutory tax rate is not given. However, because there are no permanent differences and because there are no temporary differences which are

expected to reverse at tax rates different from the current statutory rate, the effective rate for the current year must be the same as the statutory tax rate. Thus, $450,000 x 34% = $153,000.

SFAS 109 Overview

7.   (a)   SFAS 109 requires that the assets and liability method be used in accounting and reporting for temporary differences between the amount of taxable income and pretax financial income and the tax bases of assets or liabilities and their reported amounts in financial statements. Under this method, a current or deferred tax liability or asset is recognized for the current or deferred tax consequences of all events that have been recognized in the financial statements.

Temporary Differences

8.   (c)   A deferred tax *liability* should be recognized for the amount of deferred tax consequences attributable to temporary differences that will result in *taxable amounts* in future years. The liability is the amount of taxes that will be payable on those taxable amounts in future years based on the provisions of the tax law. On the other hand, a deferred tax *asset* should be recognized for the amount of deferred tax consequences attributable to temporary differences that will result in *tax deductions* in future years which will reduce taxes payable in those future years.

9.   (d)   The deferred tax liability is classified as noncurrent because it is related to the equipment and, therefore, follows the classification of the equipment. Deferred tax accounts are reported on the balance sheet as assets and liabilities, not as contra accounts.

10.   (c)   Expenses that are deductible before or after they are recognized in financial income create a difference between the tax basis of an asset or liability and its reported amount in the financial statements [SFAS 109, par. 11(b) and (d)]. These differences result in taxable or deductible amounts in a future period(s) when the reported amount of the related asset or liability is recovered or settled, respectively. Temporary differences include all existing differences that will result in taxable or deductible amounts in future years.

11.   (b)   An increase in prepaid insurance can cause an increase in deferred tax liabilities because an expense deducted this period for tax purposes but deferred for financial accounting purposes will cause future taxable amounts. An increase in rent receivable can cause an increase in deferred tax liabilities because a revenue accrued for financial accounting purposes but not recognized for tax purposes until it is collected will give rise to future taxable amounts. A deferred tax liability represents the deferred tax consequences attributable to taxable temporary differences. An increase in cumulative temporary differences giving rise to future taxable amounts results in an increase in deferred tax liabilities. An increase in warranty obligation can cause an increase in deferred tax assets rather than deferred tax liabilities. An expense accrued for financial accounting purposes but deducted for tax purposes when paid causes a temporary difference which gives rise to future deductible amounts. A deferred tax asset is the deferred tax consequences attributable to deductible temporary differences and carryforwards.

Permanent Differences

12.   (c)   No temporary differences exist at the beginning and end of the year. Therefore, the amount to be reported as income tax expense is computed by multiplying Cere's taxable income for the year by the enacted corporate tax rate for the year.

Computation of Deferred Tax Liabilities and Assets

13.   (d)   A deferred tax asset or liability is calculated by multiplying temporary differences by the enacted tax rate expected to apply to taxable income in the periods in which the deferred tax liability or asset is expected to be settled or realized.

1998-2000	$200,000 x 30% =	$60,000
2001	100,000 x 35% =	35,000
Deferred tax asset		$95,000

14.   (b)   The amount of the deferred tax asset that should be reported at 12/31/97 is computed by considering the tax effects of the temporary difference for rental income received for the one-year period beginning 7/1/97. While rental income is included in taxable income when received, it is recognized in computing financial income when earned. This causes the amount of a liability (i.e., unearned rental income) at the balance sheet date to exceed its tax basis (zero) which will result in *deductible amounts* in future years when the liability is settled. The $18,000 [i.e., $36,000 − ($36,000 x 6/12)] temporary difference as a result of the unearned rental income will reverse in 1998, and is multiplied by the enacted tax rate of 40% for 1998 to arrive at a deferred tax asset of $7,200. The entire $7,200 can be reported as a deferred tax asset at 12/31/97 because the question indicates that no valuation allowance is needed.

15. (a) The amount of the deferred tax liability to be reported is computed by considering the future tax effects of the temporary difference for depreciation. Since tax depreciation exceeded book depreciation by $25,000, this causes the reported amount of an asset to exceed its tax basis by this amount, thereby resulting in $25,000 of *taxable amounts* in future years when the asset is recovered through use or sale. The tax effects of the taxable amounts are calculated by applying the presently enacted tax rate of 35% for later years, resulting in a current deferred tax liability at of $8,750 (i.e., $25,000 x 35%). The $10,000 of nondeductible book expenses are related to permanent differences. Although the nondeductible book expenses are recognized in financial accounting income, they do not have tax consequences. Therefore, they do not give rise to temporary differences. Thus, the nondeductible book expenses do not affect the calculation of the deferred tax liability.

16. (a) The deferred tax liability balance represents the amount of taxes expected to be paid in the future when installment receivables are collected. (The revenue from installment sales has already been included in the financial statements but will not be reported for tax purposes until the related receivables are collected.) The appropriate current balance of the related deferred tax liability is computed as follows:

	Amount	Rate	Deferred Tax Liab.
Future taxable amounts			
1998 and 1999	$125,000	30%	$37,500
2000	100,000	25%	25,000
Deferred tax liability			$62,500

17. (b) To determine the current portion of income tax expense, taxable income is multiplied by the current enacted corporate income tax rate. $140,000 x 40% = $56,000.

18. (c) Since both temporary items are non-current, the amount of the deferred tax liability to be reported is computed by considering the future tax effects of the cumulative net taxable type temporary differences. ($25,000 − $10,000) x 40% = $6,000. Being the first year of operations, the temporary differences originating in the current year are the cumulative temporary differences existing at the balance sheet date.

19. (c) The deferred income tax liability is calculated by considering the tax effects of the temporary differences for contract income. The $650,000 [($300,000 + $600,000 + $850,000) − ($400,000 + $700,000)] of contract income recognized in the financial statements in excess of that included in taxable income results in *taxable amounts* in future years. The amount of tax for the taxable amounts is calculated by applying the enacted tax rate for later years of 25%, resulting in a deferred income tax liability of $162,500 (i.e., $650,000 x 25%).

20. (d) According to SFAS 109, an expense deducted for tax purposes in a period prior to the period in which it is deducted for financial statement purposes will cause a temporary difference which will result in a future taxable amount. The $9,500 temporary difference will reverse and cause a taxable amount in the following year. The enacted tax rate of 25% for future years is multiplied by the $9,500 taxable amount to arrive at a current deferred tax liability of $2,375.

21. (c) The revenues recognized in financial income in 1997 that will not be included in taxable income until 1998 represent a future taxable amount. The deferred tax liability that should be reported at 12/31/97 for the temporary difference is computed by multiplying the taxable amount scheduled for 1998 by the enacted tax rate for 1998 ($12,000 x 25% = $3,000).

22. (b) The amount of the deferred tax asset is computed by considering the tax effects of the temporary difference for accrued product warranty costs. While product warranty costs are accrued in computing financial income, they are deductible for tax purposes only when they are paid. This causes the amount of a liability (i.e., product warranty liability) to exceed its tax basis (zero) which will result in *deductible amounts* in future years when the liability is settled. A deferred tax asset should be recognized for the expected tax benefits of the deductible amounts. Because taxable income is expected in all future years, the enacted tax rates for particular years are used to tax effect the individual deductible amounts scheduled to occur in each of those years. Therefore, Black should report a deferred tax asset of $85,000 [30% ($100,000 + $50,000 + $50,000) + 25% ($100,000)].

23. (d) The calculation to determine a deferred tax effect is based on a future tax rate, which in this problem is 40%. Thus, 40% of the $250,000 difference is $100,000. Because the financial reporting basis exceeded the tax basis, the $100,000 represents the amount of tax expected to be paid in future years as a result of the turn-around of this temporary difference. This is shown on the balance sheet as a deferred tax *liability*.

24. (b) The proceeds from the officer's life insurance policy is a tax-exempt revenue; therefore, no current or future tax consequences will result and

no deferred taxes are to be recorded for this "permanent difference." Deferred taxes are recorded only for temporary differences. The $120,000 ($370,000 – $250,000) temporary difference due to depreciation is the only temporary difference existing at the balance sheet date. The tax rate that is used to measure the deferred tax consequences is the enacted tax rate(s) expected to apply to taxable income in the years that this temporary difference reverses. Thus, the $39,000 related deferred tax liability at 12/31/97 is computed as follows:

	Amount	Rate	Deferred Tax Liab.
Future taxable amounts:			
Depreciation			
1998-1999	$90,000	35%	$31,500
2000-2001	$30,000	25%	7,500
Deferred tax liability			$39,000

25. (a)   Interest income on municipal obligations is a tax-exempt revenue; therefore, no current or future tax consequences will result and no deferred taxes are to be recorded for this "permanent difference." Deferred taxes are recorded only for temporary differences. The $150,000 ($550,000 – $400,000) temporary difference due to depreciation is the only temporary difference existing at the balance sheet date and it is to reverse equally over the next three years which means it will result in future taxable amounts of $50,000 each ($150,000 ÷ 3) in 1998, 1999, and 2000. Noll expects to report taxable income in all future periods; therefore, the future taxable amounts are tax effected at the rates scheduled for individual future years. The $40,000 related deferred tax liability is computed as follows:

	Amount	Rate	Deferred Tax Liab.
Future taxable amounts:			
Depreciation			
1998	$ 50,000	30%	$15,000
1999-2000	$100,000	25%	25,000
Deferred tax liability			$40,000

26. (d)   Under SFAS 109, deferred income tax expense or benefit is calculated using the asset and liability method. Under this approach, deferred income tax expense or benefit is equal to sum of the net changes in deferred taxes assets and deferred tax liabilities on the balance sheet. Answers (a) and (b) are incomplete. Deferred income tax expense or benefit is equal to sum of the net changes in both deferred taxes assets and deferred tax liabilities. Answer (c) describes the amount of total income tax expense, assuming no estimated payments have been made.

27. (b)   At the end of year 1, a cumulative difference exists which is equal to the contract profit recognized on the income statement in year 1. The cumulative difference is to result in future taxable amounts so a deferred tax liability is established for an amount equal to the cumulative temporary difference multiplied by the tax rate enacted for the future year(s) in which the temporary difference is expected to reverse. In year 2, half of the cumulative temporary difference reverses because of the recognition of a loss to offset half of the profit reported in year 1. Assuming no change in enacted future tax rates, this reversal results in a decrease in the related deferred tax liability account. Therefore, at the end of year 2, Cody has a deferred tax liability balance equal to half of the balance that was in that account at the end of year 1.

TAX RATES USED

28. (b)   A deferred tax liability is computed at the date of the financial statements by applying the provisions in the tax law to measure the deferred tax consequences of temporary differences that will result in taxable amounts in each future year. *Enacted* changes in tax laws and rates that are scheduled for a particular future year (or years) are used to measure a liability for the deferred tax consequences of taxable amounts that will arise in that year (or years). Tax laws and rates for the current year are used if no changes have been enacted for future years.

29. (a)   A temporary difference caused by the excess of depreciation taken for tax purposes over the depreciation reported for financial statement purposes will result in taxable amounts in the periods the temporary difference reverses. The deferred tax liability related to this temporary difference at the end of year 2 is calculated by scheduling the taxable amounts that are to occur in each individual future year because of the temporary difference and by applying presently enacted tax rates for each of those years to the amount of taxable amounts scheduled for those years. Deferred tax accounts are classified as current or noncurrent based on the classification of a related asset or liability. Depreciation relates to plant assets which are a noncurrent asset classification. Hence, the entire related deferred tax liability is a noncurrent liability.

DEFERRED TAX EXPENSE

30. (c)   Deferred income tax expense reported for a period is determined by the net change during the year in the deferred tax accounts on the balance sheet. For Quinn, the elimination of the beginning $9,000 net deferred tax asset and the creation of the

ending $21,000 ($70,000 cumulative taxable differences x 30% effective income tax rate) net deferred tax liability results in $30,000 of deferred income expense for 1994.

31. (c) The deferred portion of Clark's provision for income taxes (which means the deferred portion of income tax expense) is determined by the net change during the year in deferred tax accounts on the balance sheet. The temporary difference due to depreciation will result in taxable amounts in future years; the temporary difference due to accrued warranty expense will result in deductible amounts in future years. The appropriate amount of deferred taxes is computed as follows:

	Amount	Rate	Deferred Tax Accounts
Future taxable amounts:			
Depreciation expense			
1998	$ 80,000	30%	$ 24,000
1999-2000	120,000	25%	30,000
Deferred tax liability			$ 54,000
Future deductible amounts:			
Warranty expense			
1998	$ 10,000	30%	$ 3,000
1999-2000	40,000	25%	10,000
Deferred tax asset			$ 13,000

Deferred tax liability	$ 54,000
Deferred tax asset	(13,000)
Tax expense—deferred	$ 41,000

The net deferred tax liability is $41,000 [i.e., $54,000 + $(13,000)]. There is no mention of a beginning balance of deferred taxes; therefore, the entry to record the $54,000 deferred tax liability and the $13,000 deferred tax asset will involve a credit to Deferred Tax Liability for $54,000, a debit to Deferred Tax Asset for $13,000, and a debit to Income Tax Expense for $41,000. This debit to expense represents *deferred income tax expense*, and it is referred to as the *deferred portion of the provision for income taxes*.

32. (a) The amount of deferred tax benefit to be applied against current income tax expense is computed by considering the tax effects of the temporary difference for accrued product warranty costs. While product warranty costs are accrued in computing financial income, they are deductible for tax purposes only when they are paid. This causes the amount of liability (i.e., product warranty liability) to exceed its tax basis (zero) which will result in *deductible amounts* in future years when the warranty liability is settled. A deferred tax asset should

be recognized for the tax benefit of the future deductible amounts. Therefore, Lobo should report a deferred tax asset of $18,000 ($60,000 x 30%). There is no apparent need for a valuation allowance against that deferred tax asset; Lobo expects to operate profitably in the future. Lobo had no temporary differences in prior years. Therefore, the recognition of the deferred tax asset of $18,000 requires a debit to Deferred Tax Asset and a credit to Income Tax Expense for $18,000. The credit to the expense account is called a *deferred tax benefit* of $18,000 to be applied against current income tax expense (current tax expense is computed by multiplying the taxable income figure by the current tax rate). The premiums on officers' life insurance and the interest revenue on municipal bonds do not affect the recognition of the deferred tax asset because they are events recognized in financial statements that do not have tax consequences. The insurance premiums are an expense that is not tax deductible, and the interest received on municipal bonds is revenue that is exempt from taxation.

33. (c) The amount to be reported as 1994 current tax expense is computed by multiplying 1994 taxable income by the 1994 effective income tax rate (i.e., $650,000 x 30% = $195,000).

34. (c) In 1993, Mobe should have recorded an income tax receivable of $90,000 (i.e., $300,000 x 30%) for the amount to be realized as a refund of taxes paid in 1992, based on the carryback of 1993 losses. Mobe would not likely have recorded the tax effects of the $400,000 loss carryforward ($700,000 loss less $300,000 carried back) because, in accordance with FASB 109, the measurement of deferred tax assets is reduced, if necessary, by the amount of any tax benefits that are not expected to be realized. Being a young company with a substantial loss in its second year and that loss being more than twice the net income of the first year, it was probably considered that *more likely than not* some portion or all of the deferred tax asset of $120,000 ($400,000 x 30%) would not be realized and the valuation reduced to $0. Thus, in 1994, the total tax expense would be equal to the current tax expense as follows:

Operating income for 1994	$1,200,000
Less: Operating loss carryforward	(400,000)
Net taxable income	$ 800,000
Effective tax rate	x 30%
Current tax expense 1994	$ 240,000

VALUATION ALLOWANCE

35. (c)   Shin's income tax expense is calculated as follows:

Income taxes payable	$13,000
Plus: Deferred tax expense due to valuation allowance (10% X $20,000)	2,000
Less: Deferred tax benefit due to increase in deferred tax asset ($20,000 – $15,000)	(5,000)
Total income tax expense	$10,000

36. (b)   Under SFAS 109, a deferred tax asset is to be recognized for the future benefits of a loss carryforward. Therefore, Dodd will increase income by $54,000 ($180,000 x 30% future tax rate) when the benefits of the NOL carryforward are recorded in 1997 by a debit to Deferred Tax Asset and a credit to Benefits of Loss Carryforward (a component of income tax expense on the income statement). No valuation allowance is required (which would reduce the deferred tax asset and the described impact on income) because the company expects the benefits of the loss carryforward to be realized in the future. In addition, the potential gain of $100,000 (i.e., $200,000 offer – $100,000 carrying amount) from the possible sale of the patent should *not* be recognized in 1997. Dodd Corp. has not sold the patent as of December 31, 1997; it is only considering whether to sell the patent. The excess of fair value over book value of the patent does serve, however, as some positive evidence in evaluating the realizability of the deferred tax asset related to the tax loss carryforward.

37. (d)   A deferred tax asset is to be recognized for the future tax benefits of a loss carryforward ($90,000 x 30% future tax rate = $27,000). A valuation allowance is to be established only if it is more likely than not that a portion or all of the asset will not be realized. Dorr expects to realize the asset and does not need a valuation allowance.

ENACTED CHANGE IN TAX LAW OR RATES

38. (d)   SFAS 109, par. 27, states, "Deferred tax liabilities and assets shall be adjusted for the effect of a change in tax laws or rates. The effect shall be included in income from continuing operations for the period that includes the enactment date."

BALANCE SHEET PRESENTATION

39. (d)   Deferred taxable temporary differences create deferred tax liabilities. SFAS 109 requires that deferred tax items are classified as current or noncurrent based on the related asset or liability.

Since the related item is noncurrent, the deferred tax liability would be noncurrent.

40. (a)   Under SFAS 109, deferred tax liabilities and assets shall be classified on the balance sheet as net current or net noncurrent based on the classification of the related asset or liability. The deferred tax liability resulting from the temporary difference related to equipment would be all noncurrent because equipment is in a noncurrent classification. The deferred tax asset resulting from the warranty accrual will be part current and part noncurrent because of the classification of the warranty obligation. The deferred compensation liability is all noncurrent so the related deferred tax asset is all noncurrent. Apparently only 1/3 of the total installment receivables are in a current classification so only 1/3 of the related deferred tax liability is current. Deferred taxes would be computed and classified as follows (in 000's):

Temporary diff.	Future taxable (ded.) amounts	Tax rate	Deferred tax liab. (asset)	Classification
Depreciation	$ 10	30%	$3	Noncurrent
Warranty accrual	(10)	30%	(3)	Current
Warranty accrual	(10)	30%	(3)	Noncurrent
Deferred comp.	(15)	30%	(4.5)	Noncurrent
Installment sales	10	30%	3	Current
Installment sales	20	30%	6	Noncurrent
Net	$ 5		$1.5	

Rom's accounts are to be netted as follows:

Current	Noncurrent
$ (3)	$ 3
3	(3)
$ 0	(4.5)
	6
	$ 1.5

41. (b)   The balance of the deferred tax asset and the deferred tax liability would be determined as follows:

Temporary difference	Future taxable (deductible) amount	Tax rate	Deferred tax liability (asset)
Installment sale	$1,500,000	30%	$ 450,000
Accrued costs	(2,100,000)	30%	(630,000)

The classification of each deferred tax account is based on the classification of the related asset or liability for financial reporting. The deferred tax liability arising from the installment sale is 1/3 current ($450,000 ÷ 3 = $150,000) and 2/3 noncurrent because the related receivable is classified as 1/3 current asset and 2/3 noncurrent (it arose from the sale of an investment and not in the ordinary course of its main business). The deferred tax asset arising from the accrual of warranty costs is one-third current ($630,000 ÷ 3 = $210,000) and two-thirds noncurrent because the related warranty obligation is 1/3 current (one-third of the warranty liability comes due within one year of the balance sheet date). Therefore, $150,000 + $(210,000) = $(60,000) current and $300,000 + $(420,000) = $(120,000) noncurrent.

42. (b) In a classified balance sheet, deferred tax assets and liabilities are to be reported in a net current and a net noncurrent amount. The classification of an individual deferred tax account is based on the classification of the related asset or liability for financial reporting. In the problem, the deferred income tax liability of $15,000 related to a noncurrent asset should be netted with the deferred income tax asset of $3,000 related to a noncurrent liability and be reported as a noncurrent liability of $12,000. The deferred income tax asset of $8,000 related to a current liability would be reported as a current asset. Answer (a) failed to net the noncurrent asset and the noncurrent liability and ignored the current asset. Answers (c) and (d) disregarded the current and noncurrent natures.

43. (d) Deferred tax liabilities and assets are to be classified as current or noncurrent, based on the classification of the related asset or liability (if any) for financial reporting. Therefore, in the question at hand, the $75,000 deferred tax liability should be reported as noncurrent because there is a related asset classified as noncurrent, and the $25,000 deferred tax asset should be reported as current because there is a related asset classified as current. Deferred tax liabilities and assets are to be reported in a *net* current and a *net* noncurrent amount.

INCOME STATEMENT PRESENTATION

44. (b) Except for certain areas such as business combinations and quasi-reorganizations, the manner of reporting the tax benefits of an operating loss carryforward or carryback is determined by the source of the income or loss in the current year and *not* by the source of the operating loss carryforward or taxes paid in a prior year. Thus, for example, the tax benefit of an operating loss carryforward reduces income tax expense from continuing operations if realization of the tax benefit results from income from continuing operations; likewise, that tax benefit is reported as an extraordinary item if realization of the tax benefit results from an extraordinary gain.

45. (a) Except for certain areas such as business combinations and quasi-reorganizations, the manner of reporting the tax benefits of an operating

loss carryforward or carryback is determined by the source of income or loss in the current year and not by the source of the operating loss carryforward or taxes paid in a prior year (SFAS 109, par. 37). Therefore, the tax benefit of the operating loss in question reduces income tax expense from income from continuing operations because the realization of the tax benefit results from income from continuing operations. Likewise, for example, the tax benefit would have been reported as an extraordinary item if realization of the tax benefit resulted from an extraordinary gain.

46. (a) SFAS 109, par. 35, states, "Income tax expense or benefit for the year shall be allocated among continuing operations, discontinued operations, extraordinary items, and items charged or credited directly to shareholders' equity" such as prior period adjustments, certain changes in accounting principles, and changes in market values of investments in marketable equity securities classified as noncurrent assets.

47. (c) The provision for income taxes is computed as follows:

Income before income taxes and extraordinary item	$ 900,000
Less: Nontaxable gain on life insurance coverage	(100,000)
Income before taxes and taxable extraordinary item	800,000
Applicable tax rate	x 30%
Provision for income taxes	$ 240,000

COMMON STOCK INVESTMENTS

48. (a) The question involves a temporary difference because the investor recognizes investment income for financial purposes based on its equity in the investee's earnings, whereas for income tax purposes, investment income is recognized when cash dividends are received. SFAS 109 requires that deferred income taxes be recorded on this temporary difference which will result in a future taxable amount. The increase in the investors' deferred income tax liability for this temporary difference is computed as follows:

Equity in investee's earnings recognized in financial accounting	$180,000
Less: Dividends received	(30,000)
Temporary difference before consideration of dividends-received deduction	150,000
Less: Dividends-received deduction applicable to temporary difference ($150,000 x 80%)	(120,000)
Taxable portion of temporary difference	30,000
Times: Presently enacted tax rate for future periods	x 30%
Deferred tax liability	$ 9,000

49. (d) This question involves a temporary difference because the investor recognizes investment income for financial purposes based on its equity in the investee's earnings, whereas for tax purposes, investment income is recognized on the cash basis when dividends are received. SFAS 109 requires that deferred taxes be recorded on this temporary difference. In this question, we are told to ignore the 80% dividends-received deduction that the investor would be permitted. The increase in the investor's deferred income tax liability for this temporary difference is computed as follows:

Equity in investee's earnings recognized in financial accounting ($225,000 x 40%)	$ 90,000
Less: Dividends received ($75,000 x 40%)	(30,000)
Temporary difference (without consideration of the dividends-received deduction)	60,000
Times: Presently enacted tax rate for future periods	x 30%
Increase in deferred tax liability	$ 18,000

PERFORMANCE BY SUBTOPICS

Each category below parallels a subtopic covered in Chapter 13. Record the number and percentage of questions you correctly answered in each subtopic area.

Reconciliation of Pretax Financial Income & Taxable Income

Question #	Correct √
1	
2	
3	
4	
5	
6	
# Questions	6

Correct _____
% Correct _____

SFAS 109 Overview

Question #	Correct √
7	
# Questions	1

Correct _____
% Correct _____

Temporary Differences

Question #	Correct √
8	
9	
10	
11	
# Questions	4

Correct _____
% Correct _____

Permanent Differences

Question #	Correct √
12	
# Questions	1

Correct _____
% Correct _____

Computation of Deferred Tax Liabilities & Assets

Question #	Correct √
13	
14	
15	
16	
17	
18	
19	
20	
21	
22	
23	
24	
25	
26	
27	
# Questions	15

Correct _____
% Correct _____

Tax Rates Used

Question #	Correct √
28	
29	
# Questions	2

Correct _____
% Correct _____

Deferred Tax Expense

Question #	Correct √
30	
31	
32	
33	
34	
# Questions	5

Correct _____
% Correct _____

Valuation Allowance

Question #	Correct √
35	
36	
37	
# Questions	3

Correct _____
% Correct _____

Enacted Change in Tax Law or Rates

Question #	Correct √
38	
# Questions	1

Correct _____
% Correct _____

Balance Sheet Presentation

Question #	Correct √
39	
40	
41	
42	
43	
# Questions	5

Correct _____
% Correct _____

Income Statement Presentation

Question #	Correct √
44	
45	
46	
47	
# Questions	4

Correct _____
% Correct _____

Common Stock Investments

Question #	Correct √
48	
49	
# Questions	2

Correct _____
% Correct _____

OTHER OBJECTIVE FORMAT SOLUTION

SOLUTION 13-2 INCOME TAXES (5 points)

1. (B)   When an asset is depreciated faster for tax purposes than it is depreciated for financial accounting purposes, the temporary difference results in a deferred tax liability. In other words, the current amount due for taxes is less because of the larger depreciation deduction for tax purposes. Temporary differences of this type reverse themselves over time, and the entity has a deferred tax liability in the meantime.

2. (A)   When revenue is received in advance, the temporary difference results in a deferred tax asset. For tax purposes, the revenue is taxable in the period the related cash is received. The revenue is not included in the computation of financial income until the period in which it is earned. In other words, a larger amount of taxes is due for the current period, and is similar to a prepaid expense.

3. (C)   Interest received on an investment in tax-exempt securities is a permanent difference because tax-exempt income is recognized in the financial statements, but does not have tax consequences under the regular U.S. tax system. Therefore, this difference will not reverse in future tax periods.

4. (A)   Costs of guarantees and warranties that are estimated and accrued for financial reporting create a temporary difference that results in a deferred tax asset. Such items will result in deductible amounts in future years for tax purposes when the liability is settled. This is similar to a prepaid expense in that both situations result in assets.

5. (G)   Current tax expense for the year ended April 30, 1995, is calculated as follows:

Taxable income	$600,000
Tax rate	x 20%
Current tax expense	$120,000

6. (M)   Cumulative temporary differences at April 30, 1996, are calculated as follows:

Temporary differences, 4/30/95	$200,000
Temporary differences, 4/30/96	100,000
Cumulative temporary differences	$300,000

7. (B)   Deferred tax expense for the year ended April 30, 1996, is calculated as follows:

Deferred tax liability, 4/30/96	$ 75,000
Deferred tax liability, 4/30/95	(40,000)
Deferred tax expense, 1996	$ 35,000

8. (H)   The deferred tax liability at April 30, 1997, is calculated as follows:

Cumulative temporary differences	$450,000
Tax rate	x 30%
Deferred tax liability	$135,000

PROBLEM/ESSAY SOLUTIONS

SOLUTION 13-3 TEMPORARY DIFFERENCES

a.

Rayne Co.
SCHEDULE OF INTEREST EXPENSE
For the Year Ended December 31, 1997

Note payable [1]	$ 6,600
Capital lease obligation [2]	4,750
Bonds payable [3]	26,900
Total interest expense	$38,250

[1]   1,800 (90,000 × 8% × 3/12) + 4,800 (80,000 × 8% × 9/12)
[2]   10% × 47,500 (62,500 − 15,000)
[3]   538,000 × 10% × ½

b.   To: Dunn
       From: Green
       Re: Accounting for income taxes

Below is a brief overview of accounting for income taxes in accordance with FASB 109.

The objectives of accounting for income taxes are to recognize (a) the **amount of taxes payable or refundable for the current year**, and (b) **deferred tax liabilities and assets** for the **estimated future tax consequences** of temporary differences and carryforwards. Temporary differences are **differences between the tax basis of assets or liabilities** and their **reported amounts in the financial statements** that will result in taxable or deductible amounts in future years.

Deferred tax assets and liabilities are measured based on the provisions of enacted tax law; the effects of future changes in the tax law or rates are not anticipated. The measurement of deferred tax assets is reduced, if necessary, by a valuation allowance to reflect the net asset amount that is more likely than not to be realized. Deferred income tax expense or benefit is measured as the change during the year in an enterprise's deferred tax liabilities and assets.

SOLUTION 13-4 SINGLE STEP INCOME STATEMENT/RECONCILIATION OF FINANCIAL AND TAXABLE INCOMES

A.

Powell Corp.
INCOME STATEMENT
For the Year Ended June 30, 1997

Revenues:		
Machine sales	$750,000	
Service revenues	250,000	
Interest revenue	10,000	
Total revenues		$1,010,000
Expenses:		
Cost of sales—machines	425,000	
Cost of services	100,000	
Administrative expenses	300,000	
Research and development expenses	110,000	
Interest expense	5,000	
Loss from asset disposal	40,000	
Current income tax expense [1]	6,000	
Deferred income tax expense [2]	4,500	
Total expenses and losses		(990,500)
Income before extraordinary gain		19,500
Extraordinary gain, net of income taxes of $75,000		175,000
Net income		$ 194,500
Earnings (loss) per share:		
Income before extraordinary gain [3]		($0.40)
Net income		$0.47

Editors' Note:
[1] $425,000 + $100,000 + $300,000 + $110,000 + $5,000 + 40,000 = $980,000. ($1,010,000 − $980,000 + $5,000 −$15,000) x .30 = $6,000.
[2] $15,000 x .30 = $4,500.
[3] ($19,500 − $100,000) / 200,000 = ($0.40)

b.

Net income	$ 194,500
Add: Taxes on extraordinary gain	75,000
Provision for income taxes	10,500
Financial statement income before income taxes	280,000
Permanent difference—officer's life insurance	5,000
Temporary difference—excess of tax over financial statement depreciation	(15,000)
Taxable income	$ 270,000

Education Requirements

Most states (and other jurisdictions) now require candidates to obtain 150 semester hours of education prior to taking the examination. Jurisdictions with 150-hour requirements may have alternate options available for candidates. Naturally, this information is subject to change. Contact the jurisdiction in question for all applicable requirements to sit for the exam.

The following jurisdictions have 150-hour requirements that are not yet effective.

State	Effective Date	State	Effective Date
Arizona	June 30, 2004	Minnesota	July 1, 2006
California	January 1, 2002	New Mexico	July 1, 2004
Maine	October 2, 2002	New York	August 1, 2009
Massachusetts	July 1, 2002	Oklahoma	July 1, 2003
Michigan	July 1, 2003	Virginia	Jan 1, 2006

Some jurisdictions with 150-hour requirements may substitute experience for some education. Some may allow candidates to sit for the exam without the experience required for the license. Two of these are California and Pennsylvania.

Colorado, Delaware, New Hampshire, Vermont, and the Virgin Islands currently don't have a 150-hour requirement.

SELECT HOT•SPOTS™ VIDEO DESCRIPTIONS

CPA 2035 FASB 109: Accounting for Income Taxes

Bob Monette provides comprehensive coverage of the temporary and permanent differences between financial and taxable income, current tax liability, current tax expense, deferred tax assets and liabilities, what to do when future tax rates differ from current tax rates, and how to report the various income tax-related accounts in the financial statements.

CPA 2033 FASB 95: Statement of Cash Flows

Bob Monette provides comprehensive coverage of both the direct and indirect methods of preparing the Statement of Cash Flows, with detailed explanations of the operating, investing, and financing sections of the statement and easy ways of remembering just what goes in each. In addition, learn when, where, and how to include non-cash transactions.

CPA 3267 EPS & Everything Else

Comprehensive coverage of earnings per share as required by FASB 128, including basic and diluted EPS, and the treasury stock and if-converted methods. Other topics include ratio analysis, price level accounting, foreign operations, partnerships, and personal financial statements.

CPA 2020 Consolidations

Bob Monette discusses the cost and equity methods of accounting for investments in subsidiaries, the purchase method of consolidation, and intercompany transactions. Candidates will learn the accounting rules, journal entries, and how to eliminate the effect of intercompany transactions.

Call our customer representatives toll-free at 1 (800) 874-7877 for more details about videos.

CHAPTER 14

STATEMENT OF CASH FLOWS

CHAPTER 14

STATEMENT OF CASH FLOWS

I. STANDARDS OF FINANCIAL ACCOUNTING AND REPORTING

A. SCOPE

A business enterprise that provides a set of financial statements that reports both financial position and results of operations should also provide a statement of cash flows for each period for which results of operations are provided.

B. PURPOSE

1. PROVIDE INFORMATION The primary purpose of a statement of cash flows is to provide relevant information about the cash receipts and cash payments of an enterprise during a period.

2. USE OF INFORMATION The information provided in a statement of cash flows helps investors, creditors, and others to assess the following:

    a. The enterprise's ability to generate positive future net cash flows

    b. The enterprise's ability to meet its obligations, its ability to pay dividends, and its needs for external financing

    c. The reasons for differences between net income and associated cash receipts and payments

    d. The effects on an enterprise's financial position of both its cash and noncash investing and financing transactions during the period

3. INFORMATION TO REPORT To achieve its purpose of providing information to help investors, creditors, and others make these assessments, a statement of cash flows should report the cash effects during a period of an enterprise's operations, its investing transactions, and its financing transactions. Related disclosures should report the effects of investing and financing transactions that affect an enterprise's financial position, but do **not** directly affect cash flows during the period.

C. FOCUS ON CASH AND CASH EQUIVALENTS

1. CHANGE IN CASH A statement of cash flows should explain the change during the period in cash and cash equivalents.

2. CASH EQUIVALENTS DEFINITION For purposes of SFAS 95, cash equivalents are short-term, highly liquid investments that are both (a) readily convertible into known amounts of cash and (b) so near their maturity that they present insignificant risk of changes in value because of changes in interest rates.

Generally, only investments with original maturities to the entity holding the investment of *three months or less* qualify under this definition. Examples include Treasury bills, commercial paper, and money market funds.

3. INVESTMENTS IN CASH EQUIVALENTS Cash purchases and sales of investments considered to be cash equivalents generally are part of the enterprise's cash management activities rather than part of its operating, investing, and financing activities, and details of those transactions need **not** be reported in a statement of cash flows.

4. **CASH EQUIVALENTS POLICY** An enterprise should establish a policy concerning which short-term, highly liquid investments that satisfy the definition in 2., above, are treated as cash equivalents. An enterprise's policy for determining which items are treated as cash equivalents should be disclosed.

D. CONTENT AND FORM OF THE STATEMENT

1. **CLASSIFICATION OF CASH RECEIPTS AND PAYMENTS** A statement of cash flows should classify cash receipts and cash payments as resulting from investing, financing, or operating activities. A statement of cash flows should report the following:

   a. **NET CASH** Net cash provided or used by operating, investing, and financing activities

   b. **NET EFFECT** The net effect of those flows on cash and cash equivalents during the period in a manner that reconciles beginning and ending cash and cash equivalents

2. **REPORTING CASH FLOWS FROM OPERATING ACTIVITIES**

   a. **DIRECT METHOD**

   (1) Under this method, enterprises are encouraged to report major classes of *gross* cash receipts and *gross* cash payments and their arithmetic sum—the net cash flow from operating activities. At a minimum, the following classes of operating cash receipts and payments should be separately reported:

      (a) Cash collected from customers

      (b) Interest and dividends received

      (c) Other operating cash receipts, if any

      (d) Cash paid to employees and other suppliers of goods or services, including suppliers of insurance, advertising, and the like

      (e) Interest paid

      (f) Income taxes paid

      (g) Other operating cash payments, if any

   (2) Enterprises are encouraged to provide further breakdowns of operating cash receipts and payments that they consider meaningful and feasible; for example, a retailer or manufacturer might decide to further divide cash paid to employees and suppliers into payments for costs of inventory and payments for selling, general, and administrative expenses. If the direct method of reporting net cash flow from operating activities is used, a reconciliation of net income to net cash flow from operating activities should be provided in a separate schedule.

   b. **INDIRECT METHOD** Net cash flow from operating activities may also be reported under the indirect method by adjusting net income to reconcile it to net cash flow from operating activities. That requires adjusting net income to remove the effects of the following:

   (1) All deferrals of past operating cash receipts and payments, such as changes during the period in inventory and deferred income

   (2) All accruals of expected operating cash receipts and payments, such as changes during the period in receivables and payables

(3) Items whose cash effects are investing cash flows, such as depreciation and gains and losses on sales of property, plant, and equipment and discontinued operations

(4) Items whose cash effects are financing cash flows, such as gains and losses on extinguishment of debt

c. **RECONCILE NET INCOME** The reconciliation of net income to net cash flow from operating activities should separately report all major classes of reconciling items. The reconciliation may be either reported within the statement of cash flows or provided in a separate schedule, with the statement of cash flows reporting only the net cash flow from operating activities. In addition, if the indirect method is used, amounts of interest paid (net of amounts capitalized) and income taxes paid during the period should be provided in related disclosures.

3. **REPORTING CASH FLOWS FROM INVESTING AND FINANCING ACTIVITIES** Both investing cash inflows and outflows and financing cash inflows and outflows should be reported **separately** in a statement of cash flows. For example, outlays for acquisitions of property, plant, and equipment should be reported separately from proceeds from sale of property, plant, and equipment; proceeds of borrowings should be reported separately from repayments of debt; and proceeds from issuing stock should be reported separately from outlays to reacquire the enterprise's stock.

E. **INFORMATION ABOUT NONCASH INVESTING AND FINANCING ACTIVITIES**
Information about all investing and financing activities of an enterprise during a period that affects recognized assets or liabilities, but does **not** result in cash receipts or cash payments in the period, should be reported in related disclosures. Examples of noncash investing and financing transactions are: converting debt to equity; acquiring assets by assuming *directly related liabilities*, such as purchasing a building by incurring a mortgage to the seller; obtaining an asset by entering into a capital lease; and exchanging noncash assets or liabilities for other noncash assets or liabilities. If a transaction is part cash and part noncash, only the cash portion should be reported in a statement of cash flows.

F. **CASH FLOW PER SHARE**
Financial statements should not report an amount of cash flow per share.

II. **CLASSIFICATION OF RECEIPTS AND PAYMENTS**

A. **CASH FLOWS FROM OPERATING ACTIVITIES**

1. **NET INCOME RELATED** Cash flows from operating activities are generally the cash effects of transactions and other events that enter into the determination of net income. Operating activities generally involve producing and delivering goods and providing services.

2. **CASH INFLOWS FROM OPERATING ACTIVITIES**

a. Cash receipts from sales of goods or services, including receipts from collection or sale of accounts receivable and both short- and long-term notes receivable from customers arising from those sales

b. Cash receipts from returns *on* loans, other debt instruments of other entities, and equity securities—interest and dividends

c. Cash receipts from sales and maturities of trading securities, in accordance with SFAS 115

d. All other cash receipts that do not stem from transactions defined as investing or financing activities, such as amounts received to settle lawsuits; proceeds of insurance settlements except for those that are directly related to investing or financing activities, such as from destruction of a building; and refunds from suppliers

3. **CASH OUTFLOWS FOR OPERATING ACTIVITIES**

   a. Cash payments to acquire materials for manufacture or goods for resale, including principal payments on accounts and both short- and long-term notes payable to suppliers for those materials or goods

   b. Cash payments to other suppliers and employees for other goods or services

   c. Cash payments to governments for taxes

   d. Cash payments to lenders and other creditors for interest

   e. Cash payments for purchases of trading securities, per SFAS 115

   f. All other cash payments that do not stem from transactions defined as investing or financing activities, such as payments to settle lawsuits, cash contributions to charities, and cash refunds to customers

B. **CASH FLOWS FROM INVESTING ACTIVITIES**

   1. **INVESTING ACTIVITIES**

      a. Making and collecting loans.

      b. Acquiring and disposing of property, plant, and equipment, and other productive assets (assets held for or used in the production of goods or services by the enterprise other than materials that are part of the enterprise's inventory).

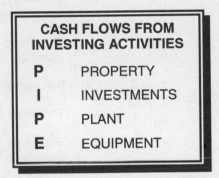

CASH FLOWS FROM INVESTING ACTIVITIES

P PROPERTY

I INVESTMENTS

P PLANT

E EQUIPMENT

   c. Purchases, sales, and maturities of debt and equity available-for-sale and held-to-maturity securities, in accordance with SFAS 115; and other investments in equity securities not covered by SFAS 115. SFAS 115 does not apply to investments in equity securities accounted for under the equity method nor to investments in consolidated subsidiaries.

   2. **CASH INFLOWS FROM INVESTING ACTIVITIES** Receipts from disposing of loans; debt or equity instruments; or property, plant, and equipment including directly related proceeds of insurance settlements, such as the proceeds of insurance on a building that is damaged or destroyed.

      a. Receipts from collections or sales of loans made by the enterprise and of other entities' debt instruments (other than cash equivalents) that were purchased by the enterprise and held as available-for-sale or held-to-maturity securities.

      b. Receipts from sales of equity instruments of other enterprises, held as available-for-sale securities or other equity securities not covered by SFAS 115.

      c. Receipts from sales of property, plant, and equipment, and other productive assets.

   3. **CASH OUTFLOWS FOR INVESTING ACTIVITIES**

      a. Disbursements for loans made by the enterprise.

      b. Payments to acquire debt and equity instruments of other entities, to be held as available-for-sale or held-to-maturity securities, or other equity securities not covered by SFAS 115.

    c. Payments at the time of purchase, or soon before or after purchase, to acquire property, plant, and equipment, and other productive assets.

        (1) Generally, only advance payments, the down payment, or other amounts paid at the time of purchase or soon before or after purchase of property, plant, and equipment and other productive assets are *investing cash outflows.*

        (2) Generally, principal payments on seller-financed debt directly related to a purchase of property, plant, and equipment or other productive assets are *financing cash outflows.*

C. CASH FLOWS FROM FINANCING ACTIVITIES

1. FINANCING ACTIVITIES

> | CASH FLOWS FROM FINANCING ACTIVITIES | |
> | --- | --- |
> | **PRINC** | DEBT PRINCIPAL |
> | **DIV** | PAY DIVIDENDS |
> | **I** | ISSUE STOCK |
> | **TS** | TREASURY STOCK |

    a. Obtaining resources from owners and providing them with a return on, and a return of, their investment.

    b. Borrowing money and repaying amounts borrowed, or otherwise settling the obligation.

    c. Obtaining and paying for other resources obtained from creditors on long-term credit.

2. CASH INFLOWS FROM FINANCING ACTIVITIES

    a. Proceeds from issuing equity instruments (e.g., common and preferred stock).

    b. Proceeds from issuing bonds, mortgages, notes, and from other short- or long-term borrowing.

3. CASH OUTFLOWS FOR FINANCING ACTIVITIES

    a. Payments of dividends or other distributions to owners, including outlays to reacquire the enterprise's equity instruments (e.g., treasury stock).

    b. Repayments of amounts borrowed.

    c. Other principal payments to creditors who have extended long-term credit.

III. PREPARATION OF THE STATEMENT

A. APPROACHES TO PREPARATION

In simple situations, efficient preparation of the statement of cash flows may be accomplished by analysis of transactions and other events, the income statement, the statement of retained earnings, and comparative balance sheets. More complex problems may require a more systematic approach to the preparation of the statement, such as the T-account method or the worksheet method. However, these methods are merely aids in preparing the statement; no formal entries are made in the company's books.

NOTE: Use of these methods is **not required** to solve CPA Exam problems but may be helpful.

B. STEPS IN PREPARING THE STATEMENT

1. CASH AND CASH EQUIVALENTS Determine the change in cash and cash equivalents for the period.

2. OPERATING ACTIVITIES Determine net cash flow from operating activities either by the direct method or the indirect method.

3. **NONOPERATING ACCOUNTS** Analyze changes in the nonoperating accounts to determine the effect on cash. Investing and financing activities affecting cash are reported in the statement; significant noncash investing and financing activities are reported in related disclosures.

4. **PRESENTATION GUIDELINES**

    a. **FORMAT** Present the above information using the following format for the statement of cash flows:

        (1)   Net cash flow from operating activities—direct method or indirect method

        (2)   Net cash flow from investing activities

        (3)   Net cash flow from financing activities

        (4)   Net increase (decrease) in cash and cash equivalents

        (5)   Cash and cash equivalents at beginning of year

        (6)   Cash and cash equivalents at end of year

    b. **DISCLOSURES** Report significant noncash investing and financing activities in related disclosures. In addition, disclose the enterprise's policy for determining which items are treated as cash equivalents.

    c. **RECONCILIATION OF NET INCOME** If the direct method of reporting net cash flow from operating activities is used, provide a reconciliation of net income to net cash flow from operating activities in a separate schedule.

    d. **INTEREST AND INCOME TAXES** If the indirect method is used, amounts of interest paid (net of amounts capitalized) and income taxes paid during the period should be provided in related disclosures.

IV. ILLUSTRATIVE PROBLEM

A. GIVEN INFORMATION

EXHIBIT 1 ♦ FINANCIAL STATEMENTS

Wolverine Company INCOME STATEMENT DATA For the Year Ended December 31, 20X8		
Sales		$242,807
Gain on sale of available-for-sale securities		2,400
Equity in earnings of 30% owned company		5,880
Gain on sale of land		10,700
		261,787
Cost of sales	$138,407	
General and administrative expenses	22,010	
Depreciation	1,250	
Interest expense	1,150	
Income taxes	34,952	(197,769)
Net income		$ 64,018
(continued on next page)		

14-7

Wolverine Company
COMPARATIVE BALANCE SHEET
December 31

Assets	20X8	20X7	Change
Cash	$ 49,400	$ 25,300	$ 24,100
Available-for-sale securities	7,300	16,500	(9,200)
Accounts receivable	50,320	25,320	25,000
Allowance for uncollectible accounts	(1,000)	(1,000)	--
Inventory	48,590	31,090	17,500
Investment in 30% owned company	67,100	61,220	5,880
Land	18,700	40,000	(21,300)
Building	79,100	79,100	--
Equipment	81,500	--	81,500
Less accumulated depreciation	(16,250)	(15,000)	(1,250)
Total Assets	$ 384,760	$262,530	$122,230
Liabilities			
Accounts payable	$ 17,330	$ 21,220	$ (3,890)
Income taxes payable	4,616	--	4,616
Bonds payable	115,000	50,000	65,000
Less unamortized discount	(2,150)	(2,300)	150
Deferred tax liability	846	510	336
Stockholders' Equity			
Preferred stock	--	30,000	(30,000)
Common stock	110,000	80,000	30,000
Retained earnings	139,118	83,100	56,018
Total Liabilities and Stockholders' Equity	$ 384,760	$262,530	$122,230

1. On January 8, 20X8, the company sold marketable equity securities for cash. These securities had a cost of $9,200.

2. The company's preferred stock is convertible into common stock at a rate of one share of preferred for two shares of common. The preferred stock and common stock have par values of $2 and $1, respectively.

3. On July 17, 20X8, three acres of land were sold for cash of $32,000.

4. On September 3, 20X8, the company purchased equipment for cash.

5. On November 10, 20X8, bonds payable were issued by the company at par for cash.

6. On December 15, 20X8, the company declared and paid an $8,000 dividend to common stockholders.

7. No dividends were received during 20X8 from the 30% owned investee.

8. For purposes of the statement of cash flows, the company considers all highly liquid debt instruments purchased with a maturity of three months or less to be cash equivalents.

9. **REQUIRED:** Prepare a statement of cash flows for the Wolverine Company.

B. **DETERMINATION OF CHANGE IN CASH AND CASH EQUIVALENTS**

The increase in cash and cash equivalents is $24,100. The marketable equity securities are not considered to be cash equivalents. Cash equivalents are short-term, highly liquid investments, such as Treasury bills, commercial paper, and money market funds.

C. **DETERMINATION OF NET CASH FLOW FROM OPERATING ACTIVITIES**

This amount is determined by using either the direct method or the indirect method.

1. **DIRECT METHOD** Under this method, enterprises report major classes of gross cash receipts and gross cash payments and their arithmetic sum—the net cash flow from operating activities. When the direct method is used, a reconciliation of net income to net cash flow from operating activities should be provided in a separate schedule. Presented below are the Wolverine Company's cash flows from operating activities for the year ended December 31, 20X8, using the direct method.

EXAMPLE 1 ♦ DIRECT METHOD OF DETERMINING NET CASH PROVIDED BY OPERATING ACTIVITIES

Wolverine Company
CASH FLOWS FROM OPERATING ACTIVITIES
For the Year Ended December 31, 20X8
Increase (Decrease) in Cash and Cash Equivalents

Cash flows from operating activities:	
Cash received from customers	$ 217,807 [1]
Cash paid for inventory	(159,797) [2]
Cash paid for general and administrative expenses	(22,010)
Interest paid	(1,000) [3]
Income taxes paid	(30,000) [4]
Net cash provided by operating activities	$ 5,000

COMPUTATIONS:

[1] Cash received from customers is determined by subtracting the increase in accounts receivable from sales; the increase in accounts receivable represents sales that were not collected in cash. It is important to note that under the direct method, the allowance for uncollectible accounts is not used to determine cash collected from customers.

Sales	$242,807
Less: Increase in accounts receivable	(25,000)
Cash received from customers	$217,807

[2] The cash paid for inventory is determined as follows. First, the increase in inventory is added to cost of sales to determine inventory purchases for the period. Second, the decrease in accounts payable is added to inventory purchases to determine cash payments for inventory.

Cost of sales	$138,407
Add: Increase in inventory	17,500
Inventory purchases	155,907
Add: Decrease in accounts payable	3,890
Cash paid for inventory	$159,797

(continued on next page)

14-9

[3] The bond discount amortization increased interest expense but did not involve an outflow of cash; therefore, it must be subtracted from interest expense to determine cash payments for interest.

Interest expense	$ 1,150
Less: Bond discount amortization	(150)
Interest paid	$ 1,000

[4] The increase in income taxes payable increased current income tax expense, but did not involve an outflow of cash. The increase in the deferred tax liability caused the recognition of deferred income tax expense, but also did not involve an outflow of cash. Therefore, the increases in those liabilities are subtracted from income tax expense to determine income taxes paid.

Income tax expense	$ 34,952
Less: Increase in income taxes payable	(4,616)
Increase in deferred tax liability	(336)
Income taxes paid	$ 30,000

2. **INDIRECT METHOD** Net cash flow from operating activities is reported under this method by converting net income to net cash flow from operating activities. Presented below are the Wolverine Company's cash flows from operating activities for the year ended December 31, 20X8, using the indirect method.

EXAMPLE 2 ♦ INDIRECT METHOD OF DETERMINING NET CASH PROVIDED BY OPERATING ACTIVITIES

Wolverine Company
CASH FLOWS FROM OPERATING ACTIVITIES
For the Year Ended December 31, 20X8
Increase (Decrease) in Cash and Cash Equivalents

Net income			$ 64,018
Adjustments to reconcile net income to			
net cash provided by operating activities:			
Depreciation	$ 1,250	[1]	
Bond discount amortization	150	[1]	
Deferred income taxes	336	[1]	
Gain on sale of available-for-sale securities	(2,400)	[2][7]	
Gain on sale of land	(10,700)	[2]	
Equity in earnings of equity method investee			
in excess of cash dividends	(5,880)	[2]	
Increase in net accounts receivable	(25,000)	[3]	
Increase in inventory	(17,500)	[4]	
Decrease in accounts payable	(3,890)	[5]	
Increase in income taxes payable	4,616	[6]	
Total adjustments			(59,018)
Net cash provided by operating activities [8]			$ 5,000

EXPLANATIONS:

[1] To convert net income to net cash flow from operating activities, the noncash charges to income for depreciation, bond discount amortization, and deferred income taxes must be added back to net income because those items did not involve an outflow of cash.

(continued on next page)

[2] The noncash credits to income for the gain on sale of available-for-sale securities, the gain on sale of land, and the equity in earnings of equity method investee in excess of cash dividends received must be deducted from net income for this conversion because those items did not produce an inflow of cash.

[3] Accounts Receivable—The $25,000 [i.e., ($50,320 – $1,000) – ($25,320 – $1,000)] increase in <u>net</u> accounts receivable represents sales that were not collected in cash. This amount must be deducted to convert net income to net cash flow from operating activities. Under the indirect method, the allowance for uncollectible accounts is used to determine the change in <u>net</u> accounts receivable during the period.

[4] Inventories—The increase in inventories is an operating use of cash; the incremental investment in inventories reduced cash without increasing cost of sales. This amount must be deducted to convert net income to net cash flow from operating activities.

[5] Accounts Payable—The decrease in accounts payable is due to cash payments for inventory exceeding the amount of inventory purchases. This amount must be deducted to convert net income to net cash flow from operating activities.

[6] Income Taxes Payable—The increase in income taxes payable represents current income tax expense not paid out in cash. This amount must be added to convert net income to net cash flow from operating activities.

[7] The Available-for-Sale Securities account is not an operating asset; therefore, the net change in the account is not used to convert net income to net cash flow from operating activities.

[8] When the indirect method is used, amounts of interest paid (net of amounts capitalized) and income taxes paid during the period should be provided in related disclosures.

D. ANALYSIS OF NONOPERATING ACCOUNTS

1. **MARKETABLE EQUITY SECURITIES** The proceeds from the sale resulted in an $11,600 cash inflow due to an investing activity. The $2,400 gain on the sale is a noncash credit to income; therefore, it does not involve an inflow of cash. The gain on the sale is not used to determine net cash flow from operating activities under the direct method (See B.1., above). If the indirect method is used, the gain is deducted from net income to determine net cash flow from operating activities. The sale of the marketable equity securities was recorded as follows:

Cash (to balance)	11,600	
Available-for-Sale Securities (cost from additional information)		9,200
Gain on Sale (from income statement)		2,400

2. **EQUITY METHOD INVESTMENT** The increase in the account of $5,880 represents Wolverine's equity in the investee's earnings for 20X8 since no cash dividends were received from the investee in 20X8. This amount is a noncash credit to income and, therefore, is not used to determine net cash flow from operating activities under the direct method (See B.1., above). If the indirect method is used, this amount is deducted from net income to determine net cash flow from operating activities.

3. **LAND** The decrease in the account is due to the sale of land. The proceeds from the sale resulted in a $32,000 cash inflow due to an investing activity. The $10,700 gain on the sale is a noncash credit to income; therefore, it does not represent an inflow of cash. The gain on the sale is not used to determine net cash flow from operating activities under the direct

method (See B.1., above). If the indirect method is used, the gain is deducted from net income to determine net cash flow from operating activities.

4. **EQUIPMENT** The $81,500 ($81,500 – $0) purchase of equipment for cash is a cash outflow due to an investing activity.

5. **ACCUMULATED DEPRECIATION** There were no disposals of plant assets during the year; therefore, the $1,250 increase in the account is due to additional depreciation expense. Depreciation is a noncash expense; it does not involve an outflow of cash. The depreciation is not used to determine net cash flow from operating activities if the direct method is used. If the indirect method is used, the depreciation is added to net income to determine net cash flow from operating activities.

6. **BONDS PAYABLE** The $65,000 ($115,000 – $50,000) proceeds from the issuance of bonds payable is a cash inflow due to a financing activity.

7. **UNAMORTIZED BOND DISCOUNT** The bond discount amortization is a noncash expense; it does not involve an outflow of cash. The bond discount amortization is not used to determine net cash flow from operating activities if the direct method is used. If the indirect method is used, the bond discount amortization is added to net income to determine net cash flow from operating activities. Interest expense for the year was recorded as follows:

Interest Expense (from income statement)	1,150
Bond Discount ($2,300 – $2,150)	150
Cash (to balance)	1,000

8. **DEFERRED TAX LIABILITY** The $336 increase in the deferred tax liability resulted in the recognition of $336 of deferred income tax expense. The deferred income tax expense is a noncash expense; it does not involve an outflow of cash. The deferred income taxes are not used to determine net cash flow from operating activities if the direct method is used. If the indirect method is used, the deferred income taxes are added to net income to determine net cash flow from operating activities.

9. **PREFERRED AND COMMON STOCK** The conversion of $30,000 of preferred stock into common stock is a noncash financing transaction; therefore, it is reported in related disclosures to the statement.

10. **RETAINED EARNINGS** The increase in retained earnings for the year can be explained as follows:

Retained earnings, 1/1/X8	$ 83,100
Add: Net income for 20X8	64,018
	147,118
Less: Cash dividends declared in 20X8	(8,000)
Retained earnings, 12/31/X8	$139,118

a. The cash dividends were *paid* in 20X8 and, therefore, are an $8,000 cash outflow due to a financing activity. If the dividends had been declared in 20X8, but not paid in 20X8, they would **not** have been reported in the statement of cash flows because their declaration would not have affected cash.

b. Neither the declaration or issuance of a stock dividend nor the appropriation of retained earnings affects the enterprise's assets or liabilities; therefore, these transactions are not investing or financing transactions and need **not** be reported in related disclosures to the statement.

E. **DIRECT METHOD**

Based on the preceding analysis, presented below is the Wolverine Company's statement of cash flows for the year ended December 31, 20X8, using the direct method of reporting cash flows from operating activities. Note that the reconciliation of net income to net cash provided by operating activities on the direct-method statement is identical to the data reported in the statement under the heading "Cash Flow from Operating Activities" under the indirect method. (See the shaded areas.)

EXHIBIT 2 ♦ DIRECT METHOD STATEMENT OF CASH FLOWS

Wolverine Company		
STATEMENT OF CASH FLOWS		
For the Year Ended December 31, 20X8		
Increase (Decrease) in Cash		
Cash flows from operating activities:		
Cash received from customers	$ 217,807	
Cash paid for inventory	(159,797)	
Cash paid for general and administrative expenses	(22,010)	
Interest paid	(1,000)	
Income taxes paid	(30,000)	
Net cash provided by operating activities		$ 5,000
Cash flows from investing activities:		
Proceeds from sale of land	32,000	
Proceeds from sale of available-for-sale securities	11,600	
Purchase of equipment for cash	(81,500)	
Net cash used in investing activities		(37,900)
Cash flows from financing activities:		
Dividends paid	(8,000)	
Proceeds from issuance of bonds payable	65,000	
Net cash provided by financing activities		57,000
Net increase in cash		24,100
Cash at beginning of year		25,300
Cash at end of year		$ 49,400
Reconciliation of net income to net cash provided by operating activities:		
Net income		$ 64,018
Adjustments to reconcile net income to net cash provided by		
operating activities:		
Depreciation	$ 1,250	
Bond discount amortization	150	
Deferred income taxes	336	
Gain on sale of available-for-sale securities	(2,400)	
Gain on sale of land	(10,700)	
Equity in earnings of equity method investee in		
excess of cash dividends	(5,880)	
Increase in net accounts receivable	(25,000)	
Increase in inventory	(17,500)	
Decrease in accounts payable	(3,890)	
Increase in income taxes payable	4,616	
Total adjustments		(59,018)
Net cash provided by operating activities		$ 5,000
Supplemental schedule of noncash investing and financing activities:		
Additional common stock was issued upon the conversion of $30,000 of preferred stock.		
Disclosure of Accounting Policy—For purposes of the statement of cash flows, the Company considers all highly liquid debt instruments purchased with a maturity of three months or less to be cash equivalents.		

F. **INDIRECT METHOD**

Based on the preceding analysis, presented below is the Wolverine Company's statement of cash flows for the year ended December 31, 20X8, using the indirect method of reporting cash flows from operating activities.

EXHIBIT 3 ◆ INDIRECT METHOD STATEMENT OF CASH FLOWS

Wolverine Company
STATEMENT OF CASH FLOWS
For the Year Ended December 31, 20X8
Increase (Decrease) in Cash

Cash flows from operating activities:		
Net income		$ 64,018
Adjustments to reconcile net income to net cash provided by operating activities:		
Depreciation	$ 1,250	
Bond discount amortization	150	
Deferred income taxes	336	
Gain on sale of available-for-sale securities	(2,400)	
Gain on sale of land	(10,700)	
Equity in earnings of equity method investee in excess of cash dividends	(5,880)	
Increase in net accounts receivable	(25,000)	
Increase in inventory	(17,500)	
Decrease in accounts payable	(3,890)	
Increase in income taxes payable	4,616	
Total adjustments		(59,018)
Net cash provided by operating activities		5,000
Cash flows from investing activities:		
Proceeds from sale of land	32,000	
Proceeds from sale of available-for-sale securities	11,600	
Purchase of equipment for cash	(81,500)	
Net cash used in investing activities		(37,900)
Cash flows from financing activities:		
Dividend paid	(8,000)	
Proceeds from issuance of bonds payable	65,000	
Net cash provided by financing activities		57,000
Net increase in cash		24,100
Cash at beginning of year		25,300
Cash at end of year		$ 49,400

Supplemental disclosures of cash flow information:

Cash paid during the year for:	
Interest (net of amount capitalized)	$ 1,000
Income taxes	30,000

Supplemental schedule of noncash investing and financing activities:

Additional common stock was issued upon the conversion of $30,000 of preferred stock.

Disclosure of Accounting Policy—For purposes of the statement of cash flows, the company considers all highly liquid debt instruments purchased with a maturity of three months or less to be cash equivalents.

CHAPTER 14—STATEMENT OF CASH FLOWS

PROBLEM 14-1 MULTIPLE CHOICE QUESTIONS (76 to 95 minutes)

1. Mend Co. purchased a three-month U.S. Treasury bill. Mend's policy is to treat as cash equivalents all highly liquid investments with an original maturity of three months or less when purchased. How should this purchase be reported in Mend's statement of cash flows?
a. As an outflow from operating activities
b. As an outflow from investing activities
c. As an outflow from financing activities
d. Not reported   (11/95, FAR, #47, 6129)

2. Deed Co. owns 2% of Beck Cosmetic Retailers. A property dividend by Beck consisted of merchandise with a fair value lower than the listed retail price. Deed in turn gave the merchandise to its employees as a holiday bonus. How should Deed report the receipt and distribution of the merchandise in its statement of cash flows?
a. As both an inflow and outflow for operating activities
b. As both an inflow and outflow for investing activities
c. As an inflow for investing activities and outflow for operating activities
d. As a noncash activity (11/92, Theory, #21, 3454)

ITEMS 3 THROUGH 7 are based on the following:

Flax Corp. uses the direct method to prepare its statement of cash flows. Flax's trial balances at December 31, 1991 and 1990, are as follows:

| | December 31 | |
	1991	1990
Debits:		
Cash	$ 35,000	$ 32,000
Accounts receivable	33,000	30,000
Inventory	31,000	47,000
Property, plant, and equipment	100,000	95,000
Unamortized bond discount	4,500	5,000
Cost of goods sold	250,000	380,000
Selling expenses	141,500	172,000
General and administrative expenses	137,000	151,300
Interest expense	4,300	2,600
Income tax expense	20,400	61,200
	$756,700	$976,100

Credits:		
Allowance for uncollectible accounts	$ 1,300	$ 1,100
Accumulated depreciation	16,500	15,000
Trade accounts payable	25,000	17,500
Income taxes payable	21,000	27,100
Deferred income taxes	5,300	4,600
8% callable bonds payable	45,000	20,000
Common stock	50,000	40,000
Additional paid-in capital	9,100	7,500
Retained earnings	44,700	64,600
Sales	538,800	778,700
	$756,700	$976,100

- Flax purchased $5,000 in equipment during 1991.
- Flax allocated one-third of its depreciation expense to selling expenses and the remainder to general and administrative expenses.

What amounts should Flax report in its statement of cash flows for the year ended December 31, 1991, for the following:

3. Cash collected from customers?
a. $541,800
b. $541,600
c. $536,000
d. $535,800   (11/92, PI, #9, 3242)

4. Cash paid for goods to be sold?
a. $258,500
b. $257,500
c. $242,500
d. $226,500   (11/92, PI, #10, 3243)

5. Cash paid for interest?
a. $4,800
b. $4,300
c. $3,800
d. $1,700   (11/92, PI, #11, 3244)

6. Cash paid for income taxes?
a. $25,800
b. $20,400
c. $19,700
d. $15,000   (11/92, PI, #12, 3245)

7. Cash paid for selling expenses?
a. $142,000
b. $141,500
c. $141,000
d. $140,000   (11/92, PI, #13, 3246)

8. Which of the following information should be disclosed as supplemental information in the statement of cash flows?

	Cash flow per share	Conversion of debt to equity
a.	Yes	Yes
b.	Yes	No
c.	No	Yes
d.	No	No

(5/95, FAR, #49, 5585)

9. Which of the following is **not** disclosed on the statement of cash flows when prepared under the direct method, either on the face of the statement or in a separate schedule?
a. The major classes of gross cash receipts and gross cash payments.
b. The amount of income taxes paid.
c. A reconciliation of net income to net cash flow from operations.
d. A reconciliation of ending retained earnings to net cash flow from operations.

(11/95, FAR, #48, 6130)

ITEMS 10 THROUGH 12 are based on the following:

The differences in Beal Inc.'s balance sheet accounts at December 31, 1997 and 1996 are presented below:

Assets	Increase (Decrease)
Cash and cash equivalents	$ 120,000
Short-term, Available-for-sale investments	300,000
Accounts receivable, net	--
Inventory	80,000
Long-term, Available-for-sale investments	(100,000)
Plant assets	700,000
Accumulated depreciation	--
	$1,100,000

Liabilities and Stockholders' Equity	
Accounts payable and accrued liabilities	(5,000)
Dividends payable	160,000
Short-term bank debt	325,000
Long-term debt	110,000
Common stock, $10 par	100,000
Additional paid-in capital	120,000
Retained earnings	290,000
	$1,100,000

The following additional information relates to 1997:

- Net income was $790,000.
- Cash dividends of $500,000 were declared.
- Building costing $600,000 and having a carrying amount of $350,000 was sold for $350,000.
- Equipment costing $110,000 was acquired through issuance of long-term debt.
- A long-term investment was sold for $135,000. There were no other transactions affecting long-term investments.
- 10,000 shares of common stock were issued for $22 a share.

In Beal's 1997 statement of cash flows,

10. Net cash provided by operating activities was
a. $1,160,000.
b. $1,040,000.
c. $ 920,000.
d. $ 705,000.   (11/91, PI, #5, amended, 2393)

11. Net cash used in investing activities was
a. $1,005,000.
b. $1,190,000.
c. $1,275,000.
d. $1,600,000.   (11/91, PI, #6, amended, 2394)

12. Net cash provided by financing activities was
a. $ 20,000.
b. $ 45,000.
c. $150,000.
d. $205,000.   (11/91, PI, #7, amended, 2395)

ITEMS 13 AND 14 are based on the following:

In preparing its cash flow statement for the year ended December 31, 1994, Reve Co. collected the following data:

Gain on sale of equipment	$ (6,000)
Proceeds from sale of equipment	10,000
Purchase of A.S. Inc. bonds (par value $200,000)	(180,000)
Amortization of bond discount	2,000
Dividends declared	(45,000)
Dividends paid	(38,000)
Proceeds from sale of treasury stock (carrying amount $65,000)	75,000

In its December 31, 1994 statement of cash flows,

13. What amount should Reve report as net cash used in investing activities?
a. $170,000
b. $176,000
c. $188,000
d. $194,000 (5/95, FAR, #47, 5583)

14. What amount should Reve report as net cash provided by financing activities?
a. $20,000
b. $27,000
c. $30,000
d. $37,000 (5/95, FAR, #48, 5584)

15. During 1995, Beck Co. purchased equipment for cash of $47,000, and sold equipment with a $10,000 carrying value for a gain of $5,000. How should these transactions be reported in Beck's 1995 statement of cash flows?
a. Cash outflow of $32,000.
b. Cash outflow of $42,000.
c. Cash inflow of $5,000 and cash outflow of $47,000.
d. Cash inflow of $15,000 and cash outflow of $47,000. (11/97, FAR, #7, 6487)

16. In a statement of cash flows, if used equipment is sold at a gain, the amount shown as a cash inflow from investing activities equals the carrying amount of the equipment
a. Plus the gain.
b. Plus the gain and less the amount of tax attributable to the gain.
c. Plus both the gain and the amount of tax attributable to the gain.
d. With **no** addition or subtraction. (11/93, Theory, #41, 4546)

17. Alp Inc. had the following activities during 1997:

- Acquired 2,000 shares of stock in Maybel Inc. for $26,000
- Sold an investment in Rate Motors for $35,000 when the carrying amount was $33,000
- Acquired a $50,000, 4-year certificate of deposit from a bank (During the year, interest of $3,750 was paid to Alp.)
- Collected dividends of $1,200 on stock investments

In Alp's 1997 statement of cash flows, net cash used in investing activities should be
a. $37,250.
b. $38,050.
c. $39,800.
d. $41,000. (5/91, PI, #11, amended, 1237)

18. Karr Inc. reported net income of $300,000 for 1992. During 1992, Karr sold equipment costing $25,000, with accumulated depreciation of $12,000, for a gain of $5,000. In December 1992, Karr purchased equipment costing $50,000 with $20,000 cash and a 12% note payable of $30,000. Depreciation expense for the year was $52,000. Changes occurred in several balance sheet accounts as follows:

Equipment	$25,000 increase
Accumulated depreciation	40,000 increase
Note payable	30,000 increase

In Karr's 1992 statement of cash flows, net cash used in investing activities should be
a. $ 2,000.
b. $12,000.
c. $22,000.
d. $35,000. (11/93, PI, #7, 4376)

19. Data regarding Ball Corp.'s investment in available-for-sale marketable equity securities follow:

	Cost	Fair Value
December 31, 1994	$150,000	$130,000
December 31, 1995	150,000	160,000

Differences between cost and fair values are considered temporary. The decline in fair value was considered temporary and was properly accounted for at December 31, 1994. Ball's 1995 statement of cash flows would report
a. The receipt of dividends as an investing activity.
b. The receipt of dividends as a financing activity.
c. Purchases of securities as an investing activity.
d. The increase in value as an operating activity. (5/91, PI, #18, amended, 0869)

20. In a statement of cash flows, which of the following would increase reported cash flows from operating activities using the direct method? (Ignore income tax considerations.)
a. Dividends received from investments
b. Gain on sale of equipment
c. Gain on early retirement of bonds
d. Change from straight-line to accelerated depreciation (5/92, Theory, #7, 2699)

ITEMS 21 AND 22 are based on the following:

A company acquired a building, paying a portion of the purchase price in cash and issuing a mortgage note payable to the seller for the balance.

21. In a statement of cash flows, what amount is included in investing activities for the above transaction?
a. Cash payment
b. Acquisition price
c. Zero
d. Mortgage amount   (5/90, Theory, #27, 9052)

22. In a statement of cash flows, what amount is included in financing activities for the above transaction?
a. Cash payment
b. Acquisition price
c. Zero
d. Mortgage amount   (5/90, Theory, #28, 9053)

23. In a statement of cash flows, proceeds from issuing equity instruments should be classified as cash inflows from
a. Lending activities.
b. Operating activities.
c. Investing activities.
d. Financing activities.   (11/89, Theory, #29, 1913)

24. During 1997, Teb Inc. had the following activities related to its financial operations:

Payment for the early retirement of
   long-term bonds payable
   (carrying amount $740,000) $750,000
Distribution in 1997 of cash dividend
   declared in 1996 to preferred
   shareholders   62,000
Carrying amount of convertible
   preferred stock in Teb, converted
   into common shares   120,000
Proceeds from sale of treasury stock
   (carrying amount at cost, $86,000)   95,000

In Teb's 1997 statement of cash flows, net cash used in financing activities should be
a. $717,000.
b. $716,000.
c. $597,000.
d. $535,000.   (5/91, PI, #10, amended, 1236)

25. Fara Co. reported bonds payable of $47,000 at December 31, 1992, and $50,000 at December 31, 1993. During 1993, Fara issued $20,000 of bonds payable in exchange for equipment. There was no amortization of bond premium or discount during the year. What amount should Fara report in its 1993 statement of cash flows for redemption of bonds payable?
a. $ 3,000
b. $17,000
c. $20,000
d. $23,000   (5/94, FAR, #50, 4865)

26. During 1992, Xan Inc. had the following activities related to its financial operations:

Payment for the early retirement of long-
   term bonds payable (carrying amount
   $370,000) $375,000
Distribution in 1992 of cash dividend
   declared in 1991 to preferred
   shareholders   31,000
Carrying amount of convertible preferred
   stock in Xan, converted into common
   shares   60,000
Proceeds from sale of treasury stock
   (carrying amount at cost, $43,000)   50,000

In Xan's 1992 statement of cash flows, net cash used in financing operations should be
a. $265,000.
b. $296,000.
c. $356,000.
d. $358,000.   (11/93, PI, #8, 4377)

27. On July 1, 1992, Dewey Co. signed a 20-year building lease that it reported as a capital lease. Dewey paid the monthly lease payments when due. How should Dewey report the effect of the lease payments in the financing activities section of its 1992 statement of cash flows?
a. An inflow equal to the present value of future lease payments at July 1, 1992, less 1992 principal and interest payments.
b. An outflow equal to the 1992 principal and interest payments on the lease.
c. An outflow equal to the 1992 principal payments only.
d. The lease payments should **not** be reported in the financing activities section.
    (11/93, Theory, #42, 4547)

28. In a statement of cash flows, which of the following items is reported as a cash outflow from financing activities?

I. Payments to retire mortgage notes
II. Interest payments on mortgage notes
III. Dividend payments

a. I, II, and III
b. II and III
c. I only
d. I and III   (5/91, Theory, #31, 1902)

29. Lino Co.'s worksheet for the preparation of its 1992 statement of cash flows included the following:

	December 31	January 1
Accounts receivable	$29,000	$23,000
Allowance for uncollectible accounts	1,000	800
Prepaid rent expense	8,200	12,400
Accounts payable	22,400	19,400

Lino's 1992 net income is $150,000. What amount should Lino include as net cash provided by operating activities in the statement of cash flows?
a. $151,400
b. $151,000
c. $148,600
d. $145,400   (11/93, PI, #5, 4374)

30. Karr Inc. reported net income of $300,000 for 1992. During 1992, Karr sold equipment costing $25,000, with accumulated depreciation of $12,000, for a gain of $5,000. In December 1992, Karr purchased equipment costing $50,000 with $20,000 cash and a 12% note payable of $30,000. Depreciation expense for the year was $52,000. Changes occurred in several balance sheet accounts as follows:

Equipment	$25,000 increase
Accumulated depreciation	40,000 increase
Note payable	30,000 increase

In Karr's 1992 statement of cash flows, net cash provided by operating activities should be
a. $340,000.
b. $347,000.
c. $352,000.
d. $357,000.   (11/93, PI, #6, 4375)

31. Duke Co. reported cost of goods sold as $270,000 for 1992. Additional information is as follows:

	December 31	January 1
Inventory	$60,000	$45,000
Accounts payable	26,000	39,000

If Duke uses the direct method, what amount should Duke report as cash paid to suppliers in its 1992 statement of cash flows?
a. $242,000
b. $268,000
c. $272,000
d. $298,000   (11/93, PI, #9, 4378)

32. Rory's Co.'s prepaid insurance was $50,000 at December 31, 1997, and $25,000 at December 31, 1996. Insurance expense was $20,000 for 1997 and $15,000 for 1996. What amount of cash disbursements for insurance would be reported in Rory's 1997 net cash flows from operating activities presented on a direct basis?
a. $55,000
b. $45,000
c. $30,000
d. $20,000   (11/90, PII, #17, amended, 1238)

33. In its 1996 income statement, Kilm Co. reported cost of goods sold of $450,000. Changes occurred in several balance sheet accounts as follows:

Inventory	$160,000 decrease
Accounts payable—suppliers	40,000 decrease

What amount should Kilm report as cash paid to suppliers in its 1996 cash flow statement, prepared under the direct method?
a. $250,000
b. $330,000
c. $570,000
d. $650,000   (5/97, FAR, #3, 6475)

34. A company's accounts receivable decreased from the beginning to the end of the year. In the company's statement of cash flows (direct method), the cash collected from customers would be
a. Sales revenues plus accounts receivable at the beginning of the year.
b. Sales revenues plus the decrease in accounts receivable from the beginning to the end of the year.
c. Sales revenues less the decrease in accounts receivable from the beginning to the end of the year.
d. The same as sales revenues.
                          (11/88, Theory, #34, 9054)

35. The following information was taken from the 1990 financial statements of Planet Corp.:

Accounts receivable, January 1, 1990	$ 21,600
Accounts receivable, December 31, 1990	30,400
Sales on account and cash sales	438,000
Uncollectible accounts	1,000

No accounts receivable were written off or recovered during the year. If the direct method is used in the 1990 statement of cash flows, Planet should report cash collected from customers as
a. $447,800.
b. $446,800.
c. $429,200.
d. $428,200.   (5/91, PI, #8, 1234)

36. A company's wages payable increased from the beginning to the end of the year. In the company's statement of cash flows (direct method), the cash paid for wages would be

a. Salary expense plus wages payable at the beginning of the year.
b. Salary expense plus the increase in wages payable from the beginning to the end of the year.
c. Salary expense less the increase in wages payable from the beginning to the end of the year.
d. The same as salary expense.

(5/88, Theory, #31, 1935)

37. Would the following be added back to net income when reporting operating activities' cash flows by the indirect method?

	Excess of treasury stock acquisition cost over sales proceeds (cost method)	Bond discount amortization
a.	Yes	Yes
b.	No	No
c.	No	Yes
d.	Yes	No

(11/91, Theory, #21, 2529)

38. In a statement of cash flows (indirect method), which of the following are subtracted from net income to determine net cash flow from operating activities?

	Increase in accrued interest payable	Depreciation expense
a.	Yes	Yes
b.	Yes	No
c.	No	Yes
d.	No	No

(Editors, 1966)

OTHER OBJECTIVE FORMAT QUESTIONS

PROBLEM 14-2 (7 to 10 minutes)

PROBLEM NUMBER 14-2 consists of 4 items. Select the **best** answer for each item.

On July 1, 1997, Ring Co. issued $250,000, 14% bonds payable at a premium. The bonds are due in ten years. Interest is payable semiannually every June 30 and December 31. On December 31, 1997 and June 30, 1998, Ring made the semiannual interest payments due and recorded interest expense and amortization of bond premium.

With the proceeds of the bond issuance, Ring retired other debt. Ring recorded a gain on the early extinguishment of the other debt.

REQUIRED: ITEMS 1 THROUGH 4 describe amounts that will be reported in Ring's 1997 statement of cash flows prepared using the indirect method or disclosed in the related notes. For each item, select from the following list where the amount should be reported or disclosed. An answer may be selected once, more than once, or not at all.

Statement of Cash Flows Items	
O	Operating Activities
I	Investing Activities
F	Financing activities
S	Supplemental schedule

1. Proceeds received from sale of bonds

2. Interest paid

3. Amortization of bond premium

4. Gain on early extinguishment of debt
(11/98, FAR, OOF #2, Part 2, 6746-6749)

PROBLEM 14-3 (25 to 30 minutes)

Following are selected balance sheet accounts of Zach Corp. at December 31, 1991 and 1990, and the increases or decreases in each account from 1990 to 1991. Also presented is selected income statement information for the year ended December 31, 1991, and additional information.

Selected balance sheet accounts	1991	1990	Increase (Decrease)
Assets:			
Accounts receivable	$ 34,000	$ 24,000	$ 10,000
Property, plant, and equipment	277,000	247,000	30,000
Accumulated depreciation	(178,000)	(167,000)	(11,000)
Liabilities and stockholder's equity:			
Bonds payable	49,000	46,000	3,000
Dividends payable	8,000	5,000	3,000
Common stock, $1 par	22,000	19,000	3,000
Additional paid-in capital	9,000	3,000	6,000
Retained earnings	104,000	91,000	13,000

Selected income statement information for the year ended December 31, 1991

Sales revenue	$155,000
Depreciation	33,000
Gain on sale of equipment	13,000
Net income	28,000

Additional information:

- Accounts receivable relate to sales of merchandise.
- During 1991, equipment costing $40,000 was sold for cash.
- During 1991, $20,000 of bonds payable were issued in exchange for property, plant, and equipment. There was no amortization of bond discount or premium.

REQUIRED:

ITEMS a THROUGH e represent activities that will be reported in Zach's statement of cash flows for the year ended December 31, 1991. The following two responses are required for each item.

- Determine the amount that should be reported in Zach's 1991 statement of cash flows.
- Using the list below, determine the category in which the amount should be reported in the statement of cash flows.

O. Operating activity
I. Investing activity
F. Financing activity

ITEMS TO BE ANSWERED:

a. Cash collections from customers (direct method)
b. Payments for purchase of property, plant, and equipment
c. Proceeds from sale of equipment
d. Cash dividends paid
e. Redemption of bonds payable   (5/92, PI, #65)

PROBLEM 14-4 (15 to 25 minutes)

The condensed trial balance of Probe Co., a publicly held company, has been adjusted except for income tax expense.

Additional information:

- During 1997 equipment with an original cost of $50,000 was sold for cash, and equipment costing $125,000 was purchased.
- On January 1, 1997, bonds with a par value of $500,000 and related premium of $75,000 were redeemed. The $1,000 face value, 10% par bonds had been issued on January 1, 1988, to yield 8%. Interest is payable annually every December 31 through 2007.
- Probe's tax payments during 1997 were debited to Income Taxes Payable. In 1996 Probe recorded a deferred income tax liability of $42,000 based on temporary differences of $120,000 and an enacted tax rate of 35%. Probe's 1997 financial statement income before income taxes was greater than its 1997 taxable income, due entirely to temporary differences, by $60,000. Probe's cumulative net taxable temporary differences at December 31, 1997, were $180,000. Probe's enacted tax rate for the current and future years is 30%.

- 60,000 shares of common stock, $2.50 par, were outstanding on December 31, 1996. Probe issued an additional 80,000 shares on April 1, 1997.

- There were no changes to retained earnings other than dividends declared.

Probe Co.
CONDENSED TRIAL BALANCE

	12/31/97 Balances Dr. (Cr.)	12/31/96 Balances Dr. (Cr.)	Net change Dr. (Cr.)
Cash	$ 473,000	$ 817,000	$ (344,000)
Accounts receivable, net	670,000	610,000	60,000
Property, plant, and equipment	1,070,000	995,000	75,000
Accumulated depreciation	(345,000)	(280,000)	(65,000)
Dividends payable	(25,000)	(10,000)	(15,000)
Income taxes payable	35,000	(150,000)	185,000
Deferred income tax liability	(42,000)	(42,000)	---
Bonds payable	(500,000)	(1,000,000)	500,000
Unamortized premium on bonds	(71,000)	(150,000)	79,000
Common stock	(350,000)	(150,000)	(200,000)
Additional paid-in capital	(430,000)	(375,000)	(55,000)
Retained earnings	(185,000)	(265,000)	80,000
Sales	(2,420,000)		
Cost of sales	1,863,000		
Selling and administrative expenses	220,000		
Interest income	(14,000)		
Interest expense	46,000		
Depreciation	88,000		
Loss on sale of equipment	7,000		
Gain on extinguishment of bonds	(90,000)		
	$ 0	$ 0	$ 300,000

REQUIRED:

For each transaction in items a through f, the following two responses are required:

- Determine the amount to be reported in Probe's 1997 statement of cash flows prepared using the indirect method.

- Select from the list below where the specific item should be separately reported on the statement of cash flows prepared using the indirect method.

O. Operating
I. Investing
F. Financing
S. Supplementary information
N. Not reported on Probe's statement of cash flows

ITEMS TO BE ANSWERED:

a. Cash paid for income taxes
b. Cash paid for interest
c. Redemption of bonds payable
d. Issuance of common stock
e. Cash dividends paid
f. Proceeds from sale of equipment

(11/94, FAR, #3, 75-80, amended)

PROBLEMS/ESSAY QUESTIONS

PROBLEM 14-5 (40 to 50 minutes)

Presented below are the balance sheet accounts of Kern Inc. as of December 31, 1998 and 1997, and their net changes.

Assets	1998	1997	Net change
Cash	$ 471,000	$ 307,000	$ 164,000
Marketable equity securities, at cost	150,000	250,000	(100,000)
Allowance to reduce marketable equity securities to market	(10,000)	(25,000)	15,000
Accounts receivable, net	550,000	515,000	35,000
Inventories	810,000	890,000	(80,000)
Investment in Word Corp., at equity	420,000	390,000	30,000
Property, plant, and equipment	1,145,000	1,070,000	75,000
Accumulated depreciation	(345,000)	(280,000)	(65,000)
Patent, net	109,000	118,000	(9,000)
Total assets	$3,300,000	$3,235,000	$ 65,000

Liabilities and Stockholders' Equity	1998	1997	Net change
Accounts payable and accrued liabilities	$ 845,000	$ 960,000	$(115,000)
Note payable, long-term	600,000	900,000	(300,000)
Deferred tax liability	190,000	190,000	--
Common stock, $10 par value	850,000	650,000	200,000
Additional paid-in capital	230,000	170,000	60,000
Retained earnings	585,000	365,000	220,000
Total liabilities and stockholder's equity	$3,300,000	$3,235,000	$ 65,000

Additional information:

- On January 2, 1998, Kern sold equipment costing $45,000, with a carrying amount of $28,000, for $18,000 cash.

- On March 31, 1998, Kern sold one of its marketable equity security holdings for $119,000 cash. There were no other transactions involving marketable equity securities.

- On April 15, 1998, Kern issued 20,000 shares of its common stock for cash at $13 per share.

- On July 1, 1998, Kern purchased equipment for $120,000 cash.

- Kern's net income for 1998 is $305,000. Kern paid a cash dividend of $85,000 on October 26, 1998.

- Kern acquired a 20% interest in Word Corp.'s common stock during 1995. There was no goodwill attributable to the investment which is appropriately accounted for by the equity method. Word reported net income of $150,000 for the year ended December 31, 1998. No dividend was paid on Word's common stock during 1998.

REQUIRED: Prepare a statement of cash flows for Kern Inc. for the year ended December 31, 1998, using the indirect method. A worksheet is **not** required.   (11/89, PI, #5, amended, 3422)

PROBLEM 14-6 (40 to 50 minutes)

Presented below are the condensed statements of financial position of Linden Consulting Associates as of December 31, 1997 and 1996, and the condensed statement of income for the year ended December 31, 1997.

Linden Consulting Associates
CONDENSED STATEMENTS OF FINANCIAL POSITION
December 31, 1997 and 1996

	1997	1996	Net change increase (decrease)
Assets			
Cash	$ 652,000	$ 280,000	$372,000
Accounts receivable, net	446,000	368,000	78,000
Investment in Zach Inc., at equity	550,000	466,000	84,000
Property and equipment	1,270,000	1,100,000	170,000
Accumulated depreciation	(190,000)	(130,000)	(60,000)
Excess of cost over book value of investment in Zach Inc. (net)	152,000	156,000	(4,000)
Total assets	$2,880,000	$2,240,000	$640,000
Liabilities and Partners' Equity			
Accounts payable and accrued expenses	$ 320,000	$ 270,000	$ 50,000
Mortgage payable	250,000	270,000	(20,000)
Partners' equity	2,310,000	1,700,000	610,000
Total liabilities and partners' equity	$2,880,000	$2,240,000	$640,000

Linden Consulting Associates
CONDENSED STATEMENT OF INCOME
For the Year Ended December 31, 1997

Fee revenue	$ 2,664,000
Operating expenses	(1,940,000)
Operating income	724,000
Equity in earnings of Zach, Inc. (net of $4,000 amortization of excess of cost over book value)	176,000
Net income	$ 900,000

Additional information:

- On December 31, 1996, partners' capital and profit sharing percentages were as follows:

	Capital	Profit sharing %
Garr	$1,020,000	60%
Pat	680,000	40%
	$1,700,000	

- On January 1, 1997, Garr and Pat admitted Scott to the partnership for a cash payment of $340,000 to Linden Consulting Associates as the agreed amount of Scott's beginning capital account. In addition, Scott paid a $50,000 cash bonus directly to Garr and Pat. This amount was divided $30,000 to Garr and $20,000 to Pat. The new profit sharing arrangement is as follows:

Garr	50%
Pat	30%
Scott	20%

- On October 1, 1997, Linden purchased and paid for an office computer costing $170,000, including $15,000 for sales tax, delivery, and installation. There were no dispositions of property and equipment during 1997.

- Throughout 1997, Linden owned 25% of Zach Inc.'s, common stock. As a result of this ownership interest, Linden can exercise significant influence over Zach's operating and financial policies. During 1997, Zach paid dividends totaling $384,000 and reported net income of $720,000. Linden's 1997 amortization of excess of cost over book value in Zach was $4,000.

- Partners' drawings for 1997 were as follows:

Garr	$280,000
Pat	200,000
Scott	150,000
	$630,000

Questions
14-24

REQUIRED:

a. Using the direct method, prepare Linden's statement of cash flows for the year ended December 31, 1997.

b. Prepare a reconciliation of net income to net cash provided by operating activities.

c. Prepare an analysis of changes in partners' capital accounts for the year ended December 31, 1997. (11/90, PI, #5, amended)

ESSAY 14-7 (5 to 7 minutes)

On June 30, 1988, Corval Co. issued 15-year 12% bonds at a premium (effective yield 10%). On November 30, 1991, Corval transferred both cash and property to the bondholders to extinguish the entire debt. The fair value of the transferred property equaled its carrying amount. The fair value of the cash and property transferred exceeded the bonds carrying amount. [Ignore income taxes.]

REQUIRED:

How should Corval report the effects of the November 30, 1991, transaction in its statement of cash flows using the indirect method?
(11/92, Theory, #3d, 6195)

SOLUTION 14-1 MULTIPLE CHOICE ANSWERS

CASH AND CASH EQUIVALENTS

1. (d) The exchange of cash for a cash equivalent is not reported on the Statement of Cash Flows.

STATEMENT CONTENT & FORM

2. (d) The receipt and distribution of the merchandise affected recognized assets but did not result in cash receipts or cash payments in the period. Hence, it should be reported in the statement of cash flows as a noncash activity.

3. (d) Accounts receivable have increased by $3,000 (i.e., $33,000 – $30,000) from the beginning to the end of the year, which means that cash collected from customers is less than the sales revenues reported on the accrual basis by this amount. Thus, the amount of cash collected from customers is $535,800 (i.e., $538,800 – $3,000). (It is important to note that since the direct method is used to determine cash flows from operating activities, the Allowance for Uncollectible Accounts is not be netted against Accounts Receivable in determining cash collected from customers.)

4. (d) Inventories have decreased by $16,000 (i.e., $47,000 – $31,000) from the beginning to the end of the year, which means that inventory purchases were less than cost of goods sold by this amount. Thus, the amount of inventory purchases is $234,000 (i.e., $250,000 – $16,000). Accounts payable have increased by $7,500 (i.e., $25,000 – $17,500) from the beginning to the end of the year, which means that cash payments for inventories

were less than inventory purchases by this amount. Thus, the amount of cash paid for inventories is $226,500 (i.e., $234,000 – $7,500).

5. (c) Unamortized bond discount decreased by $500 (i.e., $5,000 – $4,500) from the beginning to the end of the year. The bond discount amortization decreases net income (because of the increase in interest expense) but has no affect on cash. Therefore, the amount of cash paid for interest is $3,800 (i.e., $4,300 – $500).

6. (a) Since income taxes payable decreased from the beginning to the end of the year, the amount of cash paid for income taxes is greater than income tax expense reported on an accrual basis by this amount. The increase in deferred income taxes is a noncash expense (i.e., it increases income tax expense but has no affect on cash), therefore it is subtracted from income tax expense to determine the amount of cash paid for income taxes.

Income tax expense	$20,400
Add: Decrease in income taxes payable ($27,100 – $21,000)	6,100
Less: Increase in deferred income taxes ($5,300 – $4,600)	(700)
Cash paid for income taxes	$25,800

7. (c) The amount of cash paid for selling expenses is determined as follows:

Selling expenses	$141,500
Less: Allocated portion of depreciation expense [($16,500 – $15,000) ÷ 3]	(500)
Cash paid for selling expenses	$141,000

DISCLOSURES

8. (c) SFAS 95, par. 33, states, "Financial statements shall not report an amount of cash flow per share." The conversion of debt to equity is a noncash financing activity because the transaction affects the enterprise's liabilities but it does not result in cash receipts or payments during the period. The conversion of debt to equity should be disclosed as supplemental information in the statement of cash flows (*ibid.*, par. 32).

9. (d) A reconciliation of ending retained earnings to net cash flow from operations is not disclosed on the Statement of Cash Flows under either method. The major classes of gross cash receipts and payments, the amount of income taxes paid, and a reconciliation of net income to net cash flow from operations all appear on the face of the Statement of Cash Flows or in a separate schedule when the direct method is used.

CLASSIFICATION

10. (c) There was no change in the balance of the Accumulated Depreciation account in 1997. Therefore, 1997 depreciation expense equals the amount of accumulated depreciation removed from the account due to the sale of the building (i.e., $600,000 - $350,000 = $250,000). Net cash provided by operating activities is determined as follows:

Net income		$ 790,000
Adjustments to reconcile net income		
to net cash provided by operating activities:		
Depreciation expense	$ 250,000	
Gain on sale of long-term		
investment ($135,000		
proceeds – $100,000 cost)	(35,000)	
Increase in inventories	(80,000)	
Decrease in accounts payable	(5,000)	130,000
Net cash provided by operating activities		$ 920,000

11. (a) The net cash used in investing activities is determined as follows:

Purchase of short-term, available-for-sale	
investments	$ (300,000)
Proceeds from sale of long-term investment	135,000
Proceeds from sale of building	350,000
Purchase of plant assets (see below)	(1,190,000)
Net cash used in investing activities	$ (1,005,000)

The purchases of plant assets for cash is determined as follows:

Net increase in plant assets during 1997 (given)	$ 700,000
Add: Cost of building sold during 1997	600,000
Less: Cost of equipment acquired through issuance	
of long-term debt (i.e., a noncash investing	
and financing transaction)	(110,000)
Purchases of plant assets for cash during 1997	$ 1,190,000

12. (d) The net cash provided by financing activities is determined as follows:

Cash dividends paid in 1997 ($500,000 – $160,000)	$ (340,000)
Proceeds from issuance of common stock	
(10,000 x $22)	220,000
Proceeds from short-term bank debt	325,000
Net cash provided by financing activities	$ 205,000

13. (a) If an exam question does not specify that a debt or equity investment is a cash equivalent or classed as a trading security, then the cash flows from the purchase, sale, or maturity should be classed as cash flows from investing activities. The net cash used in investing activities is computed as follows:

Purchase of bond investment	$180,000
Proceeds from sale of equipment	(10,000)
Net cash used in investing activities	$170,000

14. (d) The net cash provided by financing activities is computed as follows:

Proceeds from sale of treasury stock	$ 75,000
Dividends paid	(38,000)
Net cash provided by financing activities	$ 37,000

INVESTING ACTIVITIES

15. (d) The purchase of equipment is reported as a cash outflow of $47,000 and the receipt of $15,000 cash from the sale of equipment ($10,000 carrying value plus the gain of $5,000) is reported as a cash inflow of $15,000 in the investing activities section of the statement of cash flows. Investing cash inflows and outflows should be reported separately in a statement of cash flows.

16. (a) In the statement of cash flows, proceeds from the sale of used equipment should be reported as a cash inflow due to an investing activity. Since the equipment was sold at a gain, the amount of the proceeds would equal the equipment's carrying amount plus the gain recognized on disposal. The income tax effect of the gain on disposal does not affect the amount reported in the investing section because all income taxes are to be classified as an operating activity on a statement of cash flows (see SFAS 95, par. 91-92).

17. (d) The cash receipts from interest ($3,750) and dividends ($1,200) are cash inflows from operating activities (SFAS 95, par. 27). The net cash used in investing activities is computed as follows:

Payment to acquire 2,000 shares of Maybel stock	$ (26,000)
Proceeds from sale of investment in Rate Motors	35,000
Payment to acquire a certificate of deposit from a bank	(50,000)
Net cash used in investing activities	$ (41,000)

18. (a) In order to compute the net cash used in investing activities, the proceeds Karr received from the sale of the equipment must be computed. The carrying amount of the equipment sold was $13,000 (i.e., $25,000 cost minus $12,000 accumulated depreciation). Since the sale resulted in $5,000 gain, the proceeds Karr received from the sale were $18,000 (i.e., $13,000 carrying amount of equipment plus $5,000 gain recognized). Karr reports the $18,000 proceeds from the sale of the equipment as a cash inflow due to an investing activity in the statement of cash flows. In addition, Karr purchased equipment costing $50,000 with $20,000 cash and a 12% note payable of $30,000. Since this transaction is part cash and part noncash, only the cash portion is reported in the statement of cash flows. Karr reports the $20,000 paid at the time of purchase to acquire the equipment as a cash outflow due to an investing activity. Therefore, the net cash used in investing activities is computed as follows:

Cash paid at time of purchase to acquire equipment	$ 20,000
Less: Proceeds received from sale of equipment	(18,000)
Net cash used in investing activities	$ 2,000

19. (c) For available-for-sale securities, the cash flow statement shows purchasing activities as an investing activity. Receipt of dividends and interest is always reported as an operating activity. For trading securities, purchases, sales, and maturities are classified as operating activities.

20. (a) Cash dividends received from investments produce a cash inflow due to operating activities so they increase the reported cash flow from operating activities using the direct method. The proceeds from the sale of equipment are to be classified as an inflow from investing activities; any associated gain on the sale will not impact the reported cash flows from operating activities using the direct method. The payment to retire bonds is a cash outflow due to financing activities; any associated gain will not impact the reported cash flows from operating activities using the direct method. A change from the straight-line method to an accelerated depreciation method does not affect cash nor does it impact the computation of net cash flows from operating activities using the direct method.

21. (a) To answer this question, we will reconstruct separate journal entries for:

The portion of the building acquired by issuing the mortgage note payable to the seller:

Building	XX	
Mortgage Note Payable		XX

The portion of the building acquired by paying cash:

Building	XX	
Cash		XX

The portion of the building acquired by issuing the mortgage note payable to the seller (i.e., a seller-financed debt) is a noncash investing and financing activity. This portion of the transaction affects the enterprise's recognized assets and liabilities but it does not result in cash receipts or cash payments in the period. Therefore, this portion of the transaction should be reported in related disclosures and not in the body of the statement of cash flows. The portion of the building acquired by paying cash should be reported as a cash outflow due to an investing activity. Cash outflows for investing activities include payments at the time of purchase to acquire property, plant, and equipment.

FINANCING ACTIVITIES

22. (c) The portion of the building acquired by paying cash should be reported as a cash outflow due to an investing activity. The portion of the building acquired by issuing the mortgage note payable to the seller (i.e., a seller-financed debt) is a noncash investing and financing activity. This portion of the transaction affects the enterprise's recognized assets and liabilities but it does not result in cash receipts or cash payments in the period. Therefore, this portion of the transaction should be reported in related disclosures and not in the body of the statement of cash flows.

23. (d) Cash inflows from financing activities are (1) proceeds from issuing equity instruments and (2) proceeds from issuing bonds, mortgages, notes, and from other short- or long-term borrowing (SFAS 95, par. 19).

24. (a) Cash inflows from financing activities include proceeds from issuing equity securities (e.g., treasury stock). Cash outflows for financing activities include payments of dividends and repayments of amounts borrowed. The conversion of the preferred stock into common shares is a *noncash* financing activity. Thus, the net cash used in financing activities is computed as follows:

Payment for early retirement of bonds payable	$ (750,000)
Cash dividend paid	(62,000)
Proceeds from reissuance of treasury stock	95,000
Net cash used in financing activities	$ (717,000)

25. (b) The amount reported in Fara Co.'s 1993 statement of cash flows for redemption of bonds payable can be determined by the following analysis of the Bonds Payable account for 1993:

Bonds Payable			
		$47,000	Balance, 1/1/93 (given)
Bonds payable redeemed	$17,000	20,000	Issuance of new bonds (given)
		$50,000	Balance, 12/31/93 (given)

26. (c) Cash inflows from financing activities include proceeds from issuing equity securities (e.g., treasury stock). Cash outflows for financing activities include payments of dividends and repayments of amounts borrowed. The conversion of the preferred stock into common stock is a *noncash* financing activity. Therefore, the net cash used in financing operations is computed as follows:

Payment for early retirement of bonds payable	$ (375,000)
Payment of preferred stock dividend	(31,000)
Proceeds from sale of treasury stock	50,000
Net cash used in financing operations	$ (356,000)

27. (c) Capital lease payments are comprised of interest expense and a reduction of principal. Cash outflows for financing activities include principal payments to creditors who have extended long-term credit (SFAS 95, par. 20). Therefore, the amount of the capital lease payments that consist of principal payments is reported in the statement of cash flows as a cash outflow for financing activities. Cash outflows for operating activities include cash payments to lenders and other creditors for interest (par. 23). Therefore, the amount of the capital lease payments that consist of interest payments should be reported as a cash outflow for operating activities in the statement of cash flows.

28. (d) Per SFAS 95, cash outflows from financing activities include payments of amounts borrowed and payments of dividends to owners. Interest payments, interest receipts, and dividends received are all operating activities.

OPERATING ACTIVITIES

29. (a) The increase in net accounts receivable represents sales that were not collected in cash; therefore, this amount must be subtracted from net income to compute net cash from operating activities. The decrease in prepaid rent expense represents expenses recognized that were not paid in cash, and thus must be added for the adjustment. The increase in accounts payable represents purchases that were not paid out in cash, and thus must be added for the adjustment. Net cash provided by operating activities is computed as follows:

Net income		$ 150,000
Adjustments:		
Increase in net accounts receivable [($29,000 – $1,000) – ($23,000 – $800)]	$(5,800)	
Decrease in prepaid rent expense ($12,400 – $8,200)	4,200	
Increase in accounts payable ($22,400 – $19,400)	3,000	1,400
Net cash provided by operating activities		$ 151,400

30. (b) Depreciation is a noncash expense; therefore, it is added back to net income to compute net cash provided by operating activities. The gain on the sale of equipment was added to determine net income, but it did not represent an inflow of cash. Therefore, the gain must be subtracted for the adjustment. Net cash provided by operating activities is computed as follows:

Net income		$ 300,000
Adjustments:		
Depreciation expense	$52,000	
Gain on sale of equipment	(5,000)	47,000
Net cash provided by operating activities		$ 347,000

31. (d) Inventories have increased by $15,000 (i.e., $60,000 – $45,000) from the beginning to the end of the year, which means that inventory purchases were greater than cost of goods sold by this amount. Thus, the amount of inventory purchases is $285,000 (i.e., $270,000 + $15,000). Accounts payable have decreased by $13,000 (i.e., $39,000 – $26,000) from the beginning to the end of the year, which means that cash payments for inventories were greater than inventory purchases by this amount. Therefore, the amount of cash paid to suppliers for inventories is $298,000 (i.e., $285,000 + $13,000).

32. (b) The cash disbursements for insurance can be determined as follows:

Insurance expense for 1997	$ 20,000
Increase in prepaid insurance ($50,000 – $25,000)	25,000
Cash disbursements for insurance in 1997	$ 45,000

DIRECT METHOD

33. (b) Cash paid to suppliers is calculated as follows:

Cost of sales	$ 450,000
Less: Decrease in inventory	(160,000)
Inventory purchases	290,000
Add: Decrease in accounts payable	40,000
Cash paid to suppliers	$ 330,000

34. (b) Accounts receivable have decreased from the beginning to the end of the year, which means that cash collected from customers is greater than sales revenues reported on an accrual basis. The cash collected from customers is determined by adding the decrease in accounts receivable from the beginning to the end of the year to sales revenues.

35. (c)   Accounts receivable have increased by $8,800 (i.e., $30,400 − $21,600) from the beginning to the end of the year, which means that cash collected from customers is less than the sales revenues reported on the accrual basis by this amount. Thus, the amount of cash collected from customers is $429,200 (i.e., $438,000 − $8,800). (It is important to note that since the direct method is used to determine cash flows from operating activities, the Allowance for Uncollectible Accounts is not used in determining cash collected from customers.)

36. (c)   Wages payable have increased from the beginning to the end of the year, which means that a portion of the salaries has not been paid. Therefore, wages paid are less than salary expense reported on an accrual basis by the amount of the increase in wages payable from the beginning to the end of the year.

INDIRECT METHOD

37. (c)   When using the cost method, an excess of treasury stock acquisition cost over sales proceeds is recorded by a charge to an additional paid-in capital account or to the Retained Earnings account, *not* an income statement account. Therefore, this "loss" is *not* an adjustment in converting net income on an accrual basis to net cash provided by operating activities. The amortization of bond discount decreases net income (because of the increase in interest expense) but has no effect on cash. Thus, it is added to net income when using the indirect method of computing net cash provided by operating activities.

38. (d)   When accrued interest payable increases during a period, interest expense on a cash basis is less than interest expense on an accrual basis, because cash interest payments are less than interest expense reported on an accrual basis. To convert net income to net cash flow from operating activities, the increase in accrued interest payable must be added. Depreciation is a noncash expense which was deducted in arriving at net income. Thus, it must be added back to net income to determine net cash flow from operating activities.

PERFORMANCE BY SUBTOPICS

Each category below parallels a subtopic covered in Chapter 14. Record the number and percentage of questions you correctly answered in each subtopic area.

Cash and Cash Equivalents

Question #	Correct √
1	

Questions   1

Correct _____
% Correct _____

Statement Content & Form

Question #	Correct √
2	
3	
4	
5	
6	
7	

Questions   6

Correct _____
% Correct _____

Disclosures

Question #	Correct √
8	
9	

Questions   2

Correct _____
% Correct _____

Classification

Question #	Correct √
10	
11	
12	
13	
14	

Questions   5

Correct _____
% Correct _____

Investing Activities

Question #	Correct √
15	
16	
17	
18	
19	
20	
21	

Questions   7

Correct _____
% Correct _____

Financing Activities

Question #	Correct √
22	
23	
24	
25	
26	
27	
28	

Questions   7
Correct _____
% Correct _____

Operating Activities

Question #	Correct √
29	
30	
31	
32	

Questions   4

Correct _____
% Correct _____

Direct Method

Question #	Correct √
33	
34	
35	
36	

Questions   4

Correct _____
% Correct _____

Indirect Method

Question #	Correct √
37	
38	

Questions   2

Correct _____
% Correct _____

OTHER OBJECTIVE FORMAT SOLUTIONS

SOLUTION 14-2 CLASSIFICATION & DISCLOSURE

1. F   The proceeds received from the sale of bonds are reported in the financing section of the statement of cash flows.

2. S   Under the indirect method, interest paid is provided in related disclosures. The net income amount shown in the operating section is net of interest paid and income taxes paid; so separate disclosure is needed for the statement to reflect this information.

3. O   Under the indirect method, amortization of bond premium is shown in the statement of cash flows as an adjustment to net income in the operating section.

4. O   Under the indirect method, items whose cash effects are financing cash flows, such as gain on early extinguishment of debt, are shown in the statement of cash flows as adjustments to net income in the operating section.

SOLUTION 14-3 DIRECT METHOD

a. $145,000, O.   Accounts receivable have increased from the beginning to the end of the year, which means that cash collections from customers is less than sales revenues. The cash collections from customers is determined by subtracting the increase in accounts receivable from the beginning to the end of the year from sales revenues (i.e., $155,000 – $10,000 = $145,000). In the statement of cash flows, cash collections from customers are reported as cash inflows from *operating* activities.

b. $50,000, I. The payments for property, plant, and equipment are determined as follows:

Plant assets, 12/31/91		$277,000
Plant assets, 12/31/90	$247,000	
Less Cost of equipment sold for cash	(40,000)	
Add: Plant assets acquired in exchange for bonds payable	20,000	
Plant assets before consideration of 1991 purchases		227,000
Plant assets purchased for cash (forced)		$ 50,000

In the statement of cash flows, payments for property, plant, and equipment are reported as cash outflows for *investing* activities.

c. $31,000, I.   In order to determine the proceeds from the sale of equipment, the accumulated depreciation on the equipment sold must first be determined, as follows:

Depreciation for 1991	$ 33,000
Less: Net increase in accumulated depreciation for 1991	(11,000)
Accumulated depreciation on equipment sold	$ 22,000

The proceeds from the sale of the equipment can now be determined as follows:

Cost of equipment sold	$ 40,000
Less: Accumulated depreciation on equipment sold	(22,000)
Carrying amount of equipment sold	18,000
Gain on sale of equipment	13,000
Proceeds from sale of equipment	$ 31,000

In the statement of cash flows, proceeds from the sale of equipment are reported as cash inflows from *investing* activities.

d. $12,000, F.   The amount of cash dividends paid is determined as follows:

Net income for 1991	$ 28,000
Less: Increase in retained earnings for 1991	(13,000)
Dividends declared in 1991	15,000
Less: Increase in dividends payable for 1991	(3,000)
Cash dividends paid in 1991	$ 12,000

In the statement of cash flows, cash dividends paid are reported as cash outflows for *financing* activities.

e. $17,000, F.   The cash paid for the redemption of bonds payable is determined as follows:

Bonds payable issued in exchange for plant assets	$20,000
Less: Increase in bonds payable	(3,000)
Cash paid for redemption of bonds payable	$17,000

In the statement of cash flows, cash payments for the redemption of bonds payable are reported as cash outflows for *financing* activities.

SOLUTION 14-4 INDIRECT METHOD

a. $185,000, S.   The problem states that the accounts included in Probe's condensed trial balance have not yet been adjusted for income tax expense and that Probe's income tax payments during 1997 were debited to Income Taxes Payable. Therefore, the amount of cash paid for income taxes is the decrease in the Income Taxes Payable account. In the statement of cash flows prepared using the indirect method, amounts of payments for income taxes are reported in supplementary information.

b. $50,000, S.   The cash paid for interest is determined as follows:

Decrease in unamortized premium on bonds payable	79,000
Decrease in unamortized premium on bonds payable due to extinguishment of bonds payable	(75,000)
Decrease in unamortized premium on bonds payable due to amortization of premium	4,000
Add: Interest expense recognized during 1997	46,000
Cash paid for interest during 1997	$50,000

Amortization of premium on bonds payable decreases the amount of interest expense recognized. Therefore, the amount of amortization of premium on bonds payable must be added to the amount of interest expense recognized to determine the amount of payments for interest. In the statement of cash flows prepared using the indirect method, amounts of payments for interest (net of amounts capitalized) are reported in supplementary information.

c. $485,000, F. The cash payment for redemption of bonds payable is determined as follows:

Face amount of bonds payable redeemed	$500,000
Premium on bonds payable redeemed	75,000
Carrying amount of bonds payable redeemed	575,000
Pretax gain on early extinguishment	(90,000)
Cash paid for redemption of bonds payable	$485,000

In the statement of cash flows, payments for redemption of bonds payable are reported as cash outflows for financing activities.

d. $255,000, F. The proceeds from issuance of common stock is determined as follows:

Increase in Common Stock account (80,000 shares x $2.50 par value)	$200,000
Increase in Additional Paid-In Capital account	55,000
Proceeds from issuance of common stock	$255,000

In the statement of cash flows, proceeds from issuance of common stock are reported as cash inflows from financing activities.

e. $65,000, F. Since Probe's revenue and expense accounts are included in the condensed trial balance, they have not yet been closed to Retained Earnings. Therefore, the $80,000 decrease in Retained Earnings is due entirely to the declaration of cash dividends during 1997. Since the Dividends Payable account increased by $15,000 during 1997, the amount of cash dividends paid in 1997 is $65,000 (i.e., $80,000 – $15,000). In the statement of cash flows, cash dividends payments are reported as cash outflows for financing activities.

f. $20,000, I. To determine the proceeds from the sale of equipment, the accumulated depreciation on the equipment sold must first be computed as follows:

Depreciation expense for 1997	$88,000
Less: Net increase in accumulated depreciation for 1997	(65,000)
Accumulated depreciation on equipment sold	$23,000

The proceeds from the sale of equipment can now be determined as follows:

Cost of equipment sold	$50,000
Less: Related accumulated depreciation	(23,000)
Carrying amount of equipment sold	27,000
Less: Loss on sale of equipment	(7,000)
Proceeds from sale of equipment	$20,000

In the statement of cash flows, proceeds from the sale of equipment are reported as cash inflows from investing activities.

PROBLEMS/ESSAY SOLUTIONS

SOLUTION 14-5 INDIRECT METHOD

Kern Inc.
STATEMENT OF CASH FLOW
For the Year Ended December 31, 1998
Increase (Decrease) in Cash

Cash flows from operating activities:		
Net income	$ 305,000	
Adjustments to reconcile net income to net cash provided by operating activities:		
Depreciation	82,000	[1]
Amortization of patent	9,000	
Loss on sale of equipment	10,000	
Equity in income of Word Corp.	(30,000)	[2]
Gain on sale of marketable equity securities	(19,000)	
Decrease in allowance to reduce marketable equity securities to market	(15,000)	
Increase in accounts receivable	(35,000)	
Decrease in inventories	80,000	
Decrease in accounts payable and accrued liabilities	(115,000)	
Net cash provided by operating activities		$ 272,000
Cash flows from investing activities:		
Sale of marketable equity securities	$ 119,000	
Sale of equipment	18,000	
Purchase of equipment	(120,000)	
Net cash provided by investing activities		17,000
Cash flows from financing activities:		
Issuance of common stock	$ 260,000	[3]
Cash dividend paid	(85,000)	
Payment on note payable	(300,000)	
Net cash used in financing activities		(125,000)
Net increase in cash		164,000
Cash at beginning of year		307,000
Cash at end of year		$ 471,000

<u>Explanation of amounts</u>:

[1]	Net increase in accumulated depreciation for 1998	$ 65,000
	Accumulated depreciation on equipment sold	17,000
	Depreciation for 1998	$ 82,000
[2]	Reported net income for 1998	$ 150,000
	Kern's ownership	x 20%
	Equity in income of Word Corp. for 1998	$ 30,000
[3]	Issuance of common stock 4/15/98, issued 20,000 shares for cash at $13 per share	$ 260,000

SOLUTION 14-6 DIRECT METHOD/ANALYSIS OF CHANGES IN PARTNERS' CAPITAL ACCOUNTS

a.

Linden Consulting Associates
STATEMENT OF CASH FLOWS
For the Year Ended December 31, 1997
Increase (Decrease) in Cash

Cash flows from operating activities:

Cash received from customers		$ 2,586,000 [1]	
Cash paid to suppliers and employees		(1,830,000) [2]	
Dividends received from affiliate		96,000	
Net cash provided by operating activities			$ 852,000

Cash flows from investing activities:

Purchased property and equipment		(170,000)

Cash flows from financing activities:

Principal payment of mortgage payable	(20,000)	
Proceeds for admission of new partner	340,000	
Drawings against partners' capital accounts	(630,000)	
Net cash used in financing activities		(310,000)

Net increase in cash	372,000
Cash at beginning of year	280,000
Cash at end of year	$ 652,000

Explanation of amounts:

[1]	Fee revenue		$ 2,664,000
	Less ending accounts receivable balance		(446,000)
	Add beginning accounts receivable balance		368,000
			$ 2,586,000

[2]	Operating expenses		$ 1,940,000
	Less depreciation	$ 60,000	
	Ending accounts payable balance	320,000	(380,000)
	Add beginning accounts payable balance		270,000
			$ 1,830,000

b. Reconciliation of net income to net cash provided by operating activities:

Net income		$900,000
Adjustments to reconcile net income to net cash		
provided by operating activities:		
Depreciation and amortization	$ 64,000	
Undistributed earnings of affiliate	(84,000) [1]	
Change in assets and liabilities:		
Increase in accounts receivable	(78,000)	
Increase in accounts payable and accrued expenses	50,000	
Total adjustments		(48,000)
Net cash provided by operating activities		$852,000

Explanation of amount:

[1]	Linden's share of Zach, Inc.'s:	
	Reported net income for 1997 (25% x $720,000)	$ 180,000
	Cash dividends paid for 1997 (25% of $384,000)	(96,000)
	Undistributed earnings for 1997	$ 84,000

c.

Linden Consulting Associates
ANALYSIS OF CHANGES IN PARTNERS' CAPITAL ACCOUNTS
For the Year Ended December 31, 1997

	Total	Garr	Pat	Scott
Balance, December 31, 1996	$1,700,000	$1,020,000	$680,000	$ --
Capital investment	340,000	--	--	340,000
Allocation of net income	900,000	450,000	270,000	180,000
Balance before drawings	2,940,000	1,470,000	950,000	520,000
Drawings	630,000	280,000	200,000	150,000
Balance, December 31, 1997	$2,310,000	$1,190,000	$750,000	$370,000

SOLUTION 14-7 INDIRECT METHOD

The **gross** amount of the **extraordinary loss** is **added** to **net income** under cash flows from **operating activities**. The **cash payment** is reported as a cash **outflow** from **financing activities**.

Corval should **disclose** details of the **noncash elements** of the transaction either on the **same page** as the statement cash flows or in the **notes to the financial statements**.

CHAPTER 15

FINANCIAL STATEMENT ANALYSIS & EARNINGS PER SHARE

CHAPTER 15

FINANCIAL STATEMENT ANALYSIS & EARNINGS PER SHARE

I. FINANCIAL ANALYSIS

A. DEFINITION

Financial statement analysis is an attempt to evaluate a business entity for financial and managerial decision-making purposes. In order to draw valid conclusions about the financial health of an entity, it is essential to analyze and compare specific types and sources of financial information. This analysis would include (1) a review of the firm's accounting policies, (2) an examination of recent auditors' reports, (3) analysis of footnotes and other supplemental information accompanying the financial statements, and (4) the examination of various relationships among items presented in financial statements (i.e., ratio analysis).

B. PURPOSE

Financial ratios measure elements of the firm's operating performance and financial position so that internal as well as industry-wide comparisons can be made on a consistent basis. Ratio analysis provides an indication of the firm's financial strengths and weaknesses and generally should be used in conjunction with other evaluation techniques. Ratio analysis is used primarily to draw conclusions about the solvency, operational efficiency, and profitability of a firm.

II. RATIO ANALYSIS

A. EVALUATION OF SOLVENCY

1. **SHORT-TERM SOLVENCY** Short-term solvency is the ability of a firm to meet its current obligations as they mature. The following ratios may be of primary interest to short-term creditors.

   a. **WORKING CAPITAL**

   $$Current\ Assets - Current\ Liabilities$$

   Comments: Represents assets financed from long-term capital sources that do not require near-term payment. The greater the amount of working capital, the greater the cushion of protection available to short-term creditors, and the greater assurance that short-term debts will be paid when due.

   b. **CURRENT RATIO**

   $$\frac{Current\ Assets}{Current\ Liabilities}$$

   Comments: This is a primary test of the overall solvency of the enterprise and its ability to meet current obligations from current assets. When the current ratio exceeds 1.0 to 1.0, an equal increase in current assets and current liabilities decreases the ratio. When the current ratio is less than 1.0 to 1.0, an equal increase in current assets and current liabilities increases the ratio.

   c. **ACID-TEST OR QUICK RATIO**

   $$\frac{Cash + Marketable\ Securities + Net\ Receivables}{Current\ Liabilities}$$

Comments: This ratio provides a more severe test of immediate solvency by eliminating inventories and prepaid expenses (current assets that are not quickly converted into cash).

d. **DEFENSIVE-INTERVAL RATIO**

$$\frac{Cash + Marketable\ Securities + Net\ Receivables}{Average\ Daily\ Cash\ Expenditures}$$

Comments: This ratio estimates the number of days that the company can meet its basic operational costs. The average daily cash expenditures can be approximated by reducing total expenses for the year by noncash charges (e.g., depreciation, amortization of intangibles) and dividing this amount by 365.

2. **LONG-TERM SOLVENCY** Long-term solvency is the ability to meet interest payments, preferred dividends, and other fixed charges. Similarly, long-term solvency is a required precondition for the repayment of principal.

a. **DEBT TO EQUITY**

$$\frac{Total\ Liabilities}{Owners'\ Equity}$$

Comments: This ratio provides a measure of the relative amounts of resources provided by creditors and owners.

b. **TIMES INTEREST EARNED**

$$\frac{Income\ Before\ Income\ Taxes\ and\ Interest\ Charges}{Interest\ Charges}$$

Comments: Measures the ability of the firm to meet its interest payments. Income taxes are *added* back to net income because the ability to pay interest is not dependent on the amount of income taxes to be paid, since interest is tax deductible.

c. **TIMES PREFERRED DIVIDENDS EARNED**

$$\frac{Net\ Income}{Annual\ Preferred\ Dividend\ Requirement}$$

Comments: Measures the adequacy of current earnings for the payment of preferred dividends.

B. **OPERATIONAL EFFICIENCY**
Operational efficiency is the ability of the business entity to generate income as well as its efficiency and effectiveness in using the assets employed.

1. **RECEIVABLES TURNOVER**

$$\frac{Net\ Credit\ Sales}{Average\ Net\ Receivables}$$

Comments: This ratio provides an indication of the efficiency of credit policies and collection procedures, and of the quality of the receivables. Average net receivables include trade notes receivable. Average net receivables is generally determined by adding the beginning and ending net receivables balances and dividing by two.

2. **NUMBER OF DAYS' SALES IN AVERAGE RECEIVABLES**

$$\frac{360}{Receivables\ Turnover}$$

Comments: Tests the average number of days required to collect receivables. Some analysts prefer to use 365, 300, or 250 as the number of business days in the year.

3. **INVENTORY TURNOVER**

$$\frac{Cost\ of\ Goods\ Sold}{Average\ Inventory}$$

Comments: Indicates the number of times inventory was acquired and sold (or used in production) during the period. It can be used to detect inventory obsolescence or pricing problems. Average inventory is generally determined by adding the beginning and ending inventories and dividing by two.

4. **NUMBER OF DAYS' SUPPLY IN AVERAGE INVENTORY**

$$\frac{360}{Inventory\ Turnover}$$

Comments: Indicates the number of days inventory is held before it is sold. Some analysts prefer to use 365, 300, or 250 as the number of business days in the year.

- The number of days' supply in average (ending) inventory can also be computed in the following manner:

$$\frac{Average\ (Ending)\ Inventory}{Average\ Daily\ Cost\ of\ Goods\ Sold}$$

Average daily cost of goods sold is determined by dividing cost of goods sold by the number of business days in the year (e.g., 365, 360, 300, or 250).

5. **LENGTH OF OPERATING CYCLE**

$$\begin{array}{ccc} Number\ of\ days'\ sales & & Number\ of\ days'\ supply \\ in\ average\ receivables & + & in\ average\ inventory \end{array}$$

Comments: Measures the average length of time from the purchase of inventory to the collection of cash from its sale.

C. **PROFITABILITY AND INVESTMENT ANALYSIS RATIOS**

1. **BOOK VALUE PER COMMON SHARE**

$$\frac{Common\ Stockholders'\ Equity}{Number\ of\ Common\ Shares\ Outstanding}$$

To determine common stockholders' equity, preferred stock is subtracted from total stockholders' equity at the greater of its *liquidation*, par or stated value. Cumulative preferred stock dividends in *arrears* are also similarly subtracted. Treasury stock affects the denominator as the number of common shares outstanding is *reduced*.

Comments: This ratio measures the amount that common shareholders would receive if all assets were sold at their carrying amounts and if all creditors were paid. When balance sheet valuations do not approximate fair values, the importance of this ratio is diminished.

2.   BOOK VALUE PER PREFERRED SHARE

$$\frac{Preferred\ Stockholders'\ Equity}{Number\ of\ Preferred\ Shares\ Outstanding}$$

Preferred stockholders' equity is comprised of (a) preferred stock at the greater of its *liquidation*, par or stated value and (b) cumulative preferred stock dividends in arrears.

Comments: This ratio measures the amount that preferred shareholders would receive if the company were liquidated on the basis of the amounts reported on the balance sheet.

3.   RETURN ON TOTAL ASSETS

$$\frac{Net\ Income + Interest\ Expense\ (Net\ of\ Tax)}{Average\ Total\ Assets}$$

Comments: This ratio provides a measure of the degree of efficiency with which resources (total assets) are used to generate earnings.

4.   RETURN ON COMMON STOCKHOLDERS' EQUITY

$$\frac{Net\ Income - Preferred}{Average\ Common\ Stockholders'\ Equity}$$

Comments: Measures the rate of earnings on resources provided by common stockholders. Common stockholders' equity is measured as indicated in 1., above. Average common stockholders' equity is generally determined by adding beginning and ending common stockholders' equity and dividing by two.

- Successful use of *leverage* is where a company earns more by the use of borrowed money than it costs to use the borrowed funds. When compared to the return on total assets, the return on common stockholders' equity measures the extent to which leverage is being employed for or against the common stockholders. When the return on common stockholders' equity is greater than the return on total assets, leverage is positive and common stockholders benefit.

5.   RETURN ON STOCKHOLDERS' EQUITY

$$\frac{Net\ Income}{Average\ Stockholders'\ Equity}$$

Comments: Measures the rate of earnings on resources provided by all stockholders (i.e., common and preferred). Average stockholders' equity is generally determined by adding beginning and ending stockholders' equity and dividing by two.

6.   EARNINGS PER SHARE

$$\frac{Net\ Income - Preferred\ Dividends}{Average\ Number\ of\ Common\ Shares\ Outstanding}$$

Comments: Measures the ability to pay dividends to common stockholders by measuring profit earned per share of common stock. (Earnings per share will be discussed thoroughly later in this chapter.)

7.   PRICE-EARNINGS RATIO

$$\frac{Market\ Price\ Per\ Common\ Share}{Earnings\ Per\ Common\ Share}$$

Comments: A measure of whether a stock is relatively cheap or relatively expensive based on its present earnings.

8. DIVIDEND PAYOUT RATIO

$$\frac{Cash\ Dividend\ Per\ Common\ Share}{Earnings\ Per\ Common\ Share}$$

Comments: This ratio represents the percentage of earnings per share distributed to common stockholders in cash dividends. A low ratio would probably indicate the reinvestment of profits by a growth-oriented firm.

9. YIELD ON COMMON STOCK

$$\frac{Dividend\ Per\ Common\ Share}{Market\ Price\ Per\ Common\ Share}$$

Comments: Measures cash flow return on common stock investment.

D. OTHER FACTORS IN RATIO ANALYSIS
When computing a ratio, remember to consider the following:

1. Net or gross amounts (e.g., receivables)

2. Average for the period or year-end (e.g., receivables, inventories, common shares outstanding)

3. Adjustments to income (e.g., interest, income taxes, preferred dividends)

III. EARNINGS PER SHARE

A. OVERVIEW
SFAS 128, *Earnings Per Share,* requires the presentation of basic and diluted earnings per share, and describes the calculations and how EPS data should be reported.

B. APPLICABILITY
Earnings per share data are required to be included in the financial statements of entities with publicly held common stock or potential common stock, if those securities trade in a public market. Potential common stock includes securities such as options, warrants, convertible securities, and contingent stock agreements.

C. DEFINITIONS

1. EARNINGS PER SHARE (EPS) The amount of earnings attributable to each share of common stock. Note that EPS is computed for common stock only, **not** for preferred stock.

2. DILUTION (DILUTIVE) Reduction in earnings per share due to the *assumed* conversion or exercise of certain securities into common stock.

3. ANTIDILUTION (ANTIDILUTIVE) Increase in earnings per share or decrease in loss per share.

4. BASIC EARNINGS PER SHARE (BASIC EPS) The amount of earnings for the period available to each share of common stock outstanding during the reporting period.

5. DILUTED EARNINGS PER SHARE (DILUTED EPS) The amount of earnings for the period available to each share of common stock outstanding during the reporting period and to each share that would have been outstanding assuming the issuance of common shares for all dilutive potential common shares outstanding during the reporting period.

6. **CONVERTIBLE SECURITY** A security that is convertible into another security based on a conversion rate.

D. BASIC EPS

1. **FORMULA** Basic EPS is computed by dividing income available to common stockholders (IAC) by the weighted-average number of shares outstanding during the period. Shares issued during the period and shares reacquired during the period are weighted for the portion of the period they were outstanding.

$$\text{Basic EPS} = \frac{\text{Income Available to Common Stockholders}}{\text{Weighted Average Number of Shares Outstanding}}$$

EXAMPLE 1 ♦ BASIC EPS

If IAC is $100,000 and the weighted average number of shares of common stock outstanding is 250,000 shares, basic EPS is:

$$\frac{\$100,000}{250,000} = \$.40$$

2. **NUMERATOR** The numerator for basic EPS is fairly simple to determine. The income number used for basic EPS is *income from continuing operations* adjusted for the claims by senior securities. Senior security claims generally refer to preferred stock and are adjusted in the period earned.

a. All preferred stock dividends declared reduce income to arrive at IAC.

b. Cumulative preferred stock dividends of the current period, even though not declared, also reduce income to arrive at IAC.

c. Dividends on common stock are **not** used in determining EPS.

EXAMPLE 2 ♦ IAC—NONCUMULATIVE PREFERRED STOCK

Corporation A has 10,000 shares of $100 par, noncumulative, 3% dividend, participating preferred stock. Net income has been $100,000 for each of the last four years. Dividends of $30,000 were paid in 20X1, zero in 20X2, $50,000 in 20X3, and $60,000 in 20X4. Income available to the common stockholders would be:

Year	Net Income	Preferred Dividends Earned	IAC
20X1	$100,000	$30,000	$ 70,000
20X2	$100,000	–	$100,000
20X3	$100,000	$50,000	$ 50,000
20X4	$100,000	$60,000	$ 40,000

EXAMPLE 3 ♦ IAC—CUMULATIVE PREFERRED STOCK

Refer to the facts of Example 1, except that the preferred stock is cumulative. IAC would be:

Year	Net Income	Preferred Dividends Earned	IAC
20X1	$100,000	$30,000	$70,000
20X2	$100,000	$30,000*	$70,000
20X3	$100,000	$30,000**	$70,000
20X4	$100,000	$50,000***	$50,000

*   The dividends in arrears are earned in 20X2.
** The $50,000 declared in 20X3 are $30,000 in arrears from 20X2 and $20,000 of the $30,000 earned in 20X3.
*** The $60,000 declared in 20X4 are $10,000 in arrears from 20X3, $30,000 earned in 20X4, and $20,000 participation by the preferred stockholders in 20X4.

3. **DENOMINATOR** The denominator is the weighted-average number of shares outstanding during the period. For basic EPS, this number will include shares outstanding the entire period, shares issued during the period, and shares where all of the conditions of issuance have been met.

    a. **ISSUE OR REACQUIRE STOCK** Issuance of stock and reacquisition of stock during the period changes the ownership structure and the shares only participate in earnings for the time that the stock is outstanding. For example, if a shareholder holds 10,000 shares the entire period and another shareholder purchases 10,000 in the middle of the year, you would not expect their EPS to be the same.

    b. **STOCK DIVIDENDS AND STOCK SPLITS** Stock dividends, stock splits, and reverse stock splits change the total number of shares outstanding but not the proportionate shares outstanding. For example, an individual owning 10,000 shares of a company with 20,000 shares outstanding owns 50 percent of the stock. After a 2 for 1 stock split, ownership is 20,000 of 40,000 total shares, or still 50 percent. For this reason, stock dividends, stock splits, and reverse stock splits are reflected retroactively for all periods presented. Such changes occurring after the close of the accounting period but prior to the issuance of the financial statements are also reflected in the EPS for all periods presented.

    c. **ISSUE STOCK IN A BUSINESS COMBINATION** The effect of common stock issued in a business combination consummated during the period, depends on whether the combination is accounted for as a purchase or pooling-of-interest. If the purchase method is used, the weighted average is applied from the date of combination. If the pooling-of-interest method is used, the common shares issued are given retroactive treatment for all periods presented.

EXAMPLE 4 ♦ WEIGHTED AVERAGE SHARES OF COMMON STOCK OUTSTANDING

Date	Transaction	Change in Shares from Transaction	Total Shares Outstanding
1/1	Shares outstanding		10,000
4/1	Shares issued	8,000	18,000
6/1	Shares reacquired and held in treasury	(3,000)	15,000
7/1	Issued 10% stock dividend	1,500	16,500
8/1	Shares reacquired and held in treasury	(6,000)	10,500
9/1	Shares issued	12,000	22,500
12/1	Issued 2 for 1 stock split	22,500	45,000

(continued on next page)

Total Shares Outstanding		Months Outstanding		Stock Dividend		Stock Split		Weighted Average
10,000	x	3/12	x	1.10	x	2	=	5,500
18,000	x	2/12	x	1.10	x	2	=	6,600
15,000	x	1/12	x	1.10	x	2	=	2,750
16,500	x	1/12			x	2	=	2,750
10,500	x	1/12			x	2	=	1,750
22,500	x	3/12			x	2	=	11,250
45,000	x	1/12					=	3,750
Weighted average number of shares outstanding								34,350

Note: The stock dividend and stock split are applied retroactively to the beginning of the year from the date declared.

E.   DILUTED EPS

1.   OBJECTIVE The objective of reporting diluted EPS is to measure the performance of an entity over the reporting period while giving effect to all dilutive potential common shares that were outstanding during the period.

2.   DILUTIVE SECURITY With diluted EPS, the first step is to determine if a security is dilutive. A security is dilutive if the inclusion of the security in the computation of EPS results in a smaller EPS or increases the loss per share.

   a.   POTENTIALLY DILUTIVE Securities that are potentially dilutive include convertible preferred stock, convertible debt, options, warrants, participating securities, different classes of common stock, and agreements to issue these securities or shares of common stock in the future, referred to as contingently issuable shares.

   b.   ANTI-DILUTIVE SECURITIES Not all potential dilutive securities will be dilutive. When the per share effect of an individual security is greater than the total per share effect, the security is anti-dilutive. Anti-dilutive securities are excluded from diluted EPS. Thus it is necessary to calculate the per share effect of each potentially dilutive security and include only those which have a dilutive effect.

   c.   CATEGORIES OF POTENTIALLY DILUTIVE SECURITIES Potentially dilutive securities are grouped into the following categories:

      (1)   Convertible securities where the if-converted method is used

      (2)   Options, warrants, and their equivalents where the treasury stock method is used

      (3)   Contingently issuable shares

3.   IF-CONVERTED METHOD Convertible securities may or may not be converted. If they are converted, they become common stock. The if-converted method assumes that they are converted; in other words, pretend that convertible securities are converted. The pretend conversion may impact the IAC and the weighted-average number of common shares outstanding.

   a.   NUMERATOR

      (1)   CONVERTIBLE DEBT If the enterprise has convertible debt, the conversion would mean that the company does not have the interest expense for the debt and should be added back to income to arrive at IAC. The interest expense adjustment should be net of tax and increases income or decreases the loss for

the period. If the tax amount impacts a nondiscretionary item such as bonuses, a further adjustment is necessary.

(2) **CONVERTIBLE PREFERRED STOCK** If convertible preferred stock is assumed to be exercised, the entity would not have the corresponding preferred dividends, and income from continuing operations would not be reduced for preferred dividends. These adjustments do not have nondiscretionary or tax effects.

b. **DENOMINATOR** Assuming convertible securities are converted to common stock increases the weighted average number of common shares outstanding.

EXAMPLE 5 ♦ IF-CONVERTED METHOD

A company has IAC of $2,000,000 and weighted average common shares outstanding of 1,000,000. The company has a convertible bond that is convertible into 100,000 shares. This bond has been outstanding for the entire year, and the company reported $40,000 in related interest expense. The company has a profit-sharing plan of 10% of net income and a 40% tax rate. Additionally, the company has convertible preferred stock that is convertible into 50,000 common shares, and $125,000 of dividends were earned on this preferred stock during the period.

Basic EPS is calculated as follows:

$$\frac{\$2,000,000}{1,000,000} \qquad \$ \ \ 2.00$$

The effects of the convertible debt are:

Effect on IAC:

Interest expense	$ 40,000
Increase in profit-sharing if converted	(4,000)
	$ 36,000
Tax effect ($36,000 x 40%)	(14,400)
Increase to IAC	$ 21,600

Effect on weighted average common shares:
Additional shares issued if converted; increases the weighted average

100,000

Per share effect:

$$\frac{\$ \ 21,600}{100,000} \qquad \$ \ \ \ .216$$

The convertible debt has a dilutive effect since the per share effect is less than basic EPS.

The effects of the convertible preferred stock are:

Effect on IAC:
Dividends on preferred stock added back to IAC

$125,000

Effect on weighted average common shares:
Additional shares issued if converted; increases the weighted average

50,000

Per share effect:

$$\frac{\$125,000}{50,000} \qquad \$ \ \ 2.50$$

The convertible preferred stock is anti-dilutive since $2.50 is greater than $2.00.

Diluted EPS is calculated as follows:

$$\frac{\$2,000,000 + \$ \ 21,600}{1,000,000 + \ \ 100,000} = \frac{2,021,600}{1,100,000} \qquad \$ \ \ 1.838$$

Note: The adjustments for the convertible debt assumed converted are made because they are dilutive. No adjustments are made for the convertible preferred stock because they are anti-dilutive.

4. **TREASURY STOCK METHOD** Holders of options and warrants can exercise these securities for specified amounts of cash and receive common stock. The treasury stock method assumes that this cash is used to repurchase treasury stock at the average market price, and the net effect on the shares of common stock outstanding is the difference between the shares issued and the shares purchased.

   a. **APPLIED SEPARATELY** The treasury stock method is applied separately to each option and warrant to determine if the individual option or warrant is dilutive. Since the effect of options and warrants is only a denominator effect for the net additional shares that are issued, the per share effect of each option or warrant is $.00.

   b. **DILUTIVE VS. ANTI-DILUTIVE** If the average market price is higher than the exercise price, the item is "in the money," and the options or warrants are dilutive. If the average market price is less than the exercise price, the options or warrants are anti-dilutive.

EXAMPLE 6 ♦ TREASURY STOCK METHOD

A company has IAC of $100,000 and 250,000 weighted-average common stock outstanding for the period. The average market price of the common stock is $22 per share. The following options and warrants are outstanding:

	Options	Warrants-Series A	Warrants-Series B
Shares of Common Stock Issuable	10,000	5,000	7,000
Exercise price per share	$20	$15	$24

Step 1 - Determine if the options and warrants are dilutive

Options: Market ($22) > Exercise ($20)	Dilutive
Warrants - Series A: Market ($22) > Exercise ($15)	Dilutive
Warrants - Series B: Market ($22) < Exercise ($24)	Anti-Dilutive

Step 2 - Determine the incremental shares for dilutive securities

Options:

Additional Shares of Common Stock		10,000
Less: Treasury Stock Purchased		
Proceeds (10,000 shares x $20)	$200,000	
Divided by market price	÷ 22	(9,091)
Incremental Shares		909
Per Share Effect	0 / 909	$ .00

Warrants - Series A:

Additional Shares of Common Stock		5,000
Less: Treasury Stock Purchased		
Proceeds (5,000 shares x $15)	$ 75,000	
Divided by market price	÷ 22	(3,409)
Incremental Shares		1,591
Per Share Effect	0 / 1,591	$ .00

(continued on next page)

Step 3 - Calculate Basic and Diluted EPS

Item	IAC	Shares	EPS
Basic EPS	$100,000	250,000	$.400
Warrants-Series A	0	1,591	
	$100,000	251,591	$.397
Options	0	909	
Diluted EPS	$100,000	252,500	$.396

5. **CONTINGENTLY ISSUABLE SHARES** Contingent issuances involve the meeting of specific conditions for the issuance of additional shares.

    a.   **PASSAGE OF TIME CONTINGENCY** If the contingency involves only the passage of time, the securities are assumed issued and are used in computing diluted EPS.

    b.   **CONTINGENCY NOT MET** If the contingency has not been met, the number of shares that would be issued if the contingency had been met at the end of the contingency period is used in computing diluted EPS.

    c.   **FUTURE MARKET PRICE CONTINGENCY** The number of shares contingently issuable may depend on the market price of the stock at a future date. In this case, computations of EPS should reflect the number of shares which would be issuable based on the market price at the close of the reporting period. For example, assume a company had a plan to issue 20,000 shares if the market price was $15 per share, 30,000 shares if the market price was $20 per share, and 50,000 shares if the market price was $30 per share. If the market price for the current period was $17 per share, EPS should show the 20,000 contingently issuable shares.

    d.   **EARNINGS CONTINGENCY** If the contingency is contingent on attainment or maintenance of earnings at a certain level, the number of shares would be considered outstanding and used in computing diluted EPS if the earnings amount is currently being achieved.

6. **CALCULATION OF DILUTED EPS** Diluted EPS should reflect the maximum dilution of all potentially dilutive securities that have a dilutive effect. To accomplish this, the security with the smallest individual per share effect is first introduced into total EPS and additional securities are introduced until either all dilutive securities are included or further introduction would be anti-dilutive.

EXAMPLE 7 ♦ CALCULATION OF DILUTED EPS

A company has the following earnings and securities:

Net income for the period	$100,000
Weighted average common shares outstanding	75,000
Dividends on preferred stock earned	$ 5,000
Series A Convertible Bonds	
Face amount and carrying value	$ 40,000
Interest rate	10%
Number of shares issuable	10,000

(continued on next page)

Series B Convertible Bonds	
Face amount and carrying value	$ 60,000
Interest rate	12%
Number of shares issuable	4,400

Options	
Number of shares issuable	7,500
Exercise price	$ 25
Market price	$ 35

Warrants	
Number of shares issuable	2,500
Exercise price	$ 32

The tax rate is 30% and there are no nondiscretionary items.

Step 1 - Determine Basic EPS

Net income	$100,000
Preferred dividends earned	(5,000)
IAC	$ 95,000

$$\frac{\text{IAC}}{\text{Weighted-average shares outstanding}} = \frac{\$95,000}{75,000} \qquad \$ \, 1.2667$$

Step 2 - Determine the per share effect of each dilutive security

Series A Convertible Bonds

Adjustment to IAC:	
Interest expense	$ 4,000
Taxes	(1,200)
Adjustment to IAC (increase)	$ 2,800

Adjustment to weighted-average shares (increase):	
Number of shares issuable	10,000

Per share effect:

$$\frac{\text{Adjustment to IAC}}{\text{Adjustment to weighted-average shares}} = \frac{\$ 2,800}{10,000} \qquad \$ \quad .28$$

Series B Convertible Bonds

Adjustment to IAC:	
Interest expense	$ 7,200
Taxes	(2,160)
Adjustment to IAC (increase)	$ 5,040

Adjustment to weighted-average shares (increase):	
Number of shares issuable	4,400

Per share effect:

$$\frac{\text{Adjustment to IAC}}{\text{Adjustment to weighted-average shares}} = \frac{\$5,040}{4,400} \qquad \$ \, 1.1455$$

(continued on next page)

Options:

Additional Shares of Common Stock			7,500
Less: Treasury Stock Purchased			
Proceeds (7,500 shares x $25)		$187,500	
Divided by market price		÷ 35	(5,357)
Incremental Shares			2,143
Per Share Effect		0	$ .00
		2,143	

Warrants:

Additional Shares of Common Stock			2,500
Less: Treasury Stock Purchased			
Proceeds (2,500 shares x $32)		$ 80,000	
Divided by market price		÷ 35	(2,286)
Incremental Shares			214
Per Share Effect		0	$ .00
		214	

Step 3 - Begin with the most dilutive security and include all with a dilutive effect

Item	IAC	Shares	EPS
Basic EPS	$95,000	75,000	$ 1.2667
Options	0	2,143	
	$95,000	77,143	$ 1.2315
Warrants	0	214	
	$95,000	77,357	$ 1.2281
Series A Bonds	2,800	10,000	
Diluted EPS	$97,800	87,357	$ 1.1195

NOTE: The EPS number is adjusted for the most dilutive effect. Since the per share effect ($0.28) of the Series A Bonds is less than the previously calculated EPS number ($1.2281) the Series A Bonds are dilutive. However, the per share effect of the Series B Bonds ($1.1455) is greater than the previously calculated EPS number ($1.1195), and the security is excluded because it is anti-dilutive. The options are included first because they are more dilutive than the warrants.

F.   PRESENTATION IN THE FINANCIAL STATEMENTS

1.   INCOME STATEMENT OR NOTES

a.   **INCOME STATEMENT**   EPS is reported on the face of the income statement for income from continuing operations and net income.

b.   **INCOME STATEMENT OR NOTES**   An entity that reports a discontinued operation, an extraordinary item, or the cumulative effect of an accounting change in a period is required to present EPS amounts for those line items either on the face of the income statement or in the notes to the financial statements.

c.   **ALL PERIODS PRESENTED**   EPS data is required to be presented for all periods for which an income statement or summary of earnings is presented.

2.   SIMPLE CAPITAL STRUCTURE

a.   **DEFINITION**   An entity has a simple capital structure if it has only common stock outstanding and has no dilutive securities.

b.   **REPORTING REQUIREMENTS**   An entity with a simple capital structure is required to present only basic EPS.

3. **COMPLEX CAPITAL STRUCTURE** EPS reporting is more involved if the reporting enterprise has a complex capital structure.

    a. **DEFINITION** An entity's capital structure is complex if it has dilutive securities. Dilutive securities dilute earnings per common share.

    b. **DUAL PRESENTATION** An entity with a complex capital structure is required to present both basic and diluted EPS for income from continuing operations and for net income on the face of the income statement with equal prominence, and for each component of income, including discontinued operations, extraordinary items, and cumulative effects of accounting changes, either on the income statement or in the notes to the financial statements. If the capital structure is complex for any of the periods presented, dual presentation must be provided for all the periods presented.

EXAMPLE 8 ◆ INCOME STATEMENT PRESENTATION OF EPS

Assume that the following income statement information is presented:

Income from Continuing Operations	$100,000
Discontinued Operations	(40,000)
Income before Extraordinary Item	$ 60,000
Extraordinary Item—Gain on Debt Extinguishment	25,000
Net income	$ 85,000

The company has only convertible cumulative 8% preferred stock with a par value of $100,000, that would require 5,000 shares of common stock, if converted. EPS would be:

Basic EPS from Continuing Operations

Income from continuing operations		$100,000
Preferred dividends earned		(8,000)
IAC		$ 92,000
$\dfrac{\text{IAC}}{\text{Weighted average common shares (assumed)}}$	$\dfrac{\$92,000}{40,000}$	$ 2.30

Per share effect of Preferred Stock

Effect on IAC ($100,000 x 8%)		$ 8,000
Effect on weighted-average shares		5,000
Per share effect:		
$\dfrac{\text{Effect on IAC}}{\text{Effect on weighted-average}}$	$\dfrac{\$8,000}{5,000}$	$ 1.60

Diluted EPS

Item	IAC	Shares	EPS
Basic EPS	$ 92,000	40,000	$ 2.30
Preferred Stock	8,000	5,000	
	$100,000	45,000	$ 2.22

(continued on next page)

Basic EPS for Other Income Items

Item	IAC	Shares	EPS
Basic EPS	$ 92,000	40,000	$ 2.30
Discontinued Operations	(40,000)	0	
EPS for Income Before EI	$ 52,000	40,000	$ 1.30
Extraordinary Item	25,000	0	
EPS for Net Income	$ 77,000	40,000	$ 1.93

Diluted EPS for Other Income Items

Item	IAC	Shares	EPS
Basic EPS	$ 92,000	40,000	$ 2.30
Preferred Stock	8,000	5,000	
EPS for Income from Cont. Op	$100,000	45,000	$ 2.22
Discontinued Operations	(40,000)	0	
EPS for Income Before EI	$ 60,000	45,000	$ 1.33
Extraordinary Item	25,000	0	
EPS for Net Income	$ 85,000	45,000	$ 1.89

EPS information would be presented as (if the company chose to display all EPS information on the face of the income statement):

	Income	Basic EPS	Diluted EPS
Income from Continuing Operations	$100,000	$ 2.30	$2.22
Discontinued Operations	(40,000)	(1.00)	(.89)
Income before Extraordinary Item	60,000	1.30	1.33
Extraordinary Item—Gain on Debt Extin.	25,000	.63	.56
Net income	$ 85,000	$1.93	$1.89

NOTE: The diluted EPS amount for income for extraordinary items is greater than the basic EPS. The effect of the convertible preferred stock is included in all computations if it is dilutive in computing EPS for continuing operations.

4. **DISCLOSURE REQUIREMENTS** SFAS 128 requires the following disclosures:

a. A reconciliation of the numerators and the denominators of the basic and diluted per share computations for income from continuing operations. In this way, the financial statement reader can see the per share impact of each security.

b. The effect that has been given to preferred dividends in determining the income available to common stockholders.

c. Securities that could potentially dilute basic EPS in a future period, but that were antidilutive in the current period.

d. A description of any transaction that occurs after the end of the period, but before the issuance of the financial statements that would have materially changed the number of common shares or potential common shares outstanding at the end of the period if the transaction had occurred before the end of the period. Examples would include issuance or acquisition of common shares, issuance or exercise/conversion of warrants, options, or convertible securities.

CHAPTER 15—FINANCIAL STATEMENT ANALYSIS & EARNINGS PER SHARE

PROBLEM 15-1 MULTIPLE CHOICE QUESTIONS (100 to 125 minutes)

1. North Bank is analyzing Belle Corp.'s financial statements for a possible extension of credit. Belle's quick ratio is significantly better than the industry average. Which of the following factors should North consider as a possible limitation of using this ratio when evaluating Belle's creditworthiness?
a. Fluctuating market prices of short-term investments may adversely affect the ratio.
b. Increasing market prices for Belle's inventory may adversely affect the ratio.
c. Belle may need to sell its available-for-sale investments to meet its current obligations.
d. Belle may need to liquidate its inventory to meet its long-term obligations. (R/99, FAR, #4, 6773)

2. What effect would the sale of a company's trading securities at their carrying amounts for cash have on each of the following ratios?

	Current ratio	Quick ratio
a.	No effect	No effect
b.	Increase	Increase
c.	No effect	Increase
d.	Increase	No effect

(11/95, FAR, #58, 6140)

3. In analyzing a company's financial statements, which financial statement would a potential investor primarily use to assess the company's liquidity and financial flexibility?
a. Balance sheet
b. Income statement
c. Statement of retained earnings
d. Statement of cash flows (11/94, FAR, #5, 5270)

4. At December 30, 1993, Vida Co. had cash of $200,000, a current ratio of 1.5:1 and a quick ratio of .5:1. On December 31, 1993, all cash was used to reduce accounts payable. How did these cash payments affect the ratios?

	Current ratio	Quick ratio
a.	Increased	Decreased
b.	Increased	No effect
c.	Decreased	Increased
d.	Decreased	No effect

(5/94, FAR, #60, 4875)

5. Heath Co.'s current ratio is 4:1. Which of the following transactions would normally increase its current ratio?
a. Purchasing inventory on account
b. Selling inventory on account
c. Collecting an account receivable
d. Purchasing machinery for cash

(11/92, Theory, #38, 3471)

6. Zenk Co. wrote off obsolete inventory of $100,000 during 1991. What was the effect of this write-off on Zenk's ratio analysis?
a. Decrease in current ratio but **not** in quick ratio
b. Decrease in quick ratio but **not** in current ratio
c. Increase in current ratio but **not** in quick ratio
d. Increase in quick ratio but **not** in current ratio

(5/92, PII, #18, 2650)

7. Gil Corp. has current assets of $90,000 and current liabilities of $180,000. Which of the following transactions would improve Gil's current ratio?
a. Refinancing a $30,000 long-term mortgage with a short-term note.
b. Purchasing $50,000 of merchandise inventory with a short-term account payable.
c. Paying $20,000 of short-term accounts payable.
d. Collecting $10,000 of short-term accounts receivable. (11/91, PII, #19, 2467)

8. Are the following ratios useful in assessing the liquidity position of a company?

	Defensive-interval ratio	Return on stockholders' equity
a.	Yes	Yes
b.	Yes	No
c.	No	Yes
d.	No	No

(11/90, Theory, #10, 1755)

9. Which of the following ratios is(are) useful in assessing a company's ability to meet currently maturing or short-term obligations?

	Acid-test ratio	Debt-to-equity ratio
a.	No	No
b.	No	Yes
c.	Yes	Yes
d.	Yes	No

(5/89, Theory, #37, 9055)

10. Barr Co. has total debt of $420,000 and stockholders' equity of $700,000. Barr is seeking capital to fund an expansion. Barr is planning to issue an additional $300,000 in common stock and is negotiating with a bank to borrow additional funds. The bank is requiring a debt-to-equity ratio of .75. What is the maximum additional amount Barr will be able to borrow?
a. $225,000
b. $330,000
c. $525,000
d. $750,000

(11/95, FAR, #59, 6141)

11. The following information pertains to Ali Corp. as of and for the year ended December 31, 1997:

Liabilities	$ 60,000
Stockholders' equity	500,000
Shares of common stock issued and outstanding	10,000
Net income	30,000

During 1997, Ali's officers exercised stock options for 1,000 shares of stock at an option price of $8 per share. What was the effect of exercising the stock options?
a. Debt-to-equity ratio decreased to 12%
b. Earnings per share increased by $0.33
c. Asset turnover increased to 5.4%
d. No ratios were affected

(5/92, PII, #17, amended, 2649)

ITEMS 12 AND 13 are based on the following data:

Apex Corporation
SELECTED FINANCIAL DATA
Year Ended December 31, 19XX

Operating income	$ 900,000
Interest expense	(100,000)
Income before income tax	800,000
Income tax expense	(320,000)
Net income	480,000
Preferred stock dividends	(200,000)
Net income available to common stockholders	$ 280,000

12. The times interest earned ratio is
a. 2.8 to 1.
b. 4.8 to 1.
c. 8.0 to 1.
d. 9.0 to 1.

(11/86, PI, #56, 9056)

13. The times preferred dividend earned ratio is
a. 1.4 to 1.
b. 1.7 to 1.
c. 2.4 to 1.
d. 4.0 to 1.

(11/86, PI, #57, 1263)

ITEMS 14 AND 15 are based on the following:

At December 31, 1992, Curry Co. had the following balances in selected asset accounts:

	1992	Increase over 1991
Cash	$ 300	$100
Accounts receivable, net	1,200	400
Inventory	500	200
Prepaid expenses	100	40
Other assets	400	150
Total assets	$2,500	$890

Curry also had current liabilities of $1,000 at December 31, 1992, and net credit sales of $7,200 for the year then ended.

14. What is Curry's acid-test ratio at December 31, 1992?
a. 1.5
b. 1.6
c. 2.0
d. 2.1

(5/93, PII, #15, 4123)

15. What was the average number of days to collect Curry's accounts receivable during 1992?
a. 30.4
b. 40.6
c. 50.7
d. 60.8

(5/93, PII, #16, 4124)

ITEMS 16 THROUGH 18 are based on the following:

Selected data pertaining to Lore Co. for the calendar year 1994 is as follows:

Net cash sales	$ 3,000
Cost of goods sold	18,000
Inventory at beginning of year	6,000
Purchases	24,000
Accounts receivable at beginning of year	20,000
Accounts receivable at end of year	22,000

16. The accounts receivable turnover for 1994 was 5.0 times. What were Lore's 1994 net credit sales?
a. $105,000
b. $107,000
c. $110,000
d. $210,000

(5/95, FAR, #58, 5594)

17. What was the inventory turnover for 1994?
a. 1.2 times
b. 1.5 times
c. 2.0 times
d. 3.0 times

(5/95, FAR, #59, 5595)

18. Lore would use which of the following to determine the average days' sales in inventory?

	Numerator	Denominator
a.	365	Average inventory
b.	365	Inventory turnover
c.	Average inventory	Sales divided by 365
d.	Sales divided by 365	Inventory turnover

(5/95, FAR, #60, 5596)

19. On December 31, 1997, Northpark Co. collected a receivable due from a major customer. Which of the following ratios would be increased by this transaction?
a. Inventory turnover ratio
b. Receivable turnover ratio
c. Current ratio
d. Quick ratio (5/92, Theory, #48, amended, 2741)

20. Which of the following ratios should be used in evaluating the effectiveness with which the company uses its assets?

	Receivables turnover	Dividend payout ratio
a.	Yes	Yes
b.	No	No
c.	Yes	No
d.	No	Yes

(11/89, Theory, #37, 1762)

21. During 1989, Rand Co. purchased $960,000 of inventory. The cost of goods sold for 1989 was $900,000, and the ending inventory at December 31, 1989 was $180,000. What was the inventory turnover for 1989?
a. 6.4
b. 6.0
c. 5.3
d. 5.0 (11/90, PI, #57, 1253)

22. Selected information from the accounting records of Dalton Manufacturing Company is as follows:

Net sales for 1997	$1,800,000
Cost of goods sold for 1997	1,200,000
Inventories at December 31, 1996	336,000
Inventories at December 31, 1997	288,000

Assuming there are 300 working days per year, what is the number of days' sales in average inventories for 1997?

a. 78
b. 72
c. 52
d. 48 (11/83, PI, #18, amended, 1267)

23. The following computations were made from Clay Co.'s 1997 books:

Number of days' sales in inventory	61
Number of days' sales in trade accounts receivable	33

What was the number of days in Clay's 1997 operating cycle?
a. 33
b. 47
c. 61
d. 94 (5/92, PII, #16, amended, 2648)

24. Which of the following ratios are useful for evaluating the effectiveness with which the company uses its assets?

	Acid-test (quick) ratio	Price-earnings ratio
a.	Yes	Yes
b.	Yes	No
c.	No	No
d.	No	Yes

(5/88, Theory, #38, 1767)

25. Hoyt Corp.'s current balance sheet reports the following stockholders' equity:

- 5% cumulative preferred stock, par value $100 per share; 2,500 shares issued and outstanding — $250,000
- Common stock, par value $3.50 per share; 100,000 shares issued and outstanding — 350,000
- Additional paid-in capital in excess of par value of common stock — 125,000
- Retained earnings — 300,000

Dividends in arrears on the preferred stock amount to $25,000. If Hoyt were to be liquidated, the preferred stockholders would receive par value plus a premium of $50,000. The book value per share of common stock is
a. $7.75.
b. $7.50.
c. $7.25.
d. $7.00. (11/91, PII, #3, 2451)

26. Frey Inc. was organized on January 2, 1997, with the following capital structure:

- 10% cumulative preferred stock, par value $100 and liquidation value $105; authorized, issued and outstanding 1,000 shares $100,000
- Common stock, par value $25; authorized 100,000 shares; issues and outstanding 10,000 shares 250,000

Frey's net income for the year ended December 31, 1997, was $450,000, but no dividends were declared. How much was Frey's book value per preferred share at December 31, 1997?
a. $100
b. $105
c. $110
d. $115 (5/85, PI, #14, amended, 1265)

27. The following data pertain to Cowl Inc. for the year ended December 31, 1994:

Net sales	$ 600,000
Net income	150,000
Total assets, January 1, 1994	2,000,000
Total assets, December 31, 1994	3,000,000

What was Cowl's rate of return on assets for 1994?
a. 5%
b. 6%
c. 20%
d. 24% (11/95, FAR, #60, 6142)

28. Successful use of leverage is evidenced by a
a. Rate of return on investment greater than the rate of return on stockholders' equity.
b. Rate of return on investment greater than the cost of debt.
c. Rate of return on sales greater than the rate of return on stockholders' equity.
d. Rate of return on sales greater than the cost of debt. (11/91, Theory, #17, 2525)

29. The following data pertain to Thorne Corp. for the calendar year 1997:

Net income	$240,000
Dividends paid on common stock	120,000
Common stock outstanding (unchanged during year)	300,000 shares

The market price per share of Thorne's common stock at December 31, 1997, was $12. The price-earnings ratio at December 31, 1997, was

a. 9.6 to 1.
b. 10.0 to 1.
c. 15.0 to 1.
d. 30.0 to 1. (11/89, PI, #57, amended, 1255)

30. How are dividends per share for common stock used in the calculation of the following?

	Dividend per share payout ratio	Earnings per share
a.	Numerator	Numerator
b.	Numerator	Not used
c.	Denominator	Not used
d.	Denominator	Denominator

(5/87, Theory, #40, 9057)

31. Deck Co. had 120,000 shares of common stock outstanding at January 1, 1998. On July 1, 1998, it issued 40,000 additional shares of common stock. Outstanding all year were 10,000 shares of nonconvertible cumulative preferred stock. What is the number of shares that Deck should use to calculate 1998 earnings per share?
a. 140,000
b. 150,000
c. 160,000
d. 170,000 (R/00, FAR, #9, 6904)

32. In computing the weighted-average number of shares outstanding during the year, which of the following midyear events must be treated as if it had occurred at the beginning of the year?
a. Declaration and distribution of stock dividend.
b. Purchase of treasury stock.
c. Sale of additional common stock.
d. Sale of preferred convertible stock.
(5/98, FAR, #5, 6608)

33. Ute Co. had the following capital structure during 1996 and 1997:

Preferred stock, $10 par, 4% cumulative, 25,000 shares issued and outstanding	$ 250,000
Common stock, $5 par, 200,000 shares issued and outstanding	1,000,000

Ute reported net income of $500,000 for the year ended December 31, 1997. Ute paid no preferred dividends during 1996 and paid $16,000 in preferred dividends during 1997. In its December 31, 1997, income statement, what amount should Ute report as earnings per share?
a. $2.42
b. $2.45
c. $2.48
d. $2.50 (11/95, FAR, #45, amended, 6127)

34. The following information pertains to Jet Corp.'s outstanding stock for 1997:

Common stock, $5 par value
Shares outstanding, 1/1/97	20,000
2-for-1 stock split, 4/1/97	20,000
Shares issued, 7/1/97	10,000

Preferred stock, $10 par value, 5% cumulative
Shares outstanding, 1/1/97	4,000

What are the number of shares Jet should use to calculate 1997 earnings per share?
a. 40,000
b. 45,000
c. 50,000
d. 54,000   (5/93, PI, #60, amended, 4099)

35. Timp, Inc. had the following common stock balances and transactions during 1997:

01/01/97	Common stock outstanding	30,000
02/01/97	Issued a 10% common stock dividend	3,000
03/01/97	Issued common stock in a pooling of interests	9,000
07/01/97	Issued common stock for cash	8,000
12/31/97	Common stock outstanding	50,000

What was Timp's 1997 weighted average shares outstanding?
a. 40,000
b. 44,250
c. 44,500
d. 46,000   (5/92, PI, #59, amended, 2631)

36. Strauch Co. has one class of common stock outstanding and no other securities that are potentially convertible into common stock. During 1996, 100,000 shares of common stock were outstanding. In 1997, two distributions of additional common shares occurred: On April 1, 20,000 shares of treasury stock were sold, and on July 1, a 2-for-1 stock split was issued. Net income was $410,000 in 1997 and $350,000 in 1996. What amounts should Strauch report as earnings per share in its 1997 and 1996 comparative income statements?

	1997	1996
a.	$1.78	$3.50
b.	$1.78	$1.75
c.	$2.34	$1.75
d.	$2.34	$3.50

(11/91, PI, #60, amended, 2448)

37. On January 31, 1998, Pack, Inc. split its common stock 2 for 1, and Young, Inc. issued a 5% stock dividend. Both companies issued their December 31, 1997, financial statements on March 1, 1998. Should Pack's 1997 earnings per share (EPS) take into consideration the stock split, and should Young's 1997 EPS take into consideration the stock dividend?

	Pack's 1997 EPS	Young's 1997 EPS
a.	Yes	No
b.	No	No
c.	Yes	Yes
d.	No	Yes

(11/92, Theory, #23, amended, 3456)

38. On June 30, 1996, Lomond, Inc. issued twenty $10,000, 7% bonds at par. Each bond was convertible into 200 shares of common stock. On January 1, 1997, 10,000 shares of common stock were outstanding. The bondholders converted all the bonds on July 1, 1997. The following amounts were reported in Lomond's income statement for the year ended December 31, 1997:

Revenues	$977,000
Operating expenses	(920,000)
Interest on bonds	(7,000)
Income before income tax	50,000
Income tax at 30%	(15,000)
Net income	$ 35,000

What amount should Lomond report as its 1997 basic earnings per share?
a. $2.50
b. $2.85
c. $2.92
d. $3.50   (5/92, PI, #60, amended, 2632)

39. West Co. had earnings per share of $15.00 for 1997, before considering the effects of any convertible securities. No conversion or exercise of convertible securities occurred during 1997. However, possible conversion of convertible bonds would have reduced earnings per share by $0.75. The effect of possible exercise of common stock options would have increased earnings per share by $0.10. What amount should West report as diluted earnings per share for 1997?
a. $14.25
b. $14.35
c. $15.00
d. $15.10   (11/95, FAR, #46, amended, 6128)

40. Dilutive stock options would generally be used in the calculation of

	Basic earnings per share	Diluted earnings per share
a.	No	No
b.	No	Yes
c.	Yes	Yes
d.	Yes	No

(11/88, Theory, #33, amended, 9062)

41. When computing diluted earnings per share, convertible securities are
a. Ignored.
b. Recognized whether they are dilutive or anti-dilutive.
c. Recognized only if they are anti-dilutive.
d. Recognized only if they are dilutive.

(11/93, Theory, #16, amended, 4521)

42. Dunn, Inc. had 200,000 shares of $20 par common stock and 20,000 shares of $100 par, 6%, cumulative, convertible preferred stock outstanding for the entire year ended December 31, 1997. Each preferred share is convertible into five shares of common stock. Dunn's net income for 1997 was $840,000. For the year ended December 31, 1997, the diluted earnings per share is
a. $2.40.
b. $2.80.
c. $3.60.
d. $4.20.

(5/87, PI, #58, amended, 1289)

ITEMS 43 AND 44 are based on the following information relating to the capital structure of Parke Corporation:

	December 31	
	1996	1997
Outstanding shares of:		
Common stock	90,000	90,000
Preferred stock, convertible into		
30,000 shares of common	30,000	30,000
10% convertible bonds, convertible		
into 20,000 shares of common	$1,000,000	$1,000,000

During 1997, Parke paid $45,000 dividends on the preferred stock, which was earned in 1997. Parke's net income for 1997 was $980,000 and the income tax rate was 40%.

43. For the year ended December 31, 1997, basic EPS is
a. $10.89.
b. $10.39.
c. $ 8.17.
d. $ 7.79.

(11/85, PI, #54, amended, 1294)

44. For the year ended December 31, 1997, diluted EPS is
a. $9.82.
b. $8.29.
c. $7.71.
d. $7.43.

(11/85, PI, #55, amended, 1295)

45. In determining earnings per share, interest expense, net of applicable income taxes, on convertible debt that is dilutive should be
a. Added back to net income for basic EPS, and ignored for diluted EPS.
b. Ignored for basic EPS, and added back to net income for diluted EPS.
c. Deducted from net income for basic EPS, and ignored for fully diluted EPS.
d. Deducted from net income for both basic EPS and diluted EPS.

(5/91, Theory, #29, amended, 1974)

46. The if-converted method of computing earnings per share data assumes conversion of convertible securities as of the
a. Beginning of the earliest period reported (or at time of issuance, if later).
b. Beginning of the earliest period reported (regardless of time of issuance).
c. Middle of the earliest period reported (regardless of time of issuance).
d. Ending of the earliest period reported (regardless of time of issuance).

(11/87, Theory, #33, 2006)

ITEMS 47 AND 48 are based on the following:

Mann, Inc. had 300,000 shares of common stock issued and outstanding at December 31, 1996. On July 1, 1997, an additional 50,000 shares of common stock were issued for cash. Mann also had unexercised stock options to purchase 40,000 shares of common stock at $15 per share outstanding at the beginning and end of 1997. The average market price of Mann's common stock was $20 during 1997.

47. What is the number of shares that should be used in computing basic earnings per share for the year ended December 31, 1997?
a. 325,000
b. 335,000
c. 360,000
d. 365,000

(5/85, PI, #51, amended, 1296a)

48. What is the number of shares that should be used in computing diluted earnings per share for the year ended December 31, 1997?
a. 325,000
b. 335,000
c. 360,000
d. 365,000   (5/85, PI, #51, amended, 1296b)

49. Cox Corporation had 1,200,000 shares of common stock outstanding on January 1, and December 31, 1997. In connection with the acquisition of a subsidiary company in June 1996, Cox is required to issue 50,000 additional shares of its common stock on July 1, 1998, to the former owners of the subsidiary. Cox paid $200,000 in preferred stock dividends in 1997, and reported net income of $3,400,000 for the year. Cox's diluted earnings per share for 1997 should be

a. $2.83.
b. $2.72.
c. $2.67.
d. $2.56.   (5/84, PI, #49, amended, 1299)

50. Earnings per share data should be reported in the financial statements for

	Cumulative effect of a change in accounting principle	An extraordinary item
a.	Yes	No
b.	Yes	Yes
c.	No	Yes
d.	No	No

          (11/91, Theory, #16, amended, 2524)

OTHER OBJECTIVE FORMAT QUESTION

PROBLEM 15-2 (15 to 25 minutes)

ITEMS a THROUGH f are based on the following:

Daley Inc. is consistently profitable. Daley's normal financial statement relationships are as follows:

I.	Current ratio	3 to 1
II.	Inventory turnover	4 times
III.	Total debt/total assets ratio	0.5 to 1

REQUIRED:

FOR ITEMS a THROUGH f, determine whether each 1992 transaction or event increased, decreased, or had no effect on each of the 1992 ratios. For each ratio choose only one of the three alternatives.

ITEMS TO BE ANSWERED:

a. Daley issued a stock dividend.

b. Daley declared, but did not pay, a cash dividend.

c. Customers returned invoiced goods for which they had not paid.

d. Accounts payable were paid on December 31, 1992.

e. Daley recorded both a receivable from an insurance company and a loss from fire damage to a factory building.

f. Early in 1992, Daley increased the selling price of one of its products that had a demand in excess of capacity. The number of units sold in 1991 and 1992 was the same.   (5/93, Theory, #61-66)

PROBLEM/ESSAY QUESTIONS

PROBLEM 15-3 (20 to 25 minutes)

Mason Corporation's capital structure is as follows:

	December 31	
	1997	1996
Outstanding shares of:		
Common stock	336,000	300,000
Nonconvertible preferred stock	10,000	10,000
8% convertible bonds	$1,000,000	$1,000,000

The following additional information is available:

- On September 1, 1997, Mason sold 36,000 additional shares of common stock.
- Net income for the year ended December 31, 1997, was $750,000.
- During 1997, Mason paid dividends of $3.00 per share on its nonconvertible preferred stock.
- The 8% convertible bonds are convertible into 40 shares of common stock for each $1,000 bond.

- Unexercised stock options to purchase 30,000 shares of common stock at $22.50 per share were outstanding at the beginning and end of 1997. The average market price of Mason's common stock was $36 per share during 1997. The market price was $33 per share at December 31, 1997.

- Warrants to purchase 20,000 shares of common stock at $38 per share were attached to the preferred stock at the time of issuance. The warrants, which expire on December 31, 2002, were outstanding at December 31, 1997.

- Mason's effective income tax rate was 40% for 1996 and 1997.

REQUIRED (Show supporting computations in good form, and round earnings per share to the nearest penny):

a. Compute the number of shares which should be used for the computation of basic earnings per share for the year ended December 31, 1997.

b. Compute the basic earnings per share for the year ended December 31, 1997.

c. Compute the number of shares which should be used for the computation of diluted earnings per share for the year ended December 31, 1997.

d. Compute the diluted earnings per share for the year ended December 31, 1997.

(11/81, PI, #5b, amended)

ESSAY 15-4 (15 to 25 minutes)

Columbine Co. issued 10-year convertible bonds on October 1, 1996. Each $1,000 bond is convertible, at the holder's option, into 20 shares of Columbine's $25 par value common stock. The bonds were issued at a premium when the common stock traded at $45 per share. After payment of interest on October 1, 1998, 30% of the bonds were tendered for conversion when the common stock was trading at $57 per share. Columbine used the book value method to account for the conversion.

REQUIRED:

a. How should Columbine determine whether to include the convertible bonds in computing 1996 diluted earnings per share?

b. How does the inclusion of convertible bonds affect the computation of 1996 diluted earnings per share? (5/92, Theory, #3b, amended, 6196)

SOLUTION 15-1 MULTIPLE CHOICE ANSWERS

SOLVENCY

1. (a) The quick ratio is calculated by dividing the total of cash, marketable securities, and net receivables by current liabilities. Fluctuating market prices may cause the marketable securities in the numerator to decrease, thus creating an adverse effect on the quick ratio. Because inventory is not included in the quick ratio, increasing inventory market prices would have no effect on the quick ratio. The quick ratio provides a measure to help North evaluate if Belle has sufficient liquid assets, such as available-for-sale investments, to meet its current obligations. The quick ratio does not include inventory or long-term obligations.

2. (a) The sale of a company's trading securities at their carrying amounts for cash has no effect on either ratio. Both the trading securities and cash are current assets, thus the current asset amount does not change in the current ratio (current assets divided by current liabilities). The numerator of the quick ratio is cash plus marketable securities plus

net receivables; so cash increases for the same amount that marketable securities decreases.

3. (a) The balance sheet is the financial statement that should be primarily used to assess a company's liquidity and financial flexibility (SFAC 5, par. 24). The balance sheet, however, provides an incomplete picture of either a company's liquidity or financial flexibility, unless it is used in conjunction with at least a cash flow statement (*ibid*).

4. (a) When the current ratio is greater than 1:1, any decrease in current liabilities, even when accompanied by a decrease in current assets by an equal amount, will cause an increase in the current ratio. When the quick ratio is less than 1:1, any decrease in quick assets, even when accompanied by a decrease in current liabilities by an equal amount, will cause a decrease in the quick ratio.

5. (b) Current assets increase when inventory is sold on account at a profit because the increase in accounts receivable exceeds the related decrease in the inventory account. Since the current

ratio is computed by dividing current assets by current liabilities, selling inventory on account at a profit would increase the current ratio. The purchase of inventory on account increases both current assets and current liabilities by equal amounts. When the current ratio is greater than 1:1, an equal increase in both current assets and current liabilities will decrease the ratio. The collection of an account receivable takes place entirely within current assets. Therefore, the total amounts of current assets and current liabilities do not change as a result of the collection. Purchasing machinery for cash decreases current assets. Thus, the current ratio decreases as a result of this transaction.

6. (a)   The current ratio is computed by dividing current assets by current liabilities. The write-off of the inventory reduces current assets, the numerator of the current ratio, thereby decreasing the ratio. The quick ratio is computed by dividing cash, short-term marketable securities, and net receivables by current liabilities. Since inventory is not used in the calculation of the quick ratio, the ratio is not effected by the write-off of the inventory.

7. (b)   The purchase of the merchandise inventory with a short-term account payable increases both current assets and current liabilities by $50,000. Since Gil's current ratio before this transaction was less than 1.0 (i.e., $90,000 ÷ $180,000 = .5 to 1), increasing both current assets and current liabilities by the same amount increases the current ratio [i.e., ($90,000 + $50,000) ÷ ($180,000 + $50,000) = .61 to 1]. The current ratio is computed as follows:

$$Current\ ratio = \frac{Current\ assets}{Current\ liabilities}$$

8. (b)   The defensive-interval ratio is a liquidity ratio and the return on stockholders' equity is a profitability (performance) ratio. The defensive-interval ratio is computed by dividing defensive assets (cash, marketable securities, and net receivables) by projected daily expenditures from operations. Projected daily expenditures are computed by dividing cost of goods sold plus selling and administrative expenses and other ordinary cash expenses by 365 days. This ratio measures the time span a firm can operate on present liquid assets without resorting to revenues from a future period.

9. (d)   The acid-test (quick) ratio is a measure for assessing short-term liquidity risk; it measures a company's ability to meet its currently maturing or short-term obligations. On the other hand, the debt-to-equity ratio is a measure for assessing long-term liquidity risk; it measures the portion of assets being provided by creditors and the portion of assets being provided by the stockholders of a firm.

10. (b)   The maximum additional amount Barr will be able to borrow is $330,000, calculated as follows:

Current stockholders' equity	$ 700,000
Anticipated sales of stock	300,000
Total projected stockholders' equity	$1,000,000

Maximum debt-to-equity ratio: MD/$1,000,000 = .75

Maximum debt ($1,000,000 x .75)	$ 750,000
Less: current debt	(420,000)
Additional Barr may borrow	$ 330,000

11. (a)   During 1997, the exercise of the stock options increased Ali's total assets and total stockholders' equity by $8,000 (i.e., 1,000 x $8). The debt to equity ratio is computed by dividing total liabilities by total stockholders' equity. Therefore, the exercise of the stock options decreased the debt to equity ratio to 12% (i.e., $60,000 ÷ $500,000) because it increased total stockholders' equity, the denominator of the ratio, but did not affect total liabilities, the numerator of the ratio. Earnings per share (EPS) is computed by dividing net income to common stockholders by the weighted average number of common shares outstanding. The exercise of the stock options increased the weighted average number of common shares outstanding, the denominator of the earnings per share ratio, but did not affect net income to common stockholders, the numerator of the ratio, thereby decreasing 1997 EPS. Asset turnover is computed by dividing sales by average total assets. Since the exercise of the stock options increased total assets, Ali's asset turnover would decrease as a result of the exercise of the stock options.

12. (d)   The times-interest-earned (TIE) ratio measures an entity's ability to meet its interest payments. Note that income taxes are not subtracted from operating income because interest is tax deductible.

$$\frac{TIE}{Ratio} = \frac{\substack{Income\ before\\interest\ \&\\taxes}}{\substack{Interest\\expense}} = \frac{\$900,000}{\$100,000} = \textbf{9.0 to 1}$$

13. (c)   The times-preferred-dividend-earned (TPDE) ratio measures an entity's ability to meet preferred dividend payments. Because dividends are not tax deductible, this ratio is computed on the basis of net income (i.e., after income taxes).

$$\text{TPDE Ratio} = \frac{\text{Net income}}{\text{Preferred dividends}} = \frac{\$480,000}{\$200,000} = \textbf{2.4 to 1}$$

14. (a) The acid-test ratio is computed by dividing cash, short-term marketable securities, and net receivables by current liabilities.

$$\text{Acid-test ratio} = \frac{\text{Cash} + \text{Marketable securities} + \text{Net receivables}}{\text{Current liabilities}}$$

$$= (\$300 + \$0 + \$1,200) \div \$1,000 = \textbf{1.5}$$

OPERATIONAL EFFICIENCY

15. (c) To compute the average number of days to collect accounts receivable, the number of days in the year is divided by the accounts receivable turnover ratio for the year, as follows:

$$\text{Accounts receivable turnover ratio} = \frac{\text{Net credit sales}}{\text{Average net accounts receivable}}$$

$$= \frac{\$7,200}{[(\$1,200 - \$400) + \$1,200] \div 2}$$

$$= 7.2 \text{ times}$$

$$\text{Average number of days to collect accounts receivable} = \frac{\text{Number of days in year}}{\text{Accounts receivable turnover ratio}}$$

$$= 365 \div 7.2 = \textbf{50.7 days}$$

16. (a) Cash sales are not used to compute the accounts receivable turnover. The accounts receivable turnover ratio is computed by dividing net credit sales by average accounts receivable. Therefore, 1994 net credit sales can be computed as follows:

Average accounts receivable, [($20,000 + $22,000) ÷ 2]	$ 21,000
Accounts receivable turnover	x 5.0
Net credit sales	$105,000

17. (c) To compute the inventory turnover for 1994, the inventory at the end of 1994 must first be determined. The inventory turnover for 1994 can then be computed.

Inventory, 1/1/94	$ 6,000
Plus: Purchases	24,000
Goods available for sale	30,000
Less: Cost of goods sold	(18,000)
Inventory, 12/31/94	$ 12,000

$$\text{Inventory turnover} = \frac{\text{Cost of goods sold}}{\text{Average inventory}}$$

$$= \frac{\$18,000}{(\$6,000 + \$12,000) \div 2} = \textbf{2.0 times}$$

18. (b) The average days' sales in inventory is computed by dividing the number of days in the year (numerator) by the inventory turnover ratio (denominator).

19. (b) The collection of the receivable due from a major customer reduces net average receivables, the denominator of the ratio, thereby increasing the ratio. Neither cash nor accounts receivables are used in computing the inventory turnover ratio. Although the collection of an account receivable affects the composition of current assets, the numerator of the current ratio, the total amount of current assets is unchanged. The collection of an account receivable increases cash and decreases accounts receivable; thus, the total amount of the numerator of the quick ratio (i.e., cash + marketable securities + net receivables) is unchanged. The receivable turnover ratio is determined as follows:

$$\text{Receivable turnover} = \frac{\text{Net credit sales}}{\text{Net average receivables}}$$

20. (c) The receivables turnover is computed by dividing net credit sales by net average receivables. This calculation provides information related to how effectively an enterprise uses its assets because it provides a measure of how many times the receivables have been turned into cash during the year. The dividend payout ratio is computed by dividing dividends per common share by earnings per share. This ratio is an index showing whether an enterprise pays out most of its earnings in dividends or reinvests the earnings internally; it provides no information related to how effectively the enterprise uses its assets.

21. (b) To determine the inventory turnover for 1989, the beginning inventory at January 1, 1989, must first be determined by working backwards through the cost of goods sold schedule. The inventory turnover for 1989 can then be computed.

Cost of goods sold, 1989	$ 900,000
Add: Ending inventory, 12/31/89	180,000
Goods available for sale	1,080,000
Less: Purchases, 1989	(960,000)
Beginning inventory, 1/1/89	$ 120,000

$$\text{Inventory turnover} = \frac{\text{Cost of goods sold}}{\text{Average inventory}}$$

$$= \frac{\$900,000}{(\$120,000 + \$180,000) \div 2} = \textbf{6.0 times}$$

22. (a) The number of days' sales in average inventory is determined as follows:

$$\text{Number of days sales in average inventories} = \frac{\text{Average inventory}}{\text{Cost of goods sold} \div 300 \text{ business days}}$$

$$\frac{(\$336,000 + \$288,000) \div 2}{\$1,200,000 \div 300} \quad \frac{\$312,000}{\$4,000} = \textbf{78 days}$$

23. (d) The operating cycle is the average length of time that it takes to sell an inventory item and to collect the cash from the sale. The number of days in Clay's 1997 operating cycle is determined as follows:

Number of days' sales in inventory	61
Number of days' sales in accounts receivable	33
Number of days in Clay's 1997 operating cycle	94

24. (c) Neither ratio is useful for evaluating the effectiveness with which the company uses its assets. The acid-test (quick) ratio is a measure for assessing short-term liquidity risk; it measures a company's ability to meet its short-term obligations. The price-earnings ratio measures the relationship between the market price of a share of stock and the stock's current earnings per share.

PROFITABILITY

25. (d) The book value per common share is calculated as total stockholders' equity less preferred stockholders' equity, divided by the number of common shares outstanding. The liquidating value of the preferred stock of $300,000 ($250,000 par value + $50,000 premium) is used to determine preferred stockholders' equity because that amount exceeds the par value of the preferred stock. The cumulative preferred stock dividends in arrears of $25,000 is also used in determining preferred stockholders' equity because they must be paid before any dividends can be paid on the common shares.

$$\frac{\text{Book value per common share}}{} = \frac{\text{Stockholders' equity} - \text{Preferred stockholders' equity}}{\text{Common shares outstanding}}$$

$$\frac{\$1,025,000^* - (\$300,000 + \$25,000)}{100,000} = \$7.00$$

* $250,000 + $350,000 + $125,000 + $300,000

26. (d) The book value per preferred share is the portion of stockholders' equity distributable to preferred stockholders in the event of liquidation, divided by the number of preferred shares outstanding. For Frey Inc., the calculation would be as follows:

$$\frac{\text{Book value per preferred share}}{} = \frac{\text{Liquidation value} + \text{Dividends in arrears}}{\text{Preferred shares outstanding}}$$

$$\frac{(\$105 \times 1,000 \text{ sh.}) + (10\% \times \$100,000)}{1,000 \text{ shares}} = \$115 \text{ share}$$

27. (b) Cowl's rate of return on assets for 1994 is calculated as follows:

Rate of Return on Assets = Net Income ÷ Average Total Assets

$$\frac{\$150,000}{(\$2,000,000 + \$3,000,000) / 2} = \$150,000 \div \$2,500,000 = 6\%$$

28. (b) Successful use of leverage is where you can earn more by the use of borrowed money than it costs to use the borrowed funds. This is evidenced by a rate of return on investment that is greater than the cost of debt. Answer (a) is incorrect because the reason that the rate of return on stockholders' equity is less than the rate of return on investment is because the cost of borrowing exceeds the rate of return on investment (unsuccessful use of leverage). Answers (c) and (d) are not measures of successful use of leverage.

29. (c) To determine the price-earnings ratio on common stock, the earnings per share must first be computed, as follows:

$$\frac{\text{Earnings per share}}{} = \frac{\text{Net income} - \text{Preferred dividend requirement}}{\text{Weighted average common shares}}$$

$$= \frac{\$240,000 - \$0}{300,000} = \$.80$$

$$\frac{\text{Price earnings ratio}}{} = \frac{\text{Market price per share}}{\text{Earnings per share}} \quad \frac{\$12.00}{\$.80} = 15.0 \text{ to } 1$$

30. (b) Dividends per share for common stock are used in the numerator of the dividend per share payout ratio, but are not used in computing earnings per share. The dividend per share payout ratio and earnings per share are determined as follows:

$$\frac{\text{Dividend per share payout ratio}}{} = \frac{\text{Cash dividends per common share}}{\text{Earnings per share}}$$

$$\frac{\text{Earnings per share}}{} = \frac{\text{Net income to common stockholders}}{\text{Weighted average common shares outstanding}}$$

BASIC EPS

31. (a) For EPS, the denominator is the weighted-average number of common shares outstanding during the period. This number will include common shares outstanding the entire period, shares issued during the period, and shares where all of the conditions of issuance have been met. Deck Co. will calculate their number of shares as follows:

Common shares outstanding on January 1, 1998		120,000
Add: Common shares issued on July 1, 1998	40,000	
Times weight factor for shares issued in July (1/2 year)	x 50%	20,000
Weighted-average number of shares outstanding for 1998		140,000

In this case, there is no need for a separate diluted EPS adjustment because the preferred stock is not convertible.

32. (a)   In computing the weighted-average number of shares outstanding, stock dividends, stock splits, and reverse stock splits are reflected retroactively, because they change the total number of shares outstanding but not the proportionate shares outstanding. The purchase of treasury stock, the sale of additional common stock and preferred convertible stock affect the total number of shares and the proportionate shares outstanding. These shares participate in earnings for only the time the stock is outstanding.

33. (b)   Basic EPS, with a simple capital structure, is equal to net income minus the preferred dividends declared or the dividend preference on cumulative preferred stock for the current period (even though not declared) divided by the number of shares of common stock and common stock equivalents outstanding. ($500,000 – $10,000) / 200,000 = $2.45. The cumulative preferred's $10,000 dividend preference for 1996 that was paid in 1997 is not included in the calculation. The preferred dividends for the current year are included in the calculation, regardless of whether they have been paid.

34. (b)   Stock splits are given retroactive recognition in the computation of EPS. Shares issued must be weighted averaged according to the length of time they are outstanding. Since the preferred stock is nonconvertible, it does not affect the number of shares used to calculate EPS. The weighted average number of common shares outstanding during 1997, determined as follows, should be used to calculate 1997 earnings per share.

1/1	Common shares outstanding	20,000
4/1	Common shares issued due to 2-for-1 stock split	20,000
7/1	Common shares issued for cash (10,000 x 6/12)	5,000
	Weighted average common shares, 12/31/97	45,000

35. (d)   Stock dividends and common shares issued to effect a pooling of interest business combination are given retroactive recognition in the computation of EPS (i.e., the shares are assumed outstanding for the entire period regardless of when they were issued). The weighted average number of

common shares outstanding during 1997 is computed as follows:

1/1	Common shares outstanding	30,000
2/1	Common shares issued due to 10% stock dividend	3,000
3/1	Common shares issued in a pooling of interests	9,000
7/1	Common shares issued for cash (8,000 x 6/12)	4,000
	Weighted average common shares, 12/31/97	46,000

36. (b)   Earnings per share for 1997 and 1996 is $1.78 ($410,000 ÷ 230,000 shares) and $1.75 ($350,000 ÷ 200,000 shares), respectively. Stock dividends, stock splits, and reverse splits are given retroactive recognition in the computation of EPS for all periods presented. To compute EPS for 1997 and 1996, the weighted average number of common shares outstanding must be computed for each respective year.

	1997	1996
Common shares outstanding at 1/1	100,000	100,000
Sale of additional shares, 4/1/97 (20,000 x 9/12)	15,000	
2-for-1 stock split, 7/1/97		
(1996: 100,000 x 100%)		100,000
(1997: 115,000 x 100%)	115,000	
Weighted average common shares outstanding	230,000	200,000

37. (c)   Stock dividends, stock splits, and reverse splits consummated after the close of the period but before completion of the financial report are given retroactive recognition in the computation of EPS. The per share computations are based on the new number of shares because the reader's primary interest is presumed to be related to the current capital structure.

38. (c)   To reflect the actual conversion on July 1, 4,000 additional common shares are added to the 10,000 common shares outstanding since the beginning of the year, resulting in 12,000 weighted average common shares outstanding computed as follows:

$$10,000 \times 6/12 = 5,000$$
$$14,000 \times 6/12 = 7,000$$
$$12,000$$

Basic EPS is calculated by dividing the net income of $35,000 by the 12,000 weighted average common shares outstanding to yield $2.92 per share.

DILUTED EPS

39. (a)   Dilutive securities are included in the calculation of diluted EPS; thus, the convertible bonds would be included, reducing EPS of $15.00

by $0.75. Antidilutive securities are excluded from dilutive EPS; thus, the options are not included.

40. (b) Stock options should be used in the calculation of diluted EPS if the effect is dilutive (their inclusion has the effect of decreasing the EPS amount or increasing the loss per share amount otherwise computed).

41. (d) Convertible securities are only included in the computation of diluted EPS for any period for which their effect is dilutive.

42. (b) Earnings per share (EPS) is computed by dividing net income less preferred stock dividends by the weighted average shares of common stock outstanding. Diluted EPS adjusts this calculation to reflect all potentially dilutive securities. The convertible preferred stock is assumed converted at the beginning of the year. The preferred stock dividend of $120,000 (20,000 x $100 x 6%) is added back to the numerator (canceling out its original subtraction) and the 100,000 (20,000 x 5) shares of converted common stock are added to the denominator.

$$\frac{\$840,000 \; Net \; income}{200,000 \; Common \; + \; 100,000 \; Convertible \; preferred} = \$2.80$$

43. (b) Basic earnings per share (EPS) is computed by dividing net income less preferred stock dividends by the weighted average common shares of stock outstanding, as follows:

$$\frac{\$980,000 - 45,000}{90,000} = \$10.39$$

44. (d) Diluted EPS is computed in the same manner as basic EPS except that all convertible securities are assumed to be converted (if dilutive) and the numerator is adjusted accordingly. Therefore, diluted EPS is computed as follows:

$$\frac{\$980,000 \; NI \; + \; [\$100,000 \; (interest) - \$40,000 \; (tax)]}{90,000 \; (common) \; + \; 30,000 \; (convertible \; preferred) \; + \; 20,000 \; (convertible \; bonds)} = \$7.43$$

45. (b) Convertible debt is not included in the calculations of basic EPS. The interest expense is added back to net income in determining diluted EPS.

46. (a) Dilutive convertible securities are included in EPS computations under the if-converted method. Under that method, the security is assumed to have been converted at the beginning of the earliest period reported (or at time of issuance, if later).

47. (a) The number of shares used in computing basic EPS is the weighted average calculated as follows:

Common shares outstanding throughout period	300,000
Additional shares issued 7/1/97 (50,000 x 6/12)	25,000
CS outstanding for basic EPS computation	325,000

48. (b) The number of shares used in computing diluted EPS is calculated as follows:

Weighted average used for basic EPS	325,000
Options pretended exercised	40,000
Less treasury stock pretended purchased (40,000 x $15)/$20	(30,000)
Shares used in diluted EPS calculation	335,000

49. (d) If shares are to be issued in the future upon the mere passage of time, they should be considered as outstanding for the computation of EPS. Therefore, the diluted EPS for Cox would be calculated as follows:

$$\frac{NI - Preferred \; Dividend}{Outstanding \; Shares + Contingent \; Shares} = EPS$$

$$\frac{\$3,400,000 - \$200,000}{1,200,000 + 50,000} = \$2.56$$

FINANCIAL STATEMENT PRESENTATION

50. (b) Earnings per share amounts should be reported on the face of the income statement or in the notes to the financial statements for a discontinued operation, an extraordinary item, and the cumulative effect of an accounting change.

PERFORMANCE BY SUBTOPICS

Each category below parallels a subtopic covered in Chapter 15. Record the number and percentage of questions you correctly answered in each subtopic area.

Solvency

Question #	Correct √
1	
2	
3	
4	
5	
6	
7	
8	
9	
10	
11	
12	
13	
14	

Questions   14

Correct _____
% Correct _____

Operational Efficiency

Question #	Correct √
15	
16	
17	
18	
19	
20	
21	
22	
23	
24	

Questions   10

Correct _____
% Correct _____

Profitability

Question #	Correct √
25	
26	
27	
28	
29	
30	

Questions   6

Correct _____
% Correct _____

Basic EPS

Question #	Correct √
31	
32	
33	
34	
35	
36	
37	
38	

Questions   8

Correct _____
% Correct _____

Diluted EPS

Question #	Correct √
39	
40	
41	
42	
43	
44	
45	
46	
47	
48	
49	

Questions   11

Correct _____
% Correct _____

Financial Statement Presentation

Question #	Correct √
50	

Questions   1

Correct _____
% Correct _____

OTHER OBJECTIVE FORMAT SOLUTION

SOLUTION 15-2 RATIO ANALYSIS

a. The effect of the issuance of the stock dividend on the three ratios is as follows:

- Current Ratio—The current ratio is computed by dividing current assets by current liabilities. Since the issuance of the stock dividend was recorded entirely within Daley's stockholders' equity accounts, it had no effect on the amount of Daley's current assets or current liabilities. Thus, it also **had no effect** on Daley's current ratio.

- Inventory Turnover—The inventory turnover ratio is computed by dividing cost of goods sold by average inventory. Since the issuance of the stock dividend was recorded entirely within Daley's stockholders' equity accounts, it had no effect on the amount of Daley's cost of goods sold or average inventory. Thus, it also **had no effect** on Daley's inventory turnover ratio.

- Total Debt/Total Assets Ratio—Since the issuance of the stock dividend was recorded entirely within Daley's stockholders' equity accounts, it had no effect on the amount of Daley's total assets or total liabilities. Thus, it also **had no effect** on Daley's total debt/total assets ratio.

b. The effect of the declaration of the cash dividend on the three ratios is as follows:

- Current Ratio—The current ratio is computed by dividing current assets by current liabilities. The declaration of the cash dividend increased current liabilities, the denominator of the current ratio. Therefore, Daley's current ratio **decreased** as a result of the declaration of the cash dividend.

- Inventory Turnover—The inventory turnover ratio is computed by dividing cost of goods sold by average inventory. Since the declaration of the cash dividend had no effect on the amount of Daley's cost of goods sold or average inventory, it also **had no effect** on Daley's inventory turnover ratio.

- Total Debt/Total Assets Ratio—The declaration of the cash dividend increased total debt, the numerator of the ratio. Therefore, Daley's total debt/total assets ratio **increased** as a result of the declaration of the cash dividend.

c. The effect of the customer returns on the three ratios is as follows:

- Current Ratio—The current ratio is computed by dividing current assets by current liabilities. Assuming that the goods had been sold at a profit, the customer returns decreased current assets—the numerator of the current ratio—because the amount of the decrease to accounts receivable exceeded the amount of the increase to merchandise inventory. Therefore, Daley's current ratio **decreased** as a result of the customer returns.

- Inventory Turnover—The inventory turnover ratio is computed by dividing cost of goods sold by average inventory. The customer returns decreased cost of goods sold (the numerator of the ratio) and increased average inventory (the denominator of the ratio). Therefore, Daley's inventory turnover ratio **decreased** as a result of the customer returns.

- Total Debt/Total Assets Ratio—Assuming that the goods had been sold at a profit, the customer returns decreased total assets—the denominator of the ratio—because the amount of the decrease to accounts receivable exceeded the amount of the increase to merchandise inventory. Therefore, Daley's total debt/total assets ratio **increased** as a result of the customer returns.

d. The effect of the payment on the three ratios is as follows:

- Current Ratio—The current ratio is computed by dividing current assets by current liabilities. The payment of the accounts payable decreased current liabilities and current assets by an equal amount; therefore, since Daley's current ratio was greater than 1:1 (i.e., 3.0 to 1), Daley's current ratio **increased** as a result of the payment of the accounts payable.

- Inventory Turnover—The inventory turnover ratio is computed by dividing cost of goods sold by average inventory. Since the payment of the accounts payable had no effect on the amount of Daley's cost of good sold or average inventory, it also **had no effect** on Daley's inventory turnover ratio.

- Total Debt/Total Assets Ratio—The payment of the accounts payable decreased total debt and total assets by an equal amount; therefore, since the total debt/total assets ratio was less than 1:1 (i.e., 0.5 to 1), the ratio **decreased** as a result of the payment of the accounts payable.

e. Daley recorded both a receivable from an insurance company and a loss from fire damage to a factory building. The effect on the three ratios as a result of these events is as follows:

- Current Ratio—The current ratio is computed by dividing current assets by current liabilities. The recording of the receivable from the insurance company increased current assets, the numerator of the current ratio. Therefore, Daley's current ratio **increased** as a result of the recording of the receivable from the insurance company.

- Inventory Turnover—The inventory turnover ratio is computed by dividing cost of goods sold by average inventory. Since the recording of the receivable from the insurance company and the loss from fire damage to the factory building had no effect on the amount of Daley's cost of goods sold or average inventory, they also **had no effect** on Daley's inventory turnover ratio.

- Total Debt/Total Assets Ratio—Daley recorded a loss from the fire damage to the factory building. Therefore, the amount of the receivable recorded from the insurance company was less than the carrying amount of the building (or portion thereof) removed from the accounts. This decreased total assets, the denominator of the ratio. Therefore, Daley's total debt/total assets ratio **increased** as a result of these events.

f. Daley increased the selling price of one of its products that had a demand in excess of capacity. The number of units sold in 1991 and 1992 was the same. The effect of increased selling price on the three ratios is as follows:

- Current Ratio—The current ratio is computed by dividing current assets by current liabilities. Daley increased the selling price of a product that had a demand in excess of capacity. The number of units of the product sold in 1991 and 1992 was the same. Therefore, Daley was more profitable in 1992 than 1991. The increased profits increased retained earnings, which in turn increased total stockholders' equity; therefore, since the increase in the selling price of the product had no effect on total liabilities, total assets must have increased. Since noncurrent assets would not be affected by the increase in the product's selling price, current assets—the numerator of the current ratio—must have increased. Therefore, Daley's current ratio **increased** as a result of the increase in the selling price of the product.

- Inventory Turnover—The inventory turnover ratio is computed by dividing cost of goods sold by average inventory. Since the increase in the selling price of the product had no effect on the amount of Daley's cost of goods sold or average inventory, it also **had no effect** on Daley's inventory turnover ratio.

- Total Debt/Total Assets Ratio—Daley increased the selling price of one of its products that had a demand in excess of capacity. The number of units sold in 1991 and 1992 was the same.

Therefore, Daley was more profitable in 1992 than 1991. The increased profits increased retained earnings, which in turn increased total stockholders' equity. Since the increase in the selling price of the product increased total stockholders' equity while having no effect on total liabilities, it also increased total assets, the denominator of the ratio. Therefore, Daley's total debt/total assets ratio **decreased** as a result of the increase in the selling price of the product.

PROBLEM/ESSAY SOLUTIONS

SOLUTION 15-3 COMPREHENSIVE EPS PROBLEM

a.
Mason Corporation
NUMBER OF SHARES FOR COMPUTATION OF BASIC EARNINGS PER SHARE
For Year Ended December 31, 1997

Dates	Shares	Months outstanding	Weighted shares
Jan. 1 - Aug. 31	300,000	x 8/12	200,000
Sept. 1, sold additional shares	336,000	x 4/12	112,000
Weighted average number of shares outstanding			312,000

b.
Mason Corporation
COMPUTATION OF BASIC EARNINGS PER SHARE
For Year Ended December 31, 1997

Income:	
Net income	$750,000
Deduct dividends paid on preferred stock (10,000 shares x $3)	(30,000)
Net income, adjusted	$720,000
Number of shares (from Part **a.**)	÷312,000
Basic earnings per share	$ 2.31

c.
Mason Corporation
NUMBER OF SHARES FOR COMPUTATION OF DILUTED EARNINGS PER SHARE
For Year Ended December 31, 1997

Weighted average number of shares outstanding (from Part a.)	312,000
Common stock equivalents from stock options—dilutive*	11,250
Shares assumed to be issued upon conversion of convertible bonds ($1,000,000 ÷ $1,000 = 1,000 bonds x 40)	40,000
Total number of shares for diluted EPS computation	363,250

*Calculations:

Shares that would be issued upon exercise of options	30,000
Cash proceeds that would be realized upon exercise [30,000 shares x $22.50 (option price) = $675,000]	
Treasury shares that could be purchased [$675,000 ÷ $36 (average market price)]	(18,750)
Dilutive common stock equivalents	11,250

d.
Mason Corporation
COMPUTATION OF DILUTED EARNINGS PER SHARE
For Year Ended December 31, 1997

Income:	
Net income	$750,000
Deduct dividends paid on preferred stock (10,000 shares x $3)	(30,000)
Add interest expense (net of income tax effect) on convertible bonds [$1,000,000 x 8% x (1.0 – .40 tax rate)]	48,000
Net income, adjusted	$768,000
Number of shares (from Part **c.**)	÷363,250
Diluted earnings per share	$ 2.11

SOLUTION 15-4 CONVERTIBLE BONDS

a. If the bonds are **dilutive**, they are **included** in computing Columbine's 1996 diluted earnings per share.

b. Both **earnings and number of shares** are affected by including the convertible bonds in computing diluted earnings per share. **Interest expense** on convertible bonds, **net of income taxes**, is **added to net income**. The **number of shares outstanding** is **increased by** the number of shares **potentially issuable on conversion** (number of bonds times 20), **multiplied by** the **proportion of the year** that the **bonds were outstanding** (one-quarter).

CHAPTER 16

FINANCIAL REPORTING & CHANGING PRICES

CHAPTER 16

FINANCIAL REPORTING & CHANGING PRICES

I. OVERVIEW

A. OPTIONAL DISCLOSURE

A business enterprise that prepares its financial statements in U.S. dollars and in conformity with U.S. generally accepted accounting principles is encouraged, though not required, to disclose supplementary information on the effects of changing prices. SFAS 89, *Financial Reporting and Changing Prices*, provides guidelines of measurement and presentation for such disclosure.

B. DEFINITIONS

The following terms are defined in SFAS 89:

1. **CURRENT COST/CONSTANT PURCHASING POWER ACCOUNTING** A method of accounting based on measures of current cost or lower recoverable amount in units of currency, each of which has the same general purchasing power. For operations in which the dollar is the functional currency, the general purchasing power of the dollar is used, and the Consumer Price Index for All Urban Consumers (CPI-U) is the required measure of purchasing power.

2. **CURRENT MARKET VALUE** The amount of cash, or its equivalent, expected to be derived from the sale of an asset, net of costs required to be incurred as a result of the sale.

3. **HISTORICAL COST ACCOUNTING** The generally accepted method of accounting used in the primary financial statements that is based on measures of historical prices without restatement into units, each of which has the same general purchasing power.

4. **HISTORICAL COST/CONSTANT PURCHASING POWER ACCOUNTING** A method of accounting based on measures of historical prices in units of a currency, each of which has the same general purchasing power.

5. **INCOME FROM CONTINUING OPERATIONS** Income after applicable income taxes but excluding the results of discontinued operations, extraordinary items, the cumulative effect of accounting changes, purchasing power gains and losses on monetary items, and increases and decreases in the current cost or lower recoverable amount of nonmonetary assets and liabilities.

6. **MONETARY ASSET** Money or a claim to receive a sum of money, the amount of which is fixed or determinable without reference to future prices of specific goods or services.

7. **MONETARY LIABILITY** An obligation to pay a sum of money, the amount of which is fixed or determinable without reference to future prices of specific goods and services.

8. **PURCHASING POWER GAIN OR LOSS ON NET MONETARY ITEMS** The net gain or loss determined by restating in units of constant purchasing power the opening and closing balances of, and transactions in monetary assets and liabilities.

9. **RECOVERABLE AMOUNT** Current worth of the net amount of cash expected to be recoverable from the use or sale of an asset.

10. **VALUE IN USE** The amount determined by discounting the future cash flows (including the ultimate proceeds of disposal) expected to be derived from the use of an asset at an appropriate rate that allows for the risk of the activities concerned.

C.   MONETARY AND NONMONETARY ITEMS

1.   **MONETARY ASSETS** Monetary assets are defined as money or a claim to receive a sum of money, the amount of which is fixed or determinable without reference to future prices of specific goods or services.

EXHIBIT 1 ♦ MONETARY ASSETS

Time Deposits	Cash on hand and demand bank deposits
Bonds (other than convertible)	Foreign currency—on hand and claims to
Accounts and notes receivable	Preferred stock (nonconvertible and non-participating)
Loans to employees	Allowance for uncollectible accounts/notes receivable
Long-term receivables	Advances to unconsolidated subsidiaries
Refundable deposits	Cash surrender value of life insurance
Deferred tax assets	Advances to supplier—not on a fixed price contract

2.   **NONMONETARY ASSETS**

a.   Goods held primarily for resale or assets held primarily for direct use in providing services for the business of the enterprise.

b.   Claims to cash in amounts dependent on future prices of specific goods or services.

c.   Residual rights such as goodwill or equity interests.

EXHIBIT 2 ♦ NONMONETARY ASSETS

Investment in common stocks (in most circumstances)
Inventories (other than inventories used on contracts)
Property, plant, and equipment (PP&E)
Accumulated depreciation of PP&E
Purchase commitments—portion paid on fixed-price contracts
Patents, trademarks, licenses, and formulas
Goodwill
Other intangible assets and deferred charges

3.   **ASSETS REQUIRING INDIVIDUAL ANALYSIS**

a.   **PREFERRED STOCK (CONVERTIBLE OR PARTICIPATING) AND CONVERTIBLE BONDS** If the market values the security primarily as a bond, it is monetary; if it values the security primarily as stock, it is nonmonetary.

b.   **INVENTORIES USED ON CONTRACTS** If the future cash receipts on the contracts will not vary due to future changes in specific prices, they are monetary. Goods used on contracts to be priced at market upon delivery are nonmonetary.

c.   **PENSION, SINKING, AND OTHER FUNDS UNDER AN ENTERPRISE'S CONTROL** The specific assets in the fund should be classified as monetary or nonmonetary.

4.   **MONETARY LIABILITIES** Monetary liabilities are obligations to pay a sum of money, the amount of which is fixed or determinable without reference to future prices of specific goods or services.

EXHIBIT 3 ♦ MONETARY LIABILITIES

Account and notes payable	Obligations payable in foreign currency
Accrued expenses payable	Customer advances—not on fixed price contracts
Cash dividends payable	Accrued losses on firm purchase commitments
Refundable deposits	Bonds payable and other long-terms debt
Convertible bonds payable	Unamortized premium or discount and prepaid interest
Deferred tax	on bonds or notes payable

5. NONMONETARY LIABILITIES

a. Obligations to furnish goods or services in quantities that are fixed or determinable without reference to changes in prices.

b. Obligations to pay cash in amounts dependent on future prices of specific goods or services.

EXHIBIT 4 ♦ NONMONETARY LIABILITIES

Sales commitments—portion collected on fixed-price contracts
Obligations under warranties
Deferred investment tax credits
Minority interests in consolidated subsidiaries

6. LIABILITIES REQUIRING SPECIAL ANALYSIS Liabilities requiring special analysis include deferred revenue. If an obligation to furnish goods or services is involved, deferred revenue is nonmonetary.

7. STOCKHOLDERS' EQUITY—PREFERRED STOCK Capital stock of the enterprise or of its consolidated subsidiaries subject to mandatory redemption at fixed amounts is considered a monetary item. Therefore, preferred stock, which is fixed in terms of dollars to be paid in liquidation, is classified as a monetary item.

D. PRESENTATION GUIDELINES FOR SUGGESTED SUPPLEMENTARY INFORMATION

1. FIVE-YEAR SUMMARY OF SELECTED FINANCIAL DATA Enterprises are encouraged to provide information for each of the five most recent years for net sales and other operating revenues; income from continuing operations on a current cost basis; the purchasing power gain or loss on net monetary items; the increase or decrease in the current cost or lower recoverable amount of inventory and property, plant, and equipment, net of inflation; the aggregate foreign currency translation adjustment on a current cost basis, if applicable; net assets at year-end on a current cost basis; income per common share from continuing operations on a current cost basis; cash dividends declared per common share; and the market price per common share at year-end.

2. ADDITIONAL DISCLOSURES FOR THE CURRENT YEAR If income from continuing operations on a current cost/constant purchasing power basis would differ significantly from that reported in the primary financial statements, enterprises are encourage to provide information about the current cost basis on the components, including the cost of goods sold, and the depreciation, depletion, and amortization expense. The information may be presented in a statement format or in a reconciliation format.

The enterprise is also encouraged to disclose separate amounts for the current cost of lower recoverable amount at the end of the current year of inventory and PPE; the increase or decrease in current cost or lower recoverable amount before and after adjusting for the effects of inflation of inventory and PPE for the current year; the principal types of information used to calculate the current cost of inventory, PPE, cost of goods sold, and depreciation depletion, and amortization expense; and any differences between the depreciation methods, estimates of useful lives, and salvage values of assets used for calculations of current cost/constant purchasing power depreciation and the methods and estimates used for calculations of depreciation in the primary financial statements.

II. MEASUREMENT OF SUGGESTED SUPPLEMENTARY INFORMATION

A. INVENTORY AND PROPERTY, PLANT, AND EQUIPMENT
Current cost amounts of inventory and property, plant, and equipment (PP&E) are measured as follows:

1. **INVENTORY AT CURRENT COST OR LOWER RECOVERABLE AMOUNT AT THE MEASUREMENT DATE**
The current cost of inventory owned by an enterprise is the current cost of purchasing the goods concerned or the current cost of the resources required to produce the goods concerned (including an allowance for overhead), whichever would be applicable in the circumstances of the enterprise.

EXAMPLE 1 ♦ CURRENT COST OF INVENTORY

Rice Wholesaling Corp. accounts for inventory on a FIFO basis. There were 8,000 units in inventory on January 1, 20X6. Costs were incurred and goods purchased as follows during 20X6.

20X6	Historical costs	Units purchased	Units sold
1st quarter	$ 410,000	7,000	7,500
2nd quarter	550,000	8,500	7,300
3rd quarter	425,000	6,500	8,200
4th quarter	630,000	9,000	7,000
	$2,015,000	31,000	30,000

Rice estimates that the current cost per unit of inventory was $57 at January 1, 20X6, and $71 at December 31, 20X6.

REQUIRED: Determine the amount of December 31, 20X6 inventory to be reported in Rice's voluntary supplementary information restated into current cost.

SOLUTION:

Units in inventory, 1/1/X6	8,000
Units purchased during 20X6	31,000
Units available for sale	39,000
Units sold during 20X6	(30,000)
Units in inventory, 12/31/X6	9,000
Times: Current cost per unit, 12/31/X6	x $71
Current cost of inventory, 12/31/X6	$639,000

NOTE: The FIFO inventory cost flow method used for the primary financial statements is irrelevant to the computation of the current cost of the year-end inventory.

2. **PROPERTY, PLANT, AND EQUIPMENT AT THE CURRENT COST OR LOWER RECOVERABLE AMOUNT OF THE ASSETS' REMAINING SERVICE POTENTIAL AT THE MEASUREMENT DATE** The current cost of PP&E owned by an enterprise is the current cost of acquiring the same service potential as embodied by the asset owned; the information used to measure current cost reflects whatever method of acquisition would be currently appropriate in the circumstances of the enterprise. The current cost of a used asset may be calculated as follows:

a. By measuring the current cost of a new asset that has the same service potential as the used asset when it was new (the current cost of the asset as if it were new) and deducting an allowance for depreciation.

b. By measuring the current cost of a used asset of the same age and in the same condition as the asset owned.

c. By measuring the current cost of a new asset with a different service potential and adjusting that cost for the value of the difference in service potential due to differences in life, output capacity, nature of service, and operating costs.

EXAMPLE 2 ♦ CURRENT COST OF PROPERTY, PLANT, & EQUIPMENT

Details of Poe Corp.'s plant assets at December 31, 20X6, are as follows:

Year acquired	Percent depreciated	Historical cost	Estimated current cost
20X4	30	$200,000	$280,000
20X5	20	60,000	76,000
20X6	10	80,000	88,000

Poe calculated depreciation at 10% per annum, using the straight-line method. A full year's depreciation is charged in the year of acquisition. There were no disposals of plant assets.

REQUIRED: Determine the net current cost (after accumulated depreciation) of the plant assets at December 31, 20X6, to be reported in Poe's voluntary supplementary information restated into current cost.

SOLUTION:

Year	Estimated current cost	Percent not depreciated	Net current cost
20X4	$280,000	70%	$196,000
20X5	76,000	80%	60,800
20X6	88,000	90%	79,200
Net current cost of plant assets at 12/31/X6			$336,000

B. RECOVERABLE AMOUNT

Recoverable amount is the current worth of the net amount of cash expected to be recoverable from the use or sale of an asset.

1. **MEASUREMENT** It may be measured by considering the value in use or current market value of the asset concerned. Value in use is used to determine recoverable amount of an asset if immediate sale of the asset is not intended. Current market value is used to determine recoverable amount only if the asset is about to be sold.

2. **GROUPING OF ASSETS** If the recoverable amount for a group of assets is judged to be materially and permanently lower than the current cost amount, the recoverable amount is used as a measure of the assets and of the expense associated with the use or sale of the assets. Decisions on the measurement of assets at their recoverable amount need not be made by considering assets individually unless they are used independently of other assets.

EXAMPLE 3 ♦ CURRENT COST OR LOWER RECOVERABLE AMOUNT OF INVENTORY AND PP&E

At December 31, 20X7, Jannis Corp. owned two assets as follows:

	Equipment	Inventory
Current cost	$100,000	$80,000
Recoverable amount	95,000	90,000

REQUIRED: Determine the amount of total assets that Jannis should report in voluntarily disclosed supplementary information about current cost at December 31, 20X7.

SOLUTION:

Equipment	$ 95,000	(Recoverable amount lower than current cost)
Inventory	80,000	(Current cost lower than recoverable amount)
Total assets at 12/31/X7	$175,000	

C. INCOME FROM CONTINUING OPERATIONS

An enterprise presenting the minimum information encouraged by SFAS 89 shall measure income from continuing operations on a current cost basis as follows:

1. **COST OF GOODS SOLD** Cost of goods sold at current cost or lower recoverable amount at the date of sale. To compute cost of goods sold on a current cost basis, multiply the number of units sold by the average current cost of the units during the period. (Average current cost of the units during the period is the sum of the current cost of the units at the beginning and the end of the period, divided by two.)

EXAMPLE 4 ♦ CURRENT COST OF COST OF GOODS SOLD

Refer to the facts in Example 1 for Rice Wholesaling Corp.

REQUIRED: Determine the cost of goods sold for 20X6 restated into current cost.

SOLUTION:

Average current cost per unit, 20X6 [($57 + $71) ÷ 2]	$ 64
Units sold, 20X6	x 30,000
Cost of goods sold, average current cost, 20X6	$1,920,000

NOTE: The FIFO inventory cost flow method used for the primary financial statements is irrelevant to the current cost computation of the cost of goods sold for the year.

2. **DEPRECIATION/DEPLETION/AMORTIZATION EXPENSE** Depreciation, depletion, and amortization expense of PP&E on the basis of the *average* current cost of the assets' service potential or lower recoverable amount during the period of use. To compute depreciation on a current cost basis, divide the average current cost of the plant asset during the period by its estimated useful life. (Average current cost of the plant asset is the sum of the current cost of the plant asset at the beginning and the end of the period, divided by two.)

EXAMPLE 5 ♦ DEPRECIATION EXPENSE BASED ON AVERAGE CURRENT COST

Kerr Company purchased a machine for $115,000 on January 1, 20X5, the company's first day of operations. At the end of the year, the current cost of the machine was $125,000. The machine has no salvage value, a five-year life, and is depreciated by the straight-line method.

REQUIRED: For the year ended December 31, 20X5, determine the amount of the current cost depreciation expense that would appear in voluntary supplementary current cost information.

SOLUTION:

Average current cost for 20X5 ($115,000 + $125,000) ÷ 2]	$120,000
Estimated useful life	÷ 5
Current cost depreciation for 20X5	$ 24,000

3. **OTHER REVENUES/EXPENSES AND GAINS/LOSSES** Other revenues, expenses, gains, and losses may be measured at the amounts included in the primary income statement.

D. **CHANGE IN THE CURRENT COSTS OF INVENTORY AND PP&E, NET OF INFLATION**
The increase or decrease in the current cost amounts of inventory and property, plant, and equipment represents the difference between the measures of the assets at their entry dates for the year and the measures of the assets at their exit dates for the year.

1. **ENTRY DATE** Entry date means the beginning of the year or the date of acquisition, whichever is applicable.

2. **EXIT DATE** Exit date means the end of the year or the date of use or sale, whichever is applicable.

3. **INFLATION COMPONENT** The inflation component of the increase in current cost amount is the difference between the nominal dollar and constant dollar measures.

E. **RESTATEMENT OF CURRENT COST INFORMATION INTO UNITS OF CONSTANT PURCHASING POWER**
Enterprises that do not have significant foreign operations are to use the CPI-U to restate current costs into units of constant purchasing power.

F. **PURCHASING POWER GAIN OR LOSS ON NET MONETARY ITEMS**
The purchasing power gain or loss on net monetary items is the net gain or loss determined by restating in units of constant purchasing power the opening and closing balances of, and transactions in, monetary assets and monetary liabilities.

1. **ECONOMIC SIGNIFICANCE** The economic significance of monetary assets and liabilities depends heavily on the general purchasing power of money, although other factors may affect their significance. The economic significance of nonmonetary items depends heavily on the value of specific goods and services.

2. **GAINS** Purchasing power gains result from holding

a. **MONETARY LIABILITIES DURING INFLATION** Monetary liabilities during a period of inflation because the obligations will be settled with dollars that have less purchasing power.

b. **MONETARY ASSETS DURING DEFLATION** Monetary assets during a period of deflation because a fixed amount of money will purchase more goods and services following a period of deflation.

3. **LOSSES** Purchasing power losses result from holding

    a. **MONETARY ASSETS DURING INFLATION** Monetary assets during a period of *inflation* because the fixed amount of money will purchase *fewer* goods and services following a period of inflation.

EXAMPLE 6 ♦ PURCHASING POWER LOSS ON NET MONETARY ITEMS

Lang Co.'s monetary assets exceeded monetary liabilities by $3,000 at the beginning of 20X7 and $4,000 at the end of 20X7. On January 1, the general price level was 125. On December 31, the general price level was 150.

REQUIRED: Determine the amount of Lang's 20X7 purchasing power gain or loss on net monetary items.

SOLUTION:

	Nominal Dollars	Conversion Factor	Restated into 20X7 Dollars
Net monetary assets, 1/1/X7	$3,000	150/125	$ 3,600
Change in net monetary assets during 20X7	1,000	*	1,000
Balance in net monetary assets, 12/31/X7	$4,000	150/150	(4,000)
Purchasing power loss on net monetary assets			$ 600

*Assumed to be in average 20X7 dollars.

    b. **MONETARY LIABILITIES DURING DEFLATION** Monetary liabilities during a period of *deflation* because the obligation will be settled with dollars that have *more* purchasing power.

4. **HOLDING NONMONETARY ITEMS** The holding of *nonmonetary* items during a period of changing prices does **not** give rise to purchasing power gains or losses.

EXHIBIT 5 ♦ PURCHASING POWER GAINS AND LOSSES

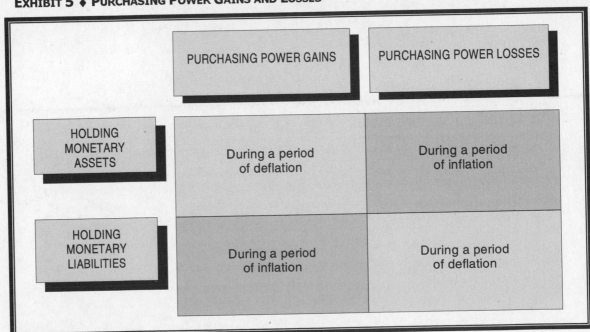

G.   HOLDING GAINS AND LOSSES ON NONMONETARY ASSETS
Current cost financial statements measure and report both *realized* and *unrealized* holding gains and losses on *nonmonetary* assets.

1.   **REALIZED HOLDING GAINS/LOSSES** Realized holding gains and losses occur when the non-monetary asset has been *sold* or *consumed* in the earnings process. An increase in the current cost of inventory items sold is an example of a realized holding gain.

2.   **UNREALIZED HOLDING GAINS/LOSSES** Unrealized holding gains and losses occur when the nonmonetary asset is *held* from period to period. A decrease in the current cost of inventory items on hand is an example of an unrealized holding loss.

CHAPTER 16—FINANCIAL REPORTING & CHANGING PRICES

PROBLEM 16-1 MULTIPLE CHOICE QUESTIONS (30 to 38 minutes)

1. Financial statements prepared under which of the following methods include adjustments for both specific price changes and general price-level changes?
a. Historical cost/nominal dollar
b. Current cost/nominal dollar
c. Current cost/constant dollar
d. Historical cost/constant dollar
(11/95, FAR, #57, 6139)

2. DeeCee Co. adjusted its historical cost income statement by applying specific price indexes to its depreciation expense and cost of goods sold. DeeCee's adjusted income statement is prepared according to
a. Fair value accounting.
b. General purchasing power accounting.
c. Current cost accounting.
d. Current cost/general purchasing power accounting. (11/93, Theory, #2, 4507)

3. During a period of inflation, the specific price of a parcel of land increased at a lower rate than the consumer price index. The accounting method that would measure the land at the highest amount is
a. Historical cost/nominal dollar.
b. Current cost/nominal dollar.
c. Current cost/constant dollar.
d. Historical cost/constant dollar.
(5/90, Theory, #3, 1910)

4. The following assets were among those that appeared on Baird Co.'s books at the end of the year:

Demand bank deposits	$650,000
Net long-term receivables	400,000
Patents and trademarks	150,000

In preparing constant dollar financial statements, how much should Baird classify as monetary assets?
a. $1,200,000
b. $1,050,000
c. $ 800,000
d. $ 650,000 (5/90, PII, #50, 1245)

5. The following items were among those that appeared on Rubi Co.'s books at the end of 1997:

Merchandise inventory	$600,000
Loans to employees	20,000

What amount should Rubi classify as monetary assets in preparing constant dollar financial statements?
a. $0
b. $ 20,000
c. $600,000
d. $620,000 (5/89, PII, #13, amended, 1247)

6. A company that wishes to disclose information about the effect of changing prices in accordance with Statement of Financial Accounting Standards No. 89, *Financial Accounting and Changing Prices,* should report this information in
a. The body of the financial statements.
b. The notes to the financial statements.
c. Supplementary information to the financial statements.
d. Management's report to shareholders.
(11/94, FAR, #4, 5269)

7. In its financial statements, Hila Co. discloses supplemental information on the effects of changing prices in accordance with Statement of Financial Accounting Standards No. 89, *Financial Reporting and Changing Prices.* Hila computed the increase in current cost of inventory as follows:

Increase in current cost (nominal dollars)	$15,000
Increase in current cost (constant dollars)	$12,000

What amount should Hila disclose as the inflation component of the increase in current cost of inventories?
a. $ 3,000
b. $12,000
c. $15,000
d. $27,000 (5/94, FAR, #58, 4873)

8. Manhof Co. prepares supplementary reports on income from continuing operations on a current cost basis in accordance with FASB Statement No. 89, *Financial Reporting and Changing Prices.* How should Manhof compute cost of goods sold on a current cost basis?
a. Number of units sold times average current cost of units during the year.
b. Number of units sold times current cost of units at year end.
c. Number of units sold times current cost of units at the beginning of the year.
d. Beginning inventory at current cost plus cost of goods purchased less ending inventory at current cost. (11/92, Theory, #40, 3473)

9. Information with respect to Bruno Co.'s cost of goods sold for 1997 is as follows:

	Historical cost	Units
Inventory, 1/1/97	$ 1,060,000	20,000
Production during 1997	5,580,000	90,000
	6,640,000	110,000
Inventory, 12/31/97	(2,520,000)	(40,000)
Cost of goods sold	$ 4,120,000	70,000

Bruno estimates that the current cost per unit of inventory was $58 at January 1, 1997 and $72 at December 31, 1997. In Bruno's supplementary information restated into average current cost, the cost of goods sold for 1997 should be
a. $5,040,000.
b. $4,550,000.
c. $4,410,000.
d. $4,060,000.   (11/89, PI, #59, amended, 1246)

ITEMS 10 AND 11 are based on the following data:

In a period of rising general price levels, Pollard Corp. discloses income on a current cost basis in accordance with FASB Statement No. 89, *Financial Reporting and Changing Prices*

10. Compared to historical cost income from continuing operations, which of the following conditions increases Pollard's current cost income from continuing operations?
a. Current cost of equipment is greater than historical cost.
b. Current cost of land is greater than historical cost
c. Current cost of cost of goods sold is less than historical cost.
d. Ending net monetary assets are less than beginning net monetary assets.
     (5/92, Theory, #4, 2696)

11. Which of the following contributes to Pollard's purchasing power loss on net monetary items?
a. Refundable deposits with suppliers
b. Equity investment in unconsolidated subsidiaries
c. Warranty obligations
d. Wages payable   (5/92, Theory, #5, 2697)

12. During a period of inflation in which an asset account remains constant, which of the following occurs?
a. A purchasing power gain, if the item is a monetary asset.
b. A purchasing power gain, if the item is a nonmonetary asset.
c. A purchasing power loss, if the item is a monetary asset.
d. A purchasing power loss, if the item is a nonmonetary asset.   (5/94, FAR, #59, 4874)

13. When computing purchasing power gain or loss on net monetary items, which of the following accounts is classified as nonmonetary?
a. Advances to unconsolidated subsidiaries
b. Allowance for uncollectible accounts
c. Unamortized premium on bonds payable
d. Accumulated depreciation of equipment
     (11/93, Theory, #1, 4506)

14. Could current cost financial statements report holding gains for goods sold during the period and holding gains on inventory at the end of the period?

	Goods sold	Inventory
a.	Yes	Yes
b.	Yes	No
c.	No	Yes
d.	No	No

     (5/91, Theory, #2, 1894)

15. The following information pertains to each unit of merchandise purchased for resale by Vend Co.:

	March 1, 1991	December 31, 1991
Purchase price	$ 8	
Selling price	12	$ 15
Price level index	110	121
Replacement cost		10

Under current cost accounting, what is the amount of Vend's holding gain on each unit of this merchandise?
a. $0
b. $0.80
c. $1.20
d. $2.00   (5/92, PII, #13, 2645)

SOLUTION 16-1 MULTIPLE CHOICE ANSWERS

DEFINITIONS

1. (c) Financial statements prepared under the current cost/constant dollar method of accounting include adjustments for both specific price changes and general price-level changes. Historical cost/nominal dollar is the generally accepted method of accounting based on measures of historical prices without restatement. Current cost/nominal dollar is a method of accounting in which adjustments for specific price changes are made but not for general price-level changes. Historical cost/constant dollar

is a method of accounting in which adjustments are not made for specific price changes but are made for general price-level changes.

2. (c) DeeCee adjusts the depreciation and cost of goods sold reported in the historical cost income statement by applying specific price indexes to these amounts. Therefore, DeeCee's adjusted income statement is prepared using current cost accounting. The income statement is not prepared using fair value accounting because only depreciation expense and cost of goods sold are restated by applying specific price indexes. The income statement is not prepared using general purchasing power accounting because DeeCee's historical costs are not remeasured into units of a currency with the same general purchasing power. The income statement is not prepared using current cost/general purchasing power accounting because amounts are not remeasured into units of a currency with the same general purchasing power.

3. (d) During a period of inflation, the specific rate of the parcel of land increased at a *lower rate* than the consumer price index. Therefore, the land would be reported at the highest amount under the historical cost/constant dollar method of accounting, since the land, a nonmonetary asset, would be reported at its historical cost measured in constant dollars. Under the historical cost/nominal dollar method of accounting, the land would be reported at its historical cost in the financial statements. The historical cost of the land would not be remeasured to reflect the change in the general purchasing power of the dollar that occurred during the period of inflation. The current cost/nominal dollar and current cost/constant dollar methods require that the land be reported at its current cost which is less than the amount that would be reported for the historical cost of the land measured in constant dollars because the specific price of the parcel of land increased at a *lower rate* than the consumer price index.

4. (b) Monetary assets represent a claim to receive a fixed sum of money or an amount determinable without reference to future prices of specific goods and services. The demand bank deposits and net long-term receivables are monetary assets as they represent claims to receive a fixed sum of money, the amounts of which can be determined without reference to future prices of specific goods and services. All assets that are not monetary are nonmonetary. The patents and trademarks do not represent a claim to receive cash, and hence are classified as nonmonetary assets.

5. (b) Monetary assets represent a claim to receive a fixed sum of money or an amount

determinable without reference to future prices of specific goods and services. All assets that are not monetary are nonmonetary. The merchandise inventory does not represent a claim to receive cash, and hence is classified as a nonmonetary asset. The loans to employees is a monetary asset as it does represent a claim to receive a fixed sum of money, the amount of which can be determined without reference to future prices of specific goods and services.

PRESENTATION

6. (c) A company disclosing voluntary information about the effect of changing prices should report this information in the supplementary information to the financial statements (SFAS 89, par. 3). This information should not be reported in the body of the financial statements, the notes to the financial statements, or management's report to shareholders.

INCREASE/DECREASE IN CURRENT COSTS

7. (a) Under SFAS 89, the "inflation component" of the increase in the current cost amount is defined as the difference between the nominal dollars and constant dollars measures.

CURRENT COST INCOME FROM CONTINUING OPERATIONS

8. (a) To compute cost of goods sold on a current cost basis, multiply the number of units sold by the average current cost of the units during the year. (Average current cost of the units during the year is the sum of the current cost of the units at the beginning and the end of the year, divided by two.)

9. (b) The cost of goods sold is restated into average current cost as follows:

Average current cost per unit, 1997 [($58 + $72) ÷ 2]	$ 65
Times: Units sold, 1997	x 70,000
Cost of goods sold, average current cost, 1997	$4,550,000

10. (c) When current cost of goods sold is less than historical cost, current cost income from continuing operations will be greater than historical cost income from continuing operations. More depreciation expense will be included in current cost income from continuing operations than historical cost income from continuing operations when the current cost of equipment is greater than historical cost. Until the land is sold, the difference in its current cost and historical cost will not affect either current cost or historical cost income from continuing operations. A purchasing power loss occurs when ending net monetary assets are less than beginning net monetary assets for a period in which there were

rising general price levels. Purchasing power gains and losses are not included in either current cost or historical cost income from continuing operations.

PURCHASING POWER GAIN/LOSS

11. (a) An entity suffers purchasing power losses in a period of rising general price levels from holding monetary assets. A monetary asset is money or a claim to receive a sum of money, the amount of which is fixed or determinable without reference to future prices of specific goods and services. A refundable deposit with a supplier is a monetary asset. An equity investment in unconsolidated subsidiaries is a nonmonetary asset. Warranty obligations are nonmonetary liabilities. Wages payable is a monetary liability. An entity would have purchasing power gains in a period of rising general price levels from holding monetary liabilities.

12. (c) Purchasing power *losses* result from holding monetary assets during a period of inflation because the fixed amount of money will purchase fewer goods and services following a period of inflation. The holding of nonmonetary items during a period of changing prices does not give rise to purchasing power gains or losses.

13. (d) In classifying balance sheet accounts as monetary or nonmonetary, a valuation account is classified the same as the account to which it relates. Accumulated depreciation on equipment is classified as nonmonetary because it is a valuation account to equipment, which is nonmonetary. Advances to unconsolidated subsidiaries is a receivable, and thus is monetary. Allowance for uncollectible accounts is a valuation allowance to accounts receivable, which is monetary. Premium on bonds payable is a valuation account to bonds payable, which is monetary.

HOLDING GAIN/LOSS

14. (a) An increase in the current cost of inventory items sold is a realized holding gain. An increase in the current cost of inventory items on hand is an unrealized holding gain. Current cost financial statements will measure and report both realized and unrealized holding gains (SFAS 89, par. 34).

15. (d) Under current cost accounting, the amount of holding gain on a unit of inventory is the increase in current cost from holding the inventory from period to period. The inventory in question was purchased at $8 per unit in 1991 and has a replacement cost of $10 on December 31, 1991. Therefore, under current cost accounting, Vend has a holding gain of $2 ($10 – $8) on each unit of the inventory.

PERFORMANCE BY SUBTOPICS

Each category below parallels a subtopic covered in Chapter 16. Record the number and percentage of questions you correctly answered in each subtopic area.

Definitions

Question #	Correct √
1	
2	
3	
4	
5	
# Questions	5

# Correct	_____
% Correct	_____

Presentation

Question #	Correct √
6	
# Questions	1

# Correct	_____
% Correct	_____

Increase/Decrease in Current Costs

Question #	Correct √
7	
# Questions	1

# Correct	_____
% Correct	_____

Current Cost Income From Continuing Operations

Question #	Correct √
8	
9	
10	
# Questions	3

# Correct	_____
% Correct	_____

Purchasing Power Gain/Loss

Question #	Correct √
11	
12	
13	
# Questions	3

# Correct	_____
% Correct	_____

Holding Gain/Loss

Question #	Correct √
14	
15	
# Questions	2

# Correct	_____
% Correct	_____

CHAPTER 17

FOREIGN OPERATIONS

CHAPTER 17

FOREIGN OPERATIONS

I. TRANSLATION OF FOREIGN CURRENCY FINANCIAL STATEMENTS

A. GAAP

SFAS 52, *Foreign Currency Translation*, deals with two main subjects: (1) translation of foreign currency financial statements and (2) foreign currency transactions, which include foreign currency forward exchange contracts.

B. OBJECTIVES OF TRANSLATION

1. Provide information that is generally compatible with the expected economic effects of a rate change on an enterprise's cash flows and equity.

2. Reflect in consolidated statements the financial results and relationships of the individual consolidated entities as measured in their **functional currencies** in conformity with U.S. generally accepted accounting principles.

C. FUNCTIONAL CURRENCY

The assets, liabilities, and operations of a foreign entity should be measured in its functional currency.

1. **DEFINITION** An entity's functional currency is the currency of the primary economic environment in which the entity operates; normally, that is the currency of the environment in which an entity primarily generates and expends cash. An entity's functional currency is basically a matter of fact. In some cases, however, the nature of a foreign entity's operations is such that its functional currency is not clearly determinable. Section V. of this chapter provides a series of factors that should be considered in determining an entity's functional currency.

2. **DETERMINING FUNCTIONAL CURRENCY** The functional currency of a foreign entity may be its **local currency**, the **U.S. dollar**, or **another foreign currency**.

   a. **LOCAL CURRENCY IS THE FUNCTIONAL CURRENCY** Where a foreign operation is relatively self-contained (i.e., most activities are performed independently of the parent company) and integrated within one country, the entity's functional currency will be the local currency. In this case, **translation** of financial statements from the functional currency into the parent's reporting currency (e.g., the U.S. dollar) will be required.

   b. **U.S. DOLLAR IS THE FUNCTIONAL CURRENCY** Where the foreign operation is, in essence, an extension of the parent's U.S. operations (e.g., a sales branch that purchases all its inventory from the U.S. home office, in U.S. dollars), the functional currency will be the U.S. dollar.

      (1) If the foreign entity's books are kept in the local currency, then **remeasurement** into U.S. dollars will be required as indicated in E., below. A gain or loss from remeasurement will be included in the foreign entity's **income from continuing operations**.

      (2) If the foreign entity keeps its books in U.S. dollars, then its trial balance can be directly incorporated into the reporting entity's financial statements. Transactions denominated in foreign currency will result in foreign currency gains and losses. The **net** gain or loss will be **the same** as the remeasurement gain or loss. In other words, if the functional currency of the foreign entity is the U.S.

dollar, the aggregate net gain or loss from exchange rate fluctuations will be the same regardless of whether the foreign entity keeps its books in the local currency or in U.S. dollars.

c. **ANOTHER FOREIGN CURRENCY IS THE FUNCTIONAL CURRENCY** A foreign entity may keep its books in the local currency (i.e., "recording currency"), yet have another foreign currency as functional currency. In this case, remeasuring of the recording currency statements into functional currency will be required. Once the statements have been remeasured into the functional currency, then translation into U.S. dollars is required.

EXAMPLE 1 ♦ FUNCTIONAL CURRENCY

> Americana Inc., a U.S. company, owns 100% of the stock of Frenchie's, a self-contained subsidiary incorporated in France. Frenchie's records all its transactions in French francs, even though the bulk of its operations are conducted in Germany (i.e., the German mark is the functional currency). In order to prepare its consolidated financial statements, Americana will first **remeasure** the French francs statements into German marks and then **translate** them into U.S. dollars.

3. **HIGHLY INFLATIONARY ECONOMIES** Where a foreign country's cumulative inflation rate over the three-year period preceding the date of financial statements is approximately 100% or more, the local currency is not considered stable enough to be the functional currency. In this case, the reporting currency (e.g., the U.S. dollar) will be the functional currency, and **remeasurement** will be required.

D. **COMPUTATION**

1. **CONFORM TO U.S. GAAP** Prior to translation, the foreign currency statements must be conformed to U.S. GAAP and be measured in the functional currency of the foreign entity (otherwise, remeasurement into the functional currency is required).

2. **RATES** Foreign currency financial statements should be translated by means of the following rates:

   a. **ALL ASSETS AND LIABILITIES** Current exchange rate at the balance sheet date.

   b. **REVENUES AND EXPENSES** Conceptually, the exchange rate at the time the revenue or expense was recognized. However, due to the impracticability of this where rates change frequently, a **weighted-average** exchange rate for the period may be used.

   c. **CONTRIBUTED CAPITAL** Historical exchange rate.

   d. **RETAINED EARNINGS** The translated amount of retained earnings for the prior period (i.e., beginning retained earnings), plus (less) net income (loss) at the weighted-average rate, less dividends declared during the period, at the exchange rate when declared.

3. **REPORTING TRANSLATION ADJUSTMENTS** Translation of foreign currency statements as indicated above will result in a **translation adjustment**. This translation adjustment is reported in other comprehensive income. It should **not** be included in the determination of net income.

4. **SALE OR DISPOSAL OF INVESTMENT IN FOREIGN ENTITY** The translation adjustments accumulated in other comprehensive income should be removed using a reclassification adjustment and reported as part of the gain or loss on the disposal of the investment.

EXHIBIT 1 ♦ FUNCTIONAL CURRENCY

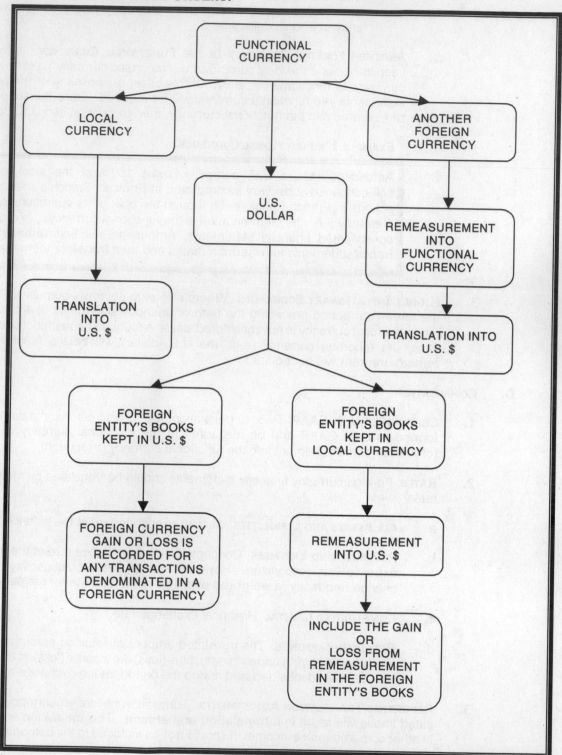

EXAMPLE 2 ♦ COMPUTATION

Americana Inc., a U.S. corporation, owns 100% of the outstanding common stock of Kaiser Ltd., a German company. Kaiser's financial statements for the year ending December 31, 20X1 are reproduced below.

KAISER LTD.
Balance Sheet
December 31, 20X1

	(000's, German marks)
Assets	
Cash	150 DM
Accounts receivable	200
Inventory	450
Plant and equipment (net)	1,200
Total assets	2,000 DM
Liabilities and Equity	
Accounts payable	100 DM
Notes payable	500
Common stock	400
Additional paid-in capital	300
Retained earnings	700
Total liabilities and equity	2,000 DM

KAISER LTD.
Income Statement
For the Year Ended December 31, 20X1

	(000's, German marks)
Sales	400 DM
Cost of goods sold	(150)
Gross margin	250
Operating expenses	(100)
Net income	150 DM

The following information is also available:

• On August 31, 20X1, Kaiser paid a 50,000 DM dividend.
• Kaiser's translated retained earnings as of January 1, 20X1, was $600,000.
• The exchange rate when Americana acquired its investment in Kaiser was 1 DM = U.S. $1.
• Exchange rate data for 20X1:

January 1	1 DM = $.95
August 31	1 DM = $.90
December 31	1 DM = $.80
20X1 average	1 DM = $.85

REQUIRED: Translate Kaiser's financial statements.

(continued on next page)

SOLUTION:

Assets	Balance Sheet (000's)		
	Marks	Rate	U.S. Dollars
Cash	150 DM	$ .80/DM	$ 120.0
Accounts receivable	200	$ .80/DM	160.0
Inventory	450	$ .80/DM	360.0
Plant and equipment (net)	1,200	$ .80/DM	960.0
Total assets	2,000 DM		$1,600.0

Liabilities and Equity	Balance Sheet (000's)		
	Marks	Rate	U.S. Dollars
Accounts payable	100 DM	$ .80/DM	$ 80.0
Notes payable	500	$ .80/DM	400.0
Common stock	400	$1.00/DM	400.0
Additional paid-in capital	300	$1.00/DM	300.0
Retained earnings	700	*	682.5
Translation adjustment (bal. fig.)**	--		(262.5)
Total liabs. and equity	2,000 DM		$1,600.0

* Translated retained earnings (RE) equals beginning RE as previously translated, plus net income at a weighted average rate, less dividends, at the rate in effect when declared.

** The translation adjustment is reported in other comprehensive income.

Beginning RE (from information above)	$600,000
Net income (below)	127,500
Dividends (50,000 DM x $.90/DM)	(45,000)
Translated RE, Dec. 31, 20X1	$682,500

	Income Statement (000's)		
	Marks	Rate	U.S. Dollars
Sales	400 DM	$ .85/DM	$ 340.0
Cost of goods sold	(150)	$ .85/DM	(127.5)
Operating expenses	(100)	$ .85/DM	(85.0)
Net income	150 DM		$ 127.5

E. REMEASUREMENT INTO FUNCTIONAL CURRENCY

1. **BEFORE TRANSLATION** If an entity does not maintain its books in its functional currency, **remeasuring** into the functional currency is required prior to **translation** into the reporting currency (i.e., the U.S. dollar). If the functional currency is the same as the reporting currency, remeasurement will eliminate the need for translation (i.e., the statements will be remeasured into U.S. dollars, and thus no translation will be required).

2. **PURPOSE OF REMEASUREMENT** The remeasuring process should achieve the same result as if the books had been initially recorded in the functional currency.

    a. This requires the remeasuring of certain accounts (nonmonetary items) at **historical rates**. All other accounts are remeasured at **current rates**.

    b. The remeasuring process will result in exchange gains and losses. The net gain or loss from **remeasurement** should be recognized in **income from continuing operations** for the current period.

    c. The following items should be remeasured at historical rates:

(1) Marketable securities carried at cost

(2) Inventories carried at cost

(3) Prepaid expenses such as insurance, advertising, and rent

(4) Property, plant, and equipment

(5) Accumulated depreciation on property, plant, and equipment

(6) Patents, trademarks, licenses, formulas, goodwill, and other intangible assets

(7) Common stock and preferred stock carried at issuance price

(8) Revenues and expenses related to nonmonetary items; for example,

    (a) Cost of goods sold

    (b) Depreciation of property, plant, and equipment

    (c) Amortization of certain intangible items such as patents

EXAMPLE 3 ♦ REMEASUREMENT INTO FUNCTIONAL CURRENCY

Figueras S.A. is a Spanish sales subsidiary formed on January 1, 20X1, and is 100 percent owned by Americana Inc. Management has determined that Figueras S.A. is, in fact, a foreign extension of Americana's operations, and thus, its functional currency is the U.S. dollar. The following additional information is available.

- No dividends were paid by Figueras S.A. during 20X1.
- Inventories are carried at weighted-average cost.
- Figueras' office is located in a building purchased on May 5, 20X1.
- Figueras' trial balance (in pesetas) is reproduced in column (1) of the trial balance.
- Exchange rate information for 20X1 follows:

January 1	1 peseta	=	$1.00
May 5		=	$ .98
December 31		=	$ .90
Average 20X1		=	$ .95

Based on the preceding information, Figueras' accounts have been **remeasured** as indicated in column (3) of the trial balance. The remeasured balance sheet and income statement are presented below.

FIGUERAS S.A.
Remeasured Balance Sheet (000's)

Assets		Liabilities	
Cash	$ 180	Accounts payable	$ 270
Inventory	475	Mortgage payable	540
Office building, net	784		810
		Equities	
		Common stock	350
		Retained earnings	279 *
			629
Total assets	$1,439	Total liabilities & equity	$1,439

* Same as NI, since 20X1 was the first year of operations, and no dividends were paid.

(continued on next page)

FIGUERAS S.A.
Trial Balance (000's)
Dr. (Cr.)

Assets	(1) Pesetas	(2) Rate	(3) U.S. Dollars
Cash	200	$ .90/P	$ 180
Inventory (w. avg. cost)	500	.95/P	475
Office building (net)	800	.98/P	784
Total assets	1,500		1,439

Liabilities	(1) Pesetas	(2) Rate	(3) U.S. Dollars
Accounts payable	(300)	.90/P	(270)
Mortgage payable	(600)	.90/P	(540)
Total liabilities	(900)		(810)

Equity			
Common stock	(350)	1.00/P	(350)
Retained earnings	0	*	0 *
Total equity	(350)		(350)

Operations			
Sales	(700)	.95/P	(665)
Cost of goods sold	350	.95/P	332.5
General and administrative	100	.95/P	95
Exchange gain (to balance)	--		(41.5)
Total debits and credits	0		$ 0

* Because 20X1 was the first year of operations, the beginning RE balance is zero. Had the company been in operation for more than a year, the RE balance as **remeasured at the end of the prior year** would have been the amount entered in column (3).

FIGUERAS S.A.
Remeasured Income Statement (000's)

Sales	$665.0
Cost of goods sold	(332.5)
General and administrative	(95.0)
Exchange gain (from trial balance)	41.5
Net income	$279.0

II. FOREIGN CURRENCY TRANSACTIONS

A. GENERAL PROVISIONS

1. Foreign currency transactions are transactions denominated in a currency other than the entity's functional currency. Foreign currency transactions may produce receivables or payables that are fixed in terms of the amount of foreign currency that will be received or paid.

2. A change in exchange rates between the functional currency and the currency in which a transaction is denominated increases or decreases the expected amount of functional currency cash flows upon settlement of the transaction. That increase or decrease in expected functional currency cash flows is a foreign currency **transaction gain or loss** that generally should be included as a component of **income from continuing operations** for the period in which the exchange rate changes.

3. Likewise, a transaction gain or loss (measured from the **transaction date** or the most recent intervening balance sheet date, whichever is later) realized upon settlement of a foreign

currency transaction generally should be included as a component of **income from continuing operations** for the period in which the transaction is settled.

4. The exceptions to this requirement for inclusion in net income of transaction gains and losses are set forth in III. B., below.

5. For other than forward exchange contracts, the following should apply to all foreign currency transactions of an enterprise and its investees.

a. At the date a transaction is recognized, each asset, liability, revenue, expense, gain, or loss arising from the transaction should be measured and recorded in the functional currency of the recording entity by use of the exchange rate in effect at that date.

b. At each balance sheet date, recorded balances that are denominated in a currency other than the functional currency of the recording entity should be adjusted to reflect the current exchange rate. These adjustments should be currently recognized as transaction gains or losses and reported as a component of **income from continuing operations**.

EXAMPLE 4 ♦ EXCHANGE RATES

On November 1, 20X1, Americana Inc. purchased equipment from an unrelated French company for 10,000 francs, payable on January 30, 20X2. The following exchange rate information is available:

November 1, 20X1	1 franc	=	$.30
December 31, 20X1		=	.32
January 30, 20X2		=	.33

Americana would account for this transaction as follows:

Nov. 1, 20X1:

Equipment	3,000	
Note Payable (10,000FR x $.30/FR)		3,000

Dec. 31, 20X1:

Exchange Loss [10,000FR x ($.32/FR – $.30/FR)]	200	
Note Payable		200

The $200 transaction loss from November 1, 20X1 to December 31, 20X1 is included as a component of income from continuing operations for 20X1.

Jan. 30, 20X2:

Note Payable ($3,000 + $200)	3,200	
Exchange Loss (to balance)	100	
Cash (10,000FR x $.33/FR)		3,300

The $100 transaction loss from December 31, 20X1 to January 30, 20X2 is included as a component of income from continuing operations for 20X2.

NOTE: The recorded amount of the equipment is not affected by exchange rate fluctuations between the date of purchase and the date of payment.

B. FORWARD EXCHANGE CONTRACTS

1. A **forward exchange contract** (forward contract) is an agreement to exchange different currencies at a specified future date and at a specified rate (the **forward rate**). A forward contract is a foreign currency **transaction**.

2. A gain or loss (whether or not deferred) on a forward contract, except a speculative forward contract (see 4., below), should be computed by multiplying the foreign currency amount of the forward contract by the difference between the **spot rate** at the **balance sheet date** and the **spot rate** at the **date of inception of the forward contract** (or the spot rate last used to measure a gain or loss on that contract for an earlier period). The **spot rate** is the exchange rate for immediate delivery of currencies exchanged.

3. The **discount or premium on a forward contract** should be accounted for **separately** from the gain or loss on the contract and generally should be **amortized** over the **life of the forward contract**. The discount or premium on a forward contract is the foreign currency amount of the contract multiplied by the difference between the contracted forward rate and the spot rate at the date of inception of the contract.

EXAMPLE 5 ♦ DISCOUNT OR PREMIUM ON A FORWARD CONTRACT

On November 1, 20X1, Americana Inc. contracted with The Money Exchange Ltd. for the delivery of 10,000 French francs in 3 months, at a rate of .3015. At the date the contract was entered into, the exchange rate was 1 franc = $.3. At the balance sheet date, the value of the franc had risen to $.32. On January 30, 20X2, the franc was worth $.33. Americana would post the journal entries below. Note that all entries are posted in U.S. $ (e.g., the 3,000 debit posted on November 1 represents the translated value in U.S. $ of 10,000 francs).

Nov. 1, 20X1:

Francs Due From Broker	3,000	
Deferred Forward Contract Cost	15	
Payable to Broker		3,015

Dec. 31, 20X1:

Francs Due From Broker	200	
Exchange Gain		200
Forward Contract Expenses ($15 x 60/90)	10	
Deferred Forward Contract Cost		10

Jan. 30, 20X2:

Payable to Broker	3,015	
Investment in Francs	3,300	
Franc Due From Broker		3,200
Cash		3,015
Exchange Gain		100
Forward Contract Expense	5	
Deferred Forward Contract Cost		5

NOTE: In this Example, the cumulative gain on the forward exchange contract (i.e., $300) would offset the **loss** recognized in Example 4. Thus by entering into the forward exchange contract Americana, in fact, protected itself from future exchange losses.

4. A gain or loss on a **speculative forward contract** (that is, a contract that does not hedge an exposure) should be computed by multiplying the foreign currency amount of the forward contract by the difference between the forward rate available for the remaining maturity of the contract and the contracted forward rate (or the forward rate last used to measure a gain or loss on that contract for an earlier period). No separate accounting recognition is given to the discount or premium on a speculative forward contract.

III. FOREIGN CURRENCY HEDGES

A. DESIGNATION OF HEDGE
In accordance with SFAS 133, an entity may designate the following types of hedges of foreign currency exposure:

1. **FAIR VALUE HEDGE** A fair value hedge of an unrecognized firm commitment or an available-for-sale security.

2. **CASH FLOW HEDGE** A cash flow hedge of a forecasted foreign-currency-denominated transaction or a forecasted intercompany foreign-currency-denominated transaction.

3. **HEDGE OF A NET INVESTMENT IN A FOREIGN OPERATION** A derivative instrument or a non-derivative financial instrument that may give rise to a foreign currency transaction gain or loss can be designated as hedging the foreign currency exposure of a net investment in a foreign operation.

B. REPORTING HEDGING GAINS AND LOSSES

1. **FOREIGN CURRENCY FAIR VALUE HEDGE** The gain or loss on the hedging instrument designated as a fair value foreign currency hedge is recognized currently in **earnings**. The gain or loss on the hedged item adjusts the carrying amount of the hedged item and is recognized currently in earnings. If the hedged item is an available-for-sale security, the recognition of gain or loss in earnings rather than in other comprehensive income is an exception to the normal accounting treatment of gains and losses on available-for-sale securities, in order to offset the gain or loss on the hedging instrument that is reported in current earnings.

2. **FOREIGN CURRENCY CASH FLOW HEDGE** The **effective portion** of the gain or loss on a derivative designated as a cash flow hedge is reported in **other comprehensive income**, and the ineffective portion is reported in earnings. Effectiveness is defined as the degree that the gain (loss) for the hedging instrument offsets the loss (gain) on the hedged item.

3. **HEDGE OF A NET INVESTMENT IN A FOREIGN OPERATION** The gain or loss on a hedging derivative instrument, or the foreign currency transaction gain or loss on a nonderivative hedging instrument, that is designated as and is effective as an economic hedge, of the net investment in a foreign operation is reported in **other comprehensive income**, as part of the cumulative translation adjustment, to the extent it is effective as a hedge.

IV. INCOME TAX CONSEQUENCES OF RATE CHANGES

A. FOREIGN CURRENCY TRANSACTIONS
Exchange gains or losses from an entity's **foreign currency transactions** that are included in taxable income of an earlier or later year than the year in which they are recognized in financial income result in **temporary differences**.

B. FOREIGN CURRENCY FINANCIAL STATEMENT TRANSLATION ADJUSTMENTS
These adjustments should be accounted for as **temporary differences** under the provisions of APB 23 and SFAS 109.

V. DETERMINATION OF THE FUNCTIONAL CURRENCY

A. DEFINITION
The functional currency is the foreign currency or parent's currency that most closely correlates with the following economic indicators.

B.   CASH FLOW INDICATORS

    1.   FOREIGN CURRENCY Cash flows related to the foreign entity's assets and liabilities are primarily in the foreign currency and do not directly impact the parent company's cash flows.

    2.   PARENT'S CURRENCY Cash flows related to the foreign entity's assets and liabilities directly impact the parent's cash flows on a current basis and are readily available for remittance to the parent company.

C.   SALES PRICE INDICATORS

    1.   FOREIGN CURRENCY Sales prices for the foreign entity's products are not primarily responsive on a short-term basis to changes in exchange rates but are determined more by local competition or local government regulation.

    2.   PARENT'S CURRENCY Sales prices for the foreign entity's products are primarily responsive on a short-term basis to changes in exchange rates; for example, sales prices are determined more by worldwide competition or by international prices.

D.   SALES MARKET INDICATORS

    1.   FOREIGN CURRENCY There is an active local sales market for the foreign entity's products, although there also might be significant amounts of exports.

    2.   PARENT'S CURRENCY The sales market is mostly in the parent's country or sales contracts are denominated in the parent's currency.

E.   EXPENSE INDICATORS

    1.   FOREIGN CURRENCY Labor, materials, and other costs for the foreign entity's products or services are primarily local costs, even though there also might be imports from other countries.

    2.   PARENT'S CURRENCY Labor, materials, and other costs for the foreign entity's products or services, on a continuing basis, are primarily costs for components obtained from the country in which the parent company is located.

F.   FINANCING INDICATORS

    1.   FOREIGN CURRENCY Financing is primarily denominated in foreign currency, and funds generated by the foreign entity's operations are sufficient to service existing and normally expected debt obligations.

    2.   PARENT'S CURRENCY Financing is primarily from the parent or other dollar-denominated obligations, or funds generated by the foreign entity's operations are not sufficient to service existing and normally expected debt obligation without the infusion of additional funds from the parent company. Infusion of additional funds from the parent company for expansion is not a factor, provided funds generated by the foreign entity's expanded operations are expected to be sufficient to service that additional financing.

G.   INTERCOMPANY TRANSACTIONS AND ARRANGEMENTS INDICATORS

    1.   FOREIGN CURRENCY There is a low volume of intercompany transactions, and there is not an extensive interrelationship between the operations of the foreign entity and the parent company. However, the foreign entity's operations may rely on the parent's or affiliates' competitive advantages, such as patents and trademarks.

2. **PARENT'S CURRENCY** There is a high volume of intercompany transactions and there is an extensive interrelationship between the operations of the foreign entity and the parent company. Additionally, the parent's currency generally would be the functional currency if the foreign entity is a device or shell corporation for holding investments, obligations, intangible assets, etc., that could readily be carried on the parent's or an affiliate's books.

Wondering how you can prepare for OOAF questions?

Some candidates who are otherwise confident about the exam are overwhelmed by other objective answer format (OOAF or OOF) questions. The following tips are designed to help you increase your confidence when presented with these lengthy questions.

As you progress through your study plan, answer an OOAF question from each major topic; waiting until the last month leaves you little time to prepare for this question type. The more uncomfortable that you are with OOAF questions, the more important this becomes. You might not realize that you are uncomfortable with OOAF questions, if you don't try answering some of them.

After answering an OOAF question (using the suggested time limit) and checking your answers, reflect on the question. If you had trouble with some aspect, evaluate whether you need to review the material, refine your answering technique, or merely gain confidence with this format.

- Did you feel pressured for time? If you in fact didn't have enough time, this may indicate you need to review the text again. As you become more familiar with the material, your speed will increase. A shortage of time may also indicate a need to consider techniques to answering OOAF questions. Specific information about OOAF question answering techniques is in the **Practical Advice** appendix.

- If you felt pressured for time, but actually had time to finish the question, answer several more OOAF questions using the suggested time limit. This experience will help you learn not to be intimidated by this format.

Once you know the content, you will be able to prepare a response regardless of the question format. Exam time is limited and you don't want the pressure of time considerations to distract you from providing your best answer to questions. To reduce the pressure, remember that you must earn 75 points to pass—the answer format that you use to earn those 75 points doesn't matter. Practice more OOAF questions that cover topics that have high point value; be prepared to answer an OOAF question in any topic area.

Remember, with the techniques and information in your material,

A passing score is well within reach!

CHAPTER 17—FOREIGN OPERATIONS

PROBLEM 17-1 MULTIPLE CHOICE QUESTIONS (54 to 68 minutes)

1. In preparing consolidated financial statements of a U.S. parent company with a foreign subsidiary, the foreign subsidiary's functional currency is the currency
a. In which the subsidiary maintains its accounting records.
b. Of the country in which the subsidiary is located.
c. Of the country in which the parent is located.
d. Of the environment in which the subsidiary primarily generates and expends cash.

(R/99, FAR, #16, 6785)

2. Certain balance sheet accounts of a foreign subsidiary of Rowan Inc., at December 31, 1997, have been translated into U.S. dollars as follows:

	Translated at	
	Current rates	Historical rates
Note receivable, long-term	$240,000	$200,000
Prepaid rent	85,000	80,000
Patent	150,000	170,000
	$475,000	$450,000

The subsidiary's functional currency is the currency of the country in which it is located. What total amount should be included in Rowan's December 31, 1997 consolidated balance sheet for the above accounts?
a. $450,000
b. $455,000
c. $475,000
d. $495,000

(5/90, PII, #44, amended, 9059)

3. A foreign subsidiary's functional currency is its local currency, which has not experienced significant inflation. The weighted average exchange rate for the current year would be the appropriate exchange rate for translating

	Sales to customers	Wages expense
a.	No	No
b.	Yes	Yes
c.	No	Yes
d.	Yes	No

(5/92, Theory, #39, 2732)

4. Park Co.'s wholly owned subsidiary, Schnell Corp., maintains its accounting records in German marks. Because all of Schnell's branch offices are in Switzerland, its functional currency is the Swiss franc. Remeasurement of Schnell's 1994 financial statements resulted in a $7,600 gain, and translation of its financial statements resulted in an $8,100 gain. What amount should Park report as a foreign exchange gain in its income statement for the year ended December 31, 1994?
a. $0
b. $ 7,600
c. $ 8,100
d. $15,700

(5/95, FAR, #31, 5567)

5. The following trial balance of Trey Co. at December 31, 1993, has been adjusted except for income tax expense:

	Dr.	Cr.
Cash	$ 550,000	
Accounts receivable, net	1,650,000	
Prepaid taxes	300,000	
Accounts payable		$ 120,000
Common stock		500,000
Additional paid-in capital		680,000
Retained earnings		630,000
Foreign currency translation adjustment	430,000	
Revenues		3,600,000
Expenses	2,600,000	
	$5,530,000	$5,530,000

Additional information:

• During 1993, estimated tax payments of $300,000 were charged to prepaid taxes. Trey has not yet recorded income tax expense. There were no differences between financial statement and income tax income, and Trey's tax rate is 30%.

• Included in accounts receivable is $500,000 due from a customer. Special terms granted to this customer require payment in equal semi-annual installments of $125,000 every April 1 and October 1.

In Trey's December 31, 1993 balance sheet, what amount should be reported as total retained earnings?
a. $1,029,000
b. $1,200,000
c. $1,330,000
d. $1,630,000

(11/94, FAR, #9, 5274)

6. Gains resulting from the process of translating a foreign entity's financial statements from the functional currency, which has not experienced significant inflation, to U.S. dollars should be included as a(an)
a. Other comprehensive income item.
b. Deferred credit.
c. Component of income from continuing operations.
d. Extraordinary item.
(11/85, Theory, #21, amended, 9060)

7. When remeasuring foreign currency financial statements into the functional currency, which of the following items would be remeasured using historical exchange rates?
a. Inventories carried at cost
b. Marketable equity securities reported at market values
c. Bonds payable
d. Accrued liabilities (11/93, Theory, #36, 4541)

8. A balance arising from the translation or remeasurement of a subsidiary's foreign currency financial statements is reported in the consolidated income statement when the subsidiary's functional currency is the

	Foreign currency	U.S. dollar
a.	No	No
b.	No	Yes
c.	Yes	No
d.	Yes	Yes

(5/90, Theory, #22, 2088)

9. Gains from remeasuring a foreign subsidiary's financial statements from the local currency, which is not the functional currency, into the parent company's currency should be reported as a(an)
a. Deferred foreign exchange gain.
b. Other comprehensive income item.
c. Extraordinary item, net of income taxes.
d. Part of continuing operations.
(11/90, Theory, #39, amended, 2087)

10. On October 1, 1992, Velec Co., a U.S. company, contracted to purchase foreign goods requiring payment in francs one month after their receipt at Velec's factory. Title to the goods passed on December 15, 1992. The goods were still in transit on December 31, 1992. Exchange rates were one dollar to 22 francs, 20 francs, and 21 francs on October 1, December 15, and December 31, 1992, respectively. Velec should account for the exchange rate fluctuation in 1992 as

a. A loss included in net income before extraordinary items.
b. A gain included in net income before extraordinary items.
c. An extraordinary gain.
d. An extraordinary loss. (5/93, Theory, #34, 4222)

11. Hunt Co. purchased merchandise for £300,000 from a vendor in London on November 30, 1992. Payment in British pounds was due on January 30, 1993. The exchange rates to purchase one pound were as follows:

	Nov. 30, 1992	Dec. 31, 1992
Spot-rate	$1.65	$1.62
30-day rate	1.64	1.59
60-day rate	1.63	1.56

In its December 31, 1992 income statement, what amount should Hunt report as foreign exchange gain?
a. $12,000
b. $ 9,000
c. $ 6,000
d. $0 (11/93, PI, #49, 4418)

12. Fogg Co., a U.S. company, contracted to purchase foreign goods. Payment in foreign currency was due one month after the goods were received at Fogg's warehouse. Between the receipt of goods and the time of payment, the exchange rates changed in Fogg's favor. The resulting gain should be included in Fogg's financial statements as a(an)
a. Component of income from continuing operations.
b. Extraordinary item.
c. Deferred credit.
d. Component of other comprehensive income.
(11/95, FAR, #32, amended, 6114)

13. On September 1, 1990, Cano & Co., a U.S. corporation, sold merchandise to a foreign firm for 250,000 francs. Terms of the sale require payment in francs on February 1, 1991. On September 1, 1990, the spot exchange rate was $.20 per franc. At December 31, 1990, Cano's year-end, the spot rate was $.19, but the rate increased to $.22 by February 1, 1991, when payment was received. How much should Cano report as foreign exchange gain or loss in its 1991 income statement?
a. $0
b. $2,500 loss
c. $5,000 gain
d. $7,500 gain (11/91, PI, #46, 2434)

14. On November 15, 1997, Celt Inc., a U.S. company, ordered merchandise F.O.B. shipping point from a German company for 200,000 marks. The merchandise was shipped and invoiced to Celt on December 10, 1997. Celt paid the invoice on January 10, 1998. The spot rates for marks on the respective dates are as follows:

November 15, 1997	$.4955
December 10, 1997	.4875
December 31, 1997	.4675
January 10, 1998	.4475

In Celt's December 31, 1997 income statement, the foreign exchange gain is
a. $9,600.
b. $8,000.
c. $4,000.
d. $1,600.   (11/90, PI, #38, amended, 1334)

15. Ball Corp. had the following foreign currency transactions during 1997:

• Merchandise was purchased from a foreign supplier on January 20, 1997, for the U.S. dollar equivalent of $90,000. The invoice was paid on March 20, 1997, at the U.S. dollar equivalent of $96,000.

• On July 1, 1997, Ball borrowed the U.S. dollar equivalent of $500,000 evidenced by a note that was payable in the lender's local currency on July 1, 1999. On December 31, 1997, the U.S. dollar equivalents of the principal amount and accrued interest were $520,000 and $26,000, respectively. Interest on the note is 10% per annum.

In Ball's 1997 income statement, what amount should be included as foreign exchange loss?
a. $0
b. $ 6,000
c. $21,000
d. $27,000   (11/90, PI, #43, amended, 1335)

16. On September 22, 1994, Yumi Corp. purchased merchandise from an unaffiliated foreign company for 10,000 units of the foreign company's local currency. On that date, the spot rate was $.55. Yumi paid the bill in full on March 20, 1995, when the spot rate was $.65. The spot rate was $.70 on December 31, 1994. What amount should Yumi report as a foreign currency transaction loss in its income statement for the year ended December 31, 1994?
a. $0
b. $ 500
c. $1,000
d. $1,500   (5/95, FAR, #32, 5568)

17. On July 1, 1996, Clark Company borrowed 1,680,000 local currency units (LCUs) from a foreign lender, evidenced by an interest bearing note due on July 1, 1997, which is denominated in the currency of the lender. The U.S. dollar equivalent of the note principal was as follows:

Date	Amount
7/1/96 (date borrowed)	$210,000
12/31/96 (Clark's year end)	240,000
7/1/97 (date repaid)	280,000

In its income statement for 1997, what amount should Clark include as a foreign exchange gain or loss?
a. $70,000 gain
b. $70,000 loss
c. $40,000 gain
d. $40,000 loss   (5/86, PI, #56, amended, 1341)

18. Shore Co. records its transactions in U.S. dollars. A sale of goods resulted in a receivable denominated in Japanese yen, and a purchase of goods resulted in a payable denominated in French francs. Shore recorded a foreign exchange gain on collection of the receivable and an exchange loss on settlement of the payable. The exchange rates are expressed as so many units of foreign currency to one dollar. Did the number of foreign currency units exchangeable for a dollar increase or decrease between the contract and settlement dates?

	Yen exchangeable for $1	Francs exchangeable for $1
a.	Increase	Increase
b.	Decrease	Decrease
c.	Decrease	Increase
d.	Increase	Decrease

(11/91, Theory, #18, 2526)

ITEMS 19 THROUGH 21 are based on the following:

On December 12, 1991, Imp Co. entered into three forward exchange contracts, each to purchase 100,000 francs in 90 days. The relevant exchange rates are as follows:

	Spot rate	Forward rate (for March 12, 1992)
December 12, 1991	$.88	$.90
December 31, 1991	.98	.93

19. Imp entered into the first forward contract to hedge a purchase of inventory in November 1991, payable in March 1992. At December 31, 1991, what amount of foreign currency transaction gain should Imp include in income from this forward contract?

a. $0
b. $ 3,000
c. $ 5,000
d. $10,000　　　　　(11/92, PI, #48, 3281)

20. Imp entered into the second forward contract to hedge a commitment to purchase equipment being manufactured to Imp's specifications. At December 31, 1991, what amount of foreign currency transaction gain should Imp include in income from this forward contract?

a. $0
b. $ 3,000
c. $ 5,000
d. $10,000　　　　　(11/92, PI, #49, 3282)

21. Imp entered into the third forward contract for speculation. At December 31, 1991, what amount of foreign currency transaction gain should Imp include in income from this forward contract?

a. $0
b. $ 3,000
c. $ 5,000
d. $10,000　　　　　(11/92, PI, #50, 3283)

22. The following information pertains to Flint Co.'s sale of 10,000 foreign currency units under a forward contract dated November 1, 1991, for delivery on January 31, 1992:

	11/1/91	12/31/91
Spot rates	$0.80	$0.83
30-day future rates	0.79	0.82
90-day future rates	0.78	0.81

Flint entered into the forward contract in order to speculate in the foreign currency. In Flint's income statement for the year ended December 31, 1991, what amount of loss should be reported from this forward contract?

a. $400
b. $300
c. $200
d. $0　　　　　(5/92, PI, #52, 2623)

23. Post Inc. had a credit translation adjustment of $30,000 for the year ended December 31, 1997. The functional currency of Post's subsidiary is the currency of the country in which it is located. Additionally, Post had a receivable from a foreign customer payable in the local currency of the customer. On December 31, 1996, this receivable for 200,000 local currency units (LCUs) was correctly included in Post's balance sheet at $110,000. When the receivable was collected on February 15, 1997, the United States dollar equivalent was $120,000. In Post's 1997 consolidated income statement, how much should be reported as foreign exchange gain?

a. $0
b. $10,000
c. $30,000
d. $40,000　　　　　(11/86, PI, #43, amended, 1340)

24. Fay Corp. had a realized foreign exchange loss of $15,000 for the year ended December 31, 1997, and must also determine whether the following items will require year-end adjustment:

• Fay had an $8,000 loss resulting from the translation of the accounts of its wholly owned foreign subsidiary for the year ended December 31, 1997.

• Fay had an account payable to an unrelated foreign supplier payable in the supplier's local currency. The U.S. dollar equivalent of the payable was $64,000 on the October 31, 1997, invoice date, and it was $60,000 on December 31, 1997. The invoice is payable on January 30, 1998.

In Fay's 1997 consolidated income statement, what amount should be included as foreign exchange loss?

a. $11,000
b. $15,000
c. $19,000
d. $23,000　　　　　(5/90, PI, #52, amended, 1336)

25. Which of the following should be reported in accumulated other comprehensive income?

a. Discount on convertible bonds that are common stock equivalents.
b. Premium on convertible bonds that are common stock equivalents.
c. Cumulative foreign exchange translation loss.
d. Organization costs.
　　　　　(11/93, Theory, #14, amended, 4519)

26. On October 1, 1992, Mild Co., a U.S. company, purchased machinery from Grund, a German company, with payment due on April 1, 1993. If Mild's 1992 operating income included no foreign exchange transaction gain or loss, then the transaction could have

a. Resulted in an extraordinary gain.
b. Been denominated in U.S. dollars.
c. Caused a foreign currency gain to be reported as a contra account against machinery.
d. Caused a foreign currency translation gain to be reported in other comprehensive income.
　　　　　(11/93, Theory, #35, amended, 4540)

27. The functional currency of Nash Inc.'s subsidiary is the French franc. Nash borrowed French francs as a partial hedge of its investment in the subsidiary. In preparing consolidated financial statements, Nash's translation loss on its investment in the subsidiary exceeded its exchange gain on the borrowing. How should the effects of the loss and gain be reported in Nash's consolidated financial statements?

a. The translation loss less the exchange gain is reported in other comprehensive income.
b. The translation loss less the exchange gain is reported in net income.
c. The translation loss is reported in other comprehensive income and the exchange gain is reported in net income.
d. The translation loss is reported in net income and the exchange gain is reported in other comprehensive income.

(5/92, Theory, #38, amended, 2731)

ESSAY QUESTION

ESSAY 17-2 (15 to 25 minutes)

Jay Co.'s 1990 consolidated financial statements include two wholly owned subsidiaries, Jay Co. of Australia (Jay A) and Jay Co. of France (Jay F). Functional currencies are the U.S. dollar for Jay A and the franc for Jay F.

REQUIRED:

a. What are the objectives of translating a foreign subsidiary's financial statements?

b. How are gains and losses arising from translating or remeasuring of each subsidiary's financial statements measured and reported in Jay's consolidated financial statements?

c. FASB Statement No. 52 identifies several economic indicators that are to be considered both individually and collectively in determining the functional currency for a consolidated subsidiary. List three of those indicators.

d. What exchange rate is used to incorporate each subsidiary's equipment cost, accumulated depreciation, and depreciation expense in Jay's consolidated financial statements? (5/91, Theory, #5, 3597)

SOLUTION 17-1 MULTIPLE CHOICE ANSWERS

TRANSLATION OF FOREIGN CURRENCY FINANCIAL STATEMENTS

1. (d) An entity's functional currency is the currency of the primary economic environment in which the entity operates. Normally, that is the currency of the environment in which an entity primarily generates and expends cash. The functional currency of a foreign entity may be its local currency, the U.S. dollar, or another foreign currency. Where a foreign operation is relatively self-contained and integrated within one country, the entity's functional currency will be the local currency. Where the foreign operation is, in essence, an extension of the parent's U.S. operations, the functional currency will be the U.S. dollar. A foreign entity may keep its books in the local currency, yet have another foreign currency as functional currency; in which case remeasurement of the recording currency statements into functional currency will be required.

2. (c) Since the subsidiary's functional currency is the currency of the country in which it is located, all of its assets are translated at the *current rate* (i.e., the exchange rate in effect at the balance sheet date).

3. (b) Since the foreign subsidiary's functional currency is its local currency, which has not experienced significant inflation, it is appropriate to *translate* the amounts of its revenues, expenses, gains, and losses at a weighted average exchange rate for the period (SFAS 52, par. 11 and 12).

4. (b) Park's foreign subsidiary does not maintain its accounting records in its functional currency (the Swiss franc). Therefore, the financial statements of the foreign subsidiary must be remeasured. The $7,600 remeasurement gain is reported in income from continuing operations. The $8,100 translation gain is reported in other comprehensive income. Translation gains and losses are not reported in income.

5. (c) Under SFAS 52, the foreign currency translation adjustment should not be included in determining net income. Instead, it should be reported in other comprehensive income. The amount to be reported as retained earnings in the 12/31/93 balance sheet is determined as follows:

Revenues	$ 3,600,000
Less: Expenses	(2,600,000)
Income before income taxes	1,000,000
Less: Income taxes ($1,000,000 x 30%)	(300,000)
Net income for 1993	700,000
Add: Retained earnings, 1/1/93	630,000
Retained earnings, 12/31/93	$ 1,330,000

6. (a) Under SFAS 52, *Foreign Currency Translation*, if an entity's functional currency is the foreign currency, which has not experienced significant inflation, translation adjustments result from the process of *translating* that entity's financial statements into the reporting currency. Translation adjustments ("gains" or "losses") should not be included in net income but should be included in other comprehensive income.

REMEASUREMENT INTO FUNCTIONAL CURRENCY

7. (a) Per SFAS 52, *Foreign Currency Translation*, if an entity does not maintain its books in its functional currency, remeasurement into the functional currency is required prior to translation into the reporting currency (i.e., the parent company's currency). In this process, nonmonetary balance sheet items are remeasured using historical exchange rates. Hence, inventories carried at cost should be remeasured using historical exchange rates because it is cited as an example of a nonmonetary balance sheet item in SFAS 52. Answers (b), (c), and (d) are monetary items. Monetary balance sheet items are remeasured using the current exchange rate.

8. (b) The functional currency of a foreign entity may be its local currency (i.e., the foreign currency) or the reporting currency (e.g., the U.S. dollar). If the functional currency is the foreign currency, the foreign currency financial statements must be *translated* into U.S. dollars. The translation adjustments which result from this process are not reported in the consolidated income statement but are reported in other comprehensive income. If the functional currency is the U.S. dollar, the foreign currency financial statements must be *remeasured* into U.S. dollars. The foreign exchange gains/losses which result from this process are reported in the consolidated income statement.

9. (d) If an entity does not maintain its books in its functional currency, *remeasuring* into the functional currency is required prior to *translation* into the reporting currency (i.e., the parent company's currency). The remeasuring process will result in exchange gains and losses. The net gain or loss should be recognized in income from continuing operations.

FOREIGN CURRENCY TRANSACTIONS

10. (b) The payable resulting from the merchandise purchased from the foreign supplier is denominated in a foreign currency. Therefore, changes in the relative value of the dollar and the foreign currency will result in exchange gains or losses which should be recognized in income from continuing operations in the period they occur. Velec should not have recorded the purchase, and the related payable, until 12/15/92, the date title to the goods passed to Velec. At that date, the exchange rate was one dollar to 20 francs. At 12/31/92, the exchange rate was one dollar to 21 francs. Since the exchange rate of francs to one U.S. dollar increased from the date the payable was recorded to the end of the year (i.e., each U.S. dollar could purchase 1 additional franc), Velec realized a foreign exchange gain in 1992 which should be included in income from continuing operations in 1992.

11. (b) Whenever a transaction is denominated (i.e., payable) in a foreign currency, changes in the translation rate (i.e., the spot rate) of the foreign currency with respect to the entity's functional currency (i.e., the dollar in this case) will result in a gain or loss. The gain or loss should be recognized in income in the period(s) the rate changes, and the related asset or liability (i.e., accounts payable in this case) should be adjusted accordingly. The foreign exchange gain recognized in 1992 is computed as follows:

Initial obligation, 11/30/92, in U.S. dollars (£300,000 x $1.65)	$ 495,000
Amount payable, 12/31/92, in U.S. dollars (£300,000 x $1.62)	(486,000)
Foreign exchange gain recognized in 1992	$ 9,000

12. (a) A change in exchange rates between the functional currency and the currency in which the transaction is denominated increases or decreases the expected amount of functional currency cash flows upon a settlement of the transaction. That increase or decrease in expected functional currency cash flows is a foreign currency transaction gain or loss that generally should be included as a component of income from continuing operations for the period in which the transaction is settled.

13. (d) Whenever a transaction is denominated (i.e., payable) in a foreign currency, changes in the translation rate of the foreign currency with respect to the entity's functional currency (i.e., the dollar in this case) will result in a transaction gain or loss. The gain or loss should be included in the determination of net income in the period(s) the rate changes, and the related asset or liability (i.e., accounts receivable in this case) should be adjusted accordingly. Likewise, if the transaction is finally settled at a rate different from that reflected in the related asset or liability, gain or loss should also be recognized. The transaction loss and gain recognized in 1990 and 1991, respectively, are determined as follows:

Initial obligation, 9/1/90, in U.S. dollars (250,000 francs x $.20)	$ 50,000
Amount receivable, 12/31/90 (250,000 francs x $.19)	(47,500)
Foreign exchange loss recognized, 1990	$ 2,500

Amount receivable, 12/31/90 (above)	$ 47,500
Amount of settlement, 2/1/91 (250,000 francs x $.22)	(55,000)
Foreign exchange gain recognized, 1991	$ (7,500)

14. (c) Whenever a *transaction* is denominated (i.e., payable) in a foreign currency, changes in the translation rate of the foreign currency with respect to the entity's functional currency (i.e., the dollar in this case) will result in a transaction gain or loss. The gain or loss should be recognized in income in the period(s) the rate changes, and the related asset or liability (i.e., accounts payable in this case) should be adjusted accordingly. Likewise, if the transaction is finally settled at a rate different from that reflected in the related asset or liability, gain or loss will also be recognized. The purchase and the related payable should not have been recorded until 12/10/97, because no liability had been incurred until the merchandise was shipped (i.e., the merchandise was ordered F.O.B. shipping point). The foreign exchange gains recognized in 1997 and 1998, respectively, are determined as follows:

Initial obligation, 12/10/97, in U.S. dollars (200,000 marks x $.4875)	$ 97,500
Amount payable, 12/31/97 (200,000 marks x $.4675)	(93,500)
Foreign exchange gain recognized, 1997	$ 4,000

Amount payable, 12/31/97 (above)	$ 93,500
Amount of settlement, 1/10/98 (200,000 marks x $.4475)	(89,500)
Foreign exchange gain recognized, 1998	$ 4,000

15. (d) The payables resulting from the merchandise purchased from the foreign supplier and the borrowing are *transactions* denominated in a foreign currency. The payable from the merchandise purchased was recorded at $90,000 on 1/20/97. It was paid on 3/20/97 at the U.S. dollar equivalent of $96,000, resulting in a $6,000 foreign exchange

loss. The payable from the borrowing was recorded at $500,000 at 7/1/97. Accrued interest on the borrowing was $25,000 (i.e., $500,000 x 10% x 6/12) at 12/31/97. At 12/31/97, the U.S. dollar equivalents of the principal amount and accrued interest were $520,000 and $26,000, respectively, resulting in an additional $21,000 [i.e., ($520,000 + $26,000) − ($500,000 + $25,000)] foreign exchange loss. Thus, the foreign exchange loss recognized in the 1997 income statement is $27,000 (i.e., $6,000 + $21,000).

16. (d) Whenever a transaction is denominated (i.e., payable) in a foreign currency, changes in the translation rate of the foreign currency with respect to the entity's functional currency (i.e., the dollar in this case) will result in a transaction gain or loss. The gain or loss should be included in the determination of net income in the period(s) the rate changes, and the related asset or liability (i.e., accounts payable in this case) should be adjusted accordingly. The transaction loss recognized in 1994 is determined as follows:

Accounts payable, 12/31/94, in U.S. dollars (10,000 local currency units x $.70)	$ 7,000
Initial obligation, 9/22/94, in U.S. dollars (10,000 local currency units x $.55)	(5,500)
Foreign exchange loss recognized, 1994	$ 1,500

17. (d) A transaction gain or loss (measured from the transaction date or most recent balance sheet date, whichever is later) is realized upon settlement of a foreign currency transaction. In 1997, a *loss* of $40,000 (i.e., $240,000 − $280,000) is recorded due to the additional amount that must be repaid since the last balance sheet date.

18. (b) To record a foreign exchange gain on collection of the receivable, the exchange rate of Japanese yen to one U.S. dollar must have decreased. For instance, assume a receivable for 1,000 yen and an exchange rate of 10 yen to 1 dollar at the contract date. If the exchange rate changed to 5 yen to 1 dollar, the 1,000 yen when collected could be converted into 200 US dollars at the settlement date. This $200 is twice the $100 that could have been obtained from the conversion of currency at the contract date (1,000 ÷ 10 = $100). To record an exchange loss on settlement of the payable, the exchange rate of French francs to one dollar must have decreased. For example, assume a payable for 1,000 francs and an exchange rate of 10 francs to 1 dollar at the contract date. If the exchange rate changed to 5 francs to 1 dollar, the 1,000 francs paid at the settlement date required more US dollars than would have been required at the date of contract (1,000 ÷ 5 = $200 at date of

settlement versus 1,000 ÷ 10 = $100 at date of contract).

FORWARD EXCHANGE CONTRACT

19. (d) A forward exchange contract is an agreement to exchange different currencies at a specified future date and at a specified rate (the forward rate). A forward contract is a foreign currency transaction. Therefore, a gain or loss on a forward contract is included in determining income from continuing operations in accordance with the requirements for other foreign currency transactions (subject to exceptions for certain intercompany transactions, certain hedges of net investments, and foreign currency commitments, which are deferred). The gain or loss realized on a forward exchange contract, other than a speculative forward contract, is computed by multiplying the foreign currency amount of the contract by the difference between the *spot* rate at the balance sheet date and the *spot* rate at the inception of the contract (or the spot rate last used to measure a gain or loss on that contract for an earlier period). Therefore, the foreign currency transaction gain that should be recognized in income from the forward contract to hedge a prior purchase of inventory is $10,000, determined as follows:

Foreign currency units to be purchased under forward contract	100,000
Times: Excess of spot rate at the balance sheet date over the spot rate at the inception of the contract ($.98 – $.88)	x $.10
Foreign currency transaction gain recognized in income in 1991 from the forward contract	$ 10,000

20. (d) Since the forward contract is not a speculative forward contract, the gain realized on the contract is computed by multiplying the foreign currency amount of the contract by the difference between the spot rate at the balance sheet date and the spot rate at the inception of the contract (or the spot rate last used to measure a gain or loss on that contract for an earlier period).

Foreign currency units to be purchased under forward contract	100,000
Times: Excess of spot rate at the balance sheet date over the spot rate at the inception of the contract ($.98 – $.88)	x $.10
Foreign currency transaction gain realized in 1991 from the contract	$ 10,000

21. (b) A gain or loss on a *speculative forward exchange contract* is included in determining income from continuing operations in accordance with the requirements for other foreign currency transactions. A gain or loss on a speculative forward contract is computed by multiplying the foreign currency

amount of the contract by the difference between the forward rate available for the remaining maturity of the contract and the contracted forward rate (or the forward rate last used to measure a gain or loss on that contract for an earlier period). Thus, the amount of gain that Imp should report in 1991 for the speculative forward contract is determined as follows:

Foreign currency units to be purchased under speculative forward contract	100,000
Times: Excess of forward rate available for remaining portion of contract and the contracted forward rate ($.93 – $.90)	x $.03
Foreign currency transaction gain recognized in income in 1991	$ 3,000

22. (a) A forward exchange contract (forward contract) is an agreement to exchange different currencies at a specified future date and at a specified rate (the forward rate). A forward contract is a foreign currency *transaction*. Therefore, a gain or loss on a forward contract is included in determining net income in accordance with the requirements for other foreign currency transactions (subject to exceptions for certain intercompany transactions and certain hedges of net investments and foreign currency commitments, which are deferred). A gain or loss on a speculative forward contract (that is, a contract that does not hedge an exposure) is computed by multiplying the foreign currency amount of the contract by the difference between the forward rate available for the remaining maturity of the contract and the contracted forward rate (or the forward rate last used to measure a gain or loss on that contract for an earlier period). Therefore, the amount of loss that Flint should report in 1991 for the speculative forward contract is determined as follows:

Foreign currency units under speculative forward contract	10,000
Times: Excess of forward rate available for the remaining maturity of the contract and the contracted forward rate ($0.82 – $0.78)	x $.04
Loss on forward contract to be recognized in 1991	$ 400

TRANSACTION GAINS & LOSSES

23. (b) Translation adjustments relating to foreign subsidiaries are *not* included in the determination of consolidated income. These adjustments are reported in other comprehensive income. Post's receivable from a foreign customer was denominated in a foreign currency; therefore, changes in the relative value of the dollar and the foreign currency results in exchange gains or losses, which are included in the determination of net income. The recorded amount of the receivable was $110,000 and it was settled for $120,000; thus, Post

recognizes a $10,000 foreign exchange gain in this transaction.

24. (a) The payable to the unrelated foreign supplier is a *transaction* denominated in a foreign currency. The payable was initially recorded at $64,000. It was included in the December 31, 1997 balance sheet at $60,000. The decrease in the payable represents a $4,000 transaction gain which is recognized in income from continuing operations in 1997. On the other hand, the $8,000 loss resulting from the *translation* of the accounts of the foreign subsidiary is not recognized in the 1997 income statement. Translation gains and losses are reported in other comprehensive income. The reported foreign exchange loss is determined as follows:

Foreign exchange loss before adjustment	$15,000
Gain on transaction denominated in a foreign currency	(4,000)
Foreign exchange loss for 1997	$11,000

25. (c) Under SFAS 52, *Foreign Currency Translation*, if an entity's functional currency is a foreign currency which has not experienced significant inflation, translation adjustments result from the process of translating that entity's financial statements into the reporting currency. Translation adjustments should not be included in determining net income but should be reported in other comprehensive income. A cumulative foreign exchange translation loss would be reported in accumulated other comprehensive income as a stockholders' equity contra account. A discount or premium on bonds payable should be reported as part of the related liability for bonds payable in the balance sheet. Organization costs should be reported as an intangible asset in the balance sheet.

26. (b) Foreign currency transactions are transactions denominated in a currency other than the entity's functional currency. Hence, no foreign currency transaction gain or loss would occur if the purchase of the machinery by the U.S. company is denominated in U.S. dollars. Foreign exchange transaction gains and losses are recognized as a component of income from continuing operations in the period they occur.

27. (a) *Translation* adjustments should not be included in determining net income but should be reported in other comprehensive income. Gains and losses on foreign currency transactions that are designated as, and are effective as, economic hedges of a net investment in a foreign entity should not be included in determining net income but should be reported in the same manner as translation adjustments. Therefore, the translation loss less the transaction gain should be reported in other comprehensive income in Nash's consolidated financial statements.

PERFORMANCE BY SUBTOPICS

Each category below parallels a subtopic covered in Chapter 17. Record the number and percentage of questions you correctly answered in each subtopic area.

Translation of Foreign Currency Financial Statements
Question # / Correct√: 1, 2, 3, 4, 5, 6 — # Questions 6, # Correct, % Correct

Remeasurement Into Functional Currency
Question # / Correct√: 7, 8, 9 — # Questions 3, # Correct, % Correct

Foreign Currency Transactions
Question # / Correct√: 10, 11, 12, 13, 14, 15, 16, 17, 18 — # Questions 9, # Correct, % Correct

Forward Exchange Contract
Question # / Correct√: 19, 20, 21, 22 — # Questions 4, # Correct, % Correct

Transaction Gains & Losses
Question # / Correct√: 23, 24, 25, 26, 27 — # Questions 5, # Correct, % Correct

ESSAY SOLUTION

SOLUTION 17-2 VARIOUS ASPECTS OF FOREIGN CURRENCY FINANCIAL STATEMENTS

a. The objectives of translating a foreign subsidiary's financial statements are to:

- Provide information that is generally compatible with the expected economic effects of a rate change on a subsidiary's cash flows and equity.
- Reflect the subsidiary's financial results and relationships in **single currency consolidated financial statements**, as measured in its **functional currency** and in **conformity with GAAP**.

b. Applying different exchange rates to the various financial statement accounts causes the restated statements to be unbalanced. The amount required to bring the restated statements into balance is termed the gain or loss from the translation or remeasurement. The gain or loss arising from remeasuring Jay A's financial statements is reported in the consolidated income statement. The gain or loss arising from translating Jay F's financial statements is reported in other comprehensive income.

c. The functional currency is the foreign currency or parent's currency that most closely correlates with the following economic indicators:

- Cash flow indicators
- Sales price indicators
- Sales market indicators
- Expense indicators
- Financing indicators
- **Intercompany transactions and arrangement indicators**

d. All accounts relating to **Jay A's** equipment are remeasured by the **exchange rate prevailing** between the **U.S. and Australian dollars** at the **time equipment** was **purchased**.

All accounts relating to **Jay F's** equipment are translated by the **current exchange rates** prevailing between the **U.S. dollar and French franc**. For the **equipment cost** and **accumulated depreciation**, this is the current exchange rate at **December 31, 1990**. **Depreciation expense** is translated at the rate prevailing on the **date the depreciation expense** was **recognized** or an appropriate **weighted average** exchange rate **for 1990**.

CHAPTER 18

PARTNERSHIPS & PERSONAL FINANCIAL STATEMENTS

CHAPTER 18

PARTNERSHIPS & PERSONAL FINANCIAL STATEMENTS

I. PARTNERSHIP FORMATION

A. UNIFORM PARTNERSHIP ACT

A majority of states have adopted the **Uniform Partnership Act** (UPA) which defines a partnership as an association of two or more persons to carry on, as co-owners, a business for profit. In addition to setting forth the legal rights and liabilities of the partners, the UPA has some impact on accounting for partnership transactions. Accounting for partnerships should therefore comply with the legal requirements as set forth by the UPA (e.g., liquidation payments to partnership creditors before any distribution to partners) or other applicable state laws, as well as complying with the partnership agreement itself.

B. IDENTIFIABLE ASSETS CONTRIBUTED

All identifiable assets (e.g., cash, inventory, land, patents, etc.) contributed to the partnership are recorded by the partnership at their **fair values** (i.e., book values are ignored). All liabilities that the partnership assumes are recorded at their present values. If a partner contributes a noncash asset to the partnership (e.g., land or equipment) subject to a mortgage, the contributing partner's capital account is credited for the **fair value** of the noncash asset **less the mortgage assumed by the partnership**.

EXAMPLE 1 ♦ IDENTIFIABLE ASSETS CONTRIBUTED

Alice and Brenda form a partnership: Alice contributes cash of $60,000; Brenda contributes a building with a fair value of $90,000 subject to a mortgage loan of $30,000.

REQUIRED: The initial journal entry made to record the formation of the partnership.

SOLUTION:

Cash	60,000	
Building	90,000	
Mortgage Loan on Building		30,000
Alice, Capital		60,000
Brenda, Capital ($90,000 – $30,000)		60,000

C. UNIDENTIFIABLE ASSETS CONTRIBUTED

In the formation of a partnership, one or more of the partners may contribute an unidentifiable asset (e.g., managerial expertise or personal business reputation). Unidentifiable assets can be as valuable to the partnership as identifiable assets, such as cash, inventory, patents, and equipment. When one or more partners contribute unidentifiable assets, the formation of the partnership may be recorded under the **bonus** method or the **goodwill** method.

1. **BONUS METHOD** The bonus method assumes that unidentifiable assets contributed to the partnership do **not** constitute a partnership asset with a measurable cost. Under this approach, only identifiable assets contributed to the partnership, such as cash, inventory, patents, and equipment are recognized by the partnership. The bonus method allocates invested capital, equal to the fair value of the identifiable net assets contributed to the partnership, to the partners according to a specified ratio.

EXAMPLE 2 ♦ BONUS METHOD

Alice and Brenda form a partnership. Alice contributes cash of $40,000 and her considerable managerial expertise; Brenda contributes a building with a fair value of $90,000 subject to a mortgage loan of $30,000. Alice and Brenda are to be given equal capital balances.

REQUIRED: The initial journal entry to record the formation of the partnership using the bonus method.

SOLUTION:

Cash	40,000	
Building	90,000	
Mortgage Loan on Building		30,000
Alice, Capital		50,000
Brenda, Capital		50,000

The bonus method does not consider Alice's managerial expertise to be a partnership asset with a measurable cost. The bonus method allocates the $100,000 [i.e., ($40,000 + $90,000) – $30,000] of invested capital to Brenda and Alice equally. Alice is receiving a capital bonus of $10,000 from Brenda because she is given a capital balance of $50,000, although she has only contributed identifiable assets of $40,000 to the partnership.

2. **GOODWILL METHOD** The goodwill method assumes that unidentifiable assets contributed to the partnership constitute a partnership asset with a measurable cost. Under this approach, all assets contributed to the partnership, such as cash, inventory, patents, equipment, and managerial expertise are recognized by the partnership. The goodwill method credits the contributing partner's capital account for the fair value of the identifiable and unidentifiable assets contributed to the partnership, less the amount of any liabilities assumed by the partnership.

EXAMPLE 3 ♦ GOODWILL METHOD

Same situation as in Example 2.

REQUIRED: The initial journal entry to record the formation of the partnership using the goodwill method.

SOLUTION:

Cash	40,000	
Building	90,000	
Goodwill	20,000	
Mortgage Loan on Building		30,000
Alice, Capital		60,000
Brenda, Capital		60,000

The goodwill method considers Alice's managerial expertise to be a partnership asset with a measurable cost. Since Alice is to be given a $60,000 capital balance while only contributing identifiable assets with a fair value of $40,000, an implied value of $20,000 can be assigned to her managerial expertise. The goodwill method capitalizes the apparent value of Alice's contribution. Brenda is given a $60,000 capital balance, equal to the fair value of the building she contributed to the partnership less the mortgage assumed by the partnership (i.e., $90,000 – $30,000).

D. OWNERS' EQUITY ACCOUNTS

The **capital** account is an equity account used to account for permanent withdrawals, additional contributions and net income or loss. Other important accounts include the **drawing** account and **loans to or from partners**. The **drawing** account is used to account for normal withdrawals. It is closed at the end of the period into the capital account. **Loan accounts** are established for amounts intended as loans, rather than as additional capital investments. In liquidation proceedings, a loan to or from a partner is in essence treated as a decrease or increase to the partner's capital account, respectively.

II. DIVISION OF PROFITS AND LOSSES

A. TYPES OF METHODS

Various methods exist for the division of partnership profits and losses, including the following:

1. **EQUALLY OR SPECIFIED RATIO** Equally or in accordance with a specified ratio set forth in the partnership agreement

2. **CAPITAL BALANCE** According to the ratio of partners' capital balances as of a particular date or according to their weighted-average capital balances for the period

3. **SALARY BONUS** According to the portions to be consumed as salaries or bonuses

B. SELECTING A METHOD

The method of division to be used in any given situation is generally the method specified in the partnership agreement. This agreement must always be consulted first, since it is legally binding on the partners.

1. **NO ARRANGEMENT SPECIFIED** If no profit and loss sharing arrangement is specified in the partnership agreement, the UPA requires that profits and losses be shared equally.

2. **NO ARRANGEMENT FOR LOSSES** If the agreement specifies how profits are to be shared but is silent as to losses, losses are to be shared in the same manner as profits.

C. OWNERSHIP INTERESTS

Notice that the profit and loss sharing ratio is totally independent of the partners' ownership interests. Thus, for instance, two partners may have ownership interests of 60% and 40% but share profits and losses equally.

EXAMPLE 4 ♦ DIVISION OF PROFITS

Foreman, Cramer, and Ramsey are partners in a going concern with capital accounts at the beginning of the period of $40,000, $24,000, and $28,000, respectively. The partnership agreement states the following:

a. All partners are to receive interest of 6% on beginning capital balances.
b. Cramer is to receive a $4,000 annual salary and Ramsey a $5,000 annual salary.
c. The remaining income is to be divided

Foreman	30%
Cramer	25%
Ramsey	45%

REQUIRED: Assuming partnership income was $25,000; and Foreman, Cramer, and Ramsey had drawings of $2,000, $1,000, and $2,000 respectively; compute the ending capital balances of each partner.

(continued on next page)

SOLUTION:

	Foreman	Cramer	Ramsey	Total
Beginning capital balances	$40,000	$24,000	$28,000	$ 92,000
6% interest on beginning capital balances	2,400	1,440	1,680	5,520
Salaries		4,000	5,000	9,000
Division of remaining income ($25,000 – $5,520 – $9,000)	3,144	2,620	4,716	10,480
Capital balances before drawings	45,544	32,060	39,396	117,000
Drawings	(2,000)	(1,000)	(2,000)	(5,000)
Ending capital balances	$43,544	$31,060	$37,396	$112,000

III. ADMISSION OF A NEW PARTNER

A. OVERVIEW

A new partner may be admitted to the partnership by purchasing the interest of one or more of the existing partners or by contributing cash or other assets (i.e., investment of additional capital).

B. PURCHASE OF INTEREST

When a new partner enters the partnership by purchasing the interest of an existing partner, the price paid for that interest is irrelevant to the partnership accounting records because it is a private transaction between the buyer and seller. The assets and liabilities of the partnership are not affected. The capital account of the new partner is recorded by merely relabeling the capital account of the old partner. The following journal entry is made:

Capital, A (old partner)	XX	
Capital, B (new partner)		XX

EXAMPLE 5 ♦ PURCHASE OF PARTNERSHIP INTEREST

Henry and Gerald are partners with capital accounts of $40,000 and $60,000, respectively. Rocky purchases Henry's interest for $50,000.

REQUIRED: Record the journal entry on the partnership books.

SOLUTION:

Henry, Capital	40,000	
Rocky, Capital		40,000

After Rocky's purchase, total partnership capital continues to equal $100,000 (i.e., $40,000 + $60,000).

C. ADMISSION BY INVESTMENT OF ADDITIONAL ASSETS

A new partner may be granted an interest in the partnership in exchange for contributed identifiable assets and/or goodwill (e.g., business expertise, an established clientele, etc.). The admission of the new partner and contribution of assets may be recorded on the basis of the **bonus** method or the **goodwill** method.

1. **BONUS METHOD** The bonus method assumes that unidentifiable assets contributed do not constitute a partnership asset with a measurable cost. Admittance of a new partner involves debiting cash or other identifiable assets for the fair value of the assets contributed and crediting the new partner's capital for the agreed (i.e., purchased) percentage of total capital. Total capital equals the **carrying amount** of the net assets prior to admittance of the new partner, plus the fair value of the identifiable assets contributed by the new partner. A difference between the fair value of the identifiable assets contributed and the interest granted to the new partner results in the recognition of a **bonus**.

a. **NO BONUS RECOGNIZED** When an incoming partner's capital account (ownership interest) is to be equal to the fair value of the identifiable assets contributed, the partnership books merely debit cash or other assets and credit capital for this amount.

EXAMPLE 6 ♦ NO BONUS RECOGNIZED

Henry and Gerald are partners with capital accounts of $40,000 and $60,000, respectively; income and losses are shared equally (50%). Rocky is granted a 1/3 interest in the partnership in exchange for $50,000.

REQUIRED: Record this transaction in the partnership books. Show computations.

SOLUTION: Following the admittance of Rocky, the identifiable net assets of the partnership will have a carrying amount of $150,000 ($40,000 + $60,000 + $50,000). One-third of this amount, or $50,000, is assigned to Rocky's capital account. Since this is equal to the fair value of the identifiable assets contributed by Rocky ($50,000), no bonus results.

Cash (or other identifiable assets, as appropriate)	50,000	
Rocky, Capital (1/3 x $150,000)		50,000

After Rocky's admission, total partnership capital equals the carrying amount of the identifiable net assets of the partnership (i.e., $40,000 + $60,000 + $50,000 = $150,000).

b. **BONUS TO THE OLD PARTNERS** When the fair value of the identifiable assets contributed by an incoming partner exceeds the amount of ownership interest to be credited to the capital account, the old partners recognize a bonus equal to this excess. This bonus is allocated on the basis of the same ratio used for income allocation (unless otherwise specified in the partnership agreement). Recording involves crediting the old partners' capital accounts for the allocated amounts of the bonus.

EXAMPLE 7 ♦ BONUS TO OLD PARTNERS

Same as Example 6, except Rocky invests $56,000 for a 1/3 interest. The partnership records admissions of new partners under the **bonus** method.

REQUIRED: Record the admission of Rocky.

SOLUTION: Since Rocky has contributed $56,000, the total capital of the new partnership equals $156,000. Rocky's 1/3 interest of this new total is $52,000. The $4,000 excess of identifiable assets contributed by Rocky over his initial capital balance is divided among the old partners as a bonus on the basis of their profit and loss sharing ratio. The journal entry is as follows:

Cash	56,000	
Henry, Capital ($4,000 x 50%)		2,000
Gerald, Capital ($4,000 x 50%)		2,000
Rocky, Capital		52,000

After Rocky's admission, Henry's and Gerald's capital balances are $42,000 (i.e., $40,000 + $2,000) and $62,000 (i.e., $60,000 + $2,000), respectively, and total partnership capital equals the recorded amount of the identifiable net assets of the partnership (i.e., $42,000 + $62,000 + $52,000 = $156,000).

c. **BONUS GRANTED TO NEW PARTNER** An incoming partner may contribute identifiable assets having a fair value less than the partnership interest granted to that new partner. Similarly, the new partner may not contribute any identifiable assets at all. The incoming partner is therefore presumed to contribute an unidentifiable asset, such as managerial expertise or personal business reputation. In this case, a bonus is granted to the new partner, and the capital accounts of the old partners are reduced on the basis of their profit and loss ratio.

EXAMPLE 8 ♦ BONUS TO NEW PARTNER

Same as in Example 6, except Rocky is to contribute only $44,000 in exchange for his 1/3 ownership interest.

REQUIRED: Record the admission of Rocky.

SOLUTION: Since Rocky contributes $44,000, the total net assets of the new partnership will be $144,000. Rocky's 1/3 share of this is $48,000.

The $4,000 difference between the fair value of the identifiable assets contributed by Rocky ($44,000) and the amount to be credited to him ($48,000) is allocated among the old partners in accordance with their profit and loss sharing ratio. The journal entry is as follows:

Cash	44,000	
Henry, Capital ($4,000 x 50%)	2,000	
Gerald, Capital ($4,000 x 50%)	2,000	
Rocky, Capital		48,000

After Rocky's admission, Henry's and Gerald's capital balances are $38,000 (i.e., $40,000 – $2,000) and $58,000 (i.e., $60,000 – $2,000), respectively, and total partnership capital equals the recorded amount of the identifiable net assets of the partnership (i.e., $38,000 + $58,000 + $48,000 = $144,000).

2. **GOODWILL METHOD** This method attempts to revalue the net worth of the partnership on the basis of the fair value of assets received in exchange for a percentage ownership interest. Following the admission of the new partner, the total capital (i.e., net worth) of the partnership is revalued to approximate its fair value. Existing identifiable assets must be revalued at their fair value; any excess valuation implied in the purchase price is recorded as goodwill.

    a. **GOODWILL ATTRIBUTABLE TO OLD PARTNERS** When a new partner's asset contribution is greater than the ownership interest he or she is to receive, the excess assets are accounted for as goodwill attributable to the old partners.

EXAMPLE 9 ♦ GOODWILL TO OLD PARTNERS

Same as Example 6, except Rocky contributes and is credited with $56,000 for a 1/3 interest.

REQUIRED: Record the admission of Rocky under the goodwill method.

SOLUTION: If Rocky is to be credited with a 1/3 interest for $56,000, the implied capital (total fair value) of the partnership is $168,000 (i.e., $56,000 x 3). The $12,000 difference between the actual capital ($156,000) and the implied capital ($168,000) is recorded as goodwill attributable to the old partners in accordance with their profit and loss sharing ratio (50% each as stated above). The following journal entries are required:

Goodwill	12,000	
Henry, Capital		6,000
Gerald, Capital		6,000
Cash	56,000	
Rocky, Capital		56,000

After Rocky's admission, Henry's and Gerald's capital balances are $46,000 (i.e., $40,000 + $6,000) and $66,000 (i.e., $60,000 + $6,000), respectively, and total partnership capital equals the fair value of the net assets of the partnership (i.e., $46,000 + $66,000 + $56,000 = $168,000).

b. **GOODWILL ATTRIBUTABLE TO NEW PARTNER** When a new partner's identifiable asset contribution is **less** than the ownership interest he or she is to receive, the excess capital allowed to the new partner is considered as goodwill attributable to him or her. This assumes that the recorded amounts of the old partners' capital accounts adequately reflect the fair value of the partnership's assets; otherwise, write off the excess carrying amount.

EXAMPLE 10 ♦ GOODWILL TO NEW PARTNER

Same as Example 6 except that Rocky invests $44,000 for a 1/3 interest.

REQUIRED: Record the admission of Rocky.

SOLUTION: If Rocky is to receive a 1/3 interest for $44,000, the old partners are to have a 2/3 interest. If 2/3X = $100,000 (old partners' capital), the implied value for 100% is $150,000 (100,000 ÷ 2/3). Thus, Rocky's capital will be $50,000 consisting of $44,000 contributed and $6,000 goodwill. The journal entry is as follows:

Cash	44,000	
Goodwill	6,000	
Rocky, Capital		50,000

After Rocky's admission, Henry's and Gerald's capital balances are $40,000 and $60,000, respectively, and total partnership capital equals the fair value of the net assets of the partnership (i.e., $40,000 + $60,000 + $50,000 = $150,000).

IV. WITHDRAWAL OF A PARTNER

A. OVERVIEW

Admission of a new partner is not the only manner by which a partnership can undergo a change in composition. Over the life of any partnership, partners may leave the organization. Thus, some method of establishing an equitable settlement of the withdrawing partner's interest in the business property is necessary. The withdrawal of a partner is generally recorded using either the **bonus** method or the **goodwill** method.

B. BONUS METHOD

The difference between the balance of the withdrawing partner's capital account and the amount he or she is paid is the amount of the "bonus." The "bonus" is allocated among the remaining partners' capital accounts in accordance with their profit and loss ratios. Although the partnership's identifiable assets may be revalued to their fair value at the date of withdrawal, any goodwill implied by an excess payment to the retiring partner is **not** recorded.

EXAMPLE 11 ♦ WITHDRAWAL, BONUS METHOD

On May 1, 20X1, the balance sheet for the partnership of Able, Baker, and Cain, together with their respective profit and loss ratios, was as follows:

Assets, at cost	$200,000	Accounts Payable	$ 20,000
		Able, Capital (20%)	40,000
		Baker, Capital (20%)	50,000
		Cain, Capital (60%)	90,000
			$200,000

Able has decided to retire from the partnership. By mutual agreement, the assets are to be adjusted to their fair value of $260,000 at May 1, 20X1. It was agreed that the partnership would pay Able $60,000 for Able's partnership interest. No goodwill is to be recorded.

(continued on next page)

REQUIRED: Record this transaction and determine the balances of Baker's and Cain's capital accounts after Able's retirement.

SOLUTION: The entry to adjust the partnership assets to their fair value is as follows:

Identifiable Assets ($260,000 – $200,000)	60,000	
Able, Capital ($60,000 x 20%)		12,000
Baker, Capital ($60,000 x 20%)		12,000
Cain, Capital ($60,000 x 60%)		36,000

After this entry, Able has a capital balance of $52,000 ($40,000 + $12,000).

Under the bonus method, the additional payment of $8,000 ($60,000 payment – $52,000 capital balance) made to Able is recorded as a decrease in the remaining partners' capital accounts. As Baker and Cain in the past have been receiving 20% and 60% of all profits and losses, respectively, 25% [.2 ÷ (.2 + .6)] of this reduction is allocated to Baker and 75% [.6 ÷ (.2 + .6)] of this reduction is allocated to Cain, as follows:

Able, Capital	52,000	
Baker, Capital (25% x $8,000)	2,000	
Cain, Capital (75% x $8,000)	6,000	
Cash		60,000

After the entry:

Baker's capital balance is $60,000 ($50,000 + $12,000 – $2,000).
Cain's capital balance is $120,000 ($90,000 + $36,000 – $6,000).

C. **GOODWILL METHOD**

The partners may elect to record the implied goodwill in the partnership based on the payment to the withdrawing partner. The amount of the implied goodwill is allocated to all of the partners in accordance with their profit and loss ratios. After the allocation of the implied goodwill of the partnership, the balance in the withdrawing partner's capital account should equal the amount he or she is to receive in final settlement of his or her interest.

EXAMPLE 12 ♦ WITHDRAWAL, GOODWILL METHOD

Same as Example 11 except that goodwill is to be recorded in the transaction, as implied by the excess payment to Able.

REQUIRED: Record this transaction and determine the balances of Baker's and Cain's capital accounts after Able's retirement.

SOLUTION: The entry to adjust the partnership assets to their fair value is the same as the above.

Identifiable Assets ($260,000 – $200,000)	60,000	
Able, Capital ($60,000 x 20%)		12,000
Baker, Capital ($60,000 x 20%)		12,000
Cain, Capital ($60,000 x 60%)		36,000

After this entry, Able has a capital balance of $52,000 ($40,000 + $12,000).

Able's capital account must be increased by $8,000 to equal her $60,000 cash distribution. To accomplish this, goodwill is recognized for some amount, of which, $8,000 represents 20%, Able's profit and loss percentage. Therefore, the amount of goodwill to be recorded is $40,000 ($8,000 ÷ 20%). The entries to record the implied goodwill of the partnership and the payment to Able in final settlement of her interest are as follows:

(continued on next page)

Goodwill	40,000	
Able, Capital ($40,000 x 20%)		8,000
Baker, Capital ($40,000 x 20%)		8,000
Cain, Capital ($40,000 x 60%)		24,000
Able, Capital ($52,000 + $8,000)	60,000	
Cash		60,000

After the entry:

Baker's capital balance is $70,000 ($50,000 + $12,000 + $8,000).
Cain's capital balance is $150,000 ($90,000 + $36,000 + $24,000).

V. LIQUIDATION OF PARTNERSHIP

A. OVERVIEW

Liquidation is the process of converting partnership assets into cash and distributing the cash to creditors and partners. Frequently, the sale of partnership assets will not provide sufficient cash to pay both creditors and partners. The creditors have priority on any distribution. The basic rule is that no distribution is made to any partner until all possible losses and liquidation expenses have been paid or provided for. An individual prematurely distributing cash to a partner whose capital account later shows a deficit may be held personally liable if the insolvent partner is unable to repay such a distribution. The proceeds of a liquidation may be distributed in a **lump sum** after all assets have been sold and all creditors satisfied, or the proceeds may be distributed to partners in **installments** as **excess** cash becomes available.

- In liquidation proceedings, a loan **to** a partner from the partnership is treated as a **decrease** to the partner's capital account. A loan **from** a partner to the partnership is treated as an **increase** to the partner's capital account.

B. LUMP-SUM DISTRIBUTION

The **first** step in the liquidation process is to sell all noncash assets and allocate the resulting gain or loss to the capital accounts of the partners in accordance with their profit and loss sharing ratio. The **second** step is to satisfy the liabilities owing to creditors other than partners. The **third** step is to satisfy liabilities owing to partners other than for capital and profits. The **final** step is to distribute any cash remaining to the partners for capital and finally for profits. Any deficiency (i.e., debit balance) in a solvent partner's capital will require that partner to contribute cash equal to the debit balance. If the deficient partner is insolvent, the debit balance must be absorbed by the remaining partners (usually in accordance with their profit and loss sharing ratio). A lump-sum liquidation is illustrated by Example 13.

EXAMPLE 13 ♦ LUMP-SUM DISTRIBUTION

The balance sheet of the XYZ Partnership is reproduced below. A loss of $108,000 is realized on the sale of noncash assets. The profit-loss ratio is indicated in parentheses next to each partner's capital account. The partnership is to be liquidated and excess cash, if any, is to be distributed to the partners in a lump sum.

XYZ Partnership
Balance Sheet

Cash	$ 22,000	Liabilities	$ 18,000
Other assets	128,000	Capital: (P/L ratio)	
		X (50%)	44,000
Total assets	$150,000	Y (30%)	44,000
		Z (20%)	44,000
		Total liabilities and capital	$150,000

(continued on next page)

REQUIRED: Provide a schedule showing the liquidation of assets and distribution of proceeds to creditors and partners.

SOLUTION:

XYZ Partnership
Liquidation Statement

	Cash	Other Assets	Liabs.	X(50%)	Capital Y(30%)	Z(20%)
Balances before realization	$ 22,000	$128,000	$18,000	$44,000	$44,000	$44,000
Sale of assets at loss of $108,000	20,000	(128,000)		(54,000)	(32,400)	(21,600)
Balances after realization	42,000	$ 0	18,000	(10,000)	11,600	22,400
Payment of liabilities	18,000)		(18,000)			
Balances	24,000		$ 0	(10,000)	11,600	22,000
Distribution of X's deficit	0			10,000	(6,000)	(4,000)
Balances	24,000			$ 0	5,600	18,400
Final distribution of cash	(24,000)				(5,600)	(18,400)
Balances	$ 0				$ 0	$ 0

C. INSTALLMENT DISTRIBUTIONS

The liquidation of a partnership may take place over a period of several months. Installment distributions may be made to partners on the basis of a **Schedule of Safe Payments**, in conjunction with a **Liquidation Schedule** similar to the one used for lump-sum liquidations. The Schedule of Safe Payments takes a conservative approach to the distribution by assuming that noncash assets are worthless; thus no distribution may be made to partners on the basis of the value of partnership assets, until the assets are sold. An installment distribution of liquidation proceeds is illustrated by Example 14.

EXAMPLE 14 ♦ INSTALLMENT DISTRIBUTIONS

Refer to the balance sheet and other data given in Example 13 for the XYZ partnership. In addition, assume that liquidation of partnership assets took place as per the schedule below. Disposal expenses to be incurred during the liquidation period were estimated at $5,000; this amount is to be held in escrow until the final liquidation.

XYZ Partnership
Liquidation of Assets

Date	Carrying Amount	Sale Price	(Loss)
June 24	$ 40,000	$ 5,000	$ (35,000)
July 7	60,000	13,000	(47,000)
August 3	28,000	2,000	(26,000)
	$128,000	$20,000	$ (108,000)

REQUIRED: What is the "safe" amount of cash that may be distributed to each partner following each sale of partnership noncash assets? Show supporting schedule(s).

(continued on next page)

SOLUTION:

XYZ Partnership
Liquidation Statement

	Cash	Other Assets	Liabs.	Capital X(50%)	Y(30%)	Z(20%)
Balances before realization	$ 22,000	$ 128,000	$ 18,000	$ 44,000	$ 44,000	$ 44,000
June 24 sale	5,000	(40,000)		(17,500)	(10,500)	(7,000)
Balance	27,000	88,000	18,000	26,500	33,500	37,000
Liabilities paid	(18,000)		(18,000)			
Balance	9,000	88,000	$ 0	26,500	33,500	37,000
Cash distribution*	(4,000)					(4,000)
Balance	5,000	88,000		26,500	33,500	33,000
July 7 sale	13,000	(60,000)		(23,500)	(14,100)	(9,400)
Balance	18,000	28,000		3,000	19,400	23,600
Cash distribution*	(13,000)				(1,400)	(11,600)
Balance	5,000	28,000		3,000	18,000	12,000
August 3 sale	2,000	(28,000)		(13,000)	(7,800)	(5,200)
Payment of liquidation costs	(5,000)			(2,500)	(1,500)	(1,000)
Balance	2,000	$ 0		(12,500)	8,700	5,800
Allocation of debit balance	0			12,500	(7,500)	(5,000)
Balance	2,000			$ 0	1,200	800
Cash distribution**	(2,000)				(1,200)	(800)
	$ 0				$ 0	$ 0

*   See accompanying Schedule of Safe Cash Distribution.

** Note that final cash distribution may be made on the basis of balances shown in the partners' capital accounts, since all assets have been sold and liabilities paid.

XYZ Partnership
Schedule of Safe Cash Distribution

Date	Description	Capital Balances X(50%)	Y(30%)	Z(20%)	Total(100%)
June 25	Acct. bal. following sale of assets & pmt. of liabilities**	$ 26,500	$ 33,500	$ 37,000	$ 97,000
	Estimated cost of disposal	(2,500)	(1,500)	(1,000)	(5,000)
	Balance	24,000	32,000	36,000	92,000
	Maximum loss possible	(44,000)	(26,400)	(17,600)	(88,000)
	Balance	(20,000)	5,600	18,400	4,000
	Allocation of debit balance	20,000	(12,000)	(8,000)	
	Balance	$ 0	(6,400)	10,400	4,000
	Allocation of debit balance		6,400	(6,400)	
	Safe cash distribution*		$ 0	$ 4,000	$ 4,000
July 7	Acct. bal. following sale of fixed assets**	$ 3,000	$ 19,400	$ 23,600	$ 46,000
	Max. loss possible (including $5,000 est. expense)	(16,500)	(9,900)	(6,600)	(33,000)
		(13,500)	9,500	17,000	13,000
	Allocation of debit balance	13,500	(8,100)	(5,400)	
	Safe cash distribution*	$ 0	$ 1,400	$ 11,600	$ 13,000

*   To Liquidation Statement.
** From Liquidation Statement.

VI. PERSONAL FINANCIAL STATEMENTS

A. OVERVIEW

The reporting entity for personal financial statements is an individual, a husband and wife, or a family. The statements may be prepared for the purpose of obtaining credit, to assist the individual with financial or tax planning, to satisfy disclosure requirements of public officials, etc.

B. REQUIRED STATEMENTS

The primary focus of users of personal financial statements is on assets and liabilities. Therefore, the basic personal financial statement is the **statement of financial condition**. In addition, a **statement of changes in net worth** is usually presented.

1. **STATEMENT OF FINANCIAL CONDITION** This statement presents the estimated current values of assets, the estimated current amounts of liabilities, the estimated income taxes on the differences between the estimated current amounts of assets and liabilities and their tax bases and net worth at a specified date.

2. **STATEMENT OF CHANGES IN NET WORTH** This statement presents the major sources of increases and decreases in net worth.

Neither the **income statement** nor the **statement of cash flows** pertains to personal financial statements.

C. PRESENTATION

1. **ACCRUAL BASIS** Present on the accrual basis, not the cash basis.

2. **ASSETS AND LIABILITIES** List assets and liabilities by order of liquidity and maturity, not on a current and noncurrent basis.

D. VALUATION

Present assets at their estimated **current values** and liabilities at their estimated **current amounts**.

1. **ESTIMATED CURRENT VALUE OF ASSETS** The amount at which the item could be exchanged between a willing, well-informed buyer and seller, neither of whom is compelled to sell or buy. Estimated selling costs (if material) should be deducted to arrive at current values.

2. **ESTIMATED CURRENT AMOUNT OF LIABILITIES** The lower of the following:

    a. The discounted amount of cash to be paid

    b. The amount at which the liability could be currently discharged

3. **SOP 82-1 GUIDANCE** SOP 82-1 provides specific guidance on determining the current values of assets and current amounts of liabilities.

    a. **RECEIVABLES** Discounted cash flow

    b. **MARKETABLE SECURITIES** Quoted market prices

    c. **OPTIONS** Quoted market prices, if available

    d. **INVESTMENT IN LIFE INSURANCE** Cash value less outstanding loans

    e. **INVESTMENT IN CLOSELY HELD BUSINESS** Liquidation value, multiple of earnings, appraisal, or discounted cash flow

f. **REAL ESTATE** Current value based on sales of similar property in area, appraisals, or discounted cash flow (also, see E., below)

g. **INTANGIBLE ASSETS** Discounted cash flow

h. **FUTURE INTERESTS (NONFORFEITABLE RIGHTS)** Discounted cash flow

i. **PAYABLES AND OTHER LIABILITIES** Discounted cash flow or discharge amount if less than discounted amount

j. **INCOME TAXES PAYABLE** Unpaid taxes from prior periods and the estimated taxes payable for the current period based on year-to-date taxable income reduced by withholdings and estimated tax payments to date

E. BUSINESS INTERESTS

Business Interests that constitute a large part of an individual's total assets should be shown as a **single amount** equal to the estimated **current value** of the business interest separate from other assets. For instance, a significant interest in a closely held corporation should be presented separately from equity investments in other corporations at its estimated current value.

F. NONSEPARATE LIMITED BUSINESS ACTIVITIES

The estimated current value of assets and estimated current amount of liabilities of limited business activities not conducted as a separate business entity should be presented **separately**. For instance, a **real estate investment** generally should be presented as **two amounts**: the estimated current value of the real property and the estimated amount of the mortgage debt on the property.

G. NONCANCELABLE COMMITMENTS

Noncancelable Commitments to pay future sums should be presented as liabilities at their discounted amounts only if the commitment: (1) is for a fixed or determinable amount; (2) is not contingent on others' life expectancies or the occurrence of a particular event, such as disability or death; and (3) does not require future performance of service by others.

H. INCOME TAXES

A provision should be made for estimated income taxes on the differences between the estimated current values of assets, the current amounts of liabilities, and their respective tax bases.

1. **COMPUTATION** Compute as if the estimated value of all assets had been realized and all liabilities had been paid at their estimated current amounts at the date of the financial statements, based on tax law and regulations then applicable.

2. **PRESENTATION** Present in the statement of financial condition **between** liabilities and net worth.

EXAMPLE 15 ♦ INCOME TAXES

The estimated current values of Hagan's personal assets at December 31, 20X1, totaled $800,000, with tax bases aggregating $500,000. The estimated current amounts of Hagan's personal liabilities at December 31, 20X1, totaled $170,000, with tax bases aggregating $200,000. Hagan's 20X1 effective income tax rate was 30%.

REQUIRED: Determine the amount of estimated income taxes that should be provided for the difference between the estimated current values of assets, the current amounts of liabilities, and their respective tax bases in Hagan's personal statement of financial condition at December 31, 20X1.

(continued on next page)

SOLUTION:

Excess of current values of assets over current amounts of liabilities ($800,000 – $170,000)	$630,000
Tax bases of net assets ($500,000 – $200,000)	300,000
	330,000
Times: 20X1 effective income tax rate	x 30%
Amount of estimated income taxes to be provided for the excess of the estimated current value of assets, the current amounts of liabilities, and their respective tax bases	$ 99,000

CPA Exam Week Checklist

WHAT TO PACK FOR EXAM WEEK:

1. CPA exam registration material.

2. Hotel confirmation.

3. Cash and/or a major credit card.

4. Alarm clock—Don't rely on a hotel wake-up call.

5. Comfortable clothing that can be layered to suit varying temperatures.

6. A watch.

7. Appropriate review materials, pencils, erasers, and pencil sharpener.

8. Healthy snack foods.

EVENINGS BEFORE EXAM SECTIONS:

1. Read through your Bisk Education chapter outlines for the next day's section(s).

2. Eat lightly and monitor your intake of alcohol and caffeine. Get a good night's rest.

3. Do **not** try to cram. A brief review of your notes will help to focus your attention on important points and remind you that you are well prepared, but too much cramming can shatter your self-confidence. If you have reviewed conscientiously, you are already well-prepared for the CPA exam.

THE MORNING OF EACH EXAM SECTION:

1. Eat a satisfying breakfast. It will be several hours before your next meal. Eat enough to ward off hunger, but not so much that you feel uncomfortable.

2. Dress appropriately. Wear layers you can take off to suit varying temperatures in the room.

3. Take ample supplies of permissible materials (may vary by jurisdiction).

4. Arrive at the exam center thirty minutes early. Check in as soon as you are allowed to do so.

More helpful exam information is included in the **Practical Advice** appendix in this volume.

CHAPTER 18—PARTNERSHIPS & PERSONAL FINANCIAL STATEMENTS

PROBLEM 18-1 MULTIPLE CHOICE QUESTIONS (66 to 83 minutes)

1. Avers and Smith formed a partnership on July 1, 1998. Avers contributed cash of $50,000. Smith contributed property with a $36,000 carrying amount, a $40,000 original cost, and a fair value of $80,000. The partnership assumed the $35,000 mortgage attached to the property. What should Smith's capital account be on July 1, 1998?
a. $36,000
b. $40,000
c. $45,000
d. $80,000   (11/98, FAR, #9, 6736)

2. On May 1, 1998, Cobb and Mott formed a partnership and agreed to share profits and losses in the ratio of 3:7, respectively. Cobb contributed a parcel of land that cost him $10,000. Mott contributed $40,000 cash. The land was sold for $18,000 on May 1, 1998, immediately after formation of the partnership. What amount should be recorded in Cobb's capital account on formation of the partnership?
a. $18,000
b. $17,400
c. $15,000
d. $10,000   (5/89, PII, #9, amended, 1308)

3. Abel and Carr formed a partnership and agreed to divide initial capital equally, even though Abel contributed $100,000 and Carr contributed $84,000 in identifiable assets. Under the bonus approach to adjust the capital accounts, Carr's unidentifiable asset should be debited for
a. $46,000.
b. $16,000.
c. $ 8,000.
d. $0.   (5/91, PII, #1, 1300)

4. Cor-Eng Partnership was formed on January 2, 1991. Under the partnership agreement, each partner has an equal initial capital balance accounted for under the goodwill method. Partnership net income or loss is allocated 60% to Cor and 40% to Eng. To form the partnership, Cor originally contributed assets costing $30,000 with a fair value of $60,000 on January 2, 1991, while Eng contributed $20,000 in cash. Eng's initial capital balance in Cor-Eng is
a. $20,000.
b. $25,000.
c. $40,000.
d. $60,000.   (11/92, PII, #48, 3382)

5. The Low and Rhu partnership agreement provides special compensation to Low for managing the business. Low receives a bonus of 15 percent of partnership net income before salary and bonus, and also receives a salary of $45,000. Any remaining profit or loss is to be allocated equally. During 1997, the partnership had net income of $50,000 before the bonus and salary allowance. As a result of these distributions, Rhu's equity in the partnership would
a. Increase.
b. Not change.
c. Decrease the same as Low's.
d. Decrease.   (5/89, Theory, #12, amended, 1994)

6. Red and White formed a partnership in 1992. The partnership agreement provides for annual salary allowances of $55,000 for Red and $45,000 for White. The partners share profits equally and losses in a 60/40 ratio. The partnership had earnings of $80,000 for 1993 before any allowance to partners. What amount of these earnings should be credited to each partner's capital account?

	Red	White
a.	$40,000	$40,000
b.	$43,000	$37,000
c.	$44,000	$36,000
d.	$45,000	$35,000 (5/94, FAR, #36, 4851)

7. The partnership agreement of Axel, Berg & Cobb provides for the year-end allocation of net income in the following order:

- First, Axel is to receive 10% of net income up to $100,000 and 20% over $100,000.
- Second, Berg and Cobb each are to receive 5% of the remaining income over $150,000.
- The balance of income is to be allocated equally among the three partners.

The partnership's 1990 net income was $250,000 before any allocations to partners. What amount should be allocated to Axel?
a. $101,000
b. $103,000
c. $108,000
d. $110,000   (11/91, PII, #11, 2459)

8. During 1994, Young and Zinc maintained average capital balances in their partnership of $160,000 and $100,000, respectively. The partners receive 10% interest on average capital balances, and residual profit or loss is divided equally. Partnership profit before interest was $4,000. By what amount should Zinc's capital account change for the year?

a. $ 1,000 decrease
b. $ 2,000 increase
c. $11,000 decrease
d. $12,000 increase   (11/95, FAR, #23, 6105)

9. The Flat and Iron partnership agreement provides for Flat to receive a 20% bonus on profits before the bonus. Remaining profits and losses are divided between Flat and Iron in the ratio of 2 to 3, respectively. Which partner has a greater advantage when the partnership has a profit or when it has a loss?

	Profit	Loss
a.	Flat	Iron
b.	Flat	Flat
c.	Iron	Flat
d.	Iron	Iron

(11/91, Theory, #15, 2523)

10. Kern and Pate are partners with capital balances of $60,000 and $20,000, respectively. Profits and losses are divided in the ratio of 60:40. Kern and Pate decided to form a new partnership with Grant, who invested land valued at $15,000 for a 20% capital interest in the new partnership. Grant's cost of the land was $12,000. The partnership elected to use the bonus method to record the admission of Grant into the partnership. Grant's capital account should be credited for

a. $12,000.
b. $15,000.
c. $16,000.
d. $19,000.   (5/93, PII, #19, 4127)

11. In the Adel-Brick partnership, Adel and Brick had a capital ratio of 3:1 and a profit and loss ratio of 2:1, respectively. The bonus method was used to record Colter's admittance as a new partner. What ratio would be used to allocate, to Adel and Brick, the excess of Colter's contribution over the amount credited to Colter's capital account?

a. Adel and Brick's new relative capital ratio
b. Adel and Brick's new relative profit and loss ratio
c. Adel and Brick's old capital ratio
d. Adel and Brick's old profit and loss ratio

(5/92, Theory, #35, 2728)

12. Blau and Rubi are partners who share profits and losses in the ratio of 6:4, respectively. On May 1, 1998, their respective capital accounts were as follows:

Blau	$60,000
Rubi	50,000

On that date, Lind was admitted as a partner with a one-third interest in capital and profits for an investment of $40,000. The new partnership began with total capital of $150,000. Immediately after Lind's admission, Blau's capital should be

a. $50,000.
b. $54,000.
c. $56,667.
d. $60,000.   (11/89, PII, #19, amended, 1307)

13. At December 31, 1997, Reed and Quinn are partners with capital balances of $40,000 and $20,000, and they share profit and loss in the ratio of 2:1, respectively. On this date Poe invests $17,000 cash for a one-fifth interest in the capital and profit of the new partnership. Assuming that goodwill is **not** recorded, how much should be credited to Poe's capital account on December 31, 1997?

a. $12,000
b. $15,000
c. $15,400
d. $17,000   (11/86, PI, #36, amended, 1312)

14. Eagle and Falk are partners with capital balances of $45,000 and $25,000, respectively. They agree to admit Robb as a partner. After the assets of the partnership are revalued, Robb will have a 25% interest in capital and profits, for an investment of $30,000. What amount should be recorded as goodwill to the original partners?

a. $0
b $ 5,000
c. $ 7,500
d. $20,000   (5/98, FAR, #4, 6607)

15. Dunn and Grey are partners with capital account balances of $60,000 and $90,000, respectively. They agree to admit Zorn as a partner with a one-third interest in capital and profits, for an investment of $100,000, after revaluing the assets of Dunn and Grey. Goodwill to the original partners should be

a. $0.
b. $33,333.
c. $50,000.
d. $66,667.   (5/91, PII, #2, 1301)

ITEMS 16 AND 17 are based on the following:

16. On June 30, 1998, the condensed balance sheet for the partnership of Eddy, Fox, and Grimm, together with their respective profit and loss sharing percentages, was as follows:

Assets, net of liabilities	$320,000	Eddy, capital (50%)	$160,000
		Fox, capital (30%)	96,000
		Grimm, capital (20%)	64,000
			$320,000

Hamm is admitted as a new partner with a 25% interest in the capital of the new partnership for a cash payment of $140,000. Total goodwill implicit in the transaction is to be recorded. Immediately after admission of Hamm, Eddy's capital account balance should be

a. $280,000.
b. $210,000.
c. $160,000.
d. $140,000.   (11/88, PI, #27, amended, 9063)

17. Assume instead that Hamm is not admitted as a new partner and that Eddy decided to retire from the partnership and by mutual agreement is to be paid $180,000 out of partnership funds for his interest. Total goodwill implicit in the agreement is to be recorded. After Eddy's retirement, what are the capital balances of the other partners?

	Fox	Grimm
a.	$ 84,000	$56,000
b.	$102,000	$68,000
c.	$108,000	$72,000
d.	$120,000	$80,000

(11/88, PI, #26, 9064)

18. Allen retired from the partnership of Allen, Beck, and Chale. Allen's cash settlement from the partnership was based on new goodwill determined at the date of retirement plus the carrying amount of the other net assets. As a consequence of the settlement, the capital accounts of Beck and Chale were decreased. In accounting for Allen's withdrawal, the partnership could have used the

	Bonus method	Goodwill method
a.	No	Yes
b.	No	No
c.	Yes	Yes
d.	Yes	No

(5/90, Theory, #17, 1984)

19. When Mill retired from the partnership of Mill, Yale, and Lear, the final settlement of Mill's interest exceeded Mill's capital balance. Under the bonus method, the excess
a. Was recorded as goodwill.
b. Was recorded as an expense.

c. Reduced the capital balances of Yale and Lear.
d. Had **no** effect on the capital balances of Yale and Lear.   (11/94, FAR, #35, 5297)

ITEMS 20 AND 21 are based on the following:

The following condensed balance sheet is presented for the partnership of Alfa and Beda, who share profits and losses in the ratio of 60:40, respectively:

Cash	$ 45,000	Accounts payable	$ 120,000
Other assets	625,000	Alfa, capital	348,000
Beda, loan	30,000	Beda, capital	232,000
	$ 700,000		$ 700,000

20. The assets and liabilities are fairly valued on the balance sheet. Alfa and Beda decide to admit Capp as a new partner with a 20% interest. No goodwill or bonus is to be recorded. What amount should Capp contribute in cash or other assets?
a. $110,000
b. $116,000
c. $140,000
d. $145,000   (5/95, FAR, #23, 5559)

21. Instead of admitting a new partner, Alfa and Beda decide to liquidate the partnership. If the other assets are sold for $500,000, what amount of the available cash should be distributed to Alfa?
a. $255,000
b. $273,000
c. $327,000
d. $348,000   (5/95, FAR, #24, 5560)

22. On January 1, 1998, the partners of Cobb, Davis, and Eddy, who share profits and losses in the ratio of 5:3:2, respectively, decided to liquidate their partnership. On this date the partnership condensed balance sheet was as follows:

Cash	$ 50,000	Liabilities	$ 60,000
Other assets	250,000	Cobb, capital	80,000
	$300,000	Davis, capital	90,000
		Eddy, capital	70,000
			$300,000

On January 15, 1998, the first cash sale of other assets with a carrying amount of $150,000 realized $120,000. Safe installment payments to the partners were made the same date. How much cash should be distributed to each partner?

	Cobb	Davis	Eddy
a.	$15,000	$51,000	$44,000
b.	$40,000	$45,000	$35,000
c.	$55,000	$33,000	$22,000
d.	$60,000	$36,000	$24,000

(5/87, PI, #33, amended, 1310)

23. The following condensed balance sheet is presented for the partnership of Smith and Jones, who share profits and losses in the ratio of 60:40, respectively:

Other assets	$ 450,000	Accounts payable	$ 120,000
Smith, loan	20,000	Smith, capital	195,000
	$ 470,000	Jones, capital	155,000
			$ 470,000

The partners have decided to liquidate the partnership. If the other assets are sold for $385,000, what amount of the available cash should be distributed to Smith?
a. $136,000.
b. $156,000.
c. $159,000.
d. $195,000. (5/94, FAR, #37, 4852)

24. Which statements are usually included in a set of personal financial statements?
a. A statement of net worth and an income statement.
b. A statement of financial condition and a statement of changes in net worth.
c. A statement of net worth, an income statement, and a statement of cash flows.
d. A statement of financial condition, a statement of changes in net worth, and a statement of cash flows. (5/98, FAR, #2, 6605)

25. At May 31, 1997, Quay owned a $10,000 whole-life insurance policy with a cash-surrender value of $4,500, net of loans of $2,500. In Quay's May 31, 1997, personal statement of financial condition, what amount should be reported as investment in life insurance?
a. $ 4,500
b. $ 7,000
c. $ 7,500
d. $10,000 (5/98, FAR, #3, 6606)

26. The following information pertains to an insurance policy that Barton owns on his life:

Face amount	$100,000
Accumulated premiums paid up to December 31, 1991	8,000
Cash value at December 31, 1991	12,000
Policy loan	3,000

In Barton's personal statement of financial condition at December 31, 1991, what amount should be reported for the investment in life insurance?
a. $97,000
b. $12,000
c. $ 9,000
d. $ 8,000 (11/92, PII, #59, 3393)

27. Quinn is preparing a personal statement of financial condition as of April 30, 1995. Included in Quinn's assets are the following:

- 50% of the voting stock of Ink Corp. A stock-holders' agreement restricts the sale of the stock and, under certain circumstances, requires Ink to repurchase the stock. Quinn's tax basis for the stock is $430,000, and at April 30, 1995, the buyout value is $675,000.
- Jewelry with a fair value aggregating $70,000 based on an independent appraisal on April 30, 1995, for insurance purposes. This jewelry was acquired by purchase and gift over a 10-year period and has a total tax basis of $40,000.

What is the total amount at which the Ink stock and jewelry should be reported in Quinn's April 30, 1995, personal statement of financial condition?
a. $470,000
b. $500,000
c. $715,000
d. $745,000 (11/95, FAR, #55, 6137)

28. The following information pertains to Smith's personal assets and liabilities at December 31, 1990:

	Historical cost	Estimated current values	Estimated current amounts
Assets	$500,000	$900,000	
Liabilities	100,000		$80,000

Smith's 1990 income tax rate was 30%. In Smith's personal statement of financial condition at December 31, 1990, what amount should be reported as Smith's net worth?
a. $294,000
b. $420,000
c. $694,000
d. $820,000 (11/91, PII, #16, 2464)

29. A business interest that constitutes a large part of an individual's total assets should be presented in a personal statement of financial condition as
a. A separate listing of the individual assets and liabilities at cost.
b. Separate line items of both total assets and total liabilities at cost.
c. A single amount equal to the proprietorship equity.
d. A single amount equal to the estimated current value of the business interest. (11/95, FAR, #54, 6136)

30. At December 31, 1990, Ryan had the following noncancellable personal commitments:

Pledge to be paid to County Welfare
Home 30 days after volunteers paint
the walls and ceiling of the Home's
recreation room $ 5,000
Pledge to be paid to City Hospital on the
recovery of Ryan's comatose sister   25,000

What amount should be included in liabilities in Ryan's personal statement of financial condition at December 31, 1990?
a. $0
b. $ 5,000
c. $25,000
d. $30,000   (11/91, PII, #15, 2463)

31. For the purpose of estimating income taxes to be reported in personal financial statements, assets and liabilities measured at their tax bases should be compared to assets and liabilities measured at their

	Assets	Liabilities
a.	Estimated current value	Estimated current amount
b.	Historical cost	Historical cost
c.	Estimated current value	Historical cost
d.	Historical cost	Estimated current amount

(5/94, FAR, #53, 4868)

32. Which of the following statements is correct regarding the provision for income taxes in the financial statements of a sole proprietorship?
a. The provision for income taxes should be based on business income using individual tax rates.
b. The provision for income taxes should be based on business income using corporate tax rates.
c. The provision for income taxes should be based on the proprietor's total taxable income, allocated to the proprietorship at the percentage that business income bears to the proprietor's total income.
d. No provision for income taxes is required.
(5/94, FAR, #38, 4853)

33. In personal financial statements, how should estimated income taxes on the excess of the estimated current values of assets over their tax bases be reported in the statement of financial condition?
a. As liabilities
b. As deductions from the related assets
c. Between liabilities and net worth
d. In a footnote disclosure only
(5/92, Theory, #50, 2743)

PROBLEM

PROBLEM 18-2 (25 to 35 minutes)

On January 1, 1998, the partners of Allen, Brown, and Cox, who share profits and losses in the ratio of 5:3:2, respectively, decide to liquidate their partnership. The partnership trial balance at this date is as follows:

	Debit	Credit
Cash	$ 18,000	
Accounts receivable	66,000	
Inventory	52,000	
Machinery & equip., net	189,000	
Allen, loan	30,000	
Accounts payable		$ 53,000
Brown, loan		20,000
Allen, capital		118,000
Brown, capital		90,000
Cox, capital		74,000
	$355,000	$355,000

The partners plan a program of piecemeal conversion of assets in order to minimize liquidation losses. All available cash, less an amount retained to provide for future expenses, is to be distributed to the partners at the end of each month. A summary of the liquidation transactions for January 1998 is as follows:
a. $51,000 was collected on accounts receivable; the balance is uncollectible.
b. $38,000 was received for the entire inventory.
c. $2,000 liquidation expenses were paid.
d. $50,000 was paid to outside creditors, after offset of a $3,000 credit memorandum received on January 11, 1998.
e. $10,000 cash was retained in the business at the end of the month for potential unrecorded liabilities and anticipated expenses.

REQUIRED:

Prepare a schedule to compute safe installment payments to the partners as of January 31, 1998. Show supporting computations in good form.
(5/82, PI, #4, amended)

SOLUTION 18-1 MULTIPLE CHOICE ANSWERS

FORMATION

1. (c) All identifiable assets contributed to a partnership are recorded by the partnership at their fair values. All liabilities that the partnership assumes are recorded at their present values. The contributing partner's capital account is credited for the fair value of the noncash asset less the mortgage assumed by the partnership. Smith's capital account would be the fair value of the property of $80,000 less the mortgage assumed by the partnership of $35,000, for a balance of $45,000.

2. (a) In the formation of a partnership, often one or more of the partners will contribute noncash assets to the business such as inventory, land, or equipment. Retaining the recorded cost for such assets would be inequitable to any partner investing appreciated property. Therefore, the contribution of noncash assets to a partnership should be recorded based on fair values.

3. (d) Carr must have made an intangible contribution to the partnership because Abel and Carr have agreed to divide initial capital equally, even though Carr contributed less in identifiable assets ($84,000 < $100,000). Because the bonus method is used to record the formation of the partnership, and the bonus method assumes that an intangible contribution does not constitute a partnership asset with a measurable cost, no unidentifiable asset (i.e., goodwill) is recognized by the partnership. Thus, the journal entry to record the formation of the partnership under the bonus method would adjust the capital accounts of the two partners without recognizing goodwill, as follows:

Identifiable Assets		
($100,000 + $84,000)	184,000	
Abel, Capital ($184,000 x 50%)		92,000
Carr, Capital ($184,000 x 50%)		92,000

4. (d) Under the partnership agreement, each partner has an equal initial capital balance accounted for under the goodwill method. Cor is given an initial capital balance of $60,000, equal to the fair value of the identifiable assets Cor contributed to the partnership. Eng is also given an initial capital balance of $60,000. Since Eng only contributed identifiable assets with a fair value of $20,000, Eng must have also contributed an unidentifiable asset (i.e., goodwill) with a fair value of $40,000. The journal entry to record the formation of the partnership under the goodwill method would be as follows:

Cash	20,000	
Identifiable Noncash Assets	60,000	
Goodwill	40,000	
Cor, Capital		60,000
Eng, Capital		60,000

DIVISION OF PROFITS AND LOSSES

5. (d) The decrease in Rhu's equity in the partnership is determined as follows:

Partnership profit prior to distributions	$ 50,000
Less: Bonus to Low (15% x $50,000)	(7,500)
Salary to Low	(45,000)
Residual partnership loss	(2,500)
Times: Rhu's loss percentage	x 50%
Decrease in Rhu's equity in partnership	$ (1,250)

6. (b) The partnership profits are allocated to Red and White as follows:

	Partnership profit	Red	White
Partnership profit prior to salary allowances	$ 80,000		
Deduct salary allowances	(100,000)	$55,000	$45,000
Residual partnership loss	$ (20,000)		
60% of loss allocated to Red		(12,000)	
40% of loss allocated to White			(8,000)
Credit to each partner's capital account		$43,000	$37,000

7. (c) The portion of partnership profit allocated to Axel is computed as follows:

	Partnership profit	Allocation to Axel
Profit prior to distribution	$250,000	
Deduct bonus to Axel [($100,000 x 10%) + ($250,000 – 100,000) x 20%]	(40,000)	$ 40,000
Less: Bonuses to Berg and Cobb [$250,000 – ($150,000 + $40,000)] x 5% x 2]	(6,000)	
Residual partnership profit	$204,000	
1/3 of residual allocated to Axel		68,000
Profit allocated to Axel		$108,000

8. (a) Young received $16,000 ($160,000 x 10%) and Zinc received $10,000 ($100,000 X 10%) for the interest on average capital balances. This makes the residual loss $22,000 ($4,000 – $16,000 – $10,000). As the residual loss is evenly divided between the two partners, Zinc gets $11,000 of loss. Zinc's interest allowance less Zinc's portion of the residual loss is the change in Zinc's capital balance. $10,000 – $11,000 = $1,000 decrease.

9. (b) When there is a profit, Flat receives 20% of the profits before the bonus and 40% of the remaining 80% (i.e., 32%), for a total of 52% of the profits. In loss situations, Flat receives only 40% of the loss. Thus Flat has a greater advantage whether the partnership has a profit or loss.

ADMISSION AND WITHDRAWAL OF PARTNERS

10. (d) Under the bonus method, the total capital of the new partnership will equal the sum of the original partners' capital balances plus the fair value of the identifiable asset (i.e., land) contributed by the new partner. Immediately after admission, the balance of the new partner's capital account equals the total capital of the new partnership multiplied by the new partner's capital interest. After Grant's admission into the partnership, Kern's capital account balance would be $57,600 (i.e., $60,000 − $2,400), and Pate's capital account balance would be $38,400 (i.e., $40,000 − $1,600).

Original partnership capital ($60,000 + $20,000)	$80,000
Fair value of identifiable asset contributed by Grant	15,000
Total recorded capital of new partnership	95,000
Grant's capital interest	x 20%
Credit to Grant's capital account	$19,000

Land (fair value)	15,000	
Kern, Capital ($4,000 x 60%)	2,400	
Pate, Capital ($4,000 x 40%)	1,600	
Grant, Capital		19,000

To record Grant's admission into the partnership.

11. (d) Under the bonus method, the excess of the partner's contribution over the amount credited to the new partner's capital account is viewed as a bonus to the original partners. The bonus is allocated to the original partners based upon their old profit and loss ratio.

12. (b) Because the total capital of the partners following the admission of Lind will be equal to the sum of the original partners' capital balances plus the cash contributed by Lind (i.e., $60,000 + $50,000 + $40,000 = $150,000), no goodwill is recognized. The balance of Blau's capital account immediately after Lind's admission is determined as follows:

Capital balance before Lind's admission		$60,000
Credit to Lind's capital account for 1/3		
of new partnership capital		
($150,000 x 1/3)	$ 50,000	
Less: Cash contributed by Lind	40,000	
Bonus to Lind from Blau and Rubi	10,000	
Times: Blau's share of bonus		
[60% ÷ (60% + 40%)]	x 60%	
Decrease in Blau's capital account		(6,000)
Capital balance after Lind's admission		$54,000

13. (c) Because no goodwill is to be recognized, the total capital of the partnership following the admission of Poe will be equal to the sum of the original partners' capital balances plus the cash contributed by Poe. Poe's capital account will be credited for one-fifth of this total amount.

Original partnership capital ($40,000 + $20,000)	$60,000
Cash contributed by Poe	17,000
Total (new) partnership capital	77,000
Percent credited to Poe	x .20
Poe's capital account	$15,400

14. (d) In the goodwill method of recording the admission of a new partner, the assets are revalued at their fair values and any excess valuation implied in the purchase price is recorded as goodwill. Robb's 25% interest for an investment of $30,000 implies that total net assets are valued at $120,000 ($30,000/25%) and the goodwill is determined as follows:

Net assets	$120,000
Less: Robb investment	(30,000)
Eagle capital	(45,000)
Falk capital	(25,000)
Goodwill	$ 20,000

15. (c) The goodwill method looks upon this transaction as an indication that the partnership possesses an actual value of $300,000 (i.e., $100,000 ÷ 1/3) after Zorn's admission. Since, even with Zorn's investment, the partnership is reporting only $250,000 (i.e., $60,000 + $90,000 + $100,000) in net assets, a valuation adjustment of $50,000 is required. This adjustment is recorded as goodwill and would be allocated to Dunn and Grey, the original partners, by their respective profit and loss sharing percentages (not provided in this question).

16. (b) The goodwill method looks upon this transaction as an indication that the partnership possesses an actual value of $560,000 ($140,000 ÷ 25%) after Hamm's admission. Since, even with Hamm's investment, the partnership is reporting only $460,000 ($320,000 + $140,000) in net assets, a valuation adjustment of $100,000 is required. This adjustment is recorded as goodwill and is allocated to the original partners—Eddy, Fox, and Grimm—by their respective profit and loss sharing percentages. Immediately after admission of Hamm, Eddy's capital account balance is $210,000 ($160,000 + $50,000).

Goodwill	100,000	
Eddy, Capital ($100,000 x 50%)		50,000
Fox, Capital ($100,000 x 30%)		30,000
Grimm, Capital ($100,000 x 20%)		20,000

Hamm's investment of $140,000 is recorded as follows:

Cash	140,000	
Hamm, Capital		140,000

17. (c) The goodwill method looks upon this transaction as an indication that the partnership possesses an actual value of $360,000 ($180,000 ÷ 50%) prior to Eddy's retirement. Since the partnership is reporting only $320,000 in net assets, a valuation adjustment of $40,000 is required. This adjustment is recorded as goodwill and is allocated to Eddy, Fox, and Grimm by their respective profit and loss sharing percentages. Immediately after Eddy's retirement, Fox's capital account balance should be $108,000 ($96,000 + $12,000) and Grimm's capital account balance should be $72,000 ($64,000 + $8,000).

Goodwill	40,000	
Eddy, Capital ($40,000 x 50%)		20,000
Fox, Capital ($40,000 x 30%)		12,000
Grimm, Capital ($40,000 x 20%)		8,000

The payment of $180,000 to Eddy is recorded as follows:

Eddy, Capital ($160,000 + $20,000)	180,000	
Cash		180,000

18. (d) Allen, the withdrawing partner, is to receive cash or other assets equal to his current capital balance plus his share of unrecorded goodwill. If the bonus method were to be used to account for this transaction, the payment made to Allen for his share of the unrecorded goodwill would be recorded as a *decrease* in the remaining partners' capital accounts. If the goodwill method were to be used to account for the withdrawal, a revaluation of partnership assets would be required. This adjustment would be recorded on the partnership's books as goodwill and allocated among the existing partners (i.e., Allen, Beck, and Chale) by their respective profit and loss sharing percentages, thereby *increasing* their respective capital accounts. Since the capital accounts of the remaining partners (i.e., Beck and Chale) decreased as a result of the settlement, the withdrawal could only have been recorded using the bonus method.

19. (c) The final settlement of Mill's interest exceeded his capital balance. The excess payment represents Mill's share of the unrecorded goodwill of the partnership. Under the bonus method, this excess payment would be recorded as a decrease in the remaining partners' capital accounts.

20. (d) Capp's contribution is calculated as follows:

Total current capital ($348,000 + $232,000)	$ 580,000
Divided by: Percentage current capital is of new total capital (100% – Capp @ 20%)	÷ 80%
Total new capital, including Capp	$ 725,000
Less: Alfa & Beda Capital (current capital)	(580,000)
Capp's contribution for 20% interest	$ 145,000

LIQUIDATION

21. (b) Distributions are calculated as follows:

Total Cash to Distribute:

Cash	$ 45,000
Plus: Sale of other assets	500,000
Less: Accounts payable to settle	(120,000)
Total available cash	$ 425,000

Distribution of Available Cash:	Alfa(60%)	Beda(40%)
Beginning capital	$348,000	$ 232,000
Reduce Beda capital for loan		(30,000)
Allocate loss on sale of assets per profit and loss sharing ratio ($625,000 – 500,000)	(75,000)	(50,000)
Distribution of cash	$273,000	$ 152,000

22. (a) The maximum possible loss assumes that nothing will be received from the disposition of the remaining $100,000 of other assets. The cash to be distributed to each partner is determined as follows (in 000's):

	Cash	Other assets	Liabs.	Cobb 50%	Davis 30%	Eddy 20%
Balances before realization	$ 50	$ 250	$ 60	$ 80	$ 90	$ 70
1/5/98 sale	120	(150)		(15)	(9)	(6)
Balance	170	100	60	65	81	64
Liabs. paid	(60)		(60)			
Balance	110	100	0	65	81	64
Maximum loss possible		(100)		(50)	(30)	(20)
Safe cash distribution	$110	$ 0	$ 0	$ 15	$ 51	$ 44

23. (a) Smith's capital balance of $195,000 is reduced by his $20,000 loan *from* the partnership ($195,000 – $20,000). The cash available to be distributed to each partner is computed as follows (in 000's):

	Cash	Other assets	Liabs.	Smith (60%)	Jones (40%)
Balances before realization	$ 0	$ 450	$ 120	$175	$155
Sale of other assets	385	(450)	0	(39)	(26)
Balances after realization	385	$ 0	$ 120	$136	$ 129
Payment of liabilities	(120)		(120)	0	0
Balances	$ 265		$ 0	$136	$ 129

PERSONAL FINANCIAL STATEMENTS

24. (b) The primary focus of users of personal financial statements is on assets and liabilities. Therefore, the basic personal financial statements are the statement of financial condition and the statement of changes in net worth. An income statement and a statement of cash flows are generally not included in a set of personal financial statements.

25. (a) According to SOP 82-1, in personal financial statements, the investment in life insurance is the cash surrender value less outstanding loans.

26. (c) Personal financial statements should present assets at their estimated current values. SOP 82-1 provides specific guidance that an investment in life insurance should be reported in the statement of financial condition as an asset for the cash value of the policy, less the amount of any loans against it ($12,000 – $3,000 = $9,000).

27. (d) The buyout value in the repurchase agreement is used as a measure of the current value of the stock. The total amount of Ink stock and jewelry reported in Quinn's April 30, 1995 personal statement of financial condition is:

Ink Corp. stock, at estimated current value	$ 675,000
Jewelry at estimated current value	70,000
Total	$745,000

28. (c) The statement of financial condition presents the estimated current value of assets, the estimated current amounts of liabilities, the estimated income taxes on the differences between the estimated current amounts of assets and liabilities and their tax bases and the resulting net worth.

Estimated current values of assets		$ 900,000
Less:	Estimated current amounts of liabilities	(80,000)
	Estimated income taxes on the differences between the estimated current values of assets, the current amounts of liabilities, and their tax bases	(126,000)*
Estimated net worth		$ 694,000

* [($900,000 – $80,000) – ($500,000 – $100,000)] x 30%

29. (d) In a personal statement of financial condition, a business interest that constitutes a large part of an individual's total assets should be shown as a single amount equal to the estimated current value of the business interest, per SOP 82-1.

30. (a) Under SOP 82-1, par. 28, noncancellable commitments to pay future sums should be presented as liabilities at their discounted amounts only if the commitment: (1) is for a fixed or determinable amount; (2) is not contingent on others' life expectancies or the occurrence of a particular event, such as disability or death; and (3) does not require future performance of service by others. Thus, neither pledge should be reported as a liability in Ryan's personal statement of financial condition. The pledge to be paid to the County Welfare Home requires *future performance of service by others* (i.e., the volunteers must paint the walls and ceiling of the Home's recreation room). The pledge to be paid to the City hospital is *contingent on the occurrence of a particular event* (i.e., the recovery of Ryan's comatose sister).

31. (a) Personal financial statements should contain a provision for estimated income taxes based on the differences between the estimated current value of assets, the current amount of liabilities, and their respective tax bases.

32. (d) A sole proprietorship pays no income taxes. Instead, any business related income taxes are reported and paid by the individual proprietor. Therefore, the financial statements of the sole proprietorship need not include a provision for income taxes.

33. (c) Personal financial statements should report a provision for estimated income taxes on the difference between the current value of assets, the current amount of liabilities, and their respective tax bases in the statement of financial condition between liabilities and net worth. The amount is computed as if the estimated current value of all assets had been realized and all liabilities had been paid at their estimated current amounts at the date of the financial statements, based on tax law and regulations then applicable.

PERFORMANCE BY SUBTOPICS

Each category below parallels a subtopic covered in Chapter 18. Record the number and percentage of questions you correctly answered in each subtopic area.

Formation

Question #	Correct √
1	
2	
3	
4	
# Questions	4
# Correct	
% Correct	

Division of Profits and Losses

Question #	Correct √
5	
6	
7	
8	
9	
# Questions	5
# Correct	
% Correct	

Admission and Withdrawal of Partners

Question #	Correct √
10	
11	
12	
13	
14	
15	
16	
17	
18	
19	
20	
# Questions	11
# Correct	
% Correct	

Liquidation

Question #	Correct √
21	
22	
23	
# Questions	3
# Correct	
% Correct	

Personal Financial Statements

Question #	Correct √
24	
25	
26	
27	
28	
29	
30	
31	
32	
33	
# Questions	10
# Correct	
% Correct	

PROBLEM SOLUTION

SOLUTION 18-2 PARTNERSHIP LIQUIDATION

Allen, Brown, and Cox Partnership
COMPUTATION OF SAFE INSTALLMENT PAYMENTS TO PARTNERS
January 31, 1998

		Residual Equities		
	Total	Allen	Brown	Cox
Profit and loss ratio	100%	50%	30%	20%
Computation of January installment				
Preliquidation balances				
Capital	$282,000	$118,000	$ 90,000	$ 74,000
Add (deduct) loans	(10,000)	(30,000)	20,000	--
	272,000	88,000	110,000	74,000
Deduct January losses				
(Schedule 1)	(28,000)	(14,000)	(8,400)	(5,600)
Predistribution balances	244,000	74,000	101,600	68,400
Deduct potential losses				
(Schedule 1)	(199,000)	(99,500)	(59,700)	(39,800)
	45,000	(25,500)	41,900	28,600
Deduct potential loss—				
Allen's debit balance				
(Brown 3/5; Cox 2/5)	--	25,500	(15,300)	(10,200)
Safe payments to partners	$ 45,000	$ 0	$ 26,600	$ 18,400

Schedule 1   Computation of Actual and Potential Liquidation Losses
January 1998

	Actual losses	Potential losses
Collection of accounts receivable ($66,000 – $51,000)	$15,000	
Sale of inventory ($52,000 – $38,000)	14,000	
Liquidation expenses	2,000	
Gain resulting from January credit memorandum offset against payments to creditors	(3,000)	
Machinery and equipment, net		$189,000
Potential unrecorded liabilities and anticipated expenses		10,000
Totals	$28,000	$199,000

Writing Skills Content

Answers to selected essay responses from Business Law & Professional Responsibilities, Auditing, and Financial Accounting & Reporting sections are used to assess candidates' writing skills. **Five percent** of the points available on each of these sections are allocated to writing skills. Effective writing skills include the following six characteristics:

1. Coherent organization.

2. Conciseness.

3. Clarity.

4. Use of standard English.

5. Responsiveness to the requirements of the question.

6. Appropriateness for the reader.

Due to the importance of writing skills, we discuss these six characteristics in the **Practical Advice** and the **Accounting for 5%** sections of this volume.

CHAPTER 19

INVESTMENTS IN EQUITY SECURITIES

CHAPTER 19

INVESTMENTS IN EQUITY SECURITIES

I. ACCOUNTING FOR INVESTMENTS IN EQUITY SECURITIES

A. INVESTMENTS

Investments are assets that may be acquired for future income potential, appreciation, or control over the investee. As such, they generally occupy an auxiliary position in relation to a firm's primary activities. Investments may be classified as either temporary or long-term.

1. **TEMPORARY** Temporary investments are those that meet two tests: (a) marketability, and (b) intention by management to dispose of the investment for cash or other current assets if the need arises.

2. **LONG-TERM** Long-term investments are all other investments not meeting these two criteria. Investments in the form of common or preferred stock represent an equity interest in the investee, and are discussed in this chapter.

B. CERTAIN INVESTMENTS IN DEBT AND EQUITY SECURITIES (SFAS 115)

Accounting for Certain Investments in Debt And Equity Securities (SFAS 115), does **not** apply to investments in equity securities accounted for by the equity method, nor to investments in consolidated subsidiaries.

C. METHODS OF ACCOUNTING

An investment in the equity securities of a corporation confers upon the investor the right to share in the earnings of the investee. If the investment is in the voting common stock of the investee, the investor is also entitled to participate, at least indirectly, in the management of the investee. The degree of influence that the investor is deemed to have over the investee by virtue of the investment determines the method of accounting for the investment. When a company owns stock in another corporation, its investment should be accounted for under one of three methods, as follows:

1. **COST METHOD** The cost method is appropriate where the investor is **not** deemed to have a significant level of influence over the investee by virtue of the investment (generally, less than 20% ownership of the outstanding common stock). In this case, income will be recognized as cash dividends are received, and the investment will be accounted for as required by SFAS 115.

2. **EQUITY METHOD** The equity method is required where the investor is deemed to have significant influence over the investee by virtue of the investment, but consolidated financial statements are not appropriate (generally 20%-50% ownership of the outstanding common stock). Under the equity method, the investor recognizes as income its pro rata share of the investee's earnings, while cash dividends received reduce the carrying amount of the investment. APB 18, *The Equity Method of Accounting for Investments in Common Stocks,* provides accounting and reporting standards.

3. **CONSOLIDATED FINANCIAL STATEMENTS** Consolidated financial statements are required by ARB 51, *Consolidated Financial Statements*, when a company owns more than 50% of the voting stock of another firm, with few exceptions. SFAS 141, *Business Combinations*, provides accounting and reporting standards.

4. **COMPARISON** Under the cost method, the investor recognizes dividends as income when received. Under the equity method, an investor recognizes as income its share of an investee's earnings or losses in the periods in which they are reported by the investee. The

equity method is more consistent with accrual accounting than is the cost method, because the equity method recognizes income when earned rather than when dividends are received.

EXHIBIT 1 ♦ ACCOUNTING FOR INVESTMENTS

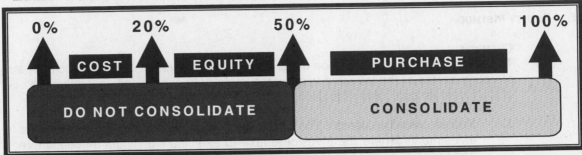

II. COST METHOD

A. CRITERIA

The cost method is appropriate when the investor is **not** deemed to be able to exercise significant influence over the investee by virtue of the investment. Significant influence is generally defined as ownership of 20% or more of the voting stock of the investee. However, other factors such as participation in policy-making or directorship may also indicate significant influence. The cost method is usually required in the following situations:

1. **NONVOTING STOCK** The investment is in nonvoting stock, such as preferred stock.

2. **LESS THAN 20% OWNERSHIP** The number of shares of voting common stock owned represent less than 20% of the common stock outstanding.

3. **TEMPORARY** The investment is of a temporary nature.

B. APPLICATION

1. **UPON ACQUISITION** Upon acquisition, the investment is recorded at cost. "Cost" also includes broker's fees and other direct costs of acquisition. In a lump-sum purchase, the purchase price is allocated to the various types of securities on the basis of their relative fair values.

2. **TRADING AND AVAILABLE-FOR-SALE SECURITIES** Investments in equity securities are classified as either (1) trading securities or (2) available-for-sale securities. Changes in fair value (at year-end) are recorded through a valuation allowance account's addition or subtraction for both unrealized holding gains and losses. For trading securities, these changes are reported in current income. For available-for-sale securities, these changes are reported in other comprehensive income. Dividends received are accounted for in current income.

3. **INVESTMENT ACCOUNT** The investment account is not adjusted to reflect the investor's share of the investee's earnings or dividend distributions of earnings subsequent to acquisition. An adjustment must be made, however, for liquidating dividends (i.e., dividend distributions in excess of earnings subsequent to acquisition). Stock dividends and splits are recorded only by a memo entry, the carrying amount of the investment being allocated to the total number of shares owned.

4. **STOCK RIGHTS** If "stock rights" are received (rights to buy additional shares usually received to satisfy the investor's preemptive right to maintain its existing level of ownership in the investee), the carrying amount of the investment should be allocated between the investment and the rights. The allocation should be based on the ratio of the market value of the stock to the market value of the rights. This procedure is also used for the receipt of stock warrants. A stock warrant is physical evidence of stock rights.

5. **UPON DISPOSAL** Upon disposal, a realized gain or loss should be recognized to the extent that the proceeds received differ from the carrying amount of the investment. The carrying amount of the shares sold may be determined by specific identification, FIFO, or the average method.

III. EQUITY METHOD

A. CRITERIA

The equity method is based upon the premise that the investor owns a sufficiently large proportion of voting shares of the investee to allow the investor to exert significant influence over the policies of the investee, particularly the dividend policy.

1. **SIGNIFICANT INFLUENCE** The equity method of accounting for investments is required for investments where the investor is able to exercise significant influence over the operating and financial policies of the investee by virtue of the investment. If 20% or more of the outstanding voting stock of the investee is owned by the investor, a presumption of significant influence exists. Significant influence may be indicated by the following:

a. Representation on the board of directors

b. Participation in policy-making decisions

c. Level of intercompany transactions or dependency

d. Concentration of ownership in the hands of a small group of stockholders

2. **CONSOLIDATION** ARB 51, *Consolidated Financial Statements* (as amended by SFAS 94, *Consolidation of All Majority-Owned Subsidiaries*), requires consolidation of all majority-owned subsidiaries, unless control is temporary or control does not rest with the majority owner. The equity method is not a valid substitute for consolidation.

B. EXCEPTIONS TO THE USE OF THE EQUITY METHOD

There are exceptions to APB 18's presumption that an investor owning 20% or more of the voting stock of an investee has "significant influence" over the investee. These exceptions are as follows: (1) the investment is temporary, or (2) the investment is operating in a foreign country where severe operating restrictions exist. Additionally, FASB Interp. 35, *Criteria for Applying the Equity Method of Accounting for Investments in Common Stock*, indicates sample situations where the 20% ownership presumption may be overcome.

1. **NO SIGNIFICANT INFLUENCE** Opposition by the investee, such as litigation or complaints to governmental regulatory authorities, challenges the investor's ability to exercise significant influence.

2. **BY AGREEMENT** The investor and investee sign an agreement under which the investor surrenders significant rights as a shareholder.

3. **OTHER OWNERS** Majority ownership of the investee is concentrated among a small group of shareholders who operate the investee without regard to the views of the investor.

4. **LACK OF INFORMATION** The investor needs or wants more financial information to apply the equity method than is available to the investee's other shareholders (for example, the investor wants quarterly financial information from an investee that publicly reports only annually), tries to obtain that information, and fails.

5. **NO REPRESENTATION** The investor tries and fails to obtain representation on the investee's board of directors.

C.   APPLICATION

1.   **UPON ACQUISITION** Upon acquisition, the investment should be recorded at cost. If the investor owned less than 20% of the voting stock of the investee and subsequently increased the ownership percentage to 20% or more, the equity method should be retroactively applied. APB 18 requires a retroactive adjustment to the investor's Investment and Retained Earnings accounts.

2.   **SUBSEQUENT TO ACQUISITION** Subsequent to acquisition, the investment in common stock and the investment income accounts must be periodically adjusted in a manner analogous to a consolidated investment. Both the income recognized and the change in owners' equity under the equity method are exactly the same as would be reported in consolidated financial statements. This is why the equity method is sometimes referred to as a "one line consolidation." In the succeeding paragraphs, we present an outline of the steps an investor would follow in applying the equity method.

a.   **INVESTEE'S EARNINGS** Periodically, the investor recognizes its share of the investee's earnings. This is done by debiting the Investment account and crediting Investment Income for an amount proportionate to the ownership interest. The investor's share of investee earnings or losses should be computed after deducting any cumulative preferred dividends of the investee. If the investor also owns shares of preferred stock, the investor should account for them under the cost method because they are nonvoting securities. Income on preferred stock would be recorded simply as dividend income as the preferred dividends are declared. Finally, when the investor's and the investee's fiscal years do not coincide, the investor may report its share of investee income from the most recent financial statements of the investee, so long as the time lag is consistent from period to period.

b.   **DIVIDENDS** Dividends declared by the investee represent a distribution of earnings previously recognized. Recording their declaration by the investor involves debiting a receivable and crediting the Investment account, since the distribution reduces the owners' equity of the investee. Dividends declared by the investee do not affect the Investment Income account.

c.   **GOODWILL** The price paid for the common stock of the investee will seldom, if ever, equal the book value of the shares acquired. Any excess purchase price over the underlying equity is usually regarded as purchased goodwill.

d.   **EXCESS PURCHASE PRICE** Specific investee assets may have fair values that differ from their book values. Any excess purchase price identified directly with individual assets (e.g., inventory, buildings, equipment, patents) having a limited useful life should be amortized over the appropriate time period. The proper entry is to debit Investment Income and credit the Investment account for the amortization amount. The opposite entry is made if the fair value of the asset is less than its book value.

e.   **INTERCOMPANY PROFITS AND LOSSES** Intercompany profits and losses should be eliminated until realized. For instance, assume Investee Co. sells inventory to Investor, Inc., and recognizes a profit on the sale. Assume further that at year-end Investor has not resold a portion of this inventory. Investor, Inc., must then reduce both its share of Investee Co.'s income and its Investment account by an amount equal to its share of the intercompany profits contained in the ending inventory.

f.   **INTERCOMPANY RECEIVABLES AND PAYABLES** Intercompany receivables and payables between affiliates should not be eliminated unless the requirements for consolidation are met (i.e., > 50% ownership).

g.   **CAPITAL TRANSACTIONS** Investee's capital transactions should be accounted for as if the investee were a consolidated subsidiary. For instance, a sale by the investee of its common stock to third parties, at a price greater than book value, results in an increase in the carrying amount of the investment and a corresponding increase in the investor's additional paid-in capital. No income is recorded if the investee declares stock dividends or splits since the investor continues to own the same portion of the investee as before the stock split or dividend. The investor needs only to make a memo entry.

h. **DEFERRED INCOME TAXES** Deferred income taxes should be recognized for the temporary difference caused by the difference between the income recognized using the equity method and the dividends received from the investee. Corporate shareholders that own 20% or more (but less than 80%) of the stock of the distributing corporation are allowed an 80% dividend deduction. This portion of the dividends received is an event recognized in the financial statements that does not have a tax consequence because it is exempt from taxation. Events that do not have tax consequences do not give rise to temporary differences and are often referred to as "permanent differences."

i. **CHANGES IN THE MARKET VALUE OF COMMON STOCK** Changes in the market value of the investee's common stock do **not** affect the Investment account or the Investment Income account.

EXAMPLE 1 ♦ APPLICATION OF THE EQUITY METHOD

On January 2, 20X1, Company R purchased 20% of the outstanding common stock of Company E for $25,000. The owners' equity section of Company E at the time of acquisition is summarized below. Assume any excess of the purchase price over the book value of the securities acquired is attributable to goodwill. Company E's net income for 20X1 was $10,000. Cash dividends amounting to $4,000 were declared and paid. During the year, Company E sold inventory to R for $8,000, recording a $2,000 profit on the sale; 50% of this inventory ($4,000) had not been resold by Company R at year-end.

Company E Owners' Equity, Jan. 2, 20X1:

Common stock ($1 par)	$ 10,000
Additional paid-in capital	40,000
Retained earnings	50,000
Book value of net assets	$100,000

REQUIRED: Provide all entries made by Company R to record the acquisition and subsequent accounting for its investment in Company E, in accordance with APB 18. Show all computations.

SOLUTION: NOTE: To facilitate understanding, all entries and related computations have been keyed to match the corresponding text above.

Entry to record acquisition of the 20% interest (2,000 shares) in E's common stock outstanding (III.C.1.).

Investment in E	25,000	
Cash		25,000

Entry to record R's share of E's net income for 20X1 (III.C.2.a.).

Investment in E (20% x $10,000)	2,000	
Investment Income		2,000

(continued on next page)

Entry to reduce the investment in E for the amount of the dividend distribution received (III.C.2.b.).

Cash ($4,000 x 20%)	800	
Investment in E		800

Calculation of the amount of the investment considered to be goodwill (III.C.2.c.).

Purchase price of E's common stock		$ 25,000
Co. E's owners' equity (net assets)	$100,000	
Book value of interest acquired	x 20%	(20,000)
Excess cost over book value (goodwill)		$ 5,000

Entry to adjust income and the investment account for Co. R's share of intercompany unrealized profits (III.C.2.e.).

Investment Income	200*	
Investment in E		200

*COMPUTATIONS: E's profit on sale of inventory to R	$ 2,000
Sale price of inventory	÷ 8,000
E's gross margin ratio	25%
R's ending inventory (in dollars)	x 4,000
E's recorded profit on R's ending inventory	1,000
R's percentage ownership in E	x 20%
R's share of unrealized intercompany profit	$ 200

EXAMPLE 2 ◆ CHANGES FROM THE EQUITY METHOD

Refer to the facts in Example 1. On January 6, 20X2, E sold 4,000 additional shares of common stock.

REQUIRED: Provide the appropriate entry(ies) made by Co. R to adjust its investment in Co. E if the shares were sold at: (a) $10.60/sh., (b) $12.00/sh., (c) $8.00/sh.

SOLUTION:

(III.C.2.g.)

(a) Memo entry to record change in ownership from 20% to 14.29% (1/7).*

(b)	Investment in Co. E	800*	
	Additional Paid-In Capital		800
(c)	Additional Paid-In Capital	1,486*	
	Investment in Co. E		1,486

*COMPUTATIONS: Book Value of Common Stock Prior to Sale

Common stock ($1 par)			$10,000
Additional paid-in capital			40,000
RE:	Beginning retained earnings	$50,000	
	20X1 Net income	10,000	
	20X1 Dividends	(4,000)	56,000
Total stockholders' equity, Co. E			106,000
Common shares outstanding			÷10,000
Book value per common share			$ 10.60

(continued on next page)

Co. R's Increase (Decrease) in Additional Paid-In Capital

	(a)	(b)	(c)
Common stock sale price	$ 10.60	$ 12.00	$ 8.00
Co. E owners' equity prior to sale	$ 106,000	$ 106,000	$ 106,000
4,000 sh. sold ($1 par)	4,000	4,000	4,000
Additional paid-in capital	38,400	44,000	28,000
E owners' equity subsequent to sale	148,400	154,000	138,000
R % ownership subsequent to sale (2,000 sh. ÷ 14,000 sh.)	x 1/7	x 1/7	x 1/7
R interest subsequent to sale	21,200	22,000	19,714
Co. R interest prior to sale ($106,000 x 20%)	(21,200)	(21,200)	(21,200)
Increase (decrease) in APIC	$ 0	$ 800	$ (1,486)

NOTE: As a result of the E's issuance of additional stock, R's ownership has dropped below 20% (to 14.29%) and, thus, from this point onward, the investment in E must be accounted for under the cost method.

3. **CHANGES FROM THE EQUITY METHOD** Upon disposal of an equity method investment, the investor should recognize a gain or loss equal to the difference between the carrying amount of the investment and its sale price. Note that the carrying amount of the investment must be adjusted to the date of disposal. If, as a result of a partial disposal, the ownership percentage becomes less than 20%, the investor should stop accruing its share of investee income. A change in the method of accounting must be made to the cost method. The cost basis for accounting purposes is the carrying amount of the investment at the date of the change. Any dividends in future years that exceed the investor's share of the investee's income for such future years (i.e., liquidating dividends) should be applied to reduce the investment account.

4. **CHANGES TO THE EQUITY METHOD** Where the investor's level of ownership increases, so that use of the equity method is required, the investment account, results of operations, and retained earnings of the investor must be retroactively adjusted. This adjustment must be consistent with the accounting for a step-by-step subsidiary acquisition. The amount of the adjustment to prior periods is for the difference between the amounts that were recognized in prior periods under the cost method and the amounts that would have been recognized if the equity method had been used.

EXAMPLE 3 ♦ CHANGES TO THE EQUITY METHOD

On January 2, 20X0, Amsted Corp. purchased 10% of the outstanding shares of Cable Co. common stock for $250,000 cash. On January 2, 20X2, Amsted Corp. purchased an additional 20% of Cable Co.'s stock for $600,000 cash. Now having a 30% interest, Amsted Corp. must use the equity method. Cable Co.'s net income and dividends paid are as follows:

Year	Cable Co. net income	Cable Co. dividends paid to Amsted
20X0	$250,000	$10,000
20X1	500,000	15,000
20X2	600,000	60,000

REQUIRED: Show Amsted's journal entry recorded for the January 2, 20X2 transaction reflecting retroactively the change from the cost method to the equity method.

(continued on next page)

19-8

SOLUTION:

Investment in Cable Co. Stock   650,000
    Cash   600,000
    Retained earnings   50,000*

	20X0	20X1	Total
*COMPUTATIONS:			
Amsted Corp. equity in earnings of Cable Co., 10%	$ 25,000	$ 50,000	$ 75,000
Dividends received	(10,000)	(15,000)	(25,000)
Prior period adjustment	$ 15,000	$ 35,000	$ 50,000

5. **LOSSES** A loss in the value of an equity method investment should be recognized if such loss is other than temporary. A loss in value may be evidenced by a poor earnings record, inability to recover the carrying amount of the investment, or similar causes. An investor should reduce its investment for its pro rata share of investee losses. However, if the investee continuously reports net losses, the investor should discontinue applying the equity method after the investment has been written down to zero. The investor should then record his or her share of further investee losses by memo entry only. If the investee becomes profitable in the future, the investor should resume applying the equity method only after its share of net income equals its share of net losses not previously recognized.

6. **FINANCIAL STATEMENT PRESENTATION** The investor's investment in common stock should be disclosed as a single line item on the balance sheet. The investor's share of investee's earnings is disclosed as a single line item on the income statement. An **exception** arises for investee's extraordinary items and prior period adjustments. If material, these items should be separately reported in the investor's financial statements.

D. **SUMMARY**
The following T-accounts briefly summarize some of the significant effects upon the investment and investment income accounts related to the above discussions of the equity method.

EXHIBIT 2 ♦ T-ACCOUNT SUMMARY OF THE EQUITY METHOD

Equity Investment in X Co. (balance sheet)	
Original cost of investment Pro rata share of investee's income since acquisition Retroactive adjustment due to change from cost to equity method (dr. or cr.)	Pro rata share of investee's losses since acquisition Pro rata share of investee's dividends declared Disposal of investee stock

Investment Income, X Co. (income statement)	
Pro rata share of investee's losses since acquisition	Pro rata share of investee's income since acquisition

NOTE: The investment income account is _not_ affected by dividends declared by the investee.

Time Management

Approximately 10% of the multiple choice questions in every section of every exam given after November 1995 are questions that are being pretested. These questions are **not** included in candidates' final grades; they are presented only so that the Board of Examiners may evaluate them for effectiveness and possible ambiguity.

The Scholastic Achievement Test and the Graduate Record Exam both employ similar but not identical strategies. Those tests include an extra section, which is being pretested, and test-takers do not know which section is the one that will not be graded. On the Uniform CPA Examination, however, the extra questions are mixed in among the graded questions.

This makes time management even more crucial. Candidates who are deciding how much time to spend on a difficult multiple choice question must keep in mind that there is a 10% chance that the answer to the question will not affect them either way. Also, candidates should not allow a question that seems particularly difficult or confusing to shake their confidence or affect their attitude towards the rest of the test; it may not even count.

This experimental 10% will work against candidates who are not sure whether or not they have answered enough questions to earn 75%. Candidates should try for a safety margin, so that they will have accumulated enough correct answers to pass, even though some of their correctly answered questions will not be scored.

CHAPTER 19—INVESTMENTS IN EQUITY SECURITIES

PROBLEM 19-1 MULTIPLE CHOICE QUESTIONS (44 to 55 minutes)

1. Peel Co. received a cash dividend from a common stock investment. Should Peel report an increase in the investment account if it uses the cost method or the equity method of accounting?

	Cost	Equity
a.	No	No
b.	Yes	Yes
c.	Yes	No
d.	No	Yes

(11/93, Theory, #9, 4514)

2. Green Corp. owns 30% of the outstanding common stock and 100% of the outstanding non-cumulative nonvoting preferred stock of Axel Corp. In 2002, Axel declared dividends of $100,000 on its common stock and $60,000 on its preferred stock. Green exercises significant influence over Axel's operations. What amount of dividend revenue should Green report in its income statement for the year ended December 31, 2002?

a. $0
b. $30,000
c. $60,000
d. $90,000   (5/92, PI, #42, amended, 2613)

3. Pal Corp.'s 2002 dividend income included only part of the dividend received from its Ima Corp. investment. The balance of the dividend reduced Pal's carrying amount for its Ima investment. This reflects that Pal accounts for its Ima investment by the

a. Cost method, and only a portion of Ima's 2002 dividends represent earnings after Pal's acquisition.
b. Cost method, and its carrying amount exceeded the proportionate share of Ima's market value.
c. Equity method, and Ima incurred a loss in 2002.
d. Equity method, and its carrying amount exceeded the proportionate share of Ima's market value. (11/92, Theory, #30, amended, 3463)

4. An investor uses the cost method to account for an investment in common stock classified as an available-for-sale security. Dividends received this year exceeded the investor's share of investee's undistributed earnings since the date of investment. The amount of dividend revenue that should be reported in the investor's income statement for this year would be

a. The portion of the dividends received this year that were in excess of the investor's share of investee's undistributed earnings since the date of investment.
b. The portion of the dividends received this year that were **not** in excess of the investor's share of investee's undistributed earnings since the date of investment.
c. The total amount of dividends received this year.
d. Zero.   (11/91, Theory, #10, amended, 2518)

5. Wood Co. owns 2,000 shares of Arlo, Inc.'s 20,000 shares of $100 par, 6% cumulative, nonparticipating preferred stock, and 1,000 shares (2%) of Arlo's common stock. During 2004, Arlo declared and paid dividends of $240,000 on preferred stock. No dividends had been declared or paid during 2003. In addition, Wood received a 5% common stock dividend from Arlo when the quoted market price of Arlo's common stock was $10 per share. What amount should Wood report as dividend income in its 2004 income statement?

a. $12,000
b. $12,500
c. $24,000
d. $24,500   (5/95, FAR, #29, amended, 5565)

6. Cobb Co. purchased 10,000 shares (2% ownership) of Roe Co. on February 12, 2003. Cobb received a stock dividend of 2,000 shares on March 31, 2003, when the carrying amount per share on Roe's books was $35 and the market value per share was $40. Roe paid a cash dividend of $1.50 per share on September 15, 2003. In Cobb's income statement for the year ended October 31, 2003, what amount should Cobb report as dividend income?

a. $98,000
b. $88,000
c. $18,000
d. $15,000   (11/93, PI, #48, amended, 4417)

7. Information pertaining to dividends from Wray Corp.'s common stock investments for the year ended December 31, 2002, follows:

- On September 8, 2002, Wray received a $50,000 cash dividend from Seco, Inc., in which Wray owns a 30% interest. A majority of Wray's directors are also directors of Seco.
- On October 15, 2002, Wray received a $6,000 liquidating dividend from King Co. Wray owns a 5% interest in King Co.
- Wray owns a 2% interest in Bow Corp., which declared a $200,000 cash dividend on November 27, 2002, to stockholders of record on December 15, 2002, payable on January 5, 2003.

What amount should Wray report as dividend income in its income statement for the year ended December 31, 2002?
a. $60,000
b. $56,000
c. $10,000
d. $ 4,000   (11/92, PI, #44, amended, 3277)

8. For the last 10 years, Woody Co. has owned cumulative preferred stock issued by Hadley, Inc. During 2002, Hadley declared and paid both the 2002 dividend and the 2001 dividend in arrears. How should Woody report the 2001 dividend in arrears that was received in 2002?
a. As a reduction in cumulative preferred dividends receivable
b. As a retroactive change of the prior period financial statements
c. Include, net of income taxes, after 2002 income from continuing operations
d. Include in 2002 income from continuing operations   (5/92, Theory, #43, amended, 2736)

9. Moss Corp. owns 20% of Dubro Corp.'s preferred stock and 80% of its common stock. Dubro's stock outstanding at December 31, 2003, is as follows:

10% cumulative preferred stock	$100,000
Common stock	700,000

Dubro reported net income of $60,000 for the year ended December 31, 2003. What amount should Moss record as equity in earnings of Dubro for the year ended December 31, 2003?
a. $42,000
b. $48,000
c. $48,400
d. $50,000   (11/94, FAR, #15, amended, 5280)

10. On January 2, 2003, Well Co. purchased 10% of Rea, Inc.'s outstanding common shares for $400,000. Well is the largest single shareholder in Rea, and Well's officers are a majority on Rea's board of directors. Rea reported net income of $500,000 for 2003, and paid dividends of $150,000. In its December 31, 2003 balance sheet, what amount should Well report as investment in Rea?
a. $450,000
b. $435,000
c. $400,000
d $385,000   (11/94, FAR, #16, amended, 5281)

11. On January 2, 2003, Kean Co. purchased a 30% interest in Pod Co. for $250,000. On this date, Pod's stockholders' equity was $500,000. The carrying amounts of Pod's identifiable net assets approximated their fair values, except for plant and equipment whose fair value exceeded its carrying amount by $200,000. The plant and equipment's remaining useful life is 10 years. Pod reported net income of $100,000 for 2003, and paid no dividends. Kean accounts for this investment using the equity method. In its December 31, 2003 balance sheet, what amount should Kean report as investment in subsidiary?
a. $210,000
b. $220,000
c. $270,000
d. $274,000   (5/94, FAR, #19, amended, 4834)

12. Pare, Inc. purchased 10% of Tot Co.'s 100,000 outstanding shares of common stock on January 2, 2002, for $50,000. On December 31, 2002, Pare purchased an additional 20,000 shares of Tot for $150,000. There was no goodwill as a result of either acquisition, and Tot had not issued any additional stock during 2002. Tot reported earnings of $300,000 for 2002. What amount should Pare report in its December 31, 2002 balance sheet as investment in Tot?
a. $170,000
b. $200,000
c. $230,000
d. $290,000   (11/93, PI, #14, amended, 4383)

13. When the equity method is used to account for investments in common stock, which of the following affect(s) the investor's reported investment income?

	A change in market value of investee's common stock	Cash dividends from investee
a.	Yes	Yes
b.	Yes	No
c.	No	Yes
d.	No	No

(5/96, FAR, #2, 6275)

14. On January 1, 2002, Point, Inc. purchased 10% of Iona Co.'s common stock. Point purchased additional shares bringing its ownership up to 40% of Iona's common stock outstanding on August 1, 2002. During October 2002, Iona declared and paid a cash dividend on all of its outstanding common stock. How much income from the Iona investment should Point's 2002 income statement report?

a. 10% of Iona's income for January 1 to July 31, 2002, plus 40% of Iona's income for August 1 to December 31, 2002
b. 40% of Iona's income for August 1 to December 31, 2002 only
c. 40% of Iona's 2002 income
d. Amount equal to dividends received from Iona
(11/93, Theory, #8, amended, 4513)

15. On July 1, 2002, Denver Corp. purchased 3,000 shares of Eagle Co.'s 10,000 outstanding shares of common stock for $20 per share. On December 15, 2002, Eagle paid $40,000 in dividends to its common stockholders. Eagle's net income for the year ended December 31, 2002, was $120,000, earned evenly throughout the year. In its 2002 income statement, what amount of income from this investment should Denver report?

a. $36,000
b. $18,000
c. $12,000
d. $ 6,000   (5/93, PI, #43, amended, 4084)

ITEMS 16 THROUGH 18 are based on the following:

Grant, Inc. acquired 30% of South Co.'s voting stock for $200,000 on January 2, 2003. Grant's 30% interest in South gave Grant the ability to exercise significant influence over South's operating and financial policies. During 2003, South earned $80,000 and paid dividends of $50,000. South reported earnings of $100,000 for the six months ended June 30, 2004, and $200,000 for the year ended December 31, 2004. On July 1, 2004, Grant sold half of its stock in South for $150,000 cash. South paid dividends of $60,000 on October 1, 2004.

16. Before income taxes, what amount should Grant include in its 2003 income statement as a result of the investment?

a. $15,000
b. $24,000
c. $50,000
d. $80,000   (11/95, FAR, #26, amended, 6108)

17. In Grant's December 31, 2003, balance sheet, what should be the carrying amount of this investment?

a. $200,000
b. $209,000
c. $224,000
d. $230,000   (11/95, FAR, #27, amended, 6109)

18. In its 2004 income statement, what amount should Grant report as gain from the sale of half of its investment?

a. $24,500
b. $30,500
c. $35,000
d. $45,500   (11/95, FAR, #28, amended, 6110)

19. Sage, Inc. bought 40% of Adams Corp.'s outstanding common stock on January 2, 2002, for $400,000. The carrying amount of Adams' net assets at the purchase date totaled $900,000. Fair values and carrying amounts were the same for all items except for plant and inventory, for which fair values exceeded their carrying amounts by $90,000 and $10,000, respectively. The plant has an 18-year life. All inventory was sold during 2002. Goodwill, if any, will be tested for impairment each year. During 2002, Adams reported net income of $120,000 and paid a $20,000 cash dividend. What amount should Sage report in its income statement from its investment in Adams for the year ended December 31, 2002?

a. $48,000
b. $42,000
c. $36,000
d. $32,000   (5/92, PI, #40, amended, 2611)

20. Park Co. uses the equity method to account for its January 1, 2002, purchase of Tun, Inc.'s common stock. On January 1, 2002, the fair values of Tun's FIFO inventory and land exceeded their carrying amounts. How do these excesses of fair values over carrying amounts affect Park's reported equity in Tun's 2002 earnings?

	Inventory excess	Land excess
a.	Decrease	Decrease
b.	Decrease	No effect
c.	Increase	Increase
d.	Increase	No effect

(5/91, Theory, #20, amended, 2015)

21. Birk Co. purchased 30% of Sled Co.'s outstanding common stock on December 31, 2000 for $200,000. On that date, Sled's stockholders' equity was $500,000, and the fair value of its identifiable net assets was $600,000. On December 31, 2000, what amount of goodwill should Birk attribute to this acquisition?
a. $0
b. $20,000
c. $30,000
d. $50,000   (R/00, FAR, #4, 6899)

22. Band Co. uses the equity method to account for its investment in Guard, Inc. common stock. How should Band record a 2% stock dividend received from Guard?
a. As dividend revenue at Guard's carrying value of the stock.
b. As dividend revenue at the market value of the stock.
c. As a reduction in the total cost of Guard stock owned.
d. As a memorandum entry reducing the unit cost of all Guard stock owned. (R/99, FAR, #8, 6777)

PROBLEM/ESSAY QUESTIONS

PROBLEM/ESSAY 19-2 (15 to 25 minutes)

Johnson, an investor in Acme Co., asked Smith, CPA, for advice on the propriety of Acme's financial reporting for two of its investments. Smith obtained the following information related to the investments from Acme's December 31, 2002, financial statements:

• 20% ownership interest in Kern Co., represented by 200,000 shares of outstanding common stock purchased on January 2, 2002, for $600,000.

• 20% ownership interest in Wand Co., represented by 20,000 shares of outstanding common stock purchased on January 2, 2002, for $300,000.

• On January 2, 2002, the carrying values of the acquired shares of both investments equaled their purchase price.

• Kern reported earnings of $400,000 for the year ended December 31, 2002, and declared and paid dividends of $100,000 during 2002.

• Wand reported earnings of $350,000 for the year ended December 31, 2002, and declared and paid dividends of $60,000 during 2002.

• On December 31, 2002, Kern's and Wand's common stock were trading over-the-counter at $18 and $20 per share, respectively.

• The investment in Kern is accounted for using the equity method.

• The investment in Wand is accounted for as available-for-sale securities.

Smith recalculated the amounts reported in Acme's December 31, 2002, financial statements, and determined that they were correct. Stressing that the information available in the financial statements was limited, Smith advised Johnson that, assuming Acme properly applied generally accepted accounting principles, Acme may have appropriately used two different methods to account for its investments in Kern and Wand, even though the investments represent equal ownership interests.

REQUIRED:

a. Prepare a detailed memorandum from Smith to Johnson supporting Smith's conclusion that, under generally accepted accounting principles, correctly applied, Acme may have appropriately used two different methods to account for its investments representing equal ownership interests.

b. Prepare a schedule indicating the amounts Acme should report for the two investments in its December 31, 2002, balance sheet and statement of income and comprehensive income. Show all calculations. Ignore income taxes.

Do not discuss SFAS No. 115, *Accounting for Investments in Certain Debt and Equity Securities.*

(11/98, FAR, Essay #2, amended, 6750)

ESSAY 19-3 (15 to 25 minutes)

Since Grumer Co.'s inception, Monroe Co. has owned 18% of Grumer's outstanding common stock. Monroe provides three key management personnel to Grumer and purchased 25% of Grumer's output during 2002. Grumer is profitable. On January 2, 2003, Monroe purchased additional common stock to finance Grumer's expansion, thereby becoming a 30% owner. Grumer's common stock does not have a quoted market price. The stock has always been issued at its book value, which is assumed to approximate its fair value.

REQUIRED:

a. In general, distinguish between investor income reporting under the cost method and under the equity method. Which method is more consistent with accrual accounting? Why?

b. Prior to January 2, 2003, what specific factors should Monroe have considered in determining the appropriate method of accounting for its investment in Grumer?

c. For purposes of your answer to **c.** only, assume Monroe used the cost method in accounting for its investment in Grumer prior to January 2, 2003. Describe the book adjustments required on January 2, 2003, when Monroe became owner of 30% of the outstanding common stock of Grumer.

(11/90, Theory, amended, #2, 3544)

SOLUTION 19-1 MULTIPLE CHOICE ANSWERS

COST METHOD

1. (a) The receipt of a cash dividend from a common stock investment should not be reported as an increase in the Investment account under either the cost or the equity method of accounting. Under the cost method of accounting, (1) dividends received up to the investor's share of the investee's earnings subsequent to the date of the investment are recorded as dividend income, and (2) dividends received in excess of the investor's share of the investee's earnings since the date of the investment represent a liquidating dividend and are recorded as a decrease to the Investment account. Under the equity method, the receipt of a cash dividend from the investee is always recorded as a decrease to the Investment account.

2. (c) The investment in the *nonvoting* preferred stock must be accounted under the cost method because Green does not have the ability to significantly influence the financial and operating policies of the investee by virtue of the preferred stock investment. Therefore, the $60,000 dividend declared on the preferred stock is reported as dividend revenue by Green. The 30% investment in the common stock should be accounted for under the equity method because Green has the ability to exercise significant influence over the investee by virtue of the investment. Under the equity method, the investor recognizes as income its share of the investee's earnings in the periods in which they are reported by the investee. These amounts are

recognized as equity in the earnings of the investee and not as dividend revenue.

3. (a) Dividend income is not recognized under the equity method of accounting for investments in common stock. Under this method, the investor's share of dividends declared by the investee reduce the carrying amount of the investment. Pal recognized dividend income from the investment in 2002. Hence it must account for the investment by the cost method. Under this method, investment income reported for the year is usually the investor's share of dividends declared by the investee during the year. The exception is where the investor's share of dividends declared by the investee exceeds the investor's share of investee earnings subsequent to the date of the investment. In this case, the excess amount represents a liquidating dividend that is recorded as a reduction of the carrying amount of the investment and not as dividend income. Since only part of the dividends that Pal received in 2002 was recorded as dividend income, only a portion of the 2002 dividends represent earnings subsequent to the date of Pal's investment (i.e., the balance of the 2002 dividends represent liquidating dividends).

4. (b) When the cost method is used to account for investments in common stock, dividends received up to the investor's share of the investee's earnings subsequent to the date of investment are recorded as dividend income. Dividends received in excess of the investor's share of the investee's earnings since the date of investment represent a

liquidating dividend and should be recorded as a decrease to the investment account.

5. (c) Wood owns 10% of Arlo's preferred stock and would have received $24,000 ($240,000 dividends × 10%) in dividends in 2004 on this preferred stock. Although this amount represents the dividend preference for 2003, due to the 6% cumulative feature of the stock, as well as for 2004, the revenue is not recognized until the dividends are actually declared in 2004. Per ARB 43, Ch. 7, stock dividends received are not recognized as income because they are not a distribution, division, or severance of the corporate assets.

6. (c) Cobb owns only a 2% interest in Roe. Thus, Cobb does not have the ability to exercise significant influence over Roe by virtue of the investment, and the investment should be accounted for under the cost method. Therefore, Cobb should report the cash dividend received from Roe as dividend income. No income is recognized from the receipt of the stock dividend from Roe, since Cobb's proportionate interest in Roe has not changed and Roe's underlying assets and liabilities have also not changed. Therefore, the amount that Cobb should report as dividend income is computed as follows:

Shares of Roe purchased 2/12/03	10,000
Add: Shares of Roe from stock dividend, 3/31/03	2,000
Shares of Roe held, 9/15/03	12,000
Times: Cash dividend per share	x $1.50
Dividend income for year ended 10/31/03	$18,000

7. (d) Of the dividends listed, only the $4,000 (i.e., $200,000 x 2%) cash dividend receivable from Bow should be reported as dividend income. Wray owns only a 2% interest in Bow; thus, Wray does not have the ability to exercise significant influence over Bow by virtue of the investment. Therefore, the investment should be accounted for under the cost method. The cash dividend received from Seco should be recorded as a reduction of the carrying amount of the investment in Seco reported in Wray's balance sheet because the investment should be accounted for under the equity method (i.e., Wray owns a 30% interest in Seco and a majority of Wray's directors are also directors of Seco). The liquidating dividend received from King should be recorded as a reduction of the carrying amount of the investment in King reported in Wray's balance sheet.

8. (d) The preferred stock investment should be accounted for under the cost method since it is highly unlikely that the investor has the ability to exercise significant influence over the operating and financial policies of the investee by virtue of the

investment. Preferred stock is usually nonvoting. Under the cost method, dividends are normally not recognized as income until they are declared by the investee. By definition, dividends in arrears have not yet been declared. Dividend income is a component of income from continuing operations.

EQUITY METHOD

9. (a) Since Moss owns 80% of Dubro's common stock, the common stock investment should be accounted for under the equity method because Moss has the ability to exercise significant influence over the financial and operating policies of Dubro by virtue of the size of this investment. Since Dubro has outstanding cumulative preferred stock, Moss should compute its share of earnings (losses) after deducting Dubro's preferred dividends, whether or not such dividends are declared [APB 18]. Thus, the amount that Moss should record as equity in earnings of Dubro for 2003 from the common stock and preferred stock investments is determined as follows:

Equity in earnings of Dubro due to common stock investment:	
Dubro's net income for 2003	$ 60,000
Less: 2003 cumulative preferred stock dividend preference ($100,000 x 10%)	(10,000)
Dubro's 2003 earnings applicable to common shareholders	50,000
Times: Percentage of common shares owned by Moss	x 80%
Due to common stock investment	40,000
Equity in earnings of Dubro due to preferred stock investment [($100,000 x 10%) x 20%]	2,000
Equity in earnings of Dubro for 2003	$ 42,000

10. (b) Although Well does not own 20% or more of Rea's common shares, Well should use the equity method to account for its investment in Rea because it can exercise significant influence over the operating and financial policies of Rea. Therefore, the carrying amount of the investment at 12/31/03 is determined as follows:

Purchase price, 1/2/03	$400,000
Add: Well's share of Rea's 2003 income ($500,000 x 10%)	50,000
Less: Well's share of 2003 dividends paid ($150,000 x 10%)	(15,000)
Carrying amount of investment, 12/31/03	$435,000

11. (d) Since Kean owns a 30% interest in Pod, the investment should be accounted for under the equity method. Under the equity method, the carrying amount of the investment is increased for Kean's share of Pod's income and decreased for Kean's share of any dividends paid by Pod. Also, the carrying amount of the investment is reduced by the yearly amortization of any payment in excess of carrying amount of assets acquired. To determine

the carrying amount of Kean's investment in Pod at 12/31/03, the original cost of the investment must first be allocated. The carrying amount of the investment at 12/31/03 may then be determined.

Purchase price	$ 250,000
Percentage of carrying amount acquired ($500,000 x 30%)	(150,000)
Payment in excess of carrying amount of net assets acquired	100,000
Excess payment associated with plant and equipment ($200,000 x 30%)	(60,000)
Goodwill	$ 40,000

Purchase price	$ 250,000
Add: 30% of Pod's $100,000 net income	30,000
Less: Amortization of excess paid for plant and equipment ($60,000 ÷ 10 years)	(6,000)
Investment carrying amount, 12/31/03	$ 274,000

12. (c) When Pare purchased an additional 20,000 shares of Tot at 12/31/02, it increased its investment in Tot's common stock from 10% to 30%. Thus, at 12/31/02, Pare gained the ability to exercise significant influence over the financial and operating policies of Tot and accordingly should report its investment in Tot using the equity method in its 12/31/02 balance sheet. The change from the cost method of reporting the investment in Tot to the equity method should be made by retroactively restating all prior periods in which the investment was held as if the equity method were used from inception. Thus, Pare should report the investment in Tot in its 12/31/02 balance sheet at $230,000, the sum of the amounts paid for Tot's shares (i.e., $50,000 and $150,000) and Pare's equity in Tot's reported earnings for 2002 (i.e., $300,000 x 10%).

13. (d) Under the equity method of accounting for investments in common stock, the investment is recorded at cost. Changes in the market value of the investee's common stock do not affect the Investment account or the Investment Income account. The investor recognizes as income its share of the investee's earnings or losses in the periods in which they are reported by the investee. Dividends declared by the investee represent a distribution of earnings previously recognized and, thus, do not affect the Investment Income account.

14. (a) On 8/1/02, when Point increased its investment in Iona's common stock from 10% to 40%, Point gained the ability to exercise significant influence over the financial and operating policies of Iona and accordingly should report its investment using the equity method. The change from the cost method to the equity method should be made by retroactively restating all prior periods in which the investment was held as if the equity method were used from inception. Therefore, the amount Point

should report as income from the Iona investment in its 2002 income statement is 10% of Iona's income from 1/1/02 to 7/31/02, plus 40% of Iona's income for 8/1/02 to 12/31/02.

15. (b) This investment should be accounted for under the equity method because Denver's purchase of 30% (i.e., 3,000 ÷ 10,000) of Eagle's common stock gives Denver the ability to exercise significant influence over the operating and financial policies of Eagle by virtue of the size of the investment. Denver should recognize investment income only for its share of Eagle's net income subsequent to the date of the investment. While dividends declared by Eagle reduce the carrying amount of the investment, they do not affect the amount of investment income that Denver recognizes. Therefore, Denver should report income from the equity method investment of $18,000 (i.e., $120,000 x 6/12 x 30%).

16. (b) As Grant has 20% or more ownership in South, the amount of investment income in Grant's income statement is Grant's percentage of ownership times South's earnings. $80,000 x 30% = $24,000.

17. (b) As Grant has 20% or more ownership in South, the carrying amount of the investment is the original purchase price plus Grant's share in South's earnings ($80,000 x 30% = $24,000), less the dividends paid to Grant ($50,000 x 30% = $15,000). $200,000 + $24,000 − $15,000 = $209,000.

18. (b) The balance in Grant's Investment in South account at the beginning of 2004 is $209,000. Grant has equity in South's earnings of $30,000 ($100,0000 x 30%), which increases the investment account. South did not pay any dividends during the first six months of 2004, so the balance in Investment in South is $239,000 at the date of sale. Half of the investment was sold, so half of the balance in the account is Grant's carrying value for the stock sold ($239,000 x 50% = $119,500). The gain is the sale price less the carrying value ($150,000 − $119,500 = $30,500).

19. (b) The common stock investment should be accounted for under the equity method since Sage has the ability to exercise significant influence over the operating and financial policies of Adams by virtue of the investment. To determine Sage's reported amount of equity in income in Adams, the cost of the investment must first be allocated. The amount that Sage should report in its income statement from its investment in Adams can then be determined. The cash dividends paid by Adams to Sage reduce the carrying amount of the investment

in Sage's balance sheet. They do not effect Sage's reported amount of equity in income in Adams.

Purchase price	$ 400,000
Percentage of carrying amount acquired ($900,000 x 40%)	(360,000)
Cost in excess of carrying amount of net assets acquired	40,000
Excess payment associated with specific assets:	
Plant assets ($90,000 x 40%)	(36,000)
Inventory ($10,000 x 40%)	(4,000)
Goodwill	$ 0

Sage's interest in Adams net income ($120,000 x 40%)	$ 48,000
Less: Amortization of excess payment associated with plant assets ($36,000 ÷ 18)	(2,000)
Excess payment associated with inventory sold	(4,000)
Equity in income of Adams	$ 42,000

20. (b) When using the equity method, a difference between the cost of the investment and the amount of underlying equity in net assets of an investee should be accounted for as if the investee were a consolidated subsidiary [APB 18]. In a consolidated situation, the excess of the investee's FIFO inventory over its carrying amount would have been charged to cost of goods sold while the excess of the fair value of the land over its carrying amount

would not affect consolidated income because land is not depreciated. Thus, the excess of the fair value of Tun's FIFO inventory over its carrying amount would decrease Park's reported equity in Tun's earnings but the excess of the fair value of Tun's land over its carrying amount would have no effect on Park's reported equity in Tun's earnings.

21. (b) Purchased goodwill is recognized and recorded at an amount equal to the excess of the cost of the enterprise acquired over the fair value of the identifiable net assets. Purchased goodwill is calculated as follows:

Purchase price of 30% of Sled Co's O/S common stock		$ 200,000
Less: Fair value of identifiable net assets of Sled Co.	$600,000	
Times percentage acquired by Birk Co.	x 30%	(180,000)
Goodwill attributable to the acquisition		$ 20,000

22. (d) Stock dividends are recorded as memorandum entries only, reducing the unit cost of the stock owned. No dividend revenue is recorded and the total cost of the stock owned remains the same.

PERFORMANCE BY SUBTOPICS

Each category below parallels a subtopic covered in Chapter 19. Record the number and percentage of questions you correctly answered in each subtopic area.

Cost Method

Question #	Correct √
1	
2	
3	
4	
5	
6	
7	
8	
# Questions	8
# Correct	_____
% Correct	_____

Equity Method

Question #	Correct √
Question #	Correct √
9	
10	
11	
12	
13	
14	
15	
16	
17	
18	
19	
20	
21	
22	
# Questions	14
# Correct	_____
% Correct	_____

PROBLEM/ESSAY SOLUTIONS

SOLUTION 19-2 INVESTMENTS

a.

To: Johnson
From: Smith, CPA
Re: Acme Co. Investments in Kern Co. and Wand Co.

The purpose of this memorandum is to explain to you that although Acme's investment in Wand and Kern represent equal ownership interests of 20%, the use of different accounting methods may be appropriate under generally accepted accounting principles.

Under those principles, Acme must use the equity method to account for an investment if Acme's ownership interest allows it to exercise significant influence over the investee company.

Generally, an investor is presumed to be able to exercise significant influence when it has an ownership interest of 20% or more, and is presumed to be unable to exercise significant influence when it has an ownership interest of less than 20%. However, either presumption may be overcome by predominant evidence to the contrary. The determination of whether an investor can exercise significant influence is not always clear and often requires judgment in light of such factors as an investor's representation on the investee's board of directors, participation in policymaking activities, and/or the extent of ownership as compared to that investee's other shareholders.

Acme used the equity method to account for its investment in Kern which indicates that its 20% ownership interest allowed it to exercise significant influence over Kern's operating and financial policies.

Acme accounted for its investment in Wand as available-for-sale securities. Apparently, despite its 20% ownership interest, there was evidence that Acme could not exercise significant influence over Wand's operating and financial policies, hence, Acme did not use the equity method to account for its investment in Wand.

b.   **Kern**

Balance Sheet—Acme reported its investment in Kern at a carrying amount of $660,000

Calculations:
Equity in earnings = $80,000 ($400,000 x 20%)
Dividend rec'd = $20,000 ($100,000 x 20%)

Carrying amount = $600,000 + $80,000 − $20,000

Statement of Income and Comprehensive Income

Acme's equity in Kern's earnings $80,000

Calculation:
$400,000 x 20%

Wand

Balance Sheet—Acme reported its investment in Wand at a fair value of $400,000

Calculation:
20,000 shares x $20 per share

Statement of Income and Comprehensive Income

Dividend income $12,000

Calculation:
$60,000 x 20%

Unrealized gain $100,000

Calculation:
$400,000 − $300,000

SOLUTION 19-3 EQUITY METHOD

a. Under the **cost method**, the investor **recognizes dividends as income when received**. Under the **equity method**, an investor **recognizes as income its share of an investee's earnings or losses** in the periods in which they are reported by the investee. The amount recognized as **income is adjusted for any change in the difference between investment cost and underlying equity in net assets** at the investment date. The **equity method** is more consistent with **accrual accounting** than is the cost method, because the equity method **recognizes income when earned** rather than when dividends are received.

b. Monroe should have assessed whether it could have **exerted significant influence** over Grumer's operating and financial policies. Monroe did not own **20%** or more of Grumer's **voting stock** (which would have given the refutable presumption that it could exercise **significant influence**); however, the ability to exercise significant influence may be **indicated by other factors** such as Monroe's provisions of three key management **personnel** and **purchase** of 25% of Grumer's **output**.

c.   On becoming a 30% owner of Grumer, Monroe should use the **equity method** to account for its **investment**. As of January 2, 1998, Monroe's investment and **retained earnings** accounts must be **adjusted retroactively** to show balances as if the equity method had been used from the initial pur-chase date. Both accounts should be increased by 18% of Grumer's undistributed income since forma-tion. [In this case, no adjustment to the undistributed income is necessary since the stock was issued at its book value which was assumed to approximate its fair value.]

Using Audio Tutor to Study

Actively listen to the audio tapes, taking notes if convenient. In the Audio Tutor product, the lecturers supplement the content in this material with the insight gained from years of CPA review experience.

If you are strong in a topic, your audio review and question drill may be sufficient. If your strength is moderate in a topic, you might find that reading the related text before listening to the audio tapes is helpful. If you are weak in a topic, one successful strategy is to listen to the audio tapes, read the book, and then listen to the audio tapes again.

FYI: The Audio Tutor tapes have similar content as the Hot*Spot, Intensive, and online video lectures, but they are not exactly the same. Audio Tutor and this book have topics arranged in essentially the same chapters, although material might be organized differently within the chapters.

Call a customer service representative for more details about Audio Tutor.

_____

CHANGE ALERTS

SFAS 141, *Business Combinations*

In June 2001, the FASB released SFAS 141, *Business Combinations,* requiring that the purchase method of accounting be used for all business combinations initiated after June 30, 2001. Use of the pooling-of-interests method is prohibited. This statement supersedes APB Opinion No. 16, *Business Combinations,* and SFAS 38, *Accounting for Preacquisition Contingencies of Purchased Enterprises.*

Many of the provisions related to the application of the purchase method were not changed. However, accounting for business combinations is changed by this statement in the following significant respects:

- The purchase method is the only method of accounting for business combinations

- Intangible assets must be recognized as assets apart from goodwill if they meet one of two criteria: (1) the contractual-legal criterion or (2) the separability criterion. Previously, separate recognition of intangible assets was required when they could be identified and named.

- Additional disclosures are required, including the primary reasons for the combination and the allocation of the purchase price paid to the assets and liabilities assumed by major balance sheet caption.

- When the amounts of goodwill and intangible assets acquired are significant, disclosure of additional information is required, such as the amount of goodwill by reportable segment and the amount of the purchase price assigned to each major intangible asset class.

SFAS 142, *Goodwill and Other Intangible Assets*

In June 2001, the FASB released SFAS 142, *Goodwill and Other Intangible Assets,* changing the accounting for goodwill from an amortization method to an impairment-only approach. Amortization of goodwill, including goodwill recorded in past business combinations, ceases upon adoption of SFAS 142, which for companies with calendar year ends, will be January 1, 2002.

CHAPTER 20

CONSOLIDATED FINANCIAL STATEMENTS

CHAPTER 20

CONSOLIDATED FINANCIAL STATEMENTS

I. BUSINESS COMBINATIONS

A. OVERVIEW

Consolidated Financial Statements (ARB 51) states, "…consolidated statements are more meaningful than separate statements and are usually necessary for a fair presentation when one of the companies in the group directly or indirectly has a controlling financial interest in the other companies" (par. 1). All majority-owned subsidiaries—all companies in which a parent has a controlling financial interest through **direct** or **indirect** ownership of a **majority voting interest** (i.e., > 50 percent)—should be consolidated, unless specifically exempted.

1. **DEFINITION** A *business combination* occurs when an entity acquires net assets or equity interests of one or more other businesses and obtains control over that entity or entities.

2. **CHAIN OF INTERESTS** On occasion, intercorporate stock ownership arrangements may indicate a chain of interests (e.g., A owns 80 percent of B, B owns 60 percent of C) the product of which (e.g., 80% x 60% = 48%) does not represent control of the lower level subsidiary, where control is defined in terms of the 50 percent stock ownership minimum. In this instance, the preparation on consolidated statements is warranted, notwithstanding the 48 percent indirect interest of A Company in C Company. The product of the percentages of stock ownership in the chain is not a determinant in establishing a minimal condition for preparation of consolidated financial statements.

3. **EXCEPTIONS** SFAS 94, *Consolidation of All Majority-Owned Subsidiaries*, provides that a majority-owned subsidiary should **not** be consolidated if (1) control is likely to be *temporary* or (2) control does **not** rest with the majority owner, for example, if the subsidiary is in legal reorganization or in bankruptcy or operates under foreign exchange restrictions, controls, or other governmentally imposed uncertainties so severe that they cast significant doubt on the parent's ability to control the subsidiary. Consolidation of majority-owned subsidiaries is required even if they have "nonhomogeneous" operations, a large minority interest, or a foreign location.

B. PURCHASE METHOD

1. **PURCHASE METHOD REQUIRED** According to SFAS 141, *Business Combinations*, business combinations initiated after June 30, 2001, must be accounted for under the purchase method.

2. **RECORDING NET ASSETS ACQUIRED** The acquiring corporation records the net assets acquired at the sum of the FV of the consideration given and direct costs incurred as a result of the purchase. Any excess of the purchase price over the FV of the net identifiable assets is recorded as goodwill.

3. **GOODWILL** Goodwill must be tested for impairment at least annually. Goodwill is impaired if carrying value exceeds the fair value.

C. POOLING OF INTERESTS METHOD

1. **WHEN POOLING ALLOWED** Business combinations initiated before June 30, 2001, that were exchanges of common stock for common stock and met several conditions, were allowed to be accounted for by the pooling of interests method. Even though new combinations must be accounted for under the purchase method, consolidated companies that have been

accounted for under the pooling method will continue to be consolidated using the pooling method.

2. **SUMMARY OF POOLING** The pooling method accounts for a combination of two firms as a union of the ownership interests of two previously separated groups of stockholders. No sale or purchase is deemed to have occurred and no new goodwill is recorded. The assets and liabilities of the combining firms continue to be carried at their recorded amounts. The income of the constituents are combined and restated for each period presented. Consolidated financial statements for the year the combination is effected should be presented as if the combination had taken place at the **beginning** of the period.

II. CONSOLIDATED FINANCIAL STATEMENTS IMMEDIATELY FOLLOWING ACQUISITION

A. ACQUISITION
The acquisition of a controlling interest in a company may be effected in different manners.

1. **ASSETS** The acquiring corporation may negotiate with management to obtain the assets (and assume the liabilities) of the company being acquired in exchange for cash, securities, or other consideration. Upon consummation, the acquired company ceases to exist as a separate economic, legal, and accounting entity. The surviving corporation records in its books the assets and liabilities of the acquired company. Note that this results in automatic consolidation for the current and subsequent periods, since the assets and liabilities of both companies are recorded in the same set of books.

2. **EQUITY INTERESTS** An acquiring corporation may acquire ownership (or control) of a subsidiary by obtaining all (or a majority) of its outstanding common stock. The separate legal entity of the subsidiary is preserved. Likewise, the subsidiary continues to maintain its own separate set of books. For financial reporting purposes, however, the two companies may be viewed as a single reporting entity, in accordance with ARB 51; this creates the need for consolidated financial statements.

B. RECORDING THE COMBINATION (PURCHASE METHOD)

1. **RECORD INVESTMENT** The investment in the acquired corporation is recorded at the sum of the fair value of the consideration given or the net assets received, whichever is more clearly determinable, and the direct acquisition costs.

2. **ASSIGN AMOUNTS TO ASSETS AND LIABILITIES ACQUIRED**

   a. **MARKETABLE SECURITIES** at fair values

   b. **RECEIVABLES** at present values of amounts to be received determined at appropriate current interest rates, less allowances for uncollectibility and collection costs

   c. **INVENTORIES**

      (1) **FINISHED GOODS AND MERCHANDISE** at estimated selling prices less the sum of the costs of disposal and a reasonable profit allowance for the selling effort of the acquiring entity

      (2) **WORK IN PROCESS** at the costs in (1) above plus the costs to complete

      (3) **RAW MATERIALS** at current replacement costs

   d. **PLANT AND EQUIPMENT**

      (1) **TO BE USED** at current replacement cost for similar capacity

(2) **To Be Sold** at fair value less cost to sell

e. **Intangible Assets**

(1) **Goodwill and Deferred Income Taxes Previously Recorded by the Acquired Entity** not recognized by the acquiring entity

(2) **Arising From Contractual or Legal Rights** at estimated fair values

(3) **Other Intangibles Separable From Entity** at estimated fair values, apart from goodwill

(4) **Other Intangibles Not Separable** not recognized separate from goodwill

Exhibit 1 ♦ Examples of Intangible Assets Recognized

1. Marketing-Related Intangible Assets—Trademarks, tradenames, service marks, collective marks, certification marks, trade dress (unique color, shape, or package design), newspaper mastheads, internet domain names, noncompetition agreements

2. Customer-Related Intangible Assets—Customer lists, order or production backlog, customer contracts and related customer relationships, noncontractual customer relationships

3. Artistic-Related Intangible Assets—Plays, operas, ballets, books, magazines, newspapers, other literary works, musical works such as compositions, song lyrics, advertising jingles, pictures, photographs, video and audiovisual material, including motion pictures, music videos, television programs

4. Contract-Based Intangible Assets—Licensing, royalty, and standstill agreements; advertising, construction, management, service or supply contracts; lease agreements; construction permits; franchise agreements; operating and broadcast rights; use rights such as drilling, water air, mineral, timber cutting, and route authorities; servicing contracts such as mortgage servicing contracts; employment contracts

5. Technology-Based Intangible Assets—Patented technology; computer software and mask works; unpatented technology; databases, including title plants; trade secrets, such as secret formulas, processes, recipes

f. **Other Assets Such as Land, Natural Resources, and Nonmarketable Securities** at appraised values

g. **Accounts and Notes Payable, and Long-Term Debt** at present values of amounts to be paid determined at appropriate current interest rates

h. **Liabilities and Accruals** at present values of amounts to be paid determined at appropriate current interest rates

i. **Preacquisition Contingencies** at fair value if the fair value can be determined during the allocation period. If not, the contingency is included if information available prior to the end of the allocation period indicates that it is probable that one or more future events will occur to confirm the existence of the asset, liability, or impairment; and the amount can be reasonably estimated.

3. **Purchase Price Exceeds FV** If the purchase price exceeds the net of the amounts assigned to assets acquired and liabilities assumed, the excess is recognized as goodwill.

4. **FV EXCEEDS PURCHASE PRICE**

    a. **REDUCE ASSET AMOUNTS** If the purchase price is less than the net of the amounts assigned to assets acquired and liabilities assumed, the excess is allocated as a pro rata reduction of the acquired asset amounts, except financial assets other than investments accounted for by the equity method, assets to be disposed of by sale, deferred tax assets, prepaid assets relating to pension or other postretirement benefit plans, and any other current assets.

    b. **EXTRAORDINARY GAIN** If any excess remains after reducing to zero the acquired asset amounts, the remaining excess shall be recognized as an extraordinary gain. This gain is recognized in the period in which the business combination is completed.

5. **ACQUISITION COSTS** Direct acquisition costs incurred (e.g., fees of finders and consultants, cost of furnishing information to stockholders) must be capitalized as part of the total purchase price. Indirect and general expenses related to the acquisition are expensed as incurred.

6. **EQUITY SECURITIES ISSUED** If the purchaser issues its own equity securities as part of the consideration, these must be credited to paid-in capital on the basis of their fair value. Costs of registering and issuing equity securities are a reduction of the otherwise determinable fair value of the securities (i.e., a reduction of additional paid-in capital).

7. **PURCHASE OF LESS THAN 100 PERCENT INTEREST** A purchase of less than 100 percent interest in a business at a price exceeding the book value of the proportionate interest acquired should **not** result in the recognition of "implied value" based on the purchase price and the percentage ownership acquired.

    a. Generally, identifiable assets are adjusted to FV only to the extent of the proportionate interest acquired.

    b. If the consideration paid exceeds the FV of identifiable net assets, identifiable assets would be presented in the consolidated balance sheet at an amount determined as follows:

Original BV + [% ownership x (FV − BV)].

EXAMPLE 1 ♦ ALLOCATION OF PURCHASE PRICE

Purchaser Inc., acquired for cash the assets and liabilities of the Acquired Co. Acquired's balance sheet prior to its dissolution is reproduced below. Book values are assumed to approximate FV except where otherwise indicated.

	BV	FV (if different)
Cash	$ 3,000	
Accounts receivable	8,000	
Inventories	22,000	$20,000
Held-to-maturity securities	50,000	55,000
Property, plant, and equipment, net (PPE)	60,000	50,000
Land	20,000	28,000
Total assets	$163,000	

(continued on net page)

Current liabilities	$	4,000
Long-term liabilities		20,000
C/S, $10 par		30,000
APIC		50,000
R/E		59,000
Total liabs. and equity		$163,000

REQUIRED: Determine the amounts assigned to the individual assets and liabilities acquired if the purchase price were the following:

a. $160,000
b. $120,000
c. $ 60,000

SOLUTION:

			Assigned Cost		
Item, Dr. (Cr.)	FV		Case a.	Case b.	Case c.
Cash	$ 3,000		$ 3,000	$ 3,000	$ 3,000
Accounts receivable	8,000		8,000	8,000	8,000
Inventories	20,000		20,000	20,000	20,000
Held-to-maturity securities	55,000		55,000	55,000	55,000
Current liabilities	(4,000)		(4,000)	(4,000)	(4,000)
Long-term liabilities	(20,000)		(20,000)	(20,000)	(20,000)
Total net FV, excluding PPE & land	$ 62,000				
Purchase price			$160,000	$120,000	$ 60,000
Net FV above			(62,000)	(62,000)	(62,000)
Excess (deficit) purchase price			98,000	58,000	(2,000)
Allocate to noncurrent assets and/or goodwill:					
PPE, net	$ 50,000		(50,000)	(37,179)*	0
Land	$ 28,000		(28,000)	(20,821)*	0
Goodwill (Extraordinary Income)			$ 20,000	$ 0	$ (2,000)

*COMPUTATIONS:

$$PPE: \frac{\$50,000}{\$50,000 + \$28,000} \times \$58,000 = \mathbf{\$37,179} \qquad Land: \frac{\$28,000}{\$50,000 + \$28,000} \times \$58,000 = \mathbf{\$20,821}$$

EXAMPLE 2 ♦ RECORDING THE PURCHASE OF 100% INTEREST

Refer to the balance sheet and FV's provided for Acquired Co. in Example 1. Assume that the acquisition price consisted of the following: $100,000 cash, 5,000 shares of Purchaser, Inc. ($3 par, $10 FV), and $10,000 paid for legal fees and commissions directly related to the purchase.

REQUIRED: Record the transaction in Purchaser's books.

SOLUTION:

Investment in Sub (balancing figure)	160,000	
Cash ($100,000 + $10,000)		110,000
C/S, $3 Par (5,000 x $3)		15,000
APIC [(5,000 x $10) – $15,000 par]		35,000

NOTE: If the $10,000 paid was for registration fees, APIC would be recorded at $25,000 ($35,000 – $10,000) and the investment in subsidiary would be recorded at $150,000 (the balancing figure).

EXAMPLE 3 ♦ PURCHASE OF LESS THAN 100% INTEREST

Refer to the balance sheet and FV information provided in Example 1. Assume that the transaction involved the acquisition by Purchaser, Inc., of 80% of Acquired's common stock outstanding, in exchange for $128,000 cash.

REQUIRED:

a. Record the investment in Purchaser's books.
b. Determine the adjustments needed if the carrying amounts of individual assets are to reflect FV only to the extent of proportionate ownership acquired (proprietary theory).
c. Present a consolidation worksheet starting with the separate balance sheets of the two companies given in the first two columns of Solution c. below. Show eliminating entries and the consolidated balance sheet.

SOLUTION:

a. Investment in Sub   128,000
       Cash   128,000

b.

Item	80% x (FV – BV)			Adjustment
Assets				
Cash	80% x ($ 3,000	–	3,000)	= $ 0
A/R	80% x ($ 8,000	–	8,000)	= 0
Inventories*	80% x ($ 20,000*	–	22,000)	= (1,600)
HTM Securities	80% x ($ 55,000	–	50,000)	= 4,000
PPE	80% x ($ 50,000	–	60,000)	= (8,000)
Land	80% x ($ 28,000	–	20,000)	= 6,400

Item	80% x (FV – BV)			Adjustment
Liabilities				
Current liabilities	80% x ($ 4,000	–	4,000)	= 0
Long-term liabilities	80% x ($ 20,000	–	20,000)	= 0
Net identifiable assets	80% x ($140,000	–	139,000)	= $ 800

Purchase price		$ 128,000
FV of net assets	$140,000	
% ownership	x 80%	
FV of 80% net assets		(112,000)
Goodwill		$ 16,000

---

* For illustration purposes only; if inventories are overvalued by $2,000, a write-down for that <u>entire</u> amount should be recorded in Acquired's books.

(continued on next page)

c.

Assets	Balance Sheets Purchaser*	Balance Sheets Acquired	Eliminations Dr.	Eliminations Cr.	Minority Interest (20%)	Consolidated Balance Sheet Dr.	Consolidated Balance Sheet Cr.
Cash	$ 20,000	$ 3,000				$ 23,000	
A/R	35,000	8,000				43,000	
Inventories	32,000	22,000		(2) $ 1,600		52,400	
HTM securities	80,000	50,000	(2) $ 4,000			134,000	
PPE (net)	150,000	60,000		(2) 8,000		202,000	
Land	40,000	20,000	(2) 6,400			66,400	
Invest. in sub (80% int.)	128,000			(1) 111,200			
				(2) 16,800			
Goodwill			(2) 16,000			16,000	
Total	$485,000	$163,000					
Liab. & Equity							
Cur. liabs.	$ 25,000	$ 4,000					$ 29,000
Long-term liabs.	40,000	20,000					60,000
C/S, $3 par (P)	90,000						90,000
APIC (P)	160,000						160,000
R/E (P)	170,000						170,000
C/S, $10 par (S)		30,000	(1) 24,000		$ 6,000		
APIC (S)		50,000	(1) 40,000		10,000		
R/E (S)		59,000	(1) 47,200		11,800		
Minority interest					(27,800)		27,800
Total	$485,000	$163,000	$137,600	$137,600	$ 0	$536,800	$536,800

---

* All P's balance sheet amounts, except **Investment in Sub**, are arbitrary.

WORKSHEET ENTRIES:
(1) To eliminate 80% of subsidiary's owners' equity account balances.
(2) To adjust assets to FV and record purchased goodwill.

III. CONSOLIDATED FINANCIAL STATEMENTS SUBSEQUENT TO ACQUISITION

A. CONSOLIDATION PROCEDURES

Subsequent to a business combination, the newly affiliated companies continue to maintain their separate accounting records. Furthermore, the eliminations and adjustments made as part of the consolidation procedures are **not** entered into the books of any of the companies; these adjustments are simply "worksheet entries" that are never formally journalized.

1. **FREQUENCY OF CONSOLIDATION PROCEDURES** As a result, consolidation procedures must be performed every period in which financial statements are presented. Generally, the parent company carries its interest in a subsidiary in a single account, "Investment in Subsidiary." This account is generally carried under one of two methods: the *cost* method or the *equity* method.

2. **FINAL RESULT OF CONSOLIDATION PROCEDURES** Consolidation procedures are partly determined by the consolidation method used. However, the final result, (the consolidated statements themselves) must be the same regardless of how the investment is carried on the parent's books.

B.   PURCHASE OF A SUBSIDIARY

When a subsidiary is purchased during a year, there are alternative methods of dealing with the results of its operations in the consolidated income statement.

1.   PREFERABLE METHOD The preferable method is to include the subsidiary in the consolidation as though it had been acquired at the beginning of the period and then deduct near the bottom of the consolidated income statement the preacquisition portion of earnings applicable to each block of stock.

2.   ALTERNATIVE METHOD The alternative method is to include in the consolidated statement only the subsidiary's revenues and expenses subsequent to the date of acquisition.

C.   DISPOSAL OF A SUBSIDIARY

Where an investment in a subsidiary is disposed of during the year, it is preferable to omit from consolidated statements all details of the subsidiary's operations and to merely show the equity of the parent in the earnings of the subsidiary prior to disposal as a separate line in the income statement (equity method).

D.   PURCHASE METHOD CONSOLIDATIONS

Consolidation procedures involve the following:

1.   ADJUST THE CARRYING AMOUNT OF INVESTMENT Entries to adjust the carrying amount of the investment to the equity method balance.

2.   ELIMINATE CAPITAL AND INVESTMENT ACCOUNTS Entries to eliminate the subsidiary's capital accounts (except for minority interest, if any), and the parent's investment account.

3.   ADJUST FOR DEPRECIATION ON EXCESS PURCHASE PRICE OVER BOOK VALUE OF ASSETS

4.   ELIMINATE INTERCOMPANY TRANSACTIONS Entries to eliminate intercompany balances and unrealized intercompany gains and losses.

EXAMPLE 4 ♦ PURCHASED SUBSIDIARY, COST METHOD

The December 31, 20X5 trial balances of Purchasing Inc., (P) and The Subsidiary Corporation (S) are reproduced in the first two columns of the worksheet in the solution, below. Purchasing acquired its 80% interest in the common stock of Subsidiary on January 1, 20X3, for $150,000 cash. At the time of acquisition, the recorded amounts of all assets and liabilities of Subsidiary were deemed to approximate their FV, except equipment, which was undervalued by $50,000 in S's books. The equipment has an estimated remaining useful life of 10 years, and it has been depreciated on an SL basis. S has not issued or retired stock since its incorporation. P carries its investment in S under the cost method.* Net income and dividend distributions for S have been as follows:

Year	Net Income	Dividends Declared
20X3	$15,000	$ 8,000
20X4	13,000	10,000
20X5	16,000	5,000
	$44,000	$23,000

---

* The **equity** method is generally required for **unconsolidated** investments exceeding 20% ownership; since the investment in S is to be consolidated, however, it is permissible for P to use the **cost method** for internal purposes.

(continued on next page)

REQUIRED: Provide elimination entries to consolidate the financial statements of P and S. Show all computations.

SOLUTION: These steps are necessary before attempting to complete the consolidation worksheet.

Step 1: Determine the net book value of S at the time of the 80% stock acquisition by P.

Beg. R/E + NI – Divids. = End R/E

$$\text{Beg. R/E} = \text{End R/E} - \text{NI} + \text{Divids.}$$
$$= \$79,000 - (\$15,000 + \$13,000) + (\$8,000 + \$10,000)$$
$$= \underline{\$69,000}$$

Beg. R/E	$69,000
C/S	20,000 (from trial balance)
Net BV Co. S (1/1/X3)	$89,000

Step 2: Determine amount of excess cost over BV of identifiable assets and purchased goodwill, if any.

Purchase price	$150,000
Less: BV of net assets acquired [$89,000 (Step 1) x .80]	(71,200)
Excess cost over BV of net assets acquired	78,800
Attributable to equipment ($50,000 x .80)	(40,000)
Goodwill	$ 38,800

Step 3: Determine amount of depreciation on excess purchase price over book value.

Excess FV over BV, equipment (Step 2)	$ 40,000
Useful life	÷ 10 years
Depreciation on excess	$ 4,000 /year

Consolidation Worksheet, 80% Ownership, Cost Method Purchase Investment

	Trial Balance Dr. (Cr.) P	S	Eliminations Dr.	Cr.	Consolidated Income Statement Dr. (Cr.)	Minority Interest Dr. (Cr.)	Controlling R/E Dr. (Cr.)	Consolidated Balance Sheet Dr.	Cr.
Current assets	50,000	15,000						65,000	
Equipment	200,000	120,000	[3] 40,000	[5] 12,000				348,000	
Investment in S	150,000		[4] 8,000	[2] 16,000					
				[2] 63,200					
				[3] 78,800					
Goodwill			[3] 38,800					38,800	
Liabilities	(70,000)	(25,000)							95,000
C/S, $1 par (P)	(100,000)								100,000
R/E, Jan. 1, 20X5 (P)	(131,000)		[5] 8,000	[4] 8,000			(131,000)		
C/S, $2 par (S)		(20,000)	[2] 16,000			(4,000)			
R/E, Jan. 1, 20X5 (S)		$(79,000)	[2] 63,200			(15,800)			
Revenues	$(255,000)	(71,000)			(326,000)				
Expenses	160,000	55,000	[5] 4,000		219,000				
Subsidiary dividend income	(4,000)		[1] 4,000						
Dividends declared		5,000		[1] 4,000		1,000			
	$ 0	$ 0	182,000	182,000					
Consolidated NI					(107,000)		(107,000)		
Minority NI, 20% x (71,000 – 55,000)						(3,200)	3,200		
Minority interest						(22,000)			22,000
R/E, controlling interest							(234,800)		234,800
								451,800	451,800

WORKSHEET ENTRIES:

[1] To eliminate current year dividends.

[2] To eliminate 80% of S equity balances.

[3] To record goodwill and excess valuation of equipment, as determined in **Step 2**, above.

[4] To adjust investment account and R/E for S income and dividends during 20X3-20X4. (80% x R/E) = 80% x ($79,000 – $69,000) = $8,000.

[5] To record accumulated depreciation (3 years) and current year expense.

EXAMPLE 5 ♦ PURCHASED SUBSIDIARY, EQUITY METHOD

The situation is the same as for Example 4, except that P maintains its investment in S under the **equity method** of accounting for investments. The trial balances of P and S are provided in Exhibit 5, below. Note that while S's trial balance is the same as in Example 4, P's trial balance shows different amounts for the Investment in S account and Subsidiary Income account. This is the result of accounting for the investment in S under the equity method.

REQUIRED: Same as Example 4.

SOLUTION: A basic understanding of the **equity** method of accounting for common stock investments is essential in solving this problem. Before attempting to work through the elimination entries required, you should carefully study the T-account analysis of P's Investment in Sub, Investment Income, and R/E accounts, as illustrated below. While this step is not necessary in solving the problem, it will facilitate the solution and increase your understanding of consolidations.

T-Account Analysis of Investment in S

Investment in S				Subsidiary Income				R/E			
(a)	150,000	18,400	(c)	(e)	4,000	12,800	(b)	(d)	8,000	22,400	(b)
(b)	35,200	8,000	(d)							116,600	(f)
		4,000	(e)								
bal.	154,800	12/31/X5		12/31/X5		8,800 bal.		1/1/X5		131,000 bal.	

Entries:

(a) To record acquisition cost of 80% interest in S (credit to cash for same amount not shown).

(b) To record parent's share of S's cumulative NI for years 20X3-X5 (80% x $44,000). Note, the beginning (i.e., 1/1/X5) balance of R/E has been credited for P's portion of the earnings for 20X3 and 20X4 [80% x ($15,000 + $13,000)]. The portion of NI reported by S in 20X5 (80% x $16,000 = $12,800) has been credited to Subsidiary Income, but is properly not reflected in the beginning (1/1/X5) balance of R/E.

(c) This entry represents the reduction in the carrying amount of the investment due to dividends declared by S during 20X3-X5 (80% x $23,000).

(d) These entries reduce the investment for the amount of depreciation of the excess cost over BV, for the years 20X3 and 20X4. Note, debit to R/E for similar reasons as in (b), above.

(e) Current year additional depreciation—credit Investment account, as in (d), above, and charge Subsidiary Income.

(f) This is not an entry or a balancing figure. It represents P's balance in R/E not including the income recognized from S. This figure may be independently determined by an analysis of P's cost method R/E, $131,000 (see worksheet in Example 4, above). Under the cost method, R/E would have been increased by dividends received from S in prior years. Subtracting these dividends, we obtain $116,600 [$131,000 – 80% x ($8,000 + $10,000)]. NOTE: The R/E balance, $131,000 credit is the same as shown in the "Controlling Interest" column (i.e., after adjustments) of the cost-method worksheet (see Example 4).

(continued on next page)

Consolidation Worksheet, 80% Ownership, Equity-Adjusted Purchase Method

	Trial Balance Dr. (Cr.)		Eliminations		Consolidated Income Statement	Minority Interest	Controlling R/E	Consolidated Balance Sheet	
	P	S	Dr.	Cr.	Dr. (Cr.)	Dr. (Cr.)	Dr. (Cr.)	Dr.	Cr.
Current assets	50,000	15,000						65,000	
Equipment	200,000	120,000	[3] 40,000	[4] 12,000				348,000	
Investment in S	154,800		[1] 4,000	[1] 12,800					
			[4] 12,000	[2] 16,000					
				[2] 63,200					
				[3] 78,800					
Goodwill			[3] 38,800					38,800	
Liabilities	(70,000)	(25,000)							95,000
C/S, $1 par (P)	(100,000)								100,000
R/E, Jan. 1, 20X5 (P)	(131,000)						(131,000)		
C/S, $2 par (S)		(20,000)	[2] 16,000			(4,000)			
R/E, Jan. 1, 20X5 (S)		(79,000)	[2] 63,200			(15,800)			
Revenues	(255,000)	(71,000)			(326,000)				
Expenses	160,000	55,000	[4] 4,000		219,940				
Subsidiary income	(8,800)		[1] 12,800	[4] 5,940					
Dividends declared		5,000		[1] 4,000		1,000			
	$ 0	$ 0	190,800	190,800					
Consolidated NI					(107,000)		(107,000)		
Minority NI, 20% x (71,000 − 55,000)						(3,200)	3,200		
Minority interest						(22,000)			22,000
R/E, controlling interest							(234,800)		234,800
								451,800	451,800

Worksheet entries:
[1] To reverse current year subsidiary income (80% x $16,000) and dividends (80% x $5,000).
[2] To eliminate 80% of S capital account balances.
[3] To record goodwill and write-up equipment to FV at time of acquisition.
[4] To record accumulated depreciation and current year expense.

E. POOLING METHOD CONSOLIDATIONS

1. Consolidation procedures are similar to those for purchase method subsidiaries for adjusting the carrying amount of the investment eliminating capital and investment accounts, and eliminating intercompany transactions.

2. The assets and liabilities of the combining entities are carried at their recorded amounts.

3. The income of the companies are combined and restated for each period presented.

F. DISCLOSURE REQUIREMENTS
The notes to the financial statements of a combined entity in the period in which a material business combination is completed should include the following information.

1. The name and brief description of the acquired entity and the percentage of voting equity interests acquired

2. The primary reasons for the acquisition and a description of the factors contributing to any recognition of goodwill

3. The period for which the results of operations of the acquired entity are included in the combined income statement

4. The cost of the acquired entity and, if applicable, the number and assigned value of shares of equity interests issued or issuable

5. A condensed balance sheet disclosing the amount assigned to each major asset and liability caption of the acquired entity at the acquisition date

6. Contingent payments, options or commitments and projected accounting treatment upon occurrence of the contingencies

7. The amount of purchased research and development assets acquired and written off in the period as having no alternative future use and the line item in the income statement that includes that amount

8. The description and reasons for any purchased price allocation, if any, that has not been finalized—in subsequent periods, the nature and amount of the adjustments must be disclosed

9. If the amounts assigned to goodwill or to other intangible assets acquired are significant in relation to the total purchase, the following must be disclosed.

    a. For intangible assets subject to amortization, the amount assigned, the amount of residual value, and the weighted-average amortization period must be disclosed.

    b. For intangible assets not subject to amortization, the total amount assigned and the amount assigned to any major intangible asset class must be disclosed

    c. For goodwill, the total amount and the amount that is expected to be deductible for tax purposes must be disclosed. In addition, if the combined entity is required to disclose segment information, the amount of goodwill by reportable segment must be disclosed, unless not practicable

10. If a series of individually immaterial business combinations completed during the period are material in the aggregate, the number and brief description of entities acquired and the aggregate costs and amounts involved must be disclosed.

11. If the combined entity is a public business enterprise, the following supplemental information of a pro forma basis must be included:

    a. Results of operations for the current period (and prior period if comparative statements are presented) as though the business combination had been completed at the beginning of the period (or prior period); and

    b. At a minimum, the information shall display revenue, income before extraordinary items and the cumulative effect of accounting changes, net income, and earnings per share.

IV. TRANSACTIONS BETWEEN AFFILIATED COMPANIES

A. INTERCOMPANY RECEIVABLES, PAYABLES, AND LOANS

1. **RECEIVABLES AND PAYABLES** Originate from intercompany transactions such as the sale of inventory and fixed assets or the rendering of services. These receivables and payables appear in the affiliated company's trial balance at the end of the period; note, however, that no asset or liability exists outside the consolidated group. Elimination of the receivable/payable simply involves a "worksheet entry" reversing the original recording.

2. **INTERCOMPANY LOANS** These must also be eliminated from consolidated statements, in a manner similar to that used for receivables and payables, above. In addition, interest income and expense and interest accruals must be eliminated.

EXAMPLE 6 ♦ INTERCOMPANY LOANS

Co. P lent $10,000 on June 1, 20X1 to Co. S, its 90% owned subsidiary. The note is to be repaid on May 30, 20X2, together with 12% interest. The partial trial balances of P and S are reproduced below:

	P	S
Assets	$ XXX	$ XX
Note receivable—S	10,000	
Accrued interest on note	600	
Investment in S	XXX	
Liabilities	(XX)	(XX)
Note payable—P		(10,000)
Accrued interest on note		(600)
C/S	(XXXX)	(XXX)
R/E	(XXX)	(XX)
Sales revenue	(50,000)	(20,000)
Interest revenue	(600)	0
Expenses	36,000	17,000
Interest expense		600
	$ 0	$ 0

REQUIRED:

a.   Provide the elimination entries related to the intercompany note.
b.   Based on the facts given, compute consolidated net income. Allocate to controlling and minority interest.

SOLUTION:

a.   (1)   Notes Payable   10,000
           Accrued Interest Payable   600
                 Notes Receivable   10,000
                 Accrued Interest Receivable   600
           To eliminate intercompany receivable/payable and related accrued interest.

     (2)   Interest Income   600
                 Interest Expense   600
           To eliminate interest income and expense on intercompany notes.

b.

	P	S	Consolidated
Sales Revenue (CR)	$(50,000)	$(20,000)	$(70,000)
Expenses	36,000	17,000	53,000
Minority interest in NI,			
10% ($20,000 – $17,000 – $600)*			240
Controlling interest in NI			$(16,760)

---

*   Note that whereas interest is not an expense for the <u>consolidated</u> entity, it is nevertheless a cost of doing business for S. It must be included in S's net income in order to determine the minority interest in S's net income.

B.   INTERCOMPANY SALES OF INVENTORY
Intercompany sales of merchandise create three problems.

1.   SALES AND COST OF GOODS SOLD   The sale and CGS are recorded twice: first, the seller records a sale and related CGS as the merchandise is "sold" to the affiliated buyer; secondly, the buyer resells the goods to outsiders, also recording a sale and CGS. For consolidated purposes, however, it is obvious that only one sale has occurred.

2. **GROSS PROFIT** When one company sells merchandise to its affiliate at a price above cost, the ending inventory of the buyer contains an element of unrealized gross profit. The gross profit is not realized to the economic entity until it is sold to outsiders. The preparation of consolidated financial statements requires that unrealized gross profit be eliminated.

3. **MINORITY INTEREST** Minority interest in the subsidiary's income must be based on the sales and CGS originally reported by the subsidiary. As was the case in interaffiliate interest income and expense, the minority income should reflect the expense incurred (or revenues obtained) in intercompany transactions. The sale, however, may not be recognized until after the goods have been sold to an outside buyer.

EXAMPLE 7 ♦ INTERCOMPANY SALES OF INVENTORY

Parent sells merchandise to its 90% owned Sub at 25% above cost. The following chart summarizes the transactions in intercompany sales at year-end:

	Parent's sales price (= cost to Sub)	Cost	Parent's gross profit	
Beginning inventory 1/1/X1	$ 50,000	$ 40,000	$10,000	(realized)
Sales	200,000	160,000	40,000	
Total	250,000	200,000	50,000	
Ending inventory 12/1/X1	(75,000)	(60,000)	(15,000)	(unrealized)
Cost of goods sold	$175,000	$140,000	$35,000	

REQUIRED: Provide the consolidation elimination entries.

SOLUTION:

(1) R/E   10,000
         CGS   10,000
To adjust beginning R/E and CGS for the overstated beginning inventory.

(2) Sales   200,000
         Purchases   200,000
To eliminate intercompany sales and purchases.

(3) CGS   15,000
         Inventory   15,000
To eliminate unrealized gross profit in ending inventory.

C. INTERCOMPANY SALES OF FIXED ASSETS

Sales of fixed assets between members of an affiliated group may result in the recognition of gain or loss by the seller, if the selling price differs from the carrying amount of the asset. Again, no gain or loss has taken place for the consolidated entity; assets have merely been transferred from one set of books to another. Additional complications result from the fact that the buyer of the asset will record it in its books at the agreed upon purchase price; subsequent depreciation charges will be based upon this purchase price, thus requiring adjustment. In summary, an interaffiliate sale of fixed assets involves the following:

1. **CARRYING AMOUNT** In the year of sale, restore the carrying amount of the asset to its original BV and eliminate the gain (loss) recorded by the seller.

2. **DEPRECIATION** For each period, adjust depreciation expense and accumulated depreciation to reflect the original BV of the asset.

3. **RETAINED EARNINGS** For periods subsequent to the year of sale, R/E must be adjusted to eliminate the gain (loss) contained therein.

a.   If the parent is the seller, controlling interest R/E absorbs the entire adjustment.

b.   If a less than 100 percent owned subsidiary is the seller, the adjustment to R/E should be allocated to the controlling and minority interests on the basis of their ownership ratio.

EXAMPLE 8 ♦ INTERCOMPANY SALE OF DEPRECIABLE ASSETS

Parent sells machinery for $1,500 to its wholly owned subsidiary. The machinery cost Parent $2,000 and accumulated depreciation at date of sale was $1,000. Parent had been depreciating the machinery on the SL method over a 10-year life. Sub continues this depreciation method.

REQUIRED: Provide the elimination entries at the end of years 1 and 2.

SOLUTION:

Year 1	Gain on Intercompany Sale of Assets	500	
	Machinery	500	
	Accumulated Depreciation		1,000

To eliminate gain and restore asset and accumulated depreciation accounts to their original balances.

	Accumulated Depreciation	100*	
	Depreciation Expense		100*

To adjust consolidated depreciation charges.

* Computed as follows: Gain	$500	
÷ Life remaining to buyer	÷ 5	years
Deprec. elimination per year	$100	

Year 2	Retained Earnings	400	
	Machinery	500	
	Accumulated Depreciation		800
	Depreciation Expense		100

NOTE: The **debit** to RE is $400 ($500 − $100). Thus, the yearly **indirect increase** in consolidated income (from decreasing depreciation expense) will cause the $500 gain to be fully recognized by the seller by the end of the fifth year, when the asset is fully depreciated.

D.   **INTERCOMPANY BONDS**

1.   **DIRECT SALE AND PURCHASE** A direct sale and purchase of bonds between affiliates poses problems similar to the interaffiliate lending and borrowing transactions discussed in subsection A. Intercompany receivables and payables (including accrued interest) must be eliminated, as well as interest income/expense. Note that in a direct acquisition of bonds, no gain or loss results to either party, even if a premium or discount is involved, since the net carrying amount of the bond liability on the issuer's books will always equal the bond investment amount on the purchaser's books.

2.   **AFFILIATED GROUPS** A member of an affiliated group may issue its bonds to outsiders. These bonds may then be purchased from the outside parties by a second affiliate. Note the following:

a.   For consolidated purposes, the bonds have been retired, since they are no longer held by outsiders.

b.   A gain or loss will typically result from the acquisition by the second affiliate, in the open market, of bonds originally issued by the first affiliate to outsiders. This occurs because the FV of the bonds at the time of reacquisition is likely to be different than the carrying amount of the bond obligation on the books of the issuer. No gain or loss is recorded by the individual affiliates, yet a gain or loss on retirement must be recognized at the consolidated level.

c. This gain or loss will be periodically recognized by the issuer as the difference between interest expense to the issuer and interest income to the purchaser. Upon maturity of the bond issue, the entire consolidated gain (loss) realized at the time of reacquisition of the bond will have been amortized and no further adjustments will be necessary.

EXAMPLE 9 ♦ DIRECT SALE OF BONDS

Parent purchases $100,000 bonds from Sub on December 31, 20X1. The bonds' stated interest rate is 10%. Parent pays $110,000 for the bonds. The effective interest rate of the bonds is 8%.

REQUIRED: Prepare the consolidation elimination entry at the date of the transaction and at December 31, 20X2.

SOLUTION: At the date of the transaction the following journal entries were made on the books of the acquirer and the issuer.

Acquirer (Parent)			Issuer (Sub)		
Investment in Bonds	110,000		Cash	110,000	
Cash		110,000	Bonds Payable		100,000
			Premium on Bonds		10,000

The consolidation elimination entry required is

Bond Premium	10,000	
Bonds Payable	100,000	
Investment in Bonds		110,000

During the first year the following journal entries would be made to record income and expenses:

Acquirer			Issuer		
Cash	10,000		Interest Expense	8,800*	
Interest Income		8,800*	Bond Premium	1,200	
Bond Investment		1,200	Cash		10,000

* Interest income or expense = Effective interest rate x Net carrying amount (8% x $110,000).

The consolidation elimination entries required at the end of 20X2 are as follows:

Interest Income	8,800	
Interest Expense		8,800
Bonds Payable	100,000	
Bond Premium	8,800	
Investment in Bonds		108,800

EXAMPLE 10 ♦ BONDS ORIGINALLY ISSUED TO THIRD PARTIES (AT FACE AMOUNT)

P owns a 90% interest in S, which it acquired several years ago in a transaction accounted for as a pooling (i.e., the recorded amounts in S's books were preserved). P accounts for its investment in S under the equity method. No intercompany sales of fixed assets or inventories have taken place. Additionally,

- On January 1, 20X1, S issued to outsiders $100,000, 8%, 10-year bonds at face amount. Interest is paid annually, on December 30.

- On January 1, 20X3, P bought the entire bond issue, when the prevailing interest rate for that type of bond was 12%.

- Operating income before interest charges and revenue was as follows:

	P	S
20X3	$55,000	$33,000
20X4	60,000	30,000

REQUIRED: Provide elimination entries <u>and</u> allocate consolidated income to the minority and controlling interest for (a) 20X3, and (b) 20X4. Ignore income taxes.

SOLUTION: For **consolidated** purposes, the bonds have been **retired**. A gain is calculated and recognized as follows:

$100,000 x P (8, 12%)	$40,388	P(8, 12%) = PV of $1 in 8 years at 12%, .40388
$ 8,000 x P_A (8, 12%)	39,741	P_A(8, 12%) = PV of $1 annuity, 8 years at 12%, 4.96763
	$80,129	

Carrying amount of bonds in S books	$100,000
Less: Price paid by P to acquire bonds	(80,129)
Gain (extraordinary) on retirement	$ 19,871

a. The following entries would have been made by P and S during 20X3:

P			S		
Cash	8,000		Interest Expense	8,000	
Invest in S Bonds	1,615		Cash		8,000
Interest Income		9,615			

Elimination entries are illustrated by the following partial consolidation worksheet:

	P Dr. (Cr.)	S Dr. (Cr.)	Eliminations Dr.	Eliminations Cr.	Consolidated Income Statement Dr. (Cr.)
Invest. in S bonds ($80,129 + $1,615)	81,744			81,744	
Bonds payable		(100,000)	100,000		
Operating income (excluding interest)	(55,000)	(33,000)			(88,000)
Interest income	(9,615)			9,615	
Interest expense		8,000		8,000	
Gain on retirement of S bonds				19,871	(19,871)
			109,615	109,615	
Consolidated NI (Cr)					(107,871)

Minority interest, 10% ($33,000 − $8,000 − $1,615 + $19,871)* $ 4,326

Controlling interest, $55,000 + $9,615 + (90% x $43,256) 103,545

$107,871

---

* The entire gain on retirement is allocated to S, and interest expense is adjusted to reflect the current rate (12%). To understand the reasoning behind this, assume two transactions:

(1) S retires $100,000 BV bonds at a cost of $80,129, realizing a $19,871 gain.

(2) S reissues debt for $80,129 at face value. The interest rate on this debt is the prevailing rate, or 12%; therefore, interest expense for 20X3 is $8,000 + $1,615 = $9,615 (i.e., 12% x $80,129).

(continued on next page)

b.   The following entries would have been made by P and S during 20X4:

P		S	
Cash	8,000	Interest Expense	8,000
Bond Investment	1,809	Cash	8,000
Interest Income			
($81,744 x 12%)	9,809		

	P	S	Eliminations		Consolidated Income Statement
	Dr. (Cr.)	Dr. (Cr.)	Dr.	Cr.	Dr.(Cr.)
Invest. in S bonds					
(81,744 + 1,809)	83,553			83,553	
Bonds payable		(100,000)	100,000		
Operating income					
(excluding interest)	(60,000)	(30,000)			(90,000)
Interest income	(9,809)			9,809	
Interest expense		8,000		8,000	
Retained earnings, P	(XXX)			16,430*	
Retained earnings, S		(XX)		1,826*	
			109,809	109,809	
Consolidated NI (Cr)					(90,000)

Minority interest, 10% x ($30,000 – $8,000 – $1,809) $ 2,019
Controlling interest, $60,000 + $9,809 + (90% x $20,191)   87,981
                                                                     $ 90,000

---

* Consolidated R/E must include the gain on retirement of the bonds ($19,871) less the amount amortized prior to 20X4 ($1,615 additional interest expense charged to S in 20X3, see part a, above). The remaining adjustment to R/E of $18,256 is allocated to the controlling and minority interests in proportion to their ownership percentage.

EXAMPLE 11 ♦ BONDS ORIGINALLY ISSUED TO THIRD PARTIES AT AN AMOUNT DIFFERENT FROM FACE VALUE

On January 1, 20X1, S issued to outside parties $100,000, 8% bonds to yield 9% and due to mature on December 30, 20X4. The bonds were purchased by P on January 1, 20X3, when the prevailing interest rate for that type of bond was 12%. Operating income before interest charges and revenues was as follows:

	P	S
20X3	$80,000	$35,000
20X4	90,000	38,000

REQUIRED: Provide the consolidation worksheet entries to eliminate the intercompany bonds and allocate consolidated net income to the minority and controlling interests for (a) 20X3, and (b) 20X4. Ignore income taxes.

SOLUTION:

Bond issue price, Jan. 1, 20X1:
$100,000	x P (n = 4, i = 9%; .70843)	$ 70,843
$ 8,000	x P$_A$ (n = 4, i = 9%; 3.23975)	25,918
Issue price		96,761
Face amount		100,000
Discount		$ 3,239

(continued on next page)

Table 1—S Discount Amortization Schedule

Date	Cash payment	Interest expense	Amortization	Carrying amount
Jan. 1, 20X1	$8,000	$8,707	$707	$ 96,761
Dec. 30, 20X1	8,000	8,772	772	97,468
Dec. 30, 20X2	8,000	8,842	842	99,082
Dec. 30, 20X4	8,000	8,918*	918	100,000

*$1 difference due to rounding

Consolidated gain on retirement:

$100,000 x P (n = 2, i = 12%; .79720)	$79,720
$ 8,000 x P$_A$ (n = 2, i = 12%; 1.6900)	13,520
Retirement price	93,240
Carrying amount in S books (Table 1)	98,240
Gain on retirement	$ 5,000

Table 2—P Discount Amortization Schedule

Date	Cash payment	Interest expense	Amortization	Carrying amount
Jan. 1, 20X3				$ 93,240
Dec. 30, 20X3	$8,000	$11,189	$3,189	96,429
Dec. 30, 20X4	8,000	11,571	3,571	100,000

a. 20X3 Partial Consolidation Worksheet

	P Dr. (Cr.)	S Dr. (Cr.)	Eliminations Dr.	Eliminations Cr.	Consolidated Income Statement Dr.(Cr.)
Investment in S bonds (Table 2)	96,429			96,429	
Bonds payable		(100,000)	100,000		
Discount (Table 1)		918		918	
Operating income (Cr) (excluding interest)	(80,000)	(35,000)			(115,000)
Int. income (Table 2)	(11,189)			11,189	
Int. expense (Table 1)		8,842		8,842	
Gain on retirement				5,000	(5,000)
			111,189	111,189	
Consolidated NI (Cr)					(120,000)
Minority interest, 10% ($35,000 – $11,189* + $5,000)					$ 2,881
Controlling interest, $80,000 + $11,189 + 90% ($28,810)					117,119
					$ 120,000

* See note following consolidated worksheet in Example 10, above. Computed by applying effective rate at time of purchase by P to the net payable (i.e., 12% x $93,240 = $11,189).

(continued on next page)

b.   20X4 Partial Consolidation Worksheet

	P Dr. (Cr.)	S Dr. (Cr.)	Eliminations Dr.	Eliminations Cr.	Consolidated Income Statement Dr.(Cr.)
Investment in S bonds (Table 2)	100,000			100,000	
Bonds payable		(100,000)	100,000		
Operating income (Cr) (excluding interest)	(90,000)	(38,000)			(128,000)
Int. income (Table 2)	(11,570)			11,570	
Int. expense (Table 1)		8,917	11,570	8,917	
R/E, P	(XXXX)			2,388*	
R/E, S		(XX)		265*	
			111,570	111,570	
Consolidated NI (Cr)					(128,000)
Minority interest, 10% ($38,000 − $11,570)					$ 2,643
Controlling interest, $90,000 + $11,570 + 90% ($26,430)					125,357
					$ 128,000

*Computation of adjustment to R/E:

Gain on requirement of S bonds		$ 5,000
Less: 20X3 amortization:		
Interest expense, S	$ 8,842	
Interest income, P	(11,189)	(2,347)
Unamortized gain, adjust beginning R/E		$ 2,653
Minority interest, 10%		$ 265
Controlling interest, 90%		2,388
		$ 2,653

V.   SUBSIDIARY ENTITY RECORDS

A.   TRADITIONAL

Our review of business combinations has focused on (1) the recording by the parent company and (2) the required consolidation procedures. Historically, where separate incorporation is maintained, the subsidiary's financial records are not affected by either the acquisition or the consolidation.

B.   PUSH-DOWN ACCOUNTING

Under push-down accounting, however, the subsidiary records purchase price allocations and subsequent amortization. The subsidiary records the allocations attributed to its identifiable net assets (e.g., inventory, land, building, equipment) and goodwill with a balancing entry to an Additional Paid-In Capital account. Every year thereafter, the subsidiary recognizes depreciation expense, as appropriate, on these various allocations.

1.   **SIMPLICITY OF CONSOLIDATION** Because the allocations and amortization are already entered into the records of the subsidiary, the use of push-down accounting simplifies the consolidation process.

2.   **BETTER INTERNAL REPORTING** In addition, push-down accounting provides better internal reporting. Since the subsidiary's separate figures may include additional depreciation expense resulting from the purchase, the net income reported by the subsidiary is a good representation of the impact that the acquisition has on the earnings of the business combination.

VI. COMBINED FINANCIAL STATEMENTS

A. USE

There are circumstances where combined financial statements (as distinguished from consolidated statements) of commonly controlled companies are likely to be more meaningful than their separate statements. Combined financial statements are often prepared for a group of related companies (e.g., a group of unconsolidated subsidiaries) or a group of commonly controlled companies (e.g., one individual owns a controlling interest in several corporations that are related in their operations). Consolidated statements are not appropriate if there is no investment by one affiliate in another to eliminate.

B. PROCEDURES

Combined financial statements are prepared by combining the individual companies' financial statement classifications into one set of financial statements.

1. INTERCOMPANY ISSUES Intercompany transactions, balances, and profits or losses are eliminated in the same manner as in consolidated statements.

2. OTHER ISSUES If there are problems in connection with such matters as minority interests, foreign operations, different fiscal periods, or income taxes, they are treated in the same manner as in consolidated statements.

CHAPTER 20—CONSOLIDATED FINANCIAL STATEMENTS

PROBLEM 20-1 MULTIPLE CHOICE QUESTIONS (112 to 140 minutes)

1. Consolidated financial statements are typically prepared when one company has a controlling financial interest in another **unless**
a. The subsidiary is a finance company.
b. The fiscal year-ends of the two companies are more than three months apart.
c. Such control is likely to be temporary.
d. The two companies are in unrelated industries, such as manufacturing and real estate.
(5/94, FAR, #7, 4822)

2. When a parent-subsidiary relationship exists, consolidated financial statements are prepared in recognition of the accounting concept of
a. Reliability.
b. Materiality.
c. Legal entity.
d. Economic entity. (5/93, Theory, #5, 4193)

3. Penn, Inc., a manufacturing company, owns 75% of the common stock of Sell, Inc., an investment company. Sell owns 60% of the common stock of Vane, Inc., an insurance company. In Penn's consolidated financial statements, should consolidation accounting or equity method accounting be used for Sell and Vane?
a. Consolidation used for Sell and equity method used for Vane
b. Consolidation used for both Sell and Vane
c. Equity method used for Sell and consolidation used for Vane
d. Equity method used for both Sell and Vane
(11/92, Theory, #31, 3464)

4. In a business combination, how should long-term debt of the acquired company generally be reported under each of the following methods?

	Pooling of interest	Purchase
a.	Fair value	Carrying amount
b.	Fair value	Fair value
c.	Carrying amount	Fair value
d.	Carrying amount	Carrying amount

(11/95, FAR, #52, 6134)

5. On June 30, 2002, Pane Corp. exchanged 150,000 shares of its $20 par value common stock for all of Sky Corp.'s common stock. At that date, the fair value of Pane's common stock issued was equal to the book value of Sky's net assets. Both corporations continued to operate as separate businesses, maintaining accounting records with years ending December 31. Information from separate company operations follows:

	Pane	Sky
Retained earnings—12/31/01	$3,200,000	$925,000
Net income—six months ended 6/30/02	800,000	275,000
Dividends paid—3/25/02	750,000	--

What amount of retained earnings would Pane report in its June 30, 2002, consolidated balance sheet?
a. $5,200,000
b. $4,450,000
c. $3,525,000
d. $3,250,000 (5/93, PI, #8, amended, 4050)

6. In a business combination accounted for as a pooling
a. Income is combined only from date of combination, **not** for prior periods presented.
b. Income is combined for all periods presented.
c. After the combination, balance sheet amounts are carried at fair market value.
d. Direct acquisition costs are recorded as part of the cost of the investment.
(11/93, Theory, #12, 4517)

7. Which of the following statements is supportive of the pooling of interests method in accounting for a business combination?
a. Bargaining between the parties is based on current values for assets and liabilities.
b. Stockholder groups remain intact but combine.
c. Goodwill is generally a part of any acquisition.
d. A portion of the total cost is assigned to individual assets acquired on the basis of their fair value. (11/93, Theory, #13, 4518)

8. A business combination is accounted for as a pooling of interests. In the consolidated balance sheet, the following component(s) of stockholders' equity may be less than the sum of those same components of the merging companies

	Retained earnings	Contributed capital
a.	No	No
b.	Yes	No
c.	No	Yes
d.	Yes	Yes

(11/90, Theory, #5, 2020)

ITEMS 9 THROUGH 11 are based on the following:

On January 2, 2004, Pare Co. purchased 75% of Kidd Co.'s outstanding common stock. Selected balance sheet data at December 31, 2004, is as follows:

	Pare	Kidd
Total assets	$420,000	$180,000
Liabilities	$120,000	$ 60,000
Common stock	100,000	50,000
Retained earnings	200,000	70,000
	$420,000	$180,000

During 2004, Pare and Kidd paid cash dividends of $25,000 and $5,000, respectively, to their shareholders. There were no other intercompany transactions.

9. In its December 31, 2004, consolidated statement of retained earnings, what amount should Pare report as dividends paid?
a. $ 5,000
b. $25,000
c. $26,250
d. $30,000   (11/95, FAR, #49, amended, 6131)

10. In Pare's December 31, 2004, consolidated balance sheet, what amount should be reported as minority interest in net assets?
a. $0
b. $ 30,000
c. $ 45,000
d. $105,000   (11/95, FAR, #50, amended, 6132)

11. In its December 31, 2004, consolidated balance sheet, what amount should Pare report as common stock?
a. $ 50,000
b. $100,000
c. $137,500
d. $150,000   (11/95, FAR, #51, amended, 6133)

12. In a business combination accounted for as a purchase, the appraised values of the identifiable assets acquired exceeded the acquisition price. How should the excess appraised value be reported?
a. As negative goodwill
b. As extraordinary gain
c. As a reduction of the values assigned to non-current assets and extraordinary gain for any unallocated portion
d. As positive goodwill
        (11/95, FAR, #53, amended, 6135)

13. A business combination is accounted for properly as a purchase. Direct costs of combination, other than registration and issuance costs of equity securities, should be
a. Capitalized as a deferred charge and amortized.
b. Deducted directly from the retained earnings of the combined corporation.
c. Deducted in determining the net income of the combined corporation for the period in which the costs were incurred.
d. Included in the acquisition cost to be allocated to identifiable assets according to their fair values.
        (5/95, FAR, #53, 5589)

ITEMS 14 AND 15 are based on the following:

On January 1, 2003, Owen Corp. purchased all of Sharp Corp.'s common stock for $1,200,000. On that date, the fair values of Sharp's assets and liabilities equaled their carrying amounts of $1,320,000 and $320,000, respectively. During 2003, Sharp paid cash dividends of $20,000. Selected information from the separate balance sheets and income statements of Owen and Sharp as of December 31, 2003, and for the year then ended follows:

	Owen	Sharp
Balance sheet accounts		
Investment in subsidiary	$1,300,000	--
Retained earnings	1,240,000	560,000
Total stockholders' equity	2,620,000	1,120,000
Income statement accounts		
Operating income	420,000	200,000
Equity in earnings of Sharp	120,000	--
Net income	400,000	140,000

14. In Owen's 2003 consolidated income statement, what amount should be reported for amortization of goodwill?
a. $0
b. $12,000
c. $18,000
d. $20,000   (5/94, FAR, #55, amended, 4870)

15. In Owen's December 31, 2003 consolidated balance sheet, what amount should be reported as total retained earnings?
a. $1,240,000
b. $1,360,000
c. $1,380,000
d. $1,800,000   (5/94, FAR, #56, amended, 4871)

16. On September 1, 2000, Phillips, Inc. issued common stock in exchange for 20% of Sago, Inc.'s outstanding common stock. On July 1, 2002, Phillips issued common stock for an additional 75% of Sago's outstanding common stock. Sago continues in existence as Phillips' subsidiary. Phillips uses the purchase method in this consolidation. How much of Sago's 2002 net income should be reported as accruing to Phillips?
a. 20% of Sago's net income to June 30 and all of Sago's net income from July 1 to December 31
b. 20% of Sago's net income to June 30 and 95% of Sago's net income from July 1 to December 31
c. 95% of Sago's net income
d. All of Sago's net income
(5/93, Theory, #6, amended, 4194)

17. PDX Corp. acquired 100% of the outstanding common stock of Sea Corp. in a purchase transaction. The cost of the acquisition exceeded the fair value of the identifiable assets and assumed liabilities. The general guidelines for assigning amounts to the inventories acquired provide for
a. Raw materials to be valued at original cost.
b. Work in process to be valued at the estimated selling prices of finished goods, less both costs to complete and costs of disposal.
c. Finished goods to be valued at replacement cost.
d. Finished goods to be valued at estimated selling prices, less both costs of disposal and a reasonable profit allowance. (5/93, Theory, #7, 4195)

18. On November 30, 2002, Parlor, Inc. purchased for cash at $15 per share all 250,000 shares of the outstanding common stock of Shaw Co. At November 30, 2002, Shaw's balance sheet showed a carrying amount of net assets of $3,000,000. At that date, the fair value of Shaw's property, plant, and equipment exceeded its carrying amount by $400,000. In its November 30, 2002 consolidated balance sheet, what amount should Parlor report as goodwill?
a. $750,000
b. $400,000
c. $350,000
d. $0 (5/93, PI, #25, amended, 4067)

19. Penn Corp. paid $300,000 for the outstanding common stock of Star Co. At that time, Star had the following condensed balance sheet:

	Carrying amounts
Current assets	$ 40,000
Plant and equipment, net	380,000
Liabilities	200,000
Stockholders' equity	220,000

The fair value of the plant and equipment was $60,000 more than its recorded carrying amount. The fair values and carrying amounts were equal for all other assets and liabilities. What amount of goodwill, related to Star's acquisition, should Penn report in its consolidated balance sheet?
a. $20,000
b. $40,000
c. $60,000
d. $80,000 (5/93, PII, #8, 4117)

20. A 70%-owned subsidiary company declares and pays a cash dividend. Under the purchase method, what effect does the dividend have on the retained earnings and minority interest balances in the parent company's consolidated balance sheet?
a. No effect on either retained earnings or minority interest
b. No effect on retained earnings and a decrease in minority interest
c. Decreases in both retained earnings and minority interest
d. A decrease in retained earnings and **no** effect on minority interest
(11/92, Theory, #34, amended, 3467)

ITEMS 21 AND 22 are based on the following:

On January 1, 2007, Dallas, Inc. purchased 80% of Style, Inc.'s outstanding common stock for $120,000. On that date, the carrying amounts of Style's assets and liabilities approximated their fair values. During 2007, Style paid $5,000 cash dividends to its stockholders. Summarized balance sheet information for the two companies follows:

	Dallas 12/31/07	Style 12/31/07	Style 01/01/07
Investment in Style (equity method)	$132,000		
Other assets	138,000	$115,000	$100,000
	$270,000	$115,000	$100,000
Common stock	$ 50,000	$ 20,000	$ 20,000
Additional paid-in capital	80,250	44,000	44,000
Retained earnings	139,750	51,000	36,000
	$270,000	$115,000	$100,000

21. What amount should Dallas report as earnings from subsidiary in its 2007 income statement?
a. $12,000
b. $15,000
c. $16,000
d. $20,000 (5/92, PI, #6, amended, 2573)

22. What amount of total stockholders' equity should be reported in Dallas' December 31, 2007 consolidated balance sheet?
a. $270,000
b. $286,000
c. $362,000
d. $385,000   (5/92, PI, #7, amended, 2574)

23. Pride, Inc. owns 80% of Simba, Inc.'s outstanding common stock. Simba, in turn, owns 10% of Pride's outstanding common stock. What percentage of the common stock cash dividends declared by the individual companies should be reported as dividends declared in the consolidated financial statements?

	Dividends declared by Pride	Dividends declared by Simba
a.	90%	0%
b.	90%	20%
c.	100%	0%
d.	100%	20%

(11/91, Theory, #9, 2517)

ITEMS 24 THROUGH 27 are based on the following:

The separate condensed balance sheets and income statements of Purl Corp. and its wholly owned subsidiary, Scott Corp., are as follows:

BALANCE SHEETS
December 31, 2002

Assets	Purl	Scott
Current assets	$ 310,000	$ 135,000
Property, plant, and equipment (net)	625,000	280,000
Investment in Scott (equity method)	400,000	--
Total assets	$ 1,335,000	$ 415,000

Liabilities and Stockholders' Equity		
Current liabilities	$ 270,000	$ 125,000
Stockholders' equity		
Common stock ($10 par)	300,000	50,000
Additional paid-in capital	--	10,000
Retained earnings	765,000	230,000
Total stockholders' equity	1,065,000	290,000
Total liabilities and stockholders' equity	$1,335,000	$415,000

INCOME STATEMENTS
For the Year Ended December 31, 2002

	Purl	Scott
Sales	$ 2,000,000	$ 750,000
Cost of goods sold	1,540,000	500,000
Gross margin	460,000	250,000
Operating expenses	260,000	150,000
Operating income	200,000	100,000
Equity in earnings of Scott	70,000	--
Income before income taxes	270,000	100,000
Provision for income taxes	60,000	30,000
Net income	$ 210,000	$ 70,000

Additional information:

- On January 1, 2002, Purl purchased for $360,000 all of Scott's $10 par, voting common stock. On January 1, 2002, the fair value of Scott's assets and liabilities equaled their carrying amount of $410,000 and $160,000, respectively, except that the fair values of certain items identifiable in Scott's inventory were $10,000 more than their carrying amounts. These items were still on hand at December 31, 2002.

- During 2002, Purl and Scott paid cash dividends of $100,000 and $30,000, respectively. For tax purposes, Purl receives the 100% exclusion for dividends received from Scott.

- There were no intercompany transactions, except for Purl's receipt of dividends from Scott and Purl's recording of its share of Scott's earnings.

- Both Purl and Scott paid income taxes at the rate of 30%.

In the December 31, 2002 consolidated financial statements of Purl and its subsidiary:

24. Total current assets should be
a. $455,000.
b. $445,000.
c. $310,000.
d. $135,000.   (5/91, PI, #13, amended, 9073)

25. Total assets should be
a. $1,750,000.
b. $1,460,000.
c. $1,350,000.
d. $1,325,000.   (5/91, PI, #14, amended, 9074)

26. Total retained earnings should be
a. $985,000.
b. $825,000.
c. $795,000.
d. $765,000.   (5/91, PI, #15, amended, 9075)

27. Net income should be
a. $270,000.
b. $210,000.
c. $190,000.
d. $170,000.   (5/91, PI, #16, amended, 9076)

28. On August 31, 2007, Wood Corp. issued 100,000 shares of its $20 par value common stock for the net assets of Pine, Inc., in a business combination accounted for by the purchase method. The market value of Wood's common stock on August 31 was $36 per share. Wood paid a fee of $160,000 to the consultant who arranged this acquisition. Costs

of registering and issuing the equity securities amounted to $80,000. No goodwill was involved in the purchase. What amount should Wood capitalize as the cost of acquiring Pine's net assets?
a. $3,600,000
b. $3,680,000
c. $3,760,000
d. $3,840,000   (5/91, PII, #13, amended, 1269)

29. Company J acquired all of the outstanding common stock of Company K in exchange for cash. The acquisition price exceeds the fair value of net assets acquired. How should Company J determine the amounts to be reported for the plant and equipment and long-term debt acquired from Company K?

	Plant and equipment	Long-term debt
a.	K's carrying amount	K's carrying amount
b.	K's carrying amount	Fair value
c.	Fair value	K's carrying amount
d.	Fair value	Fair value

(11/90, Theory, #4, 2019)

30. On December 31, 2007, Saxe Corporation was merged into Poe Corporation. In the business combination, Poe issued 200,000 shares of its $10 par common stock, with a market price of $18 a share, for all of Saxe's common stock. The stockholders' equity section of each company's balance sheet immediately before the combination was:

	Poe	Saxe
Common stock	$3,000,000	$1,500,000
Additional paid-in capital	1,300,000	150,000
Retained earnings	2,500,000	850,000
	$6,800,000	$2,500,000

In the December 31, 2007 consolidated balance sheet, additional paid-in capital should be reported at
a. $ 950,000.
b. $1,300,000.
c. $1,450,000.
d. $2,900,000.   (11/89, PI, #10, amended, 1275)

31. A subsidiary, acquired for cash in a business combination, owned inventories with a market value different than the carrying amount as of the date of combination. A consolidated balance sheet prepared immediately after the acquisition would include this difference as part of
a. Deferred credits.
b. Goodwill.
c. Inventories.
d. Retained earnings.   (11/86, Theory, #3, 2034)

ITEMS 32 THROUGH 34 are based on the following:

Selected information from the separate and consolidated balance sheets and income statements of Pare, Inc. and its subsidiary, Shel Co., as of December 31, 2004, and for the year then ended is as follows:

Balance sheet accts	Pare	Shel	Consolidated
Accounts receivable	$ 52,000	$ 38,000	$ 78,000
Inventory	60,000	50,000	104,000
Income statement accts			
Revenues	$ 400,000	$ 280,000	$ 616,000
Cost of goods sold	(300,000)	(220,000)	(462,000)
Gross profit	100,000	60,000	154,000

Additional information:

During 2004, Pare sold goods to Shel at the same markup on cost that Pare uses for all sales.

32. What was the amount of intercompany sales from Pare to Shel during 2004?
a. $ 6,000
b. $12,000
c. $58,000
d. $64,000   (5/95, FAR, #50, amended, 5586)

33. At December 31, 2004, what was the amount of Shel's payable to Pare for Intercompany sales?
a. $ 6,000
b. $12,000
c. $58,000
d. $64,000   (5/95, FAR, #51, amended, 5587)

34. In Pare's consolidating worksheet, what amount of unrealized intercompany profit was eliminated?
a. $ 6,000
b. $12,000
c. $58,000
d. $64,000   (5/95, FAR, #52, amended, 5588)

35. Sun, Inc. is a wholly owned subsidiary of Patton, Inc. On June 1, 2003, Patton declared and paid a $1 per share cash dividend to stockholders of record on May 15, 2003. On May 1, 2003, Sun bought 10,000 shares of Patton's common stock for $700,000 on the open market, when the book value per share was $30. What amount of gain should Patton report from this transaction in its consolidated income statement for the year ended December 31, 2003?
a. $0
b. $390,000
c. $400,000
d. $410,000   (11/94, FAR, #56, amended, 5317)

36. In its financial statements, Pare, Inc. uses the cost method of accounting for its 15% ownership of Sabe Co. At December 31, 2003, Pare has a receivable from Sabe. How should the receivable be reported in Pare's December 31, 2003 balance sheet?
a. The total receivable should be reported separately.
b. The total receivable should be included as part of the investment in Sabe, without separate disclosure.
c. Eighty-five percent of the receivable should be reported separately, with the balance offset against Sabe's payable to Pare.
d. The total receivable should be offset against Sabe's payable to Pare, without separate disclosure. (5/94, FAR, #16, amended, 4831)

37. Perez, Inc. owns 80% of Senior, Inc. During 2007, Perez sold goods with a 40% gross profit to Senior. Senior sold all of these goods in 2007. For 2007 consolidated financial statements, how should the summation of Perez and Senior income statement items be adjusted?
a. Sales and cost of goods sold should be reduced by the intercompany sales.
b. Sales and cost of goods sold should be reduced by 80% of the intercompany sales.
c. Net income should be reduced by 80% of the gross profit on intercompany sales.
d. No adjustment is necessary.
(11/93, Theory, #11, amended, 4516)

38. Port, Inc. owns 100% of Salem, Inc. On January 1, 2007, Port sold Salem delivery equipment at a gain. Port had owned the equipment for two years and used a five-year straight-line depreciation rate with no residual value. Salem is using a three-year straight-line depreciation rate with no residual value for the equipment. In the consolidated income statement, Salem's recorded depreciation expense on the equipment for 2007 will be decreased by
a. 20% of the gain on sale.
b. 33-1/3% of the gain on sale.
c. 50% of the gain on sale.
d. 100% of the gain on sale.
(5/93, Theory, #4, amended, 4192)

39. Clark Co. had the following transactions with affiliated parties during 2007:

• Sales of $60,000 to Dean, Inc., with $20,000 gross profit. Dean had $15,000 of this inventory on hand at year end. Clark owns a 15% interest in Dean and does not exert significant influence.

• Purchases of raw materials totaling $240,000 from Kent Corp., a wholly owned subsidiary. Kent's gross profit on the sale was $48,000. Clark had $60,000 of this inventory remaining on December 31, 2007.

Before eliminating entries, Clark had consolidated current assets of $320,000. What amount should Clark report in its December 31, 2007 consolidated balance sheet for current assets?
a. $320,000
b. $317,000
c. $308,000
d. $303,000 (5/93, PI, #9, amended, 4051)

40. Wright Corp. has several subsidiaries that are included in its consolidated financial statements. In its December 31, 2002 trial balance, Wright had the following intercompany balances before eliminations:

	Debit	Credit
Current receivable due from Main Co.	$ 32,000	
Noncurrent receivable from Main	114,000	
Cash advance to Corn Corp.	6,000	
Cash advance from King Co.		$ 15,000
Intercompany payable to King		101,000

In its December 31, 2002 consolidated balance sheet, what amount should Wright report as intercompany receivables?
a. $152,000
b. $146,000
c. $ 36,000
d. $0 (5/93, PI, #14, amended, 4056)

41. Wagner, a holder of a $1,000,000 Palmer, Inc. bond, collected the interest due on March 31, 2003, and then sold the bond to Seal, Inc. for $975,000. On that date, Palmer, a 75% owner of Seal, had a $1,075,000 carrying amount for this bond. What was the effect of Seal's purchase of Palmer's bond on the retained earnings and minority interest amounts reported in Palmer's March 31, 2003 consolidated balance sheet?

	Retained earnings	Minority interest
a.	$100,000 increase	$0
b.	$ 75,000 increase	$ 25,000 increase
c.	$0	$ 25,000 increase
d.	$0	$100,000 increase

(5/92, PI, #4, amended, 2571)

ITEMS 42 AND 43 are based on the following:

Scroll, Inc., a wholly owned subsidiary of Pirn, Inc., began operations on January 1, 2002. The following information is from the condensed 2002 income statements of Pirn and Scroll:

	Pirn	Scroll
Sales to Scroll	$100,000	$ --
Sales to others	400,000	300,000
	500,000	300,000
Cost of goods sold:		
Acquired from Pirn	--	(80,000)
Acquired from others	(350,000)	(190,000)
Gross profit	150,000	30,000
Depreciation	(40,000)	(10,000)
Other expenses	(60,000)	(15,000)
Income from operations	50,000	5,000
Gain on sale of equipment		
to Scroll	(12,000)	--
Income before income taxes	$ 38,000	$ 5,000

Additional information:

• Sales by Pirn to Scroll are made on the same terms as those made to third parties.

• Equipment purchased by Scroll from Pirn for $36,000 on January 1, 2002, is depreciated using the straight-line method over four years.

42. In Pirn's December 31, 2002, consolidating worksheet, how much intercompany profit should be eliminated from Scroll's inventory?
a. $30,000
b. $20,000
c. $10,000
d. $ 6,000   (5/92, PI, #8, amended, 2575)

43. What amount should be reported as depreciation expense in Pirn's 2002 consolidated income statement?
a. $50,000
b. $47,000
c. $44,000
d. $41,000   (5/92, PI, #9, amended, 2576)

44. Parker Corp. owns 80% of Smith, Inc.'s common stock. During 2007, Parker sold Smith $250,000 of inventory on the same terms as sales made to third parties. Smith sold all of the inventory purchased from Parker in 2007. The following information pertains to Smith and Parker's sales for 2007:

	Parker	Smith
Sales	$1,000,000	$ 700,000
Cost of sales	(400,000)	(350,000)
	$ 600,000	$ 350,000

What amount should Parker report as cost of sales in its 2007 consolidated income statement?
a. $750,000
b. $680,000
c. $500,000
d. $430,000   (5/92, PI, #11, amended, 2578)

45. During 2007, Pard Corp. sold goods to its 80%-owned subsidiary, Seed Corp. At December 31, 2007, one-half of these goods were included in Seed's ending inventory. Reported 2007 selling expenses were $1,100,000 and $400,000 for Pard and Seed, respectively. Pard's selling expenses included $50,000 in freight-out costs for goods sold to Seed. What amount of selling expenses should be reported in Pard's 2007 consolidated income statement?
a. $1,500,000
b. $1,480,000
c. $1,475,000
d. $1,450,000   (11/91, PI, #53, amended, 2441)

46. On January 1, 2007, Poe Corp. sold a machine for $900,000 to Saxe Corp., its wholly owned subsidiary. Poe paid $1,100,000 for this machine, which had accumulated depreciation of $250,000. Poe estimated a $100,000 salvage value and depreciated the machine on the straight-line method over 20 years, a policy which Saxe continued. In Poe's December 31, 2007 consolidated balance sheet, this machine should be included in cost and accumulated depreciation as

	Cost	Accumulated depreciation
a.	$1,100,000	$300,000
b.	$1,100,000	$290,000
c.	$ 900,000	$ 40,000
d.	$ 850,000	$ 42,500

(5/91, PI, #7, amended, 1268)

47. Water Co. owns 80% of the outstanding common stock of Fire Co. On December 31, 2007, Fire sold equipment to Water at a price in excess of Fire's carrying amount, but less than its original cost. On a consolidated balance sheet at December 31, 2007, the carrying amount of the equipment should be reported at
a. Water's original cost.
b. Fire's original cost.
c. Water's original cost less Fire's recorded gain.
d. Water's original cost less 80% of Fire's recorded gain.   (11/90, Theory, #2, amended, 2017)

48. P Co. purchased term bonds at a premium on the open market. These bonds represented 20 percent of the outstanding class of bonds issued at a discount by S Co., P's wholly owned subsidiary. P intends to hold the bonds until maturity. In a consolidated balance sheet, the difference between the bond carrying amounts in the two companies would be

a. Included as a decrease to retained earnings.
b. Included as an increase to retained earnings.
c. Reported as a deferred debit to be amortized over the remaining life of the bonds.
d. Reported as a deferred credit to be amortized over the remaining life of the bonds.

(5/90, Theory, #2, 2021)

49. Combined statements may be used to present the results of operations of

	Companies under common management	Commonly controlled companies
a.	No	Yes
b.	Yes	No
c.	No	No
d.	Yes	Yes

(5/93, Theory, #8, 4196)

50. For which of the following reporting units is the preparation of combined financial statements most appropriate?

a. A corporation and a majority-owned subsidiary with nonhomogeneous operations
b. A corporation and a foreign subsidiary with non-integrated homogeneous operations
c. Several corporations with related operations with some common individual owners
d. Several corporations with related operations owned by one individual

(11/91, Theory, #8, 2516)

51. Which of the following items should be treated in the same manner in both combined financial statements and consolidated statements?

	Different fiscal periods	Foreign operations	Minority interest
a.	No	No	No
b.	No	Yes	Yes
c.	Yes	Yes	Yes
d.	Yes	No	No

(11/89, Theory, #40, amended, 2026)

52. The following information pertains to shipments of merchandise from Home Office to Branch during 2007:

Home Office's cost of merchandise	$160,000
Intracompany billing	200,000
Sales by Branch	250,000
Unsold merchandise at Branch on December 31, 2007	20,000

In the combined income statement of Home Office and Branch for the year ended December 31, 2007, what amount of the above transactions should be included in sales?

a. $250,000
b. $230,000
c. $200,000
d. $180,000

(11/92, PII, #60, amended, 3394)

53. Ahm Corp. owns 90% of Bee Corp.'s common stock and 80% of Cee Corp.'s common stock. The remaining common shares of Bee and Cee are owned by their respective employees. Bee sells exclusively to Cee, Cee buys exclusively from Bee, and Cee sells exclusively to unrelated companies. Selected 2007 information for Bee and Cee follows:

	Bee Corp.	Cee Corp.
Sales	$130,000	$91,000
Cost of sales	100,000	65,000
Beginning inventory	None	None
Ending inventory	None	65,000

What amount should be reported as gross profit in Bee and Cee's combined income statement for the year ended December 31, 2007?

a. $26,000
b. $41,000
c. $47,800
d. $56,000

(5/92, PII, #20, amended, 2652)

ITEMS 54 AND 55 are based on the following:

Nolan owns 100% of the capital stock of both Twill Corp. and Webb Corp. Twill purchases merchandise inventory from Webb at 140% of Webb's cost. During 2002, merchandise that cost Webb $40,000 was sold to Twill. Twill sold all of this merchandise to unrelated customers for $81,200 during 2002. In preparing combined financial statements for 2002, Nolan's bookkeeper disregarded the common ownership of Twill and Webb.

54. By what amount was unadjusted revenue overstated in the combined income statement for 2002?

a. $16,000
b. $40,000
c. $56,000
d. $81,200

(5/91, PII, #19, amended, 1270)

55. What amount should be eliminated from cost of goods sold in the combined income statement for 2002?

a. $56,000
b. $40,000
c. $24,000
d. $16,000   (5/91, PII, #20, amended, 1271)

56. Mr. Cord owns four corporations. Combined financial statements are being prepared for these corporations, which have intercompany loans of $200,000 and intercompany profits of $500,000.

What amount of these intercompany loans and profits should be included in the combined financial statements?

	Intercompany	
	Loans	Profits
a.	$200,000	$0
b.	$200,000	$500,000
c.	$0	$0
d.	$0	$500,000 (11/90, PI, #60, 1273)

OTHER OBJECTIVE FORMAT QUESTIONS

PROBLEM 20-2 (45 to 55 minutes)

Presented below are selected amounts from the separate unconsolidated financial statements of Poe Corp. and its 90%-owned subsidiary, Shaw Co., at December 31, 2002. Additional information follows:

	Poe	Shaw
Selected income statement amounts		
Sales	$ 710,000	$ 530,000
Cost of goods sold	490,000	370,000
Gain on sale of equipment	--	21,000
Earnings from investment in subsidiary	63,000	--
Interest expense	--	16,000
Depreciation	25,000	20,000
Selected balance sheet amounts		
Cash	$ 50,000	$ 15,000
Inventories	229,000	150,000
Equipment	440,000	360,000
Accumulated depreciation	(200,000)	(120,000)
Investment in Shaw	191,000	--
Investment in bonds	100,000	--
Discount on bonds	(9,000)	--
Bonds payable	--	(200,000)
Common stock	(100,000)	(10,000)
Additional paid-in capital	(250,000)	(40,000)
Retained earnings	(402,000)	(140,000)
Selected statement of retained earnings amounts		
Beginning balance, December 31, 2001	$ 272,000	$ 100,000
Net income	210,000	70,000
Dividends paid	80,000	30,000

Additional information:

- On January 2, 2002, Poe, Inc. purchased 90% of Shaw Co.'s 100,000 outstanding common stock for cash of $155,000. On that date, Shaw's stockholders' equity equaled $150,000 and the fair values of Shaw's assets and liabilities equaled their carrying amounts.
- On September 4, 2002, Shaw paid cash dividends of $30,000.

- On December 31, 2002, Poe recorded its equity in Shaw's earnings.

REQUIRED:

a.   ITEMS 1 THROUGH 3.   Items 1 through 3, below, represent transactions between Poe and Shaw during 2002.   Determine the dollar amount effect of the consolidating adjustment on 2002 consolidated income before considering minority interest.   Ignore income tax considerations.

Items to be answered:

1. On January 3, 2002, Shaw sold equipment with an original cost of $30,000 and a carrying value of $15,000 to Poe for $36,000. The equipment had a remaining life of three years and was depreciated using the straight-line method by both companies.

2. During 2002, Shaw sold merchandise to Poe for $60,000, which included a profit of $20,000. At December 31, 2002, half of this merchandise remained in Poe's inventory.

3. On December 31, 2002, Poe paid $91,000 to purchase 50% of the outstanding bonds issued by Shaw. The bonds mature on December 31, 2008, and were originally issued at par. The bonds pay interest annually on December 31 of each year, and the interest was paid to the prior investor immediately before Poe's purchase of the bonds.

b.   ITEM 4. Determine the amount recorded by Poe as amortization of goodwill for 2002.

c.   Items 5 through 16.   Items 5 through 16, below, refer to accounts that may or may not be included in Poe and Shaw's consolidated financial statements. The list of responses refers to the various possibilities of those amounts to be reported in Poe's consolidated financial statements for the year ended December 31, 2002. Consider all transactions stated in items 5 through 16 in determining your answer. Ignore income tax considerations.

Items to be answered:
5. Cash
6. Equipment
7. Investment in subsidiary
8. Bonds payable
9. Minority interest
10. Common stock
11. Beginning retained earnings
12. Dividends paid
13. Gain on retirement of bonds
14. Cost of goods sold
15. Interest expense
16. Depreciation expense

Responses to be selected:
A. Sum of amounts on Poe and Shaw's separate unconsolidated financial statements
B. Less than the sum of amounts on Poe and Shaw's separate unconsolidated financial statements but not the same as the amount on either
C. Same as amount for Poe only
D. Same as amount for Shaw only
E. Eliminated entirely in consolidation
F. Shown in consolidated financial statements but not in separate unconsolidated financial statements
G. Neither in consolidated nor in separate unconsolidated financial statements

(11/93, PII, amended, #5)

PROBLEMS/ESSAY QUESTIONS

ESSAY 20-3 (15 to 25 minutes)

On September 1, 2007, Plains Corp. acquired all of Sox Corp.'s outstanding stock for cash. The fair value of Sox's net assets was less than the purchase price but greater than the net carrying amount. During November 2007, Plains sold goods to Sox at a price that included its normal markup. At December 31, 2007, 20% of these goods remained in Sox's inventory. The separate legal entities were maintained and Sox uses push-down accounting for its separate financial statements.

REQUIRED:

Ignore income tax considerations when answering all questions.

a. 1. Specify three reasons for preparing consolidated financial statements that present operating results, cash flows, and financial position as if a parent company and its subsidiaries were a single entity.

2. What changes in Plains' September 1, 2007 consolidated balance sheet will result from this acquisition?

3. In preparing Plains' December 31, 2007 consolidated financial statements, what adjustments or eliminations are required as a consequence of the intercompany sales?

b. In preparing separate financial statements immediately after acquisition (September 1, 2007), what is the effect of the purchase on the balance sheet of:

1. Plains?
2. Sox (which uses push-down accounting)?

(5/92, Theory, #4, amended, 6197)

PROBLEM 20-4 (40 to 50 minutes)

The December 31, 2002 condensed balance sheets of Pym Corp. and its 90% owned subsidiary, Sy Corp., are presented in the worksheet provided.

Additional information follows:

- Pym's investment in Sy was purchased for $1,200,000 cash on January 1, 2002, and is accounted for by the equity method.

- At January 1, 2002, Sy's retained earnings amounted to $600,000, and its common stock amounted to $200,000.

- Sy declared a $1,000 cash dividend in December 2002, payable in January 2003.

- As of December 31, 2002, Pym had not recorded any portion of Sy's 2002 net income or dividend declaration.

- Sy borrowed $100,000 from Pym on June 30, 2002, with the note maturing on June 30, 2003, at 10% interest. Correct accruals have been recorded by both companies.

- During 2002, Pym sold merchandise to Sy at an aggregate invoice price of $300,000, which included a profit of $60,000. At December 31, 2002, Sy had not paid Pym for $90,000 of these purchases, and 5% of the total merchandise purchased from Pym still remained in Sy's inventory.

- Pym's excess cost over book value of Pym's investment in Sy has appropriately been identified as goodwill.

REQUIRED:

Complete the worksheet provided for Pym Corp. and its subsidiary, Sy Corp., at December 31, 2002. A formal consolidated balance sheet and journal entries are not required.   (11/87, PII, #5, amended)

Pym Corp. and Subsidiary
CONSOLIDATED BALANCE SHEET WORKSHEET
December 31, 2002

	Pym Corp.	Sy Corp.	Adjustments & Eliminations		Consolidated
			Debit	Credit	
Assets					
Cash	75,000	15,000			
Accounts and other current receivables	410,000	120,000			
Merchandise inventory	920,000	670,000			
Plant and equipment (net)	1,000,000	400,000			
Investment in Sy Corp.	1,200,000				
Totals	3,605,000	1,205,000			
Liabilities and Stockholders' Equity					
Accounts payable and other current liabilities	140,000	305,000			
Common stock ($10 par)	500,000	200,000			
Retained earnings	2,965,000	700,000			
Totals	3,605,000	1,205,000			

PROBLEM 20-5 (60 to 70 minutes)

On April 1, 2007, Jared, Inc., purchased 100% of the common stock of Munson Manufacturing Company for $5,850,000 and 20% of its preferred stock for $150,000. At the date of purchase the book and fair values of Munson's assets and liabilities were as follows:

	Book Value	Fair Value
Cash	$ 200,000	$ 200,000
Notes receivable	85,000	85,000
Accounts receivable, net	980,000	980,000
Inventories	828,000	700,000
Land	1,560,000	2,100,000
Machinery and equipment	7,850,000	10,600,000
Accumulated depreciation	(3,250,000)	(4,000,000)
Other assets	140,000	50,000
	$8,393,000	$10,715,000
Notes payable	$ 115,000	$ 115,000
Accounts payable	400,000	400,000
Subordinated 7% debentures	5,000,000	5,000,000
Preferred stock; noncumulative, nonparticipating, par value $5 per share; authorized, issued, and outstanding 150,000 shares	750,000	--
Common stock; par value $10 per share; authorized, issued, and outstanding 100,000 shares	1,000,000	--
Additional paid-in capital (common stock)	122,000	--
Retained earnings	1,006,000	--
	$8,393,000	

Additional Information:

By the year-end, December 31, 2007, the following transactions had occurred:

- The balance of Munson's net accounts receivable at April 1, 2007, had been collected.
- The inventory on hand at April 1, 2007, had been charged to cost of sales. Munson used a perpetual inventory system in accounting for inventories.
- Prior to 2007, Jared had purchased at face value $1,500,000 of Munson's 7% subordinated debentures. These debentures mature on October 31, 2013, with interest payable annually on October 31.
- As of April 1, 2007, the machinery and equipment had an estimated remaining life of six

years. Munson uses the straight-line method of depreciation. Munson's depreciation expense calculation for the nine months ended December 31, 2007, was based upon the old depreciation rates.

- The other assets consist entirely of long-term investments made by Munson and do **not** include any investment in Jared.
- During the last nine months of 2013, the following intercompany transactions occurred between Jared and Munson:

Intercompany sales:

	Jared to Munson	Munson to Jared
Net sales	$158,000	$230,000
Included in purchaser's inventory at December 31, 2007	36,000	12,000
Balance unpaid at December 31, 2007	16,800	22,000

Jared sells merchandise to Munson at cost. Munson sells merchandise to Jared at regular selling price including a normal gross profit margin of 35 percent. There were **no** intercompany sales between the two companies prior to April 1, 2007.

Accrued interest on intercompany debt is recorded by both companies in their respective accounts receivable and accounts payable accounts.

- The account, "Investment in Munson Manufacturing Company," includes Jared's investment in Munson's debentures and its investment in the common and preferred stock of Munson.

REQUIRED:

Complete the worksheet to prepare the consolidated trial balance for Jared, Inc., and its subsidiary, Munson Manufacturing Company, at December 31, 2007. Show computations in good form where appropriate to support worksheet entries.

Jared's revenue and expense figures are for the twelve-month period while Munson's are for the last nine months of 2007. You may assume that both companies made all the adjusting entries required for separate financial statements unless stated to the contrary. Round all computations to the nearest dollar. **Ignore income taxes.**

(5/74, PII, amended, #5)

Jared, Inc., and Subsidiary
WORKSHEET TO PREPARE CONSOLIDATED TRIAL BALANCE
December 31, 2007

	Jared, Inc. Dr.(Cr.)	Munson Mfg. Co. Dr.(Cr.)	Adjustment and Eliminations Debit	Credit	Consolidated Balances Dr.(Cr.)
Cash	$ 822,000	$ 530,000			
Notes receivable	--	85,000			
Accounts receivable, net	2,758,000	1,368,400			
Inventories	3,204,000	1,182,000			
Land	4,000,000	1,560,000			
Machinery and equipment	15,875,000	7,850,000			
Acc. depr.—mach. and equip.	(6,301,000)	(3,838,750)			
Buildings	1,286,000	--			
Acc. depr.—buildings	(372,000)	--			
Investment in Munson Manufacturing Company	7,500,000	--			
Other assets	263,000	140,000			
Notes payable	--	(115,000)			
Accounts payable	(1,364,000)	(204,000)			
Long-term debt	(10,000,000)	--			
Subordinated debentures—7%	--	(5,000,000)			
Preferred stock	--	(750,000)			
Common stock	(2,400,000)	(1,000,000)			
Additional paid-in capital	(240,000)	(122,000)			
Retained earnings	(12,683,500)	--			
Retained earnings	--	(1,006,000)			
Sales	(18,200,000)	(5,760,000)			
Cost of sales	10,600,000	3,160,000			
Selling, G&A expenses	3,448,500	1,063,900			
Depr. exp.—mach. and equip.	976,000	588,750			
Depr. exp.—buildings	127,000	--			
Interest revenue	(105,000)	(1,700)			
Interest expense	806,000	269,400			
	$ 0	$ 0			

SOLUTION 20-1 MULTIPLE CHOICE ANSWERS

BUSINESS COMBINATIONS

1. (c) A majority-owned subsidiary should **not** be consolidated if (1) control is likely to be temporary or (2) control does not rest with the majority owner, for example, if the subsidiary is in legal reorganization or in bankruptcy or operates under foreign exchange restrictions, controls, or other governmentally imposed uncertainties so severe that they cast significant doubt on the parent's ability to control the subsidiary. Consolidation of majority-owned subsidiaries is required even if they have

"nonhomogeneous" operations, a large minority interest, or a foreign location.

2. (d) Consolidated financial statements should be prepared to present the financial position and operating results of the two separate organizations (i.e., parent company and subsidiary) as if only a single entity existed. Although legally the companies may remain separate, the control of all decision making is now held by a single party which indicates that only one economic entity exists. Reliability pertains to whether accounting information represents what it purports to represent, and is coupled with an assurance for the user that it involves the magnitude of an omission or misstatement of accounting information that, in light of the surrounding circumstances, makes it probable that the judgment of a reasonable person relying on the information would have been changed or influenced by the omission or misstatement. Although the parent and subsidiary are separate legal entities, they are presented as one economic entity in the consolidated financial statements.

3. (b) Penn should use consolidation accounting for both Sell and Vane. Penn has a controlling financial interest in Sell through direct ownership of a majority voting interest (i.e., 75%). The intercorporate stock ownership arrangement with respect to Vane indicates a chain of interests, the product of which (i.e., 75% x 60% = 45%) does not represent control of the lower level subsidiary, where control is defined in terms of the 50% stock ownership minimum. In this instance, the preparation of consolidated statements is warranted, notwithstanding the 45% indirect interest of Penn in Vane. Clearly the question of control relates to direct share ownership. Control is confirmed by the percentages of stock owned independently by Penn (i.e., 75%) and Sell (i.e., 60%). Significantly, while the product of equities in the chain are factors in the determination of consolidated net income and consolidated retained earnings, it is not a determinant in establishing a minimal condition for preparation of consolidated financial statements. There is no evidence that control of Sell or Vane is temporary or doesn't rest with Penn.

4. (c) In a business combination under the pooling of interest method, assets and liabilities of the acquired company generally are reported at their carrying amounts. In a business combination under the purchase method, the identifiable assets of the acquired company and the liabilities assumed are recorded at their fair values.

5. (d) In the consolidated statements at the date at which a purchase method business combination occurs, the balances reported for the consolidated stockholders' equity accounts equal the balances of the parent company's stockholders' equity accounts. The subsidiary's stockholders' equity accounts are eliminated through consolidation so that only the asset and liability accounts of the subsidiary remain to be combined with the parent company accounts. Therefore, consolidated retained earnings is $3,250,000 (i.e., $3,200,000 + $800,000 – $750,000), the retained earnings for Pane (i.e., the parent company) at that date.

POOLING METHOD

6. (b) In a business combination accounted for as a pooling of interests, income is combined for all periods presented. In a pooling of interests, the recorded assets and liabilities of the parties are carried forward at their recorded amounts. Direct costs related to effecting a business combination accounted for by the pooling-of-interests method should be deducted from the net income of the resulting combined corporation for the period in which the costs are incurred. Pooling of interests is no longer allowed for new business combinations in accordance with SFAS 141. Prior business combinations accounted for as pooling of interests continue to be accounted for as pooling of interests.

7. (b) One of the most important arguments in support of the pooling-of-interests method is that a business combination is simply an aggregation of previously separated ownership interests. The recorded assets and liabilities of the parties are carried forward to the combined corporation at their recorded amounts. Answers (a), (c), and (d) are supportive arguments of the purchase method of accounting for a business combination.

8. (b) The stockholders' equities of the separate companies are combined as part of a pooling of interests. If the amount of outstanding shares of stock of the combined corporation at par or stated value exceeds the total amount of capital stock of the separate combining companies, the excess should be deducted first from combined additional paid-in capital (APIC) and then from the combined retained earnings (APB 16). Thus, APIC and retained earnings might decrease, but contributed capital would stay the same or increase.

PURCHASE METHOD

9. (b) The amount that was paid by Kidd to Pare (75% x $5,000) is eliminated on a consolidated statement of retained earnings and the amount paid to minority shareholders reduces the Minority Interest balance.

10. (b) Kidd's net assets are $180,000 − $60,000 = $120,000. $120,000 x 25% = $30,000.

11. (b) Pare reports the same amount of common stock as it did before the purchase. No new Pare common stock was issued for the purchase. Pare's Kidd common stock is not Pare common stock.

12. (c) Under the purchase method, current assets and noncurrent marketable securities of the acquired company are always recorded at their fair values and all liabilities assumed are recorded at their fair value (present value). If the purchase price is less than the fair value of the identifiable net assets, any excess purchase price paid after recording the above items is allocated among the remaining noncurrent assets on the basis of their fair value. If the purchase price is less than the net fair value of said items, then extraordinary gain is recorded, and the remaining noncurrent assets are carried at a basis of zero.

13. (d) The acquisition cost of a company acquired in a business combination accounted for by the purchase method includes direct costs of combination, other than registration and issuance costs of equity securities. The acquisition cost of the "purchased" company is allocated to the identifiable assets acquired according to their fair values.

14. (a) Goodwill is no longer amortized, per SFAS 142.

15. (a) Under the purchase method, consolidated retained earnings are comprised solely of the *parent's* retained earnings at the balance sheet date since the subsidiary's owners' equity accounts are eliminated in the process of consolidation.

16. (b) When a business combination is accounted for as a purchase, the parent company accrues its equity in the subsidiary's earnings that occur subsequent to the date of the investment. Therefore, in 2002, Phillips should accrue 20% of Sago's net income from January 1 to June 30, and 95% of Sago's net income from July 1 to December 31.

17. (d) The general guidelines for assigning amounts to inventories acquired in a purchase method business combination provide for finished goods to be valued at estimated selling prices, less both costs of disposal and a reasonable profit allowance. The guidelines provide for raw materials to be valued at current replacement cost, and work in process to be valued at estimated selling prices,

less (1) costs to complete, (2) costs of disposal, and (3) a reasonable profit allowance.

18. (c) Goodwill is the excess of the investment cost over the fair value of the identifiable net assets acquired. The amount of goodwill to be reported is determined as follows:

Investment cost (250,000 x $15)		$ 3,750,000
Carrying amount of identifiable net assets	$3,000,000	
Fair value of plant assets in excess of carrying amount	400,000	
Less fair value of identifiable net assets acquired		(3,400,000)
Goodwill to be reported		$ 350,000

19. (a) Goodwill is the excess of the investment cost over the fair value of the identifiable net assets acquired. The amount of goodwill is determined as follows:

Purchase price		$ 300,000
Current assets	$ 40,000	
Plant and equipment, net ($380,000 + $60,000)	440,000	
Fair value of identifiable assets acquired	480,000	
Less: Liabilities assumed	(200,000)	
Fair value of identifiable net assets acquired		(280,000)
Goodwill		$ 20,000

20. (b) Under the purchase method, the amount of consolidated retained earnings is equal to the parent company's retained earnings because the subsidiary's stockholders' equity accounts are eliminated in the consolidation process. Thus, the cash dividend declared by the subsidiary has no effect on consolidated retained earnings. The minority interest balance reported in the consolidated statements is based upon the balances of the subsidiary's stockholders' equity accounts. Since the cash dividend declared by the subsidiary decreases the amount of the subsidiary's retained earnings, the minority interest balance reported in the consolidated balance sheet decreases.

21. (c) During the year, the subsidiary's retained earnings increased by $15,000 (i.e., $51,000 − $36,000). Since the subsidiary declared and paid a $5,000 cash dividend, the subsidiary's net income was $20,000 (i.e., $15,000 + $5,000). Since at the date of the 80% purchase, the carrying amount of the subsidiary's assets and liabilities approximated their fair values, the parent company's earnings from the subsidiary is $16,000 (i.e., $20,000 x 80%).

22. (a) The equity method accrues subsidiary earnings in the exact manner as is effected by the

consolidation process. Thus, total consolidated stockholders' equity will equal the total stockholders' equity reported by the parent company (assuming no intercompany transactions).

23. (a) With regard to Simba's dividends, 80% are eliminated in the consolidation because of intra-company ownership and the other 20% are charged against the minority interest. Thus, 0% of the dividends declared by Simba are to be reported in the consolidated financial statements. Normally, 100% of Pride's dividends would appear as dividends declared in the consolidated financial statements. However, because Simba owns 10% of Pride's stock, Simba's dividend income will be eliminated against Pride's dividends declared in the consolidation process and only 90% of the dividends declared by Pride will be reported as dividends declared in the consolidated financial statements.

24. (a) At the date of combination, Purl must allocate the cost of its investment in the subsidiary to the assets acquired and the liabilities assumed. Because there are no reciprocal or intercompany accounts at year end, the amount of consolidated current assets at that date is the sum of Purl's current assets at carrying amounts ($310,000) and Scott's current assets at fair values ($135,000 + $10,000 inventory adjustment) for a total of $455,000.

25. (b) Purl's investment in subsidiary account is *not* included in total consolidated assets because it is *eliminated* in the consolidation process. The amount of total consolidated assets is determined as follows:

Purchase price		$ 360,000
Fair value of identifiable assets ($410,000 + $10,000 inventory adjustment)	$420,000	
Fair value of liabilities	160,000	
Fair value of identifiable net assets	260,000	
Percentage acquired	x 100%	
Fair value of identifiable net assets acquired		(260,000)
Goodwill		$ 100,000

Consolidated current assets (see above solution)	$ 455,000
Purl's plant assets at carrying amounts (net)	625,000
Scott's plant assets at fair values (net)	280,000
Goodwill	100,000
Total consolidated assets	$1,460,000

26. (d) The equity method accrues subsidiary earnings and recognizes the amortization associated with the acquisition cost in the exact manner as is effected by the consolidation process. Thus, total consolidated retained earnings will equal the retained earnings reported by the parent company (assuming no intercompany transactions).

27. (b) The equity method accrues subsidiary earnings and recognizes the amortization associated with the acquisition cost in the exact manner as is effected by the consolidation process. Thus, the consolidated reported net income will equal the reported net income reported by the parent company (assuming no intercompany transactions).

28. (c) Wood's investment in Pine should be recorded at the fair value of the common shares issued to effect the combination. The bargained exchange price is $3,600,000 since the mode of payment by Wood will be 100,000 shares of its common stock having a fair value of $36 per share. In addition, Wood will pay a $160,000 finder's fee to a consultant who arranged the acquisition. Any direct costs of the combination, such as the finder's fee, are included, along with the bargained exchange price, in calculating the total acquisition cost because such costs are a necessary element in carrying out an acquisition. On the other hand, the $80,000 cost of registering and issuing the common stock is considered to be a cost of the securities rather than a cost of the acquisition. As such, the $80,000 should be accounted for as a reduction in the additional paid-in capital figure of the issued shares. Thus, the acquisition cost of the investment is $3,760,000 ($3,600,000 + $160,000).

29. (d) The acquisition corporation should allocate the cost of the acquired company to the assets acquired and the liabilities assumed. All identifiable assets acquired and liabilities assumed should be assigned a portion of the cost of the company, normally equal to their fair values at the date of acquisition. The excess of the acquisition price over the fair value of the net identifiable assets acquired should be recorded as goodwill.

30. (d) The additional paid-in capital (APIC) to be reported in the consolidated balance sheet is equal to the parent's APIC at that date. The subsidiary's stockholders' equity accounts are *eliminated* through consolidation so that only the asset and liability accounts of the subsidiary remain to be combined with the parent company accounts.

Poe's APIC before merger	$ 1,300,000
Increase in APIC from common stock issued to effect the combination [200,000 x ($18 – $10)]	1,600,000
Consolidated APIC,	$ 2,900,000

31. (c) Under the purchase method, a consolidated balance sheet prepared immediately after the acquisition would include the assets of the subsidiary at their fair values.

INTERCOMPANY TRANSACTIONS

32. **(d)** Intercompany sales are eliminated in the preparation of consolidated financial statements. The amount of intercompany sales can be computed by subtracting consolidated revenues from the sum of the revenues reported in the separate financial statements of Pare and Shel [i.e., ($400,000 + $280,000) − $616,000 = $64,000].

33. **(b)** Intercompany payables and receivables are eliminated in the preparation of consolidated financial statements. The amount of Shel's payable to Pare for intercompany sales can be computed by subtracting the amount reported for consolidated accounts receivable from the sum of the accounts receivable reported in the separate financial statements of Pare and Shel [i.e., ($52,000 + $38,000) − $78,000 = $12,000].

34. **(a)** Unrealized profit on intercompany inventory transactions is eliminated in the preparation of consolidated financial statements. The amount of unrealized intercompany profit from inventory transactions is computed by subtracting the amount reported for consolidated inventory from the sum of inventory reported in the separate financial statements of Pare and Shel [i.e., ($60,000 + $50,000) − $104,000 = $6,000].

35. **(a)** When parent shares are obtained by a subsidiary, no gain or loss is reported from the transaction in the consolidated income statement. Any dividends paid to the subsidiary on this stock are eliminated in the consolidation process because they are considered intercompany cash transfers.

36. **(a)** The total receivable from Sabe should be separately reported in Pare's financial statements since Sabe is not a subsidiary of Pare (i.e., Pare has only a 15% interest in Sabe). Pare would have to own a majority voting interest (i.e., > 50%) in Sabe in order for Sabe to be considered a subsidiary.

37. **(a)** The sale of inventory between two affiliates triggers the individual accounting systems for both companies. Revenue will duly be recorded by the seller while the purchase will simultaneously be entered into the accounts of the acquiring company. However, from a consolidated perspective, neither a sale nor a purchase has occurred. Therefore, the amount reported as sales in the consolidated income statement must be reduced by the full amount of the intercompany sales. In recording the sale of the inventory to the purchasing affiliate, the selling affiliate recognized cost of goods sold based upon its acquisition cost. The purchasing affiliate later recognized cost of goods sold equal to the amount of the intercompany sale when it later resold all of these goods to unaffiliated customers. Once again, from a consolidated perspective, the sale to the purchasing affiliate did not occur. Thus, the cost of the goods sold to unaffiliated customers should be based upon the cost of the goods to the selling affiliate. Therefore, the amount reported as cost of goods sold in the consolidated income statement should also be reduced by the full amount of the intercompany sales because this is the amount of cost of goods sold recognized by the purchasing affiliate.

38. **(b)** In the consolidated balance sheet, the cost of the machine and its accumulated depreciation must be based upon the cost of the machine to the consolidated entity. Likewise, consolidated depreciation expense must be reduced by the excess depreciation recorded by the purchasing affiliate. Since the machine's useful life on the date of sale is 3 years, Salem's depreciation expense must be decreased by 1/3, or 33-1/3%, of the gain for consolidated purposes.

39. **(c)** When one company sells merchandise to an affiliate at a price above cost, the ending inventory of the buyer contains an element of unrealized gross profit. The gross profit is not realized to the economic entity until the inventory is sold to an unaffiliated company. The preparation of the consolidated financial statements requires that the unrealized gross profit be eliminated from inventory. Dean is not an affiliate of Clark because Clark cannot exercise significant influence over Dean by virtue of its investment (i.e., Clark owns only a 15% interest in Dean). Therefore, no elimination entry should be made for the transaction with Dean. Therefore, the amount that Clark should report in the consolidated balance sheet for current assets is determined as follows:

Consolidated current assets before elimination entries	$ 320,000
Less: Unrealized gross profit on intercompany inventory transfer to wholly-owned subsidiary [($60,000 ÷ $240,000) x $48,000]	(12,000)
Consolidated current assets to be reported in consolidated balance sheet	$ 308,000

40. **(d)** Consolidated financial statements should not include any intercompany payables, receivables, and advances pertaining to consolidated subsidiaries.

41. **(a)** An investment by one member of a consolidated group of companies in the bonds of another member of that group is, in substance, the same thing as the purchase by a member of its own bonds. Although the bonds cannot physically be retired, since two separate entities are involved in the transaction, from a consolidated viewpoint, the transaction is treated as a constructive retirement of the bonds to the extent of the investment in the bonds. Thus, the consolidated financial statements will reflect any gain or loss on the retirement of bonds in the year of purchase. This is true despite the fact that the books of the affiliates involved in the transaction continue to reflect the Investment in Bonds and Bond Payable accounts, respectively. Thus, the consolidated entity in question recognizes a gain of $100,000 (i.e., $1,075,000 carrying amount of bond – $975,000 cost to subsidiary) on the bond retirement. Gains and losses on the early retirement of bonds can only be reflected on the books of the issuer. Thus, Palmer, the parent company, is attributed the entire $100,000 gain on the retirement, thereby increasing consolidated Retained Earnings by the same amount. Since no portion of the gain on retirement is attributed to the subsidiary, the amount reported in the consolidated financial statements for the 25% minority interest in the subsidiary is unaffected by the intercompany bond transaction.

42. (d) When one company sells merchandise to an affiliate at a price above cost, the ending inventory of the purchasing affiliate contains an element of unrealized gross profit. The gross profit is not realized to the economic entity until the inventory is sold to an unaffiliated company. The unrealized gross profit in inventory must be eliminated in the preparation of consolidated financial statements. The amount of unrealized intercompany profit in ending inventory that should be eliminated for the consolidation in question is determined as follows:

Scroll's ending inventory acquired from Pirn ($100,000 – $80,000)	$20,000
Times: Pirn's gross profit percentage [100% – ($350,000 ÷ $500,000)]	x 30%
Unrealized intercompany profit in Scroll's ending inventory	$ 6,000

43. (b) The cost of the equipment to the purchasing affiliate exceeds the carrying amount of the equipment to the consolidated entity by the gain recognized on the sale by the selling affiliate. Consolidated depreciation expense must be based upon the cost of the equipment to the consolidated entity. Therefore, consolidated depreciation expense must be reduced by the excess depreciation recorded by the purchasing affiliate [i.e., ($40,000 + $10,000) – ($12,000 ÷ 4) = $47,000].

44. (c) Parker, in recording the sale of the inventory to its subsidiary, Smith, recognized cost of goods sold of $100,000 [i.e., $250,000 x ($400,000 ÷ $1,000,000)]. In recording the later sale of the same inventory to an unrelated customer, Smith recognized cost of goods sold of $250,000. However,

from a consolidated perspective, the sale to Smith (the affiliated company) did not occur. Therefore, the amount to be reported as cost of goods sold in the consolidated income statement is $500,000 (i.e., $400,000 + $350,000 – $250,000).

45. (d) No portion of the $50,000 of freight costs on the intercompany inventory transfer should be reported as selling expenses in the consolidated income statement. Although this expense is "freight-out" to Pard, for consolidated purposes this is not freight-out to a buyer. It is part of the inventory cost and when the related goods are sold, the freight costs will increase the amount reported as cost of goods sold in the consolidated income statement.

46. (a) In the consolidated balance sheet, the cost of the machine and its accumulated depreciation must be based upon the cost of the machine to the consolidated entity. Therefore, the machine is reported at its cost to the consolidated entity of $1,100,000, and thus, the balance of the machine's accumulated depreciation is $300,000 [$250,000 + ($1,100,000 – $100,000) ÷ 20].

47. (c) Consolidated statements should not include gain or loss on transactions among the companies in the group. Any intercompany profit or loss on assets remaining within the group should be eliminated and is not affected by the existence of a minority interest. Therefore, the carrying amount of the equipment should be reported at the cost of the equipment to the purchasing affiliate (Water) less the entire gain recorded by the selling affiliate (Fire).

48. (a) To the consolidated entity, the acquisition of an affiliate's debt from an outside party is the equivalent of retiring the obligation. Therefore, the consolidated entity must immediately recognize any difference between the price paid and the carrying amount of the bonds as a gain or loss. The consolidated entity would recognize a loss from the acquisition because the price paid for the bonds exceeded their carrying amount on the affiliate's books (i.e., the bonds were originally issued at a discount and were purchased in the open market at a premium). The loss that the consolidated entity recognizes would be included in the consolidated balance sheet as a decrease to retained earnings. Answer (b) would be correct only if the consolidated entity recognized a gain from the purchase of the bonds. The consolidated entity must immediately recognize any difference between the price paid and the carrying amount of the bonds as a gain or loss; the gain or loss cannot be reported as a deferred credit or debit, respectively, to be amortized over the remaining life of the bonds.

COMBINED FINANCIAL STATEMENTS

49. **(d)** Combined financial statements may be used to present the financial position and results of operations of commonly controlled companies, such as a group of unconsolidated subsidiaries. They might also be used to combine the financial statements of companies under common management.

50. **(d)** There are circumstances where combined financial statements (as distinguished from consolidated financial statements) of commonly controlled companies are likely to be more meaningful than their separate statements. Examples of such circumstances are: (1) where one individual owns a controlling interest in several corporations which are related in their operations, (2) to present the financial position and the results of operations of a group of unconsolidated subsidiaries, and (3) to combine the financial statements of companies under common management.

51. **(c)** In combined financial statements, if there are problems in connection with minority interests, foreign operations, different fiscal periods, or income taxes, they should be treated in the same manner as in consolidated statements.

52. **(a)** Any sale of inventory between a home office and a branch will trigger the individual accounting systems of both units. Revenue will be duly recorded by the seller while the purchase will simultaneously be entered into the accounts of the acquirer. However, from a combined perspective, neither a sale nor a purchase has occurred. Thus, only the $250,000 of sales by Branch should be included in the combined income statement; the intracompany billing of $200,000 should be eliminated in preparing the statement.

53. **(b)** Because Bee sells exclusively to Cee, from a combined perspective, the only sales that have occurred are the sales of Cee to unrelated companies, which total $91,000. Of the $130,000 in intercompany "sales" from Bee to Cee, half (or $65,000) remained in Cee's ending inventory and the other half (or $65,000) were sold. However,

from a combined perspective, the combined cost of the ending inventory and the cost of sales is only $100,000, not $130,000. The additional $30,000 represents intercompany profits, which are eliminated in the combined statements. The $100,000, in the combined statements, is allocated half to cost of sales and half to ending inventory; based on the ratio of ending inventory and cost of sales of Cee. The amount of gross profit that should be reported in the combined income statement is calculated as follows:

Gross Sales	$ 91,000
Cost of Sales	(50,000)
Gross Profit	$ 41,000

54. **(c)** Any sale of inventory made between two commonly controlled companies will trigger the individual accounting systems for both companies. Revenue will be duly recorded by the seller while the purchase will simultaneously be entered into the accounts of the acquiring company. However, from a combined perspective, neither a sale nor a purchase has occurred. Thus, all intercompany sales must be eliminated from the combined financial statements. Since the intercompany sale was not eliminated in preparing the combined financial statements, unadjusted revenue is overstated by $56,000 ($40,000 x 140%).

55. **(a)** In recording the sale of the inventory to Twill, Webb recognized cost of goods sold of $40,000. In recording the later sale of the same inventory to an unrelated customer, Twill recognized cost of goods sold of $56,000 ($40,000 x 140%). However, from a combined perspective, the sale to Twill did not occur, and thus the cost of the goods sold to the unaffiliated company is $40,000. Therefore, $56,000 should be eliminated from cost of goods sold in the combined income statement.

56. **(c)** Where combined statements are prepared for a group of related companies, such as a group of unconsolidated subsidiaries or a group of commonly controlled companies, intercompany transactions and profits or losses should be eliminated (ARB 51).

PERFORMANCE BY SUBTOPICS

Each category below parallels a subtopic covered in Chapter 20. Record the number and percentage of questions you correctly answered in each subtopic area.

Business Combinations

Question #	Correct √
1	
2	
3	
4	
5	
# Questions	5
# Correct	
% Correct	

Pooling Method

Question #	Correct √
6	
7	
8	
# Questions	3
# Correct	
% Correct	

Purchase Method

Question #	Correct √
9	
10	
11	
12	
13	
14	
15	
16	
17	
18	
19	
20	
21	
22	
23	
24	
25	
26	
27	
28	
29	
30	
31	
# Questions	23
# Correct	
% Correct	

Intercompany Transactions

Question #	Correct √
32	
33	
34	
35	
36	
37	
38	
39	
40	
41	
42	
43	
44	
45	
46	
47	
48	
# Questions	17
# Correct	
% Correct	

Combined Financial Statements

Question #	Correct √
49	
50	
51	
52	
53	
54	
55	
56	
# Questions	8
# Correct	
% Correct	

OTHER OBJECTIVE FORMAT SOLUTIONS

SOLUTION 20-2 CONSOLIDATED FINANCIAL STATEMENTS

1. **$14,000 decrease.** The intercompany sale of the equipment resulted in an unrealized gain of $21,000 ($36,000 proceeds received − $15,000 carrying amount) to Shaw, that must be eliminated from consolidated net income. In addition, consolidated net income must be increased by $7,000 [($36,000 cost to Poe ÷ 3) − ($15,000 carrying amount to Shaw ÷ 3)] to eliminate the excess depreciation recorded by Poe, because consolidated depreciation expense must be based upon the cost of the equipment to the consolidated entity. Therefore, the dollar amount effect of the consolidating adjustment for the intercompany sale of equipment on consolidated net income before considering minority interest is computed as follows:

Unrealized gain recognized by Shaw from sale of equipment	$21,000
Less: Excess depreciation recognized by Poe	(7,000)
Dollar amount of consolidating adjustment for intercompany transfer of equipment	$14,000

2. **$10,000 decrease.** When one company sells merchandise to an affiliate at a price above cost, the ending inventory of the purchasing affiliate contains an element of unrealized gross profit. The gross profit is not realized to the economic entity until the inventory is sold to an unaffiliated company, and thus must be eliminated in the preparation of consolidated financial statements. The dollar amount effect of the consolidating adjustment for the intercompany sale of inventory on consolidated net income before considering minority interest is computed as follows:

Poe's 12/31 inventory acquired from Shaw ($60,000 x 50%)	$30,000
Times: Shaw's gross profit percentage ($20,000 ÷ $60,000)	x 1/3
Unrealized intercompany profit in Poe's 12/31 inventory to be eliminated from consolidated net income	$10,000

3. **$9,000 increase.** To the consolidated entity, the acquisition of an affiliate's debt from an outside party is the equivalent of retiring the obligation. Therefore, the consolidated entity must immediately recognize any difference between the price paid and

the carrying amount of the bonds retired as a gain or loss. The dollar amount effect of the consolidating adjustment for the intercompany bond transaction on consolidated net income before considering minority interest is computed as follows:

Carrying amount of Shaw's bonds purchased by Poe	$100,000
Price Poe paid for bonds	(91,000)
Dollar amount of adjustment for gain recognized by consolidated entity on retirement of debt	$ 9,000

4. $-0-. Goodwill is not amortized, in accordance with SFAS 142.

5. A   No consolidating entry affects the Cash account. Therefore, the amount to be reported for cash in the consolidated financial statements is the sum of the amounts on Poe's and Shaw's separate unconsolidated financial statements.

6. B   The amount reported for equipment in consolidated financial statements must be based upon the cost of the equipment to the consolidated entity. Therefore, due to the intercompany sale of equipment, the amount to be reported for equipment in the consolidated financial statements must be decreased by $6,000, the excess of the equipment's $36,000 cost to Poe (the purchasing affiliate) over the equipment's cost of $30,000 to both Shaw and the consolidated entity. Thus, the amount to be reported for equipment in the consolidated financial statements is $794,000 [i.e., ($440,000 − $6,000) + $360,000]. This amount is less than the sum of the amounts on Poe's and Shaw's separate unconsolidated financial statements but not the same as the amount on either [i.e., $794,000 < ($440,000 + $360,000)].

7. E   The Investment in Subsidiary account is eliminated entirely in the consolidation process so that the subsidiary's individual assets and liabilities can be combined with the parent company accounts.

8. B   To the consolidated entity, the acquisition of 50% of Shaw's outstanding bonds by Poe from an outside party is the equivalent of retiring the bonds. Thus, the amount to be reported for bonds payable in the consolidated financial statements is $100,000 [i.e., $0 + ($200,000 x 50%)]. This amount is less than the sum of the amounts on Poe's and Shaw's separate unconsolidated financial statements but not the same as the amount on either [i.e., $100,000 < ($0 + $200,000)].

9. F   While no amount is reported for minority interest in the separate unconsolidated financial statements of Poe and Shaw, an amount for minority interest must be presented in the consolidated

balance sheet because Poe did not acquire complete ownership of Shaw.

10. C   The subsidiary's stockholders' equity accounts are eliminated through consolidation so that only the asset and liability accounts of the subsidiary remain to be combined with the parent company accounts. Therefore, the amount to be reported for common stock in the consolidated financial statements is the same as the amount as reported for Poe in its separate unconsolidated financial statements.

11. C   The subsidiary's stockholders' equity accounts are eliminated through consolidation so that only the asset and liability accounts of the subsidiary remain to be combined with the parent company accounts. Therefore, the amount to be reported for beginning retained earnings in the consolidated financial statements is the same as the amount as reported for Poe in its separate unconsolidated financial statements.

12. C   The subsidiary's stockholders' equity accounts are eliminated through consolidation so that only the asset and liability accounts of the subsidiary remain to be combined with the parent company accounts. Therefore, the amount to be reported for dividends paid in the consolidated financial statements is the same as the amount reported for Poe in its separate unconsolidated financial statements.

13. F   To the consolidated entity, the acquisition of Shaw's bonds by Poe from an outside party is the equivalent of retiring the bonds. The consolidated entity includes the excess of the $100,000 carrying amount of the bonds over the $91,000 price paid by Poe as a $9,000 gain on the early extinguishment of debt in consolidated net income. The gain on the retirement of the bonds is reported in the consolidated financial statements but not in the separate unconsolidated financial statements of Poe and Shaw.

14. B   In recording the intercompany sale of the inventory to Poe, Shaw recognized cost of goods sold of $40,000 (i.e., $60,000 − $20,000). From a consolidated perspective, the sale to Poe (the affiliated company) did not occur. Thus, consolidated cost of goods sold must be decreased by $40,000 as a result of the intercompany sale. In recording the later sale of half of the same inventory to an unaffiliated customer, Shaw recognized cost of goods sold of $30,000 (i.e., $60,000 x 50%). Consolidated cost of goods sold, however, must be based upon the cost of the inventory to the consolidated entity (i.e., $40,000). Thus, the amount of

consolidated cost of goods sold that should be recognized from the sale of half of the inventory to the unaffiliated customer is $20,000 (i.e., $40,000 x 50%). Thus, consolidated cost of goods sold must be decreased by $10,000 (i.e., $30,000 − $20,000), the excess of the amount of cost of goods sold recognized by Shaw on the sale to the unaffiliated customer over the amount that should be recognized by the consolidated entity. Therefore, consolidated cost of goods sold must be decreased by $50,000 (i.e., $40,000 + $10,000). Thus, the amount to be reported for cost of goods sold in the consolidated financial statements is $810,000 (i.e., $490,000 + $370,000 − $40,000 − $10,000). This amount is less than the sum of the amounts on Poe's and Shaw's separate unconsolidated financial statements, but not the same as the amount on either [i.e., $810,000 < ($490,000 + $370,000)].

15. D (A is also correct.) Poe purchased bonds issued by Shaw on 12/31. The bonds pay interest annually on December 31 of each year, and the interest was paid to the prior investor immediately before Poe's purchase of the bonds.

Thus, no consolidating entry affects the Interest Expense account. Therefore, since Poe did not report any interest expense, the amount to be reported for interest expense in the consolidated financial statements is the same as the amount reported for Shaw in its separate unconsolidated financial statements.

16. B Consolidated depreciation expense must be based upon the cost of depreciable plant assets to the consolidated entity. Therefore, consolidated depreciation expense must be decreased by $7,000 [i.e., ($36,000 cost to Poe ÷ 3) − ($15,000 carrying amount to Shaw ÷ 3)] to eliminate the excess depreciation recorded by Poe, the purchasing affiliate. Thus, the amount to be reported for depreciation expense in the consolidated financial statements is $38,000 [i.e., ($25,000 − $7,000) + $20,000]. This amount is less than the sum of the amounts on Poe's and Shaw's separate unconsolidated financial statements but not the same as the amount on either [i.e., $38,000 < ($25,000 + $20,000)].

PROBLEM/ESSAY SOLUTIONS

SOLUTION 20-3 CONSOLIDATED FINANCIAL STATEMENTS

a. 1. Consolidated operating results, cash flows, and financial position are prepared, as if a parent company and its subsidiaries are a single entity, to provide information that:

- Reflects the operating results, financial status, and central management ties that bind the companies into a **single economic and financial unit.**
- Is **representationally faithful and fair**, without the biases caused by exclusions or netting of data.
- Is **comparable** with information about other economic entities regardless of the companies' legal framework.
- Is **relevant and complete for investors** and other parties basing decisions on the data.

2. Plains' September 1, 2007, consolidated balance sheet is changed by **including all of Sox's identifiable assets and liabilities at their fair values,** and **cash is decreased by the purchase price**. The **excess of purchase price over the fair value of the net assets acquired is reported as goodwill**.

3. The effect of the intercompany sales is eliminated from Plains' December 31, 2007, consolidated financial statements by:

- **Reducing sales by the amount of the intercompany sales.**
- **Reducing ending inventory by the markup on goods sold by Plains and still held by Sox.**
- **Reducing cost of goods sold for the difference between the amounts of the two previous adjustments.**

b. 1. The effects on Plains' September 1, 2007, balance sheet are the **establishment of an investment in Sox** and a **decrease in cash equal to the purchase price**.

2. Using push-down accounting, all of **Sox's assets and liabilities**, including goodwill, are **restated to reflect their fair values on September 1, 2002**. The **retained earnings balance is eliminated**. **Additional paid-in capital is adjusted** for the difference arising from the restatement of the asset and liability balances and the elimination of retained earnings.

SOLUTION 20-4 CONSOLIDATED FINANCIAL STATEMENTS—PURCHASE

Pym Corp. and Subsidiary
CONSOLIDATED BALANCE SHEET WORKSHEET
December 31, 2002

	Pym Corp.	Sy Corp.	Adjustment and Eliminations Debit	Adjustment and Eliminations Credit	Consolidated
Assets					
Cash	75,000	15,000			90,000
Accounts and other current receivables	410,000	120,000	[b] 900	[e] 900 [f] 5,000 [g] 100,000 [i] 90,000	335,000
Merchandise inventory	920,000	670,000		[h] 3,000	1,587,000
Plant and equipment (net)	1,000,000	400,000			1,400,000
Investment in Sy Corp.	1,200,000		[a] 90,900	[b] 900 [c] 480,000 [d] 810,000	
Goodwill			[c] 480,000		480,000
Totals	3,605,000	1,205,000			3,892,000
Liabilities and Stockholders' Equity					
Accounts payable and other current liabilities	140,000	305,000	[e] 900 [f] 5,000 [g] 100,000 [i] 90,000		249,100
Common stock ($10 par)	500,000	200,000	[d] 200,000		500,000
Retained earnings	2,965,000	700,000	[d] 700,000 [h] 3,000	[a] 90,900	3,052,900
Minority interest, 10%				[d] 90,000	90,000
Totals	3,605,000	1,205,000	1,670,700	1,670,700	3,892,000

Explanation of Adjustments & Eliminations:

[a] To record net income of Sy corp. accruing to Pym Corp.

Sy Corp.'s retained earnings at 12/31/02	$ 700,000
Sy Corp.'s retained earnings at 1/1/02	(600,000)
Increase in retained earnings after dividend declaration	100,000
Add dividend declaration	1,000
Sy Corp.'s net income for the year ended 12/31/02	101,000
Pym Corp.'s share, 90%	$ 90,900

[b] To record Pym Corp.'s share of dividend declared by Sy Corp., 90% of $1,000 $ 900

[c] To record goodwill

Purchase price of 90% of Sy Corp.'s common stock		$1,200,000
Sy Corp.'s book value at 1/1/02		
Common stock	$200,000	
Retained earnings	600,000	
Total	$800,000	
Pym Corp.'s share, 90%		(720,000)
Goodwill		$ 480,000

[d] To eliminate 90% of Sy Corp.'s book value and record minority interest

Common stock	$ 200,000
Retained earnings at 12/31/02	700,000
Total	$ 900,000
Pym Corp.'s share, 90%	$ 810,000
Minority interest, 10%	90,000
Total	$ 900,000

FINANCIAL ACCOUNTING & REPORTING

[e] To eliminate intercompany dividend
receivable and payable
90% of $1,000 ... $ 900

[f] To eliminate intercompany accrued
interest $100,000 @ 10% x ½ year ... $ 5,000

[g] To eliminate intercompany loan ... $ 100,000

[h] To eliminate intercompany profit in
Sy Corp.'s 12/31 inventory
Sales from Pym Corp. to Sy Corp. ... $ 300,000
5% remaining in Sy Corp.'s 12/31
inventory ... $ 15,000
Multiply by 20% (60,000 ÷ 300,000) ... $ 3,000

[i] To eliminate intercompany trade
accounts receivable and payable ... $ 90,000

SOLUTION 20-5 CONSOLIDATED FINANCIAL STATEMENTS—PURCHASE

Jared, Inc., and Subsidiary
WORKSHEET TO PREPARE CONSOLIDATED TRIAL BALANCE
December 31, 2007

	Jared, Inc. Dr.(Cr.)	Munson Mfg. Co. Dr.(Cr.)	Adjustment and Eliminations Debit	Credit	Consolidated Balances Dr.(Cr.)
Cash	$ 822,000	$ 530,000			$ 1,352,000
Notes receivable	--	85,000			85,000
Accounts receivable, net	2,758,000	1,368,400		$ 17,500 [6]	4,070,100
				38,800 [7]	
Inventories	3,204,000	1,182,000		4,200 [8]	4,381,800
Land	4,000,000	1,560,000	$ 540,000 [1]		6,100,000
Machinery and equipment	15,875,000	7,850,000	2,750,000 [1]		26,475,000
Acc. depr.—mach. and equip.	(6,301,000)	(3,838,750)		750,000 [1]	$ (11,126,000)
				236,250 [5]	
Buildings	1,286,000	--			1,286,000
Acc. depr.—buildings	(372,000)	--			(372,000)
Investment in Munson Mfg. Co.	7,500,000	--		2,322,000 [1]	
				1,400,000 [3]	
				2,128,000 [2]	
				1,500,000 [6]	
				150,000 [4]	
Other assets	263,000	140,000		90,000 [1]	313,000
Excess of cost over FV of net assets acquired			1,400,000 [3]		1,400,000
Notes payable	--	(115,000)			(115,000)
Accounts payable	(1,364,000)	(204,000)	17,500 [6]		(1,511,700)
			38,800 [7]		
Long-term debt	(10,000,000)	--			(10,000,000)
Subordinated debentures—7%	--	(5,000,000)	1,500,000 [6]		(3,500,000)
Preferred stock	--	(750,000)	150,000 [4]		(600,000)
Common stock	(2,400,000)	(1,000,000)	1,000,000 [2]		(2,400,000)
Additional paid-in capital	(240,000)	(122,000)	122,000 [2]		(240,000)
Retained earnings	(12,683,500)	--			(12,683,500)
Retained earnings	--	(1,006,000)	1,006,000 [2]		
Sales	(18,200,000)	(5,760,000)	388,000 [7]		(23,572,000)
Cost of sales	10,600,000	3,160,000	4,200 [8]	388,000 [7]	13,248,200
				128,000 [1]	
Selling, G&A expenses	3,448,500	1,063,900			4,512,400
Depr. exp.—mach. and equip.	976,000	588,750	236,250 [5]		1,801,000
Depr. exp.—buildings	127,000	--			127,000
Interest revenue	(105,000)	(1,700)	78,750 [9]		(27,950)
Interest expense	806,000	269,400		78,750 [9]	996,650
	$ 0	$ 0	$9,231,500	$ 9,231,500	$ 0

Jared, Inc., and Subsidiary
CONSOLIDATING ENTRIES
December 31, 2007
(Not Required)

	Debit	Credit
[1] Land	540,000	
Machinery and equipment	2,750,000	
Other assets		90,000
Accumulated depreciation— machinery & equipment		750,000
Investment in Munson Manufacturing Company		2,322,000
Cost of sales		128,000

To adjust Munson's assets to fair value at date of purchase.

	Debit	Credit
[2] Common Stock	1,000,000	
Additional Paid-in Capital (Common)	122,000	
Retained Earnings	1,006,000	
Investment in Munson Manufacturing Company		2,128,000

To eliminate Jared's investment in Munson's equity at date of purchase.

	Debit	Credit
[3] Excess of Cost Over FV of Net Assets Acquired	1,400,000	
Investment in Munson Manufacturing Company		1,400,000

To record excess of cost over fair value of Munson's net assets at date of purchase as follows:

COMPUTATION

Purchase price (common stock)		$ 5,850,000
Less: Adj. of Munson's assets to FV (J/E No. 1)	$ 2,322,000	
Elimination of investment in Munson's equity (J/E No. 2)	2,128,000	(4,450,000)
Excess		$ 1,400,000

	Debit	Credit
[4] Preferred Stock	150,000	
Investment in Munson Manufacturing Company		150,000

To eliminate Jared's investment in Munson's preferred stock at date of purchase.

	Debit	Credit
[5] Depr. exp.—Mach. and Equip.	236,250	
Acc. Depr.—Mach. and Equip.		236,250

To adjust to fair value at date of purchase.

COMPUTATION

Mach. and Equip.—		
$10,600,000 – 4,000,000 ÷ 6 years =		$ 1,100,000
Depr. exp. for nine months ($1,100,000 x 9/12)		$ 825,000
Depreciation expense per books		(588,750)
Adjustment		$ 236,250

	Debit	Credit
[6] Subordinated Debentures 7%	1,500,000	
Accounts Payable	17,500	
Investment in Munson Mfg. Co.		1,500,000
Accounts Rec. Net		17,500

To eliminate intercompany bonds and related accrued interest for two months.

	Debit	Credit
[7] Accounts Payable	38,800	
Sales	388,000	
Accounts Rec. Net		38,800
Cost of Sales		388,000

To eliminate intercompany sales and unpaid balances at December 31, 2007.

	Debit	Credit
[8] Cost of Sales	4,200	
Inventories		4,200

To eliminate intercompany profit (35%) in Jared's inventory at December 31, 2007 ($12,000 x 35% = $4,200).

	Debit	Credit
[9] Interest Revenue	78,750	
Interest Expense		78,750

To eliminate intercompany interest expense and revenue on debentures for nine months. ($105,000 x 9/12 = $78,750)

What is this I've been hearing about the computerized exam?

The AICPA is in the process of converting the CPA exam into a "computerized" exam. Currently, candidates read questions from a printed page, darken ovals on a machine-readable sheet for the objective answers, and write essay answers on lined paper. To some extent, the exam is already computerized; the objective answers are machine-graded.

The next step in this conversion is likely to be essentially the same exam, with candidates reading questions from, and entering answers into, a personal computer. Before this happens, laws in many jurisdictions must change to allow this format, among other things.

The examination division has targeted November 2003 as the date for this next stage. There may be only pilot groups who sit for the computerized exam in November 2003. Candidates are unlikely to have much say in whether they will be part of a pilot group.

As we go to press, the AICPA has not yet decided most details; even the implementation date is subject to change. There has been some discussion regarding eliminating essay questions from the exam, in order that the entire exam may be computer-graded. When the exam becomes "computerized," Bisk Education will provide necessary details in its updating supplements, just as it provides information regarding new pronouncements, laws, and other related material.

Because the details of the computerized exam are subject to change, we don't recommend that candidates wait to take the exam in order, say, to avoid the essay questions. After waiting, candidates may find that the computerized exam has essay questions after all.

FYI: A further step in the conversion to a computerized exam may involve the computer selecting additional sets of questions based on a candidate's responses to a first set of questions. As opposed to current types of essay questions, candidates instead may complete research tasks (given a CD-ROM library) and express conclusions in written form.

Candidates interested in learning more about the computerized exam should contact the AICPA. As we go to press, the AICPA web-site (www.aicpa.org) has an exposure draft available for downloading. However, do not confuse time spent learning about proposals for the computerized exam with review time. Bisk Education's updating supplements will include a concise summary of need-to-know information for candidates, when it becomes relevant to passing the exam.

APPENDIX A
FINAL EXAMINATION

NUMBER 1 MULTIPLE CHOICE QUESTIONS (120 to 150 minutes)

1. Under Statement of Financial Accounting Concepts No. 2, which of the following is an ingredient of the primary quality of reliability?
a. Understandability
b. Verifiability
c. Predictive value
d. Materiality

2. Under Statement of Financial Accounting Concepts No. 5, which of the following items would cause earnings to differ from comprehensive income for an enterprise in an industry **not** having specialized accounting principles?
a. Unrealized loss on investments in available-for-sale marketable equity securities
b. Unrealized loss on investments in trading marketable equity securities
c. Loss on exchange of similar assets
d. Loss on exchange of dissimilar assets

3. According to the FASB conceptual framework, which of the following statements conforms to the realization concept?
a. Equipment depreciation was assigned to a production department and then to product unit costs.
b. Depreciated equipment was sold in exchange for a note receivable.
c. Cash was collected on accounts receivable.
d. Product unit costs were assigned to cost of goods sold when the units were sold.

4. Reporting inventory at the lower-of-cost-or-market is a departure from the accounting principle of
a. Historical cost.
b. Consistency.
c. Conservatism.
d. Full disclosure.

5. In 2001, Cromwell Corporation bought 30,000 shares of Fleming Corporation's listed stock for $300,000, and included it in the trading securities portfolio. In November 2002, when the market value declined to $200,000, Cromwell changed its classification from trading to available-for-sale. In January 2003, before Cromwell's 2002 year-end statements were issued, the market value of the Fleming stock had risen to $230,000. How much should Cromwell recognize as a loss in its determination of net income for 2002?

a. $0
b. $ 30,000
c. $ 70,000
d. $100,000

6. Based on the aging of its accounts receivable at December 31, 2002, Drury Company determined that the net realizable value of the receivables at that date is $95,000. Additional information is as follows:

Accounts receivable at 12/31/02	$110,000
Allowance for doubtful accounts at 1/1/02—credit balance	16,000
Accounts written off as uncollectible at 9/30/02	12,000

Drury's bad debt expense for the year ended December 31, 2002, was
a. $11,000.
b. $13,000.
c. $15,000.
d. $19,000.

7. Trans Co. had the following balances at December 31, 2002:

Cash in checking account	$ 35,000
Cash in money market account	75,000
U. S. Treasury bill, purchased 11/1/2002, maturing 1/31/2003	350,000
U. S. Treasury bill, purchased 12/1/2002, maturing 3/31/2003	$400,000

Trans's policy is to treat as cash equivalents all highly-liquid investments with a maturity of three months or less when purchased. What amount should Trans report as cash and cash equivalents in its December 31, 2002, balance sheet?
a. $110,000
b. $385,000
c. $460,000
d. $860,000

8. On December 31, 2001, Jet Co. received two $10,000 notes receivable from customers in exchange for services rendered. On both notes, interest is calculated on the outstanding principal balance at the annual rate of 3% and payable at maturity. The note from Hart Corp., made under customary trade terms, is due in nine months and the note from Maxx Inc. is due in five years. The market interest rate for similar notes on December 31, 2001, was 8%. The compound interest factors to convert future values into present values at 8% follow:

Present value of $1 due in nine months: .944
Present value of $1 due in five years: .680

At what amounts should these two notes receivable be reported in Jet's December 31, 2001 balance sheet?

	Hart	Maxx
a.	$ 9,440	$6,800
b.	$ 9,652	$7,820
c.	$10,000	$6,800
d.	$10,000	$7,820

9. On December 31, 2001, Kern Company adopted the dollar value LIFO inventory method. All of Kern's inventories constitute a single pool. The inventory on December 31, 2001, using the dollar value LIFO inventory method was $600,000. Inventory data for 2002 are as follows:

12/31/02 inventory at year-end prices $780,000
Relevant price index at year-end
  (base year 2001) 120

Under the dollar value LIFO inventory method, Kern's inventory at December 31, 2002, would be
a. $650,000.
b. $655,000.
c. $660,000.
d. $720,000.

10. The replacement cost of an inventory item is below the net realizable value and above the net realizable value less the normal profit margin. The original cost of the inventory item is above the replacement cost and below the net realizable value. As a result, under the lower-of-cost-or-market method, the inventory item should be valued at the
a. Replacement cost.
b. Original cost.
c. Net realizable value.
d. Net realizable value less the normal profit margin.

11. Under the retail inventory method, freight-in would be included in the calculation of the goods available for sale for which of the following?

	Cost	Retail
a.	No	No
b.	No	Yes
c.	Yes	No
d.	Yes	Yes

12. On December 28, 2003, Kerr Manufacturing Co. purchased goods costing $50,000. The terms were F.O.B. destination. Some of the costs incurred in connection with the sale and delivery of the goods were as follows:

Packaging for shipment $1,000
Shipping 1,500
Special handling charges 2,000

These goods were received on December 31, 2003. In Kerr's December 31, 2003 balance sheet, what amount of cost for these goods should be included in inventory?
a. $54,500
b. $53,500
c. $52,000
d. $50,000

13. Bren Co.'s beginning inventory at January 1, 2003, was understated by $26,000, and its ending inventory was overstated by $52,000. As a result, Bren's cost of goods sold for 2003 was
a. Understated by $26,000.
b. Overstated by $26,000.
c. Understated by $78,000.
d. Overstated by $78,000.

14. In an arm's-length transaction, Company A and Company B exchanged nonmonetary assets with **no** monetary consideration involved. The exchange did culminate an earning process for both Company A and Company B, and the fair values of the nonmonetary assets were both clearly evident. The accounting for the exchange should be based on the
a. Fair value of the asset surrendered.
b. Fair value of the asset received.
c. Recorded amount of the asset surrendered.
d. Recorded amount of the asset received.

15. Wells Company purchased a machine on January 1, 1999, for $480,000. At the date of acquisition, the machine had an estimated useful life of six years with no salvage value. The machine is being depreciated on the straight-line basis. On January 1, 2002, Wells determined, as a result of additional information, that the machine had an estimated useful life of eight years from the date of acquisition with no salvage value. An accounting change was made in 2002 to reflect this additional information. What is the amount of depreciation expense on this machine for the year ended December 31, 2002?
a. $0
b. $30,000
c. $48,000
d. $60,000

16. On January 1, 1997, Victor Company purchased for $85,000 a machine having a useful life of ten years and an estimated salvage value of $5,000. The machine was depreciated by the straight-line method. On July 1, 2002, the machine was sold for $45,000. For the year ended December 31, 2002, how much gain should Victor record on the sale?
a. $0
b. $1,000
c. $4,000
d. $6,750

17. On January 1, 1998, Vick Company purchased a trademark for $400,000, having an estimated useful life of 16 years. In January 2002, Vick paid $60,000 for legal fees in a successful defense of the trademark. Trademark amortization expense for the year ended December 31, 2002, should be
a. $0.
b. $25,000.
c. $28,750.
d. $30,000.

18. Should the following fees associated with the registration of an internally developed patent be capitalized?

	Legal fees	Registration fees
a.	Yes	Yes
b.	Yes	No
c.	No	Yes
d.	No	No

19. An activity that would be expensed currently as research and development costs is the
a. Testing in search for or evaluation of product or process alternatives.
b. Adaptation of an existing capability to a particular requirement or customer's need as a part of continuing commercial activity.
c. Legal work in connection with patent applications or litigation, and the sale or licensing of patents.
d. Engineering follow-through in an early phase of commercial production.

20. For the issuer of a ten-year term bond, the amount of amortization using the interest method would increase each year if the bond was sold at a

	Discount	Premium
a.	No	No
b.	Yes	Yes
c.	No	Yes
d.	Yes	No

21. When the issuer of bonds exercises the call provision to retire the bonds, the excess of the cash paid over the carrying amount of the bonds should be recognized separately as a(an)
a. Extraordinary loss.
b. Extraordinary gain.
c. Loss from continuing operations.
d. Loss from discontinued operations.

22. When the cash proceeds from a bond issued with detachable stock purchase warrants exceeds the sum of the par value of the bonds and the fair value of the warrants, the excess should be credited to

a. Additional paid-in capital.
b. Retained earnings.
c. Premium on bonds payable.
d. Detachable stock warrants outstanding.

23. Strand Inc., provides an incentive compensation plan under which its president receives a bonus equal to 10% of the corporation's income in excess of $200,000 before income tax but after deduction of the bonus. If income before income tax and bonus is $640,000 and the tax rate is 40%, the amount of the bonus would be
a. $40,000.
b. $44,000.
c. $58,180.
d. $64,000.

24. Dix Company operates a retail store and must determine the proper December 31, 2002, year-end accrual for the following expenses:

- The store lease calls for fixed rent of $1,200 per month, payable at the beginning of the month, and additional rent equal to 6% of net sales over $250,000 per calendar year, payable on January 31 of the following year. Net sales for 2002 are $450,000.

- An electric bill of $850 covering the period 12/16/02 through 1/15/03 was received January 22, 2003.

- A $400 telephone bill was received January 7, 2003, covering:

Service in advance for Jan. 2003	$150
Local and toll calls for Dec. 2002	250

In its December 31, 2002, balance sheet, Dix should report accrued liabilities of
a. $15,075.
b. $13,100.
c. $12,825.
d. $12,675.

25. Cobb Company sells appliance service contracts agreeing to repair appliances for a two-year period. Cobb's past experience is that, of the total dollars spent for repairs on service contracts, 40% is incurred evenly during the first contract year and 60% evenly during the second contract year. Receipts from service contract sales for the two years ended December 31, 2002, are as follows:

2001	$500,000
2002	600,000

Receipts from contracts are credited to unearned service contract revenue. Assume that all contract sales are made evenly during the year. What amount should Cobb report as unearned service contract revenue at December 31, 2002?
a. $360,000
b. $470,000
c. $480,000
d. $630,000

26. On November 1, 2002, Beni Corp. was awarded a judgment of $1,500,000 in connection with a lawsuit. The decision is being appealed by the defendant, and it is expected that the appeal process will be completed by the end of 2003. Beni's attorney feels that it is highly probable that an award will be upheld on appeal, but that the judgment may be reduced by an estimated 40%. In addition to footnote disclosure, what amount should be reported as a receivable in Beni's balance sheet at December 31, 2002?
a. $1,500,000
b. $ 900,000
c. $ 600,000
d. $0

27. On June 1, 2002, Ichor Company entered into a ten-year noncancellable lease with Gillie, Inc., for a machine owned by Gillie. The machine had a fair value of $180,000 at inception of the lease. Ownership of the machine is transferred to Ichor upon expiration of the lease. The present value of the ten $30,000 annual lease payments, based on Ichor's incremental borrowing rate of 12%, is $190,000. The lease agreement specifies that all executory costs are assumed by Ichor. How much should Ichor record as an asset and corresponding liability at the inception of the lease?
a. $0
b. $180,000
c. $190,000
d. $300,000

28. On December 31, 2002, Pell, Inc., sold a machine to Flax, and simultaneously leased it back for one year. Pertinent information at this date is as follows:

Sales price	$360,000
Carrying amount	315,000
Estimated remaining useful life	12 years
Present value of lease rentals ($3,000 for 12 months @ 12%)	34,100

At December 31, 2002, how much should Pell report as deferred revenue from the sale of the machine?
a. $0
b. $10,900
c. $34,100
d. $45,000

29. The excess of the subscription price over the par value of nonredeemable preferred stock subscribed should be recorded as
a. A liability.
b. Additional paid-in capital.
c. Retained earnings.
d. Revenue.

30. Ten thousand (10,000) shares of a common stock with a par value of $20 per share were initially issued at $25 per share. Subsequently, two thousand (2,000) of these shares were purchased as treasury stock at $30 per share. Assuming that the par value method of accounting for treasury stock transactions is used, what is the effect of the purchase of the treasury stock on each of the following?

	Additional paid-in capital	Retained earnings
a.	Decrease	Increase
b.	Decrease	Decrease
c.	Increase	Decrease
d.	Increase	No effect

31. How would the declaration of a 10% stock dividend by a corporation affect each of the following on its books?

	Retained earnings	Total stockholders' equity
a.	Decrease	Decrease
b.	Decrease	No effect
c.	No effect	Decrease
d.	No effect	No effect

32. Compensation cost should be recognized in the income statement of each period in which services are rendered for a compensatory stock option plan for which the date of grant and the measurement date are

	Different	Identical
a.	No	No
b.	No	Yes
c.	Yes	Yes
d.	Yes	No

33. The following costs were incurred by Griff Co., a manufacturer, during 2002:

Accounting and legal fees	$ 25,000
Freight-in	175,000
Freight-out	160,000
Officers' salaries	150,000
Insurance	85,000
Sales representatives' salaries	215,000

What amount of these costs should be reported as general and administrative expenses for 2002?
a. $260,000
b. $550,000
c. $635,000
d. $810,000

34. Flint Corporation elected early adoption of SFAS No. 144, Accounting for the Impairment or Disposal of Long-Lived Assets. On February 2, Flint Corp.'s board of directors voted to discontinue operations of its frozen food division and to sell the division's assets on the open market as soon as possible. The division reported net operating losses of $20,000 in January and $30,000 in February. On February 26, sale of the division's assets resulted in a gain of $90,000. What amount of gain from disposal of a business segment should Flint recognize in its income statement for the three months ended March 31?
a. $0
b. $40,000
c. $60,000
d. $90,000

35. Strand, Inc., incurred the following infrequent losses during 2002:

A $90,000 write-down of equipment leased to others.
A $50,000 adjustment of accruals on long-term contracts.
A $75,000 loss from a major strike by employees.

In its 2002 income statement, what amount should Strand report as total infrequent losses that are **not** considered extraordinary?
a. $215,000
b. $165,000
c. $140,000
d. $125,000

36. A change in the salvage value of an asset depreciated on a straight-line basis and arising because additional information has been obtained is
a. An accounting change that should be reported in the period of change and future periods if the change affects both.
b. An accounting change that should be reported by restating the financial statements of all prior periods presented.
c. A correction of an error.
d. Not an accounting change.

37. Pro forma effects of retroactive application would usually be reported on the face of the income statement for a
a. Correction of error.
b. Change in entity.
c. Change in accounting estimate.
d. Change in accounting principle.

38. On December 31, 2002, Rapp Co. changed inventory cost methods to FIFO from LIFO for financial statement and income tax purposes. The change will result in a $175,000 increase in the beginning inventory at January 1, 2002. Assuming a 30% income tax rate, the cumulative effect of this accounting change reported in the income statement for the year ended December 31, 2002, is
a. $175,000.
b. $122,500.
c. $ 52,500.
d. $0.

39. A development stage enterprise
a. Issues an income statement that shows only cumulative amounts from the enterprise's inception.
b. Issues an income statement that is the same as an established operating enterprise, but does **not** show cumulative amounts from the enterprise's inception as additional information.
c. Issues an income statement that is the same as an established operating enterprise, and shows cumulative amounts from the enterprise's inception as additional information.
d. Does **not** issue an income statement.

40. Casey Corp. entered into a troubled debt restructuring agreement with First State Bank. First State agreed to accept land with a carrying amount of $85,000 and a fair value of $120,000 in exchange for a note with a carrying amount of $185,000. Disregarding income taxes, what amount should Casey report as extraordinary gain in its income statement?
a. $0
b. $ 35,000
c. $ 65,000
d. $100,000

41. An inventory loss from a market price decline occurred in the first quarter, and the decline was not expected to reverse during the fiscal year. However, in the third quarter the inventory's market price recovery exceeded the market decline that occurred in the first quarter. For interim financial reporting, the dollar amount of net inventory should
a. Decrease in the first quarter by the amount of the market price decline and increase in the third quarter by the amount of the decrease in the first quarter.
b. Decrease in the first quarter by the amount of the market price decline and increase in the third quarter by the amount of the market price recovery.
c. Decrease in the first quarter by the amount of the market price decline and **not** be affected in the third quarter.
d. Not be affected in either the first quarter or the third quarter.

42. Green Company, which began operations on January 1, 2002, appropriately uses the installment method of accounting. The following information is available for 2002:

Gross profit on sales	40%
Deferred gross profit at 12/31/02	$240,000
Cash collected, including down payments	450,000

What is the total amount of Green's installment sales for 2002?
a. $ 600,000
b. $ 690,000
c. $ 850,000
d. $1,050,000

43. Marr Construction Company has consistently used the percentage-of-completion method. On January 10, 2001, Marr began work on a $6,000,000 construction contract. At the inception date, the estimated cost of construction was $4,500,000. The following data relate to the progress of the contract:

Income recognized at 12/31/02	$ 600,000
Cost incurred 1/10/01 through 12/31/02	3,600,000
Estimated cost to complete at 12/31/02	1,200,000

How much income should Marr recognize for the year ended December 31, 2002?
a. $300,000
b. $525,000
c. $600,000
d. $900,000

44. On February 12, 2002, VIP Publishing, Inc. purchased the copyright to a book for $15,000 and agreed to pay royalties equal to 10% of book sales, with a guaranteed minimum royalty of $60,000. VIP had book sales of $800,000 in 2002. In its 2002 income statement, what amount should VIP report as royalty expense?
a. $60,000
b. $75,000
c. $80,000
d. $95,000

45. Busy Corp. prepared the following reconciliation between pretax accounting income and taxable income for the year ended December 31, 2002:

Pretax accounting income	$ 250,000
Taxable income	(150,000)
Difference	$ 100,000

Analysis of difference:	
Interest on municipal bonds	$ 25,000
Excess of tax over book depreciation	75,000
	$ 100,000

Busy's effective income tax rate for 2002 is 30%. The depreciation difference will reverse in equal amounts over the next three years at an enacted tax rate of 40%. In Busy's 2002 income statement, what amount should be reported as the current portion of its provision for income taxes?
a. $45,000
b. $67,500
c. $75,000
d. $82,500

46. According to FASB Statement No. 109, *Accounting for Income Taxes*, justification for the method of determining periodic deferred tax expense is based on the concept of
a. Matching of periodic expense to periodic revenue.
b. Objectivity in the calculation of periodic expense.
c. Recognition of assets and liabilities.
d. Consistency of tax expense measurements with actual tax planning strategies.

47. Which of the following should be recognized for the amount of deferred tax consequences attributable to temporary differences that will result in taxable amounts in future years?

	Deferred tax asset	Deferred tax liability
a.	Yes	Yes
b.	Yes	No
c.	No	Yes
d.	No	No

48. In a statement of cash flows, if used equipment is sold at a loss, the amount shown as a cash inflow from investing activities equals the carrying amount of the equipment
a. Less the loss and plus the amount of tax attributable to the loss.
b. Less both the loss and the amount of tax attributable to the loss.
c. Less the loss.
d. With **no** addition or subtraction.

49. In 2002, a tornado completely destroyed a building belonging to Holland Corp. The building cost $100,000 and had accumulated depreciation of $48,000 at the time of the loss. Holland received a cash settlement from the insurance company and reported an extraordinary loss of $21,000. In Holland's 2002 cash flow statement, the net change reported in the cash flows from investing activities section should be a
a. $10,000 increase.
b. $21,000 decrease.
c. $31,000 increase.
d. $52,000 decrease.

50. Brock Corp.'s transactions for the year ended December 31, 2002 included the following:

- Acquired 50% of Hoag Corp.'s common stock for $225,000 cash which was borrowed from a bank.
- Issued 5,000 shares of its preferred stock for land having a fair value of $400,000.
- Issued 500 of its 11% debenture bonds, due 2005, for $490,000 cash.
- Purchased a patent for $275,000 cash.
- Paid $150,000 toward a bank loan.
- Sold investment securities for $995,000.

Brock's net cash provided by investing activities for 2002 was
a. $370,000.
b. $495,000.
c. $595,000.
d. $770,000.

51. Lyon Company's net accounts receivable were $1,000,000 at December 31, 2001, and $1,200,000 at December 31, 2002. Net cash sales for 2002 were $400,000. The accounts receivable turnover for 2002 was 5.0. Lyon's net sales for 2002 were
a. $11,000,000.
b. $ 6,400,000.
c. $ 6,000,000.
d. $ 5,900,000.

52. The following items were among those that appeared on Roth Co.'s books at the beginning and end of the year:

Demand bank deposits	$500,000
Net long-term receivables	300,000
Deferred income tax assets	100,000

In preparing constant purchasing power financial statements, how much should Roth classify as monetary assets?
a. $500,000
b. $600,000
c. $800,000
d. $900,000

53. A December 15, 2001, purchase of goods was denominated in a currency other than the entity's functional currency. The transaction resulted in a payable that was fixed in terms of the amount of foreign currency, and was paid on the settlement date, January 20, 2002. The exchange rates between the functional currency and the currency in which the transaction was denominated changed between the transaction date and December 31, 2001, and again between December 31, 2001, and January 20, 2002. Both exchange rate changes resulted in gains. The amount of the gain that should be included in the 2002 financial statements would be
a. The gain from December 31, 2001, to January 20, 2002.
b. The gain from December 15, 2001, to January 20, 2002.
c. The gain from December 15, 2001, to December 31, 2002.
d. Zero.

54. Certain balance sheet accounts in a foreign subsidiary of Ross Company at December 31, 2002, have been remeasured into United States dollars as follows:

	Remeasured at	
	Current rates	Historical rates
Accounts receivable		
long-term	$120,000	$100,000
Prepaid insurance	55,000	50,000
Copyright	75,000	85,000
	$250,000	$235,000

What total should be included in Rose's balance sheet at December 31, 2002, for the above items?
a. $235,000
b. $240,000
c. $250,000
d. $255,000

55. On June 30, 2001, Lomond, Inc. issued twenty $10,000, 7% bonds at par. Each bond was convertible into 200 shares of common stock. On January 1, 1997, 10,000 shares of common stock were outstanding. The bondholders converted all the bonds on July 1, 2002. The following amounts were reported in Lomond's income statement for the year ended December 31, 2002:

Revenues	$977,000
Operating expenses	920,000
Interest on bonds	7,000
Income before income tax	50,000
Income tax at 30%	15,000
Net income	$ 35,000

What amount should Lomond report as its 2002 basic earnings per share?
a. $2.50
b. $2.85
c. $2.92
d. $3.50

56. The following condensed balance sheet is presented for the partnership of Axel, Barr, and Cain, who share profits and losses in the ratio of 4:3:3, respectively:

Cash	$100,000		Liabilities	$150,000
Other assets	300,000		Axel, capital	40,000
	$400,000		Barr, capital	180,000
			Cain, capital	30,000
				$400,000

The partners agreed to dissolve the partnership after selling the other assets for $200,000. Upon dissolution of the partnership, Axel should have received
a. $0.
b. $40,000.
c. $60,000.
d. $70,000.

57. Personal financial statements should include which of the following statements?

	Financial condition	Changes in net worth	Cash flows
a.	No	Yes	Yes
b.	Yes	No	No
c.	Yes	Yes	No
d.	Yes	Yes	Yes

58. Cobb Co. purchased 10,000 shares (2% ownership) of Roe Co. on February 12, 2003. Cobb received a stock dividend of 2,000 shares on March 31, 2003, when the carrying amount per share on Roe's books was $35 and the market value per share was $40. Roe paid a cash dividend of $1.50 per share on September 15, 2003. In Cobb's income statement for the year ended October 31, 2003, what amount should Cobb report as dividend income?

a. $98,000
b. $88,000
c. $18,000
d. $15,000

59. On November 30, 2002, Parlor, Inc. purchased for cash at $15 per share all 250,000 shares of the outstanding common stock of Shaw Co. At November 30, 2002, Shaw's balance sheet showed a carrying amount of net assets of $3,000,000. At that date, the fair value of Shaw's property, plant, and equipment exceeded its carrying amount by $400,000. In its November 30, 2002 consolidated balance sheet, what amount should Parlor report as goodwill?

a. $750,000
b. $400,000
c. $350,000
d. $0

60. Perez, Inc. owns 80% of Senior, Inc. During 2007, Perez sold goods with a 40% gross profit to Senior. Senior sold all of these goods in 2007. For 2007 consolidated financial statements, how should the summation of Perez and Senior income statement items be adjusted?

a. Sales and cost of goods sold should be reduced by the intercompany sales.
b. Sales and cost of goods sold should be reduced by 80% of the intercompany sales.
c. Net income should be reduced by 80% of the gross profit on intercompany sales.
d. No adjustment is necessary.

OTHER OBJECTIVE FORMAT QUESTIONS

NUMBER 2 (15 to 25 minutes)

Number 2 consists of 10 items to be reported on Chem Co.'s 2005 financial statements.

ITEM 61 THROUGH 70 are based on the following:

- Accounts receivable at December 31, 2004, were $100,000 before allowance for uncollectible accounts of $10,000. Sales to customers on account (excluding credit card sales) during 2005 were $1,810,000, and collections from customers, excluding recoveries, totaled $1,795,000. During 2005, accounts receivable of $45,000 were written off and $17,000 were recovered. An aging of the accounts receivable at December 31, 2005, indicated that $15,000 may be uncollectible.

- Chem accepts credit cards for payments for sales, and deposits the credit card slips in the bank, which credits Chem's account with the amount of the sale less a 4% commission. For 2005 credit card sales, Chem received proceeds of $600,000, net of commission.

- During 2005, Chem was involved in a tax dispute with the IRS. At December 31, 2005, tax advisor believed that an unfavorable outcome was probable. A reasonable estimate of additional tax payments was between $45,000 and $95,000, but $60,000 was the best estimate in that range.

- One of Chem's product lines carries a two-year warranty against defects. Based on past experience, warranty costs are estimated at 4% of sales. During 2005, sales of this product totaled $500,000 and warranty costs of $6,000 were incurred and paid.

- On July 1, 2005, Chem issued an 8%, $1,000,000 bond at a discount of $160,000 to yield 10%. The bond is due on June 30, 2020, and pays interest annually on June 30. Chem applies the effective interest method on an annual basis to amortize the discount.

- Chem's 2005 income before income taxes was $300,000. Due to temporary differences, its taxable income was $260,000. During 2005, Chem made estimated tax payments of $45,000. Chem reported deferred tax liabilities of $15,000 and $3,000 at December 31, 2005, and 2004, respectively. Chem is subject to a 30% tax rate.

REQUIRED:

FOR ITEMS 61 THROUGH 70, determine the amount to be reported in Chem's 1995 financial statements.

61. Accounts receivable (excluding credit card sales).
62. Allowance for uncollectible accounts.
63. Uncollectible accounts expense.
64. Credit card commission expense.
65. Estimated liability for tax assessment.
66. Estimated liability for warranty.
67. Bond interest payable.
68. Bond interest expense.
69. Federal income taxes currently payable.
70. Deferred income tax expense.

NUMBER 3 (40 to 50 minutes)
The following information pertains to Sparta Co.'s defined benefit pension plan.

Discount rate	8%
Expected rate of return	10%
Average service life	12 years

At January 1, 2002:

Projected benefit obligation	600,000
Fair value of pension plan assets	720,000
Unrecognized prior service cost	240,000
Unamortized prior pension gain	96,000

At December 31, 2002:

Projected benefit obligation	910,000
Fair value of pension plan assets	825,000

Service cost for 2002 was $90,000. There were no contributions made or benefits paid during the year. Sparta's unfunded accrued pension liability was $8,000 at January 1, 2002. Sparta uses the straight-line method of amortization over the maximum period permitted.

REQUIRED:

a. FOR ITEMS 71 THROUGH 75, calculate the amounts to be recognized as components of Sparta's unfunded accrued pension liability at December 31, 2002.

AMOUNTS TO BE CALCULATED:

71. Interest cost.
72. Expected return on plan assets.
73. Actual return on plan assets.
74. Amortization of prior service costs.
75. Minimum amortization of unrecognized pension gain.

b. FOR ITEMS 76 THROUGH 80, determine whether the component increases (I) or decreases (D) Sparta's unfunded accrued pension liability.

ITEMS TO BE ANSWERED:

76. Service cost.
77. Deferral of gain on pension plan assets.
78. Actual return on plan assets.
79. Amortization of prior service costs.
80. Amortization of unrecognized pension gain.

PROBLEM/ESSAY QUESTIONS

NUMBER 4 (15 to 25 minutes)

Boulder Company appropriately changed its depreciation method for its production machinery from the double-declining balance method to the production method effective January 1, 2002.

In addition, effective January 1, 2002, Boulder appropriately changed the salvage values used in computing depreciation for its office equipment.

On December 31, 2002, Boulder appropriately changed the specific subsidiaries constituting the group of companies for which consolidated financial statements are presented.

REQUIRED:

a. Identify any accounting changes in the three situations described above. For each accounting change identified, indicate whether Boulder should show:

- The cumulative effect of a change in accounting principle in net income of the period of change.
- Pro forma effects of retroactive application for all prior periods presented currently.
- Restatement of the financial statements of all prior periods presented currently.

b. 1. Why are accounting principles, once adopted, normally continued?

2. What is the rationale for disclosure of a change from one generally accepted accounting principle to another generally accepted accounting principle?

NUMBER 5 (15 to 25 minutes)

At the beginning of the year, Patrick Company acquired a computer to be used in its operations. The computer was delivered by the supplier, installed by Patrick, and placed into operation. The estimated useful life of the computer is five years, and its estimated residual (salvage) value is significant.

During the year, Patrick received cash in exchange for an automobile that was purchased in a prior year.

REQUIRED:

a. 1. What costs should Patrick capitalize for the computer?

2. What is the objective of depreciation accounting? **Do not discuss specific methods of depreciation.**

b. What is the rationale for using accelerated depreciation methods?

c. How should Patrick account for and report the disposal of the automobile?

NUMBER 6 (20 to 30 minutes)

The following information relates to the obligations of Villa Watch Co. as of December 31, 2002:

- Accounts payable for goods and services purchased on open account amounted to $35,000 at December 31, 2002.
- On December 15, 2002, Villa declared a cash dividend of $.05 per common share, payable on January 12, 2003, to shareholders of record as of December 31, 2002. Villa had 1,000,000 shares of common stock issued and outstanding throughout 2002.
- On December 30, 2002, Villa entered into a six-year capital lease on a warehouse and made the first annual lease payment of $100,000. Villa's incremental borrowing rate was 12%, and the interest rate implicit in the lease, which was known to Villa, was 10%. The rounded present value factors for an annuity due for six years are 4.6 at 12% and 4.8 at 10%.
- On July 1, 2002, Villa issued $500,000, 8% bonds for $440,000 to yield 10%. The bonds mature on June 30, 2008, and pay interest annually every June 30. At December 31, 2002, the bonds were trading on the open market at 86 to yield 12%. Villa uses the effective interest method.
- Villa's 2002 pretax financial income was $850,000 and its taxable income was $600,000. The difference is due to $100,000 of permanent differences and $150,000 of temporary differences related to noncurrent assets. At December 31, 2002, Villa had cumulative taxable differences of $300,000 related to noncurrent assets. Villa's effective tax rate is 30%. Villa made no estimated tax payments during the year.

- Contingency information:

  — Villa has been named a liable party for toxic waste cleanup on its land, and must pay an as-yet undetermined amount for environmental remediation activities.

  — An adjoining landowner, Clear Toothpaste Co., sold its property because of possible toxic contamination of the water supply and resulting potential adverse public reaction toward its product. Clear sued Villa for damages. There is a reasonable possibility that Clear will prevail and be awarded between $250,000 and $600,000.

  — As a result of comprehensive risk assessment, Villa has discontinued rockslide insurance for its warehouse, which is located at the base of a mountain. The warehouse has never sustained rockslide damage, and the probability of sustaining future damage is only slight.

REQUIRED:

a. Prepare the liabilities section of Villa's December 31, 2002, balance sheet.

b. Discuss the information Villa is required to disclose, either in the body of the financial statements or the notes thereto, related to bonds payable and capital leases included in the liabilities presented above.

c. Explain how Villa should account for each contingency in its 2002 financial statements. Discuss the theoretical justification for each accounting treatment.

SOLUTION 1 MULTIPLE CHOICE ANSWERS (1 point each; 60 points total)

1. **(b)** Verifiability and representational faithfulness are the two ingredients of reliability.

2. **(a)** Under SFAC 5, unrealized loss on investments in available-for-sale marketable equity securities is a component of comprehensive income but is *not* a component of earnings. Unrealized loss on investment in trading marketable equity securities, loss on exchange of similar assets, and loss on exchange of dissimilar assets are all items that are included in earnings (and therefore are *also* components of comprehensive income).

3. **(b)** Per SFAC 6, par. 143, "Realization in the most precise sense means the process of converting noncash resources and rights into money and is most precisely used in accounting and financial reporting to refer to sales of assets for cash or *claims to cash.*" Thus, the sale of the depreciated equipment for a note (i.e., a claim to cash) conforms to the realization concept. None of the transactions in the other choices involve the conversion of a noncash resource or right into cash or claims to cash.

4. **(a)** The accounting principle of historical cost requires assets as well as liabilities to be recorded and carried on the books at cost. Therefore, reporting inventory at the lower-of-cost-or-market is a departure from this principle.

5. **(d)** The security should be transferred from trading to available-for-sale (AFS) at market value with the gain or loss recognized at transfer and without reversing any previously recognized gain or loss. As a trading security, unrealized gain or loss is included in net income, so the first decline of $100,000 is included in the determination of net income. As an AFS security, the unrealized gain or loss would be recognized in other comprehensive income, not in the determination of net income.

6. **(a)** Since the accounts receivable balance at 12/31 is $110,000 and the net realizable value at that date is $95,000, the allowance for doubtful accounts must have a 12/31 balance of $15,000.

Allowance for Doubtful Accounts		
	$16,000	Balance, 1/1 (given)
Write-offs $12,000	11,000	Bad debt expense (required)
	$15,000	Balance, 12/31

7. **(c)** The $400,000 U.S. Treasury bill purchased 12/01/02 and maturing 3/31/03 is not included as a cash equivalent because the maturity was more than three months at the time of purchase.

Cash and cash equivalents reported at December 31, 2002, are as follows:

Cash in checking account	$ 35,000
Cash in money market account	75,000
U.S. Treasury Bills, purchased 11/1/02, maturing 1/31/03	350,000
Total cash & cash equivalents	$460,000

8. **(d)** Both notes were received on the balance sheet date. Since the note receivable from Hart arose from a transaction with a customer in the normal course of business and is due in customary trade terms not exceeding one year, it can be reported at its face amount of $10,000 despite the fact that the 3% stated interest rate of the note differs from the prevailing market interest rate of 8% for similar notes at the date of the transaction [APB 21, par 3(a)]. On the other hand, the note receivable from Maxx, which also arose from a transaction with a customer in the normal course of business, is due in five years (i.e., more than one year). Therefore, the note from Maxx cannot be reported at its face amount because the 3% stated interest rate of the note differs from the prevailing market interest rate of 8% for similar notes at the date of the transaction. Because neither the fair value of the services performed by Jet nor the fair value of the note received from Maxx is indicated, the note should be reported at its present value, determined by discounting all future cash payments of the note at the prevailing (i.e., market) rate of interest for a note of this type. Therefore, the note receivable from Maxx should be reported at $7,820, determined as follows:

Principal amount	$10,000
Interest on outstanding principal balance due on maturity date [($10,000 x 3%) x 5]	1,500
Amount due on maturity date	11,500
Present value factor of $1 at 8% for 5 periods	x .680
Present value of note received from Maxx	$ 7,820

9. **(c)** The ending inventory of Kern Company is calculated as follows:

12/31/02 inventory at year-end prices	$780,000
Conversion factor to base year (2001)	÷ 1.2
12/31/02 inventory at base-year prices	650,000
Base year inventory layer (12/31/01)	(600,000)
Inventory increase at base year prices	50,000
Conversion factor to current year prices	x 1.2
2002 inventory layer	$ 60,000
Base year inventory layer (2001)	$600,000
2002 inventory layer	60,000
Valuation of ending inventory, 12/31/02	$660,000

10. **(a)** ARB 43, Chap. 4, requires valuation of inventory items at the lower of cost or replacement cost (commonly referred to as market). For purposes of this rule, however, market cannot exceed

the net realizable value (ceiling) of the good (i.e., selling price less expected costs to sell), and market should not be less than this net realizable value reduced by an allowance for a normal profit margin (floor). In this problem, the replacement cost is between the ceiling and floor amounts, and so it is compared to cost. Because the original cost is greater than replacement cost, the item will be carried at replacement cost.

11. (c)   Under the retail inventory method, the cost of the ending inventory is determined by multiplying the retail value of the ending inventory by the cost/retail ratio of the goods available for sale (if the weighted average, LCM method is used). For purposes of the cost/retail fraction, "cost" is defined in the usual manner, to include freight-in, handling charges, etc. "Retail," on the other hand, is simply the retail value of the goods, that is, the amount at which it can be expected to sell them. Freight-in and other incidental acquisition costs do not determine the retail value of the inventory.

12. (d)   The term *F.O.B. destination* means free on board at destination; that is, the goods are shipped to their destination without charge to the buyer. Thus, the costs incurred in connection with the sale and delivery of the goods (i.e., packaging for shipment, shipping, and special handling charges) are borne by the seller. Thus, Kerr's cost of the goods purchased is $50,000.

13. (c)   An understatement of beginning inventory understates the cost of goods available for sale, thereby understating cost of goods sold. An overstatement of ending inventory also understates cost of goods sold. Therefore, cost of goods sold for 2003 is understated by the sum of the understatement of beginning inventory and the overstatement of ending inventory.

14. (a)   Under the general rule of APB 29, *Accounting for Nonmonetary Transactions*, the cost of a nonmonetary asset acquired in exchange for a nonmonetary asset is the fair value of the surrendered asset (par. 18). The fair value of the asset received will be used as the recording amount only if it is more clearly evident than fair the value of the asset surrendered. The Opinion provides for recording based on the recorded amount of the asset surrendered only where the exchange "...is not essentially the culmination of an earning process." Even then, the recording amount should not exceed the fair value of the asset received. An exchange is not in "culmination of an earning process" where its purpose is merely to facilitate the sale of merchandise to third parties, or where the exchange involves similar productive assets.

15. (c)   A change in accounting estimate is accounted for prospectively; that is, the new estimate is reflected in the current and subsequent periods. Thus, in this problem, depreciation for 2002 and subsequent years will be determined by dividing the carrying amount of the asset by the new estimated remaining life.

Cost of machine	$ 480,000
Accumulated depreciation, SL [($480,000 ÷ 6) x 3 years]	(240,000)
Carrying amount as of Jan. 1, 2002	240,000
Estimated remaining life (8 – 3)	÷ 5
Depreciation expense, 2002	$ 48,000

16. (c)   The machine had a depreciable basis of $80,000 ($85,000 cost – $5,000 salvage value) and was depreciated at a rate of $8,000 per year ($80,000 ÷ 10-year useful life). At the time of sale, Victor depreciated the machine for 5.5 years and its carrying amount was equal to $41,000, i.e., [$85,000 – (5.5 x $8,000)]. Thus a $4,000 gain ($45,000 – $41,000) should be recognized.

17. (d)

Amortization of original cost ($400,000 ÷16 years)	$25,000
Amortization of legal defense cost,	
($60,000 ÷ 12 remaining years)	5,000
Total amortization expense, 2002	$30,000

18. (a)   The legal and registration fees associated with the registration of the patent will benefit the patent over its entire useful life and, therefore, should be capitalized and amortized over such useful life in a systematic and rational manner.

19. (a)   Paragraph 9 of SFAS 2, *Accounting for Research and Development Costs*, provides a listing of activities that typically will be classified as research and development (R&D). "Testing in search for or evaluation of product or process alternatives" is included in this list. Conversely, the items described in answers (b), (c), and (d) are included in the listing of activities generally **not** considered R&D, in paragraph 10.

20. (b)   When a bond is issued at a discount, the interest expense each year is based on the carrying amount of the bond (face amount less unamortized discount) and is equal to the sum of the cash paid as interest and the amortization of the discount. In each subsequent year the carrying amount of the bond is greater, and the interest expense is greater, because it is based upon the carrying amount of the bond. The interest expense remains equal to the sum of the cash paid as interest and the amortization of the discount. Since the cash paid remains constant and the interest expense increases each year, the amortization of the discount must also increase each year. When a

bond is issued at a premium, the interest expense is based upon the carrying amount of the bond (face amount plus unamortized premium) and is equal to the difference between the cash interest paid and the amortization of the premium. Each year the carrying amount of the bond decreases and the interest expense decreases. Since each year the interest expense decreases while the cash paid out remains constant, the amortization of the premium must increase each year.

21. (a)   When a debt security is reacquired prior to its maturity date (except through conversion into equity securities by the holder), it is considered an early extinguishment [APB 26, par. 3(a)]. Early extinguishments of debt are always classified as extraordinary (SFAS 4, par. 8). If upon retirement the cash paid is greater than the carrying amount of the bonds, a loss is incurred.

22. (c)   The proceeds from the sale of debt with stock purchase warrants should be allocated between the two instruments based on the relative fair values of the debt security without the warrants and the warrants themselves. The portion of the proceeds so allocated to the warrants is accounted for as paid-in capital. The remainder is allocated to the face amount of the bond, and to the extent remaining, to premium on bonds payable.

23. (a)   The amount of the bonus can be determined algebraically as follows, where B = Bonus:

$$B = .10(\$640,000 - \$200,000 - B)$$
$$B = .10(\$440,000 - B)$$
$$B = \$44,000 - .1B$$
$$1.1 B = \$44,000$$
$$B = \underline{\$40,000}$$

24. (d)   Accrued liabilities amount to $12,675, determined as follows:

Rent surcharge ($450,000 – $250,000) x .06	$12,000
Electricity, $850 ÷ 2	425
Phone, December 2002	250
	$12,675

25. (d)   All contract sales are made *evenly* during the year. Using the midpoint of each year of July 1, the last 6 months of the 2001 service contract sales have yet to be earned (7/1/01 to 12/31/02 is 18 months earned), and the last 18 months of the 2002 service contract sales are also unearned (7/1/02 to 12/31/02 is 6 months earned). Cobb's past experience is that of the total dollars spent for repairs on service contracts, 40% is incurred evenly during the first 12 months of the contract and 60% during the second 12 months of the contract.

Service contract sales, 2001					$500,000
To be earned last six months of contract (60% ÷ 2)				x	.30
Unearned 2001 service contract revenue					150,000
Unearned 2002 service contract revenue:					
Service contract sales—1997		$600,000			
To be earned months 7-12					
of contract (40% ÷ 2)	.20				
To be earned months 13-24					
of contract (all 60%)	.60	x	.80		480,000
Unearned service contract revenue, 12/31/02					$630,000

26. (d)   SFAS 5 provides that gain contingencies are not accrued before realization. Thus, no gain can be accrued until the lawsuit is settled. The gain contingency should be disclosed in the footnotes in the financial statements.

27. (b)   Because ownership of the machine is transferred to the lessee upon expiration of the lease, SFAS 13 provides that the lessee account for the lease as a capital lease. As a result, the lessee, at the inception of the lease, records the asset and the corresponding liability at an amount equal to the lesser of the asset's fair value at the inception date or the present value of the minimum lease payments, or $180,000.

28. (a)   Gains or losses on sale-leaseback transactions are generally deferred and amortized over the term of the lease. There are two exceptions to this general rule: (1) where the seller-lessee retains only a minor portion of the use of the property, or (2) where the seller-lessee retains more than a minor portion of the use but less than substantially all. For purposes of these tests, a minor portion is defined as 10% or less of the use of the asset; thus, if the present value of lease rentals during the leaseback period is 10% or less than the fair value of the property, the seller-lessee is deemed to have retained only a minor interest in the property (SFAS 28, par. 3). In this case, the sale and leaseback are accounted for as two separate transactions (i.e., the entire gain is recognized upon sale of the property). In this problem, the present value of the lease payments ($34,100) was less than 10% of the fair value of the property (i.e., 10% of $360,000 = $36,000).

29. (b)   The answer to this question can be easily derived by simply writing the standard journal entry to record the issuance of stock on a subscription basis.

Cash ("down payment")	XX	
Subscriptions Receivable (remainder of purchase price)	XX	
Preferred Stock Subscribed (par value)		XX
Additional Paid-In Capital (to balance)		XX

30. (b)   Under the par value method, treasury stock purchased is recorded at par. If the acquisition price is greater than par, the excess is charged-off pro rata to additional paid-in capital (APIC) and the balance (if any) to retained earnings. Retained earnings are never increased from the purchase or reissuance of treasury stock. On the facts of this question, the following journal entries would be made. As entry (2) indicates, the purchase of the treasury stock at $30 per share would reduce both APIC and retained earnings.

(1)	Cash (10,000 x $25)	250,000	
	Common Stock, $20 par		200,000
	Additional Paid-In Capital (PIC)		50,000
(2)	Treasury Stock (2,000 x $20)	40,000	
	Additional PIC (2,000 x $5)	10,000	
	Retained Earnings (to balance)	10,000	
	Cash		60,000

31. (b)   The declaration of a 10% stock dividend would be recorded as in Entry (1). The distribution of the shares is recorded as in Entry (2). Entry (1) reduces Retained Earnings but total stockholders' equity remains unchanged because paid-in capital accounts are credited for the same amount. Entry (2) has no effect on either Retained Earnings or total stockholders' equity because it is recorded entirely within paid-in capital.

(1)	Retained Earnings (shares x FMV)	XX	
	Common Stock Dividend		
	Distributable (shares x PV)		XX
	Additional Paid-In Capital (to balance)		XX
(2)	Common Stock Dividend Distributable		
	(shares x PV)	XX	
	Common Stock (shares x PV)		XX

32. (c)   Compensation costs in stock option plans should be recognized as an expense of one or more periods in which an employee performs services. The grant or award may specify the period or periods during which the employee performs services. Whether or not the measurement date is later than the date of grant, an employer should record the compensation expenses each period from the date of grant to the date of measurement (APB 25, par. 13).

33. (a)   The freight-in cost is an inventoriable cost. The freight-out cost and the sales representatives' salaries should both be reported as selling expenses.

Accounting and legal fees	$ 25,000
Officers' salaries	150,000
Insurance	85,000
General and administrative expenses	$260,000

34. (b)   SFAS 144, para. 43 states, "In the period in which a component of an entity either has been disposed of or is classified as held for sale, the income statement of a business enterprise for current and prior periods shall report the results of operations of the component…in discontinued operations...in the periods(s) in which they occur." Flint Corp.'s gain from disposal of its frozen food division is computed as follows:

Gain from sale of division assets on Feb 26	$ 90,000
Less: Operating loss during the fiscal year	(50,000)
Gain on disposal of segment, before	
income taxes	$ 40,000

The operating loss of $20,000 in January would not have been included in the calculation under APB Opinion No. 30, because it was before the measurement date. APB 30 was superceded by SFAS 144.

35. (a)   APB 30 provides that (1) the write-down or write-off of receivables, inventories, equipment leased to others, or intangible assets, (2) adjustments of accruals on long-term contracts, and (3) the effects of a strike, including those against competitors and major suppliers, should not be reported as extraordinary items. Therefore, the total amount of infrequent losses not considered extraordinary is $215,000 (i.e., $90,000 + $50,000 + $75,000).

36. (a)   Changes in accounting estimates, such as a change in the salvage value of an asset, are required to be accounted for prospectively; that is, in the current and future periods affected (APB 20, par. 31). Previously issued financial statements are only restated to reflect prior period adjustments, a change in the reporting entity, and some special changes in accounting principle. A change in an accounting estimate is not the correction of an error. A change in estimate is one of the three types of accounting changes identified by Opinion 20.

37. (d)   The pro forma effects of a retroactive application of most changes in accounting principle are shown on the face of the income statement (APB 20, par. 21). A correction of an error is reflected as an adjustment to the opening balance of retained earnings. A change in entity also requires restatement of prior period statements. A change in estimate is handled on a prospective basis. No retroactive adjustment is made for a change in estimate.

38. (d)   A change from LIFO to another inventory method is a change in accounting principle that should be reported *retroactively* by applying the new method in restatements of prior periods and adjusting the beginning balance of *retained earnings* (APB 20, par. 27)

39. (c)   A development stage enterprise is required to issue the same financial statements presenting the same basic information as an established operating enterprise. SFAS 7, *Accounting and Reporting by Development Stage Enterprises*, also requires certain additional disclosures, including cumulative revenues and expenses from the enterprise's inception.

40. (c)   Casey should report as extraordinary gain the difference between the obligation settled ($185,000) and the fair value of the asset transferred ($120,000), for a total extraordinary gain of $65,000. As an added note, Casey will also report ordinary gain of $35,000, which is the difference between the fair value ($120,000) and carry amount ($85,000) of the land.

41. (a)   APB 28, par. 14(c), states that inventory losses from market declines that cannot be reasonably expected to be restored in the fiscal year should not be deferred beyond the interim period in which the decline occurs. Hence, the inventory should decrease in the interim period in which the loss occurred (i.e., the first quarter) by the amount of the market price decline. Recoveries of such losses on the same inventory in later interim periods of the same fiscal year through market price recoveries should be recognized as gains in the later interim period, thus increasing the inventory balance. Such gains should not exceed previously recognized losses.

42. (d)   Total installment sales is $1,050,000, i.e., $600,000 + $450,000 cash. The total amount of Green's installment sales for 2002 is determined as follows:

$$\text{Deferred profit at 12/31/02} = \text{Profit margin ratio} \times \text{Installment sales receivable at 12/31/02}$$

Substitute and solve for installment sales receivable at 12/31/02 (or ISR)

$240,000 = 40\% \times \text{ISR}$
$\text{ISR} = \$240,000 \div 40\% = \$600,000$

43. (a)   Under the percentage-of-completion method, the gross profit recognized in 2002 is determined by multiplying the estimated total gross profit of the contract by the estimated percentage-of-completion and then subtracting the gross profit previously recognized.

Contract price		$ 6,000,000
Less: Estimated total costs:		
Actual costs incurred	$3,600,000	
Estimated costs to complete	1,200,000	(4,800,000)
Estimated total gross profit		1,200,000
Times: Estimated percentage-of-completion:		
Actual costs incurred	3,600,000	
Estimated total costs	÷4,800,000	x 75%
Gross profit recognizable to date		900,000
Less: Gross profit previously recognized		(600,000)
Gross profit recognized in 2002		$ 300,000

44. (c)   Under the royalty agreement, VIP incurs royalty expense equal to 10% of book sales, with a guaranteed minimum royalty of $60,000. Therefore, in its 2002 income statement, VIP should recognize royalty expense of $80,000 [($800,000 x 10%) > $60,000].

45. (a)

Future taxable amounts originating	$ 75,000
Enacted future tax rate	40%
Deferred tax expense for 2002	$ 30,000

Total tax expense = Effective tax rate x Pretax financial income
Total tax expense = 30% x $250,000
Total tax expense = $75,000

Total tax expense	$ 75,000
Deferred tax expense	(30,000)
Current tax expense	$ 45,000

46. (c)   Per SFAS 109, par. 16, "An enterprise shall recognize a deferred tax liability or asset for all temporary differences...." After computing the balances of deferred tax accounts at a balance sheet date, the amount of deferred income tax expense is computed by determining the change required during the period in the deferred tax asset and liability accounts. That change is a by-product of the amount of deferred taxes (asset and/or liability) to be reported on the balance sheet at the balance sheet date. The method prescribed in SFAS 109 is often called the "liability" method or the "asset-liability" method.

47. (c) A deferred tax *liability* should be recognized for the amount of deferred tax consequences attributable to temporary differences that will result in *taxable amounts* in future years. The liability is the amount of taxes that will be payable on those taxable amounts in future years based on the provisions of the tax law. On the other hand, a deferred tax *asset* should be recognized for the amount of deferred tax consequences attributable to temporary differences that will result in *tax deductions* in future years which will reduce taxes payable in those future years.

48. (c) In the statement of cash flows, the proceeds from the sale of used equipment should be reported as a cash inflow due to an investing activity. The amount of proceeds would equal the equipment's carrying amount less the loss recognized on disposal. The tax effect of the loss on disposal will *not* affect the amount reported in the investing section because all income taxes are to be classified as an operating activity on a statement of cash flows (see SFAS 95, par. 91-92).

49. (c) Since the cash settlement is due to the destruction of a building, it is reported as a cash inflow due to an investing activity [SFAS 95, par. 22(c)]. The cash settlement received from the insurance company is computed as follows (work backwards through the computation):

Cash settlement received from insurance company (forced)		$ 31,000
Carrying amount of building at time of involuntary conversion:		
Cost (given)	$100,000	
Accumulated depreciation	(48,000)	(52,000)
Loss on involuntary conversion (given)		$(21,000)

50. (b) The purchase of the investment securities for cash which was borrowed from a bank is *not* a noncash investing and financing transaction because the asset was not acquired by assuming a directly related liability. Examples of acquiring assets by assuming directly related liabilities include purchasing a building by incurring a mortgage to the seller and obtaining an asset by entering into a capital lease. On the other hand, the acquisition of the land by issuing preferred stock is a noncash investing and financing transaction. The proceeds from the issuance of the bonds payable and payment toward the bank loan are to be classified as financing activities.

Purchase of investment securities for cash	$ (225,000)
Purchase of a patent for cash	(275,000)
Proceeds from sale of investment securities	995,000
Net cash provided by investing activities	$ 495,000

51. (d) The accounts receivable turnover ratio equals the total credit sales for the year divided by the average of the beginning and ending accounts receivable balances. The average accounts receivable balance equals $1,100,000 [i.e., ($1,000,000 + $1,200,000) ÷ 2], and credit sales equal $5,500,000 (i.e., 5.0 x $1,100,000). Thus, total sales are equal to $5,900,000 (i.e., $5,500,000 credit sales + $400,000 cash sales).

52. (d) Monetary assets include cash, contractual claims to a fixed amount of cash in the future such as accounts receivable, and investments that pay a fixed amount of interest or dividends and will be repaid at a fixed amount in the future. SFAS 89, *Financial Reporting and Changing Prices*, indicates that a deferred tax asset should be classified as monetary.

Demand bank deposits	$ 500,000
Net long-term receivables	300,000
Deferred income tax assets	100,000
Total monetary assets	$ 900,000

53. (a) The purchase of the goods, with the corresponding payable, is a transaction denominated in a foreign currency which will result in a transaction gain or loss whenever the exchange rate changes between the transaction date and the settlement date (or year-end, if earlier). According to SFAS 52, par. 15, transaction gains and losses must be recognized in income from continuing operations in the period they occur (subject to exceptions for certain intercompany transactions and certain hedges of net investments and foreign currency commitments, which are deferred). Therefore, the amount of the gain that should have been included in the 2001 financial statements is the gain from the 12/15/01 transaction date to 12/31/01. The amount of the gain that should be included in the 2002 financial statements is the gain from 12/31/01 to the 1/20/02 settlement date.

54. (d) SFAS 52 specifies the rates to be used to remeasure various assets as follows:

Long-term accounts receivable	Current rate	$ 120,000
Prepaid insurance	Historical rate	50,000
Copyright	Historical rate	85,000
		$ 255,000

55. (c) To reflect the actual conversion on July 1, 4,000 additional common shares are added to the 10,000 common shares outstanding since the beginning of the year, resulting in 12,000 weighted average common shares outstanding computed as follows:

$$10,000 \times 6/12 \ = \ 5,000$$
$$14,000 \times 6/12 \ = \ \underline{7,000}$$
$$\underline{12,000}$$

Basic EPS would be calculated by dividing net income of $35,000 by the 12,000 weighted average common shares outstanding to yield $2.92 per share.

56. (a) Barr receives $150,000 from the dissolution of the partnership. Axel and Cain receive no cash upon dissolution. The cash to be distributed to each partner is computed as follows:

| | | | | | Capital | |
| | | | | Axel | Barr | Cain |
Description	Cash	Other assets	Liabs.	40%	30%	30%
Balances before realization	$ 100	$ 300	$ 150	$ 40	$180	$ 30
Sale of other assets	200	(300)		(40)	(30)	(30)
Balances after realization	300	$ 0	150	$ 0	150	$ 0
Payment of liabilities	(150)		(150)			
Balances	$ 150		$ 0		$150	

57. (c) Personal financial statements should include a statement of financial condition and a statement of changes in net worth. Neither the statement of cash flows nor the income statement pertain to personal financial statements.

58. (c) Cobb owns only a 2% interest in Roe. Thus, Cobb does not have the ability to exercise significant influence over Roe by virtue of the investment, and the investment should be accounted for under the cost method. Therefore, Cobb should report the cash dividend received from Roe as dividend income. No income is recognized from the receipt of the stock dividend from Roe, since Cobb's proportionate interest in Roe has not changed and Roe's underlying assets and liabilities have also not changed. Therefore, the amount that Cobb should report as dividend income is computed as follows:

Shares of Roe purchased 2/12/03	10,000
Add: Shares of Roe from stock dividend, 3/31/03	2,000
Shares of Roe held, 9/15/03	12,000
Times: Cash dividend per share	x $1.50
Dividend income for year ended 10/31/03	$18,000

59. (c) Goodwill is the excess of the investment cost over the fair value of the identifiable net assets acquired. The amount of goodwill to be reported is determined as follows:

Investment cost (250,000 x $15)		$ 3,750,000
Carrying amount of identifiable net assets	$3,000,000	
Fair value of plant assets in excess of carrying amount	400,000	
Less fair value of identifiable net assets acquired		(3,400,000)
Goodwill to be reported		$ 350,000

60. (a) The sale of inventory between two affiliates triggers the individual accounting systems for both companies. Revenue will duly be recorded by the seller while the purchase will simultaneously be entered into the accounts of the acquiring company. However, from a consolidated perspective, neither a sale nor a purchase has occurred. Therefore, the amount reported as sales in the consolidated income statement must be reduced by the full amount of the intercompany sales. In recording the sale of the inventory to the purchasing affiliate, the selling affiliate recognized cost of goods sold based upon its acquisition cost. The purchasing affiliate later recognized cost of goods sold equal to the amount of the intercompany sale when it later resold all of these goods to unaffiliated customers. Once again, from a consolidated perspective, the sale to the purchasing affiliate did not occur. Thus, the cost of the goods sold to unaffiliated customers should be based upon the cost of the goods to the selling affiliate. Therefore, the amount reported as cost of goods sold in the consolidated income statement should also be reduced by the full amount of the intercompany sales because this is the amount of cost of goods sold recognized by the purchasing affiliate.

OTHER OBJECTIVE FORMAT QUESTION SOLUTIONS

SOLUTION 2 (1 point each; 10 points total)

61. $70,000.

Beginning A/R	$ 100,000
Sales on account	1,810,000
Less: Collections	(1,795,000)
Less: A/R written off	(45,000)
A/R December 31, 2005	$ 70,000

62. $15,000. As given in the problem, an aging of accounts receivable indicated that $15,000 may be uncollectible.

63. $33,000. The uncollectible accounts expense is the amount by which the allowance for uncollectible accounts must be adjusted to arrive at the year-end balance of $15,000, as follows:

Allowance For Uncollectible Accounts

		Bal. 12/31/04 (given)	10,000
A/R written off (given)	45,000	Recovered (given)	17,000
Bal. Before adj.	18,000		
		Adjustment (forced)	33,000
		Bal. 12/31/05 (given)	15,000

64. $25,000.   Credit card sales less 4% commissions equals proceeds of $600,000.   Let credit card sales = C; commissions = 4%C.

$$C - 4\%C = \$600,000$$
$$96\%C = \$600,000$$
$$C = \$625,000$$
$$4\%(\$625,000) = \underline{\$ 25,000}$$

65. $60,000. The tax dispute with the IRS is a contingent liability. When contingent liabilities are probable and the loss can be reasonably estimated, the estimated loss should be accrued. If only a range of possible loss can be estimated and no amount in the range is a better estimate than the others, the minimum amount in the range should be accrued.   In this case, however, $60,000 was the best estimate in the range and should be the amount that is accrued.

66. $14,000.

2005 Sales	$500,000
Warranty cost experience	x 4%
2005 Warranty expense	20,000
Less: Warranty costs incurred	(6,000)
Estimated warranty liability	$ 14,000

67. $40,000.

Face amount of bond	$1,000,000
Face rate of bond	x 8%
Interest for full year	80,000
July 1 - Dec. 31, 2005	x 6/12
Bond interest payable 12/31/05	$ 40,000

68. $42,000.

Face amount of bond	$1,000,000
Less: Bond discount	(160,000)
Bond carrying amount	840,000
Effective interest rate	x 10%
Interest expense for full year	84,000
July 1 - Dec. 31, 2005	x 6/12
Bond interest expense 2005	$ 42,000

69. $33,000.

Taxable income	$ 260,000
Tax rate	x 30%
Income taxes payable	78,000
Less: Estimated payments	(45,000)
Income taxes currently payable	$ 33,000

70. $12,000.

Income before income taxes	$ 300,000
Less: Taxable income	(260,000)
Temporary differences	40,000
Tax rate	x 30%
Deferred income tax expense	$ 12,000

This answer is confirmed by the difference of $12,000 in deferred tax liabilities at December 31, 2005, and 2004 ($15,000 − $3,000 = $12,000), which is the adjustment required to recognize deferred income tax expense.

SOLUTION 3 (1 point each; 10 points total)

71. $48,000. Interest cost included in net pension cost is determined as the increase in the projected benefit obligation due to the passage of time (SFAS 87, par. 22). Thus, the amount of interest cost that Sparta should include in the calculation of 2002 net pension cost is computed as follows:

Projected benefit obligation, 1/1/02	$600,000
Times: Discount rate at which pension benefits could be effectively settled	x 8%
Interest cost for 2002	$ 48,000

72. $72,000. The expected return on plan assets is determined based on the expected long-term rate of return on plan assets and the market-related value of plan assets. The market-related value of plan assets is either fair value or a calculated value that recognizes changes in fair value in a systematic and rational manner over not more than five years (SFAS 87, par. 30). Therefore, Sparta's expected return on plan assets for 2002 is computed as follows:

Fair value of plan assets, 1/1/02	$720,000
Times: Expected rate of return	x 10%
Expected return on plan assets for 2002	$ 72,000

73. **$105,000.** For a funded plan, the actual return on plan assets is determined based on the fair value of plan assets at the beginning and the end of the period, adjusted for contributions and benefit payments (SFAS 87, par. 23). Therefore, since there were no contributions made or benefits paid during 2002, the actual return on Sparta's plan assets is $105,000 (i.e., $825,000 – $720,000), the increase in the fair value of plan assets in 2002.

74. **$20,000.** Prior service cost is the increase in the projected benefit obligation at the date of a plan amendment (or initiation of a plan). Prior service cost is amortized during the future service periods of those employees active at the date of the amendment (or initiation) who are expected to receive benefits under the plan. Since the amortization of prior service cost can be quite complex, a straight-line method that amortizes the cost over the average remaining service life of the active participants is acceptable. Therefore, the amount of prior service cost that Sparta should include in the calculation of 2002 net pension cost is $20,000 (i.e., $240,000 ÷12).

75. **$2,000.** The minimum amortization of unrecognized pension gain that Sparta should include in the calculation of net pension cost is determined, as of the beginning of the year, as either the amount by which the unrecognized pension gain exceeds 10 percent of the projected benefit obligation or the market-related value of plan assets divided by the average remaining service period of active employees expected to receive benefits under the plan, whichever is greater.

Unrecognized pension gain, 1/1/02	$ 96,000
Less: Ten percent of fair value of plan assets (i.e., the market-related value of plan assets), 1/1/02 ($720,000* x 10%)	(72,000)
Excess of unrecognized pension gain over 10% of the greater of the projected benefit obligation or the market-related value of plan assets at 1/1/02	24,000
Divide by: Average service life	÷ 12
Minimum amortization of unrecognized pension gain, 2002	$ 2,000

*   At 1/1/02, the fair value of plan assets exceeds the projected benefit obligation (i.e., $720,000 > $600,000).

76. **(I)** Service cost is the actuarial present value of benefits attributed by the pension benefit formula to employee service during that period (SFAS 87, par. 21). Since service cost increases net pension cost, it also increases the unfunded accrued pension liability.

77. **(I)** Since the deferral of the gain on pension plan assets increases net pension cost, it also increases the unfunded pension liability.

78. **(D)** Since the actual return on plan assets decreases net pension cost, it also decreases the unfunded accrued pension liability.

79. **(I)** Since the amortization of prior service costs increases net pension cost, it also increases the unfunded accrued pension liability.

80. **(D)** Since the amortization of unrecognized pension gain decreases net pension cost, it also decreases the unfunded accrued pension liability.

PROBLEM/ESSAY SOLUTIONS

SOLUTION 4 (5 points total)

a. (3 points) Boulder's change in depreciation method is a change in accounting principle. This change in accounting principle should show the cumulative effect of a change in accounting principle in net income of the period of change, and the pro forma effects of retroactive application for all prior periods presented currently. Financial statements of prior periods should not be restated.

Boulder's change in salvage values is a change in accounting estimate. Boulder would not report a cumulative effect, nor pro forma effects, nor would prior period financial statements be restated.

Boulder's change in the specific subsidiaries constituting the group of companies for which consolidated financial statements are presented is a change in reporting entity. Neither the cumulative effect nor the pro forma effects of the change should be reported. However, financial statements of prior periods presented currently should be restated.

b. 1. (1 point) Consistent use of accounting principles from one accounting period to another enhances the comparability of accounting information across accounting periods and, thus, increases the usefulness of financial statements.

2. (1 point) If a change in accounting principle occurs, the nature and effect of a change in accounting principle should be disclosed to avoid misleading financial statement users. Disclosure is required because there is a presumption that an accounting principle once adopted should not be changed in accounting for events and transactions of a similar type.

SOLUTION 5 (5 points total)

a. 1. (1 point) The capitalized cost for the computer includes all costs reasonable and necessary to prepare it for its intended use. Examples of such costs are the cash purchase price, delivery, installation, testing, and set up.

2. (1 point) The objective of depreciation accounting is to allocate the depreciable cost of an asset over its estimated useful life in a systematic and rational manner. This process matches the depreciable cost of the asset with revenues generated from its use. Depreciable cost is the capitalized cost less its estimated residual (salvage) value.

b. (1 point) The rationale for using accelerated depreciation methods is based on the following assumptions:

- An asset is more productive in the earlier years of its estimated useful life. Therefore, larger depreciation charges in the earlier years would be matched against the larger revenues generated in the earlier years.
- An asset may become technologically obsolete prior to the end of its originally estimated useful life. The risk associated with estimated long-term cash flows is greater than the risk associated with near-term cash flows. Accelerated depreciation recognizes this condition.

c. (2 points) Patrick should record depreciation expense to the date of disposal. Recording depreciation updates the carrying amount of the automobile. If the carrying amount of the automobile (capitalized cost less accumulated depreciation) differs from the cash proceeds from the disposal, a gain or loss results. Patrick should report gain or loss on disposal as part of income from continuing operations.

SOLUTION 6 (10 points total)

a. (3 points)

Villa Co.
BALANCE SHEET—LIABILITIES SECTION
December 31, 2002

Accounts payable	$ 35,000	
Accrued interest payable	20,000	[2]
Income taxes payable	180,000	[3]
Dividends payable	50,000	
Current portion, long-term debt	62,000	[1]
Total current liabilities	347,000	
Capital lease payable, less $62,000 current portion	318,000	[1]
Bonds payable	442,000	[2]
Deferred tax liability	90,000	[3]
Total liabilities	$1,197,000	

[1] $100,000 × 4.8 = $480,000
$480,000 − $100,000 = $380,000
$380,000 × 10% = $ 38,000
$100,000 − $38,000 = $ 62,000
$380,000 − $62,000 = $318,000

[2] 500K × 8% × ½ = 20K
440K × 10% × ½ = 20K
440K + (22K − 20K) = 442,000

[3] 600K × 30% = 180K
300K × 30% = 90K

b. (4 points) Villa should disclose the following information about the capital leases, either in the body of the financial statements or in the notes thereto:

- The gross amount of assets recorded under the capital leases, presented by major classes. This information may be combined with owned assets.
- Future minimum lease payments as of the balance sheet date, in the aggregate and for each of the five succeeding years.
- A general description of the leasing arrangement, including the existence and terms of renewal, escalation clauses, and restrictions imposed by the lease agreements.

Villa should disclose the following information about the bonds payable, either in the body of the financial statements or in the notes thereto:

- The face amount.
- The nature and terms of the bonds and a discussion of their credit and market risk, cash requirements, and related accounting policies.
- The fair value of the bonds and the method used to estimate their fair value. The price at which the bonds are trading is the most reasonable estimate of their fair value at December 31, 2002.

c. (3 points) Villa should account for each contingency in a slightly different way because the likelihood of Villa's incurring a loss differs in each situation.

For the toxic waste cleanup, a loss has been incurred. In the notes to its financial statements, Villa should disclose the nature of the loss on cleanup and indicate that an estimate of the loss, or range of the loss, cannot be made. No accrual should be made because the loss cannot be reasonably estimated and accrual of an uncertain amount would impair the integrity of the financial statements.

With regard to Clear's claim it is only reasonably possible, and not probable, that Villa will have to pay. Accordingly, Villa should not accrue the loss. Villa should disclose the existence and nature of Clear's claim in the notes to its financial statements. Disclosure should include an estimate of the potential range of loss.

Regarding the lack of rockslide insurance, no asset has been impaired and no liability has been incurred. Accordingly, Villa should not accrue a loss. Since the likelihood of a rockslide is remote, disclosure of the uninsured risk, while permitted, is not required.

APPENDIX B
PRACTICAL ADVICE

Your first step toward an effective CPA Review program is to **study** the material in this appendix. It has been carefully developed to provide you with essential information that will help you succeed on the CPA exam. This material will assist you in organizing an efficient study plan and will demonstrate effective techniques and strategies for taking the CPA exam.

SECTION ONE: GENERAL COMMENTS ON THE CPA EXAM

The difficulty and comprehensiveness of the CPA exam is a well-known fact to all candidates. However, success on the CPA exam is a **reasonable**, **attainable** goal. You should keep this point in mind as you study this appendix and develop your study plan. A positive attitude toward the examination, combined with determination and discipline, will enhance your opportunity to pass.

PURPOSE OF THE CPA EXAM

The CPA exam is designed as a licensing requirement to measure the technical competence of CPA candidates. Although licensing occurs at the State Board level, it is a uniform exam with national acceptance. Generally, passing the CPA exam in one jurisdiction allows a candidate to obtain a reciprocal certificate or license if they meet all the requirements imposed by the jurisdiction from which reciprocity is being sought.

State Boards also rely upon other means to ensure that candidates possess the necessary technical and character attributes, including interviews, letters of reference, affidavits of employment, ethics examinations, and educational requirements. Addresses of state boards are listed in this section of the **Practical Advice** appendix or (along with applicable links) on the web site of the National Association of the State Boards of Accountancy (http://www.nasba.org).

Generally speaking, the CPA exam is essentially an academic examination that tests the breadth of material covered by good accounting curricula. It also emphasizes the body of knowledge required for the practice of public accounting. It is to your advantage to take the exam as soon as possible after completing the formal education requirements. We also recommend that you study for the entire examination the first time you take it, since there is a **synergistic** learning effect to be derived through preparing for all four parts. That is, all sections of the exam share some common subjects (particularly Financial Accounting & Reporting, Accounting & Reporting, and Auditing); so as you study for one section, you are also studying for the others.

EXAMINATION SCHEDULE AND FORMAT

The CPA exam is given twice a year, on Wednesday and Thursday of the first week of May and November. AICPA-scheduled exam dates are May 8 and 9, 2002, and November 6 and 7, 2002. Unofficial projections for 2003 are May 7 and 8 as well as November 5 and 6. As the exam is becoming further computerized, projections past November 2002 are subject to greater uncertainty than in the past.

The four sections of the exam cover the following:

1. **Business Law & Professional Responsibilities**—This section covers the legal implications of business transactions generally confronted by CPAs, and the CPA's professional responsibility to the public and the profession (formerly covered in the Auditing section). This section's name is frequently abbreviated as BLPR. (3 hours)

2. **Auditing**—This section covers the generally accepted auditing standards, procedures, and related topics. The CPA's professional responsibility is no longer tested in this area. This section's name is frequently abbreviated as AUD. (4½ hours)

3. **Accounting & Reporting-Taxation, Managerial, and Governmental and Not-for-Profit Organizations**—This section covers federal taxation, managerial accounting, and accounting for governmental and nonprofit organizations. This section consists of multiple choice and other objective format questions only. This section has no essay questions or problems. This section's name is frequently abbreviated as ARE. (3½ hours)

4. **Financial Accounting & Reporting**—This section covers generally accepted accounting principles for business enterprises. This section's name is frequently abbreviated as FARE. (4½ hours)

The examination has the following formats and times:

Section	Format Multiple Choice	Format Other Objective Answer Formats	Format Essays or Problems	Day and Time			Duration	
BLPR	50-60%	20-30%	20-30%	Wed.	9:00	-12:00	3	hours
Auditing	50-60%	20-30%	20-30%	Wed.	1:30	- 6:00	4 1/2	hours
ARE	50-60%	40-50%	---	Thur.	8:30	-12:00	3 1/2	hours
FARE	50-60%	20-30%	20-30%	Thur.	1:30	- 6:00	4 1/2	hours
							15 1/2	hours

CONDITIONAL STATUS

You will receive four scores. A passing score for each section is 75. Individual Boards of Accountancy may grant conditional status to those candidates who receive a passing grade in some, but not all, sections. Some Boards of Accountancy grant conditional status to candidates who pass only one section, while other Boards require that at least two sections be passed before conditional status is awarded. Many Boards require a minimum grade in the sections failed to receive conditional credit for the sections passed. Candidates should check with their State Board of Accountancy concerning details on conditional status.

ATTORNEYS' WAIVER

Some Boards of Accountancy may waive the Business Law section for members of the state bar. Once again, candidates should check with their particular state Board of Accountancy concerning this matter.

WRITING SKILLS CONTENT

Answers to selected essay responses from Business Law & Professional Responsibilities, Auditing, and Financial Accounting & Reporting sections will be used to assess candidates' writing skills. Additional information regarding writing skills is included in the **Accounting for 5%** section of those volumes. Five percent of the points available on each of these sections will be allocated to writing skills. Effective writing skills include the following six characteristics:

1. Coherent organization
2. Conciseness
3. Clarity
4. Use of standard English
5. Responsiveness to the requirements of the question
6. Appropriateness for the reader

REFERENCE MATERIALS

All the material you need to review to pass the CPA exam is in your Bisk Education *CPA Comprehensive Review* texts! However, should you desire more detailed coverage in any area, you should consult the actual promulgations. Individual copies of recent pronouncements are available from the FASB or AICPA. To order materials from the **FASB** or **AICPA** contact:

FASB Order Department
P.O. Box 5116
Norwalk, CT 06856-5116
Telephone (203) 847-0700

AICPA Order Department
P.O. Box 1003
New York, NY 10108-1003
Telephone (800) 334-6961
www.aicpa.org

The FASB offers a student discount that varies depending on the publication. The AICPA offers a 30% educational discount, which students may claim by submitting proof of their eligibility (e.g., copy of ID card or teacher's letter). AICPA members get a 20% discount and delivery time is speedier because members may order by phone.

THE NONDISCLOSED EXAM

The Uniform CPA Examination is nondisclosed. This means that candidates are not allowed to keep (or receive) their examination booklets after the test. Candidates are also required to sign a statement of confidentiality in which they promise not to reveal questions or answers. After the exam, only the Institute will have access to the tests themselves. (The AICPA releases a small number of questions with unofficial answers from each nondisclosed exam.) Bisk Education's editors will continue to update our diagnostic tests for your convenience, with questions based upon the representative items, items from previously disclosed tests, and the teaching expertise of our editors.

BACKGROUND

The AICPA made this change (beginning May 1996), in order to increase consistency, facilitate possible future computer administration of the test, and improve examination quality by pretesting questions. Because the examination is no longer completely changed every year, statistical equating methods will be more relevant, and the usefulness of specific questions as indicators of candidates' knowledge can be tested.

EFFECTS ON TIME MANAGEMENT

Approximately 10% of the multiple choice questions in every section of every nondisclosed exam are questions that are being pretested. These questions are not included in candidates' final grades; they are presented only so that the Board of Examiners may evaluate them for effectiveness and possible ambiguity. The Scholastic Achievement Test and the Graduate Record Exam both employ similar but not identical strategies: those tests include an extra section that is being pretested, and test-takers do not know which section is the one which will not be graded. On the Uniform CPA Examination, however, the extra questions are mixed in among the graded questions. This makes time management even more crucial. Candidates who are deciding how much time to spend on a difficult multiple choice question must keep in mind that there is a 10% chance that the answer to the question will not affect them either way. Also, candidates should not allow a question that seems particularly difficult or confusing to shake their confidence or affect their attitude towards the rest of the test; it may not even count. This experimental 10% works against candidates who are not sure whether they have answered enough questions to earn 75%. Candidates should try for a safety margin, so that they will have accumulated enough correct answers to pass, even though some of their correctly answered questions will not be scored.

POST-EXAM DIAGNOSTICS

The AICPA Board of Examiners' Advisory Grading Service provides boards of accountancy with individual diagnostic reports for all candidates along with the candidates' grades. The accountancy boards may mail the diagnostic reports to candidates along with their grades. Candidates should contact the state board in their jurisdiction to find out its policy on this issue. A sample of a diagnostic report is in Section Five of this appendix. As before, grades are mailed approximately 90 days after the examination.

DISCUSSING THE EXAM

Remember that candidates are required to sign a statement of confidentiality in which they promise not to reveal questions or answers. Due to the nondisclosure requirements, Bisk Education's editors are no longer able to address questions about specific examination questions, although we continue to supply help with similar study problems and questions in our texts.

QUESTION RE-EVALUATION

Candidates who believe that an examination question contains errors that will affect the grading should fax their complaint to the AICPA Examinations Division, at (201) 938-3443, within 4 days after taking the examination. The Advisory Grading Service asks candidates to be as precise as possible about the question and their reason for believing that it should be re-evaluated, and, if possible, to supply references to support their position. Since candidates are no longer able to keep or discuss the examination questions, it is important to remember as much detail as possible about a disputed question.

STATE BOARDS OF ACCOUNTANCY

Certified Public Accountants are licensed to practice by individual State Boards of Accountancy. Application forms and requirements to sit for the CPA exam should be requested from your individual State Board. IT IS EXTREMELY IMPORTANT THAT YOU COMPLETE THE APPLICATION FORM CORRECTLY AND RETURN IT TO YOUR STATE BOARD BEFORE THE SPECIFIED DEADLINE. Errors and/or delays may result in the rejection of your application. Be extremely careful in filling out the application and be sure to enclose all required materials. In many states, applications must be received by the State Board at least ninety days before the examination date. Requirements as to education, experience, internship, and other matters vary. If you have not already done so, take a moment to call the appropriate State Board for specific and current requirements. Complete the application in a timely manner. Some states arrange for an examination administrator, such CPA Examination Services [a division of the National Association of State Boards of Accountancy (NASBA), (800) CPA-EXAM (272-3926)] or Continental Examination Services [(800) 717-1201], to handle candidate registration, examination administration, etc.

It may be possible to sit for the exam in another state as an out-of-state candidate. Candidates wishing to do so should also contact the State Board of Accountancy in the state where they plan to be certified. NASBA has links (**http://www.nasba.org**) to many state board sites.

Approximately one month before the exam, check to see that your application to sit for the exam has been processed. DON'T ASSUME THAT YOU ARE PROPERLY REGISTERED UNLESS YOU HAVE RECEIVED YOUR CANDIDATE ID NUMBER.

The AICPA publishes a booklet entitled *Information for CPA Candidates*, usually distributed by State Boards of Accountancy to candidates upon receipt or acceptance of their applications. To request a complimentary copy, contact your **State Board** or the **AICPA**, Examination Division, 1211 Avenue of the Americas, New York, NY 10036. The information contained in this booklet is also available on the AICPA's web site: www.aicpa.org.

CONTACTING YOUR STATE BOARD

CPA Examination Services, a division of the National Association of State Boards of Accountancy (NASBA) administers the examination for 25 states. Contact CPA Examination Services at (800) CPA-EXAM (272-3926), (615) 880-4250, or www.nasba.org.

CO	CT	DE	GA	HI	IA	IN	KS	LA	MA	ME	MI	
MO	NJ	NM	NY	OH	PA	PR	RI	SC	TN	VA	VT	WA

Continental Testing Services at (800) 717-1201 administers the examination for WI.

Following are the telephone numbers for the boards in the other states.

AK	(907) 465-2580	IL	(217) 333-1565	NH	(603) 271-3286
AL	(334) 242-5700	KY	(502) 595-3037	NV	(775) 786-0231
AR	(501) 682-1520	MD	(410) 333-6322	OK	(405) 521-2397
AZ	(602) 255-3648	MN	(651) 296-7937	OR	(503) 378-4181
CA	(916) 263-3680	MS	(601) 354-7320	SD	(605) 367-5770
DC	(202) 442-4461	MT	(406) 841-2388	TX	(512) 305-7850
FL	(352) 333-2500	NC	(919) 733-4222	UT	(801) 359-4417
GU	(671) 477-1050	ND	(800) 532-5904	VI	(340) 773-2226
ID	(208) 334-2490	NE	(402) 471-3595	WV	(304) 558-3557
				WY	(307) 777-7551

The web sites for the state boards that administer the exam themselves are listed below. Each address has www. as a prefix, except WY.

AK	dced.state.ak.us/occ/pcpa.htm	MT	discoveringmontana.com/dli/bsd
AL	asbpa.state.al.us	NE	nol.org/home/BPA
AZ	accountancy.state.az.us	NV	accountancy/state.nv.us
AR	state.ar.us/asbpa	NH	state.nh.us/accountancy
CA	dca.ca.gov/cba	NC	state.nc.us/cpabd
DC	dcra.org/acct/newboa.shtm	ND	state.nd.us/ndsba
FL	myflorida.com	OK	state.ok.us/~oab
GU	guam.net/gov/gba	OR	boa.state.or.us/boa.html
ID	state.id.us/boa	SD	state.sd.us/dcr/accountancy
IL	illinois-cpa-exam.com/cpa.htm	TX	tsbpa.state.tx.us
KY	state.ky.us/agencies/boa	UT	commerce.state.ut.us
MD	dllr.state.md.us/license/occprof/account.html	VI	usvi.org/dlca/liscensing/cpa.html
MN	boa.state.mn.us	WV	state.wv.us/wvboa
MS	msbpa.state.ms.us	WY	cpaboard.state.wy.us

The Bisk Education web site (**www.cpaexam.com**) has several links to state boards and NASBA. These numbers and addresses are subject to change without notice. Bisk Education doesn't assume responsibility for their accuracy.

TEN ATTRIBUTES OF EXAMINATION SUCCESS

1. **Positive Mental Attitude**
2. **Development of a Plan**
3. **Adherence to the Plan**
4. **Time Management**
5. **Knowledge**

6. **Examination Grading**
7. **Solutions Approach™**
8. **Examination Strategies**
9. **Focus on Ultimate Objective—Passing!**
10. **Examination Confidence**

We believe that successful CPA candidates possess these ten characteristics that contribute to their ability to pass the exam. Because of their importance, we will consider each attribute individually.

1. Positive Mental Attitude

Preparation for the CPA exam is a long, intense process. A positive mental attitude, above all else, can be the difference between passing and failing.

2. Development of a Plan

The significant commitment involved in preparing for the exam requires a plan. We have prepared a Study Plan in the preceding "Getting Started" section. Take time to read this plan. Whether you use our "Study Plan" or create your own, the importance of this attribute can't be overlooked.

3. Adherence to the Plan

You cannot expect to accomplish a successful and comprehensive review without adherence to your study plan.

4. Time Management

We all lead busy lives, and the ability to budget study time is a key to success. We have outlined steps to budgeting time in the **Personalized Training Plan** found in the "Getting Started" section.

5. Knowledge

There is a distinct difference between understanding the material and knowing the material. A superficial understanding of accounting, auditing, and business law is not enough. You must know the material likely to be tested on the exam. Your Bisk Education text is designed to help you acquire the working knowledge that is essential to exam success.

6. Examination Grading

An understanding of the CPA exam grading procedure will help you to maximize grading points on the exam. Remember that your objective is to score 75 points on each section. Points are assigned to individual questions by the grader who reads your exam. In essence, your job is to satisfy the grader by writing answers that closely conform to the grading guide. In Section Two, we explain AICPA grading procedures and show you how to tailor your answer to the grading guide and thus earn more points on the exam.

7. Solutions Approach™

The Solutions Approach™ is an efficient, systematic method of organizing and solving questions found on the CPA exam. This Approach will permit you to organize your thinking and your written answers in a logical manner that will maximize your exam score. Candidates who do not use a systematic answering method often neglect to show all their work on difficult problems or essays—work that could earn partial credit if it were presented to the grader in an orderly fashion. The Solutions Approach™ will help you avoid drawing "blanks" on the exam; with it, you always know where to begin.

Many candidates have never developed an effective problem-solving methodology in their undergraduate studies. The "cookbook" approach, in which students work problems by following examples, is widespread among accounting schools. Unfortunately, it is not an effective problem-solving method for the CPA exam or for problems you will encounter in your professional career. Our Solutions Approach™ teaches you to derive solutions independently, without an example to guide you.

Our **Solutions Approach™** and grader orientation skills, when properly developed, can be worth at least 10 to 15 points for most candidates. These 10 to 15 points can often make the difference between passing and failing.

The **Solutions Approach™** for objective questions, problems, and essays is outlined in Section Three. Examples are worked and explained.

8. Examination Strategies

You should be familiar with the format of the CPA exam and know exactly what you will do when you enter the examination room. In Section Four, we discuss the steps you should take from the time you receive the test booklet, until you hand in your answer sheet. Planning in advance how you will spend your examination time will save you time and confusion on exam day.

9. Focus on Ultimate Objective—Passing!

Your primary goal in preparing for the CPA exam is to attain a grade of 75 or better on all sections and, thus, **pass the examination**. Your review should be focused on this goal. Other objectives, such as learning new material or reviewing old material, are important only insofar as they assist you in passing the exam.

10. Examination Confidence

Examination confidence is actually a function of the other nine attributes. If you have acquired a good working knowledge of the material, an understanding of the grading system, a tactic for answering the problems or essays, and a plan for taking the exam, you can go into the examination room **confident** that you are in control.

SECTION TWO: EXAMINATION GRADING ORIENTATION

The CPA exam is prepared and graded by the AICPA Examinations Division. It is administered by the various State Boards of Accountancy.

An understanding of the grading procedure will help you maximize grading points on the CPA exam. Remember that your objective is to pass the exam. You cannot afford to spend time on activities that will not affect your grade, or to ignore opportunities to increase your points. The following material abstracted from the *Information for CPA Candidates* booklet summarizes the important substantive aspects of the Uniform CPA Examination itself and the grading procedures used by the AICPA.

SECURITY

The examination is prepared and administered under tight security measures. The candidates' anonymity is preserved throughout the examination and grading process. Unusual similarities in answers among candidates are reported to the appropriate State Boards.

OBJECTIVE QUESTIONS

Objective questions consist of four-option, multiple-choice questions and other objective answer formats, which include: yes-no, true-false, matching, and questions requiring a numerical response. Objective questions are machine graded. Thus, you will accomplish nothing (and only waste time) by writing explanations beside your answers—only the blackened response is considered by the optical scanner. It is also important to understand that there is **no grade reduction** for incorrect responses to objective questions—your total objective question grade is determined solely by the number of correct answers. Thus, you **should answer every question**. If you do not know the answer, make an intelligent guess.

There are two or three formats for questions on each section of the CPA exam. In the past, difficulty points were assigned to these parts as a means of curving the entire section. This no longer occurs. Instead, difficulty points are assigned to the exam as a whole, not to each individual question. The point to remember is to avoid getting "bogged down" on one answer. Move along and answer **all** the questions. This helps you avoid leaving questions unanswered or panic-answering questions due to poor budgeting of test time.

PROBLEMS AND ESSAY QUESTIONS

Problems and essay questions are graded by CPAs and AICPA staff members, using the following procedures as described in the *Information for CPA Candidates* booklet:

FIRST GRADING

The first grading is done by graders assigned to individual questions. For example, each problem and essay in the Financial Accounting & Reporting section will be graded by a different grader. A grader assigned to a single question, that will be graded during the full grading session of six or seven weeks, becomes an expert in the subject matter of the question and in the evaluation of the candidates' answers. Thus, grading is objective and uniform.

The purpose of the first grading is to separate the candidates' papers into three groups: obvious passes, marginal, and obvious failures.

SECOND GRADING

Upon completion of the first grading, a second grading is done by reviewers. Obvious passes and failures are subjected to cursory reviews as part of the grading controls. Marginal papers, however, receive an extensive review.

The graders who make the extensive reviews have had years of experience grading the CPA Examination. They have also participated in the development of the grading bases and have access to item analysis for objective questions, identifying concepts as discriminating (those included by most candidates passing the exam) or as rudimentary (those included by candidates both passing and failing the exam). An important indicator of the competence of the candidate is whether grade points were earned chiefly from discriminating concepts or from rudimentary concepts.

THIRD GRADING

After the papers have been through the second grading for all parts of the examination, the resultant grades are listed by candidate number and compared for consistency among subjects. For example, if a candidate passes two subjects and receives a marginal grade in a third, the marginal paper will receive a third grading in the hope that the candidate, now identified as possessing considerable competence, can have the paper raised to a passing grade by finding additional points for which to grant positive credit. This third grading is done by the section head or a reviewer who did not do the second grading of the paper.

FOURTH GRADING

The Director of Examinations applies a fourth grading to papers that have received the third grading but have grades that are inconsistent. The Director knows that the papers have already been subjected to three gradings, and that it would be difficult to find additional points for which the candidates should be given credit. Obviously, very few candidates are passed in this manner, but this fourth grading assures that marginal candidates receive every possible consideration.

Problem Example—Grading Guide

Points are assigned to Financial Accounting & Reporting problems on the basis of **check figures**. That is, the grader checks your answer against a list of key figures from throughout the unofficial answer. It is **extremely important** that you turn in all scratch sheets with supporting computations for practice problems. The grader will be able to give you credit for alternative methods of calculation if he or she can trace your answer. You may also receive partial credit, even if you have mathematical mistakes, if the grader can verify that your procedures were correct. Note that you need not include **all** possible check figures to receive full credit on a question. The total number of grading bases exceeds the point value of the question. For example, a 10-point question may have 16 or more grading bases. Thus, a candidate would not have to provide all the check figures to get the maximum available points. Conversely, a candidate cannot receive more points even if he or she provides more than 16 check figures.

To illustrate the grading procedure, we will develop a hypothetical grading guide for a question adapted from a past examination. We will assume that the question is worth 15 points, and each part is worth 5 points. Here is the question:

Example 1—Sample Problem

The Printing Company is listed on the New York Stock Exchange. The market value of its common stock was quoted at $10 per share at December 31, 20X7, and 20X6. Printing's balance sheet at December 31, 20X7, and 20X6, and statement of income and retained earnings for the years then ended are presented below.

Printing Company
BALANCE SHEET

	December 31,	
	20X7	20X6
Assets		
Current assets:		
Cash	$ 3,500,000	$ 3,600,000
Trading securities	13,000,000	11,000,000
Accounts receivable, net of allowance for doubtful accounts	105,000,000	95,000,000
Inventories, lower of cost or market	126,000,000	154,000,000
Prepaid expenses	2,500,000	2,400,000
Total current assets	250,000,000	266,000,000
Property, plant, and equipment, net of accumulated depreciation	311,000,000	308,000,000
Investments, at equity	2,000,000	3,000,000
Long-term receivables	14,000,000	16,000,000
Patents and other intangibles, net of accumulated amortization	13,000,000	15,000,000
Total assets	$590,000,000	$608,000,000
Liabilities and Stockholders' Equity		
Liabilities		
Current liabilities:		
Notes payable	$ 5,000,000	$ 15,000,000
Accounts payable and accrued expenses	63,500,000	76,000,000
Payments due within one year on long-term debt	6,500,000	7,000,000
Total current liabilities	75,000,000	98,000,000
Long-term debt	169,000,000	180,000,000
Deferred income tax liability	83,000,000	75,000,000
Total liabilities	$327,000,000	$353,000,000
Stockholders' Equity		
Common stock, par value $1.00 per share; authorized 20,000,000 shares; issued and outstanding 10,000,000 shares	10,000,000	10,000,000
5% cumulative preferred stock, par value $100.00 per share; $100.00 liquidating value; authorized 50,000 shares; issued and outstanding 40,000 shares	4,000,000	4,000,000
Additional paid-in capital	107,000,000	107,000,000
Retained earnings	142,000,000	134,000,000
Total stockholders' equity	263,000,000	255,000,000
Total liabilities and stockholders' equity	$590,000,000	$608,000,000

Printing Company
STATEMENT OF INCOME AND RETAINED EARNINGS

	Year ended December 31,	
	20X7	20X6
Net sales	$600,000,000	$500,000,000
Costs and expenses:		
Cost of goods sold	490,000,000	400,000,000
Selling, general and administrative expenses	73,000,000	66,000,000
Total costs and expenses	563,000,000	466,000,000
Income before income taxes	37,000,000	34,000,000
Income taxes	16,800,000	15,800,000
Net income	20,200,000	18,200,000
Retained earnings at beginning of period	134,000,000	126,000,000
Dividends on common stock	12,000,000	10,000,000
Dividends on preferred stock	200,000	200,000
Retained earnings at end of period	$142,000,000	$134,000,000

Required:

Based on the above information, compute (for 20X7 only) the following:

1. Current (working capital) ratio.
2. Quick (acid-test) ratio.
3. Number of days' sales in average receivables, assuming a business year consisting of 300 days and all sales on account.
4. Inventory turnover.
5. Book value per share of common stock.
6. Earnings per share on common stock.
7. Price-earnings ratio on common stock.
8. Dividend-payout ratio on common stock.

Unofficial Answer:

1. Current (working capital) ratio:

$$\frac{\text{Total current assets}}{\text{Total current liabilities}} = \frac{\$250,000,000}{\$\ 75,000,000} = \underline{3.33 \text{ to } 1}$$

2. Quick (acid-test) ratio:

$$\frac{\text{Total quick (acid-test) assets}}{\text{Total current liabilities}} = \frac{\$121,500,000}{\$\ 75,000,000} = \underline{1.62 \text{ to } 1}$$

3. Number of days' sales in average receivables:

$$\frac{\text{Average accounts receivable}}{\text{Sales on account} \div 300 \text{ business days}} = \frac{\$100,000,000}{\$\ \ \ 2,000,000} = \underline{50 \text{ days}}$$

4. Inventory turnover:

$$\frac{\text{Cost of goods sold}}{\text{Average inventories}} = \frac{\$490,000,000}{\$\ \ 140,000,000} = \underline{3.50 \text{ to } 1}$$

5. Book value per share of common stock:

$$\frac{\substack{\text{Total stockholders' equity less} \\ \text{liquidating value of preferred stock}}}{\substack{\text{Common shares issued and outstanding} \\ \text{at December 31, 20X7}}} = \frac{\$259,000,000}{10,000,000} = \underline{\$25.90}$$

6. Earnings per share on common stock:

$$\frac{\substack{\text{Net income less dividends} \\ \text{on preferred stock}}}{\substack{\text{Average common shares issued} \\ \text{and outstanding during 20X7}}} = \frac{\$20,000,000}{10,000,000} = \underline{\$2.00}$$

7. Price-earnings ratio on common stock:

$$\frac{\text{Market value of common stock}}{\text{Earnings per share on common stock}} = \frac{\$10.00}{\$\ 2.00} = \underline{5 \text{ to } 1}$$

8. Dividend-payout ratio on common stock:

$$\frac{\text{Dividends on common stock}}{\substack{\text{Net income less dividends on} \\ \text{preferred stock}}} = \frac{\$12,000,000}{\$20,000,000} = \underline{60\%}$$

The grading guide consists of a list of check figures from the unofficial answer. Each figure is assigned a point, or more than one point if it is particularly important or fundamental. A point is also given on many questions for neatness and clarity of answer (including the use of proper formats, schedules, etc.). A hypothetical grading guide for our sample question is illustrated below.

A grading guide similar to the one in Example 2 is attached to every candidate's paper, with the check figures or grading bases for each question. Each check figure in the answer increases the candidate's grade. The candidate's total grade for the question is easily determined by converting raw points, using a conversion chart. For example, a candidate who provides 14 of the 16 check figures for the questions would earn a grade of 9 for the answer.

Example 2—Grading Guide for Sample Problem

STATE _____

CANDIDATE NO. _____

	POINTS	KEY WORD CONCEPTS	POINTS	ANSWER
1.	1	Total current assets / Total current liabilities	1	3.33 to 1
2.	1	Total quick (acid-test) assets / Total current liabilities	1	1.62 to 1
3.	1	Average accounts receivable / Sales on account ÷ 300 business days	1	50 days
4.	1	Cost of goods sold / Average Inventories	1	3.50 to 1
5.	1	Total stockholders' equity less liquidating value of preferred stock / Common shares issued and outstanding at December 31, 20X7	1	$25.90
6.	1	Net income less dividends on preferred stock / Average common shares issued and outstanding during 20X7	1	$2.00
7.	1	Market value of common stock / Earnings per share on common stock	1	5 to 1
8.	1	Dividends on common stock / Net income less dividends on preferred stock	1	60%
Total	8		8	

GRADE CONVERSION CHART: POINTS TO GRADE

POINTS	1	2	3	4	5 6	7 8	9 10	11 12	13 14	15 16
GRADE	1	2	3	4	5	6	7	8	9	10

You should notice that the unofficial answer closely conforms to the grading guide, making the grader's task simple. In turn, the unofficial answer also conforms to the format of the question. That is, each answer is numbered and lettered to correspond to the requirements. This should be your standard format.

ESSAY QUESTION EXAMPLE—GRADING GUIDE

Points are assigned to essay questions on the basis of **key concepts**. A key concept is an idea, thought, or option that can be clearly defined and identified. Through a grading of sample papers, a list of key concepts related to each question is accumulated. These key concepts become the **grading bases** for the question. That is, your answer will be scored according to the number of key concepts it contains. Note that you need not include **all** possible key concepts to receive full credit on a question. The total number of grading bases exceeds the point value of the question. For example, a 10-point question may have 15 or more grading bases. Thus, a candidate would not have to provide all the key concepts to get the maximum available points. Conversely, a candidate cannot receive more points even if he or she provides more than 10 key concepts.

To illustrate the grading procedure and the importance of using key concepts in your answers, we will develop a hypothetical grading guide for a question adapted from a past Auditing exam. We will assume that the entire question is worth 10 points.

Example 3—Sample Essay

Taylor Company, a household appliances dealer, purchases its inventories from various suppliers. Taylor has consistently stated its inventories at the lower of cost **(FIFO)** or market.

Required:

a. Taylor is considering alternate methods of accounting for the cash discounts it takes when paying its suppliers promptly. From a theoretical standpoint, discuss the acceptability of each of the following methods:

1. Financial income when payments are made.
2. Reduction of cost of goods sold for period when payments are made.
3. Direct reduction of purchase cost.

b. Identify the effects on both the balance sheet and the income statement of using the LIFO inventory method instead of the FIFO method over a substantial time period when purchase prices of household appliances are rising. State why these effects take place.

c. Why is the lower of cost-or-market rule used for valuing inventories when the FIFO method is used?

Unofficial Answer to Part b

Now let's look at the unofficial answer to one part of the question, Part **b**. Notice that we have underlined the key concepts in the answer. Later, as we develop a grading guide for the answer, you will see the importance of using key concepts to tailor your answer to parallel the grading guide.

b. Inventories would be **lower** using the LIFO inventory method instead of the FIFO method over a substantial time period when purchase prices of household appliances are rising, because the **inventories are at the oldest (lower) purchase prices** instead of the most recent (higher) purchase prices. Correspondingly, the **cost of goods sold would be higher** because the cost of goods sold is at **more recent** (higher) purchase prices instead of older (lower) purchase prices. Consequently, **net income and retained earnings would be lower**.

More cash flow would generally be available using the LIFO inventory method instead of the **FIFO** method because **taxable income is decreased**, resulting generally in accrual and payment of lower income taxes. Correspondingly, **Income tax expense would generally be lower**.

The grading guide consists of a list of the key concepts relevant to the question, both in key word form and in a detailed phrase. Each concept is assigned a point (more than one point if it is particularly important or fundamental). A point is also given on many questions for neatness and clarity of answer (including the use of proper formats, schedules, etc.). A hypothetical grading guide for our sample question is illustrated below.

Example 4—Grading Guide for Sample Essay Part b.

STATE_____

CANDIDATE NO._____

POINTS   KEY WORD CONCEPTS

2	Inventories lower:
1	Inventories at lower (oldest) purchase prices.
2	CGS higher:
1	CGS at higher (most recent) purchase prices
1	Net income and R/E lower
1	Greater cash flow:
1	Decrease in taxable income results in lower income tax expense.
_1_	Neatness and clarity
10	

GRADE CONVERSION CHART: POINTS TO GRADE

GRADE	1	2	3	4	5
POINTS	1	2 3	4 5	6 7	8 9 10

IMPORTANCE OF KEY CONCEPTS

A grading guide similar to the one in Example 4 is attached to every candidate's paper, with the key concepts or grading bases for each question. On the first grading, answers may be scanned first for key words, then read carefully to ascertain that no key concepts were overlooked. Each key concept in the answer increases the candidate's grade. The candidate's total grade for the question is easily determined by converting raw points, using a conversion chart. For example, a candidate who earns 8 of the 10 possible points for key concepts for this question would earn a grade of 5 for the answer. The process is repeated by the second grader and subsequent graders if necessary (i.e., borderline papers).

The point you should notice is that **key concepts earn points**. The unofficial answer closely conforms to the grading guide, making the grader's task simple. In turn, the unofficial answer also conforms to the format of the question. That is, each answer is numbered and lettered to correspond to the requirements. This should be your standard format.

There are two more points you should observe as you study the unofficial answer for our example. First, the answer is written in standard English, with clear, concise sentences and short paragraphs. A simple listing of key words is **unacceptable**; the concepts and their interrelationships must be logically presented. Secondly, remember that the unofficial answer represents the most acceptable solution to a question. This is not to say, however, that alternative answers are not considered. During the accumulation of grading bases, many concepts are added to the original "correct answer." Additionally, a paper that is near the passing mark receives a third (and perhaps fourth) grading, at which time individual consideration is given to the merits of each answer.

Parenthetically, we should mention that all the Bisk Education *CPA Review* essays and problems are solved using the unofficial AICPA answers. Thus, you have ample opportunity to accustom yourself to the favored answer format.

IMPORTANCE OF WRITING SKILLS

At least two essay responses will be graded for writing skills. A response is defined as a part of an essay. Therefore, if an essay question has a **Part a** and a **Part b,** it has two responses. The two responses graded for writing skills may be from the same question or from different questions. Either way, they will be totally independent topics requiring different technical knowledge. Five percent of the candidate's grade for the essay portion of the exam will be allocated to writing skills. For more coverage of this area, refer to the section of your book entitled **Accounting for 5%**.

GRADING IMPLICATIONS FOR CPA CANDIDATES

To summarize this review of the AICPA's grading procedure, we can offer the following conclusions that will help you to **satisfy the grader** and maximize your score:

1. Attempt an answer on every question.

2. Do not explain answers to multiple choice questions or other objective answer formats.

3. Respond directly to the requirements of the questions.

4. Use of a well-chosen example is an easy way of expressing an understanding of the subject or supporting a conclusion.

5. Use schedules and formats favored by the AICPA examiners.

6. Answer all requirements.

7. Develop a **Solutions Approach™** to each question type.

8. Essay questions:

   Label your solutions parallel to the requirements.

   Offer reasons for your conclusions.

   Emphasize key words by underlining them.

   Separate grading concepts into individual sentences or paragraphs.

   Do **not** present your answer in outline format.

9. Allocate your examination time based on AICPA point value.

10. Write neatly and legibly to avoid demerits.

_____

SECTION THREE: THE SOLUTIONS APPROACH™

The **Bisk Education Solutions Approach™** is an efficient, systematic method of organizing and solving questions found on the CPA exam. Remember that all the knowledge in the world is worthless unless you can get it down on paper. Conversely, a little knowledge can go a long way if you use a proper approach. The **Solutions Approach™** was developed by our Editorial Board in 1971; all subsequently developed stereotypes trace their roots from the original "Approach" that we formulated. Our **Solutions Approach™** and grader orientation skills, when properly developed, can be worth at least 10 to 15 points for most candidates. These 10 to 15 points often make the difference between passing and failing.

We will suggest a number of steps for deriving a solution that will help maximize your grade on the exam. Although you should remember the important steps in our suggested approach, don't be afraid to adapt these steps to your own taste and requirements. When you work the questions at the conclusion of each chapter, make sure you use your variation of the **Solutions Approach™**. It is also important for you to attempt to pattern the organization and format of your written solution to the unofficial answer reprinted after the text of the questions. However, DO NOT CONSULT THE UNOFFICIAL ANSWER UNTIL YOU FINISH THE QUESTION. The worst thing you can do is look at old questions and then turn to the answer without working the problem. This will build false confidence and provide **no** skills in developing a **Solutions Approach™**. Therefore, in order to derive the maximum number of points from an essay solution, you should **first** apply the **Solutions Approach™** to reading and answering the question, and **secondly**, write an essay answer using an organization and format identical to that which would be used by the AICPA in writing the unofficial answer to that essay question.

Solutions Approach™ for Problems

Our **six steps** are as follows:

1. Scan the text of the problem. Determine the particular topic area. Do not write anything anywhere—simply **scan**.
2. Study the problem requirements and obtain a clear understanding of what is required. **Underline** specific requirements.
3. Visualize the solution format and plan how you are going to work the problem before you start. **Know** the types of schedules and formats used by the AICPA in their unofficial answers.
4. Carefully study the text of the problem. Underline important data. Perform intermediate calculations, such as depreciation schedules and interest calculations, that will be used in your final solution.
5. Prepare the solution in a neat and orderly fashion. Clearly label computations, intermediary solutions, assumptions made, and supporting schedules.
6. Proofread and edit your solution, looking for math errors and unreasonable results. Be careful of changing things during the last few minutes of the exam; your first impressions are often correct.

To illustrate how the **Solutions Approach™** can be applied to a computational problem, we want to consider a problem adapted from a past examination. The problem appears in Example 5 and the unofficial answer appears in Example 6.

Example 5—Sample Problem (Estimated time—40 to 50 minutes)

Kern Inc. had the following long-term receivable account balances at December 31, 2002:

Note receivable from the sale of an idle building	$750,000
Note receivable from an officer	200,000

Transactions and other information relating to Kern's long-term receivables follows:

- The $750,000 note receivable is dated May 1, 2002, bears interest at 9%, and represents the balance of the consideration Kern received from the sale of its idle building to Able Co. Principal payments of $250,000 plus interest are due annually beginning May 1, 2003. Able made its first principal and interest payment on May 1, 2003. Collection of the remaining note installments is reasonably assured.

- The $200,000 note receivable is dated December 31, 2000, bears interest at 8%, and is due on December 31, 2005. The note is due from Frank Black, president of Kern Inc., and is collateralized by 5,000 shares of Kern's common stock. Interest is payable annually on December 31, and all interest payments were made through December 31, 2003. The quoted market price of Kern's common stock was $45 per share on December 31, 2003.

- On April 1, 2003, Kern sold a patent to Frey Corp. in exchange for a $100,000 noninterest bearing note due on April 1, 2005. There was no established exchange price for the patent, and the note had no ready market. The prevailing interest rate for this type of note was 10% at April 1, 2003. The present value of $1 for two periods at 10% is 0.826. The patent had a carrying amount of $40,000 at January 1, 2003, and the amortization for the year ended December 31, 2003 would have been $8,000. Kern is reasonably assured of collecting the note receivable from Frey.

- On July 1, 2003, Kern sold a parcel of land to Barr Co. for $400,000 under an installment sale contract. Barr made a $120,000 cash down payment on July 1, 2003, and signed a four-year 10% note for the $280,000 balance. The equal annual payments of principal and interest on the note will be $88,332, payable on July 1 of each year from 2004 through 2007. The fair value of the land at the date of sale was $400,000. The cost of the land to Kern was $300,000. Collection of the remaining note installments is reasonably assured.

Required:

Prepare the following and show supporting computations:

a. Long-term receivables section of Kern's December 31, 2003, balance sheet.

b. Schedule showing current portion of long-term receivables and accrued interest receivable to be reported in Kern's December 31, 2003, balance sheet.

c. Schedule showing interest revenue from long-term receivables and gains recognized on sale of assets to be reported in Kern's 2003 income statement.

APPLYING THE SOLUTIONS APPROACH™

In **Step 1**, you quickly scan the text of the problem: You will ascertain that it is a note receivable problem. You will also get a general idea of the type of information given.

In **Step 2**, you study the requirements to determine exactly what is called for. As we have said before, this step is extremely important in computational problems since you do not want to do more work than you have to. You should read all of the requirements so you can see how they relate. However, in working the problem, you will have to concentrate on individual requirements.

In **Step 3**, you visualize the format of your solution and plan the steps you will go through.

In **Step 4**, you return to the text and read it carefully, looking for the information you need. For example, in **Part a** you know that you need all the long-term receivables at the balance sheet date. Knowing what you need makes it easier to read the text and to make the intermediate calculations you will need for your solution. Underline important data.

In **Step 5**, you prepare the solution in a format similar to the unofficial answer. Note the clarity of the answer. The grader can easily follow it through. However, remember that whoever prepared the unofficial answer did not do so under examination conditions. Given plenty of time, you too could present your solution in that manner. However, because you will not have the time, your primary goal should be to make your answer resemble and contain, as nearly as possible, the form and content of the unofficial answer. This is why we emphasize that you must practice developing a Solutions Approach under strict examination conditions in advance of the exam.

Even though you will be pressed for time, you should still strive for clarity. Abbreviations will help. For example, you may want to abbreviate note receivable as "NR" or "Long-term portion of 9% note receivable" could be abbreviated "LT portion 9% NR @ 12/31/03." If you think there is any chance the grader may not understand an abbreviation you use, you should define it, possibly at the top or bottom of the page, and reference this definition the first time you use the abbreviation in each answer.

Finally, note how the unofficial answers explain the computations. For example, in this solution, the actual computations used to arrive at the required answers are listed. It is very important that you give the grader every opportunity to give credit for all your work.

In **Step 6**, you should review your solution for obvious errors or omissions. For example, you may have forgotten to answer the last requirement or forgotten to label your calculations.

Example 6—Sample Problem Unofficial Answer

a.

Kern Inc.
LONG-TERM RECEIVABLES SECTION OF BALANCE SHEET
December 31, 2003

9% note receivable from sale of idle building, due in annual installments of $250,000 to May 1, 2005, less current Installment	$250,000	[1]
8% note receivable from officer, due December 31, 2005, collateralized by 5,000 shares of Kern Inc. common stock with a fair value of $225,000	200,000	
Noninterest bearing note from sale of patent, net of 10% imputed interest, due April 1, 2005	88,795	[2]
Installment contract receivable, due in annual installments of $88,332 to July 1, 2007, less current installment	219,668	[3]
Total long-term receivables	$758,463	

b.

Kern Inc.
SELECTED BALANCE SHEET ACCOUNTS
December 31, 2003

Current portion of long-term receivables:		
Note receivable from sale of idle building	$250,000	[1]
Installment contract receivable	60,332	[3]
Total	$310,332	
Accrued interest receivable:		
Note receivable from sale of idle building	$ 30,000	[4]
Installment contract receivable	14,000	[5]
Total	$ 44,000	

c.

Kern Inc.
INTEREST REVENUE FROM LONG-TERM RECEIVABLES
AND GAINS RECOGNIZED ON SALE OF ASSETS
For the year ended December 31, 2003

Interest revenue:

Note receivable from sale of idle building	$ 52,500	[6]
Note receivable from sale of patent	6,195	[2]
Note receivable from officer	16,000	[7]
Installment contract receivable from sale of land	14,000	[5]
Total interest revenue	$ 88,695	

Gains recognized on sale of assets:

Patent		
Land	$ 44,600	[8]
	100,000	[9]
Total gains recognized	$144,600	

Explanation of Amounts:

[1] Long-term portion of 9% note receivable at 12/31/03

Face amount, 5/1/02	$ 750,000
Less installment received 5/1/03	(250,000)
Balance, 12/31/03	500,000
Less installment due 5/1/04	(250,000)
Long-term portion, 12/31/03	$ 250,000

[2] Noninterest bearing note, net of imputed interest at 12/31/03

Face amount, 4/1/03	$ 100,000
Less imputed interest [$100,000 – $82,600 ($100,000 x 0.826)]	(17,400)
Balance, 4/1/03	82,600
Add interest earned to 12/31/03 [$82,600 x 10% x 9/12]	6,195
Balance, 12/31/03	$ 88,795

[3] Long-term portion of installment contract receivable at 12/31/03

Contract selling price, 7/1/03	$ 400,000
Less cash down payment	(120,000)
Balance, 12/31/03	280,000
Less installment due 7/1/04 [$88,332 – $28,000 ($280,000 x 10%)]	(60,332)
Long-term portion, 12/31/03	$ 219,668

[4] Accrued interest—note receivable, sale of idle building at 12/31/03

Interest accrued from 5/1 to 12/31/03 [$500,000 x 9% x 8/12]	$ 30,000

[5] Accrued interest—installment contract at 12/31/03

Interest accrued from 7/1 to 12/31/03 [$280,000 x 10% x 6/12]	$ 14,000

[6] Interest revenue—note receivable, sale of idle building, for 2003

Interest earned from 1/1 to 5/1/03 [$750,000 x 9% x 4/12]	$ 22,500
Interest earned from 5/1 to 12/31/03 [$500,000 x 9% x 8/12]	30,000
Interest revenue	$ 52,500

[7] Interest revenue—note receivable, officer, for 2003

Interest earned 1/1 to 12/31/03 [$200,000 x 8%]	$ 16,000

[8] Gain recognized on sale of patent

Stated selling price		$ 100,000
Less imputed interest		(17,400) [2]
Actual selling price		82,600
Less cost of patent (net)		
Carrying amount 1/1/03	$ 40,000	
Less amortization 1/1 to 4/1/03 [$8,000 x 1/4]	(2,000)	(38,000)
Gain recognized		$ 44,600

[9] Gain recognized on sale of land

Selling price	$ 400,000
Less cost	(300,000)
Gain recognized	$ 100,000

Solutions Approach™ for Essay Questions

Our **six steps** are as follows:

1. Scan the text of the question for an overview of the subject area and content of the question.
2. Study the question requirements slowly and thoroughly. Underline portions of the requirements as needed.
3. Visualize the unofficial answer format based on the requirements of the question.
4. Carefully study the text of the question. Underline important data.
5. Outline the solution in key words and phrases. Be sure to respond to the requirements, telling the grader only what he or she needs to know. You must explain the reasons for your conclusions.
6. Write the solution in the proper format based upon your key word outline. Write legibly in concise, complete sentences. Do not forget to proofread and edit your solution.

To illustrate the Solutions Approach™ for essay questions, we have adapted a question from a past examination. Key words in the solution are underlined.

Example 7—Sample Essay

Bristol Company purchased land as a site for construction of a factory. Outside contractors were engaged to:

- Construct the factory.
- Grade and pave a parking lot adjacent to the factory for the exclusive use of the factory workers.

Operations at the new location began during the year and normal factory maintenance costs were incurred after production began.

Required:

a. Distinguish between capital and revenue expenditures.

b. Indicate how expenditures for each of the following should be accounted for and reported by Bristol at the time incurred and in subsequent accounting periods.

1. Purchase of land.
2. Construction of factory.
3. Grading and paving parking lot.
4. Payment of normal factory maintenance costs.

Do not discuss capitalization of interest during construction in your response.

Let's look at the steps you go through to arrive at your solution:

In **Step 1**, you scan the question. Do not read thoroughly, simply get an overview of the subject area and content of the question. You notice the question addresses the acquisition costs of plant assets.

In **Step 2**, you study the question requirements thoroughly. **Part a** addresses capital and revenue expenditures in general, while **Part b** refers to individual expenditures. Underline key phrases and words.

In **Step 3**, you visualize the format of your solution. The solution will be in paragraph form. **Part a** will define capital and revenue expenditures and discuss the differences between the two. **Part b** will discuss each individual expenditure and describe how each should be accounted for.

In **Step 4**, you carefully study the text of the question, given the requirements you want to satisfy, i.e., read the question carefully, noting the individual expenditures. You should mark important information.

In **Step 5**, you outline your answer in keyword form. This will include a description of each type of expenditure and an explanation of their differences in **Part a** along with individual analysis of each requirement in **Part b** plus additional key concepts you want to include in your final answer.

Outline Answer

a.   Capital Expenditures—future periods
       Revenue Expenditures—current period only

b.   1.   Land
            Capitalize
                 Noncurrent Asset
                 Original Cost
                 Non-depreciable

       2.   Factory Construction
            Capitalize
            Depreciate over expected life
            Apply cost to inventory through Factory Overhead
            Classification
            Factory—noncurrent
                 Inventory—current
                 Cost of Sales—expense

       3.   Parking Lot
            Capitalize
            Depreciate over the shorter of factory life or parking lot life
            Apply depreciation to inventory via factory overhead
            Classification
                 Parking Lot improvements—Noncurrent
                 Inventory—current
                 Cost of Sales—expense

       4.   Factory Maintenance—Revenue Type expenditure
            "Factory Cost" to be added to inventory cost via overhead
            Inventory—current asset
            Cost of Sales—expense

In **Step 6**, you write your solution in a format similar to the unofficial answer. Notice how clear and concise the AICPA unofficial answers are. There is no doubt as to their decision or the reasoning supporting the decision. Notice also how they answer each requirement separately and in the same order as in the question. Be sure to proofread and edit your solution.

Example 8—Sample Essay Unofficial Answer

a.   Capital expenditures **benefit future periods**. Revenue expenditures **benefit the current period only**.

b.   1.   The **purchase price** of the **land** should be **capitalized**. The land should be shown as a **noncurrent asset** on the balance sheet at its **original cost** and is **not subject to depreciation**.

       2.   The cost of constructing the factory should be **capitalized** and **depreciated** over the expected life of the factory. The **depreciation should be added to cost of inventory, via factory overhead**, as goods are produced, and **expensed as cost of sales as goods are sold**. The factory expenditures, net of accumulated depreciation, should be shown as a **noncurrent asset** on the balance sheet. Inventory should be reported as a **current asset** on the balance sheet, and cost of sales should be reported as an **expense** on the income statement.

       3.   The cost of grading and paving the parking lot should be **capitalized** and **depreciated** over the expected life of either the factory or parking lot, **whichever is shorter**. The depreciation should be **added to cost of inventory**, via factory overhead, as goods are produced, and **expensed as cost of sales as goods are sold**. The land improvement expenditures, net of accumulated depreciation, should be shown as a **noncurrent asset** on the balance sheet. Inventory should be reported as a **current asset** on the balance sheet, and cost of sales should be reported as an **expense** on the income statement.

4.   The cost of maintaining the factory once production has begun is a **"revenue type" expenditure**. However, since it is a factory cost, it should be **added to cost of inventory, via factory overhead**, as goods are produced, and **expensed as cost of sales as goods are sold**. Inventory should be reported as a **current asset** on the balance sheet, and cost of sales should be reported as an **expense** on the income statement.

SOLUTIONS APPROACH™ FOR OBJECTIVE QUESTIONS

The **Solutions Approach™** is also adaptable to objective questions. We recommend the following framework:

1.   Read the "Instructions to Candidates" section on your particular exam to determine if the AICPA's standard is the same. Generally, your objective portion will be determined by the number of correct answers with no penalty for incorrect answers.

2.   Read the question carefully, noting exactly what the question is asking. Negative requirements are easily missed. Underline key words and note when the requirement is an exception (e.g., "except for...," or "which of the following does **not**..."). Perform any intermediate calculations necessary to the determination of the correct answer.

3.   Anticipate the answer by covering the possible answers and seeing if you **know** the correct answer.

4.   Read the answers given.

5.   Select the best alternative. Very often, one or two possible answers will be clearly incorrect. Of the other alternatives, be sure to select the alternative that **best answers the question asked**.

6.   Mark the correct answer on the examination booklet itself. After completing all of the individual questions in an overall question, transfer the answers to the machine readable answer sheet with extreme care. Before you hand in your answer sheet, **go back** and double check your answers—make sure the answer is correct and make sure the sequence is correct. The AICPA uses answer sheets with varying formats; it is extremely important to follow the correct sequence (across the sheet vs. down or vice versa). READ THE INSTRUCTIONS CAREFULLY.

7.   Answer the questions in order. This is a proven, systematic approach to objective test taking. You will generally be limited to a maximum of 2 minutes per multiple choice question. Under no circumstances should you allow yourself to fall behind schedule. If a question is too difficult, too long, or is a multiple question fact situation, be sure you remain cognizant of the time you are using. If after a minute or so you feel that it is too costly to continue on with a particular question, select the letter answer you tentatively feel is the best answer and go on. Return to these questions at a later time and attempt to finally answer them when you have time for more consideration. If you cannot find a better answer when you return to the question, use your preliminary answer because your first impressions are often correct. However, as you read other question(s), if something about these subsequent questions or answers jogs your memory, return to the previous tentatively answered question(s) and make a note of the idea for later consideration (time permitting).

A particularly challenging format is a group of objective questions based on one hypothetical situation. In this case, you should skim all the related questions (but not answer possibilities) before you begin answering, since an overall view of the problem will guide you in the work you do.

Note also that many incorrect answer choices are based on the erroneous application of one or more items in the text of the question. Thus, it is extremely important to **anticipate** the answer before you read the alternatives. Otherwise, you may be easily persuaded by an answer choice that is formulated through the incorrect use of the given data.

Let's consider a multiple choice question adapted from a past examination.

Example 9—Sample Objective Question

Jel Co., a consignee, paid the freight costs for goods shipped from Dale Co., a consignor. These freight costs are to be deducted from Jel's payment to Dale when the consignment goods are sold. Until Jel sells the goods, the freight costs should be included in Jel's

a. Cost of goods sold.
b. Freight-out costs.
c. Selling expenses.
d. Accounts receivable.

APPLYING THE SOLUTIONS APPROACH

Let's look at the steps you should go through to arrive at your objective question solution.

In **Step 1**, you must carefully read the "**Instructions**" that precede your particular objective CPA exam portion.

In **Step 2**, you must read the question and its requirements carefully. Look out for questions that require you to provide those options **not** applicable, **not** true, etc...

In **Step 3**, you must anticipate the correct answer **after** reading the question **but before** reading the possible answers.

In **Step 4**, you must read the answer carefully and select the alternative that best answers the question asked. Ideally, the best alternative will immediately present itself because it roughly or exactly corresponds with the answer you anticipated before looking at the other possible choices.

In **Step 5**, you select the best alternative. If there are two close possibilities, make sure you select the **best** one in light of the **facts** and **requirements** of the question.

In **Step 6**, you must make sure you accurately mark the **correct answer** in the proper sequence. If **anything** seems wrong, stop, go back and double check your answer sheet. As a fail safe mechanism, circle the correct letter on the exam sheet first, before you move it to the answer sheet.

In **Step 7**, you must make sure you answer the questions on the answer sheet in order, with due regard to time constraints.

Example 10—Sample Objective Question Solution

The answer is (d). The consignee will be reimbursed for the freight costs after the sale of the consignment goods by reducing the payment to the consignor. An amount that will be reimbursed in the future represents a receivable. The other answers are incorrect because an amount that will be reimbursed in the future should not be recorded as an expense.

BENEFITS OF THE SOLUTIONS APPROACH™

The **Solutions Approach™** may seem cumbersome the first time you attempt it; candidates frequently have a tendency to write as they think. It should be obvious to you that such a haphazard approach will result in a disorganized answer. The Solutions Approach™ will help you write a solution that parallels the question requirements. It will also help you recall information under the pressure of the exam. The technique assists you in directing your thoughts toward the information required for the answer. Without a Solutions Approach™, you are apt to become distracted or confused by details that are irrelevant to the answer. Finally, the Solutions Approach™ is a **faster** way to answer exam questions. You will not waste time on false starts or rewrites. The approach may seem time-consuming at first, but as you become comfortable using it, you will see that it actually saves time and results in a better answer.

We urge you to give the **Solutions Approach™** a good try by using it throughout your CPA review. As you practice, you may adapt or modify it to your own preferences and requirements. The important thing is to develop a system so that you do not approach exam questions with a storehouse of knowledge that you can not put down on paper.

SECTION FOUR: EXAMINATION STRATEGIES

The CPA exam is more than a test of your knowledge and technical competence. It is also a test of your ability to function under psychological pressure. You could easily be thrown off balance by an unexpected turn of events during the days of the exam. Your objective is to avoid surprises and eliminate hassles and distractions that might shake your confidence. You want to be in complete control so that you can concentrate on the exam material, rather than the exam situation. By taking charge of the exam, you will be able to handle pressure in a constructive manner. The keys to control are adequate preparation and an effective examination strategy.

OVERALL PREPARATION

Advance preparation will arm you with the confidence you need to overcome the psychological pressure of the exam. As you complete your comprehensive review, you will cover most of the material that will be tested on the exam; it is unlikely that an essay, problem, or series of objective questions will deal with a topic you have not studied. But if an unfamiliar topic **is** tested, you will not be dismayed because you have learned to use the **Solutions Approach™** to derive the best possible answer from the knowledge you possess. Similarly, you will not feel pressured to write "perfect" answers, because you understand the grading process. You recognize that there is a limit to the points you can earn for each answer, no matter how much you write.

The components of your advance preparation program have previously been discussed in this appendix. Briefly summarizing, they include:

1. Comprehensive review materials such as your Bisk Education CPA Review Program.

2. A method for pre-review and ongoing self-evaluation of your level of proficiency.

3. A study plan that enables you to review each subject area methodically and thoroughly.

4. A **Solutions Approach™** for each type of examination question.

5. An understanding of the grading process and grader orientation skills.

CPA EXAM STRATEGIES

The second key to controlling the exam is to develop effective strategies for the days during which the exam is given. Your objective is to avoid surprises and frustrations so that you can focus your full concentration on the questions and your answers.

You should be familiar with the format of the CPA exam and know exactly what you will do when you enter the examination room. Remember to carefully read the instructions on the cover page of the exam booklet AND for each problem. Disregarding the instructions may mean loss of points.

On the following pages, we discuss the steps you should take from the time you receive the test booklet until the time you hand in your booklet. Planning in advance how you will spend your examination time will save you time and confusion on exam day.

INVENTORY OF THE EXAMINATION

You should spend the first few minutes of the exam surveying the exam booklet and planning your work. **Do not** plunge head-first into answering the questions without a plan of action. You do not want to risk running out of time, becoming frustrated by a difficult question, or losing the opportunity to answer a question that you could have answered well. Your inventory should take no longer than five minutes. The time you spend will help you "settle in" to the examination and develop a feel for your ability to answer the questions.

1. Carefully read the "Instructions to Candidates" on the cover page.

2. Note the number of questions/problems on the cover page.

3. Once permission is given, go through the booklet and see what topics each question covers. Jot down the topics and devise a time schedule on the front cover, forming a table of contents.

ORDER OF ANSWERING QUESTIONS

Once you have completed your inventory of the exam, the next step is to develop an order for answering the objective questions and problems/essays. We recommend that you begin with the objective questions and then proceed to the problems/essays, beginning with the problem/essay that you feel is the least difficult.

Objective questions comprise a majority of the point value of each section. Because of their objective nature, the correct solution is listed as one of the answer choices. By solving these questions, not only do you gain confidence, but they often involve the same or a related topic to that covered in one of the problems or essays.

A very effective and efficient manner of answering the objective questions is to make **two passes** through the questions. On the first pass, you should answer those questions that you find the easiest. If you come across a question that you find difficult to solve, mark it and proceed to the next one. This will allow you to avoid wasting precious time and will enable your mind to clear and start anew on your **second pass**. On the second pass, you should go back and solve those questions you left unanswered on the first pass. Some of these questions you may have skipped over without an attempt, while in others you may have been able to eliminate one or two of the answer choices. Either way, you should come up with an answer on the second pass, even if you have to guess! After completing all of the individual questions in an overall question, transfer the answers to the machine readable answer sheet with extreme care. Simply make note of those questions that gave you difficulty and then proceed to the problems or essays.

Each **problem** should be worked through to the end using the **Solutions Approach™**. All schedules and calculations should be labeled before leaving the problem. However, leave a problem if you get stuck and return to it later with a fresh perspective.

Essay questions should be worked only through the key word outlines on the first pass. Then return to write your essay solution with a fresh look at the question.

EXAMINATION TIME BUDGETING

You must **plan** how you will use your examination time and adhere faithfully to your schedule. If you budget your time carefully, you should be able to answer all parts of all questions. To demonstrate a realistic time budget, refer again to the time parameters in the examination booklet.

The time limitation on the exam is 4½ hours for the Financial Accounting & Reporting section. You should subtract five minutes for your initial inventory on each section. Assuming you will use the **Solutions Approach™** and there will be two problem/essay type questions, your time budget may be similar to the one below. The actual exam may differ from this scenario so be sure to adjust your time budget to accommodate the number and type of questions asked.

		Minutes		
	FAR	ARE	Auditing	BLPR
Inventory examination	5	5	5	5
Answer objective questions	160	190	180	120
Write problem solutions	45			
Key word outline essays	20		20	20
Write essay solutions	25		50	20
Review answers	15	15	15	15
	270	210	270	180

Your objective in time budgeting is to avoid running out of time to answer a question. Work quickly but efficiently (i.e., use the **Solutions Approach™**). Remember that when you are answering an essay question, a partial answer is better than no answer at all. If you don't write anything, how can a grader justify giving you any points?

PAGE NUMBERING

Follow all instructions on the front of each exam section. Remember to arrange your answers in numerical order and number pages consecutively. The multiple choice answer sheet should be numbered page 1 and the numbering of your other pages should start with page 2. Start every essay question on a new sheet of paper and write on one side. For problem type questions, identify and include scratch pages. Write "continued" on the bottom of sheets when another answer sheet for the same problem or essay follows.

PSYCHOLOGY OF EXAMINATION SUCCESS

As stated previously, the CPA exam is in itself a physical and mental strain. You can minimize this strain by avoiding all unnecessary distractions and inconveniences during exam week. For example:

- **Make reservations for lodging well in advance**. It's best to reserve a room for Tuesday night so that you can check in, get a good night's sleep, and locate the exam site early the next morning.

- **Stick to your normal eating, sleeping, and exercise habits**. Eat lightly before the exam, and take small candies with you for quick energy. Watch your caffeine and alcohol intake. If you are accustomed to regular exercise, continue a regular routine during exam week.

- **Visit the examination facilities before the examination** and familiarize yourself with the surroundings.

- **Arrive early for the exam**. Allow plenty of time for unexpected delays. Nothing is more demoralizing than getting caught in a traffic jam ten minutes before the exam is scheduled to begin.

- **Avoid possible distractions**, such as friends and pre-exam conversation, immediately before the exam.

- In general, **you should not attempt to study on the nights before exam sessions**. It's better to relax—go to a movie, read a novel, or watch television. If you feel you must study, spend half an hour or so going over the chapter outlines in the text.

- **Don't discuss exam answers with other candidates**. Not only have you signed a statement of confidentiality, but someone is sure to disagree with your answer, and if you are easily influenced by his or her reasoning, you can become doubtful of your own ability. Wait and analyze the entire exam yourself after you have finished all sections.

AICPA General Rules Governing Examination

1. Read carefully the identification card assigned to you; sign it; make note of your number for future reference; when it is requested, return the card to the examiner. Only the examination number on your card shall be used on your papers for the purpose of identification. The importance of remembering this number and recording it on your examination paper correctly cannot be overemphasized. If a question calls for an answer

involving a signature, **do not** sign your own name or initials.

2. Seating during the exam is assigned according to your ID number in most states.

3. Answers must be submitted on paper furnished by the Board and must be completed in the total time allotted for each subject stated on the printed examinations. Begin your answer to each question on a separate page.

4. Answers should be written in pencil using No. 2 lead. **Neatness and orderly presentation of work are important**. Credit cannot be given for answers that are illegible.

5. Use a soft No. 2 lead pencil to blacken the spaces on the answer sheets for the objective-type questions.

6. Supplies furnished by the Board shall remain its property and must be returned whether used or not. You must hand in your printed examination booklet before leaving the examination room or your examination will not be graded.

7. Any reference during the examination to books or other matters or the exchange of information with other persons shall be considered misconduct sufficient to bar you from further participation in the examination.

8. The only aids candidates are permitted to have in the examination room are pens, pencils, and erasers. Calculators will be provided. Handbags and purses must be placed on the floor at candidates' locations during the entire time they are taking the exam. Briefcases, files, books, and other material brought to the examination site by candidates must be placed in a designated area before the start of the examination.

9. The fixed time for each session must be observed by all candidates. Each period will start and end promptly. It is the candidate's responsibility to be present and ready at the start of the period and to stop writing when told to do so.

10. Candidates arriving late should not be permitted any extension of time, but may be allowed to take the examination with proctor approval.

11. Smoking is allowed only in designated areas away from the general examination area.

12. No telephone calls are permitted during the examination session.

13. Only two time warnings are given: (1) thirty minutes prior to the end of session, and (2) five minutes prior to the end of session. (Additional warnings are not considered necessary.)

CPA Exam Week Checklist

WHAT TO PACK FOR EXAM WEEK:

1. CPA exam registration material.

2. Hotel confirmation.

3. Cash and/or a major credit card.

4. Alarm clock—Don't rely on a hotel wake-up call.

5. Comfortable clothing that can be layered to suit varying temperatures.

6. A watch.

7. Appropriate review materials, pencils, erasers, and pencil sharpener.

8. Healthy snack foods.

EVENINGS BEFORE EXAM SECTIONS:

1. Read through your Bisk Education chapter outlines for the next day's section(s).

2. Eat lightly and monitor your intake of alcohol and caffeine. Get a good night's rest.

3. Do **not** try to cram. A brief review of your notes will help to focus your attention on important points and remind you that you are well prepared, but too much cramming can shatter your self-confidence. If you have reviewed conscientiously, you are already well-prepared for the CPA exam.

THE MORNING OF EACH EXAM SECTION:

1. Eat a satisfying breakfast. It will be several hours before your next meal. Eat enough to ward off hunger, but not so much that you feel uncomfortable.

2. Dress appropriately. Wear layers you can take off to suit varying temperatures in the room.

3. Take ample supplies.

4. Arrive at the exam center thirty minutes early. Check in as soon as you are allowed to do so.

WHAT TO BRING TO THE EXAM:

1. ID card—This is your official entrance permit to the exam.

2. Several sharpened No. 2 pencils, erasers, and a small pencil sharpener. Some states provide pencils and do not allow candidates to bring their own.

3. A watch.

4. Tissues, small candies, gum, and aspirin.

5. Do **not** take articles that will not be allowed in the exam room. Highlighters are not allowed.

DURING THE EXAM:

1. Always read all instructions and follow the directions of the exam administrator. If you don't understand any written or verbal instructions, or if something doesn't seem right, ASK QUESTIONS. Remember that an error in following directions could invalidate your **entire** exam.

2. Budget your time. Always keep track of the time and avoid getting too involved with one question.

3. **Satisfy the grader**. Remember that the grader cannot read your mind. You must explain every point. Focus on key words and concepts. Tell the grader what you know, don't **worry** about any points you don't know.

4. Answer every question, even if you must guess.

5. Use **all** the allotted time. If you finish a section early, go back and reconsider the more difficult questions.

6. Check the answer sheet frequently to see that the number of each answer corresponds to the number of the question you intended. Many examinees get out of sequence on the answer sheet.

7. Stop working **immediately** when time is called. You do not want to risk being disqualified just to get one last answer recorded.

8. Get up and stretch if you feel sluggish. Walk around if you are allowed. Breathe deeply; focus your eyes on distant objects to avoid eye strain. Do some exercises to relax muscles in the face, neck, fingers, and back.

9. Take enough time to write neatly and organize your answer. Legible, well-organized answers will impress the grader.

10. Remember that you are well-prepared for the CPA exam, and that you can **expect to pass**! A confident attitude will help you overcome examination anxiety.

SECTION FIVE: CONTENT SPECIFICATION OUTLINE AND FREQUENTLY TESTED AREAS

The AICPA Board of Examiners has developed a **Content Specification Outline** of each section of the exam to be tested. These outlines list the areas, groups, and topics to be tested and indicate the approximate percentage of the total test score devoted to each area. The content of the examination is based primarily on the results of two national studies of public accounting practice and the evaluation of CPA practitioners and educators.

FINANCIAL ACCOUNTING & REPORTING.

I. **Concepts and Standards for Financial Statements (20%)**

A. Financial Accounting Concepts
B. Financial Accounting Standards for Presentation and Disclosures in General Purpose Financial Statements
   1. Consolidated and Combined Financial Statements
   2. Balance Sheet
   3. Statement(s) of Income, Comprehensive Income, and Changes in Equity Accounts
   4. Statement of Cash Flows
   5. Accounting Policies and Other Notes to Financial Statements
C. Other Presentations of Financial Data
   1. Financial Statements Prepared in Conformity With Comprehensive Bases of Accounting Other Than Generally Accepted Accounting Principles
   2. Personal Financial Statements
   3. Prospective Financial Information
D. Financial Statement Analysis

II. **Recognition, Measurement, Valuation, and Presentation of Typical Items in Financial Statements in Conformity With Generally Accepted Accounting Principles (40%)**

A. Cash, Cash Equivalents, and Marketable Securities
B. Receivables
C. Inventories
D. Property, Plant, and Equipment

E. Investments
F. Intangibles and Other Assets
G. Payables and Accruals
H. Deferred Revenues
I. Notes and Bonds Payable
J. Other Liabilities
K. Equity Accounts
L. Revenue, Cost, and Expense Accounts

III. **Recognition, Measurement, Valuation, and Presentation of Specific Types of Transactions and Events in Financial Statements in Conformity With Generally Accepted Accounting Principles (40%)**

A. Accounting Changes and Corrections of Errors
B. Business Combinations
C. Cash Flow Components—Financing, Investing, and Operating
D. Contingent Liabilities and Commitments
E. Discontinued Operations
F. Earnings Per Share
G. Employee Benefits
H. Extraordinary Items
I. Financial Instruments
J. Foreign Currency Transactions and Translation
K. Income Taxes
L. Interest Costs
M. Interim Financial Reporting
N. Leases
O. Nonmonetary Transactions
P. Quasi-Reorganizations, Reorganizations, and Changes in Entity
Q. Related Parties
R. Research and Development Costs
S. Segment Reporting

AICPA NONDISCLOSED EXAMINATION SUMMARY

The following chart compiled by information released by the AICPA, provides an analysis of the AICPA Content Specification Outline coverage for the Financial Accounting and Reporting section of the 1997, 1998, and 1999 Uniform CPA Examinations. (The chart does not include information on the 2000 and 2001 exams, as the AICPA did not release enough information to complete this chart.) This summary is intended only as a study aid and should **not** be used to predict the content of future examinations.

The percentages shown on the chart indicate the subject and format of questions on each examination. For the Financial Accounting and Reporting section, 60 percent of the questions are multiple choice, 20 percent of the questions are other objective answer format (OOAF), and 20 percent are essays.

The actual number of multiple choice questions asked for each area and group of the Content Specification Outline is also provided. For example, in the November 1999 exam, under the *Concepts and Standards for Financial Statements* area, there were 5 multiple choice questions asked; of those, 1 dealt with the *Financial Accounting Concepts* group.

Financial Accounting & Reporting	Multiple Choice						OOAFs						Essays					
	N99	M99	N98	M98	N97	M97	N99	M99	N98	M98	N97	M97	N99	M99	N98	M98	N97	M97
(section totals)	(60%) 60	(60%) 60	(60%) 60	(60%) 60	(60%) 60	(60%) 60	20%	20%	20%	20%	20%	20%	20%	20%	20%	20%	20%	20%
I. Concepts & Standards for Financial Statements	5%/5	7%/7	7%/7	11%/11	14%/14	0%/0	10%	5%	3%	2%	1%	5%	5%	8%	10%	7%	5%	15%
A. Financial Accounting Concepts	1	0	2	0	0	0					1%			4%			2%	5%
B. Financial Accounting Standards for Presentation & Disclosures in General Purpose Financial Statements	0	5	3	8	12	0	10%	5%	3%	2%		5%	5%	4%	10%	7%	3%	10%
C. Other Presentations of Financial Data	4	2	2	3	2	0												
D. Financial Statement Analysis	0	0	0	0	0	0												
II. Recognition, Measurement, Valuation, & Presentation of Typical Items in Financial Statements in Conformity With GAAP	25%/25	22%/22	17%/17	19%/19	24%/24	28%/28	10%	10%	12%	18%	0%	0%	8%	8%	10%	3%	12%	5%
A. Cash, Cash Equivalents, & Marketable Securities	2	2	1	2	0	3			1%									
B. Receivables	0	2	1	2	1	2		5%									7%	
C. Inventories	3	1	2	2	2	2		5%										
D. Property, Plant, & Equipment	3	2	2	0	3	3			5%	5%								
E. Investments	2	1	0	1	0	2												
F. Intangible & Other Assets	0	1	1	1	1	1									10%		2%	
G. Payables & Accruals	2	1	1	2	2	2	5%											
H. Deferred Revenues	2	1	1	0	1	1				4%								
I. Notes & Bonds Payable	2	2	0	0	3	2			6%									
J. Other Liabilities	2	3	1	0	1	2												
K. Equity Accounts	3	2	2	3	2	3										3%		
L. Revenue, Cost, & Expense Accounts	4	4	5	6	8	5	5%			9%			8%					

III. Recognition, Measurement, Valuation, & Presentation of Specific Types of Transactions & Events in Financial Statements in Conformity With GAAP

	MultipleChoice N99 30%/30	M99 31%/31	N98 36%/36	M98 (30%)/30	N97 (22%)/22	M97 (32%)/32	OOAFs N99 0%	M99 5%	N98 5%	M98 0%	N97 19%	N97 15%	Essays M99 4%	N99 10%	N99 4%	N98 0%	N98 10%	N97 3%	M97 0%
A. Accounting Changes & Corrections of Errors	2	2	0	2	0	2			1%		4%				1%				
B. Business Combinations	3	2	2	2	1	3						5%							
C. Cash Flow Components—Financing, Investing, & Operating	0	2	2	2	3	0											3%		
D. Contingent Liabilities & Commitments	2	1	1	0	1	2													
E. Discontinued Operations	1	2	2	2	2	2		5%						3%					
F. Earnings Per Share	2	0	2	2	0	2					2%	5%						3%	
G. Employee Benefits	2	3	5	3	1	4							1%	1%					
H. Extraordinary Items	1	2	3	2	3	3											3%		
I. Financial Instruments	2	3	2	1	1	0													
J. Foreign Currency Transactions & Translation	3	2	2	1	1	2													
K. Income Taxes	2	1	3	2	2	0						5%			2%				
L. Interest Costs	2	1	0	2	0	2			4%										
M. Interim Financial Reporting	2	2	2	2	0	2					3%						4%		
N. Leases	2	1	3	0	0	2					10%								
O. Nonmonetary Transactions	1	2	1	1	2	2													
P. Quasi-Reorganizations, Reorganizations, & Changes in Entity	1	1	1	1	1	0													
Q. Related Parties	2	2	2	2	2	2								3%					
R. Research & Development Costs	0	1	2	2	2	1								3%					
S. Segment Reporting	0	1	1	1	0	1													

The distribution of points on the 1996, 1997, 1998, and 1999 exams is summarized in the following chart. The Bisk Education chapters are indicated for each topic. Specific predictions about which topics will be stressed or the type of question used to test a specific topic are mere speculation and rather useless. (The examiners try not to make the exam predictable. Candidates must know roughly the same information regardless of the type of questions.) Don't waste time with mere speculation; instead, study and be prepared!

		Chapter	M96	N96	M97	N97	M98	N98	M99	N99	Ave.
I.A	Financial Accounting Concepts	1	3	2	5	3	2	2	4	1	2.8
I.B	Finl Acctg Stand for Pres & Discl in Gen Purp F/S	*	16	17	15	15	15	16	14	15	15.4
I.C	Other Presentations of Financial Data	11,18	1	1	0	2	3	2	2	4	1.9
I.D	Financial Statement Analysis	15	0	0	0	0	0	0	0	0	0
II.A	Cash, Cash Equiv & Marketable Securities	2	2	3	3	7	2	2	2	2	2.9
II.B	Receivables	2	***10	1	2	1	2	1	2	5	3.0
II.C	Inventories	3	3	10	2	2	2	2	6	3	3.8
II.D	Property, Plant & Equipment	4	2	4	3	3	5	2	2	3	3.0
II.E	Investments	6,19	2	2	2	2	1	10	1	2	2.8
II.F	Intangible & Other Assets	5	1	2	1	1	1	1	1	5	1.6
II.G	Payables & Accruals	7	2	1	2	2	2	1	1	2	1.6
II.H	Deferred Revenues	7,8,12	1	1	1	1	4	1	1	2	1.5
II.I	Notes & Bonds Payable	6,7	1	2	2	3	3	6	2	2	2.6
II.J	Other Liabilities	7	1	0	2	1	0	1	3	2	1.3
II.K	Equity Accounts	10,18	4	4	6	5	3	7	7	3	4.9
II.L	Revenue, Cost, & Expense Accounts	**	11	8	7	8	15	5	12	9	9.4
III.A	Accounting Changes & Corrections of Errors	11	6	1	2	4	2	1	3	2	2.6
III.B	Business Combinations	20	2	5	3	1	2	2	2	3	2.5
III.C	Cash Flow Comp - Fin, Invest, & Op	14	2	2	5	3	2	2	0	0	2.3
III.D	Contingent Liabilities & Commitments	7	0	2	2	1	3	1	1	2	1.5
III.E	Discontinued Operations	11	0	2	2	2	2	2	2	4	2.0
III.F	Earnings Per Share	15	1	1	2	2	2	2	5	2	2.1
III.G	Employee Benefits	7,9	11	6	9	4	3	5	3	2	5.4
III.H	Extraordinary Items	11	2	4	3	3	2	3	3	2	2.8
III.I	Financial Instruments	2	2	3	0	1	4	2	3	2	2.1
III.J	Foreign Currency Transactions & Translation	17	1	1	2	1	1	2	2	3	1.6
III.K	Income Taxes	13	4	4	5	2	2	3	2	2	3.1
III.L	Interest Costs	4,7	1	2	2	0	2	4	1	2	1.8
III.M	Interim Financial Reporting	11	2	1	2	3	2	2	2	2	2.0
III.N	Leases	8	1	2	2	10	4	3	1	2	3.1
III.O	Nonmonetary Transactions	4	2	2	2	2	1	1	2	1	1.6
III.P	Quasi-Reorg, Reorgan, & Changes in Entity	10	0	1	0	1	1	1	1	1	0.8
III.Q	Related Parties	8,11	2	1	2	2	2	2	2	2	1.9
III.R	Research & Development Costs	5	1	1	1	2	2	2	1	3	1.6
III.S	Segment Reporting	11	0	1	1	0	1	1	1	3	1.0
			100	100	100	100	100	100	100	100	100

*1,2,7,9,10,11,12,14,15,16,20

**2,3,4,5,7,8,11,12,15,19,20

***May 96 II.B. 10 points: Ch2=4,7=2,6=2,13=2. Not all the points were on the topic of receivables.

SECTION SIX:
AUTHORITATIVE PRONOUNCEMENTS CROSS-REFERENCES

FINANCIAL ACCOUNTING & REPORTING

Pronouncement	Bisk Education Chapter Number(s)	Accounting Research Bulletins
ARB 43	1, 2, 3, 7, 10, 11	Restatement and Revision of Accounting Research Bulletins
ARB 45	12	Long-Term Construction-Type Contracts
ARB 51	20	Consolidated Financial Statements

Pronouncement	Bisk Education Chapter Number(s)	Accounting Principles Board Opinions
APB 2 & 4	13	Accounting for the Investment Credit
APB 6	4, 10	Status of Accounting Research Bulletins
APB 9	1, 11	Reporting the Results of Operations
APB 10	1, 10, 11, 12	Omnibus Opinion—1966
APB 12	10	Omnibus Opinion—1967
APB 14	6	Convertible Debt and Debt Issued With Stock Purchase Warrants
APB 18	13, 19, 20	The Equity Method of Accounting for Investments in Common Stock
APB 20	11, 13	Accounting Changes
APB 21	2, 6, 7	Interest on Receivables and Payables
APB 22	10, 11, 16	Disclosure of Accounting Policies
APB 23	13, 17	Accounting for Income Taxes—Special Areas
APB 25	10	Accounting for Stock Issued to Employees
APB 26	6, 7	Early Extinguishment of Debt
APB 28	11, 13	Interim Financial Reporting
APB 29	4	Accounting for Nonmonetary Transactions
APB 30	1, 11	Reporting the Results of Operations—Reporting the Effects of Disposal of a Segment of a Business, and Extraordinary, Unusual, and Infrequently Occurring Events and Transactions

Pronouncement	Bisk Education Chapter Number(s)	Statements of Financial Accounting Standards
SFAS 2	5	Accounting for Research & Development Costs
SFAS 3	11	Reporting Accounting Changes in Interim Financial Statements
SFAS 4	6, 7, 11	Reporting Gains and Losses From Extinguishment of Debt
SFAS 5	7, 12, 20	Accounting for Contingencies
SFAS 6	7	Classification of Short-Term Obligations Expected to Be Refinanced
SFAS 7	11	Accounting & Reporting by Development Stage Enterprises
SFAS 13	8	Accounting for Leases
SFAS 15	7	Accounting by Debtors and Creditors for Troubled Debt Restructurings
SFAS 16	11	Prior Period Adjustments
SFAS 22	8	Changes in the Provisions of Lease Agreements Resulting From Refundings of Tax-Exempt Debt

Pronouncement	Bisk Education Chapter Number(s)	Statements of Financial Accounting Standards
SFAS 23	8	Inception of the Lease
SFAS 27	8	Classification of Renewals or Extensions of Existing Sales-Type or Direct Financing Leases
SFAS 28	8	Accounting for Sales With Leasebacks
SFAS 29	7	Determining Contingent Rentals
SFAS 34	4	Capitalization of Interest Cost
SFAS 37	13	Balance Sheet Classification of Deferred Income Taxes
SFAS 42	4	Determining Materiality for Capitalization of Interest Cost
SFAS 43	7	Accounting for Compensated Absences
SFAS 45	12	Accounting for Franchise Fee Revenue
SFAS 47	6, 7	Disclosure of Long-Term Obligations
SFAS 48	12	Revenue Recognition When Right of Return Exists
SFAS 49	7	Accounting for Product Financing Arrangements
SFAS 52	17	Foreign Currency Translation
SFAS 57	11	Related Party Disclosures
SFAS 58	4	Capitalization of Interest Cost in Financial Statements That Include Investments Accounted for by the Equity Method
SFAS 62	4	Capitalization of Interest Cost in Situations Involving Certain Tax-Exempt Borrowings and Certain Gifts and Grants
SFAS 64	6	Extinguishments of Debt Made to Satisfy Sinking-Fund Requirements
SFAS 68	5	Research and Development Arrangements
SFAS 78	6, 7	Classification of Obligations That Are Callable by the Creditor
SFAS 84	6	Induced Conversions of Convertible Debt
SFAS 86	5	Accounting for the Costs of Computer Software to Be Sold, Leased, or Otherwise Marketed
SFAS 87	9	Employers' Accounting for Pensions
SFAS 88	7, 9	Employers' Accounting for Settlements and Curtailments of Defined Benefit Pension Plans and for Termination Benefits
SFAS 89	1, 16	Financial Reporting and Changing Prices
SFAS 91	8	Accounting for Nonrefundable Fees and Costs Associated with Originating or Acquiring Loans and Initial Direct Costs of Leases
SFAS 94	19, 20	Consolidation of All Majority-Owned Subsidiaries
SFAS 95	1, 14	Statement of Cash Flows
SFAS 98	8	Accounting for Leases—Sale-Leaseback Transactions Involving Real Estate; Sales-Type Leases of Real Estate; Definition of the Lease Term; Initial Direct Costs of Direct Financing Leases
SFAS 102	14	Statement of Cash Flows—Exemption of Certain Enterprises and Classification Cash Flows From Certain Securities Acquired for Resale

Pronouncement	Bisk Education Chapter Number(s)	Statements of Financial Accounting Standards
SFAS 104	14	Statement of Cash Flows—Net Reporting of Certain Cash Receipts and Cash Payments and Classification of Cash Flows From Hedging Transactions
SFAS 106	9	Employers' Accounting for Postretirement Benefits Other Than Pensions
SFAS 107	2	Disclosures About Fair Value of Financial Statements
SFAS 109	13	Accounting for Income Taxes
SFAS 110	9	Reporting by Defined Benefit Pension Plans of Investment Contracts
SFAS 112	7	Employers' Accounting for Postemployment Benefits
SFAS 114	2	Accounting by Creditors for Impairment of a Loan
SFAS 115	2, 19, 20	Accounting for Certain Investments in Debt and Equity Securities
SFAS 116	4	Accounting for Contributions Received and Contributions Made
SFAS 118	2	Accounting by Creditors for Impairment of a Loan—Income Recognition and Disclosures
SFAS 121	4	Accounting for the Impairment of Long-Lived Assets and for Long-Lived Assets to be Disposed Of
SFAS 123	10	Accounting for Stock-Based Compensation
SFAS 126	2	Exemption from Certain Required Disclosures about Financial Instruments for Certain Nonpublic Entities
SFAS 128	15	Earnings Per Share
SFAS 129	10	Disclosure of Information about Capital Structure
SFAS 130	1, 2, 9, 11, 17	Reporting Comprehensive Income
SFAS 131	11	Disclosures about Segments of an Enterprise and Related Information
SFAS 132	9	Employers' Disclosures about Pensions and Other Postretirement Benefits
SFAS 133	2, 7, 11, 17	Accounting for Derivative Instruments and Hedging Activities
SFAS 137	2, 7, 11, 17	Deferral of Effective Date of FASB 133
SFAS 138	2	Accounting for Certain Derivative Instruments and Certain Hedging Activities (amends SFAS 133)
SFAS 140	2, 7	Accounting for Transfers and Servicing of Financial Assets and Extinguishments of Liabilities
SFAS 141	19, 20	Business Combinations
SFAS 142	5, 20	Goodwill and Other Intangible Assets
SFAS 143	7	Accounting for Asset Retirement Obligations
SFAS 144	4, 11	Accounting for Impairment or Disposal of Long-Lived Assets

Pronouncement	Bisk Education Chapter Number(s)	Statements of Financial Accounting Concepts
SFAC 1	1	Objectives of Financial Reporting by Business Enterprises
SFAC 2	1	Qualitative Characteristics of Accounting Information
SFAC 5	1	Recognition and Measurement in Financial Statements of Business Enterprises
SFAC 6	1, 10, 11	Elements of Financial Statements
SFAC 7	1	Using Cash Flow Information and Present Value in Accounting Measurements

Interpretation No.	Pronouncement	FASB Interpretations
No. 1	APB 20	Accounting Changes Related to the Cost of Inventory
No. 4	SFAS 2	Applicability of SFAS 2 to Business Combinations Accounted for by the Purchase Method
No. 6	SFAS 2	Applicability of SFAS 2 to Computer Software
No. 7	SFAS 7	Applying SFAS 7 in Financial Statements of Established Operating Enterprises
No. 8	SFAS 6	Classification of a Short-Term Obligation Repaid Prior to Being Replaced by a Long-Term Security
No. 14	SFAS 5	Reasonable Estimation of the Amount of Loss

Interpretation No.	Pronouncement	FASB Interpretations
No. 18	SFAS 28	Accounting for Income Taxes in Interim Periods
No. 19	SFAS 13	Lessee Guarantee of the Residual Value of Leased Property
No. 20	APB 20	Reporting Accounting Changes under AICPA Statements of Position
No. 21	SFAS 13	Accounting for Leases in a Business Combination
No. 24	SFAS 13	Leases Involving Only Part of a Building
No. 26	SFAS 13	Accounting for Purchase of a Leased Asset by the Lessee During the Term of the Lease
No. 27	SFAS 13 & APB 30	Accounting for a Loss on a Sublease
No. 28	APB 25	Accounting for Stock Appreciation Rights and Other Variable Stock Option or Award Plans
No. 30	APB 29	Accounting for Involuntary Conversions of Nonmonetary Assets to Monetary Assets
No. 34	SFAS 5	Disclosure of Indirect Guarantees of Indebtedness of Others
No. 35	APB 18	Criteria for Applying the Equity Method of Accounting for Investments in Common Stock
No. 37	SFAS 52	Accounting for Translation Adjustments Upon Sale of Part of an Investment in a Foreign Entity
No. 38	APB 25	Determining the Measurement Date for Stock Option, Purchase, and Award Plans Involving Junior Stock
No. 39	APB 10 & SFAS 105	Offsetting of Amounts Related to Certain Contracts
No. 41	APB 10	Offsetting of Amounts Related to Certain Repurchase and Reverse Repurchase Agreements
No. 42	SFAS 116	Accounting for Transfers of Assets in Which a Not-for-Profit Organization is Granted Variance Power
No. 44	APB 25	Accounting for Certain Transactions Involving Stock Compensation

---

From the AICPA's *Information for CPA Candidates*:

"Candidates are responsible for knowing accounting and auditing pronouncements, including the governmental and not-for-profit organizations areas, six months after a pronouncement's *effective* date, unless early application is permitted. When early application is permitted, candidates are responsible for knowing the new pronouncement six months after the *issuance* date. In this case, candidates are responsible for knowing both the old and new pronouncements until the old pronouncement is superseded.

APPENDIX C
ACCOUNTING FOR 5%

CONTENTS

INTRODUCTION

Before skipping this appendix, review at least the following writing samples and the "Writing an Answer to an Exam Question" starting on page C-5. Be sure to take the Diagnostic Quiz on C-8.

To assess candidates' writing skills, answers to selected essay responses from Business Law & Professional Responsibilities, Auditing, and Financial Accounting & Reporting sections will be used. Five percent of the points available on each of these sections will be allocated to writing skills. If you are not convinced that the five points in a section will make a significant difference, consider this: of the passing grades in each section, the vast majority are scored at 75, the minimum. For many candidates, therefore, writing skills may determine whether or not they pass a section.

If an essay question is divided into parts a, b, and c, for example, each of these parts is considered a separate response. It is possible that only one of these three parts will be graded for writing skills. However, at least two responses from each section will be used for this assessment. These responses may or may not be from the same question, but they will cover different technical areas. If a question is graded differently for writing skills, then the number of points allocated to the technical concepts of the essay is reduced so that the total number of points per question does not change.

The AICPA considers the following six characteristics to constitute effective writing and will make its evaluations of candidates' writing skills based on these criteria:

1. **COHERENT ORGANIZATION.** Does each paragraph begin with a topic sentence? Are ideas arranged logically, and do they flow smoothly?

2. **CONCISENESS.** Are complete thoughts presented in the fewest possible words?

3. **CLARITY.** Are sentences constructed properly? Are meanings and reasons clear? Are proper technical terminology and key words and phrases used?

4. **STANDARD ENGLISH.** Is your work free of nonstandard usage; that is, does it demonstrate proper spelling, punctuation, capitalization, diction, and knowledgeable usage choices?

5. **RESPONSIVENESS TO THE REQUIREMENTS OF THE QUESTION.** Make sure your answers respond directly to the question and are not broad discourses on the general subject.

6. **APPROPRIATENESS FOR THE READER.** If not otherwise mentioned in the question, you should assume that the reader is a CPA. Questions asking that you write something for a client or anyone else with less technical knowledge should be answered with that particular audience in mind.

> When writing your exam answers, write on **every other line only**. This will give you space for editing.

Accounting for 5% has been designed primarily to help CPA candidates polish their writing skills. Beyond this purpose, we hope that it will continue to serve as a useful reference in the future.

WRITING SKILLS SAMPLES

The following problems taken from past exams are answered in various ways to illustrate good, fair, and poor writing skills.

Essex Company has a compensation plan for future vacations for its employees. What conditions must be met for Essex to accrue compensation for future vacations?   FAR Problem—From Chapter 7—Liabilities

GOOD: Essex must accrue compensation for future vacations if all of the following criteria are met. Essex's obligation relating to employees' rights to receive compensation for future vacations is attributable to employees' services already rendered. The obligation relates to rights that vest or accumulate. Payment of the vacation benefits is probable. The amount can be reasonably estimated.

EXPLANATION: This essay is coherent, concise, and well organized. The first sentence uses the wording of the question to introduce the elements of the answer. Each point is then made clearly and concisely. There are no unnecessary words or elements. The language and vocabulary are appropriate, and there are no mistakes in grammar or spelling.

FAIR: In order for Essex to accrue compensation for future vacations, they must attribute their obligation to employees services already rendered, recognize that the obligation relates to vested and accumulated rights, and that payment is probable and the amount can be reasonably estimated.

EXPLANATION: This passage is also coherent and concise; however, it lacks the clarity and detail of the previous answer. The language is appropriate, but the grammatical construction is somewhat weak.

POOR: It is based on accrual. The employees must have vested or accumulated rights. They must be able to estimate amounts of compensation and their payment. Vested rights means that the employer must pay the employees even if he is fired or quits.

EXPLANATION: This answer is so poorly worded and disorganized as to be virtually incoherent. There are also some grammar mistakes. The final sentence is additional information but not necessary to answer the question.

PARAGRAPHS

The kind of writing you do for the CPA exam is called **expository writing** (writing in which something is explained in straightforward terms). Expository writing uses the basic techniques we will be discussing here. Other kinds of writing (i.e., narration, description, argument, and persuasion) will sometimes require different techniques.

Consider a paragraph as a division of an essay that consists of one or more sentences, deals with one point, and begins on a new, indented line. Paragraphs provide a way to write about a subject one point or one thought at a time.

Usually, a paragraph begins with a **topic sentence**. The topic sentence communicates the main idea of the paragraph, and the remainder of the paragraph explains or illuminates that central idea. The paragraph sometimes finishes with a restatement of the topic sentence. This strategy is easily read by the exam graders.

Often the topic sentence of the first paragraph is the central idea of the entire composition. Each succeeding paragraph then breaks down this idea into subtopics with each of the new topic sentences being the central thought of that subtopic.

Let's take a look at a simple paragraph to see how it's put together.

> The deductibility of home mortgage interest has been under recent review by Congress as a way to raise revenue. There have been two major reasons for this scrutiny. First, now that consumer interest is nondeductible and investment interest is limited to net investment income, taxpayers have been motivated to rearrange their finances to maximize their tax deductions. Second, most voters do not own homes costing more than $500,000 and, therefore, putting a cap on mortgage loans does not affect the mass of voters. Given the pressure to raise revenue, two major changes have occurred in this area.

The first sentence of the example is the **topic sentence**. The second sentence introduces the supporting examples which appear in the next two sentences beginning with *first* and *second*. The final sentence of the paragraph acts as a preview to the contents of the next paragraph.

Now, let's examine the makeup of a single paragraph answer to a Business Law Exam essay question.

> Question: Dunhill fraudulently obtained a negotiable promissory note from Beeler by misrepresentation of a material fact. Dunhill subsequently negotiated the note to Gordon, a holder in due course. Pine, a business associate of Dunhill, was aware of the fraud perpetrated by Dunhill. Pine purchased the note for value from Gordon. Upon presentment, Beeler has defaulted on the note.
>
> Required: Answer the following, setting forth reasons for any conclusions stated.
>
> 1. What are the rights of Pine against Beeler?
> 2. What are the rights of Pine against Dunhill?

Examples of possible answers:

> 1.   The rights of Pine against Beeler arise from Pine's having acquired the note from Gordon, who was a holder in due course. Pine himself is not a holder in due course because he had knowledge of a defense against the note. The rule wherein a transferee, not a holder in due course, acquires the rights of one by taking from a holder in due course is known as the "shelter rule." Through these rights, Pine is entitled to recover the proceeds of the note from Beeler. The defense of fraud in the inducement is a personal defense and not valid against a holder in due course.

The first sentence of the paragraph is the topic sentence in which the basic answer to the question is given. The third and fourth sentence explains the rule governing Pine's rights. (The *shelter rule* would be considered a *key phrase* in this answer.) The final sentence of the paragraph is not really necessary to answer the question but was added as an explanation of what some might mistakenly believe to be the key to the answer.

> 2.   As one with the rights of a holder in due course, Pine is entitled to proceed against any person whose signature appears on the note, provided he gives notice of dishonor. When Dunhill negotiated the note to Gordon, Dunhill's signature on the note made him secondarily liable. As a result, if Pine brings suit against Dunhill, Pine will prevail because of Dunhill's secondary liability.

The first sentence of this paragraph restates the fact that Pine has the rights of a holder in due course and what these rights mean. The second sentence explains what happened when Dunhill negotiated the note, and the third sentence states the probable outcome of these results.

Note that in both answers 1. and 2., the sentences hang together in a logical fashion and lead the reader easily from one thought to the next. This is called *coherence*, a primary factor in considerations of conciseness and clarity.

TRANSITIONS

To demonstrate how to use **transitions** in a paragraph to carry the reader easily from one thought or example to another, let's consider a slightly longer and more detailed paragraph. The transitions are indicated in italics.

A concerted effort to reduce book income in response to AMT could have a significant impact on corporations. *For example,* the auditor-client relationship may change. *Currently,* it isn't unusual for corporate management to argue for higher rather than lower book earnings, *while* the auditor would argue for conservative reported numbers. Such a corporate reporting posture may change as a consequence of the BURP adjustment. *Furthermore,* stock market analysts often rely on a price/earnings ratio. Lower earnings for essentially the same level of activity may have a significant effect on security prices.

The first sentence of the paragraph is the topic sentence. The next sentence, beginning with the transition *for example,* introduces the example with a broad statement. The following sentence, beginning with *currently,* gives a specific example to support the basic premise. The sentence beginning *furthermore* leads us into a final example. Without these transitions, the paragraph would be choppy and lack coherence.

What follows is a list of some transitions divided by usage. We suggest you commit some of these to memory so that you will never be at a loss as to how to tie your ideas together.

TRANSITIONAL WORDS AND PHRASES

One idea plus one idea:

again	equally important	in addition	likewise	similarly
also	finally	in the same fashion	moreover	third
and	first	in the same respect	next	thirdly
and then	further	last	second	too
besides	furthermore	lastly	secondly	

To show time or place:

after a time	at that time	immediately	presently	thereafter
after a while	at the same time	in due time	second	thereupon
afterwards	before	in the meantime	shortly	to the left
as long as	earlier	lately	since	until
as soon as	eventually	later	soon	when
at last	finally	meanwhile	temporarily	while
at length	first	next	then	
	further	of late		

To contrast or qualify:

after all	at the same time	however	nevertheless	on the other hand
although true	but	in any case	nonetheless	otherwise
and yet	despite this fact	in contrast	notwithstanding	still
anyway	for all that	in spite of	on the contrary	yet

To introduce an illustration

for example	in particular	incidentally	specifically	to illustrate
for instance	in other words	indeed	that is	
in fact	in summary	namely	thus	

To indicate concession		To indicate comparison:
after all	I admit	in a likewise manner
although this may be	naturally	likewise
at the same time	of course	similarly
even though		

WRITING AN ANSWER TO AN EXAM QUESTION

Now that we have examined the makeup of an answer to an exam question, let's take an actual question from a past Business Law Exam and see how to go about writing a clear, comprehensive answer, step by step, sentence by sentence. A question similar to the one that follows would very likely be one the examiners would choose to grade writing skills.

QUESTION:

Bar Manufacturing and Cole Enterprises were arch rivals in the high technology industry, and both were feverishly working on a new product that would give the first to develop it a significant competitive advantage. Bar engaged Abel Consultants on April 1, 1983, for one year, commencing immediately, at $7,500 a month to aid the company in the development of the new product. The contract was oral and was consummated by a handshake. Cole approached Abel and offered them a $10,000 bonus for signing, $10,000 a month for nine months, and a $40,000 bonus if Cole was the first to successfully market the new product. In this connection, Cole stated that the oral contract Abel made with Bar was unenforceable and that Abel could walk away from it without liability. In addition, Cole made certain misrepresentations regarding the dollar amount of its commitment to the project, the state of its development, and the expertise of its research staff. Abel accepted the offer.

Four months later, Bar successfully introduced the new product. Cole immediately dismissed Abel and has paid nothing beyond the first four $10,000 payments plus the initial bonus. Three lawsuits ensued: Bar sued Cole, Bar sued Abel, and Abel sued Cole.

REQUIRED: Answer the following, setting forth reasons for any conclusions stated.

Discuss the various theories on which each of the three lawsuits is based, the defenses that will be asserted, the measure of possible recovery, and the probable outcome of the litigation.

COMPOSING AN ANSWER:

<u>Analyze</u> requirements.

<u>Plan</u> on one paragraph for each lawsuit. Each paragraph will contain four elements: theory, defenses, recovery, and outcome.

PARAGRAPH ONE:

STEP 1: Begin with the first lawsuit mentioned, Bar vs. Cole. Write a topic sentence that will sum up the theory of the suit.

   Topic sentence: Bar's lawsuit against Cole will be based upon the intentional tort of wrongful interference with a contractual relationship.

STEP 2: Back up this statement with law and facts from the question scenario.

   The primary requirement for this cause of action is a valid contractual relationship with which the defendant knowingly interferes. This requirement is met in the case of Cole.

STEP 3: State defenses.

The contract is not required to be in writing since it is for exactly one year from the time of its making. It is, therefore, valid even though oral.

STEP 4: Introduce subject of recovery (damages).

Cole's knowledge of the contract is obvious.

STEP 5: Explain possible problems to recovery.

The principal problem, however, is damages. Since Bar was the first to market the product successfully, it would seem that damages are not present. It is possible there were actual damages incurred by Bar (for example, it hired another consulting firm at an increased price).

STEP 6: Discuss possible outcome.

It also might be possible that some courts would permit the recovery of punitive damages since this is an intentional tort.

PARAGRAPH ONE COMPLETED:

Bar's lawsuit against Cole will be based upon the intentional tort of wrongful interference with a contractual relationship. The primary requirement for this cause of action is a valid contractual relationship with which the defendant knowingly interferes. The requirement is met in the case of Cole. The contract is not required to be in writing since it is for exactly one year from the time of its making. It is, therefore, valid even though oral. Cole's knowledge of the contract is obvious. The principal problem, however, is damages. Since Bar was the first to market the product successfully, it would seem that damages are not present. It is possible there were actual damages incurred by Bar (for example, it hired another consulting firm at an increased price). It also might be possible that some courts would permit the recovery of punitive damages since this is an intentional tort.

PARAGRAPH TWO:

STEP 1: Discuss second lawsuit mentioned, Bar vs. Abel. Write a topic sentence that will sum up the theory of the suit.

Topic sentence: Bar's cause of action against Abel would be for breach of contract.

STEP 2: State defenses. [Same as for first paragraph; this could be left out.]

The contract is not required to be in writing since it is for exactly one year from the time of its making. It is, therefore, valid even though oral.

STEP 3: Introduce subject of recovery (damages).

Once again, [*indicating similarity and tying second paragraph to first*] damages would seem to be a serious problem.

STEP 4: Explain possible problems to recovery.

Furthermore, punitive damages would rarely be available in a contract action. Finally, Bar cannot recover the same damages twice.

STEP 5: Discuss possible outcome.

Hence, if it proceeds against Cole and recovers damages caused by Abel's breach of contract, it will not be able to recover a second time.

PARAGRAPH TWO COMPLETED:

Bar's cause of action against Abel would be for breach of contract. [The contract is not required to be in writing since it is for exactly one year from the time of its making. It is, therefore, valid even though oral.] Once again, damages would seem to be a serious problem. Furthermore, punitive damages would rarely be available in a contract action. Finally, Bar cannot recover the same damages twice. Hence, if it proceeds against Cole and recovers damages caused by Abel's breach of contract, it will not be able to recover a second time.

PARAGRAPH THREE:

STEP 1: Discuss third lawsuit mentioned, Abel vs. Cole. Write a topic sentence that will sum up the theory of the suit.

> **Topic sentence:** Abel's lawsuit against Cole will be based upon fraud and breach of contract.

STEP 2: State defenses.

> There were fraudulent statements made by Cole with the requisite intent and that were possibly to Abel's detriment. The breach of contract by Cole is obvious.

STEP 3: Back up these statements with law and facts from the question scenario.

> However, the contract that Cole induced Abel to enter into and which it subsequently breached was an illegal contract, that is, one calling for the commission of a tort.

STEP 4: Explain possible problems to recovery and possible outcome.

> Therefore, both parties are likely to be treated as wrongdoers, and Abel will be denied recovery.

PARAGRAPH THREE COMPLETED:

Abel's lawsuit against Cole will be based upon fraud and breach of contract. There were fraudulent statements made by Cole with the requisite intent and that were possibly to Abel's detriment. The breach of contract by Cole is obvious. However, the contract that Cole induced Abel to enter into and which it subsequently breached was an illegal contract, that is, one calling for the commission of a tort. Therefore, both parties are likely to be treated as wrongdoers, and Abel will be denied recovery.

PARAGRAPH EDITING:

After you have written your essay, go back over your work to check for the six characteristics that the AICPA will be looking for; coherent organization, conciseness, clarity, use of standard English, responsiveness to the requirements of the question, and appropriateness to the reader.

DIAGNOSTIC QUIZ

The following quiz is designed to test your knowledge of standard English. The correct answers follow the quiz, along with references to the sections that cover that particular area. By identifying the sections that are troublesome for you, you will be able to assess your weaknesses and concentrate on reviewing these areas. If you simply made a lucky guess, you'd better do a review anyway.

CIRCLE THE CORRECT CHOICE IN THE BRACKETS FOR ITEMS 1 THROUGH 17.

1. The company can assert any defenses against third party beneficiaries that [they have/it has] against the promisee.

2. Among those securities [which/that] are exempt from registration under the 1933 Act [are/is] a class of stock given in exchange for another class by the issuer to its existing stockholders without the [issuer's/issuer] paying a commission.

3. This type of promise will not bind the promisor [as/because/since] there is no mutuality of obligation.

4. Under the cost method, treasury stock is presented on the balance sheet as an unallocated reduction of total [stockholders'/stockholders/stockholder's] equity.

5. Jones wished that he [was/were] not bound by the offer he made Smith, while Smith celebrated [his/him] having accepted the offer.

6. [Non-cash/Noncash] investing and financing transactions are not reported in the statement of cash flows because the statement reports only the [affects/effects] of operating, investing, and financing activities that directly [affect/effect] cash flows.

7. Since [its/it's] impossible to predict the future and because prospective financial statements can be [effected/affected] by numerous factors, the accountant must use [judgment/judgement] to estimate when and how conditions are [likely/liable] to change.

8. A common format of bank reconciliation statements [is/are] to reconcile both book and bank balances to a common amount known as the "true balance."

9. Corporations, clubs, churches, and other entities may be beneficiaries so long as they are sufficiently identifiable to permit a determination of [who/whom] is empowered to enforce the terms of the trust.

10. None of the beneficiaries [was/were] specifically referred to in the will.

11. Either Dr. Kline or Dr. Monroe [have/has] been elected to the board of directors.

12. The letter should be signed by Bill and [me/myself].

13. Any trust [which/that] is created for an illegal purpose is invalid.

14. When the nature of relevant information is such that it cannot appear in the accounts, this [principal/principle] dictates that such relevant information be included in the accompanying notes to the financial statements. Financial reporting is the [principal/principle] means of communicating financial information to those outside an entity.

15. The inheritance was divided [between/among] several beneficiaries.

16. Termination of an offer ends the offeree's power to [accept/except] it.

17. The consideration given by the participating creditors is [their/there] mutual promises to [accept/except] less than the full amount of [their/there] claims. Because [their/there] must be such mutual promises [between/among] all the participating creditors, a composition or extension agreement requires the participation of at least two or more creditors.

FOLLOW INSTRUCTIONS FOR ITEMS 18 THROUGH 20.

18. The duties assigned to the interns were to accompany the seniors on field work assignments and the organization and filing of the work papers.

    Fix this sentence so that it will read more smoothly. _____

    _____

    _____

19. Circle the correct spelling of the following pairs of words.

    liaison laison   privilege priviledge   paralleled paraleled

    achieve acheive   occasion occassion   accommodate accomodate

20. Each set of brackets in the following example represents a possible location for punctuation. If you believe a location needs no punctuation, leave it blank; if you think a location needs punctuation, enter a comma, a colon, or a semicolon.

    If the promises supply the consideration [ ] there must be a mutuality of obligation [ ] in other words [ ] both parties must be bound.

ANSWERS TO DIAGNOSTIC QUIZ

Each answer includes a reference to the section that covers what you need to review.

1.	it has	Pronouns—Antecedents, p. C-27.
2.	that; is; issuer's	Subordinating Conjunctions, p. C-30; Verbs—Agreement, p. C-23; Nouns—Gerunds, p. C-26.
3.	because	Subordinating Conjunctions, p. C-30.
4.	stockholders'	Possessive Nouns, p. C-25.
5.	were; his	Verbs, Mood, p. C-22; Nouns—Gerunds, p. C-26.
6.	Noncash; effects; affect	Hyphen, p. C-20; Syntax: Troublesome Words, p. C-13.
7.	it's; affected; judgment, likely	Syntax: Troublesome Words, p. C-13; Spelling: Troublesome Words, p. C-22; Diction: List of Words, p. C-11.
8.	is	Verbs—Agreement, p. C-23.
9.	who	Pronouns, Who/Whom, p. C-26.
10.	were	Verbs—Agreement with Each/None, p. C-24.
11.	has	Verbs—Agreement, p. C-23.
12.	me	Pronouns, that follow prepositions, p. C-27.
13.	that	Subordinating Conjunctions, p. C-30.
14.	principle; principal	Syntax: Troublesome Words, p. C-12.
15.	among	Diction: List of Words, p. C-10.
16.	accept	Syntax: Troublesome Words, C-12

17.   their; accept; their; there; among;   Syntax: Troublesome Words, p. C-12; Diction: List of Words, p. C-10.

18.   Two possible answers: Parallelism: p. C-15.

The duties assigned to the interns were *accompanying* the seniors on field work assignments and *organizing* and filing the work papers.
or
The duties assigned to the interns were to accompany the seniors on field work assignments and *to organize* and *file* the work papers.

19.   In every case, the **first choice** is the correct spelling.
                                  Refer to Spelling: Troublesome Words, p. C-21.

20.   If the promises supply the consideration [,] there must be a mutuality of obligation [;] in other words [,] both parties must be bound.   Refer to Punctuation, p. C-16.

SCORING

Count one point for each item (some numbers contain more than one item) and one point for question number 18 if your sentence came close to the parallelism demonstrated by the answer choices. There are a total of 40 points.

If you scored 37-40, you did very well. A brief review of the items you missed should be sufficient to make you feel fairly confident about your grammar skills.

If you scored 33-36, you did fairly well—better than average—but you should do a thorough review of the items you missed.

If you scored 29-32, your score was average. Since "average" will probably not make it on the CPA exam, you might want to consider a thorough grammar review, in addition to the items you missed.

If you scored below average (28 or less), you **definitely** should make grammar review a high priority when budgeting your exam study time. You should consider using resources beyond those provided here.

SENTENCE STRUCTURE

A sentence is a statement or question, consisting of a subject and a predicate. A subject, at a minimum is a noun, usually accompanied by one or more modifiers (for example, "The Trial Balance"). A predicate consists, at a minimum, of a verb. Cultivate the habit of a quick verification for a subject, predicate, capitalized first word, and ending punctuation in each sentence of an essay. A study of sentence structure is essentially a study of grammar but also moves just beyond grammar to diction, syntax, and parallelism. As we discuss how sentences are structured, there will naturally be some overlapping with grammar.

DICTION

Diction is appropriate word choice. There is no substitute for a diversified vocabulary. If you have a diversified vocabulary or "a way with words," you are already a step ahead. A good general vocabulary, as well as a good accounting vocabulary, is a prerequisite of the CPA exam. Develop your vocabulary as you review for the Exam.

An important aspect of choosing the right words is knowing the audience for whom you are choosing those "perfect words." A perfect word for accountants is not necessarily the perfect word for mechanics or lawyers or English professors. If a CPA exam question asks you to write a specific document for a reader other than another accountant or CPA, you need to be very specific but less technical than you would be otherwise.

Accounting, auditing, and related areas have a certain diction and syntax peculiar unto themselves. Promulgations, for instance, are written very carefully so as to avoid possible misinterpretations or misunderstandings. Of course, you are not expected to write like this—for the CPA exam or in other situations. Find the best word possible to explain clearly and concisely what it is you are trying to say. Often the "right word" is simply just not the "wrong word," so be certain you know the exact meaning of a word before you use it. As an accountant writing for accountants, what is most important is knowing the technical terms and the "key words" and placing them in your sentences properly and effectively. Defining or explaining key words demonstrates to graders that you understand the words you are using and not merely parroting the jargon.

The following is a list of words that frequently either are mistaken for one another or incorrectly assumed to be more or less synonymous.

Among—preposition, refers to more than two
Between—preposition, refers to two; is used for three or more if the items are considered severally and individually

If only part of the seller's capacity to perform is affected, the seller must allocate deliveries *among* the customers, and he or she must give each one reasonable notice of the quota available to him or her.
Between merchants, the additional terms become part of the contract unless one of the following applies. (This sentence is correct whether there are two merchants or many merchants.)

Amount—noun, an aggregate; total number or quantity
Number—noun, a sum of units; a countable number
Quantity—noun, an indefinite amount or number

The checks must be charged to the account in the order of lowest *amount* to highest *amount* to minimize the *number* of dishonored checks.
The contract is not enforceable under this paragraph beyond the *quantity* of goods shown in such writing.

Allude—verb, to state indirectly
Refer—verb, to state clearly and directly

She *alluded* to the fact that the company's management was unscrupulous.
She *referred* to his poor management in her report.

Bimonthly—adjective or adverb; every two months
Semimonthly—adjective or adverb; twice a month

Our company has *bimonthly* meetings.
We get paid *semimonthly*.

Continual—adjective, that which is repeatedly renewed after each interruption or intermission
Continuous—adjective, that which is uninterrupted in time, space, or sequence

The *continuous* ramblings of the managing partner caused the other partners to *continually* check the time.

Cost—noun, the amount paid for an item
Price—noun, the amount set for an item
Value—noun, the relative worth, utility, or importance of an item
Worth—noun, value of an item measured by its qualities or by the esteem in which it is held

The *cost* of that stock is too much.
The *price* of that stock is $100 a share.
I place no *value* on that stock.
That stock's *worth* is overestimated.

Decide—verb, to arrive at a solution
Conclude—verb, to reach a final determination; to exercise judgment

Barbara *decided* to listen to what the accountant was saying; she then *concluded* that what he was saying was true.

Fewer—adjective, not as many; consisting or amounting to a smaller number (used of numbers; comparative of few)
Less—adjective, lower rank, degree, or importance; a more limited amount (used of quantity—for the most part)

My clients require *fewer* consultations than yours do.
My clients are *less* demanding than yours are.

Good—adjective, of a favorable character or tendency; noun, something that is good
Well—adverb, good or proper manner; satisfactorily with respect to conduct or action; adjective, being in satisfactory condition or circumstances

It was *good* [adjective] of you to help me study for the CPA exam.
The decision was for the *good* [noun] of the firm.
He performed that task *well* [adverb].
His work was *well* [adjective] respected by the other accountants.

Imply—verb, to suggest
Infer—verb, to assume; deduce

Her report seems to *imply* that my work was not up to par.
From reading her report, the manager *inferred* that my work was not up to par.

Oral—adjective, by the mouth, spoken; not written
Verbal—adjective, relating to or consisting of words
Vocal—adjective, uttered by the voice, spoken; persistence and volume of speech

Hawkins, Inc. made an *oral* agreement to the contract.
One partner gave his *verbal* consent while the other partner was very *vocal* with his objections.

State—verb, to set forth in detail; completely
Assert—verb, to claim positively, sometimes aggressively or controversially
Affirm—verb, to validate, confirm, state positively

The attorney *stated* the facts of the case.
The plaintiff *asserted* that his rights had been violated.
The judge *affirmed* the jury's decision.

SYNTAX

Syntax is the order of words in a sentence. Errors in syntax occur in a number of ways; the number one way is through hasty composition. The only way to catch errors in word order is to read each of your sentences carefully to make sure that the words you meant to write or type are the words that actually appear on the page and that those words are in the best possible order. The following list should help you avoid errors in both diction and syntax and gives examples where necessary.

TROUBLESOME WORDS

Accept—verb, to receive or to agree to willingly
Except—verb, to take out or leave out from a number or a whole; conjunction, on any other condition but that condition

Except for the items we have mentioned, we will *accept* the conditions of the contract.

Advice—noun, information or recommendation
Advise—verb, to recommend, give advice

> The *accountant advised* us to take his *advice.*

Affect—verb, to influence or change (**Note:** affect is occasionally used as a noun in technical writing only.)
Effect—noun, result or cause; verb, to cause

> The effect [noun] of Ward, Inc.'s decision to cease operations affected many people.
> He quickly *effected* [verb] policy changes for office procedures.

All Ready—adjectival phrase, completely prepared
Already—adverb, before now; previously

> Although the tax return was *all ready* to be filed, the deadline had *already* passed.

All Right; Alright—adjective or adverb, beyond doubt; very well; satisfactory; agreeable, pleasing. (Although many grammarians insist that **alright** is not a proper form, it is widely accepted.)

Appraise—verb, set a value on
Apprise—verb, inform

> Dane Corp. *apprised* him of the equipment's age, so that he could *appraise* it more accurately.

Assure—verb, to give confidence to positively
Ensure—verb, to make sure, certain, or safe
Insure—verb, to obtain or provide insurance on or for; to make certain by taking necessary measures and precautions

> The accountant assured his client that he would file his return in a timely manner.
> He added the figures more than once to *ensure* their accuracy.
> She was advised to *insure* her diamond property.

Decedent—noun, a deceased person
Descendant—noun, proceeding from an ancestor or source

> The decedent left her vast fortune to her *descendants.*

Eminent—adjective, to stand out; important
Imminent—adjective, impending

> Although he was an *eminent* businessman, foreclosure on his house was *imminent.*

Its—possessive
It's—contraction, **it is**

> The company held *its* board of directors meeting on Saturday. *It's* the second meeting this month.

Lay—verb, to place or set
Lie—verb, to recline

> He *lies* down to rest.
> He *lays* down the book.

Percent—used with numbers only
Percentage—used with words or phrases

> Each employee received 2 *percent* of the profits.
> They all agreed this was a small *percentage.*

Precedence—noun, the fact of preceding in time, priority of importance
Precedent—noun, established authority; adjective, prior in time, order, or significance

> The board of directors meeting took *precedence* over his going away.
> The president set a *precedent* when making that decision.

Principal—noun, a capital sum placed at interest; a leading figure; the corpus of an estate; adjective, first, most important
Principle—noun, a basic truth or rule

> Paying interest on the loan's *principal* [noun] was explained to the company's *principals* [noun].
> The principal [adjective] part of...
> She refused to compromise her *principles*.

Than—conjunction, function word to indicate difference in kind, manner, or identity; preposition, in comparison with (indicates comparison)
Then—adverb, at that time; soon after that (indicates time)

> BFE Corp. has more shareholders *than* Hills Corp.
> First, we must write the report, and *then* we will meet with the clients.

Their—adjective, of or relating to them or themselves
There—adverb, in or at that place

> *There* were fifty shareholders at the meeting to cast *their* votes.

MODIFIER PLACEMENT

Pay close attention to where modifiers are placed, especially adverbs such as **only** and **even**. In speech, inflection aids meaning but, in writing, placing modifiers improperly can be confusing and often changes the meaning. The modifier should usually be placed before the word(s) it modifies.

> She *almost* finished the whole report.
> She finished *almost* the whole report.
>
> *Only* she finished the report.
> She *only* finished the report.
> She finished *only* the report.

Phrases also must be placed properly, usually, but not always, following the word or phrase they modify. Often, **reading the sentence aloud** will help you decide where the modifier belongs.

> Fleming introduced a client to John with a counter-offer. (*With a counter-offer* modifies *client*, not *John*, and should be placed after *client*.)
> The accountant recommended a bankruptcy petition to the client under Chapter 7. (*Under Chapter 7* modifies *bankruptcy petition*, not *the client*, and should be placed after *bankruptcy petition*.)

SPLIT INFINITIVES

Infinitives are the root verb form (e.g., to be, to consider, to walk). Generally speaking, infinitives should not be split except when to do so makes the meaning clearer.

Awkward:	Management's responsibility is to clearly represent its financial position.
Better:	Management's responsibility is to represent its financial position clearly.
Exception:	Management's responsibility in the future is to better represent its financial position.

SENTENCE FRAGMENTS

To avoid sentence fragments, read over your work carefully. Each sentence needs at least (1) a subject and (2) a predicate.

> Unlike the case of a forged endorsement, a drawee bank charged with the recognition of its drawer-customer's signature. (The verb *is*, before the word *charged*, has been left out.)

PARALLELISM

Parallelism refers to a similarity in structure and meaning of all parts of a sentence or a paragraph. In parallelism, parts of a sentence (or a paragraph) that are parallel in meaning are also parallel in structure. Sentences that violate rules of parallelism will be difficult to read and may obscure meaning. The following are some examples of different **violations** of parallelism.

(1) A security interest can be effected through a financing statement or the creditor's taking possession of it. (The two prepositional phrases separated by **or** should be parallel.)

Corrected: A security interest can be effected through a financing statement or through possession by the creditor.

(2) The independent auditor should consider whether the scope is appropriate, adequate audit programs and working papers, appropriate conclusions, and reports prepared are consistent with results of the work performed. (The clause beginning with **whether** (which acts as the direct object of the verb **should consider**) is faulty. The items mentioned must be similarly constructed to each other.)

Corrected: The independent auditor should consider whether the scope is appropriate, audit programs and working papers are adequate, conclusions are appropriate, and reports prepared are consistent with results of the work performed.

(3) The CPA was responsible for performing the inquiry and analytical procedures and that the review report was completed in a timely manner. (The prepositional phrase beginning with **for** is faulty.)

Corrected: The CPA was responsible for performing the inquiry and analytical procedures and ensuring that the review report was completed in a timely manner.

(4) Procedures that should be applied in examining the stock accounts are as follows:
(1) Review the corporate charter...
(2) Obtain or preparing an analysis of...
(3) Determination of authorization for... (All items in a list must be in parallel structure.)

Corrected:

1. Review the corporate charter...
2. Obtain or prepare an analysis of...
3. Determine the authorization for...

There are many other types of faulty constructions that can creep into sentences—too many to detail here. Furthermore, if any of the above is not clear, syntax may be a problem for you and you might want to consider a more thorough review of this subject.

NUMBERS

1. The basic rule for writing numbers is to write out the numbers ten and under and use numerals for all the others. More formal writing may dictate writing out all round numbers and numbers under 101. Let style, context of the sentence and of the work, and common sense be your guide.

The partnership was formed 18 years ago.
Jim Bryant joined the firm four years ago.
Baker purchased 200 shares of stock.

2.   When there are two numbers next to each other, alternate the styles.

three 4-year certificates of deposit   5 two-party instruments

3.   Never begin a sentence with numerals, such as:

1989 was the last year that Zinc Co. filed a tax return.

This example can be corrected as follows:

Nineteen hundred and eighty-nine was the last year that Zinc Co. filed a tax return. (For use only in very formal writing)
or
Zinc Co. has not filed a tax return since 1989.

CAPITALIZATION

This section mentions only areas that seem to cause particular difficulties.

1.   The first word **after a colon** is capped only when it is the beginning of a complete sentence.

We discussed several possibilities at the meeting: Among them were liquidation, reorganization, and rehabilitation.
We discussed several possibilities at the meeting: liquidation, reorganization, and rehabilitation.

2.   The capitalization of titles and headings is especially tricky. In general, the first word and all other important words, no matter what length they are, should be capped. Beyond this general rule, there are several variations relating to the capitalization of pronouns. The important thing here is to pick a style and use it consistently within a single document, article, etc.

For example, the following pair of headings would both be acceptable depending on the style and consistency of style:

Securities to which SFAS 115 Applies   **or**   Securities to Which SFAS 115 Applies
Issues for Property other than Cash   **or**   Issues For Property Other Than Cash

PUNCTUATION

PERIOD

Probably the two most common errors involving periods occur when incorporating quotation marks and/or parentheses with periods.

1.   When a period is used with closing quotation marks, the period is always placed **inside**, regardless of whether the entire sentence is a quote or only the end of the sentence.

2.   When a period is used with parentheses, the period goes **inside** the closing parenthesis if the entire sentence is enclosed in parentheses. When only the last word or words is enclosed in parentheses, the period goes **outside** the closing parenthesis.

(See Chapter 38, Contracts.)
The answer to that question is in the section on contracts (Chapter 38).

EXCLAMATION POINT

An exclamation point is used for emphasis and when issuing a command. In many cases, this is determined by the author when he or she wants to convey urgency, irony, or stronger emotion than ordinarily would be inferred.

COLON

A colon is used to introduce something in the sentence—a list of related words, phrases, or items directly related to the first part of the sentence; a quotation; a **direct** question; or an example of what was stated in the first part of the sentence. The colon takes the place of **that is** or **such as** and should never be used **with** such phrases.

> The accountant discussed two possibilities with the clients: first, a joint voluntary bankruptcy petition under Chapter 7, and second,...

> The following will be discussed: life insurance proceeds; inheritance; and property.

> My CPA accounting review book states the following: "All leases that do not meet any of the four criteria for capital leases are operating leases."

Colons are used in formal correspondence after the salutation.

> Dear Mr. Bennett:
> To Whom it May Concern:

Note: When **that is** or **such as** is followed by a numeric list, it may be followed by a colon.

> When writing a sentence, if you're not sure whether or not a colon is appropriate, it probably isn't. When in doubt, change the sentence so that you're sure it doesn't need a colon.

SEMICOLON

A semicolon is used in a number of ways:

1. Use a **semicolon in place of a conjunction** when there are two or more closely related thoughts and each is expressed in a coordinate clause (a clause that could stand as a complete sentence).

    > A marketable title is one that is free from plausible or reasonable objections; it need not be perfect.

2. Use a **semicolon** as in the above example **with a conjunction** when the sentence is very long and complex. This promotes **clarity** by making the sentence easier to read.

    > Should the lease be prematurely terminated, the deposit may be retained only to cover the landlord's actual expenses or damages; *and* any excess must be returned to the tenant.

    > An assignment establishes privity of estate between the lessor and assignee; *[and]* therefore, the assignee becomes personally liable for the rent.

3. When there are commas in a series of items, use a **semicolon** to separate the main items.

    > Addison, Inc. has distribution centers in Camden, Maine; Portsmouth, New Hampshire; and Rock Island, Rhode Island.

COMMA

Informal English allows much freedom in the placement or the omission of commas, and the overall trend is away from commas. However, standard, formal English provides rules for its usage. Accounting "language" can be so complex that using commas and using them correctly and appropriately is a necessity to avoid obscurity and promote clarity. Accordingly, we encourage you to learn the basics about comma placement.

What follows is not a complete set of rules for commas but should be everything you need to know about commas to make your sentences clear and concise. Because the primary purpose of the comma is to clarify meaning, it is the opinion of the authors that in the case of a complex subject such as accounting, it is better to overpunctuate than to underpunctuate. If you are concerned about overpunctuation, try to reduce an unwieldly sentence to two or more sentences.

1. Use a comma to **separate a compound sentence** (one with two or more independent coordinate clauses joined by a conjunction).

> Gil Corp. has current assets of $90,000, but the corporation has current liabilities of $180,000.
> Jim borrowed $60,000, and he used the proceeds to purchase outstanding common shares of stock.

> **Note:** In these examples, a comma would **not** be necessary if the **and** or the **but** were not followed by a noun or pronoun (the subject of the second clause). In other words, if by removing the conjunction, the sentence could be separated into two complete sentences, it needs a comma.

2. Use a comma after an **introductory word or phrase**.

> During 1992, Rand Co. purchased $960,000 of inventory.
> On April 1, 1993, Wall's inventory had a fair value of $150,000.

> **Note:** Writers often choose to omit this comma when the introductory phrase is very short. Again, we recommend using the comma. It will never be incorrect in this position.

3. Use a comma after an **introductory adverbial clause**.

> Although insurance contracts are not required by the Statute of Frauds to be in writing, most states have enacted statutes that now require such.

4. Use commas to separate **items, phrases, or clauses in a series**.

> To be negotiable, an instrument must be in writing, signed by the maker or drawer, contain an unconditional promise or order to pay a sum certain in money on demand or at a specific time, and be payable to order or to bearer.

> **Note:** Modern practice often omits the last comma in the series (in the above example, the one before **and**). Again, for the sake of clarity, we recommend using this comma.

5. In most cases, use a comma or commas to separate **a series of adjectives**.

> Silt Co. kept their inventory in an old, decrepit, brick building.
> He purchased several outstanding shares of common stock. (*No* commas are needed.)

When in doubt as to whether or not to use a comma after a particular adjective, try inserting the word **and** between the adjectives. If it makes sense, use a comma. (In the second example, above, **several and outstanding**, or **outstanding and several** don't make sense.)

6. Use a comma or commas to set off any **word or words, phrase, or clause that interrupts the sentence** but does not change its essential meaning.

> SLD Industries, as drawer of the instrument, is only secondarily liable.

7.   Use commas to set off **geographical names** and **dates**.

        Feeney Co. moved its headquarters to Miami, Florida, on August 16, 1992.

QUOTATION MARKS

Quotation marks are used with **direct quotations; direct discourse and direct questions**; and **definitions or explanations of words**. Other uses of quotation marks are used rarely in the accounting profession and, therefore, are not discussed in this review.

HYPHEN

1.   Use a hyphen to separate words into syllables. It is best to check a dictionary, because some words do not split where you might imagine.

2.   Modern practice does not normally hyphenate prefixes and their root words, even when both the prefix and the root word begin with vowels. A common exception is when the root word begins with a capital letter or a date or number.

        prenuptial   nonexempt   semiannual
        pre-1987   nonnegotiable   non-American

3.   Although modern practice is moving away from using hyphens for **compound adjectives** (a noun and an adjective in combination to make a single adjective), clarity dictates that hyphens still be used in many cases.

        long-term investments   two-party instrument
        a noninterest-bearing note   short-term capital losses

4.   Use a hyphen **only** when the compound adjective or compound adjective-adverb **precedes the noun**.

        The well-known company is going bankrupt.
        The company is well known for its quality products.

Note: There are certain word combinations that are always hyphenated, always one word, or always two words. Use the dictionary.

5.   **Suspended hyphens** are used to avoid repetition in compound adjectives. For example, instead of having to write **himself or herself**, especially when these forms are being used repeatedly as they often must be in our newly nongender-biased world, use **him- or herself**.

        10-, 15-, and 18-year depreciation   first-, second-, and third-class

SPELLING

Just as many of us believe that arithmetic can always be done by our calculators, we also believe that spelling will be done by our word processors and, therefore, we needn't worry too much about it. There is no doubt that these devices are tremendous boons to writers and others. However, although you soon will be able to use a calculator during the CPA exam, you will not be able to use a word processor. And like it or not, you will encounter many other situations where a spell-checker will not be available to you, so you'd better be able to **spell!** Also, a spell-checker cannot tell the difference between words that you have misspelled which are nonetheless real words, such as **there** and **their**. (See the list in this section of words often confused.)

Let's hit some highlights here of troublesome spellings with some brief tips that should help you become a better speller.

1.   **IE** or **EI**? If you are still confused by words containing the **ie** or **ei** combinations, you'd better relearn those old rhymes we ridiculed in grade school.

"**i** before **e** except after **c**." (This works only for words where the ie-ei combination sounds like **ee**.)

ach**ie**ve	bel**ie**ve	ch**ie**f
c**ei**ling	rec**ei**ve	rec**ei**pt

Of course there are always **exceptions** such as:

either	neither	seize	financier

When **ie** or **ei** have a different sound than **ee**, the above rule does not apply. For example:

fr**ie**nd	s**ie**ve	effic**ie**nt
for**ei**gn	sover**ei**gn	surf**ei**t

2. **Doubling final consonants**. When an ending (**suffix**) beginning with a vowel is added to a root word that ends in a single consonant, that final consonant is **usually doubled**.

lag—lagging	bid—bidding	top—topped

    The exceptions generally fall under three rules.

    First, double only after a short vowel and **not** after a double vowel.

big—bigger	tug—tugging	get—getting
need—needing	keep—keeping	pool—pooled

    Second, a **long** vowel (one that "says its own name"), which is almost always followed by a silent **e** that must be dropped to add the suffix, is **not** doubled.

hope—hoping	tape—taped	rule—ruled

    Note: Sometimes, **as** in the first two examples above, doubling the consonants would create entirely new words.

    Third, **with** root words of two or more syllables ending in a single consonant, double the consonant **only** when the last syllable is the **stressed syllable**.

    Double: be**gin**—beginning, beginner   pre**fer**—preferred, preferring
    re**gret**—**regretted**, regrettable   ad**mit**—admitted, admittance
    Don't
    Double: pro**hib**it—prohibited, prohibitive   **ben**efit—benefited, benefiting
    de**vel**op—developing   **pref**erence—preferable

3. **Drop** the silent **e** before adding a suffix **beginning with a vowel**.

store—storing	take—taking	value—valuing

    Keep the **e** before adding a suffix **beginning with a consonant**, such as:

move—movement	achieve—achievement

    Again, there are **exceptions**.

    e: mile—mileage   dye—dyeing

    No e: argue—argument   due—duly   true—ruly

4. Change **y** to **ie** before adding **s** when it is the single final vowel.

country—countries	study—studies	quantity—quantities

Change **y** to **i** before adding other endings **except s**.

        busy—business   dry—drier   copy—copier

Exceptions: Keep **y** for the following:

        copying   studying   trying

Y is also usually preserved when it follows another vowel.

        delays   joys   played

Exceptions:

        day—daily   lay—laid   pay—paid   say—said

5.   **Forming Plurals.** The formation of some plurals does not follow the general rule of adding **s** or **es** to the singular. What follows are some of the more troublesome forms.
Some singular nouns that end in **o** form their plurals by adding **s**; some by adding **es**.

        ratio**s**   zero**s**   hero**es**   potato**es**

Many nouns taken directly from **foreign languages** retain their original plural. Below are a few of the more common ones.

        alumnus—alumni   basis—bases   crisis—crises
        criterion—criteria   datum—data   matrix—matrices

Other nouns taken directly from foreign languages have **two acceptable plural forms**: the foreign language plural and the anglicized plural. Here are some of the more common:

        medium—media, mediums   appendix—appendices, appendixes
        formula—formulae, formulas   memorandum—memoranda, memorandums

Finally, in this foreign language category are some commonly used Latin nouns that form their plurals by adding **es**.

        census—censuses   consensus—consensuses
        hiatus—hiatuses   prospectus—prospectuses

Troublesome Words: Spelling

Spelling errors occur for different reasons; probably the most common reason is confusion with the spelling of similar words. The following is a list of commonly misspelled words. You will find those you may have misspelled in taking the Diagnostic Quiz, and you may recognize others you have problems with. Memorize them. (Note: some of these words may have acceptable alternative spellings; however, the spellings listed below are the preferred form.)

accommodate	bankruptcy	irrelevant	paralleled	skillful
achieve	deferred	judgment	privilege	supersede
acknowledgment	existence	liaison	receivable	surety
balance	fulfill	occasion	resistance	trial

GRAMMAR

This section on grammar is intended to be a brief overview only. Consequently, the authors have chosen to focus on items that seem to cause the most problems. If you did not do well on the Diagnostic Quiz, you would be well advised to go over all the material in this section and consider a more thorough grammar study than provided here.

VERBS

The verb is the driving force of the sentence: it is the word or words to which all other parts of the sentence relate. When trying to analyze a sentence to identify its grammatical parts or its meaning, or when attempting to amend a sentence, you should always identify the verb or verbs first. A verb expresses action or being.

> Action: The accountant *visits* his clients regularly.
> Being: Kyle *is* an accountant.

VOICE

1. The **active voice** indicates that the subject of the sentence (the person or thing) does something. The **passive voice** indicates that the subject is acted upon.

   Active: *The accountant worked* on the client's financial statements.
   Passive: The client's financial statements *were worked on by the accountant.*

2. The most important thing to understand about voice is that it should be consistent; that is, you should avoid shifts from one voice to another, especially within the same sentence as below.

   > Taylor Corporation *hired* an independent computer programmer to develop a simplified payroll application for its new computer, and an on-line, data-based microcomputer system *was developed.*

   Use the active voice for the entire sentence:

   > Taylor Corporation *hired* an independent computer programmer to develop a simplified payroll application for its new computer, and he *developed* an on-line, data-based microcomputer system.

MOOD

1. Common errors in syntax are made when **more than one mood** is used in a single sentence. The first example that follows begins with the **imperative** and shifts to the **indicative**. The second example corrects the sentence by using the imperative in both clauses, and the third example corrects the sentence by using the indicative in both clauses. The fourth example avoids the problem by forming two sentences.

   > Pick up (imperative) that work program for me at the printer, and then we will go (indicative) to the client.
   > Pick up that work program for me at the printer, and then go to the client with me.
   > After you pick up that work program for me at the printer, we will go to the client.
   > Pick up that work program for me at the printer. Then we will go to the client.

2. There are three moods: the indicative, the imperative, and the subjunctive. We do not examine the subjunctive. Most sentences are **indicative**:

   > *The percentage-of-completion method is justified.* Declarative indicative.
   > *Is the percentage-of-completion method justified?* Interrogative indicative.

3. Sentences that give a command are called **imperative** sentences:

   > Pick up your books!
   > Be sure to use the correct method of accounting for income taxes.

TENSE

1. Tense is all about *time*. If the proper sequence of tenses is not used, confusion can arise as to what happened when. Consider:

    Not getting the raise he was expecting, John was unhappy about the additional work load. [???]
    Having not gotten the raise he was expecting, John was unhappy about the additional work load. [Much clearer]

2. The **present tense** is used to express action or a state of being that is taking place in the present. The present tense is also used to express an action or a state of being that is habitual and when a definite time in the future is stated.

    Dan *is taking* his CPA exam.
    Robin *goes* to the printer once a week.
    The new computer *arrives* on Monday.

3. The **present perfect tense** is used to indicate action that began in the past and has continued to the present.

    From the time of its founder, the CPA firm *has celebrated* April 16 with a fabulous dinner party.

4. The **future tense** is used to indicate action that takes place in the indefinite future.

    A plan of reorganization *will determine* the amount and the manner in which the creditors *will be paid*, in what form the business *will continue*, and any other necessary details.

5. The **future perfect tense** is used to indicate action that has not taken place yet but will take place before a specific future time.

    Before Susan arrives at the client's office, the client *will have prepared* the documents she needs.

6. The **past tense** is used to indicate an action that took place in the past. The **past tense** is also used to indicate a condition or state occurring at a specific time in the past.

    The predecessor auditor *resigned* last week.
    The company *contacted* its auditor the first of every new year.

7. The **past perfect tense** is used to indicate an action that is completed before another action that also took place in the past.

    The work load *had been* so heavy that she was required to work overtime. (Not *was*)

AGREEMENT

1. The first element of agreement to examine is **verb** and **subject**. These two components must agree **in number**. Number is just one of several things to consider when examining the agreement of the components of a sentence.

2. The subject of the sentence is the noun or pronoun (person, place, or thing) doing the action stated by the verb (in the case of the active voice) or being acted upon by the verb (in the case of the passive voice). Although the subject normally precedes the verb, this is not always the case. Thus, you must be able to identify sentence elements no matter where they happen to fall. This is not a difficult matter, at least most of the time. Consider:

    (1) Lewis, Bradford, Johnson & Co. [is or are] the client with the best pay record.

    (2) For me, one of the most difficult questions on the exam [was or were] concerned with correcting weaknesses in internal controls.

In both examples, the first choice, the singular verb form, is correct. In sentence (1), Lewis, Bradford, Johnson & Co. is considered singular in number because we are talking about the company, not Lewis, Bradford, and Johnson per se. In sentence (2), the verb is also singular because **one** is the subject of the sentence, not **questions**. **Questions** is the object of the preposition **of**. If this seems confusing, rearrange the sentence so that the prepositional phrase appears first, and the agreement of subject and verb will be clearer. Thus:

Of the most difficult questions, one *was concerned* with correcting weaknesses in internal controls.

We will address special problems associated with prepositional phrases in other sections.

3.　Beware of the word **number**. When it is preceded by the word **the**, it is always singular, and when it is preceded by the word **a**, it is always plural.

The number of listings generated by the new EDP system *was* astounding.
A number of listings *were generated* by the new EDP system.

4.　A **compound subject**, even when made up of nouns singular in number, always takes a plural verb.

The balance sheet, the independent auditor's report, and the quarterly report *are lying* on the desk. (Not *is lying*)

5.　Continuing now with **compound subjects**, let's address the problem of when there are two or more subjects—one (or more) singular and one (or more) plural. When the sentence contains subjects connected by **or** or **nor**, or **not only...but also**, the verb should agree with the subject nearer to the verb.

Either the auditors or the partner *is going* to the client.
Not only the partner but also the auditors *are going* to the client.

In the case of the first example above, which sounds awkward, simply switch the order of the subjects **(the partner; the auditors)** and use the verb **are going** to make it read better.

6.　When one subject is **positive** and one is **negative**, the verb always agrees with the positive.

The partner, and not the auditors, *is going* to the client.
Not the partner but the auditors frequently *go* to the client.

7.　You should use **singular verbs** with the following: **each, every, everyone, everybody, anyone, anybody, either, neither, someone, somebody, no one, nobody,** and **one**.

Anybody who wants to go *is* welcome.
Neither the accountant nor the bookkeeper ever *arrives* on time.
One never *knows* what to expect.

> Watch out for the words **each** and **none**. They can trip up even careful writers.

8.　Improper placement of **each** in the sentence will confuse the verb agreement.

The balance sheet, the income statement, and the statement of cash flows each [*has/have*] several errors.

In this example, we know that the verb must be **has** (to agree with **each**), but then again, maybe it should be **have** to agree with the subjects. The problem is that we have a sentence with a compound subject that must take a plural verb, but here it is connected with a singular pronoun (each). This is a very common error. This particular example may be fixed in one of two ways. First, if the word **each** is not really necessary in the sentence, simply drop it. Second, simply place the word **each** in a better position in the sentence. In the example below, placing the word **each** at the end of the sentence properly connects it to **errors**; also it no longer confuses verb agreement.

The balance sheet, the income statement, and the statement of cash flows *have* several errors *each*.

9. The word **none** has special problems all its own. Not too many years ago, it was the accepted rule that every time **none** was the subject of the sentence, it should take a **singular verb**. Most modern grammarians now agree that the plural may be used when followed by a prepositional phrase with a plural object (noun) or with an object whose meaning in the sentence is plural.

   None of the statements *were* correct.

   When **none** stands alone, some purists believe it should take the singular and others believe that the plural is the proper form when the meaning conveys plurality. Consequently, in the following example, either the singular or plural is generally acceptable.

   All the financial statements had been compiled, but none *was* **or** *were* correct.

   When in doubt, use **not one** in place of **none** (with a singular verb, of course).

NOUNS

Nouns are people, places, and things and can occur anywhere in the sentence. Make sure that, when necessary, the nouns are the same in number.

   Do the exercises at the end of each chapter by answering the *questions* true or false. (Not singular *question*)
   At the end of the engagement, everyone must turn in their *time sheets*. (Not singular *time sheet*)

POSSESSIVE NOUNS

1. The basic rule for making a **singular noun** possessive is to add an **apostrophe and an s.** If a singular noun ends in s, **add apostrophe and an s**. To make a **plural noun** possessive, add an **apostrophe alone** when the plural ends in **s** or an **apostrophe and an s** when the plural does not end in an **s**.

Singular:	client*'s*	system*'s*	beneficiary*'s*	*Chris'*
Plural:	client*s'*	system*s'*	beneficiarie*s'*	

2. A common area of difficulty has to do with **ownership**, that is, when two or more individuals or groups are mentioned as owning something. If the ownership is **not common** to all, apostrophes appear after each individual or group. If the ownership **is common** to all, only the last individual or group in the series takes an apostrophe.

Not common to all:	The accountant's and the attorney's offices...
Common to all:	Robert, his brother, and their sons' company...

   Most of the confusion associated with possessives seems to be with the plural possessive. Remember to make the noun **plural** first and **possessive** second.

3. Modern usage tends to make possessive forms into adjectives where appropriate. Thus:

   Company's (possessive) management becomes *company* (adjective) management.
   A *two weeks'* (possessive) vacation becomes a *two weeks* or *two-week* (both adjectives) vacation.

   In most instances, either the possessive form or the adjectival form is acceptable. Go with the form that seems most appropriate for that particular sentence.

GERUNDS

1.   A gerund is a verb changed to a noun by adding **ing**. A noun preceding a gerund must be possessive so that it may be construed as **modifying the noun**.

> *Caroline's telecommuting* was approved by the partner.

In this example, the subject of the sentence is **telecommuting**, not Caroline or Caroline's. Since we know that nouns cannot modify nouns, Caroline must become **Caroline's** to create a possessive form that can modify the noun **telecommuting**.

2.   The same holds true for **gerunds** used as **objects of prepositions**:

> The partner objected to *Caroline's telecommuting*.

In this example, **telecommuting** is the object of the preposition **to**. Caroline's is an appositive (or possessive) form modifying **telecommuting**.

PRONOUNS

Like Latin where most words have "cases" according to their function in the sentence, English **pronouns** also have cases. Sometimes you may be aware that you are using a case when determining the proper form of the pronoun and sometimes you may not.

> *He* met *his* partner at *their* office.

1.   Let's begin by tackling everybody's favorite: **who** and **whom**. We're going to take some time reviewing this one since it seems to be a major area of confusion. There is little or no confusion when **who** is clearly the **subject** of the sentence:

> *Who* is going with us?

And little or no confusion when **whom** is clearly (1) the **object** of the sentence or (2) the **object** of the preposition.

> (1)   Jenny audited *whom*? *Whom* did Jenny audit?

> (2)   Jenny is working for *whom*? For *whom* is Jenny working?

If you are having difficulty with **questions**, try changing them into declarative sentences (statements) and substituting another pronoun. Thus: Jenny audits **them** (objective), obviously not **they** (subjective), or Jenny is working for **her**, obviously not **she**.

---

2.   **Who** or **whoever** is the subjective case, and **whom** or **whomever** is the objective case. Common errors occur frequently in two instances: (1) when **who or whoever** is interrupted by a parenthetical phrase and (2) when an entire clause is the subject of a preposition.

> (1)   *Whoever* she decides is working with her should meet her at six o'clock.

In this example, **she decides** is a parenthetical phrase (one that could be left out of the sentence and the sentence would still be a complete thought). When you disregard **she decides**, you can see that **whoever** is the subject of the sentence, not **she**. The error occurs when **she** is believed to be the subject and **whomever**, the object of **decides**.

> (2)   Jenny will work with *whoever* shows up first.

This example represents what seems the most problematic of all the areas relating to who or whom. We have been taught to use the objective case after the preposition (in this case **with**). So why isn't **whomever** the correct form in this example? The answer is that it would be the correct form if the sentence ended with the word **whomever**. (**Whomever** would be the object of the preposition **with**.) In this case, it is not the last word but, rather, it is the **subject** of the clause **whoever shows up first**.

> Again, make the substitution of another pronoun as a test of whether to use the subjective or objective case.

Let's look at a few more examples. See if you are better able to recognize the correct form.

(1) I'm sure I will be comfortable with [*whoever/whomever*] the manager decides to assign.

(2) To [*who/whom*] should she speak regarding that matter?

(3) He always chooses [*whoever/whomever*] in his opinion is the best auditor.

(4) She usually enjoys working with [*whoever/whomever*] the partner assigns.

(5) [*Who/Whom*] should I ask to accompany me?

Let's see how well you did.

(1) **Whomever** is correct. The whole clause after the preposition **with** is the object of the preposition, and **whomever** is the object of the verb **to assign**. Turn the clause around and substitute another pronoun. Thus, **the manager decides to assign** *him*.

(2) **Whom** is correct. **Whom** is the object of the preposition **to**. Make the question into a declarative sentence and substitute another pronoun. Thus, **She should speak to** *him* **regarding that matter**.

(3) **Whoever** is correct. The entire clause **whoever is the best auditor** is the object of the main verb **chooses**. **Whoever** is the subject of that clause. **In his opinion** is a parenthetical phrase and doesn't affect the rest of the sentence.

(4) **Whomever** is correct. The entire clause **whomever the partner assigns** is the object of the preposition **with**, and **whomever** is the object of the verb **assigns**. Again, turn the clause around and substitute another pronoun. Thus, **the partner assigns** *him*.

(5) **Whom** is correct. **Whom** is the object of the main verb **ask**. Turn the question into a regular declarative sentence and substitute another pronoun. Thus, **I should ask** *her* **to accompany me**.

3. Pronouns that follow prepositions are always in the **objective case**, except when serving as the subject of a clause, as discussed above. The most popular misuse occurs when using a pronoun after the preposition **between**. (**I, he, she, they,** are never used after **between**, no matter where the prepositional phrase falls in the sentence.)

> Between you and me, I don't believe our client will be able to continue as a going concern.
> That matter is strictly between her and them.

ANTECEDENTS

1. An antecedent is the word or words for which a pronoun stands. Any time a pronoun is used, its antecedent must be clear and agree with the word or words for which it stands.

> *The accountant* placed *his* work in the file.

In this example, **his** is the pronoun with **the accountant** as its antecedent. **His** agrees with **the accountant** in person and number. **His** is used so as not to repeat **the accountant**.

2. Confusion most often occurs when using indefinite pronouns such as **it, that, this,** and **which**.

> The company for *which* he works always mails *its* paychecks on Friday.

In this example, the pronouns **which** and **its** both clearly refer to **the company**. Consider the next example. Since it is not clear what the antecedent for **it** is, we can't tell for sure whether the company or the paycheck is small.

> The company always mails my paycheck on Friday and *it* is a small one.

3. So far in our discussion of antecedents, we have talked about agreement in person. We have not addressed agreement in **number**. The following examples demonstrate pronouns that **do not agree** in number with their antecedents.

    > The company issued quarterly financial reports to *their* shareholders. (*Its* is the correct antecedent to agree in number with *company*.)

    > Each of the methods is introduced on a separate page, so that the student is made aware of *their* importance. (*Its* is the correct antecedent to agree in number with *each*.) **Note: Importance** refers to **each**, the subject of the sentence, not to **methods**, which is the object of the preposition **of**.

4. When a pronoun refers to singular antecedents that are connected by **or** or **nor**, the pronoun should be **singular**.

    > Joe or Buddy has misplaced *his* workpapers.
    > Neither Joe nor Buddy has misplaced *his* workpapers.

5. When a pronoun refers to a singular and a plural antecedent connected by **or** or **nor**, the pronoun should be **plural**.

    > Neither Joe nor his associates can locate *their* workpapers.

6. Pronouns must also agree with their antecedents in **gender**. Because English language has no way of expressing gender-neutral in pronoun agreement, it has been the custom to use **his** as a convenience when referring to both sexes. To avoid this "gender bias" in writing, there is a growing use of a more cumbersome construction in order to be more politically correct.

    > **Old:** When a new partner's identifiable asset contribution is less than the ownership interest *he* is to receive, the excess capital allowed *him* is considered as goodwill attributable to *him*.

    > **New:** When a new partner's identifiable asset contribution is less than the ownership interest *he or she* is to receive, the excess capital allowed *the new partner* is considered as goodwill attributable to *him or her*.

    You will note in the above example that **he or she (he/she)** and **him or her (him/her)** have been used only once each and the antecedent **new partner** has been repeated once.

The idea is to not overload a single sentence with too many repetitions of each construction. When it seems that **he/she** constructions are overwhelming the sentence, repeat the noun antecedent where possible, even if it sounds a bit labored.

---

7. **Reflexive pronouns** are pronouns that are used for **emphasizing their antecedents** and should **not be used as substitutes** for regular pronouns. The reflexive pronouns are **myself, yourself, himself, herself, itself, ourselves, yourselves, and themselves.**

    > The financing is being handled by the principals *themselves.* (Demonstrates emphasis)
    > The partner *himself* will take care of that matter. (Demonstrates emphasis)
    > My associate and *I* accept the engagement. (Not my associate and *myself*...)
    > I am fine; how about *you*? (Not how about *yourself*?)

ADJECTIVES AND ADVERBS

1. Most of us understand that adjectives and adverbs are **modifiers**, but many of us can't tell them apart. In fact, there are many words that can be used as either depending on their use. Consequently, differentiating adjectives from adverbs is really not very important as long as you know how to use them. Understanding, however, that **adjectives modify nouns or pronouns**, and **adverbs modify verbs** and adjectives will help you choose the correct form.

    > Falcone Co. purchased *two* computers from Wizard Corp., a very *small* manufacturer. (*two* is an adjective describing the noun *computers, very* is an adverb modifying the adjective *small*, and *small* is an adjective describing the noun *manufacturer.*)

    > Acme advised Mason that it would deliver the appliances on July 2 as *originally* agreed. (*originally* is an adverb describing the verb *agreed.*)

2. In writing for the CPA exam, avoid colloquial uses of the adjectives **real** and **sure**. In the following examples, adverbs are called for.

    > I am *very* (not *real*) sorry that you didn't pass the exam.
    > He will *surely* (not *sure*) be glad if he passes the exam.

3. **Comparisons** using adjectives frequently present problems. Remember that when comparing two things, the **comparative** (often **er**) form is used, and when comparing more than two, the **superlative** (often **est**) form is used.

    > This report is *larger* than the other one.
    > This report is the *largest* of them all.
    > This report is *more* detailed than the others.
    > This report is the *most* detailed of them all.

4. **Articles** are adjectives. **An** precedes most vowels, but when the vowel begins with a **consonant sound**, we should use **a**.

    > *a* usual adjustment...
    > *a* one in a million deal...

    Similarly, when **a** or **an** precedes abbreviations or initials, it is the next **sound** that we should consider, not the next letter. In other words, if the next sound is a vowel sound, **an** should be used. Usually, your reader will be reading the abbreviations or initials and not the whole term, title, etc.

    > *An S.A.* will be used to head up the field work on this engagement.
    > *An F.O.B.* contract is a *contract* indicating that the seller will bear that degree of risk and expense that is appropriate to the F.O.B. terms.

CONJUNCTIONS

There are three types of conjunctions: coordinating, subordinating, and correlative.

COORDINATING CONJUNCTIONS

Coordinating conjunctions are conjunctions that connect equal elements in a sentence. These conjunctions include **and, but, for, yet, so, or,** and **nor**. Examples of common problems involving coordinating conjunctions:

1. Leaving out the **and**, leading to difficulties with comprehension and clarity.

    > The accountant studied some of management's representations, marked what she wanted to discuss in the meeting. (The word *and* should be in the place of the comma.)

Mike's summer job entails opening the mail, stamps it with a dater, routing it to the proper person. (Should be: ...opening the mail from other offices, *stamping* it with a dater, *and* routing it to the proper person. **This example also demonstrates a lack of parallelism,** which is addressed in an earlier section.)

2. Omission of **and** is correct when the sentence is a compound sentence (meaning that it contains two independent clauses), in which case a semicolon takes the place of **and**. When the semicolon is used, the ideas of each independent clause should be closely related.

The security is genuine; it has not been materially altered.

3. Although the rules for **or** and **nor** have become less strict over time, you should understand proper usage for the sake of comprehension and clarity. Most of us are familiar with **either...or** and **neither...nor**:

Either the creditor must take possession *or* the debtor must sign a security agreement that describes the collateral.

The company would neither accept delivery of the water coolers, nor pay for them, because Peterson did not have the authority to enter into the contract.

SUBORDINATING CONJUNCTIONS

Subordinating conjunctions are conjunctions that introduce subordinate elements of the sentence. The most common and the ones we want to concentrate on here are **as, since, because, that, which, when, where,** and **while.**

1. **AS; SINCE; BECAUSE**

Because is the only word of the three that **always** indicates cause. **Since** usually indicates **time** and, when introducing adverbial clauses, may mean either **when** or **because**. **As** should be avoided altogether in these constructions and used only for comparisons. We strongly recommend using the exact word to avoid any confusion, especially when clarity is essential.

Attachment of the security interest did not occur because Pix failed to file a financing statement. (Specifically indicates *cause*.)
Green has not paid any creditor since January 1, 1992. (Specifically indicates *time*.)

The following example is a typical misuse of the conjunction **as** and demonstrates why **as** should not be used as a substitute for **because**:

As the partners are contributing more capital to the company, the stock prices are going up.

The meaning of this sentence is ambiguous. Are the stock prices going up **while** the partners are contributing capital or are the stock prices going up **because** the partners are contributing more capital?

2. **THAT; WHICH**

Many people complain about not understanding when to use **that** and when to use **which** more than just about anything else. The rule to follow requires that you know the difference between a restrictive and a nonrestrictive clause. A **restrictive clause** is one that must remain in the sentence for the sentence to make sense. A **nonrestrictive** clause is one that may be removed from a sentence and the sentence will still make sense.

That is used with restrictive clauses; *which* is used with nonrestrictive clauses.

(1) An accountant who breaches his or her contract with a client may be subject to liability for damages and losses *which* the client suffers as a direct result of the breach.

(2) As a result, the accountant is responsible for errors resulting from changes *that* occurred between the time he or she prepared the statement and its effective date.

(3) A reply *that* purports to accept an offer but which adds material qualifications or conditions is not an acceptance; rather, it is a rejection and a counter-offer.

In example (1) above, the clause beginning with **which** is nonrestrictive (sentence would make sense without it). In examples (2) and (3), the clauses that follow **that** are restrictive (necessary for the meaning of the sentence).

> If you can put commas around the clause in question, it is usually nonrestrictive and thus takes **which**. Occasionally, there will be a fine line between what one might consider restrictive or nonrestrictive. In these cases, make your choice based on which sounds better and, if there is another **which** or **that** nearby, let that help your decision. (Unless truly necessary, don't have two or three uses of **which** or two or three uses of **that** in the same sentence.)

3. **WHEN; WHERE**

The most common incorrect usage associated with these words occurs when they are used to define something.

(1) Exoneration is *where* the surety takes action against the debtor, which seeks to force the debtor to pay his or her debts.

(2) A fiduciary relationship is *where* the agent acts for the benefit of the principal.

(3) Joint liability is *when* all partners in a partnership are jointly liable for any contract actions against the partnership.

The above three examples are **faulty constructions**. The verb **to be** (**is**, in this case) must be followed by a predicate adjective (an adjective modifying the subject) or a predicate nominative (a noun meaning the same as the subject), **not** an adverbial phrase or clause. These sentences should be rewritten as follows:

(1) Exoneration is *an action* by the surety against the debtor, which seeks to force the debtor to pay his or her debts.

(2) A fiduciary relationship is *the association* of the agent and the principal whereby the agent acts for the benefit of the principal.

(3) Joint liability is *the liability* of all partners in a partnership for any contract actions against the partnership.

4. **WHILE**

Formerly, **while** was acceptable only to denote time. Modern practice accepts **while** and **although** as nearly synonymous. In example (1), either while or although is acceptable. In example (2), **while** is **not** a proper substitution for **although**.

(1) *While/Although* Acme contends that its agreement with Mason was not binding, it is willing to deliver the goods to Mason.

(2) Under a sale or return contract, the sale is considered as completed *although* it is voidable at the buyer's election.

CORRELATIVE CONJUNCTION

The third type of conjunction is the **correlative conjunction**. We have briefly mentioned and presented examples of **either ... or** and **neither ... nor** earlier in connection with nouns, verbs, and agreement. Now we want to discuss these correlatives in connection with **parallelism**.

1.   **Not only** should be followed by **but (also)**.

In determining whether a mere invitation or an offer exists, the courts generally will look *not only* to the specific language *but also* to the surrounding circumstances, the custom within the industry, and the prior practice between the parties.

2.   Watch out for **placement of correlatives**. Faulty placement leads to faulty construction and obstructs clarity.

The lawyer *either* is asked to furnish specific information *or* comment as to where the lawyer's views differ from those of management.

Below is the same sentence in much clearer form. Note that the phrases introduced by *either* and *or* are now in parallel construction: *either to furnish ... or to comment*.

The lawyer is asked *either* to furnish specific information *or to* comment as to where the lawyer's views differ from those of management.

———————————

APPENDIX D
COMPOUND INTEREST TABLES

TABLE 1—FUTURE VALUE OF $1

$FV = PV(1 + r)^n$

r = interest rate; n = number of periods until valuation; PV = $1

$n = 1$	1%	2%	3%	4%	5%	6%	7%	8%	10%	12%	15%	20%	25%
1	1.010000	1.020000	1.030000	1.040000	1.050000	1.060000	1.070000	1.080000	1.100000	1.120000	1.150000	1.200000	1.250000
2	1.020100	1.040400	1.060900	1.081600	1.102500	1.123600	1.144900	1.166400	1.210000	1.254400	1.322500	1.440000	1.562500
3	1.030301	1.061208	1.092727	1.124864	1.157625	1.191016	1.225043	1.259712	1.331000	1.404928	1.520875	1.728000	1.953125
4	1.040604	1.082432	1.125509	1.169859	1.215506	1.262477	1.310796	1.360489	1.464100	1.573519	1.749006	2.073600	2.441406
5	1.051010	1.104081	1.159274	1.216653	1.276282	1.338226	1.402552	1.469328	1.610510	1.762342	2.011357	2.488320	3.051758
6	1.061520	1.126162	1.194052	1.265319	1.340096	1.418519	1.500730	1.586874	1.771561	1.973823	2.313061	2.985984	3.814697
7	1.072135	1.148686	1.229874	1.315932	1.407100	1.503630	1.605781	1.713824	1.948717	2.210681	2.660020	3.583181	4.768372
8	1.082857	1.171659	1.266770	1.368569	1.477455	1.593848	1.718186	1.850930	2.143589	2.475963	3.059023	4.299817	5.960464
9	1.093685	1.195093	1.304773	1.423312	1.551328	1.689479	1.838459	1.999005	2.357948	2.773079	3.517876	5.159781	7.450581
10	1.104622	1.218994	1.343916	1.480244	1.628895	1.790848	1.967151	2.158925	2.593743	3.105848	4.045558	6.191737	9.313226
11	1.115668	1.243374	1.384234	1.539454	1.710339	1.898299	2.104852	2.331639	2.853117	3.478550	4.652391	7.430084	11.64153
12	1.126825	1.268242	1.425761	1.601032	1.795856	2.012197	2.252192	2.518170	3.138428	3.895976	5.350250	8.916101	14.55192
13	1.138093	1.293607	1.468534	1.665074	1.885649	2.132928	2.409845	2.719624	3.452271	4.363493	6.152788	10.69932	18.18989
14	1.149474	1.319479	1.512590	1.731676	1.979932	2.260904	2.578534	2.937194	3.797498	4.887112	7.075706	12.83918	22.73737
15	1.160969	1.345868	1.557967	1.800943	2.078928	2.396558	2.759032	3.172169	4.177248	5.473566	8.137062	15.40702	28.42171
16	1.172579	1.372786	1.604706	1.872981	2.182875	2.540352	2.952164	3.425943	4.594973	6.130394	9.357621	18.48843	35.52714
17	1.184304	1.400241	1.652848	1.947900	2.292018	2.692773	3.158815	3.700018	5.054471	6.866041	10.76126	22.18611	44.40892
18	1.196147	1.428246	1.702433	2.025816	2.406619	2.854339	3.379932	3.996019	5.559917	7.689965	12.37545	26.62333	55.51115
19	1.208109	1.456811	1.753506	2.106849	2.526950	3.025599	3.616528	4.315701	6.115909	8.612761	14.23177	31.94800	69.38894
20	1.220190	1.485947	1.806111	2.191123	2.653298	3.207135	3.869684	4.660957	6.727500	9.646293	16.36654	38.33760	86.73618
22	1.244716	1.545980	1.916103	2.369919	2.925261	3.603537	4.430402	5.436540	8.140275	12.10031	21.64475	55.20615	135.5253
24	1.269735	1.608437	2.032794	2.563304	3.225100	4.048934	5.072367	6.341180	9.849733	15.17863	28.62518	79.49685	211.7582
26	1.295256	1.673418	2.156591	2.772470	3.555673	4.549383	5.807353	7.396353	11.91818	19.04007	37.85680	114.4755	330.8723
28	1.321291	1.741024	2.287928	2.998703	3.920129	5.111687	6.648839	8.627106	14.42099	23.88387	50.06562	164.8447	516.9879
30	1.347849	1.811362	2.427262	3.243397	4.321942	5.743491	7.612255	10.06266	17.44940	29.95992	66.21178	237.3763	807.7936
32	1.374941	1.884541	2.575083	3.508059	4.764942	6.453386	8.715271	11.73708	21.11378	37.58172	87.56509	341.8219	1262.177
34	1.402577	1.960676	2.731905	3.794316	5.253348	7.251025	9.978113	13.69013	25.54767	47.14251	115.8048	492.2236	1972.152
36	1.430769	2.039887	2.898278	4.103932	5.791816	8.147252	11.42394	15.96817	30.91268	59.13557	153.1519	708.8019	3081.488
38	1.459527	2.122299	3.074783	4.438813	6.385478	9.154252	13.07927	18.62527	37.40435	74.17966	202.5434	1020.675	4814.825
40	1.488864	2.208040	3.262038	4.801021	7.039989	10.28572	14.97446	21.72452	45.25926	93.05096	267.8636	1469.772	7523.164
45	1.564811	2.437854	3.781596	5.841176	8.985008	13.76461	21.00245	31.92045	72.89049	163.9876	538.7694	3657.262	22958.88
50	1.644632	2.691588	4.383906	7.106683	11.46740	18.42015	29.45703	46.90161	117.3909	289.0022	1083.658	9100.439	70064.92
100	2.704814	7.244646	19.21863	50.50494	131.5013	339.3020	867.7164	2199.761	13780.61	83522.24	117×10^4	828×10^5	491×10^7

EXAMPLE 1 ♦ FUTURE VALUE OF A SINGLE SUM

REQUIRED: Find the future value of a $100 certificate of deposit at 8% for three years, (A) compounded annually and (B) compounded quarterly.

SOLUTION A: Let   Principal = P = $100,   Interest Rate = r = 8%,   Period = n = 3 years
Future Value Interest Factor at r Rate for n Periods = FVIF(r, n)
Future Value = FV = P x FVIF(r, n)

FVIF(8%, 3 years) = 1.2597 (from Table 1)

FV = $100 x 1.2597 = $125.97

SOLUTION B: Let   Principal = P = $100
Interest Rate = r = 8% ÷ 4 quarters = 2%, Period = n = 12 quarters
Future Value Interest Factor at r Rate for n Periods = FVIF(r, n)
Future Value = FV = P x FVIF(r, n)

FVIF(2%, 12 quarters) = 1.2682 (from Table 1)

FV = $100 x 1.2682 = $126.82

TABLE 2—PRESENT VALUE OF $1

$$PV = \frac{FV}{(1 + r)^n}$$

r = discount rate; n = number of periods until payment; FV = $1

	1%	2%	3%	4%	5%	6%	7%	8%	10%	12%	15%	20%	25%
n = 1	0.990099	0.980392	0.970874	0.961538	0.952381	0.943396	0.934579	0.925926	0.909091	0.892857	0.869565	0.833333	0.800000
2	0.980296	0.961169	0.942596	0.924556	0.907029	0.889996	0.873439	0.857339	0.826446	0.797194	0.756144	0.694444	0.640000
3	0.970590	0.942322	0.915142	0.888996	0.863838	0.839619	0.816298	0.793832	0.751315	0.711780	0.657516	0.578704	0.512000
4	0.960980	0.923845	0.888487	0.854804	0.822702	0.792094	0.762895	0.735030	0.683013	0.635518	0.571753	0.482253	0.409600
5	0.951466	0.905731	0.862609	0.821927	0.783526	0.747258	0.712986	0.680583	0.620921	0.567427	0.497177	0.401878	0.327680
6	0.942045	0.887971	0.837484	0.790315	0.746215	0.704961	0.666342	0.630170	0.564474	0.506631	0.432328	0.334898	0.262144
7	0.932718	0.870560	0.813092	0.759918	0.710681	0.665057	0.622750	0.583490	0.513158	0.452349	0.375937	0.279082	0.209715
8	0.923483	0.853490	0.789409	0.730690	0.676839	0.627412	0.582009	0.540269	0.466507	0.403883	0.326902	0.232568	0.167772
9	0.914340	0.836755	0.766417	0.702587	0.644609	0.591898	0.543934	0.500249	0.424098	0.360610	0.284262	0.193807	0.134218
10	0.905287	0.820348	0.744094	0.675564	0.613913	0.558395	0.508349	0.463194	0.385543	0.321973	0.247185	0.161506	0.107374
11	0.896324	0.804263	0.722421	0.649581	0.584679	0.526788	0.475093	0.428883	0.350494	0.287476	0.214943	0.134588	0.085899
12	0.887449	0.788493	0.701380	0.624597	0.556837	0.496969	0.444012	0.397114	0.318631	0.256675	0.186907	0.112157	0.068719
13	0.878663	0.773033	0.680951	0.600574	0.530321	0.468839	0.414964	0.367698	0.289664	0.229174	0.162528	0.093464	0.054976
14	0.869963	0.757875	0.661118	0.577475	0.505068	0.442301	0.387817	0.340461	0.263331	0.204620	0.141329	0.077887	0.043980
15	0.861349	0.743015	0.641862	0.555265	0.481017	0.417265	0.362446	0.315242	0.239392	0.182696	0.122894	0.064905	0.035184
16	0.852821	0.728446	0.623167	0.533908	0.458112	0.393646	0.338735	0.291890	0.217629	0.163122	0.106865	0.054088	0.028147
17	0.844378	0.714163	0.605016	0.513373	0.436297	0.371364	0.316574	0.270269	0.197845	0.145644	0.092926	0.045073	0.022518
18	0.836017	0.700159	0.587395	0.493628	0.415521	0.350344	0.295864	0.250249	0.179859	0.130040	0.080805	0.037561	0.018014
19	0.827740	0.686431	0.570286	0.474642	0.395734	0.330513	0.276508	0.231712	0.163508	0.116107	0.070265	0.031301	0.014412
20	0.819544	0.672971	0.553676	0.456387	0.376889	0.311805	0.258419	0.214548	0.148644	0.103667	0.061100	0.026084	0.011529
22	0.803396	0.646839	0.521892	0.421955	0.341850	0.277505	0.225713	0.183941	0.122846	0.082643	0.046201	0.018114	0.007379
24	0.787566	0.621722	0.491934	0.390121	0.310068	0.246979	0.197147	0.157699	0.101526	0.065882	0.034934	0.012579	0.004722
26	0.772048	0.597579	0.463695	0.360689	0.281241	0.219810	0.172195	0.135202	0.083905	0.052521	0.026415	0.008735	0.003022
28	0.756836	0.574375	0.437077	0.333477	0.255094	0.195630	0.150402	0.115914	0.069343	0.041869	0.019974	0.006066	0.001934
30	0.741923	0.552071	0.411987	0.308319	0.231377	0.174110	0.131367	0.099377	0.057309	0.033378	0.015103	0.004213	0.001238
32	0.727304	0.530633	0.388337	0.285058	0.209866	0.154957	0.114741	0.085200	0.047362	0.026609	0.011420	0.002926	0.000792
34	0.712973	0.510028	0.366045	0.263552	0.190355	0.137912	0.100219	0.073045	0.039143	0.021212	0.008635	0.002032	0.000507
36	0.698925	0.490223	0.345032	0.243669	0.172657	0.122741	0.087535	0.062625	0.032349	0.016910	0.006529	0.001411	0.000325
38	0.685153	0.471187	0.325226	0.225285	0.156605	0.109239	0.076457	0.053690	0.026735	0.013481	0.004937	0.000980	0.000208
40	0.671653	0.452890	0.306557	0.208289	0.142046	0.097222	0.066780	0.046031	0.022095	0.010747	0.003733	0.000680	0.000133
45	0.639055	0.410197	0.264439	0.171198	0.111297	0.072650	0.047613	0.031328	0.013719	0.006098	0.001856	0.000273	0.000044
50	0.608039	0.371528	0.228107	0.140713	0.087204	0.054288	0.033948	0.021321	0.008519	0.003460	0.000923	0.000110	0.000014
100	0.369711	0.138033	0.052033	0.019800	0.007604	0.002947	0.001152	0.000455	0.000073	0.000012	0.000001	0.000000	0.000000

Note: The future value factor is equal to 1 divided by the present value factor.

EXAMPLE 2 ♦ PRESENT VALUE OF A SINGLE SUM

REQUIRED: Find the present value of $100 paid three years from now if the market rate of interest is 8% (A) compounded annually and (B) compounded quarterly.

SOLUTION A: Let   Principal = P = $100,   Interest Rate = r = 8%, Period = n = 3 years
Present Value Interest Factor at r Rate for n Periods = PVIF(r, n)
Present Value = PV = P x PVIF(r, n)

PVIF(8%, 3 years) = 0.7938 (from Table 2)

PV = $100 x 0.7938 = $79.38

SOLUTION B: Let   Principal = P = $100,   Interest Rate = r = 2%, Period = n = 12 quarters
Present Value Interest Factor at r Rate for n Periods = PVIF(r, n)
Present Value = PV = P x PVIF(r, n)

PVIF(2%, 12 quarters) = 0.7885 (from Table 2)

PV = $100 x 0.7885 = $78.85

TABLE 3—FUTURE VALUE OF ANNUITY OF $1 IN ARREARS

$$FV = \frac{(1 + r)^n - 1}{r}$$

r = interest rate; n = number of payments

n	1%	2%	3%	4%	5%	6%	7%	8%	10%	12%	15%	20%	25%
n = 1	1.000000	1.000000	1.000000	1.000000	1.000000	1.000000	1.000000	1.000000	1.000000	1.000000	1.000000	1.000000	1.000000
2	2.010000	2.020000	2.030000	2.040000	2.050000	2.060000	2.070000	2.080000	2.100000	2.120000	2.150000	2.200000	2.250000
3	3.030100	3.060400	3.090900	3.121600	3.152500	3.183600	3.214900	3.246400	3.310000	3.374400	3.472500	3.640000	3.812500
4	4.060401	4.121608	4.183627	4.246464	4.310125	4.374616	4.439943	4.506112	4.641000	4.779328	4.993375	5.368000	5.765625
5	5.101005	5.204040	5.309136	5.416323	5.525631	5.637093	5.750739	5.866601	6.105100	6.352847	6.742381	7.441600	8.207031
6	6.152015	6.308121	6.468410	6.632976	6.801913	6.975318	7.153291	7.335929	7.715610	8.115189	8.753738	9.929920	11.25879
7	7.213535	7.434283	7.662462	7.898294	8.142009	8.393838	8.654021	8.922803	9.487171	10.08901	11.06680	12.91590	15.07349
8	8.285670	8.582969	8.892336	9.214226	9.549109	9.897468	10.25980	10.63663	11.43589	12.29969	13.72682	16.49908	19.84186
9	9.368527	9.754628	10.15911	10.58280	11.02656	11.49132	11.97799	12.48756	13.57948	14.77566	16.78584	20.79890	25.80232
10	10.46221	10.94972	11.46388	12.00611	12.57789	13.18079	13.81645	14.48656	15.93742	17.54873	20.30372	25.95868	33.25290
11	11.56683	12.16872	12.80780	13.48635	14.20679	14.97164	15.78360	16.64549	18.53117	20.65458	24.34928	32.15042	42.56613
12	12.68250	13.41209	14.19203	15.02581	15.91713	16.86994	17.88845	18.97713	21.38428	24.13313	29.00167	39.58050	54.20766
13	13.80933	14.68033	15.61779	16.62684	17.71298	18.88214	20.14064	21.49530	24.52271	28.02911	34.35192	48.49660	68.75957
14	14.94742	15.97394	17.08632	18.29191	19.59863	21.01507	22.55049	24.21492	27.97498	32.39260	40.50471	59.19592	86.94947
15	16.09690	17.29342	18.59891	20.02359	21.57856	23.27597	25.12902	27.15211	31.77248	37.27971	47.58041	72.03511	109.6868
16	17.25786	18.63929	20.15688	21.82453	23.65749	25.67253	27.88805	30.32428	35.94973	42.75328	55.71748	87.44213	138.1086
17	18.43044	20.01207	21.76159	23.69751	25.84037	28.21288	30.84022	33.75023	40.54470	48.88367	65.07510	105.9306	173.6357
18	19.61475	21.41231	23.41443	25.64541	28.13239	30.90565	33.99903	37.45024	45.59917	55.74971	75.83636	128.1167	218.0446
19	20.81090	22.84056	25.11687	27.67123	30.53900	33.75999	37.37896	41.44626	51.15909	63.43968	88.21181	154.7400	273.5558
20	22.01900	24.29737	26.87037	29.77808	33.06596	36.78559	40.99549	45.76196	57.27500	72.05244	102.4436	186.6880	342.9447
22	24.47159	27.29898	30.53678	34.24797	38.50521	43.39229	49.00574	55.45675	71.40275	92.50258	137.6317	271.0307	538.1011
24	26.97346	30.42186	34.42647	39.08260	44.50200	50.81557	58.17667	66.76476	88.49733	118.1552	184.1679	392.4843	843.0330
26	29.52563	33.67091	38.55304	44.31174	51.11345	59.15638	68.67647	79.95441	109.1818	150.3339	245.7120	567.3773	1319.489
28	32.12910	37.05121	42.93092	49.96758	58.40258	68.52811	80.69769	95.33883	134.2099	190.6989	327.1041	819.2233	2063.951
30	34.78489	40.56808	47.57542	56.08494	66.43885	79.05818	94.46078	113.2832	164.4940	241.3327	434.7452	1181.882	3227.174
32	37.49407	44.22703	52.50276	62.70147	75.29883	90.88978	110.2182	134.2135	201.1378	304.8477	577.1005	1704.110	5044.710
34	40.25770	48.03380	57.73018	69.85791	85.06696	104.1838	128.2588	158.6267	245.4767	384.5210	765.3655	2456.118	7884.609
36	43.07688	51.99437	63.27594	77.59831	95.83633	119.1209	148.9135	187.1021	299.1268	484.4631	1014.346	3539.010	12321.95
38	45.95272	56.11494	69.15945	85.97034	107.7095	135.9042	172.5610	220.3159	364.0435	609.8305	1343.622	5098.374	19255.30
40	48.88637	60.40198	75.40126	95.02551	120.7998	154.7620	199.6351	259.0565	442.5926	767.0914	1779.091	7343.858	30088.66
45	56.48108	71.89271	92.71986	121.0294	159.7002	212.7435	285.7493	386.5056	718.9048	1358.230	3585.129	18281.31	91831.50
50	64.46318	84.57940	112.7969	152.6671	209.3480	290.3359	406.5289	573.7701	1163.909	2400.018	7217.718	45497.20	280255.7
100	170.4814	312.2323	607.2877	1237.624	2610.025	5638.368	12381.66	27484.51	137796.1	696010.5	783×10^4	414×10^6	196×10^8

Note: To convert from this table to values of an annuity in advance, determine the annuity in arrears factor above for one more period and subtract 1.

EXAMPLE 3 ♦ FUTURE VALUE OF AN ANNUITY IN ARREARS

REQUIRED: Jones plans to save $300 a year for three years. If Jones deposits money at the end of each period in a savings plan that yields 24%, how much will Jones have at the end of the three years if Jones deposits (A) $75 at the end of each quarter? (B) $25 at the end of every month?

SOLUTION A: Let Payment = P = $75, Interest Rate = r = 6%, Period = n = 12 quarters
Future Value of an Annuity Factor at r Rate for n Periods = FVAF(r, n)
Future Value of the Annuity = FVA = P x FVAF(r, n)

FVAF(6%, 12 quarters) = 16.8699 (from Table 3)

FVA = $75 x 16.8699 = $1,265.24

SOLUTION B: Let Payment = P = $25, Interest Rate = r = 2%, Period = n = 36 months
Future Value of an Annuity Factor at r Rate for n Periods = FVAF(r, n)
Future Value of the Annuity = FVA = P x FVAF(r, n)

FVAF(2%, 36 months) = 51.9944 (from Table 3)

FVA = $25 x 51.9944 = $1,299.86

TABLE 4—PRESENT VALUE OF ANNUITY OF $1 IN ARREARS

$$PV = \frac{1 - (1 + r)^{-n}}{r} \qquad r = \text{discount rate}; \; n = \text{number of payments}$$

	1%	2%	3%	4%	5%	6%	7%	8%	10%	12%	15%	20%	25%
n = 1	0.990099	0.980392	0.970874	0.961538	0.952381	0.943396	0.934579	0.925926	0.909091	0.892857	0.869565	0.833333	0.800000
2	1.970395	1.941561	1.913470	1.886095	1.859410	1.833393	1.808018	1.783265	1.735537	1.690051	1.625709	1.527778	1.440000
3	2.940985	2.883883	2.828611	2.775091	2.723248	2.673012	2.624316	2.577097	2.486852	2.401831	2.283225	2.106482	1.952000
4	3.901966	3.807729	3.717098	3.629895	3.545950	3.465106	3.387211	3.312127	3.169865	3.037349	2.854978	2.588735	2.361600
5	4.853431	4.713459	4.579707	4.451822	4.329477	4.212364	4.100197	3.992710	3.790787	3.604776	3.352155	2.990612	2.689280
6	5.795476	5.601431	5.417192	5.242137	5.075692	4.917325	4.766540	4.622880	4.355261	4.111407	3.784483	3.325510	2.951424
7	6.728195	6.471991	6.230283	6.002055	5.786374	5.582381	5.389289	5.206370	4.868419	4.563756	4.160419	3.604592	3.161139
8	7.651678	7.325481	7.019692	6.732745	6.463213	6.209794	5.971299	5.746639	5.334926	4.967640	4.487321	3.837160	3.328911
9	8.566017	8.162237	7.786109	7.435332	7.107821	6.801692	6.515232	6.246888	5.759024	5.328250	4.771584	4.030966	3.463129
10	9.471305	8.982585	8.530203	8.110896	7.721735	7.360087	7.023582	6.710082	6.144567	5.650223	5.018768	4.192472	3.570503
11	10.36763	9.786848	9.252625	8.760477	8.306415	7.886875	7.498674	7.138964	6.495061	5.937699	5.233712	4.327060	3.656403
12	11.25508	10.57534	9.954004	9.385074	8.863252	8.383844	7.942686	7.536078	6.813692	6.194374	5.420619	4.439217	3.725122
13	12.13374	11.34837	10.63496	9.985648	9.393573	8.852683	8.357651	7.903776	7.103356	6.423549	5.583147	4.532681	3.780098
14	13.00370	12.10625	11.29607	10.56312	9.898641	9.294984	8.745468	8.244237	7.366687	6.628168	5.724475	4.610567	3.824078
15	13.86505	12.84926	11.93793	11.11839	10.37966	9.712249	9.107914	8.559479	7.606080	6.810864	5.847370	4.675473	3.859262
16	14.71787	13.57771	12.56110	11.65230	10.83777	10.10590	9.446649	8.851369	7.823709	6.973986	5.954235	4.729560	3.887410
17	15.56225	14.29187	13.16612	12.16567	11.27407	10.47726	9.763223	9.121638	8.021553	7.119631	6.047161	4.774634	3.909928
18	16.39827	14.99203	13.75351	12.65930	11.68959	10.82760	10.05909	9.371887	8.201412	7.249670	6.127965	4.812195	3.927943
19	17.22601	15.67846	14.32380	13.13394	12.08532	11.15812	10.33560	9.603600	8.364920	7.365777	6.198231	4.843496	3.942354
20	18.04555	16.35143	14.87747	13.59033	12.46221	11.46992	10.59401	9.818148	8.513564	7.469444	6.259331	4.869580	3.953883
22	19.66038	17.65805	15.93692	14.45112	13.16300	12.04158	11.06124	10.20074	8.771541	7.644646	6.358663	4.909431	3.970485
24	21.24339	18.91393	16.93554	15.24696	13.79864	12.55036	11.46933	10.52876	8.984744	7.784316	6.433771	4.937104	3.981111
26	22.79520	20.12104	17.87684	15.98277	14.37519	13.00317	11.82578	10.80998	9.160945	7.895660	6.490564	4.956323	3.987911
28	24.31644	21.28127	18.76411	16.66306	14.89813	13.40616	12.13711	11.05108	9.306566	7.984423	6.533508	4.969668	3.992263
30	25.80771	22.39646	19.60044	17.29203	15.37245	13.76483	12.40904	11.25778	9.426914	8.055184	6.565979	4.978936	3.995048
32	27.26959	23.46833	20.38877	17.87355	15.80268	14.08404	12.64655	11.43500	9.526376	8.111594	6.590533	4.985373	3.996831
34	28.70267	24.49859	21.13184	18.41120	16.19290	14.36814	12.85401	11.58693	9.608575	8.156565	6.609098	4.989842	3.997972
36	30.10751	25.48884	21.83225	18.90828	16.54685	14.62099	13.03521	11.71719	9.676508	8.192414	6.623107	4.992046	3.998702
38	31.48466	26.44064	22.49246	19.36786	16.86789	14.84602	13.19347	11.82887	9.732652	8.220994	6.633752	4.995101	3.999169
40	32.83469	27.35548	23.11477	19.79277	17.15909	15.04630	13.33171	11.92461	9.779051	8.243777	6.641778	4.996598	3.999468
45	36.09451	29.49016	24.51871	20.72004	17.77407	15.45583	13.60552	12.10840	9.862807	8.282516	6.654293	4.998633	3.999826
50	39.19612	31.42361	25.72976	21.48219	18.25593	15.76186	13.80075	12.23349	9.914814	8.304499	6.660514	4.999451	3.999943
100	63.02888	43.09835	31.59891	24.50500	19.84791	16.61755	14.26925	12.49432	9.999274	8.333234	6.666661	5.000000	4.000000

Note: To convert from this table to values of an annuity in advance, determine the annuity in arrears factor above for one less period and add 1.

EXAMPLE 4 ♦ PRESENT VALUE OF AN ANNUITY IN ARREARS AND PRESENT VALUE OF AN ANNUITY DUE

REQUIRED: Smith can make annual mortgage payments (not including taxes, etc.) of $4,800. How much can Smith borrow at 8% interest and repay in 20 years: (A) making 20 equal payments at the end of the year? (B) making 20 equal payments at the beginning of the year?

SOLUTION A: Let   Payment = P = $4,800, Interest Rate = r = 8%, Period = n = 20 years
Present Value of an Annuity Factor at r Rate for n Periods = PVAF(r, n)
Present Value of the Annuity = PVA = P x PVAF(r, n)

PVAF(8%, 20 years) = 9.8181 (from Table 4)

Loan = PVA = $4,800 x 9.8181 = $47,126.88

SOLUTION B: Let   Payment = P = $4,800, Interest Rate = r = 8%, Period = n = 20 years
Present Value of an Annuity Factor at r Rate for n Periods = PVAF(r, n)
Present Value of the Annuity in Advance = PVAA = P x [PVAF(r, n - 1) + 1]

PVAF(8%, 19 years) = 9.6036 (from Table 4)

Loan = PVAA = $4,800 x (9.6036 + 1) = $50,897.28

EXAMPLE 5 ♦ CAPITAL LEASE OBLIGATION

Alpha Company has a 10 year capital lease with an implicit interest rate of 8%. The $40,000 payments are made at the beginning of each year.

REQUIRED: What is the capital lease obligation (the present value of the lease payments)?

SOLUTION: Let   Payment = P = $40,000,   Interest Rate = r = 8%,   Period = n = 10 years
Present Value of an Annuity Factor at r Rate for n Periods = PVAF(r, n)
Present Value of the Annuity in Advance = PVAA = P x [PVAF(r, n - 1) + 1]

PVAF(8%, 9 years) = 6.246888 (from Table 4)

Capital Lease Obligation = PVAA = $40,000 x (6.246888 + 1) = $289,875.52

This is the same as: Capital Lease Obligation

= Initial Payment   + PVA (where r = 8%, n = 9)
= Initial Payment   + P x PVAF(8%, 9)
= $40,000   + $40,000 x 6.246888
= $289,875.52

EXAMPLE 6 ♦ INTERNAL RATE OF RETURN

Beta Company is considering the purchase of a machine for $12,500. Beta expects a net year-end cash inflow of $5,000 annually over the machine's 3-year life. [The IRR is that rate at which NPV = 0. For more information on internal rate of return (IRR) and net present value (NPV), see Chapter 26 in the ARE volume.]

REQUIRED: What is this project's approximate internal rate of return?

SOLUTION: This example involves a present single sum and an annuity. The present value of the single sum paid today is $12,500. In this situation, NPV is the present value of the purchase price (P) less the present value of the future annual cash inflow (PVA).

Let   Single Payment = P = $12,500   Interest Rate = r = ?
Annual Cash Inflow = A = $5,000   Period = n = 3 years
Present Value of an Annuity Factor at r Rate for n Periods = PVAF(r, n)

NPV = P - PVA   and   NPV = 0   Thus,   P - PVA = 0

PVA = A x PVAF(r, n)   so   P - [A x PVAF(r, n)] = 0 or
                        P = A x PVAF(r, n)   or
                        P / A = PVAF(r, n)   and substituting known values:
      $12,500 / $5,000 = PVAF(r, 3 years)   or
                           PVAF(r, 3 years) = 2.5

Looking in the 3 period row of Table 4, we find the interest rate that produces the interest factor closest to 2.5 is in the 10% column. (Examiners generally narrow the field somewhat by supplying half a dozen values instead of a whole table, but they frequently also provide values from tables that are misleading. For instance, they may supply future values of annuities or present values of single sums.)

PVAF(8%, 3 years) = 2.577097   rounds to 2.6
PVAF(10%, 3 years) = 2.486852   rounds to 2.5   Thus, r (or IRR) is about <u>10%</u>.
PVAF(12%, 3 years) = 2.401831   rounds to 2.4

INDEX

Writing Skills Content

Answers to selected essay responses from Business Law & Professional Responsibilities, Auditing, and Financial Accounting & Reporting sections are used to assess candidates' writing skills. **Five percent** of the points available on each of these sections are allocated to writing skills. Effective writing skills include the following six characteristics:

1. Coherent organization.

2. Conciseness.

3. Clarity.

4. Use of standard English.

5. Responsiveness to the requirements of the question.

6. Appropriateness for the reader.

Due to the importance of writing skills, we discuss these six characteristics in the **Practical Advice** and the **Accounting for 5%** sections of this volume.

COLLEGE REP PROGRAM

Hiring on Your Campus Now!

Join our national team of future CPAs...and earn while you learn

Many future CPAs start preparing for the CPA Exam during their college years and need information about their options before they graduate. With more than 31 years of exam preparation and educational development experience, Bisk recognizes that accounting students who study with our materials serve as our very best advertisement on college campuses. Why are our student representatives so important to us? Because our reps are always so impressed with the quality of our materials that they gladly spread the word about Bisk CPA Review to their friends, professors and fellow accounting students. Our college reps tell us that they're proud to represent us, because they have first-hand proof that our products really work.

The BENEFITS & REWARDS TO YOU

Excellent exam preparation support & award-winning CPA Review materials

- Use our materials to study for your accounting classes, and watch your grades improve dramatically.

- Pass the CPA Exam the *first* time you sit with Bisk's proven CPA Review System – used by Elijah Watt Sells Award Gold Medal winners, Paul Ito and Stephanie Seiberg, who scored the highest in the nation on the CPA Exam. In the last 8 years, the University of South Florida, which uses Bisk materials, was ranked more often than any other university as one of the top 5 schools in the nation for students with advanced degrees passing all sections of the CPA Exam.

- Call our toll-free editorial and technical support help lines anytime.

A generous compensation plan
- A complete CPA Review absolutely FREE, saving thousands of dollars!
- You have opportunities to earn generous commissions and extra bonuses.

A competitive edge in today's tough job market
- You receive valuable career credentials for your resume.
- Our materials help you achieve the grades and exam scores that prospective employers want to see.

We invite you to join our nationwide network of college representatives today! For information on how to become a Bisk College Representative on your campus...

Call Toll-Free 1-800-874-0540

Internet www.cpaexam.com/nia
Email infonia@cpaexam.com
Fax 1-813-621-7565

Bisk CPA Review · 9417 Princess Palm Avenue · Tampa, FL 33619-8313

Bisk
cpa review